• Movies Released Since 1990 •

What Can We Watch Tonight?

A Family Guide to Movies

Buy or Rent with Confidence

Ted Baehr

with Dr. Tom Snyder

ZONDERVAN™

GRAND RAPIDS, MICHIGAN 49530 USA

This book is joyfully dedicated to Jesus, our Lord and Savior,
Lili, my beautiful wife,
Peirce, James, Robert, and Evelyn, my wonderful children, and
Ted "Bob 'Tex' Allen" Baehr, my loving father and a truly great actor.

ZONDERVAN™

What Can We Watch Tonight?
Copyright © 2003 by Theodore Baehr

Requests for information should be addressed to:

Zondervan, *Grand Rapids, Michigan 49530*

Library of Congress Cataloging-in-Publication Data

Baehr, Theodore.
    What can we watch tonight? : a family guide to movies / Ted Baehr.— 1st ed.
      p. cm.
    Includes index.
    ISBN 0-310-24770-5
    1. Motion pictures—Moral and ethical aspects.   2. Motion pictures—Religious aspects—
Christianity.   3. Motion pictures—Reviews. 4. Television and family.   I. Title.
PN1995.5.B29   2003
791.43'75–dc'1

                                                     2003008404

All Scripture quotations, unless otherwise indicated, are taken from the *Holy Bible: New International Version*®. NIV®. Copyright © 1973, 1978, 1984 by International Bible Society. Used by permission of Zondervan. All rights reserved.

Scripture quotations marked KJV are taken from the King James Version.

Published in association with the literary agency of The Envoy Group, 11125 North La Canada #151, Oro Valley, AZ 85737.

Interior design by Susan Ambs

Printed in the United States of America

03 04 05 06 07 08 09 /❖ DC/ 10 9 8 7 6 5 4 3 2 1

CONTENTS

What Can We Watch Tonight?   7

Part 1: Before Reading the Movie Reviews

Chapter 1: Learning to Have Media Wisdom   13

Chapter 2: Because Children and Adults See It Differently   31

Chapter 3: Asking the Right Questions   53

Chapter 4: Glossary and Explanation of
    Review Ratings   83

Part 2: A Decade of Movie Reviews
Including Lists of the Best and Worst of Each Year

1990   91

1991   123

1992   155

1993   191

1994   229

1995   267

1996   305

1997   343

1998   383

1999   423

2000   463

2001   505

The first half of 2002   547

Conclusion   569

Epilogue   571

Acceptability Index   573

MPAA Rating Index   581

Genre Index   589

Movie Titles, Actors, and Directors Index   599

Acknowledgments   621

WHAT CAN WE WATCH TONIGHT?

What can I watch tonight with my family?

What can I watch tonight with my wife?

What can we watch when we invite our friends over this weekend?

These are the kinds of questions that we receive often at *Movieguide: A Biblical Guide to Movies and Entertainment*. Our *www.movieguide.org* website helps, but even so, many people continue to ask for a book they can take to their video store. Since 250 to 300 major movies are released every year in movie theaters and several hundred more are direct to video, most Christians need help making wise choices.

What Can We Watch Tonight hopes to answer this important question for the home. It hopes to do this in a couple of ways.

First, *What Can We Watch Tonight* is made up of reviews of the most popular and influential movies of the last ten years (1990–2001 with a set of reviews for the first six months of 2002) that are found in the "Favorites" section of most rental stores. *What Can We Watch Tonight* does not claim to be exhaustive, but in its selections it hopes to bring to the attention of the reader those movies that truly made a mark on a specific year (some of which will not be family oriented, but will be apparent as you read the rest of this book).

Second, each review will indicate whether a movie is for the family, for a mature audience (adults), or whether it is not recommended because of its lack of morality, but is included in the guide because it had such a strong effect on our culture's thinking and attitudes at that particular time. Standard symbol indications for the amount of violence, offensive language, and sex will be used in each of the three categories, as well as the date, director, actor information, and name of studio. A wide variety is included because of the possible effect on culture or a possible recommendation against viewing.

Third, the adapted *Movieguide* review will be a comprehensive analysis of the movie and a commentary on the value of its message—valuable as a communicator of truth and conveyer of a Christian or moral message, or its importance to culture and how it makes a comment at the time it was made as well as its influence on children at different stages of development. This covers the basic plot ("Does this sound like a movie I'd like?") and the effect on our children and culture ("Is this of interest to me and does it comment on things I need to be aware of?").

Fourth, the book will cover movies of the 1990s in addition to the first half of 2002. Each year will have a section, with the final section being 2002.

Fifth, the book will list the best movies for families and the best movies for mature audiences. These movies are not only well made, but they are also refreshingly free of the excessive sex, violence, and foul language of years past. However, it must be noted that most of the best films for mature audiences deal with strong subject matter and caution, or even extreme caution, is advised. Please note that there are several three star (☆ ☆ ☆) movies that make it into our best films for families and best films for mature audiences because they had good moral values and acceptability as well as good entertainment value. It is our prayer that the movie industry will make more and more recommendable movies and that they will remove all offensive elements in them.

Finally, *What Can We Watch Tonight* will list the twenty worst films of each year with a headline that will indicate why the movie was chosen. Please note that these films have been chosen not necessarily because they have sex, violence, nudity, or profanity, but because they have a worldview that is antithetical to the biblical worldview. They communicate philosophies that in the final analysis are anti-human and anti-God and that can only lead to disaster. Some of these movies are very entertaining and liked by many Christians. Furthermore, many of them have positive values interwoven with their negative messages. Therefore, this list is to help you wrestle with the theological issues involved and to help others with the false philosophies in these movies.

DISTINCTIVES

It is self-evident that movie review books share common features that distinguish them from other literary genres. That said, *What Can We Watch Tonight* is easily distinguished from secular review books because of its clear Christian worldview, which offers families of faith and values the ability to make wise entertainment decisions.

Furthermore, it is distinguished from other Christian review books by its comprehensive approach to reviewing using the *Movieguide* method, which analyzes movies in terms of clear-cut standards and theological perspectives. This includes the obvious offensive elements such as foul language, sex, violence, the entertainment value, the worldview, the theology, and much more.

Large segments of the 135 million people who go to church each week frequent movies in theaters and rent movies at the video store. Furthermore, 92 percent of Christian youths see the same movies at the theaters and rent the same movies at the video store as their non-Christian contemporaries, according to Barna Research. Over 90 percent of the teenagers say that movies are their favorite leisure time activity (60 percent rank TV as their second choice with 39 percent opting for music and 18 percent for the Internet). These youths watch 50 movies a year in theaters and 50 videos a year.

Now you can patronize the video rental store without being in a quandary as to what to rent for an evening's entertainment depending on the audience in your living room. This book also helps you make your own decisions, rather than making decisions for you. *What Can We Watch Tonight* represents your concerns and worldview and not the libertine, amoral, or even immoral views of secular and non-Christian critics. At *Movieguide,* we constantly receive letters from people who feel deceived by other critics.

Furthermore, this book understands and takes into consideration the stages of development of your children so you can make wise movie and video[1] selections for your children at each age level.

---

1. Please note that video movies may change to DVDs as the technology shift occurs. At present video movies is still a term collectively referring to everything rented at a rental store.

THE APPROACH

What Can We Watch Tonight analyzes movies in the comprehensive manner of the *Movieguide* reviews. *Movieguide* tries not to play traffic cops with a thumbs up or thumbs down. Rather, *Movieguide* provides the information to allow the readers to make the decisions. Using Dr. Ted Baehr's method, *Movieguide* tries to look at each movie in these ways:

- *Aesthetically* by looking at the artistic value of the movie and by looking at how well the movie is made just as other reviewers do.
- *Emotively* by looking at how it captures and amuses the audience as entertainment and amusement.
- *Semantically* by looking at the individual elements, such as words, nudity, and incidents of violence, and their meanings just as many parents do.
- *Syntactically* by looking at how the elements of the film come together and how the pieces and characters relate to each other just as many teenagers and single adults do.
- *Propositionally* by looking at what the movie is communicating as summarized in the premise of the movie.
- *Generically* by comparing it to other movies in its genre.
- *Thematically* by looking at the themes that are present in the movie.
- *Morally* by looking at its moral perspective and content.
- *Biblically* by looking at the biblical perspective and biblical principles in the movie.
- *Systematically* by looking at how the movie relates to other movies.
- *Economically* by looking at how it does at the box office and how its box office gross compares to other movies.
- *Intellectually* by looking at how the movie fulfills its goals and premise.
- *Sociologically* by looking at how the movie relates to culture and society.
- *Politically* by looking at the political perspective of the movie.
- *Cognitively* by looking at the age group to whom the movie is marketed, the age group for whom it is suitable, and how it will impact a particular age group.
- *Psychologically* by looking at how the movie deals with mind and soul.
- *Historically* by looking at how accurate the movie is in presenting history.
- *Sexually* by looking at how the movie deals with sex and sexual relationships.
- *Philosophically* by looking at the philosophical perspective and the worldview of the movie.
- *Ontologically* by looking at how the movie deals with the nature of being.
- *Epistemologically* by looking at how the movie deals with the nature of knowing.
- *Spiritually* by looking at how the movie deals with God, faith, and religion.

If *What Can We Watch Tonight* is interesting or helpful to you, *please* tell your friends, relatives, and all the people you know about it!

BEFORE READING THE MOVIE REVIEWS

CHAPTER 1

LEARNING TO HAVE MEDIA WISDOM

STORYTELLING AND MYTHMAKING

Telling stories is at the heart of much of our entertainment media. It is the essence of the mass media influence in today's culture—the most powerful genre of mass communication. Jesus told stories called "parables" in order to help people understand the kingdom of God. Hollywood tells stories through film, television, video, CD-ROMs, radio, and other modes.

Our *Movieguide* editor, Dr. Tom Snyder, notes in his book *Myth Conceptions*,

> Stories matter deeply. They make a profound difference in our lives. They bring us laughter, tears, and joy. They stimulate our minds and stir our imaginations. They help us to escape our daily lives for a while and visit different times, places, and people. They can arouse our compassion or empathy, spur us toward truth and love, or sometimes even incite us toward hatred or violence.... Different kinds of stories satisfy different needs. For example, a comedy evokes a different response from us than a tragedy. A hard-news story on page one affects us differently than a human interest story in the magazine section or a celebrity profile next to the movie listings.... Although different stories satisfy different needs, many stories share common themes, settings, character types, situations, and other recurrent patterns. They may even possess a timeless, universal quality.[1]

Many stories focus on one individual—a heroic figure who overcomes trials and tribulations to defeat some kind of evil or to attain some positive goal. By looking at the differences among stories, we can examine the motifs, meanings, values, and principles that each story evokes. And in observing their common patterns, we can gain insights into truth, reality, human nature, and the spirit of the imagination.

Every story also has a worldview—a way of viewing reality, truth, the universe, the human condition, and the supernatural world. A story can have a Christian worldview, which shows people's need for salvation through faith in Jesus Christ, or it can have a secular, humanist worldview that explicitly or implicitly rejects the Christian worldview. By examining the worldview of a story or film, we can determine the moral, philosophical, social, psychological, spiritual, theological, and aesthetic message that the story conveys. We can also examine in this light the emotions that the story evokes.

This leaves us with an important question: How are we to judge whether a particular movie or television program is appropriate for our families or children? By what standards do we select a film? Furthermore, how can we protect ourselves and our families from destructive influences in the media while at the same time view what is good and helpful?

THE PROBLEM

Thousands of scientific studies and case studies have shown the powerful influence that the entertainment media has on people's cognitive development and behavior—especially on children, teenagers, and young people, who represent the biggest audience. By the time he or she is seventeen years old, a child will have spent at least 40,000 hours watching movies, videos, and TV programs, playing video games, listening to music, and reading popular books and news stories. In contrast, he or she will have spent only 11,000 hours in school, 2,000 hours with his or her parents, and 800 hours in church, if attended! That's about 2,353 hours of media consumption per year for the average child. Of those 2,353 hours each year, current figures indicate that only 20 percent of these—about 471 hours—will feature a solid, strong, or very strong moral worldview, and up to 7 percent—about 165 hours—will feature a solid, strong, or very strong redemptive or Christian worldview. Just who is teaching our youth is demonstrated in the following chart:[2]

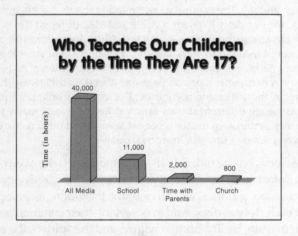

Early in 2001 the surgeon general of the United States agreed with four top medical groups—the American Medical Association, the American Academy of Pediatrics, the American Psychological Association, and the American Academy of Child and Adolescent Psychiatry—as well as with countless psychological and neurological experts, that violence in the mass media is contributing to increased violent behavior among children and teenagers.[3] In addition, many scientific studies from other sources, such as education professor Diane Levin, author of *Remote Control Childhood? Combating the Hazards of Media Culture,*[4] and psychologists such as Dr. Victor Cline, Dr. Stanley Rachman, Dr. Judith Reisman, and Dr. W. Marshall[5] have found that viewing sexual images in the media leads to increased sexual activity among children and teenagers and increased deviant behavior, including rape. A recent Dartmouth Medical School study of New England middle-school students, reported by the National Cancer Institute, found that viewing drug use in movies and TV programs leads to increased drug use among children.[6]

A new, long-term study released in 2002 demonstrates the negative effects of today's popular visual media on children, teenagers, and young adults. Published in the journal *Science*, the study found that teenagers and young adults who watch more than one hour of television and/or videos daily are more likely to commit violent crimes and other forms of aggressive behavior. The study, led by Jeffrey G. Johnson of Columbia University and the New York State Psychiatric Institute, followed children in 707 families in northern New York State for seventeen years. Adolescents and young adults who watch television for more than seven hours per week are 16 to 200 percent more likely to commit an aggressive act in later years. The study found a link between violence and viewing any television, not just violent programming. "The evidence has gotten to the point where it's overwhelming," Johnson reported.[7]

These studies demonstrate that movies such as *Hannibal, From Hell, Scream, American Pie 2, Jason X, Queen of the Damned*, and the Harry Potter series, and television programs such as *The Sopranos, The West Wing, Temptation Island*, and *Will and Grace* can have a tremendously negative impact on the lives of children and teenagers, as well as their parents, families, friends, and teachers. These types of movies and programs are nothing more than visual terrorism.

POWERFUL EMOTIONAL IMAGES

Movies and television programs are powerful tools of communication. They plant emotional images in our minds, influence our purchases and our lifestyles, and direct our hopes and dreams.

Gary Smalley, president of Today's Family, a nonprofit counseling center, has pointed out that while altering a person's actions or attitudes has always been difficult, a 1942 Walt Disney release demonstrated the power of movies to change people's lives and the world around us. Disney's animated movie *Bambi* created an image that went straight to the heart of its viewers, including grown men who hunt. Almost overnight this film nearly bankrupted the deer-hunting industry. Smalley notes,

> The year before the film was released, deer hunting in the United States was a $9.5 million business. But when one particularly touching scene was shown—that of a yearling who sees his mother gunned down by a hunter—there was a dramatic change in men's attitudes. The following season, hunters spent only $4.1 million on tags, permits, and hunting trips![8]

We may applaud this use of the emotive power of film to save wildlife, but we cannot overlook the power of film to negatively affect people and our civilization as well. The heinous power of photographs was dramatically brought to the world's attention by Dr. James Dobson's television interview with Ted Bundy, just hours before Bundy was executed in Florida's electric chair. During this interview, Bundy acknowledged that pornography had played a critical role in leading him to murder as many as twenty-eight young women and children. Reflecting on the many years he'd spent in prison with violent criminals, Bundy observed, "Without exception, every one of them was deeply involved with pornography—without question, without exception—deeply influenced and consumed by an addiction to pornography. The FBI's own study on serial homicide shows that the most common interest among serial killers is pornography."

What is even more disturbing is David Scott's vast compendium of scientific information entitled "Pornography: Its Effects on Family, Community, and Culture," which shows that rapists report a preference for "soft-core" films before seeking out a victim. R-rated feature films often fall into this category (for example, *Fatal Attraction* and *Skin Deep*).

Dr. Victor Cline's research has shown that the exposure of randomly selected male college students to sexually suggestive theatrical movies increases their aggressive behavior toward women, and decreases both male and female sensitivity to rape and the plight of the victim. Both males and females, after viewing this type of material, judge a female rape victim to be less injured, less worthy, and more responsible for her own plight.

Furthermore, Dr. Cline has found that pornographic and violent images are locked into the viewer's brain by the release of the adrenal chemical called epinephrine when the viewer is emotionally or sexually aroused. These images are almost impossible to erase. So conditioned, the susceptible viewer seeks aggressively to act out these images in his or her own life to fulfill his or her desire to experience the release that comes with arousal.

The key word in Dr. Cline's findings is "susceptible." Studies conducted by the Annenberg Institute at the University of Pennsylvania have found that the majority of people viewing a violent or sexual television program or film seem to be unaffected by what they see. Twenty to thirty percent of those viewing the same television program or film become paranoid, depressed, and see themselves as the victim. However, 7 to 11 percent of those viewing the program or film are mainlined by what they see in that they want to go out and replicate or mimic the actions of the protagonist in the program. The 1987 Attorney General's Commission on Pornography carefully details the conclusive research demonstrating that sex and violence in films and on television leads to rape, child abuse, and increased divorce rates in our society.[9]

This breakdown into three types of responses seems to hold true whether the program in question is an advertisement selling beer, a religious program seeking to make conversions, or a violent program depicting rape. Most who view it will be unaffected, but a significant percentage will be "mainlined," in the sense that they will want a beer if they are susceptible to beer, they will convert if they are susceptible to the religious message, or they will want to rape someone if they are susceptible to that message. These categories often overlap, although sometimes they are mutually exclusive.

The most definitive studies on this mainlining effect of television programs and movies relate to teenage suicide. Studies conducted at Columbia University and the University of California at San Diego conclusively demonstrated that movies, television programs, and even news reports involving teenage suicide led to a 7 percent increase in the number of teenage suicides during the week following such programming.

Soon after these findings appeared in the prestigious *New England Journal of Medicine*, several movies and television programs came out focusing on teenage suicide. This is irresponsible behavior, which frequently hides behind a specious distortion of the constitutional right to free speech—a right that has clear constitutional limits. For instance, you are not allowed yell "fire" in a theater, joke about bombs at an airport x-ray machine, or advertise cigarettes on television.

In fact, those who yell the loudest about free speech have yelled the loudest that Christians do not have a right to teach biblical principles in public schools or pray before a high school football game. How Christians have come to accept this perverse worldview—that it is all right to show women being mutilated in the name of free speech while it is forbidden to proclaim the Good News in strife-ridden schools—exemplifies the cunning of the adversary and the passivity of the church.

WE CAN'T IGNORE MOVIES

No matter what we do, we can't ignore movies or any other products of the mass media. If we avoid movies in the theater, they will soon be on broadcast television.

Even the films we would most like to avoid because they are violent or sexually suggestive have a way of confronting us directly or indirectly. Many Christians confide that they have seen some of the worst films that the industry has to offer. Some who try to protect their family find that their children see such films at a friend's house, in school, or somewhere else where parents have little or no control. One friend confided that he had home-schooled his children and thoroughly insulated them, only to discover that they saw an X-rated movie at a friend's house.

In his powerful death-row television interview with Dr. James Dobson, Ted Bundy confessed, regarding his addiction to pornography,

> We are your sons and we are your husbands, and we grew up in regular families. Pornography can reach out and snatch a kid out of any house today. It snatched me out of my home twenty, thirty years ago.... As dedicated as my parents were—and they were diligent in protecting their children—and as good a Christian home as we had—and we had a wonderful Christian home—there is no protection against the kind of influences that are loose in society.

Bundy's statements can also be applied to movies. There is no way to retreat into a secure, insulated environment.

INSATIABLE

David Puttnam, former president of Columbia Pictures and producer of *Chariots of Fire*, noted in an interview with Bill Moyers that once people are exposed to the spectacle of blood and sex, they want more and more as they become hardened to the titillation of the last violent or sexual act they saw. Just as a drug addict, whose body becomes less and less responsive to a drug, keeps looking for the rush he experienced during his first use of that drug, those who are addicted to the sex and violence in films seek increasing doses to appease their lust. This is one aspect of man's sin nature.

Since the days of the bloody sports in the Roman Colosseum, people have demanded increasing decadence with each voyeuristic exposure to the violation of moral taboos. In reference to the Colosseum, Mr. Puttnam noted that the insatiable lust of the public prompted the spectacle of gladiators fighting each other to deteriorate into a bloody show of gladiators slaughtering unarmed innocents, and the spectacle of a woman having sex with an ass degenerated into the act of a woman having sex with several animals. As Mr. Puttnam stated, someone in Hollywood must say "Stop!" before we go the way of the Roman Empire.[10]

WHEN GOOD MEN DO NOTHING

> *The only thing necessary for the triumph of evil is for good men to do nothing.*
>
> —*Edmund Burke*

The way to stop this proliferation of prurient films and television programs is to follow the biblical mandate and take every thought in the mass media captive for Christ. By supporting the good and rejecting the bad, Christians *can* make a difference.

Movies and television programs are a sensitive subject, however. The legalism of some Christians has prompted them to reject storytelling, drama, and entertainment, even though the Bible exalts all three. In some ways, such legalism resembles that of David's wife Michal, the daughter of Saul, who disapproved of David's dancing before the Lord when he brought the Ark of the Covenant into Jerusalem.

Survey after survey[11] shows that Christians see the same movies and watch the same television programs as pagans. When asked whether they have seen a particular movie or television program, the same percentage of Christians and pagans answer "yes." However, when asked on the same survey whether they go to movies or watch television in general, many of those Christians will say "no." How they can see *Top Gun* and yet not go to movies is one of the unsolved mysteries of our age. In fact, World Vision has reported that Christians spend $6.60 out of every $100.00 on entertainment, while they give only $1.20 to the church (including missions and ministries).

Denouncing the media of film or television is illogical, since these media are merely tools of communication, just as the telephone is a tool of communication. Like other tools, these mass media of entertainment may be used for good or for evil.

A hammer may be used to build a church, or to hit someone. Either way it is used, the hammer is not responsible. The film *Jesus* has brought thousands of people to Jesus Christ, while *Rambo* has influenced susceptible men to go out and use machine guns to kill innocent people in the United States and England. The medium is not the problem; the misuse of the medium by sinful human beings is the problem.

A telephone may be used to communicate between family members separated by many miles, or to communicate pornography to impressionable children and susceptible adults. We are not called to stop using the telephone because someone is using it for pornography; we are called to redeem the medium by stopping the evil use of it.

Denial is part of the problem. It separates the Christian's entertainment choices from his or her moral discernment. By viewing television and movies surreptitiously, Christians insulate themselves from moral judgment. Too often they believe that a violent movie or television program will not affect them, although they know that it will affect others.

Denial short-circuits the ability to choose good entertainment and reject bad entertainment. Through the process of informed choice, however, we can make a difference. The movie industry needs money to survive. If we redirect our entertainment spending from bad entertainment to good entertainment, the industry will begin to make more good movies and fewer bad ones.

While some films present a worldview that is opposed to Christianity, others offer insight and beauty. As the renowned actor Richard Kiel points out, there are many good, entertaining movies being released, such as *Chariots of Fire, The Prince of Egypt, The Straight Story, The Princess Diaries, Spider-Man*, and *Toy Story 2*. Still, other movies contain material, such as exploitative violence and sex, impossible for Christians to see in good conscience.

PEOPLE POWER

Richard Halverson has summed up the problem in one of his pithy newsletters:

> People power! Let's face it! If people don't buy the product, it goes off the market.... If people don't buy, there is no profit.... People have the power to close down an undesirable operation ... or prosper it!

> Pornography prevails on TV, films, video tapes, magazines because they are profitable. People watch them, read them, buy them. If they didn't, they would be dead.

> Pornography prevails because it is profitable. It is profitable because people want it. That is people power!

The movie industry is the cash register of the mass media. If Christians would vote for the good and against the bad at the box office, the mass media would turn from its present trends and steer instead toward a course that would include—not exclude—Christians. Christians are the largest group within the United States, but have been overshadowed in influence by other groups because we have not acted according to biblical principles in our daily lives.

ONCE UPON A TIME...

> *Those who do not remember the past are condemned to relive it.*
> —*George Santayana*

Christians often forget that the church exerted a great influence on the entertainment industry from 1933 to 1966. For thirty-three years, every script was read by representatives of the Roman Catholic Church, the Southern Baptist Church, and the Protestant Film Office. Their job was to evaluate a movie in terms of the Motion Picture Code. If the film passed, it received the Motion Picture Code Seal and was distributed. If it didn't pass, the theaters would not screen it.

The "Short Form" of the Motion Picture Code read as follows:

The basic dignity and value of human life shall be respected and upheld. Restraint shall be exercised in portraying the taking of life.

Evil, sin, crime, and wrong-doing shall not be justified.

Detailed and protracted acts of brutality, cruelty, physical violence, torture, and abuse shall not be presented.

Indecent or undue exposure of the human body shall not be presented.

Illicit sex relationships shall not be justified. Intimate sex scenes violating common standards of decency shall not be portrayed. Restraint and care shall be exercised in presentations dealing with sex aberrations.

Obscene speech, gestures, or movements shall not be presented. Undue profanity shall not be presented.

Religion shall not be demeaned.

Words or symbols contemptuous of racial, religious, or national groups shall not be used so as to incite bigotry or hatred.

Excessive cruelty to animals shall not be portrayed, and animals shall not be treated inhumanely.[12]

During the period of the Motion Picture Code, movies containing explicit sex, violence, profanity, and blasphemy were not approved or released. Also, films were not allowed to mock a minister of religion or a person's faith (the religious persecution in Germany prompted this wise counsel). For the most part, movies and television programs communicated the true, the good, and the beautiful.

Then, in 1966, the churches voluntarily withdrew from the entertainment industry. Many of the media elite bemoaned the retreat of the churches. One prophesied, "If the salt is removed from the meat, then the meat will rot."[13] Many studio executives felt that the church involvement helped them to reach the large Christian audience in the United States, and believed that Christians would avoid films that lacked the Motion Picture Code Seal.

CENSORSHIP? OR PATRON SOVEREIGNTY?

Patron sovereignty has traditionally been regarded by Hollywood as the right of movie patrons to determine what they want to see or avoid, by their activity at the box office. When there was talk in the 1930s about government censorship (censorship as prior restraint by the government), the movie industry requested patron sovereignty in the form of the Motion Picture Code. Throughout the life of the Code and its successor, the MPAA rating system, the entertainment industry has continued to express its preference for patron sovereignty, rather than government intervention, to curb tendencies in the industry toward obscenity and violence.

When the churches retreated, the Motion Picture Association of America instituted the rating system to take the place of the Code. However, this was like letting the fox guard the henhouse, and the results were predictable.

Today, scripts are being read by feminists, Marxists, and homosexual groups such as the Alliance of Gay and Lesbian Artists, rather than by Christians. These groups award pictures and television programs that communicate their point of view, and condemn movies and television programs that disagree with their point of view. For example, one television network had to spend hundreds of thousands of dollars to reshoot and reedit a television movie so that it wouldn't offend the Alliance of Gay and Lesbian Artists.

WHOEVER CONTROLS THE MEDIA CONTROLS THE CULTURE

As a result of the influence of these anti-biblical groups, movies and television programs have become purveyors of immorality, blasphemy, and rebellion, and have influenced too many viewers to mimic the evil they see on the screen. Alan Alda noted in the movie *Sweet Liberty* that, to capture an audience, a movie must include the destruction of property (as in the car chase), rebellion against authority, and immoral sex. Of course, the audience he had in mind were the teenagers and young adults who flock to movies.

It is interesting to note that Karl Marx had only four goals in his Communist Manifesto: to abolish property, to abolish the family, to abolish the nation, and to abolish religion and morality. Marx's points concur with Alan Alda's since rebellion against authority serves the goal of abolishing the family and the nation. Since God created property rights ("Thou shalt not steal" and "Thou shalt not covet"), the family, the nation, religion, and morality, it is clear that the movie industry today, divorced from the influence of the church, is proclaiming an anti-biblical, pro-humanist agenda that appeals to an adolescent audience and undermines the fabric of our civilization.

The United States is already considered by many to be the most immoral country in the world. Movies are often reedited to include more sex and violence when released in the U.S. market. For instance, in Australia the movie *Return to Snowy River* shows the hero and heroine getting married, whereas the version released in the U.S. shows the hero and heroine going off to live with each other without being married.

The destructive power of the mass media was highlighted by the 1988 television remake of the famous movie *Inherit the Wind*, which dramatically retells the story of the famous Scopes "monkey" trial. Having seen the movie many years ago, I had forgotten that Christians won the trial, but lost the battle in the media. William Jennings Bryan defeated Clarence Darrow in court, but he was defeated by the venomous anti-Christian reporting of H. L. Mencken. As in many cases since then, the Christians won the skirmish, but lost the battle to the manipulators of the mass media.

Christians should never forget the lesson of the Scopes trial: It is futile to win the trial only to lose the battle to the power of the media. We need to claim God's victory and win the war by taking every thought captive for him.

The lesson of the Scopes trial can be best summarized by a paraphrase of John Locke, "Whoever controls the media, controls the culture." In covering the trial, the press controlled the language and communicated a strong anti-Christian bias. Society adopted that bias and moved against the Christians, even though the Christians had the law on their side. In the same manner, if those who control the language emphasize rape, pillage, and plunder, the culture will reflect those communications.

Like the Christians involved in the Scopes trial, we often forget that there is a war raging around us. It's not the one in Nicaragua, or Mozambique, or the Persian Gulf, or even in Afghanistan. It's right here in America, and it's being fought by a cunning adversary who is aiming at you, your loved ones, and your future!

This war is not taking place on the usual battlefield. It's being fought inside the minds of men, women, and children. It's a spiritual war for the souls of those who constitute our civilization, and it uses the most effective weapon ever conceived: communications.

Jesus was the Master of communications. His parables are as pertinent today as they were two thousand years ago. He knew the power of communication and how ideas shape civilizations. His Word toppled one of the most powerful civilizations in history, the Roman Empire, and it continues to transform the world today.

Though the tools of communications have changed, the words remain the same. The warfare of ideas and thoughts has exploded through the use of movies and television, revolutionizing our way of thinking. We are fighting against an enemy that is using every possible tactic to control our minds: materialism, secularism, humanism, Marxism—all the "isms" that conflict with Christianity.

We are besieged daily with an onslaught of messages that tear us apart. If not from the morning newspaper, then from the nightly news or cable television movies filled with images of drugs, illicit sex, and violence.

CARING IS THE ONLY DARING

The other side understands what is at stake. Feminist, homosexual, pro-abortion, and communist groups have banded together as Operation Prime Time to lobby the mass media to establish an anti-Christian and anti-human agenda in the entertainment industry. An instructive article in the April 8, 1988, *Wall Street Journal* discussed Norman "People for the American Way/Archie Bunker" Lear's success in opposing "the religious right" and promoting socialism through the mass media.

An in-depth portrait that appeared in the April 1988 *American Family Association Journal,* noted that Mr. Lear has united the rich, famous, and powerful against Christianity, morality, and freedom. These dilettante revolutionaries pour millions of dollars into campaigns aimed at destroying our free society and Christianity.

We cannot escape as some have tried to do. We must take a stand and resist. We are the body of Christ, and he takes his stand in us (Psalm 82:1). For too long, Christ's body has not responded to the directions of the Head, who is Jesus Christ. Now he is cleansing and disciplining us, his body.

Throughout history, God allowed his enemies to discipline his people. His enemies, the idolatrous Babylonians, carried his people into captivity (see Jeremiah). The Lord allowed Satan to scourge the righteous Job, without cause (see Job 1 and 2).

There is a growing attack on the body of Christ. The forces of the adversary are marshaled against his people. He has called us to stand for Jesus. Through him, we are more than conquerors. We must repent of any apostasy and take a stand for Jesus Christ.

WHY?

Why do surveys show that Christians too often go to bad movies while missing good ones? The answer is sin, peer pressure, curiosity, deceptive advertisements (especially on television), and a lack of guidance.

Renowned columnist Cal Thomas has pointed out that the rating system, based on secular values, doesn't help. This rating system, devised and determined by the Motion Picture Association of America, has failed to guide individuals in their choice of motion pictures. Often these ratings disuade people from watching movies that have a biblical worldview, such as *Eleni,* or ones that are worthwhile but have restrictive ratings for political, economic, or ideological motives, such as *The Killing Fields.*

Ratings are not given for content but to help the motion picture companies promote films. For example, the Billy Graham Organization requested a PG-13 rating for their movie *Caught,* although it had no overtly offensive elements and witnessed to Jesus Christ. Robert Redford asked for an R rating on *The Milagro Beanfield* because he was afraid that it was too family-oriented to attract viewers.

The elements that Christians would identify as objectionable are not the ones used by the motion picture companies to classify a movie as an R, PG, or G. In fact, some G movies are worse from a Christian perspective than some R movies. The movie *Labyrinth* is a case in point. It promotes magical thinking, which is an anathema to God, but is rated G. This book applies biblical standards to confront every aspect of a motion picture, from its premise to its photography.

Some secular reviewers have a pronounced anti-biblical, anti-religious, and anti-Christian bias. Often, a critic's worldview and the values he or she is advocating will be directly opposed to Christianity. Christians need information from a biblical perspective to make godly viewing decisions. We need to reclaim the entertainment industry by uniting to support the true, the good, and the beautiful while opposing the immoral messages of the Adversary's entertainment machine. Most of all, we need to know what is good and what isn't.

Christians prefer wholesome movies and programs, but have had no one to help direct them and their families away from immoral entertainment toward moral, uplifting movies. We seek to meet this need in *What Can We Watch Tonight.*

GOOD NEWS

What Can We Watch Tonight reviews movies from a sound biblical perspective to help you make an informed decision about which movies to see and which to avoid. While some Christians choose not to watch any movies, over two-thirds of the born-again, evangelical and/or charismatic Christians in this country watch what non-Christians watch. Helping these individuals choose good movies is an important ministry. If Christians redirect their entertainment dollars away from immoral entertainment toward moral movies, producers will take notice and produce movies and programs for us.

What Can We Watch Tonight includes reviews of both good and bad movies. You will find a detailed review of each movie to help you decide why you would want to see or avoid a movie. Best of all, the detailed reviews provide a biblical perspective toward each movie to help you develop your own biblical world-view and discernment. By using discernment in your family's choice of movies and entertainment, you are casting your vote for Hollywood to make better movies, either by your financial support—when you buy tickets to good movies or rent good videos—or by your withholding financial support—when you refuse to spend money on bad movies.

The leaders of two large entertainment companies have already recognized the impact of *Movieguide* and *What Can We Watch Tonight*, and have asked us to help them understand what needs to be done to make movies and television programs more acceptable to the Christian audience. By acting on the recommendations in this book, you can make a difference.

SEEK THE GOOD, THE TRUE, AND THE BEAUTIFUL

A prisoner wrote us a revealing letter that underlines both the problem and the solution. Like him, we need to seek guidance to protect ourselves, our families, and our friends from the adversary.

> Dear Friends,
>
> I've read about the work of Ted Baehr and your *Movieguide* service in this month's issue of Focus on the Family's magazine *Citizen* (January 1989).
>
> I'm in prison in New York State. I'm forty years old, and my wife Jennifer and I have a three-year-old son, Alexander. I am also free in our Lord and born again.
>
> . . . Recently I was elected as an alternate to our prison liaison committee. One task of the liaison committee is to choose the movies we prisoners see. I must confess that for too long I didn't pay much attention to movies. I felt (back then) that I was being "liberal" and "modern." "After all," I used to say, "it's 'only' a movie." But over the years I've grown more and more upset by what I see on the screen. This has been especially true since Alexander was born. . . . I've become uncomfortable to sit in an auditorium filled with those of us convicted of crimes, and to be shown films showcasing violence, drugs, and assorted corruptions.
>
> But what worries me more than the visual things (bombs, shootings, nude bodies) are the mental messages. Even supposed comedies promote divorce, random sex, drugs, vulgarities, dishonesty.

I'm writing to request a subscription to your guide.... First, I'd like to read it myself and share it with Jennifer. I'd like to use it so we can choose our family entertainment more wisely. Second, I'd like to use it to attempt to influence the men here to alter the type of films we've been seeing.

There are more Christians in prison than you might suspect. And there are good men of other faiths too. Maybe such men are not in the majority here (or anywhere)—but they exist.

One problem all of us face is being unaware of suitable alternatives.... We can rent alternatives, but first someone must know what alternatives exist.

... I believe that good things are contagious. That good movies on positive topics will help us all feel better. That films about loving spouses and loyalty and faith will appeal to us all. Because deep down, who wants to be brainwashed into expecting divorce and violence and lies?

I believe that God works powerful good through every little effort we make. If we make the effort to find better films, I trust in the Lord to influence our hearts.

... A person's location here or there isn't what determines if he's lost—it's how far we are from Jesus in our hearts that does. The need is great here. What better place to begin?

You're doing something important. And you can help shape young minds and hearts—and inspire some of us less young adults also. God bless you all.

Name withheld

We appreciate this heartfelt plea and recognize the need of prisoners throughout the United States to have guidance in their choice of videos. Movies influence audiences for good or for evil. Individuals, especially those who are prone to violence, desperately need guidance to steer them away from movies that influence audiences negatively.

THE SOLUTION: MEDIA WISDOM

Parents need to teach their children and teenagers how to be media-wise, intelligent consumers, rather than passive couch potatoes.

We must understand

- the influence of the entertainment media,
- our children's cognitive development,
- the grammar of the entertainment media, and
- our moral, spiritual values and teach them to our children.

"Understanding the influence of the entertainment media" might also be called *"breaking the bonds of denial."* Dale Kunkel, professor at the University of

California, Santa Barbara, points out that after thousands of intensive studies in this area, only one significant researcher still denies the influence of the media, and that researcher last did real research in this area in the mid-1980s.[14] In the wake of the Columbine High School massacre, CBS president Leslie Moonves put it bluntly, "Anyone who thinks the media have nothing to do with this is an idiot" (Associated Press, 19 May 1999). Thus, the American Psychological Association's report on media violence concludes, "There is absolutely no doubt that those who are heavy viewers of violence demonstrate increased acceptance of aggressive attitudes and increased aggressive behavior."

The entertainment industry is made up of seven major studios and many independents. The major studios consistently control 95 percent or more of the box office. They also control most of the other mass media of entertainment. The seven major studios also control the Motion Picture Association of America (MPAA), which rates the movies according to age groups: G, PG, PG-13, R, and NC-17. Because the major studios control the organization that rates their movies, the past few years have seen an increase in PG-13 and R ratings so that more explicit sex, nudity, violence, foul language, vulgarity, and other immorality can be marketed to your children and teenagers.

Those seven studios are run by executives who administrate, finance, and distribute movies. It is important to keep in mind that the industry is made up of a small number of key "players" (as Hollywood calls them). Their decisions affect not only the U.S. but the world as well, as many areas of the world have come under the influence of Hollywood and its interpretation of the American experience. Thus, with regard to movies, there are about thirty financial and studio persons who can green-light projects, and about three hundred key players—executive producers as well as a few directors and actors—who can easily get movies made by the major studios.

Each idea for a movie, however, originates from an executive producer (and/or a production company, who could have deals going with several studios). In a sense, each movie is an independent unit that is brought together by an executive producer who attaches to the project the director and stars and seeks financing from investors as well as the studios. The studio's major role is that of distribution—getting prints to the theatres and doing the publicity to bring the audiences there. Production and distribution budgets for major movies now average more than $76 million, according to the Motion Picture Association of America, which is owned by the major studios. One movie in the year 2000 had a $250 million cross-marketing budget, according to *The Los Angeles Times*.

The executive producer is thus the initiator and the motivating factor to getting a movie made. The movie starts with the story idea and the script. Sometimes writers are commissioned to write a script from an idea that a producer has, but often the writers write scripts they would like to have produced and "pitch" the idea to the producers. The director takes the script and the budget and, working with the actors and his crew, turns the idea into a reality on celluloid. In many cases the director is a hired hand, but often a director will also be a writer and a producer.

Of course, the media is not the whole problem but only one part of the equation that could be summed up with the sage biblical injunction found in 1 Corinthians 15:33, "Do not be misled: 'Bad company corrupts good character.'" This is the message of the surgeon general's report concerning youth violence. Bad company corrupts good character, whether that bad company is gangs, peer pressure, or the violent and vulgar works of popular culture.

"Breaking the bonds of denial" also means noting that there are a lot of good media out there, which we honor every March at the *Movieguide* Annual Faith and Values Awards Gala and Report to the Entertainment Industry in Los Angeles. Since we started the Annual Faith and Values Awards Gala ten years ago, the number of movies with worthwhile moral, redemptive, and even Christian content has more than tripled! We can alert you and your families— including the children, teenagers, and young adults in your household—to the better and best movies and television programs that are out there: movies such as *Toy Story 2*, *Monsters, Inc.*, *The Rookie*, *The Princess Diaries*, *On the Line*, *Return to Me*, *Remember the Titans*, *Spider-man*, *My Dog Skip*, *Shrek*, *Joshua*, *Chicken Run*, *Jimmy Neutron: Boy Genius*, and *The Basket*, and TV series such as *Touched by an Angel*, *Jag*, *Doc*, and *Seventh Heaven*.

The second step in media wisdom is *to understand the susceptibility of children at each stage of cognitive development*. Not only do children see the media differently at each stage of development, but also different children are susceptible to different stimuli. For instance, you might not want your younger children to see *Monsters, Inc.*, *Shrek*, or *The Lord of the Rings*, while *Toy Story 2* and *Jimmy Neutron: Boy Genius* are safer for them. Or you might want your teenager to avoid a movie such as *The Family Man*, but would allow him or her to see something like *The Princess Diaries*, *Return to Me*, or *The Lord of the Rings*. As the research of the National Institute of Mental Health showed many years ago, some children want to copy media violence, some are susceptible to other media influences, some become afraid, and many just become desensitized. Just as an alcoholic would be inordinately tempted by a beer commercial, so the propensity for susceptibility plays an important part in what kind of media will influence your child at each stage of development.

The third part of media wisdom is *to understand the grammar of the media* so that you can deconstruct and critique what you are watching by asking the right questions. Children spend the first fourteen years of their lives learning grammar according to sixteenth-century technology—the written word. They need to be taught the grammar of the twenty-first century—technology. They need to know how aspects of different media work and influence them, and how to ask the right questions such as

- "Who is the hero?"
- "What kind of role model is the hero?"
- "Who is the villain?"
- "What kind of message does his character convey?"

- "How much sex and violence is in the mass media product?"
- "What is the premise, or proposition, that drives the narrative?"
- "What worldviews and values is the movie or program teaching?"
- "How does the movie or program treat Christians, Jews, religion, and political ideologies such as conservatism, liberalism, socialism, fascism, Marxism, and environmentalism?"
- "Does good triumph over evil?"
- "Would you be embarrassed to sit through this movie or television program with your parents, children, God, or Jesus Christ?"

As we noted in the introduction, there are not only different types of stories, there are also recurrent, archetypal, universal, and transcendent patterns, motifs, images, character types, themes, values, and principles within stories. Some kinds of stories are more visually oriented while other stories are more literary or theatrical. Also, most stories embody the cultural ideals of a people and their society and give expression to deep, commonly shared, even transcendent emotions and rational or irrational ideas. Every story has a worldview: a way of viewing reality, truth, the universe, the human condition, and the supernatural world. The theology of the storyteller or storytellers helps shape the worldview of the story. Thus, every worldview has a doctrine of God, a doctrine of man, a doctrine of salvation, a doctrine of the church, a doctrine of history and the future, a doctrine of the nature of reality (including a doctrine of nature or creation and a doctrine of supernatural forces), and a doctrine of knowledge (including a doctrine of truth).

Harry Potter and the Sorcerer's Stone, for instance, has an occult, New Age worldview that subtly encourages children to dabble in witchcraft and sorcery. As such, it indirectly, and sometimes directly, teaches a nature-based, polytheistic religion that confuses the spiritual world of God with the natural or physical world, has no doctrine of salvation or forgiveness for sin, and believes human nature is basically good instead of inherently sinful (as the Bible teaches), among other things.

In May of 2002, a nationwide poll of teenagers between the ages of 13 and 19, conducted on behalf of WisdomWorks Ministries, revealed that 41 percent of American teens—roughly nine million 13- to 19-year-olds—are very interested in the occult, supernatural content of the Harry Potter books and movies. Of that number, 53 percent of the teens most likely to be exposed to that occult, supernatural material are between the ages of 13 and 14. Fifty percent are "A" students, 49 percent describe themselves as "stressed out," 49 percent attend a youth group frequently, and 45 percent are Caucasian. This poll clearly shows the dangers of letting your children consume such cultural artifacts as the Harry Potter books or movies without proper parental and spiritual guidance.

In contrast to the Harry Potter series, Part One of *The Lord of the Rings* reflects a Christian understanding of reality. In Middle Earth there is a clear distinction between right and wrong and there is clear accountability to a sovereign, holy God who is Lord of the universe. Here, wielding vast supernatural power is seen as a temptation that should be shunned and best left up to God. *The Fellowship of the Ring* also provides your family with characters they can emulate, characters such as Gandalf the Grey, the kindly, supernatural being who dispenses wisdom and has a good sense of humor, not unlike God or Jesus Christ. He states, "We cannot change what has been. It is what we do with the days we have that matters." Furthermore, he tells Frodo, "Don't be so free to deal in death and judgment." In other words, don't try to play God, which is the opposite of the "do what thou wilt" occult philosophy of the Harry Potter series. And there is the character Frodo himself, who humbly takes up the cross of "ring-bearer" so that he can stop the forces of darkness from obtaining awesome powers of evil.

Finally, children need to *understand your values* in order to ask the right questions and evaluate the answers they get. If the hero wins by murdering and mutilating, your children need to apply godly values, which may or may not see the hero's actions as heroic or commendable. Families have an easier time with number four, because they can apply their deeply held religious beliefs to evaluate the media. Even so, media literacy and values education are two of the fastest growing areas in the academic community, as educators realize that something is amiss.

Dr. Ted Baehr, chairman of the Christian Film and Television Commission, speaks to education associations worldwide, presenting his deeply held Christian beliefs he uses to evaluate the questions that need to be asked. He trains and equips Christian groups to immerse themselves in a biblical worldview so that they can help their children and grandchildren to "know before they go," to choose the good and reject the bad.

Of course, there is much more to teaching media wisdom. Reading to your children five minutes a day is a most effective tool, according to University of Wisconsin research. Parents should read the Bible to their children. Jesus Christ quoted the Hebrew Scriptures, saying, "Man does not live on bread alone, but on every word that comes from the mouth of the Lord" (Deuteronomy 8:3).

Encourage your children to prepare their own rating system and then let them adhere to it. You might also have your children review the media they consume by writing up their answers to the questions listed on pages 27–28. Encourage your children to create their own stories, plays, paintings, sculptures, movies, and television programs.

As Theodore Roosevelt taught, if we educate a man's mind but not his heart, we have an educated barbarian. Media wisdom involves educating the heart so that it will make the right decisions.

We pray that this book will help you and your children.

> *I, the Lord, have called you in righteousness; I will take hold of your hand. I will keep you and will make you to be a covenant for the people and a light for the Gentiles, to open eyes that are blind, to free captives from prison and to release from the dungeon those who sit in darkness.*
>
> *—Isaiah 42:6–7*

NOTES

1. Tom Snyder, *Myth Conceptions: Joseph Campbell and the New Age* (Grand Rapids: Baker, 1995), 17.
2. *Movieguide*, 2002.
3. See "Joint Statement on the Impact of Entertainment Violence on Children," Congressional Public Health Summit, 26 July 2000, *www.aap.org*. (*Movieguide* is happy to provide copies of this statement as well as articles and position papers.)
4. See *abcnews.com*, accessed 9 April 2001.
5. Ted Baehr, *The Media-Wise Family* (Colorado Springs: Chariot Victor, 1998), 87–110. Contact us for articles on the effect of sexual content in entertainment mass media.
6. Press release, National Cancer Institute, 23 March 2001.
7. Jeffrey Johnson et al., "Television Viewing and Aggressive Behavior During Adolescence and Adulthood," *Science Magazine* 295 (29 March 2002): 2468–71.
8. Gary Smalley and John Trent, *The Language of Love* (Pomona, Calif.: Focus on the Family, 1988), 20.
9. *Attorney General's Commission on Pornography: Final Report* (Washington, D.C.: U.S. Department of Justice, 1986).
10. *Bill Moyers' World of Ideas: David Putnam* (PBS, 12 September 1988).
11. A Barna Research poll has shown conclusively that there is no difference between the viewing habits of those who claim Jesus Christ as Lord and those who do not.
12. "The Short Form" is the 1956 condensed circulation of the original *A Code to Govern the Making of Motion and Talking Pictures* (New York City, 1948).
13. The George Heimrich Collection of the archives of the Protestant Film Office in the possession of Christian Film & Television Commission ministry and Dr. Ted Baehr.
14. Dale Kunkel, "Evidence on Media Violence Still Stands," *Los Angeles Times*, 6 November 2000, F3.

CHAPTER 2

BECAUSE CHILDREN AND ADULTS SEE IT DIFFERENTLY

But if anyone causes one of these little ones who believe in me to sin, it would be better for him to have a large millstone hung around his neck and to be drowned in the depths of the sea.

—Matthew 18:6

TEACHING CHILDREN TO BE MEDIA-WISE

Dear Ted,

My daughter, Sarah, is nine years old and, like the majority of children in her school, she was captivated by the *Pokemon* craze as it unfolded. She avidly collected the cards and bought the game. My wife, Val, and I became concerned as we realized that Sarah was a little too obsessed with the whole thing. We heard that children were actually stealing cards from one another, selling them at ridiculous prices, or swapping them under duress. An unhealthy atmosphere was developing.

We talked to Sarah about this, explaining the Christian perspective and asking her to get rid of the cards. While she listened to what we said, she could not quite bring herself to part with the cards or stop playing the game.

Our concern grew as time went by. One day I visited your web site after learning about it through Christian Vision. I read your report on the forthcoming *Pokemon* film, and this increased my concern. I showed Sarah your site and left her to read the review.

That same evening she came to us and said that she had decided to swap all of her *Pokemon* cards with her friends for other things. We were extremely pleased that she had made this decision, but Val was concerned that the cards, while leaving Sarah's possession, would still be used by others. However, she decided not to say anything and wait and see. The next morning Sarah met us at the top of the stairs and opened her hand to show a lot of torn paper. At first we couldn't think what was in her hands, but then we realized that she had torn up the *Pokemon* cards. We were thrilled that one so young could appreciate the effect of the craze and make her own decision.

So, thank you, Ted, for your web site and the truth it shares. You certainly made a difference in our family life.

Terry Bennett
Director of Operations
Christian Vision

CHRISTIAN VISION

A few years back the evening news broadcast a story about a babysitter in Dallas, Texas, who had molested the baby she was supposed to be caring for. The parents, who had become suspicious of the sitter, installed a hidden camera in their living room. The evening news showed what the parents saw: the baby-sitter starting to undress in front of the baby. The news anchors were horrified and wondered how the parents had failed to check this sitter's credentials. The news team closed by remarking that this type of abuse probably occurred more often than anyone knew.

They were right. There is one babysitter who is constantly abusing millions of our children. That babysitter is a television set, which is often attached to a VCR. No one fires this babysitter or brings criminal charges against it, nor do many people try to rehabilitate it.

No matter how much we condemn the mass media for influencing the behavior of our children, we must admit that there are several accomplices in this tragedy. They include churches that don't instruct parents how to teach their children discernment, and parents who allow their children to watch television, go to movies, or surf the Internet without adequate supervision or training in the necessary discernment skills.

SEEK UNDERSTANDING

Understanding why and how the mass media affect children and adults is an extremely important step in protecting your children and helping them to develop the necessary critical thinking skills and discernment. Many scientists have argued that there is such a significant body of evidence on the connection between the content of the mass media (such as violence) and behavior (especially aggressive behavior) that researchers should move beyond accumulating further evidence and focus on the processes responsible for this relationship. Recent research has focused on developing theories that explain why and how that relationship exists.

BIG

Many of the theories that have developed involve the stages of cognitive development of children. Although there are many factors common to all ages of development, there are also unique distinctions between each stage of child development that require different treatment with regard to exposure to and training about the mass media.

Children often see the world and the media quite differently than adults do. Parents generally look at television programs *semantically*, in terms of the mean-ing of what is said or what is happening. Children see *syntactically*, in terms of the action and special effects in the program. Thus, with regard to music a mother will say to her child, "Did you hear the lyrics in that awful song?" And the child will respond, "Ah Mom, I don't listen to the words. Did you hear the rhythm and the beat?"

This generation gap was highlighted when Mr. Rogers of *Mr. Rogers' Neighborhood* was talking to a class of little children and a little girl asked him how he got out of the television set to be with them that day. He said that he was never in the television set and carefully explained how TV worked. Then he asked the girl if she understood him. She said "Yes; but, how are you going to get back into the TV so I can watch you this afternoon?"

GROWING PAINS

Cognitive development is often directly impacted by the mass media, especially television. It is important to understand that cognition is not thinking; rather, thinking is part of cognition, and cognition itself is the process of knowing, which philosophers and theologians call *epistemology*. Cognitive development is similar to building a house step-by-step from a blueprint, or adding colors to our mental palette, or installing an operating system in a computer so that the computer can then perform the tasks that you direct it to do.

Each of these tasks must be done correctly and in the right order or the result will be disastrous. The human operating system develops over many years in a series of stages. Each stage has unique characteristics and each stage must develop properly.

Once when I was teaching at an Ivy League graduate school, a woman in the audience shrieked because her toddler had picked up a sharp instrument and was about to put it in his mouth. After quickly taking the sharp tool away the mother started to lecture him.

After the wave of concern in the room died down, I pointed out that toddlers are in the sensation stage of cognitive development: they learn through their senses. Taking the object away from her child was the right thing to do, but lecturing the toddler would have no effect because the toddler was not at a stage of development where he could understand the logic of her arguments. Thus, I noted, toddlers have to be protected by their parents and cannot be expected to make wise decisions when they are presented with dangerous situations.

When you pass from one stage of development to another, you tend to forget what the previous stage was like. When my six-year-old son, Robby, was frightened by a thunderstorm, my eleven-year-old, Peirce, tried to get his younger brother to be quiet by telling him to "shut up." When this compassionate request didn't work, Peirce told Robby that the reason for the thunderstorm was that God was angry at him. Of course, this only aggravated Robby's fears. I pointed out to Peirce that Robby was affected by the storm very differently than he was because Robby was in the imagination stage of development—his imagination was predominant and he was less able to sort out the difference between fact and fiction.

I reminded Peirce about the time he had a friend stay overnight when he was nine years old, and the friend had nightmares all night long. The next morning I asked the young boy what was bothering him, and he said that his father had taken him to see the R-rated movie *Total Recall*, an extremely violent movie. The boy said that he didn't like the scene where Arnold Schwarzenegger shoots Sharon Stone, who is posing as his wife, and says, "Consider that a divorce." When I called his father to tell him of the fears expressed by his son, he replied that his son was a man and that he took his son to a lot of R-rated movies. I noted that his son was in the imagination stage of cognitive development and was incapable of dealing with the violence in many R-rated movies. I said that taking him to see these films was like putting him on the front line of psychological and spiritual warfare just like sending children into battle without adequate training and before they are big enough to carry their weapons. Three months later the father called to say that I was right and that he could see that his son was disturbed by the movies to which he had taken him.

FIVE SEASONS

To understand why children are affected by the mass media, we need first to understand cognitive development itself. In the late 1970s, building on the research of the renowned child psychologist Jean Piaget,[1] television researcher Robert Morse[2] adapted Piaget's stages of cognitive growth so that they can be more effectively applied to research concerning the mass media.

Each stage represents a growing differentiation between the person and the object. At the youngest stages a child assumes that he is the center of the universe, and sees everything as an extension of himself. The saying "out of sight, out of mind" takes on a very concrete meaning with respect to the baby. When something is removed from his field of vision, he will act as if that something no longer exists. As we mature, however, we begin to see things not as projections of ourselves, but as distinct and different, and we act differently toward them.

Every child goes through the following stages:

The sensation stage[3] (approximately infant to age two): The child's sole means of processing reality is his or her senses. Children at this stage think that they are the center of the universe—that something exists only if they can see it, and that everything around them serves them.

The imagination stage[4] (approximately ages two to seven years old): The child's cognition is dedicated to the acquisition of representational skills such as language, mental imagery, drawing, and symbolic play. It is limited by being serial and one-dimensional. During this stage the child has a very active imagination, often confusing fact and fiction.

The concrete operational stage (approximately ages seven to eleven years old): The child acquires the ability of simultaneous perception of two points of view, enabling him or her to master quantities, relations, and classes of objects. At this stage there is a strong correspondence between the child's thoughts and reality. He or she assumes that his or her thoughts about reality are accurate, and distorts facts to fit what he or she thinks.

The reflection or formal operations stage (approximately ages twelve to fifteen years old): Abstract thought gains strength. In this stage there is still incomplete differentiation as a result of the adolescent's inability to conceptualize the thoughts of others, as exemplified by the assumption that other people are as obsessed with his or her behavior and appearance as he or she is. For example, if he has a pimple and walks into a room filled with friends, he will usually think that everyone is looking at his pimple. In this stage, the adolescent still has difficulty conceptualizing the consequences of his actions. He or she will therefore often take risks without regard to the consequences.

The relationship stage: The adolescent grows into a mature adult; there is complete differentiation. At this stage the individual understands that others are different and accepts those differences by learning to relate to others. Furthermore, the individual is able to conceptualize the consequences of his or her actions and take the necessary steps to reduce the risks.

BABES IN TOYLAND

Research has confirmed these stages and shown that younger children are less able to integrate pieces of information or narration from stories and then draw inferences from such information.[5] Younger children react to direct violence but not to suspense. Children in the concrete stage of cognitive development are more upset by suspense than direct violence. Thus, little children will get bored by a movie such as *Jaws*, which is mostly suspense, while older children may be traumatized by it.

During the imagination stage, when children have trouble distinguishing between fact and fiction, children are uniquely susceptible to what they see on television and in movies.

THE PROGRAM

Teenagers in the reflection stage of development often have difficulty thinking about the consequences of their actions and are more vulnerable to the influence of movies and television programs than mature adults. In fact, research has shown that teenagers are physiologically limited in their ability to focus on the consequences of their actions. Perhaps this is why teenagers are willing to take such great risks. When the movie *The Program* was released, several teenagers mimicked the main characters by lying down in the middle of the road to prove their courage. Some of these teenagers were seriously injured and some were killed.

One national radio personality commented that these teenagers were really "stupid." However, one of the teenagers that died was at the top of his class. What the radio personality did not understand is that these teenagers were in a stage of development when they were the most impulsive and the least able to consider the consequences of their actions. Like most of us, the radio personality didn't remember what it was like to be in a previous stage of cognitive development.

The borders between these stages depend on the child. Some children never mature beyond an early stage of cognitive development. These children and adults may be very smart in some ways while cognitively immature, like Raymond in *Rainman*. Furthermore, there may be incomplete development or advanced development. However the vast majority of children will fit within the norm.

FROM PSYCHO TO SEVEN

Research shows that children in the imagination stage of cognitive development are more frightened by different types of stimuli and events than are older children.[6] Researchers Barbara J. Wilson, Daniel Lynn, and Barbara Randall have examined the harmful effects of graphic horror on children and discovered the following important distinctions:[7]

Visual versus non-visual threat: The principle of perceptual dependence suggests that younger children are likely to be frightened by films with visually frightening creatures like witches and monsters. Older children will focus more on conceptual qualities, such as the motives of a character,[8] and are likely to be more upset by an evil, normal-looking character or by an unseen threat than by a benign but grotesque character. *The Wizard of Oz* is more frightening for younger children than for older children; while older children are more frightened by movies such as *Poltergeist* and *Jaws*, which rely more on non-visual threats.

Reality versus fantasy: Younger children are unable to fully distinguish between reality and fantasy.[9] Although the terms "real" and "make-believe" may be used in conversation, younger children do not understand the implications of these terms. The notion that a character or an event is "not real" has little impact on a younger child's emotions. Therefore, fantasy offerings involving events that could not possibly happen are more frightening to younger children, whereas fictional programs involving events that could happen are more frightening to older children.[10]

Abstract versus concrete events: A concrete threat is explicit and tangible. For example, an evil character might attack a victim. In contrast, abstract threats must be inferred from information in the plot. Examples might include movies about evil conspiracies, or disasters such as poisonous gases. Younger children have difficulty drawing inferences from entertainment and are more likely to focus on explicit rather than implicit cues in the plot.[11] They will be more frightened by a movie depicting a concrete threat than by one involving an intangible or obscure hazard.

Threat versus victim focus: Also, cognitive stages are distinguished by the degree to which the scenes concentrate on the actual threat versus the victim's emotional reactions to the threat. Movies that require viewer involvement and focus primarily on the victims' emotional reactions are less upsetting for younger children than for older children. *Jaws* is a good example because the viewer often sees only the upper bodies of the victims as they are attacked by the unseen shark.

Children experience fear reactions to horror entertainment, and exposure to large amounts of violence can produce either desensitization or imitation. Since all human beings want to cope with the problems they face, the child may try to immerse him- or herself in the problem (horror movie, violence, or whatever) so he or she can come up with a solution. This immersion in unpleasant media is a form of cognitive dissonance reduction.

More important than the sheer amount of mass media horror and violence children watch is the way in which even small amounts of violence are portrayed.[12] Therefore, as Comstock and Paik have found, "a number of contextual features of violence are critical determinants of whether such depictions will facilitate aggressive behavior."[13] According to Wilson, Lynn, and Randall, these contextual features include

Reward versus punishment associated with violence: Violent depictions for which the aggressor is rewarded are most likely to produce imitation effects or foster attitudes supportive of aggression.[14] Characters need not be explicitly rewarded for such effects to occur. As long as there is no punishment associated with a violent act, young viewers will often imitate such depictions.[15] The lack of punishment is a reward for such behavior. Much media violence is portrayed without negative consequences; neither perpetrators nor victims suffer much, and the perpetrator is often rewarded for antisocial actions.[16]

The timing of the reward or punishment has important developmental implications.[17] In many movies, the perpetrator receives material rewards immediately after performing an aggressive act. Punishment, however, is typically delivered toward the end of the movie. Since younger children are less able than older children to coherently link scenes together and draw inferences from them,[18] younger children are more likely than older children to perceive the violence as acceptable and to imitate such behavior when rewards are immediate and punishment is delayed in a movie.

The degree of reality of violence: Violence perceived to be realistic is more likely to be imitated and used as a guide for behavior.[19] Older children are better able to distinguish reality from fantasy and are more emotionally responsive to programs that depict realistic events. Thus, older children are affected more by violent movies that feature events that are humanly possible. Younger children are responsive to both realistic and unrealistic violence as long as the acts are concrete and visual.

The nature of the perpetrator: Children are more likely to imitate models who are perceived as attractive or interesting.[20] Children who strongly identify with violent media characters are more likely to be aggressive themselves than are those who do not identify with such characters.[21]

Younger children are more likely to focus on the consequences of a character's behavior in determining whether the character is "good" or "bad," whereas older children focus more on the character's motives.[22] Such age differences are presumably due to the fact that motives are typically presented early in a plot so that the viewer must be able to draw inferences in order to link them to subsequent behaviors. Therefore, younger children will be more likely to emulate bad characters as long as they are rewarded, whereas older children presumably will be cognizant of the characters' motives in selecting role models.

Justified violence: Violence that is portrayed as justified is more likely to be imitated.[23] A common theme in many movies is the portrayal of a hero who is forced to be violent because his job demands it (e.g., *Dirty Harry*) or because he must retaliate against an enemy (e.g., *Rambo*). Although the message may be ultimately prosocial (e.g., "don't be a criminal"), the moral is conveyed in a violent context.

In one experiment examining "mixed messages,"[24] children viewed either a purely prosocial cartoon or a cartoon that contained a prosocial message delivered through justified violence. Kindergartners were more likely to hurt than to help a peer after watching the prosocial-aggressive cartoon. Moreover, both younger and older children showed less understanding of the moral lesson when it was conveyed in the context of violence versus no violence. A hero who commits violence for some "good" cause is likely to be a confusing and negative role model for both younger and older children.

Similarity of movie situations and characters to viewer: Viewers are more likely to imitate media violence if cues in the program are similar to those in real life.[25] Also, children are likely to imitate models who are similar to themselves.[26] Thus, movies depicting children as violent are more problematic than those involving violent adults. Preschool and early elementary school children focus on younger characters who are violent, whereas preteens and teenagers attend more to aggressive teenage characters.

Amount of violence: Although the way in which violence is portrayed is more critical than the amount of violence in facilitating aggressive behavior, the sheer amount and explicitness of the violent content is important with regard to the viewer's emotions. Excessive exposure to violence may produce a "psychological blunting" of normal emotional responses to violent events. Children who are heavy viewers of television violence show less physiological arousal to a clip of filmed violence than light viewers.

In one experiment, children who watched a violent film were subsequently less likely to seek help when the other children became disruptive and violent. Thus, exposure to media violence leads to a lack of responsiveness to real-life aggression.[27]

DANGEROUS MINDS

Television researcher Robert Morse has found that the very medium of television, apart from the content of what is being shown and communicated (such as the perverse sex and violence that is the subject of so much research), can cause severe cognitive problems when viewed in excess.[28] Morse notes that the medium of television is effective at converting (e.g., from one product to another or one point of view to another), motivating (e.g., to buy a product that you may not need), and informing (e.g., the news).[29] The result is that many viewers can be converted from one product to another and even from one political candidate to another, as evidenced by the voter swings after the Carter-Reagan and Bush-Clinton television debates.[30] Many viewers are influenced to look at the world in the way television does, since their information about the world is filtered through the unique nature of the television medium. Morse has found that television is very effective at transmitting emotions and concrete physical information or facts to the viewer, but he also found that it is deficient in promoting or affecting cognitive growth.[31] Cognitive growth is the process by which we come to understand something so well that we set up structures to use that thing which we now know and the structure we have developed to think and reason. For example, a baby can look at a door and learn to call it a door without understanding what it is. Only after the child plays with the door, opening and closing it, will the child come to know what a door is and experience cognitive growth.

Through exhaustive testing, the producers of *Sesame Street* found that the children who watched *Sesame Street* would often acquire words from the program that they could repeat but did not understand; they were unable to use those words correctly or to use them in reasoning. Perhaps this problem arose because *Sesame Street* used a "distracter machine" with a test audience to insure that viewers' minds did not wander from the program. Researchers would watch the test audience to see when they looked away from the *Sesame Street* program at the distracter machine. At those points in the program where the test audience was distracted, the producers inserted a technical effect such as a pan, fade, camera move, or dissolve, or an action to hold the attention of the audience. Thus, the producers guaranteed that there was no time to stop, review, react, dialogue, and concentrate.

Thus, television is extremely effective at propelling powerful emotional images into the viewer's mind in real time, with no time for the viewer to reflect, react, or review the information he or she is receiving—processes absolutely necessary for cognitive development.

The very act of watching is harmful to the cognitive development of children and, as a consequence, adversely influences their moral, social, emotional, and religious development. Television also "debilitates an important cognitive function in adults, the one that permits abstract reasoning—and hence related capacities for moral decision making, learning, religious growth, and psychological individualization."[32] At the same time as television inhibits cognitive growth, research shows that children "habituate" to repetitive light-stimuli (flickering light, dot patterns, limited eye movement). When habituation occurs, the brain decides that there is nothing of interest going on—at least nothing that anything can be done about—and virtually quits processing information. In particular, the left brain "common internegative area" goes into a kind of holding pattern, and television viewing reaches the level of somnambulism, similar to being hypnotized.[33] In these ways excessive television watching can be harmful apart from the content.

THE TWILIGHT ZONE

Children who are heavy users of television demonstrate a decreased capacity for creative imagination, concentration, and delayed gratification. With regard to imagination, they are less able to form "mental pictures," and they engage in less "imaginative play." With regard to concentration, children become "lazy readers" of "non-books" with greatly decreased attention spans (you have to exercise concentration or it atrophies). With regard to delayed gratification, the children have less tolerance for getting into a book or other activities.

The symbolic function, perception, and abstract reasoning capacities are damaged in a manner that resembles dyslexia. The rapid increase in reading disabilities, or dyslexia, in the United States may in part be attributed to heavy television viewing. Television inhibits eye movement and thereby the acquisition of reading skills.

With respect to adults, Morse reports that television saps the cognitive strength, analogous to the situation in nursing homes where inactivity leads to cognitive impairment. After an hour or two of television watching, people come away cranky, irritable, tired, and reactive.[34]

DUMB AND DUMBER

By posing the right question, John Rosemond helps us to understand Morse's findings with regard to children:

> The next time your child watches television, look at him instead of the screen. Ask yourself, "What is he doing?" Better yet, since the chances are he won't be doing much of anything, ask yourself, "What is he not doing?"
>
> He is not . . .

- scanning.
- practicing motor skills, gross or fine.
- practicing eye-hand coordination.
- using more than two senses.
- asking questions.
- exploring.
- exercising initiative or imagination.
- being challenged.
- solving problems.
- thinking analytically.
- exercising imagination.
- practicing communication skills.
- being either creative or constructive.

> Also, because of television's insidious "flicker," (every four seconds, on the average, the picture changes) television does not promote long-term attention.
>
> Lastly, because the action shifts constantly and capriciously backward, forward and laterally in time . . . television does not promote logical sequential thinking.
>
> So what? Interestingly, the deficiencies noted above are characteristic of learning-disabled children—children who don't seem able to "get it all together" when it comes to learning how to read and write.[35]

THE DUMBING DOWN OF AMERICA

In its first international assessment of educational progress, the Educational Testing Service of Princeton, New Jersey, tested students from six countries on the effects of television.[36] The results were shocking. The more students watch television, the lower their academic performance. Thirteen-year-olds in the U.S. watch TV the most and rank last in mathematics and near the bottom in science. South Korean students outperform all others academically and by wide margins in mathematics. They watch television less and do more homework than their counterparts in the U.S. Students in Canada, Spain, the United Kingdom, and Ireland watch more television than the South Korean students and less than the American students.

A ten-year study of more than one thousand children from inner-city Manchester, England, showed that infants who were exposed to too much television experienced severe speech and language difficulties.[37] These children were unable to understand their own names, the names of their family members, or of simple objects. By age three, they spoke like two-year-olds. Dr. Sally Ward, author of the study, warned that parents who let the television babysit their children may be unwittingly damaging their infants' communication skills.

Especially vulnerable to excessive exposure to television is the skill of "mapping"—pointing at an object and following the child's focus of attention as he pronounces the word. This skill is crucial for teaching speech. Children who focus on the visual effects of television are unable to focus on anything else. Ward cautions that infants under one year old should be exposed to no television, while preschoolers should be limited to one hour a day.[38]

DR. SPOCK

If you ask children if they would rather have spinach or ice cream, they will ask for ice cream. If you ask them if they want to go to school or stay home and play, they will choose to stay home and play.

This seemed absurdly obvious until *USA Today* started a column with young adolescents reviewing movies—some unsuitable for the ages of the reviewers. When I wrote a letter to the paper about this problem, they replied that these children like to watch these movies.

A comprehensive study found that teenagers prefer to learn by (1) movies, (2) music, and (3) videos—in that order.[39] Please note that teachers didn't even rate consideration. The question is: Do we want to educate our children or pander to their entertainment choices?

HONEY, I SHRUNK THE KIDS

By contributing to cognitive impairment, television has a deleterious effect on a child's moral, social, emotional, and religious development.[40] With regard to social and emotional development, a child needs dramatic play to develop in these areas, but dramatic play, as we have noticed, is inhibited by television. Watching social interaction on television is not enough because a child must do or act, not just observe, or there will be impairment of social and emotional development.

In the case of psychological maturation, the necessary function of suppressing detrimental functions of the libido is impaired, since television (and the other mass media) indulge these detrimental functions.

With regard to religious development, impairment of the symbolic function results in the "clogging of the filters of religious perception," so that the child's doorway to experience of the transcendent is blocked.[41] Television watching causes the viewer to see reality or the nature of being (ontology) as illusory or nominalistic, whereas Christianity is posited on a real ontology or nature of being because God created a real world in which real events occur independent of our consciousness and our imaginations. Therefore, television inhibits a Christian ontology and worldview.

COMING OF AGE

Looking at the stages of cognitive development with respect to the major religious systems, there are some interesting analogies.

In the first *sensation* period, there is no differentiation between the child and the object. The child is basically solipsistic. She acts as if she is not only the center of the universe but also as if nothing exists unless she is aware of it. This stage is very similar to monism and any of the monistic religious systems, such as some forms of Buddhism, Hinduism, and New Age beliefs, where all is one and all is consciousness.

The child in this stage is a god, demanding and thinking that the world is ordered according to his whim. Others are merely there to serve him. Many people can recall a state of mind where they thought that they were the universe or all was within their mind. Drugs and Eastern meditation can induce this state. (Most Eastern meditation focuses inward, whereas Christian meditation focuses outward on God and on his Word.) Also, by retarding cognitive development, television can induce this solipsistic state and inhibit the cognitive growth into a more mature stage.

In the *imagination* stage there is some differentiation, though the child has difficulty distinguishing between fantasy and reality and assumes that every-thing is sentient and conscious. The child will often attribute anthropomorphic or human thoughts to the dog or cat, and the child will get totally caught up in fantasy when playing pretend games, even to the point of temper tantrums.

This stage recalls polytheistic religious systems, such as animism, some forms of Hinduism, spiritism, and most New Age beliefs that attribute consciousness to everything and assume that everything is sentient. Much of the mass media can also induce this stage of cognitive development. Many movies, television programs, and other entertainment media overtly promote polytheism. Horror movies and children's films based on magical thinking are particularly prone to polytheistic and nominalistic worldviews.

In the *concrete* stage the child acquires the ability of simultaneous perception of two points of view so that he or she can master quantities, relations, and classes of objects. At this stage there is such a strong correspondence between the child's thoughts and reality, she assumes that her thoughts about reality are accurate and distorts the facts to fit what she thinks. This tends to be a more materialistic period, where things take on value, especially money, and peer pressure is great. Children in this stage stop assuming that everyone thinks as they do, and start worrying that they are too different. To compensate, they form peer groups, cliques, and even gangs. This stage is similar to any of the materialistic religions or political systems, such as socialism and Marxism, where friends and even gangs protect the individual from the now differentiated world. Since material things mean so much, power is used to get what the child wants, as contrasted with his wishing for what he wants in the earlier, more nominalistic stages. In using power, espe-cially in gangs, children can be very cruel during this period.

In the *reflection* or *formal operations* stage, abstract thought gains strength and the person learns to accept the fact that others are different. The child in this stage moves away from power to get what he or she wants toward legalism. He or she will enforce rules, claim rights, and judge others to protect, promote, and establish him- or herself. This stage is similar to the legalistic theistic religions, such as Islam, where a person begins to understand the other, including the ultimate "other" who is God, but does not have a relationship of love and trust with the other. In the name of "the other," the child will take great risks.

In the *relationship* stage the adolescent grows into complete differentiation. The person understands that others are different, accepts those differences, and learns to relate to and even love others. Relationships gain predominance over possessions in this stage of cognitive development. Clearly, this stage is similar to the relationship with God in grace-oriented, theistic Christianity. The person in this stage learns to love God and others and begins to understand the love of God as manifest in Jesus Christ.

CLUES

Observational learning theory suggests that children imitate modeled behavior.[42] Researchers have found that when a young viewer watches a violent television episode, he will store that behavior in his brain. Later in his life, when a situation arises similar to what he watched on television, the viewer may retrieve and mimic the violent act once viewed.

Dr. Victor Cline reports that the more intelligent and imaginative the viewer is, the more susceptible he or she is to mimicking and becoming addicted to the viewed behavior. Cline found the vast majority of criminals behind bars for sexual crimes are intelligent—as was Ted Bundy. In the last interview before his execution, serial killer Bundy described in detail to Dr. James Dobson the stages of addiction that he experienced to become a killer, starting with an attraction to 1950's soft-core pornography, material that was much milder than what is being shown in most movies and television programs today.

Attitude-change theory suggests that when some children watch a great deal of violent television these children develop a favorable attitude toward aggressive behavior and come to see violent behavior as normal and even acceptable.[43] This research also found that other children are anesthetized or desensitized by the same overloading process.

VIRTUAL SOCIOPATHS

Another area of research on the influence of the mass media on children and adults is false memory syndrome, unchained memories, memory therapy, and associated psychological insights that have captured the national imagination.

One area of life that most likely contributes to the false memory syndrome is the tremendous amount of movie and television sex, violence, and occultism that has filled the minds of youth over the years. Nefarious films and other mass media have planted images in the minds of our youth that they have processed in the same manner as the daily activities in which they engage. However, unlike the many daily activities which are repetitive and dull, most of these entertaining movies and television programs are a potent and often cognitively dissonant, if not traumatic, brew of emotive visual and audile messages that lodge in the nooks and crannies of the child's memory, waiting to invade their dreams and consciousness.

Recent research indicates that the minds of our youth are overflowing with movies and television programs that they confuse with reality and history. Everyday examples abound, from the woman who saw the movie *Independence Day* and afterwards told a reporter that she believes the government is hiding a flying saucer, to those who saw the movie *The Wind and the Lion* and assume that this historical incident involved a beautiful woman and a dashing desert chieftain, rather than the real characters—an old Greek immigrant and a Moroccan thief.

Memory therapists have been able to induce adults to fabricate a childhood history from disjointed memories. Regrettably, some of these adults have acted upon these false memories.

Whether they are from a therapist or the mass media, these false memories interfere with cognitive development, reasoning, and common sense. The individuals who are confused by these false memories, just as a computer is confused by viruses, may develop psychoses and neuroses and attribute those symptoms to child abuse, or even lifelong tendencies. Regrettably, these individuals could become tomorrow's deviants, killers, rapists, or Ted Bundys.

Worse, a large portion of society could be suffering from the false memories planted by the thousands of hours of entertainment most people watch. As noted, by the time they are seventeen years old, most children have viewed at least 200,000 to 400,000 sexual acts, from touching to kissing to fornication; 100,000 to 200,000 acts of violence; and 17,000 to 33,000 murders. All this and more is lodged in their memory as part of the fabric of their daily life. How many confuse their memories of fact and fantasy is open to question, but almost everyone has a story of some young person whose view of recent history was not based on facts but on a television or movie revision of those facts.

Walter Reich, in his article "The Monster in the Mists," sadly points out:

> The institution of memory deserves all the respect and protection it can get. One indication of how vulnerable to manipulation it already is can be appreciated from the fact that holocaust deniers have managed to receive, in recent years, a respectful hearing on college campuses and elsewhere, despite the existence of mountains of first-hand and traumatic memories of the holocaust provided by many thousands of survivors—memories that don't have to be recovered because they are all too vividly, and all to persistently, remembered.[44]

Perhaps we have moved from George Santayana's insight that "Those who do not remember the past are condemned to relive it," to a more terrifying social condition: those who confuse the past with false memories are condemned to live out those false memories in reality. Perhaps our biggest problem is the false memories that are giving our society cultural Alzheimer's. In the end "a man's memory is all that stands in the way of chaos."[45]

RUSH

Watching fighting or other violence can make the mind believe that it is about to engage in life-threatening activity. The body will often respond by releasing adrenal epinephrine into the bloodstream, giving the viewer an adrenal rush without the threat of actual violence. Watching sexual activity and nudity makes the mind think that the person is about to mate, so the body releases hormones that can often cause an addictive adrenal rush without the psychological burdens attendant to most human relationships. These physiological phenomena will engage and attract the viewer, often causing him or her to want more and more exposure to the stimuli that cause such artificial physical stimulation.

Psychologist James L. McGaugh posits that memories of experiences that occur at times of emotional arousal are locked into the brain by the chemical epinephrine and are difficult to erase.[46] This research may partly explain pornography's addictive effects. As Dr. Victor Cline notes, "Powerful sexually arousing memories of experiences from the past keep intruding themselves back on the mind's memory screen, serving to stimulate and erotically arouse the viewer. If he masturbates to these fantasies he reinforces the linkage between sexual arousal and orgasm, with the particular scene repeatedly rehearsed on his memory screen.[47] So conditioned, the susceptible viewer may seek to aggressively act out these images in his own life to fulfill his desire to experience the release that comes with arousal.[48] Scientists have discovered that mass media violence leads to aggressive behavior by overstimulating children. The more intense and realistic the violent scene, the more likely it is to be encoded, stored in the memory, and later retrieved as model behavior.

Another study showed that boys who watch a great deal of violent programming may exhibit less physiological arousal when shown new violent programs than do boys who regularly watch less violent fare.[49] This study seems to explain why consumers of mass media sex and violence need more and more prurient fare or more and more violent fare. Of course, all of this can add up to addiction (best summed up by the phrase the "plug-in drug" as applied to television) because most of the offerings of the mass media are emotive, not intellectual, pursuits.

The impact of excessive movie and television sex and violence on teenagers is aggravated by the fact that their raging hormones give them a predisposition to seek arousal. They are subject to tremendous peer and media pressure at an age when fitting in with their peers is extremely important, even if fitting in means rebelling against their parents. They have a predisposition to seek out movies and programs that arouse them. Some are so aroused they seek to replicate the emotive sexual or violent situations portrayed in the movie or television program in their own lives.

HOLLYWOOD IDOLS

In her book *Soft Porn Plays Hardball*, Dr. Judith A. Reisman writes that in 1948 there was an "incident of impotence of only 0.4% of the males under 25, and less than 1% of the males under 35 years of age."[50] By 1970 almost all of the male population "experienced impotence at some time, and chronic or repeated impotence probably affects about 30 to 40% of men at any given time."[51] The research of Dr. Reisman and others demonstrates that much of this impotence is due to the increase in pornography in the mainstream mass media, which makes males dependent on visualizing pornographic images in order to make love to their wives. In other words, they are engaged in autoeroticism, not in a relationship with their wives.

One pastor insisted that he didn't believe that pornography was bad and that he and his wife always used pornography to make love. Several years later, he declared himself to be a homosexual. It is clear that the pornography corrupted his sexual cognition and drove him further and further into autoeroticism.

At a church where I once preached, the pastor told me that his married daughter had received a *Victoria's Secret* catalog in the mail and had left it on her bed. When she came back to her room, she saw her five-year-old son staring at the pictures in the catalog of seminude women. After a while the boy looked up at his mother and exclaimed, "I want a mommy like that." She immediately understood that her boy had been attracted to an image that was nothing like her and had replaced her as the ideal with an image. To a degree he had even transferred his love for her to an idol.

DEEPEST FEELINGS AND ULTIMATE CONCERNS

The mass media influence not only our behavior but also our beliefs. Therefore it is important to realize that religion is alive and well in the mass media—though it is not the predominantly Christian faith of our founding fathers. It is, instead, a cacophony of ill-conceived religions such as materialism, consumerism, eroticism, hedonism, naturalism, humanism, cynicism, stoicism, the cult of violence (that used to pay homage to the war-god Mars), and a multitude of other modern variations on pagan practices that now vie for renewed homage in the mass media.

These religions, many of which can trace their roots back to long discredited ancient cults, have their rituals, beliefs, values, signs, metaphysics, cosmologies, ontologies, epistemologies, and ultimate meanings played out in programs, commercials, and movies with ritualistic regularity. On any given night on prime-time television, we may find happy Buddhist monks hawking athletic gear, or Hollywood stars touting the virtues of astrology.

Of course, materialists might quibble that their beliefs exclude anything but the natural, and Buddhists might intone that they are nontheistic. But as philosopher Ludwig Feuerbach has observed, even "atheism ... is the secret of religion itself; [in] that religion itself, not indeed on the surface, but fundamentally, not in intention or according to its own supposition, but in its heart, in its essence, believes in nothing else than the truth and divinity of human nature."[52] Feuerbach's contention grasps the essence of many anthropocentric (man-centered) religions. For some in the dream world of the entertainment media, "sex is the mysticism of materialism and the only possible religion in a materialistic society," as the prominent British broadcaster Malcolm Muggeridge has incisively observed.[53] For others, harking back to the rituals of ancient cultures of the Mediterranean with their temples of sport, "modern bodybuilding is ritual, religion, sport, art, and science, awash in Western chemistry and mathematics. Defying nature, it surpasses it."[54]

For millions, in a manner not too dissimilar from pagan sacrifices, novelist E. L. Doctorow's words are apropos: "Murders are exciting and lift people into a heart-beating awe as religion is supposed to do, after seeing one in the street, ... people will cross themselves and thank God for the gift of their stuporous lives, old folks will talk to each other over cups of hot water with lemon, because murders are enlivened sermons to be analyzed and considered and relished, they speak to the timid of the dangers of rebellion."[55] Theologian Paul Tillich noted that "your god is that reality which elicits from you your deepest feelings and ultimate concerns," and "religion is the state of being grasped by an ultimate concern, a concern which qualifies all other concerns as preliminary and which itself contains the answer to the question of a meaning of our life."[56] British playwright J. M. Barrie summarizes that "one's religion is whatever he is most interested in."[57] The Internet, computer games, prime-time entertainment television, movies, and popular music have become a religion for too many, especially some of those employed in the entertainment industry.

SPIRITUAL WARFARE

The cognitive/psychological and physiological influence of the mass media has a spiritual impact. The images of the mass media that tug at our desires, seduce our thoughts, and lodge in our memories are the demons of our age. They claw at our consciousness and entice us to do things we would not otherwise do—whether to buy a product we don't need, or worse.

Just as the sovereign Lord uses films such as *Chariots of Fire* and *Ben Hur* to bring people to Jesus Christ, the adversary is using the mass media to inflame the lust of our eyes and the lust of our flesh because he wants us to worship him, or if not him, then ourselves or the creation or even the media itself—anything other than our Creator.

As the prophet Isaiah noted with such prescience in discussing the foolishness of worshiping the idols of his age: "No one stops to think, no one has the knowledge or understanding to say, '. . . Shall I bow down to a block of wood?' He feeds on ashes, a deluded heart misleads him; he cannot save himself, or say, 'Is not this thing in my right hand a lie?'" (Isaiah 44:19–20). Of course, Isaiah is talking about the little household idols of wood, but he could be talking about the TV remote control or the mouse used to peruse the Internet.

We often forget there is a war raging around us. It is a war being waged inside our minds, a spiritual war for our souls. The adversary is using every possible tactic to control our minds: materialism, secularism, humanism, and all the other "isms" that conflict with Christianity. He is using the most effective weapons to win: the power of the mass media of entertainment. Through corrupt movies and television programs of our age, the adversary is fueling our sinful propensity to lust and hooking us on our desires. Once hooked, he drags us down to hell.

VIRTUAL ABUSE

Many parents play an unconscious role in this tragedy by taking children to unacceptable movies or by allowing them to watch unacceptable movies and television programs at home. These parents forget that if a child is being entertained, then his or her real needs are seldom discerned. These children need attention—not entertainment.

Those who say that children must be exposed to the "reality" of the entertainment media ignore the susceptibility of children, the ability of human beings to learn from secondary sources, and the unreal nature of the mass media. While animals learn from experiencing primary sources, humans can learn from secondary sources. An animal has to stick its foot in a trap to know what a trap is, but a human being can learn what a trap is from another person, a book, or another secondary source. Thus, a person does not have to commit murder to know that murder is wrong, nor adultery to know that adultery is wrong. In fact, one does not have to watch a murder to know that murder is wrong. Those who say that one has to experience something to know if it is right or wrong do not understand how human beings learn, and they are inadvertently dumbing down our youth. If every child had to learn everything experientially, knowledge and civilization would never progress.

TRUTH OR CONSEQUENCES

Since 1966 (the year the church abandoned Hollywood), violent crime has increased in the United States of America by 560 percent; illegitimate births have increased by 419 percent; divorces rates have quadrupled; the percentage of children living in single-parent homes has tripled; the teenage suicide rate has increased by more than 300 percent; and SAT scores have dropped almost 80 points. Rapes, murders, and gang violence have become common occurrences. While many factors have contributed to our cultural decline, it is clear that the mass media have had a significant influence on behavior.[58] A report by the Washington, D.C.-based Children's Defense Fund[59] states that every day in the United States

- 2,781 teenage girls get pregnant (an increase of about 500 percent since 1966),
- 1,115 teenage girls have abortions (an increase of about 1,100 percent since 1966),
- 1,295 teenage girls give birth,
- 2,556 children are born out of wedlock,
- 4,219 teenagers contract a sexually transmitted disease (an increase of about 335 percent since 1966),
- 5,314 teenagers are arrested, and
- 135,000 children bring a gun to school.

In 1993 researchers affiliated with the National Bureau of Economic Research and Stanford University reported in the journal *Science*[60] that America's children are fatter, more suicidal, more murderous, and scored lower on standardized tests in recent years than in the 1960s.

More shocking is the fact that 98 percent of the American public was literate in 1900, while today only 60 percent of all Americans are functionally literate.

The biblical foundations of our society are cracking. Disaster looms in front of us. Yet, in spite of the clear correlation between violence in the mass media and violence on the street, very few people are shouting "Stop!" The growing American tolerance for brutal sex and violence in the mass media suggests the proverbial frog who calmly dies as he is slowly brought to a boil; whereas the frog dropped into a boiling pot jumps out.

DELIVERANCE

Protection from powerful negative spirits begins with the awareness of the subtle effect that other individuals, groups, and even the media often exert on us. Following such awareness, we need to recognize that God wants to and will deliver us from the demons of our age:

> *As for you, you were dead in your transgressions and sins, in which you used to live when you followed the ways of this world and of the ruler of the kingdom of the air, the spirit who is now at work in those who are disobedient. All of us also lived among them at one time, gratifying the cravings of our sinful nature and following its desires and thoughts. Like the rest, we were by nature objects of wrath. But because of his great love for us, God, who is rich in mercy, made us alive with Christ even when we were dead in transgressions—it is by grace you have been saved. And God raised us up with Christ and seated us with him in the heavenly realms in Christ Jesus, in order that in the coming ages he might show the incomparable riches of his grace, expressed in his kindness to us in Christ Jesus. For it is by grace you have been saved, through faith—and this not from yourselves, it is the gift of God—not by works, so that no one can boast. For we are God's workmanship, created in Christ Jesus to do good works, which God prepared in advance for us to do.*
>
> *—Ephesians 2:1–10*

Once he has saved us from the spirits of our age, we need to walk in the Spirit of God and renew our minds according to the Bible. As Paul states in his letter to the Romans, "I beseech you therefore, brethren, by the mercies of God, that ye present your bodies a living sacrifice, holy, acceptable unto God, which is your reasonable service. And be not conformed to this world: but be ye transformed by the renewing of your mind, that ye may prove what is that good, and acceptable, and perfect, will of God" (12:1–2 KJV).

In addition, if we discover compromise in our lives, we need to repent, turn away from it, and seek the Lord with all our hearts. We also need to break off any associations not of God and renounce any ungodly spirits. Then we must avoid any further spiritual oppression by staying in the Word of God daily, walking in the Spirit of God, and using the spiritual armor God has given us through Jesus Christ. Thus we can enjoy the provision Christ has made for us to walk in him and not give way to the evil that surrounds us, for "greater is he that is in you than he that is in the world" (1 John 4:4 KJV).

In all of this, it is important to remember that God is sovereign: We are more than conquerors in Jesus Christ, and God gives us the victory. This is the essence of the Good News, that we need not despair and can rest and rejoice in him. "Rejoice in the Lord always. I will say it again: Rejoice! Let your gentleness be evident to all. The Lord is near. Do not be anxious about anything, but in everything, by prayer and petition, with thanksgiving, present your requests to God. And the peace of God, which transcends all understanding, will guard your hearts and your minds in Christ Jesus" (Philippians 4:4–7).

The magnificent glory of God's loving grace, which we meet in Jesus Christ, is magnified when we perceive the harsh reality of the judgment that awaits those who reject Jesus as Lord and Savior. Delivered from the judgment they deserve, those who know his salvation cannot keep on sinning, for "No one who continues to sin has either seen him or known him" (1 John 3:6).

NOTES

1. See Jean Piaget, *The Origins of Intelligence in Children*, trans. Margaret Cook (New York: Norton, 1963), and David Elkind, *Children and Adolescents: Interpretive Essays on Jean Piaget* (New York: Oxford University Press, 1970).
2. Ted Baehr, *The Media-Wise Famly* (Colorado Springs: Chariot Victor, 1998), 115–17.
3. Piaget called this the "sensorimotor period."
4. Piaget called this the "preoperational period."
5. Barbara J. Wilson, Daniel Lynn, and Barbara Randall, "Applying Social Science Research to Film Ratings: A Shift from Offensiveness to Harmful Effects," *Journal of Broadcasting and Electronic Media* 34, no. 4 (Fall 1990): 443–68, citing C. R. Schmidt, S. R. Schmidt, and S. M. Tomalis, "Children's Constructive Processing and Monitoring of Stories Containing Anomalous Information," *Child Development* 55 (1984): 2056–71; and J. H. Thompson and N. A. Myers, "Inferences and Recall at Ages Four and Seven," *Child Development* 56 (1985): 1134–44.
6. Ibid., citing J. Cantor and G. G. Sparks, "Children's Fear Responses to Mass Media: Testing Some Piagetian Predictions," *Journal of Communication* 34, no. 2 (1984): 90–103; G. G. Sparks, "Developmental Differences in Children's Reports of Fear Induced by Mass Media," *Child Study Journal* 16 (1986): 55–66; G. G. Sparks and J. Cantor, "Developmental Differences on Fright Responses to a Television Program Depicting a Character Transformation," *Journal of Broadcasting and Electronic Media* 30 (1986): 309–23; and B. J. Wilson and J. Cantor, "Developmental Differences in Empathy with a Television Protagonist's Fear," *Journal of Experimental Child Psychology* 39 (1985): 284–99.
7. Ibid.
8. Ibid., citing C. Hoffner and J. Cantor, "Developmental Differences in Responses to a Television Character's Appearance and Behavior," *Developmental Psychology* 21 (1985): 1065–74.
9. Ibid., citing P. Morison and H. Gardner, "Dragons and Dinosaurs: The Child's Capacity to Differentiate Fantasy from Reality, *Child Development* 49 (1978): 642–48.
10. Ibid., citing Sparks, "Developmental Differences in Children's Reports," 55–66.
11. Ibid., citing W. A. Collins, "Interpretation and Inference in Children's Television Viewing," in *Children's Understanding of Television: Research on Attention and Comprehension*, ed. J. Bryant and D. R. Anderson (New York: Academic Press, 1983) 125–50.
12. Ibid., citing G. Comstock and H. J. Paik, "Television and Children: A Review of Recent Research," ERIC Document Reproduction Service No. XX (Syracuse, N.Y.: Syracuse University, 1987).
13. Ibid.
14. Ibid., citing A. Bandura, "Influence of Models' Reinforcement Contingencies on the Acquisition of Imitative Responses," *Journal of Personality and Social Psychology* 1 (1965): 589–95; A. Bandura, D. Ross, and S. A. Ross, "Vicarious Reinforcement and Imitative Learning," *Journal of Abnormal and Social Psychology* 67 (1963) : 601–7; M. A. Rosekrans and W. W. Hartup, "Imitative Influences of Consistent and Inconsistent Response Consequences to a

Model on Aggressive Behavior in Children," *Journal of Personality and Social Psychology* 7 (1967): 429–34.

15. Ibid., citing Bandura, "Influence of Models' Reinforcement," 589–95.
16. Ibid., citing Wilson, Lynn, and Randall, "Applying Social Science Research," 443–68.
17. Ibid., citing Bandura, "Influence of Models' Reinforcement," 589–95.
18. Ibid., citing Collins, "Interpretation and Inference," 125–50.
19. Ibid., citing C. K. Atkin, "Effects of Realistic TV Violence vs. Fictional Violence on Aggression," *Journalism Quarterly* 60 (1983): 615–21; S. Feshbach, "The Role of Fantasy in the Response to Television," *Journal of Social Issues* 32 (1976): 71–85.
20. Ibid., citing A. Bandura, *Social Foundations of Thought and Action: A Social Cognitive Theory* (Englewood Cliffs, N.J.: Prentice-Hall, 1986).
21. Ibid., citing L. R. Huesmann, K. Lagerspetz, and L. D. Eron, "Intervening Variables in the TV Violence-Aggression Relation: Evidence from Two Countries," *Developmental Psychology* 20 (1984): 746–75.
22. Ibid., citing Collins, "Interpretation and Inference," 125–50.
23. Ibid., citing L. Berkowitz, "Some Aspects of Observed Aggression," *Journal of Personality and Social Psychology* 2 (1965): 359–69; T. P. Meyer, "Effects of Viewing Justified and Unjustified Real Film Violence on Aggressive Behavior," *Journal of Personality and Social Psychology* 23 (1972): 21–29.
24. Ibid., citing M. A. Liss, L. C. Reinhardt, and S. Fredricksen, "TV Heroes: The Impact of Rhetoric and Deeds," *Journal of Applied Developmental Psychology* 4 (1983): 175–87.
25. Ibid.
26. Ibid., citing Bandura, *Social Foundations*.
27. Ibid.
28. Robert W. Morse, *The TV Report* (New York: The Regional Religious Educational Coordinators of the Episcopal Church, 1978).
29. Ibid. For an interesting insight into the power of television to perform these functions see Laurel Leff, "TV Comes to Town; Fads and New Wants Come Along with It," *Wall Street Journal*, 2 October 1979, p. 1.
30. According to a report by the Roper Organization, Inc., entitled, "Evolving Public Attitudes Toward Television and Other Mass Media 1959–1980," after the televised Carter-Reagan debates, 36 percent of those surveyed who voted for Reagan reported that the debates had influenced their voting decision. These and other research findings may be obtained from the Television Information Office, 745 Fifth Avenue, New York, NY 10022.
31. Morse, *The TV Report*.
32. Ibid.
33. Morse, *The TV Report*, citing the research of an Australian National University psychological research team headed by Merrelyn and Fred Emery.
34. Ibid.
35. John Rosemond, "Pre-Schoolers Who Watch TV Show Symptoms of Learning Disabilities," *The Atlanta Constitution*, 16 November 1983, B12.
36. The first international assessment of educational progress, 1989, Educational Testing Service of Princeton, N.J.

37. Abbie Jones, "When the Telly Is On, Babies Aren't Learning," *Chicago Tribune,* 10 March 1996, sec. 13, p. 1.
38. Ibid.
39. A Youth Specialties survey, April 1995.
40. See Lawrence Kohlberg, "Stage and Sequence: The Cognitive-Developmental Approach to Socialization," *Handbook of Socialization and Research* (New York: Rand McNally, 1969): 391.
41. Morse, *The TV Report*, 107.
42. "The UCLA Television Violence Monitoring Report," UCLA Center for Communication Policy, September 1995.
43. Ibid.
44. Walter Reich, "The Monster in the Mists," *New York Times,* 15 May 1994. On Sunday, May 15, 1994, the *New York Times* ran at least four articles—including a lengthy, cover-page critique of three new books—on the subject of long-buried memories, including "The Monster in the Mists" and a report entitled "Father Wins Suit Against Memory Therapists." The *Atlanta Journal/Constitution* followed suit with several articles, as did other papers around the country.
45. Ibid.
46. James L. McGaugh, "Preserving the Presence of the Past," *American Psychologist* (Feb. 1983): 161.
47. Ibid.
48. Ibid.
49. V. B. Cline, R. G. Croft, and S. Courrier, "Desensitization of Children to Television Violence," *Journal of Personality and Social Psychology* (1973), cited by The UCLA Television Violence Monitoring Report, UCLA Center for Communication Policy, September, 1995.
50. Judith A. Reisman, *Soft Porn Plays Hardball* (Lafayette: Huntington, 1991), 56.
51. Ibid.
52. Ludwig Feuerbach, *The Essence of Christianity* (New York: Harper, 1957), preface.
53. "Muggeridge Through the Microphone: The American Way of Sex," BBC1 television broadcast, 21 October 1965 (London: British Broadcasting Corporation, 1967).
54. Camille Paglia, "Alice in Muscle Land," *Boston Globe,* 27 January 1991; reprinted in *Sex, Art, and American Culture* (New York: Knopf, 1992).
55. E. L. Doctorow, *Billy Bathgate* (New York: Random House, 1989), chapter 19.
56. Paul Tillich, *Christianity and the Encounter of the World Religions* (New York: Columbia University Press, 1963), ch. 1.
57. J. M. Barrie, "Kate, in the Twelve-Pound Look" (1910).
58. William J. Bennett, "Quantifying America's Decline," *Wall Street Journal*, 15 March 1993.
59. Quoted in *Movieguide*, Vol. VI, 10: 910524.
60. Quoted in *Movieguide*, Vol. VII, 3: 920214.
61. Quoted by Edward E. Ericson Jr., "Solzhenitsyn—Voice from the Gulag," *Eternity*, October 1985, 23–24.

CHAPTER 3

ASKING THE RIGHT QUESTIONS

They shall teach my people the difference between the holy and the unholy and cause them to discern between the unclean and the clean.

—*Ezekiel 44:23*

"AIN'T NOTHING LIKE THE REAL THING"

Dear Mr. Baehr,

I wanted to let you know how much I appreciate your ministry. We have just signed up as members of your on-line service. Just prior to that, I was searching the web on [another purportedly Christian website] and looking at the movie reviews. I began to write down the names of the movies they listed as "good" in content and movies that had received three or more stars. As believers, my family has a rule that we will not view anything rated PG-13 or "lower." Since we rid ourselves of cable, I was excited to see that [this purportedly Christian website] had several movies listed as "OK" for Christian viewing that I would not have dreamed of watching previously. Then the Holy Spirit kicked in and reminded me that I am to be holy as God is holy. In other words, I began to feel convicted.

I ran a "test" on the movie reviews and searched for *The Cider House Rules*, a movie that disgusted me. To my dismay, the reviewers who were giving a "thumbs up" on the movies I was listing, gave *The Cider House Rules* a big "thumbs up," with no regard to the content of the movie whatsoever. I proceeded to throw my list in the garbage and shared with my husband how discouraged I was with the so-called "Christian" reviews on [that website].

It was then he pointed me to your website, after hearing one of your reviews on radio. We immediately signed up and were thrilled to see the *Cider House* movie listed as "abhorrent."

Thank you for giving us a tool to choose wisely what we allow in our hearts and minds. We want to be pleasing to God, and we pray he blesses you and your ministry for helping us to do so.

Name withheld

Parents must be equipped to teach their children discernment. Many, of course, have no idea how to do so, beyond removing the television set. While that may be a good idea, stories abound of children who became addicted to sex and violence across the street at a neighbor's house, or who were the victims of someone else who was addicted to sex and violence.

There are no quick fixes in the matter of teaching discernment. You have to teach your children what the problem is, why there is a problem, what the impact of entertainment is on them, how to look at different media differently, and how to ask the right questions in order to understand what is going on in a given entertainment product. In other words, you must equip your children with the intellectual, cognitive, and spiritual tools to deal with the mass media.

Too many people tend to reduce the entertainment media issues to matters of sex and violence, even though sex and violence are only parts of the problem. False gods and doctrines, which beckon to us with so much deadly appeal, are often more dangerous.

DESCRIBING THE ELEPHANT

To teach discernment, you must understand that while many parents primarily look at the entertainment media semantically—in terms of the sex, violence, nudity, and profanity content—many children look at the entertainment media syntactically—in terms of the rhythm, action, adventure, and special effects. So parents and children talk *at* each other about the entertainment media, not *to* each other.

A father might say to his son, "Did you hear the horrible lyrics in that music?" The son might reply, "No, but did you hear the riff, the rhythm, and the beat?"

Children are not immune to the messages of the mass media, but it is the syntactical elements of those messages that most influence them. Try asking a younger child what she is watching on television. Quite often she will say, "I don't know." Ask the child what the program is about and often she will repeat, "I don't know."

However, pay attention to the child's actions, and you will often see her mimicking the behavior she is watching. Or, later she will ask for a product that was advertised with the program.

THUMBS UP

One set of keys to media literacy is to teach your children to analyze the mass media product by deciphering, decoding, and detecting meaning in the media communication and then to compare and evaluate that meaning with a biblical worldview. By helping them learn to ask good questions, you can help your children broaden their perspective and develop discernment as they review, critique, and report on what they see and hear.

One of the most important keys to developing the biblical discernment needed to choose good entertainment is asking the right questions. The entertainment media are loaded with messages. Learning how to discover these messages helps you appreciate the movies and television programs you watch, the games you play, the music you listen to, and the mass media information sources upon which you rely.

Asking the right questions about the entertainment media requires media literacy and a working knowledge of how the medium in question communicates and entertains. Developing discernment requires comparing the messages you discover from the questions you ask with the standards and principles of a Christian worldview.

Ascertainment questions help us isolate elements, evidence, meaning, point of view, and worldview in a particular media product. The answers to these ascertainment questions can then be compared to the biblical standard.

A Christian worldview requires the wisdom that comes from a fear of the Lord, the understanding that comes from a personal knowledge of Jesus Christ, and a solid knowledge of Scripture.

We will look briefly at those elements that make up powerful dramatic entertainment. This analysis will be framed as a series of questions to guide you to ask the right questions about the entertainment product you, your children, and your friends view. These questions will help you look beneath the surface of an entertainment product to determine whether you and God's written Word[1] agree with the messages the media product communicates.

This call to action requires our active viewing and listening. As we learn to identify these elements, we become able to discern the subtle ways in which seemingly innocuous material molds our thinking. This is especially important for Christian parents.

For the reasons stated in the introduction, I will focus on movies and videos, but the principles apply and are easily adapted to other media. Stimulating children to interact with their entertainment media experience, rather than simply absorbing it, is crucial.

But, first . . .

On the way to the video store, brainstorm with your child for prior knowledge about the story or content matter. This gives you an opportunity to share a short description of the movie's plot and characters. Before the film begins you can encourage children to imagine the characters and what could happen. If the child's thinking is activated prior to the passive activity of watching, he or she can engage in the story and learn from the plot on the screen.

Prior to viewing, to facilitate active viewing:

- Talk about the title, the images, and ideas about the plot.
- Predict the character types and action in the film.
- Ask what your children know that they can bring to the film.
- Use *What Can We Watch Tonight* as an introduction to the film.
- Plan to stop the video to predict a character's actions or twists in the plot. Don't stop too often, however, as this will disrupt the rhythm of the film. (*Hint:* Set the timer so that if you or older children see something worth discussing in the video, you can easily return to that section after the movie.)

ELEMENTAL AND EVIDENTIARY QUESTIONS

The first set of questions we will ask are known as elemental and evidentiary questions. These deal with elements of the mass media product that are easily ascertained. Most of these questions help us to find out facts about the product with which most thinking people will agree. It should be clear after reviewing these questions that there are many other questions we can and should ask in order to be media-literate and discerning.

These are key questions to ask your child after watching a movie. They're sure to help launch an animated discussion. It is important to set a tone that supports the child's responses and creative impressions of the story.

Ascertainment Question: Who is the hero?

Usually the easiest question for anyone, including children, to answer about a movie, television program, computer game, stage play, book, or story is, Who is the hero or heroine? Of course, when we are confronted by some modern literature wherein the reader realizes that he is the hero (or the hero doesn't exist), or if we probe beyond the character's name to find out his characteristics, then this question becomes much more complex.

Many dramatists[2] talk not about the main character in the story, whom most people would consider the hero, but rather about the character who forces the action, whom the dramatists call the protagonist. From a dramatist's point of view, the villain—such as Judas in the Passion story—can be the protagonist if he forces the action, whereas the hero, Jesus, may be the antagonist because he opposes the protagonist. Even so, our main character, in this case Jesus, remains the hero because he triumphs over his opponent(s).

For our purposes we can conclude that in most cases, especially as far as popular entertainment is concerned, the hero is the main character who is the focus of the story. Using this insight, most children can find the hero in most entertainment media products.

However, knowing the name of the hero is not enough. To understand who the hero is we must analyze the hero's "bone structure." The bone structure of any character is the combination of all the characteristics that make up the character. In analyzing a character's bone structure we need to look at the following: his physical characteristics, his background, his psychological characteristics, and his religious characteristics.

As a guide to the impact a hero has on a story, the following reminders of the archetypal story genre are helpful:

> In a mythic or apocalyptic story such as *The Ten Commandments*, God triumphs, or the hero triumphs because of an act of God.

> In the heroic story such as *High Noon*, the hero triumphs because he or she is superior.

> In the high ironic story, such as *Forrest Gump*, the hero triumphs because of a quirk of fate or circumstances.

> In the low ironic story, such as *Death of a Salesman*, the hero fails because of a quirk of fate or circumstances.

> In the demonic story, which includes not only many horror films but also psychological movies and political films such as *The Diary of Anne Frank*, the hero is hopelessly overwhelmed by evil.

In the next movie, television program, story, or game with which you interact, locate the hero or heroine and describe his or her character traits.

Discernment Question: What kind of role model is the hero?

After locating the hero or heroine in the entertainment product, and identifying his or her character traits, you need to discern whether or not he or she is a worthy role model. It is not safe to assume that the heroes of today's movies are the positive role models we want for our impressionable children. Even where the premise is positive and the morals reflect a Christian worldview, we must ask the question: Is the hero compatible with the biblical role model?

A comparison of the three characters of action-star Sylvester Stallone—Rocky, Rambo, and Cobra (one of his lesser known, later characters)—illustrates the different messages that a hero can communicate through his or her character traits in movies with basically the same premise:

Rocky is an ironic hero who loves his family, prays, and tries to do the right thing, although he is reduced to using brute force to prove his worth and win in our complex modern society. Rocky's use of force in the boxing ring is mitigated by the fact that he prays before each fight, demonstrating his reliance on God and not on his own prowess. (Note that in *Rocky 4*, Rocky steps out of character and pursues vengeance for its own sake.)

Rambo is a haunted man who strikes out at the country (the United States) that abandoned him to die in Vietnam and tries to rescue his buddies who have suffered a similar fate. Rambo has lost faith in everyone and ends up by asking why the rug of faith was pulled out from under him by the country he loved. He uses brute force out of anger and frustration in order to triumph.

Cobra is a killing machine who sets himself up as judge and jury. He is the ultimate humanist, a product of Ayn Rand, Nietzsche, and Hobbes, who exhibits the solipsistic heresy of titanism.

The Last Temptation of Christ pushed the desecration of the hero one step further. Never before in history had moviemakers declared war on Jesus. Here are excerpts from notes taken by Evelyn Dokovic, of the *Morality in Media* newsletter, at a screening of *The Last Temptation of Christ*:[3]

> Judas berates Jesus for making crosses that are used by the Romans to kill Jews. As they talk, Jesus indicates that he is struggling. (Viewer observation: Jesus is weak, confused, fearful, doesn't know who he is, from time to time falls on the ground in a faint after hearing voices. He doesn't know if the voices come from God or the devil.)

> Jesus seems to be helping them crucify the man. He revives and says he wants God to hate him. He makes crosses because he wants God to hate him.

> The viewer sees a bare-breasted woman sitting at a well. Jesus proceeds on his way to Mary Magdalene's house. He has to wait in line to get in. When he does the room is filled with men sitting down, watching Mary have sex with a customer. Jesus sits down and watches, too.

> Jesus says: "I'm a liar, a hypocrite. I'm afraid of everything. Do you want to know who my God is? They're fear. Lucifer is inside me. He tells me I am not a man, but the Son of Man, more the Son of God, more than that, God."

> Jesus is walking with his wives (bigamy) and children, and stops to listen to a preacher—St. Paul. He is telling the people that Jesus of Nazareth was the Son of God, that he was tortured and crucified for our sins, and that three days later he rose from the dead.

Jesus screams, "Liar." Jesus tells Paul that he is Jesus, asks why he is telling these lies. Jesus says: "I was saved. I have children." Paul tells him to look around him and see how unhappy the people are. Their only hope is the resurrected Jesus. Paul says: "They need God. If I have to crucify you, I'll crucify you. If I have to resurrect you, I'll resurrect you. My Jesus is more important than you are. I'm glad I met you. Now I can forget about you."

This hero is evil and this movie is blasphemy. To think that Jesus, the Word, who was in the beginning, through whom all things were made, who is God, was lusting in his holy heart for one of his creations is grotesque and horrifying (see John 1). This film desecrates the sinless Lamb of God, who cleansed us through his death and resurrection. *The Last Temptation of Christ* is the ultimate desecration of the hero, even though the premise says that good triumphs over evil.

Subsidiary Discernment Questions

- If the hero is not a moral character, how would the story change if the hero were a moral character?
- How would you tell the story from another character's viewpoint?
- Do you know anyone like the hero?
- Is there a character in the Bible who is like the hero? Who is it? What is his or her story?

Ascertainment Question: Who is the villain?

As in the case of the hero, you need to identify the villain and his character traits. In most entertainment products the villain is easy to identify, but there are exceptions.

To identify the villain, it is helpful to recall the four basic plots:

1. Man against man
2. Man against nature
3. Man against himself
4. Man against the supernatural or the subnatural

In the remake of *Cape Fear,* the villain does not say he is a Christian, but he has Bible verses tattooed on his body and he spouts contemporary Christian code words in a malevolent manner. You need to look at all the attributes of character to see if he is supposed to be a Christian.

Once you have identified the villain, you should list his character traits in the same manner that you did with the hero. You will want to list physical characteristics, background, psychological characteristics, and religious characteristics.

Since the demise of the motion picture and television codes, many media products have portrayed those who are moral as prudes, nerds, kooks, and psychopaths. One of the first of these was *Midnight Cowboy* (1969), which portrayed a street preacher as a sleazy homosexual who leads the hero into homosexual prostitution. The movie *Criminal Law* (1989) went further by portraying pro-lifers, who do not think that babies should be murdered in their mothers' wombs, as psychopathic killers.

In *South Park*, the mother is the villain, and the devil is one of the heroes. In *Dances with Wolves*, the villains are the American settlers and the U.S. Cavalry. The heroes are the Indians. In *The Bear*, the villains are the hunters and the heroes are the bears. In *Old Gringo*, the Americans are the bad guys and the Mexicans are the good guys.

In contrast, in the 1996 film adaptation of *Richard III*, the archetypal villain is truly evil, so much so that his mother tells him that he has abandoned God.

Discernment Question:
What kind of a message does the character of the villain communicate?

As Christians, we need to analyze the character of the villain to determine whether he, she, or they are being used to attack a biblical worldview. If so, we may want to protest this anti-Christian bigotry and perhaps even boycott the movie in question.

Ascertainment Question:
How much violence is there in the mass media product?

Violence in the entertainment media is a critical problem because of its influence on children and susceptible individuals. It is important to know how much violence is in a mass media product. Many contemporary movies and television programs push the limits of violence.

Looking at the content of some movies will help you to understand the severity of the situation:

The movie *Freddy's Dead: The Final Nightmare* shows

- multiple grotesque murders and violence in dream sequences,
- a wooden rod rammed through a man's ear,
- the deforming and exploding of a character's head,
- a man impaled on a bed of nails,
- blood dripping or gushing from doors, ceilings, and a television set,
- stabbings and slashings,
- amputation of fingers and ears, and
- recurrent intense depictions of child abuse and molestations by parents.

In *People Under the Stairs*, the content included

- sadistic violence, including a woman bound by wrists inside a torture chamber,
- people hit with cement blocks,
- a tongue cut out,
- a girl being chased with a meat cleaver,
- a woman's stomach impaled with a knife,
- a pit bull attacking intruders,
- body mutilation,
- a gory corpse hanging on a rack,

- electric shock,
- a man shot and hurled down stairs,
- a child forced into boiling water,
- a man punched in the groin,
- gasoline poured into an inhabited chamber and set aflame,
- a sword impaled into a dog,
- a man being poked in the eye,
- crude references to genitals,
- sexual jokes,
- a child likened to a prostitute,
- talk of "tricks," tarot cards, and voodoo dolls that embody the souls of victims,
- crack and drug addicts,
- distortion of Psalm 23,
- an occurrence of breaking and entering,
- sadomasochistic dress, and
- cannibalism.

Something must be done to curb this level of violence in movies. The most effective stand you can make is to become informed before you go: read *Movieguide* and avoid such movies with abhorrent material. Since teenagers are the most likely to attend these types of movies, it is important to help them understand why they need to make godly choices before they view any of the modern mass media.

Discernment Question:
How is violence presented in the mass media product?

The emotive heart of drama is conflict, and the ultimate conflict ends in violence. The Bible is full of violence and the gospel story has one of the most violent scenes imaginable: the crucifixion of Jesus Christ. The presentation of violence in the entertainment media is not always bad and is sometimes necessary. It is, however, critical to protect young children from such violence and to identify how it is presented in the entertainment product so you can discern whether it is necessary and furthers the good and the true.

Ron Maxwell, director of *Gettysburg*, said that while violence was essential to the storyline of the movie, he purposely avoided porno-violence, with its excessive blood, guts, and gore. His discretion made *Gettysburg* a better movie, and one that could reach a broader audience.

Discernment Question: How is love portrayed?

The beauty of God's love is wonderful, yet most movies reduce love to one-night sexual relationships, tedious ordeals, eternal battles, or homosexual coupling. This desecration of love should be an anathema to God's people.

The Scarlet Letter contends that adulterous love is honorable. The movie *Kids* suggests that promiscuous sex, posing as love, is acceptable among young teenage children. *The War of the Roses* suggests that marriage is war, while the

Disney movie *Ruthless People* depicts the husband trying to murder his wife, while the wife is trying to blackmail the husband. *Desert Hearts* portrays a woman getting a divorce and discovering that lesbian love is better than heterosexual love. *Accidental Tourist* is based on the premise that self-indulgence is more important than love. *Naked Lunch, The Incredibly True Adventure of Two Girls in Love, Bound, Philadelphia,* and *Birdcage* all present homosexual lust as love.

Many horror movies capture an audience by luring them with the thought of forbidden lust, such as necrophilia (fornication with the dead) and bestiality (fornication with animals). However, horror films are not the only films that extol forbidden fruit. The Disney comedy *Splash* treats bestiality in a humorous way by having the hero fall in love with a mermaid. Bestiality is not funny and is condemned by God. Many movies suggest, or even promote, the idea of sex with a child.

On the other hand, the most memorable and profitable movies are usually carefully crafted character studies that portray love in a wholesome, biblical, uplifting light, movies such as *Tender Mercies* and *Sense and Sensibility.*

Ascertainment Question: How much sex is in the mass media product?

In 1995 there were thirty-six movies produced that had excessive sexual content. These films earned on average less than $1 million at the box office. Two of the biggest-budget Hollywood sex films, *Showgirls* and *Striptease,* bombed at the box office and lost millions of dollars, despite mammoth advertising campaigns. In 1996 the average box office for the six movies with strong homosexual content was a pitiful $705,302. Since the average Hollywood movie costs $54 million to produce and market, one has to wonder why the industry continues to try to force such products on the public. In 1995, movies with strong Christian content earned on average 2,400 percent more at the box office than movies with excessive sexual content.

An example of the excess of sexual content in some Hollywood movies is the critically acclaimed movie *Naked Lunch.* This movie contains twelve obscenities and six profanities, a woman shooting insecticide into her breast, grotesque giant bugs with talking anuses, a woman ripping open her body, women shot in the head, "mugwump" monsters with dripping and squirting phalluses on their heads, graphic fornication, adultery, reference to sexually transmitted diseases and fellatio, transvestism, homosexual kissing, lesbian and homosexual copulation, male and female nudity, surrealistic and overt depictions of genitalia, witchcraft, graphic drug use, drug-induced hallucinations, and alcohol consumption.

Many such movies garner the applause of the secular critics and film festivals around the world, but do not get much of an audience.

Discernment Question: How is the family portrayed?

Contemporary movies that build up the family, such as the pro-life, pro-family, pro-marriage, pro-fatherhood *Father of the Bride,* are rare. Instead, today's movies tend to lift up homosexuality, promote free love, downplay marriage, portray motherhood as psychopathic, and show husbands and dads as irresponsible. Such movies attack the basic building block of our society: the family.

The content of two antifamily movies with family MPAA ratings is very instructive:

> *Addams Family Values* (PG-13) depicts children dropping a cannonball on their baby sibling, dropping a guillotine blade on their baby sibling, dropping their baby sibling from the roof of a house, burning their summer camp, and starting to burn a girl at the stake, while a nurse tries to electrocute her husband, bomb her husband, and electrocute the family. The movie also portrays extreme graphic violence at the camp; suggests sadomasochism, sadism, and perverse sex and fornication; makes occult references throughout the movie; and mocks Christianity.

> In *The Brady Bunch* (PG), there is frequent sexual innuendo; an older woman flirts with young boys; a lesbian girl has a crush on an unsuspecting friend; and the family's nonreligious, clean-living morality is mocked.

The Bible is very clear about the importance of the family. The family is the focal point of God's economy and governance. God created the family and ordained it as the basic unit of government along with self-government, the church, and civil government. The family is much more important than the state.

Ascertainment Questions: Are religion, the church, people of faith, and/or Christians portrayed in the mass media product?

Being able to identify religion, the church, and people of faith and/or Christians in an entertainment media product is an extremely important aspect of discerning viewing. Religion is alive and well in the entertainment media, especially on prime-time network fiction television. But it is not the predominantly Christian faith of our founding fathers. It is, instead, a cacophony of ill-conceived religions such as materialism, consumerism, eroticism, hedonism, naturalism, humanism, cynicism, stoicism, the cult of violence (that used to pay homage to the war-god Mars), and a multitude of other modern variations on pagan practices. These religions—many of which can trace their roots back to long discredited ancient cults—have their rituals, beliefs, values, signs, metaphysics, cosmologies, ontologies, and epistemologies played out with ritualistic regularity on programs, commercials, and music videos. On any given night on television we may find happy Hollywood stars touting the virtues of astrology, while Madonna embraces a religious statue that comes alive.

Many in Hollywood recognize the religious significance of their work. Joe Eszterhas, author of the movie *Showgirls*, claimed that his pornographic film was a religious experience.

Discernment Question:
How are religion, Christians, and the church portrayed?

All too often in contemporary movies, religion, individual believers, and the church are portrayed as evil, weak, insincere, obsequious, corrupt, or foolish.

Though it had nothing to do with the premise, a series of morning prayer meetings were inserted into the mediocre movie *Head Office*, which caricatures

Christians as neo-Nazis who pray in German accents for world conquest. Woody Allen's movie *Hannah and Her Sisters* mocks Christianity, Roman Catholicism, and Hinduism.

As Christians, we may think mocking other religions is funny, but the truth is that mocking false doctrines is a sign of hubris and not of a godly desire to lift up the Truth, who is Jesus the Christ. As history has constantly proven, mockery will lead to disaster. For example, Hitler began his campaign against the Jews by mocking them in grotesque cartoons.

The good news is that there are more and more movies that lift up Jesus Christ and commend the church—movies such as *Dead Man Walking*, *The Preacher's Wife*, *Return to Me*, and *The Patriot*.

Subsidiary Discernment Questions

- Does one or more of the characters play the role of God?
- Did you see anything supernatural? Who was the source: God or Satan? Or were you not sure? (Ask God to show you.)
- Does good win over evil?
- Does the winning side use spiritual power not from God? (Remember, if supernatural power is not from God, it is demonic. Frequent exposure tends to bring unquestioning acceptance, so be careful.)
- Are magic, spells, fortune-telling, spiritism (contacting the spirit world or functioning as a medium between the living and the dead, as in *Ghost*) presented as a means to happy living? Might they build a dangerous fascination with paganism and a desire to experiment?

Ascertainment Question: How is the world or the environment in which the story takes place portrayed?

The environment in which a story, song, or entertainment event takes place has an immense impact on the audience. Because every communication excludes what it does not include, its omissions create powerful secondary messages in the mind of the audience. Editing, close-ups, reverse shots, and other camera techniques can distort the meaning of a scene and the way we look at the world.

To understand how the media influence by excluding material, look through the viewfinder of a camera and note how you can completely change the mode and the message of a scene by what you include and what you exclude within the frame of the picture. Let your children do the same and you will help them to develop a critical media literacy skill.

One college student wanted to become an anthropologist because of a beautiful picture of a temple in Bali. When I recognized the location and told the student that the temple was surrounded by a gas station and urban blight, his perspective changed.

Research has shown that the background environment of an entertainment media product has a tremendous impact on the worldview of the children. It is important that we are aware of how the media product is portraying the world so we can counter any misconceptions the product might create.

Since a camera excludes everything beyond its field of view, television journalism is technically biased in its reporting. Yet the viewer interprets what he or she sees as the truth. The camera is typically used to implode the subject matter by focusing tightly around one aspect that makes the shot appear larger than life. This distorts the real-world environment.

In other words, the camera does lie.

The entertainment industry often distorts the way we look at the world. The next time you watch a movie or television, pay close attention to how the world or environment in which the story takes place is portrayed. Although the environment in which the story is set may not be the focus of your attention as you watch or listen, the environment will send you distinct messages that influence how you look at the world and the subject matter of the entertainment product.

Subsidiary Ascertainment Questions:
Where did the story take place? How do you know?

Children need to be aware that movies are staged—that props and scenery are used to set a story in a particular time and place. These questions will help your child realize that, for example, a horse and carriage signal that a story is set in the past. As children begin to notice such details, their movie viewing will become a richer experience.

Subsidiary Ascertainment Question:
How is language used in the mass media product?

Closely related to the environmental ascertainment and discernment questions is the question of how language is used in a mass media product. A definitive study by Timothy Jay entitled *Cursing in America*[4] found that only 7 percent of American people curse on the job and only 12 percent curse in their leisure time. Yet many movies and television programs would lead us to believe that Americans curse all the time and that our language is full of profanity and obscenity. It may be rare to hear cursing in your local grocery store or mall, but turn on your TV, radio, or go to the movies, and you will hear a constant barrage of cursing.

One school of Marxist thought considered language as a weapon with which to attack the bourgeois society in which we live.[5] In the years *Movieguide* has been tracking language in movies, we have found that the more foul language is included in a movie, the worse it will do at the box office.

Subsidiary Ascertainment Question: What special effects were used to create the setting and environment of the entertainment product?

This question helps demystify the entertainment media product so that children can see that it is pretend—that it is all created. Children can be unsettled by even seemingly innocent things in an entertainment media product. Therefore it is important to emphasize that some movies, television programs, and other mass media products are fantasy.

If your child is very young, you might ask questions such as the following:

- How do you think they made that character fly without getting hurt?
- What pretend things were the characters doing?

Many young children will try to duplicate what they see, so it is wise to point out what is not real.

Discernment Question:
How are government and business portrayed?

This question belongs as a subset of the question "How is the world portrayed?" But because so many movies attack republican governments and promote socialism and communism, it behooves us to pay close attention to the way a movie portrays government. Furthermore, to really identify the worldview that is being foisted upon us by a media product, we should also ask, "How is private enterprise portrayed in this movie?"

Studies by Lichter, Rothman, and Lichter show[6] the vast majority of those involved in the entertainment industry believe in socialism, which believes that the state, not God, is the savior of mankind.

At the very root of socialism and communism is a negation of God's Law—the Ten Commandments—particularly the first, since the state is being elevated to a position higher than God; the eighth, because the redistribution of property by the state is stealing from those less powerful than the state, who are forced to give up their property against their will; and the tenth, because the premise of socialism and communism is based on the politics of envy or coveting that which belongs to someone else. A movie that lifts up the state as savior and attacks the individual and his God-given rights is, in fact, promoting a very anti-Christian worldview.

Salvador is a particularly coarse example of a movie aimed at promoting the goals of socialist revolutionaries. The rebels are a nice bunch of young people with no weapons except their good cause, and the hero makes it clear that he hates all authority, especially American.

Another extreme example is *Remo Williams: The Adventure Begins*, a fascist fantasy wherein mystical, humanistic violence is used to defend the Big Brother State from unscrupulous free-enterprise capitalists. The savior is an ancient Korean martial-arts master who can walk on water. Regrettably, this savior is dedicated to serving Big Brother and death. Many people become infected by the virus of the corrupt mystic statism in such movies; therefore we need to be aware of these deceptions and be prepared to rebuke them.

The opposite view, that the state is always the villain, as represented in the movies *JFK* and *Nixon*, is also wrong. In a similar vein, *Fat Man and Little Boy* suggests that the United States government was immoral for creating and employing the atomic bomb to end World War II. *Independence Day*, for all its many good points, goes in the opposite direction and suggests that internationalism is the key to harmony and world peace.

Statism, in whatever form it takes—fascism, communism, or national socialism—is a punishment for rejecting God and seeking salvation from men. This is the key to the impoverishment of every totalitarian state, including the former Soviet Union with all its natural wealth. Salvation can never be found in the state, but tyranny can.

Forrest Gump and *Braveheart* are two very successful examples of movies that adhere to a biblical view. *Forrest Gump* shows the foolishness of the self-appointed revolutionaries; while *Braveheart* demonstrates the principle of *Lex Rex*, which holds that even the king has no right to violate God's Law.

Examining how government and private enterprise are portrayed will help us to cut through the hidden political agendas of many films.

Discernment Question:
How is history treated in the media product?

Any familiarity with world history will convince us that those who forget the past are doomed to repeat it. When the media revises the past to suit their worldview, it is a very serious issue for the future of our civilization.

Much revisionism has been devoted to whitewashing the Holocaust. Those who deal in this area of revisionism are anxious to remove the memory of the Holocaust from the annals of history by claiming that the gas chambers could not have killed so many people and that the death camps were actually work camps with good sanitary conditions.

While *Schindler's List* accurately portrays the horror of the Holocaust, *The English Patient* whitewashes the real history of its Nazi hero, extols adultery, and promotes euthanasia.

Any thinking person understands the threat of revising history to remove the memory of the Holocaust, but few object to the wholesale revision of any history that supports our republican democracy and Christian heritage. In her book *The Rewriting of America's History*, historian Catherine Millard has chronicled the removal of Christian quotes and information from our national monuments by the U.S. Park Service and the removal of the Christian writings of our founding fathers from the Library of Congress.[7] This book gives a frightening look at how the revisionists are trying to remove all traces of Christianity from our society.

WORLDVIEW QUESTIONS

We now move out of the evidentiary world toward the philosophical foundations and perspectives that the mass media feed us over the impulse waves. In order to establish a meaningful biblical agenda, we need first to distinguish between differing worldviews and humankind's relation between ourselves, our world, and God.

The term *discernment* has a much deeper meaning than identifying discrepancies between "good" and "bad" viewing, which is to see the differences between the two elements and to make an educated decision. We are here to build discernment, and discernment involves our entire process of thinking, feeling, and knowing so that we are able to recognize a piece of media or information as moral, ethical, and holy or as information that does not follow the laws of God and his plan for our lives.

The second set of questions we will ask are "worldview" questions. These deal with the underlying elements of the mass media products, which must be ascertained by looking at the dynamic interfaces between the evidentiary elements. These elements help us to understand and discern the philosophical and theological messages that the product is communicating.

Ascertainment Question:
What is the premise of the movie?

If you understand the premise of an entertainment product, then you will understand the ultimate message the product is communicating to the audience. The premise drives the story to its conclusion. Whether or not the audience is conscious of the premise, the message is implanted in their minds.

The storyline logically proves the premise. If the premise of the mass media product is that "good triumphs over evil," then the storyline has to tell in a logical manner how the good hero triumphs over the evil villain, or the story will fail to capture the audience.

Without a clear-cut premise, no idea is strong enough to carry a story through to a logical conclusion.[8] If there is no clear-cut premise, the characters will not come alive. A badly worded or false premise will force the mass media-maker[9] to fill space with irrelevant material. A mass media product with more than one premise is confusing because it goes in more than one direction. A premise that says too much is ambiguous, and therefore says nothing. A premise that does not take a position is ambivalent and also says nothing.

In most cases, a mass media-maker will not be able to produce a successful entertainment product based on a premise that he or she does not believe. No one premise expresses the totality of universal truth, and every premise is limiting. For example, poverty does not always lead to crime, but if the mass media-maker has chosen the premise that poverty leads to crime, he or she must prove it.

Some sample premises are as follows:

- God's love triumphs over death. (*Dead Man Walking*)
- Great faith triumphs over death. (*Lady Jane*)
- Love conquers death. (*Romeo and Juliet*)
- Great faith triumphs over despotism. (*Braveheart*)
- Ruthless ambition destroys itself. (*Macbeth*)
- Strength defeats evil. (*Rambo*)
- Human cunning defeats inhuman evil. (*Alien*)
- God triumphs over self-centeredness. (*The Preacher's Wife*)
- God's call triumphs over bondage. (*Trip to Bountiful*)

The premise can be found by analyzing the story. In *Driving Miss Daisy*, an elderly woman has alienated all those around her. Motivated by his Christian faith, her black chauffeur gives his life to help her, ignoring her cruelty and demeaning barbs. In the end she recognizes that he is her only friend. This heart-warming story has the incredibly powerful premise that Christian virtues bring reconciliation, redemption, and love into a person's life.

Finding the premise will help your children develop cause-and-effect thinking, which is so important in understanding a story. Another way of finding the premise is to ask: Why did the story end the way it did?

Discernment Question:
Does the premise agree with, or conflict with, a biblical worldview?

Once you find the premise, you need to evaluate whether or not the premise is consistent with a biblical worldview. If the premise of the media product does not square with a biblical worldview, then you need to question the message the product is leaving in the minds of the audience.

The premise of *Rambo* has led to senseless violence and bullying because too many impressionable viewers end up believing that might makes right. *Rambo* demonstrates that strength, not goodness, triumphs over evil. The eternal truth is that God's love alone secures the victory over the forces of evil, as the classic movie *Ben Hur* clearly demonstrates.

Ascertainment Question:
How is the premise solved?

It is quite possible that the premise can agree with the biblical worldview, but the way that premise is solved may be anti-Christian, immoral, or evil. If this is the situation, then the media product is not acceptable viewing for Christians.

In many movies, good triumphs over evil but only by means of magic. So while the premise ("good triumphs over evil") agrees with the biblical world-view, the method by which the premise is resolved (magic) is anti-biblical. These movies are suspect for anyone who does not understand that all magic is evil. If magic is applied as a literary device that condemns the manipulation of the supernatural for personal gain and upholds Jesus and God's grace, as in the Chronicles of Narnia, then the redemptive aspect of the story will make the movie acceptable.

Subsidiary Ascertainment Question:
What is the plot of the media product? What is the media product about?

Part and parcel of identifying the premise is to identify the plot. To do so you need to identify the "five Ws"—who, what, where, when, and why. Always attempt to identify in the film as many of these as you think need to be answered. Often, it is a good idea to try to do this in one or two sentences.

Identifying the plot will help you to identify the premise and help your children to understand the story. Asking this straightforward question helps you find out whether your children understand a movie's main ideas. This question will also prompt children to recall details and incidents in sequence—two important thinking skills. Concerned about question formation techniques and the taxonomy of thought, education specialists stress the importance of asking questions deeply (instead of widely) to explore knowledge, comprehension, application, analysis, synthesis, and evaluation.

Subsidiary Discernment Question:
What images and/or sounds best summarize the media product?

A sound-image schema can help you discover recurring themes and under-lying principles in the media product. Ask your children to state one sound or image that relates to the story and discuss different suggestions from the family.

Subconscious sounds and images recite themselves over and over in the mind like an unwanted mantra. (Of course, no Christian wants any mantra, especially one placed in our minds by a media product.)

Children constantly repeat songs from commercials such as McDonald's advertisements. Ask them to think about the songs and what they mean. Most children will come to the conclusion that they do not want to be singing songs that manipulate them.

If these ideas are explored on a conscious level, we can then make decisions about their appropriateness. We can choose to accept the song and dance or reject the negative images in the name of God.

Ascertainment and Discernment Questions:
What moral statements does the media product make, and do these moral statements agree or conflict with a biblical worldview?

Besides having a premise that drives the story to its logical conclusion, many media products make one or more moral statements. *Batman Forever* is based on the premise that cunning intelligence (as represented by Batman) triumphs over evil, and thus concurs with the biblical statements that "A double minded man is unstable in all his ways" (James 1:8 KJV), "Pride goeth before destruction, and an haughty spirit before a fall" (Proverbs 16:18 KJV), and a person should not "take revenge, . . . but leave room for God's wrath, for it is written: 'It is mine to avenge; I will repay,' says the Lord" (Romans 12:19).

Sometimes the premise of a media product is anti-Christian, while the moral basis agrees with a biblical worldview. The premise of *Labyrinth*, that a strong will defeats evil, is contrary to the biblical worldview; however, the primary moral statement of *Labyrinth*—that possessions are worthless when compared to the value of the life of another human being—agrees with God's written Word.

Ascertainment and Discernment Questions:
How is evil portrayed, and how does the portrayal of evil in the media product compare with the biblical view of evil?

Heretical doctrine can most often be traced to an incorrect view of evil. This is the case with humanism, which sees man as basically good and minimizes evil and sin, or with New Age religions, which see evil as simply an illusion, or with occultism and Satanism, which view evil as being as strong as, if not stronger than, the ultimate good who is God. It is critical to an orthodox Christian worldview that evil be presented for what it is—real, not illusory or imaginary—and that Jesus is proclaimed as Victor over evil.

Sweet Liberty portrays the archetypal humanist view of evil: Neither God nor evil is a factor; everything is acceptable in the right context; and human actions have no consequences. *The Craft* portrays evil as having tremendous power and says that the teenage heroine can only succeed by participating in an occult power wherein evil witches also draw their strength. The *Star Wars* movies show evil as being simply the other side of the good, with the Force—the god of *Star Wars*—being ambiguous and ambivalent. *Agnes of God* distorts the gospel by making evil good and by portraying the nun, Agnes, as a spiritist who talks to departed spirits and who worships the powers of the air. All of these movies demean the reality of our sinful situation and negate the Truth of God—his sovereign goodness and his victory on the cross.

However, there are many movies that take a biblical view of evil and good, from classics such as *The Sound of Music* to more recent movies such as *Spider-Man* or *First Knight*, which has one of the best portraits of a biblical view of good and evil ever presented in a movie.

Ascertainment and Discernment Questions:
How is reality portrayed, and how does the presentation of reality in the media product compare to the biblical norm?

The question as to how reality is presented in the media product is the classic ontological question (*ontology* is the study of the nature of being, reality, or existence): What is the nature of being, which is reality, presented in the mass media product?

For Christians and Jews the biblical view toward reality is that we live in a real world, created by the real God, wherein there are real problems, pain, and suffering that we cannot ignore or wish away. For those of us who are Christians, the creator God has saved us from real evil, sin, and death through the real death and resurrection of his Son, Jesus the Christ, who was really God and really man. Any other ontology, or view of the nature of being, denies the gospel.

Classical Buddhism considers reality to be an illusion and the ultimate reality to be nonbeing, which means that there is no evil and no need for redemption.

Christian Science believes that the sinful, fallen world as we know it is only mortal mind, while reality is divine mind, which is similar to the good universal consciousness of New Age religions.

In like manner, Hinduism and many New Age and pagan religions see reality as an illusion, or "maya." These nominalists (*nominalism* holds that the things in the world are only names, not real things) believe that reality is merely a fiction, not a real creation by the real, transcendent God of the Bible. This ontology denies the reality of sin and the need for salvation.

A nominalist premise blurs the line between imagination and reality. But evil is real, and to deny its reality by saying that it is only a dream or an illusion denies the need for Jesus' death on the cross to save us from our sins and from sin itself.

Hindus ignore the sick and hurting people around them because they believe that such sickness is maya and that nothing is real. Therefore Hindu holy men will pass a dying street urchin, with the explanation that his suffering is only an illusion and his karma, while Mother Teresa will pick the child up and take it to a hospital.

A universalist worldview suggests that Jesus is not the only way to salvation. If that were the case, then it was futile for Jesus to suffer a vicious death on the cross. The universalist worldview makes a mockery of the reality of Jesus' suffering, death, and resurrection, and reduces Jesus to a liar or a madman, rather than the "Way, the Truth, and the Life" (as C. S. Lewis so aptly noted).[10]

Another branch of the New Age and pagan religions see the world as made up of many gods and spiritual forces. Such polytheistic ontology sees reality as a cacophony of myriad spiritual forces.

While Christians and Jews believe we live in a real world, they do not subscribe to the materialistic view of humanists and Communists—that all that exists is the material world and the spiritual world is merely an invention of deluded minds. On this basis Christians and Jews have explored the world and the laws of the universe, and thereby developed civilization. Pagans, however, remained in a barbaric fear of venturing forth into the unknown and were unable to develop scientifically.

Every movie has an ontology, whether the producer, writer, or director knows it or not. The funny and poignant movie *Groundhog Day* presents a nominalistic ontology in its story that is contrary to the Word of God. It has a moral conclusion, however, that makes it worth watching.

Movies with a magical premise, such as *Aladdin*, usually present a nominalistic ontology. However, it is interesting that the movie *The Lion King* has an ontology in which there are real consequences for young Simba's actions—real death and real solutions that require his taking responsibility.

Subsidiary Ascertainment and Discernment Questions:
How does the media product present knowledge, and how does this presentation compare with the biblical norm?

How do we know that anything exists? This question is often phrased: How do you know that a tree fell in the forest if no one, including yourself, sees it?

Christians and Jews believe in a real epistemology, which means that they know because God tells them. God has told us that his laws govern all creation, including the forest, so we know that the life and death of trees occurs because trees are subject to his laws.

Many media products, especially horror films, posit that we cannot know, and therefore we are trapped in an unpredictable and frightening world. Other media products, such as Sartre's famous play *No Exit*, take an existentialist perspective that one cannot know, so life is essentially meaningless.

In *Groundhog Day* there is the unique combination of ontological nominalism and epistemological realism. Even though the days repeat themselves in a very unreal fashion, the hero knows that they repeat themselves and adjusts his actions accordingly. However, no one else can, so the other characters are trapped in the nominalistic universe.

Subsidiary Ascertainment and Discernment Questions:
What is the cosmology of the media product, and how does that presentation compare with the biblical norm?

Christians and Jews believe that God created the universe, therefore the universe is governed by his laws of creation. Since he has informed us that he is good, we can trust those laws of creation and explore the universe with confidence.

In contrast, many media products have an evolutionary cosmology, which means that nothing is certain and everything is ultimately pointless. Thus, you need to understand the cosmology of a media product to make discerning entertainment choices.

Ultimate Ascertainment Question and Discernment Questions:
What is the worldview of the media product, and how does it compare with a biblical worldview?

Developing a biblical worldview involves much more than a particular perspective or filter. Your worldview defines your approach to all areas of thought, including mass media, education, politics, religion, law, and government. It is the task of the viewer to examine the messages and assumptions that the entertainment industry imparts, and to ask questions that will pierce through thinking that is inconsistent with biblical principles. Parents have this opportunity to teach their children how to probe beneath these assumptions and to test their truth or validity against the Word of God.

When looking at a media product, ask the basic philosophical questions:

- What is the nature of reality?
- What can we know about reality?
- What is the nature and purpose of humanity?
- How do we decide what is good or evil?
- In what does a human find value?
- What is the relationship of the individual to God? to self? to nature?
- Is truth relative or is it absolute, regardless of the era or culture?
- How does the hero live his life justly?

Every media product reflects and projects the broader culture in which we live. The entertainment industry often regards the problematic elements in their media product as a problematic element of our society as a whole.

The entertainment industry evades criticism by appealing to the First Amendment and by claiming that we cannot judge a media product out of the context of our culture. Clearly, these are specious evasions. We need to view the world through God's Word, not view God's Word through the eyes of the world. We need to be media literate and familiar with a biblical worldview, then compare the worldviews of the media products we encounter with that biblical worldview.

Ascertainment Question:
Is there any redeeming value?

A media product may not have a biblical worldview and still be redemptive. *Nothing in Common* tells the story of an egocentric young advertising executive who pushes everyone around and plays with every woman he meets. In the end, however, he gives up his job and fast-paced life to take care of his sick father. He makes a decision for love that costs him everything in the world's eyes, but gives him back his father and a new appreciation of life.

Surprisingly, his boss lets him leave work to take care of his father with the insight that "there has been only one perfect son," or so he had been told. *Nothing in Common* tells the story of a man who has been moved by the power of love from selfishness to selfless giving—a very redemptive message.

It is very rare that a film can have a redemptive element that will transcend the negative elements. Some children's films, such as *The Dirt Bike Kid* do transcend their negative parts because those parts are treated lightly, with deference and a lack of conviction as storytelling devices, while the redemptive elements of love, courage, and integrity is emphasized. If a motion picture does transcend its parts because of some redemptive element, then we need to be aware of both the good and the bad in the movie so that we can discuss it honestly and rebut any negative elements that may be detrimental to our Christian worldview.

REFLECTION QUESTIONS

Reflection Question: Would you be embarrassed to sit through the movie with your parents, your children, or Jesus?

When we are alone or with a friend, we often deceive ourselves regarding the true nature of a movie or television program. If we ignore the faults in a movie, we will slowly be conditioned to accept, if not condone, a non-Christian point of view.

There are many other questions we could ask in evaluating a motion picture, but they all may be boiled down to the question, *Would we like our loved ones to be inundated by the messages being communicated by this movie?*

Reflection Questions: What was your favorite part, and why did you like that part so much?

Here you're guiding children to think about how the mass media product relates to real life. Most important, you're boosting a child's self-esteem. Any time you ask children their opinion, you build their confidence tremendously.

Reflection Question: If you were an actor in this movie, what character would you be?

Children usually love to think about the character they identify with most, or would most like to be. Your child's responses can give you insights into his or her wishes and concerns. Children are prone to accept role models and to accept the underlying belief systems that these models exercise and demonstrate. In this discussion, a parent can expose worldviews and value systems that are inconsistent and even dangerous.

Subsidiary Reflection Question: Would you do what that character did, or would you have done things differently?

This question gets children thinking about the plausibility of characters' actions. It's important to invite your child to consider whether a character's action was the right choice. Mass media product makers sometimes manipulate a character's choice just to make the entertainment product more exciting. Children should know that this kind of thing goes on in Hollywood.

Reflection Questions: What did you like about the hero/heroine? What things were important to the hero/heroine? Are those things important to you?

Get children to explore the association between the character and their own lives. This helps children become aware of why they like a character—was it because the character made them feel good, or because he or she did something they could do? Mass media products made for children often communicate positive values of honesty, loyalty, and so on. If your child responds to your questions with answers such as, "Well, she was a good friend to him and believed in him no matter what," this will tell you that your child is picking up on values. Together, with biblical guidance, you can discuss a full range of solutions to the problem this character faced and possible remedies for his or her future problems.

Reflection Questions: What feelings did you have as you watched or listened to this media product? Did you feel sad, mad, or scared? Did your feelings change? If so, when?

Can your child identify what he is feeling? Does the child realize that it is the media product and the storyline that makes him feel that way? It is important for parents to explore this because children need to put a name to their feelings—especially younger children, who might not know where their feelings are coming from. Asking children questions such as these after seeing a movie helps them identify the source of their emotions.

There are many other questions we could ask to evaluate a mass media product, but they all boil down to how we want our loved ones to be affected by messages communicated by the mass media. If we care about others and about the Lord Jesus, we will take a stand against anything communicated that undermines a biblical worldview and mocks our Lord and Savior Jesus Christ. Anything less than standing on his Word denies our relationship with him.

SEASONS

Through Their Eyes and Ears

Beyond asking the right questions to help your children develop discernment about the mass media of entertainment, you need to understand the perspectives or methods of evaluative media viewing and listening that your children possess. You will then be able to guide them through the different levels of critical viewing.

Our perspectives shape the way we look at and understand a media product. By viewing the media through these various perspectives or filters, we are better able to comprehend and analyze its message and how the message influences us and others.

Our children develop perspectives of critical viewing that reflect their cognitive levels as they grow and mature. A young child in the imagination stage perceives and extracts a different message from mass media than older children in the concrete stage and even teenagers growing into adulthood.

Try to picture what they are seeing through their eyes at the various cognitive levels, and introduce them to other perspectives appropriate to their cognitive level. You can use these methods of critical viewing with your children to understand how they examine media messages and to teach them to dissect the message. This is an opportunity for you and your children to better understand the workings of the mass media of entertainment together.

Role Models

The first stage of cognitive development, as we have discussed, is the sensation stage (approximately from infancy to age two). During this time the child's sole means of processing reality is his or her senses. Children in this stage think that they are the center of the universe and that everything around them serves them.

Most children in the sensation stage of cognitive development look at the entertainment media aesthetically—in terms of how interesting and attractive it is to watch or hear.

Young children may not pick up on the emotional elements in a movie or television program, and certainly will miss the message of the lyrics of a song. They often toddle around, oblivious to a very emotive scene occurring in a television program or movie, much to the chagrin of their parents. They will, however, note and respond to the emotional state of their parents.

Though not cognizant of the various aspects of a particular media product, young children do absorb what they see and hear and can repeat songs and remember images. Therefore they need to be protected from those mass media products that will leave negative images in their minds. Furthermore, because the mass media will model behavior for them, and they will copy that behavior, parents must be careful about the products to which they are exposed.

If you are watching or listening with a very young child during this stage who can talk, ask, "What do you see?" "What do you hear?" Then help the child understand what he or she is seeing and hearing.

For parents, this is often an easier stage than the next. Because it is clear to the parent that a child at this stage sees the world differently, most parents are careful in their guidance of the cognitive development of such young children. Regrettably, when the child starts to talk fluently, a parent will often forget that the child perceives the world differently, and will treat the child like an adult.

Imagine

The next stage of cognitive development is the imagination or preoperational stage, which spans the period from two to seven years of age. In this stage the child's cognition is dedicated to the acquisition of representational skills such as language, mental imagery, drawing, and symbolic play—and limited by being serial and one-dimensional. During this stage, the child has a very active imagination, often confusing fact and fiction.

While the terms "real" and "make-believe" are used by younger children, they do not understand the implications of these terms. Thus, the notion that a character or an event is "not real" will have little impact on a younger child's emotions.

Younger children in the imagination stage of cognitive development look at the entertainment media aesthetically, syntactically—in terms of the characters, action, and special effects[11]—and emotively—in terms of how it excites and amuses them.

Younger children focus on the individual elements of a movie, such as acts of violence, a character's costume and outward appearance, and the landscape or setting. They tend to see each image as isolated, so each event in the program is taken at face value.

At this cognitive stage, the child does not integrate the images to create a dramatic story with a moral or happy ending. They are viewing the movie syntactically—looking at each element such as action, the special effects, the camera angle. The picture tells the story, much like an advertisement page in a magazine. Therefore, most documentaries and lectures do not hold their attention no matter how amusing or interesting the topic.

Aware of this, advertisers design toy-product advertisements using quick camera clips and sharp angle transitions. If they can keep your child's attention long enough, the child will remember the product, and you will hear about this product the next time you enter the store.

The mass media serve two functions in a household: to inform and to persuade. The media are extremely adept at persuasion and commercialization. Therefore, as the audience, we must become more savvy in our ability to think critically. Commercials using icons of the family to sell a long-distance carrier, images of survival protection to sell recreational vehicles, and the promise of sexual attraction to promote a certain brand of toothpaste are rampant in the advertisement industry. Though many of these tactics are identifiable, we can be easily caught up emotionally and allow such messages to sway our opinions and perspectives.

At a young age children can develop an awareness of the emotive quality of critical viewing. Television programs, movies, the Internet, and news media are all worthwhile places to get meaningful information, but much of this information is saturated with an emotive influential agenda. Christians need to discern when this agenda is sincere or when it is used to manipulate. Manipulation tries to change our feelings or persuade us away from the truth, while sincerity comes from the liberating truth of God.

Since younger children actively view a movie or program for its presentation, encourage them to look at the film for its aesthetic value as well. You can ask them to describe the different camera angles and lighting in a scene: "Why was this scene so bright and happy?" "Why was that scene so dark and gloomy?"

Your child will develop discernment as he or she discovers what you appreciate and find to be attractive in a video. Videos are helpful because you can stop the tape and go back to places that you feel were presented honestly and well-produced.

Viewing a program aesthetically means understanding its presentation. Now is an appropriate time to interest your child in what is artistic and what is not. If the presentation is honest and not biased, as a parent you can use this opportunity to instill these ideals in your children. When they are older, you will be able to hear them share these ideals back to you.

Some movies that appeal to this age group are *Babe*, *Charlotte's Web*, *Lassie*, *Mickey's Christmas Carol*, *The Muppets Take Manhattan*, and *Stuart Little 2*. These movies are child-friendly, low on violence, and provide positive role models. Regrettably, most of them are animation or fantasies—categories that play upon the child's inability to separate fact from fiction. Therefore you need to ask your child discernment questions, such as "Can animals talk?" to help them develop an understanding of the difference between fact and fantasy as they move into the next stage of cognitive development.

Some children persist in the imagination stage longer than others, and some develop patterns of thought that are conducive to ontological nominalism, or magical thinking, based on what they view and their susceptibility.

Keep in mind that during this stage even psychologically healthy preschool children tend to indiscriminately imitate all that they see and hear, whether the characters are good guys or bad guys, and whether the long-term consequences of the actions are positive or negative. They have very little ability to choose what is imitation-worthy and what isn't. For this reason, in choosing an entertainment product for young children, we should look for as many imitation-worthy acts as possible. Children need to learn to deal with tragedy and with bad people eventually, but the more their preschool years, particularly the early preschool years, can be filled with positive models, the better off they will be.

In this regard, it is extremely important to avoid exposing young children to acts of violence that are easy to imitate. In *The Wizard of Oz*, Dorothy's killing the witch by accidentally pouring water on her does not inspire much real-life imitation in young children. The kicks and karate chops seen in *Teenage Mutant Ninja Turtles*, by contrast, are easily imitated by young children.

Just the Facts

The next stage is the concrete operational stage, which spans ages seven to eleven. In this stage the child becomes able to simultaneously perceive two points of view and is able to master quantities, relations, and classes of objects. At this stage, there is such a strong correspondence between the child's thoughts and reality that he or she assumes these thoughts about reality are accurate and distorts the facts to fit what he or she thinks.

Children in the concrete stage of cognitive development look at the entertainment media

- conceptually—in terms of the storyline, character motivations, and basic concepts;
- emotionally—in terms of the emotional response of the characters;
- realistically—in terms of the realism of the events portrayed; and
- legalistically—in terms of whether the perpetrator is rewarded or punished.

In this stage, the child is starting to appreciate the nonvisual threat. Younger children are likely to be frightened by visually frightening creatures like witches and monsters, while older children will focus more on conceptual qualities, such as the motives of a character.[12] Indeed, older children are likely to be more upset by an evil, normal-looking character or by an unseen threat than by a benign but grotesque character. Thus younger children are more likely to be frightened by *The Wizard of Oz* and *The Incredible Hulk*, while older children are more frightened by movies such as *Poltergeist* and *Jaws*, which rely more on nonvisual threats.

Children in this stage are more attuned to realism in the plot and the victim's emotional reactions to the threat. Violent depictions for which the aggressor is rewarded are most likely to produce imitation effects or foster attitudes supportive of aggression.[13] Also, as long as there is no punishment associated with a violent act, young viewers have been shown to imitate such depictions.[14]

Children in this stage are more likely to respond to characters who are attractive.[15] In determining whether the character is "good" or "bad," this age group tends to focus more on the character's motives.[16]

Violence that is justified is more likely to be imitated,[17] such as the hero who is forced to be violent because his job demands it (e.g., *Dirty Harry*) or because he must retaliate against an enemy (e.g., *Batman*).

Children in this stage are more likely to imitate models portrayed as similar to themselves,[18] especially if cues in the program are similar to those in real life.[19] Children in this stage need to be helped to compare what they see with biblical models. Ask them questions that will cause them to make these comparisons, such as "How does the character relate to what God teaches us about what is right and wrong to do?"

Older Children in the Reflection Stage

In the reflection stage, which spans ages twelve to fifteen, abstract thought gains strength, though there is still incomplete differentiation as a result of the adolescent's inability to conceptualize the thoughts of others—exemplified by the assumption that other people are equally obsessed with his or her behavior and appearance (such as a pimple). Since the adolescent still has difficulty conceptualizing the consequences of his actions, he will often take risks without regard to consequences.

In this stage, the adolescent will perceive the media product

- semantically—by looking at the individual elements such as words, nudity, and violence and their meanings;
- propositionally—by looking at what the program or movie is communicating as summarized in the premise;
- thematically—by looking at the themes that are present;
- sociologically—by looking at how it relates to culture and society; and
- systemically—by looking at how it relates to other productions in a similar genre.

The reflection stage is an excellent time for helping your children develop critical viewing habits. At this age, they can look deeply at the content of a story and learn about plot, character, and setting. This will also strengthen their reading skills throughout their lives. They can also learn to look at a movie's language and make decisions about what is appropriate and what is out-of-character or not useful for a character.

In the reflection stage, the child desires deeply to make decisions and solve problems but wants approval from his or her parents in the process. As a parent, you have a prime opportunity to help lay a valuable foundation for your children to rely on as they grow.

As children grow older they become able to evaluate entertainment media through higher levels of critical thinking. Children at the reflection stage of cognitive development are beginning to understand the content, language, and drama of a story. Since older children are developing the ability to make inferences between a cowboy's black hat and his dark nature or actions, parents can foster this progress by discussing a story semantically.

Adults tend to overlook some elements of a story when they know the story has a happy ending. Such is the case in the Walt Disney animated feature *Aladdin*. The main theme of the story is that love triumphs over evil. One such evil is Aladdin's own deceit, as the character Aladdin is a thief. A good discernment question to ask one's child in this case would be, "Was it wrong for Aladdin to steal?" Most younger children will say "no," but your adolescent should begin to understand the complexity of Aladdin's character and be able to condemn the stealing while understanding that he learns that he has to be honest in order to achieve his heart's desire.

From the story's plot, characters, and setting we can summarize its premise. Children at this cognitive level are just developing the ability to integrate the elements of a story to deduce its basic assumptions or to view the program or movie propositionally.

Although this is a challenging task for many children, you can use a video box to help. Have your children read the description of the movie on the video cover before they view. What do you already know about the story? the characters? What is the conflict that needs to be solved? How will the conflict be solved? Here is a way to quiz your children and yourself about the nature of the movies you bring into your home: Does the solution to the conflict have a biblical answer or a secular, ungodly answer?

Because many plots are written by non-Christians or people with an unbiblical belief system, many movies and television stories end without a redemptive or positive resolution. Many of today's writers assume that there is no escape from evil, no release from sin, and no basis for true hope. Though I suggest that you do not subject your family to this type of mass media of entertainment on purpose, there is a valuable distinction between the light of God and the darkness of the world. If you choose to view a movie and then through critical analysis discover the story's premise to be lacking in biblical grace, here is a wonderful time to share with developing minds what God can do with this situation. Now you are set to discuss the ways God could influence the characters to change hearts. How would you solve this conflict? What do you feel is a Christian response?

While older children are looking for the meaning of a story, you can help them use the themes inherent in a program or movie to draw out the overall premise. Themes such as color (a dark character dressed in black or a positive character dressed in white) are beneficial to children in the cognitive stage. Directors use lighting and foreshadowing to disclose information that aids the audience in discovering a story's meaning. By critically viewing the program or movie thematically, you can look at how the program's themes shape our impression of the premise.

Teenagers in the Reflection Stage

In the relationship stage, adolescents grow into mature adults and progress toward complete differentiation. Adults understand that others are different, and accept those differences by learning to relate to others. Furthermore, the adult is able to conceptualize the consequences of his or her actions and take the necessary steps to reduce the risks.

Teenagers and adults are able to view the media product

- ontologically—by looking at how the media product deals with the nature of being,
- epistemologically—by looking at how it deals with the nature of knowing,
- morally—by looking at its moral perspective and content, and
- philosophically—by looking at the philosophical perspective and the worldview.

As children develop, their cognitive powers of reasoning and thinking grow tremendously and they become capable of using the concept of "not." If all has gone well, when they become teenagers they will be able to appreciate the fact that in works like *Hamlet* and *Oedipus Rex*, the violent acts are tragic and horrible with terrible consequences, and perhaps their repulsion for violence will increase rather than decrease. A teenager should be able to identify with certain characters in a work of fiction and want to become more like them and less like other characters. This is the stage where all our previous questions come into play and where full media literacy and discernment can be achieved.

However, because teenagers are still immature in many ways other than cognitive development, they are susceptible to the appeal of today's movie theaters, videos, and cable-TV channels. It is therefore advisable to help them understand the impact of the mass media and to teach and encourage them to reflect on the biblical principles that apply.

Teenagers hate to be manipulated. They need to understand that Satan is trying to manipulate them in his quest for their minds and hearts. He is constantly endeavoring to get them to think his thoughts and act his ways. From gratuitous profanity in otherwise innocuous story scripts, to rock 'n' roll radio, to steamy scenes in dramatic films and vulgar comedy, a humanistic philosophy is being presented. Christian young people need to recognize this and shun it.

Before your teenager rents a video, plops down in front of the TV for some mindless entertainment, or even considers going to a theater with friends to see the latest film (in a theater where you have no control over what comes before your eyes), ask yourself these questions:

- Does good triumph over evil?
- Is the primary appeal to the flesh? (1 Peter 1:13)
- Will this use of the media allow you to control what they watch and hear, and thus bring every thought under captivity of Christ? (Proverbs 4:23–27)
- Will there be an anti-biblical philosophy, unwholesome music, and compromised standards that will wear them down, make them doubt what they believe, or tempt them to sin? (Isaiah 55:7)

- Will they be tired when they are watching or listening? Are they likely to let their mental guard down?

Perhaps substitution of another medium such as uplifting music or a good book would be more to the glory of God (Philippians 4:8).

While the rest of society is making TV and movies the standard against which they measure and make moral choices, Christians should not. The fact that someone else tries to legitimize an action or practice by presenting it in an attractive package does not lessen the Christian's responsibility to make the Word of God the main source of his values.

By and large, the mass media is discretionary. We are able to control what we put before our eyes by the way we use it or don't use it. Here are some general guidelines:

- Don't watch just because the television set is there or the video cover looks good.
- Don't watch out of boredom; instead read, exercise, play a game, or listen to good music.
- Set priorities, and make the media a lower priority.

In previous centuries "entertainment" was a once-in-a-while pastime. Someone might read aloud or play a musical instrument, and there might be an occasional visit to the theater. Today's use of the media has gone far beyond this level. It is not separate from the daily routine, it *is* the daily routine.

God's standards have not changed. He calls us to bring each thought into captivity and to be good stewards of the time he gives us on this earth. Remember, the goal is to bring every thought into captivity: This is a lifelong challenge and an eternal command.

By ourselves we can't resist the devil's schemes. However, God, who is far greater than Satan, has already won the war. When we know and follow him, he makes us "more than conquerors" in Christ.

NOTES

1. God's Word is Jesus Christ (John 1). God's written Word is the Bible. God's written Word was used often by the Reformers to emphasize the relation between God the Father, God the Son, and his Holy Scripture.
2. Lajos Egri wrote the definitive text about scriptwriting, *The Art of Dramatic Writing*—a must-read for anyone interested in scriptwriting. This is the primary text used at USC, UCLA, and other premiere film and television schools.
3. Evelyn Dokovic, *Morality in Media* newsletter, August 1988.
4. Timothy Jay, *Cursing in America* (Philadelphia: John Benjamins, 1992).
5. Professor Marcuse, a famous Marxist at the Sorbonne, advocated using language as a weapon. He inspired many renowned Communist revolutionaries in the twentieth century. Even Jane Fonda studied with him.
6. See S. Robert Lichter, Stanley Rothman, and Linda Lichter, *The Media Elite* (Maryland: Adler & Adler, 1986). See also Donald Wildmon, *The Home*

Invaders (Wheaton, Ill.: Victor Books, 1985), 18–23, for an excellent analysis of the Lichter-Rothman studies.

7. Catherine Millard, *Rewriting of America's History* (Camp Hill, Penn.: Christian Publications, 1991).

8. Lajos Egri, *The Art of Dramatic Writing* (New York: Simon & Schuster, 1946, 1960), 6.

9. The term "mass media-maker" is used here to refer to all persons responsible for authoring a movie, including the screenwriter, the director, the producer, the executive producer, and so forth.

10. C. S. Lewis, *Mere Christianity* (New York: MacMillan, 1943), 56.

11. From a media producer's point of view, the "syntactical aspect" of the media product refers to how the elements come together and how the pieces and characters relate to each other. Here, however, we are focusing on how these elements relate to the young viewer or listener.

12. Barbara J. Wilson, Daniel Lynn, and Barbara Randall, "Applying Social Science Research to Film Ratings: A Shift from Offensiveness to Harmful Effects," *Journal of Broadcasting and Electronic Media* 34, no. 4 (Fall 1990): 443–68; C. Hoffner and J. Cantor, "Developmental Differences in Responses to a Television Character's Appearance and Behavior," *Developmental Psychology* 21 (1985) : 1065–74.

13. Ibid., citing A. Bandura, "Influence of Models' Reinforcement Contingencies on the Acquisition of Imitative Responses," *Journal of Personality and Social Psychology* 1 (1965): 589–95; A. Bandura, D. Ross, and S. A. Ross, "Vicarious Reinforcement and Imitative Learning," *Journal of Abnormal and Social Psychology* 67 (1963) : 601–7; M. A. Rosekrans and W. W. Hartup, "Imitative Influences of Consistent and Inconsistent Response Consequences to a Model on Aggressive Behavior in Children," *Journal of Personality and Social Psychology* 7 (1967): 429–34.

14. Ibid., citing Bandura, "Influence of Models' Reinforcement."

15. Ibid., citing Bandura, *Social Foundations*.

16. Ibid., citing Collins, "Interpretation and Inference."

17. Ibid., citing L. Berkowitz, "Some Aspects of Observed Aggression," *Journal of Personality and Social Psychology* 2 (1965) : 359–69 and T. P. Meyer, "Effects of Viewing Justified and Unjustified Real Film Violence.," *Journal of Personality and Social Psychology* 23 (1972) : 21–29.

18. Ibid., citing Bandura, *Social Foundations*.

19. Ibid., citing M. A. Liss, L. C. Reinhardt, and S. Fredrickesen, "TV Heroes: The Impact of Rheteric and Deeds," *Journal of Applied Developmental Psychology* 4 (1983): 175-87.

CHAPTER 4

GLOSSARY AND EXPLANATION OF REVIEW RATINGS

QUALITY RATINGS

☆☆☆☆ Excellent
☆☆☆ Good
☆☆ Fair
☆ Poor

Quality Ratings refer to the production values in the movie, its entertainment quality, and whether the movie fulfills what it sets out to do. A four-star rating does not guarantee that the movie will meet our criteria for what makes a truly great work of art. That will depend on one's moral and spiritual values, issues that our Acceptability Ratings address (see below).

ACCEPTABILITY RATINGS

+4 Exemplary: Is based on a biblical, usually Christian, worldview; no questionable elements whatsoever.
+3 Moral: Some minor questionable elements.
+2 Good: Moderately questionable elements.
+1 Worthwhile: Discernment required for young children.
−1 Caution: Discretion advised for older children.
−2 Extreme Caution: Discretion advised for adults.
−3 Excessive: Excessive sex, violence, immorality, and/or worldview problems.
−4 Abhorrent: Intentional blasphemy, evil, gross immorality, and/or worldview problems.

The Acceptability Ratings take into account cognitive stages of development, moral issues, and theological issues. These ratings are designed to help parents with children and the media-wise adult viewer. They are based on a traditional view of the Bible and Christianity. Some movies receive positive ratings because they fit a biblical worldview of ethical monotheism, even though they contain little explicit Christian content. The ultimate evaluation of a movie depends on one's moral and spiritual values. Those values depend on one's worldview and philosophy of life, humanity, the universe, and the supernatural.

Most people understand that something can be very high in entertainment quality and abhorrent in acceptability. Teenagers understand this all too well and constantly argue, "But, Dad, it's a great movie." Along the same line, Hitler was a great orator, but almost all of what he said was evil. God gives people talent, which they can use for good or evil. Thus, some highly entertaining movies are evil, such as the Nazi movie *I Accuse*, which won top prize at the Venice Film Festival and convinced many German people to approve the Holocaust, or so-called "mercy killing."

Our approach has been extremely effective with teenagers and youth. It helps them develop media wisdom rather than sow the seeds of rebellion by helping them to analyze, understand, discern, and then choose wisely.

CONTENT RATINGS AND ABBREVIATIONS

Ab	—anti-biblical, anti-Christian, or anti-Jewish worldview or elements
AC	—anti-Communist worldview
ACap	—anti-capitalism, anti-wealth, politics of envy
AP	—anti-patriotism or anti-Americanism
A	—alcohol use or abuse
B	—biblical or moral worldview, principles, perspective, or character
b	—minor occurences of biblical morality
C	—Christian worldview or elements, gospel witness, or positive reference to Jesus Christ
c	—minor occcurences of Christian elements
Cap	—capitalism
Co	—communism
D	—substance abuse
E	—environmentalism or environmentalist worldview
Ev	—evolutionary worldview or elements
Fe	—feminist worldview or elements
FM	—free-market elements
FR	—non-Christian worldview or false religions
H	—humanist worldview or humanism (incl. Marxism, communism, socialism, etc.)
Ho	—homosexual worldview or homosexuality (incl. sodomy and lesbianism)
I	—internationalist worldview or elements
L	—few obscenities and profanities (1–9)
LL	—several obscenities and profanities (10–25)
LLL	—numerous obscenities and profanities (more than 25)
M	—miscellaneous (gambling, revenge, theft, blackmail, etc.)
N	—naturalistic nudity (not in a sexual context)
NN	—partial or brief nudity
NNN	—extensive nudity
O	—occult worldview, occult elements, or Satanism
P	—patriotic worldview or elements
Pa	—pagan worldview or elements
PC	—politically correct worldview or elements

Ro   —romantic, idealistic worldview or elements
RH   —revisionist history
S   —implied adultery, promiscuity, or sexual immorality
SS   —depicted adultery, promiscuity, or sexual immorality
SSS   —graphic adultery, promiscuity, or sexual immorality
So   —socialist worldview or elements
V   —brief or action violence
VV   —moderate violence
VVV   —extreme or graphic violence

TRADITIONAL LITERARY GENRES (5-STEP SCALE)

1. *Mythic:* The triumph of God or gods.
2. *Heroic:* The triumph of man by his own means.
3. *High Ironic:* The triumph of man by a quirk of fate.
4. *Low Ironic:* The failure of man by a quirk of fate.
5. *Demonic:* The triumph of evil, demons, etc.

ANTI-CHRISTIAN WORLDVIEWS[1]

Humanism: Humanism posits man as the measure of all things. Modern humanism, however, is not just an anthropocentric or man-centered system. Accepting (as a matter of good faith!) the definition of humanism posited by "A Humanist Manifesto,"[2] modern humanism (unlike traditional or Christian humanism) proposes that only the material world exists—there is no supernatural or nonmaterial world, no God, no gods, and usually no alien "others." Man has no soul. He is just a "meat machine" that has "evolved" according to some form of Darwinism. Modern humanism always has a strong anti-supernatural bias. Marx said that his communism was the ultimate humanism, and advocated that a humanist society should abolish religion, family, nation, and private property.

Romanticism: Man is essentially good and noble, and civilization (by which Rousseau, the "father" of Romanticism, meant Christianity) corrupts man. Man is controlled by his "heart" and emotions, not by his intellect or logical mind. Paganism and mob-rule are related to Romanticism, though Romanticism is more consistent and avoids totemism, or belief in a mystical relationship between the emblem of a family, clan, or ancestor. Romanticism is not related to the idea of romance, but is an idealistic worldview.

Paganism: Eclectic, "anything goes" worship of whatever gods or nontraditional belief system a person desires to worship (or a mixture of belief systems), apart from any Christian or biblical values, in contrast to an organized system such as Shintoism. Sensual pleasure and material goods are often, but not always, the main goal in life. Paganism often leads to hedonism, anarchy, or a fascist dictatorship. It often involves spiritism—the use of magic or worship of many false gods, often singling out one of the gods for special worship or lifelong devotion. Includes what is sometimes called "New Age" religion.

GLOSSARY

The following is a brief glossary of terms.

Profanity: Language that profanes or defiles that which is sacred. Usually refers to taking the Lord Jesus' name in vain.

Blasphemy: Language or actions that curse, revile, mock, or blaspheme God, the Holy Spirit, Jesus, or the church.

Obscenity: Foul, disgusting, offensive, and lewd language.

Discernment: The word *discern* means "to see or understand the difference; to make distinction; as, to discern between good and evil, truth and falsehood."[3] *Discernment* is "the act of discerning ... the power or faculty of the mind, by which it distinguishes one thing from another, as truth from falsehood, virtue from vice."[4] Discernment implies an "acuteness of judgment" and can be seen as "the power of perceiving the differences of things or ideas and their relations and tendencies."[5] As Noah Webster pointed out in the first edition of his *American Dictionary of the English Language*, "the errors of youth often proceed from the want of discernment."[6]

Wisdom: The word "wisdom" can be defined as "the right use of knowledge" or "the choice of laudable ends and of the best means to accomplish them."[7] However, after defining "wisdom" in that manner, Noah Webster notes that

> this is wisdom in act, effect, or practice. If wisdom is to be considered as a faculty of the mind, it is the faculty of discerning or judging what is most just, proper and useful, and if it is to be considered as an acquirement, it is the knowledge and use of what is best, most just, most proper, most conducive to prosperity or happiness. Wisdom in the first sense, or practical wisdom, is nearly synonymous with discretion. It differs somewhat from prudence, in this respect; prudence is the exercise of sound judgment in avoiding evils; wisdom is the exercise of sound judgment either in avoiding evils or attempting good. Prudence then is a species, of which wisdom is the genus.[8]

Knowledge: Noah Webster defines *knowledge* as "a clear and certain perception of that which exists, or of truth and fact."[9]

Understanding: "The faculty of the human mind by which it apprehends the real state of things presented to it, or by which it receives or comprehends the ideas which others express and intend to communicate. The understanding is also called the intellectual faculty. It is the faculty by means of which we obtain a great part of our knowledge. Luke 24, Ephesians 1."[10]

Mass media: The Concise Columbia Encyclopedia defines *mass media* as

> [A] comprehensive term embracing television, radio, motion pictures, and large-circulation newspapers and magazines. It refers to much more than the journalistic aspects of the instruments of popular communication. The mass media often function as the locus of social control and the source of popular culture. They help create historical events, teach values, and by virtue of the huge commercial enterprises they represent, affect the viability of free societies.[11]

In this book, the term *mass media* refers to the industry and process of communicating with a large audience. Thus, "mass media" refers to the mass medium of television in the sense of the means of communicating with a large audience and the television industry involved in such communication. Furthermore, it refers to much more than just journalism, encompassing the entire industry involved in communicating to and entertaining a large number of people.

Entertainment: Amusement, pleasure, or instruction, derived from conversation, discourse, argument, oratory, music, dramatic performances, etc.; the pleasure which the mind receives from anything interesting, and which holds or arrests the attention. Something that amuses, pleases, or diverts, especially a performance or show.[12]

Mass media of entertainment: The "mass media of entertainment" is that section of the mass media which is focused on entertainment. However, it can be argued that all of the mass media is concerned with entertainment and that journalism in the mass media such as television is merely another form of entertainment.

Amuse: "To entertain the mind agreeably; to occupy or detain attention with agreeable objects, whether by singing, conversation, or a show of curiosities."[13]

Culture: The *Concise Columbia Encyclopedia* notes that in anthropology *culture* is

> The way of life of a human society, transmitted from one generation to the next by learning (of language and other symbolic media) and by experience. Cultural universals include social organization, religion, structure, economic organization, and material culture (tools, weapons, clothing). The spread of culture traits (customs, ideas, attitudes) among groups by direct or indirect contact is called diffusion. The general stages in cultural evolution are nomadic food gathering (as in the Old and Middle Stone Age); settled food producing (New Stone Age); and urban dwelling.[14]

The Culture Wars: The *culture wars* are the battle for the way of life of our society, our fundamental beliefs, and how we function. Will we continue as a Christian society or will we descend into a new barbarism?

Pagan: Anyone who is not a Christian or Jew; a heathen who has no religion, or a hedonist.

Media literacy: The ability to access, analyze, interpret, and create media messages. The ability to access must include everything from owning media delivery devices (TV, radio, computer, VCR, etc.) to understanding how to turn them on and use them to deliver messages. One cannot "access" a VCR if one does not now how to connect the various wires and operate the controls.

To *analyze* is to comprehend not only the storyline or language of a program but also how it may have been put together. Understanding the media requires some exposure to and comprehension of the way it was made.

Interpretation looks at the basis for the story and the agenda that may be part of its underlying message. If the program is sponsored by the XYZ company, one can assume they expect their views to be promoted, probably not only in the advertisements but also in the story. In some cases, the agenda of the production company is promoted regardless of the advertisers. Some networks have stated that the programs they produce are intended to appeal to the "real world" of singles who live together, adults who accept divorce as an option, and homosexual viewers. They stretch the bounds of acceptable programming every season.

Creating media material can help people understand what to look for in the media we watch. When teenagers use a video camera to make a ten-minute film, the choice of camera angles, script, actors, sets, and scenery all become important factors.

Now that you have the background information, you're ready to read the movie reviews from 1990 to the first half of 2002.

NOTES

1. See Dr. Ted Baehr's book, *The Media-Wise Family*, 248–68.
2. "A Humanist Manifesto," *The New Humanist* V1, no. 3 (May/June 1993): 1–5.
3. Noah Webster, *An American Dictionary of the English Language*, 1st ed. (New York: Foundation for American Christian Education, 1993).
4. Ibid.
5. Ibid.
6. Ibid.
7. Ibid.
8. Ibid.
9. Ibid.
10. Ibid.
11. *The Concise Columbia Encyclopedia* is licensed from Columbia University press. Copyright © 1995 by Columbia University Press. All rights reserved.
12. Webster, *An American Dictionary*.
13. Ibid.
14. *The Concise Columbia Encyclopedia*.

A Decade of Movie Reviews

Including Lists of the Best and Worst of Each Year

1990 MOVIES

Heartwarming

THE ADVENTURES OF MILO AND OTIS

Quality: ☆☆☆☆   Acceptability: +4

WARNING CODES:
Language: None
Violence: None
Sex: None
Nudity: None

RATING: G
GENRE: Children's animal adventure
INTENDED AUDIENCE: Children
RUNNING TIME: 80 minutes
NARRATION: Dudley Moore
DIRECTOR: Masanori Hata
PRODUCERS: Masaru Kakutani and Satoru Ogata
WRITER: Mark Saltzman
DISTRIBUTOR: Columbia Pictures
BRIEF SUMMARY:
The Adventures of Milo and Otis is a heartwarming, live-action movie narrated by Dudley Moore about a mischievous kitten named Milo and his friend, a pug-nosed pup named Otis. Milo and Otis begin their life in a barnyard. One day Milo is swept downriver by the current. Otis follows, hoping to rescue the feline. Once Milo is rescued, they discover it is not easy to get back to the farm. Their adventures include close encounters with everything from a fox to a clam. Some funny and a few scary moments occur as they are chased by a bear, pecked by gulls, and saved by a sea turtle. As they make their way home, the seasons change. So do Milo and Otis.

Director Hata said of *Milo and Otis*, "I wanted to make an animal film that would delight and warm the hearts of all who saw it . . . , the only characters of which would be animals and the setting of which would be timeless and priceless. . . . I also wanted the film to be a celebration of life." This he has done with beautiful photography, a great musical score, the versatile Dudley Moore, and, of course, the animals themselves. What a pleasure to have a perfect film for the little ones that adults will enjoy as well.

CONTENT ANALYSIS: (BBB) Moral worldview with nothing objectionable.

Vivid Allegory

AKIRA KUROSAWA'S DREAMS

Quality: ☆☆☆☆   Acceptability: +3

WARNING CODES:
Language: None
Violence: *
Sex: None
Nudity: None

RATING: PG
GENRE: Fantasy/Drama
INTENDED AUDIENCE: Adults
RUNNING TIME: 120 minutes
LANGUAGE: Japanese
STARRING: Akira Terao, Mitsunori Isaki, Toshihiko Nakano, Hisashi Igawa, Chosuke Ikariya, Mitsuko Baisho, Mieko Harada, and Martin Scorsese
DIRECTOR: Akira Kurosawa
DISTRIBUTOR: Warner Brothers
BRIEF SUMMARY:
Dreams is a vivid, cautionary allegory about the fate of mankind and the planet. The two-hour feature involves eight separate dream sequences from director Kurosawa's own slumber: one from his childhood, another from adolescence, and the remaining six from his adult life. The stories run the gamut from the lyrical to

the nightmarish. The filmmaker's overriding concern is man's current abuse of nature, the fear of nuclear holocaust, and its aftermath. There are also excursions into other fantasies, but the main motifs are a nostalgic cry for a way of life that respects nature and an emphatic, anguished struggle against the death, both of the individual and of the planet.

Akira Kurosawa's Dreams misses the complete joy of knowing the Truth that will set you free; however, the film is worth seeing, as Mr. Kurosawa splashes the screen with sumptuous colors and awesome images and demonstrates once again his classic storytelling skills. This is a reflective film, not the action-adventure fare that most Americans crave. In many ways it is a masterpiece of filmmaking and a great opportunity to gain a profound insight into the mind of one of the world's great filmmakers.

CONTENT ANALYSIS: (FRFRFR) Shinto worldview and symbolism.

Delightful but Flawed

ALMOST AN ANGEL

Quality: ☆☆☆   Acceptability: −2

WARNING CODES:
  Language: **
  Violence: **
  Sex: None
  Nudity: None
RATING: PG
GENRE: Comedy
INTENDED AUDIENCE: Teens and adults
RUNNING TIME: 96 minutes
STARRING: Paul Hogan, Elias Koteas, and Linda Kozlowski
DIRECTOR: John Cornell
PRODUCER: John Cornell
WRITER: Paul Hogan
DISTRIBUTOR: Paramount Pictures
BRIEF SUMMARY:
Small-time burglar Terry Dean gets hit on the head and wakes up "almost an angel." First, Dean apologizes to the Almighty, "I planned to get very religious before I died." God gives him another chance to do good deeds. Visiting a church, he contributes $62,000 (from his last bank job). Soon, Dean starts reading the Bible and looking for signs from heaven. Dean meets Steve, a paraplegic. Steve is filled with self-pity, but Dean proves to Steve that he is still a man despite the wheelchair. In gratitude, Steve invites Dean home to meet his sister, Rose. Steve and Rose are involved in a run-down recreation center for teens. Dean provides George, a wealthy patron, with signs from God to persuade him to give generously.

Unfortunately, *Almost an Angel* contains profanity, but Dean apologizes to the Lord for taking his name in vain. Also, the theology is flawed: Salvation is through Jesus Christ, not through good deeds; God does not give persons a second chance after death; and we do not come back as angels. Overall, *Almost an Angel* is a delightful movie that will not only entertain but will possibly help viewers choose a new perspective on life.

CONTENT ANALYSIS: (BB, C, Ab, L, V, M) Moral worldview with some Christian and anti-Christian elements; several obscenities and profanities; violence, breaking and entering, and bank robbery.

Nightmarish

ARACHNOPHOBIA

Quality: ☆☆☆   Acceptability: −2

WARNING CODES:
  Language: **
  Violence: * *
  Sex: None
  Nudity: *
RATING: PG-13
GENRE: Horror/Thriller/Comedy
INTENDED AUDIENCE: Older teens and adults

RUNNING TIME: 105 minutes
STARRING: Jeff Daniels, Julian Sands, Harley Jane Kozak, and John Goodman
DIRECTOR: Frank Marshall
PRODUCERS: Kathleen Kennedy and Richard Vane
WRITERS: Don Jakoby, Stephen Metcalfe, and Wesley Strick
DISTRIBUTOR: Walt Disney Company/Buena Vista Distribution
BRIEF SUMMARY:
While on an expedition to Venezuela, Dr. Atherton discovers a new species of spider. Measuring eight inches, the predatory arachnid is highly poisonous, fearsomely intelligent, and has an "attack" attitude. The spider kills a photographer and hitches a ride in his coffin to a small California town. The spider then mates, to produce deadly soldier spiders. To escape big-city life, another doctor, Dr. Ross, moves his medical practice to a perfect town to raise a family. Unfortunately, Ross loses his first two patients to spider bites. With the townsfolk dying like flies, Dr. Atherton comes to help Ross and Delbert McClintock, the exterminator, formulate a plan. In a climactic finish, Ross overcomes his arachnophobia to battle the militant arachnid one-on-one.

Arachnophobia tries to do for spiders what *Jaws* did for sharks. Though laughter is balanced with chills, the chills are too intense for all but the most robust. Unfortunately, much humor is derived from the expressions of the victims at time of death. The camera work and music are good, even spectacular at times. Unless you enjoy scary thrillers laced with profanity and obscenity, you should avoid *Arachnophobia*. You could have nightmares for weeks.

CONTENT ANALYSIS: (HH, LL, VV, N, M) Humanist worldview; twenty-four obscenities and profanities; violence; brief partial female nudity; and uses death as a basis for humor.

Powerful Family Saga

AVALON

Quality: ☆☆☆☆   Acceptability: +2

WARNING CODES:
  Language: *
  Violence: None
  Sex: None
  Nudity: None

RATING: PG
GENRE: Drama
INTENDED AUDIENCE: All ages
RUNNING TIME: 125 minutes
STARRING: Armin Mueller-Stahl, Elizabeth Perkins, Leo Fuchs, Aidan Quinn, Lou Jacobi, Joan Plowright, and Kevin Pollak
DIRECTOR: Barry Levinson
PRODUCER: Mark Johnson
WRITER: Barry Levinson
DISTRIBUTOR: Tri-Star Pictures
BRIEF SUMMARY:
Spanning the years 1914 through the late 1960s, this powerful, pro-family saga is about the Krachinsky family, Jewish immigrants who move to the mythically symbolic Avalon section of Baltimore, Maryland. With the advent of television, they open up a TV store. They succeed, enabling the elder, Sam, to move to the suburbs. Thus, with the pursuit of the American dream, the demise of the traditional family begins. It is illustrated by the family leaving their dinner to watch one of those new TV commercials. Sam tries to keep the family intact, but he eventually resigns as patriarch. When the turnout at his wife's funeral is low, he laments, "This is not the family." Finally Sam goes to reside in an old-folks home. "I came to America in 1914," he notes. "It was the most beautiful place I'd ever seen." Tellingly, the great-grandson is captivated by a TV program, rather than the words of one who is speaking truth.

Avalon is an extremely enlightening, entertaining movie, reflecting a time when news of a pregnancy was *good* news. There is great honor for America and an equal value placed on family and heritage. Four profanities and six obscenities (i.e., *hell*) comprise all that may be considered offensive.

CONTENT ANALYSIS: (BB, L) Moral worldview; four profanities and six obscenities.

Provocative and Engrossing

AWAKENINGS

Quality: ☆☆☆☆   Acceptability: +2

WARNING CODES:

Language: *
Violence: None
Sex: None
Nudity: None

RATING: PG-13
GENRE: Medical drama
INTENDED AUDIENCE: Adults
RUNNING TIME: 121 minutes
STARRING: Robert De Niro, Robin Williams, and Julie Kavner
DIRECTOR: Penny Marshall
PRODUCERS: Walter Parkes and Lawrence Lasker
WRITER: Steve Zaillian
BASED ON: The novel by Oliver Sacks
DISTRIBUTOR: Columbia Pictures
BRIEF SUMMARY:
Based on Dr. Oliver Sacks's book about his attempts to revive ten catatonic patients in 1969, *Awakenings* is about the experiences of Dr. Malcolm Sayers, a neurologist in charge of the catatonic patients at the Bronx Hospital. Believing they are not brain-dead but need to be revived, Sayers tries the experimental drug L-dopa on Leonard Lowe, who has been catatonic for thirty years. Leonard comes to life, awakened from when he went to sleep at age ten. He begins experiencing many things—such as shaving and falling in love—for the first time and keeps his doctor up late into the night talking. The other

nine patients also "awaken." The drug, however, begins to lose its effectiveness. Leonard consciously begins to deteriorate. "Has it all been worthwhile?" the doctor asks himself. *Awakenings* leaves the answer for the viewer to determine.

The dignity of human existence is upheld; however, no mention is made of a sovereign God. The movie is about being joyous about life and grateful for what you take for granted. Since the doctor, a recluse, also lives in a shell, there are two awakenings, Leonard's and Sayers's. Williams and De Niro give outstanding performances. *Awakenings* is a thought-provoking and engrossing movie.

CONTENT ANALYSIS: (C, B, O, L) Christian worldview with moral elements; Ouija board used as clinical tool and one obscenity.

Pure Fun

BACK TO THE FUTURE III

Quality: ☆☆☆   Acceptability: +1

WARNING CODES:

Language: *
Violence: *
Sex: None
Nudity: None

RATING: PG
GENRE: Western/Science fiction
INTENDED AUDIENCE: Teens
RUNNING TIME: 90 minutes
STARRING: Michael J. Fox, Christopher Lloyd, Thomas F. Wilson, Mary Steenburgen, and Lea Thompson
DIRECTOR: Robert Zemeckis
PRODUCERS: Bob Gale and Neil Canton
WRITER: Bob Gale
DISTRIBUTOR: Universal Pictures
BRIEF SUMMARY:
Marty, who's been left in 1955, takes an 1885 letter from Doc Brown to his 1955 counterpart. The letter says that the time machine has been buried, and warns them not to come after him. However,

when Marty and Doc uncover an article describing Doc's death in 1885, Marty goes after his friend. The DeLorean is unearthed, and Marty travels to the Old West. Marty locates Doc, but the DeLorean runs out of gas. They devise a plan to use a locomotive to push it up to time-breakaway speed. Doc is reluctant to leave because he has fallen in love with Clara, a schoolteacher who shares his passion for science and Jules Verne.

It is pure fun as the characters race against the clock in the final moments to get back to the future. There are also some great lines. Doc's zany inventions create an element of comedy, as do Marty's clichés. Also, Marty learns not to let name-calling affect his judgment. Unfortunately, six obscenities occur, but no profanities. There is some violence, but it is relevant to the storyline. The movie concludes in 1985 with Doc announcing that no one's future has yet been written. He exhorts Marty, "Make it whatever you want ... make it a good one."

CONTENT ANALYSIS: (Ro, B, LL, VV) Romantic worldview with moral elements; six obscenities; and some violence, including gunfights and a barroom brawl.

Mean-Spirited Attack on Children

CHILD'S PLAY 2

Quality: ☆☆   Acceptability: −4

WARNING CODES:

Language: ***
Violence: ***
Sex: None
Nudity: None

RATING: R
GENRE: Horror
INTENDED AUDIENCE: Teens and adults
RUNNING TIME: 84 minutes
STARRING: Alex Vincent, Jenny Aguter, Gerrit Graham, and Christine Elise

PRODUCER: David Kirschner
WRITER: Don Mancini
DIRECTOR: John Lafia
DISTRIBUTOR: Universal Pictures
BRIEF SUMMARY:
At the end of *Child's Play*, Chucky was decapitated and burned to a crisp. In *Child's Play 2*, he returns from Mattel Hell reassembled by his designers as evidence in a court case. Chucky is a "Good Guy," one of a series of childlike, talking dolls. However, Chucky turns out to be an aberration, doggedly tracking down his former owner, little Andy Barclay. Chucky wants to possess Andy's soul, thereby attaining life. As Chucky pursues Andy to consummate his evil purpose, he gleefully murders anyone in his path. Chucky meets his waterloo at the close of *Child's Play 2* when he is demolished in the Good Guy factory where he began his wretched life.

This is an evil film bound to give nightmares to any child who sees it and many adults as well. It took the reviewer two hours to regain composure from the film's emotional bombardment of graphic, explicit gore, violence, murder, and the accompanying sound effects. The message is anti-child. As Chucky admits, "I hate kids." Don't waste your time on *Child's Play 2*, if you value your mental health.

CONTENT ANALYSIS: (OOO, LL, VVV) Occult worldview; several dozen obscenities and some profanities; graphic, explicit gore, violence, and murder.

The Journey of Faith

CHINA CRY

Quality: ☆☆☆☆   Acceptability: +1

WARNING CODES:

Language: None
Violence: **
Sex: *
Nudity: None

RATING: PG-13
GENRE: Drama
INTENDED AUDIENCE: Families
RUNNING TIME: 103 minutes
STARRING: Julia Nickson-Soul, Russel Wong, James Shigeta, France Nuyen, and Philip Tan
DIRECTOR: James Collier
PRODUCER: Don Parker
WRITER: James Collier
DISTRIBUTOR: The Penland Company
BRIEF SUMMARY:

China Cry is about the making of a Christian. Adopted by a prominent family in Shanghai in 1941, little Sung Neng Yee is treated like a princess until the bombs drop and the Japanese seize her house. After the defeat of the Japanese, Sung Neng Yee joins the Communists, believing they are the liberators of China. All goes well until she falls in love with Lam Cheng Shen from Hong Kong. Communist officials decide to break her of any bourgeois tendencies. During the next few years, in which she marries and has three children, she is subjected to excruciating persecution.

When she calls out to God for salvation, miracles follow. She bargains for her husband and daughter's release to Hong Kong and is sent to hard labor, where she begins agitating for her own release. *China Cry* is director Collier's best since *The Hiding Place.* The camera work evokes the Orient. Al Kasha's superb music heightens the drama. Thus, the audience shares in Nora Neng Yee Lam's (the girl the story is based on) sorrows and her victories. This is one of the ten best films of the year. Not only does it expose the senseless humanism of communism, but it reveals the journey of faith that produces an exemplary Christian life. *China Cry* is a must-see for everyone.

CONTENT ANALYSIS: (CCC, VV, S) Christian worldview; violence; and love story.

Richly Textured

CINEMA PARADISO

Quality: ☆☆☆☆　　　Acceptability: +1

WARNING CODES:
  Language: *
  Violence: None
  Sex: **
  Nudity: *
RATING: Not rated
GENRE: Drama
INTENDED AUDIENCE: Adults
RUNNING TIME: 123 minutes
LANGUAGE: Italian
STARRING: Philippe Noiret, Jacques Perrin, Salvatore Cascio, and Marco Leonardi
DIRECTOR: Giuseppe Tornatore
DISTRIBUTOR: Miramax
BRIEF SUMMARY:

Cinema Paradiso is a richly textured film that celebrates the role of movies and the way they shape and change our lives.

When Salvatore diVitto receives word in his Rome apartment that his old friend Alfredo has died, his thoughts return to the small Sicilian village of Giancaldo, where he grew up. When Salvatore was a child, Alfredo had been the town's projectionist at the Cinema Paradiso. Quoting dialogue from movies as though imparting wisdom from the Scriptures, Alfredo reveals the cherished mysteries of the old films that foster the imagination of the fatherless Salvatore.

Salvatore also recalls the innocence and insatiable curiosity of childhood, the church where he was an altar boy, the anguish of first love, and, most of all, memories of Alfredo.

Such collective reverie is orchestrated around the rituals of moviegoing that the director appears to be suggesting that cinema once, in an age before TV, had a role similar to that of the church. Despite this, the film is a lot of fun, especially the humorous idiosyncrasies of Italian village life. To the faint of heart, all the previously edited kissing scenes are presented to the viewer at the end.

Unfortunately, this fine Italian film is marred by some obscenities, promiscuity, and brief, naturalistic female nudity. With little editing, this film could have been recommended.

CONTENT ANALYSIS: (RoRo, LL, SS, N) Romantic worldview; some obscenities; promiscuity; and brief female nudity.

Fidelity, Nobility, and Love

CYRANO DE BERGERAC

Quality: ✰✰✰✰   Acceptability: +4

French with English subtitles
WARNING CODES:
  Language: None
  Violence: None
  Sex: None
  Nudity: None
RATING: PG
GENRE: Romantic tragedy
INTENDED AUDIENCE: All ages
RUNNING TIME: 135 minutes
STARRING: Gerard Depardieu, Jacques Weber, Anne Brochet, Vincent Perez, Roland Bertin, Philippe Morier-Genoud, and Philippe Volter
DIRECTOR: Jean-Paul Rappeneau
PRODUCERS: Rene Cleitman and Michel Seydoux
WRITERS: Jean-Paul Rappeneau and Jean-Claude Carriere
BASED ON: The play by Edmond Rostand
DISTRIBUTOR: Orion Classics
BRIEF SUMMARY:
In seventeenth-century France, Cyrano De Bergerac, imbued with wit and wisdom but deprived of good looks by his enormous nose, falls in love with Roxanne. His handsome friend Christian is equally smitten by Roxanne; however, Christian lacks the skills to woo her. He uses Cyrano to compose letters, which he

sings to win Roxanne for himself. Roxanne falls for the letters and declares to Christian that she loves him for his soul and would love him even if he were ugly. Christian is killed in battle, and for fourteen years Cyrano protects Christian's memory. The truth is revealed as Cyrano is wounded on his way to visit Roxanne. The resolution of this unrequited love story is one of the greatest moments in the history of drama.

Fidelity, nobility, and love weave wonderfully throughout the film, which is awash with the beauty of the original French, aptly subtitled by author Anthony Burgess. There is nothing objectionable—only the sweeping majesty of the countryside and the fierceness of love and commitment so lacking in most films these days. The film is recommended for lovers of all ages.

CONTENT ANALYSIS: (RoRo, B) Romantic worldview with moral elements and nothing objectionable.

Most Blatant Revision of American History

DANCES WITH WOLVES

Quality: ✰   Acceptability: −2

WARNING CODES:
  Language: **
  Violence: ***
  Sex: **
  Nudity: *
RATING: PG-13
GENRE: Drama/Action/Adventure
INTENDED AUDIENCE: Adults
RUNNING TIME: 224 minutes
STARRING: Kevin Costner, Mary McDonnell, Charles Rocket, Graham Greene, Rodney Grant, Floyd Westerman, and Robert Pastorelli
DIRECTOR: Kevin Costner
PRODUCERS: Jim Wilson and Kevin Costner
WRITER: Michael Blake
DISTRIBUTOR: Orion Pictures

BRIEF SUMMARY:

Lieutenant John Dunbar's exhibitionism elevates him to Civil War hero. Given the choice of any post, Dunbar opts for the unspoiled frontier of the 1860s. At the frontier, "St. Francis of the New Age" Dunbar befriends a wolf and a Sioux tribe. Dunbar gets caught in the crossfire between the evil whites and the heroic Indians. The movie implies that the Sioux were faultless, while the Pawnee were murderers and the whites were rotten; however, the Sioux's action (armed with stolen rifles) against the Pawnee was just as brutal as the advance of the U.S. Army.

Dances with Wolves is Kevin Costner's confused tribute to idealized Indians. This self-indulgent rehash of Rousseau's absurd noble savage theory does not bode well for Costner's career as a director, philosopher, or historian. Costner has no idea that all men are sinners who need Jesus' saving grace. Entangled in the pretentious storyline is Dunbar's corny narration. The anachronisms are also annoying. What is worse is that *Dances with Wolves* is a three-hour yawner. It would be best to pass on this film that continually steps on the audience's toes with its two left feet.

CONTENT ANALYSIS: (PaPa, Rh, LL, VVV, SS, NN, M) Pagan worldview with revisionist history; six profanities and twelve obscenities; theft and extreme violence; promiscuity, fornication, and rear female nudity.

Too Ironic

DICK TRACY

Quality: ☆☆☆   Acceptability: +1

WARNING CODES:

Language: *
Violence: **
Sex: *
Nudity: *

RATING: PG
GENRE: Fantasy/Crime/Drama

INTENDED AUDIENCE: All ages except young children
RUNNING TIME: 195 minutes
STARRING: Warren Beatty, Madonna, Al Pacino, Dustin Hoffman, William Forsythe, James Caan, Mandy Patinkin, Paul Sorvino, Glenne Headly, Seymour Cassel, Charles Durning, Ed O'Ross, R. G. Armstrong, and Dick Van Dyke
DIRECTOR: Warren Beatty
PRODUCER: Warren Beatty
WRITERS: Jim Cash and Jack Epps Jr.
BASED ON: The comic strip created by Charles Gould
DISTRIBUTOR: Walt Disney Company/Buena Vista Distribution
BRIEF SUMMARY:

Dick Tracy evokes the comic strip, but its ironic worldview saps the moral perspective that sustained the strip. Detective Dick Tracy goes after Big Boy, who wants to control the city, and finds an ally in "Kid," a young orphan. Tracy appeals to Breathless Mahoney, a singer in Big Boy's Club Ritz, to testify. Breathless then tries to get the detective to question his love for Tess Trueheart. Blank offers to rub out Tracy in exchange for 10 percent of Big Boy's business. Thus, when Tess disappears and Tracy goes looking for her, he is framed for the murder of the D.A. Tracy thwarts Blank's double-cross, but Big Boy escapes with Tess. Tracy then comes to the rescue.

The music is operatic, and the scenes move quickly. The movie contains a few pro-family moments, and underscores the importance of role models in children's lives. Unfortunately, much of the conversation between Breathless and Tracy contains offensive sexual innuendos. However, Madonna is no Mae West and, clad in a see-through dress, she will alienate parents with children. Also, Beatty's acting has not improved since *Ishtar*, so instead of carrying the movie, he is merely the central persona. Overall, the villains dominate the action and the drama. With their sagging skins, warped skulls, and hunched backs, the villains may give children nightmares. Older audiences will find the movie tame and boring in spots. Parents will want to exercise caution because of the frightening makeup, the semi-nudity, and the profanity uttered by the urchin.

CONTENT ANALYSIS: (HH, M, L, VV, S, N) Ironic humanist worldview with moral elements; one profanity and one obscenity; gunfire and violence (no blood is shown); a see-through, sexually provocative dress and sexual innuendos.

Animated Adventure

DUCKTALES: THE MOVIE— TREAURES OF THE LOST LAMP

Quality: ☆☆☆   Acceptability: +2

WARNING CODES:

Language: None
Violence: *
Sex: None
Nudity: None

RATING: G
GENRE: Animation
INTENDED AUDIENCE: Children
RUNNING TIME: 75 minutes
VOICES: June Foray, Joan Gerber, Richard Libertini, Christopher Lloyd, Chuck McCann, Terry McGovern, Rip Taylor, Russi Taylor, and Alan Young
DIRECTOR: Bob Hathcock
PRODUCER: Bob Hathcock
WRITER: Alan Burnett
DISTRIBUTOR: Walt Disney Company/Buena Vista Distribution
BRIEF SUMMARY:
Crash-landing into ancient ruins, Scrooge McDuck, his three nephews— Huey, Dewey, and Louie—and his niece, Wendy, uncover a map that leads to the famed treasure of Collie Baba. The evil wizard Merlock orders his cowardly flunkie, Dijon, to guide the McDucks.

Finding the treasure, Scrooge gives a worthless-looking lamp to Wendy moments before Merlock steals the booty. Back at McDuck mansion, the grand-nephews rub the lamp, and out comes a boy-duck genie. The genie warns them that Merlock must not get the lamp. After much adventure, Merlock gets the lamp, but thanks to a trusty slingshot, the lamp is knocked from Merlock's hands.

Some Christians will find *DuckTales* unsuitable because it suggests that magic is an accepted part of life. Other Christians will explain to their children that God warns us to stay away from magic. There are good messages in the movie, as when the genie states that it is better to be a boy than a genie and Scrooge vows he'll never make another wish. *DuckTales* is the best scripted and animated of this year's animated features. Children of all ages will enjoy this adventure, putting pressure on Christian parents to take their offspring. Since this is a light movie, you may want to discuss the movie with your children ahead of time and then enjoy the picture.

CONTENT ANALYSIS: (PaPa, OO) Ancient myths woven together with the New Age notion that magic is an accepted fabric of society and everyday occurrence.

Too Much Innuendo

EDWARD SCISSORHANDS

Quality: ☆☆☆   Acceptability: −2

WARNING CODES:

Language: **
Violence: **
Sex: *
Nudity: None

RATING: PG-13
GENRE: Drama/Fantasy
INTENDED AUDIENCE: Young adults
RUNNING TIME: 110 minutes

STARRING: Winona Ryder, Johnny Depp, and Dianne Wiest
DIRECTOR: Tim Burton
PRODUCER: Denise Di Novi
WRITERS: Caronie Thompson and Tim Burton
DISTRIBUTOR: 20th Century Fox
BRIEF SUMMARY:

Edward Scissorhands portrays an innocent who struggles to adjust in a fallen world. When Avon lady Peg Boggs makes her rounds, she persuades Edward to come live with her. Edward's creator died before he could give Edward hands, so he makes do with scissorhands. Edward's fame spreads as he sculptures shrubbery, trims dogs, and cuts ladies' hair. Peg's neighbor tries to seduce Edward, and Peg's daughter and her boyfriend involve him in a theft. The police catch poor Edward. Peg's husband tries to teach Edward about ethics by asking him what he would do if he found a satchel of money and gives him three choices. Edward chooses to give the money to loved ones. Edward, in his innocence, is all heart. Because of the theft and—according to the seductress—attempted rape, the neighborhood turns against Edward, so he flees to the safety of his mansion.

While *Edward Scissorhands* is a funny film with an imaginative plot, it offers a subtle commentary on the human race. If only the violence, blatant sexual innuendos, and foul language had been cut from *Edward Scissorhands,* it would have been better suited to most viewers' agendas.

CONTENT ANALYSIS: (CC, Pa, Ro, LL, VV, SS, A, M) Strange Christian incarnational allegory with New Age and romantic elements; ten obscenities and profanities; violence; sexual innuendos; drinking; and breaking and entering.

Slapstick Stunts

ERNEST GOES TO JAIL

Quality: ★★☆   Acceptability: +2

WARNING CODES:
  Language: None
  Violence: *
  Sex: None
  Nudity: None
RATING: PG
GENRE: Comedy
INTENDED AUDIENCE: Children
RUNNING TIME: 81 minutes
STARRING: Jim Varney, Gailard Sartain, Bill Byrge, and Barbara Bush
DIRECTOR: John Cherry
PRODUCER: Stacy Williams
WRITER: Charlie Cohen
DISTRIBUTOR: Walt Disney Company/Buena Vista Distribution
BRIEF SUMMARY:

The know-it-all Ernest works as a janitor in a bank. The president wants to fire the goofball, but Charlotte, his assistant, argues on Ernest's behalf. Ernest is then overjoyed when he's given jury duty. However, the defendant notices that Ernest is a dead ringer for jailed crime boss Felix Nash. The defendant strikes a deal with Nash, and a plan is hatched to switch the two look-alikes. When the jurors are taken to view the scene of the crime, Ernest is snatched from the crowd and locked up, while his notorious double joins the jury and sneaks away to freedom. Ernest is destined for the electric chair, but he is not as easy to kill as one would suspect.

This is a clean movie with no sex or foul language. There's a lot of mock violence, but it's pure slapstick. For example, while working as the night janitor, Ernest fights for his life with a runaway, frenzied floor polisher. Other stunts have Ernest hanging from a crystal chandelier and being "spun dry" in his own invention of a human washing machine. No child will take these gags seriously, but they can be overwhelming for adults. *Ernest Goes to Jail* has a lot of production value and good acting, though the script is definitely aimed at the very young.

CONTENT ANALYSIS: (BB, V) Moral worldview and mock-violence.

Masterfully Scary

EXORCIST 3: LEGION

Quality: ✫✫✫✫   Acceptability: −2

WARNING CODES:
  Language: *
  Violence: ***
  Sex: None
  Nudity: None
RATING: R
GENRE: Horror from a biblical perspective
INTENDED AUDIENCE: Adults
RUNNING TIME: 105 minutes
STARRING: George C. Scott, Ed Flanders, Brad Dourif, Viveca Lindfors, and Scott Wilson
DIRECTOR: William Peter Blatty
PRODUCER: Carter DeHaven
WRITER: William Peter Blatty
BASED ON: The novel by William Peter Blatty
DISTRIBUTOR: 20th Century Fox
BRIEF SUMMARY:
Exorcist 3 is the real sequel to the 1973 original, set in Georgetown seventeen years later. Police detective Kinderman, who was involved with his good friends Father Dyer and Father Merrin in the exorcism seventeen years earlier, is now faced with a series of grisly murders of priests. Kinderman is about to have his skepticism shaken to the core. A decapitated body is found with the markings of the "Zodiac" murderer, executed fifteen years ago. Father Dyer is admitted to the hospital for tests. The next morning, his body is discovered with his head removed. The confrontations between Kinderman and the antagonist, a demon-possessed mental patient, reach new levels of intensity for audiences.

The movie will leave you reeling by the climax. It is a film that uses skill and craftsmanship to attain high levels of excellence from all areas—direction, scripting, acting, and production. Almost all the violence takes place off-screen and little obscene language is used. This is a thriller which uses suspense, not carnage, to grab the audience. Also to be commended is the way the film attests to the power of Jesus Christ and his power over Satan. Jesuit-educated Blatty has created a masterpiece. However, because this may be one of the most frightening movies ever made, adults should exercise extreme caution before seeing *Exorcist 3: Legion*. Children should definitely not see it.

CONTENT ANALYSIS: (CCC, O, L, VV) Christian worldview with demonic manifestations; two profanities and two obscenities; violence includes decapitations, mutilations, and murder, but is not gory or graphic.

Powerful Tragedy

THE FIELD

Quality: ✫✫✫✫   Acceptability: −2

WARNING CODES:
  Language: *
  Violence: **
  Sex: *
  Nudity: None
RATING: PG-13
GENRE: Drama
INTENDED AUDIENCE: Adults
RUNNING TIME: 107 minutes
STARRING: Tom Berenger, Richard Harris, John Hurt, Sean Bean, Frances Tomelty, and Brenda Flicker
DIRECTOR: Jim Sheridan
PRODUCER: Steve Morrison and Noel Pearson
ADAPTED FROM: *The Field*, a play by John B. Keane
DISTRIBUTOR: Avenue Pictures
BRIEF SUMMARY:
The Field is a tragedy about jealousy and pagan consciousness warring with

Christian morality. Bull McCabe's life in the 1930s is threatened when an Irish-American businessman wants to purchase land the McCabes have worked for generations. Bull dominates his rural Irish village by force of will. For years his family has leased a grassy field on which a small herd of cattle graze. When its owner sells the parcel to an outsider, Bull is driven to madness. He is also tortured by the suicide of his eldest son eighteen years earlier. Since the death, Bull's wife has neither slept nor spoken with him. He also remembers the nineteenth-century famine that decimated the land. Bull resents those who fled to the New World. The American represents those émigrés who return to build their wealth upon what has been achieved through the sweat and blood of Bull's family. Thus, the struggle over the field leads to murder.

The Field is about the pagan west of Ireland. There is a brooding sense of violence pervading the film that is tempered with a feminine tenderness and compassion. Be forewarned of a graphic murder scene. Immediately afterwards, Bull confesses before God.

CONTENT ANALYSIS: (CC, Pa, LL, V, SS, M) Christian storyline in a pagan setting; several obscenities and a few profanities; murder, revenge, and implied fornication.

Half Right

FLATLINERS

Quality: ☆☆☆   Acceptability: −3

WARNING CODES:
  Language: **
  Violence: **
  Sex: **
  Nudity: **
RATING: R
GENRE: Drama/Fantasy/Thriller
INTENDED AUDIENCE: Adults

RUNNING TIME: 120 minutes
STARRING: Kiefer Sutherland, Julia Roberts, Kevin Bacon, William Baldwin, and Oliver Platt
DIRECTOR: Joel Schumacher
PRODUCER: Michael Douglas and Rick Bieber
WRITER: Peter Filardi
DISTRIBUTOR: Columbia Pictures
BRIEF SUMMARY:
Med student Nelson recruits four friends for a daring experiment to see what lies beyond life. They stop their hearts until the monitors read nothing but flat lines. Minutes later, armed with medical equipment, the team revives them. Soon after Nelson's experience, the supernatural begins to intrude upon his reality. After Joe is revived, his sexual conquests haunt him. A childhood schoolmate David scorned materializes to give him the same treatment. Rachel is hounded by her father's apparition. David realizes they have brought back manifestations of their past sins. David seeks out his victim, now an adult, to ask for forgiveness. Rachel grants forgiveness to her father's apparition. Nelson, however, decides to die a second time so that he can fight his assailant on equal ground.

Flatliners affirms the biblical doctrine that man needs forgiveness for his sins, but overlooks the fact that nothing you do can put you right with God. Only Jesus Christ "is the atoning sacrifice for our sins" (1 John 2:2). The filmmakers vaguely suggest this message in the sets and dialogue. Unfortunately, *Flatliners* overflows with profanity, obscenity, fornication, nudity, attempted murder, and gross scenes of cadavers, which could have been avoided without diminishing the power of the movie. *Flatliners* is not an edifying movie for Christian families. However, you may want to pray that pagans who see the movie will come to know the true forgiveness for our sins, which is only available through Jesus Christ.

CONTENT ANALYSIS: (C, Pa, O, LL, VV, SS, NN, M) Christian worldview marred by pagan and occult elements; many profanities and obscenities; attempted murder and scenes with cadavers; fornication, crude sexual innuendos, and nudity.

God's Wonderful Creation

FOR ALL MANKIND

Quality: ✩✩✩✩   Acceptability: +3

WARNING CODES:
  Language: *
  Violence: None
  Sex: None
  Nudity: None

RATING: G
GENRE: Documentary
INTENDED AUDIENCE: All ages
RUNNING TIME: 75 minutes
NARRATED BY: The Apollo astronauts
DIRECTOR: Al Reinert
PRODUCER: Al Reinert
WRITER: Al Reinert
DISTRIBUTOR: Apollo Associates, through NASA
BRIEF SUMMARY:
Detailing the lunar explorations of the late sixties and the seventies, *For All Mankind* is a superb documentary from NASA. The film, narrated by the astronauts, documents what they saw and said during their voyages. The story moves from launchpad to splashdown. Rather than describe the missions separately, the film assembles memorable moments from each. Thus, the launch phase is a composite of all the launches. For seventy-five minutes the viewer lives within a space suit, floats in weightlessness, eats from plastic packs, and learns how to use the bathroom in zero gravity. From the lunar orbit, there is a clear view of Earth, a tiny blue marble within the vastness of space. The awesome work of the Creator is visible,

and some of the insightful dialogue refers to the work and grace of God, affirming the words of Genesis 1:1.

A wonderful triumph of cinematography, the film is an excellent teaching opportunity to explain to children how the world and universe came into existence. (Two instances of mildly crude language almost go unnoticed.) *For All Mankind* is informative, entertaining, and great fun.

CONTENT ANALYSIS: (CC, L) Christian worldview and two minor vulgarities.

Sharp Comedy

THE FRESHMAN

Quality: ✩✩✩✩   Acceptability: −1

WARNING CODES:
  Language: *
  Violence: *
  Sex: None
  Nudity: None

RATING: PG
GENRE: Comedy
INTENDED AUDIENCE: Adults
RUNNING TIME: 95 minutes
STARRING: Marlon Brando, Matthew Broderick, Bruno Kirby, Penelope Ann Miller, Frank Whaley, Maximillian Schell, and Pamela Payton-Wright
DIRECTOR: Andrew Bergman
PRODUCER: Mike Lobell
WRITER: Andrew Bergman
DISTRIBUTOR: TriStar
BRIEF SUMMARY:
Considering its ambitions to make a statement about saving the earth's endangered species, *The Freshman* is not very successful in stirring emotions about that subject. The comedy, however, is extremely sharp and funny. Marlon Brando does a great job of spoofing his Godfather persona.

The story is about a freshman film student at NYU who has no money to buy books, and the alleged mafia kingpin who befriends him. The student falls for the daughter of this man, who sends the young man on a bizarre errand that leads to comic results.

The comedy in *The Freshman* is mostly inoffensive, but the dialogue includes a few profanities and obscenities. Also, the story involves robbery and deception. The filmmakers spoof bureaucratic environmentalist officers from the government, however, so there are some positive aspects to the movie's thematic structure.

CONTENT ANALYSIS: (H, LL, M) Humanist worldview; few profanities and six obscenities; robbery and deception.

Worst Attractive Presentation of Spiritism

GHOST

Quality: ☆☆   Acceptability: –3

WARNING CODES:

Language: **
Violence: **
Sex: **
Nudity: None

RATING: PG-13
GENRE: Romantic comedy/Horror
INTENDED AUDIENCE: Adults
RUNNING TIME: 128 minutes
STARRING: Patrick Swayze, Demi Moore, and Whoopi Goldberg
DIRECTOR: Jerry Zucker
PRODUCER: Lisa Weinstein
EXECUTIVE PRODUCERS: Howard W. Koch and Steven-Charles Jaffe
WRITER: Bruce Joel Rubin
DISTRIBUTOR: Paramount Pictures
BRIEF SUMMARY:

This romantic comedy is about Sam Wheat and his girlfriend, Molly Jensen, who are renovating their new flat. When Sam is murdered, his spirit lingers and he becomes determined to communicate with Molly. Sam calls on Oda Mae Brown,

a medium. The psychic is astonished to discover that her powers work, but no one believes her because of her record as a conartist. Sam and Oda Mae work together to get the goods on Carl, Sam's fellow banker and drug launderer, who murdered him. When Oda closes Carl's bank account, Carl plans to kill Molly. With Molly's life in danger, Oda Mae becomes a reluctant liaison for the two lovers.

This tiresome premise of after-death deeds has been featured many times before. Christians therefore must be all the more diligent in explaining that God warns us that the medium who consults the dead is detestable to the Lord (Deuteronomy 18:11–12). *Ghost* even goes one abhorrent step further when Sam learns from "shadow monsters" that he has to focus his power by possessing Oda Mae's body so he can talk to Molly. The movie's spiritism is combined with profanities, obscenities, and promiscuity.

CONTENT ANALYSIS: (OOO, RoRo, LL, VV, SS, M) Occult worldview with romantic elements and spiritism; many profanities and obscenities; murder, promiscuity, and revenge.

Memorable but Flawed

THE GODFATHER, PART III

Quality: ☆☆☆☆   Acceptability: –2

WARNING CODES:

Language: ***
Violence: ***
Sex: **
Nudity: None

RATING: R
GENRE: Crime/Drama
INTENDED AUDIENCE: Adults
RUNNING TIME: 162 minutes
STARRING: Al Pacino, Diane Keaton, Talia Shire, Andy Garcia, Eli Wallach, Joe Mantegna, Bridget Fonda, George Hamilton, and Sofia Coppola
DIRECTOR: Francis Ford Coppola

PRODUCER: Gray Frederickson
WRITERS: Mario Puzo and Francis Ford Coppla
DISTRIBUTOR: Paramount Pictures
BRIEF SUMMARY:

Don Michael Corleone opens *Godfather III* in New York City, two decades after the events that concluded *Godfather II*, with the profound insight, "The only wealth in this world is children." Now old, diabetic, and racked with guilt, Don Michael tries to atone for his sins by taking his family into legitimate business. During the crisis of the film, Don Michael prays and swears by the lives of his children that if given a chance to redeem himself he will sin no more. However, in acquiescing to the young, would-be Godfather's desire for revenge, he continues the cycle that results in the death of his only daughter. The irony is that he must return to the blood-and-violence philosophy to absolve himself of Godfatherhood.

The scarlet thread of familial covenant is brilliantly seamed into all three films. In each, the Corleone covenant goes awry, and blood is shed because covenants have been broken. *Godfather III* has the same rich-toned look as its predecessors. Unfortunately, Sophia Coppola's acting leaves much to be desired, ministers of the church are portrayed as thieves and murderers, and the movie, though often brilliant, drags at times. However, some of the dialogue is the most memorable in the history of film, such as when Michael tells Vincent, "Don't hate your enemy. It clouds your judgment."

CONTENT ANALYSIS: (AbAb, C, LLL, VVV, SS, M) Anti-Christian worldview with positive Christian elements; many obscenities and profanities; graphic murder and violence; incest and implied fornication.

Crazy White People

THE GODS MUST BE CRAZY II

Quality: ☆☆☆   Acceptability: +2

WARNING CODES:
  Language: None
  Violence: None
  Sex: None
  Nudity: None

RATING: PG
GENRE: Comedy
INTENDED AUDIENCE: All ages
RUNNING TIME: 98 minutes
STARRING: N!Xau, Lena Farugia, and Hans Strydom
DIRECTOR: Jamie Uys
PRODUCER: Boet Troskie
WRITER: Jamie Uys
DISTRIBUTOR: Columbia Pictures
BRIEF SUMMARY:

N!Xau finds himself again with crazy white people who do not seem to understand nature. Flying overhead, a city woman and her pilot get their small plane caught in a tree. Meanwhile, N!Xau loses his two sons to illegal bounty hunters. The boys have fun, though, escaping from the truck while on the move. Back at the crippled plane, the woman manages to get the aircraft into the air, but leaves the pilot behind. Both have humorous run-ins with the natives and nature as they attempt to reunite. The story progresses in a humorous vein, with N!Xau coming to the aid of the collapsed pilot. In a tongue-in-cheek James Bond ending, the plane touches down with a parachute covering the girl and the pilot as they kiss.

The film's premise seems to indicate that a "primitive" culture is better than ours. Although it is true that our Western civilization can be "out of touch," true peace between men and between man and nature can only be achieved through Jesus Christ. This back-to-nature philosophy ignores the fact that all men are sinners. However, this is a fun movie that allows the audience to laugh at itself and reminds the audience that no one should take themselves too seriously. As the film shows through N!Xau, having one's family together is of greatest importance.

CONTENT ANALYSIS: (RoRo, PaPa) Romantic worldview with pagan elements and nothing else objectionable (except for one minor occurrence of impropriety in dress).

Lying Has Consequences

GREEN CARD

Quality: ☆☆☆☆   Acceptability: -2

WARNING CODES:

  Language: *
  Violence: None
  Sex: *
  Nudity: None

RATING: PG-13
GENRE: Romantic comedy
INTENDED AUDIENCE: Adults
RUNNING TIME: 110 minutes
STARRING: Gerard Depardieu, Andie MacDowell, Bebe Neuwirth, Gregg Edelman, and Robert Prosky
DIRECTOR: Peter Weir
PRODUCER: Peter Weir
WRITER: Peter Weir
DISTRIBUTOR: Walt Disney Company/Buena Vista Distribution
BRIEF SUMMARY:

In this romantic comedy, a French ruffian who longs for a new identity in the United States marries an American woman, Bronte Parrish, in order to get his INS green card. Bronte wants an exclusive apartment with a botanical garden that is only available to married couples. Anton arranges their civil marriage, so George gets his green card, Bronte her apartment, and they part—intending never to see each other again. However, immigration officials decide to investigate. Comic complications abound when they are forced to live together to rehearse a history of their lives together to convince the INS that they are truly married. Bronte loves plants and distrusts people. George came out of the Paris street gangs,

smokes, and eats red beef. Bronte considers him oafish. George considers her effete. Being opposites, they fall in love. The ending, however, is not all wine and roses.

Green Card is a masterpiece of filmmaking. Between peals of laughter, there are moments of insight into human character that prove the premise that getting to know someone makes one recognize the value of the other. Also, *Green Card* emphasizes that lying has consequences. Although they share an apartment for forty-eight hours, commendably, Bronte and George do not have a sexual relationship. Unfortunately, there is some profanity and sexual innuendo. With its magnificent acting and music, *Green Card* delightfully demonstrates the fact that you can't judge a book by its cover.

CONTENT ANALYSIS: (BB, C, L) Moral worldview with Christian elements; three obscenities and four exclamatory profanities.

Outstanding Masterpiece

HAMLET

Quality: ☆☆☆☆   Acceptability: +1

WARNING CODES:

  Language: *
  Violence: **
  Sex: *
  Nudity: None

RATING: PG
GENRE: Dramatic tragedy
INTENDED AUDIENCE: Teens and adults
RUNNING TIME: 135 minutes
STARRING: Mel Gibson, Glenn Close, Alan Bates, Paul Scofield, Ian Holm, and Helena Bonham Carter
DIRECTOR: Franco Zeffirelli
PRODUCER: Dyson Lovell
WRITERS: Christopher Devore and Franco Zeffirelli
BASED ON: The play by William Shakespeare

DISTRIBUTOR: Warner Brothers

BRIEF SUMMARY:

In this version of *Hamlet*, Franco Zeffirelli directs Mel Gibson as the melancholy Dane and gives us a masterpiece. The opening scene of the king's funeral establishes Hamlet's agonizing relationship with his mother who has become his "father's brother's wife" when his father has been dead only two months. Hamlet also struggles to avenge his father's murder. One of Shakespeare's most outstanding tragedies, *Hamlet* overflows with memorable lines. Treachery, intrigue, and violence abound as Hamlet seeks revenge. He feigns madness, gives up his love for Ophelia, and kills the obnoxious Polonius. He cleverly plans "a play within a play" to "catch the conscience of the king" and out-fences the treacherous Laertes, only to die by a poisoned sword.

Hamlet is such a well-produced movie that modern audiences can relate to Hamlet's agonizing problems. Mel Gibson is believable and superb as Hamlet. Zeffirelli has trimmed the four-hour epic into an entertaining film that captures the essence of the play. Of course, there are graphic sexual innuendos and Elizabethan oaths. Even so, Shakespeare had a strong Christian value system. Therefore, when sin is covered over, the outcome is tragic, as we see in *Hamlet*. Zeffirelli's *Hamlet* is a must for every person who wants to be really entertained.

CONTENT ANALYSIS: (C, BB, O, L, VV, S) Christian worldview with moral elements and some occult plot devices; Elizabethan oaths; murder; some violence; and sexual innuendos.

Most Virulent Attack on Jews and Christians

THE HANDMAID'S TALE

Quality: ☆☆☆☆   Acceptability: −4

WARNING CODES:

Language: ***

Violence: **

Sex: ***

Nudity: **

RATING: R

GENRE: Drama/Tragedy

RUNNING TIME: 109 minutes

INTENDED AUDIENCE: Adults

STARRING: Natasha Richardson, Robert Duvall, Faye Dunaway, Elizabeth McGovern, and Aidan Quick

DIRECTOR: Volker Schlondorff

BASED ON: The novel by Margaret Atwood

DISTRIBUTOR: Cinecom Entertainment

BRIEF SUMMARY:

Set at the turn of the century, fundamentalists have overthrown the government and replaced it with a repressive society. Reading is outlawed. Minorities have been sent to work camps while white women are forced into the roles of wives, domestics, and childbearers. Most women are infertile due to pesticides and other toxins. Those capable of childbearing are deemed "handmaids" and are assigned to the Commanders. Kate tries to escape to Canada, but gets caught and is sent to a training center where she is forced to become a handmaid. She is renamed Offred and assigned to Fred and his wife, Serena Joy, a former television evangelist. The three engage in a sexual ceremony. If Offred fails to become pregnant, she will be doomed to clean up toxic waste until her death.

This film is a blatant example of anti-Christian bigotry, which will only promote religious persecution. Such bigotry must be rebuked and condemned. Some of the key points of refutation:

• Throughout history strong Christian commitment has brought civilization, freedom, and toleration to nations, while humanism has resulted in totalitarianism and genocide.

- Christianity is the root of our republican democracy.
- Justice and mercy are at the heart of God's Law, while humanism gave birth to Marxism and national socialism.
- It would be impossible for Christians, controlled by God's Holy Spirit, to institute a repressive society.
- Renewing one's mind and seeking wisdom, knowledge, and understanding are at the heart of biblical Christianity.
- Christianity values individuality because God created and loves each individual, while humanism has always sought conformity.

CONTENT ANALYSIS: (HHH, AbAbAb, LLL, VV, SSS, NN) Very strongly humanist, anti-Jewish, anti-Christian worldview with blasphemous distortions of Scripture; many profanities and obscenities; extreme violence; adultery, lesbianism, and female nudity.

Love Triumphs over Alienation

HOME ALONE

Quality: ✰✰✰✰   Acceptability: +1

WARNING CODES:

Language: *
Violence: **
Sex: *
Nudity: None

RATING: PG
GENRE: Comedy/Drama
INTENDED AUDIENCE: Older children and teens
RUNNING TIME: 98 minutes
STARRING: Macaulay Culkin, Joe Pesci, Catherine O'Hara, Daniel Stern, and John Heard
DIRECTOR: Chris Columbus

PRODUCER: John Hughes
WRITER: John Hughes
DISTRIBUTOR: 20th Century Fox
BRIEF SUMMARY:

Home Alone is the story about eight-year-old Kevin who has to cope with a pair of bumbling burglars when his family accidentally leaves him behind for Christmas vacation. Having been justly disciplined the night before, Kevin awakens a few days before Christmas and discovers his family gone. For once, precocious Kevin does not have to answer to anyone. His family travels to Paris and discovers Kevin is missing. His mom tries frantically to change her ticket, but all flights are full. Meanwhile, Kevin does the laundry, says "grace," and eats dinner by candlelight. When he overhears burglars planning to break into the house on Christmas Eve, Kevin plans his battle strategy. He goes to a carol service at a nearby church and returns home before the break-in. When the burglars arrive, they slip and fall, one burns his hands, the other loses his shoes and, because of the mayhem, they have second thoughts about the robbery.

Home Alone is a delightful movie with good acting and a generous supply of humor. An intriguing plot emphasizes prayer, repentance, and reconciliation, and the movie is so well crafted that it is virtually seamless. Unfortunately, there is some bad language, slight sexual innuendo, and frequent humorous slapstick violence. Kevin attends church and helps reconcile an old man with his estranged family. Best of all, Kevin learns from his experience not to be afraid and to be thankful for his family. In the end, love triumphs over alienation.

CONTENT ANALYSIS: (CC, B, L, VV, S) Christian worldview including prayer, repentance, church, and reconciliation of an old man with his estranged family; some bad language; frequent humorous slapstick violence; and slight sexual innuendo.

Gripping Adventure

THE HUNT FOR RED OCTOBER

Quality: ☆☆☆☆   Acceptability: +1

WARNING CODES:
  Language: **
  Violence: **
  Sex: None
  Nudity: None
RATING: PG
GENRE: Thriller
INTENDED AUDIENCE: Adults
RUNNING TIME: 135 minutes
STARRING: Sean Connery, Alec Baldwin, Scott Glenn, James Earl Jones, Sam Neill, Joss Ackland, Tim Curry, and Rip Torn
DIRECTOR: John McTiernan
PRODUCER: Mace Neufield
WRITER: Larry Ferguson and Donald Stewart
BASED ON: The novel by Tom Clancy
DISTRIBUTOR: Paramount Pictures
BRIEF SUMMARY:
Set in November 1984, Dr. Jack Ryan, CIA, has learned about the existence of a new Soviet submarine, the *Red October*. This nuclear sub can approach any target undetected. *Red October* is captained by Marko Ramius, a brilliant Soviet officer. However, Ramius kills the executive officer and heads for America's eastern seaboard. When Washington learns that a Soviet submarine has been dispatched to sink *Red October*, they assume that Ramius is planning a nuclear attack against the U.S. The nuclear submarine USS *Dallas* is dispatched. An intense chase begins. Ryan, however, voices his belief that a defection might be planned. The Soviets are aware of this, which is the real reason they want to destroy the sub. Ryan races against the clock to reach the *Red October* before it is too late.

This is a gripping adventure with a great plot that accurately conveys a wide range of emotions and courage. The technical features are outstanding in every way. As Ramius, Sean Connery does an excellent job. Unfortunately, the offensive elements include six profanities, several minor obscenities, a few shootings, and one instance of violence where a man's head is smashed against the floor.

CONTENT ANALYSIS: (C, B, LL, VV) Redemptive worldview with moral elements; some profanities and obscenities; one instance of brutal violence.

Educational Documentary

IN THE BLOOD

Quality: ☆☆☆☆   Acceptability: +3

WARNING CODES:
  Language: None
  Violence: None
  Sex: None
  Nudity: *
RATING: PG
GENRE: Documentary
INTENDED AUDIENCE: All ages
RUNNING TIME: 90 minutes
FEATURING: Robin Hurt, President Theodore Roosevelt, Tyssen Butler, Larry Wilson, Greg Martin, and Harry Muller
DIRECTOR: George Butler
PRODUCER: George Butler
EXECUTIVE PRODUCERS: William E. Simon and R. L. Wilson
DISTRIBUTOR: Deutchman Company
BRIEF SUMMARY:
"The only thing that's going to save the game in Africa is hunting." A paradox? Maybe not, according to filmmaker George Butler, who, convinced that hunting results in conservation, set out to make the first feature film ever about hunting. *In the Blood* is "a figurative and literal safari into the past in search of a future." The film retraces two safaris. The first is a yearlong safari that Theodore Roosevelt made with his son,

Kermit, in 1909 through eastern Africa, recorded using the first movie camera ever in the region. The second is a 1986 hunt in which Roosevelt's grandson, Ted, embarked with a small group of hunters to explore the relationship between hunting and conservation.

Government-controlled economies have had the worst environmental records, whether the totalitarian regimes of Eastern Europe or the authoritarian regimes of Africa. For instance, elephants in the public parks throughout most of Africa have been hunted almost to extinction. However, in those areas where the elephant is owned, their owners protect them as with any other livestock. People do better economically, while the elephant does better ecologically.

Motivating intelligent people to stewardship, the film educates people about the benefits of hunting, and "bring[s] hunters and preservationists together within the conservationist movement." Butler speaks passionately of selective hunting. The film's music is a mix of old and new, and represents a rich tapestry of African sounds. In the Blood is for all lovers of animals and natural resources. In fact, you will want to see In the Blood to gain a deeper understanding of the issues.

CONTENT ANALYSIS: (BB, N) Moral worldview with brief native nudity. Some scenes of animals eating other animals may be too intense for little ones.

Strong Values, Fair Quality

JETSONS: THE MOVIE

Quality: ☆☆   Acceptability: +4

WARNING CODES:
Language: None
Violence: None
Sex: None
Nudity: None
RATING: G
GENRE: Animated comedy
INTENDED AUDIENCE: Children
RUNNING TIME: 81 minutes

VOICES: George O'Hanlon, Penny Singleton, Tiffany, Don Messick, Jean VanderPyl, Mel Blanc, and Patrick Zimmerman
DIRECTORS: William Hanna and Joseph Barbera
PRODUCERS: William Hanna and Joseph Barbera
WRITER: Dennis Marks
DISTRIBUTOR: Universal Pictures
BRIEF SUMMARY:
Jetsons: The Movie will captivate five-year-olds, but may bore seven-year-olds. Elroy has just perfected his elevator shot and Judy has been asked out by rock star Cosmic Cosmo, when George receives a promotion that will relocate him to the Spacely Sprockets orbiting asteroid. No one wants to go but, upon arrival Elroy finds a new spaceball team, Judy has a new boyfriend, and everybody makes friends with the aliens. George is kidnapped, so Elroy leads a rescue party, which finds his father held captive by the Grungies who live in the asteroid. To save their city from the mining equipment, they sabotage the plant. Ashamed, Mr. Spacely hires the Grungies to produce Spacely Sprockets.

The Jetsons does contain a friendly lecture on environmentalism, which does not drift into paganism or one-worldism but extols the positive virtues of stewardship. Loving your neighbor and the importance of respecting your father are also emphasized. The film is a vehicle for other moral statements as well. Too bad the picture is not very entertaining. The animation is typical Saturday-morning cartoon fare. In all, Jetsons: The Movie is acceptable, but could have been better.

CONTENT ANALYSIS: (B, E) Moral worldview with some environmentalism.

Stirring

THE LONG WALK HOME

Quality: ☆☆☆☆   Acceptability: +1

WARNING CODES:

Language: *
Violence: *
Sex: None
Nudity: None

RATING: PG
GENRE: Drama
INTENDED AUDIENCE: Adults
RUNNING TIME: 97 minutes
STARRING: Sissy Spacek, Whoopi Goldberg, Dwight Schultz, Ving Rhames, and Dylan Baker
DIRECTOR: Richard Pearce
PRODUCERS: Howard W. Koch Jr. and David Bell
WRITER: John Cork
DISTRIBUTOR: Miramax Films
BRIEF SUMMARY:
Miriam Thompson is a devoted Alabama wife and mother. She knows her place in society and exists to be served. Odessa is her maid. An intelligent woman, she exists to serve. Their relationship is disrupted when the Reverend Martin Luther King calls for the 1955 black boycott of the Montgomery bus line following the arrest of Rosa Parks, who refuses to give up her seat to a white passenger. Odessa is not a crusader, but she is devoted to her family, so she endures a daily nine-mile walk to keep her job. Miriam decides to do the unthinkable: to pick up her housekeeper at her home. Miriam's friends are appalled, but Miriam shrugs it off. Finally, her husband, Norman, forbids Miriam to drive Odessa to work. Odessa asks, "What's scaring you, Mrs. Thompson?" which causes Miriam to take a stand that will forever affect her position in the community.

A triumphant drama, *The Long Walk Home* is a gentle example of how ordinary people can bring about extraordinary change when they demonstrate courage and sacrifice without yielding to the temptation of hatred, violence, and revenge. The film depicts the faith of black Christians as they attempt to sustain the Montgomery protest. The story gently builds to an emotional crescendo, catching the audience unprepared for its ultimate stirring impact.

CONTENT ANALYSIS: (CCC, BB, L, V) Christian worldview with moral elements; six obscenities and two light exclamatory profanities; some violence.

Heroic Examples

MEMPHIS BELLE

Quality: ☆☆☆☆   Acceptability: −1

WARNING CODES:

Language: *
Violence: **
Sex: *
Nudity: None

RATING: PG-13
GENRE: War drama
INTENDED AUDIENCE: Adults
RUNNING TIME: 105 minutes
STARRING: Matthew Modine, Eric Stoltz, Sean Astin, Harry Connick Jr., Reed Edward Diamond, Tate Donovan, David Strathairn, and John Lithgow
DIRECTOR: Michael Caton-Jones
PRODUCERS: David Puttnam and Catherine Wyler
WRITER: Monte Merrick
DISTRIBUTOR: Warner Brothers
BRIEF SUMMARY:
This drama depicts the final, twenty-fifth mission of ten World War II airmen who fly the B-17 bomber, the *Memphis Belle.* If they survive, they will become part of a publicity drive to stimulate war-bond sales and boost flagging morale. The time is May 16, 1943, and the target is Bremen, Germany. Scarcely out of their teens, the crew's experiences mold them into an effective fighting force and into a caring family. When Colonel Derringer, the army's PR man, arrives to extol the crew of the *Memphis Belle,* the CO complains that Derringer should not extol one crew over others. During the flight, various planes are shot down until the

Memphis Belle becomes the lead. The pilot spends precious extra time waiting for the clouds to lift to avoid bombing a school.

This is a well-produced movie with an outstanding script, good acting, and excellent photography. The action shots as the planes wheel and dive are breathtaking. Worth mentioning is the crew's singing of "Amazing Grace" on takeoff. Even though this is a war film, there is little bad language. There is, however, an instance of drunkenness and off-screen promiscuity. The film's outstanding virtue is its premise: A man's word is more important than his life. We can all benefit from such heroic examples as these.

CONTENT ANALYSIS: (CC, B, L, VV, S, A) Christian worldview with moral elements; few profanities and obscenities; wartime violence; off-screen sexual promiscuity; and drunkenness.

A Subtle Undertone of Rebellion

MR. AND MRS. BRIDGE

Quality: ✰✰✰✰   Acceptability: −2

WARNING CODES:

   Language: *
   Violence: *
   Sex: **
   Nudity: **

RATING: PG-13
GENRE: Drama/Comedy
INTENDED AUDIENCE: Adults
RUNNING TIME: 127 minutes
STARRING: Paul Newman, Joanne Woodward, Blythe Danner, Simon Callow, Kyra Sedgewick, Robert Sean Leonard, and Margaret Welsh
DIRECTOR: James Ivory
PRODUCER: Ismail Merchant
WRITER: Ruth Prawer Jhabvala
BASED ON: The novels *Mrs. Bridge* and *Mr. Bridge* by Evan Connell
DISTRIBUTOR: Miramax
BRIEF SUMMARY: *Mr. and Mrs. Bridge* follows a middle-class marriage through the mid-1930s

and 1940s. Walter and India Bridge are rooted in Kansas City society. They find that modern life, sexual freedom, psychoanalysis, and the women's movement are crashing in on them. Mr. Bridge expresses his love by providing for his family. This only goes so far, as his wife feels underappreciated, while his children are rebellious. After years of unhappiness, the children go their separate ways. The constrictions of a one-sided relationship take their toll on Mrs. Bridge. She knows there is more to life, yet cannot reach out beyond the existence that has been given her.

Mr. and Mrs. Bridge grants the Bridges the dignity they worked to achieve, and Woodward gives a wonderful performance as the cheery, but unhappy Mrs. Bridge. However, the movie has a subtle undertone of discontent and rebellion, implying that divorce would liberate Mrs. Bridge. In fact, the only solution for the Bridges is a new life in Christ. This is a beautiful film, but beware the wiles of the adversary, for God tells us in Hebrews 13:5: "[Let your] conversation [be] without covetousness; [and be] content with such things as ye have" (KJV).

CONTENT ANALYSIS: (H, L, V, SS, NN, A) Humanist worldview; five obscenities and two profanities; implied suicide; sexual immorality; female frontal nudity in magazine; and use of moderate alcohol.

Entertaining and Reflective

MR. DESTINY

Quality: ✰✰✰   Acceptability: −2

WARNING CODES:

   Language: ***
   Violence: *
   Sex: * *
   Nudity: None

RATING: PG-13
GENRE: Comedy
INTENDED AUDIENCE: Teens

RUNNING TIME: 90 minutes

STARRING: Jim Belushi, Michael Caine, Hart Bochner, Rene Russo, Linda Hamilton, and Jon Lovitz

DIRECTOR: James Orr

PRODUCERS: James Orr and Jim Cruickshank

WRITERS: James Orr and Jim Cruickshank

DISTRIBUTOR: Touchstone Pictures

BRIEF SUMMARY:

Mr. Destiny is a reflective, entertaining comedy. For twenty years Larry believed his life would have been better if he hadn't struck out during his high school championship baseball game. Then Larry meets Mr. Mike Destiny, who tells him he has the power to show him just how different his life really would have been. Larry suddenly becomes a company president, married to the owner's daughter, living in a mansion. However he soon discovers the dark side of his new status. Money and prestige have replaced family and friends. In wanting to return to his former life, Larry shows maturity and reflects contentment with his lot in life. Of course, this is a biblical principle: "Godliness with contentment is great gain.... For the love of money is a root of all kinds of evil" (1 Timothy 6:6–10).

Although it starts off slowly, *Mr. Destiny* develops into an enjoyable movie. There are some objectionable scenes involving sexual innuendo, several profanities, and too many obscenities. The movie seeks to answer everyone's question, "What if I had taken another direction in my life—how different would my life be now?"

CONTENT ANALYSIS: (BB, C, LLL, V, SS) Morality tale with redemptive elements; many obscenities and eight profanities; brief violence; and sexual innuendo.

Beautiful, Epic Film

MOUNTAINS OF THE MOON

Quality: ☆☆☆   Acceptability: +1

WARNING CODES:

Language: *
Violence: **
Sex: *
Nudity: **

RATING: R

GENRE: Epic drama/Adventure

INTENDED AUDIENCE: Adults

RUNNING TIME: 135 minutes

STARRING: Patrick Bergen, Iain Glen, Fiona Shaw, Richard E. Grant Bernard Hill, and Omar Sharif

DIRECTOR: Bob Rafelson

PRODUCER: Daniel Melnick

WRITERS: Bob Rafelson and William Harrison

BASED ON: The novel *Burton and Speke* by William Harrison

DISTRIBUTOR: TriStar

BRIEF SUMMARY:

This fascinating portrayal of the hardships faced by nineteenth-century explorers opens on the East African coast in 1854, when Sir Richard Burton teams up with John Speke to search for the source of the Nile. Their safari endures a lion attack, a warrior's lance piercing Burton's face, a bug rendering Speke deaf in one ear, the loss of men, and imprisonment. Speke is allowed to leave, and returns claiming to have found the source, which he names Lake Victoria. The ailing Burton, who insists the source must be a basin of lakes, makes his way home as best he can. When Speke is killed in a hunting accident just before a debate sponsored by the Geographic Society, Burton is moved with compassion and repudiates his theory in support of Speke's. Twelve years later Lake Victoria is confirmed as the source of the Nile.

This beautiful, epic film is a graphic history lesson propelled by the relationships and the question of motives. Why did Speke betray Burton? For glory, it would seem. Burton's motive, instead, was to be truthful, which is ironic since he is lost spiritually. There is some intense violence. Brief nudity and obscenities are also objectionable. Overall, *Mountains of the Moon* is recommended with caution for mature audiences.

CONTENT ANALYSIS: (C, B, L, V, S, NN) Mild Christian worldview with moral elements; some obscenities; tribal violence; and brief female nudity with implied promiscuity.

Redemptive Masterpiece

PATHFINDER

Quality: ☆☆☆☆   Acceptability: −1

WARNING CODES:
  Language: None
  Violence: * *
  Sex: None
  Nudity: *
RATING: Not rated
GENRE: Action/Adventure
INTENDED AUDIENCE: Adults
RUNNING TIME: 88 minutes
LANGUAGE: Lapp with subtitles
STARRING: Mikkel Gaup, Helgi Skulason, Nils Utsi, and Svein Scharffenberg
  DIRECTOR: Nils Gaup
  PRODUCER: John M. Jacobsen
  WRITER: Nils Gaup
  DISTRIBUTOR: International Film Exchange
BRIEF SUMMARY:
This story about a boy who seeks to avenge a family massacre has been passed down in Lapland from generation to generation for almost a thousand years. A thousand years ago in frozen Lapland, sixteen-year-old Algin returns from hunting to find that Tchude warriors have killed his family. Algin watches from a hill, but he is discovered. He flees to a nearby camp. Algin asks the Lapps to fight, but no one listens. Algin stays behind to avenge his family. Raste, the *noaidi*, or spiritual leader, tells the

boy he must never let revenge control his soul. Three Lapps, who join forces with Algin, are slaughtered in a surprise attack. Suddenly, Raste appears and instructs the boy to escape while he distracts the warriors. To save Raste, Algin offers to guide them to the Lapp settlement. The chief accepts, and the raiding party moves out. However, Algin has devised a secret plan that may save them all—if it works.

With a battle between good and evil and a choice between right and wrong, the film reflects basic Judeo-Christian principles, such as "Do not repay evil with evil." Viewed allegorically, Algin serves as a Christ-figure who, as one Lapp says, "gave his life that we might live." At film's end, one Lapp woman says, "We will always have a pathfinder," which is reminiscent of Psalm 48:14: "He will be our guide even to the end."

The sweeping imagery of the original legend is captured breathtakingly. With superb editing and acting, this beautiful film will entertain and edify. Incidentally, *Pathfinder* was an Academy Award nominee for best foreign language film in 1988.

CONTENT ANALYSIS: (CCC, O, VV, NN) Strong Christian allegory with superstitious beliefs relative to the story; some violence and blood, though not gratuitous; brief female nudity.

Partially Insightful

POSTCARDS FROM THE EDGE

Quality: ☆☆☆   Acceptability: −2

WARNING CODES:
  Language: ***
  Violence: None
  Sex: *
  Nudity: None
RATING: R
GENRE: Comedy/Drama
INTENDED AUDIENCE: Adults

RUNNING TIME: 100 minutes

STARRING: Meryl Streep, Shirley MacLaine, Dennis Quaid, Gene Hackman, and Richard Dreyfus

DIRECTOR: Mike Nichols

PRODUCERS: Mike Nichols and John Calley

WRITER: Carrie Fisher

BASED ON: The novel by Carrie Fisher

DISTRIBUTOR: Columbia Pictures

BRIEF SUMMARY:

Postcards from the Edge is about a mother-daughter relationship set against the backdrop of Hollywood. While working on a movie, Suzanne Vale, an actress in her thirties, experiences a drug overdose and is brought to a rehabilitation unit. Once Suzanne checks out, she is informed that she can only return to the set if she consents to her mother, Doris, staying with her for the duration of the movie. Suzanne agrees, but the problems they've had soon begin to resurface. Even the daughter's drug problem is shown to be connected with her mother's drinking problem. All this comes to a head, and a heartfelt talk between mom and daughter ensues.

The interplay between mother and daughter is humorous and insightful in this good "slice-of-life" script. The issues of coming to terms with dysfunctional family patterns are clearly shown. However, *Postcards* may have too much reality and not enough entertainment. Anyone really interested in these issues may want to read *My Mother/My Self* instead. Unfortunately, obscenities and profanities occur, as well as implied promiscuity, an instance of effeminacy, substance abuse, and sexual innuendo. The movie comes to the right conclusion by focusing on relationships as the key to recovery and restoration. Christians know, however, that complete restoration can be found only in Jesus Christ.

CONTENT ANALYSIS: (B, LLL, SS, DD) Moral worldview; thirty obscenities and three profanities; implied promiscuity, effeminacy, sexual innuendo; and substance abuse.

Most Subtle Attack on Biblical Morality

PRETTY WOMAN

Quality: ☆☆☆   Acceptability: –2

WARNING CODES:

Language: **
Violence: *
Sex: **
Nudity: **

RATING: R

GENRE: Romantic drama/Comedy

INTENDED AUDIENCE: Adults

RUNNING TIME: 120 minutes

STARRING: Richard Gere, Julia Roberts, Laura San Giacomo, Hector Elizondo, and Ralph Bellamy

DIRECTOR: Garry Marshall

PRODUCER: Laura Ziskin

WRITER: J. F. Lawton

DISTRIBUTOR: Touchstone Pictures

BRIEF SUMMARY:

In this Pygmalion story, Edward Lewis is a wealthy financier who can't have a meaningful relationship with a woman. One day he meets Vivian, a prostitute who is trying to improve her life. Edward invites Vivian to several business functions. She is transformed into a woman of society. Vivian falls in love with this man who has treated her with respect. Edward then begins to show twinges of conscience when he has second thoughts about his latest hostile takeover. Edward's intentions are dealt a blow when his friend reminds Edward that Vivian is nothing but a prostitute and tries to destroy the relationship. In the end, Edward must decide how much he really respects Vivian. Will it be enough to fall in love with her?

The movie has few obscenities, but there are several sexual innuendos. The relationship is more intimate than physical, but due to the element of immorality, extreme caution is advised. With many funny scenes, the script is excellent. Edward and Vivian's relationship is about the rebuilding of self-worth. Christ gave us an example of this when he restored the woman caught in adultery. However, Jesus declared to the woman, "Go now and leave your life of sin," a point not touched upon in *Pretty Woman*.

CONTENT ANALYSIS: (RoRo, LL, V, SS, NN) Romantic worldview; obscenities; promiscuity; prostitution, sexual innuendos; and brief nudity.

Heroic Role Model

QUIGLEY DOWN UNDER

Quality: ✩✩✩   Acceptability: +1

WARNING CODES:

Language: **
Violence: **
Sex: None
Nudity: None

RATING: PG-13
GENRE: Western
INTENDED AUDIENCE: Teens and adults
RUNNING TIME: 120 minutes
STARRING: Tom Selleck, Alan Rickman, and Laura San Giacomo
DIRECTOR: Simon Wincer
PRODUCERS: Stanley O'Toole and Alex Rose
WRITERS: John Hill, Tracy Keenan Wynn, and Ian Jones
DISTRIBUTOR: MGM-UA
BRIEF SUMMARY:
In the 1860s, Matthew Quigley, an American cowboy, is brought to Australia by Elliott Marston. Upon arriving, Quigley rescues Crazy Cora, who is being commandeered by Marston's men. In her demented state, she believes he is the husband who abandoned her. Arriving at the ranch, Quigley finds that Marston hired him as

a sharpshooter to kill Aborigines. When Quigley refuses, Marston's men drag him and Cora into the outback to die. Quigley kills Marston's men and heads off with Cora. They almost perish but are rescued by Aborigines. Marston sends his men to kill Quigley, only to have them bested. Finally Marston and two of his men face Quigley in a classic shoot-out.

Quigley Down Under is a classic Western with a unique setting and twist, in that Quigley defends the Aborigines against the greedy whites. Unfortunately there are a few references to magic, some obscenities, and the Aborigines are romanticized. However, these imperfections are outweighed by the fact that Quigley is a positive, heroic role model. In addition, the photography is beautiful, the dialogue pithy, and the characters are well drawn. Though the shoot-out is predictable, the story is entertaining.

CONTENT ANALYSIS: (B, Pa, OO, LL, VV) Moral worldview; twelve obscenities; murder, moderate violence; and references to magic and superstition.

Hope and Perseverance Triumph

THE RESCUERS DOWN UNDER

With the special featurette
The Prince and the Pauper

Quality: ✩✩✩✩   Acceptability: +4

WARNING CODES:

Language: None
Violence: *
Sex: None
Nudity: None

RATING: G
GENRE: Animated action/Adventure
INTENDED AUDIENCE: Families
RUNNING TIME: main feature 77 minutes, featurette 24 minutes
VOICES: Bob Newhart, Eva Gabor,

George C. Scott, and Tristan Rogers; featurette: Wayne Allwine, and Tony Anselmo

DIRECTORS: Hendel Butoy and Michael Gabriel; featurette: George Scribner

PRODUCERS: Tom Schumacher; featurette: Dan Rounds

WRITERS: James Douglas Cox, Karey Kirkpatrick, Byron Simpson, and Joseph Ranft; featurette: Gerrit Graham, Samuel Graham, and Chris Hubbel

DISTRIBUTOR: Walt Disney Company/Buena Vista Distribution

BRIEF SUMMARY:

The Disney studios still know how to make quality children's fare, and prove it here by giving us two beautifully animated films on the same bill.

The twenty-four-minute featurette, *The Prince and the Pauper,* is inspired by the Mark Twain classic. It takes place at a time in England when the great king is ill. As a result, the captain of the guard terrorizes the countryside. Peasant Mickey Mouse, a double for the prince, agrees to change places with the prince since the prince envies the beggar's freedom. The captain discovers the switch and throws the prince in jail. However, with help from Goofy, Pluto, and Donald Duck, the prince squares off against the treacherous captain in a duel of swordsmanship. The action is fast and furious as good triumphs over evil. The animation, done in the classic majestic style, is so good that even individual snowflakes look like the real thing.

In *The Rescuers Down Under,* Cody, an Australian boy, frees a golden eagle, but is taken prisoner by McLeach, a poacher who wants to know where to find the bird's nest. Radio signals from military mice get the word to mouse agents Bernard and Miss Bianca, who team up with Wilbur, a fun-loving albatross. They are guided into the Australian outback by Jake, a Crocodile Dundee-type kangaroo mouse. McLeach imprisons Cody with animals destined to be made into belts and purses. Then he frees him under the pretense that the eagle is dead, so he can follow him since Cody is concerned about the eggs. Thus, McLeach captures the mother eagle, then sets out to throw Cody into a crocodile pit. Can our heroes stop the ruthless poacher in time?

Disney animators have created spectacular settings, memorable characters, and lots of adventure. Noteworthy is the way that realistic movements have been captured and mimicked. Biblical principles, such as perseverance and teamwork, are exemplified. Hope is set up as a standard. All ends well, with Jake saying to Bernard, "Well done, mate." Adults who appreciate good animation and brisk storytelling will do well to watch *The Rescuers Down Under* and *The Prince and the Pauper* with their families.

CONTENT ANALYSIS: (BB, VV) Moral worldview with some action violence.

Compelling Real-Life Drama

REVERSAL OF FORTUNE

Quality: ☆☆☆☆   Acceptability: −1

WARNING CODES:
  Language: **
  Violence: *
  Sex: *
  Nudity: None
RATING: R
GENRE: Drama
INTENDED AUDIENCE: Adults
RUNNING TIME: 110 minutes
STARRING: Glenn Close, Jeremy Irons, and Ron Silver
DIRECTOR: Barbet Schroeder
PRODUCER: Pressman and Oliver Stone
WRITER: Alan Dershowitz
BASED ON: The novel by Alan Dershowitz
DISTRIBUTOR: Warner Brothers

BRIEF SUMMARY:

Flying over the mansions of Newport, the camera swoops into a hospital and rests on comatose Sunny Von Bulow, who describes her comas and the conviction of her husband, Claus. Von Bulow asks Harvard law professor Alan Dershowitz to handle his appeal. Von Bulow suggests that Sunny's children framed him. Dershowitz enlists his best law students to overturn the conviction. Claus reveals Sunny's spoiled discontent and her use of drugs. Because of her strong will and the fact that she paid the bills, nobody tried to stop her from destroying herself. Near the end, Dershowitz cautions Von Bulow: "The court has dismissed the legal charge against you, but you'll have to deal with the moral charge."

Reversal of Fortune is a well-crafted film with magnificent acting. The unique plot devices capture the viewer's attention, both emotionally and intellectually. There is little bad language; however, this is a real-life drama, and the subject matter is strong. As Dershowitz points out, Claus is a scapegoat. If only those involved in this case had come to know Jesus, who is the propitiation for our sins, this drama could have moved beyond pathos to the heart of Truth.

CONTENT ANALYSIS: (BB, LL, V, S) Moral worldview; numerous obscenities, few profanities; violence; and references to adultery.

New Age Solutions to Evil

TEENAGE MUTANT NINJA TURTLES

Quality: ☆☆☆   Acceptability: −2

WARNING CODES:

Language: **
Violence: **
Sex: None
Nudity: None
RATING: PG

GENRE: Fantasy/Action/Comedy
INTENDED AUDIENCE: Children and teens
RUNNING TIME: 93 minutes
STARRING: Judith Haag, Elias Koteeas, James Saito, Raymond Serra, and Corey Feldman
DIRECTOR: Steve Barron
PRODUCERS: Kim Dawson, Simon Fields, David Chan, and Graham Cottle
WRITERS: Bobby Herbeck and Todd W. Langen
DISTRIBUTOR: New Line Cinema
BRIEF SUMMARY:

In New York City, Ninja warriors terrorize citizens. Shredder, a karate master from Japan, recruits teenage boys (who feel their parents don't want them) by giving them a sense of worth and then trains them to steal. Opposing Shredder are the teenage mutant ninja turtles: Donatello, Raphael, Michelangelo, and Leonardo. They are guided by Splinter, a rat who is a master of ninjitsu. All the animals were once normal, but when they walked through radioactive waste in the sewers, they acquired human qualities. Splinter is captured by the evil Shredder, and it's the turtles to the rescue! Splinter disposes of Shredder by dropping him from a rooftop into a garbage truck, where he is crushed by its trash compactor.

The turtles' power includes telepathy and visualization. Splinter teaches the turtles that by using the powers of their minds, they can do anything. Children will not discern occultism so subtly presented, or the film's underlying theme that the only way to solve conflict is by beating someone to a pulp. The "good" turtles use that which is evil to overcome evil (a non-biblical premise). Finally, to put obscenity into a movie targeted for children is disturbing to say the least. We recommend that no younger than older teenagers watch it.

CONTENT ANALYSIS: (PaPaPa, LL, VV, M) New Age teachings of telepathy and visualization; six obscenities; violence, theft; and police characterized as incompetent.

Love Conquers Difficult Situations

THREE MEN AND A LITTLE LADY

Quality: ☆☆☆☆   Acceptability: +1

WARNING CODES:
  Language: *
  Violence: None
  Sex: *
  Nudity: None
RATING: PG
GENRE: Comedy
INTENDED AUDIENCE: Teens and adults
RUNNING TIME: 104 minutes
STARRING: Tom Selleck, Steve Guttenberg, Ted Danson, and Nancy Travis
  DIRECTOR: Emile Ardolino
  PRODUCERS: Ted Field and Robert W. Cort
  WRITERS: Charlie Peters, Sara Parriott, and Josann McGibbon
  BASED ON: The novel *Trois Hommes et un Couffin* by Coline Serreau
  DISTRIBUTOR: Walt Disney Company/Buena Vista Distribution
  BRIEF SUMMARY:
In this sequel to *Three Men and a Baby*, five years have passed since baby Mary was deposited by mother Sylvia on the doorstep of father Jack and his two bachelor roommates. The fivesome now share a New York brownstone. Mary is placed in preschool, but experiences distress over having such a different family from the other kids. Sylvia, an actress, is offered an opportunity to appear on the London stage in a play directed by Edward, who is trying to win her hand in marriage. Jack, feeling obligated, proposes marriage, but Sylvia refuses. Sylvia loves Peter, but Peter has been hurt in the past, so he doesn't pursue

marriage. Frustrated, Sylvia accepts Edward's proposal. The doting dads go to great lengths to stop the wedding and bring the little lady back home to where she belongs.

Three Men and a Little Lady is wonderfully humorous and marvelously well-acted. There are no bedroom scenes or even near nudity, just four obscenities. Although such a convoluted family situation seems like a setup for undermining families, the premise of *Three Men and a Little Lady* proves the opposite: Monogamous marriage and having children by your spouse-for-life is the highest social order, and love conquers difficult situations.

CONTENT ANALYSIS: (CC, L, S) Christian worldview; four obscenities; implied promiscuity, and sexual innuendo.

A Parable Filled with Insights

TO SLEEP WITH ANGER

Quality: ☆☆☆☆   Acceptability: +1

WARNING CODES:
  Language: *
  Violence: None
  Sex: None
  Nudity: None

RATING: PG
GENRE: Comedy/Drama
INTENDED AUDIENCE: Adults
RUNNING TIME: 110 minutes
STARRING: Danny Glover, Paul Butler, Mary Alice, Richard Brooks, Carl Lumbly, Vonetta McGee, and Sheryl Lee Ralph
  DIRECTOR: Charles Burnett
  PRODUCERS: Caldecot Chubb, Thomas S. Byrnes, and Darin Scott
  WRITER: Charles Burnett
  DISTRIBUTOR: Samuel Goldwyn
  BRIEF SUMMARY:
To Sleep with Anger is a thought-provoking comedy about a middle-class

black family—father Gideon and mother Susie, with their two sons, Junior and Babe. From the South, they have relocated to Los Angeles and are starting to unravel. Into their home comes Harry, an unexpected visitor from back home, who exploits the family's tensions. Harry is both charmer and menace, teaching the youngest son to cheat one moment, quoting Pushkin the next, all while the family goes to church and gets baptized. When Gideon takes ill, the church prays over him. Sick of Harry's evil influence, Susie asks him to leave. Babe wants to go with Harry. A scuffle ensues between Babe and Junior, ending with reconciliation. Then, comically, things begin to change.

To Sleep with Anger is a parable filled with insights into human behavior. Reveling in the old man, Harry stands in contrast to the new life, which is characterized by reform, responsibility, and church attendance. The characters in this all-black cast are believable and realistic. This is an entertaining film that many will enjoy. Please note a slight caution for eight minor obscenities.

CONTENT ANALYSIS: (CCC, L) Strong Christian worldview and eight obscenities.

Taking a Stand for Righteousness

WEAPONS OF THE SPIRIT

Quality: ☆☆☆☆   Acceptability: +4

WARNING CODES:
  Language: None
  Violence: None
  Sex: None
  Nudity: None

RATING: Not rated
GENRE: Documentary
INTENDED AUDIENCE: Adults
RUNNING TIME: 90 minutes
STARRING: Not applicable
DIRECTOR: Pierre Sauvage
PRODUCER: Pierre Sauvage
WRITER: Pierre Sauvage
DISTRIBUTOR: 1st Run Features
BRIEF SUMMARY:
This documentary by Pierre Sauvage chronicles the achievement of a village that took a stand for righteousness. Sauvage, who is Jewish, was born in 1944 in the French village Le Chambon-sur-Lignon, where his parents were being sheltered from the National Socialists. As an adult, he goes back to discover why this village took such risks: some 5,000 Jews were saved from the Nazis by some 5,000 Christians. The film details the history of the unorganized resistance in Le Chambon. One of the most moving aspects of the film is the obvious humility in obedience to biblical principles demonstrated by the villagers. When asked why they risked death to hide so many Jews, the villagers respond simply: "It needed to be done," or "Christ said to love your neighbor."

Why did this "conspiracy of goodness" emerge in Le Chambon? Most villagers are Huguenots who, for more than four centuries, were a Protestant minority in Catholic France, often persecuted for their faith. Why was Le Chambon the only Huguenot village to take a community stand against the deportation of 75,000 Jews to the death camps? The village pastor encouraged resistance to the Nazi regime, using the "weapons of the Spirit" designated in 2 Corinthians 10:4–5.

With much Scripture, the film is beautifully and lovingly crafted. It provides a wonderful look at the testimony created by simple obedience to the Word of God.

CONTENT ANALYSIS: (CCC) Very strong and overt Christian worldview with nothing objectionable.

Encounters with the Occult

THE WITCHES

Quality: ☆☆☆   Acceptability: −2

WARNING CODES:

Language: *
Violence: None
Sex: None
Nudity: None
RATING: PG
GENRE: Fantasy/Adventure
INTENDED AUDIENCE: Adults
RUNNING TIME: 92 minutes
STARRING: Anjelica Huston, Mai Zetterling, and Jasen Fisher
DIRECTOR: Nicolas Roeg
PRODUCER: Mark Shivas
EXECUTIVE PRODUCER: Jim Henson
WRITER: Alan Scott
BASED ON: The novel by Roald Dahl
DISTRIBUTOR: Warner Brothers
BRIEF SUMMARY:
Norwegian grandma Helga tells young Luke about witches: Ruled by the Grand High Witch, a servant of Satan, witches look like ordinary people and have one purpose—to kill children. Luke moves to England with Helga when his parents are killed in an accident. Checking into a hotel hosting a prevention-of-cruelty-to-children convention, Luke hides in a room full of convention women. They pull off their masks, revealing themselves to be ugly witches. The High Witch gives an order: Every child will be destroyed through candy laced with a formula that turns children into mice. The witches discover Luke, feed him the potion, and cackle as he shrinks into a mouse. Mouse Luke and Helga swipe the formula and pour it into the witches' soup. The witches change into mice, which the hotel staff eliminates. One witch, who does not eat the soup, has a change of heart and turns Luke back into a boy.

The special effects are good, the transformations not too frightening, and Luke as a mouse borders on the lovable. However, these ideas about witches are something no children need fill their minds with. God warns us to stay away from the occult: "Anyone who does these things is detestable to the Lord" (Deuteronomy 18:12).

CONTENT ANALYSIS: (PaPaPa, L) Witchcraft and one profanity.

Self-Destructive Genius

WHITE HUNTER, BLACK HEART

Quality: ☆☆☆☆   Acceptability: −2

WARNING CODES:
Language: **
Violence: **
Sex: None
Nudity: None
RATING: PG
GENRE: Drama
INTENDED AUDIENCE: Adults
RUNNING TIME: 112 minutes
STARRING: Clint Eastwood, Jeff Fahey, George Dzundra, Marisa Berenson, and Alun Armonstrong
DIRECTOR: Clint Eastwood
PRODUCER: Clint Eastwood
WRITER: Peter Viertel, James Bridges, and Burt Kennedy
DISTRIBUTOR: Warner Brothers
BRIEF SUMMARY:
Based on Peter Viertel's 1953 novel about his experiences with director John Huston while filming *The African Queen*, this tale is a somber look into the complex nature of the oft-revered, highly problematic filmmaker. *White Hunter, Black Heart* takes place mostly in Africa, as John Wilson prepares for his next movie. On the verge of bankruptcy, Wilson realizes that he needs a hit to survive. Self-assured and cocky, he plans for the filming, but something else begins to dominate his life. In fact, the movie is only a ploy to undertake his real mission, to bag a bull elephant. Contemptuous of the people around him, Wilson is only interested in shooting with his rifle, not a camera. When the rains come, the movie's start is delayed by days. Wilson continues to

track his trophy. He is about to come to terms with himself.

The movie captures the grand backdrop of Africa, yet is essentially a study of man's inner self. There is much to analyze in Eastwood's portrayal, though his mimicking of Huston's mannerisms are somewhat forced. The inner turmoil of a self-destructive genius overshadows the difficulties of shooting a movie in a logistically impossible place. Wilson is a man whose psychological needs are so great that he sets the definitions by which others must act within his own life. Huston was noted for a salty, caustic manner, which Eastwood has captured. However, the profane and obscene language is objectionable.

CONTENT ANALYSIS: (HH, LL, VV) Humanist worldview; profanities, obscenities, and violence.

☆☆☆ THE BEST FILMS OF 1990 ☆☆☆

Headline	Title
Outstanding Masterpiece	*Hamlet*
Provocative and Engrossing	*Awakenings*
Compelling Real-Life Drama	*Reversal of Fortune*
Fidelity, Nobility, and Love	*Cyrano De Bergerac*
The Journey of Faith	*China Cry*
Taking a Stand for Righteousness	*Weapons of the Spirit*
A Parable Filled with Insights	*To Sleep with Anger*
Stirring	*The Long Walk Home*
Powerful Family Saga	*Avalon*
Heroic Examples	*Memphis Belle*
Love Triumphs over Alienation	*Home Alone*
Lying Has Consequences	*Green Card*
Hope and Perseverance Triumph	*The Rescuers Down Under*
God's Wonderful Creation	*For All Mankind*
Redemptive Masterpiece	*Pathfinder*

☆☆☆ THE TWENTY MOST UNBEARABLE FILMS OF 1990 ☆☆☆

Headline	Title
Worst Attack on Jews and Christians	*The Handmaid's Tale*
Worst Attack on Jesus Christ	*Jesus of Montreal*
Worst Libertine Art Film	*Henry and June*
Worst Blatant Marxist Propaganda	*Havana*
Worst Mean-Spirited Attack on Children	*Child's Play 2*
Worst Shameful Promotion of Adultery	*Enemies, a Love Story*
Worst Revision of American History	*Dances with Wolves*
Worst Spiritism	*Ghost*
Worst Attack on Biblical Morality	*Pretty Woman*
Worst Promotion of Sodomy	*Longtime Companion*
Worst Promotion of Satanism	*The First Power*
Worst Promotion of Murder	*Henry: Portrait of a Serial Killer*
Worst Obscene Portrayal of Cruelty	*The Cook, the Thief, His Wife and Her Lover*
Worst Anti-Christian Bigotry	*Blaze*
Worst Mockery of Christianity	*Nuns on the Run*
Worst Demented Violence	*Leatherface: Texas Chainsaw Massacre III*
Worst Art Film	*Vincent and Theo*
Worst Diatribe	*Graffiti Bridge*
Worst Sexual Violence	*Wild at Heart*
Worst Occult Movie Aimed at Children	*Ghost Dad*

Wholesome Family Message

ALL I WANT FOR CHRISTMAS

Quality: ☆☆☆☆   Acceptability: +1

WARNING CODES:
  Language: *
  Violence: None
  Sex: None
  Nudity: *
RATING: G
GENRE: Comedy
INTENDED AUDIENCE: All ages
RUNNING TIME: 92 minutes
STARRING: Thora Birch, Ethan Randall, Harley Jane Kozak, Lauren Bacall, Jamey Sheridan, Kevin Nealon, and Leslie Nielsen
DIRECTOR: Robert Lieberman
PRODUCER: Stan Rogow
WRITERS: Thom Eberhardt and Richard Kramer
DISTRIBUTOR: Paramount Pictures
BRIEF SUMMARY:
All I Want for Christmas is an uplifting film that opens with a church-school choir singing "God Rest Ye Merry Gentlemen." After choir practice, thirteen-year-old Ethan takes his seven-year-old sister, Hallie, home. All they want for Christmas is for their divorced parents to remarry. Evidently, Mike and Catherine O'Fallon's problems began when, disgusted with his yuppie lifestyle, Mike purchased a diner in lower Manhattan. Catherine refused to sacrifice her lifestyle and moved in with her mother. Now Catherine is planning to marry Tony, though he is uncomfortable with her children. Hallie visits the "real" Santa at Macy's and requests that her parents remarry. Knowing that Santa isn't real, Ethan enlists Stephanie to help make Hallie's Christmas wish come true by con-cocting a well-meaning but mischievous scheme.

The wholesome pro-family message in *All I Want for Christmas* will appeal to all generations. Six-year-old Robbie Baehr has proclaimed enthusiastically, "I liked it all. This is a good movie. It's like real life." With surprises at every turn, including a *Miracle on 34th Street* ending, *All I Want for Christmas* unfolds with vir-tually flawless directing, editing, and act-ing performances.

CONTENT ANALYSIS: (BB, CC, L, N,) Biblical theme and positive refer-ences to Jesus Christ; three borderline exclamations; and an abstract painting of a nude woman at museum.

Grotesque

BARTON FINK

Quality: ☆☆☆   Acceptability: −2

WARNING CODES:
  Language: ***
  Violence: **
  Sex: **
  Nudity: *
RATING: R
GENRE: Drama
INTENDED AUDIENCE: Adults
RUNNING TIME: 116 minutes
STARRING: John Turturro, John Goodman, Judy Davis, and John Mahoney
DIRECTOR: Joel Coen
PRODUCERS: Ethan Coen and Graham Place
WRITER: Ethan Coen
DISTRIBUTOR: 20th Century Fox Film Corporation
BRIEF SUMMARY:
Barton Fink is a 1940s playwright who is brought to Hollywood by Capital

Studios after his successful Broadway debut. He experiences a hell dominated by the inverted values of the movie industry, complete with a neighborly psychopathic killer. In conformity to the Communist fashion, Bart wants to pen the struggles of the common man. He checks into the eerie Hotel Earl and is greeted by the pallid hotel clerk who climbs out of a trap door in the floor. Chief executive Jack Lipnik assigns Bart to construct a wrestling script. Mr. Lipnik is a Jewish-American godfather who can't read. As Bart struggles with writer's block, he befriends an acclaimed writer with a drinking problem, W. P. Mayhew, and his mistress/secretary. Bart is corrupted by his new friends, including "Mad Man Mundt," who sets the story ablaze with murder and pyromania.

Barton Fink is the slow, surrealistic tale of a man who is compromised by incompetent Hollywood executives, a lush who enjoys a success that isn't rightfully his, and a psychopath who deceives him into thinking they can be friends. This is not entertainment. It is an "inside" joke about Hollywood filled with arrogance, an unappealing hero, disgusting language, and bloody grotesqueries.

CONTENT ANALYSIS: (H, BB, Ab, LLL, VV, SS, N, A, D) Humanist worldview with some anti-Christian content and some moral messages; forty-nine obscenities and fifty-one profanities; murder, bloody cadaver, arson, wrestling, and a gun fired between a man's eyes; implied fornication; nude woman on man's tie; and alcoholism.

Strong Redemptive Fairy Tale

BEAUTY AND THE BEAST

Quality: ☆☆☆☆   Acceptability: +3

WARNING CODES:
Language: None
Violence: *
Sex: None

Nudity: None
RATING: G
GENRE: Animated fantasy
INTENDED AUDIENCE: All ages
RUNNING TIME: 84 minutes
VOICES: Angela Landsbury, Robby Benson, Paige O'Hara, Jerry Orbach, Jesse Corti, Rex Everhart, David Ogden Stiers, Richard White, Bradley Pierce, and Jo Anne Worley
DIRECTORS: Gary Trousdale and Kirk Wise
PRODUCER: Don Hahn
WRITER: Linda Woolverton
BASED ON: The classic fairy tale by Madame Gabrielle de Villeneuve
DISTRIBUTOR: Buena Vista/Disney
BRIEF SUMMARY:

Disney's musical fantasy *Beauty and the Beast* brings to life the classic fairy tale of the Beast who must convince Belle to look beyond appearances to break the spell before he is destroyed by the vengeful Gaston. In eighteenth-century France, Belle reads books to escape Gaston, who is intent on marrying her. One day, Belle's father, Maurice, leaves town on a journey, is caught in a storm, stumbles onto the Beast's castle, and is taken prisoner. When the horse returns, Belle sets out to rescue her father. Arriving at the Beast's castle, she agrees to take Maurice's place. She befriends the enchanted staff: a perky teapot, a hot-blooded candelabra, and a tightly wound clock. She also discovers the heart of a prince beneath Beast's exterior. Meanwhile, Gaston leads a mob to the castle for a climactic confrontation.

A masterpiece in filmmaking, *Beauty and the Beast* revives the age-old tale with new dimensions that are only possible with animation. Moviegoers young and old will appreciate this tale, which reminds us that appearances can be deceiving, for true beauty is spiritual. Also, the tale of Belle's willingness to lay down her life for others points out that love, not force, conquers all.

CONTENT ANALYSIS: (CCC, BBB, O, V) Very strong Christian worldview with very strong moral values, plus evil enchantress rebuked. Some very young children might be frightened by Belle's father held prisoner in the Beast's castle, Maurice being lost in the woods, a mob attack on the Beast's castle during a spring thunderstorm, the Beast's slightly gruesome physique, and by the premise that certain people and objects are under an enchantress's magic spell. However, these elements are so well thought out that it is doubtful that they will scare the average young child. Moreover, the themes of self-sacrifice, looking beyond appearances, and love are biblical. There are also Christian images of angels in parts of the movie.

Worst Psychic Silliness

BILL AND TED'S BOGUS JOURNEY

Quality: ☆☆   Acceptability: −4

WARNING CODES:

> Language: *
> Violence: *
> Sex: *
> Nudity: None

RATING: PG-13
GENRE: Comedy/Adventure
INTENDED AUDIENCE: Teens
RUNNING TIME: 98 minutes
STARRING: Alex Winter and Keanu Reeves
DIRECTOR: Peter Hewitt
PRODUCER: Scott Kroof
WRITERS: Chris Matheson and Ed Soloman
DISTRIBUTOR: Orion Pictures
BRIEF SUMMARY:
In *Bill and Ted's Bogus Journey*, two dim-witted guitar players embark on an occult odyssey to save the world from their robotic replicas. The year is A.D. 2691, and Bill and Ted have established a university.

A villain plots to send two robotic replicas of Bill and Ted back in time to rid the world of them. Back in the 1990s, Bill and Ted mistake their evil twins for their future selves and end up being murdered. They come face-to-face with the grim reaper and knock him unconscious. They overhear the twins plotting to murder their girlfriends. They alert the police by possessing the bodies of two cops and then crash a séance. A satanic chant sends the two into a "bad karma" hell. Their only option is to beat the reaper at a game. After a few games, the reaper takes them to heaven to petition God. Bill and Ted ask "God" to help them save the world from their oppressors.

Describing their travels as "bogus" is accurate. *Bill and Ted's Bogus Journey* counterfeits heaven and hell with occultism and foolishness. Someday, these misfits will come face-to-face with the Creator they mocked in their movie. God will not accept their absurd answers to the meaning of life. Instead, he will only consider whether or not they accepted Jesus Christ as Lord and Savior before they died.

CONTENT ANALYSIS: (PaPa, L, V, S, O, Ab) Pagan worldview; five obscenities; enemy interrogation, murder; implied rape, gazing upon woman's breasts, transvestism (female turns out to be male); use of crystals, channeling, and hell depicted as bad karma (past experiences haunting you after death); out-of-body experiences, appearance of grim reaper, demon possession, calling upon dead in séance, graphic depictions of demons and hell, repeated use of hand signal for devil worship (index and ring finger curled under, other fingers pointing up), chanting an occult spell from *Book of Evil*; and unbiblical depictions of God and heaven (heaven's "most intelligent beings" are two fat, hairy chimpanzee creatures with huge rear cheeks).

Realistic Portrayal of Christianity

BLACK ROBE

Quality: ☆☆☆☆   Acceptability: −2

WARNING CODES:
  Language: None
  Violence: ***
  Sex: ***
  Nudity: **
RATING: R
GENRE: Historical drama
INTENDED AUDIENCE: Adults
RUNNING TIME: 101 minutes
STARRING: Lothaire Bluteau,
August Schellenberg, Aden Young,
Sandrine Holt, and Tantoo Cardinal
  DIRECTOR: Bruce Beresford
  PRODUCER: Robert Lantos
  WRITER: Brian Moore (based upon
his novel)
  DISTRIBUTOR: Samuel Goldwyn
  BRIEF SUMMARY:
  Black Robe, directed by Bruce
Beresford (Driving Miss Daisy), relates
the story of a seventeenth-century
French Jesuit priest who goes to New
France (Quebec) in an effort to convert
the Indians in 1634. Set in the Quebec
wilderness, the magnificent film Black
Robe opens in 1634 as Jesuit Father
Laforgue sets out to travel 1,500 miles to
a Huron mission outpost, guided by a
handful of Algonquins, led by chief
Chomina; his wife; his daughter,
Annuka; and his young son. A French
carpenter, Daniel, accompanies them.
Soon, Daniel and Annuka fornicate.
Daniel tells Father Laforgue that the
Indians "share everything without question." Father Laforgue replies that "they
should question." The Iroquois attack,
kill the chief's wife and son, and wound
the chief. Annuka uses her sexuality to
escape. Father Laforgue arrives at the
mission only to find the priest dying and
the Indians decimated by fever. The
Indians plead with him to baptize
them. He contends they must first understand Jesus Christ, but finally relents.
Abandoning their brutal ways, they are
soon annihilated by the Iroquois.
  The masterful direction, sensitive performances, and remarkable cinematography create a film that forces the viewer
to ponder the struggle between paganism and Christianity. Regrettably, the
prospective viewer does have to consider the naturalistic sex and brutal torture scenes before he deems Black Robe a
movie to see.
  CONTENT ANALYSIS: (CCC, B,
VVV, SSS, O, NN) A strong Christian
worldview, a biblical theme of giving up
one's life for others, and a realistic portrayal of Christianity with portrayal of
pagan beliefs of the Indians; extreme
violence and torture inflicted on their
captives by the Indians, several graphic
fornication scenes, sexual fondling; and
partial upper female nudity.

Most Demented Revenge on the Church

CAPE FEAR

Quality: ☆☆☆   Acceptability: −4

WARNING CODES:
  Language: ***
  Violence: ***
  Sex: ***
  Nudity: None
RATING: R
GENRE: Thriller
INTENDED AUDIENCE: Adults
RUNNING TIME: 128 minutes
STARRING: Robert De Niro, Nick
Nolte, Jessica Lange, Gregory Peck,
Robert Mitchum, Martin Balsam, and
Juliette Lewis
  DIRECTOR: Martin Scorsese
  PRODUCER: Barbara De Fina
  EXECUTIVE PRODUCERS:
Kathleen Kennedy and Frank Marshall
  WRITERS: John D. MacDonald and
James R. Webb
  DISTRIBUTOR: Universal Pictures

BRIEF SUMMARY:

Cape Fear, a suspenseful remake of the 1962 thriller, is directed by Martin Scorsese and contains cameo appearances by Gregory Peck and Robert Mitchum from the original cast. Robert De Niro portrays the rapist and ex-con who terrorizes the lawyer responsible for his imprisonment.

Characterized by foreboding evil, this remake of the 1962 *Cape Fear* shocks viewers to the point of numbness. When lethal sexual psychopath Max Cady is released from prison after fourteen years, he plots revenge against the man who put him there, prosecutor Sam Bowden, who now has a private practice. Cady stalks Bowden's family—his wife and his fifteen-year-old daughter. The family dog is poisoned, then Cady plagues Bowden's wife with obscene phone calls. Bowden tries to have him arrested, but since Cady has not broken the law, the attempt fails. Cady nearly seduces Bowden's daughter when he tells her he is her new drama teacher in a deserted theatre. Bowden and his family travel to a houseboat on the Cape Fear River. Cady follows and terrorizes them. During a storm, Bowden and Cady struggle for supremacy.

Cape Fear is a well-crafted film. The suspense keeps the viewer on the edge of his seat, especially during the bloody, graphic, violent rape scene. De Niro is convincing as a fiendish sexual psychopath. He spouts biblical epithets and uses Christian terminology so as to distort the biblical meaning. What a travesty characters like this make of the precious gospel of Jesus Christ!

CONTENT ANALYSIS: (AbAbAb, LLL, VVV, SSS, Ab, M) Anti-Christian worldview with psychopathic killer portrayed as a demented, tormented Christian spouting biblical epithets; at least fifteen gross profanities and numerous obscenities; extreme sexual violence, including a graphic rape scene with implied mutilation (however, woman is partially clothed); and a revenge motif by convicted rapist.

Do-Your-Own-Thing Pabulum

CITY SLICKERS

Quality: ☆☆☆   Acceptability: −2

WARNING CODES:
  Language: ***
  Violence: *
  Sex: *
  Nudity: None
RATING: PG-13
GENRE: Comedy
INTENDED AUDIENCE: Adults
RUNNING TIME: 112 minutes
STARRING: Billy Crystal, Bruno Kirby, Daniel Stern, Jack Palance, Helen Slater, Josh Mostel, Kyle Secor, and Patricia Wettig
DIRECTOR: Ron Underwood
PRODUCER: Irby Smith
WRITERS: Lowell Ganz and Babaloo Mandel
DISTRIBUTOR: Columbia Pictures
BRIEF SUMMARY:

As an antidote to midlife crisis, three New Yorkers go on a cattle drive from New Mexico to Colorado and learn about life, love, and smelly animals. Mitch Robbins, turning thirty-nine, is depressed until Ed and Phil ask him to join them on a two-week cattle drive vacation. Trail boss Curly presides over these vacationers as a tough cowboy who disdains city slickers. Much of what you've seen in Westerns turns up as satire in *City Slickers*: the stampede, the duel, and the art of lassoing, to name a few. There are also those things you haven't seen on the trail, like mobile phones and discussions about VCRs. (Definitely not for the squeamish is a live-calf delivery.)

Unlike *Blazing Saddles* (essentially an inane movie), the satire in *City Slickers* gives way to philosophical musings. Unfortunately, the message turns out to be the humanistic "do your own thing." For those who know the Truth, the secret of life is found in Jesus, and the best day of life is that day we "cross over from death to life" (John 5:24). The film rebukes the idea of adultery, but cannot be recommended due to over seventy instances of obscenity or profanity, humanism, and its tilt toward sexually lewd jokes.

CONTENT ANALYSIS: (HH, B, LLL, V, S, H, M) Humanist worldview with moral elements; forty-four obscenities and twenty-seven profanities; some Western violence; sexually lewd joking and comments; unflattering portrayal of a marriage; brief rear male nudity; and drunkenness.

Passion without Repentance

THE COMMITMENTS

Quality: ☆☆☆   Acceptability: −2

WARNING CODES:
  Language: ***
  Violence: **
  Sex: *
  Nudity: None
RATING: R
GENRE: Drama
INTENDED AUDIENCE: Teens and adults
RUNNING TIME: 118 minutes
STARRING: Robert Arkins, Angeline Ball, Johnny Murphy, and Andrew Strong
DIRECTOR: Alan Parker
PRODUCERS: Lynda Miles and Roger Randall-Cutler
WRITERS: Dick Clement and Ian LeFrenais
BASED ON: The novel by Roddy Doyle
DISTRIBUTOR: 20th Century Fox

BRIEF SUMMARY:
Committing themselves to be "the saviors of soul," a group of young Irishmen form "The Commitments" to vocalize the passion of soul in this portrait of modern Dublin ravaged by socialism. Managing the band is Jimmy Rabbitte, a young music lover who brings together seven guys and three girls to form a soul band The Commitments. Jimmy tells them that the Irish are "the blacks of Europe," so they should have soul. One band member, "Joey-the-Lips," feels called of God to perform with the group. Boasting of his previous performances with B.B. King, Otis Redding, and Joe Tex, and professing to be a Christian, Joey seduces all three female band members. The band concludes that "soul music is sex, isn't it?"

Unfortunately, the band's "soul" has no spirit. Their passion is without repentance, so it only leads to their downfall. Thus, the movie shows how a lack of commitment will unravel even this talented band. Furthermore, the "f–" word peppers every other word of dialogue, detracting from *The Commitments'* intriguing portrait of Irish living, including Irish expressions, style, customs, architecture, and the socialist blight that has wasted Ireland.

CONTENT ANALYSIS: (Pa, Ab, C, LLL, VV, S, A, D, M) Pagan worldview with Christian and anti-Christian elements; swearing on Bible, 194 obscenities, and 23 profanities; fistfighting, violent brawls, and whacking man on head with garbage can; audible off-camera fornication, seduction, sexual gestures; hypocrisy, Christian band member portrayed as gigolo, Mariolatry, and worship of Elvis Presley (see Exodus 34:14).

Too Many Mixed Signals

CURLY SUE

Quality: ☆☆☆   Acceptability: +1

WARNING CODES:
  Language: **

Violence: *
Sex: None
Nudity: None
RATING: PG
GENRE: Comedy
INTENDED AUDIENCE: All ages, but recommended audience is ten years old and up
RUNNING TIME: 101 minutes
STARRING: Jim Belushi, Kelly Lynch, and Allison Porter
DIRECTOR: John Hughes
PRODUCER: John Hughes
WRITER: John Hughes
DISTRIBUTOR: Warner Brothers
BRIEF SUMMARY:
Curly Sue begins in wintry Chicago, where homeless Bill and his eight-year-old foster child, Curly Sue, look for an easy target for a good meal. Bill has Sue clobber him with a stick and throws himself in front of a Mercedes driven by attorney Doris. The two get their meal. The next day, Doris happens to hit Bill again—this time for real. She takes the bathless twosome to her penthouse and calls a doctor to assess Bill's condition. He needs rest, the doctor tells Doris. Doris's attorney boyfriend comes tripping into her apartment at night and heads for the guest room. When Sue sees him, she screams. He disdains sheltering homeless people, but Doris tells him to get out.

Curly Sue is a well-crafted movie with uplifting moments such as Sue's singing "The Star-Spangled Banner" in a Shirley Temple-like voice. While the cinematography portrays the plight of homeless people, the plot is not credible. Also, the film contains profanities and slapstick violence. *Curly Sue* sends too many mixed signals, along with a confused premise and therefore cannot be highly recommended.

CONTENT ANALYSIS: (Pa, LL, V, A, D, B) Pagan worldview; seven profanities, ten obscenities; slapstick violence; and some alcohol abuse.

Spoiled Bucolic Comedy

DOC HOLLYWOOD

Quality: ☆☆☆   Acceptability: −2

WARNING CODES:
Language: *
Violence: *
Sex: None
Nudity: None
RATING: PG-13
GENRE: Comedy
INTENDED AUDIENCE: Teens and adults
RUNNING TIME: 104 minutes
STARRING: Michael J. Fox, Julie Warner, Bridget Fonda, Woody Harrelson, and George Hamilton
DIRECTOR: Michael Caton-Jones
PRODUCER: Susan Solt
WRITERS: Price and Daniel Pines
DISTRIBUTOR: Warner Brothers
BRIEF SUMMARY:
Heading for Beverly Hills to practice plastic surgery, Ben Stone is an ambitious young medical doctor who smashes into a fence on the outskirts of Grady, Georgia, when he misses the freeway. He is sentenced to forty-eight hours of community service at Grady Memorial Hospital. The town leaders want to keep him in Grady, fearing that the elderly Dr. Hogue might die any minute. Life in Grady is not so bad, however, especially after Ben sees Vilulu skinny-dipping in the river. Winning the affections of the townspeople, Ben performs various minor "emergencies," from removing a fishhook from a man's finger to reading letters for an illiterate family. After a few days, Ben and Lu share a romantic rowboat trip together around the lake at the Grady Squash Festival. They are tempted to fornicate, but he stops, noting, "I want this to be more than a one-night stand."

Doc Hollywood, with its *Green Acre*-ish storyline, could have been a wholesome portrayal of community living. Unfortunately, profanity, obscenity, nudity, and scatological humor spoil the picture. *Doc Hollywood* shows how the perverse mindset in Hollywood can mess up a cute movie with a commendable plot by adding unnecessary objectionable elements.

CONTENT ANALYSIS: (B, C, L, N, M) Morality tale with Christian elements; nineteen obscenities; six profanities, scatological humor; and nudity.

Learning the Golden Rule

THE DOCTOR

Quality: ☆☆☆☆   Acceptability: –1

WARNING CODES:

Language: **
Violence: None
Sex: None
Nudity: None

RATING: PG-13
GENRE: Drama
INTENDED AUDIENCE: Adults
RUNNING TIME: 122 minutes
STARRING: William Hurt and Christine Lahti
DIRECTOR: Randa Haines
PRODUCERS: Laura Ziskin and Edward S. Feldman
WRITER: Robert Caswell
BASED ON: The book by Ed Rosenbaum, M.D.
DISTRIBUTOR: Buena Vista/Disney
BRIEF SUMMARY:
The Doctor begins as heart surgeon Jack rescues a man who attempted suicide. To celebrate, he sings, "Why don't we get drunk and f–!" as he dances about the room. Jack counsels the interns not to become emotionally involved with their patients. Suffering from a sore throat and a cough, Jack visits Dr. Abbott. Clinically cold, Dr. Abbott enables Jack to realize how a patient must feel when treated with indifference. When Dr. Abbott schedules him for a biopsy, Jack experiences the horrors of dealing with doctors and medical institutions. Jack's tumor is malignant. In chemotherapy, Jack meets June, another patient with an inoperable tumor. Through June, who prays, dances, and eats chocolate, Jack sorrowfully realizes that his medical practice was built upon a wrong premise and learns to treat others with sensitivity and respect.

Medicine and the Golden Rule come together in *The Doctor,* which highlights Luke 6:31: "Do to others as you would have them do to you." Regrettably, a few profanities and obscenities soil the moral messages. *The Doctor* could have been a great movie with an exemplary message, but the script doesn't do the story justice, though it still has much to offer an audience.

CONTENT ANALYSIS: (C, B, LL) Christian worldview with a biblical premise of repentance and grace marred by twenty-five obscenities and a few profanities.

Most Idolatrous Glorification

THE DOORS

Quality: ☆☆☆   Acceptability: –4

WARNING CODES:

Language: ***
Violence: **
Sex: ***
Nudity: ***

RATING: R
GENRE: Musical biography/ Documentary
INTENDED AUDIENCE: Adults
RUNNING TIME: 140 minutes
STARRING: Val Kilmer, Meg Ryan, Kevin Dillon, Kyle MacLachlan, Frank Whaley, and Kathleen Quinlan
DIRECTOR: Oliver Stone
PRODUCER: A. Kitman Ho
WRITER: Oliver Stone
DISTRIBUTOR: TriStar

BRIEF SUMMARY:

Set in the 1960s, *The Doors* is about rock idol Jim Morrison. In the desert, Morrison and his friends get stoned. Morrison kisses a huge snake and encounters his medium. Thus, "The Doors" are born. Through their songs, Morrison informs the world of his demonic vision. Morrison elicits an inspired frenzy in his fans. Patricia, a trendy reporter, seduces him. After they make love, Patricia introduces him to a satanic ritual. They slit their wrists and drink mingled blood. Concerts follow, with a memorable one in Miami: Numerous women dance naked as a tripped-out Morrison sings filthy lyrics before shedding his clothes. In 1971, a disenchanted Morrison travels to Paris to start anew as a poet. At twenty-seven years old, he suffers a fatal heart attack.

The Doors is an extremely powerful, well-constructed film that openly glorifies Morrison. How tragic that the images one remembers consist primarily of Morrison's revolting, immoral behavior and of his being stoned from drugs and alcohol. *The Doors* can only provide impressionable young people with despicable examples of immorality, rebelliousness, drugs, and the occult. What Morrison reaped was an untimely death, a reminder that the "wages of sin is death."

CONTENT ANALYSIS: (OOO, LLL, VV, SSS, NNN, A, D) Occult worldview with occult elements and Satan worship; eighty obscenities and twenty profanities; extreme violence; graphic sexual immorality and fornication; and complete female and male nudity; frequent, excessive drug and alcohol abuse.

Affirming Family Values

FATHER OF THE BRIDE

Quality: ✰✰✰✰   Acceptability: +1

WARNING CODES:

Language: *
Violence: None
Sex: *
Nudity: None

RATING: PG
GENRE: Comedy
INTENDED AUDIENCE: Adults
RUNNING TIME: 105 minutes
STARRING: Steve Martin, Diane Keaton, Kimberly Williams, George Newbern, and Martin Short
DIRECTOR: Charles Shyer
PRODUCERS: Sandy Gallin, James Orr, Jim Cruickshank, and Cindy Williams
WRITERS: Frances Goodrich, Albert Hackett, Nancy Meyers, and Charles Shyer
DISTRIBUTOR: Buena Vista/Disney
BRIEF SUMMARY:

Returning from a semester of architectural study in Rome, twenty-two-year-old Annie Banks announces her engagement to a youth she met abroad. Her mother is thrilled, but the news wreaks havoc on the soon-to-be father of the bride in this updated modernization of Vincente Minnelli's 1950 MGM classic. The wedding becomes a comic foil for the story, with father George objecting to everything and everyone (from the prospective groom and in-laws to out-of-town wedding guests)—especially how expensive it all is. George's hysteria seems to be fueled by his intense devotion to Annie and fear of losing his identity once she is gone. He is not ready for the parenting part of his life to end.

Steve Martin is funny yet poignant in this role. Memorable scenes include a Tom Jones imitation and George's snooping around in his future in-law's house. Adding to George's troubles is a foppish wedding coordinator. Refreshingly, *Father of the Bride* affirms old-fashioned family values, though there is one exclamatory profanity and sexual innuendo. Aside from these flaws, *Father of the Bride* is a heartwarming father-daughter story that reflects family life in the 1990s.

CONTENT ANALYSIS: (B, C, L, S) A biblical theme of love overcoming all adversity, positive pro-family and pro-church messages; one exclamatory pro-fanity, reference to condoms, and parents talking about fornicating before marriage.

Needs Some Work

FLIGHT OF THE INTRUDER

Quality: ☆☆☆   Acceptability: −2

WARNING CODES:
  Language: ***
  Violence: **
  Sex: *
  Nudity: None
RATING: PG-13
GENRE: War/Action/Adventure
INTENDED AUDIENCE: Adults and young adults
RUNNING TIME: 115 minutes
STARRING: Danny Glover, Willem Dafoe, Brad Johnson, Rosanna Arquette, and Tom Sizemore
DIRECTOR: John Milius
PRODUCER: Mace Neufeld
WRITERS: Robert Dillon and David Shaber
BASED ON: The novel by Stephen Coonts
DISTRIBUTOR: Paramount Pictures
BRIEF SUMMARY:
Set on an aircraft carrier, this adventure is about U.S. Navy men flying above North Vietnam in 1972. Lt. Grafton flies the A-6 Intruder, a low altitude bomber. When Grafton returns from a disastrous mission in which his bombardier is killed, he begins having second thoughts about their effectiveness, since the squadron leader has restricted bombing to tree clusters. Lt. Commander Cole, an ace bombardier, is then assigned to fly with Grafton.

Grafton asks Cole to join him in an unauthorized raid on a missile depot in Hanoi. Grafton and Cole bomb a power plant and a stockpile of SAM missiles, only to return to an angry Camparelli. The charges are dropped when President Nixon issues orders to bomb all restricted targets.

In the tradition of the classic war movies, *Flight of the Intruder* is about men keeping faith with each other. Those who believe America's mistake was the half-hearted way it waged the war will find much to like in the picture. Unfortunately, the movie gets off to a slow start and it resorts to using over seventy-five instances of obscenity and profanity. Cole's comment that "flying is not as grat-ifying as killing" is particularly disturb-ing. Thus, while the patriotic sentiments in the movie about the Vietnam War may be on target, the characters and storyline need a bit of work.

CONTENT ANALYSIS: (B, LLL, VV, S, M) Moral worldview; fifty-three obscenities, twenty-three profanities; violence (some of it graphic); fornication, sexually immoral references; racial innu-endo, and a man urinating in coffee cup.

Excessive New Age Sex and Scatology

THE FISHER KING

Quality: ☆☆☆   Acceptability: −3

WARNING CODES:
  Language: ***
  Violence: ***
  Sex: *
  Nudity: **
RATING: R
GENRE: Drama
INTENDED AUDIENCE: Adults
RUNNING TIME: 137 minutes
STARRING: Robin Williams, Jeff Bridges, Mercedes Ruehl, and Amanda Plummer
DIRECTOR: Terry Gilliam

PRODUCERS: Debra Hill and Lynda Obst

WRITER: Richard LaGravenese

DISTRIBUTOR: TriStar Pictures

BRIEF SUMMARY:

Misconstruing the flippant advice of WNOU disk jockey Jack Lucasimo, a psychopath opens fire on seven people before taking his own life in the movie *The Fisher King*. To survive, the fired DJ shacks up with a busty video-store owner. Three years later, Jack wanders off to commit suicide. At a bridge, on the verge of suicide, two teenagers knock him senseless with a bat and douse him with gasoline. Suddenly a gang of vagabonds comes to his rescue. The next morning, Jack awakens in a candlelit shrine of religious pictures, cooking ware, and discarded memorabilia. He is greeted by Perry, a schizophrenic hobo he recognizes from the night before. Perry tells Jack that his excrement appointed him on a knightly quest to recapture the Holy Grail. Later, Jack learns that Perry witnessed his wife being murdered by the psychopath Jack incited, and never overcame the horror.

Although *The Fisher King* is well-acted and thought-provoking, this off-beat update of the classic medieval Holy Grail myth suffers from a nominalistic ontology that confuses reality with fantasy, and an overabundance of objectionable content that includes everything from perverse violence to scatological visions.

CONTENT ANALYSIS: (C, LLL, VVV, NN, S, A, D, Ab, B, M) Christian worldview about Holy Fool; fifty-four obscenities, seven profanities; man knocked senseless with baseball bat and doused with gasoline, suicide and suicide attempt, street person ignited with cigarette lighter (extinguished), bleeding man covered with manure, psychotic murder, and blood oozing on victims; men engaged in nude "cloud gazing" (genitalia visible), implied fornication, sexual foreplay, cohabitation, crude references to male erection, cleavage, sexual innuendo, DJ jokes about having sex with teenager, transvestitism, discussion of bowel movements, sexually suggestive positions, and schizophrenic makes sexual advances; smoking marijuana, drug-induced dementia; guzzling whiskey; belief in reincarnation, catatonic schizophrenic behavior, delusions, and schizophrenic calls himself "janitor of God"; idolatry, and blasphemy; and breaking and entering.

Most Deceptive Feminist Presentation

FRIED GREEN TOMATOES

Quality: ☆☆☆   Acceptability: −3

WARNING CODES:

Language: **
Violence: **
Sex: *
Nudity: None

RATING: PG-13

GENRE: Drama

INTENDED AUDIENCE: Adults

RUNNING TIME: 130 minutes

STARRING: Kathy Bates, Jessica Tandy, Mary Stuart Masterson, Mary-Louise Parker, Cicely Tyson, and Chris O'Donnell

DIRECTOR: Jon Avnet

PRODUCER: Jon Avnet

WRITER: Fannie Flagg

DISTRIBUTOR: Universal Pictures

BRIEF SUMMARY:

In *Fried Green Tomatoes*, Evelyn Couch can't pry her husband from the TV. While visiting a nursing home, she listens to Ninny Threadgoode's tales about life sixty years ago with Idgie Threadgoode and her friend Ruth Jamison. In flashbacks, we find that Idgie "liberates" Ruth into the exciting world of drinking, gambling, fighting, and stealing. When Ruth marries a wife-beating racist, Idgie threatens death to the husband unless he leaves. The women open a café, and the husband returns. He threatens everyone and then disappears. When Ruth dies, we learn that her husband was killed by a black employee. To dispose of the body, Idgie mixed it into the café's barbecue sauce. (This cannibalism is treated as a clever joke.) In the end, Evelyn brings Ninny Threadgoode (really Idgie) home with her.

Fried Green Tomatoes is a tacky effort to dress up worn-out feminist clichés in ruffled sleeves and southern drawls. According to the film, to be liberated means to drink, gamble, fight, get a job, and tell men where to get off, or cannibalize them if they don't. The church is mocked, and the local preacher's only redeeming act is lying at Idgie's trial in order to save her.

CONTENT ANALYSIS: (FeFe, C, LL, VV, S, A, D, Ab, Ho, M, B) Feminist worldview with negative stereotype of minister and church in general and some positive references to God; four obscenities, eight profanities; boy run over by a train; another boy's arm cut off by train, murder; three beatings, including wife abuse; smoking, drinking, and gambling portrayed as liberating; lying shown as beneficial, hints of lesbianism, radical feminism, and use of deceased villain's remains in a barbecue sauce treated as humorous.

Love Thy Neighbor

THE GIANT OF THUNDER MOUNTAIN

Quality: ✰✰✰✰   Acceptability: +2

WARNING CODES:
  Language: None
  Violence: *
  Sex: None
  Nudity: None
RATING: G
GENRE: Action/Adventure
INTENDED AUDIENCE: Families

RUNNING TIME: 88 minutes
STARRING: Richard Kiel, Jack Elam, Marianne Rogers, Foster Brooks, Noley Thornton, William Sanderson, and Bart the Bear
DIRECTOR: James Robinson
PRODUCER: Joseph Raffill
WRITERS: Tony Lozito and Richard Kiel
DISTRIBUTOR: New Generation
BRIEF SUMMARY:
Set in California in the late 1800s, *The Giant of Thunder Mountain* is about the giant Eli who shuns people because they make fun of his size. Two young brothers, Ben and Tommy, find Eli's cabin and run off with one of his carvings. The next day they set out to return the stolen item and are followed by their little sister, Amy. Amy approaches Eli, and he appreciates the return of his carving. Tommy and Ben then discover some gold nuggets. Hezekiah Crow, a carnival operator, learns from Amy where they found their nuggets. The next day, Amy and Eli go to view the sequoia trees just as Hezekiah and his brood come looking for Eli's gold. They knock Tommy unconscious, put Ben in a gunnysack, and search the cabin for the gold. Meanwhile, the children's mother discovers them missing. A posse forms for a rescue mission. At the same time, Amy and Eli are being stalked by a grizzly, and the stage is set for the exciting ending.

The Giant of Thunder Mountain is recommended for the whole family. The music is excellent, the children are terrific actors, and the story tells an important message: We need to love our neighbor as ourselves. It is full of moral messages, including the fact that we should not judge people by their physical appearance.

CONTENT ANALYSIS: (B, C, V) Biblical story with positive references to Christianity and some violence.

Engrossing and Provocative

GRAND CANYON

Quality: ☆☆☆☆   Acceptability: −2

WARNING CODES:
   Language: ***
   Violence: **
   Sex: *
   Nudity: *
RATING: R
GENRE: Drama
INTENDED AUDIENCE: Adults
RUNNING TIME: 134 minutes
STARRING: Danny Glover, Kevin Kline, Steve Martin, Mary McDonnell, Mary-Louise Parker, and Alfre Woodard
   DIRECTOR: Lawrence Kasdan
   PRODUCERS: Lawrence Kasdan, Charles Okun, and Michael Grillo
   WRITERS: Lawrence and Meg Kasdan
   DISTRIBUTOR: 20th Century Fox Pictures
   BRIEF SUMMARY:
In *Grand Canyon*, woven among various relationships, is an exploration of the nature of evil, the brevity of life, and miraculous interventions on our behalf. A number of storylines develop and crisscross seamlessly. Mack, a successful attorney, and his wife, Claire, struggle with their fifteen-year-old son's impending autonomy. When Mack's car breaks down, a tow-truck driver named Simon saves him from a street gang. Meanwhile, Mack's friend Davis is a movie producer victimized by violence. After years of producing slasher flicks, the tables are turned. Adding to Mack's troubles is his secretary, who tempts him with an affair. As the story unfolds, the characters ponder the possibility that divine appointments take place at life's critical moments.

Grand Canyon has a variety of meanings, one of which is the Colorado landmark as a reminder that a benevolent power, far greater than human effort,

ambition, or evil, is much at work in the world. With excellent acting, writing, and directing, *Grand Canyon* is a superior, engrossing, and satisfying film. Drawbacks include the occasional intense language, brief nudity in a dream sequence, a faint nominalistic undertone, and two short glimpses of surgery that may startle the unwary.

CONTENT ANALYSIS: (B, LLL, VV, N, S) Though pointing toward a Creator God who intervenes in our lives, *Grand Canyon* is weighed down by fifty obscenities and three profanities; also a man shot in the leg, graphic views of surgery, female nudity, and an adulterous relationship (discussed rather than shown).

Most Heavy-Handed Hollywood Propaganda

GUILTY BY SUSPICION

Quality: ☆☆   Acceptability: −4

WARNING CODES:
   Language: ***
   Violence: *
   Sex: None
   Nudity: None
RATING: PG-13
GENRE: Drama
INTENDED AUDIENCE: Adults
RUNNING TIME: 105 minutes
STARRING: Robert De Niro, Annette Bening, George Wendt, Sam Wanamaker, Patricia Wettig, Ben Piazza, and Gailard Sartain
   DIRECTOR: Irwin Winkler
   PRODUCER: Arnon Milchan
   WRITER: Irwin Winkler
   DISTRIBUTOR: Warner Brothers
   BRIEF SUMMARY:
Guilty by Suspicion focuses on fictional director David Merrill, whose career crashes in 1951 when he refuses to testify against his friends before the House of Un-American Activities Committee (HUAC). The director falls victim to blacklisting by studio chiefs who once

vied for his services. David is subpoenaed in 1952. Lashing out at the HUAC chairman, David states he will testify only about himself. He winds up with a prison term along with the "Hollywood Ten."

The real Hollywood Ten were card-carrying members of the Communist Party that was controlled by the mass-murdering Soviet Leader Josef Stalin. In the film, the leftists are portrayed as naïve, when, in fact, the Hollywood Reds were committed to destroying the government of the United States. Furthermore, after the dust settled, the conservatives were blacklisted while the liberals went back to work. It is up to Christians to set the record straight by objecting to films that poison the wells of history.

CONTENT ANALYSIS: (Co, HHH, LLL, V, AAA) Communist worldview; sixty-four obscenities, twenty-four profanities; brief violence; excessive use of alcohol; and suicide.

Putting Family above Work

HOOK

Quality: ✩✩✩✩   Acceptability: +1

WARNING CODES:
  Language: *
  Violence: *
  Sex: None
  Nudity: None
RATING: PG
GENRE: Fantasy
INTENDED AUDIENCE: Older children and adults
RUNNING TIME: 144 minutes
STARRING: Dustin Hoffman, Robin Williams, and Julia Roberts
DIRECTOR: Steven Spielberg
PRODUCER: Frank Marshall, Kathleen Kennedy, and Gerald Molen
WRITER: Jim Hart
CONCEPT BASED IN PART ON: *Peter Pan* by J. M. Barrie
DISTRIBUTOR: TriStar (Amblin Entertainment)

BRIEF SUMMARY:
In Steven Spielberg's *Hook*, Captain Hook returns to wreak revenge on a grown-up Peter Pan. The thirty-five-year-old Peter Banning; his wife, Moira; his eleven-year-old son, Jack; and his seven-year-old daughter, Maggie, travel to London to visit the ninety-two-year-old Wendy. When the adults attend an evening event where Wendy is to be honored by the orphanage where she found Peter, the children are left alone at home. Hook finds them and carries them off—leaving a ransom note pirate-style. The rest of the story revolves around Peter regaining his sense of joy and courage, and taking on Hook—a process abetted by the feisty Tinkerbell.

Hook has its flaws, which are quickly lost in the tidal wave of imagination that sweeps the story along. However, the message is one that every father needs to hear: If dads don't spend time with their children when they are young, the adversary will steal their hearts when they grow older. Only when Peter learns to put his family before his work can he save his children from Hook. This is an old-fashioned idea, and not politically correct. Furthermore, the sets and the acting are superb. By helping our children to understand the difference between make-believe and reality, we can welcome *Hook* as a delightful escape into Never Never Land.

CONTENT ANALYSIS: (B, C, L, V, A, D) There is a prominent biblical theme as well as several biblical messages; however, there is some "borderline" vulgar language (including slight sexual innuendo), violence in Captain Hook's sword fights, swordplay, and substance abuse (alcohol) in scene with somewhat tipsy Peter.

Exposing the Evils of Communism

THE INNER CIRCLE

Quality: ✩✩✩✩   Acceptability: −2

WARNING CODES:

Language: **
Violence: *
Sex: *
Nudity: None

RATING: R
GENRE: Drama
INTENDED AUDIENCE: Older teens and adults
RUNNING TIME: 137 minutes
STARRING: Tom Hulce, Lolita Davidovich, Bob Hoskins, Alexandre Zbruev, and Bess Meyer
DIRECTOR: Andrei Konchalovsky
PRODUCER: Claudio Bonivento
WRITER: Andrei Konchalovsky
DISTRIBUTOR: Columbia Pictures
BRIEF SUMMARY:

The Inner Circle deftly exposes Josef Stalin's reign of terror. In 1938, Ivan is a projectionist who loves the "worker's paradise" and Stalin in spite of wretched living conditions and the sudden arrest of his Jewish neighbors, which leaves their four-year-old daughter, Katya, an orphan. Soon Ivan, married to the beautiful Anastasia, is hauled into the Kremlin in the middle of the night. As it turns out, his skills are needed for a film-showing for Stalin, who loved American movies. He lands a job as the Kremlin's projectionist. Meanwhile, Anastasia seeks out Katya. Ivan is mortified since her parents were purged by the Party. Anastasia asks Ivan whom he loves the most—her or Stalin? Ivan doesn't hesitate: "Stalin." Ivan's subservience ultimately leads to Anastasia's undoing at the evil hands of KGB boss Beria. Though he loses his wife, Ivan is able to take redemptive action on behalf of Katya.

The Inner Circle is at once fascinating history, intense drama, and a strong warning of the folly of worshiping a political leader as a secular god. Despite some scattered objectionable language, it should be seen by every American. It teaches that esteeming any man or government above God is a sure route to chaos and disaster.

CONTENT ANALYSIS: (BB, LL, S, V, AC) Moral worldview with an accurate revealing of anti-Communism; fourteen obscenities and one profanity; an on-screen sexual encounter (between newly-weds, without nudity); a man violently strikes his head against a wall; and implied sexual immorality.

Love Overcomes Adversity

LITTLE MAN TATE

Quality: ☆☆☆☆   Acceptability: −2

WARNING CODES:

Language: *
Violence: *
Sex: *
Nudity: None

RATING: PG
GENRE: Drama
INTENDED AUDIENCE: Older children and up
RUNNING TIME: 99 minutes
STARRING: Adam Hann-Byrd, Jodie Foster, Dianne Wiest, and Harry Connick Jr.
DIRECTOR: Jodie Foster
PRODUCERS: Scott Rudin and Peggy Rajski
WRITER: Scott Frank
DISTRIBUTOR: Orion Pictures
BRIEF SUMMARY:

Little Man Tate begins as seven-year-old Fred realizes he is different from other elementary schoolers. While others play ball, he sketches figures on the sidewalk. He is fascinated with art history and tinkers classical sonatas on the piano. Unfortunately, he is plagued with stomach ulcers and insomnia, being obsessed with things out of his control such as world hunger and homelessness. Fred's only friend is his cocktail waitress mom, Dede. Dede allows Fred to spend his summer at an "Odyssey of the Mind" workshop being held at an Ivy League college. In college, Fred whizzes through quantum physics, but misses Dede's gentle, loving touch.

Little Man Tate is a remarkably well-crafted film with a biblical theme of self-sacrifice and love overcoming adversity. Watching Fred's brilliant yet lonely existence unfold before our eyes, one can't help but marvel at the complexity of the human mind. Indirectly, *Little Man Tate* admonishes us to "study to show thyself approved unto God." Regrettably, the film contains some offensive language, some disrespect for elders, and a child walking in on a couple fornicating (though this scene is brief with no nudity).

CONTENT ANALYSIS: (B, C, L, V, S) Moral worldview with a biblical theme of self-sacrifice and love overcoming adversity marred by eleven obscenities, nine profanities, use of middle-finger signal, name-calling, and verbal disrespect for elders; child walks in on a couple fornicating (brief) and a child is born out of wedlock.

A Cautionary Tale of Comeuppance

MISTER JOHNSON

Quality: ✩✩✩✩   Acceptability: −1

WARNING CODES:
  Language: *
  Violence: *
  Sex: *
  Nudity:
RATING: PG-13
GENRE: Drama
INTENDED AUDIENCE: Adults
RUNNING TIME: 97 minutes
STARRING: Pierce Brosnan, Maynard Eziashi, Edward Woodward, and Beati Edney
DIRECTOR: Bruce Beresford
PRODUCER: Michael Fitzgerald
WRITER: William Boyd
BASED ON: The novel by Joyce Cary

DISTRIBUTOR: Avenue Pictures
BRIEF SUMMARY:
Set in colonial British West Africa in the early 1920s, *Mister Johnson* is about a young Nigerian who worships Mother England. Mister Johnson clerks for an English district officer, Harry Rudbeck, who is determined to build a hundred-mile-long road through the African bush. When Harry runs out of funds, Johnson suggests using revenues from other sources. When an English official arrives and finds the ledger discrepancies, Rudbeck is forced to let Johnson go. Mister Johnson next works for Sargy Gollup, the racist proprietor of a general store. Johnson throws a party, inviting all his friends to the general store. The noise wakes Gollup, who breaks up the party. When Gollup confronts him, Johnson slugs him. This costs Johnson his job.

Mister Johnson examines British colonialism and its mixed effects on a nation. The vast African terrain, the engaging native rhythms, and the superb acting provide a fascinating, often amusing, glimpse into a society on the threshold of sweeping change. In addition, the biblical adage, "Be sure your sin will find you out" in Numbers 32:23 (KJV), probably applies best to the disarming and feckless Mister Johnson as he meets his comeuppance at the film's end.

CONTENT ANALYSIS: (B, C, L, V, S) This cautionary biblical tale is marred by five obscenities and profanities, some violence, some racial slurs in context of the historical time and place, and some sexual references and innuendos.

Loving Memories of a Christian Mother

MY FATHER'S GLORY and MY MOTHER'S CASTLE

Quality: ✩✩✩✩   Acceptability: +1

WARNING CODES:
  Language: *
  Violence: None

Sex: None
Nudity: None
RATING: G
GENRE: Drama
INTENDED AUDIENCE: Adults
RUNNING TIME: *My Father's Glory*,
105 minutes; *My Mother's Castle*, 98
Minutes
LANGUAGE: French
STARRING: Philippe Caubere,
Nathalie Roussel, Didier Pain, Therese
Liotard, Julien Ciamaca, and Victorien
Delmare
DIRECTOR: Yves Robert
PRODUCER: Alain Poire
WRITERS: Jerome Tonnere, Louis
Nucera, and Yves Robert
BASED ON: The novel *Souvenirs* by
Marcel Pagnol
DISTRIBUTOR: Orion Classics
BRIEF SUMMARY:
My Father's Glory and *My Mother's
Castle* are Yves Robert's two charming
film adaptations of the loving memoirs
of Marcel Pagnol, novelist, playwright,
filmmaker, schoolteacher, and translator.
Born in Aubagne, France, on February
28, 1895, Marcel spent his childhood in
Marseilles. The first film, *My Father's
Glory*, is based on his years of adolescent
passage, mainly the vacation time the
family spent in the mountains, when
Pagnol gained a deeper love and understanding of his father, Joseph. *My
Mother's Castle* focuses on the relationship of preteen Marcel with his mother,
Augustine. The "castle" is a modest
summer house, a sanctuary where the
family frolics. Uncle Jules is a dynamic
Christian who says to Joseph at
Christmas, "I begged him [God] to grace
you with his presence and give you the
gift of faith."
These two movies are filled with a
gentle liveliness as Pagnol struggles with
his mother's religion versus "the miracles
of science" espoused by his father. Joseph
had extraordinary knowledge of the natural sciences, but he did not know the

Creator God. Resembling Impressionist
paintings, both films communicate the
character of Provence, reinforced by a
wonderful musical score. The fine, warm
depiction of Marcel's mother contrasts
sharply with Hollywood's portrayal of
women as sex objects and is another reason these are exceptional films. It is a biblical representation of a Christian mother,
an ideal that every mother should try to
emulate.
CONTENT ANALYSIS: (CC, B, L, N)
A biblical representation of the mother, a
believing Christian, and of the family,
with positive references to Christianity;
a few mild obscenities, nude little boys
washing outside presented in an innocent, naturalistic, inoffensive manner,
and a mother breastfeeding her baby in
a natural, inoffensive style.

Families Are Important

MY GIRL

Quality: ✰✰✰✰   Acceptability: +1

WARNING CODES:
Language: *
Violence: *
Sex: None
Nudity: None

RATING: PG
GENRE: Tragic comedy
INTENDED AUDIENCE: Mature
children and up
RUNNING TIME: 102 minutes
STARRING: Macaulay Culkin, Anna
Chlumsky, Dan Aykroyd, and Jamie
Lee Curtis
DIRECTOR: Howard Zieff
PRODUCER: Brian Grazer
WRITER: Laurice Elehhwany
DISTRIBUTOR: Columbia Pictures
BRIEF SUMMARY:
My Girl is a biblical perspective
toward coming-of-age. Growing up in
Madison, Pennsylvania, during the
1970s is hard for eleven-year-old Vada
Sultenfuss, since her house is also the

funeral parlor. Harry, her father, is a dour mortician who seems to spend more time with his "patients" than with his daughter. Surrounded by death, Anna is convinced she is about to die and frequently drags her best friend, Thomas J. Senett, to the doctor. What Anna suffers from most is the lack of a mother, since her mother died in childbirth. This is the void that Shelly has the chance of filling when she becomes the makeup person at the mortuary. What seems to be a happily-ever-after comedy, however, turns to tragedy, and Anna and her father must deal with a more serious problem than her hypochondria.

My Girl emphasizes that fathers must take time to understand their children and that families are important. In fact, the family, dating, fathers, mothers, and the pastor are portrayed positively in this heartwarming film. *My Girl* has a number of positive points and only a few negative ones. If about three foul words and a hippie poem were cut, we could give it our unqualified recommendation.

CONTENT ANALYSIS: (CC, B, L, VV) Positive references to Christianity and a biblical perspective of coming-of-age; a few objectionable words and the death of a child, which could upset some children.

A Great Beginning

THE NEVERENDING STORY II: THE NEXT CHAPTER

Quality: ☆☆☆   Acceptability: +1

WARNING CODES:
  Language: None
  Violence: *
  Sex: None
  Nudity: None
RATING: PG
GENRE: Fantasy
INTENDED AUDIENCE: Ages eight and up

RUNNING TIME: 90 minutes
STARRING: Jonathan Brandis, Kenny Morrison, Clarissa Burt, John Wesley Shipp, Martin Umbach, Alexandra Johnes, Helena Mitchell, and Thomas Hill
DIRECTOR: George Miller
PRODUCER: Dieter Geissier
WRITER: Karin Howard
BASED ON: The novel *Die Unendliche Geschict* by Michael Ende
DISTRIBUTOR: Warner Brothers
BRIEF SUMMARY:
In *The NeverEnding Story II: The Next Chapter*, the hero is motherless Bastian Bux who has been disgraced at school for lacking courage. Bastian looks in an antique store for a book on courage. Picking up *The NeverEnding Story*, he hears voices whisper, "Bastian! Help us!" At home, Bastian falls into one of the illustrations and soon is gliding through Fantasia. Unaware that he is Fantasia's last hope in the struggle against the sorceress Xayide, Bastian must rescue the imprisoned empress. The movie features joyous reunions with his lovable cohorts from the original. Not so much a next chapter as a revised version of the first, the theme is that tales of the imagination are vital to avoid catastrophe. Only when Bastian sacrifices his childhood can he take the plunge back into reality.

The movie has fabulous animatronics and exotic sets. There are humorous overtones, allegorical items of interest, a suspenseful battle between good and evil, and only the mildest touch of violence; however, it may be too intense for little ones. There are also hints of New Age nominalism in the film, but this can be a great opening to explain the Good News of Jesus Christ to children, so discussion is advised.

CONTENT ANALYSIS: (PaPa, O, V) Nominalism and some New Ageism within the framework of fictional fantasy; some depictions of monsters may be too intense for little ones.

Clever but Marred

ONLY THE LONELY

Quality: ☆☆☆☆   Acceptability: −2

WARNING CODES:
Language: **
Violence: None
Sex: *
Nudity: None
RATING: PG-13
GENRE: Romantic comedy
INTENDED AUDIENCE: Adults
RUNNING TIME: 104 minutes
STARRING: John Candy, Maureen O'Hara, Ally Sheedy, Anthony Quinn, Jim Belushi, Kevin Dunn, Bert Remsen, and Milo O'Shea
DIRECTOR: Chris Columbus
PRODUCERS: John Hughes and Hunt Lowry
WRITER: Chris Columbus
DISTRIBUTOR: 20th Century Fox
BRIEF SUMMARY:
Only the Lonely is a clever romantic comedy about Danny Muldoon, a Chicago cop whose courting of a mortician's shy daughter is impeded by his domineering Irish mother, Rose. Danny drives a mortuary wagon for the Chicago police department. One day, he sees Theresa, who paints the faces of corpses to resemble famous celebrities. The Sicilian-born Theresa endures much derision from prejudiced Rose, but stands up for herself. Danny loves Theresa but fears marriage, since Rose makes him feel guilty. Finally Danny proposes marriage. However, both bride and groom give in to their fears once again, and are "no shows" for the wedding.

As dreams fade, one realizes a point is being wonderfully made about gathering one's resolve. This is moviemaking at its finest. The biblical perspective that "a man will leave his father and mother and be united to his wife" is resoundingly proclaimed in *Only the Lonely*. However, the film falters by advocating sex before marriage. Also, Danny's on-the-job partner makes offensive comments and lewd jokes. Considering the thirty-six instances of profanity and obscenity, *Only the Lonely* merits extreme caution.

CONTENT ANALYSIS: (H, LL, S, M) Humanist worldview; twenty-three obscenities and thirteen profanities; sexual innuendos, lewd joking; implied promiscuity; lying; and deception.

Business Matters

OTHER PEOPLE'S MONEY

Quality: ☆☆☆   Acceptability: −2

WARNING CODES:
Language: **
Violence: None
Sex: *
Nudity: None
RATING: R
GENRE: Drama
INTENDED AUDIENCE: Adults
RUNNING TIME: 103 minutes
STARRING: Danny DeVito, Penelope Ann Miller, Gregory Peck, Piper Laurie, and Dean Jones
DIRECTOR: Norman Jewison
PRODUCERS: Davina Belling, Ellen M. Krass, Kelley Baker, Sarah Miller Hayward, Norman Jewison, and Ric Kidney
WRITER: Alvin Sargent
DISTRIBUTOR: Warner Brothers
BRIEF SUMMARY:
In *Other People's Money*, when "Larry the Liquidator" Garfield attempts to take over New England Wire and Cable Company and replace their product with advanced fiber optics, the debt-free manufacturer clings to its old-fashioned values. At stake are a community's way of life and greenbacks, as stockholders cast their vote at a showdown meeting. Fighting for Wire and Cable are Andrew Jorgenson, the chief executive who recalls the hard work put

into making the company what it is today. Larry Garfield is a billionaire with other people's money. Larry's liquidation target looks easy, but he finds himself pitted against a formidable opponent: Kate Sullivan, a curvaceous, hard-boiled attorney. Larry lusts after Kate. What starts out as drama becomes soap suds, as Larry asks Kate to marry him.

Other People's Money suggests that traditional business practices are not necessarily cost-effective or beneficial to society. In spite of Larry's fiscal cleverness, he fails to realize that "the love of money is the root of all evil" (1 Timothy 6:10 KJV). Also discomforting are his sexual advances to Kate and his presumptuous statements.

CONTENT ANALYSIS: (Pa, LL, S, A, D, M, B) Pagan worldview; twenty-seven obscenities, two profanities, crude references to genitalia, bribe offered in exchange for sexual favors, suggestively eating food while musing about sex, lust, cohabitation, and seductive dress; alcohol consumption; greed, love of money, and gluttony.

Worst Anti-Christian Horror Movie

PEOPLE UNDER THE STAIRS

Quality: ☆　　　　　Acceptability: −4

WARNING CODES:
　Language: *
　Violence: ***
　Sex: *
　Nudity: None
RATING: R
GENRE: Horror
INTENDED AUDIENCE: Adults
RUNNING TIME: 102 minutes
STARRING: Brandon Adams, Everett McGill, Wendy Robie, and A. J. Langer
DIRECTOR: Wes Craven
PRODUCERS: Marianne Maddalena and Stuart M. Besser
WRITER: Wes Craven
DISTRIBUTOR: Universal Pictures

BRIEF SUMMARY:
Unable to pay rent or provide medical attention for his sick mother, thirteen-year-old Fool and his mentor, Leroy, break into their landlord's mansion to steal his antique gold coins, only to discover the ghoulish people under the stairs. These prisoners are salesmen, repair people, and thieves who are forced to live inside tunneled chambers of this electrically locked mansion. The misfits look to Fool for a way of escape. After Leroy is murdered, Fool enlists the help of Alice, the landlord's abused daughter. Looney "Daddy" and "Mommy" landlord stalk Fool and the others with their pit bull, machine gun, and meat cleaver. Trigger-happy Daddy occasionally removes his hood to gnaw his victims' flesh.

People Under the Stairs brings to mind Jesus' words: "Father, forgive them; for they do not know what they are doing" (Luke 23:34). The film is another bigoted Hollywood attack on Christianity, depicting Daddy and Mommy landlord as "Christians" who operate a torture chamber while deceiving people into thinking they are law-abiding citizens. Intelligent Americans will be offended by this attack on Christianity, which breeds religious hatred and stereotyping.

CONTENT ANALYSIS: (Ab, Pa, O, L, VVV, S, A, D, M) Anti-Christian, pagan worldview distorting the twenty-third Psalm with occult elements such as tarot cards and voodoo dolls that embody the souls of victims; fifty-nine obscenities and seven profanities; sadistic violence (woman bound by wrists inside torture chamber, people hit with cement blocks, tongue cut out, chasing girl with meat cleaver, knife impaled in woman's stomach, pit bull attacks intruders, bodily mutilation, gory corpse hanging on rack, electric shock, man shot and hurled down stairs, child forced into boiling water, man punched in groin, gasoline poured inside inhabited chamber and ignited, sword impaled into dog, and man poked in eye); crude references to genitals, sexual jokes, child likened to prostitute, talk of "tricks," drug addicts, breaking and entering, sadomasochistic dress, and cannibalism.

Worst Promotion of Adultery

PRINCE OF TIDES

Quality: ☆☆☆   Acceptability: –3

WARNING CODES:
Language: ***
Violence: ***
Sex: ***
Nudity: **

RATING: R
GENRE: Drama
INTENDED AUDIENCE: Adults
RUNNING TIME: 132 minutes
STARRING: Barbra Streisand, Nick Nolte, Blythe Danner, Kate Nelligan, Jeroen Krabbe, and Jason Gould
DIRECTOR: Barbra Streisand
PRODUCER: Barbra Streisand
WRITERS: Becky Johnson and Pat Conroy
BASED ON: The novel by Pat Conroy
DISTRIBUTOR: Columbia Pictures
BRIEF SUMMARY:
The Prince of Tides is about a high school football coach, Tom, and a New York psychiatrist brought together by the suicide attempt of Tom's twin sister, Savannah. Tom comes to New York to discover the reason for Savannah's depression. As Tom sits in Dr. Lowenstein's office day after day recalling his past, he uncovers the roots of his own traumas. His father, a shrimper, and his mother, an unconventional housewife, both come across as heavies. Along the way, Tom and the doctor start to fornicate. The film's climax occurs as Tom thinks of the word "Callanwolde," which unlocks not only Savannah's psyche but Tom's as well.

Although The Prince of Tides is a well-crafted movie with competent acting and some beautiful cinematography, the theme of adultery is unacceptable. If Tom and Lowenstein learned from their affair, we could be encouraged, but regrettably, even though they return to their respective mates at film's end, neither shows any remorse or guilt. Also, the extreme profanity in this film is deplorable. Further, Prince of Tides contains some graphic scenes where two children are raped.

CONTENT ANALYSIS: (Pa, LLL, VVV, NN, SSS) Pagan worldview; over twenty-seven obscenities and twenty-six profanities; graphic rapes of children and mother; graphic murder with knife plunged into victim and a lot of blood; partial nudity in sex scenes, several adulterous sexual encounters, and an overall adulterous affair.

Powerful Insight

PRISONERS OF THE SUN

Quality: ☆☆☆   Acceptability: –2

WARNING CODES:
Language: *
Violence: **
Sex: None
Nudity: None

RATING: R
GENRE: Drama
INTENDED AUDIENCE: Adults
RUNNING TIME: 108 minutes
STARRING: Bryan Brown, George Takei, Sokyu Fujita, Terry O'Quinn, John Bach, Toshi Shioya, John Clarke, and Deborah Unger
DIRECTOR: Stephen Wallace
PRODUCERS: Charles Waterstreet, Denis Whitburn, and Brian A. Williams
WRITERS: Denis Whitburn and Brian A. Williams
DISTRIBUTOR: Skouras Pictures
BRIEF SUMMARY:
In World War II the Japanese seized Ambon Island, capturing 1,100 Australian troops. At the war's end, only 300 prisoners survived. As Prisoners of

the Sun opens, Australian troops recapture Ambon and uncover mass graves of mutilated prisoners. Unfortunately, all trial witnesses are seriously ill or dead. Vice Admiral Takahashi is acquitted. POW camp manager Captain Ikeuchi is incriminated by a POW victim who dies before cross-examination. Lieutenant Hideo Tanaka, a Christian, surrenders to the Australians to expedite justice. The audience learns that he complained about the inhumane treatment of POWs to his supervisors. To silence his complaints, Tanaka was forced to execute four Australian fliers. Tanaka testifies that Captain Ikeuchi was a vicious murderer and that Vice Admiral Takahashi gave orders to mistreat the POWs. Unfortunately, Ikeuchi commits suicide and Takahashi is long gone, leaving Tanaka to pay for their crimes. Tanaka goes to face a firing squad at peace with God about his eternal destiny.

Overall, *Prisoners of the Sun* is well written, acted, and directed. The film respects Tanaka's Christian faith and presents a powerful insight into biblical morality, although it is tough to watch Tanaka being executed.

CONTENT ANALYSIS: (CC, B, L, VV) Christian worldview with moral elements; a few obscenities; brief but intense prison camp violence, decapitation, hara-kiri, and a firing squad.

Tortured by Theological Confusion

THE RAPTURE

Quality: ✩✩✩   Acceptability: −2

WARNING CODES:
   Language: *
   Violence: None
   Sex: ***
   Nudity: ***
RATING: R
GENRE: Drama
INTENDED AUDIENCE: Adults
RUNNING TIME: 100 minutes

STARRING: Mimi Rogers, David Duchovny, Patrick Bauchau, Kimberly Cullum, Will Patton, and Terri Hanauer
DIRECTOR: Michael Tolkin
PRODUCERS: Nick Wechsler, Nancy Tenenbaum, and Karen Koch
WRITER: Michael Tolkin
DISTRIBUTOR: Fine Line Features
BRIEF SUMMARY:

In *The Rapture*, Sharon is a telephone operator who engages in orgies to relieve her boredom. She overhears coworkers talking about the "end times." Later, she questions two evangelists about Jesus. Finally Sharon lets God into her heart, marries Randy, and they have a daughter, Mary. Years later, an ex-employee kills Randy, and Sharon becomes preoccupied with the return of Christ. Sharon shoots Mary to get her into heaven. Sheriff Foster takes Sharon to jail. The Rapture begins and Mary appears and begs her mother to love God. Sharon can't love a God who didn't do what she wanted him to do. Mary and the sheriff are taken up to be with Jesus Christ. Sharon condemns herself to hell forever.

The dialogue in *The Rapture* is skillfully crafted to counter every argument against faith in God. It is reminiscent of evangelistic films, except that it has extremely pornographic opening scenes. It is aimed at the pagans who need to think about their salvation. Regrettably, Sharon is so obsessed with the "end times" and confused in her theology that she fails to do God's will here and now. *The Rapture* also contains extensive nudity with explicit sex scenes.

CONTENT ANALYSIS: (CC, AbAb, L, VV, NNN, SSS) Christian worldview with strong verbal presentation of the gospel, but the dramatic realization has cultic undertones; five obscenities and a profanity (character was subsequently rebuked for taking Christ's name in vain); and extensive nudity with explicit sex scenes.

A Poignant Story of Repentance and Forgiveness

REGARDING HENRY

Quality: ☆☆☆☆   Acceptability: −1

WARNING CODES:
  Language: *
  Violence: *
  Sex: *
  Nudity: None
RATING: PG-13
GENRE: Drama
INTENDED AUDIENCE: Adults
RUNNING TIME: 108 minutes
STARRING: Harrison Ford and
Annette Bening
  DIRECTOR: Mike Nichols
  PRODUCER: Robert Greenhut
  WRITER: Jeffrey Abrams
  DISTRIBUTOR: Paramount Pictures
  BRIEF SUMMARY:
  In *Regarding Henry*, Henry Turner has
a beautiful wife, an eleven-year-old
daughter, a Manhattan penthouse, and a
law career. He ruthlessly defends a local
hospital in a malpractice suit brought by
an elderly couple. Thanks to his defense,
the hospital is found innocent. That
evening, a vagrant demands Henry's
money. Since Henry only has pocket
change on him, the thug shoots Henry in
the head and chest. The gun wound renders him an invalid. With complete loss
of memory and most of his motor skills,
Henry begins physical therapy. With the
help of his therapist, Henry is able to go
home. Remembering is slow and painful.
Once home, his wife and daughter help
him remember his past. Henry discovers
truth he suppressed. He was having an
adulterous affair. His past sins disgust
him and he repents. Furthermore, his
family still loves him. This unconditional
acceptance gives Henry a fresh chance to
start life over again.
  Regarding Henry is to be commended
for rebuking selfishness and reaffirming
the family. However, the saving knowledge of Jesus Christ is understated in this
otherwise poignant, well-produced story
of repentance, forgiveness, and grace.
  CONTENT ANALYSIS: (C, B, L, V, S)
A poignant story of repentance, forgiveness, and grace; ten obscenities, eight
profanities; man gets shot in head by
thief; sexual humor and discussions of
adulterous relationships.

Thematically Problematic

ROBIN HOOD:
PRINCE OF THIEVES

Quality: ☆☆☆☆   Acceptability: −2

WARNING CODES:
  Language: *
  Violence: **
  Sex: *
  Nudity: *
RATING: PG-13
GENRE: Adventure/Drama
INTENDED AUDIENCE: Older
teens and adults
RUNNING TIME: 143 minutes
STARRING: Kevin Costner, Morgan
Freeman, Christian Slater, Alan
Rickman, and Mary Elizabeth
Mastrantonio
  DIRECTOR: Kevin Reynolds
  PRODUCERS: Pen Densham, John
Watson, and Richard B. Lewis
  WRITERS: Pen Densham and John
Watson
  DISTRIBUTOR: Warner Brothers/
Morgan Creek
  BRIEF SUMMARY:
  In the swashbuckling *Robin Hood:
Prince of Thieves*, based on a twelfth-
century ballad, Robin Hood and his
merry men steal from the rich and give to
the poor. Opening in Jerusalem at the
time of the Third Crusade (A.D. 1190) led
by King Richard I the Lion-Heart, Robin
is being held in an enemy prison. He
escapes with the help of Azeem, a Turk,
who returns to England with him. Soon

Robin learns of his father's death by the evil Sheriff of Nottingham. Robin and Azeem flee into Sherwood Forest, where they encounter Little John and his cohorts. Robin and Azeem join the band and proceed to rob the wealthy people entering Sherwood Forest. They even rob Friar Tuck, who joins them and contributes some ribald humor to the plot.

Robin Hood has good cinematography, sets, costuming, and few objectionable elements. One flaw is the graphic attempted seduction of Marian by the sheriff. Also, to call Robin the "Prince of Thieves" equates him with the devil (who he is not!), and the premise of robbing from the rich to give to the poor is anti-biblical. Actually, Robin is fighting for the legitimate authority of King Richard I against the usurpers, Prince John and the Sheriff of Nottingham. Before you see *Robin Hood*, you may want to rent the 1938 movie *Adventures of Robin Hood* featuring Errol Flynn to help understand the metaphors in the original story. Our heroes should not be thieves (even those who exchange the Christian archetypes of history for the gilded fools of the New Age) but those who represent the legitimate authority of Jesus the Christ.

CONTENT ANALYSIS: (Pa, Ab, O, L, VV, S, N, M) Pagan worldview with sheriff's fortune-teller and soothsaying; a few obscenities and profanities; graphic battle violence; some attempted seduction scenes; brief rear male nudity; anti-biblical ideas about stealing and thievery (film title and premise); and robbing from people for revenge.

Triumphant Heroism

THE ROCKETEER

Quality: ✩✩✩✩   Acceptability: +1

WARNING CODES:

Language: *
Violence: **
Sex: None
Nudity: None

RATING: PG
GENRE: Adventure
INTENDED AUDIENCE: Older children and adults
RUNNING TIME: 108 minutes
STARRING: Billy Campbell, Jennifer Connelly, Alan Arkin, Timothy Dalton, and Paul Sorvino
DIRECTOR: Joe Johnston
PRODUCERS: Lawrence Gordon, Charles Gordon, and Larry Franco
WRITERS: Danny Bilson, Paul De Meo, and Frank Darabont
DISTRIBUTOR: Buena Vista Pictures
BRIEF SUMMARY:
Strapping a flame-spewing, wing-tipped metallic gizmo to his back, the rocketeer takes off flying when envious goons and Nazis attempt to steal his futuristic equipment with a secret plan to rule the world. *The Rocketeer* begins in 1938 when Cliff Secord, a stunt pilot, and "Peevy," his inventive mentor, find a rocket pack and test-run it on a mannequin. The mannequin zooms into the sky and returns with its head burnt off. Meanwhile, gangsters as well as Feds search for the rocket. Cliff's actress-girlfriend, Jenny Blake, is cast for a role in "The Laughing Bandit." Later, on the set of "The Laughing Bandit," Neville Sinclair, the lead and one of the gangsters looking for the rocket, overhears Cliff talking about the rocket. At Cliff's airfield, a clown's flying plane takes a nosedive, and the rocketeer soars through clouds to swoop the clown out of his seat just before his plane crashes. As a result, Cliff becomes hunted by the Feds and Neville's Mafia goons, who want the rocket.

The Rocketeer is an excellent, very entertaining movie, one of the most fun movies you'll ever see. Best of all, good triumphs over evil. This movie also has endearing characters, colorful scenery, great atmosphere, and exciting, sometimes hilarious special effects. Billy Campbell's sensitive portrayal of Cliff Secord enables the viewer to experience all of the wonder, excitement, fear, and suspense that his character does. Jennifer Connelly is also wonderful. *The Rocketeer*'s only detraction is some violence, but it is mostly action oriented, aimed toward older children and adults who are young at heart.

CONTENT ANALYSIS: (BBB, L, VV, A, D) Decency, integrity, and chastity triumph over evil in this action adventure yarn marred only by four minor obscenities, some violence (shooting scenes, explosions, wrecks, fighting, and interrogation scenes), slight sexual innuendo, and a woman drugged with chloroform hankie.

Good, Clean, Wholesome Fun

SHIPWRECKED

Quality: ☆☆☆☆   Acceptability: +4

WARNING CODES:
  Language: None
  Violence: None
  Sex: None
  Nudity: None

RATING: PG
GENRE: Action/Adventure
INTENDED AUDIENCE: Ages eight and up
RUNNING TIME: 99 minutes
STARRING: Stian Smestad and Gabriel Byrne
DIRECTOR: Nils Gaup
PRODUCER: John M. Jaccobsen
WRITERS: Nils Gaup, Bob Foss, Greg Dinner, and Nick Theil
BASED ON: The novel *Hakoon Haakonson* by O. V. Flack-Ytter
DISTRIBUTOR: Buena Vista
BRIEF SUMMARY:
Shipwrecked is a classic adventure about a fourteen-year-old Norwegian named Hakon who sails on a merchant ship in 1859 to earn money in order to save his family's farm. Hakon is befriended by Jens, the boatswain. A pirate named Merrick is disguised as an officer and takes control of the ship after poisoning the captain. At Sydney, an orphan named Mary stows away. A hurricane maroons Hakon on an island, where he finds a cave full of treasures. Figuring that Merrick will be back for his treasures, Hakon booby-traps the island. Spying smoke on a nearby island, Hakon paddles over to find that Mary and Jens have been washed ashore. The trio return and don't have to wait long before the pirates sail into view. It is fun watching them trying to outsmart the buccaneers.

The period feel is excellent, the effects are majestic, and the shots at sea are superb. The suspense is good too. There are humorous moments as well. The film shouldn't be rated PG. No one is killed except the captain, and his crew commits his body to the deep with a Christian prayer and hymn. *Shipwrecked* is good, clean, wholesome fun, and will leave you with warm feelings of the value of family, responsibility, and bravery.

CONTENT ANALYSIS: (B, C) Biblical worldview, pro-Christian prayer and other moral, pro-family elements.

Learning to Love and Forgive

STEP KIDS

Quality: ☆☆☆☆   Acceptability: −1

WARNING CODES:
  Language: **
  Violence: *
  Sex: *
  Nudity: None

RATING: PG
GENRE: Comedy
INTENDED AUDIENCE: Adolescents and adults
RUNNING TIME: 110 minutes
STARRING: Hillary Wolf, Griffin Dunne, Margaret Whitton, and Ben Savage
DIRECTOR: Joan Micklin Silver
PRODUCERS: Melissa Goddard and Peter Morgan

WRITER: Frank Mugavero
DISTRIBUTOR: New Line Cinema
BRIEF SUMMARY:

In *Step Kids*, fifteen-year-old Laura sees herself as unwanted by her family consisting of her mother, Millie, who favors stepsister, Corinne; her indifferent stepfather, Keith; pretty, fourteen-year-old Corinne, who treats Laura like dirt; and stepbrothers chubby, thirteen-year-old Kurt; know-it-all, ten-year-old Sam; and bright, twenty-one-year-old Josh, who lives in a lakeside cabin. Her father, David, lives with his mistress, Stephanie (pregnant with his twins), and his three-year-old daughter, Jessie, lives with his "last" wife, Barbara. Fed up with being ignored, Laura goes to the lake. When her family comes for her, she hitches a ride with the Smiths, a happy family who prays and reaches out to her in acceptance and love. Hilarity prevails as everyone assembles at the lake while the search for Laura continues. Laura returns and discovers they care about her.

Step Kids is an enjoyable, believable comedy. With good acting, a complex plot, and vivid photography, the film, despite some obscenities, a robbery, and implied promiscuity, is worth seeing if these flaws are discerned and compared with biblical principles. Laura and the members of her family learn from their experiences to love and forgive one another.

CONTENT ANALYSIS: (C, B, LL, V, S, M) Positive portrayals of Christians and a biblical theme of reconciliation are marred by ten obscenities, one profanity, some minor violence when Laura hits a girl in the face, implied sexual immorality (woman pregnant outside of marriage), and a convenience-store robbery.

Funny Depiction of a Mean Spirit

TATIE DANIELLE

Quality: ☆☆☆☆   Acceptability: −2

WARNING CODES:
Language: *
Violence: None
Sex: *
Nudity: None
RATING: Not rated
GENRE: Comedy
INTENDED AUDIENCE: Adults
RUNNING TIME: 110 minutes
LANGUAGE: French
STARRING: Tsilla Chelton, Catherine Jacob, Isabelle Nanty, Neige Dolsky, and Eric Prat
DIRECTOR: Etienne Chatiliez
PRODUCER: Charles Gassot
WRITER: Florence Quentin
DISTRIBUTOR: Prestige (a division of Miramax Films)
BRIEF SUMMARY:

As this French comedy opens, Tatie Danielle is living out her final years with her housekeeper, Odile, and her attack dog. She deliberately tramples Odile's flowers and sics her dog on the mailman. Bored, she gives Odile the job of cleaning the chandelier. Sure enough, Odile falls and breaks her neck, so Tatie has to move to Paris, where her nephew, Jean-Pierre, lives. She refuses her grandnephew's pictures, leaves him on the playground, and kicks the family dog. When she ruins a dinner party, the family hires Sandrine to look after Tatie. When Sandrine smacks her, Tatie learns to behave. They clash again, and Sandrine quits. Tatie sets the house on fire, landing herself in the hospital. Tatie escapes with the aid of Sandrine, and everyone is glad to be rid of the geriatric sadist.

While there is some obscenity and a scene where Tatie barges in on Jean-Pierre and his wife in bed, there is much to recommend in *Tatie Danielle*, a movie that defines the concept of mean-spirited. The subtitles do not detract from the laughs, which are good and plenty. It is encouraging that Jean-Pierre and Catherine exhort an unwed mother to carry her baby to term despite her difficult situation.

CONTENT ANALYSIS: (B, L, S, M) Moral worldview; some obscenities; brief sexual situations; and meanness.

Ultimately Forgettable

TEENAGE MUTANT NINJA TURTLES II: THE SECRET OF THE OOZE

Quality: ☆☆   Acceptability: −2

WARNING CODES:
  Language: None
  Violence: **
  Sex: None
  Nudity: None
RATING: PG
GENRE: Comedy/Action/Martial arts
INTENDED AUDIENCE: Teens and up
RUNNING TIME: 88 minutes
STARRING: Paige Turco, David Warner, Ernie Rayes Jr., Kevin Clash, Raymond Serra, and Toshishiro Obata
ANIMATRONIC TURTLES CREATED BY: Jim Henson Associates
DIRECTOR: Michael Pressman
PRODUCERS: Thomas K. Gray and Kim Dawson
WRITER: Todd W. Langen
DISTRIBUTOR: New Line Cinema
BRIEF SUMMARY:
In *Teenage Mutant Ninja Turtles II*, those four ninja-fighting turtles, Raphael, Leonardo, Michelangelo, and Donatello, face Shredder, the leader of a teenage gang who resurfaces from a landfill and vows revenge. At a toxic-waste site, TV reporter April interviews the professor who created radioactive "ooze" fifteen years prior. Splinter, the Turtles' rat mentor, realizes it is the same ooze that gave him and the four baby turtles their amazing strength and human powers years ago. Shredder forces the professor to mutate a wolf and snapping turtle into super beasts. The Turtles grab the professor, hoping he can come up with an anti-

dote. Shredder ingests the ooze to become a monster.

Although well made with no language problems, *Ninja Turtles II* sends the same message as the last picture: Solve your problems by beating your opponents to a pulp. The movie encourages children to develop fighting skills. The National Association for the Education of Young Children has said that the Ninja Turtles has brought violence to the classroom. Also, there is a distressing amount of Eastern mysticism and New Age thought in the film. Overall, the film is forgettable.

CONTENT ANALYSIS: (PaPa, VV, M) Pagan worldview with Eastern mysticism and New Age reference; comic-book violence; and revenge.

Distorted Views

TERMINATOR 2: JUDGMENT DAY

Quality: ☆☆☆   Acceptability: −3

WARNING CODES:
  Language: ***
  Violence: ***
  Sex: None
  Nudity: None
RATING: R
GENRE: Science fiction
INTENDED AUDIENCE: Older teens and adults
RUNNING TIME: 137 minutes
STARRING: Arnold Schwarzenegger, Linda Hamilton, Edward Furlong, and Robert Patrick
DIRECTOR: James Cameron
PRODUCER: James Cameron
WRITERS: James Cameron and William Wisher
DISTRIBUTOR: TriStar Pictures
BRIEF SUMMARY:
The title, *Terminator 2: Judgment Day*, refers to an August 29, 1997, nuclear holocaust that wipes out three billion people. Schwarzenegger's cyborg, reconstituted as a good guy, must protect teenage

future hero John Connor (born of the Connor-Reese liaison in 1984 *Terminator*) from alien forces. Connor's mother, Sarah, languishes at a hospital for the insane in California, talking about "terminators" and the world being destroyed in a nuclear holocaust. A policeman comes to John's foster parents' house and the chase is on, since he is the evil terminator who wants to kill John. He is also Schwarzenegger's deadly antagonist. According to *Terminator 1*, Connor is destined to lead the humans against the machines on August 29, 1997. Fortunately for John, Schwarzenegger comes to his rescue.

Although *Terminator 2* is the ultimate in sci-fi films, with dazzling special effects, it has a downside. The distorted view of women and mothers is deplorable, and the film contains considerable violence that provides a terrible role model for children. Also, the pace slows to the point of boredom, the message becomes garbled, and Schwarzenegger's role switch is quite unbelievable.

CONTENT ANALYSIS: (Ab, LLL, VVV) Anti-biblical philosophy; forty obscenities and fifteen profanities; extreme and graphic violence; and sexual innuendo.

Most Overrated Exhibition of Feminism

THELMA AND LOUISE

Quality: ☆☆   Acceptability: −3

WARNING CODES:
Language: ***
Violence: **
Sex: **
Nudity: None
RATING: R
GENRE: Action/Drama
INTENDED AUDIENCE: Adults
RUNNING TIME: 129 minutes
STARRING: Geena Davis, Susan Sarandon, Harvey Keitel, Michael Madsen, Christopher McDonald, and Brad Pitt

DIRECTOR: Ridley Scott
PRODUCERS: Ridley Scott and Mimi Polk
WRITER: Callie Khouri
DISTRIBUTOR: MGM/UA
BRIEF SUMMARY:
In *Thelma and Louise*, Thelma, a bored housewife, and Louise, a waitress, sneak off in a '66 T-Bird convertible for a getaway weekend. The girls stop at a honky-tonk for some dancing and drinking. Louise foils a rape attempt against Thelma, then shoots and kills the assailant. Fleeing the scene, Thelma and Louise try to figure out what to do. Louise opts for Mexico. Thelma phones her husband, Darryl, and then agrees to go. A hitchhiker joins them and after fornicating with Thelma, teaches her how to rob a convenience store. When the hitchhiker absconds with Louise's cash, Thelma robs a store. The offenses pile up as the desperadoes run roadblocks. Eventually, with half the army in pursuit, their luck runs out when they come to the Grand Canyon.

Unbelievably, the viewer is asked to sympathize with these lamebrained, gullible characters. Thelma and Louise are despicable characters, amoral losers, who give us nothing to like. *Thelma and Louise* continues the assault on marriage, which is mocked through innuendo and slander. The surrealistic scenery is the one good thing to say about the picture. The movie glorifies ugliness, yet it will probably be described by others as "high art."

CONTENT ANALYSIS: (FeFe, LLL, SS, VV, A, D, M) Feminist worldview; 112 obscenities and 55 profanities; adultery, fornication, attempted rape, and sexual immorality; murder, suicide, and violence; alcohol and substance abuse, drunkenness; theft and mocking of police authority.

An Act of Conscience

URANUS

Quality: ☆☆☆☆   Acceptability: −2

WARNING CODES:

Language: **
Violence: *
Sex: **
Nudity: None

RATING: Not rated
GENRE: Drama
INTENDED AUDIENCE: Adults
RUNNING TIME: 100 minutes
LANGUAGE: French
STARRING: Gerard Depardieu, Michel Blanc, Philippe Noiret, and Florence Darel
DIRECTOR: Claude Berri
PRODUCER: Pierre Grunstein
WRITERS: C. Berri and Arlette Langman
BASED ON: The novel by Marcel Ayme
DISTRIBUTOR: Prestige
BRIEF SUMMARY:
Uranus, an extremely well-crafted, quality film, marred by a brief scene of fornication with no nudity, turns out to be a story of espionage and intrigue following World War II. The movie is set in a village in France just after its liberation from Nazi occupation at the end of the war. The Communists control the police and are trying to find and execute "collaborators." Many families share housing. Mr. Archambaud, a De Gaulle supporter, hosts a Communist official and his family as well as Professor Watrin. Watrin conducts school in the tavern operated by Leopold, an ignorant, bighearted man who is engrossed in the children's studies and fancies himself a poet. A Communist accuses him of hiding Mr. Loin, a collaborator, which lands Leopold in jail. Mr. Archambaud hides Loin (the house has apartments), since he opposes the drive to execute those who may have collaborated simply to survive. Mr. Archambaud's act of conscience is inspiring. When it becomes known that the accusation against Leopold is false, the party members cover up their wrongdoing.

Despite unfortunate outcomes for some characters, *Uranus* is uplifting because those with a conscience are the winners, while lovers of power suffer shame. Life is uncertain, though we sense that good will prevail. Furthermore, *Uranus* is a film of quality. Though there is no nudity, sadly there is brief fornication and implied adultery.

CONTENT ANALYSIS: (B, AC, LL, SS, V, A, D) Moral worldview with anti-Communist theme and some biblical elements; twenty obscenities, brief fornication, implied adultery, murder, and alcohol abuse.

Inspired Lunacy for Mature Audiences

WHAT ABOUT BOB?

Quality: ☆☆☆   Acceptability: −1

WARNING CODES:

Language: **
Violence: *
Sex: None
Nudity: None

RATING: PG-13
GENRE: Comedy
INTENDED AUDIENCE: Teens and adults
RUNNING TIME: 99 minutes
STARRING: Bill Murray, Richard Dreyfuss, Julie Hagerty, Charles Korsmo, and Kathryn Erbe
DIRECTOR: Frank Oz
PRODUCER: Laura Ziskin and Bernie Williams
WRITERS: Tom Schulman, Alvin Sargent, and Laura Ziskin
DISTRIBUTOR: Buena Vista
BRIEF SUMMARY:
Bill Murray pulls out all the stops in *What About Bob* to create a neurotic character so obsessed he follows his shrink on vacation. Bob Wiley is a New York nutcase. Author of a best-selling self-help book *Baby Steps*, Dr. Leo Marvin is Bob's last chance. However, the diffident doctor goes on vacation with his family.

Panic-stricken, Bob ferrets out the doctor's serene vacation paradise. Dr. Marvin is less than thrilled. Lunacy prevails as Bob turns the tables on their already shaky professional relationship. When Dr. Marvin resorts to "death therapy," the question arises as to who is really crazy and who isn't.

If *What About Bob* is meant to be an attack on psychiatry and self-help books, then in an uproariously funny manner it succeeds. The only problem with *What About Bob* are some early outbursts of obscenity that Bob utters to prove that he's not faking a profanity complex. He later resorts to the same tactic to win the friendship of Marvin's son, Sigmund (to continue the Freudian analogy, the daughter's name is Anna). Had these elements been deleted, the film could be recommended to almost all ages, but as it is, it cannot.

CONTENT ANALYSIS: (B, LL, V) Moral satire; twenty-one obscenities, five profanities; and some violence.

Learning Useful Lessons

WHITE FANG

Quality: ☆☆☆☆   Acceptability: +1

WARNING CODES:
  Language: *
  Violence: *
  Sex: None
  Nudity: None
RATING: PG
GENRE: Animal/Action/Adventure
INTENDED AUDIENCE: Families (except littlest ones)
RUNNING TIME: 107 minutes
STARRING: Ethan Hawke, Klaus Maria Brandauer, Seymore Cassel, James Remar, and Susan Hogan
DIRECTOR: Randal Kleiser
PRODUCER: Marykay Powel
WRITERS: Jeanne Rosenberg, Nick Thiel, and David Fallon
BASED ON: The novel by Jack London

DISTRIBUTOR: Buena Vista
BRIED SUMMARY:
Based on the classic novel by Jack London, *White Fang* was filmed amid the breathtaking scenery of Alaska. In 1898, Jack Conroy comes to the harsh Alaskan wilderness to search for his father's gold mine. The young explorer meets his father's buddy, Alex Larson, who agrees to take Jack to his father's claim. They set out by dogsled, and we see a half-wolf swiping fish for her pup. When wolves kill the mother, Indians find the pup and name him White Fang. When Jack is trapped by a grizzly, White Fang intervenes. Later, an unsavory lot teach the wolf-dog to fight in illegal dogfights. White Fang meets his match in a brutal bulldog, but Jack intervenes in the nick of time. Having reached his father's claim and begun digging for gold, the boy returns with the wolf-dog to the cabin to transform White Fang's nature. Jack's ordeal is far from over. Bringing a bag of gold for testing, Jack and White Fang are followed by evildoers.

If you like dogs and lessons about responsibility, love, and loss, you'll like *White Fang*. The action is well edited and handled tastefully. Its message reflects biblical values. Disney knows how to capture God's creation on screen. It could have stood on its own as a G-rated picture, but due to a few obscenities, the movie is rated PG.

CONTENT ANALYSIS: (B, L, V) A biblical worldview of coming-of-age, marred only by nine obscenities, two profanities, and some violence to represent the conflicts in the story.

Learning to Live with Limitations

WILD HEARTS CAN'T BE BROKEN

Quality: ☆☆☆☆   Acceptability: +1

WARNING CODES:
  Language: None
  Violence: None

Sex: None
  Nudity: None
RATING: G
GENRE: Biographical drama/Adventure
INTENDED AUDIENCE: Families
RUNNING TIME: 88 minutes
STARRING: Gabrielle Anwar, Michel Schoeffling, and Cliff Robertson
DIRECTOR: Steve Miner
PRODUCER: Matt Williams
WRITERS: Matt Williams and Oley Sassone
DISTRIBUTOR: Buena Vista
BRIEF SUMMARY:
Wild Hearts Can't Be Broken is the true, inspirational story of Sonora Webster, a stunt-rider at Atlantic City's Steel Pier amusement pier during the Great Depression, who continued to perform after an accident left her permanently blind. Orphaned and about to become a ward of the state, sixteen-year-old Sonora runs away to answer an ad for a diving horse girl. W. F. Carver already has Marie; however, he hires Sonora as a stable hand. Sonora captures the heart of Carver's son, Al, who trains her. Sonora gets her chance when Marie dislocates a shoulder, but a rift between father and son drives Al away. Al returns and reconciles with his father, having negotiated a contract with Atlantic City's Steel Pier amusement pier. On the way there, the elder Carver dies. Al publicly proposes marriage to Sonora as she climbs the tower platform, but tragedy strikes.

Wild Hearts Can't Be Broken moves beyond the coming-of-age theme to incorporate a real-life tragedy. Sonora learns she must fit reality to her dreams. Interestingly, all three players in the film have wild hearts. Even more interesting is that all are broken as they are reconciled with one another and learn to live with their limitations.

CONTENT ANALYSIS: (C, B, M) A Christian biblical worldview advocating courage, repentance, forgiveness, and humility, marred only by early adolescent rebellion and stubbornness.

★★★ THE BEST 1991 FILMS FOR FAMILIES ★★★

Headline	Title
Strong Redemptive Fairy Tale	*Beauty and the Beast*
Loving Memories of a Christian Mother	*My Father's Glory* and *My Mother's Castle*
Putting Family above Work	*Hook*
Learning to Live with Limitations	*Wild Hearts Can't Be Broken*
Affirming Family Values	*Father of the Bride*
Good, Clean, Wholesome Fun	*Shipwrecked*
Triumphant Heroism	*The Rocketeer*
Learning Useful Lessons	*White Fang*
Wholesome Family Message	*All I Want for Christmas*
Love Thy Neighbor	*The Giant of Thunder Mountain*

★★★ THE BEST 1991 FILMS FOR MATURE AUDIENCES ★★★

Headline	Title
Families Are Important	*My Girl*
Realistic Portrayal of Christianity	*Black Robe*
Exposing the Evils of Communism	*The Inner Circle*
Funny Depiction of a Mean Spirit	*Tatie Danielle*
Love Overcomes Adversity	*Little Man Tate*
A Poignant Story of Redemption and Forgiveness	*Regarding Henry*
Learning the Golden Rule	*The Doctor*
An Act of Conscience	*Uranus*
Learning to Love and Forgive	*Step Kids*
A Cautionary Tale of Comeuppance	*Mister Johnson*

★★★ THE TWENTY MOST UNBEARABLE FILMS OF 1991 ★★★

Headline	Title
Worst Promotion of Sodomy (Tie)	*Poison* and *Paris Is Burning*
Worst Attack on Christian Missionaries	*At Play in the Fields of the Lord*
Worst Demented Revenge on the Church	*Cape Fear*
Worst Adaptation of Great Literature	*Prospero's Books*
Worst Deceptive Feminist Presentation	*Fried Green Tomatoes*
Worst Promotion of Scientology	*Defending Your Life*
Worst Idolatrous Glorification of Evil	*The Doors*
Worst Communist Propaganda	*Guilty by Suspicion*
Worst Feminism	*Thelma and Louise*
Worst Bomb	*Hudson Hawk*
Worst Exhibitionism	*Truth or Dare*
Worst Ridicule of the Church	*The Pope Must Die*
Worst Promotion of Adultery	*Prince of Tides*
Worst Occult Movie of the Year	*The Butcher's Wife*
Worst Transgender Depiction	*Switch*
Worst Politically Correct Adultery	*Jungle Fever*
Worst Psychic Silliness	*Bill and Ted's Bogus Journey*
Worst Evil Joke on Moviegoers	*Freddy's Dead: The Final Nightmare*
Worst Perverted Movie	*Whore*
Worst Anti-Christian Horror Movie	*People Under the Stairs*

Slightly Revisionist

1492: CONQUEST OF PARADISE

Quality: ☆☆☆   Acceptability: −2

WARNING CODES:
  Language: **
  Violence: ***
  Sex: *
  Nudity: **
  RATING: PG-13
  GENRE: Adventure/Drama
  INTENDED AUDIENCE: Adults
  RUNNING TIME: 154 minutes
  STARRING: Gerard Depardieu, Armande Assante, Sigourney Weaver, Angela Molina, Fernando Rey, Tcheky Karyo, Frank Langella, and Michael Wincott
  DIRECTOR: Ridley Scott
  PRODUCERS: Ridley Scott and Alain Goldman
  WRITER: Roselyne Bosch
  DISTRIBUTOR: Paramount Pictures
  BRIEF SUMMARY:
The film *1492: Conquest of Paradise* is an ambitious treatment of the voyages of Christopher Columbus. In the midst of the Spanish Inquisition, Columbus is granted an opportunity at the University of Salamanca to speak his case for sailing across the Atlantic to China. His theories are regarded as heretical by everyone except for Sanchez, advisor to Queen Isabella. Eventually, Isabella finances his expedition. Columbus sets sail and, weeks later, discovers an island paradise. He leaves thirty-nine men behind and sails back to report to Isabella. Although disappointed at the lack of gold, Isabella authorizes another voyage. When the second expedition arrives, they find that the original group has been murdered by the natives. When a rebellion ensues, Columbus prevails, but word gets back to Spain of the disarray in the colony, and he is recalled and imprisoned. Years later, he is freed and allowed to return to explore the mainland.

The Columbus of *1492: Conquest of Paradise* is a man of contradictions who wants to bring God to the New World, yet struggles with his own faith, curses God, and has two sons out of wedlock. Even though *1492: Conquest of Paradise* is a well-photographed film, it has some shortfalls including scantily clothed natives and violence. Regrettably, *1492: Conquest of Paradise* falls short of giving credit to the God, who inspired Columbus, and it often implies that paganism is just as good as, if not better than, Christianity.

CONTENT ANALYSIS: (Pa, Ab, C, B, RH, LL, VVV, S, NN) Positive references to paganism and native religious practices; many derogatory references to Christianity, deceitful clergy, some cursing of God; some positive references that Columbus is on a mission for God; revisionist history; six obscenities and four profanities. Graphic, bloody battles with swords, arrows, and spears, including man's hand being severed; men discuss sexual desire for native women; upper female nudity, and scantily clad natives.

Truth Triumphs

ALADDIN

Quality: ☆☆☆☆   Acceptability: +2

WARNING CODES:
  Language: None
  Violence: **
  Sex: None
  Nudity: None

RATING: G
GENRE: Animated fairy tale
INTENDED AUDIENCE: Families
RUNNING TIME: 90 minutes
VOICES: Scott Weinger, Linda Larkin, Robin Williams, Jonathan Freeman, Frank Welker, Gilbert Gottfried, and Douglas Seale
DIRECTORS: John Musker and Ron Clements
PRODUCERS: John Musker and Ron Clements
WRITERS: Ron Clements, John Musker, Ted Elliot, and Terry Rossio
DISTRIBUTOR: Walt Disney Pictures
BRIEF SUMMARY:
Aladdin follows the rags-to-riches story of a resourceful young "diamond in the rough" who is recruited by the Sultan's evil vizier, Jefar, to help retrieve a magical lamp from deep within the Cave of Wonders. Aladdin gets possession of the lamp and conjures up a wisecracking Genie, who offers him three wishes. Wanting to impress Princess Jasmine but fearing to be honest, Aladdin has the Genie turn him into the magnificent Prince Ali, only to find that the Princess rejects this false face as readily as she has rejected other arrogant suitors. Thus, the fundamental message of *Aladdin* is the importance of accurately representing oneself, rather than putting on pretensions.

Aladdin, like *Beauty and the Beast*, uses magic liberally as a plot device, but the movie's moral context provides a responsible balance. Also, the name of Allah is used as an Arabian cultural touchstone and not as a religious endorsement. Brilliant characterizations combine with state-of-the-art animation to bring *Aladdin* to vibrant life. Particularly impressive is Robin Williams's virtuoso performance as the voice of the Genie. Like the best animated classics, *Aladdin*'s humor will appeal to both children and adults. However, some scenes (such as the emergence of the Cave of Wonders and Jefar's turning into a huge snake) are intense and may frighten young children. Fortunately, these scenes are few. *Aladdin* is a sure hit and a sweet cinematic confection, bursting with kinetic energy and firmly grounded in the message of the importance of personal honesty and integrity.

CONTENT ANALYSIS: (B, O, C, VV) Truth triumphs in the movie *Aladdin*, which contains classic fairy-tale magic, including hypnotism, levitation (of the magic-carpet variety), a Genie who grants wishes, an evil sorcerer who turns into a snake, as well as some violence; however, these magical elements are clearly shown to be inferior and unsatisfying compared to true love and personal honesty, which includes repentance and forgiveness. Some scenes, such as the conjuring of the Cave of Wonders, may be too intense for some young children.

Dark Biblical Allegory

BATMAN RETURNS

Quality: ☆☆☆☆   Acceptability: −2

WARNING CODES:
  Language: *
  Violence: ***
  Sex: *
  Nudity: None

RATING: PG
GENRE: Action/Adventure
INTENDED AUDIENCE: Teenagers and adults
RUNNING TIME: 126 minutes
STARRING: Michael Keaton, Danny DeVito, Michelle Pfeiffer, Christopher Warren, Michael Gough, and Pat Hingle
DIRECTOR: Tim Burton
PRODUCERS: Jon Peters, Peter Gruber, Benjamin Meiniker, and Michael Uslan
WRITER: Daniel Waters
DISTRIBUTOR: Warner Brothers Distributing Corporation

BRIEF SUMMARY:

Batman Returns is a gripping, artistic adventure full of bathos that pits the Dark Knight of Gotham City against Penguin, Catwoman, and mega-millionaire Max Shreck. Though very entertaining and less risqué than its predecessor, *Batman Returns* is still a dark film, mixing subtle sadomasochism with revenge, innuendo, and a perverse twist of the story of Moses. The story begins as baby Penguin is rejected by his parents and set adrift in a basket in the sewer. Weaned by black-beaked friends and filled with revenge, Penguin wants to kill every first-born child. Therefore, he embarks on his diabolical plan to destroy Gotham City and its savior, Batman. However, Batman faces an even greater challenge from the Penguin's ally, the lethally seductive Catwoman.

Batman Returns will lure many teenagers and adults. Not only is it engaging and well produced, it also does not have extensive offensive language and overt sex. However, it is a dark film filled with violence, vengeance, and perverse innuendo. While few parents will keep their teenagers away from *Batman Returns*, discernment of the film-noir aspects of the movie is highly recommended. In fact, discerning Christians could use its storyline as a springboard for presenting the gospel and man's need for forgiveness.

CONTENT ANALYSIS: (B, C, L, VVV, S, M, Ab) The theme that the wages of sin is death, combined with biblical allegory and anti-abortion undertones, is marred by six obscenities, constant violence (cutting down villains, machine guns concealed in Batmobile, hurling villains off buildings, metallic flying disks, electrocution, machine-gun umbrella, car wrecks, explosions, physical assault, murder, fistfights, shootings, destruction of property, circus flame thrower, and use of stun gun), and sado-masochistic overtones (Catwoman's leather bodysuit, use of bullwhip to hurl victims to floor, and razor-like talons on hands to claw victims); sexual innuendo; revenge, rejection; and distortions of biblical story of Moses.

Doggone Heartwarming!

BEETHOVEN

Quality: ☆☆☆☆   Acceptability: +3

WARNING CODES:
  Language: *
  Violence: *
  Sex: None
  Nudity: None

RATING: PG
GENRE: Comedy
INTENDED AUDIENCE: All ages
RUNNING TIME: 87 minutes
STARRING: Charles Grodin, Bonnie Hunt, and Dean Jones
DIRECTOR: Brian Levant
PRODUCERS: Joe Medjuck and Michael C. Grass
WRITERS: Edmond Dantes and Amy Holden
DISTRIBUTOR: MCA-Universal
BRIEF SUMMARY:

In the movie *Beethoven*, George Newton meets his nemesis in the form of a St. Bernard puppy named Beethoven. Since Beethoven's owner never claims him, the Newtons keep the cuddly puppy. However, Beethoven begins to grow and grow, and the bags of puppy chow get bigger and bigger. Furthermore, George finds his shoes destroyed as Beethoven teethes on them, and has to contend with Beethoven's bathroom habits. So, when the veterinarian hints that St. Bernards' dispositions change in time to the point where they can turn on people, George is determined to rid himself of the dog. However, Beethoven proves to be a wonderful friend and companion to George's family. The dramatic tension builds to a climax with the result that Beethoven emerges as George's champion, and they grow to love and respect one another.

Beethoven is a family movie—refreshing, funny, exciting, and heartwarming as each member of the Newton family learns from their new pet and from each other about love, understanding, and acceptance.

CONTENT ANALYSIS: (B, C, L, V) *Beethoven* emphasizes love, understanding, and acceptance; few exclamatory obscenities and some slapstick violence.

Suspenseful

THE BODYGUARD

Quality: ☆☆☆   Acceptability: −2

WARNING CODES:
  Language: ***
  Violence: **
  Sex: *
  Nudity: None
RATING: R
GENRE: Thriller/Drama
INTENDED AUDIENCE: Older teenagers and adults
RUNNING TIME: 130 minutes
STARRING: Kevin Costner, Whitney Houston, Bill Cobbs, Gary Kemp, and Michelle Richards
  DIRECTOR: Mick Jackson
  PRODUCERS: Lawrence Kasdan, Kevin Costner, and Jim Wilson
  WRITER: Lawrence Kasdan
  DISTRIBUTOR: Warner Brothers
BRIEF SUMMARY:
In *The Bodyguard*, rock star Rachel Merritt reluctantly hires bodyguard Frank Farmer to protect her from an obsessed fan. The bodyguard's number one rule is his willingness to lay down his life for the life of his client. Through a series of swift-moving events, the bodyguard has various opportunities to prove his rule. One night, however, he and Rachel spend the night together, and he tells her the next morning that he confused his life with his job, and it will not happen again. At film's end, Farmer discovers the would-be assailant's identity and saves Rachel's life.

Well crafted and acted, *The Bodyguard* can be commended for its overall premise. Kevin Costner fits the role of the bodyguard perfectly with his understated, concise, and sparse dialogue. The film moves well with suspense building to the climax. Two significant elements need to be pointed out: the first is Nikki's (Rachel's sister) singing "Jesus Loves Me" outside on a beautiful morning, and later, at her funeral, we hear her singing it again as her voice hovers over the hearse carrying her body. The second element consists of a clergyman being called on to pray during a Congressional meeting near the film's end. However, be aware that the movie is marred by obscenity and profanity, several violent scenes, implied fornication (although nothing is shown), many scenes of drinking, and the theme of jealousy.

CONTENT ANALYSIS: (B, C, LLL, VV, S, A, D, M) A dedication to laying down one's life for others; twenty-five obscenities, twenty-three profanities; several violent fighting scenes with considerable blood, gore, and murder; implied scene of fornication (but nothing shown); scenes of drinking in bars and other places; and theme of jealousy throughout the film.

Achievement in the Face of Adversity

A BRIEF HISTORY OF TIME

Quality: ☆☆☆☆   Acceptability: + 2

WARNING CODES:
  Language: None
  Violence: None
  Sex: None
  Nudity: None
RATING: G
GENRE: Documentary

INTENDED AUDIENCE: Older children to adults
RUNNING TIME: 80 minutes
FEATURING: Errol Morris
DIRECTOR: David Hickman
PRODUCER: David Hickman
WRITER: Stephen Hawking
DISTRIBUTOR: Triton Pictures
BRIEF SUMMARY:

A Brief History of Time is a fascinating documentary about Stephen Hawking, the brilliant physicist who has Lou Gehrig's disease. Hawking occupies the mathematics professorship at Cambridge University once held by Isaac Newton. In the film, director Errol Morris explores Hawking's story and his speculations about the universe. During his youth Hawking chose theoretical physics because he didn't want to bother learning any more facts than necessary. However, troubled by a loss of coordination at twenty-one, he learned he had Lou Gehrig's disease, which robs its victims of the ability to move, without loss of intellect. Given thirty months to live, Hawking plunged into an analysis of the ultimate questions about the universe.

A Brief History of Time continues through the eyes of family, friends, and coworkers as Hawking ponders whether the universe has a purpose, limits, and a Designer. His brilliance sputters as he approaches the Truth, and even after thirty years, Hawking rejects God. Even so, Hawking inspires us to make the most of our days on earth.

CONTENT ANALYSIS: (H, Ev, B) Naturalistically slanted observations on the origin of the universe; inspiring portrait of achievement in the face of adversity.

The Movie That Started It All

BUFFY THE VAMPIRE SLAYER

Quality: ☆☆   Acceptability: –3

WARNING CODES:
  Language: *
  Violence: **
  Sex: None
  Nudity: None
RATING: PG-13
GENRE: Comedy
INTENDED AUDIENCE: Teenagers and adults
RUNNING TIME: 86 minutes
STARRING: Kristy Swanson, Luke Perry, Donald Sutherland, Paul Rubens, and Rutger Hauer
DIRECTOR: Fran Rubel Kuzui
PRODUCERS: Sandy Gallin, Carol Baum, and Fran Rubel Kuzui
WRITER: Joss Whedon
DISTRIBUTOR: 20th Century Fox/Sandollar/Kuzui Enterprises
BRIEF SUMMARY:

Buffy is a vacuous, mall-crawling valley girl. However, a centuries-old man named Merick tells Buffy that she is the "chosen one," having "the mark of the coven," and under Merick's training she is transformed into Buffy the Vampire Slayer. It seems that a particularly persistent bloodsucker named Lothos and his sidekick have staked out suburban Los Angeles as their new territory. Merick has appeared to awaken Buffy's latent paranormal skills and coach her in battle against the vampires. They are joined by a scruffy dropout auto mechanic named Pike. Thus, Buffy is drawn into a final showdown at the senior prom.

Buffy the Vampire Slayer is mercifully short on blood and gore, compared to other vampire comedies. Most of the action consists of martial arts, back flips, and wooden stakes driven through vampires. Regrettably, the movie involves reincarnation and the vampire premise itself—an unspeakable evil and perversion. *Buffy the Vampire Slayer* also offers negative characterizations of adults. In fact, the film is merely another stereotypical teen flick, only a little short on profanity, violence, and immorality.

CONTENT ANALYSIS: (O, Ab, L, VV) Vampirism, reincarnation, unbiblical concept of "slayer" with "the mark of the coven" who is "chosen" to terminate vampires; Merick states he will go to heaven when the vampires are destroyed, establishing an unbiblical idea of salvation; five obscenities, two profanitie; martial-arts violence, stakes through chests, and vampire electrocuted.

Epic Grandeur

CHRISTOPHER COLUMBUS: THE DISCOVERY

Quality: ☆☆☆☆   Acceptability: –1

WARNING CODES:

Language: None
Violence: **
Sex: *
Nudity: *

RATING: PG-13
GENRE: Historical epic
INTENDED AUDIENCE: Older teenagers and adults
RUNNING TIME: 120 minutes
STARRING: George Corraface, Marlon Brando, and Tom Selleck
DIRECTOR: John Glen
PRODUCERS: Alexander and Ilya Salkind
WRITER: John Briley and Mario Puza
DISTRIBUTOR: Warner Brothers
BRIEF SUMMARY:
Filled with epic grandeur, *Christopher Columbus: The Discovery* begins in Portugal years before Columbus's voyage in 1492. After failing to convince the king, Columbus goes to Spain and pleads with King Ferdinand and Queen Isabella, telling her: "I want to take the gospel into all the world as well as find a new route to the Indies." His opposition comes from a priest, who warns Columbus that his dream is refuted by St. Augustine. Columbus shows that Augustine was wrong in this regard, alienating the priests. Nevertheless, Columbus persuades Isabella, who desires to see the heathen become Christians. To assemble a crew, Columbus even enlists prisoners by guaranteeing their freedom. One sailor frequently reads aloud from the Bible during the voyage.

Of course, Columbus's journey was successful. The outstanding cinematography and positive portrait of Columbus's faith in God is truly remarkable, and the light of the gospel flares across the screen. However, there is implied sexual impropriety, some violence and native nudity, although no offensive language. *Christopher Columbus: The Discovery* is reminiscent of the golden age of Hollywood.

CONTENT ANALYSIS: (C, B, S, VV, N) Focused on Christian character, gospel witness, positive references to Jesus Christ, and a biblical worldview. The film is slightly marred by implied sexual impropriety, some brief violent episodes, and native nudity (upper female).

Icy Escapades

THE CUTTING EDGE

Quality: ☆☆☆   Acceptability: –2

WARNING CODES:

Language: **
Violence: None
Sex: *
Nudity: None

RATING: PG
GENRE: Drama
INTENDED AUDIENCE: Older teens
RUNNING TIME: 97 minutes
STARRING: D. B. Sweeney, Moira Kelly, Roy Dotrice, and Terry O'Quinn
DIRECTOR: Paul Michael Glaser
PRODUCERS: Ted Field, Karen Murphy, and Robert Cort
WRITER: Tony Gilroy
DISTRIBUTOR: MGM/Pathe

BRIEF SUMMARY:

In *The Cutting Edge,* when former U.S. Olympic hockey player Doug Brewer sustains an injury, he takes up figure skating with Kate, a temperamental partner, to train for the U.S. Olympic team. Kate treats Doug shabbily, directing caustic remarks toward him. Kate's miserable treatment continues for a few months, with Doug trying to get even with her. At Christmas, however, Doug brings Kate a cherished shirt from a fellow hockey player, while Kate gives him a copy of *Great Expectations.* Doug appears disturbed at the New Year's party, when he meets Kate's fiancé, Hal, who has an MBA from Harvard. However, by the time of the Olympic tryouts in Chicago, they achieve an undeniable artistry on the ice. As they celebrate, Kate gets drunk. When Doug helps her to her room, Kate turns on him, they quarrel, and he leaves in a huff. To retaliate, Doug spends the night with another skater. The feud continues until the night of the final trials.

The Cutting Edge has much to recommend it: dazzling skating and costumes, a credible and interesting plot, and fairly good acting. Regrettably, Doug's committing fornication, Kate's getting drunk, and the generally bad language fatally mar the film.

CONTENT ANALYSIS: (Pa, LL, S, A, D) Pagan worldview; twenty-five obscenities, several profanities; implied fornication; drinking and drunkenness.

A Stirring Moral Lesson

DARK HORSE

Quality: ☆☆☆   Acceptability: +3

WARNING CODES:

Language: *
Violence: None
Sex: None
Nudity: None
RATING: PG

GENRE: Drama
INTENDED AUDIENCE: Families
RUNNING TIME: 98 minutes
STARRING: Ed Begley Jr., Mimi Rogers, Samantha Eggar, and Donovan Leitch
DIRECTOR: David Hemmings
PRODUCERS: Alan Glaser, Tab Hunter, and Bonnie Sugar
WRITER: Janet Maslin
DISTRIBUTOR: Republic Pictures
BRIEF SUMMARY:

Following her mother's death in the film *Dark Horse,* fourteen-year-old Allison Mills faces a new school. However, she also has to face her new situation without the support of her workaholic father. As a result, she finds herself in juvenile court. The judge sentences Allison to ten weekends of community service on a horse ranch where the children are disabled, but in their determination and steadfastness, they learn to ride the horses. Allison befriends the children and a racehorse, Jet, who is recuperating at the ranch after an injury. Jet seems temperamental, yet Allison earns his trust. Her grades in school improve, and she even nurses Jet back to health. Regrettably, while taking Jet back to his owner, Allison and the veterinarian have an accident. Allison finds herself confined to a wheelchair and may never walk again. Moreover, Jet may have to be put to sleep. Allison gains strength from the disabled children and Jet, who recovers from the accident. However, one final incident tests Allison's strength to walk.

This film brings to mind the scriptural idea of losing one's life in order to find it (Luke 17:33), since only in the service of others did Allison find her life. *Dark Horse* provides young people with a positive example. It is an entertaining, moral film that will challenge, encourage, and stir your emotions.

CONTENT ANALYSIS: (B, C, L) A moral lesson that one has to lose one's life by giving to others in order to find it, marred by five profanities and two obscenities.

Loving Family Portrait

DAUGHTERS OF THE DUST

Quality: ✰✰✰✰   Acceptability: +2

WARNING CODES:

Language: None
Violence: None
Sex: None
Nudity: None

RATING: Not rated
GENRE: Poetic drama
INTENDED AUDIENCE: Adults
RUNNING TIME: 112 minutes
STARRING: Cora Lee Day, Adisa Anderson, and Trula Hoosier
DIRECTOR: Julie Dash
PRODUCERS: Julie Dash and Arthur Jafa
WRITER: Julie Dash
DISTRIBUTOR: Kino International Release
BRIEF SUMMARY:

In *Daughters of the Dust*, filmmaker Julie Dash achieves a poetic lyricism in this imaginative African American history. Set in 1902 on the islands off the coast of Georgia, the Peazant clan holds a farewell reunion. The decision has been made to leave their home on the island and to join mainland U.S.A. in the twentieth century. Each member, dressed in his Sunday finery, presents himself for the photographer who records the event. Basically, three "daughters" tell the history of the Peazant family. Also present are Viola and Haagar. Viola has just returned from the mainland, where she has been converted to Christ. Now she sees the error of Gullah superstitions and warns the others of their consequences. Haagar is self-educated, sharp-tongued, and believes in assimilation.

Although *Daughters of the Dust* is often hard to follow from the standpoint of history, it presents a tapestry of swirling vignettes that are superimposed on each other, while the characters dance from one scene to another. Dash has captured something quite wonderful in this film as she creates some breathtaking visual imagery and a dreamy, spellbinding mood all at the same time.

CONTENT ANALYSIS: (C, O) A loving portrait of an African American Gullah family that shows the tension between generations and spiritism vis-à-vis Christianity.

Stirring Tale of Self-Sacrifice

A DAY IN OCTOBER

Quality: ✰✰✰✰   Acceptability: +3

WARNING CODES:

Language: **
Violence: **
Sex: *
Nudity: None

RATING: PG
GENRE: Drama
INTENDED AUDIENCE: Adults
RUNNING TIME: 102 minutes
LANGUAGE: Danish
STARRING: D. B. Sweeny, Kelly Wolf, Daniel Benzali, Ole Lemmeke, and Tovah Feldshuh
DIRECTOR: Kenneth Madsen
PRODUCERS: Just Betzer and Philippe Rivier
WRITER: Damian F. Slattery
DISTRIBUTOR: Castle Hill
BRIEF SUMMARY:

A Day in October tells how the resistance smuggled 7,500 Jews out of Denmark the night before the Nazis planned to haul them off to concentration camps. In Copenhagen, Denmark, September 1943, Niels Jensen leads an attack on a German munitions factory. Wounded, Niels barely escapes. Sara Kublitz, a Jewish girl, finds Niels and hides him. Her mother, Emma, brings him into the house. When her father,

Solomon, the bookkeeper at the factory, finds the mutilated bodies of Niels's friends, he agrees to carry a bomb into the factory. When the factory blows up, Niels and the Kublitzes flee. Soloman and Emma find out that in two days the Nazis will arrest every Jew in Denmark. Niels stows the Kublitzes and some other Jews in a brick plant, planning to send them to neutral Sweden by fishing boat.

A Day in October is a magnificent film that contrasts man's nobility with his fallen nature. Throughout the film, the Kublitzes grow in faith. The acting, directing, and cinematography are superb. Regrettably, there are four profanities and implied promiscuity. While the love story is not credible, A Day in October is one of those rare movies that deserves to be commended.

CONTENT ANALYSIS: (C, B, LL, VV, S, M) Christian worldview about a stirring tale of self-sacrifice with respect for Judaism and Christianity, marred by four profanities (mostly exclamatory), two obscenities, some wartime violence (not gruesome but gut wrenching), implied promiscuity, smoking, and alcohol consumption.

Exposing Evil

THE DISTINGUISHED GENTLEMAN

Quality: ☆☆☆☆   Acceptability: –2

WARNING CODES:
  Language: ***
  Violence: None
  Sex: *
  Nudity: None
RATING: PG
GENRE: Comedy
INTENDED AUDIENCE: Adults
RUNNING TIME: 112 minutes
STARRING: Eddie Murphy, Lane Smith, Sheryl Lee Ralph, and Joe Don Baker
DIRECTOR: Jonathan Lynn

PRODUCER: Marty Kaplan
WRITER: Marty Kaplan
DISTRIBUTOR: Hollywood Pictures/Walt Disney Company
BRIEF SUMMARY:
The Distinguished Gentleman, starring Eddie Murphy as con man Thomas Jefferson Johnson, makes fun of conniving politicians and uninformed voters as Johnson fakes his identity and gets elected to Congress. Once in Congress, Johnson feels right at home with the other like-minded members of Congress in their deceitful and dishonest ways. However, his conscience is awakened through one of his constituents, and he finds himself going against not only powerful lobbying groups but Congress itself. Johnson, in a clever TV denouement in which congressional malefactors are photographed and caught at their own game, exposes the evils of the system and aids his constituents in a battle against the huge power conglomerate.

The Distinguished Gentleman shows Eddie Murphy at his best with a minimum of offensive language—for him—(thirty-five obscenities and at least three profanities) and only one gratuitous, unneeded sex scene. The movie exposes a painful truth: Congressional decadence along with a Machiavellian penchant for doing the expedient thing (the end justifies the means), instead of decent and just action. The film also fits neatly into an extremely rare genre, that of true and well-done satire—a political one at that—and is reinforced by competent acting and excellent cinematography and direction, all of which combine to make the movie a genuine spoof of our political system.

CONTENT ANALYSIS: (B, C, LLL, S, M) Justice triumphs in this comedy with positive references to Christianity and Jesus Christ; marred by thirty-five obscenities and three profanities; brief scene of fornication (no nudity), sexual innuendo, bribery, and confidence games.

Quietly Redemptive

EFFICIENCY EXPERT

Quality: ☆☆☆☆   Acceptability: +3

WARNING CODES:
Language: *
Violence: None
Sex: None
Nudity: None

RATING: PG
GENRE: Comedy/Drama
INTENDED AUDIENCE: Adults
RUNNING TIME: 95 minutes
STARRING: Anthony Hopkins, Ben Mendelsohn, Toni Collette, Alwyn Kurts, and Dan Wyllie
DIRECTOR: Mark Joffe
PRODUCERS: Richard Brennan and Timothy White
WRITERS: Max Dann and Andrew Knight
DISTRIBUTOR: Miramax
BRIEF SUMMARY:
Efficiency Expert is a quietly redemptive story. In this Australian production, Anthony Hopkins plays Wallace, an efficiency expert who helps the owners of large factories engineer huge layoffs. However, his next assignment is a small moccasin factory owned by Mr. Ball. Mr. Ball's employees are a family who love and care for one another. After a few days, Wallace concludes that a large number of workers must be let go or the business will go belly up. However, he begins to have second thoughts as he witnesses the devotion of Mr. Ball's people to their boss and the kindness they extend to him as well. Before long, Wallace repents, restores his marriage, breaks with his unscrupulous partner, and looks for creative ways to turn the company around.

Efficiency Expert makes its points with subtlety, gentleness, and sly humor. It is a Frank Capra tale told in whispers. Its opening exposition requires some patience, a commodity unfortunately in short supply among audiences jaded by shock, schlock, and hyperkinetic editing. However, it deserves to be seen and supported for its warm embrace of the virtues of generosity and kindness. Seek it out and tell a few friends about it.

CONTENT ANALYSIS: (C, B, L) A positive portrayal of unselfishness and caring attitudes in a business setting, marred by three mild obscenities and one profanity.

Unconditional Love

ENCHANTED APRIL

Quality: ☆☆☆☆   Acceptability: +1

WARNING CODES:
Language: None
Violence: None
Sex: None
Nudity: None

RATING: PG
GENRE: Romantic comedy
INTENDED AUDIENCE: Older teens and adults
RUNNING TIME: 95 minutes
STARRING: Joan Plowright, Miranda Richardson, Polly Walker, and Alfred Molina
DIRECTOR: Mike Newell
PRODUCER: BBC Productions in association with Greenpoint Films
WRITER: Peter Barnes
BASED ON: The novel by Elizabeth Von Arnim
DISTRIBUTOR: Miramax
BRIEF SUMMARY:
Enchanted April begins in England, when Lotty Wilkins sees an ad for an Italian castle available for rent during the month of April. Depressed by England's weather and her husband who seems not to care about her, she views this as an opportunity to get away. Unable to pay all the rent, Lotty convinces a fellow churchgoer, Rose Arbuthnot, to share the expenses. Rose is also having husband problems and sees

this trip as a form of escape. A third woman, Lady Caroline, views most men as only interested in her good looks and money. A fourth companion, the elderly Mrs. Fisher, is preoccupied with her fond memories. Alone at first, the women relish their freedom. However, soon Lotty invites her husband, Mellersh, to share in her happiness. As it turns out, Lotty's love brings the best out of Mellersh, who discovers his own love for Lotty. When Rose's husband shows up, he too reciprocates. Suffice it to say that this paradise has a similar effect on both Lady Caroline and Mrs. Fisher.

The only thing missing from this paradise is God himself, a point worth noting since there are numerous references to our Lord in the beginning of the film. However, *Enchanted April* has a redemptive message: We should love others unconditionally without expecting anything in return. Furthermore, good writing, directing, and cinematography combine to make this film a visual masterpiece.

CONTENT ANALYSIS: (CC, B, C, S) Christian worldview proclaiming that only unconditional love, where we expect nothing in return, can make us happy. *Enchanted April* has some positive references to our Lord and no objectionable elements except for Rose's "extramarital" interest in another man, which never culminates in a romance, and Rose reconciles with her husband by the end of the film.

A Personal Relationship with Jesus Christ

EYE OF THE STORM

Quality: ☆☆   Acceptability: +4

WARNING CODES:

Language: None
Violence: None
Sex: None
Nudity: None
RATING: Not rated

GENRE: Evangelistic drama
INTENDED AUDIENCE: Teenagers and adults
RUNNING TIME: 65 minutes
STARRING: Connie Sellecca, Jeff Conaway, Deborah Tucker, Cyndi James Gossett, Ken Magee, and Sasha Jenson
DIRECTOR: Robert Marcarelli
PRODUCERS: John Shepherd and Rocky Lane
WRITERS: Eric Gilliland and John Shepherd
DISTRIBUTOR: World Wide Pictures
BRIEF SUMMARY:

After a five-year hiatus, World Wide Pictures, the film division of the Billy Graham Association, released *Eye of the Storm* about Tom Edwards, a successful news anchor, who has just returned from covering Operation Desert Storm. While in the Persian Gulf, Tom saved a coworker, Pete, from injury. Now, Tom comes up with a story: What happened to the battlefield converts to Christianity? Tom discovers one soldier after another who has become more convinced of the reality of Jesus' lordship in postwar living. Meanwhile, Tom's daughter Jill has become increasingly distant. When a crisis blows open, a review of Pete's Billy Graham video footage leads to a satisfying reconciliation of father and daughter with each other and God.

Eye of the Storm occasionally portrays the sinners as more interesting than the saints. However, Jeff Conaway pulls off the conversion scenes very convincingly. Overall, *Eye of the Storm* marks a welcome reentry of World Wide Pictures into Christian filmmaking. Regrettably, unlike previous World Wide films, it was made for church release as opposed to theatrical release.

CONTENT ANALYSIS: (B, C) Positive portrayal of personal acceptance of Christ.

Flawed Epic

FAR AND AWAY

Quality: ☆☆☆ Acceptability: −2

WARNING CODES:
  Language: ***
  Violence: **
  Sex: **
  Nudity: None
RATING: PG-13
GENRE: Drama
INTENDED AUDIENCE: Adults
RUNNING TIME: 140 minutes
STARRING: Tom Cruise and Nicole Kidman
DIRECTOR: Ron Howard
PRODUCERS: Brian Grazer and Ron Howard
WRITER: Bob Dolman
DISTRIBUTOR: Universal Pictures
BRIEF SUMMARY:
Far and Away begins in Ireland in 1892, where Joseph Donnelly (Tom Cruise) works the family farm. His father returns dying from a skirmish with the landlords and tells Joseph to go to America. To avenge his father's death, Joseph visits landlord Daniel Christie. There, he falls in love with Christie's beautiful daughter Shannon. Shannon is betrothed to one of her father's cronies yet has no feelings for him. She and Joseph run away, posing as siblings. Upon arrival in Boston, they are robbed, forcing them to seek employment. Searching for Shannon, her parents and suitor arrive in America. When Shannon receives a gunshot wound, Joseph delivers her back to her parents. Heading west, Joseph reunites with Shannon on the day before the Oklahoma land rush. She is in the clutches of her suitor. As the cannon sounds, the race begins and the stakes now are not just land but love.

Far and Away pursues love as if it were an idol and portrays courtship as a game of conquest. Although billed as an epic, *Far and Away* misses the mark. Too much time is spent in Boston, and not enough on the breathtaking Great Plains. Avid Tom Cruise fans may find the film satisfying. Others will not be so enthusiastic.

CONTENT ANALYSIS: (Ro, LLL, VV, SS, A, D) This romantic movie, in which love triumphs over adversity, is marred by twenty-five obscenities and three profanities; mildly graphic gunshots, fistfights, beatings, and crude references to bodily functions, genitals, and breasts; brothel scenes, sexual innuendo; guzzling alcohol; and bar scenes.

Most Blatant Eco-Pagan Occultism for Children

FERNGULLY: THE LAST RAINFOREST

Quality: ☆☆☆ Acceptability: −4

WARNING CODES:
  Language: None
  Violence: *
  Sex: None
  Nudity: None
RATING: G
GENRE: Animated adventure
INTENDED AUDIENCE: Families
RUNNING TIME: 76 minutes
VOICES: Tim Curry, Samantha Mathis, Christian Slater, Jonathan Ward, and Robin Williams
DISTRIBUTOR: 20th Century Fox
BRIEF SUMMARY:
Ferngully: The Last Rainforest depicts a microscopic utopia inhabited by fairies and talking animals whose lives are threatened by evil land developers. The story begins with Crysta, a teenage fairy, telling us, "Only by using the magical power of nature was I able to save Ferngully." Her mentor, Magi, shows her how to make things happen—by calling upon magical powers and believing—noting that, "Everyone can call upon the magic powers of life. How you use it is up to you." Targeted for condominiums, Ferngully is being cleared. Inside a bulldozer, two oafish workers gossip and

munch on snacks. In defense of Ferngully, the community calls upon the power of nature. The movie ends on a somber note, "No Hexes ... can ever harm Ferngully again. Except the humans."

Environmental issues are rarely black and white. In presenting its one-sided argument, *Ferngully* depicts all land developers as "bad guys." How to balance the competing land uses is the question that should have been posed. Also, if mismanaged development is a problem, it won't go away with occult incantations or by releasing the force of nature. This mixed bag of New Age, occultism, and nominalism is anything but family entertainment.

CONTENT ANALYSIS: (OOO, Pa, H, VV, M) Occult worldview with inanimate objects such as trees depicted as having emotions, magical thinking, belief in "force" causes things to happen, occult incantations, spells, spirit of Hexes, witchcraft, pantheism, monism, belief in the magical power of nature, negative characterizations of demolition crew, humanism (strength from within man equips man to overcome hardships), and environmentalism; unconscious man heading for grinding leveler, man held upside down and flown away by biker fairies riding huge cockroaches, man hit on head by tree, man hit on head by giant berries, girl chased by hawk, encounter with hungry snake, and lizard wanting to eat fairy and miniature human.

Powerful Courtroom Drama

A FEW GOOD MEN

Quality: ☆☆☆☆   Acceptability: –2

WARNING CODES:
  Language: ***
  Violence: *
  Sex: None
  Nudity: None
RATING: R
GENRE: Courtroom drama

INTENDED AUDIENCE: Older teenagers and adults
RUNNING TIME: 138 minutes
STARRING: Tom Cruise, Jack Nicholson, Demi Moore, Kevin Bacon, Kiefer Sutherland, Kevin Pollack, J. T. Walsh, and James Marshall
DIRECTOR: Rob Reiner
PRODUCERS: David Brown, Rob Reiner, and Andrew Scheinman
WRITER: Aaron Sorkin
DISTRIBUTOR: Columbia Pictures
BRIEF SUMMARY:
A Few Good Men is a powerful courtroom drama that asks, "How important is the truth?" "Is it more important than saving lives?" "Is it worth risking your career?" These questions must be answered by two determined individuals—one, a power-hungry Marine colonel (played by Jack Nicholson), and the other, an undisciplined lawyer (played by Tom Cruise)—who are locked on a collision course that will destroy the weaker of the two. The plot develops around the mysterious death of a young Marine. Two Marines are accused of murdering him during an unsanctioned disciplinary action known as a "Code Red," a brutal Marine tradition designed to drill a rigid "code of honor" into recruits (whereby they learn to respect the chain of command more than their own lives).

A Few Good Men forces us to analyze our own perceptions of truth, honor, and justice. The colonel's priorities are wholly different from the lawyer's, who has no comprehension of the brutality of war. The film offers challenging performances and superb direction. Regrettably, there is an abundance of foul language and a scene of a man committing suicide. This is not a movie for children, since the issues would be difficult for them to understand.

CONTENT ANALYSIS: (B, Ab, LLL, V, A/D,) Moral worldview but authority and military discipline are questioned; negative caricatures of Christianity, thirty-six obscenities, seven profanities, man commits suicide by placing gun in mouth, and a brief scene of disorderly behavior brought on by drunkenness.

Old-Fashioned Values

FOREVER YOUNG

Quality: ☆☆☆☆   Acceptability: +1

WARNING CODES:
  Language: *
  Violence: *
  Sex: None
  Nudity: None
RATING: PG
GENRE: Fantasy/Drama
INTENDED AUDIENCE: All ages
RUNNING TIME: 102 minutes
STARRING: Mel Gibson, Isabel Glasser, Elijah Wood, and Jamie Lee Curtis
DIRECTOR: Steve Miner
PRODUCER: Bruce Davey
WRITER: J. J. Abrams
DISTRIBUTOR: Warner Brothers
BRIEF SUMMARY:
Forever Young is a heartwarming movie about Danny, a test pilot in the 1930s. The film contrasts the chivalrous lifestyle of the 1930s with the selfish cynicism of the 1990s. As the movie opens, Danny's friend, Harry, is conducting cryogenic experiments. Just when Danny wants to ask Helen to marry him, she gets hit by a car, which leaves her comatose. Danny convinces Harry to "freeze" him until Helen awakens. Sixty years later, in 1992, two young boys accidentally open Danny's cryogenic vault. Danny wakes and tries to make his way in a world devoid of the Christian values of the earlier era. Many funny, heartwarming, and tense moments follow as Danny tries to convince people he is who he says he is. Eventually his records are found and the chase is on as Danny tries to find Helen before the military turns him into an experiment.

Forever Young is a wholesome movie with an exuberant ending where love triumphs over all adversity. The film has a believable plot, excellent acting, and good pacing. Not only is there no sex, violence, or nudity, but also there is a minimum of foul language. Also, the film is loaded with positive values and emphasizes the importance of fidelity, chastity, and manners.

CONTENT ANALYSIS: (B, L, V) Love, integrity, and chastity triumph over all adversity in the delightful film marred only by three obscenities, three mild profanities, and brief violence (fistfight).

Humanist Diatribe

GLENGARRY GLEN ROSS

Quality: ☆☆☆   Acceptability: −3

WARNING CODES:
  Language: ***
  Violence: None
  Sex: None
  Nudity: None
RATING: R
GENRE: Drama
INTENDED AUDIENCE: Adults
RUNNING TIME: 100 minutes
STARRING: Al Pacino, Jack Lemmon, Alec Baldwin, Ed Harris, Alan Arkin, and Kevin Spacey
DIRECTOR: James Foley
PRODUCER: Jerry Tokofsky
WRITER: David Mamet
BASED ON: The play by David Mamet
DISTRIBUTOR: New Line Cinema
BRIEF SUMMARY:
Based on an award-winning play by David Mamet, Glengarry Glen Ross focuses on four salesmen threatened with the loss of their jobs. At a meeting of Consolidated Properties, salesmen David Moss, George Aaronanow, and Sheldon Levine are met by a hostile coordinator. Ricky Roma, a fourth salesman, is not present due to his impeccable sales

record. The coordinator castigates the men and outlines a deal: the salesman with the highest sales wins a Cadillac, the second place salesman wins steak knives, and the third place salesman gets fired. Feeling abused, these three go off into the night to deal with the situation. Rather than use old hackneyed techniques like Sheldon, or complain like Moss and Aaronanow, Ricky Roma slides up to a bar and waxes philosophical with his buyer, thus snaring a lucrative contract.

Glengarry Glen Ross is a harsh and cynical movie, without heroes or even admirable characters. These salesmen are like gangsters, except that gangsters would be more supportive of each other. Although this movie is devoid of physical violence, the constant profanity and verbal abuse is disturbing and harrowing enough. *Glengarry Glen Ross* is a waste of some admirable talent.

CONTENT ANALYSIS: (H, LLL, M, A, D) Humanist diatribe complete with 135 obscenities and 10 profanities, most presented in a context of verbal abuse; salesmen proudly use deceptive and harassing tactics to secure closings, salesmen plan to rob their company and sell valuable information to rivals, and a salesman gets intoxicated with a client and uses this camaraderie as a springboard to a sale.

Slapstick Showdown

HOME ALONE 2: LOST IN NEW YORK

Quality: ☆☆☆   Acceptability: −1

WARNING CODES:
  Language: *
  Violence: ***
  Sex: *
  Nudity: None
RATING: PG
GENRE: Comedy
INTENDED AUDIENCE: All ages

RECOMMENDED AGE: Older children
RUNNING TIME: 120 minutes
STARRING: Macaulay Culkin, Joe Pesci, Daniel Stern, Catherine O'Hara, John Heard, Brenda Fricker, Tim Curry, Eddie Bracken, and Rob Schneider
DIRECTOR: Chris Columbus
PRODUCER: John Hughes
WRITER: John Hughes
DISTRIBUTOR: 20th Century Fox
BRIEF SUMMARY:

In *Home Alone 2: Lost in New York*, Kevin McCallister (Macauley Culkin) once again separates from his vacation-bound family for a wild adventure that involves defending his favorite toy store against crooks. Although Kevin manages to stick with his family all the way to the airport, he boards the wrong plane. Arriving in New York City, Kevin checks into the ritzy Plaza Hotel, where he lives it up. Eventually, Kevin meets up with the same crooks who robbed his house the year before. He overhears them planning to rob Duncan's Toy Store at midnight on Christmas Eve. Kevin sets out to thwart their efforts, chasing them to an abandoned, booby-trapped house for a slapstick showdown that mimics the original.

Unfortunately, the violence is extreme and almost stressful to watch. While *Home Alone 2: Lost in New York* affirms man's need for fellowship, the Christmas sentiments—goodwill and friendship—regrettably melt into a muddled humanism. For many, it was not the Kevin-versus-crooks showdown that made the original movie a success but the clever storyline that affirmed family and Christian values such as responsibility, repentance, and reconciliation.

CONTENT ANALYSIS: (B, H, Pa, C, L, VVV, Ho, S, M) Biblical messages of family, giving, and friendship marred by humanistic approach to Christmas and vague New Age philosophy plus some positive references to prayer and Christianity; four obscenities, one exclamatory profanity, explicit slapstick violence such as man douses flaming head in kerosene-filled toilet causing house to explode, man electrocuted by handling faucets connected to AC/DC welder, man pierced with staples, man whacked with bricks, kerosene-saturated rope ignited while crooks climb down, missing step in ladder causes crooks to hit pavement facedown, men whacked by huge lead pipe, man hit on head with a hundred-pound bag of ready-to-mix cement, man saturated with paint, fistfights, and physical assault; boy's pun unintentionally labels hotel clerk as homosexual; boy walks past skimpily dressed prostitutes in street; petty theft and fallacies that "a good deed erases a bad one" and that Santa Claus is omnipresent.

Pro-Family Scenario

HONEY, I BLEW UP THE KID

Quality: ✫✫✫✫   Acceptability: +4

WARNING CODES:
Language: *
Violence: *
Sex: None
Nudity: None
RATING: PG
GENRE: Comedy
INTENDED AUDIENCE: All ages
RUNNING TIME: 89 minutes
STARRING: Rick Moranis, Marcia Strassman, Daniel and Joshua Shalikar, Robert Oliveri, Lloyd Bridges, and John Shea
DIRECTOR: Randall Kleiser
PRODUCERS: Albert Band and Stuart Gordon
WRITER: Thom Eberhardt
DISTRIBUTOR: Walt Disney/Buena Vista Pictures
BRIEF SUMMARY:
After inadvertently shrinking his children with a particle beam in 1989, madcap inventor Wayne Szalinski is at it again. This time Wayne's baby, Adam, wanders in front of his latest experi-

ment: an enlargement ray. Confronted by his wife, Wayne admits: "Honey, I blew up the kid." Meanwhile, their teenage son, Nick, is lovesick with his first teenage crush, a fourteen-year-old girl named Mandy. Comic complications abound when Adam's growth skyrockets. With Mom, Dad, Nick, and Mandy in hot pursuit, Adam heads for Las Vegas for a final showdown. In an attempt to restore Adam, the family develops a creative solution that involves hordes of police cars, an ice cream truck, a lullaby, an electromagnetic flux, and his mother's loving touch.

With surprises at every turn, *Honey, I Blew Up the Kid* unfolds with dynamic colors and special effects as well as brilliant execution, editing, and acting performances. As a fantastic tall tale, it presents a pro-family scenario featuring three powerful moral lessons: (1) children need moms and dads, (2) only parents have the responsibility for their children, and, (3) the world needs people who are different (even "nerdy" geniuses like Wayne). The second best family film of 1992, *Honey, I Blew Up the Kid*, with its riveting action, appeals to all generations.

CONTENT ANALYSIS: (B, V, L) Heartwarming, extremely pro-family movie marred by a smattering of slapstick violence (hitting police officer, car hangs from top of building with passengers inside, door slammed on man's nose, reckless driving, child runs through a wall, destruction of property, exploding airplane, and girl gagged and bound), and one exclamatory profanity, which could be construed as an exclamatory prayer.

Humanistic Justice

HOWARD'S END

Quality: ✫✫✫   Acceptability: −1

WARNING CODES:
Language: *
Violence: None

Sex: None
Nudity: None
RATING: PG
GENRE: Drama
INTENDED AUDIENCE: Adults
RUNNING TIME: 140 minutes
STARRING: Anthony Hopkins, Vanessa Redgrave, Helena Bonham Carter, Emma Thompson, James Wilby, and Prunella Scales
DIRECTOR: James Ivory
PRODUCER: Ismail Merchant
WRITER: Ruth Prawer Jhabvala
BASED ON: The novel by E. M. Forster
DISTRIBUTOR: Sony Classics
BRIEF SUMMARY:

Howard's End, based on the novel by E. M. Forster, begins with the rejection of young Helen Schlegel by young Mr. Wilcox, who states that he must go to Africa to learn his father's trade. The Schlegels are cosmopolitan, liberated, humane, and humanistic. In contrast, the Wilcox family is stuffy, crusty, and complex, exuding insecurity and joylessness despite its vast wealth. Mrs. Ruth Wilcox becomes a friend of Margaret Schlegel. Just before dying, Ruth Wilcox wills the summer house, Howard's End, to Margaret. The Wilcoxes get hold of the paper and destroy it to keep the house. Mr. Wilcox asks Margaret to marry him. After some time, a tired Mr. Wilcox, racked by one damaging incident after another, apportions his fortune to his heirs, and Howard's End is given to Margaret, the rightful owner.

Despite its humanistic bent, there is much that can be enjoyed about *Howard's End*, such as its beautiful photography. However, regrettably, there is also adultery and profanity. It is unfortunate that E. M. Forster would have employed his considerable talent to give such a heavy-handed endorsement of humanistic social justice, as he did in this case.

CONTENT ANALYSIS: (H, L) Humanist worldview and four profanities.

Biblical Virtues Triumph

THE LAST OF THE MOHICANS

Quality: ☆☆☆☆   Acceptability: −1

WARNING CODES:
  Language: *
  Violence: ***
  Sex: *
  Nudity: None
RATING: R
GENRE: Romance/Adventure/Drama
INTENDED AUDIENCE: Older teenagers and adults
RUNNING TIME: 122 minutes
STARRING: Daniel Day-Lewis, Madeleine Stowe, Jodhi May, Russell Means, and Steven Waddington
DIRECTOR: Michael Mann
PRODUCERS: Michael Mann and Hunt Lowry
WRITERS: Christopher Crowe and Michael Mann
BASED ON: The novel by James Fenimore Cooper
DISTRIBUTOR: 20th Century Fox
BRIEF SUMMARY:

The Last of the Mohicans, adapted from the novel by James Fenimore Cooper, is set in 1757 in upstate New York, where British and French forces struggle for supremacy of the Colonies. Major Duncan Heyward of the British army has orders to escort Cora and Alice Munro to Fort William Henry, where their father, Colonel Munro, is the commandant. Guiding them is a renegade Huron Indian, Magua. To their dismay, the party is ambushed by Iroquois. Hawkeye, nee Nathaniel Poe, a white man raised by Indians, his Mohican friend, Hingachgook, and his son, Uncas, come along in the nick of time to rescue the women and Heyward. When the party arrives at the fort, they find it under siege by the French under the command of General Montcalm. The fort falls, and Montcalm offers generous terms to the defeated British. Meanwhile, Hawkeye and Cora enjoy a tender romance.

The Last of the Mohicans is a visual delight and contains commendable performances. Despite considerable violence, the film achieves a cinematic success even though it forsakes the clear Protestant perspective of the book and leans slightly toward politically correct paganism. Even so, biblical virtues triumph in this visual masterpiece.

CONTENT ANALYSIS: (C, B, Pa, RH, Ab, L, VVV, S) Christian worldview where good triumphs over evil in this classic story marred by a subtle anti-Christian statement, slight revisionist history, and a slight leaning toward a back-to-nature paganism; two obscenities; extreme bloody violence in battles between Indians, English, and French in Colonial America; and stabbing, scalping, killing; and implied fornication.

Lifting Up Jesus Christ

LEAP OF FAITH

Quality: ☆☆☆   Acceptability: −1

WARNING CODES:
   Language: **
   Violence: None
   Sex: *
   Nudity: None
RATING: PG-13
GENRE: Drama
INTENDED AUDIENCE: Older teens and adults
RUNNING TIME: 108 minutes
STARRING: Steve Martin, Debra Winger, and Liam Neeson
DIRECTOR: Richard Pearce
PRODUCER: Richard Pearce
WRITER: Janus Cercone
DISTRIBUTOR: Paramount Pictures
BRIEF SUMMARY:

The film *Leap of Faith* deals with a con-man evangelist, Jonas (Steve Martin), who uses his skills of observation and technology to manipulate the emotions of others. His assistant, Jane, and his crew find out about audience members in order to deceive them. His adversary, Sheriff Braverman of Rustwater, Kansas, discovers that Jonas is a con and wants to get rid of him. However, the situation changes dramatically when real miracles take place in the form of the healing of a crippled boy and a drought-ending rain.

The film is well crafted and the acting is credible. Some Christians may be offended by the premise of a con man using preaching as a con game. *Leap of Faith* shows how technology can be used to manipulate people's belief and to profit the unscrupulous. However, it also shows how even those that deal in tricks cannot explain the true miracles of faith that point unequivocally to the sovereignty of God. In fact, the film rebukes those who try to use or manipulate God, while it lifts up Jesus Christ as the Great Physician and Creator God. At the film's end, a host of monarch butterflies reminds us that Jesus creates new creatures even as Jane decides to become a new person. The Angels of Mercy Gospel Choir, directed by Edwin Hawkins, provides a strong musical backdrop for the movie. Overall, *Leap of Faith* has a good message, marred only slightly by worldly language.

CONTENT ANALYSIS: (CC, B, Ab, LL, S, A, D) Christian worldview with a strong testimony to the sovereignty of God; marred by the portrait of an evangelist con man and at least twenty crude, obscene words, and a few profanities (hard to tell about some); implied sexual intercourse (one time); and alcohol abuse.

The Wages of Sin

LETHAL WEAPON 3

Quality: ☆☆☆   Acceptability: −2

WARNING CODES:

Language: **
Violence: ***
Sex: **
Nudity: None

RATING: R
GENRE: Crime/Thriller
INTENDED AUDIENCE: Older teens and adults
RUNNING TIME: 118 minutes
STARRING: Mel Gibson, Danny Glover, Rene Russo, Joe Pesci, Steve Kahan, Darlene Love, Traci Wolfe, and Daman Hines
DIRECTOR: Richard Donner
PRODUCER: Joel Silver
WRITER: Jeffrey Boam
DISTRIBUTOR: Warner Brothers
BRIEF SUMMARY:

In *Lethal Weapon 3*, the same invincible duo of Los Angeles detectives Riggs and Murtaugh try to find out why high-powered police weapons and ammunition are missing in huge quantities from police lockup and have begun to resurface on the streets, most recently in the hands of street-gang youths. In their investigation, the detectives find that the evidence points to the involvement of an ex-policeman named Jack Travis. While Internal Affairs has been following Travis for some time now, Detective Lorna Cole isn't interested in working together. What really concerns Riggs, however, is his partner's insistence on retiring, claiming he is "too old" to keep up. Will he or won't he retire? The search for the thief leads Riggs and Murtaugh many places and down many back alleys. Suffice it to say that by the end of the film, they each get what they want.

Lethal Weapon 3 has action, good timing, humor, and Detective Cole performs some spectacular karate. Moreover, Joe Pesci as Leo Getz is delightful and deserves kudos for his role. Regrettably, implied fornication mars the film, along with some objectionable language. The outcome proves that sooner or later, no matter what sins are committed, they will be exposed.

CONTENT ANALYSIS: (B, LL, VVV, SS, M) The wages of sin is death when loyalty, integrity, and love triumph. Marred by at least twenty obscenities, four profanities, violence in shootings, killings, car and vehicle crashes, implied fornication in two scenes, and the stealing of police weapons and ammunition.

Actions Have Consequences

LITTLE NEMO: ADVENTURES IN SLUMBERLAND

Quality: ☆☆☆   Acceptability: +2

WARNING CODES:

Language: None
Violence: None
Sex: None
Nudity: None

RATING: G
GENRE: Animated adventure
INTENDED AUDIENCE: All ages
RUNNING TIME: 85 minutes
VOICES: Mickey Rooney, Rene Auberjonois, Gabriel Damon, Danny Mann, Laura Mooney, Bernard Erhard, William E. Martin, Alan Oppenheimer, Michael Bell, Sidney Miller, Neil Ross, John Stephenson, Jennifer Darling, and Greg Burson
DIRECTORS: Masami Hata and William Hurtz
PRODUCER: Yutaka Fujioka
WRITERS: Chris Columbus and Richard Outten
DISTRIBUTOR: Hemdale Pictures
BRIEF SUMMARY:

Little Nemo: Adventures in Slumberland begins as Little Nemo falls asleep and journeys into Slumberland. He is welcomed by the people of Slumberland and becomes heir to the king's throne. Thus he is entrusted with the royal scepter and a mysterious key that unlocks the Forbidden Door of dangerous secrets. Nemo befriends the king's daughter, Princess Camille, and Flip, a prankster. Flip convinces Nemo to use the key to unlock whatever lurks in the dark. Hesitantly, Nemo unlocks the door and unleashes a demon. The monster kidnaps the king and takes him to Nightmareland, ruled by the Nightmare King. Nemo uses the royal scepter to free the king of Slumberland and put an end to the Nightmare World. Nemo returns as a hero and flies away with Princess Camille. Together, they dream on happily ever after.

With brilliant colors, excellent pacing, and special effects, *Little Nemo: Adventures in Slumberland* is fun for the whole family. Not only do the characters tug at your heartstrings, but they explore issues that are relevant to children, such as temptation and peer pressure. The movie shows that our actions have consequences, and that forbidden doors may open into trouble. Ultimately, this entertaining allegory may serve as a springboard for the gospel, though there is some magic present as a plot device, and a few children under eight may be frightened by the Nightmare King.

CONTENT ANALYSIS: (B, O, A, D) Biblical message that good triumphs over evil; some magic present as an allegorical plot device—not necessarily nominalistic or occult (i.e., magic key, presence of dark demon, Nightmare King, etc.); one character, Flip, smokes a cigar.

Powerful Testimony of Parental Love

LORENZO'S OIL

Quality: ☆☆☆☆   Acceptability: +1

WARNING CODES:
  Language: None
  Violence: *
  Sex: None
  Nudity: None
RATING: PG-13
GENRE: Drama

INTENDED AUDIENCE: Adults
RUNNING TIME: 129 minutes
STARRING: Susan Sarandon, Nick Nolte, Peter Ustinov, Kathleen Wilhoite, and Zach Greenberg
DIRECTOR: George Miller
PRODUCERS: George Miller and Doug Mitchell
WRITERS: George Miller and Nick Enright
DISTRIBUTOR: Universal Pictures
BRIEF SUMMARY:

Based on a true story, *Lorenzo's Oil* tells about Lorenzo Odone, a nine-year-old boy who is struck down by a rare disease called Adrenoleukodystrophy (ALD), which causes degeneration of the brain. ALD is a genetic disorder carried down from mother to male offspring. Because of ALD, Lorenzo does not have the ability to produce a certain enzyme that keeps fat from building up in his blood. Consequently, Lorenzo degenerates from a healthy, active boy into a withered, frail, hairless child who can't walk, talk, swallow, or see, and he suffers from seizures that cause him to tremble, scream, and choke. His faithful and determined parents Augusto (Nick Nolte) and Michaela (Susan Sarandon) begin conducting their own research. The couple discover an antidote, a medicinal oil. When Lorenzo adds this oil to his diet, it stabilizes the fat in his blood. By fourteen, he is able to see and communicate with simple sounds. The oil is coined "Lorenzo's Oil" and is now given to boys suffering from ALD.

Lorenzo's Oil is emotionally intense and a powerful testimony to the power of parental love and perseverance. The mother and father's love for the child serves as a pro-life role model for all of us.

CONTENT ANALYSIS: (CC, B, C, V) Christian pro-life worldview with a few positive references to Jesus Christ and graphic portrayal of ALD illness (violent seizures that cause boy to tremble, scream, and choke; bleeding from mouth; blindness; and the inability to walk, speak, and swallow).

Romanticized Portrait

MALCOLM X

Quality: ☆☆☆   Acceptability: –2

WARNING CODES:
  Language: **
  Violence: **
  Sex: **
  Nudity: None
RATING: PG-13
GENRE: Biographical drama
INTENDED AUDIENCE: Teens and adults
RUNNING TIME: 194 minutes
STARRING: Denzel Washington, Al Freeman Jr., Angela Bassett, Delroy Lindo, Albert Hall, Theresa Randle, and Kate Vernon
DIRECTOR: Spike Lee
PRODUCERS: Marvin Worth and Spike Lee
WRITERS: Arnold Perl and Spike Lee
BASED ON: The novel *The Autobiography of Malcolm X* by Alex Haley and Malcolm X
DISTRIBUTOR: Warner Brothers Pictures
BRIEF SUMMARY:
Malcolm X tells the life story of the visionary black leader, from poor child to scheming criminal to white-bashing spokesperson for the Nation of Islam to humanist espousing harmony and unity. Malcolm grows up in poverty during the 1920s in Lansing, Michigan. The death of his father lands his mother in a mental institution. In foster care, Malcolm thrives academically. However, discouraged by bigotry, Malcolm becomes involved with drugs, alcohol, theft, and fornication. Eventually, he is sentenced to eight to ten years in prison. His breakthrough comes after receiving letters from "The Honorable Elijah Muhammad, the Messenger of Islam." Malcolm finishes his prison term and begins preaching. Ironically, the movie portrays Malcolm as a kind, loving, sensitive man who is just as concerned with racial equality as he is with spreading the message of Allah.

Malcolm X overlooks the sinfulness of man and the need for divine intervention. Instead of God's plan, the movie offers a confused evangelistic plea, hailing Malcolm X as the messiah. It ends with little children around the world declaring: "I am Malcolm X!" In an offhanded way, the film's revisionist, romanticized portrait attempts to make his beliefs appealing to everyone. Careful discernment and frequent leg-stretching are musts for the three-hour-long *Malcolm X*. Although well-crafted, the movie will confuse those who have not read the book.

CONTENT ANALYSIS: (FRFRFR, Ab, RH, LL, VV, O, SS, A, D, M) An ode to Islam complete with anti-Christian remarks and Scripture twisting. Revisionist history, Islamic religious practices, racism by blacks and whites, ten obscenities, and two profanities. Malcolm X is gunned down while preaching (gory close-ups), bloody massacre, man knocked unconscious in street fight, police brutality (police drag man across steel floor), twenty days of solitary confinement, photograph of man hanging from noose, footage from John F. Kennedy's assassination, arson and destruction of property, house fire results from cocktail bomb thrown through window, and harassing phone calls. Spiritist delusion leads to conversion; fornication and adultery (mostly implied), skimpily dressed prostitutes, sexual innuendo, implied cunnilingus; illicit drug use and intoxication.

The Mighty Rewards of Hard Work

THE MIGHTY DUCKS

Quality: ☆☆☆☆   Acceptability: +2

WARNING CODES:
  Language: *
  Violence: *

Sex: None

Nudity: None

RATING: PG

GENRE: Comedy

INTENDED AUDIENCE: Ages seven and up

RUNNING TIME: 100 minutes

STARRING: Emilo Estevez, Joss Ackland, and Lane Smith

DIRECTOR: Stephen Herek

PRODUCERS: Jordan Kerner and Jon Avnet

WRITER: Steven Brill

DISTRIBUTOR: Walt Disney Pictures

BRIEF SUMMARY:

When an aggressive coach takes over a ragtag team of peewee hockey players and renames them the Mighty Ducks, they snap their losing streak and skate their way to the championships. The story begins when Gordon Bombay, a hard-nosed trial lawyer, is sentenced by a judge to community service: coaching a peewee hockey team. To Gordon's horror, he is assigned a clumsy crew of misfits that can't skate, score, or win. After several embarrassing losses, Gordon recalls when a coach made him feel miserable as a child, and he realizes that winning isn't everything and that playing hockey should be fun. What the team needs is a new attitude, coupled with vigorous training, new equipment, and a coach who believes in them. With newfound inspiration, Coach Gordon turns things around.

Mighty Ducks is an excellent choice for dads, grandpas, youth pastors, and schoolteachers to take their youngsters to see. Almost everyone will appreciate the camaraderie, humor, and riveting storyline, which tugs at our heart strings. The movie offers hope to our youth by pointing to the rewards of hard work, discipline, service, self-sacrifice, and teamwork.

CONTENT ANALYSIS: (B, L, V, M) A biblical focus on teamwork, friendship, honesty, and self-sacrifice overcoming adversity; marred by seven obscenities, one exclamatory profanit; slapstick violence (man lands on groin inside trash dumpster, hockey puck breaks car window, boy's head hit by hockey puck, fistfight, woman accidentally falls into water fountain, padded goalie tied to hockey post while hockey pucks are fired at him); youngsters occasionally disrespectful toward elders, and an attempted bribe.

Sports Comedy

MR. BASEBALL

Quality: ☆☆☆   Acceptability: −1

WARNING CODES:

Language: **

Violence: None

Sex: **

Nudity: **

RATING: PG-13

GENRE: Comedy

INTENDED AUDIENCE: Teens and adults

RUNNING TIME: 108 minutes

STARRING: Tom Selleck, Ken Takakura, and Aya Takanashi

DIRECTOR: Fred Schepisi

PRODUCER: Fred Schepisi

WRITERS: Theo Pellitier and John Junkerman

DISTRIBUTOR: Universal Pictures

BRIEF SUMMARY:

In *Mr. Baseball,* Tom Selleck stars as Jack Elliot, a rebellious, hedonistic New York Yankee, who falls into a batting slump and is traded to a Japanese baseball team. Arriving in Nagoya, Japan, Jack soon finds that his lazy Western ways collide head-on with a culture where discipline is king. His major league arrogance is soon deflated as he tries to impose American customs on an Eastern environment. It is through this humbling process, done in an inoffensive way, that the film develops a storyline. Eventually realizing that he "ain't what he used to be," Jack comes to the end of himself and gets back in shape. His hard work pays off in the climactic win over the league leader, the Giants.

The premise that pride and sloth come before a fall is the central thread developed here. However, the film is marred by Jack's sexual conquests, a condescending attitude toward women, and unnecessary shots of Jack's backside. The cinematography is good, the clash and subsequent blending of cultures is amusing, and the reconciliation that comes out of the humbling process is good. However, this film joins many others in overall mediocrity, and you may be better off spending spare time with a more edifying film.

CONTENT ANALYSIS: (B, LL, NN, SS) The biblical premise that pride and sloth come before a fall is marred by ten profanities, thirteen obscenities; complete rear male nudity, partial male frontal nudity; and fornication.

Fun Biblical Allegory

THE MUPPET CHRISTMAS CAROL

Quality: ☆☆☆☆   Acceptability: +4

WARNING CODES:

Language: None
Violence: *
Sex: None
Nudity: None

RATING: G
GENRE: Musical
INTENDED AUDIENCE: All ages
RUNNING TIME: 85 minutes
STARRING: Michael Caine
VOICES: Frank Oz, Dave Goelz, and Steve Whitmire
DIRECTOR: Brian Henson
PRODUCER: Frank Oz
WRITER: Jerry Juhl
DISTRIBUTOR: Buena Vista Pictures/Walt Disney Company
BRIEF SUMMARY:
The Muppet Christmas Carol is a live-action musical that retells the classic Dickens story with all our Muppet favorites and actor Michael Caine as Scrooge. Following the traditional story, Scrooge is beset by three ghosts who show him the past, present, and future results of his greed and bitterness. Of course, the story is a biblical allegory depicting a depraved man who repents of his selfishness, confesses his sinfulness, turns to God, and proceeds to walk in the Spirit by showing kindness and generosity to everyone.

It's fun for the whole family with plenty of finger-snapping musical numbers, breathtaking Victorian costumes and winter scenery, and surprise appearances by our Muppet favorites. Remember those two elderly grumps who sat in the balcony on the Muppet Show? They're back as Jacob and Robert Marley, Scrooge's deceased partners. Also, Kermit and Miss Piggy are back as the happily married Bob and Emily Cratchit, with piglet daughters and froggie sons, including Tiny Tim, who is handicapped. Not only is Tiny Tim part of the happy ending, but he mentions going to church as a testimony that God causes blind eyes to see and makes the lame to walk. Well, he isn't completely healed at the end but at least Scrooge comes through with a plump turkey and pays the family's mortgage. There is plenty of Muppet fun to go around in this tale.

CONTENT ANALYSIS: (CCC, B, V, M) Christian worldview with a biblical allegory of self-examination, repentance, reconciliation, and restitution containing plenty of positive references to God. There is some harmless slapstick violence (Muppet rat's tail catches fire and falls into pail of ice water, Muppets fall from window, boy hit in face, Muppet rat used as wind blower to heat stove, Muppet cat rams into door, etc.). Also, Scrooge's "ghosts" of past, present, and future serve as plot devices to expose his egocentric lifestyle and are therefore not necessarily occult.

Gavel to Gavel Comedy

MY COUSIN VINNY

Quality: ☆☆☆   Acceptability: −2

WARNING CODES:
  Language: ***
  Violence: *
  Sex: **
  Nudity: None
RATING: R
GENRE: Comedy
INTENDED AUDIENCE: Older teens and adults
RUNNING TIME: 120 minutes
STARRING: Joe Pesci, Marisa Tomei, Ralph Maccio, Fred Gwynne, Mitchell Whitfield, Lane Smith, Bruce McGill, and Austin Pendleton
  DIRECTOR: Jonathon Lynn
  PRODUCERS: Dale Launer and Paul Schiff
  WRITER: Dale Launer
  DISTRIBUTOR: 20th Century Fox
  BRIEF SUMMARY:
My Cousin Vinny opens with Bill Gambini and his friend, Stan, buying groceries in a Sac o' Suds convenience store in Alabama. On the way out, Bill steals a can of tuna. In the car, they joke about the tuna until a policeman pulls them over. Soon, they discover that they are being held for the clerk's murder at the Sac o' Suds, whereupon Bill contacts his family's lawyer, Vinny Gambini, to defend them. The fun begins as Vinny and his fiancée, Lisa, arrive in Wazoo, Alabama, in their beat-up New York car and with their obvious Brooklyn dress, speech, and mannerisms. Vinny's ignorance and talking back to the judge puts him in contempt of court—three times! Things really heat up for Bill and Stan as three "eyewitnesses" against them are brought forward at the trial. In an amazing turn of events, Cousin Vinny comes through for them.

My Cousin Vinny is really a funny movie. The acting is quite good, with Pesci and Tomei playing their roles to the hilt as jaded but naïve Brooklynites. Be forewarned, however, the language is offensive, and Vinny and Lisa, although engaged, sleep together (no fornication or nudity shown). In the final analysis, this movie will be more entertaining when it is edited for television.
  CONTENT ANALYSIS: (C, LLL, V, SS, M) Redemptive worldview with over fifty obscenities, fifteen profanities; brief violence in person being struck, implied sexual immorality; and theft.

Christian Charity

NEWSIES

Quality: ☆☆☆   Acceptability: +2

WARNING CODES:
  Language: *
  Violence: *
  Sex: None
  Nudity: None
RATING: PG
GENRE: Musical
INTENDED AUDIENCE: Families
RUNNING TIME: 121 minutes
STARRING: Christian Bale, David Moscow, Robert Duvall, Max Casella, and Ann Margret
  DIRECTOR: Kenny Ortega
  PRODUCER: Michael Finnell
  WRITERS: Bob Tzudiker, Noni White, David Fallon, and Tom Rickman
  DISTRIBUTOR: Walt Disney Company/Buena Vista Pictures
  BRIEF SUMMARY:
When publishing giant Joseph Pulitzer tries to cheat the newsboys working for his New York World News in 1899, he finds he has bitten off more than he can chew in Newsies, Disney's latest musical venture. When Pulitzer cuts costs by raising the pickup price charged the newsboys, young Jack Kelly, with the help of

David, the "brains" of the outfit, urges the newsies to strike. Unable to break the strike, Pulitzer wages a personal war on Jack and David, threatening Jack with a return to the boys' prison from which he escaped, and David with harm to his family. Still, the determined newsies fight (and sing and dance) on to a final showdown that eventually gets the sympathetic attention of President Teddy Roosevelt himself.

Newsies is one of the better family films, largely due to the strength of its performers. Unfortunately, only two of the original songs will stay with you the next day, and the disregard for the law, encouraged during the strike, is troublesome—though not graphic enough to offend most viewers. Commendable, however, is the positive portrayal of nuns who feed the boys during the opening number. Viewed with caution, *Newsies* is a film for the whole family.

CONTENT ANALYSIS: (C, B, L, V, A, D) This very positive portrayal of Christian charity is marred by three vulgarities, strike riots, and minors smoking.

Classic Tragedy

OF MICE AND MEN

Quality: ☆☆☆   Acceptability: −1

WARNING CODES:
   Language: *
   Violence: *
   Sex: *
   Nudity: None
RATING: PG-13
GENRE: Drama
INTENDED AUDIENCE: Adults
RUNNING TIME: 115 minutes
STARRING: John Malkovich, Gary Sinise, and Sharilyn Fenn
DIRECTOR: Gary Sinise
PRODUCERS: Russ Smith and Gary Sinise
WRITER: Horton Foote
BASED ON: The novel by John Steinbeck

DISTRIBUTOR: Metro Goldwyn-Mayer
BRIEF SUMMARY:
In the screen adaptation of John Steinbeck's *Of Mice and Men,* John Malkovich and Gary Sinise play Lennie and George, respectively—two manual laborers in California during the Depression era of the 1930s. The characters have a great need for each other. Because of his handicap, Lennie needs George the way a child needs a parent, and George relies on Lennie's size and strength for protection. The men have a simple dream, which they recount frequently: both of them desire a small house with some farmland. Lennie often pleads with George to retell their dream, and Lennie's favorite part is that one day he will be allowed to care for the rabbits on their little farm. Lennie has a fascination with soft animals. He (literally) smothers them with love, which eventually ends in tragedy.

The story is a tragedy—not a "feel good" movie. The film makes no attempt to modernize the story in order to make it accessible to a contemporary audience. Also, a caution is in order: It is disturbing to see Lennie's unintentional killing of animals and eventually Curley's wife, although this aspect of the film is handled discreetly.

CONTENT ANALYSIS: (B, L, S, V) Many biblical principles, such as love, friendship, honor, and compassion, are challenged by tragedy in this classic story marred by six profanities, four obscenities, and adulterous flirtation.

Beautiful Christian Parable

THE OX

Quality: ☆☆☆☆   Acceptability: +3

WARNING CODES:
   Language: *
   Violence: *
   Sex: *

Nudity: None
RATING: Not rated
GENRE: Drama
INTENDED AUDIENCE: Adults
RUNNING TIME: 92 minutes
LANGUAGE: Swedish
STARRING: Stellan Skarsgard, Ewa Froling, Lennart Hjulstrom, Max von Sydow, and Liv Ulmann
DIRECTOR: Sven Nykvist
PRODUCER: Sven Nykvist
WRITERS: Sven Nykvist and Lasse Summanen
DISTRIBUTOR: Castle Hill Productions, Inc.
BRIEF SUMMARY:
The Ox is set in a Swedish village in the 1860s, where Helge kills his boss's ox to feed his starving wife and baby. Helge's wife, Elfrida, urges him to confess but he refuses. However, the next summer, Helge confesses to the pastor and, after pleading guilty in court, is sentenced to life imprisonment. In prison, Helge repents and his faith in God and love for his wife grows. Elfrida, left with the baby and no income, succumbs to the advances of a worker in exchange for food. Soon after, she discovers she is pregnant. Six years pass, and Helge's boss finally allows for Helge's release. Helge comes home to find that his wife has borne a son. Helge storms out to find the pastor, who reminds Helge how everyone has forgiven him. Doesn't his wife deserve the same? Touched by the truth, Helge returns to and embraces his wife.

The Ox is an edifying, well-made, morally responsible film. It shows a clear demarcation between right and wrong, and retribution is presented as necessary to punish sin, just as forgiveness should follow repentance. Thus the director creates a world in which people's love for Christ gives them compassion for others, and so this beautiful Christian parable entertains while it teaches.

CONTENT ANALYSIS: (CC, B, L, M, SS, V) This realistic portrayal of Christians

in a small Swedish parish in the late 1800s communicates a message of repentance and compassion. The film is framed within a moral context, in contrast to a brief scene of violence (a stolen ox is bludgeoned to death) and off-camera adultery. This story of forgiveness triumphing over sin has two slight obscenities and seven minor profanities.

Contrived

PATRIOT GAMES

Quality: ☆☆☆   Acceptability: −2

WARNING CODES:
  Language: **
  Violence: ***
  Sex: *
  Nudity: None
RATING: R
GENRE: Action/Adventure
INTENDED AUDIENCE: Older teens and adults
RUNNING TIME: 117 minutes
STARRING: Harrison Ford, Anne Archer, Patrick Bergin, Sean Bean, Thora Birch, James Fox, James Earl Jones, and Richard Harris
DIRECTOR: Phillip Noyce
PRODUCERS: Mace Neufeld and Robert Rehme
WRITER: W. Peter Iliff and Donald Stewart
BASED ON: The novel by Tom Clancy
DISTRIBUTOR: Paramount Pictures
BRIEF SUMMARY:
The thriller *Patriot Games* promises more than it delivers as Harrison Ford plays former CIA analyst Jack Ryan, who vows to protect his wife and daughter from Irish terrorists. Vacationing in Britain with his wife and daughter, Ryan foils a group of Irish terrorists as they attempt to kidnap a member of the royal family. In doing so, he kills the brother of the vicious terrorist, Sean Miller. Miller wants

revenge, so he leads an assault against Jack's family after they return home to Maryland. To protect his family, Ryan rejoins the CIA.

Patriot Games fails to take us deep inside the clandestine organizations of the IRA and the CIA, and the terrorists come across as a sketchy lot. Due to a weak script, which prompted Tom Clancy, the author of the book upon which the movie is based, to ask to have his name taken off the credits, *Patriot Games* moves slowly in spite of some intense action. Thus, the film never quite persuades the viewer concerning its mission. Even the isolated "farmhouse" where the Ryans live and where the final confrontation comes during a stormy night when the lights suddenly go out, seems hokey, melodramatic, and contrived.

CONTENT ANALYSIS: (B, C, LL, VVV, S, M) Love for family triumphs over evil in this film complete with a positive reference to Christian prayer. It is marred by ten obscenities, eight profanities, extreme, close-up, bloody violence as people have shoot-outs and fistfights with terrorists; and the initiation of a fornication scene (no nudity) cut short by a murder.

Exposing Hollywood's Seedy Underbelly

THE PLAYER

Quality: ☆☆☆   Acceptability: −2

WARNING CODES:
  Language: ***
  Violence: *
  Sex: **
  Nudity: **
RATING: R
GENRE: Comedy/Mystery
INTENDED AUDIENCE: Adults (especially film buffs)
  RUNNING TIME: 124 minutes
  STARRING: Tim Robbins, Greta Scacchi, Fred Ward, Whoopi Goldberg,

Peter Gallagher, Cynthia Stevenson, Vincent D'Onofrio, and dozens of stars in cameos
  DIRECTOR: Robert Altman
  PRODUCERS: David Brown, Michael Tolkin, and Nick Wechsler
  WRITER: Michael Tolkin
  DISTRIBUTOR: Fine Line Features
  BRIEF SUMMARY:
  Director Robert Altman's *The Player* is a clever satire on Hollywood film production.

Griffin Mill is an executive at a major studio. A steady stream of writers "pitch" their storylines, which he wants condensed to "twenty-five words or less." From those concepts come million-dollar gambles, and his job is to hit cinematic home runs. Also he must curry favor with the stars and directors and second-guess Larry Levy, who is gunning for his position. Furthermore, Griffin starts receiving threatening cards from a writer he "never got back to." Griffin tracks down a suspect, but a scuffle results in manslaughter, though there are no witnesses. Griffin gets away with the crime in a satirical send-up of the contrived happy ending. Here Griffin is rich, secure, and satisfied—and also mean, smug, and pompous, even as he deals with a blackmailer.

The Player may be more entertaining to film buffs than to mass audiences. Regrettably, it includes harsh language, nudity, and sexual immorality. With these cautions, and fair warning that this film's purpose is exposing rather than role-modeling, anyone interested in the slippery mechanics of modern filmmaking will find *The Player* an engrossing experience, while others will find it as repulsive as Hollywood itself.

CONTENT ANALYSIS: (H, LLL, V, SS, NN) Humanist satire complete with forty-five obscenities, ten profanities, man beaten to death, brief frontal female and rear male nudity, prolonged close-up on characters' faces during sex, sexual immorality, and major character escapes responsibility for crime (though satirical intent implied).

Profound Debate on God's Justice

THE QUARREL

Quality: ☆☆☆☆   Acceptability: +4

WARNING CODES:

Language: *
Violence: None
Sex: None
Nudity: None

RATING: Not rated
GENRE: Drama
INTENDED AUDIENCE: Adults
RUNNING TIME: 85 minutes
STARRING: Saul Rubinek and R. H. Thomson
DIRECTOR: Eli Cohen
PRODUCERS: David Brandes and Kim Todd
WRITER: David Brandes
BASED ON: The story "My Quarrel with Hersh Rasseyner" by Chaim Grade
SCREENPLAY ADAPTED FROM: The play by Joseph Telushkin
DISTRIBUTOR: Apple & Honey Film Corp.
BRIEF SUMMARY:
Set in 1948 Montreal, *The Quarrel* details the resolution of an old conflict between two old friends. Chaim is a writer who has abandoned his Jewish faith. Hersh is a rabbi who has started a Yeshiva in Montreal. Both nurse the wounds of surviving the Holocaust and of the fight they had the night Chaim left the Yeshiva for a life of worldly "freedom." As the two men walk and talk, the joy of discovery gives way to old bitterness and unresolved conflicts. Chaim and Hersh enter into a passionate debate on the justice of God, which yields many challenging and profound observations. Ultimately neither man budges from his position, but still they find a moment where they can be united, dancing and singing together an old song from their Yeshiva days, at peace with the past.

The Quarrel consists of Chaim and Hersh's arguing and reminiscing. Those who see it are in for a rare treat. *The Quarrel* is a masterful film with brilliant performances. Taking the mystery of the justice of God and the nature of faith and putting them in a powerfully human context, *The Quarrel* achieves an emotional and philosophical depth that most movies fail to achieve.

CONTENT ANALYSIS: (B, L) Biblical views of man's weakness and God's justice expressed by rabbi. Two exclamatory profanities by apostatized Jewish writer.

Cultural Insights

RAISE THE RED LANTERN

Quality: ☆☆☆☆   Acceptability: −1

WARNING CODES:

Language: *
Violence: *
Sex: *
Nudity: None

RATING: PG
GENRE: Drama
INTENDED AUDIENCE: Adults
RUNNING TIME: 125 minutes
LANGUAGE: Mandarin
STARRING: Gong Li, Ma Jingwu, and He Caifei
DIRECTOR: Zhang Yimou
PRODUCER: Chiu Fu-sheng
WRITER: Ni Zhen
BASED ON: The novel by Su Tong
DISTRIBUTOR: Orion Pictures
BRIEF SUMMARY:
Nominated for an Academy Award, *Raise the Red Lantern* is a Chinese tapestry, as strong as it is delicately woven, about a young girl, Songlian, whose father has died and who, unable to tolerate her stepmother, leaves school and becomes the fourth mistress of the House of Chen

Zuoquian. There she meets the first mistress, Yuru, a neglected, embittered contemporary of the fifty-year-old Chen; the second mistress, Zhuoyun, an outwardly smiling but malevolent woman; and the third mistress, Meishan, a haughty opera singer who clashes immediately with the proud Songlian, who has usurped Meishan's position as the youngest, prettiest wife. Sensing the resentment of her servant Yan'er, who had envisioned herself as fourth mistress, Songlian turns as scathing as the rest. When Songlian feigns pregnancy, they conspire to betray her.

In a movie laden with symbolism, the red lanterns represent the wives' insignificance and the bones Chen throws them, and the castle is their prison. *Raise the Red Lantern* affords a profitable insight into another culture, in another time. A film of great beauty, it uses that beauty to reflect on the human capacity for ignorance and cruelty.

CONTENT ANALYSIS: (H, L, V, S) Humanist worldview with a beautiful and profitable insight into another culture, in another time, reflecting on the human capacity for ignorance and cruelty, slightly marred by three obscenities, sexual situations (implied), and adultery (implied).

Fishing as Metaphor

A RIVER RUNS THROUGH IT

Quality: ☆☆☆☆   Acceptability: −1

WARNING CODES:
  Language: *
  Violence: None
  Sex: *
  Nudity: **
RATING: PG-13
GENRE: Adventure/Drama
INTENDED AUDIENCE: Adults
RUNNING TIME: 123 minutes
STARRING: Craig Sheffer, Brad Pitt, Tom Skerritt, Brenda Blethyn, Emily Lloyd, and Edie McClurg
DIRECTOR: Robert Redford

PRODUCER: Jake Eberts
WRITER: Richard Friedenberg
BASED ON: The story by Norman Maclean
DISTRIBUTOR: Columbia Pictures
BRIEF SUMMARY:
A River Runs Through It centers on two brothers, their father, and the river that shapes their lives. Set in Montana between 1910 and 1935, the story uses fly-fishing as a metaphor for science, sport, religion, art, and the quest for grace that they all share. Norman and Paul Maclean are devoted to each other and to their parents, yet the tough stoicism that has been bred into them by their stern father, the Reverend Maclean (Tom Skerritt), and by the rough land has made it difficult for them to seek, accept, or offer help when needed, though Paul is in need of help. On the river, however, teaching his sons how to cast the line, to read the water, to respect the fish, the reverend initiates the boys into a discipline that links them to nature, beauty, art, and, irrevocably, to each other.

Like Robert Redford's Oscar-winning directorial debut, *Ordinary People*, *A River Runs Through It* deals with a family whose members are unable to help or communicate with one another. Redford has created a work that ties religion, family, and fishing together in an unusual and intelligent, though sometimes New Age manner.

CONTENT ANALYSIS: (B, C, Pa, L, M, NN, S) Biblical character of minister father and Protestant work ethic symbolized in fly-fishing, but with some minor New Age aspects. There are five obscenities, three profanities, brief scenes of gambling and drinking, partial male nudity, and implied fornication.

Good Triumphs over Evil

ROCK-A-DOODLE

Quality: ☆☆☆   Acceptability: +2

WARNING CODES:

Language: None
Violence: None
Sex: None
Nudity: None

RATING: G
GENRE: Animated musical adventure
INTENDED AUDIENCE: Families
RUNNING TIME: 77 minutes
VOICES: Glen Campbell, Eddie Deezen, Sandy Duncan, Ellen Greene, Phil Harris, Christopher Plummer, and Charles Nelson-Reilly
DIRECTOR: Don Bluth
PRODUCERS: Don Bluth, Gary Goldman, and John Pomeroy
WRITER: David N. Weiss
DISTRIBUTOR: Samuel Goldwyn
BRIEF SUMMARY:

Director Don Bluth, of *An American Tail* fame, recaptures his animated brilliance in *Rock-A-Doodle* and brackets it with a *Wizard of Oz* live-action opening and close. In the film, Chanticleer is a rooster who calls up the sun with his cock-a-doodle, or so reads little Edmund in his storybook. One day, while fighting evil owls, Chanticleer forgets to crow and sees the sun coming up without him. Ridiculed, Chanticleer leaves for the city. Edmund is injected into his storybook fantasy when a flood threatens the farm. Knowing that only Chanticleer can stop the rain by bringing up the sun, he tries to call the rooster, but comes face-to-face with the Grand Duke, an evil owl. Edmund is rescued by Patou, the old farm-dog, and discovers that he has been transformed into a kitten. He sets off to find Chanticleer with Patou; Peepers, an intelligent mouse; and Snipes, a wise-cracking magpie.

Rock-A-Doodle is a well-made, enjoyable, family film destined to make you laugh and cry. It is a favorite among children and their parents, as it communicates messages of friendship, love, courage, repentance, and forgiveness. While there

is some magic present, it is not nominalistic but rather used as a simple plot device in the style of C. S. Lewis.

CONTENT ANALYSIS: (BB, Pa, M) Good triumphs over evil in this cute, lightweight cartoon for children of all ages. It communicates messages of friendship, love, courage, repentance, and forgiveness. Some magic is used as a plot device, but it is not nominalistic, occult, or New Age.

A Redemptive Romp

SISTER ACT

Quality: ☆☆☆☆   Acceptability: −1

WARNING CODES:

Language: **
Violence: **
Sex: *
Nudity: None

RATING: PG
GENRE: Comedy
INTENDED AUDIENCE: Teens and adults
RUNNING TIME: 100 minutes
STARRING: Whoopi Goldberg, Maggie Smith, Harvey Keitel, Bill Nunn, Mary Wickes, Kathy Najimy, Wendy Makkena, Joe Maher, and Richard Portnow
DIRECTOR: Emile Ardolino
PRODUCER: Scott Rudin
WRITER: Paul Rudnick
DISTRIBUTOR: Buena Vista/Touchstone Pictures
BRIEF SUMMARY:

Sister Act begins in a Reno casino, where Delores belts out muzak in sequined garb. Trapped in a relationship with her married boss, Vinnie, Delores decides to leave town. On her way, she witnesses Vinnie shooting a man, and runs to the police station. To protect her, an officer hides her in a dying convent in an inner-city neighborhood. Now Delores must embrace a disciplined lifestyle. She does, and both Delores and the convent are converted. Initially selfish, when she puts others before herself, Delores finds her true self, restores the convent's choir, and revives morale. In turn, Delores gets the nuns to reach out to the community, and their faith comes alive. Delores's impact on the choir is a heartwarming sound that may convert the most stiff-necked sophisticate. As Delores says, "This is rejoicing. We are singing to the Lord."

Sister Act is a redemptive romp that affirms that Christian forgiveness and self-sacrifice do overcome adversity. It is recommended for those who want to introduce their worldly friends to the joy of real celebration. However, Delores comes out of a fallen world, which is portrayed accurately in the movie. Therefore, the film is not for pietists or little children.

CONTENT ANALYSIS: (C, B, LL, VV, S, A, D, M, Ab) Biblical messages of forgiveness, unconditional acceptance, and self-sacrifice overcoming adversity marred by eleven obscenities, murder, punching thugs in their groins in self-defense, chase scenes, fights, holding nuns hostage; implied adultery, nude sculptures, suggestive dance moves, cleavage, sexual innuendo; bar scenes, police corruption, disrespect for elders, and jumbling Bible verses out of ignorance in a makeshift prayer.

The Election of God

A STRANGER AMONG US

Quality: ☆☆☆   Acceptability: +1

WARNING CODES:

Language: *
Violence: *
Sex: None
Nudity: None

RATING: PG-13
GENRE: Drama
INTENDED AUDIENCE: Mature children and adults
RUNNING TIME: 110 minutes

STARRING: Melanie Griffith and Eric Thal
DIRECTOR: Sidney Lumet
PRODUCERS: Steve Golin, Sigurjon Sighvatsson, and Howard Rosenman
WRITER: Robert J. Avrech
DISTRIBUTOR: Hollywood Pictures/Buena Vista
BRIEF SUMMARY:

In *A Stranger Among Us*, Melanie Griffith plays a New York cop, Emily, who goes into the Hasidic Jewish community to investigate a murder. This callous policewoman discovers more than just the guilty party as she finds herself touched by the warm and ancient culture of Hasidism. Emily lives with the rabbi and his family in their intimate Hasidic environment. At first she thinks of them as a "quaint" society, but soon learns their values and traditions. In fact, the bulk of the action centers on the family, relationships, traditions, and the Sabbath, instead of the murder case. Emily believes she is in love with the rabbi's adopted son, Ariel, who will one day be the rabbi of their community. So, in one brilliant scene, he explains to her the Jewish idea that God chooses one man for every woman and that God chose the daughter of a French rabbi for him.

The ideas in *A Stranger Among Us* are scrupulously authentic. Eric Thal studied the Cabala for his performance and a Hasidic Jew was on the set at all times. It is interesting that the Disney company has brought us two films in one year (*Sister Act* and *A Stranger Among Us*) that portray a religious community with great care, love, and reverence.

CONTENT ANALYSIS: (B, L, V) A positive portrayal of Hasidic Jewish customs and biblical principles marred by four vulgarities, one profanity, and brief violence.

Violent Solutions

UNDER SIEGE

Quality: ☆☆☆   Acceptability: −2

WARNING CODES:

Language: ***
Violence: ***
Sex: None
Nudity: **

RATING: R
GENRE: Action/Thriller
INTENDED AUDIENCE: Older teens and adults
RUNNING TIME: 103 minutes
STARRING: Steven Seagal, Tommy Lee Jones, and Gary Busey
DIRECTOR: Andrew Davis
PRODUCERS: Arnon Milchan, Steven Seagal, and Steven Reuther
WRITER: J. F. Lawton
DISTRIBUTOR: Warner Brothers
BRIEF SUMMARY:
Under Siege is a fast-paced action movie about a group of nuclear terrorists highjacking the USS *Missouri,* and the ship's cook (Steven Seagal) coming to their rescue. The highjacking takes place as the USS *Missouri* embarks from Pearl Harbor on her final voyage across the Pacific to San Francisco, manned only by a skeleton crew. A group of terrorists board the battleship via helicopter, posing as entertainers for the captain's surprise birthday party. The guerrilla force takes over the ship, imprisons the crew, and kills all the high-ranking officers, including the captain. Their goal is to ransom the world using the formidable nuclear arsenal aboard the USS *Missouri,* and no one can stop them, not even the U.S. government. However, just in the nick of time Steven Seagal comes to the world's rescue.

Obviously, *Under Siege* is a violent movie. Men are gunned down by automatic weapon fire, explosions, impaled, knifed, or whacked with martial arts. Seagal's performance gives his audience what he is known for: lots of action, violence, and martial arts, but there is little substance here to nurture our souls. While Seagal's character has a noble purpose (saving the world), his methodical slaughter of the bad guys teaches us that evil can

only be overcome by more evil. In almost every instance, Seagal kills his heinous opponents in self-defense, but his actions still condone excessive murder and killing.

CONTENT ANALYSIS: (BB, LLL, VVV, NN, B) The theme is that the wages of sin is death. Twenty-two obscenities, five profanities; revenge, explicit violence (over fifty killings caused by gunfire, victim impaled by falling steel girder, use of knives and other weaponry, martial arts, explosions, destruction of property, and terrorists highjack battleship for government extortion and world anarchy); and brief upper female nudity.

Most Nihilistic Ironic Revisionism

UNFORGIVEN

Quality: ☆☆☆   Acceptability: −3

WARNING CODES:

Language: ***
Violence: ***
Sex: ***
Nudity: None

RATING: R
GENRE: Western
INTENDED AUDIENCE: Older teens and adults
RUNNING TIME: 131 minutes
STARRING: Clint Eastwood, Gene Hackman, Morgan Freeman, and Richard Harris
DIRECTOR: Clint Eastwood
PRODUCER: Clint Eastwood
WRITER: David Webb Peoples
DISTRIBUTOR: Warner Brothers
BRIEF SUMMARY:
In his film *Unforgiven,* Clint Eastwood transforms the heroic Western into an ironic tale about a killer who can't escape his past. Set in Big Whisky, Wyoming, in the 1800s, *Unforgiven* opens in a brothel where a cowboy slashes a prostitute's face while his friend watches. When Little Bill, the sheriff, merely reprimands

the culprits, the prostitutes raise money to avenge the crime. The Scofield Kid contacts William Munny, a killer who has settled down, to join him in the bounty hunt. Munny does so reluctantly having promised his late wife that his killing days were over. On the way, he picks up his partner, Ned. When they arrive, Little Bill beats Munny mercilessly. After Munny recovers, he kills one of the cowboys. Little Bill's men catch Ned and whip him to death. Meanwhile, the Kid kills the slasher. When Munny finds out about Ned, he takes on the sheriff and his cohorts.

Unforgiven portrays a hopeless, depressing, existential world, where man is at the mercy of hostile forces that force him to commit heinous crimes to survive. Though this portrait of the Old West demeans history, it does capture the despair of those modern humanists who are truly without hope. Ultimately, *Unforgiven* fails as entertainment for want of a satisfying climax. Eastwood fans who are expecting a cathartic experience will only find despair.

CONTENT ANALYSIS: (HHH, RH, LLL, VVV, SSS, A, D, H, M) Humanist, revisionist worldview, fifty-eight obscenities, seventeen profanities, excessive violence (a woman's face is slashed repeatedly with a knife, frequent shootings, beatings, kickings, etc.); fornication, sexual immorality (story revolves around Old West brothel), seminudity; drinking, drunkenness, and a revenge motif.

A Delicate Message of Faith

WHERE THE RED FERN GROWS: PART 2

Quality: ☆☆☆☆   Acceptability: +3

WARNING CODES:
Language: *
Violence: *
Sex: None

Nudity: None
RATING: G
GENRE: Romantic drama
INTENDED AUDIENCE: All ages
RUNNING TIME: 93 minutes
STARRING: Wilford Brimley, Doug McKeon, Lisa Whelchel, Adam Faraizl, and Chad McQueen
DIRECTOR: Jim McCullough
PRODUCER: William J. Immerman
WRITER: Samuel Bradford
BASED ON: The novel by Wilson Rawls
DISTRIBUTOR: Triad Family Media/Video Communications, Inc.

BRIEF SUMMARY:
A remarkable testimony of the sovereignty of God unfolds in *Where the Red Fern Grows: Part 2*. Based on the novel by Wilson Rawls, the movie opens in 1946 as two marines, Billy Coleman and Rainee Pritchard, return from World War II to the Louisiana farmhouse of Grandpa Coleman (Wilford Brimley) and Billy's sister, Sara. The story begins with a sweet reunion, though many changes have taken place. Sara is no longer a teenager; she now attends college on a scholarship. Grandpa Coleman is older and suffers from poor health. Rainee must overcome selfish ambition to win Sara's hand in marriage. Billy struggles with the issue of fairness, and how the war cost him his right leg. As the characters work through their difficulties, tragedy strikes, drawing everyone closer to God. Billy recalls a discussion about the Lord. "Did you meet him halfway?" Grandpa asked. Now Billy realizes: "It wasn't a matter of meeting God halfway. God found me and he's been there all along."

Though slow-moving, *Where the Red Fern Grows: Part 2* is a superb film, enhanced with beautiful scenery, heartfelt acting performances, and a delicate message of faith. The movie should serve as proof that movie excellence can be achieved without pathological behavior, foul language, occultism, or excessive sex and violence.

CONTENT ANALYSIS: (CC, B, L, V) Christian worldview with biblical messages of God's sovereignty, friendship, self-sacrifice, responsibility, and respect for elders and animals. Minister reads from Bible, evidence of character's faith in God, singing hymns in church. Two minor obscenities, one exclamatory profanity, and a fistfight.

☆☆☆ THE BEST 1992 FILMS FOR FAMILIES ☆☆☆

Headline	Title
Fun Biblical Allegory	The Muppet Christmas Carol
Pro-Family Scenario	Honey, I Blew Up The Kid
Truth Triumphs	Aladdin
The Mighty Rewards of Hard Work	The Mighty Ducks
Doggone Heartwarming!	Beethoven
A Delicate Message of Faith	Where the Red Fern Grows: Part 2
Slapstick Showdown	Home Alone 2: Lost in New York
Good Triumphs over Evil	Rock-A-Doodle
A Stirring Moral Lesson	Dark Horse
Actions Have Consequences	Little Nemo: Adventures in Slumberland

☆☆☆ THE BEST 1992 FILMS FOR MATURE AUDIENCES ☆☆☆

Headline	Title
A Redemptive Romp	Sister Act
Beautiful Christian Parable	The Ox
Old-Fashioned Values	Forever Young
Powerful Testimony of Parental Love	Lorenzo's Oil
Biblical Virtues Triumph	The Last of the Mohicans
Unconditional Love	Enchanted April
Profound Debate on God's Justice	The Quarrel
Stirring Tale of Self-Sacrifice	A Day in October
Loving Family Portrait	Daughters of the Dust
Quietly Redemptive	Efficiency Expert

☆☆☆ THE TWENTY MOST UNBEARABLE FILMS OF 1992 ☆☆☆

Headline	Title
Worst Adultery	Basic Instinct
Worst Demonic	Bram Stoker's Dracula
Worst Occultism for Children	Ferngully: The Last Rainforest
Worst Transvestite Movie	The Crying Game
Worst Homoerotic Drug Addiction	Naked Lunch
Worst Violent Pornography	The Bad Lieutenant
Worst Animated Sexual Fantasy	Cool World
Worst Politically Correct Adaptation	Edward II
Worst Incestuous Horror Flick	Sleepwalkers
Worst Gang Films (tie)	American Me and Juice
Worst Rape Myth	Love Crimes
Worst Glorification of Pederasty	The Lover
Worst Christian-Bashing Slasher Movie	Rampage

Headline	Title
Worst Psychotic	*Twin Peaks: Fire Walk with Me*
Worst Science Fiction Sequel	*Alien 3*
Worst Frightening for Children	*Freddie As F.R.O. 7*
Worst Revisionism	*Incident at Oglala*
Worst Racist Comedy	*White Men Can't Jump*
Worst Trivialization of Christianity	*The Favor, the Watch and the Very Big Fish*
Worst Revisionism	*Unforgiven*

Delightful but Sanitized

THE ADVENTURES OF HUCK FINN

Quality: ☆☆☆☆   Acceptability: −1

WARNING CODES:

Language: **
Violence: **
Sex: None
Nudity: None

RATING: PG
GENRE: Adventure/Drama
INTENDED AUDIENCE: All ages
RUNNING TIME: 108 minutes
STARRING: Elijah Wood, Courtney
B. Vance, Ron Perlman, and Dana Ivey
DIRECTOR: Stephen Sommers
BASED ON: *The Adventures of
Huckleberry Finn* by Mark Twain
DISTRIBUTOR: Walt Disney Company/Buena Vista Pictures
BRIEF SUMMARY:
The Adventures of Huck Finn is a delightful though sanitized rendering of Mark Twain's classic. On the banks of the Mississippi River in St. Petersburg, Missouri, twelve-year-old Huckleberry Finn (Elijah Wood) makes his home with the Widow Douglas and her sister, Miss Watson. Since Huck's mother died when he was young and his father, Pap, is a no-good bum who's out to kill him for the $600 left by his mother, Huck puts up with the "civilizing" at the Widow Douglas's house. After Pap abducts Huck to kill him, Huck has no choice but to get away. This scene is difficult to watch, and children would be upset to see Huck's father trying to kill him. Huck takes off on a small raft. Soon Huck discovers Jim, one of Widow Douglas's slaves, who wants to escape to freedom so he can buy his wife and children. Huck tries to protect Jim since there is a bounty on his head, and Jim lovingly watches over Huck.

Several hilarious episodes occur, and Twain's themes shine through the dialogue, including death and rebirth, freedom and bondage, the search for a father, and the theme of brotherhood. Slavery is a metaphor for social bondage and institutionalized injustice. Twain also gives religion a black eye in the satiric *Huckleberry Finn*. The acting, cinematography, costumes, and staging of life in nineteenth-century America are superb. Despite the detracting elements that derive from the novel, most viewers will delight in Huck's witticisms.

CONTENT ANALYSIS: (H, Ab, A, D, LL, O, VV) Anti-Christian humanism, nineteen obscenities, four nonexclamatory profanities, several violent episodes (Pap's abduction of Huck, hitting him, trying to kill him, Pap knocks woman down, slaves being beaten, fighting, shooting and killing in feud battle between the Shepherdsons and Grangerfords); alcohol drinking and drunkenness by Pap, Huck's pipe-smoking, and a ritual by Jim that appears to be satanic.

Upholding Tradition

THE AGE OF INNOCENCE

Quality: ☆☆☆☆   Acceptability: +1

WARNING CODES:

Language: *
Violence: None
Sex: *
Nudity: None

RATING: PG
GENRE: Drama

INTENDED AUDIENCE: Older teens and adults

RUNNING TIME: 139 minutes

STARRING: Daniel Day-Lewis, Michelle Pfeiffer, and Winona Ryder

DIRECTOR: Martin Scorsese

PRODUCER: Barbara De Fina

WRITERS: Jay Cocks and Martin Scorsese

BASED ON: Edith Wharton's novel

DISTRIBUTOR: Columbia Pictures

BRIEF SUMMARY:

The poignant film *The Age of Innocence* moves across the screen with the graceful elegance of circa 1870s New York haute society and manages to convey numerous mores of the society that apply universally to humanity as well. Although set in another time and era, the message of human conflict and repressed passion is timeless. Engaged to the proper May Welland, attorney Newland Archer suddenly finds himself attracted to the more exotic and interesting Countess Olenska, whose estranged husband lives in Europe. However, unbeknownst to him until the Countess is safely removed from his life, society intervenes and keeps him from throwing away his future for a fleeting affair.

Beautifully crafted and a visual delight with its authentic period sets of 1870s New York society, complete with opulent drawing rooms, ornate chandeliers, highly polished silver, and gorgeous beaded gowns, *The Age of Innocence* will abundantly reward the patient, discerning viewer. Taken from the Edith Wharton novel, the film uniquely upholds tradition and conservative values and is a careful psychological study of its characters and the temptations that confront every person. Discerning viewers will delight in paying careful attention to each word, phrase, and nuance to gain understanding of film action.

CONTENT ANALYSIS: (B, C, L, S) An exceptional film that upholds biblical standards and takes place in a time when the U.S. population operated on the basis of Christian principles. Two exclamatory profanities and suspected infidelity, but nothing shown.

Scouting for Superstars

THE AIR UP THERE

Quality: ☆☆☆☆   Acceptability: –1

WARNING CODES:
  Language: **
  Violence: *
  Sex: None
  Nudity: None

RATING: PG

GENRE: Comedy

INTENDED AUDIENCE: Older children and adults

RUNNING TIME: 107 minutes

STARRING: Kevin Bacon, Sean McCann, and Eric Menyuk

DIRECTOR: Paul Michael Glaser

DISTRIBUTOR: Hollywood Pictures/Walt Disney Company/Buena Vista Pictures

BRIEF SUMMARY:

In *The Air Up There*, Jimmy Dolan (Kevin Bacon) wants the head coaching position at his alma mater, St. Joseph's University where, while playing point guard, he once hit the winning basket in a college national championship game. Once the heir apparent to the head coaching job, Dolan is now relegated to scouting small-time high school basketball games. That is, until he sees a film at the alumni banquet documenting the progress of St. Joseph's mission to the Winabi tribe in Africa and notes, in the out-of-focus background of the missionary's film, a very tall, agile young African man slam-dunking a basketball in Air-Jordan fashion over the outstretched arms of helpless defenders. Dolan sees his chance to land a big recruit and the head coaching job, so, at his own expense, he heads for Africa.

The Air Up There is a fun, positive, enjoyable film with great acting by all involved and excellent cinematography. The directing is well done and the soundtrack is upbeat. The only down note, once again, is the relative amount of offensive language. Featuring no sex or nudity, there is even a fun, albeit somewhat predictable, surprise near the film's climax. Without the offensive language the film could be highly recommended for all ages.

CONTENT ANALYSIS: (B, C, LL, V, A, M, Pa) Biblical worldview stressing the moral principles of truth, friendship, forgiveness, ethics, and the importance of family, with positive portrait of Christianity. Fifteen obscenities, four profanities, a few vulgarities; violent scene as African village burns, mild violence in on-court basketball action; main character occasionally drinks beer, two groups bet on basketball game; and African tribal ceremony.

Sacred Encounter

ALIVE

Quality: ☆☆☆☆   Acceptability: –1

WARNING CODES:

Language: *
Violence: *
Sex: None
Nudity: None

RATING: PG-13
GENRE: Drama
INTENDED AUDIENCE: Teens and adults
RUNNING TIME: 127 minutes
STARRING: Ethan Hawke, Vincent Spano, and Josh Hamilton
DIRECTOR: Frank Marshall
BASED ON: The novel by Piers Paul Read
DISTRIBUTOR: Walt Disney Company/Buena Vista Pictures
BRIEF SUMMARY:
A true survival story, complete with heroism, prayer, and conversion, *Alive* is

about the plane full of Uraguayan rugby players that crashed in the Andes on October 13, 1972. *Alive* opens with one survivor reflecting that his time of trial high atop the mountains took him to a spiritual plane where he met "the God who is hidden"—the sovereign Creator. At first, hopes for rescue are high, but then, on the eighth day, the group learns via radio that search operations have been abandoned. Soon they decide to eat their dead comrades to survive, after someone points out that Christians believe that the soul leaves the body when a person dies. After exhausting all possibilities, two embark on a treacherous journey over the Andes to reach Chile and come back with helicopters to rescue the others—seventy days after the plane crash.

Alive is an excruciating but extremely well-directed film that captures the essence of the ordeal faced by the survivors of this catastrophe. Cannibalism is not the focus of the film, rather, faith in a living God versus religious ritual is. As the Scripture intones: "It is a dreadful thing to fall into the hands of the living God" (Hebrews 10:31).

CONTENT ANALYSIS: (B, C, L, V, Ab) A true story of prayer, faith, and self-reliance triumphing over the harshest adversity imaginable, marred by five obscenities, two profanities, and cannibalism.

Answered Prayer

BEETHOVEN'S 2ND

Quality: ☆☆☆☆   Acceptability: +2

WARNING CODES:

Language: *
Violence: None
Sex: *
Nudity: None

RATING: PG
GENRE: Comedy
INTENDED AUDIENCE: All ages

RUNNING TIME: 89 minutes

STARRING: Charles Grodin, Bonnie Hunt, Nicholle Tom, Christopher Castile, Sarah Rose Karr, Debi Mazar, Chris Penn, Maury Chaykin, and Beethoven

DIRECTOR: Rod Daniel

PRODUCERS: Ivan Reitman, Michael C. Gross, and Joe Medjuck

WRITER: Len Blum

BASED ON: Characters by Edmond Dantes and Amy Holden Jones

DISTRIBUTOR: Universal Pictures

BRIEF SUMMARY:

Beethoven's 2nd brings new meaning to the expression "puppy love" to moviegoers of all ages. *Beethoven's 2nd* finds the gentle, good-natured St. Bernard smitten by a demure, feminine ladylove, Missy. While George Newton (Charles Grodin) and his wife, Alice (Bonnie Hunt), struggle with typical financial pressures, their children face their own challenges. Budding, fifteen-year-old Ryce faces peer pressure and younger siblings, while Ted and Emily strive to be noticed and heard. The three are accomplices to Beethoven's big surprise. Moonlight and a warm snuggle mean the rediscovery of the meaning of chaos-times-four: Tchaikovsky, Chubby, Dolly, and Mo, a quartet of irresistible offspring. Trouble arises in the person of Missy's evil owner Regina, who heartlessly separates Beethoven and Missy and plots to steal the puppies. To the delight of the audience, a child's bedtime prayer is answered, and Regina is led to her just desserts by Beethoven and family.

The acting is excellent, but of highest merit is *Beethoven's 2nd*'s beautiful theme song, "The Day I Fall in Love," sung by James Ingram and Dolly Parton. Of course, Beethoven and his family steal the hearts of the audience, as lovers often do. More doesn't always mean better, but in this case it does. *Beethoven's 2nd* is more fun, more adventure, and more excitement.

CONTENT ANALYSIS: (BB, C, L, S, M) Family values and challenges, love and right choices. A no-sex, no-drugs, no-drinking message for teens, although a boyfriend attempts to corner the girl and is thwarted by Beethoven. Brief lying for the protection of the animals gives way to immediate honest replies when confronted by a parent; children show responsibility, good judgment, and logic; the Newtons are a "functional" caring family. One obscenity, some questionable song lyrics, and a brief discussion of "Where do babies come from?"—nothing graphic or explicit.

Sticking Together

BENNY AND JOON

Quality: ✩✩✩✩   Acceptability: –1

WARNING CODES:

Language: *
Violence: *
Sex: *
Nudity: None

RATING: PG

GENRE: Drama

INTENDED AUDIENCE: Teens and adults

RUNNING TIME: 98 minutes

STARRING: Aidan Quinn, Mary Stuart Masterson, and Johnny Depp

DIRECTOR: Jeremiah Checkik

DISTRIBUTOR: MGM

BRIEF SUMMARY:

Benny and Joon is the story of a brother and his disturbed sister trying to cope with adult life after the death of their parents twelve years ago. The resulting anxiety leaves Benny's sister, Joon, unable to handle much of reality. That is, until Sam comes along. This eccentric Buster Keaton clone speaks a language Joon can comprehend. As he reaches out to her, a story of love and compassion unfolds before us.

Beautifully photographed (lighting and composition) and creatively filmed (viewpoints, camera angles, etc.), *Benny and Joon* brings to life the small town of Deer Park, Washington. The soundtrack is quite diverse, but seems to fit the scenes nicely. Aidan Quinn is excellent as the responsible and devoted Benny. There is just enough fatigue in his face to show the burden he carries. Joon is portrayed by Mary Stuart Masterson in a convincing performance. Nearly stealing the show is Johnny Depp as the offbeat but highly talented and resourceful Sam. *Benny and Joon* is a delightful story of love, tragedy, and victory, the only drawbacks being the implied sexual encounter between Joon and Sam and a few obscenities. However, several positive principles are demonstrated: love, which triumphs in the end; forgiveness, exemplified when characters reconcile; friendship, when characters support each other in crisis; and commitment, as the family sticks together.

CONTENT ANALYSIS: (H, B, L, S, V, M) Humanist rendition of biblical principles with four obscenities, one profanity; mild violence in the form of a broken lamp, a brief on-camera scene from a cheap horror movie the characters are watching on video; implied fornication; and gambling.

A Lesson on Losing Gracefully

COOL RUNNINGS

Quality: ☆☆☆☆   Acceptability: −1

WARNING CODES:

Language: *
Violence: *
Sex: None
Nudity: None

RATING: PG
GENRE: Comedy
INTENDED AUDIENCE: Teens and adults
RUNNING TIME: 98 minutes
STARRING: Leon, Doug E. Doug, Rawle D. Lewis, Malik Yoba, and John Candy
DIRECTOR: Jon Turteltaub

EXECUTIVE PRODUCERS: Christopher Meledandri and Susan B. Landau
WRITERS: Lynn Siefert, Tommy Swerdlow, Michael Goldberg, and Michael Ritchie
DISTRIBUTOR: Walt Disney Company/Buena Vista Pictures
BRIEF SUMMARY:
After the disastrous outcome of a 1988 Olympic qualifying trial he was destined to win, Jamaican sprinter Derrice Bannock decides his only chance to follow in his father's footsteps to the Olympic games is as a member of the yet-to-be-formed Jamaican bobsled team, in this Disney comedy adventure *Cool Runnings*. He and four unlikely partners team up to make history as the first bobsled team from a small island country too tropical for snow or ice. They must learn to pull together as a team to have any chance of success in the bobsled competition and bring honor to their country and to themselves.

Cool Runnings is an enjoyable film, with good acting performances. The film is a bit predictable, as most people are familiar with the true story, but it is still quite enjoyable. This is a positive, family-friendly film that promotes friendship, acceptance, integrity, and teamwork, as well as the importance of the support of family. The film also teaches an excellent lesson on competition and the relative importance of winning. A small amount of relatively mild foul language mars this otherwise enjoyable film.

CONTENT ANALYSIS: (BB, L, V, A, D) Moral principles promoted, such as honesty, integrity, hard work, perseverance, self-sacrifice, redemption, and friendship; and cheating is explained as the biggest mistake of one character's life. There are nine mild obscenities, one profanity; brief violence in the form of a short fistfight; and brief alcohol consumption in a bar scene, but teammates drink soda and celebrate a toast with Coca-Cola.

Decent Common Citizen

DAVE

Quality: ☆☆☆   Acceptability: –2

WARNING CODES:
  Language: **
  Violence: None
  Sex: *
  Nudity: **
RATING: PG-13
GENRE: Comedy
INTENDED AUDIENCE: Teens and adults
RUNNING TIME: 110 minutes
STARRING: Kevin Kline, Sigourney Weaver, Frank Langella, and Ben Kingsley
  DIRECTOR: Ivan Reitman
  DISTRIBUTOR: Warner Brothers
  BRIEF SUMMARY:
Dave Kovic becomes a foil for U.S. President Bill Mitchell, who lingers at the point of death. As the story opens, Dave runs a temporary employment agency. The Secret Service is alerted to Dave's resemblance to the president, and he is tapped to fill in for the president in risky situations. Dave's job takes an unexpected turn when the president, in a sexual tryst, becomes a stroke victim. Quickly, Dave takes up residence in the White House and discovers that the president and the First Lady share only their last name. Shortly after arriving at the White House, Dave finds himself caught between the ambitions of powerful people and his own basic ideas of right and wrong. Chief of Staff Bob Alexander soon realizes that Dave will not be anyone's patsy, as his education in the intricacies of power, deception, and intrigue transforms the presidency in a succession of comic maneuvers that rekindle America's belief in the decency of the common citizen.

Dave is an enjoyable film for anyone who appreciates subtle as well as overt humor, though regretably it is marred by a couple of blatant profanities and a discreet sex scene. It is a funny, tongue-in-cheek approach to poking fun at America's time-honored political institutions. Some politically correct elements put a socialist spin on the story.

CONTENT ANALYSIS: (H, B, PC, So, LL, NN, S) A humanist worldview that makes some good biblical points but is politically correct with a hint of socialist solutions. There are ten obscenities, five profanities; a side view of male in shower (nothing shown), and a scene with couple fornicating, but nothing visible.

People Matter

DENNIS THE MENACE

Quality: ☆☆☆☆   Acceptability: +3

WARNING CODES:
  Language: None
  Violence: *
  Sex: None
  Nudity: None
RATING: PG
GENRE: Comedy
INTENDED AUDIENCE: Children and adults
RUNNING TIME: 95 minutes
STARRING: Walter Matthau, Mason Gamble, Christopher Lloyd, Joan Plowright, Lea Thompson, and Robert Stanton
  DIRECTOR: Nick Castle
  PRODUCER: John Hughes
  WRITER: John Hughes
  DISTRIBUTOR: Warner Brothers
  BRIEF SUMMARY:
With slingshot, marbles, wagon, and dog Ruff in tow, Dennis the Menace is a disaster waiting to happen, and he is headed for his favorite next-door neighbor, George Wilson. Walter Matthau is literally on the defensive as the cranky old Mr. Wilson, running for his life from the baby-toothed, towheaded "Menace,"

brought to inexhaustible life by newcomer Mason Gamble. Although a bit spoiled and undisciplined, Dennis is a lovable little rascal who sets out to explore and conquer his summertime surroundings while his mom is off at work. Mr. Wilson usually ends up paying the price for Dennis's out-of-control curiosity and quest for new knowledge. He even brings a few consequences on himself as he foolishly attempts to stay a step ahead of "the Menace." Things don't improve when Switchblade Sam (Christopher Lloyd) arrives in town looking for trouble of his own. However, he doesn't know what trouble is until he meets Dennis. It takes near tragedy to show Mr. Wilson that even though Dennis drives him crazy, Dennis gives him a reason for living.

Dennis the Menace is a harmless, entertaining, fun treat for children of all ages. The film portrays a way of life where children are still allowed to be children—happy and safe—neighbors look out for each other, and people and relationships are valued and important. Christopher Lloyd is great as the nasty villain, and Joan Plowright is everyone's dream of a grandmother.

CONTENT ANALYSIS: (B, C, V, M) A biblical worldview complete with biblical principles, neighbors helping each other, families intact and functional, and respect for authority, friendship, and responsibility. This is marred by mild, slapstick violence (tacks in fingers, people falling down and struck by objects—regrettably several times in groin area—but nothing serious), a little rowdiness (little Margaret asks Joey to close his eyes, then fools him into kissing her doll's behind); brief make-out scene involving babysitter and boyfriend; and one character smokes and steals, but answers for his crimes.

ELE, MY FRIEND

Quality: ☆☆☆   Acceptability: +2

WARNING CODES:

Language: None
Violence: *
Sex: None
Nudity: None

RATING: Not rated
GENRE: Adventure/Drama
INTENDED AUDIENCE: Children and adults
RUNNING TIME: 104 minutes
STARRING: Jacob Paul Guzman, Gazan Khan, and R. S. Shivaji
DIRECTOR: Dharan Mandrayar
PRODUCER: Dharan Mandrayar
WRITER: Dharan Mandrayar
DISTRIBUTOR: Video Communications, Inc.

BRIEF SUMMARY:
Like the boy-and-his-beast friendship in *The Black Stallion*, *Ele, My Friend* is the delightful story of a young boy, Charles, who befriends a wild elephant and ends up learning the true meaning of friendship and parental relationship. Set on a lush tea plantation in Southern India, Charles's parental home, the ten-year-old boy sneaks off to a favorite water hole where he discovers a family of elephants. Among them he finds a baby elephant, Ele, whom he befriends, and they spend many happy hours together. When his mother decides to send him to boarding school in England to become a "gentleman," Charles goes to say goodbye to Ele, only to find that some evil men have captured him. Charles proves his friendship as he pursues and saves Ele.

Beautifully photographed in the Mudmalai Wildlife Sanctuary of Southern India, and fraught with stunning images of wild elephants, *Ele, My Friend* harks back to the simple, innocent family films of Disney in the 1950s and 1960s. Devoid of politically correct ecological statements and deep, pseudo-psychological complexities, the movie is a wonderful visual treat revealing the simple friendship between a boy and a beast. Through Ele, Charles learns friendship's real meaning and also how to relate to his parents in a loving way. *Ele, My Friend* is a rare, gentle movie that will satisfy the viewer.

CONTENT ANALYSIS: (B, V, M) The story of childhood disobedience and deception that brings true repentance, i.e., a child who recognizes he has done wrong and seeks to remedy his ways; and mild violence.

Family and Friendship Are Important

African Adventures

A FAR OFF PLACE

Quality: ☆☆☆☆   Acceptability: −1

WARNING CODES:
  Language: **
  Violence: **
  Sex: None
  Nudity: None
RATING: G
GENRE: Romance/Adventure/Drama
INTENDED AUDIENCE: Older children to adults
RUNNING TIME: 100 minutes
STARRING: Reese Witherspoon, Ethan Randall, Sarel Bok, Jack Thompson, and Maximilian Schell
DIRECTOR: Mikael Salomon
PRODUCER: Kathleen Kennedy
WRITER: Robert Caswell
BASED ON: Two novels *A Story Like the Wind* and *A Far Off Place* by Laurens van der Post
DISTRIBUTOR: Walt Disney Company/Buena Vista Pictures
BRIEF SUMMARY:
Harry Winslow quickly finds that southwestern Africa is anything but "bone-dry and boring" in the politically correct adventure, *A Far Off Place.* Under duress, Harry has gone to Africa with his dad to visit lifelong friends, the Parkers. Mr. Parker works as a commissioner of wildlife. As the movie begins, Mr. Parker is struggling with the alarming problem of elephant poaching. In the predawn, while his daughter, Nonnie, and guest Harry are spending the night in a nearby cave with African friend, Xhabbo, the Parkers, and Harry's father are mercilessly killed and their house destroyed. Of course, the attackers also meant to get Harry and quick-witted Nonnie, who witnesses some of the destruction of her home. So the chase begins. Xhabbo suggests they take the least likely route to safety—a trek across the one-thousand-mile Kalahari desert.

A Far Off Place is a skillfully made and directed movie with competent acting. Movies that are this sexually wholesome are comparatively scarce. However, there is fairly graphic violence in the film, such as when the poachers kill the game warden and his wife. Furthermore, the subtle animistic and politically correct New Age philosophies set forth in the film cannot be commended. Sadly, the movie also portrays Nonnie's foul language as funny, and thus encourages it for children who might see the film. However, the movie also exemplifies the biblical principle that all-consuming greed leads to self-destruction.

CONTENT ANALYSIS: (E, PC, H, LL, VV, Pa, B) This politically correct environmental adventure story, with its sweeping African vistas, contains a surprising amount of language and violence (given the "G" rating) and is unsuitable for small children. Some positive biblical principles are marred by seven obscenities, one profanity uttered by a child, some rather vivid violence, and native African mysticism (a "tapping" ritual) and animism.

Breaking Free from Bondage

THE FIRM

Quality: ☆☆☆   Acceptability: −2

WARNING CODES:
  Language: ***

Violence: ***
Sex: *
Nudity: None
RATING: R
GENRE: Mystery/Drama
INTENDED AUDIENCE: Older teens and adults
RUNNING TIME: 154 minutes
STARRING: Tom Cruise, Gene Hackman, Jeanne Tripplehorn, Ed Harris, Holly Hunter, Hal Holbrook, and David Strathairn
DIRECTOR: Sydney Pollack
PRODUCERS: Scott Rudin, John A. Davis, and Sydney Pollack
WRITERS: David Rabe, Robert Towne, and David Rayfiel
BASED ON: The novel by John Grisham
DISTRIBUTOR: Paramount Pictures
BRIEF SUMMARY:
The Firm opens with various law firms courting Harvard Law School honors graduate Mitch McDeere (Tom Cruise). Shortly, the Memphis firm of Bendini, Lambert, and Locke discretely presents their offer in a sealed envelope, which McDeere chooses not to open. Mitch is razor sharp, ambitious, and happily married. Mitch and Abby are drawn into a sophisticated, prestigious lifestyle in which everything is provided. However, when a diving accident occurs involving some lawyers from the firm, Mitch and Abby are troubled. On a business trip, Mitch finds files that confirm his worse suspicions: The firm is a front for the Mafia, and no one has ever left the firm— alive. From this point on, Mitch develops a strategy to be the first one to leave the firm. However, the firm covers their bases to control him. On the line for Mitch is his desire to maintain his oath as a lawyer, to uphold the law, but at the same time to break free from the firm.
The Firm is a suspense-filled, well-directed movie that will keep viewers on the edge of their seats. The movie illustrates that each of us, like Mitch, has to choose whether to do the right thing or make himself rich. Regrettably, the movie is laced with obscenity, profanity, adultery, sexual immorality, and extreme violence.
CONTENT ANALYSIS: (H, B, LLL, M, S, VVV) Humanist worldview that emphasizes some biblical principles; forty-five obscenities, fifteen profanities; revenge, blackmail, fraud, and payoffs (all part of the plot). Also adultery, implied sexual immorality, and extreme violence in scenes where mob hunts intended victims.

Family Matters

FREE WILLY

Quality: ☆☆☆☆   Acceptability: +3

WARNING CODES:
Language: None
Violence: *
Sex: None
Nudity: None

RATING: PG
GENRE: Action/Adventure
INTENDED AUDIENCE: All ages
RUNNING TIME: 112 minutes
STARRING: Jason James Richter, Lori Petty, and Michael Madsen
DIRECTOR: Simon Wincer
PRODUCERS: Jenny Lew Tugend and Lauren Shuler-Donner
WRITERS: Keith A. Walker and Corey Blechman
BASED ON: The story by Keith A. Walker
DISTRIBUTOR: Warner Brothers
BRIEF SUMMARY:
In *Free Willy*, twelve-year-old Jesse is in desperate need of love and the security of a family and recognizes similar needs in his newfound friend Willy, a 7000-pound killer whale. Jesse is running from the law, as well as his last foster home, when he is caught defacing walls and windows at an adventure park. While cleaning up the mess he has made, Jesse meets Willy and is amazed

and intrigued by the enormous creature. Willy takes notice when the youngster stops his work to play his harmonica. The sound attracts the orca and an amazing friendship begins. Jesse comes to understand Willy's struggle living in the North West Adventure Park and knows there can be only one solution—to free Willy.

Jason James Richter makes his feature film debut as the troubled and rebellious Jesse. His portrayal of a hurting young boy who needs love is accurate and believable. An excellent case is made in support of the family and the undeniable benefits of keeping the family intact. Shot in the Pacific Northwest with some beautiful ocean scenes and scenic photography, this film is well made and clean, to the point of being refreshing. Even the "bad guy" isn't sadistic or twisted. The acting is adequate for the storyline. *Free Willy* is a great treat and suitable for the entire family.

CONTENT ANALYSIS: (B, C, E, V, FR, Pa) A wholesome film that emphasizes the Christian principles of love, acceptance, restitution, and redemption as well as the vital need for and importance of family and an emphasis on the proper and kind treatment of animals. Good triumphs over evil and greed; a car crashes through a gate, with no injuries; however, there is a reference to Indian lore and a boy repeats a prayer by an ancient Indian figure (this is actually a Native American Christian prayer!). Also, there is a slight anthropomorphic representation of the whale.

The Truth Will Set Us Free

THE FUGITIVE

Quality: ☆☆☆☆   Acceptability: −2

WARNING CODES:
Language: ***
Violence: **
Sex: None

Nudity: None
RATING: PG-13
GENRE: Action/Adventure
INTENDED AUDIENCE: Adults
RUNNING TIME: 130 minutes
STARRING: Harrison Ford, Tommy Lee Jones, Joe Pantoliano, Julianne Moore, and Sela Ward
DIRECTOR: Andrew Davis
PRODUCERS: Roy Huggins and Keith Barish
WRITERS: Jeb Stuart and David Twohy
DISTRIBUTOR: Warner Brothers
BRIEF SUMMARY:
Unjustly convicted of the murder of his wife, Dr. Richard Kimble is en route to prison when a fateful train crash sets him free to embark on a desperate quest to prove his innocence and expose his wife's real killer. Harrison Ford stars in *The Fugitive*, an exciting and suspenseful thriller, reminiscent of the 1960s TV series, that promises to keep viewers on the edge of their seats. Tommy Lee Jones leads the dogged chase as the cagey deputy U.S. Marshall, Sam Gerard.

The Fugitive definitely does justice to the memory of the original story, while adding a few twists and turns of its own. The photography and directing are both excellent: night scenes of the city of Chicago, chase scenes through a sewer maze, hospital trauma-room action (where a disguised Dr. Kimble changes a young boy's wrong diagnosis, thereby saving his life), and, of course, the incredible train/bus crash. There is a fair amount of foul language, provided mostly by supporting cast (further proving its needlessness), but no nudity or sex, and the violence is not gory or bloody to excess. The train crash is realistic, however, as is the aftermath of the murder scene. Kimble's dream-time memories of his deceased wife are also treated with good taste. If it were not for the foul language, *The Fugitive* would be a highly recommended adult action-thriller, although it is definitely not for children.

CONTENT ANALYSIS: (B, LLL, VV, M, PC) This "truth will set you free" tale is marred by thirty obscenities and four profanities (few of which come from the two main characters); realistically violent train wreck with severe injuries, somewhat bloody scene of aftermath of a woman's murder (but not gory), man struggles with intruder, and a fistfight scene. Deceit, deception, and murder are part of the plot, and one character wears red AIDS ribbon and button saying, "Hate Is Not a Family Value."

History Comes Alive

GETTYSBURG

Quality: ☆☆☆☆   Acceptability: −1

WARNING CODES:

Language: ***
Violence: ***
Sex: None
Nudity: None

RATING: PG
GENRE: Civil War drama
INTENDED AUDIENCE: Older teens and adults
RUNNING TIME: 261 minutes
STARRING: Tom Berenger, Martin Sheen, Stephen Lang, Richard Jordan, Jeff Daniels, Sam Elliott, C. Thomas Howell, Kevin Conway, Andrew Prine, Maxwell Caulfield, James Lancaster, Royce Applegate, and Brian Mallon
DIRECTOR: Ronald F. Maxwell
PRODUCERS: Robert Katz and Moctesuma Esparza
WRITER: Ronald F. Maxwell
BASED ON: The novel *The Killer Angels* by Michael Shaara
DISTRIBUTOR: Turner Pictures / Fine Line Cinema
BRIEF SUMMARY: Ron Maxwell's epic film *Gettysburg*, based on Michael Shaara's Pulitzer Prize-winning novel *The Killer Angels*, dramatically depicts the three most courageous days in American history, when North and South were arrayed against each other in the decisive battle fought on the Gettysburg, Pennsylvania, plains. General Robert E. Lee (Martin Sheen) believes he can end the war with a decisive victory over Federal troops by taking Gettysburg, then marching on Washington with an offer of peace. In the decisive battle, Lee orders Major General George Pickett and his division to advance across an open field in order to capture the entrenched Union forces. Pickett's division of fifteen thousand men suffers tremendous losses, and the next morning Lee's remaining army is in full retreat.

The epic movie admirably re-creates the events of those fateful days. The excellent acting and directing make history live again. The scenes reenacting Pickett's charge are believed to be the largest period-scale sequences filmed in North America since D. W. Griffith's *Birth of a Nation.* The film overflows with positive references to God and prayer. Of course, as in any epic there are moments that drag and a surplus of profanities are used by the soldiers. However, overall, *Gettysburg* is a magnificent movie that should be viewed by every American.

CONTENT ANALYSIS: (B, C, LLL, VVV) Frequent references to God and his will for our lives and frequent prayers with the theme that whatever happened at Gettysburg was God's will. Over forty obscenities and eight exclamatory profanities used by the soldiers, and war-fighting violence.

Faith without Works Is Dead

GROUNDHOG DAY

Quality: ☆☆☆☆   Acceptability: −1

WARNING CODES:

Language: *
Violence: *
Sex: *

Nudity: None
RATING: PG
GENRE: Comedy
INTENDED AUDIENCE: Older teens and adults
RUNNING TIME: 101 minutes
STARRING: Bill Murray, Andie MacDowell, Chris Elliott, and Stephen Tobolowsky
DIRECTOR: Harold Ramis
PRODUCER: Trevor Albert
WRITER: Danny Rubin
DISTRIBUTOR: Columbia Pictures
BRIEF SUMMARY:
Being forced to live the same day repeatedly, Phil Connors (Bill Murray) learns that there has to be more to life than a meaningless Groundhog Day. Set in Punxsutawney, Pennsylvania, Phil, a TV weatherman, has been sent to cover the annual Groundhog Day festivities and finds himself caught in a time warp. The alarm relentlessly wakes him with Sonny and Cher's "I Got You, Babe." Stretching in his room, Phil is set for a day of recurring incidents, no surprises, and no consequences, so he can do whatever he wants. However, experiencing all that life can offer, Phil has a change of heart and becomes the ultimate moral human being: he saves lives, spreads cheer, and acquires culture. He has learned the error of his ways—but is his goodness enough to save him?

Although *Groundhog Day* emphasizes that man desires not to be accountable for his deeds, it falsely implies that man can save himself from his sinful propensities. Even so, the film is hilarious, light-hearted, and lots of fun. In the end, the movie may remind viewers of the adage in the book of James, that "faith without works is dead." Thus, by the end of the story, Phil realizes the value of helping other people and learns to think about them before thinking about his own needs.

CONTENT ANALYSIS: (H, B, L, V, S) Humanist rendition of the biblical prin-

ciple that one can only gain one's life by giving of one's self. Slightly marred by two mild obscenities and two exclamatory profanities; moderate violence in suicide attempts in fantasy context; sexually suggestive dialogue with references to intercourse and one passionate kissing scene; two incidents referring to homosexuality; and man mentioned as being homosexual and man with stereotypical homosexual behavior.

Icy Conflict

GRUMPY OLD MEN

Quality: ☆☆☆   Acceptability: −2

WARNING CODES:
  Language: ***
  Violence: None
  Sex: *
  Nudity: None
RATING: PG-13
GENRE: Comedy
INTENDED AUDIENCE: Teens and adults
RUNNING TIME: 103 minutes
STARRING: Jack Lemmon, Walter Matthau, and Ann Margret
DIRECTOR: Donald Petrie
DISTRIBUTOR: Warner Brothers
BRIEF SUMMARY:
In *Grumpy Old Men*, John Gustafson (Jack Lemmon) and Max Goldman (Walter Matthau) are lifelong enemies living out the waning years of their lives as next-door neighbors in a small Minnesota town. Both widowed and retired, their main activity is to go ice fishing every day. When Ariel Truax (Ann-Margret) moves across the street, both men court her. Earlier, they had both dated the same woman, but John married her, and all their lives they have feuded because of it. Ariel befriends both men, but prefers John, and so the three-way love triangle becomes a reality once more. John, in love, nevertheless abandons the affections of Ariel to give Max the opportunity to even

the score between them and to have a chance at happiness.

The movie has several obscenities and profanities. There is also an implied sexual liaison, but nothing is shown. By revealing John's fifteen-year celibacy and Ariel's five-year celibacy (since the death of both their spouses), Hollywood has attempted to show restraint and personal responsibility for acts of intimacy. However, because Hollywood still doesn't understand that everything happens under the eyes of God, their union falls short of a moral sexual relationship. Even so, the acting by all three of these longtime actors—Lemmon, Matthau, and Ann-Margret—is delightful and commendable.

CONTENT ANALYSIS: (H, B, LLL, S) Humanist worldview that emphasizes some biblical principles, ten obscenities, fifteen profanities, sexual innuendo, and reference to a senior citizen's post-marital sexual encounter.

Biblical Messages

HOMEWARD BOUND: THE INCREDIBLE JOURNEY

Quality: ☆☆☆☆   Acceptability: +4

WARNING CODES:
  Language: None
  Violence: *
  Sex: None
  Nudity: None
RATING: G
GENRE: Drama
INTENDED AUDIENCE: All ages
RUNNING TIME: 84 minutes
STARRING: Robert Hays, Kim Geist, Veronica Lauren, Kevin Chevalia, and Benj Thall
VOICES: Michael J. Fox, Sally Fields, and Don Ameche
DIRECTOR: Duwayne Dunham
PRODUCERS: Donald W. Ernst and Kirk Wise
WRITERS: Caroline Thompson and Linda Woolverton
DISTRIBUTOR: Walt Disney Company/Buena Vista Pictures
BRIEF SUMMARY:

Separated from their human family, three domesticated pets brave the Pacific Northwest wilderness as they embark on a perilous mission to find their masters. An excellent family film, *Homeward Bound: The Incredible Journey* delicately affirms the importance of family, self-sacrifice, responsibility, and love. The story begins with the vacation-bound Seaver family dropping off their pets with friend Kate, who lives on a farm. Life on Kate's farm is fun for Chance, an American bulldog puppy with a big appetite and a nose for trouble; Sassy, a sophisticated Himalayan cat; and Shadow, a wise, faithful, and elderly golden retriever. Insight into animal behavior is provided through comical voiceovers for each pet. Michael J. Fox adds laughs as Chance (whose risk-taking and curiosity earns him his name), Sally Fields adds virtuous femininity as Sassy, and Don Ameche adds a seasoned, grandfatherly touch as Shadow. As the story continues, Kate leaves things in the hands of another farmer for a few days, and the pets assume they've been abandoned and attempt to find their way back home through the wilderness.

Movieguide wholeheartedly recommends *Homeward Bound: The Incredible Journey* for all ages. However, the movie contains some brief semi-violent elements that are essential to the storyline.

CONTENT ANALYSIS: (B, M, V) Biblical messages of family, self-sacrifice, love, and responsibility, slightly marred by a few instances of name-calling, a negative characterization of an overweight guard, and semi-violent elements essential to the storyline (cat falls in water and is consumed by undertow of rapids, porcupine needles stick in dog's muzzle, dog falls in ditch, and confrontations with wild animals).

Honoring Professionalism and Self-Sacrifice

IN THE LINE OF FIRE

Quality: ☆☆☆☆   Acceptability: −2

WARNING CODES:
   Language: ***
   Violence: **
   Sex: *
   Nudity: None
RATING: R
GENRE: Action/Adventure
INTENDED AUDIENCE: Older
teens and adults
RUNNING TIME: 128 minutes
STARRING: Clint Eastwood, John
Malkovich, Rene Russo, Dylan
McDermott, Gary Cole, and Fred
Dalton Thompson
   DIRECTOR: Wolfgang Petersen
   PRODUCER: Jeff Apple
   WRITER: Jeff Maguire
   DISTRIBUTOR: Columbia Pictures
   BRIEF SUMMARY:
   In the Line of Fire dramatizes the nerve-
wracking task of protecting a president
during a whirlwind campaign and serves
up a riveting duel between a tough but
vulnerable Secret Service agent and a dia-
bolically clever assassin. In the harrowing
opening sequence, we watch veteran
agent Frank Horrigan (Clint Eastwood)
save his rookie partner from execution.
Horrigan is haunted by the events of
November 22, 1963, and the nagging
remorse that a quicker reaction on his
part might have saved JFK from the infamous head wound. The traumatic memory of death in Dallas becomes a living
nightmare when Horrigan accidentally
crosses paths with the most malignant
adversary of his long career, Mitch Leary
(John Malkovich, in a searing characterization), a cruel and relentless killer who is
absolutely determined to assassinate the
president.
   One of the many strengths of *In the
Line of Fire* is its cleverness at revealing
bits and pieces of Leary's identity a little

at a time. The language, unfortunately,
becomes intense in several scenes,
although obscenity does not flow gratu-
itously throughout the film. There are
also brief outbursts of cops-and-crooks
violence. On the other hand, *In the Line of
Fire* is a great political thriller. Most
important, it honors professionalism and
self-sacrifice, qualities that have recently
been in far too short supply on the big
screen.
   CONTENT ANALYSIS: (H, B, LLL,
VV) Humanistic worldview that inadvertently emphasizes some biblical principles, thirty-eight obscenities, eighteen
profanities, multiple brief bursts of violence including approximately ten shootings and two fistfights, two women
killed when necks broken by assassin,
brief views of autopsy photos, and positive overall portrayal of Secret Service
agents as heroic professionals.

A Quiet Faith

IN THE NAME OF THE FATHER

Quality: ☆☆☆   Acceptability: −2

WARNING CODES:
   Language: ***
   Violence: **
   Sex: *
   Nudity: **
RATING: R
GENRE: Drama
INTENDED AUDIENCE: Older
teens and adults
RUNNING TIME: 133 minutes
STARRING: Daniel Day-Lewis, Pete
Postlethwaite, and Emma Thompson
   DIRECTOR: Jim Sheridan
   BASED ON: The book *Proved
Innocent* by Gerry Conlon
   DISTRIBUTOR: Universal Pictures
   BRIEF SUMMARY:
   The film *In the Name of the Father* tells
the story of Irish teenager Gerry Conlon
(Daniel Day-Lewis) who goes to London
in the 1960s to live in a hippie commune

to enjoy free love and dope. He sees his father as lacking the courage to rise above his working-class station. While Gerry visits his family in Belfast, the police raid the commune and take members in for questioning about a bombing. His friend names Gerry as the leader and, after days of interrogation, Gerry signs a false confession. When his father comes to London to get an attorney for his son, he is arrested too. Both receive life sentences. A young attorney, Ms. Pierce, takes an interest in them and, when she discovers suppressed evidence, moves to have the case retried. During the fifteen years Gerry and his father share a cell, Gerry learns how strong his father's faith is.

This is an absorbing, dramatic presentation about an innocent man's struggle to make sense of a seemingly unjust system. Although the film makes a strong statement about the roots of prejudice, the ultimate triumph of justice, and the strength of a quiet faith, the dialogue is filled with obscenity and profanity, the interrogation is intense, and physical abuse and male nudity is shown. Unfortunately, it has too many negative aspects in telling a positive story.

CONTENT ANALYSIS: (CC, B, LLL, VV, S, NN, D, Ho, M) Christian worldview with some biblical principles— father helps son and positive portrayal of faith and prayer. Ninety-four obscenities, six profanities, six vulgarities, violence in form of fighting, gun-play, man set on fire, and explosion. Implied promiscuity, male nudity, drug abuse, implied homosexuality, and ethnic prejudice.

A Rare Classic for Older Audiences

THE JOY LUCK CLUB

Quality: ✰✰✰✰   Acceptability: −2

WARNING CODES:
  Language: *
  Violence: **
  Sex: *
  Nudity: None
RATING: R
GENRE: Drama
INTENDED AUDIENCE: Older teens and adults
RUNNING TIME: 139 minutes
STARRING: Ming-Na Wen, Kieu Chinh, Tsai Chin, France Nuyen, Lisa Lu, Tamlyn Tomita, Lauren Tom, and Rosalind Chao
DIRECTOR: Wayne Wang
WRITERS: Amy Tan and Ronald Bass
BASED ON: The novel by Amy Tan
DISTRIBUTOR: Hollywood Pictures
BRIEF SUMMARY:
The Joy Luck Club tells the story of two generations of Chinese women and their American daughters. The story begins when June is invited to join the Joy Luck Club, a weekly Mahjong group. She takes her dead mother's place in the group along with her three "aunties." The three older women begin to tell her their guarded and hidden secrets, their deep hurts, and their devastating pasts in a China that maintained a strict religious and caste system that discriminated against women. June acts as a kind of reflector and sounding board as the women seek to unite past with present, Eastern culture with Western culture, and try to find a sense of peace and forgiveness from their turbulent pasts. The hopes of the mothers for the daughters they fiercely cherish spreads echoes of love throughout this entire film.

The Joy Luck Club is truly a rare and epic classic, transcending temporal, cultural, and economic birthrights. Each scene ushers the viewer majestically into the hearts and souls of these heroic Chinese women with an ever deeper admiration as their transparent lives unfold before us. The acting is excellent and each scene is flawless—together they build toward an overwhelming emotional climax. However, as might be expected, there is a great deal of violence against women and there are abusive acts against infants, women, and children.

CONTENT ANALYSIS: (C, H, O, L, S, VV, B) Christian worldview with humanist and occult elements where the heroes of this film live in unresolved grief until they reach out and look for true forgiveness and love. Seven obscenities and profanities; brief scene suggesting fornication and adultery; violence against women and those of lower social class along with jarring discrimination of them; abusive acts against infants, women, and children; mental and sexual abuse in several scenes; and one alarming scene when a terribly abused and distraught woman takes the life of her child while bathing him.

Courage in the Mouth of Danger

JURASSIC PARK

Quality: ✩✩✩✩   Acceptability: −2

WARNING CODES:
 Language: *
 Violence: ***
 Sex: None
 Nudity: None
RATING: PG-13
GENRE: Science fiction
INTENDED AUDIENCE: Families
RECOMMENDED AUDIENCE:
Older teens and adults
 RUNNING TIME: 127 minutes
 STARRING: Sam Neill, Laura Dern, Jeff Goldblum, and Richard Attenborough
 DIRECTOR: Steven Spielberg
 PRODUCERS: Kathleen Kennedy and Gerald R. Molen
 WRITERS: Michael Crichton and David Koepp
 BASED ON: The novel by Michael Crichton
 DISTRIBUTOR: Universal Pictures
 BRIEF SUMMARY:
Jurassic Park, the much-touted science fiction thriller about genetically

cloned dinosaurs—directed by Steven Spielberg and avidly promoted as a family film—turns out to be an excessively violent and frightening film that is bound to scare young children. When Jurassic Park designer John Hammond invites two scientists, his two young grandchildren, and a visiting mathematician to take a park tour to certify the safety of his new dinosaur theme park, a violent storm and a greedy computer operator shut down the computers and the electric power and place the people at the mercy of the dinosaurs, who go on a rampage stalking and eating the humans. A resolution is achieved at film's end, but not without numerous terrifying scenes in the interim. It is definitely not for children under thirteen.

Spielberg's directing must be commended for the film's realistic dinosaurs and for the technical wizardry, though the story and human characters leave much to be desired. However, perhaps like John Hammond, Steven Spielberg has gotten too caught up in the marketing of this creation and forgotten his responsibility to those who see it. It is instructive that Spielberg said that he would not take his children to see *Jurassic Park*.

CONTENT ANALYSIS: (E, B, L, VVV) Environmental message mixed with a positive though offhanded statement about creation combined with six obscenities, three profanities, and excessive frightening violence with dinosaurs on a rampage who stalk and devour people.

Surviving the Great Depression

KING OF THE HILL

Quality: ✩✩✩✩   Acceptability: −2

WARNING CODES:
 Language: *
 Violence: *
 Sex: *
 Nudity: None

RATING: PG-13

GENRE: Drama

INTENDED AUDIENCE: Teens and adults

RUNNING TIME: 109 minutes

STARRING: Jesse Bradford, Jeroen Krabbe, Lisa Eichorn, Joseph Chrest, Spalding Gray, Elizabeth McGovern, Karen Allen, and Adrien Brody

DIRECTOR: Steven Soderbergh

PRODUCER: Barbara Maltby, Albert Berger, and Ron Yerxa

WRITER: Steven Soderbergh

BASED ON: The novel by A. E. Hotchner

DISTRIBUTOR: Universal Pictures/Gramercy Pictures

BRIEF SUMMARY: Based on an autobiographical novel set in St. Louis during the Great Depression, *King of the Hill* is an exquisitely crafted and poignant tale of a boy who survives abandonment and deprivation. We first meet Aaron Kurlander, an excellent student, in his eighth-grade classroom, bluffing through a class exercise in which he claims to be linked to the rich and famous. He and his family actually live in a deteriorating hotel with other down-on-their luck individuals who fight continually to avoid eviction. Aaron's father sells decorative candles door-to-door, his mother has a worrisome cough, and to conserve their meager income the parents agree to send Aaron's brother, Sullivan, to live with a relative. When the father gets a better sales job in another state, Aaron has to remain alone in the hotel for a time. This situation taxes Aaron's resilience, but in the end the family is reunited.

While its finale is emotionally satisfying, the trials that form the core of the story may leave the viewer wrung out and make it unsuitable for children. However, there is food for thought about the value of an intact family bearing up under adversity and preserving moral values in a crisis situation. Regrettably, Aaron's lying (mainly to save face) and petty thievery are moral issues with which this film never comes to grips.

CONTENT ANALYSIS: (H, B, L, V, S) Humanistic worldview that inadvertently emphasizes some biblical principles; four profanities; sexual immorality implied; one brief fistfight, police (primarily one character) portrayed as brutal and bigoted, lying and thievery, brief view of bloody suicide victim; and the struggle of the adolescent protagonist to survive during prolonged separation from family is very intense for younger children.

Caught between Two Worlds

THE LAST ACTION HERO

Quality: ☆☆☆   Acceptability: −2

WARNING CODES:

Language: **

Violence: ***

Sex: *

Nudity: *

RATING: PG-13

GENRE: Fantasy

INTENDED AUDIENCE: Older teens and adults

RUNNING TIME: 130 minutes

STARRING: Arnold Schwarzenegger, Austin O'Brien, Art Carney, Charles Dance, Anthony Quinn, and Robert Prosky

DIRECTOR: John McTiernan

PRODUCERS: Arnold Schwarzenegger, Steve Roth, and John McTiernan

WRITERS: Zak Penn and Adam Leff

DISTRIBUTOR: Columbia Pictures

BRIEF SUMMARY: Danny Madigan (Austin O'Brien) idolizes fictional action hero Jack Slater (Arnold Schwarzenegger), and even skips school to see his movies. When an eccentric theater owner (Art Carney) gives Danny a mysterious ticket that magically transports him into the latest Jack Slater adventure film, Danny finds himself in the middle of a make-believe world where the good guys always win and all the women are gorgeous. In this movie-within-a-movie, Danny pairs up with L.A. cop Slater to find the killer of Slater's favorite second cousin. However, Danny and Slater soon have to cross over into the real world to catch the villain.

In the Jack Slater film, people are beaten, shot, blown up, set afire, and stabbed. The violence isn't graphic—no one actually sheds blood—but it is continuous. Violence is treated casually in the movie-within-a-movie and has no consequences, but when Jack and Danny step into real life, violence causes real suffering. One of the most troubling features of this movie is that Danny, only eleven years old, uses a gun in both the Jack Slater film and in reality. Although he never actually shoots anyone, he does discover that waving a gun around gets results. Besides the violence, *The Last Action Hero* also contains a moderate amount of obscenities, including one instance of the "f-word." Although imaginative and sometimes amusing, *The Last Action Hero* is not a family film.

CONTENT ANALYSIS: (H, B, LL, N, S, M, VVV) Humanistic worldview with biblical principles; over ten obscenities and three profanities; scantily glad women; sexual innuendo; political satire; and, excessive nonstop violence (although mostly without blood and gore). However, Arnold Schwarzenegger's character does say, "God, save me from all of this."

A Comical Study of Bitterness

LOST IN YONKERS

Quality: ✰✰✰✰   Acceptability: −1

WARNING CODES:

Language: *
Violence: *
Sex: *
Nudity: None
RATING: PG
GENRE: Comedy

INTENDED AUDIENCE: Older children to adults
RUNNING TIME: 114 minutes
STARRING: Richard Dreyfuss and Mercedes Ruehl
DIRECTOR: Martha Coolidge
PRODUCER: Ray Stark
WRITER: Neil Simon
DISTRIBUTOR: Columbia Pictures
BASED ON: The play by Neil Simon
BRIEF SUMMARY:
Based on Neil Simon's play, *Lost in Yonkers* presents a hilarious and sometimes sorrowful array of diverse characters who come together to love, hate, or escape. Set in 1942 Yonkers, New York, Jay and Arty are two young boys whose mother has recently died. They are forced to live with their stoic, difficult, Jewish grandmother for the summer while their father works in a scrap-metal yard. The grandmother makes her home above a candy store and has a reputation for hitting her family with her cane. The boys are greeted by their aunt Bella (Mercedes Ruehl)—a spacey remnant of a child caught in a woman's body. Aunt Bella lives with her mother, and has been ensnared by her mother's strict control. Jay and Arty adore Bella because she offers solace in the midst of bitter chaos. Aunt Gert offers comic relief as she makes humorous sounds when she speaks. Meanwhile, Uncle Louie (Richard Dreyfuss), a local thug, teaches the boys how to play cards, steal, and puff on his cigarette. When they help him escape from his enemies, they think they have accomplished something.

The artistic quality of this movie is excellent. The conflict between the characters is intensified by the grandmother's fascination for brutality. The movie contains insight into human nature. The characters are real, not stereotypical. The movie demonstrates how bitterness can destroy a person's life, and how it can defile many. Regrettably, the uncle is a poor role model for children.

CONTENT ANALYSIS: (H, L, S, V, A, D, M) Humanist worldview; crude reference to male genitalia; eight profanities and one obscenity; man steals from his mother's store; man hits boy in the face, shoot-out with gangsters, no one is killed; man kisses woman and both fall to the ground with man on top—fully clothed; one character believes that crime pays and that each person has to make a "splash" in life or be forgotten; and children are taught to steal and smoke cigarettes.

Brotherly Disputes

MAC

Quality: ✫✫✫✫   Acceptability: −2

WARNING CODES:

Language: ***
Violence: ***
Sex: *
Nudity: **

RATING: R
GENRE: Drama
INTENDED AUDIENCE: Older teens and adults
RUNNING TIME: 110 minutes
STARRING: John Turturro, Michael Badalucco, Carol Capotorto, and Katherine Borowitz
DIRECTOR: John Turturro
PRODUCERS: Nancy Tenenbaum and Brenda Goodman
WRITERS: John Turturro and Brandon Cole
DISTRIBUTOR: Samuel Goldwyn
BRIEF SUMMARY: Using house building as a metaphor for life, the film *Mac* explores the relationships between three brothers from a working-class Italian family in Queens in the early 1950s. Starring John Turturro as Mac, the film is also his directorial debut and deals with autobiographical material from Turturro's life. Turturro says of his film, "My father was a builder. He was also a great actor, the King Lear of his

day—a very expressive man in a very expressive world." After their father's death, the Vitelli brothers, under Mac's leadership, begin their own construction business. However, as the pressures of the family business take their toll on the Vitellis, each of the brothers must decide whether the memory of his father and ties to the family are more important than his own desires and dreams. Turturro clarifies that "it's a raw film influenced by the neo-realists.... These are people who would go head-to-head with each other during the morning and then have lunch together."

Despite considerable foul language and a rather distasteful bathroom scene with the three brothers performing daily functions, *Mac* is an exceptional film. The actors are superb, and the overall thrust of the plot proves powerful. Although the brothers have tremendous love and respect for each other, their difficulties with simple communication and seeing things from each other's point of view proves their undoing.

CONTENT ANALYSIS: (H, LLL, NN, S, VVV) Humanism; roughly forty crude obscenities and three profanities; partial male nudity in bathroom scene and veiled upper female nudity in bedroom scene—once with prostitute, the other within context of marriage; considerable fighting between men on various construction sites and also between brothers.

Looking for a Father Figure

THE MAN WITHOUT A FACE

Quality: ✫✫✫✫   Acceptability: −1

WARNING CODES:

Language: **
Violence: *
Sex: *
Nudity: None

RATING: PG-13
GENRE: Drama
INTENDED AUDIENCE: Adults

RUNNING TIME: 114 minutes

STARRING: Mel Gibson and Nick Stahl

DIRECTOR: Mel Gibson

PRODUCERS: Steve McEveety and Bruce Davey

WRITER: Malcolm MacRury

BASED ON: The novel by Isabelle Holland

DISTRIBUTOR: Warner Brothers

BRIEF SUMMARY: Lessons in the tender mercies of injustice—a descriptive phrase from the film *The Man Without a Face*—tells much about this bittersweet drama involving the lives of two misfits and the relationship that develops as they help each other cope with overwhelming and painful circumstances. Chuck Norstadt is a troubled, fatherless boy who befriends mysterious recluse Justin McLeod and finds the first real friend he has ever had.

The Man Without a Face is a touching and powerful story of trust, mercy, and unconditional friendship between two unlikely candidates. Mel Gibson excels in his dual role of directing and acting, as he successfully sets the mood for this drama and carries it through on screen. Twelve-year-old Nick Stahl turns in possibly the best performance of any of the current crop of big-picture "child actors." He is believable, natural, and convincing in his role. The photography is very good, the music, while not memorable, is pleasing and appropriate, and the supporting-cast members are all excellent. The only real drawback is, as usual, the unnecessarily foul language, most of which is spoken by young Chuck. When will they learn? Without the language, this would be an excellent, heartwarming, and entertaining movie.

CONTENT ANALYSIS: (C, B, LL, V, S, A, D, M) Christian worldview with biblical principles of grace, mercy, forgiveness, trust, and friendship; fifteen obscenities, four profanities, and twelve crudities; brief violence in form of verbal arguments; implied promiscuity and teenage couple interrupted in bed; young boys are offered beer by a parent and smoke cigarettes; and boy lies frequently, but character is redeemed by film's end.

The Hero Within

MANHATTAN MURDER MYSTERY

Quality: ☆☆☆☆   Acceptability: −1

WARNING CODES:

Language: **
Violence: None
Sex: None
Nudity: None

RATING: PG

GENRE: Comedy

INTENDED AUDIENCE: Adults

RUNNING TIME: 104 minutes

STARRING: Woody Allen, Diane Keaton, Alan Alda, and Angelica Houston

DIRECTOR: Woody Allen

WRITERS: Woody Allen and Marshall Brickman

PRODUCERS: Jack Rollins and Robert Greenhut

DISTRIBUTOR: TriStar

BRIEF SUMMARY:

Another Allenesque character study, *Manhattan Murder Mystery* focuses on a midlife crisis in the Big Apple. The dialogue reveals Woody Allen at his best with delicious scenes and scripting between Allen's character, Larry, and his wife, Carol. Larry and Carol's verbal exchange explores beyond the obvious to discover the many complicated layers of humanity. Dangerous flirtations between Larry and Marsha and Carol and Ted are cooled by Larry and Carol's declarations of commitment to their marriage. Despite their obvious desperation and desire for regained youth, Larry and Carol successfully spurn the advances of their would-be lovers. This is a moral triumph on the silver screen!

In the end, Allen's otherwise fearful and at best "careful" character finds the hidden "hero within." He bravely arises to the occasion as "rescuer" and regains his wife's respect and love in the process. Allen's artful use of a favorite old film clip, coupled with a room of mirrors and a "fact-is-stranger-than-fiction" dialogue climaxes with the demise of unlikely villains and a happy-ever-after ending New York style. *Manhattan Murder Mystery* ranks among the Allen Hall of Fame with *Annie Hall, Radio Days, Broadway Danny Rose,* and the *Purple Rose of Cairo.*

CONTENT ANALYSIS: (B, LL) Moral worldview; a few profanities and expressions like "Oh, God!" scattered throughout; passing vulgar comment; and, supporting characters attempt to seduce main characters into extramarital affairs without success.

Reclaiming Our Neighborhoods

THE METEOR MAN

Quality: ☆☆☆☆   Acceptability: +1

WARNING CODES:
  Language: None
  Violence: **
  Sex: *
  Nudity: None
RATING: PG-13
GENRE: Adventure/Comedy
INTENDED AUDIENCE: Teens and adults
RUNNING TIME: 95 minutes
STARRING: Robert Townsend, Bill Cosby, Robert Guillaume, James Earl Jones, Marla Gibbs, Luther Vandross, Big Daddy Kane, and Frank Gorshin
DIRECTOR: Robert Townsend
PRODUCER: Loretha Jones
WRITER: Robert Townsend
DISTRIBUTOR: Metro Goldwyn-Mayer
BRIEF SUMMARY:
The Meteor Man is a creative and energetic story about Jefferson Reed, a schoolteacher hit by a magical emerald meteor and transformed into a superhero gifted with superhuman powers and motivation to help his inner-city neighbors learn to help themselves and find the true meaning of courage. As his newly acquired Superman-like abilities are revealed, Reed becomes the hero of Castle Hill, a Washington, D.C., suburb plagued by gangs, drugs, and violence. Resolved to help clean up the neighborhood, Reed (as Meteor Man) ventures into the most troublesome areas, taking on gangs and drug-lords alike.

The quality of writing and overall sensitivity of the movie is quite revealing. After the final scene, audience members walked out of the theater with smiles on their faces. There are some violent scenes, however, and a caution is noted for children under thirteen. However, the movie is basically clean, with no foul language and little sexual content. The humor is not the usual scatological humor found in most comedies today. The high point of the movie, though, is the message that Meteor Man sends to our youth: It is time to get straight and reclaim our neighborhoods for our families. *The Meteor Man* sends a valuable message that young people need to see.

CONTENT ANALYSIS: (B, C, S, VV) Positive biblical values and Christian worldview slightly marred by one sexual innuendo and violence, but not gory.

Woman's Work

MRS. DOUBTFIRE

Quality: ☆☆☆   Acceptability: −2

WARNING CODES:
  Language: **
  Violence: None
  Sex: *
  Nudity: None
RATING: PG-13
GENRE: Comedy
INTENDED AUDIENCE: Older teens and adults

RUNNING TIME: 125 minutes

STARRING: Robin Williams, Sally Field, Pierce Brosnan, Harvey Fierstein, Polly Holliday, Lisa Jakub, Matthew Lawrence, and Mara Wilson

DIRECTOR: Chris Columbus

PRODUCERS: Marsha Garces Williams, Robin Williams, and Mark Radcliffe

WRITERS: Randi Mayem Singer and Leslie Dixon

BASED ON: The novel *Alias Madame Doubtfire* by Anne Fine

DISTRIBUTOR: 20th Century Fox

BRIEF SUMMARY: In *Mrs. Doubtfire,* when Daniel Hillard (Robin Williams) loses his acting job and then, for his son's birthday party, hires a petting zoo that wreaks havoc on his San Francisco home, his wife, Miranda, demands a divorce. Since Daniel has neither a job nor a home, the judge awards the custody of the children to Miranda in spite of Daniel's pleas. However, with the help of his homosexual brother and his lover, Daniel is transformed into Mrs. Doubtfire, so he can respond to Miranda's advertisement for a nanny and thus be close to his children. Mrs. Doubtfire gets the job, and the fun begins. She/he "burns" dinner, insists on the children doing their homework, offers grandmotherly advice to Miranda, and brings order, love, and respect to the Hillard household. Mrs. Doubtfire becomes such a favorite that, after her unveiling, each of the family wishes she/he would return, intimating that Dad is better as a woman.

Mrs. Doubtfire is a somewhat funny movie if you enjoy transvestite jokes, sexual innuendo, and foul language. Aside from the admonition in Deuteronomy 22:5: "A woman must not wear men's clothing, nor a man wear women's clothing, for the Lord your God detests anyone who does this," the movie fails to develop its full potential. Sally Field seems totally out of place, so Williams has to carry the entire movie.

CONTENT ANALYSIS: (B, LL, S, Ho, PC) Messages of the importance of both parents and of a father's love for his children is marred by: at least twelve obscenities, nine profanities (including teaching a five-year-girl how to curse), and several vulgarities; sexual innuendo and humor; Robin Williams dressed in "drag" and a homosexual lifestyle portrayed as natural.

Profound Insights

MUCH ADO ABOUT NOTHING

Quality: ☆☆☆☆   Acceptability: −1

WARNING CODES:

Language: *
Violence: *
Sex: *
Nudity: *

RATING: PG-13

GENRE: Comedy

INTENDED AUDIENCE: Older teens and adults

RUNNING TIME: 111 minutes

STARRING: Kenneth Branagh, Emma Thompson, Keanu Reeves, and Michael Keaton

DIRECTOR: Kenneth Branagh

PRODUCERS: Stephen Evans and David Parfitt

BASED ON: The play by William Shakespeare

ADAPTED BY: Kenneth Branagh

DISTRIBUTOR: Samuel Goldwyn

BRIEF SUMMARY:

William Shakespeare's witty romantic comedy *Much Ado About Nothing* sizzles and snaps from start to finish in Kenneth Branagh's innovative film, which revolves around two intertwined love stories: one mischievously funny, between Beatrice and Benedick; and the other, between Claudio and Hero, poignantly sweet. A returning soldier, Claudio, falls in love with Hero at first sight, courts her, and they plan to marry. However, Benedick and Beatrice have a "merry war with words" as they spar verbally in a continual battle of wits. On Hero and Claudio's wedding day, Hero is falsely accused of infidelity. She faints, and the wedding is called off. Some watchmen, however, soon uncover an evil plot, and all is resolved. At the movie's end, a double wedding between the two couples takes place.

Director/actor Kenneth Branagh is to be commended for a masterful job in adapting *Much Ado About Nothing* for the screen. The acting is competent and convincing, and the cinematography in and around a magnificent fourteenth-century Italian villa is breathtaking. Overflowing with humor, Christian metaphor, and profound insights into human nature, the movie can be commended for its imaginative concept and is marred only by an opening naturalistic nude bathing scene that will put this superb film off-limits to many.

CONTENT ANALYSIS: (B, C, L, N, S, V) This humorous morality play about the vicissitudes of human nature is undergirded with Christian metaphor and marred only by some mild Elizabethan obscenitie; naturalistic rear male and female nudity in bathing and dressing scene, implied sexual intercourse (but nothing shown), and some violence in the wedding scene when Claudio believes Hero has been unfaithful.

Coping with Death

MY LIFE

Quality: ☆☆☆☆   Acceptability: +1

WARNING CODES:
  Language: *
  Violence: None
  Sex: None
  Nudity: None

RATING: PG
GENRE: Drama
INTENDED AUDIENCE: Adults
RUNNING TIME: 117 minutes

STARRING: Michael Keaton, Nicole Kidman, Bradley Whitford, Queen Latifah, Michael Constantine, and Rebecca Schull
DIRECTOR: Bruce Joel Rubin
PRODUCERS: Jerry Zucker, Bruce Joel Rubin, and Hunt Lowry
WRITER: Bruce Joel Rubin
DISTRIBUTOR: Columbia Pictures
BRIEF SUMMARY:

My Life is a heartwarming story that will touch the heart of anyone who has experienced the tragedy of cancer. The movie portrays the struggles Bob and his family encounter when he discovers he has kidney cancer. His is the typical American success story with a successful business, a big house, a wonderful wife, and the awaited birth of their first child. However, Bob is not content. Discovering that he has a terminal illness, he starts to videotape his life for his unborn child. While he does this, he is forced to take a close look at himself. We are taken on a trip in which he tries to tell his yet-to-be-born son the so-called "facts of life," how to play basketball and a host of things that a father longs to share with his son. The most difficult part of his life is his relationship with his parents. As he tries to mend this relationship, however, he finally discovers himself. As he slows down to take a close look at himself, he finds tranquillity and is able to enjoy what he already possesses.

Although the lead characters are not Christian, *My Life* is an excellent movie with good moral content. Although they do not turn to Jesus Christ in their crisis, they do offer up two brief prayers. The terminal illness and subsequent videotaping of his life cause Bob to put his life in perspective, and the audience is forced to do the same through the film portrayal of Bob's life.

CONTENT ANALYSIS: (B, L, Pa) Moral worldview, six obscenities, but otherwise an excellent movie with good moral content, although the lead characters are not Christian and do not turn to God in their crisis other than to pray two brief prayers, and there is a New Age aspect to the movie.

Allegory Squandered

THE NIGHTMARE BEFORE CHRISTMAS

Quality: ☆☆☆☆   Acceptability: −1

WARNING CODES:
  Language: None
  Violence: **
  Sex: None
  Nudity: None
RATING: PG
GENRE: Animated fantasy
INTENDED AUDIENCE: Preteens and adults
RUNNING TIME: 76 minutes
VOICES: Chris Sarandon, Danny Elfman, Catherine O'Hara, William Hickey, Glenn Shadix, and Paul Rubens
  DIRECTOR: Henry Selick
  PRODUCERS: Denise Di Novi and Tim Burton
  WRITER: Tim Burton
  DISTRIBUTOR: Touchstone Pictures/Walt Disney Company
  BRIEF SUMMARY:
The Nightmare Before Christmas opens with the fantasy premise that in some far-off forest, in a small grove of trees, one can enter lands that generate the festivities of various holidays. We soon find ourselves in Halloweentown, where Jack Skellington reigns as king of the assorted, dark, evil-looking creatures of Halloween. Tired of Halloween, Jack discovers Christmastown and tries to bring it to Halloweentown, although he doesn't understand Christmas and thinks Santa is Christmas. In the hands of Jack and his cohorts, Christmas becomes distorted and evil and is in danger of being lost.

From a visual and technical standpoint, the film is brilliant. Filmed in frame-by-frame stop motion by an army of inventive and patient puppeteers, *The Nightmare Before Christmas* is eye-popping, jaw-dropping entertainment. Regrettably, the film focuses much more on Halloween than on Christmas and the screen fills up with intense visions of spooks, bogeymen, bats, bugs, and spiders. As a result, it is far too intense for younger children and anyone who has been ensnared in the occult. The film sets up a poignant allegory about the inability of those steeped in darkness to comprehend light, only to squander it on a hyperkinetic finale. How wonderful this film might have been if Jack had stumbled upon a Nativity scene in Christmastown.

CONTENT ANALYSIS: (VV, O, B) Cartoon-style, slapstick violence throughout, involving a huge collection of Halloween creatures, witches, bogeymen, spiders, bugs, etc. While the intent is comic, many images are far too intense for children under ten. Extreme caution advised, especially for any who have been involved with, or abused by, the occult, although a redemptive concept runs throughout the movie.

Extolling Christian Virtues

ONCE UPON A FOREST

Quality: ☆☆☆☆   Acceptability: +2

WARNING CODES:
  Language: None
  Violence: None
  Sex: None
  Nudity: None

RATING: G
GENRE: Animated adventure
INTENDED AUDIENCE: All ages
RUNNING TIME: 71 minutes
VOICES: Michael Crawford, Ben Vereen, Ellen Blain, Ben Gregory, Paige Gosney, and Elizabeth Moss
  DIRECTOR: Charles Grosvenor
  PRODUCERS: David Kirschner and Jerry Mills
  WRITER: Kelly Ward

BASED ON: The story by Rae Lambert

DISTRIBUTOR: 20th Century Fox

BRIEF SUMMARY:

Once Upon a Forest introduces us to four small creatures known as furlings—Abigail the mouse, Russell the hedgehog, Edgar the mole, and Michelle the badger—who, as the movie opens, say goodbye to their parents and run off to be instructed by Cornelius, a wise old badger. While they contend with each other on a river-ramble instruction, a truck carrying poison gas runs off the road, and gas leaks throughout the wood. The furlings return home to find that the gas has destroyed all the foliage and many of the animals. Michelle herself has to be rescued from the gas when she runs into her underground home to find her parents dead. Cornelius tells the three healthy furlings that Michelle needs certain herbs administered within two days to survive and that they must find a healthy meadow to find those herbs. In the end, they must work together and overcome their fears to retrieve the herbs in time. The ending will bring tears of joy to the most hardened heart.

Once Upon a Forest is a well-crafted animated film that children of all ages will love. The film avoids any New Age, occult, or humanist messages. It also emphasizes Christian virtues such as love, forgiveness, kindness, perseverance, and cooperation. Although it is environmentally concerned, the film does not take a radical position and does emphasize that we can solve our problems by working together.

CONTENT ANALYSIS: (E, C, B, H) A balanced environmental message combined with Christian virtues such as love, forgiveness, kindness, perseverance, and cooperation set in materialistic world (no references to the super- or subnatural).

Service above All

THE REMAINS OF THE DAY

Quality: ☆☆☆☆   Acceptability: +2

WARNING CODES:
Language: None
Violence: None
Sex: None
Nudity: None

RATING: PG
GENRE: Comedy of manners
INTENDED AUDIENCE: Adults
RUNNING TIME: 133 minutes
STARRING: Anthony Hopkins, Emma Thompson, James Fox, Christopher Reeve, Peter Vaughan, Hugh Grant, and Michael Lonsdale
DIRECTOR: James Ivory
PRODUCERS: Mike Nichols, John Calley, and Ismail Merchant
WRITER: Ruth Prawer Jhabvala
BASED ON: The novel by Kazuo Ishiguro
DISTRIBUTOR: Columbia Pictures
BRIEF SUMMARY:

In what constitutes a nearly perfect film, *The Remains of the Day* is filmmaking at its best. Anthony Hopkins turns in a colossal performance in his characterization of the exemplary and dedicated head butler Stevens; and Oscar-award-winning actress Emma Thompson as the head housekeeper, Miss Kenton, is outstanding as well. Stevens is head butler of Darlington Hall and hires Miss Kenton as the housekeeper. Lord Darlington, his master, hosts an international "peace" conference with delegates from various countries, including Germany, in the pre-World War II 1930s. Stevens falls in love with Miss Kenton but struggles with divulging his true feelings because of his propriety and rigid formalism. A statement Stevens gives near the movie's close says it all: "I was too busy serving to listen to the speeches."

All performances are outstanding—especially that of Hopkins, with his penetrating eyes, body language, and facial expressions—and Emma Thompson in her superb characterization of the efficient, yet forward-speaking housekeeper who tries to lead Stevens out of his rigid, decorous prison. The direction under James Ivory, the screenplay by Ruth Prawer Jhabvala, and the fine cinematography—both with exterior scenes and intimate close shots—must also be commended.

CONTENT ANALYSIS: (B, C) A positive, moral portrayal of English life in various societal levels prior to World War II, with Christian overtones and nothing objectionable.

Coming to Terms with God's Sovereignty

RUDY

Quality: ☆☆☆☆   Acceptability: −1

WARNING CODES:
Language: **
Violence: None
Sex: None
Nudity: None
RATING: PG-13
GENRE: Drama
INTENDED AUDIENCE: Older teens and adults
RUNNING TIME: 110 minutes
STARRING: Sean Astin, Ned Beaty, Charles S. Dutton, Jason Miller, Lili Taylor, and Robert Prosky
DIRECTOR: David Anspaugh
EXECUTIVE PRODUCER: Lee R. Mayes
WRITER: Angelo Pizzo
DISTRIBUTOR: TriStar Pictures
BRIEF SUMMARY:
The film *Rudy* tells about Rudy's struggle from boyhood to manhood to disprove his father's dictum that dreamers are not doers. Despite the obstacle of his size, "5 feet nothing, 100 pounds of nothing, and virtually no athletic abil-

ity," Rudy desires to play football for no less than Notre Dame. No one, including his father, his more talented brothers, his classmates, and certainly not his coach, takes him seriously. Rudy's repetitive question as to whether he has done all he can do to achieve his goal leads him into conversations with a priest, to prayer, and eventually to come to terms with his size and, in particular, with the sovereignty of God.

Rudy is a modern-day hero with an indomitable spirit. His victory against the odds makes him a real-life model, not only for his five younger brothers, but also for the viewer. Rudy accomplishes something rare in today's movies. He makes one care about even his smallest struggles. This identification is a tribute to the fine casting, acting, realistic sets, and script. Regrettably, the depiction of Catholicism is somewhat skewed, although a sovereign God is implicitly extoled; and the film is marred by some foul language, although the character using the most profanity is reformed by his girlfriend.

CONTENT ANALYSIS: (B, C, Ab, LL) A biblical view of character, the need for prayer, the sovereignty of God, and a positive view of Christianity and clergy, although some priests are portrayed as shortsighted. Fourteen obscenities and ten profanities—the character using the most profanity is reformed by his girlfriend—and a funeral scene promotes a capricious view of God.

Fun, Wholesome Entertainment

THE SANDLOT

Quality: ☆☆☆   Acceptability: +1

WARNING CODES:
Language: *
Violence: None
Sex: None
Nudity: None
RATING: PG

GENRE: Comedy
INTENDED AUDIENCE: All ages
RUNNING TIME: 101 minutes
STARRING: Mike Vitar, Tom Guiry, Karen Allen, and James Earl Jones
DIRECTOR: David Mickey Evans
PRODUCERS: Chris Zarpas, Dale De la torre, and William S. Gilmore
WRITERS: David M. Evans and Robert Gunter
DISTRIBUTOR: 20th Century Fox
BRIEF SUMMARY:
In the movie *The Sandlot*, young Scott Smalls moves to a new California neighborhood and attempts to make friends with the eight boys who play sandlot baseball. Each of the boys, including their leader, Benny, takes baseball very seriously, so when Scott finally gets his opportunity to play with them, he finds himself humiliated because he can neither catch nor throw the ball. With help he learns, but one day, after their ball is lost, Scott gets his stepfather's cherished, autographed "Babe Ruth" ball to finish the game. The ball is hit into an old, dilapidated warehouse that contains a mysterious "beast," and Scott worries about how he can retrieve the ball and save face with his stepfather. The rest of the film hinges on the boys getting the ball back and uncovering an enormous surprise lurking in the old warehouse.

Although *The Sandlot* lags in a few places, overall it maintains an even pace, builds suspense and intrigue, and humorously depicts the trials of growing up. Commendably, the film contains little that is objectionable save (regrettably) some mild obscenities and a couple of exclamatory profanities. Not wanting to divulge any further information about this delightful film, suffice it to say that *The Sandlot* is good, wholesome, family entertainment and will cause its viewers to laugh and to rejoice, wishing that more just plain good movies would come along.

CONTENT ANALYSIS: (B, L) Biblical principles are taught; five or six mild obscenities and a couple of exclamatory ("Oh, God") profanities; and a brief episode of chewing tobacco that makes the boys sick.

Saved by Grace

SCHINDLER'S LIST

Quality: ☆☆☆☆   Acceptability: –2

WARNING CODES:
  Language: ***
  Violence: ***
  Sex: ***
  Nudity: ***
RATING: R
GENRE: Holocaust drama
INTENDED AUDIENCE: Adults
RUNNING TIME: 185 minutes
STARRING: Liam Neeson, Ben Kingsley, Ralph Fiennes, Caroline Goodall, Jonathan Sagalle, and Embeth Davidtz
DIRECTOR: Steven Spielberg
PRODUCERS: Steven Spielberg, Gerald R. Molen, and Branko Lustig
WRITER: Steven Zaillian
BASED ON: The novel by Thomas Keneally
DISTRIBUTOR: Universal Pictures
BRIEF SUMMARY:
A riveting film dealing with the World War II Jewish Holocaust, *Schindler's List* will shock and astound its viewers not only with man's inhumanity to man but also with one man's triumph in the face of incredible odds. Oskar Schindler arrives in Poland in 1939 to seek his fortune. To accomplish his goal, Schindler shamelessly bribes the corrupt National Socialists (Nazis) and succeeds in acquiring a failed factory. Almost simultaneously, the Jewish population of Krakow is ordered to register. Schindler staffs his factory with unpaid Jewish workers. When the extermination of Jews in the city begins, Schindler seems determined to "rescue" as many Jews as he can by hiring them to work in his factory. He has

numerous close calls when it appears that various persons will be sent away for good to the concentration camps, but he always finds a way to get them back. When the Jews are liberated at the movie's end, Schindler has managed to save over thirteen hundred from certain death in the camps, although he weeps that he "didn't do enough."

Schindler's List is a heartrending movie about the near-extinction of the Jews in the Holocaust. Regrettably, the movie fails to clarify Schindler's faith or motivations, although Liam Neeson gives an outstanding performance. Also it is regrettable that nudity, sex, and violence detract from this important epic film. That said, the final scene where Schindler realizes that he could never be good enough despite all that he has done reveals the biblical truth that we are saved by grace through faith energized by love, not by works.

CONTENT ANALYSIS: (C, B, Ab, LLL, NNN, SSS, VVV) Redemptive biblical theme in Schindler's risking his own life to save Jews, though there are some anti-Christian references and, of course, the anti-Semitic National Socialist (Nazi) hatred of Jews. Approximately nineteen obscenities, eight profanities, and several vulgarities; extensive nudity in concentration camp scenes where Jews are paraded like cattle before their captors, and male and female nudity in several graphic sex scenes between unmarried individuals; and extreme violence in beatings, killings, and treatment of Jews.

Thoroughly Uplifting

SEARCHING FOR BOBBY FISCHER

Quality: ☆☆☆☆   Acceptability: +2

WARNING CODES:
Language: *
Violence: None
Sex: None
Nudity: None

RATING: PG
GENRE: Drama
INTENDED AUDIENCE: All ages
RUNNING TIME: 110 minutes
STARRING: Joe Mantegna, Laurence Fishburne, Joan Allen, Max Pomeranc, and Ben Kingsley
DIRECTOR: Steven Zaillian
EXECUTIVE PRODUCER: Sydney Pollack
PRODUCERS: Scott Rudin and David Wisnievitz
WRITER: Steven Zaillian
BASED ON: The book by Fred Waitzkin
DISTRIBUTOR: Paramount Pictures
BRIEF SUMMARY:
Based on a true story about seven-year-old chess prodigy Josh Waitzkin, *Searching for Bobby Fischer* begins with Josh's parents discovering his prowess at chess. The Waitzkins hire a teacher for their son and encourage him in his genius. His father tells an indifferent elementary teacher on one occasion, "He's better at this than I've ever been at anything in my life!" The bulk of the film concerns Josh's early triumphs and the adults' conflicts as Josh competes in one chess tournament after another, all of which lead to the big match where Josh has to reconcile his twin desires to win at all costs and still hold onto his humanity.

The relationship between Josh and his journalist father, Fred, is a touching one. When Fred recognizes his son's gift, he wants to encourage his son but not push him. After Josh loses an important match, his dad lets him know, "It's okay, Josh; it's just a game." Noticeably on edge, Josh retorts: "No, it isn't!" There is also a fabulous scene between Josh and his chess teacher, played wonderfully by Ben Kingsley. This movie's subject is unusual, but its themes are universal: a child's discovery of what makes him special and a parent's loving possessiveness. These qualities, combined with excellent directing, acting, and cinematography will endear *Searching for Bobby Fischer* to moviegoers. The film exemplifies the proverb "Train up a child in the way he should go: and when he is old, he will not depart from it" (Proverbs 22:6 KJV).

CONTENT ANALYSIS: (B, L) Positive father-son relationship in movie and affirming of child to bring out his best. Regrettably, two profanities mar an otherwise nearly perfect film.

Love Brings Rebirth

THE SECRET GARDEN

Quality: ☆☆☆☆   Acceptability: +2

WARNING CODES:
  Language: None
  Violence: None
  Sex: None
  Nudity: None
RATING: G
GENRE: Drama
INTENDED AUDIENCE: All ages
RUNNING TIME: 102 minutes
STARRING: Maggie Smith, Kate Maberly, Heydon Prowse, and Andrew Knott
DIRECTOR: Agnieszka Holland
PRODUCERS: Fred Fuchs, Fred Roos, and Tom Luddy
WRITER: Caroline Thompson
BASED ON: The novel by Frances Hodgson Burnett
DISTRIBUTOR: Warner Brothers
BRIEF SUMMARY:
The Secret Garden is a beautifully photographed family film based on the classic children's story by Frances Hodgson Burnett. Set in India in 1906, Mary Lennox, the young daughter of a British ambassador, is sick of her life. Mary spends her time alone, since her parents are too busy. Isolated, Mary develops a sour disposition. When her parents die suddenly, Mary sheds no tears. She is shipped to England to live with her uncle in his manor. Mrs. Medlock (Maggie Smith) treats Mary like an unwanted child. Mary finds a key that opens her deceased aunt's private garden, which has been sealed for ten years. Mary begins working to revive the "sleeping" flowers. Dickon, a local boy, helps Mary bring the garden back to life. Mary also discovers Colin, her ten-year-old cousin whose mother died when he was born and who has become a hypochondriac that fears the outside world. Mary resolves to help Colin experience more than his room.

The friendship that develops between Mary, Colin, and Dickon succeeds in transforming the claustrophobic atmosphere of the manor into a world of hope and happiness. Love prevails over despair, and life is restored to the manor. There is no offensive language in the movie, but one scene shows three children chanting a magical spell around a bonfire. According to the director, this is not intended to be witchcraft, but a children's fantasy. The film is beautifully photographed, contains interesting performances, and brings a poignant message of death and rebirth.

CONTENT ANALYSIS: (Pa, B, M) This classic children's story tells how love can overcome despair and bring rebirth to the most hardened heart. One scene shows three children chanting a magical spell around a bonfire, but according to the director this is not intended to be witchcraft but a children's fantasy. However, some of the Christian references in the novel have been deleted.

Coping with Tragedy

SHADOWLANDS

Quality: ☆☆☆☆   Acceptability: +1

WARNING CODES:
  Language: None
  Violence: None
  Sex: None
  Nudity: None
RATING: PG

GENRE: Drama

INTENDED AUDIENCE: Teens and adults

RUNNING TIME: 130 minutes

STARRING: Anthony Hopkins, Debra Winger, Joseph Mazzello, Edward Hardwicke, John Wood, and Andrew Hawkins

DIRECTOR: Richard Attenborough

PRODUCERS: Richard Attenborough and Brian Eastman

WRITER: William Nicholson

DISTRIBUTOR: Savoy Pictures

BRIEF SUMMARY:

Christian author C. S. Lewis's relationship with Joy Gresham is presented with great dignity in the movie *Shadowlands*. Anthony Hopkins portrays Professor Lewis at Oxford, who meets Joy Gresham (Debra Winger), an American poet touring England with her son. Mrs. Gresham wants to settle in London, and Lewis helps her by marrying her in a civil ceremony, thus giving her English citizenship, but then living apart. When Mrs. Lewis is diagnosed with a malignant bone tumor, Lewis assumes responsibility for her care and falls in love. In a moving scene, he brings a minister to her bedside to repeat their marriage ceremony with vows promised to God. The Lewises enjoy a satisfying but brief time together. Regrettably, in grappling with Lewis's loss, *Shadowlands* drops the ball. Unless one knows better, the final impression is that Lewis never regained a viable faith after Joy's death. The ending does, however, provide a glimpse of the joys of heaven, to which Joy has gone.

This movie's conclusion may be a sore spot for Lewis admirers and a great loss for the general public because we so rarely see intelligent portrayals of faith in contemporary films. Lewis, to be sure, did not become an agnostic in the face of this tragedy. Even so, *Shadowlands* is well worth a viewing. Had this film done as much justice to Lewis's faith as it does to his humanity, it would have been a masterpiece—not just a superb and moving love story.

CONTENT ANALYSIS: (B, C, M) Christian worldview with positive presentation of mature and sacrificial love in a married couple; however, the theme of loss of loved ones may be upsetting to children.

Hero Image

SIDEKICKS

Quality: ☆☆☆☆   Acceptability: +3

WARNING CODES:

Language: *
Violence: *
Sex: None
Nudity: None

RATING: PG

GENRE: Action/Drama

INTENDED AUDIENCE: All ages

RUNNING TIME: 110 minutes

STARRING: Jonathon Brandis, Chuck Norris, Beau Bridges, Dennis Burkley, Julia Nickson-Soul, and Joe Piscopo

DIRECTOR: Aaron Norris

PRODUCERS: Chuck Norris and Jim McIngvale

WRITER: Galen Thompson

DISTRIBUTOR: Triumph Releasing

BRIEF SUMMARY:

Sidekicks is the uplifting story of an underdog, asthmatic, high school student, Barry, who idolizes Chuck Norris and imagines fighting battles alongside him. Norris plays himself and adds that "hero" quality as he comes to Barry's rescue in several different "dream" scenarios and as a surprise at the film's end. This is a good-hearted movie that focuses on several characters who all care about Barry and want the best for him. Barry decides to take a stand against his crippling health defect and the class bully who is jealous because the most popular girl likes Barry. An old man, Mako, teaches Barry to defend himself using karate, and at the film's end Barry is vindicated in his struggles.

Sidekicks touches on several areas that deal with how we treat one another in this society and how we handle issues such as prejudice, disrespect for peers and adults, teen dating, the frustrations teenagers go through with parental relationships, and seeing dreams come true if you want them badly enough. Aside from the cartoon-like violence in the various make-believe action scenarios, the themes and characters deliver the moral lessons Barry seems to need at each particular hour. The special effects, dynamic colors, interesting plot twists, funny performances, and a great storyline make this action/adventure/comedy a bright spot as a family film. The movie is also a return to the "hero" concept—a welcome return indeed.

CONTENT ANALYSIS: (C, B, L, V) *Sidekicks* emphasizes self-esteem, achieving goals and dreams, having a hero to look up to, working hard for what you want, and teamwork. It is a family-oriented film marred by six minor obscenities and two exclamatory profanities, slapstick violence played out in several different scenarios depicting Norris fighting alongside Barry but no deaths, two scenes where boy kisses girl, bully picks on Barry until Barry fights back, and a karate tournament with competitive action.

Communicating the Love of God

SISTER ACT II

Quality: ☆☆☆☆   Acceptability: −1

WARNING CODES:
  Language: **
  Violence: None
  Sex: None
  Nudity: None
RATING: PG
GENRE: Comedy
INTENDED AUDIENCE: All ages

RUNNING TIME: 120 minutes
STARRING: Whoopi Goldberg, Kathy Najimy, Mary Wickes, Wendy Makkena, and Maggie Smith
DIRECTOR: Bill Duke
PRODUCERS: Christopher Meledandri, Scott Rudin, and Dawn Steel
WRITERS: James Orr and Jim Cruickshank
DISTRIBUTOR: Touchstone Pictures/ Walt Disney Company/Buena Vista Pictures
BRIEF SUMMARY:

Joyous, foot-stomping music that lifts the heart characterizes *Sister Act II*, the much-anticipated sequel to *Sister Act*, as Sister Mary Clarence, alias Delores (Whoopi Goldberg), and her fellow nuns work (this time) on converting some potential delinquents from St. Francis High School into happy, diligent students. The nuns persuade nightclub singer Delores to leave Las Vegas and help them at the San Francisco school of St. Francis, where the students would rather do anything than study. In time, Sister Mary Clarence gets her music class's attention. They become a choir and practice for the state competition, despite some obstacles that could spoil everything.

Sister Act II contains some outstanding musical numbers such as "His Eye Is on the Sparrow" and "Joyful, Joyful, We Adore Thee." The acting is also commendable, with Whoopi Goldberg and Maggie Smith both convincing. Regrettably, there are some borderline foul words and one profanity uttered by the contemptible school administrator. Even so, there is little to object to in this movie, which clearly communicates the love of God, the value of hard work, and the need to acquire Christian virtues— messages that every teenager and adult needs to hear. In its own joyous way, *Sister Act II* may bring some wayward soul to Jesus Christ.

CONTENT ANALYSIS: (C, LL) Overall positive Christian worldview marred by roughly thirteen obscenities, one profanity, and some minor innuendos.

Love Never Fails

SLEEPLESS IN SEATTLE

Quality: ☆☆☆☆   Acceptability: −1

WARNING CODES:
 Language: None
 Violence: None
 Sex: None
 Nudity: None
RATING: PG
GENRE: Romantic comedy
INTENDED AUDIENCE: Teens and adults
RUNNING TIME: 115 minutes
STARRING: Tom Hanks, Meg Ryan, Bill Pullman, Rosie O'Donnell, Rob Reiner, and Ross Malinger
DIRECTOR: Nora Ephron
PRODUCER: Gary Foster
WRITER: Nora Ephron
DISTRIBUTOR: TriStar Pictures
BRIEF SUMMARY:
In the film, *Sleepless in Seattle*, eight-year-old Jonah calls a talk-show host on Christmas Eve to discuss his recently widowed father's problems, while Annie, in Baltimore, hears the broadcast and begins to daydream about Sam, the boy's father. Engaged to Walter, Annie nevertheless is intrigued with Sam. She flies to Seattle hoping to meet him, but all she can say is "Hello." Later, she writes to Sam and Jonah and proposes a meeting atop the Empire State Building on Valentine's Day. Jonah manages to arrange a flight to New York so he can meet Annie. Meanwhile, Sam rushes after Jonah. Annie breaks her engagement to Walter, and then runs out the door toward the Empire State Building. Of course, the movie has a "happily ever after" ending, making it one of the hits of the decade, at least for women between the ages of twenty-five and forty-nine.

Screenwriter and director Nora Ephron says the movie pays homage to another movie, *An Affair to Remember*. She told the actors, "This is not a movie about love; it's a movie about love in the movies." The movie is well crafted, though not outstanding, with competent acting on the part of Hanks, Ryan, and, in particular, Ross Malinger, who plays eight-year-old Jonah. Admiringly, the story theme reminds one of 1 Corinthians 13:8: "Love never fails"—a refreshing theme indeed.
CONTENT ANALYSIS: (L, B, H) A couple of obscenities and at least two scenes with suggestive sexual dialogue involving eight-year-old Jonah, and a positive portrayal of father-son relationship, although the father doesn't believe in God.

Perseverance Overcomes Adversity

STRICTLY BALLROOM

Quality: ☆☆☆☆   Acceptability: −1

WARNING CODES:
 Language: None
 Violence: None
 Sex: *
 Nudity: None
RATING: PG
GENRE: Comedy
INTENDED AUDIENCE: All ages
RUNNING TIME: 94 minutes
STARRING: Paul Mercurio, Tara Morice, and Pip Mushin
DIRECTOR: Baz Luhrmann
PRODUCERS: Popsy Albert, Antoinette Albert, Tristam Miall, and Ted Albert
WRITER: Baz Luhrmann
DISTRIBUTOR: Miramax/Beyond Films
BRIEF SUMMARY:
Ballroom dancing provides the backdrop for the Australian film *Strictly Ballroom*. The story revolves around a heated dance contest involving strict rules. Scott, a twenty-one-year-old ball-

room dancing champion whose parents failed to win the coveted "Pan Pacific Grand Prix" in their youth, practices feverishly after hours when the other dance students have left the studio. Scott yearns to break away from the Dance Federation in order to dance his own steps. When his partner dumps him because she thinks his chances of winning are slim, he gets a new partner—Fran, an unpromising "ugly duckling"—for the contest. However, Scott's new partner blossoms into the Spanish beauty she was destined to become with the help of his mother's beauty aids, and the two benefit from her Spanish family's unique dance steps.

At no moment will a viewer be bored over this hilarious comedy—but you may fall off your seat in fits of laughter. The development of the characters and their relationships make this film a winner. The Australian film's world premiere was the surprise hit at Cannes in 1992. In fact, it received a fifteen-minute standing ovation at the 1992 Cannes Film Festival, as well as a great deal of critical acclaim. Furthermore, the Cannes jury awarded *Strictly Ballroom* a "Special Mention" in the Camera D'Or competition. In all, *Strictly Ballroom* is fantastic entertainment.

CONTENT ANALYSIS: (B, S, A, D) Perseverance overcomes all adversity; two extremely brief scenes suggesting sex; and one character drinks.

Somewhat Innocuous

SUPER MARIO BROS.

Quality: ☆☆☆   Acceptability: −1

WARNING CODES:
  Language: *
  Violence: **
  Sex: None
  Nudity: *
RATING: PG-13
GENRE: Comedy/Fantasy

INTENDED AUDIENCE: Teens
RUNNING TIME: 104 minutes
STARRING: Bob Hoskins, John Leguizamo, Dennis Hopper, Samantha Mathis, Fisher Stevens, Fiona Shaw, and Richard Edson
DIRECTORS: Rocky Morton and Annabel Jankel
PRODUCERS: Jake Eberts and Roland Joffe
WRITERS: Parker Bennett and Terry Runte
DISTRIBUTOR: Hollywood Pictures/Walt Disney Company/Buena Vista Pictures
BRIEF SUMMARY:
Super Mario Bros., based on the classic Nintendo video game, turns on a visit to a parallel world peopled by Dinosaurian descendants. As the film opens in Brooklyn, a cloaked woman places a mysterious basket at a convent door. The nuns marvel at the contents: a huge egg that breaks open to reveal a baby girl. The film cuts to an excavation twenty years later near the East River, where some students participate in an archaeological dig. When Daisy, the student leader at the excavation, calls for protection from the Scapelli Construction Company thugs, the Mario brothers, Mario and Luigi, come to her aid. Before long, the Mario brothers find themselves pulled through a mysterious portal into Dinohattan in a parallel dimension where reptiles have evolved into near-human-type beings. Koopa (Dennis Hopper), the diabolical tyrant of his dimension, plans to save his dying world by merging with the human world. The Mario brothers experience many far-out adventures in the phantasmagoric atmosphere of Dinohattan.

Despite superlative special effects and an imaginative set, *Super Mario Bros.* lags in places. Even Hoskins does not turn in a particularly credible performance. Furthermore, the New Age and humanistic undertones are slightly unsettling. In the final analysis, this is an innocuous action movie.

CONTENT ANALYSIS: (Pa, C, H, L, M, VV, N) A positive reference to Jesus Christ as Lord opens this good-triumphs-over-evil film marred by fewer than five obscenities, revenge motif, idea of evolution and de-evolution promulgated by villain, several violent episodes as when innocent-looking old lady jabs the Mario brothers with a vicious probe, New Age concepts in storyline such as parallel universes and psychic abilities, demonic creatures, and some skimpy costumes.

Moving Story

SWING KIDS

Quality: ✰✰✰✰   Acceptability: −1

WARNING CODES:
  Language: *
  Violence: **
  Sex: *
  Nudity: *
RATING: PG-13
GENRE: Historical drama
INTENDED AUDIENCE: Older teens and adults
RUNNING TIME: 112 minutes
STARRING: Robert Sean Leonard, Christian Bale, Frank Whaley, and Barbara Hershey
DIRECTOR: Thomas Carter
PRODUCERS: Christopher Meledandri, Mark Gordon, and John Bard Manulis
WRITER: Jonathan Marc Feldman
DISTRIBUTOR: Buena Vista Pictures/The Walt Disney Company
BRIEF SUMMARY:
In this gem of a movie, the "swing kids" are German university students living in Hamburg in 1939 who refuse to join Hitler's National Socialist cause and instead rally around swing music as the expression of their personal freedom. Carefully researched and beautifully

detailed, this historical drama of life in World War II Germany will appeal to anyone who loves history, music, dance, or wonders what it was like to live during that era. More than that, *Swing Kids* presents a realistic, moral hero and a hopeful ending that allows one to leave the theater with a renewed conviction to serve God faithfully, no matter what the cost. The movie opens with joyful jitterbugging at the Café Bismarck in Hamburg and zeros in on Peter, Thomas, and Arvid. Peter goes home to a wonderful mother, an adoring younger brother, and a senile grandmother. Peter's mom works in a factory, following her husband's untimely death six years earlier at the hands of the National Socialists (Nazis). Thomas lives the life of privilege, but his doctor father hasn't a clue about good parenting. Arvid is an intense, clubfooted musician, wholly devoted to his music.

Swing Kids is a rich tapestry of life and the struggle between good and evil that touches us all. All the actors give great performances. Echoing God's encouragement to his faithful but fearful prophet Elijah, Peter cries out, "I know who my friends are! I am not alone!" And thus it encourages us.

CONTENT ANALYSIS: (B, L, M, N, S, VV) A moving story of German teenagers struggling to do what is right in Nazi Germany, slightly marred by four obscenities and one crude reference; a night scene where three friends urinate on a propaganda poster; brief scene of schoolboys passing around postcards of partially nude women (upper-female nudity); implied promiscuity between policeman and shop owner; and realistic (but not gratuitous) violence, including four very bloody beatings, one murder by police shooting into the water, and one death shown after the fact.

Action-Packed

THE THREE MUSKETEERS

Quality: ✰✰✰✰   Acceptability: −1

WARNING CODES:
  Language: *
  Violence: **
  Sex: *
  Nudity: None
RATING: PG
GENRE: Action/Adventure
INTENDED AUDIENCE: Teens and adults
RUNNING TIME: 105 minutes
STARRING: Charlie Sheen, Kiefer Sutherland, Chris O'Donnell, Oliver Platt, Tim Curry, Rebecca DeMornay, Gabrielle Anwar, and Julie Delpy
DIRECTOR: Stephen Herek
PRODUCERS: Jordan Kerner, Joe Roth, and Roger Birnbaum
WRITER: David Loughery
BASED ON: The classic French novel by Alexandre Dumas
DISTRIBUTOR: Walt Disney Pictures/Caravan Pictures
BRIEF SUMMARY:
Determined to avenge his musketeer father's death and join the Musketeers (the king's bodyguards), young D'Artagnon sets off for Paris during the reign of King Louis XIII. The young man's bravado gets him into trouble, yet also provides an introduction to the king's protectors. The group is led by three loyal and courageous men— suave Aramis, pensive Athos, and lusty Porthos. The crux of the story revolves around a secret plot, masterminded by the evil Cardinal Richelieu, to topple the French monarchy and install himself as ruler. The nefarious cardinal unlawfully disbands the Musketeers and proceeds to attempt to sign, without King Louis's knowledge, a treaty with England. The evil plot is discovered by the three Musketeers (plus D'Artagnon), who must now fight to save France. In the process, D'Artagnon discovers who his father's real murderer is.

This is a terrific, action-packed movie for the whole family. Mocking God is duly punished in the end and values such as loyalty and courage are commended and rewarded. Because of killings related primarily to sword fights and implied licentiousness, parental discretion is advised for young children.

CONTENT ANALYSIS: (B, Ab, L, S, VV, A, D, M) Revelry scene involving drunkenness and implied sexual debauchery; threatened castration, killing (mostly through sword fights) and one graphic killing through impalement, deceitfulness (exposed in the end), and mocking God (Cardinal Richelieu is justly punished for this).

Good Conquers Evil

TOM AND JERRY: THE MOVIE

Quality: ☆☆☆☆   Acceptability: +3

WARNING CODES:
  Language: None
  Violence: *
  Sex: None
  Nudity: None
RATING: G
GENRE: Animated musical adventure
INTENDED AUDIENCE: All ages
RUNNING TIME: 80 minutes
VOICES: Richard Kind, Dana Hill, Charlotte Rae, Tony Jay, Henry Gibson, Rip Taylor, Howard Harris, Michael Bell, Edmund Gilbert, David L. Lander, and Anndi McAfee
DIRECTOR: Phil Roman
PRODUCER: Phil Roman
WRITER: Dennis Marks
DISTRIBUTOR: Turner Pictures Worldwide/Turner Entertainment Company
BRIEF SUMMARY:
After some "classic" chase scenes, Tom and Jerry's comfortable lifestyle turns topsy-turvy when a wrecking ball demolishes their home, forcing them out on the street to fend for themselves in *Tom and Jerry: The Movie*. On the streets, they

encounter a streetwise mutt, Puggsy, and his diminutive cohort Frankie Da Flea, who advise them to ignore their differences and be "friends forever." So, for the first time, Tom and Jerry talk! They befriend Robyn, who has fled her aunt Figg in search of her missing father. Aunt Figg only pretends to care about Robyn to have access to her trust fund. Eventually Tom and Jerry whisk Robyn away just in time to have Aunt Figg and her cronies follow them on the chase of a lifetime, which leads them into the able hands of a surprise hero who is sure to take care of Robyn, Tom, and Jerry forever.

Tom and Jerry: The Movie has captured the "Tom and Jerry feel" of the 1940s in a contemporary setting with brilliant backgrounds and color, excellent pacing, superb effects, and a terrific soundtrack put together by Oscar winners Henry Mancini and Leslie Bricusse. *Tom and Jerry: The Movie* is an entertaining family film with plenty of adventure and humor for all ages. It incorporates messages of friendship, teamwork, the importance of family, and the dead-end road one takes when love of money surpasses love for friends and family.

CONTENT ANALYSIS: (B, V) A biblical message of good triumphing over evil with positive messages of friendship, teamwork, and the importance of family togetherness. The film warns that the love of money is the road to unhappiness. Some cartoon slapstick violence.

Superb Adaptation

THE TRIAL

Quality: ☆☆☆☆   Acceptability: −1

WARNING CODES:

Language: *
Violence: None
Sex: *
Nudity: None

RATING: PG-13
GENRE: Comedy/Drama

INTENDED AUDIENCE: Adults
RUNNING TIME: 120 minutes
STARRING: Kyle Maclachlan, Anthony Hopkins, Jason Robards, and Jean Stapleton
DIRECTOR: David Jones
PRODUCERS: Kobi Jaeger, Reneiro Compostella, and Louis Marks
WRITER: Harold Pinter
BASED ON: The novel by Franz Kafka
DISTRIBUTOR: Capitol Films/Santa Anna Productions
BRIEF SUMMARY:

Based on the novel by Franz Kafka, *The Trial* is an intense drama telling the story of Josef K. (Kyle Maclachlan), who, on the morning of his thirtieth birthday, wakes to find himself being placed under arrest. No dull account of prison and punishment, *The Trial* chronicles the nightmare of Josef K.'s struggle to find the real reason for his unjust conviction. In this interpretation, Kafka's masterpiece takes a shockingly modern turn. Harold Pinter's powerful screenplay ensures that the audience understands the power of a Fascist state and what took place behind the Iron Curtain for seventy years. Innocent people were charged, found guilty, imprisoned, and even sent to their deaths for crimes they did not commit.

This modern adaptation of *The Trial* is a superb rendition. The original version, directed by Orson Welles in 1963, was considered by Welles to be "the best film I've ever made." This current version compares favorably with Welles's original and is outstanding in every manner: the acting is superb, the script almost impeccable, and the photography brilliant. It is an outstanding movie, but viewers take caution. Because of the intensity and complexity of the movie, it is recommended for adults only. Children under sixteen will have a difficult time understanding the concepts and dynamics.

CONTENT ANALYSIS: (AC, H, L, S) This surrealistic, anti-Fascist and anti-Communist story is marred by several expletives and sexual innuendos.

★★★ THE BEST 1993 FILMS FOR FAMILIES ★★★

Headline	Title
Biblical Messages	*Homeward Bound: The Incredible Journey*
Thoroughly Uplifting	*Searching for Bobby Fisher*
History Comes Alive	*Gettysburg*
Family Matters	*Free Willy*
Reclaiming Our Neighborhoods	*The Meteor Man*
Communicating the Love of God	*Sister Act II*
People Matter	*Dennis the Menace*
Answered Prayer	*Beethoven's 2nd*
Good Conquers Evil	*Tom and Jerry: The Movie*
A Lesson in Losing Gracefully	*Cool Runnings*

★★★ THE BEST 1993 FILMS FOR MATURE AUDIENCES ★★★

Headline	Title
Service above All	*The Remains of the Day*
Upholding Tradition	*The Age of Innocence*
Profound Insights	*Much Ado About Nothing*
The Truth Will Set Us Free	*The Fugitive*
Saved by Grace	*Schindler's List*
Coming to Terms with God's Sovereignty	*Rudy*
Love Never Fails	*Sleepless in Seattle*
Faith without Works Is Dead	*Groundhog Day*
Honoring Professionalism and Self-Sacrifice	*In the Line of Fire*
Courage in the Mouth of Danger	*Jurassic Park*

★★★ THE TWENTY MOST UNBEARABLE FILMS OF 1993 ★★★

Headline	Title
Worst Serial Killings	*Kalifornia*
Worst Gruesome Sexual Fixation	*Boxing Helena*
Worst Destroying Black Teenagers	*Poetic Justice*
Worst Turning Wives into Whores	*Indecent Proposal*
Worst Madonna Madness	*Body of Evidence*
Worst How to Murder Your Siblings	*Addams Family Values*
Worst Kinky Action Thriller	*Rising Sun*
Worst Pro-Abortion Scare Tactics	*Rain Without Thunder*
Worst Occultism for Families	*Hocus Pocus*
Worst Most Amusing Advocy for Anarchy	*Demolition Man*
Worst Pulp for Pedophiles	*A Perfect World*
Worst Normalizing Perversion	*Philadelphia*
Worst Mainstreaming Transvestites	*M. Butterfly*
Worst Anti-American Buddhist Sermon	*Heaven and Earth*
Worst Politically Correct Racism	*Bopha!*
Worst Occult Primer for Children	*Happily Ever After*
Worst Mainstreaming of Spiritism	*Heart and Souls*
Worst Anti-American Communist Propaganda	*The Panama Deception*
Worst PC Portrait of Football	*The Program*
Worst Romanticism Run Amok	*The Shadow of the Wolf*

Corny but Endearing

ANDRE

Quality: ✰✰✰   Acceptability: +1

WARNING CODES:
Language: *
Violence: *
Sex: None
Nudity: None

RATING: PG
GENRE: Drama
INTENDED AUDIENCE: Families
RUNNING TIME: 93 minutes
STARRING: Keith Carradine, Tina Majorino, Keith Szarabajk, Chelsea Field, Joshua Jackson, Shane Meier, and Aidan Pendleton
DIRECTOR: George Miller
EXECUTIVE PRODUCERS: Peter Locke and Donald Kushner
WRITER: Dana Baratta
BASED ON: The book *A Seal Called Andre* by Harry Goodridge and Lew Dietz
DISTRIBUTOR: Paramount Pictures
BRIEF SUMMARY:
Andre is the true story of a summer in 1962 and the years following as nine-year-old Toni Whitney and her father, Harry, take in a seal pup and raise it to maturity. Andre becomes part of the Whitney family, so much so that he acts almost human. Toni becomes particularly attached to Andre, and her only friends seem to be the menagerie of animals that her father has adopted. Harry is so fascinated by the seal that he soon begins to neglect the emotional needs of his family and the responsibilities of his job as harbor master in the fishing town of Rockport, Maine. Andre becomes nationally admired, but it becomes apparent that he is not suited to the harsh winters of Maine. The issue is how to care for him in the most humane way.

Andre is a corny but endearing movie, and by film's end the viewer will forgive the movie for going over the top in sap. There is a fair amount of scatological humor and some mildly offensive language, but, overall, both children and adults will love this touching and remarkable story. It is almost void of environmental preaching and is a wonderful story of love and devotion. The film's message is one we must all learn: If you love something, let it go; if it comes back, it is yours to keep.

CONTENT ANALYSIS: (B, L, V, A, M) Biblical worldview with theme of setting something or someone free if you love them, eight mild obscenities, brief fistfight, alcohol abuse, cigarette smoking by minors (not condoned), and numerous instances of scatological humor.

Biblical Parallels

ANGELS IN THE OUTFIELD

Quality: ✰✰✰   Acceptability: +1

WARNING CODES:
Language: *
Violence: None
Sex: *
Nudity: None

RATING: PG
GENRE: Comedy
INTENDED AUDIENCE: Families
RUNNING TIME: 101 minutes
STARRING: Danny Glover, Brenda Fricker, Tony Danza, Ben Johnson, Joseph Gordon-Levitt, and Christopher Lloyd
DIRECTOR: William Dear

EXECUTIVE PRODUCER: Gary Stutman

PRODUCERS: Irby Smith, Joe Roth, and Roger Birnbaum

WRITER: Holly Goldberg Sloan

DISTRIBUTOR: Buena Vista Pictures/Walt Disney Company

BRIEF SUMMARY:

Angels in the Outfield is an endearing remake of a 1951 film. In the 1994 PG-rated version, angels are dispatched to help the failing California Angels baseball team as a result of prayer from eleven-year-old Roger. Roger, having been abandoned by his father, is living in a foster care facility. After his father's sarcastic promise that they will be a "family" again when the Angels win the pennant, Roger begins seeing the celestial beings help the miserable team by assisting in miraculous plays. After he confides in the team's crusty manager, the two work together to make sure the angels have their way, and the result is a good-hearted, uplifting, biblical film.

Angels in the Outfield is packed with positive messages. The special effects are astounding and beautiful. There are, however, some elements that will warrant some discussion between Christian parents and children to make sure the portrayal of God and his kingdom is deciphered accurately amid some possibly humanistic philosophies. However, there are more parallels to the Bible than not, and the film undeniably paints the picture of a loving God. A charming film, it is regrettably marred by one minor sexual innuendo and a small amount of offensive language that is discouraged. Additionally, there is a clear contrast between answered prayer and superstition.

CONTENT ANALYSIS: (B, L, S, A, M, AB, H) Strong biblical worldview with positive depiction of angels as helpers commissioned by God in answer to prayer, four obscenities and one exclamatory profanity (barely audible), one mild sexual innuendo, alcohol use, cigarette smoking, some possible heretical viewpoints of God as questioned by young child, and humanistic approach to salvation suggested.

Crime Doesn't Pay

BABY'S DAY OUT

Quality: ☆☆   Acceptability: +1

WARNING CODES:
  Language: *
  Violence: **
  Sex: None
  Nudity: None

RATING: PG
GENRE: Comedy
INTENDED AUDIENCE: Families
RUNNING TIME: 93 minutes
STARRING: Joe Mantegna, Lara Flynn Boyle, Joe Pantoliano, Brian Haley, Cynthia Nixon, Fred Dalton Thompson, John Neville, Matthew Glave, Adam Robert Worton, and Jacob Joseph Worton
DIRECTOR: Patrick Read Johnson
EXECUTIVE PRODUCER: William Ryan
WRITER: John Hughes
DISTRIBUTOR: 20th Century Fox
BRIEF SUMMARY:

In *Baby's Day Out*, the Cotwells are the classic high-society couple with a mansion, limousine, and nanny. They decide to put Baby Bink's (their one-year-old son) picture in the paper because their friends have done the same with their kids. They select a photographer, not knowing three hoodlums have found out about the photo shoot. They pose as photographers and kidnap Baby Bink, holding him for ransom. Bink escapes and leads his kidnappers on a wild chase through the city that resembles a trip in his favorite storybook. The thugs are always one step behind, and go through excruciating slapstick injuries to catch Bink. The nanny pieces together the different locations where Bink has been spotted and figures out where he is going next.

Baby's Day Out is a younger version of *Home Alone*, done up with lots of slapstick humor and violence. Although there is a "family" look and feel to the film, with a soothing soundtrack, don't be fooled into thinking it is completely safe to let the children see without discernment. Many of the laughs are at the expense of injury to someone, with some embarrassing moments and crude remarks. The kidnappers are constantly falling off buildings and getting slammed or burned. Take a *Three Stooges* two-reeler and a *Roadrunner* cartoon, mix in a *Home Alone* theme, and you have *Baby's Day Out*.

CONTENT ANALYSIS: (B, R, L, VV, M) Traditional, biblically moral worldview (no reference to God) with a crime-doesn't-pay conclusion wherein evildoers get their just desserts. Materialistic and romantic elements, two obscenities, and nonstop slapstick-type violence.

Moral Anarchy Does Not Work

BABYFEVER

Quality: ✰✰✰   Acceptability: −1

WARNING CODES:
  Language: **
  Violence: None
  Sex: **
  Nudity: None

RATING: R
GENRE: Drama
INTENDED AUDIENCE: Adults
RUNNING TIME: 110 minutes
STARRING: Victoria Foyt, Frances Fisher, Elaine Kagan, Dinah Lenney, Zack Norman, Matt Salinger, and Eric Roberts
DIRECTOR: Henry Jaglom
PRODUCER: Judith Wolinsky
WRITERS: Henry Jaglom and Victoria Foyt
DISTRIBUTOR: Rainbow Releasing
BRIEF SUMMARY:
Babyfever sets in motion (somewhat awkwardly) a rudimentary storyline whose main purpose is to reach a fascinating main event—a baby shower in which we eavesdrop on several highly engrossing conversations about having and raising children. We hear from feminists, hedonists, traditionalists, a lesbian couple, singles, marrieds, career women, full-time homemakers, and—in two conversations—a clear-eyed evangelical Christian who is portrayed not only as fervent but also eloquent and sensitive. (How refreshing indeed it was to see a Christian portrayed with these qualities.)

For some reason, presentation of the simple plot in the first half-hour is distractingly amateurish, as though director Henry Jaglom were grinding his way through a school project. However, once the party kicks into high gear, the writing, performances, and editing are startlingly effective. What this film shows with surprising candor is the inadequacy of today's moral anarchy to serve as the basis for having and raising children. *Babyfever* will not satisfy every taste, and will probably appeal much more to women than to men. In a few spots the discussion of reproduction is frank (not lewd), however, and a handful of obscenities erupt in a couple of scenes. But overall this is one of the most interesting and original films in recent memory.

CONTENT ANALYSIS: (C, LL, SS, PC, H, Ho) Brief but positive portrayal of a Christian character, four obscenities and ten profanities, somewhat frank discussions of reproductive processes (though for the most part not lewd or offensive), sexual immorality implied, viewpoints on childbearing and child-raising from a variety of perspectives—including feminist, agnostic, homosexual, and evangelical Christian—all treated respectfully.

Timeless Tale of Hope and Faith

BLACK BEAUTY

Quality: ✰✰✰✰   Acceptability: +3

WARNING CODES:

Language: None
Violence: *
Sex: None
Nudity: None

RATING: G
GENRE: Drama
INTENDED AUDIENCE: Families
RUNNING TIME: 90 minutes
STARRING: Sean Bean, Peter
Davison, Jim Carter, Andrew Knott,
Alun Armstrong, John McEnery, Peter
Cook, Eleanor Bron, and David Thewlis

DIRECTOR: Caroline Thompson
PRODUCERS: Peter MacGregor-
Scott and Robert Shapiro
WRITER: Caroline Thompson
BASED ON: The book by Anna
Sewell
DISTRIBUTOR: Warner Brothers
BRIEF SUMMARY:

"The story of a horse's life is the story
of the people in it." Thus begins the
Warner Brothers remake of Anna Sewell's
family classic *Black Beauty*. This latest rendition is well produced, well scripted,
and destined to become a family classic in
its own right. Telling the story of the magnificent stallion and his many and varied
types of masters, the film is a beautiful
portrayal of Black Beauty's birth (portrayed very graphically), his first relationship with a trustworthy master, his
attachment to his equine carriage partner
Ginger, and the slow breakdown and
slower rebuilding of his trust for any
master. Though necessarily episodic in
nature, this is a film accessible to the
entire family.

A must-see movie for the entire family, *Black Beauty* is a sensitive and moving tale of timeless hope and faith. Told
through the use of voiceover in a first-
person narrative and using flashbacks
with backdrops of the lush English countryside, the film features very few special effects and a contemplative nature
that allows the children to enjoy the
wonder of Black Beauty's world without
the frenetic pacing that plays havoc with
cognitive development. Children of all
ages will come away with a renewed
respect for the animals that have been
entrusted to our human care.

CONTENT ANALYSIS: (C, B, V, A, M)
Christian worldview with strong moral
emphasis, animal abuse depicted (not
graphic), alcohol use, and graphic scene
of colt being born.

Money Can't Buy Happiness

BLANK CHECK

Quality: ☆☆☆   Acceptability: +2

WARNING CODES:

Language: *
Violence: *
Sex: None
Nudity: None

RATING: PG
GENRE: Comedy
INTENDED AUDIENCE: Older chil-
dren
RUNNING TIME: 90 minutes
STARRING: Brian Bonsall, Karen
Duffy, Miguel Ferrer, James Rebhorn,
Tone Loc, Michael Lerner, and Jayne
Atkinson
DIRECTOR: Rupert Wainwright
EXECUTIVE PRODUCERS: Hilary
Wayne and Blake Snyder
WRITERS: Blake Snyder and Colby
Carr
DISTRIBUTOR: Walt Disney Pic-
tures/Buena Vista Pictures
BRIEF SUMMARY:

In this *Big*-meets-*Home Alone* Disney
comedy *Blank Check*, eleven-year-old
Preston Waters just can't seem to get a
break—from his older brothers taking
over his room to a bully stealing the birthday money he got from his grandma.
That is, until a money-laundering mobster accidentally runs over Preston's
bicycle and hurriedly gives the youngster a signed blank check to cover the
damages. Once Preston realizes the

monetary significance of a signed blank check, his troubles are all over—or so he thinks. Preston has, shall we say, a "large time" with his newfound prosperity but quickly learns just how far a buck will go. The best humor occurs in scenes with Preston's driver-for-hire/confidante Henry, whose humor is matched only by his insight, ably expressed in comments like "A fool and his money are soon parted," and "Be careful what you wish for, you just might get it."

Overall, *Blank Check* is an enjoyable film with a minimum of objectionable material. There are actually several worthwhile elements in the film: money doesn't buy happiness, one's family is more precious than possessions, and a fool and his money are soon parted. While there is nothing really new here, the acting, filming, directing, and screen-writing all add up to a very decent movie the entire family will enjoy.

CONTENT ANALYSIS: (B, L, V, M) Biblical worldview in redemptive ending upholding honesty, truth, importance of family, and punishment of wrongdoing; one obscenity, one mild exclamatory profanity, a few mild vulgarities, and one obscene gesture; slapstick violence, including one man struck in the groin with baseball; criminal escapes jail and attempts to launder stolen money, but is eventually caught.

The Redemptive Power of Forgiveness

THE BROWNING VERSION

Quality: ☆☆☆☆   Acceptability: −1

WARNING CODES:
  Language: *
  Violence: None
  Sex: *
  Nudity: *
RATING: R
GENRE: Drama
INTENDED AUDIENCE: Adults

RUNNING TIME: 107 minutes
STARRING: Albert Finney, Greta Scacchi, Matthew Modine, Ben Silverstone, and Julian Sands
DIRECTOR: Mike Figgis
PRODUCERS: Ridley Scott and Mimi Polk
WRITER: Ronald Harwood
BASED ON: The play by Terence Rattigan
DISTRIBUTOR: Paramount Pictures
BRIEF SUMMARY:
The Browning Version is the story of the relationship between a young student and the retiring British schoolteacher who is forced through circumstances to come to terms with the failures in his life. The teacher, Andrew, discovers that his wife has betrayed their loveless marriage by having an affair with a young American chemistry instructor. The one bright spot in his life is the fresh-faced admiration of a young student who visits the instructor every week for one-on-one tutoring. It is through this relationship that the older man rediscovers the true value of human relationships, and thus learns to rebuild his own life and make amends to those around him.

The Browning Version is a story driven by character revelations and decisions. The director, Mike Figgis, confidently guides his actors into a kind of underplayed naturalism, and Albert Finney turns in a skillfully restrained performance that is undoubtedly one of the finest of his long career. It is refreshing to see the scriptural themes of unconditional love and the redemptive power of forgiveness played out in such a skillful manner. The film is marred, however, by the unnecessary use of a handful of obscenities sprinkled throughout the dialogue. Other than that, there is much to appreciate in *The Browning Version*.

CONTENT ANALYSIS: (C, L, N, S) Christian worldview demonstrating themes of redemption and forgiveness, six obscenities, brief naturalistic male nudity, and implied adultery (regret is clearly demonstrated).

The Folly of Pride

BULLETS OVER BROADWAY

Quality: ☆☆☆☆   Acceptability: −2

WARNING CODES:
  Language: **
  Violence: *
  Sex: *
  Nudity: None
RATING: R
GENRE: Comedy
INTENDED AUDIENCE: Adults
RUNNING TIME: 99 minutes
STARRING: Jim Broadbent, John Cusack, Harvey Fierstein, Chazz Palmineri, Mary-Louise Parker, Rob Reiner, Jennifer Tilly, Tracey Ullman, Joe Viterelli, Jack Warden, and Dianne Wiest
  DIRECTOR: Woody Allen
  PRODUCER: Robert Greenhut
  WRITERS: Woody Allen and Douglas McGrath
  DISTRIBUTOR: Miramax Films
  BRIEF SUMMARY:
  Woody Allen's film, *Bullets Over Broadway*, is a witty comedy about a young Roaring Twenties playwright, David Shayne (John Cusack), whose new "masterpiece" is to be underwritten by mobster Nick Valenti, provided the crook's dim-witted girl, Olive, gets a major role. To make matters worse, Nick assigns his toughest bodyguard, Cheech, to play watchdog for his Olive at every rehearsal. David, for all of his artistic "vision," has written dialogue so stale that even dim Olive can spot its defects. Even more aware of the need for a serious overhaul of the play is the surly Cheech, whose suggestions prove to be more useful than any ideas from the cast. David eventually realizes that this hood has a raw gift for dramatic structure, and slowly begins to tap into it.

Complications are many, but the bottom line of this film is surprisingly moral. This is, above all, a cautionary tale about the folly of pride and moral relativism. Although sexual immorality is discussed, it is not portrayed as desirable. Shot in a glowing warmth that intensifies color like an oil painting, *Bullets Over Broadway* is expertly acted by a tight ensemble cast. For grown-ups who are willing to endure some needless (but fortunately limited) foul language, there are in this film an abundance of clever lines and some provocative observations about self-defined rules of right and wrong.

CONTENT ANALYSIS: (LL, V, S, A, M) Sixteen obscenities, seven profanities, gangster shootings (not prolonged or bloody), threats of violence, sexual immorality discussed and implied (not shown), and drinking and smoking.

A Moral Hero

CLEAR AND PRESENT DANGER

Quality: ☆☆☆☆   Acceptability: −2

WARNING CODES:
  Language: ***
  Violence: **
  Sex: *
  Nudity: None
RATING: PG-13
GENRE: Action/Adventure
INTENDED AUDIENCE: Adults
RUNNING TIME: 140 minutes
STARRING: Harrison Ford, Willem Dafoe, Anne Archer, James Earl Jones, Henry Czerny, and Harris Yulin
  DIRECTOR: Phillip Noyce
  PRODUCERS: Mace Neufeld and Robert Rehme
  WRITERS: Donald Stewart, Steven Zaillian, and John Milius
  BASED ON: The novel by Tom Clancy
  DISTRIBUTOR: Paramount Pictures

BRIEF SUMMARY:

In *Clear and Present Danger* Jack Ryan (Harrison Ford) is promoted from analyst to deputy director of intelligence for the CIA and finds himself thrust into one of America's most dangerous conflicts: the war on drugs. Ryan soon draws a connection between the murder of the president's friend and a powerful Colombian drug cartel. This provides the Oval Office with striking evidence that their war on drugs is ineffective. Wanting to ensure a second term in office, the president calls for decisive action against the cartel. When Ryan uncovers illegal actions, he must decide if he will risk his career and reputation to expose the corruption.

This movie is the third Tom Clancy best-seller to be adapted into a screenplay featuring protagonist Jack Ryan, who presents many wholesome qualities. He refuses to sit still and allow the president to put innocent people in danger to further his own agenda. Ryan strives to find the truth, stands up for what is right, and opposes what is wrong. Regrettably, the movie is marred by numerous obscenities and profanities, but in the end decency, honesty, and integrity triumph over evil. With action, adventure, suspense, drama, comedy, and a moral message, *Clear and Present Danger* has it all.

CONTENT ANALYSIS: (B, PC, LLL, VV, S, A) Moral worldview with biblical and politically correct elements, twenty-seven obscenities, ten profanities one vulgarity, action violence (guns, bombs, and deaths and woman's neck is broken by killer); brief fondling and alcohol use.

Justice Triumphs

THE CLIENT

Quality: ✫✫✫✫   Acceptability: −2

WARNING CODES:

Language: ***
Violence: **
Sex: None
Nudity: None

RATING: PG-13
GENRE: Drama
INTENDED AUDIENCE: Adults
RUNNING TIME: 116 minutes
STARRING: Susan Sarandon, Tommy Lee Jones, Anthony LaPaglia, Brad Renfro, Mary-Louise Parker, Anthony Edwards, and Ossie Davis
DIRECTOR: Joel Schumacher
PRODUCERS: Arnon Milchan and Steven Reuther
WRITERS: Robert Getchell and Akiva Goldsman
BASED ON: The novel by John Grisham
DISTRIBUTOR: Warner Brothers
BRIEF SUMMARY:

In this film version of the latest John Grisham best-seller, eleven-year-old Mark and little brother Ricky could not foresee how their lives would be dramatically and irreversibly changed one hot summer morning in Memphis, Tennessee, when they sneaked down by the river to smoke cigarettes. By day's end, however, Ricky lay motionless in a coma and Mark finds himself in need of a good attorney. His picture flooding the papers and his family surrounded by police who believe he has information about a murder, Mark enlists the services of Reggie Love, Attorney at Law. This turns out to be a wise move. Heading up the investigation is U.S. Attorney "Reverend" Roy Foltrigg, a flamboyant and ambitious man not to be taken lightly.

There is no real mystery in *The Client*, as the facts unfold along with the story. Mark knows everything (therefore, so does the audience), and that is why he is in danger. However, a substantial amount of suspense and intrigue should keep adult audiences motivated until the very end of the film. Acting performances are excellent, and with no sex or nudity, and violence appropriate to the story, an overabundance of offensive language is the only negative in *The Client*, an otherwise well-made, interesting, and enjoyable film.

CONTENT ANALYSIS: (B, C, LLL, VV, A, D, M) Justice triumphs in a sinful, fallen world where Scripture is quoted and grace is acknowledged; eighty-nine obscenities, twenty-three profanities, and ten to fifteen vulgarities; moderate violence (off-screen suicide with gun, mob killer chases boy and threatens with knife, and brief gunfire); brief alcohol and drug abuse in attempted suicide; young boys smoke cigarettes; and brief glimpse of maggots in body bag.

Christian Witness

CORRINA, CORRINA

Quality: ✰✰✰✰   Acceptability: +1

WARNING CODES:
  Language: *
  Violence: None
  Sex: None
  Nudity: None
RATING: PG
GENRE: Comedy/Drama
INTENDED AUDIENCE: Families
RUNNING TIME: 116 minutes
STARRING: Whoopi Goldberg, Ray Liotta, Tina Majorino, Wendy Crewson, Larry Miller, Erica Yohn, Jenifer Lewis, Joan Cusack, and Don Ameche
DIRECTOR: Jessie Nelson
EXECUTIVE PRODUCERS: Ruth Vitale and Bernie Goldmann
WRITER: Jessie Nelson
DISTRIBUTOR: New Line Cinema
BRIEF SUMMARY:
At the center of Jessie Nelson's semi-autobiographical story, *Corrina, Corrina*, is a question: Where did Molly Singer's mother go when she died? Five-year-old Molly does not know the answer and refuses to speak to anyone for weeks after her mother's funeral. Molly's young, atheistic father professes not to share Molly's confusion, yet he watches home movies of his wife with a clear expression of longing to know what has become of her. The question remains throughout the movie and is answered in many ways by the Singers' new Christian nanny and housekeeper, Corrina, played by Whoopi Goldberg.

The message the director is sending is clear: Although Christian belief in heaven is merely a nicety, it is one that atheists should not begrudge. After all, the director seems to say, we all need to get by somehow. *Corrina, Corrina* is fine entertainment for the whole family, at least in one sense. It is a well-crafted comic drama with lots of good humor and few objectionable elements. · Although the movie itself comes up short of answers, *Corrina, Corrina* provides an excellent platform for parents to teach their children about the Christian understanding of death.

CONTENT ANALYSIS: (C, L, A, M) Christian worldview, positive portrayal of Christian character, two obscenities and three profanities, alcohol use, and mature themes of death and racism.

Wholesome Entertainment

D2: THE MIGHTY DUCKS

Quality: ✰✰✰✰   Acceptability: +2

WARNING CODES:
  Language: *
  Violence: *
  Sex: None
  Nudity: None
RATING: PG
GENRE: Comedy
INTENDED AUDIENCE: Children and adults
RUNNING TIME: 100 minutes
STARRING: Emilio Estevez, Michael Tucker, Jan Rubes, and Kathryn Erbe
DIRECTOR: Sam Weisman
PRODUCERS: Jordan Kerner and Jon Avnet
EXECUTIVE PRODUCER: Doug Claybourne
WRITER: Steven Brill

DISTRIBUTOR: Walt Disney Company/Buena Vista Pictures

BRIEF SUMMARY:

In *D2: The Mighty Ducks*, Emilio Estevez plays Gordon Bombay, a prominent hockey player whose career is stalled by an unfortunate injury. However, a hockey equipment manufacturer offers him a job as head coach for Team U.S.A. Hockey. Many of Team U.S.A.'s players were on the Mighty Ducks peewee team that he had previously coached. When extra players are added to the team, resulting in tension, Bombay ties the team together and does not allow them to separate until they can work together and move as a unit. Another problem arises when he is tempted by the material rewards of a house in Malibu, fine clothes, and other possessions that almost cause him to lose his purpose with the team. When the team loses to the Iceland team 12–1, he begins to wake up. An old friend reminds him of his convictions and urges him to follow them. When the team changes from their Team U.S.A. uniforms to their Ducks uniforms, the crowd goes wild, and he coaches the team to new heights.

The movie is a great representation of how much can be accomplished through working together as a team. Because it lacks foul language and other objectionable elements, *D2: The Mighty Ducks* is a commendable movie. It will be a hit with young people and will entertain adults as well.

CONTENT ANALYSIS: (B, L, V, M) Positive, wholesome worldview; two obscenities; typical violence associated with game of hockey (in one instance the opposing coach hits Ducks coach Bombay with a hockey stick); material things such as houses and money given to Bombay cause him temporarily to forget his priorities.

A Visual Treat

THE FLINTSTONES

Quality: ☆☆☆☆   Acceptability: +3

WARNING CODES:
  Language: *
  Violence: None
  Sex: *
  Nudity: None
RATING: PG
GENRE: Comedy
INTENDED AUDIENCE: All ages
RUNNING TIME: 92 minutes
STARRING: John Goodman, Elizabeth Perkins, Rick Moranis, Rosie O'Donnell, Kyle MacLachlan, Halle Berry, Elizabeth Taylor, Richard Moll, Jonathan Winters, and Harvey Korman
DIRECTOR: Brian Levant
PRODUCER: Bruce Cohen
EXECUTIVE PRODUCER: Steven Spielberg
WRITERS: Tom S. Parker, Jim Jennewein, and Steven E. de Souza
DISTRIBUTOR: Universal Pictures
BRIEF SUMMARY:

The Flintstones is one of those rare family films that thoroughly entertains you—whether you are five years old or fifty. Unlike most cartoons-turned-feature-films, *The Flintstones* has it all— fantastic special effects, humorous sets, endearing characters, superb acting, and a winsome plot. The plot revolves around a villainous rock-quarry executive, Cliff Vandercave, who wants to embezzle the Slate and Company Quarry by setting up a patsy Neanderthal executive whom he can manipulate into transferring funds to him and then staying around to take the rap while Cliff heads for Rockapulco. When Cliff tests the aptitude of the laborers, he finds his man in Fred Flintstone. Success goes to Fred's head, and he and Wilma begin spending money and friendships as if there were no tomorrow. The rest of this imaginative movie involves Cliff framing Fred and Fred learning that family and friendship are worth far more than money.

The Flintstones movie is full of good moral lessons, from the dictabird teaching Fred that you must read what you sign, to a clear message that you should be faithful to your spouse. Regrettably, there is one obscenity in the film and some sexual innuendo, which is clearly rebuffed.

CONTENT ANALYSIS: (B, L, S) A strong biblical worldview with several moral messages, one obscenity, and sexual innuendo that is rebuked.

God Is Good

FORREST GUMP

Quality: ☆☆☆☆   Acceptability: –1

WARNING CODES:
  Language: **
  Violence: *
  Sex: *
  Nudity: *
RATING: PG-13
GENRE: Comedy/Drama
INTENDED AUDIENCE: Adults
RUNNING TIME: 135 minutes
STARRING: Tom Hanks, Robin Wright, Gary Sinise, Mykelti Williamson, and Sally Field
  DIRECTOR: Robert Zemeckis
  PRODUCERS: Wendy Finerman, Steve Tisch, and Steve Starkey
  WRITER: Eric Roth
  DISTRIBUTOR: Paramount Pictures
BRIEF SUMMARY:
In the movie by the same name, Forrest Gump is a lovable, dim-witted hero in a picaresque tale of America during three of its most tumultuous decades (the '50s, '60s, and '70s). From Elvis Presley to JFK to President Nixon, Forrest Gump meets them all, becomes a football star, war hero, athlete, and millionaire, and in doing so gives us a comic and rueful overview of the political and social events and persons that entered into our national consciousness during these decades. Although Southerner Forrest Gump has an IQ of only 75, his optimism and generosity place him in extraordinary circumstances during extraordinary times. We travel with Forrest on his comic ventures as he becomes an All-American, joins the Army, and wins the Congressional Medal of Honor, goes on to own a conglomerate, becomes a celebrated runner, and wins his one true love.

This is a delightful adult fairy tale in the tradition of *Being There*, *Rainman*, and the Orthodox Holy Fool stories. It is well crafted in every facet, combining special-effects technology and storytelling to give us an extremely entertaining film. Tom Hanks is uncannily ingenious as Forrest. Due to the decades explored, there are gross vulgarities and obscenities, implied fornication, as well as depicted drug abuse. However, all of these lead to the overwhelming conclusion that a wanton lifestyle destroys.

CONTENT ANALYSIS: (C, B, LL, V, S, N, D, C) Christian worldview with a presupposition of God and probing references to heaven, Jesus, God's presence and will for our lives versus our will, and our fallen nature as well as a biblical perspective toward wages of sin; ten obscenities, two profanities, and several gross vulgarities; brief action violence; several instances of implied fornication; brief, partial nudity; substance abuse; and one character finds redemption in love of God.

Refreshing Family Film

GORDY

Quality: ☆☆☆   Acceptability: +3
WARNING CODES:
  Language: None
  Violence: None
  Sex: None
  Nudity: None

RATING: G
GENRE: Comedy
INTENDED AUDIENCE: All ages
RUNNING TIME: 95 minutes
STARRING: Doug Stone, James Donaldio, Deborah Hobart, Michael Roescher, Kristy Young, Tom Lester, and Tom Key
DIRECTOR: Mark Lewis
PRODUCER: Sybil Robson
WRITER: Leslie Stevens
BRIEF SUMMARY: The film *Gordy* will delight children and warm the hearts of the entire family. Gordy is a bright-eyed little piglet without a care in the world until one afternoon he discovers that his father, his mother, and his brothers and sisters have been taken away in hog trucks bound for the slaughter house. Gordy sets out on a desperate quest to find his family. In the process he is adopted by little Jinnie Sue MacAllister, who sings with her father's traveling band. The next performance is the Governor's Barbecue, where a little boy named Hanky Royce, grandson of Henry Royce, founder of Royce Industries, falls into the pool, and Gordy dives in and saves him. The news media run with the story as the Governor awards Gordy a medal. Overnight, the hero pig becomes famous and the logo of Royce Industries! When Henry dies, Hanky is named sole heir, with Gordy as the trustee. Gilbert Sipes, a scheming PR-man who wants to control Royce industries, orders his henchmen to pig-nap Gordy.

Gordy is an uplifting, refreshing family film with a comic-book quality that contains no offensive elements and plenty of insightful humor. One slight distraction, however, is that some characters played their parts "straight" while others "hammed it up." However, in the final analysis *Gordy* is a hoot and a holler—a hero pig who will entertain and enlighten children and parents.

CONTENT ANALYSIS: (B, C) Biblical, redemptive worldview stressing the importance of family relationships, emphasizing positive moral values, and showing that prayer is answered.

Flawed Redemptive Story

GUARDING TESS

Quality: ☆☆☆☆   Acceptability: −1

WARNING CODES:
  Language: **
  Violence: None
  Sex: None
  Nudity: None

RATING: PG-13
GENRE: Drama
INTENDED AUDIENCE: Older teens and adults
RUNNING TIME: 97 minutes
STARRING: Shirley MacLaine, Nicholas Cage, and Austin Pendleton
DIRECTOR: Hugh Wilson
PRODUCERS: Ned Tanen and Nancy Graham Tanen
WRITERS: Hugh Wilson and Peter Torokvei
DISTRIBUTOR: TriStar Pictures
BRIEF SUMMARY:
Guarding Tess tells the story of Special Secret Service Agent Doug Chesnic, who has been assigned to guard Tess, a former First Lady. In some deliciously humorous scenes, Doug tries to extricate himself from his humdrum post while the crafty Tess uses all of her influence with the current president to keep him on duty. The president even has some high-level meetings interrupted because of Tess, and tells Chesnic in the most profane language to try to make Tess more comfortable. Tess in turn exercises her authority imperiously by playing golf in the freezing cold, driving off without her security protection, and undertaking other irregular activities to keep Chesnic on his toes. Why she is so attached to Doug appears to be a puzzle until, while looking back at old videotapes of her husband's funeral, Tess freezes on a frame where only Agent

Chesnic shows remorse at the death of her husband. When Tess is kidnapped, Agent Chesnic is the only man for the job.

Guarding Tess is filled with laughter and some tears. Nicholas Cage as Agent Chesnic and Shirley MacLaine as Tess are brilliant. Hugh Wilson directs this piece with great authenticity and balance. However, the film's unnecessary twenty profanities and seventeen obscenities, which even degrade the office of the president, will only limit the audience appeal of this otherwise redemptive story.

CONTENT ANALYSIS: (B, LL, A, D) Redemptive worldview, twenty profanities, seventeen obscenities, and alcohol use.

Seeking Fortune and Glory

HOOP DREAMS

Quality: ☆☆☆   Acceptability: −1

WARNING CODES:
  Language: **
  Violence: *
  Sex: None
  Nudity: None

RATING: PG-13
GENRE: Sports documentary
INTENDED AUDIENCE: Teens
RUNNING TIME: 190 minutes
FEATURING: Arthur Agee and William Gates
DIRECTOR: Steve James
PRODUCERS: Gordon Quinn, Catherine Allan, Frederick Marx, Steve James, and Peter Gilbert
WRITERS: Frederick Marx and Steve James
DISTRIBUTOR: Fine Line Features
BRIEF SUMMARY:
Hoop Dreams is a documentary that does what the medium should do—it tells a story with little commentary, letting the audience be the judge. The film begins in 1987 and chronicles the lives of two inner-city African American boys from age fourteen to eighteen as each strives to reach his dream of playing for the NBA. William Gates and Arthur Agee come from supportive families and show early promise in grade school, where a scout for the prestigious St. Joseph prep school offers each young man a partial scholarship. Told in almost claustrophobic close-ups, the film quickly leads the audience to cheer for these two young men and their families. This is as much a story about their home lives as it is about the game and the coaches that shape them.

The main downside to this documentary is the focus of these young men. Basketball and the hope of fame and a great deal of money are their only goals. If they are injured or if they play poorly, they have nothing. The idea that going to school might help provide a real future never seems to enter their minds, or anyone else's for that matter. Someone, somewhere along the way, should have thought to tell them that the "system" could work for them if only they would change their focus from the distorted "fortune and glory" viewpoint that seems to prevail. Also, language, bigotry, and drug use mar the movie.

CONTENT ANALYSIS: (Pa, LL, V, A, D, C) Materialistic worldview, ten obscenities and several exclamatory profanities; off-screen violence (wife abuse) and vicious anti-white rap song; illegitimate children live with unmarried parents, alcohol use, drug dealing and use implied, and father returns to family after experiencing religious turnaround.

An Honest Man Is Good to Find

THE HUDSUCKER PROXY

Quality: ☆☆☆☆   Acceptability: −1

WARNING CODES:
  Language: *
  Violence: *
  Sex: None
  Nudity: None

RATING: PG
GENRE: Dramatic comedy
INTENDED AUDIENCE: Adults
RUNNING TIME: 105 minutes
STARRING: Tim Robbins, Jennifer Jason Leigh, Paul Newman, Charles Durning, John Mahoney, Jim True, and William Cobbs
DIRECTOR: Joel Coen
PRODUCER: Ethan Coen
EXECUTIVE PRODUCERS: Eric Fellner and Tim Bevan
WRITERS: Ethan Coen, Joel Coen, and Sam Raimi
DISTRIBUTOR: Warner Brothers
BRIEF SUMMARY:

In *Hudsucker Proxy*, it is New York City in 1958 and the president of Hudsucker Industries has just jumped to his death from the 44th floor—45th if you count the mezzanine. Why did he jump? Wasn't he happy? Why didn't he open the window first? Most importantly, what's the board supposed to do when old man Hudsucker's controlling stock is about to be released for sale to the general public for any Tom, Dick, or Harry to purchase (i.e., public takeover)? Why ... force the stock to fall in price and buy it up themselves, of course. To do that, however, they will need a new president, someone they can really push around, a patsy, a jerk, a proxy—a Hudsucker proxy, to be exact.

Not just another rehash of old-Hollywood movie styles, *The Hudsucker Proxy* is a superbly produced and technically stunning visual treat. The cinematography is dark and moody but alive with style. The actors are tremendous, not a bad performance in the entire cast, and the story, while predictable and politically correct plotwise (big business crushes innocent man who prevails against all odds with the help of coldhearted, tough career woman whose cold heart is thawed by love found in the honest, good-hearted man), is suspenseful and humorous and successfully holds the viewer's interest throughout. Don't look down to check your watch, you won't want to miss this ending.

CONTENT ANALYSIS: (H, L, V, FR, B) Light humanist, socialist worldview where fate is in control and big business is inherently evil; seven mild obscenities and five exclamatory profanities; mild, comic violence as two men fall from 44th floor, although there are no injuries shown, and several comic slaps and punches; one reference to Hindu religion and importance of karma; and biblical element of forgiveness when a man receives second chance at life and then forgives his friend.

A Captivating Movie for Older Audiences

I LOVE TROUBLE

Quality: ☆☆☆☆   Acceptability: −1

WARNING CODES:
  Language: *
  Violence: *
  Sex: *
  Nudity: *
RATING: PG
GENRE: Comedy/Mystery
INTENDED AUDIENCE: Adults
RUNNING TIME: 115 minutes
STARRING: Julia Roberts, Nick Nolte, Saul Rubinek, Robert Loggia, and Olympia Dukakis
DIRECTOR: Charles Shyer
PRODUCER: Nancy Meyers
WRITERS: Charles Shyer and Nancy Meyers
DISTRIBUTOR: Buena Vista Pictures/Walt Disney Company
BRIEF SUMMARY:

Moviegoers will not be disappointed with Disney's pairing of Julia Roberts and Nick Nolte in the entertaining and suspenseful adventure comedy, *I Love Trouble.* Two rival newspaper reporters, one a seasoned veteran and the other a fresh-faced cub, go head-to-head covering the same story involving a Chicago train wreck. With new facts emerging by the minute, our two crack reporters uncover suspicious circumstances surrounding the cause of the wreck and, in the process, stumble upon a plot involving industrial espionage. The race is on: Who will get the next scoop, and who will ultimately break the whole story?

An intriguing mystery with intense drama, I Love Trouble also provides comic relief and a romantic element in the relationship between Roberts and Nolte. Never a dull or lagging moment, the film's pace and plot development are superb, and the drama and suspense are captivating. First-rate cinematography establishes the overall continuity and style, and the story is made even easier to follow by the use of innovative cuts and edits that add to the smooth flow. I Love Trouble is an immensely enjoyable film combining intrigue, mystery, drama, and humor with superb acting and excellent production. A small amount of foul language, sexual innuendo, and implied immorality mar this otherwise enjoyable movie that is suitable mainly for adults.

CONTENT ANALYSIS: (R, L, V, S, N, M) Romantic worldview with pattern of lying to achieve agenda, but played for laughs; three obscenities, five exclamatory profanities, three vulgarities, and three sexual innuendos; brief action violence (train wreck, car chase, gunfire, and dead body, but nothing gratuitous and all necessary to plot) implied promiscuity and suggestive dancing in one scene; brief partial nudity (only back and shoulders seen briefly in one comic scene); and smoking and drinking portrayed casually, but no abuse.

Endearing Hilarity

I.Q.

Quality: ☆☆☆   Acceptability: +1

WARNING CODES:
  Language: *
  Violence: *

  Sex: None
  Nudity: None
RATING: PG
GENRE: Romance
INTENDED AUDIENCE: Teens and adults
RUNNING TIME: 96 minutes
STARRING: Meg Ryan, Tim Robbins, Walter Matthau, Charles Durning, Steve Fry, Frank Whaley, and Joseph Maher
DIRECTOR: Fred Schepisi
PRODUCERS: Scott Rudin and Sandy Gallin
WRITERS: Andrew Breckman and Michael Leeson
DISTRIBUTOR: Paramount Pictures
BRIEF SUMMARY:

The delightful comedy I.Q. finds Albert Einstein's niece caught in a romantic choice between her rational but boring fiancé and a dreamy auto mechanic. This delightful fantasy stars Meg Ryan as Einstein's niece, Catherine Boyd, a dedicated mathematician happily engaged to a stuffy, intellectual psychologist—that is until a fateful stop at a service station where she meets auto mechanic and amateur scientist Ed Walters. Their eyes meet, and the reaction is positively celestial. Although Boyd will not allow herself to fall for a "mere" mechanic, Uncle Albert takes an instant liking to the young man. He launches a plot to convince his niece that Walters is actually an undiscovered genius. The plan works all too well, and soon Uncle Albert must either tell her the truth or face rigorous questioning that may reveal his fraud.

I.Q. does not take an Einstein to guess how this endearing film will end. However, what keeps the viewer hooked is the hilarity, particularly the antics of Einstein and his lovable scientist cronies. Walter Matthau is skillful in his performance as Einstein, and Meg Ryan is perfectly believable as his mathematician niece, while maintaining an effortless girlishness throughout the film. The gorgeous cinematography reinforces the innocent 1940s feel of this good-natured picture, which even touches on such Christian themes as mortality and God's ordering the universe.

CONTENT ANALYSIS: (B, Pa, L, V, B, A) Idealistic fantasy featuring basic morality—God recognized as controlling the universe but offering no personal redemption or relationship and some nominalistic concepts broached but not illustrated; one obscenity and ten vulgarities (including eight sexual innuendos); two disturbing scenes—subjects of scientific experiments in agony, one subject sings from "Hallelujah" chorus while in extreme suffering; and brief social drinking.

Fairness, Truth, and Integrity Prevail

IRON WILL

Quality: ☆☆☆☆   Acceptability: +2

WARNING CODES:
   Language: *
   Violence: *
   Sex: None
   Nudity: None

RATING: PG
GENRE: Action/Adventure
INTENDED AUDIENCE: Teens and adults
RUNNING TIME: 110 minutes
STARRING: Mackenzie Astin, Kevin Spacey, David Ogden Stiers, and August Schellenberg
DIRECTOR: Charles Haid
PRODUCERS: Patrick Palmer and Robert Schwartz
WRITERS: John Michael Hayes, Djordje Milicevic, and Jeff Arch
DISTRIBUTOR: Buena Vista Pictures/Walt Disney Company
BRIEF SUMMARY:
Seventeen-year-old Will Stoneman puts his life on the line, along with his family's future, when he enters a grueling, 522-mile dogsled marathon from Winnipeg to St. Paul in Disney's excellent new action adventure Iron Will. The year is 1917, war looms over Europe, and the $10,000 cash prize for winning the Dog Derby could save the farm and send Will to college, not to mention rekindle his desire to live after the tragic death of his father in a sledding accident.

Like his father, Will is an excellent sledder, but to have any chance at winning this race he must not only train hard but gain the respect of his father's team of dogs, led by a beautiful white Husky named Gus. All of his training, however, cannot totally prepare Will for what he will encounter as he enters the biggest challenge of his life.

Iron Will extols the principles of fairness, truth, and integrity. These moral values prove victorious as Will overcomes the obstacles placed before him.

Iron Will is an adventure like adventures ought to be, with virtuous heroes, treacherous villains, and edge-of-the-seat action—plus some heart-tugging emotion to complete the package. Audiences will cheer young Iron Will Stoneman for his heroic effort, just as those in the film who watched him race. What a finish!

CONTENT ANALYSIS: (L, V, M, B) Two mild obscenities; adventure-type violence in form of dangerous dogsled race; a dogfight, dog attack on antagonist character, and one brief fistfight (scenes are actually more intense than violent); sponsors bet on race outcome and drink cognac (not to excess); and moral principles of fairness, truth, and integrity are exhibited and prove victorious.

Purity and Love Conquers Avarice and Pride

THE JUNGLE BOOK

Quality: ☆☆☆☆   Acceptability: +2

WARNING CODES:
   Language: *

Violence: **
Sex: *
Nudity: None
RATING: PG
GENRE: Action/Adventure
INTENDED AUDIENCE: Older children and up
RUNNING TIME: 110 minutes
STARRING: Jason Scott Lee, Sam Neill, John Cleese, Cary Elwes, and Lena Headey
DIRECTOR: Stephen Sommers
EXECUTIVE PRODUCERS: Sharad Patel, Mark Damon, and Lawrence Mortorff
WRITERS: Ronald Yanover and Mark D. Geldman
BASED ON: The book by Rudyard Kipling
DISTRIBUTOR: Buena Vista Pictures/Walt Disney Company
BRIEF SUMMARY:
This Walt Disney live-action rendition of *The Jungle Book* opens on an ancient map of India, as Major Brydon (Sam Neill) tells about traveling to a remote area of this exotic subcontinent. His entourage includes his five-year-old daughter, Kitty, and her Indian friend Mowgli. Both Kitty and Mowgli lost their mothers to untimely deaths. When the tiger Shere Khan attacks the camp, Mowgli is carried off into the jungle. There, Mowgli is befriended by a panther, a gray wolf, and a bear. Years later, a grown-up Kitty wanders into the jungle and meets Mowgli (Jason Scott Lee). Soon thereafter, Mowgli sneaks into the city to find Kitty and is thrown in prison. Kitty appeals to her father to let her teach Mowgli English. Kitty's fiancé, Captain William Boone, realizes that Mowgli knows the way to a lost treasure and wants Mowgli to lead him to it. When Mowgli flees to the jungle, Captain Boone pursues him in his greedy quest for the lost treasure.

The Jungle Book is a classic romance that has hint of a pantheistic respect for wildlife. However, its deviations from a biblical perspective are kept in abeyance by the triumph of purity and love over avarice and pride. The movie is not for little children because of the frightening battles, but is well suited for children ages eight and up. This is an entertaining movie, well worth seeing.

CONTENT ANALYSIS: (C, Ro, L, VV, S, FR, B, M) Christian premise that love, purity, and integrity triumph over evil set in a Romantic worldview; three obscenities and two vulgar references; frightening fights with python, fistfights, beatings, and minor scuffles; reference to being kicked in private parts; some references and symbols of false religions (Hinduism and pantheism); false religion rebuked; and some smoking.

Exciting and Heartwarming

LASSIE

Quality: ☆☆☆☆   Acceptability: +2

WARNING CODES:
Language: *
Violence: *
Sex: None
Nudity: None
RATING: PG
GENRE: Adventure
INTENDED AUDIENCE: Families
RUNNING TIME: 90 minutes
STARRING: Tom Guiry, Richard Farnsworth, Helen Slater, Jon Tenney, Brittany Boyd, Frederic Forrest, and Lassie
DIRECTOR: Daniel Petrie
EXECUTIVE PRODUCER: Michael Rachmil
PRODUCER: Lorne Michaels
WRITER: Matthew Jacobs, Gary Ross, and Elizabeth Anderson
BASED ON: The character "Lassie" created by Eric Knight
DISTRIBUTOR: Paramount Pictures
BRIEF SUMMARY:
"Children are supposed to have a dog—it helps them grow up right," argues seven-year-old Jennifer Turner to

her family when she finds a collie that she names Lassie left homeless by an accident in the exciting Paramount picture, *Lassie*. The Turners find Lassie as they are abandoning the big city for a small village in the Shenandoah, Virginia, countryside, but there is a question about who rescues whom at the accident, for Lassie seems to pick out Jennifer's brother, thirteen-year-old Matt, to rescue him from his rebelliousness and depression. Once they arrive in their Shenandoah home, Lassie takes Matt's headphones and forces him to chase her until he realizes the value of nature. When he does, the drama starts, for their neighbor Sam Garland has been making a fortune pasturing his sheep on Turner land. Sam determines to drive off these neighbors, and Lassie must save the day.

Director Dan Petrie does a superb job of directing this exciting and heartwarming tale. Slightly marred by six low-key obscenities and two ambivalent exclamations, *Lassie* is otherwise a stirring coming-of-age tale that involves redemption, forgiveness, courage, and all those virtues that we associate with the original *Lassie* movies.

CONTENT ANALYSIS: (C, B, L, V) Christian worldview of sacrifice, forgiveness, and redemption with several strong moral messages; six obscenities and two exclamatory profanities; and some minor action violence.

Magnificent Christian Allegory

THE LION KING

Quality: ✰✰✰✰   Acceptability: +2

WARNING CODES:
  Language: None
  Violence: *
  Sex: None
  Nudity: None
RATING: G

GENRE: Animated adventure
INTENDED AUDIENCE: Families
RUNNING TIME: 80 Minutes
VOICES: Jonathan Taylor Thomas, Matthew Broderick, James Earl Jones, Jeremy Irons, Moira Kelly, Niketa Calame, Ernie Sabella, Nathan Lane, Robert Guillaume, Rowan Atkinson, Madge Sinclair, Whoopi Goldberg, Cheech Marin, and Jim Cummings
DIRECTORS: Roger Allers and Rob Minkoff
EXECUTIVE PRODUCERS: Thomas Schumacher and Sarah McArthur
PRODUCER: Don Hahn
WRITERS: Irene Mecchi, Jonathan Roberts, and Linda Woolverton
DISTRIBUTOR: Walt Disney Pictures
BRIEF SUMMARY:

A magnificent example of Disney animation, *The Lion King* is a heroic tale of good versus evil, which embodies many Christian allegorical elements. The sinister Scar plots to kill his brother and nephew, King Mufasa and young Simba, so he can become king himself. Demonstrating incredible love and courage, King Mufasa risks his own life to save the life of his son, Simba. However, his own brother who seizes the throne ultimately kills the noble king. King Mufasa's death is a sad but necessary part of the story. Simba returns to confront his evil uncle and demonstrates his understanding of responsibility and true authority.

The Lion King conveys a clear message of hope and reconciliation and promotes a message of stewardship and enjoyment of the wonders of creation. Although there are several minor areas that call for discernment, the good far outweighs the bad. The film includes a positive portrayal of an intact family, as well as a portrait of a powerful yet humble leader willing to sacrifice for others. The humor is delightful, hilarious, and clean. The animation is stunning. A roaring success, *The Lion King* presents eternal truths in the context of an entertaining, exciting, magnificent wildlife adventure that will capture the hearts and minds of viewers of all ages.

CONTENT ANALYSIS: (C, B, V, FR) Christian allegory emphasizing death to self and selfishness, self-sacrifice, forgiveness, and overcoming hardship, featuring heroic characters driven by a moral worldview; action violence— chase by vicious animals, stampede scene, several bloodless fights, and Mufasa's death fall; and seven portrayals of false religion.

Fun

LITTLE BIG LEAGUE

Quality: ✰✰✰✰   Acceptability: –1

WARNING CODES:

Language: **
Violence: None
Sex: *
Nudity: *

RATING: PG
GENRE: Comedy
INTENDED AUDIENCE: Teens and adults
RUNNING TIME: 112 minutes
STARRING: Luke Edwards, Timothy Busfield, John Ashton, Kevin Dunn, Jonathan Silverman, Billy L. Sullivan, Miles Feulner, Ashley Crow, Dennis Farina, and Jason Robards
DIRECTOR: Andrew Scheinman
EXECUTIVE PRODUCERS: Steve Nicolaides and Andrew Bergman
PRODUCER: Mike Lobell
WRITERS: Gregory Pincus and Adam Scheinman
DISTRIBUTOR: Columbia Pictures
BRIEF SUMMARY:

In *Little Big League*, twelve-year-old Billy Heywood's friends think it is awesome that his grandfather owns the Minnesota Twins baseball team. Billy thinks it is awesome that Grandpa considers him his best friend. When Grandpa Thomas Heywood passes away unexpectedly, what do the boys think when he leaves full ownership of the major league team to grandson Billy? The answer can be found in the heartwarming and hilarious summer comedy *Little Big League*.

While good summer fun, *Little Big League* is marred somewhat by foul language and brief sexual innuendo, both of which are condemned. However, with excellent acting performances and tremendously authentic baseball action, the good far outweighs the bad. Billy honestly learns some valuable life lessons, during which we find the objectionable content. Some "grown-up" big leaguers learn a thing or two from young Billy as well, including that baseball is a game and meant to be played for fun. Take away the fun and you no longer have a game. "You guys are major leaguers!" Billy pleadingly reminds them. "You're on baseball cards! What could be better than that?" Not much, as proven by the comments from two players after experiencing Billy's magical effect on their team: "Most fun I ever had," one player says wistfully. "Only fun I ever had," nods the other. See, I told you . . . fun!

CONTENT ANALYSIS: (B, LL, S, N, M) Wholesome, moral worldview (but no reference to God)—baseball should be played for fun not for money and family portrayed as more important than wealth; ten obscenities, one profanity, and four vulgarities; implied promiscuity in off-screen pay-TV porn movie; brief scene of women in pay-TV porn movie unbuttoning their shirts and boy reprimanded for watching porn movie and promises never to watch again; boy lies to teacher once; and ballplayer chews tobacco.

Heaven Is Where Salvation Lies

LITTLE WOMEN

Quality: ✰✰✰✰   Acceptability: +3

WARNING CODES:

Language: None
Violence: None
Sex: None
Nudity: None

RATING: PG
GENRE: Romance/Drama/
Biography
INTENDED AUDIENCE: All ages
RUNNING TIME: 170 minutes
STARRING: Winona Ryder, Gabriel
Byrne, Trini Alvarado, Samantha Mathis,
Kirsten Dunst, Claire Danes, Christian
Bale, Eric Stoltz, John Neville, Mary
Wickes, and Susan Sarandon
DIRECTOR: Gillian Armstrong
PRODUCER: Denise Di Novi
WRITER: Robin Swicord
BASED ON: The novel by Louisa
May Alcott
DISTRIBUTOR: Columbia Pictures
BRIEF SUMMARY:
Little Women is the second cinematic
adaptation of Louisa May Alcott's classic
tale of the four March sisters, Meg, Jo,
Beth, and Amy, who grow up economi-
cally poor but spiritually rich to find
love, success, and happiness. The linch-
pin of the movie is Jo (she is Louis May
Alcott idealized). A restless spirit imprisoned by convention and long skirts, Jo
longs to go to college and succeed. She
directs her longings and energy into her
stories, which occasionally bring some
much-needed money to the family.
Meanwhile, her volatile nature leads her
to temperamental outbursts and abrupt,
although generous, acts (such as selling
her hair for money to send to her war-
injured father).

Director Gillian Armstrong deftly
weaves the scenes from Alcott's book
into a coherent plot, with Jo's growth
from wild girl to strong, disciplined,
accomplished young woman as the uni-
fying thread. Ryder overcomes her
sometimes-forced dialogue with a
dynamic performance. It is interesting
to note that the strong religious themes

in Alcott's book are downplayed in the
movie. The fact that Mr. March is a reverend is never mentioned, and the scene
in which the professor eloquently
defends God is not included. The
emphasis in *Little Women* is on Jo's personal growth and sisterhood. However,
the movie still makes it clear, through
its music and general theme, that salvation lies in heaven.

CONTENT ANALYSIS: (B, C) Moral
worldview with positive Christian characters and actions, strong parental figures
and chaste courtships, but no mention of
Jesus Christ.

Classy Update

LOVE AFFAIR

Quality: ☆☆☆☆   Acceptability: −1

WARNING CODES:

Language: **
Violence: None
Sex: *
Nudity: None

RATING: PG-13
GENRE: Romance/Drama
INTENDED AUDIENCE: Adults
RUNNING TIME: 101 minutes
STARRING: Warren Beatty, Annette
Bening, Katharine Hepburn, Gary
Shandling, Pierce Brosnan, Kate
Capshaw, Chloe Webb, Brenda Vaccaro,
and Harold Ramis
DIRECTOR: Glenn Gordon Caron
EXECUTIVE PRODUCER: Andrew
Z. Davis
PRODUCER: Warren Beatty
WRITERS: Robert Towne and
Warren Beatty
DISTRIBUTOR: Warner Brothers
BRIEF SUMMARY:
An update of the classic romantic
story, *Love Affair* stars Warren Beatty
and Annette Bening in the roles made
famous by Cary Grant and Deborah
Kerr in 1957's *An Affair to Remember*, as
the two people whose lives are changed

when they meet, this time, on board a transcontinental flight to Australia. Former NFL football star-turned-sportscaster, Mike Gambrill is all set to marry wealthy talk-show host Lynn Weaver. Former singer Terry McKay is all set to marry handsome, wealthy, investment bank executive Kenneth Bradley. When their plane is forced to land on a Pacific atoll, Mike and Terry experience a romantic paradigm shift and all thoughts of their impending nuptials are dashed. Will they take a chance on each other? Will they both show up in three months?

Love Affair is finely crafted with excellent performances by Beatty and Bening, plus an incredible scene-stealing performance by Katharine Hepburn; this enjoyable remake/new-version does impressive justice to its famous predecessors. A wonderfully made, warmly portrayed love story that manages to communicate without an abundance of foul language (regrettably there is some) or explicit sexual activity.

CONTENT ANALYSIS: (Ro, LL, S, A, Ho, B) Romantic, love-conquers-all viewpoint; eight obscenities, four profanities (one exclamatory), and three vulgarities; implied sexual immorality and mild references to promiscuity; frequent alcohol use and brief, near drunkenness; isolated comment in support of homosexuality; and isolated positive description of marital fidelity.

Vivid Historical Masterpiece

THE MADNESS OF KING GEORGE

Quality: ☆☆☆☆   Acceptability: −1

WARNING CODES:
  Language: *
  Violence: *
  Sex: *
  Nudity: None
RATING: Not rated
GENRE: Historical drama

INTENDED AUDIENCE: Adults
RUNNING TIME: 100 minutes
STARRING: Nigel Hawthorne, Helen Mirren, Ian Holm, Amanda Donohoe, Rupert Graves, Rupert Everett, and Charlotte Curley
DIRECTOR: Nicholas Hytner
PRODUCERS: Stephen Evans and David Parfitt
WRITER: Alan Bennett
BASED ON: The play by Alan Bennett
DISTRIBUTOR: Samuel Goldwyn
BRIEF SUMMARY:
In 1788, King George III of England (the same King George of the American Revolution!) endured a six-month bout with insanity that nearly cost him his throne. *The Madness of King George* is a film adaptation of the play about this strange interlude. When a sudden illness causes a marked change in King George's behavior, it is decided that he must be kept out of sight. The action of the film alternates between the irrational ramblings of the deranged and suffering monarch, and the battle in Parliament over whether to wait for his recovery or appoint the Prince of Wales regent in his stead. The drama culminates in a race against time as the suddenly recovered king tries to head off the appointment of his son to the power of the throne.

The Madness of King George contains ample drama due to the political intrigue of the impending succession of the prince. Also, there are numerous minor conflicts involving the touching and positive relationship between the king and the queen, the struggle between the doctor and his incorrigible patient, and the covert maneuvers of members of Parliament to retain, or attain, power. Potential offenses are very mild: typical is a scene where it is implied that the king has soiled his pants. On a technical level, the cast is excellent, and so are the directing and camera work.

CONTENT ANALYSIS: (B, L, V, S, M) Justice triumphs, four obscenities and one profanity, moderate violence in struggles to restrain the mad king, implied fornication, and political skullduggery and several scatological references.

Wild Fun, with a Caution

THE MASK

Quality: ☆☆☆☆   Acceptability: −2

WARNING CODES:

Language: **
Violence: **
Sex: *
Nudity: *

RATING: PG-13
GENRE: Comedy
INTENDED AUDIENCE: Older teens and adults
RUNNING TIME: 95 minutes
STARRING: Jim Carrey, Peter Riegert, Cameron Diaz, Richard Jeni, Peter Greene, and Max (as dog Milo)
DIRECTOR: Chuck Russell
EXECUTIVE PRODUCERS: Mike Richardson, Charles Russell, and Michael De Luca
PRODUCER: Bob Engelman
SCREENWRITER: Michael Werb
BASED ON: The story by Michael Fallon and Mark Verheiden
DISTRIBUTOR: New Line Cinema
BRIEF SUMMARY:
A timid bank clerk releases all his inhibitions when an ancient mask summons a supernatural, cartoon-like alter ego, emerging only when he wears ... the mask. Jim Carrey stars in the Dark Horse Comics fantasy as terminal niceguy Stanley Ipkiss, constantly down on his luck and always finishing last until he finds a strange-looking mask floating in the river. Edge City may never be the same once Stanley slips on the mask only to be consumed in a tornado-like whirlwind and emerge as a green-faced, zoot-suited, wild man with the biggest set of caps this side of Whoopi Goldberg.

Dazzling special effects by George Lucas's Academy Award-winning Industrial Light and Magic bring *The Mask* to life. While Jim Carrey's on-screen canine sidekick, Max, deserves an Oscar, Carrey is the real surprise. Carrey's normal shtick is perverse, obnoxious, and disgusting, but in *The Mask* his wacky style (under control with director Chuck Russell) is a perfect fit. However, this otherwise surprisingly enjoyable movie's message falls short, teaching that nice guys finish last unless they can muster up a wildly aggressive dark side able to overcome adversity and stand up for number one. With a slight change in the resolution, this would have been a more acceptable movie.

CONTENT ANALYSIS: (Pa, LL, VV, S, N, O, M) Pagan worldview in which aggressive traits are necessary for problem solving; fourteen obscenities, five profanities (exclamatory), and numerous vulgarities and sexual innuendos; shoot-outs and gunfire, fistfights, car chases, and slapstick violence—none gory; two prolonged kisses; one female character wears revealing clothing; brief occultism—one reference to ancient mask as representative of Norwegian night god of mischief, Loki; robbery and theft by main character who uses cash for partying; and dog urinates on man.

An Absolute Delight

MAVERICK

Quality: ☆☆☆☆   Acceptability: −1

WARNING CODES:

Language: ***
Violence: *
Sex: *
Nudity: *

RATING: PG-13
GENRE: Western
INTENDED AUDIENCE: Older teens and adults

RUNNING TIME: 123 minutes

STARRING: Mel Gibson, Jodie Foster, James Garner, James Coburn, and a host of well-known faces in cameos

DIRECTOR: Richard Donner

PRODUCERS: Richard Donner and Bruce Davey

WRITER: William Goldman

DISTRIBUTOR: Warner Brothers

BRIEF SUMMARY:

On his way to the biggest poker game in Old West history, Bret Maverick finds himself a few dollars short and a few inches shy of a hanging in the light-hearted and engagingly entertaining film *Maverick*. Mel Gibson stars as the smooth-talking, never-cheating, hardly-ever-bluffing gambler set on winning a half-million-dollar prize and—more important—establishing once and for all just how good he really is. The stakes are high in this first-ever, all-star riverboat poker extravaganza, and Bret Maverick is not welcome. The poker game soon turns into an adventure, however, like every other event in his life.

Action-packed and star-studded with cameos, *Maverick* is true to the form of the original TV series that ran from 1957 to 1962. Mel Gibson brings just the right blend of action, intrigue, and sly humor to the big screen *Maverick* and, as the title character originally made famous by James Garner, Gibson plays Bret Maverick like Garner did. The role fits him like a glove. Jodie Foster is extraordinary as Mrs. Annabelle Bransford, a card-playing con woman who cannot decide whether to fall in love with Maverick, hate him, or just take his wallet. James Garner rounds out a trio whose interaction on-screen is a flawless work of harmony. This combination incontestably screams for a sequel. Tainted only by foul language, *Maverick* is an otherwise absolute delight.

CONTENT ANALYSIS: (B, LLL, V, S, N, A, C, M) No strongly apparent world-view, although gambling and dishonesty practiced, but characters sing "Amazing Grace" over grave of stagecoach driver and film closes with same song; fifty-four obscenities and two profanities; Western action violence—fistfights, brief gunfights, and runaway stage; one implied sexual encounter; brief female nudity in saloon wall painting and man without shirt; brief alcohol consumption, but not by main characters; and gambling and con games.

The Value of Love, Hope, Trust

MIRACLE ON 34TH STREET

Quality: ☆☆☆☆   Acceptability: +1

WARNING CODES:

Language: *

Violence: *

Sex: *

Nudity: *

RATING: PG

GENRE: Romantic comedy

INTENDED AUDIENCE: Children and adults

RUNNING TIME: 110 minutes

STARRING: Richard Attenborough, Elizabeth Perkins, Dylan McDermott, and Mara Wilson

DIRECTOR: Les Mayfield

EXECUTIVE PRODUCER: William Ryan

WRITERS: John Hughes and George Seaton

DISTRIBUTOR: 20th Century Fox

BRIEF SUMMARY:

Miracle on 34th Street, a John Hughes remake of the 1947 Christmas classic, relates the arrival of one Kriss Kringle, a department store Santa who believes that he is the genuine article and who subsequently turns a child's perspective from skepticism and fatalism toward hope and imagination. The story begins as Dorie Walker supervises the annual Thanksgiving Day parade for Cole's Department Store. When the parade's Santa shows up drunk, Dorie hires Kriss Kringle for the job and thereby causes her six-year-old daughter, Susan, to struggle with the fact that Dorie taught her that there is no Santa Claus. While believing that Kriss is a nice old man that her mother has hired to play a role, Susan also secretly yearns for her dream of a real home with a dad and baby brother. Dorie, Susan, and Kriss are befriended by attorney and neighbor Bryan Bedford, who, like Kriss, believes that dreams can come true if you have faith in love.

This well-crafted and well-acted movie stresses the importance of family and makes the case that love, hope, and trust are more important than money. *Miracle on 34th Street* is fun family viewing if parents explain to their children that Santa is a myth, even though the film suggests that he is in some way real. Of course, the Good News is that Jesus Christ is real, and he is the reason for this wonderful season.

CONTENT ANALYSIS: (B, Pa, L, V, S, N, A, C, Ab) Biblical values triumph in this movie about faith in love and the possibility of the supernatural, three mild obscenities, Kriss Kringle punches a drunken Santa in effort to "defend his honor," false accusation of Kriss Kringle being perverted, partially exposed posterior of drunken Santa, bar scene with several drunken Santas, and relationship drawn between having faith in Santa and having faith in God.

Uniquely Clever and Wholesome

MONKEY TROUBLE

Quality: ☆☆☆☆   Acceptability: +2

WARNING CODES:
  Language: None
  Violence: *
  Sex: None
  Nudity: None

RATING: PG
GENRE: Comedy
INTENDED AUDIENCE: All ages

RUNNING TIME: 100 minutes
STARRING: Harvey Keitel, Thora Birch, Mimi Rogers, and Christopher McDonald
DIRECTOR: Franco Amurri
EXECUTIVE PRODUCER: Ridley Scott
WRITERS: Amurri and Stu Krieger
DISTRIBUTOR: New Line Cinema
BRIEF SUMMARY:
In *Monkey Trouble,* a small pet capuchin monkey steals the show. He is a laugh a minute as he chatters, grins, and races around doing his assigned tasks for Azor (Harvey Keitel), a Gypsy organ grinder and con artist. The capuchin delights the bystanders as he hops around on them, but at the same time secretly relieves them of their jewelry and loose cash. He's so good that two professional gangsters want him to work for them. However, the monkey decides to leave and takes up with nine-year-old Eva (Thora Birch), who names him Dodger. Eva is thrilled to have a pet but neglects telling her parents, who would object. In the meantime, the gangsters try to recover the monkey. The action and the fun never slow down as Eva tries to keep her parents from discovering Dodger and to elude the gangsters who are hot on her trail.

Monkey Trouble is a uniquely clever, entertaining film that will not only delight children, but Mom and Dad as well. What a joy to find this film virtually free of offensive elements! Although preoccupied with Eva's young brother, Eva's parents love her and are attentive to her needs and feelings. When Eva grows weary of deceiving her parents she consults her teacher, who says that telling the truth is a good way to make things better. With considerable difficulty, Eva teaches Dodger not to steal. The film provides fun entertainment with positive messages.

CONTENT ANALYSIS: (B, A, D, V) Uplifting, positive comedy that emphasizes family love and portrays stealing as wrong; one exclamatory profanity and one crude epithet; several scenes with Gypsy drinking whiskey; moderate violence in rough treatment of Gypsy, girl, boy, and monkey; monkey shoots gun at man; and trailer is damaged.

Worst Promotion of Psychopathic Murderers

NATURAL BORN KILLERS

Quality: ☆☆   Acceptability: −4

WARNING CODES:
  Language: ***
  Violence: ***
  Sex: ***
  Nudity: **
RATING: R
GENRE: Satire
INTENDED AUDIENCE: Adults
RUNNING TIME: 120 minutes
STARRING: Woody Harrelson, Juliette Lewis, and Tommy Lee Jones
DIRECTOR: Oliver Stone
EXECUTIVE PRODUCERS: Arnon Milchan, Thom Mount, and Oliver Stone
PRODUCERS: Jane Hamsher, Don Murphy, and Clayton Townsend
WRITERS: Quentin Tarantino, David Veloz, Richard Rutowski, and Oliver Stone
DISTRIBUTOR: Warner Brothers
BRIEF SUMMARY:
Thanks to the media, married serial killers Mickey and Malory Knox become the newest American celebrities in *Natural Born Killers*, a satire examining violence, murder, and the media. The movie also makes some comments about the devastation of abuse in the home. Sparked by abuse from Malory's father, Mickey and Malory go on a rampage killing fifty-two people. Because of the media's portrayal, they become celebrities. After they are thrown in prison, the TV show *American Maniacs* catches up with them. Taking advantage of a live TV interview, Mickey and Malory escape by using the host as a hostage.

Natural Born Killers is a chaotic and disturbing movie. There are numerous clips of TV shows, violent cartoons, demonic faces, and beasts throughout the movie. Although the premise that television is corrupting the culture is correct, the filmmakers make the statement by showing that which they condemn. Also, Mickey says he has no regrets for murdering people, and he and Malory escape without punishment. The movie is also plagued by gross obscenity and profanity, graphic on-screen violence and murder, overt sexual content, and brief nudity. Even biblical elements are misused and blasphemed. Viewers will walk away picturing the demonic and beastly images flashed before their eyes through the entire movie.

CONTENT ANALYSIS: (Pa, LLL, VVV, SSS, NN, Ab, PC, M) Nihilistic worldview with elements of New Age and Eastern mysticism (yoga practiced); 166 obscenities and 20 profanities; 37 killings shown, a plethora of slain bodies shown and many bloody, gory scenes throughout; fornication depicted, implied sexual abuse, numerous sexual innuendos, and suggested sexual acts through body language, brief male rear nudity, anti-biblical and politically correct elements, and theft.

Provocative, Entertaining, Christian Allegory

THE PRINCESS AND THE GOBLIN

Quality: ☆☆☆   Acceptability: +1

WARNING CODES:
  Language: None
  Violence: *
  Sex: None
  Nudity: None
RATING: G
GENRE: Animated fantasy
INTENDED AUDIENCE: Families
RUNNING TIME: 82 minutes
VOICES: Joss Ackland, Roy Kinnear, Rik Mayall, Peter Murray, Mollie Sudgen, William Hootkins, Claire Bloom,

Sally Ann Marsh, Peggy Mount, Victor Spinetti, Frank Rozelaar Green, Maxine Howe, Steve Lyons, and Robin Lyons

DIRECTOR: Jozsef Gemes

EXECUTIVE PRODUCERS: Steve Walsh and Marietta Daradai

WRITER: Robin Lyons

BASED ON: The book by George MacDonald

DISTRIBUTOR: Hemdale

BRIEF SUMMARY:

If C. S. Lewis was the father of modern Christian allegory, George MacDonald was the grandfather. In his story *The Princess and the Goblin* published in 1872, he set the metaphorical stage for C. S. Lewis, J. R. R. Tolkien, and modern Christian fantasy. Now Robin Lyons has done a superb and faithful job of bringing MacDonald's classic children's tale to the big screen as an animated feature. For those who have not had the delightful experience of reading the book, *The Princess and the Goblin* tells the profound story of a young princess who has to overcome her fears to help save her father's kingdom from the forces of darkness. In the process, she learns about faith, truth, and love.

Many of the biblical parallels and theological principles are self-evident in MacDonald's endearing work; however, his allegory is not as precise as C. S. Lewis's Chronicles of Narnia, and there are areas that are open to misinterpretation. In fact, because of the misuse of many biblical symbols in contemporary culture, some will be put off by MacDonald's allegory. At the time that MacDonald wrote, people understood these symbols. However, in the final analysis, *The Princess and the Goblin* is superbly crafted, exciting, and thought-provoking. Children who see this film will need a theologically mature guide to help them understand its Christian import.

CONTENT ANALYSIS: (C, B, O, V) Christian worldview, moral principles, some magic (although it is denigrated), and some cartoon violence.

Refreshingly Creative and Wholesome

PRINCESS CARABOO

Quality: ☆☆☆   Acceptability: +2

WARNING CODES:

Language: *
Violence: *
Sex: *
Nudity: None

RATING: PG

GENRE: Romantic comedy

INTENDED AUDIENCE: Teens and adults

RUNNING TIME: 94 minutes

STARRING: Jim Broadbent, Pheobe Cates, Wendy Hughes, Kevin Kline, John Lithgow, and Stephen Rea

DIRECTOR: Michael Austin

EXECUTIVE PRODUCERS: Armyan Bernstein, Tom Rosenberg, and Marc Abraham

WRITERS: Michael Austin and John Wells

DISTRIBUTOR: TriStar Pictures

BRIEF SUMMARY:

The charming romantic comedy *Princess Caraboo* is based on the true story of a mysterious peasant girl who captured the imagination, appealed to the ambition, and won the hearts of an English village. The year is 1817, and the girl appears wearing a turban and speaking only a language that is unrecognizable to all. Taken in by the aristocratic Mr. and Mrs. Worrell, she is deemed a princess and becomes the object of the attention of all of the elite, including the Prince Regent. Only the Worrells' butler, a hack journalist, and a bookish professor suspect that Princess Caraboo is an elaborate hoax, and set out to expose her. Is she a princess? Is she a charlatan?

Princess Caraboo is a refreshingly creative and wholesome family romance with standout performances by Kevin Kline as the snobbish Greek butler, Phoebe Cates as the mysterious stranger, Stephen Rae as the unconventional romantic lead reporter, and the multi-talented John Lithgow as the lovestruck professor. Slight offenses in language are the only elements that would prohibit this family romance from being certified by the Motion Picture Code. The characters are God-fearing, moral, churchgoing, and likable, and learn valuable lessons in the consequences of their actions and of true forgiveness and love. *Princess Caraboo* is a wonderful family film.

CONTENT ANALYSIS: (C, B, L, V, S, A) Subtle Christian worldview with biblical themes of actions having consequences and forgiveness being a virtue; three mild obscenities and two mild exclamatory profanities; woman bites man on the arm in self-defense and one scene with hanged men in the background; subtly implied adultery with consequences and alcohol use.

Sick Normalization of Hit Men

PULP FICTION

Quality: ☆☆☆   Acceptability: −3

WARNING CODES:
   Language: ***
   Violence: ***
   Sex: **
   Nudity: *
RATING: R
GENRE: Action/Drama
INTENDED AUDIENCE: Adults
RUNNING TIME: 165 minutes
STARRING: John Travolta, Samuel L. Jackson, Uma Thurman, Bruce Willis, Harvey Keitel, Tim Roth, Amanda Plummer, Eric Stoltz, Rosanna Arquette, and Christopher Walken
   DIRECTOR: Quentin Tarantino
   EXECUTIVE PRODUCERS:
Danny DeVito, Michael Shamberg, and Stacey Sher

WRITER: Quentin Tarantino
DISTRIBUTOR: Miramax Films
BRIEF SUMMARY:
Pulp Fiction, the eagerly awaited winner of the 1994 Cannes Film Festival's Palme D'Or, weaves the stories of two hit men and a second-rate boxer into a hard-driving, violent film that jumps back and forth between being electric and on edge, to wordy and discursive. Director Quentin Tarantino "stays with his characters," looping from end, to middle, to beginning, and back again, to deliver what is basically a day-in-the-life story. Of course, when this is a day in the life of two hit men, the workaday problems include executing three double-crossers, accidentally blowing off a friend's head, and saving the boss's wife from a drug overdose. However, "staying with his characters" also means the viewer gets the chatter, the discussions, and the inanities that go on when the characters are not blowing someone to pieces.

When all is said and done and the plot and violence are set aside, *Pulp Fiction* is really about the ordinary within the extraordinary. When Vincent and Jules are on their way to a hit, they could just as well be going to a party, the office, or on a drive in the country. They talk about McDonald's and coworkers. An odd mixture, the movie falls short of what it might have been. There is some fine cinematography, a good score, and some good dialogue. There are also some redemptive and moral elements, especially regarding the character portrayed by Bruce Willis and one of the hit men, who stops a violent robbery and apparently leaves his life of crime at the end of the story. However, the movie contains enough extreme violence, foul language, and drug use to push the boundaries of its R-rating to NC-17. Director Quentin Tarantino treats much of this degrading content in an ironic, humorous fashion, and thus nearly drowns out the redemptive themes he tries to convey.

CONTENT ANALYSIS: (PaPa, Ab, C, B, LLL, VVV, SS, Ho, N, D) Pagan worldview includes murder, violence, drug use, and blasphemy in quoting Scripture while committing murder, but with some redemptive and moral elements, including scene where man realizes that his earlier blasphemous reading of Hebrew Scripture misinterpreted the moral meaning of the verses; 348 obscenities, 35 profanities, and many racial slurs; bloody fight, people run over by car, stabbings, shootings, and murders with various weapons; oral sex implied and forced sodomy depicted; brief, partial male nudity in shower; and frequent drug use including graphic overdose and extreme close-ups of needles injecting heroin.

Exposing Fraud

QUIZ SHOW

Quality: ☆☆☆☆   Acceptability: −2

WARNING CODES:
  Language: ***
  Violence: None
  Sex: None
  Nudity: None

RATING: PG-13
GENRE: Drama
INTENDED AUDIENCE: Adults
RUNNING TIME: 129 minutes
STARRING: Rob Morrow, John Turturro, Ralph Fiennes, David Paymer, Christopher McDonald, Elizabeth Wilson, and Paul Scofield
DIRECTOR: Robert Redford
EXECUTIVE PRODUCERS: Fred Zollo, Richard Dreyfuss, and Judith James
PRODUCERS: Robert Redford, Michael Jacobs, Julian Krainin, and Michael Nozik
WRITER: Paul Attanasio
BASED ON: The book *Remembering America: A Voice from the Sixties* by Richard N. Goodwin

DISTRIBUTOR: Buena Vista Pictures/Walt Disney Company
BRIEF SUMMARY:
It is New York, 1957, and America gathers in front of the TV to witness contestants battle for fortune and fame on the most popular weekly television program in this intriguing Disney drama *Quiz Show*. Based on the true events surrounding the game show *Twenty One*, *Quiz Show* questions the mass media's willingness to manipulate and corrupt people for profit. On the immensely popular show *Twenty One*, champion Herb Stempel is on his way to financial independence when the producers decide he is no longer appealing. Keeping viewers interested, so advertisers can sell them products, requires ingenuity and creativity, so the producers ask Herb to take a dive. The new contestant, handsome professor Charles Van Doren, instantly becomes a celebrity. However, the producers convince Charles to cheat by studying the questions before each show, and Herb Stempel ignites a scandal by revealing that the show is a fraud.

The filming, directing, and acting are all well done. Rob Morrow and Ralph Fiennes, in particular, are superb as the main characters in conflict. The entire production effectively captures the feel of the late 1950s. The musical score is also fitting, featuring such timely classics as "Mac the Knife." With no sex or nudity, the only real down side is foul language.

CONTENT ANALYSIS: (B, LLL, A, D, M) Ethical worldview—truth and integrity are worth more than money and fame; twenty-one obscenities, twelve profanities, and five vulgarities; brief alcohol use and smoking; lying and deceit as shortcuts to financial gain and notoriety; and one character attempts to expose fraud but the guilty escape punishment.

Very Enjoyable Family Entertainment

RICHIE RICH

Quality: ✰✰✰✰   Acceptability: +2

WARNING CODES:
  Language: *
  Violence: *
  Sex: None
  Nudity: None
RATING: PG
GENRE: Comedy/Adventure
INTENDED AUDIENCE: Children over eight
RUNNING TIME: 107 minutes
STARRING: Macaulay Culkin, John Larroquette, Edward Herrman, Jonathan Hyde, and Christine Ebersole
DIRECTOR: Donald Petrie
PRODUCERS: Joel Silver and John Davis
SCREENPLAY BY: Tom S. Parker and Jim Jennewein
STORY BY: Neil Tolkin
BASED ON: Characters appearing in Harvey Comics
DISTRIBUTOR: Warner Brothers
BRIEF SUMMARY:
Warner Brothers serves up a delightful translation of *Richie Rich* from the comic strip to the big screen in their film starring Macaulay Culkin. Richie Rich, a boy who has everything, lives contentedly until an excursion into a blue-collar neighborhood reveals to him the one thing that he does not possess—genuine friends. Richie's unflappable valet, Cadbury, bribes a group of ragtag children to spend a day with Richie. Their initial hesitancy to befriend Richie disappears as they discover that he enjoys the same things they do. When his parents' plane goes down over the Atlantic Ocean, he needs the children's help to find his mom and dad, to run the company, and to gather evidence against executive Lawrence Van Dough, whom he suspects responsible for the plot against his parents.

Richie Rich consistently conveys the message that it is not what you have but rather how you respond to others that matters. In scene after scene, the Riches communicate their devotion to one another. Also the Riches give generously to establish shelters, hospitals, and new companies to be owned by their employees. In a biblical sense, they strive to be good stewards of their blessings. *Richie Rich* is an enjoyable and clean movie. Cleverly structured and well directed, the movie engages the viewer in its adventure and humor. Macaulay Culkin and Jonathan Hyde perform superbly.

CONTENT ANALYSIS: (B, L, V, M, Pa) Biblically moral worldview in which a family strives to be good stewards of their blessings, shares with others, and places more value on family unit than on money; one mild obscenity, one exclamatory profanity, and two mild vulgarities; some action violence and fistfighting; two characters plot to kill the Rich family and seize their wealth; and a brief allusion between adults to the signs of the zodiac, as in "What's your sign?"

Good Triumphs

THE RIVER WILD

Quality: ✰✰✰✰   Acceptability: −2

WARNING CODES:
  Language: ***
  Violence: **
  Sex: None
  Nudity: None
RATING: PG-13
GENRE: Action/Adventure
INTENDED AUDIENCE: Adults
RUNNING TIME: 110 minutes
STARRING: Meryl Streep, Kevin Bacon, David Strathairn, Joseph Mazzello, and John C. Reilly
DIRECTOR: Curtis Hanson
EXECUTIVE PRODUCERS: Ilona Herzberg and Ray Hartwick

PRODUCERS: David Foster and Lawrence Turman
WRITER: Denis O'Neill
DISTRIBUTOR: Universal Pictures
BRIEF SUMMARY:

The River Wild is a powerful tale of a couple struggling to recapture their love, save their marriage, and survive a treacherous journey down the River Wild. In a last-ditch effort to save their marriage, the Hartmans take their young son on a white-water rafting vacation. Everything goes well until the Hartmans encounter Wade and Terry. Wade holds the family at gunpoint and forces Gail (Streep) to take him and his accomplice down the life-threatening rapids. Gail must use all her skills and strength to save her family.

The River Wild is a powerful film. The most impressive element of the movie is how it captures the audience and does not let go even after the credits roll. The director does a superb job of creating a movie with suspense, action, drama, and comedy. This is a positive and uplifting movie in which good triumphs in the end and a couple's shaky marriage is revived. Regrettably, there are numerous obscenities, two shooting deaths, numerous fights as the Hartmans try to escape, and a cultural reference to the "guardian spirit" of the Indians. Overall, however, *The River Wild* is a powerful and emotional movie that will leave audiences cheering.

CONTENT ANALYSIS: (B, C, LLL, VV, A, Pa) Moral worldview in which good triumphs over evil, a marriage is reaffirmed, a family is restored, people learn to forgive each other, and a father risks his life for his family. Twenty obscenities and ten profanities; action violence that includes shootings and fights in attempts to escape; alcohol use; and references to the "guardian spirit" of Indian culture.

Mature Christian Drama

SAFE PASSAGE

Quality: ☆☆☆   Acceptability: −1

WARNING CODES:
  Language: **
  Violence: None
  Sex: *
  Nudity: None

RATING: R
GENRE: Drama
INTENDED AUDIENCE: Older teens and adults
RUNNING TIME: 100 minutes
STARRING: Susan Sarandon, Sam Shepard, Robert Sean Leonard, Nick Stahl, Jason London, Marcia Gay Harden, and Matt Keeslar
DIRECTOR: Robert Allan Ackerman
EXECUTIVE PRODUCERS: David Gale, Betsy Beers, and Ruth Vitale
PRODUCER: Gale Anne Hurd
WRITER: Deena Goldstone
BASED ON: The novel by Ellyn Bache
DISTRIBUTOR: New Line Cinema
BRIEF SUMMARY:

Safe Passage is an intelligently poignant movie about a family awaiting news of a loved one in crisis overseas, which sells itself as a genuine family drama—a look into the way a crisis puts the whole of a family's life together into relief—and delivers in a refreshingly unaffected way. Susan Sarandon stars as the concerned wife and mother in this movie that affirms the process of living and loving rather than focusing on the pathos of untimely death and grief.

The movie is, in fact, a salute to all women who have poured themselves out for their children. However, it also has the courage to communicate the impossibility of doing all things well for every child at every moment. In its faithfulness to life, *Safe Passage* does not shy away from the intense vulnerability a mother experiences by investing her heart in a child who may grow up not to appreciate or love her, and its complete honesty is its great strength. Unpretentious in dialogue and believable in structure, the movie's overall effect is quite moving. Filmmakers Ackerman and Hurd assemble a cast who artfully bring their characters to life, and the texture and colors of the film generate the warmth of home. Although many themes are mature, the issues are handled well. The movie's most profound insight just might be that the art of parenting may always be complex, but is never completely ambiguous.

CONTENT ANALYSIS: (B, LL, S, A, D, C) Moral worldview supporting traditional family unit; thirteen obscenities and four profanities; unmarried couple lives together; adult drinking, use of marijuana, reference to the Resurrection as the source of all joy, and church attendance encouraged.

Honor Thy Father

THE SANTA CLAUSE

Quality: ☆☆☆☆   Acceptability: +2

WARNING CODES:
  Language: *
  Violence: *
  Sex: None
  Nudity: None
RATING: PG
GENRE: Fantasy/Comedy
INTENDED AUDIENCE: All ages
RUNNING TIME: 95 minutes
STARRING: Tim Allen, Eric Lloyd, Judge Reinhold, Wendy Crewson, David Krumholtz, and Peter Boyle
DIRECTOR: John Pasquin
EXECUTIVE PRODUCERS: Richard Baker, Rick Messina, and James Miller
PRODUCERS: Robert Newmyer, Brian Reilly, and Jeffrey Silver
WRITERS: Leo Benvenuti and Steve Rudnick
DISTRIBUTOR: Buena Vista Pictures/The Walt Disney Company
BRIEF SUMMARY:
  It's late Christmas Eve and up on the roof there arose such a clatter that Scott Calvin and his son, Charlie, awake just in time to see a red-suited man fall off their roof and into the snow in *The Santa Clause*. Together the two are swept up in a magical fantasy when they climb aboard Santa Claus's sleigh. Tim Allen stars as a divorced dad trying to salvage his relationship with his young son. Although they soon find out where the sleigh is going, Scott does not yet realize that he is in for an abrupt career change involving a big red suit and weight gain. The card he took from Santa's pocket contained some fine print . . . a "clause," if you will. The red suit now belongs to Scott, and the job description, well . . . you can imagine!

The Santa Clause is a delightful adventure fantasy. While admittedly feel-good, light-weight fare, the movie is definitely an uplifting experience even for adults. Children squeal with delight at the sight of Santa Claus, as well as during scenes of the North Pole complete with elves played by children, and toys galore. Essentially, this movie is about a little boy who loves his dad and believes in him when no one else does. If you explain to your children the difference between fantasy and the Truth, then they can enjoy this fun fantasy without conforming to the myths of our fallen age.

CONTENT ANALYSIS: (Pa, L, V, A, PC, B, C, M) Light fantasy worldview in which Santa Claus exists if you believe; one mild obscenity, four mild exclamatory profanities, two flatulence jokes, and a few mildly crude remarks; brief, mild slapstick violence—man falls off roof; brief, implied alcohol use by adults at party; and one brief politically correct allusion to family unit including both father and stepfather; a father-son relationship is restored; and man lies to ex-wife about being late.

A Christian Hero

SQUANTO: A WARRIOR'S TALE

Quality: ☆☆☆☆   Acceptability: +3

WARNING CODES:

Language: None
Violence: *
Sex: None
Nudity: None

RATING: PG

GENRE: Historical drama/Adventure

INTENDED AUDIENCE: Teens and adults

RUNNING TIME: 100 minutes

STARRING: Adam Beach, Mandy Patinkin, Eric Schweig, and Michael Gambon

DIRECTOR: Xavier Koller

EXECUTIVE PRODUCER: Don Carmody

PRODUCER: Kathryn Galan

WRITERS: Darlene Craviotto and Bob Dolman

DISTRIBUTOR: Buena Vista Pictures/Walt Disney Company

BRIEF SUMMARY:

The exciting historical-adventure drama, *Squanto: A Warrior's Tale,* tells the amazing legend of a Native American Indian and his enslavement at the hands of English traders, his daring escape into the English countryside, and his miraculous return to his New England homeland where he risks his life for peace and helps Pilgrim settlers survive in the early 1600s. Adam Beach stars as Squanto, a brave young warrior who is captured and taken to England by deceitful traders shortly after his marriage to the beautiful princess Nakooma.

This wonderful Disney movie is free of offensive content—save for appropriate action violence—and contains an exceptionally positive portrayal of Christian belief. Friendship, selfless love, and reverence for God are portrayed beautifully. Technically speaking the photography is stunning and the action is daring and exciting. The story is wonderful, and the acting performances are outstanding. Adam Beach is the first Native American Indian to be cast in the lead role of a major motion picture, and he is phenomenal. All the elements of this fine movie work exceptionally well. *Squanto* is sure to be a top-ten pick.

CONTENT ANALYSIS: (C, V, M) Christian worldview espousing forgiveness, love for one's enemies, helping those in need, prayer, and attributing God as Creator, Sustainer, and Giver of life; action violence relative to story (nothing gory or gratuitous); and very minor elements (Indian customs) that could be interpreted loosely as spiritism, but not intended as such.

A Need for Speed

SPEED

Quality: ☆☆☆   Acceptability: −2

WARNING CODES:

Language: ***
Violence: **
Sex: None
Nudity: None

RATING: R

GENRE: Action/Drama

INTENDED AUDIENCE: Adults

RUNNING TIME: 110 minutes

STARRING: Keanu Reeves, Dennis Hopper, Sandra Bullock, Jeff Daniels, and Joe Morton

DIRECTOR: Jan De Bont

EXECUTIVE PRODUCER: Ian Bryce

PRODUCER: Mark Gordon

WRITER: Graham Yost

DISTRIBUTOR: 20th Century Fox

BRIEF SUMMARY:

Keanu Reeves stars as a cop out to save the day when a Los Angeles city bus full of passengers is rigged with a bomb set to explode when the vehicle's speed goes below fifty miles per hour in the action-packed thriller, *Speed*. As police bomb expert Jack Traven, Reeves thwarts a mad bomber's first attempt to extort $3.7 million by rescuing hostages held on an express elevator rigged with explosives.

The bomber (Dennis Hopper), angry at the missed financial opportunity, goes after Jack personally with his next scheme—the bomb planted beneath the city bus. The bomber informs Jack by phone, making him the only person with a chance to save the passengers. Thus, the race is on—a race against time, fuel, pavement, and speed.

Suspense, tension, great action, and excellent stunts abound, along with some credible acting performances. Sandra Bullock is extremely natural and believable as Annie, the stand-in bus driver without a license, and provides needed comic relief and witty dialogue. Dennis Hopper is simply the best psycho-crazy man in the business. Keanu Reeves, still sporting his tired surfer accent and said to be nervous about carrying a film, is surrounded by enough excellent work that *Speed* manages to carry itself. However, an overabundance of foul and profane language serves only to offend and distract from an otherwise truly exciting film.

CONTENT ANALYSIS: (R, LLL, VV, M) Heroic romantic worldview; sixty-two obscenities, eleven profanities, and nineteen exclamatory profanities; action violence includes numerous vehicle crashes and bomb explosions and one brief but gory stabbing murder; and two verbal references to promiscuity.

Somewhat Disappointing

STARGATE

Quality: ☆☆☆   Acceptability: −2

WARNING CODES:
  Language: *
  Violence: *
  Sex: *
  Nudity: None
RATING: PG-13
GENRE: Science fiction
INTENDED AUDIENCE: Older children and adults
RUNNING TIME: 121 minutes

STARRING: Kurt Russell, James Spader, Jaye Davidson, John Diehl, Mili Avital, Richard Kind, and Viveca Lindfors
DIRECTOR: Roland Emmerich
EXECUTIVE PRODUCER: Mario Kassar
PRODUCERS: Joel B. Michaels, Oliver Eberle, and Dean Devlin
WRITERS: Dean Devlin and Roland Emmerich
DISTRIBUTOR: Metro Goldwin-Mayer/United Artists
BRIEF SUMMARY:
James Spader and Kurt Russell team up as a nerdy Egyptologist, Dr. Daniel Jackson, and a hawkish military colonel, Jack O'Neil, in *Stargate*, a big-budget science fiction adventure that revolves around the quest to find the origin of modern civilization on Earth. A strange artifact found near Giza in Egypt turns out to be the doorway to a planet on the other side of the universe. Jackson and O'Neil use the stargate to travel to that planet, where they discover a colony of slaves ruled by the evil sun god Ra. Before they can destroy the gate, the unlikely duo must first lead the slaves in an uprising of their own (similar to the one that supposedly took place on Earth by a civilization placed here by Ra and responsible for building the pyramids), and then destroy Ra.

Stargate is heavy on expensive, well-executed, entertaining special effects and art direction, but the teaming of Russell and Spader is somewhat disappointing. There is little point at which their characters intersect, making the partnership seem inconsequential. Of course, the plotline is a bit ludicrous, but the foul language is sparse and the violence is brief. Overall, *Stargate* is a far-fetched B-movie dressed up in a blockbuster suit, with some obvious parallels to Scientology.

CONTENT ANALYSIS: (Pa, L, V, S, M) New Age/Scientology worldview; three obscenities and three profanities; several deaths (none graphic), much action violence with no blood, some deaths by gunshot, and one man is crushed (but not shown); implied fornication; and cigarette smoking and alien creatures based on Egyptian hieroglyphics.

Love Triumphs

THE SWAN PRINCESS

Quality: ☆☆☆☆   Acceptability: +3

WARNING CODES:
  Language: None
  Violence: *
  Sex: None
  Nudity: None

RATING: G
GENRE: Animated musical
INTENDED AUDIENCE: All ages
RUNNING TIME: 85 minutes
VOICES: Jack Palance, John Cleese, Steven Wright, and Sandy Duncan
DIRECTOR: Richard Rich
EXECUTIVE PRODUCERS: Jared Brown and Seldon Young
SONGS AND MUSIC BY: David Zippel and Lex De Azevedo
WRITER: Brian Nissen
DISTRIBUTOR: Nest Entertainment, Inc.
BRIEF SUMMARY:
In the lovely animated musical *The Swan Princess,* Prince Derek and Princess Odette come to life in a saga of young lovers torn apart by a sorcerer who schemes to rule their kingdom. From the credits, the movie whirls into a fairy-tale world of kings and kingdoms where "once upon a time" there were two kingdoms and two little heirs, Odette and Derek, whose parents thought it would be a good idea to join the kingdoms by marriage. Regrettably, the rotten Rothbart, an evil sorcerer who had been banished from her father's kingdom, captures the princess. Rothbart turns Odette into a swan who can only regain her human form when moonlight hits the pond where she is imprisoned. However, as soon as the moon sets—poof!—she is a swan again. Derek and a zany trio of creatures must risk their lives to save the princess.

The Swan Princess offers a fast-paced plot, luscious, dream-like scenery, and incredibly beautiful music. One gets the feeling that the animators and lyricists all had a great deal of fun creating this movie. With love triumphing over evil, the only caution is the fantasy motif replete with the sorcerer villain (the adversary) who transforms into a giant hairy bat before his demise in a final battle. The movie teaches loving others for who they are on the inside and contains exceptional music and choreography.

CONTENT ANALYSIS: (C, B, V, Pa) Christian worldview that love triumphs over adversity, with the moral theme that true love goes deeper than outward appearance; mild violence involving villain that very young children may find scary; and magic and myth.

Timeless Fairy Tale

THUMBELINA

Quality: ☆☆☆   Acceptability: +3

WARNING CODES:
  Language: None
  Violence: None
  Sex: None
  Nudity: None

RATING: G
GENRE: Animation
INTENDED AUDIENCE: All ages
RUNNING TIME: 95 minutes
VOICES: Jodi Benson, Gino Conforti, Barbara Cook, Carol Channing, Charo, and Will Ryan
DIRECTORS: Don Bluth and Gary Goldman
PRODUCERS: Don Bluth, Gary Goldman, and John Pomeroy
WRITER: Don Bluth
BASED ON: The story by Hans Christian Andersen
DISTRIBUTOR: Warner Brothers

BRIEF SUMMARY:

Thumbelina takes one on a whimsical adventure with a thumb-sized girl searching for a boy her own height. Thumbelina blossoms in a magical flower given to her mother by a Gypsy. Thumbelina's size limits her romantically until one day she meets a fairy prince and they fall in love. The prince leaves, intending to come back, and the adventure begins when Thumbelina is kidnapped by a family of frogs. The family's son, Grundel, is infatuated with Thumbelina. Thumbelina's despair is noticed by a swallow named Jacquimo, and he helps her escape. On her journey, others fall in love with her and want to keep her as their own. The only thing that keeps Thumbelina going is the thought of finding her fairy prince. When she hears that her prince has died, Thumbelina almost marries wealthy Mr. Mole, who promises her security. However, she is constrained by the love she has for her prince. In the end Thumbelina and the prince are reunited, marry, and live happily ever after.

This endearing fairy tale focuses on a beautiful young woman who desires to find the right companion. This desire points toward the bride of Christ's longing for the true Prince of Peace and the many false suitors who present themselves along life's journey. Most children will love this timeless moral fairy tale about hope and fidelity. The music, in particular, is outstanding.

CONTENT ANALYSIS: (B, O) Uplifting and moral movie with some fairy-tale magic.

An Indictment of Communism

TO LIVE

Quality: ☆☆☆☆   Acceptability: -1

WARNING CODES:

Language: *
Violence: *
Sex: None
Nudity: None

RATING: Not rated
GENRE: Drama
INTENDED AUDIENCE: Adults
RUNNING TIME: 129 minutes
LANGUAGE: Mandarin
STARRING: Ge Young, Gong Li, Niu Ben, and Guo Tao
DIRECTOR: Zhang Yimou
PRODUCER: Chiu Fusheng
WRITERS: Yu Hua and Lu Wei
BASED ON: The novel by Yu Hua
DISTRIBUTOR: Samuel Goldwyn

BRIEF SUMMARY: Zhang Yimou's *To Live* is one of the most uplifting family dramas to grace the screen in a long time. Following the lives of an average Chinese family during the turbulent decades between 1940 and 1970, *To Live* tells a classic tale of love, commitment, and hope in the face of seemingly insurmountable odds. Avoiding the over-the-top melodramatic antics common to most epic dramas, Yimou opts for a smaller canvas on which to depict the struggles of the Xu family. In Yimou's story, no family member suffers from unjust incarceration, there are no grand battle scenes, and there are no torrid affairs or bitter blood feuds. The Xu family's travails are more down-to-earth, more recognizable: finding work when jobs are scarce, finding a doctor when a child gets sick, forgiving family friends for past mistakes. For Zhang Yimou, raising a family is an epic adventure all in itself.

Mercifully devoid of sexual and violent content, but containing several obscenities and profanities, *To Live* is also one of the more accessible adult family dramas of the year. In its quiet, down-to-earth way, the film also stands as a strong indictment of Mao Tse Tung's Communist regime. So strong, in fact, that the Chinese government has placed an indefinite ban on the film's distribution and a two-year filmmaking ban on Yimou.

CONTENT ANALYSIS: (Ac, B, L, V, M) Anti-Communist worldview portraying moral elements of forgiveness and family unity (no spirituality depicted), five obscenities and three profanities; one off-screen execution and two accidents involving children; and some gambling.

Delightful Comedy

WIDOW'S PEAK

Quality: ☆☆☆☆   Acceptability: +1

WARNING CODES:
  Language: *
  Violence: None
  Sex: None
  Nudity: None
RATING: PG
GENRE: Comedy/Drama
INTENDED AUDIENCE: Teens and adults
RUNNING TIME: 106 minutes
STARRING: Mia Farrow, Joan Plowright, Natasha Richardson, Adrian Dunbar, Jim Broadbent, Anne Kent, and John Kavanagh
  DIRECTOR: John Irvin
  PRODUCER: Jo Manuel
  WRITER: Hugh Leonard
  DISTRIBUTOR: Fine Line Features
BRIEF SUMMARY: In the cozy, Irish town of Kilshannon, circa 1920s, a group of haughty and wealthy widows, lead by the imperious "Mammie" (an excellent Joan Plowright), live atop a hill called Widow's Peak, from which they hand down the town's rules of decorum and status, much to the ruin of any wayward lass, in the delightful comedy *Widow's Peak*. When Edwina Broom (Natasha Richardson), a newly arrived American widow who also happens to be young and beautiful, sets her eyes on the wealthy son of the town's ruling widow, a fierce rivalry ensues as her designs are confronted by the town's resident spinster, Kathleen O'Hare (Mia Farrow). The women take turns digging up each

other's skeletons and succeed only in destroying each other's designs for marriage. However, all is not as it seems in this intriguing tale, and in a comic, whodunit finale and a wonderful surprise ending, all parties receive their just desserts—from the haughty, controlling widows, to Kathleen and Edwina.

Marred only by a sprinkling of obscenities and the premise that deception can bring about justice (the deception is regretted), *Widow's Peak* is an otherwise wonderfully scripted, acted, and directed film, with excellent performances by Mia Farrow and Joan Plowright. It is also a beautiful film to watch, for the cinematography does justice and then some to the beautiful Irish landscape and the exquisite costuming.

CONTENT ANALYSIS: (B, L) Biblical worldview somewhat flawed by the premise that deception brings about justice, although the deception is regretted; and three obscenities.

Poignant Character Study

WRESTLING ERNEST HEMINGWAY

Quality: ☆☆☆☆   Acceptability: -2

WARNING CODES:
  Language: **
  Violence: None
  Sex: *
  Nudity: *
RATING: PG-13
GENRE: Drama
INTENDED AUDIENCE: Adults
RUNNING TIME: 122 minutes
STARRING: Robert Duvall, Richard Harris, Sandra Bullock, Shirley MacLaine, and Piper Laurie
  DIRECTOR: Randa Haines
  PRODUCERS: Todd Black and Joe Wizan
  WRITER: Steve Conrad
  DISTRIBUTOR: Warner Brothers

BRIEF SUMMARY:

Credit is due to director Randa Haines and to veteran actors Robert Duvall and Richard Harris for turning a simple act of generosity—one man giving another a shave—into one of the most poignant film scenes in recent memory.

Frank (Richard Harris) is an old salt permanently beached in a run-down seaside motel. He is the quintessential drunken ex-sailor: rarely separated from his Irish whiskey, coarse and profane, sexually amoral with four divorces strewn in his wake, and utterly alone. Banging around beaches and parks like a piece of derelict driftwood, Frank one day happens to intrude on Walt (Robert Duvall). Quiet, almost birdlike in pained shyness, Walt is a Cuban emigré who happened to be in the U.S. when Castro took over his homeland. Retired from a half century of barbering, his days are ordered on a gentle but nearly obsessive routine: morning and afternoon visits to a local café to order a bacon sandwich from Elaine (Sandra Bullock)—a pretty young waitress for whom he holds a chaste attraction—

working crossword puzzles in the park, and watching the flailing efforts of a Little League team. Even though he is sweet and pleasant, a perfect gentleman, he is as lonely as Frank. As might be expected, a friendship between such distant souls doesn't come easily, but a tentative bond develops.

Both Richard Harris and Robert Duvall are superb in *Wrestling Ernest Hemingway*, but the latter's complete, understated submersion into the character of Walt is one of the best performances of his career. As mentioned, the language is at times extremely coarse, and the lack of any spiritual frame of reference disappointing. However, with those cautions and limitations, *Wrestling Ernest Hemingway* is a poignant character study.

CONTENT ANALYSIS: (LL, N, S, A, D) Sixteen obscenities and twenty profanities, as well as several coarse references to sex (nearly all spoken by one character), brief rear male nudity, very brief fondling of female breast, and extensive alcohol use by one character (not condoned).

☆☆☆ THE BEST 1994 FILMS FOR FAMILIES ☆☆☆

Headline	Title
Heaven Is Where Salvation Lies	*Little Women*
Timeless Tale of Hope and Faith	*Black Beauty*
Magnificent Christian Allegory	*The Lion King*
Purity and Love Conquers Avarice and Pride	*The Jungle Book*
Christian Witness	*Corrina, Corrina*
Family and Friendship Are Important	*The Flintstones*
Biblical Parallels	*Angels in the Outfield*
A Christian Hero	*Squanto: A Warrior's Tale*
The Value of Love, Hope, Trust	*Miracle on 34th Street*
Honor Thy Father	*The Santa Clause*

☆☆☆ THE BEST 1994 FILMS FOR MATURE AUDIENCES ☆☆☆

Headline	Title
God Is Good	*Forrest Gump*
Exposing Fraud	*Quiz Show*
Delightful Comedy	*Widow's Peak*
Justice Triumphs	*The Client*
A Moral Hero	*Clear and Present Danger*
Good Triumphs	*The River Wild*
An Indictment of Communism	*To Live*
An Honest Man Is Good to Find	*The Hudsucker Proxy*
An Absolute Delight	*Maverick*
Vivid Historical Masterpiece	*The Madness of King George*

☆☆☆ THE TWENTY MOST UNBEARABLE FILMS OF 1994 ☆☆☆

Headline	Title
Worst Scatological Movie	*Ace Ventura*
Worst Drag Queen	*The Adventures of Priscilla, Queen of the Desert*
Worst Promotion of Teenage Rebellion	*Camp Nowhere*
Worst Explicit Sex Thriller	*Color of Night*
Worst Evil Spiritism	*The Crow*
Worst S & M Movie	*Exit to Eden*
Worst Premise	*The Favor*
Worst Mix of Spiritism and Marxism	*The House of the Spirits*
Worst Lackluster Blasphemy	*Interview with the Vampire*
Worst Slick Bigotry and Adultery	*It Could Happen to You*
Worst Concept Ever to Carry a Movie	*It's Pat*
Worst Blatant Buddhist Propaganda	*Little Buddha*
Worst Promotion of Psychopathic Murderers	*Natural Born Killers*
Worst Promotion of Prostitution	*Milk Money*
Worst Promotion of Paganism	*On Deadly Ground*
Worst Normalization of Hit Men	*Pulp Fiction*
Worst Attack on Motherhood	*Serial Mom*
Worst Promotion of Incest	*Spanking the Monkey*
Worst Comeback	*Wes Craven's Nightmare*
Worst Politically Correct Adventure Yarn	*White Fang 2: Myth of the White Wolf*

1995 MOVIES

More Bizarre

12 MONKEYS

Quality: ☆☆☆   Acceptability: −2

WARNING CODES:

Language: ***
Violence: ***
Sex: None
Nudity: *

RATING: R
GENRE: Science fiction
INTENDED AUDIENCE: Adults
RUNNING TIME: 130 minutes
STARRING: Bruce Willis, Madeline Stowe, Brad Pitt, and Christopher Plummer
DIRECTOR: Terry Gilliam
PRODUCER: Charles Roven
WRITERS: David and Janet Peoples
DISTRIBUTOR: Universal Pictures
BRIEF SUMMARY:

It is the year 2035. Time travel is the norm, and the population is viral-phobic and obsessed with the idea that they can change history. The scientists of the day choose a criminal by the name of James Cole, played by Bruce Willis, to go back to 1996 to find out the source of a deadly virus. James is lured by a promised pardon in exchange for this dubious task. The time machinery is deficient, and James finds himself in the middle of World War I. He makes it to 1996 but is taken into a mental institution. There he meets the Dr. Kathryn Railly, who joins him in searching for the source of the miserable virus. James befriends the raving Jeffrey Goines, played by Brad Pitt, who becomes the surprising link in James's search.

The movie *12 Monkeys* is the work of famed but controversial director Terry Gilliam. It is more bizarre than spell-binding, and more visual than coherent. The movie's backdrop is impressive though not lavish. The best of the movie is the final twist in the last segment of the movie. Otherwise, the end-of-the-world premise is not biblical but seen only from a human experience without religious bearings. Some unnecessary violence and male nudity also mar the movie. The moral of the story is that you cannot change time.

CONTENT ANALYSIS: (Pa, Ab, E, LLL, VVV, N, D) Anti-biblical, pagan worldview with an environmental theme where all-powerful man tries to control the world; fourteen vulgarities, nine obscenities, and four profanities; some graphic violence includes recurring shoot-out at airport, violent outburst at mental institution, two instances of thugs being brutally kicked and punched, man shot in leg, man punching woman, bloody tooth forcibly pulled out, and man shot in back; one vulgar sexual reference; four instances of male nudity in naturalistic context; cigarette smoking; and insect eating and car theft.

Race against Time

THE AMAZING PANDA ADVENTURE

Quality: ☆☆☆   Acceptability: +1

WARNING CODES:

Language: *
Violence: *
Sex: None
Nudity: *

RATING: PG
GENRE: Animal adventure
INTENDED AUDIENCE: Children

RUNNING TIME: 82 minutes
STARRING: Stephen Lang, Ryan Slater, Yi Ding, and Wang Fei
DIRECTOR: Christopher Cain
PRODUCER: Lee Rich
WRITERS: Jeff Rothberg and Laurice Elewany
DISTRIBUTOR: Warner Brothers
BRIEF SUMMARY:
In *The Amazing Panda Adventure*, Michael Tyler is an American researcher in charge of a wilderness preserve in China dedicated to the breeding and preservation of pandas. Tyler takes his job seriously and values pandas above all else, even his own son. When his son, Ryan, arrives for a visit, Michael forgets to pick him up at the airport. Michael and Ryan then go to find an injured panda who has just given birth to a cub. On finding it, they encounter poachers who shoot Michael in the leg and steal the baby panda. Michael and the mama panda are flown back to camp for medical treatment, and Ryan and Ling, a girl Chinese translator, and her grandfather go in hot pursuit of the poachers. Ryan and Ling get separated from her grandfather, and the remainder of the picture involves a race against time as the children try to flee with their own lives and reunite the starving cub to its mother so that it can feed.

This film could easily have slipped into a politically correct sermon on environmentalism, but it does not. Instead, it shows that relationships with people are more important than occupational pursuits or animals. This film does show people in their native cultures, but avoids exploring or endorsing other religions. Aside from a very brief animistic prayer, it is a charming story suitable for children that affirms the value of people, without excessive violence or foul language.

CONTENT ANALYSIS: (B, FR, L, V, N, A, M) Moral worldview with very minor Eastern religious elements; one obscenity (mild) and one profanity (exclamatory); action violence including gunfire (no blood), Panda paw caught in trap, falling in water, and kicking; upper male (boy) nudity; alcohol use; and theft.

Can-Do Patriotism

APOLLO 13

Quality: ☆☆☆☆   Acceptability: −1

WARNING CODES:
Language: ***
Violence: None
Sex: *
Nudity: None
RATING: PG
GENRE: Historical drama
INTENDED AUDIENCE: Older children to adults
STARRING: Tom Hanks, Kevin Bacon, Bill Paxton, Gary Sinise, and Ed Harris
DIRECTOR: Ron Howard
PRODUCER: Brian Grazer
EXECUTIVE PRODUCER: Todd Hallowell
WRITERS: William Broyles Jr. and Al Reinert
BASED ON: The novel *Lost Moon* by Jim Lovell and Jeffrey Kluger
DISTRIBUTOR: Universal Pictures
BRIEF SUMMARY:
Apollo 13 is a patriotic, can-do American movie. It is the familiar story (to those of us who lived through that period) of the ill-fated flight of *Apollo 13*, which blew out most of its oxygen into space halfway between the earth and the moon and barely made it back to earth. The film starts at a party at Jim and Marilyn Lovell's house as they watch Neal Armstrong take that "one giant step" onto the moon. Lovell is willing to wait until his turn on *Apollo 14*, however a physical ailment to Jim Shepperd, the commander of *Apollo 13*, moves Jim and his crew up the ladder. Days before the launch, Jim loses his crack pilot, Ken Mattingly, due to measles, and Ken is replaced by the philandering Jack Swaggert. They are joined on the crew

by Fred Haise. After a successful takeoff, an oxygen tank blows out the side of the spacecraft, putting the crew in jeopardy of dying deep in space. In an already known ending, Houston guides them safely back to earth.

This is a well-paced, exciting movie. It shows that teamwork, courage, and determination can overcome the worst of situations. If it were not for the obscenities, profanities, and noticeable lack of prayer, it would be a movie that every moral American would love.

CONTENT ANALYSIS: (B, H, LLL, S) Moral worldview that seems too anthropocentric; thirty-two obscenities and thirteen profanities; some sexual innuendo among married couple and a shower scene (no visible nudity).

Talent Rewarded

BABE

Quality: ☆☆☆☆   Acceptability: +2

WARNING CODES:

Language: *
Violence: *
Sex: None
Nudity: None

RATING: G
GENRE: Fantasy/Comedy
INTENDED AUDIENCE: All ages
VOICES: Christine Cavanaugh, Miriam Margolyes, and Danny Mann
RUNNING TIME: 91 minutes
STARRING: James Cromwell and Magda Szubanski
DIRECTOR: Chris Noonan
PRODUCERS: George Miller, Doug Mitchell, and Bill Miller
WRITERS: George Miller and Chris Noonan
DISTRIBUTOR: Universal Pictures
BRIEF SUMMARY:
On his arrival to a farm, piglet Babe explores his world with abandon. First, Babe makes friends with a duck named Ferdinand, who thinks he is a rooster.

Every morning, Ferdinand lets out a cockle-doodle-do, waking up Farmer Hoggett and his wife. Babe helps Ferdinand capture the competition: an alarm clock. Then Babe begins to develop skill as a sheepherder. The sheepdog, Rex, is infuriated and attacks Babe. Yet, in a stunning climax, Rex learns to appreciate Babe when Farmer Hoggett decides to enter Babe in a sheepherding competition. With Rex's help, Babe performs beautifully, winning him high points at the judge's table, cheers from the crowd, and the admiration of all.

Although the human actors occasionally speak, 80 percent of the soundtrack is the animals talking. With seamless computer animation, the animals appear as if they are talking quite naturally. This realism is augmented by a barnyard reminiscent of old-world charm, yet set in modern times. Created with care and tenderness, *Babe* is winsome and heartwarming. Regrettably, *Babe* contains a few mild vulgarities. On the other hand, it has many moments of purity and pleasure that will compel its viewers to love their neighbors.

CONTENT ANALYSIS: (B, L, V, M) Biblical worldview extolling love; three vulgarities and one exclamatory profanity; dogs fight and bite; pig urinates; and sheep is stolen.

Heroes Come in All Shapes and Sizes

BALTO

Quality: ☆☆☆   Acceptability: +3

WARNING CODES:

Language: None
Violence: **
Sex: None
Nudity: None

RATING: G
GENRE: Animated adventure
INTENDED AUDIENCE: All ages
VOICES: Bob Hoskins, Kevin Andersen, and Jim Cummings

DIRECTOR: Simon Wells

EXECUTIVE PRODUCERS: Steven Spielberg, Kathleen Kennedy, and Bonne Radford

PRODUCER: Stephen Hickner

WRITER: Elana Lesser

DISTRIBUTOR: Universal Pictures

BRIEF SUMMARY:

With animated vigor, *Balto* is the ultimate dog story. An unwanted, ill-treated dog turns out to be the town hero when he succeeds where others fail. In Nome, Alaska, a little girl named Rosey has just received a dogsled from her parents. She promptly harnesses her well-bred dog, Jeena, to the sled. They rush to the street to watch the annual dogsled race and see Steele, the lead dog, flash through the finish line. Soon, Steele fights with Balto, a half-breed dog-wolf, but both Rosey and Jeena sense that Balto is a special animal. Rosey becomes dangerously ill. The doctor's supply of medicine is quickly depleted, and a way must be found to obtain more, but a tremendous blizzard is raging and the closest source is six hundred miles away. Balto comes to the rescue.

Based on a true story, this humorous yet suspenseful and clever animated movie will be enjoyed by the entire family. Bring plenty of tissues too, because it is also a tearjerker of sorts. To the moviemaker's credit, there is scarcely anything inappropriate; however, some dogfights and narrow escapes may upset sensitive youngsters. *Balto* is a feel-good family movie that shows us that heroes come in different shapes and sizes and that we all have special talents that make us worthy and unique.

CONTENT ANALYSIS: (B, VV) Moral worldview uplifting the value of each individual and of risking your life for another; and moderate violence including dogfights, near drowning, falling off cliff, and other narrow escapes.

Denouncing Revenge, Pride, and Double-Mindedness

BATMAN FOREVER

Quality: ☆☆☆   Acceptability: −1

WARNING CODES:

Language: **

Violence: **

Sex: *

Nudity: None

RATING: PG-13

GENRE: Action/Adventure/Fantasy

INTENDED AUDIENCE: Teens and adults

RUNNING TIME: 120 minutes

STARRING: Val Kilmer, Tommy Lee Jones, Jim Carrey, Nicole Kidman, and Chris O'Donnell

DIRECTOR: Joel Schumacher

EXECUTIVE PRODUCERS: Benjamin Melniker and Michael E. Uslan

PRODUCERS: Tim Burton and Peter MacGregor-Scott

WRITERS: Lee Batchler and Janet Scott Batchler

DISTRIBUTORS: Warner Brothers

BRIEF SUMMARY:

Lighter and more moral than its predecessor, *Batman Forever*, starring Val Kilmer as Batman, explodes with an action-packed attack on a Gotham City bank by Two-Face Harvey Dent (Tommy Lee Jones). In the midst of the attack, Batman meets Dr. Chase Meridian (Nicole Kidman), a psychiatrist who is infatuated with Batman. Next, we find Bruce Wayne touring his research department, where he meets Edward Nygma (Jim Carrey), who shows him a "box" that sends television into people's minds. When Bruce rejects this invention as immoral, Nygma redesigns his machine to suck knowledge from the brains of Gotham's citizens into his brain and becomes the Riddler, who teams up with Two-Face to destroy Batman. Acrobat Dick Grayson turns into Batman's sidekick, Robin, after Two-Face kills his family at the circus. Batman and Robin must save Chase and bring the two villainous criminals to justice.

This film falls short on plot, but delivers on action, brilliant design, and a moody central character. It includes bloodless action violence, sexual innuendo, and an occult talisman. However, the film provides a moral worldview: Batman instructs Robin that revenge is not an answer to grief, Two-Face demonstrates that a double-minded man is unstable in all his ways, and Riddler demonstrates that pride comes before a fall. *Batman Forever* will entertain those who love comic books.

CONTENT ANALYSIS: (B, LL, VV, S, O, M) Moral worldview promoting forgiveness, healing, and condemning humanism and indecision; eleven obscenities and three vulgarities; cartoon-type action violence including several explosions, face disfigurement, personal assaults and fights, five people falling to their deaths, two people hit over the head with objects, and gunfire but no blood; some mild sexual innuendo and some characters dressed in provocative clothing; demonic-type gang members and an occult talisman; and revenge themes.

Attacking Family Values

THE BRADY BUNCH

Quality: ☆☆   Acceptability: –1

WARNING CODES:
  Language: *
  Violence: None
  Sex: *
  Nudity: None
RATING: PG
GENRE: Comedy
INTENDED AUDIENCE: Teens and adults
RELEASE: February 1995
RUNNING TIME: 90 minutes
STARRING: Shelley Long, Gary Cole, Michael McKean, Jean Smart, Christine Taylor, Jennifer Elise Cox, Olivia Hack, Christopher Daniel Barnes, Paul Sutera, Jesse Lee, and Henriette Mantel
DIRECTOR: Betty Thomas

EXECUTIVE PRODUCER: Alan Ladd Jr.
PRODUCERS: Sherwood Schwartz, Lloyd Schwartz, and David Kirkpatrick
WRITERS: Laurice Elehwany, Rick Capp, Bonnie Turner, and Terry Turner
DISTRIBUTOR: Paramount Pictures
BRIEF SUMMARY:
A campy spoof of the popular TV sitcom, *The Brady Bunch* movie stars Shelley Long in a cardboard performance. While surprisingly funny—dropping the show's '70s characterizations and dialogue into a '90s world of racy living and cynicism—it is ultimately nothing more than an extra-long sitcom itself. The plot centers around the Brady children saving the day when they learn that their parents owe $20,000 in back taxes. Complicating matters, a smarmy neighbor and real estate agent (played solidly by Michael McKean) is working to sell the block to developers and wants the Bradys out at any cost.

Regrettably, the movie equates the Brady family's basic moral decency with stupidity. Mike and Carol Brady, oblivious to innuendo, think of warm coats when Marcia's date says he has "protection." When Marcia is tossed out of a boy's car for turning down his sexual proposition, he drives away, shouting, "Bradys suck!" Also oblivious, Marcia fails to realize that her best friend is a lesbian and has a crush on her. Overall, the "Brady way" wins the day. However, their moral "perfection" is strictly human and not based in any religious conviction. Along with the amount of sexual innuendo presented, this movie is not for children. It is light, dumb fun only, for nostalgia-minded older teenagers and adults who remember the TV show.

CONTENT ANALYSIS: (Pa, B, L, S, Ho, Ab) Secularized morality; four obscenities; frequent sexual innuendo and older woman flirts with young boys;

lesbian girl has crush on unsuspecting friend; and family's nonreligious, clean-living morality is mocked but ultimately triumphs.

Lex Rex

BRAVEHEART

Quality: ☆☆☆☆   Acceptability: −2

WARNING CODES:
  Language: *
  Violence: ***
  Sex: **
  Nudity: **
RATING: R
GENRE: War drama
INTENDED AUDIENCE: Adults
RUNNING TIME: 170 minutes
STARRING: Mel Gibson, Sophie Marceau, and Patrick McGoohan
DIRECTOR: Mel Gibson
EXECUTIVE PRODUCER: Stephen McEveety
PRODUCERS: Mel Gibson, Alan Ladd Jr., and Bruce Davey
WRITER: Randall Wallace
DISTRIBUTOR: Paramount Pictures
BRIEF SUMMARY:
William Wallace (Mel Gibson) leads his fellow Scots in a heroic struggle for freedom from England's cruel rule in the movie *Braveheart*, an epic that extols liberty, condemns unjust rulers, and acknowledges God's will. Set in the thirteenth century, *Braveheart* tells about the young man whose his father and brother are killed fighting the invaders. Meanwhile, King Edward I is plotting to repopulate Scotland by reinstituting the medieval right of "prima nocta," which allows English lords to spend the first marriage nights with the wives of their subjects. Therefore, when William falls in love, he gets married in secret. When the English guards try to rape his wife and she tries to escape, her throat is slit by the English sheriff. This tragedy starts Wallace on his crusade to drive the English out of Scotland. After many successful battles he is overcome by treachery, but his cry for freedom emboldens the Scots to drive the English out.

Braveheart is a rallying cry for the supremacy of God's law over unjust governors. Regrettably, the movie is extraordinarily violent, the Scots taunt the English by exposing themselves, and there is an implicit adulterous affair. Even so, as director, star, and producer, Mel Gibson brilliantly weaves together romance, heroism, magnificent cinematography, and explosive action into a modern epic.

CONTENT ANALYSIS: (B, CCC, Pa, Ro, VVV, SS, NN, RH) Moral worldview with many positive references to Christianity, God's will, God, and Jesus, as well as some pagan and romantic elements; six obscenities, three exclamations that are clearly prayers; two obscene acts (the Scot army expose themselves to the English army at a distance); extreme violence (frequent fight scenes and battles that include stabbings, hangings, garrotings, impalings, castratings, gougings, dismemberings, and other vividly portrayed acts of violence, and several lingering shots of corpses with gaping wounds); two discrete sex scenes (one marital, one adulterous); shadowed, upper-body female nudity; and mythic revisionist history.

Most Blatant Celebration of Adultery

THE BRIDGES OF MADISON COUNTY

Quality: ☆☆☆   Acceptability: −3

WARNING CODES:
  Language: *
  Violence: None
  Sex: **
  Nudity: **
RATING: PG-13
GENRE: Romantic drama
INTENDED AUDIENCE: Adults

RUNNING TIME: 135 minutes
STARRING: Clint Eastwood and Meryl Streep
DIRECTOR: Clint Eastwood
EXECUTIVE PRODUCER: Clint Eastwood
PRODUCERS: Clint Eastwood and Kathleen Kennedy
WRITER: Richard LaGravenese
BASED ON: The novel by Robert James Waller
DISTRIBUTOR: Warner Brothers
BRIEF SUMMARY:

The Bridges of Madison County is a well-crafted but dangerous film directed by Clint Eastwood. Eastwood plays National Geographic photographer Robert Kincaid on assignment in Madison County, Iowa, who becomes involved in an adulterous affair with housewife Francesca Johnson (Meryl Streep). Told through the reading of a letter written by the recently deceased Francesca to her two, thirty-something children, the film illustrates her 1965 affair when her husband and children left for a four-day outing to the Illinois State Fair. When Kincaid asks Francesca for directions to the Roseman bridge, Francesca offers to hop in his pickup and show him the way. As he brushes her knees while accessing the glove box, the flames of lust stir within Francesca, and by day two they have begun their physical affair. As the time of her family's return approaches, Francesca must decide whether to stay in Iowa or run away with Kincaid to begin a new life with her thrilling lover.

Streep continues to present Oscar-caliber performances, while Eastwood seems wooden and old for the role of Kincaid. Yet together they do a convincing job of encouraging immorality. Acting as a two-hour endorsement of adultery, this film's portrayal of a lonely woman finding happiness in the arms of an exciting loner blatantly subverts the seventh Commandment.

CONTENT ANALYSIS: (Ro, L, SS, NN, A, D, M) Romantic worldview denying the holiness of the marriage covenant; seven obscenities and two profanities; substantial yet darkened depicted adulterous relations in bed and bathtub; upper male nudity, brief rear male nudity, and discreet female frontal nudity; alcohol use; smoking; and aimless wanderlust.

Sobering Drama

THE BROTHERS MCMULLEN

Quality: ☆☆☆   Acceptability: −2

WARNING CODES:
  Language: ***
  Violence: None
  Sex: *
  Nudity: None
RATING: R
GENRE: Drama
INTENDED AUDIENCE: Older teens and adults
RUNNING TIME: 97 minutes
STARRING: Shari Albert, Maxine Bahns, Catherine Bolz, Connie Britton, and Edward Burns
DIRECTOR: Edward Burns
PRODUCERS: Dick Disher and Edward Burns
WRITER: Ed Burns
DISTRIBUTOR: Fox Searchlight
BRIEF SUMMARY:

The Brothers McMullen are Barry, Patrick, and Jack. After their cruel, alcoholic father dies and their mother moves to Ireland to reunite with her long lost love, they use and misuse their Catholicism in New York City to deal with their own feeble love lives. Barry, a struggling screenwriter, vows to never fall in love and marry. Yet he meets a girl named Audrey, and instantly is attracted to her. Patrick, fresh out of college, gets an offer from his girlfriend's father to accept an apartment and a job. Yet, getting cold feet on "adulthood," he refuses the offer, loses his girlfriend, and shines up to a former

Catholic girl with wanderlust. Jack celebrates his beautiful wife's thirtieth birthday. They seem to have the perfect marriage, yet the marriage bed stays cool, and Jack begins to heat up other beds.

The Brothers McMullen is a directorial debut from Ed Burns, a one-time production assistant on *Entertainment Tonight*. Yet, instead of celebrity fodder, he shapes an intimate character study of three complex and compelling brothers. Unfortunately, the budget was low and it shows in the film quality and art direction. Containing many obscenities and profanities, this film shows a Catholic family that upholds its faith as much as it violates it. Addressing themes of interfaith marriage, adultery, birth control, abortion, and commitment, this frank and oftentimes sobering drama is recommended to the cautious but curious viewer.

CONTENT ANALYSIS: (B, LLL, S, A, D, M) Christian Catholic worldview that violates its faith as much as it upholds it; thirty-eight obscenities, nine profanities, ten vulgarities, and one major blasphemy; two acts of adultery and one act of promiscuity implied; alcohol use; smoking; and lying.

Worst Spiritism for Children

CASPER

Quality: ☆☆   Acceptability: −3

WARNING CODES:
  Language: **
  Violence: **
  Sex: None
  Nudity: None
RATING: PG
GENRE: Fantasy
INTENDED AUDIENCE: All ages
RUNNING TIME: 93 minutes
STARRING: Christina Ricci, Bill Pullman, Cathy Moriarty, and Eric Idle
DIRECTOR: Brad Siberling

EXECUTIVE PRODUCERS: Steven Spielberg, Gerald R. Molen, and Jeffrey A. Montgomery
PRODUCER: Colin Wilson
WRITERS: Sherri Stoner and Deanna Oliver
DISTRIBUTOR: Universal Pictures
BRIEF SUMMARY:
In *Casper*, an old mansion called Whipstaff is inherited by a money-loving villain named Carrigan. She soon discovers that her new abode is inhabited by three mean ghouls and a friendly one named Casper. After unsuccessful attempts to rid the house of its unwanted guests, she hires Dr. James Harvey, therapist to the dead, and his adolescent daughter, Kat, to perform a psychological exorcism. Dr. Harvey does this dirty work because he wishes to reconnect with his deceased wife. Kat, as well, seeks a companion to fill the gap caused by the scorn from those who scoff her father's occupation. Father and daughter move into Whipstaff and soon discover the specters. In the end, Kat gets a friend and a date for the dance, Dad gets another chance to talk with his wife, the three ghost uncles become nicer, and Casper gets a new yet brief lease on life.

Casper is a mess. It contains numerous incongruities and implausibilities within its already unbelievable premise. These problems are carried over into its treatment of the afterlife, which not only teaches a spiritist perspective, but actually degrades the value of human life. Furthermore, *Casper* contains obscenities and profanities that clearly are unnecessary and jarring to the viewer in search of some innocuous entertainment.

CONTENT ANALYSIS: (OO, LL, VV, A, Pa, OO, Ab) Spiritist worldview presenting an anti-biblical perspective toward the afterlife; eight obscenities, four vulgarities, and three profanities; slapstick violence (man comes out of haunted house with head on backwards;

car demolished; man falls down stairs; man hits head; couple falls; ghosts get beaten, squeezed, pushed shoved, drawn, and quartered; and woman falls to implied death); alcohol use; psycho-analysis of ghosts; use of pentagram, frivolous treatment of the supernatural, ghost tomfoolery, ghosts presented as real; people purportedly die to become a ghost or an angel, and the power of God is belittled when a priest is shown as unable to exorcise ghosts.

Pagan Lifestyle

CLUELESS

Quality: ☆☆☆   Acceptability: −2

WARNING CODES:

Language: **
Violence: None
Sex: *
Nudity: None

RATING PG–13
GENRE: Comedy
INTENDED AUDIENCE: Teens
RUNNING TIME: 113 minutes
DIRECTOR: Amy Heckerling
STARRING: Alicia Silverstone, Stacey Dash, and Brittany Murphy
PRODUCERS: Adam Schroeder and Barry Berg
WRITER: Amy Heckerling
DISTRIBUTOR: Paramount Pictures
BRIEF SUMMARY:
Clueless is a movie that deals with sixteen-year-old Cher's development from a clueless Beverly Hills mall shop-per into a conscientious, community-conscious teenager. This transformation ensues as she takes on two pet projects. The first is a totally selfish attempt to get her bad grades changed. Her successful matchmaking of two of her teachers impresses her lawyer father, who is unconcerned with her lack of scholar-ship. As the love-struck teachers ease up on the students, Cher's popularity with the student body is enhanced. Her sec-ond project is to rescue a transfer student from New York, save her from fashion disaster, and make her as popular as Cher and her friends. She does this by getting her into the right clothes, taking her to the right parties, and trying to find her the right guy.

This is a lighthearted comedy with some unfortunate characters that many teenagers will either identify with or rec-ognize as their own friends. From drug use, to homosexuality, to free sex and shopping sprees, this film endorses a pagan lifestyle. The picture does deliver some giggles at the lifestyle of these pampered kids, but the overall message leaves something to be desired.

CONTENT (Pa, E, Ho, PC, Ro, LL, S, A , M) Pagan worldview with elements of environmentalism, romanticism, homosexuality, and inclusions of politi-cally correct speeches and causes; eleven obscenities; implied oral sex and inter-course; teens boozing at party; teens smoking joints at party; and main char-acter held up and robbed.

Healing the Land

CRY, THE BELOVED COUNTRY

Quality: ☆☆☆   Acceptability: +2

WARNING CODES:

Language: None
Violence: **
Sex: *
Nudity: None

RATING: PG-13
GENRE: Drama
INTENDED AUDIENCE: All ages
RUNNING TIME: 120 minutes
STARRING: James Earl Jones, Richard Harris, Vusi Kunene, Leleti Khumalo, and Charles S. Dutton
DIRECTOR: Darrell James Roodt
PRODUCER: Anant Singh
WRITER: Ronald Harwood
BASED ON: The novel by Alan Paton

DISTRIBUTOR: Miramax Films

BRIEF SUMMARY:

In *Cry, the Beloved Country*, racial tensions reign in South Africa in the 1940s. Zulu Christian minister Stephen Kumalo, played by James Earl Jones, is called away to Johannesburg. He is asked to locate a local girl who moved to the city. Kumalo arrives in the city, only to learn that his sister has turned to prostitution and now has an illegitimate son. Kumalo forgives her, and searches also for his brother, John, and his son, Absalom. He finds that John has walked away from the church and is a prominent organizer in protests against whites, and that Absalom has been arrested for the murder of Arthur Jarvis, a white reformer. The murder trial has commenced, and Kumalo, a man of deep compassion for others, has to face the most difficult trial of his life.

There are few films today that touch the heart and turn the viewer to tears. This is such a film. Although slow paced, it grips the emotions. This film will convict some viewers of the injustices they throw at each other. Perhaps those watching will be moved to listen and learn from Kumalo's consistent Christlike example. Just like the good shepherd who gathers his sheep into the fold, Kumalo attempts to reunite his family. Easily transferable into our neighborhoods today, there is much we can learn from the Christian characters in this movie.

CONTENT ANALYSIS: (CCC, VV, S) Christian worldview extoling Christ; implied murder, beatings enforced by police and a hanging; implied prostitution and implied fornication resulting in illegitimacy; and thievery.

Caring Teacher

DANGEROUS MINDS

Quality: ☆☆☆   Acceptability: −2

WARNING CODES:

Language: ***

Violence: *

Sex: None

Nudity: None

RATING: R

GENRE: Drama

INTENDED AUDIENCE: Older teens and adults

RUNNING TIME: 99 minutes

STARRING: Michelle Pfeiffer, George Dzundza, Courtney B. Vance, Bruklin Harris, Renoly Santiago, and Wade Dominguez

DIRECTOR: John N. Smith

PRODUCERS: Don Simpson and Jerry Bruckheimer

WRITER: Ronald Bass

BASED ON: The novel by LouAnne Johnson

DISTRIBUTOR: Buena Vista

BRIEF SUMMARY:

The inspirational drama *Dangerous Minds* opens with ex-marine LouAnne Johnson visiting a suburban high school in northern California to inquire about a substitute teaching position. Teaching is Ms. Johnson's dream, and to her elation she is offered a full-time job at the upperclass high school. This sounds great to the green recruit, who never thought that she would walk straight from her first interview into the classroom. However, Ms. Johnson soon finds out that her group of children are jaded, rebellious "ruffians" who have absolutely no interest in listening to what she has to say. LouAnne seeks to overcome her frustration with the students by finding ways to get their attention. The teenagers slowly turn into exemplary students, but as the caring teacher seeks to make a difference in their young lives, she encounters opposition from the school's authority figures, the students' parents, the curriculum, and at times the students themselves.

The acting is superb and the absence of nudity and sex, as well as the sparsely applied violence in this film, should be commended. While not denying the rough elements of urban

America through course language, it actually provides a tasteful look of hope and the triumph of one person positively affecting the lives of many.

CONTENT ANALYSIS: (B, LLL, V, A, D) Moral worldview extolling discipline and education; twenty-five obscenities and three vulgarities; brief fistfight and implied murder (shooting); and alcohol use and implied drug use.

Repentance, Forgiveness, New Life

DEAD MAN WALKING

Quality: ✩✩✩✩   Acceptability: –1

WARNING CODES:

Language: **
Violence: **
Sex: None
Nudity: *

RATING: R
GENRE: Drama
INTENDED AUDIENCE: Adults
RUNNING TIME: 125 minutes
STARRING: Sean Penn and Susan Sarandon
DIRECTOR: Tim Robbins
EXECUTIVE PRODUCERS: Tim Belvin and Eric Fullner
WRITER: Tim Robbins
BASED ON: The book by Helen Prejean
DISTRIBUTOR: Gramercy Pictures
BRIEF SUMMARY:
Dead Man Walking is a powerful movie about a nun who becomes the spiritual advisor to an inmate on death row. Susan Sarandon plays Sister Helen Prejean, a nun who lives among the black poor in rural Louisiana. One day she is asked to write a letter to an inmate on death row. His name is Matthew Poncelet and he is convicted of murdering two teenagers. Her coworkers and friends begin to abandon her because she is siding with a "monster." Poncelet is given a date for his execution. Sister Helen decides to pay a visit to the parents of the deceased victims. Days before the execution, Sister Helen gives Poncelet a Bible and asks him to read it. He does and they talk about Jesus, but Poncelet still doesn't confess to the murders. Minutes before his execution, Poncelet accepts Christ, confesses his crimes, and apologizes to the families of the victims.

This movie may convict and challenge Christians to live out their faith boldly. Non-Christians will hear many accurate Bible references. There is a slight undercurrent of political correctness, but it is restrained. The movie does briefly show the murder scene, and there are some obscenities. This film uses Scripture in a thorough examination of an important topic, particularly in light of today's rising crime rate.

CONTENT ANALYSIS: (CCC, PC, LL, VV, N, D, M) Christian worldview where Christ, church attendance, Bible reading, repentance, service to God, and forgiveness are extolled even at a high price; mild politically correct view of capital punishment; seven obscenities and seven vulgarities; moderate violence including a point-blank shooting and rape (seen at a distance) and images of two corpses; natural female rear nudity of dead woman (seen at a distance); smoking; and hate and unforgiveness.

Pro-Family, Pro-Life, Pro-Father

FATHER OF THE BRIDE PART II

Quality: ✩✩✩✩   Acceptability: +3

WARNING CODES:

Language: *
Violence: None
Sex: *
Nudity: None

RATING: PG
GENRE: Comedy
INTENDED AUDIENCE: All ages
RUNNING TIME: 100 minutes

STARRING: Steve Martin, Diane Keaton, Kimberly Williams, and Martin Short

DIRECTOR: Charles Shyer

PRODUCER: Nancy Meyers

WRITERS: Charles Shyer and Nancy Meyers

DISTRIBUTOR: Touchstone Pictures/Walt Disney Pictures/Buena Vista Pictures

BRIEF SUMMARY:

Father of the Bride Part II is a funny, entertaining, positive portrait of a traditional family, produced with exquisite love and compassion. This pro-family, pro-father, pro-life movie will make you laugh and cry and go home feeling better about your life. It opens with George Banks (Steve Martin) discovering that his now-married daughter, Annie, is expecting a baby. Nina Banks is overjoyed, but George is distraught. Immediately, George tries to stop the aging process by exercising, dying his hair, and selling his house. Thus, the complications begin as a swarthy developer buys his house and, in his newfound energy, George discovers his wife is pregnant. Now George is not only going to be a grandfather, he is also going to be a father—again!

Thus, George's life takes its twists and turns, producing an endearing portrait of humanity in a way that has been unrivaled since *It's a Wonderful Life*. *Father of the Bride Part II* is a movie for those who have children, as well as for children who want to find out how wonderful being a father or a mother really is. The direction is flawless, the dialogue witty, and the acting superb. In fact, every element of this film has been crafted to perfection, and in the end, it lifts up the American family and the American father in a way that has never been done in a film before.

CONTENT ANALYSIS: (C, L, S, Ho) Strong Christian worldview promoting love, fatherhood, marriage, commitment, and forgiveness; ten exclamatory profanities and one colloquialism; some mild sexual allusions and two sexually ambivalent characters; and great soundtrack that includes several moral songs, including "When the Saints Go Marching In."

Pay the Price

FEAST OF JULY

Quality: ☆☆☆☆   Acceptability: −2

WARNING CODES:

Language: *
Violence: **
Sex: *
Nudity: None

RATING: R

GENRE: Drama

INTENDED AUDIENCE: Adults

RUNNING TIME: 115 minutes

STARRING: Embeth Davidtz, Tom Bell, Gemma Jones, James Purefoy, Greg Wise, Kenneth Anderson, and Ben Chaplin

DIRECTOR: Christopher Menaul

PRODUCERS: Ismail Merchant and Paul Bradley

WRITER: Christopher Neame

BASED ON: The novel by H. E. Bates

DISTRIBUTOR: Touchstone Pictures/Walt Disney Pictures/Buena Vista Pictures

BRIEF SUMMARY:

In *Feast of July*, Bella Ford is betrayed by her lover Archie Wilson. He leaves her, and she gives birth to a stillborn child. She searches for Archie, but collapses at the foot of a kind man named Mr. Wainwright. He invites her back to his home and introduces her to his wife and three sons, Jed, Matty, and Con. Bella soon becomes the object of attention from all three sons, but Con eventually wins her. Trying to forget her past, Bella goes out boating with Con. They encounter Archie Wilson fishing. When Archie taunts them, Con kills Archie. The two decide to flee to Ireland. However, when morning comes Con decides to turn himself in to the police.

Bella pleads for him not to do so, but he does. As Con faces the gallows, Bella sails off to Ireland with his unborn child.

This movie is emotionally moving because we care so much about the characters. Con and his family pray, go to church, and seem to love each other. They believe that their faith and restraint should have prevented disaster, but, like King David of old, this movie tells the story of people who want to live holy lives under God but pay the price for unbridled passions. Although the movie contains some violence and sexual situations, it is all done with great restraint. The film powerfully shows the penalty of sin within a Christian worldview.

CONTENT ANALYSIS: (B, C, L, VV, S, A, D, M) Biblical worldview emphasizing that the wages of sin is death and extoling family, prayer, and church attendance; three profanities and three obscenities (all mild); moderate violence including fighting with farm tools, hanging, man beaten to death with rock, and man strikes woman; woman gives birth; implied fornication, and briefly depicted fornication; alcohol use and one brief drunk scene; smoking; and vomiting.

Best Depiction of Kingdoms in Conflict

FIRST KNIGHT

Quality: ☆☆☆☆   Acceptability: +1

WARNING CODES:

Language: None
Violence: **
Sex: *
Nudity: None

RATING: PG-13
GENRE: Romantic drama
INTENDED AUDIENCE: Teens and adults
RUNNING TIME: 125 minutes
STARRING: Sean Connery, Richard Gere, Julia Ormond, and Ben Cross
DIRECTOR: Jerry Zucker
PRODUCERS: Jerry Zucker and Hunt Lowry

WRITERS: Lorne Cameron, David Hoselton, and William Nicholson
DISTRIBUTOR: Columbia Pictures
BRIEF SUMMARY:

Written by the same man who penned *Shadowlands*, *First Knight* presents a noble spin on the tale of King Arthur and his Knights of the Round Table. Ben Cross plays Malagant, a knight who chooses to usurp the reign of good King Arthur (Sean Connery). Richard Gere plays Lancelot, a romantic loner who travels about as a vagabond in search of adventure, including wooing Lady Guinevere (played by the beautiful Julia Ormond). Guinevere rejects Lancelot and marries King Arthur. Arthur calls the knights together to have a peace talk with Malagant. Malagant kidnaps Guinevere. Lancelot rescues Guinevere and again tells her of his love. On their return to Camelot, Lancelot kisses Guinevere goodbye and is discovered by the king, who almost condemns them for treason but doesn't carry out the judgment when Lancelot again comes to the rescue at a final confrontation with Malagant.

First Knight demonstrates integrity and truth. King Arthur realizes that God is the King of Kings and that true leadership means serving God. Guinevere realizes that even unfortunate circumstances can be used for the glory of God. And Lancelot learns true servitude. No nudity or profane language and a moral treatment of issues of war, love, and forgiveness make this movie a must-see.

CONTENT ANALYSIS: (B, CCC, Ro, VV, S, A, M) Biblical, Christian worldview with some romantic elements; moderate violence including three battle scenes with stabbing, slicing, beatings, and mild bloodletting; an adulterous kiss; alcohol consumption; and betrayal themes.

Ups and Downs

FORGET PARIS

Quality: ☆☆☆☆   Acceptability: −2

WARNING CODES:

Language: ***
Violence: *
Sex: **
Nudity: *

RATING: PG-13
GENRE: Romantic comedy
INTENDED AUDIENCE: Adults
RUNNING TIME: 95 minutes
STARRING: Billy Crystal, Debra Winger, Joe Mantegna, Cynthia Stevenson, Richard Masur, Julie Kavner, and Robert Costanzo
DIRECTOR: Billy Crystal
EXECUTIVE PRODUCER: Peter Schindler
PRODUCER: Billy Crystal
WRITERS: Billy Crystal, Lowell Ganz, and Babaloo Mandel
DISTRIBUTOR: Columbia Pictures
BRIEF SUMMARY:
"Romantic movies always leave you with the thought that the couple is going to live happily ever after. Well, happily-ever-after is a lot of hard work," says Billy Crystal, writer, director, producer, and star of the romantic comedy *Forget Paris*. Also starring Debra Winger and a host of NBA celebrities, *Forget Paris* takes a funny, poignant look at the marriage relationship. Theirs has been a relationship full of ups and downs. Life in Paris is wonderful for Ellen, a lifelong dream. Can she give it up for love? Life in the NBA is wonderful for Mickey, but Paris it ain't! There you have the basis for relational conflict, and the trouble only builds from there. Do they "Forget Paris!"—the most wonderful week in their lives—and go their separate ways? Or can they find some common ground in their crazy lives on which to build?

On the downside are some foul language and a worldly but not graphic outlook on morality. The story does support and promote marriage but doesn't give any clear reasons for it. The humor is decidedly adult, but only rarely borders on the offensive. Not just for romantics and not overloaded with humor, *Forget Paris* takes an honest look at relationships, with all the fun and all the pain.

CONTENT ANALYSIS: (Ro, LLL, V, SS, N, A, M) Somewhat romantic worldview supporting marriage; twenty-seven obscenities, three profanities (two exclamatory), and nine vulgarities; verbal outbursts from sports fans at game and reckless auto driving; implied fornication and briefly depicted intercourse (covered and marital), several sexual innuendos and much adult humor, references to masturbation, and implied use of pornography; man briefly shirtless; brief alcohol use with meal; and woman receives injections.

Unconventional Comedy

FUNNY BONES

Quality: ☆☆☆☆   Acceptability: −2

WARNING CODES:

Language: **
Violence: **
Sex: *
Nudity: None

RATING: R
GENRE: Comedy
INTENDED AUDIENCE: Older teens and adults
RUNNING TIME: 125 minutes
STARRING: Oliver Platt, Lee Evans, Oliver Reed, George Carl, Leslie Caron, and Jerry Lewis
DIRECTOR: Peter Chelsom
EXECUTIVE PRODUCER: Nicholas Frye
PRODUCERS: Simon Fields and Peter Chelsom
WRITERS: Peter Chelsom and Peter Flannery
DISTRIBUTOR: Buena Vista Pictures/Walt Disney Company
BRIEF SUMMARY:
Funny Bones is a disarmingly intelligent and unconventional comedy that

plumbs the depths of comedic psyche. It is not all funny and, at moments, becomes downright horrifying. The movie's protagonist is Tommy Fawkes, a failed comedian who has lived his entire life in the shadow of his father, George, a very famous stand-up comic. After Tommy blows his opening night in Las Vegas, he disappears to Blackpool, England, in search of new material, funny people, and a "new way of looking at life." Upon his introduction to the Parker brothers, he finds all three. In the end, it is the viewer who feels that he or she has been atop a pole for two hours, teetering at the mercy of a capricious clown.

Funny Bones is clearly a celebration of modern philosophy and psychology, intelligently posing valid questions: What does it mean to be human? What does it mean to be alive? However, it arrives at the rather standard existential and nihilistic position that all answers are relative and unknowable. Brilliant acting and excellent cinematography make the movie visually stunning and emotionally powerful, transporting the viewer to a world where all authority is corrupt and where self-preservation is the ultimate good. This kind of genius may elevate the work to the status of art, but mercifully does not and cannot make its premise true.

CONTENT ANALYSIS: (H, LL, VV, S, A, M) Humanist worldview; thirteen obscenities, three profanities, and two vulgarities; man killed by boat propeller, his feet shown floating in the water, and man beaten to death with lead pipe; implied adultery; alcohol use; and revenge and corrupt police officers.

Bittersweet Tale

GEORGIA

Quality: ✫✫✫✫   Acceptability: –2

WARNING CODES:
  Language: ***

Violence: None
Sex: **
Nudity: **

RATING: R
GENRE: Drama
INTENDED AUDIENCE: Adults
RUNNING TIME: 117 minutes
STARRING: Jennifer Jason Leigh, Mare Winningham, Ted Levine, and John Doe
DIRECTOR: Ulu Grosbard
PRODUCERS: Ulu Grosbard, Barbara Turner, and Jennifer Jason Leigh
WRITER: Barbara Turner
DISTRIBUTOR: Miramax Films
BRIEF SUMMARY:
Once again, Jennifer Jason Leigh stuns and rivets with her performance as Sadie in the film *Georgia*. The story is simple, but fraught with the human drama played out in troubled families. Georgia, played by Mare Winningham, is a popular singer, rooted in her loving family. Sadie, her sister, is constantly adrift and drunk, looking for the fame that comes so easily to Georgia. When things go wrong, Georgia is there, but her tolerance and patience are stretched. Sadie, with her raw-edged personality, mascara-laden eyes, and bloody tattoos is always on the brink of the abyss. Everyone tries to help her, but to no avail in this bittersweet tale.

The film is gripping in its interplay of deep-seated emotions between the two sisters. Even though the film is named after the character Georgia, the story is Sadie's. Jennifer Jason Leigh's portrayal of the painfully lost Sadie is testimony to her incredible talent. Both Ms. Leigh and Ms. Winningham sing in this film. Music and script blend in telling the story. Though the movie has excessive foul language and a sexual scene involving nudity, the film has a moral fiber as it elevates family loyalty and love as ultimate virtues.

CONTENT ANALYSIS: (B, LLL, SS, NN, A, S, M) Moral worldview validating family ties and love; thirty-eight obscenities and seven profanities; one sex scene and one reference to sexual activity; one brief scene of full female nudity; alcohol use and abuse; drug use and smoking; and tattoos.

Seduced by Filmmaking

GET SHORTY

Quality: ☆☆☆   Acceptability: −2

WARNING CODES:
  Language: ***
  Violence: **
  Sex: **
  Nudity: None
RATING: R
GENRE: Crime/Comedy
INTENDED AUDIENCE: Adults
RUNNING TIME: 105 minutes
STARRING: John Travolta, Gene Hackman, Rene Russo, and Danny DeVito
  DIRECTOR: Barry Sonnenfeld
  EXECUTIVE PRODUCER: Barry Sonnenfeld
  WRITER: Scott Frank
  DISTRIBUTOR: Metro Goldwyn-Mayer/United Artists
  BRIEF SUMMARY:
Get Shorty is not a very profound crime comedy, but what it lacks in substance it makes up for in pathos, although it is occasionally crude and mean spirited. Chili Palmer (John Travolta) is a mob debt collector who gives another gangster a bloody nose. Chili's godfather dies of a heart attack, leaving him without any protection against his new nemesis. Soon thereafter, Chili finds himself headed west in pursuit of some hard cash. It is only a matter of time before Chili is seduced by the excitement of filmmaking. He pitches a new script to eccentric director Harry Zimm, played by Gene Hackman. Zimm wants gangster money to fund the picture. The result is a topsy-turvy, fast-paced madcap movie with lots of twists, and lots of holes to match.

One of *Get Shorty*'s major assets is its cast. Travolta, Hackman, Russo, DeVito, and Lindo are all good in their respective roles. There are also brief appearances by Bette Midler and Penny Marshall. The film manages to convey the warm feel of a witty, funny, and poignant satire. It is marred, however, by scenes of extramarital sex, too many obscenities, excessive profanities, and chilling violence. This prevents it from being truly enjoyable. In fact, the film is irreparably soiled by all its excesses and so are its characters, the good as well as the bad.

CONTENT ANALYSIS: (Pa, LLL, VV, SS, A, D, M) Pagan worldview showcasing criminals in Hollywood; over thirty obscenities and over ten profanities; moderate violence including three murders by gunfire, man pushed over railing, and man beaten with broken bones; one extramarital sex scene with alcohol use; drug sales and use implied; and stealing, deceit, and other gangster activity.

Not Very Funny

A GOOFY MOVIE

Quality: ☆☆   Acceptability: +1

WARNING CODES:
  Language: None
  Violence: *
  Sex: None
  Nudity: None
RATING: G
GENRE: Animated adventure
INTENDED AUDIENCE: All ages
RUNNING TIME: 73 minutes
VOICES: Jason Marsden, Bill Farmer, Kellie Martin, Jenna Von Oy, Jim Cummings, Rob Paulsen, Wallace Shawn, Jo Anne Worley, Joey Lawrence, and Julie Brown
  DIRECTOR: Kevin Lima
  PRODUCER: Dan Rounds
  WRITERS: Jymn Magon, Chris Matheson, and Brian Pimental
  STORY BY: Jymn Magon

BASED ON: The cartoon series *Goof Troop*

DISTRIBUTOR: Buena Vista Pictures/Walt Disney Company

BRIEF SUMMARY:

Following in the tradition of *DuckTales*, Disney offers another movie based on one of its animated television series, *Goof Troop*. Max, PJ, Pete, and Goofy are all there, plus a few new characters in *A Goofy Movie*. Numerous cameo appearances are featured, including Mickey Mouse and Donald Duck, plus a special guest appearance by Elvis. As is the case with Disney's other full-length animated features, *A Goofy Movie* has enough songs to be considered a musical. While billed as a children's movie, children in the audience appeared not to find it very funny and seemed to laugh simply because their parents did. In this movie, Max and PJ are older than their television series counterparts, so this feature may be over the heads of younger children.

A Goofy Movie is a fine example of how *not* to be a parent. In the two father-son relationships, both fathers fail to communicate with their sons. PJ is in fear of his dad, and Goofy displays a bad example for his son, sneaking him into a rock concert and helping him continue a lie to impress his girlfriend. In the end, Max admits his lie, and the audience is treated to a typical Walt Disney happy ending. However, the lies and deception are never fully addressed, and the advantages gained by them are viewed as successes.

CONTENT ANALYSIS: (Ro, V, N, M) Romantic worldview of prevailing love but also condoning lying and deception; one vulgarity and childish name-calling (one character refers to Max and Goofy as "dorks"); action violence centered upon Goofy's poor driving skills and man gets punched; child runs loose in a department store sans diaper; and use of lies and deception to achieve desired ends, lack of respect for authority, underwear used as comic device, and dead man dances during musical number.

Taking Care of Friends

THE INDIAN IN THE CUPBOARD

Quality: ☆☆☆   Acceptability: +1

WARNING CODES:
  Language: *
  Violence: *
  Sex: None
  Nudity: None

RATING: PG

GENRE: Fantasy

INTENDED AUDIENCE: Families

RUNNING TIME: 91 minutes

STARRING: Hal Scardino, Litefoot, Lindsay Crouse, Richard Jenkins, Rishi Bhat, and David Keith

DIRECTOR: Frank Oz

PRODUCERS: Kathleen Kennedy, Frank Marshall, and Jane Sartz

WRITER: Melissa Mathison

BASED ON: The novel by Lynne Reid Banks

DISTRIBUTOR: Paramount Pictures

BRIEF SUMMARY:

In the charming family picture *The Indian in the Cupboard*, Omri receives a skateboard, a helmet, an action figure, an old wooden cupboard, and a miniature plastic Indian for his birthday. When he puts the last two together, the Indian turns into Little Bear, an eighteenth-century Iroquois man. Amazed, Omri decides to keep him. Omri discovers that anything plastic placed in the cupboard becomes real, so Omri gives Little Bear a teepee. Little Bear rejects the teepee and asks for materials to make a longhouse. In time, Omri becomes overwhelmed with meeting Little Bear's needs and so he tells his friend Patrick about the cupboard. Patrick wants to turn his plastic cowboy and horse into real creatures. He does so, and creates Boo-Hoo Boone, a crying cowboy. Boone and Little Bear start fighting, but the boys become peacemakers, and the figures become friends. Omri and Patrick realize that taking care of friends requires responsibility. After great challenges involving a schoolteacher, a rat, and an injury, the boys decide to send Little Bear and Boone back to their own times.

This story works because it refuses to condescend to children and accepts them as creative persons who face personal decisions every day. Except for very few obscenities and exclamations and mild violence, this film provides a marvelous antidote to violent and New Age summer fare.

CONTENT ANALYSIS: (B, Pa, FR, L, V) Moral worldview with a fantasy, nominalistic ontology and minor elements of Native American religions; seven obscenities (mild) and two exclamatory profanities; minor action violence including arrow and gunfire, with one arrow hitting man, and kicking a rat.

Looking for a Family

IT TAKES TWO

Quality: ☆☆☆   Acceptability: +2

WARNING CODES:
Language: *
Violence: None
Sex: None
Nudity: None
RATING: PG
GENRE: Drama
INTENDED AUDIENCE: Children
RUNNING TIME: 100 minutes
STARRING: Kirstie Alley, Steve Guttenberg, Jane Sibbett, Mary-Kate Olsen, and Ashley Olsen
DIRECTOR: Andy Tennant
PRODUCERS: Keith Samples and Mel Efros
WRITER: Deborah Dean Davis
DISTRIBUTOR: Warner Brothers
BRIEF SUMMARY:
It Takes Two tells the story of identical girls living at extremes: one is rich; the other is an orphan. Starring the Olsen twins, the movie weaves an idealistic tale where a child's fantasy of picking one's parents comes true. Amanda Lemon is an orphan. Her caseworker, Diane Barrows, would like to adopt Amanda but the "system" says no. The children's home is spending a week at a camp founded by Roger Callaway's deceased wife. Roger is engaged to Claris, a woman he doesn't love, and has a daughter identical to Amanda named Alyssa. Together, Amanda and Alyssa execute plans to stop Roger from marrying Claris and instead marry Diane.

The movie is a cute fantasy where identical young girls of diverse means are able to switch places and fix their family woes. (In this sense it is a modern *Prince and the Pauper*.) The tale is fairly clean; children can see this without the worry of parents. There is no violence, sex, or harsh language. However, the movie is pure fantasy, taking leaps of believability. The Olsen twins, fresh from *Full House* fame and eager to strut their comedic twin-power, carry off a delightful movie. Despite a fantasy storyline, the movie *It Takes Two* is a sweet, innocent film about two girls looking for a family. The movie is innocuous fun for families with small children, especially girls.

CONTENT ANALYSIS: (Ro, L, A) Romantic worldview of two identical girls able to bring together their respective "parents" romantically despite several obstacles; one obscenity, one vulgarity, and two profanities; and alcohol use implied.

Most Perverse Slander of an Important Historical Figure

JEFFERSON IN PARIS

Quality: ☆☆   Acceptability: −2

WARNING CODES:
Language: None
Violence: **
Sex: **
Nudity: None
RATING: PG-13

GENRE: Historical drama
INTENDED AUDIENCE: Adults
RUNNING TIME: 120 minutes
STARRING: Nick Nolte, Greta Scacchi, Thandie Newton, Gwyneth Paltrow, and Charlotte DeTurckheim
DIRECTOR: James Ivory
PRODUCER: Ismail Merchant
WRITER: Ruth Prawer Jhabvala
DISTRIBUTOR: Buena Vista Pictures/Walt Disney Company
BRIEF SUMMARY:

Set during the period between 1784 and 1789, in prerevolutionary Paris, *Jefferson in Paris* focuses on Ambassador Thomas Jefferson dealing with the death of his wife and the role of the United States in history. This saga opens in the mid-1800s, with the "alleged" black grandson of Thomas Jefferson, Mr. Hemmings, telling the tale of *Jefferson in Paris*. He informs us that Mr. Jefferson's relationship with the court of Louis XVI was confounded by his relationship with Maria Cosway, the wife of an English painter. After this affair, Jefferson's attention is diverted to his fourteen-year-old slave, Sally Hemmings, when the Cosways return to England. When Maria returns, she is told that, in America, masters have a "special" relationship with their slaves. When Jefferson finds that Sally is pregnant, he promises to give her and her children their freedom after he dies.

Aside from the annoying tendency of revisionists to read their mores into the history they are writing, this movie gives very little insight into Thomas Jefferson, author, statesman, scientist, architect, and philosopher. Jefferson is portrayed as a clod who is preoccupied with sex. Not only does the script fail to enlighten us, but the acting is strained. Regrettably, this mediocre movie will become a historical reference point for all who see it.
CONTENT ANALYSIS: (RH, H, VV, SS, M, C) Revisionist history with a humanist worldview; revolutionary violence including hangings, bloody head on a spike, and mob activity; adultery and fornication implied, Punch and Judy doll with oversized private male organ; perverse Punch and Judy show mocking king and queen of France; and positive reference to Catholic convent and faith.

Finish the Game

JUMANJI

Quality: ☆☆☆   Acceptability: −1

WARNING CODES:
  Language: *
  Violence: **
  Sex: None
  Nudity: None
RATING: PG
GENRE: Fantasy
INTENDED AUDIENCE: All ages
RUNNING TIME: 104 minutes
STARRING: Robin Williams, Kirsten Dunst, Bonnie Hunt, and Bradley Pierce
DIRECTOR: Joe Johnston
EXECUTIVE PRODUCERS: Ted Field, Larry Franco, and Robert W. Cort
PRODUCERS: Scott Kroopf and William Teitler
WRITER: Jonathan Hensleigh
BASED ON: The book by Chris Van Allsburg
DISTRIBUTOR: Columbia/TriStar Motion Picture Company
BRIEF SUMMARY:
In 1969, young Alan Parrish discovers a buried box on a construction site. He takes it home and discovers a board game designed for those who want to escape. He starts playing it with his friend, Sarah. She rolls a number, and giant bats attack. He rolls a number and the board reads that he must go to the jungle until someone rolls a five or an eight. He then gets sucked into the game. He is not seen again until two children start playing the game years later (the present). Understanding that they must finish the game, they evoke a

swarm of giant mosquitoes, a hungry lion, a band of vandalistic monkeys, and more. Each step brings more destruction to their home and the town until one player finishes the game, restoring Alan and Sarah to their young selves in 1969.

The production value of this movie is superb. However, it may be too scary for little children. Concerned parents will want to know if the fantasy and supernatural elements of this movie is New Age or anti-Christian. The answer is that all we know about these strange occurrences is that the game *Jumanji* makes it happen. For discerning parents, movie choices can sometimes be a jungle. *Jumanji* is a jungle. While exciting, it has its dangers, and caution is advised.

CONTENT ANALYSIS: (Pa, B, L, VV, M) Pagan worldview of fantasy game world with no spiritual or anti-Christian forces implied; moral elements of familial love; four mild obscenities and three profanities; moderate violence includes attempted lion attack, rhino stampede, carnivorous plant attempts to eat person, English hunter shoots at people, flooding, car crashes, and alligator attacks; and lying.

Grace Overcomes Misery

LES MISERABLES

Quality: ☆☆☆☆   Acceptability: –1

WARNING CODES:
Language: **
Violence: ***
Sex: **
Nudity: None
RATING: R
GENRE: Drama
INTENDED AUDIENCE: Adults
RUNNING TIME: 160 minutes
STARRING: Jean-Paul Belmondo, Michel Bounehah, Alessandra Martines, Clementine Celarie, and Salome LeLouch
DIRECTOR: Claude LeLouch

PRODUCER: Claude LeLouch
WRITER: Claude LeLouch
DISTRIBUTOR: Warner Brothers
BRIEF SUMMARY:
This magnificent movie by Claude LeLouch, *Les Miserables*, is not another film adaptation of Victor Hugo's redemptive story; instead, the movie is a unique retelling of Hugo's masterpiece using Hugo's work as a metaphor for life. The movie opens at the turn of the twentieth century with the tragic story of Henri Fortin, a chauffeur who is wrongly sent to prison. After Fortin dies, the movie follows his son, young Henri, a boxer who eventually starts a moving business. His business flourishes until he moves the Zimans, a Jewish couple escaping the German occupation of Paris during World War II. When they are betrayed and captured, Henri also falls on hard times and is brutally tortured for aiding the Zimans. Henri escapes prison by dealing with the Gestapo and eventually sees the end of the war. When the policeman realizes that Henri can testify in court to his wartime activities, he commits suicide, and Henri is blamed. Mr. Ziman escapes the farm where he has been held hostage and comes to Henri's legal defense. In the end, prayer triumphs and the misery of existence is alleviated by love and grace.

There are not enough superlatives to adequately commend the acting, camera work, music, dialogue, and set direction in *Les Miserables*. This is a wonderful work of love about lives in misery until touched by the grace, love, and knowledge of God.

CONTENT ANALYSIS: (CCC, B, H, Ro, LL, VVV, SS, M) Moral redemptive worldview marred by humanistic, Romantic, and pluralistic elements; twenty-seven obscenities including teaching a little girl to say a slang phrase that includes an obscenity; cruel acts of violence associated with war, prison, and crime, including a reenactment of the D-day invasion, several people shot

at close range, pistol whippings, strangulation, torture by submersion in water,
beatings, and falling down a well, four
suicides, and extreme domestic violence;
implied prostitution, two scenes of
implied sex, and one scene with suggested sex (the adults are clothed, with
children watching from a distance); negative reference to homosexuality; many
positive references to God, prayer, and
Jesus; and theft, graft, and treason.

Imagination Triumphs over Avarice

A LITTLE PRINCESS

Quality: ☆☆☆☆   Acceptability: +3

WARNING CODES:
   Language: None
   Violence: None
   Sex: None
   Nudity: None
RATING: G
GENRE: Adventure
INTENDED AUDIENCE: Children
RUNNING TIME: 90 minutes
STARRING: Liesel Matthews, Liam
Cunningham, and Eleanor Bron
   DIRECTOR: Alfonso Cuaron
   EXECUTIVE PRODUCERS: Alan C.
Blomquist and Amy Ephron
   PRODUCERS: Mark Johnson and
Barry Levinson
   WRITER: Richard LaGravanese
   BASED ON: The novel by Frances
Hodgson Burnett
   DISTRIBUTOR: Warner Brothers
   BRIEF SUMMARY:
   Every once in a while a movie comes
along that innocently touches the heart
and becomes a classic. Such is *A Little
Princess,* the story of a wealthy, precious,
and precocious little girl, Sara Crewe, and
her adventures at Miss Minchin's School
for Girls. It is also the tale of her father's
separation from her by the horrors of war,
her time living as an orphan, and their
subsequent triumphant reunion. Raised
in the jungles of India, young Sara lives in
a world filled with exotic experiences and

an adoring father, who is forced to leave
her at the boarding school while he goes
to fight in World War I. When he is
reported killed, Sara is reduced to
poverty until a miracle happens.
   A Little Princess is a very good technical production. Casting is impeccable,
and every character is memorable. The
story (taken from the family favorite by
the same name) is well written and the
cinematography is at times breathtaking.
The acting performances are delightful.
In this movie, magic ("believing in what
you want and yet cannot see") is portrayed as somewhat similar to what the
Bible calls faith. This is a child's innocent
representation of a source of hope in the
midst of an otherwise hopeless situation.
As such, it should not be faulted. All
ends well in this well-crafted adventure
movie.
   CONTENT ANALYSIS: (Ro, B) Romantic worldview with moral elements.

Righteousness Prevails

A MONTH BY THE LAKE

Quality: ☆☆☆☆   Acceptability: −1

WARNING CODES:
   Language: **
   Violence: *
   Sex: *
   Nudity: None
RATING: PG
GENRE: Comedy
INTENDED AUDIENCE: Adults
RUNNING TIME: 94 minutes
STARRING: Vanessa   Redgrave,
Edward Fox, Uma Thurman, and
Alesandro Gassman
   DIRECTOR: John Irvin
   PRODUCER: Robert Fox
   WRITER: Trevor Bentham
   BASED ON: The novel by H. E. Bates
   DISTRIBUTOR: Miramax Films
   BRIEF SUMMARY:
   A Month by the Lake provided a refresh-
ing vacation for moviegoers beaten down
by the offerings of the summer of 1995.

Set at a hotel on the shores of Lake Como, Italy, just prior to World War II, the movie tells the story of two aging English sojourners who finally find love. Miss Bentley squandered her youth on an affair that trapped her for fourteen years. Through it all, she developed common sense and a sense of humor. Thus, she is both amused by and attracted to Major Wilshire and tries to strike up a friendship with him, but he is attracted to a young English governess, Miss Beaumont. Into this morally upright triangle comes a handsome young Italian heir who is smitten by the elegant Miss Bentley. This young man's interest in Miss Bentley, as well as the rejection by Miss Beaumont, opens the Major's eyes to the wit and charms of Miss Bentley. In the end, they fall into each other's arms while Italian minstrels serenade them. Miss Bentley's voiceover tells us that they married, forever grateful to Miss Beaumont for bringing them together.

The direction and cinematography bring the 1930s to life. Other nuances help us to understand the heartbeat of these characters. This film will make you laugh and appreciate life. There are a few exclamations, but otherwise the film is a moral tale that subtly condemns promiscuity and deception and promotes marriage.

CONTENT ANALYSIS: (B, LL, V, S, A, D) Moral worldview that subtly condemns promiscuity and deception and promotes marriage; five mild obscenities and six exclamatory profanities; a Fascist mob chases the heroine; discussion of adultery, attempted kiss and hugging; alcohol use; and smoking.

True Worth

MR. HOLLAND'S OPUS

Quality: ☆☆☆☆   Acceptability: +2

WARNING CODES:
  Language: *
  Violence: None

  Sex: None
  Nudity: None
RATING: PG
GENRE: Drama
INTENDED AUDIENCE: All ages
RUNNING TIME: 130 minutes
STARRING: Richard Dreyfuss and Glenne Headly
DIRECTOR: Stephen Herek
EXECUTIVE PRODUCERS: Scott Kroopf and Patrick Sheane Duncan
WRITER: Patrick Sheane Duncan
DISTRIBUTOR: Buena Vista Pictures/Walt Disney Company/ Hollywood Pictures
BRIEF SUMMARY:
Mr. Holland's Opus is a poignant movie that will remind us that our lives are important and can positively affect many people. In 1965, Mr. Holland is a young composer looking for fame and fortune, who takes a job as a high school music teacher. He is awkward and scared, but students take a liking to him. His first challenge is convincing a girl that she can play the clarinet. Meanwhile, his wife announces her pregnancy. They name their son Cole, after Cole Porter, but soon discover he is nearly 100 percent deaf. Mr. Holland faces other challenges, including balancing career with family. The film climaxes as Mr. Holland gets cut out of the school budget. He fights a losing battle with the school board, yet is rewarded when an auditorium full of his students—both past and present—throw a celebration in his honor.

Anyone with a heart will be moved by the unfolding story of Mr. Holland. It elevates the value of human lives, perseverance, love of family, self-sacrifice, and marital fidelity. It shows us how one person can impact the lives of many. In today's cynical times, this film may be panned off as saccharine, but love and kindness never go out of style, and this film has fashioned these elements into a powerful story.

CONTENT ANALYSIS: (B, L, A, D, M) Moral worldview extolling love of family, marital fidelity, and self-sacrifice; four mild obscenities and three profanities; alcohol use; smoking; a student attempts to seduce teacher; and brief image of two male students holding hands.

Inhumane Treatment

MURDER IN THE FIRST

Quality: ☆☆☆☆   Acceptability: –2

WARNING CODES:

Language: ***
Violence: **
Sex: **
Nudity: **

RATING: R
GENRE: Drama
INTENDED AUDIENCE: Adults
RUNNING TIME: 120 minutes
STARRING: Kevin Bacon, Christian Slater, Gary Oldman, Embeth Davidtz, Bill Macy, Brad Douriff, and Ben Stack
DIRECTOR: Marc Rocco
PRODUCERS: Marc Frydman and Mark Wolper
WRITER: Dan Gordon
DISTRIBUTOR: Warner Brothers
BRIEF SUMMARY:
Based on historical events, *Murder in the First* is an extraordinary but intense courtroom drama centering on the inhumane treatment of prisoners behind the imposing walls of Alcatraz a half century ago. Kevin Bacon delivers an Oscar-caliber performance as a prisoner on trial for killing another inmate, and Christian Slater stars as the young public defender who ultimately puts the entire prison on trial. Initially imprisoned as a teenager for the theft of a five-dollar bill, prolonged and cruel mistreatment turns Henri into a broken man, virtually out of his mind. His rookie public defender feels compassion and determines to put an end to the prison atrocities.

Director Marc Rocco utilizes a highly visual storytelling style to complement an intelligent script. However, the most startling aspect of *Murder in the First* is Kevin Bacon's remarkable performance. In his use of both physical and vocal mannerisms to convey the utter desolation of a young man pushed beyond the limits of his endurance of suffering, he is extraordinary. Some initial depictions of prison brutality and an attempted sexual encounter mar this expertly directed movie about the importance of seeking truth and serving "the least of these" behind prison walls.

CONTENT ANALYSIS: (B, LLL, VV, SS, NN) Moral worldview portraying dedicated efforts to end inhumane treatment of prisoners at Alcatraz; twenty-three obscenities and ten profanities; intense (though limited) portrayal of prison brutality—prolonged solitary confinement, beatings, cutting prisoner with a razor (off camera), and man stabbed to death; brief depiction of attempted fornication and implied oral sex; and brief rear male nudity.

Not History

NIXON

Quality: ☆☆☆   Acceptability: –2

WARNING CODES:

Language: ***
Violence: **
Sex: *
Nudity: None

RATING: R
GENRE: Drama
INTENDED AUDIENCE: Adults
RUNNING TIME: 190 minutes
STARRING: Anthony Hopkins, Joan Allen, Powers Boothe, Ed Harris, and Bob Hoskins
DIRECTOR: Oliver Stone
PRODUCERS: Clayton Townsend, Oliver Stone, and Andrew G. Vajna

WRITERS: Stephen J. Ribele, Christopher Wilkinson, and Oliver Stone

DISTRIBUTOR: Buena Vista Pictures/Walt Disney Company/ Hollywood Pictures

BRIEF SUMMARY:

The Oliver Stone film *Nixon* is a masterful, if flawed, work about a very complex man. The movie starts with a disclaimer stating that this is not history. It then quotes the Bible verse Matthew 16:26, "For what is a man profited if he gains the whole world, and loses his own soul?" We discover Nixon's childhood in Whittier, California, and how he got to attend law school. The movie also shows Nixon's relationship with his wife, Pat, as he suffers political defeat and victory. The final hour of the movie details Nixon's victorious summit meetings with Mao Tse Tung and Leonid Brezhnev, and then quickly goes into the intricacies of the Watergate scandal. Throughout it all, Nixon broods and passes blame. In a moving final moment, alone with Kissinger in defeat, Nixon asks that they pray together. Nixon prays, "Please forgive me . . ." and finishes in tears.

Lead characters Anthony Hopkins and Joan Allen captivate. The movie depicts Nixon to be profane and obscene behind closed doors. He is depicted as a solipsist, taking responsibility for his victories but in some ways denying any involvement in his defeat. The movie is Mr. Stone's least controversial and most spiritual, although it is still flawed, excessive, and self-serving.

CONTENT ANALYSIS: (B, C, LLL, VV, S, A, D, M) Morality tale about one man's drive for success with moral elements such as marital commitment, prayer, and paying for one's sins; eighty-five obscenities, forty-three profanities, and ten vulgarities; moderate violence that comes exclusively from live war and news footage including shooting, explosions, shots of corpses; woman tries to seduce Nixon; alcohol use and abuse; smoking; and lying, gambling, and extortion.

Fooling with Nature

OUTBREAK

Quality: ☆☆☆   Acceptability: −1

WARNING CODES:
  Language: *
  Violence: **
  Sex: None
  Nudity: None

RATING: R
GENRE: Drama
INTENDED AUDIENCE: Adults
RUNNING TIME: 123 minutes
STARRING: Dustin Hoffman, Rene Russo, Morgan Freeman, Cuba Gooding, Patrick Dempsey, Kevin Spacey, and Donald Sutherland
DIRECTOR: Wolfgang Petersen
EXECUTIVE PRODUCERS: Duncan Henderson and Anne Kopelson
PRODUCERS: Arnold Kopelson, Wolfgang Petersen, and Gail Katz
WRITERS: Laurence Dworet and Robert Roy Pool
DISTRIBUTOR: Warner Brothers
BRIEF SUMMARY:

Built around the fast-paced search for an anti-serum for a new killer virus, *Outbreak* is a reasonably believable and well-made suspense drama starring Dustin Hoffman, Rene Russo, and Donald Sutherland. The movie opens with the urgent message "Please send help!" sent from a small village doubling as a mercenary camp located near the Motaba River in 1967 war-torn Zaire. While help is promised, the approaching aircraft actually contains a massively destructive incendiary device ("Operation Clean Sweep") intended to kill everyone in the camp. It succeeds . . . almost! Not killed is the deadly Motaba virus. Twenty-five years later, Dustin Hoffman as Colonel Sam Daniels, a doctor from the Army's Medical Research Institute for Infectious Diseases, must now return to the Motaba River area. Another outbreak has occurred, and it has spread to the United States.

Fast-paced and continuously interesting, *Outbreak* is well constructed and entertaining. However, the plot grows a bit thin toward the conclusion as Hoffman, in Superman fashion, leaps into action and saves nearly the entire world. Director Petersen has admitted off-camera: "I'd like for people to think, 'maybe we shouldn't be fooling with nature too much.'" However, the film does make the important point that no man, including a renegade general, is above the law.

CONTENT ANALYSIS: (B, E, L, VV, B) Moral point of view that individual government officials are not above the law; environmentalist viewpoint that man should not tamper with the earth; three obscenities, two profanities, and four vulgarities; action violence, many people die from deadly and gory disease that causes bodies to decompose; betrayal of people by U.S. government officials, and mass murder to cover up; and appeals for God's help at the end of the movie.

Love Conquers All

THE PEBBLE AND THE PENGUIN

Quality: ☆☆☆   Acceptability: +1

WARNING CODES:

Language: None
Violence: *
Sex: None
Nudity: None

RATING: G
GENRE: Animated musical adventure
INTENDED AUDIENCE: Children
RUNNING TIME: 74 minutes
VOICES: Martin Short, Jim Belushi, Tim Curry, and Annie Golden

EXECUTIVE PRODUCER: James Butterworth
PRODUCER: Russell Boland
WRITERS: Rachel Koretsky and Steve Whitestone
SCORE BY: Mark Watters
DISTRIBUTOR: Metro Goldwyn-Mayer
BRIEF SUMMARY:

Featuring original songs by Barry Manilow and Bruce Sussman and the voices of Martin Short, Jim Belushi, and Tim Curry, the animated musical adventure movie *The Pebble and the Penguin* is a lighthearted cartoon for all ages to enjoy. The movie begins on the shores of Antarctica, where male penguins must "propose" to the female penguins by presenting them with an acceptable pebble before the full moon. While Hubie has always dreamed of giving Marina a pebble, he is very shy. His friends tease him and tell him there is no way he could ever win her, especially since Drake the villain wants her too. Even though he feels hopeless, he searches for the rarest and most beautiful pebble for Marina. However, Drake finds out and sends Hubie floating away unconscious on an iceberg. It is only with the help of a new friend that Hubie makes his way back and fights for his true love.

Stressing the qualities of honor, friendship, and love, *The Pebble and the Penguin* illustrates that true love conquers all. Targeting young children with its bright animation and lively music, *The Pebble and the Penguin* is a delightful treat for any age. Regrettably, the movie also includes some minor magical thinking that must be brought to the attention of children with the instruction that faith in God—not wishing for the impossible—is the answer.

CONTENT ANALYSIS: (B, Ro, Pa, V, M) Moral worldview with romantic elements—penguin has faith that he can overcome anything in his way to win his one true love; also some magical thinking that enables a penguin to fly; brief action violence—penguins fighting and being chased by killer whales; and evil penguin seeks revenge and uses unscrupulous means to get what he wants.

True Love Overcomes Prejudice

PERSUASION

Quality: ☆☆☆☆   Acceptability: +2

WARNING CODES:
Language: *
Violence: *
Sex: None
Nudity: None
RATING: PG
GENRE: Drama
INTENDED AUDIENCE: Adults
RUNNING TIME: 103 minutes
STARRING: Amanda Root, Ciaran Hinds, Susan Fleetwood, John Woodvine, and Corin Redgrave
DIRECTOR: Roger Michell
PRODUCER: Fiona Finlay
WRITER: Nick Dear
BASED ON: The novel by Jane Austen
DISTRIBUTOR: Sony Picture Classics
BRIEF SUMMARY:
If you liked *A Room with a View*, you will enjoy *Persuasion*, a film adaptation of Jane Austen's novel. Based on poor advice, Anne Elliot throws away an opportunity to marry at the age of nineteen. Years later, her family is living in debt. They move to Bath and lease their home to Admiral Croft and his wife, the sister of Frederick Wentworth, Anne's lost love. Anne and her sister, Mary, stay behind to welcome their new tenants. To her surprise, Frederick makes an appearance. A group of family, friends, and officers decides to take a small holiday to the seaside. There, Sir William Elliot pledges his love to Anne. To sort out this new advance, Anne goes to Bath to see her family, where she abandons hopes of marriage to William or Frederick. Frederick, however, reveals his undying love for Anne in a letter. Thrilled, she goes to him, and they plan to marry, upsetting family and society expectations.

Beautifully acted and wonderfully told, the characters hold a certain realism and warmth that could easily have been stereotyped or overplayed. The dry but serviceable photography and art direction seem to suite Anne's forlornness perfectly. Dramatically, the film sustains suspense throughout. *Persuasion* demonstrates a moral rectitude, in its treatment of family, Christianity, and marriage, that is uncommon in modern cinema.

CONTENT ANALYSIS: (B, CC, L, V, A, D, M) Moral worldview extolling love, marriage, and Christian faith; two obscenities; woman has a near-fatal fall; alcohol use; smoking; and gossiping.

Worst New Age Propaganda

POCAHONTAS

Quality: ☆☆☆   Acceptability: –1

WARNING CODES:
Language: None
Violence: *
Sex: None
Nudity: None
RATING: G
GENRE: Animated fantasy
INTENDED AUDIENCE: All ages
RUNNING TIME: 80 minutes
VOICES: Irene Bedard, Mel Gibson, David Ogden Stiers, and Russell Means
DIRECTORS: Mike Gabriel and Eric Goldberg
PRODUCER: James Pentecost
WRITERS: Carl Binder, Susannah Grant, and Philip LaZebnik
DISTRIBUTOR: Walt Disney Pictures/Buena Vista
BRIEF SUMMARY:
In *Pocahontas*, John Smith and a group of English explorers set sail for America

in search of gold. Back in America, Chief Powhatan and his noble warriors celebrate a victory. One warrior claims his love for the chief's daughter, Pocahontas, and claims he wants to marry her. The chief tells his daughter, but she refuses the proposal. Instead, she goes to counsel with a talking willow tree. The tree tells her the man she will marry will carry a "spinning arrow," or compass. John Smith and Pocahontas meet, and she discovers he has the compass. They kiss, but her father sees them and attacks John Smith. Another Englishman sees the attack and kills the chief. When the tribe captures John Smith and prepares to behead him, the English crew arrives for battle. In what could have been a fatal showdown, Pocahontas interrupts and calls for peace, saving the lives of many people.

Pocahontas demonstrates that peace through negotiation is preferable to battle. The character of Pocahontas demonstrates some feminism and dishes out a little environmentalism and spiritism. The film doesn't cave into a bad-white-man/good-Indian political correctness but shows both sharing the blame equally. This film doesn't have sweeping themes and archetypal characters but does make some moral points. However, in the end many will complain that *Pocahontas* is too New Age.

CONTENT ANALYSIS: (E, FR, RH, Pa, PC, RH, V, M) A pantheistic, environmentalist worldview that mixes New Age thinking and Native American animistic religious beliefs. This is a revisionist historical tale that takes visible pains to be as politically correct and inoffensive as possible; action violence involving gunslinging and fistfighting; and romantic kissing.

Common Genius

THE POSTMAN (IL POSTINO)

Quality: ☆☆☆   Acceptability: −1

WARNING CODES:
  Language: *
  Violence: None
  Sex: *
  Nudity: **
RATING: PG
GENRE: Romantic drama
INTENDED AUDIENCE: Adults
RUNNING TIME: 105 minutes
LANGUAGE: Italian
STARRING: Massimo Troisi, Philippe Noiret, and Maria Grazia Cucinotta
DIRECTOR: Michael Radford
EXECUTIVE PRODUCER: Albert Passone
PRODUCERS: Mario and Vittorio Cecchi Gori, and Gaetano Daniele
WRITERS: Anna Pavignano, Michael Radford, Furio Scarpelli, Giacomo Scarpelli, and Massimo Troisi
BASED ON: The novel *Burning Patience* by Antonio Skarmeta
DISTRIBUTORS: Miramax Films
BRIEF SUMMARY:
The Postman presents a charming and simple story involving a shy postman named Mario Rouppolo who forges an unlikely friendship with a writer in exile, Pablo Neruda, and learns from him how to write love poetry. We discover that Mario wants to learn how to impress women, or at least one woman, so Pablo takes Mario down to the sea to inspire him. There, Pablo instructs Mario on the use of metaphors. Emboldened, Mario goes to a local business to speak with the object of his attention, beautiful Beatrice Russo. Mario sends Beatrice some verbatim poetry from the book, and Pablo rebukes him, saying, "Poetry doesn't belong to those who write it, but to those who need it." Touched by these words, Pablo assents to helping Mario, Beatrice eventually agrees to marry Mario, and Pablo returns to his native Chile.

The Postman treats tastefully and with restraint the subject of wooing women through romantic language.

(This provides a stark contrast to the much-too-blatant *Don Juan De Marco*.) All acting performances demonstrate genuine respect for the characters. The plot and storyline, though simple, provide a genuine slice of life found on this island nation. The photography, though basic, adequately complements the action. Containing little bad language and mild sexual suggestions, this Italian film presents a refreshing and relatively clean look at chivalry.

CONTENT ANALYSIS: (R, L, S, NN, A, H, M) Romantic worldview extolling marriage as its goal; three profanities (one exclamatory) and three vulgarities; mild sexual activity involving kissing and rolling a ball up the front of a woman; brief female cleavage and back nudity; pro-Communist character; and alcohol use and smoking.

Redemption and Hope

RESTORATION

Quality: ☆☆☆☆   Acceptability: –2

WARNING CODES:

Language: *
Violence: *
Sex: ***
Nudity: **

RATING: R
GENRE: Drama
INTENDED AUDIENCE: Adults
RUNNING TIME: 118 minutes
STARRING: Robert Downey Jr., Sam Neill, David Thewlis, Polly Walker, and Meg Ryan
DIRECTOR: Michael Hoffman
EXECUTIVE PRODUCER: Kip Hagopian
PRODUCERS: Cary Brokaw, Andy Paterson, and Sarah Ryan Black
WRITER: Rupert Walters
BASED ON: The novel by Rose Tremain
DISTRIBUTOR: Miramax

BRIEF SUMMARY:
In *Restoration*, seventeenth-century English history is brilliantly recounted. King Charles II, when not cavorting with his mistress Celia, worries about his ailing spaniel. The king invites doctor Robert Merivel to examine the pup. The good doctor soon finds favor with the king, and the king grants him an estate, knighthood, and a wife, Celia, on the condition that he not fall in love with her (after all, she is the king's mistress). When Merivel falls in love with Celia, he is stripped of his estate and turned out into the world. His only recourse is to find his old friend, Pearce, who is working in a Quaker insane asylum. Here, Merivel is exposed to spiritual meaning and rediscovers his profession. Dedicating himself to healing plague victims, he is eventually called to the palace where the king's mistress is ill. Dr. Merivel goes in disguise but is later recognized, and the king restores his home, wealth, and respect.

Restoration is a visually beautiful, historically correct, and meaningful movie with profound moral lessons presented in a subtle and non-preachy way. It shows some explicit sexual activity, but it offers a strong message of redemption and hope. It illustrates that being responsible for one's actions, while sometimes difficult, is the most fulfilling path we can take.

CONTENT ANALYSIS: (B, C, L, V, SSS, NN, A, M) Moral worldview demonstrating that decadence is not an acceptable way of life and with several prominent references to Jesus Christ and the gospel; two vulgarities; brief fire scene and images of the dead and dying; seduction and two brief but graphic sex scenes; upper female and rear nudity; alcohol use; and decadence, seduction, and redemptive themes.

Scottish Folktale

ROB ROY

Quality: ☆☆☆☆   Acceptability: –2

WARNING CODES:

Language: **

Violence: ***
Sex: **
Nudity: **
RATING: R
GENRE: Action/Adventure
INTENDED AUDIENCE: Older
teens and adults
RUNNING TIME: 135 minutes
STARRING: Liam Neeson, Jessica
Lange, John Hurt, Tim Roth, Eric Stoltz,
Brian Cox, and Andrew Keir
DIRECTOR: Michael Caton-Jones
EXECUTIVE PRODUCER: Michael
Caton-Jones
PRODUCERS: Peter Broughan and
Richard Jackson
WRITER: Alan Sharp
DISTRIBUTOR: United Artists
Pictures
BRIEF SUMMARY:
Rob Roy is a beautiful, epic, Scottish
folktale of love and honor, seriously
marred by a violent dark side that is por-
trayed all too vividly in the movie. The
story is set in the picturesque Scottish
highlands, where Robert Roy McGregor
supports his family by raising cattle. He
plans to enlarge his holdings by buying
more cattle with money borrowed from
the Marquis of Monrose. The plot thickens when a friend, entrusted to bring the
money to Rob Roy, is brutally stabbed
and the money stolen by Archibald
Cunningham, an associate of Monrose. To
stay out of prison, Rob can bear false witness against the Duke of Argyll, as pro-
posed by Monrose, but Rob refuses to
violate his honor. As a result, he is hunted
by the evil Cunningham, who torches
Rob's house and violates his wife. Rob
escapes only to finally meet Cunningham
in a contest for repayment and retribution.
Robert Roy McGregor takes pride in
keeping his word and honor. This is a
lesson that holds great promise, but gives
only a glimmer of light in the movie, as it
is weakened by violence and immorality.
Regrettably, the darkness in the movie

will prevent children and many adults
from enriching their knowledge about
the meaning of a personal word of honor.
Even so, the Scottish highland location
provides a breathtaking backdrop for the
excellent cinematography, acting, and
direction.
CONTENT ANALYSIS: (Ro, LL, VVV,
SS, NN, A, M) Romantic worldview;
eighteen vulgarities, and sexually suggestive language; numerous, graphic
sword stabbings, hanging suicide, large
gash sliced in man's body, drowning,
numerous shootings and brutality, stran-
gling, on-screen rape, and livestock gut-
ted; implied intercourse with prostitutes
and attempted molestation of prostitute;
nude male bathing; alcohol drinking in
bar; and references to abortion.

Cinderella Tale

SABRINA

Quality: ☆☆☆   Acceptability: −1

WARNING CODES:
Language: *
Violence: *
Sex: *
Nudity: None
RATING: PG
GENRE: Romantic comedy
INTENDED AUDIENCE: Teens and
adults
RUNNING TIME: 125 minutes
STARRING: Harrison Ford, Julia
Ormond, and Greg Kinnear
DIRECTOR: Sydney Pollack
PRODUCERS: Scott Rudin and
Sydney Pollack
WRITERS: Barbara Benedek and
David Rayfiel
BASED ON: The 1954 film written
by Billy Wilder, Samuel Taylor, and
Ernest Lehman
DISTRIBUTOR: Paramount Pictures
BRIEF SUMMARY:
Sabrina Fairchild is a pretty but plain
chauffeur's daughter, living on the

wealthy Larrabee family estate. The Larrabee family includes corporate workaholic Linus and debonair David, who plays tennis instead of going to the office. Sabrina is infatuated with David and in awe of Linus. When she returns after a year in Paris, she is sleek, poised, and stunning. Although David is engaged to the daughter of a wealthy tycoon whose business the Larrabees covet, he turns his attentions to the new Sabrina. Linus steps in to save David's pending marriage and the merger, but in the process Linus manipulates Sabrina into falling for him instead and succeeds all too well.

This modern Cinderella fairy tale is a remake of the 1954 classic. The witty screenplay energized with contemporary observations injects new charm into this old-fashioned and whimsical story. The characters are colorful and likable. This is a delightful and moral film in many ways, and promiscuity is merely implied. Some exclamatory profanities; materialistic greed and romantic love serve as major themes, though all is resolved morally in the end. On the whole, *Sabrina* provides a breath of fresh air to the torrid tumble of today's film offerings.

CONTENT ANALYSIS: (B, C, Ro, H, L, V, S, M) Moral worldview emphasizing family love, self-sacrifice, and repentance with humanist and romantic elements as well as romantic love as the focus; seven exclamatory profanities, one vulgarity, and one off-color joke; two scenes of man being punched; implied promiscuity and kissing scene in bed; and miscellaneous themes of manipulation and materialistic greed.

Deconstructing Literature and Faith

THE SCARLET LETTER

Quality: ☆   Acceptability: −4

WARNING CODES:
Language: **

Violence: ***
Sex: ***
Nudity: ***
RATING: R
GENRE: Romantic drama
INTENDED AUDIENCE: Adults
RUNNING TIME: 130 minutes
STARRING: Demi Moore, Gary Oldman, and Robert Duvall
DIRECTOR: Roland Joffe
PRODUCER: Roland Joffe
WRITER: Douglas Day Stewart
FREELY ADAPTED FROM THE NOVEL BY: Nathaniel Hawthorne
DISTRIBUTOR: Buena Vista Pictures/Walt Disney Company/Hollywood Pictures
BRIEF SUMMARY:
The Scarlet Letter is nothing like Nathaniel Hawthorne's great novel. In the movie, Demi Moore plays a plain Hester Prynne sent ahead to America by her husband to establish a home. When she starts acting like a man by buying indentured servants and real estate, the people of Boston start talking. Soon she starts flirting with Mr. Dimmesdale, the town preacher. When news arrives that Hester's husband died in an Indian attack, the reverend ravishes Hester in her barn. When her pregnancy shows, she is locked away. After the birth of her daughter, Hester must wear a scarlet letter on her breast. Hester's husband arrives—the rumor having been false—and vows to kill the offending man. When he kills a man posing as an Indian, the town decides to kill Hester, the minister, a group of witches, and some friendly Indians. At the last moment, the Indians come to their rescue.

The Scarlet Letter stars the popular Demi Moore and promises fine talent in a literary, tasteful movie. Audiences will soon discover, however, that this movie is neither literary, tasteful, moral, nor entertaining. It is boring, immoral, gratuitous in sex and nudity, and a mockery of Nathaniel Hawthorne's masterpiece. This is a poorly produced, politically correct film promoting adultery and mocking Christianity.

CONTENT ANALYSIS: (Ro, Ab, FR, RH, LL, VVV, SSS, NNN, D, M) Romantic worldview extolling adulterous affairs over biblical morality with anti-biblical portrayals of clergy and elders; revisionist historical account of early Boston and American Indian religious practices; eleven obscenities, four profanities, and extensive blasphemous remarks; extreme violence including brutal battle scene with spurting blood, attempted rape, rape, candle burned into man's eye, cutting hands against pillory pole, vivid scalping, and torture of slave girl; depicted adulterous fornication and adulterous kisses; extensive nudity including full male and full female nudity and upper female nudity; positive and negative references to witchcraft; smoking; and lying, deceit, and withholding evidence.

Christian Virtues Commended

SENSE AND SENSIBILITY

Quality: ☆☆☆☆   Acceptability: +4

WARNING CODES:
  Language: None
  Violence: None
  Sex: None
  Nudity: None
RATING: PG
GENRE: Drama
INTENDED AUDIENCE: All ages
RUNNING TIME: 135 minutes
STARRING: Emma Thompson, Alan Rickman, Kate Winslet, and Hugh Grant
DIRECTOR: Ang Lee
EXECUTIVE PRODUCER: Sydney Pollack
PRODUCER: Lindsay Doran
WRITER: Emma Thompson
BASED ON: The novel by Jane Austen
DISTRIBUTOR: Columbia Pictures

BRIEF SUMMARY:
After two hundred years, Jane Austen has become one of the popular screenwriters in Hollywood. *Sense and Sensibility*, the latest screen adaptation of her work, opens with a deathbed request: Mr. Dashwood asks his son, John, to provide for his second family who, according to the laws at that time, could not inherit his money. John, however, is beaten down and convinced otherwise by his avaricious wife, Fanny. He finally decides to give his stepmother and her three daughters—Eleanor, Marianne, and Margaret—merely a small yearly stipend. However, Mrs. Dashwood's relative Lord Middleton comes to her aid and invites her daughters to live in a cottage on his estate. Lord Middleton and his mother-in-law, Mrs. Jennings, take a strong interest in marrying off the girls. Complications in love arise, but eventually all ends well as prudence, honor, and duty triumph over sensibility.

With no more violence than a twisted ankle, no more nudity than an exposed foot, and no more sex than the snipping of a lock of hair, *Sense and Sensibility* communicates the depth of human emotions and the reasons why virtue triumphs over moral degradation. On the surface, this is a pleasant comedy of manners, but the character studies run deep into the heart of the laws of the universe and the divine Providence that governs the affairs of men.

CONTENT ANALYSIS: (CC, B) Moral Christian worldview that emphasizes prudence, honor, and duty as well as forgiveness, love, and grace; and positive view of the church and the ministry as being a worthy profession.

Heroic Virtues

TALL TALE

Quality: ☆☆☆☆   Acceptability: +2

WARNING CODES:
  Language: *
  Violence: *
  Sex: None
  Nudity: None

RATING: PG
GENRE: Western/Fantasy
INTENDED AUDIENCE: Families
RUNNING TIME: 100 minutes
STARRING: Nick Stahl, Patrick Swayze, Scott Glenn, Oliver Platt, Catherine O'Hara, Stephen Lang, and Roger Aaron Brown
  DIRECTOR: Jeremiah Chechik
  EXECUTIVE PRODUCER: Bill Badalato
PRODUCERS: Joe Roth and Roger Birnbaum
WRITERS: Steven L. Bloom and Roger Rodat
DISTRIBUTOR: Buena Vista Pictures/Walt Disney Company
BRIEF SUMMARY:
Tall Tale, Disney's clever fantasy set at the turn of the century, recounts the heroics of a boy so determined to save his family farm and the frontier way of life that he conjures up three Old West legends to come to his aid. When a land dispute leaves his father wounded and lingering between life and death, Daniel Hackett retreats to the security of his fishing boat, where he falls into a fast sleep and a startlingly realistic dream. Transported to a Texas desert, Daniel meets Old West legend Pecos Bill, who pledges his aid and recruits fellow legends Paul Bunyan and John Henry to help as well. The four head north, but before they can get there, Daniel suffers confusion and desperation and rejects the help of his legend friends. In an instant, everything disappears, and Daniel is transported to Paradise—now nothing more than a strip mine. Horrified, Daniel abruptly awakens from sleep, still in his boat tied to the dock. However, armed with all he has learned from Pecos Bill, Paul Bunyan, and John Henry, Daniel

takes a stand. When he does, something marvelous happens.

Tall Tale is a Western with lots of action, some melodrama, and almost no objectionable material. Affirming absolutes, redemption, love, and friendship, the movie is an emotive and thoughtful delight that will entertain both children and adults.

CONTENT ANALYSIS: (B, R, Pa, L, V, A, M) Moral worldview with an emphasis on biblical virtues, slightly skewed by the romantic notion that civilization and technology are corrupting forces and the inexplicable appearance of legendary people, although it is implied that they are real not magical; one mild obscenity; action violence, fistfighting, and gunplay resulting in the lost trigger fingers of several bad guys (only in self-defense); alcohol consumption in saloon; and evil plot to obtain a piece of land by any means necessary.

The Most Entertaining Moral Breakthrough in Filmmaking

TOY STORY

Quality: ☆☆☆☆   Acceptability: +3

WARNING CODES:
  Language: *
  Violence: *
  Sex: None
  Nudity: None

RATING: G
GENRE: Animated
INTENDED AUDIENCE: All ages
RUNNING TIME: 85 minutes
VOICES: Tom Hanks, Tim Allen, and Don Rickles
  DIRECTOR: John Lasseter
PRODUCER: Bonnie Arnold and Ralph Guggenheim
WRITERS: Joss Wheldon, Andrew Stanton, Joel Cohen, and Alex Sokolow
DISTRIBUTOR: Walt Disney Pictures/Buena Vista
BRIEF SUMMARY:
Toy Story is the first totally computer-animated movie. It answers the question

"What happens to my toys when I leave the room?" in a wonderful, moral, fantastic way that will capture the hearts of children of all ages. Woody is a cowboy doll, voiced by Tom Hanks, the hero in the world of Andy's toys—that is, until Andy gets Buzz Lightyear, space ranger, voiced by Tim Allen. Woody comes down with a strong case of envy, and creates a situation that causes Buzz to fall out the window. When he can't find Buzz, Andy grabs Woody to take to Planet Pizza. As Mom drives off, Buzz climbs onto the back of the car. At a gas station, Buzz and Woody are fighting so seriously that the car drives off without them. Thus, they have to start working together to get back home. On the way, however, they are commandeered by Sid, a destructive neighborhood boy who pulls the heads off dolls and blows up toys. The final chase is a masterpiece.

The movie is overflowing with heroism, virtues, and moral messages, not the least of which is that while envy can only destroy, friendship can overcome. The double entendres in the film will make it just as appealing to teenagers and adults as it is to younger children. *Toy Story* has a heart of gold. It is funny, clean, wholesome, and virtuous. It is a classic beginning to a new genre—a masterpiece that is sure to capture the imaginations of young and old alike.

CONTENT ANALYSIS: (C, L, V, M) Christian worldview where friendship and forgiveness triumph over envy and adversity; one obscure scatological reference and some sarcastic innuendos; and action violence such as blowing up toys, a dog chewing toys, and scary toys that prove to be nice guys in the end.

Faith and Forgiveness

TWO BITS

Quality: ☆☆☆☆   Acceptability: +1

WARNING CODES:
  Language: **
  Violence: **
  Sex: *
  Nudity: *
RATING: PG
GENRE: Drama
INTENDED AUDIENCE: All ages
RUNNING TIME: 93 minutes
STARRING: Mary Elizabeth Mastrantonio, Al Pacino, and Jerry Barone
  DIRECTOR: James Foley
  EXECUTIVE PRODUCERS: Joseph Stefano, Willi Baer, and David Korda
  WRITER: Joseph Stefano
  DISTRIBUTOR: Miramax Films
  BRIEF SUMMARY:
Two Bits is a charming, warm movie that highlights the relationship between an Italian grandfather and his grandson in the 1930s. Grandpa, played by Al Pacino, announces to his twelve-year-old grandson, Gennaro, that he is going to die today. Grandpa promises Gennaro that he can have a quarter when he dies because Gennaro desires to attend the new movie theater that costs twenty-five cents. Not wanting his grandfather to die, Gennaro decides to earn the money himself. He sings, works in a grocery store, and sweeps out cellars, but only makes fifteen cents. In a moving scene, Grandpa has Gennaro go to a woman he hurt long ago and ask her for forgiveness. Regrettably, by the time he earns enough money and reaches the theater, the price has gone up to fifty cents. Crestfallen, he returns home and discovers Grandfather near death. Grandfather says to Gennaro, in a whisper, to never stop wanting. Then he dies. Gennaro gets his quarter and, as he enters the theater, he hears his grandfather's voice giving him one last word of advice.

This movie is exceptional in every way. Containing some obscenities and somewhat of a works theology, it is primarily a character study emphasizing family ties, church attendance, forgiveness, and never giving up on one's dreams.

CONTENT ANALYSIS: (B, C, LL, VV, S, N) Moral worldview where churchgoing, family, and religious faith are esteemed; eleven obscenities and one profanity; fistfighting, a death, and woman hangs herself; woman attempts to seduce boy; upper male nudity; and churchgoing, sins rebuked, forgiveness themes.

Fears, Loves, Hopes, and Concerns

WAITING TO EXHALE

Quality: ☆☆☆   Acceptability:−2

WARNING CODES:
  Language: ***
  Violence: None
  Sex: ***
  Nudity: *
RATING: R
GENRE: Drama
INTENDED AUDIENCE: Adults
RUNNING TIME: 127 minutes
STARRING: Whitney Houston, Angela Bassett, Loretta Devine, Lela Rochon, and Gregory Hines
DIRECTOR: Forest Whitaker
EXECUTIVE PRODUCERS: Terry McMillan and Ronald Bass
PRODUCERS: Ezra Swerdlow and Deborah Schindler
WRITERS: Terry McMillan and Ronald Bass
BASED ON: The novel by Terry McMillan
DISTRIBUTOR: 20th Century Fox
BRIEF SUMMARY:
Waiting to Exhale is the much-anticipated film adaptation of the best-selling book by author Terry McMillan. The movie begins by showcasing Savannah, played by Whitney Houston, on New Year's Eve. She has recently moved from Denver to Phoenix to be reunited with her three friends, Bernadine, Robin, and

Gloria. As the story progresses, we begin to discover the troubles they have with men. Savannah has been asking God for years to send her a decent man. She has gotten two-timing Lionel, and a married man named Kenneth. Bernadine suffers as she discovers her husband left her for a white woman. Robin is an attractive woman who always lands men that lie and cheat. Gloria's husband leaves her, but she begins to befriend the man next door. Through the course of exactly one year, these women overcome these challenges and reveal to us their fears, loves, hopes, and concerns.

Although a "chick flick" and at times unsympathetic to men, this movie displays a remarkable amount of talent, charm, and warmth. The primary goal of these women is serving their own desires in gaining a man. The major theme of this movie is that disappointment and strife can come when we don't allow Jesus to be our sufficiency. Furthermore, there are obscenities and stark depictions of sex.

CONTENT ANALYSIS: (Ro, C, LLL, SSS, N, A, D, M) Romantic worldview with positive references to God, Jesus, prayer, and church attendance; fifty-nine obscenities and three profanities; condom use, flirting, adultery, and extensive sexual situations including implied oral sex, four depictions of sex, and two instances of implied sex; upper male nudity and woman in lingerie; alcohol use; smoking; and woman steals clothes and sets them on fire.

Lackluster Environmentalist Satire

WATERWORLD

Quality: ☆☆☆   Acceptability: −2

WARNING CODES:
  Language: **
  Violence: **
  Sex: **
  Nudity: **
RATING: PG-13

GENRE: Science fiction

INTENDED AUDIENCE: Older teens and adults

RUNNING TIME: 120 minutes

STARRING: Kevin Costner, Jeanne Tripplehorn, Dennis Hopper, Tina Majorino, and Michael Jeter

DIRECTOR: Kevin Reynolds

PRODUCERS: Charles Gordon, John Davis, and Kevin Costner

WRITERS: Peter Rader and David Twohy

DISTRIBUTOR: Universal Pictures

BRIEF SUMMARY:

Waterworld is set on a post-apocalyptic earth, where the polar ice caps have melted, cities are left underwater, and junkyard atolls and bloodthirsty nomads float atop. Kevin Costner portrays the mariner who is taken captive and discovered to be a "mutant." He has webbed toes and gills behind his ears. He is soon rescued by a lovely woman named Helen, who demands from him passage out of the junkyard village with a girl in her care named Enola, who appears to have knowledge of another world and paints figures of strange creatures (horses) and trees. Tattooed on her back is an ancient map, rumored to bear direction to Dryland, a mythical island with lots of trees and fresh water. It just so happens that many inhabitants of Waterworld would kill to find this map to paradise. These killers are called "smokers," a vigilante gang of polluting pirates. The mariner battles the smokers, rescues Enola, falls in love with Helen, and eventually finds Dryland.

Although science fiction, the film has overtones of an environmentalist satire. The villains are chain-smoking capitalists who search for Dryland in the name of "progress." Their blasphemous and violent worldview may be entertaining, but will offend some discerning viewers.

CONTENT ANALYSIS: (Ro, Pa, Ab, E, B, LL, VV, SS, NN, A, M) Mythic worldview of post-apocalyptic earth with some anti-biblical, environmentalist, pagan, and moral elements; twelve obscenities, six profanities, and one blasphemous scene; moderate violence including eight battle scenes with murders using a variety of weapons and methods (spears, machetes, machine guns, slashings, torture, and drowning); one implied scene of fornication with partial nudity, references to rape, and prostitution and pedophilia; and smoking.

Truth Triumphs

WHILE YOU WERE SLEEPING

Quality: ☆☆☆   Acceptability: +1

WARNING CODES:

Language: **
Violence: *
Sex: *
Nudity: None

RATING: PG

GENRE: Romantic comedy

INTENDED AUDIENCE: Older teens and adults

RUNNING TIME: 98 minutes

STARRING: Sandra Bullock, Bill Pullman, Peter Gallagher, Peter Boyle, Glynis Johns, and Jack Warden

DIRECTOR: Jon Turteltaub

EXECUTIVE PRODUCERS: Arthur Sarkissian and Steve Barron

PRODUCER: Roger Birnbaum

WRITERS: Fredrick Lebow and Daniel G. Sullivan

DISTRIBUTOR: Buena Vista Pictures/Walt Disney Company

BRIEF SUMMARY:

The romantic comedy *While You Were Sleeping* stars Sandra Bullock as Lucy, a Chicago Transit Authority worker who, after rescuing a man named Peter from the path of a train, finds herself mistakenly identified as his fiancée and taken in by his over-zealous family. After losing her mother at an early age, Lucy's father once told her, "Life doesn't always come out the way you plan." When an illness took her father as well, Lucy took a job with the Chicago Transit Authority. Now a young adult, she finds herself without family and with dim hopes for the future. That changes when, with Peter in a coma, his family rallies around her. The confusion and misunderstandings compound, especially when she begins to enjoy the attention and plays along. However, her motives are pure: She truly wishes to hurt no one and is willing to go on with her life and forget about the Callaghan family, if only she can figure out how.

With enough misunderstandings and confusion to keep the plot from becoming stale, this entertaining movie demands very little from the viewer. With few offensive elements other than some foul language, *While You Were Sleeping* celebrates the strengths of the family and succeeds as light and undemanding entertainment.

CONTENT ANALYSIS: (CC, LL, V, S, A, M) Christian worldview portraying a close family who attend mass together and offer prayer for healing, but behave irreverently during mass; one obscenity, seven profanities, and twelve vulgarities; brief mugging scene and man pulled from path of oncoming train; two references to male genitals; minimal alcohol and tobacco use (drinks offered at family gathering and New Year's Eve party, liquor bottles on shelf); and reference to gambling.

☆☆☆ THE BEST 1995 FILMS FOR FAMILIES ☆☆☆

Headline	Title
The Most Entertaining Moral Breakthrough in Movies	*Toy Story*
Pro-Family, Pro-Life, Pro-Father	*Father of the Bride Part II*
Best Depiction of Kingdoms in Conflict	*First Knight*
Talent Rewarded	*Babe*
Imagination Triumphs over Avarice	*A Little Princess*
True Love Overcomes Prejudice	*Persuasion*
Christian Virtues Commended	*Sense and Sensibility*
Faith and Forgiveness	*Two Bits*
Heroic Virtues	*Tall Tale*
Heroes Come in All Shapes and Sizes	*Balto*

☆☆☆ THE BEST 1995 FILMS FOR MATURE AUDIENCES ☆☆☆

Headline	Title
Lex Rex	*Braveheart*
Grace Overcomes Misery	*Les Miserables*
Repentance, Forgiveness, and New Life	*Dead Man Walking*
Righteousness Prevails	*A Month by the Lake*
Can-Do Patriotism	*Apollo 13*
True Worth	*Mr. Holland's Opus*
Common Genius	*The Postman*
Truth Triumphs	*While You Were Sleeping*
Healing the Land	*Cry, the Beloved Country*
Denouncing Revenge, Pride, and Double-Mindedness	*Batman Forever*

✰✰✰ THE TWENTY MOST UNBEARABLE FILMS OF 1995 ✰✰✰

Headline	Title
Worst Rerelease	*Belle de Jour*
Worst Family Values	*The Brady Bunch*
Worst Celebration of Adultery	*The Bridges of Madison County*
Worst Obscenities	*Casino*
Worst Spiritism for Children	*Casper*
Worst Overrated Documentary	*Crumb*
Worst Bisexual Movie	*The Doom Generation*
Worst Luring Girls into Lesbianism	*The Incredibly True Adventure of Two Girls in Love*
Worst Mix of Sex and Violence	*Jade*
Worst Slander of an Important Historical Figure	*Jefferson in Paris*
Worst Techno-Movie	*Johnny Mnemonic*
Worst Pedophile Kiddie Porn	*Kid*
Worst New Age Propaganda	*Pocahontas*
Worst New Age Evolution	*Powder*
Worst Defamation of Clergy	*Priest*
Worst Deconstruction of Literature and Faith	*The Scarlet Letter*
Worst Defamation of Christians	*Seven*
Worst Overexposure	*Showgirls*
Worst Attack on the Unborn	*Species*
Worst Drag Queen	*To Wong Foo, Thanks for Everything! Julie Newmar*

101 DALMATIANS

Quality: ☆☆☆☆   Acceptability: +2

WARNING CODES:

Language: *
Violence: *
Sex: None
Nudity: None

RATING: G
GENRE: Comedy
INTENDED AUDIENCE: All ages
RUNNING TIME: 103 minutes
STARRING: Glenn Close, Jeff Daniels, Joely Richardson, and Joan Plowright
DIRECTOR: Stephen Herek
EXECUTIVE PRODUCER: Edward F. Feldman
PRODUCERS: John Hughes and Richard Mestres
WRITER: John Hughes
DISTRIBUTOR: Walt Disney Pictures/Walt Disney Company/Buena Vista
BRIEF SUMMARY:

This live-action version of Disney's classic animated movie pushes all the right emotional buttons while upholding marriage and the sanctity of human life, as well as a high regard for animal life. Set in London, *101 Dalmatians* is about two well-rounded singles, Roger and Anita, who are brought together by their Dalmatians, Pongo and Perdita. Or, rather, their Dalmatians drag them together. When they realize that their Dalmatians are in love, they know they can't separate them, so they get married. Soon, both the human and the Dalmatian families are pregnant. Anita is a dress designer for Cruella De Vil. When Cruella sees Anita's drawings and a picture of Perdita, Cruella realizes she wants a Dalmatian-skin coat. She sets out to capture not only Perdita's puppies but a total of ninety-nine puppies to produce this coat.

This is an adorable, fast-paced movie. We could quibble with the slapstick violence but it is much less than most live-action children's fare. We could quibble with the overly intelligent animals, but they don't talk. This is clearly a fairy tale, with a beautiful church scene and bungling burglars who say that they are saved and thank God when the police finally catch them. This is one that the whole family can enjoy.

CONTENT ANALYSIS: (CC, B, L, V, A, D, PC, M) Christian worldview upholding moral principles, Jesus, salvation, marriage, and good triumphing over evil; two exclamations; slapstick violence including pratfalls, falls into slop in a barnyard, electric shock on a farm fence, falling through ice, getting hit by exhaust, and other slapstick situations; drinking by the bad guys; smoking by the villain is rebuked; and an indication that animals are intelligent beings, subtle animal rights message, and some animal "potty" jokes.

THE ADVENTURES OF PINOCCHIO

Quality: ☆☆☆   Acceptability: +1

WARNING CODES:

Language: *
Violence: *
Sex: None
Nudity: None

RATING: G
GENRE: Fairy tale

INTENDED AUDIENCE: All ages
RUNNING TIME: 96 minutes
STARRING: Martin Landau, Jonathan Taylor Thomas, Genevieve Bujold, Udo Kier, and Bebe Neuwirth
DIRECTOR: Steve Barron
EXECUTIVE PRODUCERS: Sharad Patel, Peter Locke, and Donald Kushner
PRODUCERS: Ruju Patel and Jeffrey Sneller
WRITERS: Sherry Mills, Steve Barron, Tom Benedek, and Barry Berman
BASED ON: The novel by Carlo Collodi
DISTRIBUTOR: New Line Cinema
BRIEF SUMMARY:
Produced in Italy, *The Adventures of Pinocchio* is a compelling story for children of all ages. The story opens with Geppetto carving the initials of the one he loves, Leona, on a tree in the forest. Years later he carves Pinocchio from this tree, and the puppet comes to life. Two thieves notice Pinocchio and decide to sell him to Lorenzini, the puppet master. With his conscience, Pepe the cricket, in tow, Pinocchio learns that fame is not love and that other people are more precious than gold. Geppetto goes looking for Pinocchio, thinks that the puppet has been washed out to sea, and heads after him. Meanwhile, Pinocchio causes Lorenzini to fall into his own magic potion, which turns him into Monstro, the giant fish. Pinocchio heads out after Geppetto and becomes a real boy.

This is a very well-made movie, with Martin Landau giving a superb performance. Although it is a powerful morality tale, the movie is flawed by magical elements and the fact that Pinocchio consciously lies to extend his nose so that he and Geppetto can get out of Monstro. On the other hand, the movie teaches that lying is wrong, you should love your brother, you should put others before yourself, you should not succumb to temptation, you should not be seduced by fame, and many other biblical principles.

CONTENT ANALYSIS: (BB, O, L, V, M) Moral worldview teaching several clear moral principles: you should not lie; you have to stand for your convictions; and people are more important than money. Marred by lying used to solve a plot problem and vengeful lying to get back at thieves, also some magical thinking, a reference to witch and magical elements; fairy-tale violence including punching, shoving, frightening fire sequence, frightening carnival sequence; and lying, cheating, and stealing, all rebuked.

Lest We Forget History

ANNE FRANK REMEMBERED

Quality: ☆☆☆☆　　　Acceptability: +1

WARNING CODES:
　Language: *
　Violence: *
　Sex: None
　Nudity: *
RATING: PG
GENRE: Historical documentary
INTENDED AUDIENCE: Teens and adults
RUNNING TIME: 122 minutes
VOICES: Kenneth Branagh and Glenn Close
DIRECTOR: Jon Blair
PRODUCER: Jon Blair
WRITER: Jon Blair
DISTRIBUTOR: Sony Picture Classics
BRIEF SUMMARY:
Anne Frank Remembered recalls the person of young Anne Frank, who with her family went into hiding from the National Socialists during World War II. Father Otto, born to a well-to-do family in Frankfurt, took his family to the Netherlands to escape Hitler's rule, but soon Hitler's troops arrived in the Netherlands. Otto and his family, joined by another family and friend, went into hiding. It was during this two-year

period that the thirteen-year-old Anne began writing her now-world-famous diaries. Her diary entries describe their caged lives and the growing oppression of the Jews.

Director, writer, and producer Jon Blair does an excellent job reconstructing the events that helped shape Anne's young life and tracing Anne's last tortured year before she finally died of typhus at the desolate and wind-ravaged Bergen-Belsen camp. The interviewees reveal much of Anne's personality and inner spirit. Kenneth Branagh's narration is flawless, adding to the strength of the documentary. There are gruesome scenes of the dead in mass graves, descriptions of persecution, suffering, starvation, cannibalism, beatings, and mass torture and death through gassing. However, the documentary also shows man's courage and renewed hope.

CONTENT ANALYSIS: (B, Ab, H, L, V, N, M) A moral worldview of loyalty, courage, decency, and sacrifice contrasted with the anti-Jewish and humanist worldviews that led to the horrors of the National Socialist persecution and murder of the Jews; three vulgar namecallings by National Socialist soldiers and one exclamatory profanity; grisly images of dead bodies in concentration camps, disease and suffering with descriptions of cannibalism, mass torture, murder, beatings, gassing, shooting, starvation; deprivation of clothes, medicine, and food; one reference in Anne's diary mentioning her interest in cuddling and kissing; naked bodies of the dead; and inhumane treatment and betrayal of men, women, and children.

Italian Feast for the Eyes

BIG NIGHT

Quality: ☆☆☆   Acceptability: −2

WARNING CODES:
Language: ***
Violence: *
Sex: *
Nudity: None

RATING: R
GENRE: Drama
INTENDED AUDIENCE: Adults
RUNNING TIME: 115 minutes
STARRING: Tony Shalhoub, Stanley Tucci, Minnie Driver, Isabella Rossellini, Liev Schreiber, and Campbell Scott
DIRECTORS: Campbell Scott and Stanley Tucci
EXECUTIVE PRODUCERS: Keith Samples and David Kirkpatrick
PRODUCER: Jonathan Filley
WRITERS: Joseph Tropiano and Stanley Tucci
DISTRIBUTOR: Samuel Goldwyn
BRIEF SUMMARY:
In the tradition of *Like Water for Chocolate* comes *Big Night*, a movie that brings you an Italian feast for the eyes. This low-key, bittersweet story highlights the relationship of two Italian-American brothers in the 1950s who wish to make a success in the restaurant business. Primo is an excellent chef, while his brother Secondo is the money-man. They settle in a small New Jersey town and open a restaurant called The Paradise. They get a few customers, but most go to Pascal's across the street. When Pascal tells the brothers that an Italian entertainer is coming to town, the brothers prepare for a big night of feasting. All seems set, including the wonderful dinner, until unexpected news makes for an evening quite different than anticipated.

This movie has the same charm and feeling as *The Postman*, but is set in America. The direction, editing, and music seem to be cut from the European mold. Slow yet unpredictable, it brings an artistic aesthetic to American cinema. The cinematography of the food preparation will make you drool. Regrettably, *Big Night* has many obscenities and implied sex. Likewise, some crooked practices from two businessmen demonstrate that competition can be cutthroat and vicious. Yet, connoisseurs will find good acting and good food in this movie.

CONTENT ANALYSIS: (B, LLL, V, S, A, D, M) Biblical worldview of brotherly love; twenty-two obscenities and eleven profanities; brief fight scene; implied sex; implied fornication; alcohol use; smoking; and corrupt capitalist pursuits.

Propaganda for Perversion

THE BIRDCAGE

Quality: ☆☆☆   Acceptability: −3

WARNING CODES:
Language: ***
Violence: None
Sex: None
Nudity: ***

RATING: R
GENRE: Comedy
INTENDED AUDIENCE: Adults
RUNNING TIME: 110 minutes
STARRING: Robin Williams, Gene Hackman, Nathan Lane, and Dianne Wiest
DIRECTOR: Mike Nichols
PRODUCER: Mike Nichols
WRITER: Elaine May
DISTRIBUTOR: United Artists
BRIEF SUMMARY:
Armand Goldman, played by Robin Williams, is the owner of a cross-dressing nightclub called The Birdcage. A big show is beginning and Armand is searching for his star dancer, Starina, played by Nathan Lane. Albert, a matronly looking transvestite with all the overdone female mannerisms, won't perform because he thinks that Armand is cheating on him. Into this situation walks an attractive young man named Val, Armand's son. To Armand's horror, Val announces to his father that he is going to marry a girl. This is only the beginning of the clash of moral and cultural scenarios in the film. It turns out

that Barbie, Val's fiancée, is none other than the daughter of the conservative and moralistic Senator Keeling. Armand and company make every effort to turn themselves and their apartment inside out, to turn themselves into John Wayne and Margaret Thatcher, and convince the Keelings that this is a "straight" family.

This film draws attention to the flamboyant and ridiculous side of homosexuality and the callous attitudes of those who consider themselves above moral reproof. The use of obscene props and art, phallic humor, nudity, and bad language will shock many viewers as it demonstrates the moral struggle between the homosexual and straight cultures.

CONTENT ANALYSIS: (Ho, LLL, NNN, Ab, M) Homosexual worldview; eighteen obscenities, seven vulgarities, six profanities, and one blasphemy; scene of a topless beach, female breasts, excessive bodily exposure, including both males and females in bikinis, G-strings and thongs; phallic jokes and two cases where the crucifix is referred to irreverently.

Battles the Issue of Abortion

CITIZEN RUTH

Quality: ☆☆☆   Acceptability: −2

WARNING CODES:
Language: ***
Violence: *
Sex: **
Nudity: **

RATING: R
GENRE: Comedy
INTENDED AUDIENCE: Adults
RUNNING TIME: 104 minutes
STARRING: Laura Dern, Swoosie Kurtz, Kurtwood Smith, Mary Kay Place, Burt Reynolds, and Tippi Hedren
DIRECTOR: Alexander Payne
PRODUCERS: Cary Woods and Cathy Konrad
WRITERS: Alexander Payne and Jim Taylor

DISTRIBUTOR: Miramax Films/ Buena Vista (Disney)

BRIEF SUMMARY:

Citizen Ruth tells the story of Ruth Snoops who, in the early stages of pregnancy, sniffs toxic vapors. Ruth is told by the court to get an abortion. This gets the attention of a group of Christian pro-lifers, who make Ruth a symbol of their cause, until Ruth goes to a pro-abortion group led by a lesbian couple who also see Ruth as a powerful message for their cause. As the media catches on to all of this, money is offered to Ruth from both sides. Ruth finally wises up to her own cause and schemes to turn the situation to her advantage.

This is a well-done comedy, as it battles the issue of abortion. Presenting both sides of the controversy, the movie positions anti-abortionists as godly Christians who pray and sing hymns to support their cause, denouncing abortion as sinful. There are plenty of positive references to God, but there are occasions when the film does poke fun at the Christian "baby-savers." It also shows a seamy, slick preacher. Despite its strong Christian references, the comic satire contains strong language, fornication, and profanity. While the film shows two sides to the abortion issue, it does not take a stand, leaving the issue to be resolved through Ruth Snoop's own personal insight and understanding of the issues involved.

CONTENT ANALYSIS: (CC, Ab, Ho, LLL, V, SS, NN, A, D, M) Moderate Christian worldview where Christian anti-abortionist groups fight their crusade, quote the Bible, pray, and sing hymns; contains some anti-Christian and lesbian elements; thirty obscenities, fifteen vulgarities, and thirteen profanities; mild violence involving anti- and pro-life demonstrations, use of guns in threatening situations, car crash where a small boy is hit, and toilet cistern-cover hits man on the head; promiscuity, unwanted pregnancies, and one actual and one implied sexual situation; obscured female nudity; alcohol use and abuse; substance abuse involving hazardous vapor inhalation while pregnant; and miscellaneous immorality including abortion, parental neglect, fetal abuse, stealing, and lying.

Unraveling of the Mayor

CITY HALL

Quality: ✰✰✰✰   Acceptability: −2

WARNING CODES:

Language: ***
Violence: *
Sex: None
Nudity: None

RATING: R
GENRE: Drama/Thriller
INTENDED AUDIENCE: Adults
RUNNING TIME: 120 minutes
STARRING: Al Pacino, John Cusack, Bridget Fonda, Danny Aiello, Martin Landau, and David Paymer
DIRECTOR: Harold Becker
PRODUCERS: Edward R. Pressman, Ken Lipper, Charles Mulvehill, and Harold Becker
WRITERS: Ken Lipper, Paul Schrader, Nicholas Pileggi, and Bo Goldman
DISTRIBUTOR: Castle Rock Entertainment

BRIEF SUMMARY:

In *City Hall*, New York City mayor John Pappas, played by Al Pacino, and his southern-fried deputy mayor Kevin Calhoun, played by John Cusack, have an apparently strong lock on the public's affection. Together they handle all adversity with tact. One morning, a cop and a drug dealer have a shoot-out, and a stray bullet kills a six-year-old black child. That begins the unraveling of the mayor's reign. The child was killed by a bullet from Tino Zapatti. Tino's father, Paul, is a Mafia chieftain. Abe Goodman is the mayor's able chief of staff. He sees the court file for Tino Zapatti and notices that he was let off on probation for a crime that should have put him in jail for ten to twenty years. Goodman smells a fix, which may implicate presiding judge Walter Stern. Kevin Calhoun and police benevolent attorney Marybeth Cogan do gumshoe work that uncovers the repercussions of the murders. The result is more murders and shocking evidence that implicates the mayor himself.

City Hall is excellent and professional in every way. The acting is superb. It has a tight script with a thought-provoking, rather than climactic, ending. It should be rightly noted as a movie only for adults. It is brainy and intelligent but contains a little violence and some hard language. It is a strong testament to the power of goodness over corruption.

CONTENT ANALYSIS: (B, C, LLL, V, A, D, M) Moral worldview demonstrating honesty and loyalty with some Christian elements; twenty-seven obscenities and three profanities; brief violence including two gunfire murders, an implied suicide, and image of corpse; alcohol use; smoking; mob pressure and underhanded dealings and lying.

Rejoice in All Circumstances

COLD COMFORT FARM

Quality: ☆☆☆☆   Acceptability: −1

WARNING CODES:

Language: *
Violence: *
Sex: *
Nudity: *

RATING: PG
GENRE: Comedy
INTENDED AUDIENCE: Older teens and adults
RUNNING TIME: 95 minutes
STARRING: Kate Beckinsale, Joanna Lumley, Rufus Sewell, Ian McKellen, Stephen Fry, Eileen Atkins, Sheila Burrell, Freddie Jones, and Maria Miles
DIRECTOR: John Schlesinger
PRODUCERS: Richard Broke for BBC Films and Anthony Root for Thames International
WRITER: Malcolm Bradbury
BASED ON: The novel by Stella Gibbons
DISTRIBUTOR: Gramercy Pictures
BRIEF SUMMARY:
Cold Comfort Farm throws new and wonderful light on the plight of living with relatives. Flora goes to live at Cold Comfort Farm. With a penchant for tidying up messy situations and lives, she goes about changing lives on the farm. Armed with *Vogue* and travel catalogs, she encourages the inhabitants of Cold Comfort Farm to pursue their individual ambitions: from full-time evangelist to movie star. In time, she also persuades the old matriarch of the house, heard but hardly seen, to leave her cobwebbed life and room to take on a more glamorous existence.

This film is as good-natured as is its heroine, Flora. It is relentless with wicked wit and cunning caricatures. A couple of cautionary notes include the presence of implied promiscuous sex, out-of-wedlock births, sexual innuendos, and the comic exaggeration of a preacher obsessed with the wages of sin. However, there are strong moral qualities such as positive references to Christianity, honoring the family, and an overwhelming sense of kindness from relatives. This movie makes even the most disheveled farmhand lovable and shows that literary wit can be farmed from the soggy soils of the English rural landscapes.

CONTENT ANALYSIS: (B, C, L, V, S, N, D, M) Biblical, moral worldview honoring family ties and doing good deeds with mild Christian elements including a church service and full-time evangelism, although the portrayal of a preacher obsessed with burning in hell for sins and his quivering congregation borders on mockery; two mild profanities; mild violence when old woman hits man with walking stick and hits girl with newspapers; two implied sexual situations including implied promiscuous sex and implied use of contraceptives for sexual acts, giving birth out of wedlock, and numerous sexual innuendos; woman in bathtub (not exposed) and upper male nudity; cigarette smoking; social drinking; defecation, and miscellaneous immorality.

Teaching Children Witchcraft

THE CRAFT

Quality: ✰✰   Acceptability: −4

WARNING CODES:
   Language: ***
   Violence: ***
   Sex: None
   Nudity: None
RATING: R
GENRE: Occult thriller
INTENDED AUDIENCE: Teens
RUNNING TIME: 100 minutes
STARRING: Robin Tunney, Fairuza Balk, Neve Campbell, and Rachel True
DIRECTOR: Andrew Fleming
PRODUCER: Douglas Wick
WRITERS: Peter Filardi and Andrew Fleming
DISTRIBUTOR: Columbia Pictures/Sony Pictures Entertainment
BRIEF SUMMARY:
The Craft is a special-effects propaganda piece for occultism and witchcraft. It is a diabolical lesson in witchcraft, where the "good" witch wins in the end. When Sarah moves to Los Angeles, she is drafted into a three-girl coven at her high school. By completing the fourth corner of the coven, these budding witches are able to cast spells and take revenge on their enemies. Rochelle causes the beautiful white racist to lose her hair. Sarah causes the chauvinist football hunk Chris to lose his mind over her. Bonnie gets her

wish for the healing of her disfigurement. The leader, Nancy, invites the false-god Manon (whom she claims is older, greater, and wiser than God and the devil) into herself so that she can wreak havoc on other people.

For teenagers who seek self-affirmation and are trying to establish their identity, this movie offers the hope that occult powers can give you everything you desire. Occult incantations and rituals are presented with a respect and credibility that will cause teenagers to long for these proffered powers. Yet, this is an egocentric perspective, the self-absorbed perspective of the adversary. Of course, occult powers cannot be used for good. They are evil, and this movie's promotion of them is evil. This movie should be rebuked. It will lead many impressionable children astray.

CONTENT ANALYSIS: (OOO, LLL, VVV, S, A, D, M) Occult worldview commending witchcraft, with clearly defined false doctrines, ancient occult teachings, New Age artifacts, and witchcraft; thirty-one obscenities and ten profanities; extreme violence including man hit by car, man falling through window, woman struck by lightning, needle therapy, supernatural disfigurement, blood, furniture hits girl, explosion in shop, slitting wrists, heart attack, attempted suicide, and other grotesqueries including snakes, rats, and gruesome insects attacking people; kissing, seduction, implied oral sex, implied lesbianism, and discussion of sex; alcohol use; smoking and reference to drug use; revenge themes, lying, cheating, and many occult rituals and activities.

Teamwork, Honesty, and Self-Sacrifice

D3: THE MIGHTY DUCKS

Quality: ✰✰✰   Acceptability: +1

WARNING CODES:
   Language: *

Violence: *
Sex: None
Nudity: None
RATING: PG
GENRE: Comedy
INTENDED AUDIENCE: All ages
RUNNING TIME: 100 minutes
STARRING: Emilio Estevez, Jeffrey Nordling, David Selby, Heidi Kling, and Joss Ackland
DIRECTOR: Robert Lieberman
EXECUTIVE PRODUCERS: Steven Brill and C. Tad Devlin
PRODUCERS: Jordan Kerner and Jon Avnet
WRITERS: Steven Brill and Jim Burnstein
STORY BY: Kenneth Johnson and Jim Burnstein
DISTRIBUTOR: Walt Disney Pictures/Walt Disney Company/Buena Vista Distribution
BRIEF SUMMARY:
The Mighty Ducks hit the ice and silver screen again with a winner for the whole family. Emilio Estevez returns as Gordon Bombay, who tells Ducks captain Charlie that he won't return as coach. Charley asks hard-nosed Ted Orion to take over, now that the Ducks have joined the hockey state championship school, Eaton Hall. Charlie and the team feel abandoned by Gordon. Orion is demanding and unfriendly. The varsity doesn't think that the Ducks, now the junior varsity team, are true Eaton Hall Warriors, and pull countless pranks on them. Charlie is so fed up that he decides to quit the team. When Gordon returns, Charlie joins again, submits to Orion's rules, and faces their biggest challenge yet: playing the varsity in an exhibition match.

This formulaic but crowd-pleasing movie has a little of everything—tender moments, big laughs, rivalry, romance, and of course, hockey. Most of all, this movie teaches that teamwork and sticking it out when things get tough pays off.

This movie is filled with quality morals and relevant themes for children. There are three mild obscenities and a boy tries unsuccessfully to look up a cheerleader's skirt, but that is the extent of anything bad. *D3: The Mighty Ducks* is all that it is quacked up to be.

CONTENT ANALYSIS: (B, L, V, M) Biblical, moral worldview on teamwork, friendship, honesty, and self-sacrifice overcoming adversity with positive reference to prayer; three mild obscenities and two vulgarities; mild action violence including chases, hockey fight, and threats; boy tries to look up girl's skirt; and mild rebellion themes, pranks, and vomiting.

God's Hands

DEAR GOD

Quality: ☆☆☆   Acceptability: +1

WARNING CODES:
Language: *
Violence: *
Sex: None
Nudity: None
RATING: PG
GENRE: Comedy
INTENDED AUDIENCE: Older children to adults
RUNNING TIME: 115 minutes
STARRING: Greg Kinnear, Laurie Metcalf, Maria Pitillo, Tim Conway, Roscoe Lee Browne, Jon Seda, and Hector Elizondo
DIRECTOR: Garry Marshall
PRODUCER: Steve Tisch
WRITERS: Warren Leight and Ed Kaplan
DISTRIBUTOR: Paramount Pictures
BRIEF SUMMARY:
Greg Kinnear stars as Tom Turner in this likable and winsome movie, *Dear God*. Tom is in debt, so he methodically cons innocent people out of their money. One day he is caught and brought to trial. He is sentenced to a job in the dead-

letter office of the post office. Included are letters to Elvis, the tooth fairy, and God. The office is filled with a staff of misfits, and Tom thinks he might have found a better class of people in jail. Yet they soon act together to answer letters addressed to God, and form a tight team of mercy and love. All goes well until they are charged with mail fraud and face their biggest challenge.

Technically, the movie is very good. Well cast, it shows some very fresh and original characters. The movie depicts prayer, gratitude to God, and good deeds. It tells the audience that we are God's hands and feet. It shows that serving God and doing good deeds are more important than living for selfish reasons. It is important to know that our good deeds are as filthy rags without Christ's atonement. Good deeds and giving to others is, rather, part of our worship and service to God. This movie may motivate you to good works and to learn more about God.

CONTENT ANALYSIS: (BB, C, L, V, A, D, M) Biblical, moral worldview depicting and examining faith in God, good deeds, the role of serving God, and prayer with positive depiction of Christian leaders; many positive appeals to God; nine obscenities; one brief scene where man gets punched in gut; alcohol use; smoking; and miscellaneous immorality includes conning, lying, and cheating.

Madcap Monkeyshines

DUNSTON CHECKS IN

Quality: ☆☆☆   Acceptability: +1

WARNING CODES:
  Language: *
  Violence: *
  Sex: *
  Nudity: *
RATING: PG
GENRE: Comedy
INTENDED AUDIENCE: Children

RUNNING TIME: 80 minutes
STARRING: Jason Alexander, Faye Dunaway, Eric Lloyd, and Rupert Everett
DIRECTOR: Ken Kwapis
EXECUTIVE PRODUCER: Rodney Liber
PRODUCERS: Todd Black and Joe Wizan
WRITERS: John Hopkins and Bruce Graham
DISTRIBUTOR: 20th Century Fox
BRIEF SUMMARY:
Dunston Checks In opens with young Kyle and Brian Grant playing a prank on one of the bellmen at the prestigious Majestic Hotel that their father, Robert Grant (Jason Alexander), manages. Next, Kyle hears some knocking in a trunk owned by Lord Rutledge. Lord Rutledge is really Mr. O'Malley, a thief who uses an orangutan named Dunston to rob hotel guests. That night, Dunston climbs up and into one wealthy guest's window and steals everything that glitters. However, Dunston decides that he is no longer going to serve Lord Rutledge, and hides in the air ducts. When Mr. Grant discovers that there is a monkey loose in the hotel, he calls for animal control. The madcap monkeyshines culminate on the night of the Crystal Ball. Dunston is found out, Lord Rutledge is exposed, and all ends well.

Dunston Checks In is a cute comedy destined to enthrall little children. The direction, acting, and writing are superior for this genre. Good triumphs over evil and honesty is rewarded. Discernment is required regarding the slapstick comedy. Given this caution, *Dunston Checks In* is a remarkably clean movie. There is not much more that parents could ask for on a snowy winter afternoon.

CONTENT ANALYSIS: (B, L, V, S, N, M) Moral worldview with no theological underpinning; five obscenities and one profanity; slapstick violence including children falling several stories down laundry shoot into laundry, dog falling off roof into garbage, several pratfalls, fistfight, man shot with tranquilizer gun, man hit by coconut, and miscellaneous violence; suggestive massage and suggestive cosmetic face mask removal; some cleavage and female bare back; and theft, fraud, and greed.

Noble Responsibilities

EMMA

Quality: ☆☆☆   Acceptability: +2

WARNING CODES:
Language: None
Violence: *
Sex: None
Nudity: None
RATING: PG
GENRE: Drama
INTENDED AUDIENCE: All ages
RUNNING TIME: 120 minutes
STARRING: Gwyneth Paltrow, Jeremy Northam, Toni Collette, Greta Scacchi, Polly Walker, Juliet Stevenson, and Alan Cumming
DIRECTOR: Douglas McGrath
PRODUCER: Patrick Cassavetti
WRITER: Douglas McGrath
DISTRIBUTOR: Miramax Films/ Buena Vista (Disney)
BRIEF SUMMARY:
Emma, played wonderfully by Gwyneth Paltrow, is a well-to-do young woman who has taken it upon herself to be a matchmaker to her contemporaries in early nineteenth-century England. She tries to set up the less-advantaged and slightly homely Harriet Smith with the Reverend Elton. However, the Reverend Elton confesses his love to Emma. When Emma doesn't return it, the Reverend Elton marries elsewhere. Meanwhile, Harriet turns down a marriage proposal from a kind farmer, while Emma's brother-in-law, Mr. Knightley, is looking down on Emma with ridicule. Emma next tries to pair Harriet with Frank Churchill, but fails. Harriet instead falls for Mr. Knightley, arousing Emma's jealousy, for she has grown fond of Knightley. Through frank discussions and reappearing suitors, all turns out well.

In every way, *Emma* stands apart from the normal summer fare. It is a quiet drama that isn't interested in bad weather, witness protection programs, or spies. It is interested in love and marriage. The narrow view of gentility and courtship stimulate us with a sense of chaste fun, while also giving us a sense of monotony. Without the biting and brilliant wit of a script by Emma Thompson, who also wrote the script for *Sense and Sensibility*, nor the severity and focus of the director of *Persuasion*, *Emma* stands apart as slightly flawed, but nonetheless entertaining and moral.

CONTENT ANALYSIS: (CCC, V, A) Christian worldview extolling marriage, prayer, and a favorable representation of the ministry; the word "blast" used once; one very brief scene where woman is abducted by Gypsies; and alcohol use.

Powerful Ministry to the Poor

ENTERTAINING ANGELS: THE DOROTHY DAY STORY

Quality: ☆☆☆   Acceptability: −1

WARNING CODES:
Language: ***
Violence: *
Sex: *
Nudity: *
RATING: Not rated
GENRE: Inspiration
INTENDED AUDIENCE: All ages
RUNNING TIME: 110 minutes
STARRING: Moira Kelly, Martin Sheen, Melinda Dillon, and Lenny Von Dohlen

DIRECTOR: Michael Ray Rhodes
PRODUCER: Ellwood E. Kieser
WRITER: John Wells
DISTRIBUTOR: October Films
BRIEF SUMMARY:

The Roman Catholic Paulist Productions produces a worthwhile period piece in *Entertaining Angels: The Dorothy Day Story*. A dark-eyed Moira Kelly portrays Miss Day as a feisty radical in the first quarter of the twentieth century, advocating the overthrow of most anything contrary to liberal thinking. Communism, nihilism, and the personal problems associated with sexual liberation plague the opening scenes of her early life, a foundation of depravity from which Day must be delivered. Melinda Dillon plays a nun nobody could dislike. Martin Sheen serves as Dorothy's messenger from God. These two Christians lead Dorothy into the way of the Lord. Her passion to assist the down-and-out leads Dorothy into a powerful ministry to the poor.

This movie shows a sinner saved by grace. If it did not deal with evil in its few opening scenes, we could not fully understand the uphill climb of this woman who defined the word *faithful*. It may uplift your own aspirations. It will certainly be a powerful testimony to those who look for solutions to life's problems in the leftist social movements of the age. A Communist friend tells Dorothy, when she doubts her mission and ministry, that the Communists talk about helping the poor, while, with her faith, she actually *has* helped hundreds.

CONTENT ANALYSIS: (CCC, LLL, V, S, N, A, D, H) Strong Christian worldview of woman converting to Christ and serving humanity; eighteen obscenities and five profanities; mild violence with hitting and rioting; implied fornication; seductive upper male nudity; alcohol use and abuse; smoking; and socialism.

Witness Protection

ERASER

Quality: ☆☆☆☆   Acceptability: −2

WARNING CODES:
  Language: **
  Violence: ***
  Sex: None
  Nudity: None
RATING: R
GENRE: Action/Adventure
INTENTED AUDIENCE: Teens and adults
STARRING: Arnold Schwarzenegger, Vanessa Williams, James Caan, and James Coburn
DIRECTOR: Charles Russell
EXECUTIVE PRODUCERS: Michael Tadross and Charles Russell
PRODUCERS: Arnold Kopelson and Anne Kopelson
WRITER: Tony Puryear
DISTRIBUTOR: Warner Brothers
BRIEF SUMMARY:

Arnold Schwarzenegger stars in *Eraser*, another nail-biting, big-gun thrill ride, sure to delight his fans. He plays good guy, federal marshal John Kruger, a member of an elite group called WITSEC who erase identities in the witness protection program. His latest challenge involves a woman named Lee Cullen, played by Vanessa Williams, who has a disk that implicates government officials in a secret arms deal with terrorists. Kruger successfully hides Ms. Cullen until key witnesses suddenly end up dead. Kruger finds out that his own superiors are behind this secret deal. Kruger and Cullen must run for their lives as they seek to clear their names and catch the villains.

Eraser is extremely fast paced and suspenseful. Not only does it have exciting stunts and special effects, it also has multiple witty one-liners. Parents should be aware, however, that there is excessive action violence, but it remains on an action level, with few on-screen grotesqueries. Also, the movie is marred by foul language. On the other hand, Arnold claims at one point that God's laws are not man's laws, and at another point a man of the cloth helps out the innocent Kruger and Cullen. In the final analysis, *Eraser* is a superior action picture without sex, nudity, or a vengeful protagonist.

CONTENT ANALYSIS: (B, C, LL, VVV, A, D, M) Moral worldview with some mild Christian elements about integrity triumphing over dishonesty; twenty-eight obscenities and seventeen profanities; extreme action violence including shooting, explosions, falling out of plane, hitting, kicking, cutting, and neck breaking; alcohol use; smoking; vengeance and corrupt government officials.

Political Idolatry

EVITA

Quality: ☆☆☆   Acceptability: −1

WARNING CODES:

Language: *
Violence: **
Sex: *
Nudity: None

RATING: PG-13
GENRE: Historical musical
INTENDED AUDIENCE: Older teens and adults
RUNNING TIME: 125 minutes
STARRING: Madonna, Antonio Banderas, and Jonathan Pryce
DIRECTOR: Alan Parker
PRODUCERS: Robert Stigwood, Alan Parker, and Andrew G. Vajna
WRITERS: Alan Parker and Oliver Stone
BASED ON: The musical play with lyrics by Tim Rice and music by Andrew Lloyd Webber
DISTRIBUTOR: Hollywood Pictures/Walt Disney Company/Buena Vista

BRIEF SUMMARY:

Evita is a stunning musical portrait of an impoverished, illegitimate little girl who claws her way to the top. Told solely through song, the movie does not whitewash Evita's corrupt past nor her dedication to national socialism, but features stylized images of her manipulations as she works her way to the top of the political ladder, where she meets Juan Perón. The narrator, Ché, tells us that the people were the real show and that Evita's words were empty, she stole from everyone, and took every opportunity to advance herself. Throughout the film, the music and cinematography tries to emotionally engage the audience in the political idolatry of the twentieth century.

Clearly, the point of all this is to show us how easy it is to be manipulated and how our emotions can blind us to the facts. The movie starts out with great power, but ends with a whimper. There are very few offensive elements in this movie, and it is not a pro-Fascist diatribe. The not-so-good news is that the script does not sustain the weight of all this magnificence and does not allow the actors the character growth that they need to soar. The better news is that it is a beautiful production.

CONTENT ANALYSIS: (B, C, L, VV, S, A, D, M) Moral worldview about an immoral woman, with scenes of religious and political idolatry as well as a brief, positive Christian reference; one obscenity; mild violence including soldiers attacking civilians with swords, guns, and bombs but little or no blood except in stylized aftermath pictures; frequent highly stylized sexual innuendo, including implied prostitution and implied adultery such as Evita dancing the tango with one partner after another while the narrator sings about her using men to advance her status in life; woman in nightgown; alcohol use; smoking; and miscellaneous immorality including lying, cheating, stealing, fraud, unjust political activity, and socialist thuggery.

Love One Another

A FAMILY THING

Quality: ☆☆☆   Acceptability: −1

WARNING CODES:
  Language: ***
  Violence: **
  Sex: None
  Nudity: *
RATING: PG-13
GENRE: Drama
INTENDED AUDIENCE: Adults
RUNNING TIME: 110 minutes
STARRING: Robert Duvall, James Earl Jones, Michael Beach, Irma P. Hall, and Grace Zabrinskie
DIRECTOR: Richard Pearce
EXECUTIVE PRODUCER: Michael Hausman
PRODUCERS: Robert Duvall, Todd Black, and Randa Haines
WRITERS: Billy Bob Thornton and Tom Epperson
DISTRIBUTOR: Metro Goldwyn-Mayer/United Artists
BRIEF SUMMARY:
Earl Pilcher, played by Robert Duvall, is a white racist living in Arkansas. When Earl's mother dies, she leaves him a note that states that she was not his mother. His real mother was a black maid whom his father impregnated, who died while giving birth. The note ends with a request that Earl go to Chicago to meet his half brother, Virgil, played by James Earl Jones, and accept him as family. Earl goes to Chicago, and while there experiences a clash of cultures. Virgil has nothing but contempt for Earl and his father. Earl tries to leave, but is mugged by black thugs. Alone and frightened, Earl has no choice but to turn to Virgil. In time, with the help of their benevolent Aunt T, Virgil and Earl learn to respect and even love one another.

This is a very simple movie, yet it is emotionally powerful. It focuses at a per-sonal level of what it means to be united as brothers. The answer is not found in culture or even skin color but in the love of God. Both of these men express faith in God, and learn that the meaning of their faith, as told by Aunt T, is to love one another. While excellent and moving, care should be taken in viewing this movie, as these men sometimes settle their differences with contemptuous and obscene language.

CONTENT ANALYSIS: (CC, LLL, VV, N, A, D, M) Christian worldview where brotherly love, tolerance, churchgoing, and the Lord Jesus Christ are affirmed; forty-three obscenities, six vulgarities, and one profanity that is severely rebuked; man assaulted resulting in bloodshed; very brief shot of woman giving birth; alcohol use; smoking; and lying, stealing, and racist themes.

Unveiling the Truth

FARGO

Quality: ☆☆☆   Acceptability: −2

WARNING CODES:
  Language: ***
  Violence: ***
  Sex: **
  Nudity: **
RATING: R
GENRE: Drama
INTENDED AUDIENCE: Adults
RUNNING TIME: 100 minutes
STARRING: William H. Macy, Steve Buscemi, Peter Stormare, Kristin Rudrud, and Frances McDormand
DIRECTOR: Joel Coen
EXECUTIVE PRODUCERS: Tim Bevan and Eric Fellner
PRODUCER: Ethan Coen
WRITERS: Ethan Coen and Joel Coen
DISTRIBUTOR: Gramercy Pictures
BRIEF SUMMARY: The Coen brothers have gone back to their Minnesota roots

to craft a hyper-realistic crime drama called *Fargo*. Set in Northern Minnesota, it tells the story of a botched kidnapping scheme, demonstrating the futility of crime. Jerry Lundegaard is a car salesman in Minneapolis. He has a loving family, but has recently come under severe financial difficulties. He decides to hire two thugs to kidnap his own wife and demand eighty thousand dollars. Jerry is convinced this is a solid plan. Everything goes as planned until one thug kills a policeman and two witnesses to the crime. They demand more money, and Jerry's plan unravels. Soon, small-town police chief Marge Gunderson is on the case. Observant and even-tempered, she slowly starts to discover that Jerry is behind this caper.

This story is remarkable because it has realistic and expertly acted Scandinavian characters. Realistic too is its brutality. Murders are clearly seen, sex is seen, and the thugs frequently use obscenities, but the strength of this movie doesn't rest on the brutality of the wicked. It is stirring because it shows the slow yet deliberate unveiling of the truth and the failure of evil.

CONTENT ANALYSIS: (B, LLL, VVV, SS, NN, A, M) Moral worldview clearly demonstrating that lying and crimes will be brought to justice; seventy obscenities, four vulgarities, and twenty profanities (mostly "jeez"); graphic but not pervasive violence, including attempted strangulation, assault, breaking and entering, kidnapping, several point-blank gunfire murders with bloodshed, man killed with ax implied, and grinding in wood chopper; fornication depicted; alcohol use; and smoking.

Ultralight

FLY AWAY HOME

Quality: ☆☆☆   Acceptability: −1

WARNING CODES:
  Language: *
  Violence: None
  Sex: *
  Nudity: *
RATING: PG
GENRE: Drama
INTENDED AUDIENCE: All ages
RUNNING TIME: 110 minutes
STARRING: Jeff Daniels, Anna Paquin, Dana Delany, and Terry Kinney
DIRECTOR: Carroll Ballard
EXECUTIVE PRODUCER: Sandy Gallin
PRODUCERS: John Veitch and Carol Baum
WRITERS: Robert Rodat and Vince McKewin
DISTRIBUTOR: Columbia Pictures/Sony
BRIEF SUMMARY:
Fly Away Home is based on the true story of a young girl, Amy Alden. When her mother dies, Amy must move from New Zealand to Ontario to live with her father, whom she hasn't seen since her parents divorced. Her father, Thomas, lives on a farm making garish sculptures. One day Amy finds a nest of Canadian goose eggs abandoned by their mother. The birds become a bridge that bonds Amy and her father together. Enduring threats of confiscation by local authorities, Amy and her dad devise a plan not only to teach the birds how to fly but also encourage them to fly south for the winter. With ultralight planes, Amy accompanies her father in an attempt to lead the geese to a natural wetlands habitat in the Southern U.S.

The scenery and cinematography are striking. The film succeeds as a "family friendly" film with the sad exception of three needless obscenities. The film further suffers from the unfortunate introduction of a New Age element when Thomas tries to console Amy with the adage that her mother's spirit still watches over her. There is also an implied live-in girlfriend, however the girlfriend is never shown living in the house. All in all, however, the film uplifts and encourages healthy relationships between fathers and daughters.

CONTENT ANALYSIS: (B, Pa, L, S, N) Moral worldview of family love with New Age element where deceased mother presides over the family; three obscenities; implied live-in girlfriend situation; and one scene with father standing in front yard in his underwear.

Fighting Injustice

GHOSTS OF MISSISSIPPI

Quality: ☆☆☆☆   Acceptability: –2

WARNING CODES:
  Language: ***
  Violence: **
  Sex: None
  Nudity: None
RATING: PG-13
GENRE: Historical drama
INTENDED AUDIENCE: Teens and adults
RUNNING TIME: 123 minutes
STARRING: Alec Baldwin, Whoopi Goldberg, James Woods, and Craig T. Nelson
DIRECTOR: Rob Reiner
PRODUCERS: Rob Reiner, Frederick Zollo, Nicholas Paleologos, and Andrew Scheinman
EXECUTIVE PRODUCERS: Charles Newirth and Jeff Stott
WRITER: Lewis Colick
DISTRIBUTOR: Castle Rock Entertainment
BRIEF SUMMARY: In *Ghosts of Mississippi*, set in the 1960s, a white racist is paraded as a champion after shooting Medgar Evers, the African American civil rights leader. After two hung juries result in mistrials and thirty years pass, the defendant, Byron De La Beckwith, is brought back to trial, thanks to the persistence of Myrlie Evers-Williams, the wife of the slain civil rights leader, and a courageous assistant district attorney,

Bobby DeLaughter. The story centers around DeLaughter's uphill battle and the personal consequences he and his family face when he chooses to pursue a third trial against Beckwith. Also highlighted is Myrlie Evers's relationship with DeLaughter, which evolves from frustration and suspicion into trust.

Director and producer Rob Reiner should be commended for his treatment of how family love and support can empower those who fight injustice. The acting is well done, and Woods's portrayal of the elderly Beckwith is superb. On a moral note, Beckwith makes disturbing racist statements, which he attributes to the Bible and Jesus. The movie fails to acknowledge God as the source of justice and the One with the only balm that will eternally heal our wounds. This is a probing movie marred by some brief but graphic violence and many obscenities.

CONTENT ANALYSIS: (H, B, C, Ab, LLL, VV, A, D, M) Humanist worldview in which the court system is relied on as the sole means for obtaining justice, with some moral, Christian, and anti-Christian elements; four profanities, fourteen obscenities, twenty-one vulgarities, eight blasphemies, extensive racist epithets including numerous uses of the word "nigger"; references to the Ku Klux Klan, swastikas, and death threats; fatal shooting in which children are present and video clips from the 1960s show burning crosses and violence against blacks, including beatings by police officers; woman grabs her husband's buttocks; reference to drinking too much; cigar smoking; and wife leaves husband and children, divorce; vandalism, and lying on the witness stand.

Violence, Intrigue, and Madness

HAMLET

Quality: ☆☆☆☆   Acceptability: –2

WARNING CODES:

Language: None
Violence: **
Sex: **
Nudity: *

RATING: PG-13
GENRE: Drama
INTENDED AUDIENCE: Adults
RUNNING TIME: 242 minutes
STARRING: Kenneth Branagh, Julie Christie, Billy Crystal, Gerard Depardieu, Charlton Heston, Derek Jacobi, Jack Lemmon, Rufus Sewell, Robin Williams, and Kate Winslet
DIRECTOR: Kenneth Branagh
PRODUCER: David Barron
WRITER: Kenneth Branagh
BASED ON: The play by William Shakespeare
DISTRIBUTOR: Castle Rock Entertainment
BRIEF SUMMARY:
With lavish sets and lush costume design changing the setting from medieval times to the nineteenth century, Kenneth Branagh's film version of William Shakespeare's *Hamlet* tells once more the tale of a son's revenge for the untimely death of his father at the hands of his father's brother. This story involves all levels of drama, including violence, intrigue, sex, and madness. The character of Hamlet is wrought with complexity and divisions. Hamlet is also taxed with a love interest of his own in Ophelia. In the medieval setting, Ophelia embodied everything pure and somewhat simple; however, under Branagh's direction we see her as simple but less pure. Now she is Hamlet's lover and is not as innocent, but still fragile. When she sees her father dead at the hands of her lost lover, she goes mad and ends her life.

With a strong adherence to the play's script, the movie has few instances of immoral elements, but Kenneth Branagh has added his own modern touches including lascivious sex scenes and some mildly graphic violence. The movie is not like typical Hollywood fare, but reflects more of an enactment of a play than an entertaining picture.

CONTENT ANALYSIS: (C, VV, SS, N, M) Mild Christian worldview of honorable family relationships but including revenge; intense sword fight, several poisonings, stabbing, and war; depicted sexual encounter and references to the same; natural nudity; casual drinking and drunkenness; poisoning and smoking; and revenge and paranoia.

Love One Another

HARRIET THE SPY

Quality: ☆☆☆☆   Acceptability: +1

WARNING CODES:

Language: **
Violence: *
Sex: None
Nudity: None

RATING: PG
GENRE: Drama
INTENDED AUDIENCE: Families
STARRING: Michelle Trachtenberg, Rosie O'Donnell, Vanessa Lee Chester, and Gregory Smith
DIRECTOR: Bronwen Hughes
PRODUCER: Marykay Powell
WRITERS: Douglas Petrie and Theresa Rebeck
DISTRIBUTOR: Paramount Pictures
BRIEF SUMMARY:
Harriet the Spy wants to be a writer, so she observes people and writes down everything she sees in her notebook. Golly, her nanny, encourages her with wit and wisdom. Harriet's life is turned inside out when Golly decides to leave. Just as Harriet is learning to make it on her own, her rival, Marion Hawthorne, finds Harriet's diary and reads to her classmates all of Harriet's incisive observations about them. The truth hurts, and her classmates turn against her. Finally Golly comes back to tell Harriet that she has to learn to say she is sorry. Harriet

does, and gets a different perspective on her friends.

Harriet the Spy will make you laugh and cry. It portrays the truth of childhood with such vividness that you are there once again. This is a movie you will want to take your children to see to help them understand themselves. There is one unnecessary line when Golly, who has always valued the truth, tells Harriet that she must not only apologize but also lie to restore her friendships. Actually, Harriet does not have to lie. Aside from this line and some minor foul language, this movie is a powerful morality tale. There is some childish name-calling and a few exclamations, but whatever is bad is rebuked as such. This is a movie for boys and girls. It is one of my top ten of all time.

CONTENT ANALYSIS: (B, Pa, LL, V, M) Moral worldview with one relativist statement and several references to blessings; two very mild profanities and eight very mild obscenities; childlike violence such as pushing and shoving; and teasing, lying, cheating, and stealing—all rebuked.

Purr-fectly Delightful

HOMEWARD BOUND II: LOST IN SAN FRANCISCO

Quality: ★★★   Acceptability: +2

WARNING CODES:
   Language: *
   Violence: *
   Sex: None
   Nudity: None

RATING: G
GENRE: Comedy/Fantasy
INTENDED AUDIENCE: All ages
RUNNING TIME: 85 minutes
STARRING: Robert Hays, Kim Greist, Veronica Lauren, and the voices of Michael J. Fox, Sally Field, Ralph Waite, and Sinbad
DIRECTOR: David R. Ellis

PRODUCER: Barry Jossen
WRITER: Chris Hauty
DISTRIBUTOR: Walt Disney Pictures/Buena Vista (Touchstone/Miramax/Hollywood Pictures)
BRIEF SUMMARY:
Homeward Bound II: Lost in San Francisco places the Seaver family pets Chance, Sassy, and Shadow on a homeward trek through big-city perils. The family decides to go on a camping trip in the Canadian Rockies and to take their pets. As they are being caged for the flight, the animals suspect the worst and escape at the airport as the Seavers fly off. The three agree that their only hope is to go home and wait. Meeting certain trouble, they encounter junkyard dogs, animal catchers, rushing traffic, and bad weather. When Chance is picked up by dogcatchers, Sassy, Shadow, and a pack of new friends come to the rescue. After this close call, the threesome find the Golden Gate Bridge and are almost home except for one last hair-raising scare.

Homeward Bound II: Lost in San Francisco tells the familiar story of the prodigal son. This movie has very little immoral content. Perhaps the most divisive part is the continual banter and barbs exchanged between the reckless Chance and the sensible Sassy. We also see the usual action pratfalls and adventures common to many animal movies. This movie is pure entertainment, down to its padded paws. It makes no bones about being original or cataclysmic. It is a purr-fect delight for the whole family.

CONTENT ANALYSIS: (B, L, V, M) Moral worldview extolling love of family and self-sacrifice; three "butts," one "pee-ed"; some mild obscene actions including implied dog vomiting, burping, and urinating, and one use of the Lord's name in vain; action violence including dogfights, dog chases, dogs pull on human clothes, dogs steal food, fire, truck falls into river, and near car collision; and brief shot of women in bikinis.

Love Story with Restraint

THE HORSEMAN ON THE ROOF

Quality: ☆☆☆☆   Acceptability: −2

WARNING CODES:
  Language: *
  Violence: ***
  Sex: None
  Nudity: **
RATING: R
GENRE: Drama
INTENDED AUDIENCE: Adults
RUNNING TIME: 135 minutes
STARRING: Juliette Binoche, Olivier Martinez, Pierre Arditi, and Francois Cluzet
DIRECTOR: Jean-Paul Rappeneau
EXECUTIVE PRODUCER: Bernard Bouix
PRODUCER: Rene Clietman
WRITERS: Jean-Paul Rappeneau, Nina Companeez, and Jean-Claude Carriere
DISTRIBUTOR: Miramax Films/ Buena Vista (Disney)
BRIEF SUMMARY:
The Horseman on the Roof is a beautifully told story of devotion, honor, and love set in Provence, France. The young Italian freedom fighter, Angelo Pardi, has yet to prove himself in battle or in love until Pauline de The'us, played by Juliette Binoche, reluctantly provides him with his chance to be her guardian.

An exile from Italy, Angelo gallops through the French countryside, which is overcome by a devastating plague. He rides to the plague-ridden town of Monosque, where smoking piles of bodies are being burned in the street. Attacked by a fearful crowd, he takes refuge on the rooftops. There he meets Pauline, a married woman who lives alone. Gently she convinces him to stay. Thus begins a relationship that actor Martinez describes as "a love story with restraint."

Jean-Paul Rappeneau has created a beautiful film that pays homage to the artistic vision of the novel upon which it is based. When Pauline is struck by the plague, Angelo must rub her naked body to resuscitate her. Other areas of concern are gross images of plague victims. Graphically displaying the plague-infested land of early-nineteenth-century France, this movie manages to exhilarate us with its portrayal of the human struggle to cultivate honor and love in the midst of terrifying circumstances.

CONTENT ANALYSIS: (Ro, C, L, VVV, NN, A) Romantic worldview depicting honor, Christian prayer, and the struggle to remain faithful to marriage; one profanity, one vulgarity, and one obscenity; one mention of suicide, many dead and bloated bodies, scenes of death rattle, choking emaciated person vomiting white bile, one hanged man, crow picking at the face of a corpse, two people killed by gunfire, one man beaten to death by a crowd, graphic scene of dying woman; full female nudity in natural context; and drunkenness.

God's Love Prevails

THE HUNCHBACK OF NOTRE DAME

Quality: ☆☆☆☆   Acceptability: +2

WARNING CODES:
  Language: *
  Violence: **
  Sex: *
  Nudity: None
RATING: G
GENRE: Animated musical
INTENDED AUDIENCE: Older children and adults
RUNNING TIME: 87 minutes
VOICES: Jason Alexander, Tom Hulce, Tony Jay, Paul Kandel, Charles Kimbrough, Kevin Kline, Demi Moore, David Ogden Stiers, and Mary Wickes

DIRECTORS: Gary Trousdale and Kirk Wise

PRODUCER: Don Hahn

WRITERS: Tab Murphy, Irene Mecchi, Bob Tzudiker, Noni White, and Jonathan Roberts

DISTRIBUTOR: Walt Disney Pictures

BRIEF SUMMARY:

The Hunchback of Notre Dame opens with a song from which we learn that the cathedral's bell-ringer is a mysterious outcast named Quasimodo, who is imprisoned by the evil judge Claude Frollo. Judge Frollo caused the death of Quasimodo's Gypsy mother and was forced to care for the child. Frollo forbids Quasimodo to leave the bell tower, but Quasimodo escapes to the square during the "Feast of Fools." He is pulled onto the stage by Gypsy Esmeralda, crowned King of Fools, and then tied down and pelted by villagers. Esmeralda rescues Quasimodo, but Frollo is not amused. Frollo orders Phoebus, the captain of the guard, to arrest her, but Esmeralda runs into the cathedral and claims sanctuary. Quasimodo and Phoebus team up to rescue Esmeralda, whom Judge Frollo threatens to burn at the stake.

Technically flawless, the music and artistry display gothic spirituality. Inappropriate acts include a dance by Esmeralda and Frollo's lust for Esmeralda. This is a very mature, complex movie about the battle between legalism and grace. *The Hunchback of Notre Dame* has a strong Christian worldview and displays many favorable expressions of God's grace and the church. *The Hunchback of Notre Dame* will delight animation fans, but this may not be a movie for very young children. However, it is a must-see masterpiece for older children and mature audiences, as a testimony to the Truth who offers every person sanctuary.

CONTENT ANALYSIS: (CCC, B, Ab, L, VV, S, O, M) Strong Christian worldview uplifting the inherent value of all mankind with positive reference to God, prayer, the church, resisting temptation, self-sacrifice, and exposing hypocrisy with an undercurrent of anti-nomianism; two mild profanities and several uses of the word "hellfire"; moderate action violence including burning a house, shooting arrows, one arrow strikes man, throwing rocks, breaking open cathedral door, threats of hanging, punching, dropping bricks on attackers, chasing, tripping, horse sits on man, man squishes ants, man tied down and fruit thrown at him, and attempted burning at the stake; shapely woman dances suggestively, kissing, man with shirt off, and man lusts after woman; deception and references to palm reading.

A Plethora of Biblical References

INDEPENDENCE DAY

Quality: ☆☆☆   Acceptability: −1

WARNING CODES:
Language: ***
Violence: **
Sex: *
Nudity: *

RATING: PG-13

GENRE: Science fiction

INTENDED AUDIENCE: Teens and adults

RUNNING TIME: 145 minutes

STARRING: Will Smith, Jeff Goldblum, Bill Pullman, and Mary McDonnell

DIRECTOR: Roland Emmerich

EXECUTIVE PRODUCERS: Roland Emmerich, Ute Emmerich, and William Fay

PRODUCER: Dean Devlin

WRITERS: Dean Devlin and Roland Emmerich

DISTRIBUTOR: 20th Century Fox

BRIEF SUMMARY:

Independence Day is a classic B-movie that draws on the fun, sci-fi movies of the past to weave together a thrilling story. It opens with a large, Star Wars-type spacecraft flying over the American flag on the moon. On earth, the Defense Department tells the president, and a technician named David realizes that aliens are attacking. Eventually the president strikes, but futilely. Meanwhile, the aliens destroy every major city on earth. The president discovers that the CIA has been hiding a captured saucer in New Mexico. David suggests that they upload a computer virus into the mother ship by flying the captured saucer back to the mother ship. He thinks that they can knock out the shields just long enough to allow them to destroy the aliens.

Independence Day is a fun movie. It moves with substantial emotion towards a satisfying climax. Good triumphs over evil, people are married, marriages are restored, prayer is upheld, faith is reclaimed, heroism is extolled, and environmentalism is mocked. Regrettably, the movie is peppered with foul language. Also, there is a brief scene in a strip club, a morning-after scene of a couple in bed, and some violent scenes of the alien in the laboratory. The good outweighs the bad, but the bad could have been jettisoned in space.

CONTENT ANALYSIS: (B, C, LLL, VV, S, N, A, D, M) Moral worldview with Jewish and Christian prayers and positive references to faith, marriage, and family; forty-three obscenities and twenty-two profanities; action violence including frightening scenes of aliens attacking humans as well as air battle sequences and massive damage from explosions and battle sequences; implied fornication; a brief scene in an exotic dance club of girl in halter and G-string; alcohol use; smoking; and deception and government secrets.

Friendship Triumphs

JAMES AND THE GIANT PEACH

Quality: ★★★☆   Acceptability: −1

WARNING CODES:
Language: *
Violence: *
Sex: None
Nudity: None

RATING: PG
GENRE: Animated fantasy
INTENDED AUDIENCE: All ages
RUNNING TIME: 80 minutes
VOICES: Simon Callow, Richard Dreyfuss, Jane Leeves, Joanna Lumley, and Miriam Margolyes
DIRECTOR: Henry Selick
PRODUCERS: Denise Di Novi and Tim Burton
WRITERS: Karey Kirkpatrick, Jonathan Roberts, and Steve Bloom
BASED ON: The novel by Roald Dahl
DISTRIBUTOR: Walt Disney Pictures/Buena Vista
BRIEF SUMMARY:

From the creators of *The Nightmare Before Christmas* comes Disney's *James and the Giant Peach*. Using stop-motion animation, live-action, and computer animation for a seamless mix of pure fantasy, it is a faithful adaptation of the novel by Roald Dahl. The movie starts out with James on an English beach with his parents, where they dream of going to New York City. Suddenly, a rhinoceros-shaped storm cloud charges out, destroying his parents. James goes to live with his two mean aunts, Spiker and Sponge. One day, an old man offers James a bag of magic crocodile tongues, saying they will make his dreams come true. James, excited, trips under a peach tree and spills the bag, and an enormous peach begins to grow. James crawls inside of it and discovers a group of human-sized insects. James and his new friends battle storms, sharks, skeletons, and more as they make their way to New York City.

Technically brilliant, the movie may put some people off by many scary scenes and images. *James and the Giant Peach* is a fairy tale and uses a great deal of magic to create supernatural realities. All good things stem from the grace of God, not from willpower or magic. It is an excellent movie with edge-of-your-seat entertainment. It is visually juicy and sweet, but watch out for the magical pits.

CONTENT ANALYSIS: (B, Pa, L, V, D) Moral worldview of friendship combined with ontological nominalism; two obscenities; mild action violence including scary, mean aunts, falling down stairs, falling down mountain inside of peach, shark attacks peach, shark explodes, stampeding rhinoceros, skeletons attack, and spider spins humans in web; and smoking.

Overcoming Legalism

JANE EYRE

Quality: ☆☆☆☆   Acceptability: −1

WARNING CODES:
  Language: None
  Violence: **
  Sex: None
  Nudity: None
RATING: PG
GENRE: Romance
INTENDED AUDIENCE: Adults
RUNNING TIME: 112 minutes
STARRING: William Hurt, Charlotte Gainsbourg, Joan Plowright, and Anna Paquin
  DIRECTOR: Franco Zeffirelli
  PRODUCER: Dyson Lovell
  EXECUTIVE PRODUCERS: Bob Weinstein and Harvey Weinstein
  WRITERS: Hugh Whitemore and Franco Zeffirelli
  BASED ON: The novel by Charlotte Bronte
  DISTRIBUTOR: Miramax Films/ Buena Vista (Disney)
  BRIEF SUMMARY:
  Franco Zeffirelli, who brought us *Jesus of Nazereth*, now brings us a faithful rendition of Charlotte Bronte's famous romance novel *Jane Eyre*. The film opens with little Jane being mocked by her cousins because Jane's parents died without leaving her an inheritance. She is then mistreated in a charity school, but she grows into a woman with an inner dignity. She gains employment as the governess of Adele, a young girl, at Thornfield Hall. Lord Rochester, the troubled lord of the manor, appreciates Jane's forthrightness and intelligence, but he is being courted by many eligible young women. However, under the stars, he confesses that Jane is the one he loves and asks her to marry him. In time, many unexpected, frightening, and fortuitous events turn Jane's life around.

The movie portrays some Christians as cruel legalists, although there are positive portraits of other Christians, positive references to God, and clear signs of compassion, forgiveness, and love and there is a redemptive element to the story. In the tradition of romance novels, the characters seem slightly contrived and the plot tends toward the melodramatic. Even so, Zeffirelli's superb direction has brought us a captivating movie.

CONTENT ANALYSIS: (Ro, Ab, C, B, VV, M) Romantic worldview with a negative portrait of some Christians, a positive portrait of others, and some positive references to Christianity; mean-spirited treatment of orphaned Jane, severe charity school discipline, man falls from horse, a fire, man attacked in bedroom, bloody wound depicted, woman attacks with knife and with fire, two women fall to death, and man trapped in fire; and insanity, greed, deceit, and cruelty.

Seeking Intimacy, Commitment, and Honesty

JERRY MAGUIRE

Quality: ☆☆☆   Acceptability: −2

WARNING CODES:
  Language: ***
  Violence: *
  Sex: **

Nudity: **
RATING: R
GENRE: Romantic comedy
INTENDED AUDIENCE: Adults
RUNNING TIME: 135 minutes
STARRING: Tom Cruise, Cuba Gooding Jr., Renee Zellweger, Kelly Preston, Jerry O'Connell, Regina King, and Bonnie Hunt
DIRECTOR: Cameron Crowe
PRODUCERS: James L. Brooks, Laurence Mark, Richard Sakai, and Cameron Crowe
WRITER: Cameron Crowe
DISTRIBUTOR: TriStar Pictures/Sony
BRIEF SUMMARY:
Jerry Maguire has it all—a prestigious job at Sports Management International, a gorgeous fiancée, and a large roster of clients. One night he writes a mission statement for his company suggesting a change in policy. He makes a copy for everybody in the company and gets fired. His boss, Bob Sugar, steals all of his clients but one, Rod Tidwell, a great but small wide receiver. Jerry makes an exit from SMI and is joined only by single mother Dorothy Boyd. Jerry eventually loses his fiancée and marries Dorothy, but money is tight and the marriage is rocky. When Rod gets hit hard on the playing field, this setback yields wonderful results both in Jerry's career, Rod's career, and in Jerry's marriage.

This movie tries earnestly to be likable, and most of the time it succeeds. All this sap might be unbearable if it didn't provide fascinating information about the sports world, and if it didn't show the tender and passionate quest of a man who wants to do right. Jerry wants to get away from impersonal relationships and shady deals to intimacy, commitment, and honesty. He loses everything including his fiancée and job, but finds a new and better wife and a smaller but better business. This movie contains many obscenities, some sexual situations, and nudity.

CONTENT ANALYSIS: (B, LLL, V, SS, NN, A, D, M) Moral worldview emphasizing loyalty, honesty, ethical business practices, and upholding marriage; forty-five obscenities and eight profanities; mild violence including woman slapping man and close images of nasty football tackles; briefly depicted fornication, implied fornication, and sensual kissing; briefly depicted full male and full female nudity (no genitalia showing); alcohol use and abuse; smoking; and miscellaneous immorality including unjust firing and stealing clients; and vomiting.

Father Worship

JINGLE ALL THE WAY

Quality: ☆☆☆   Acceptability: −1

WARNING CODES:
Language: *
Violence: *
Sex: None
Nudity: None
RATING: PG
GENRE: Comedy
INTENDED AUDIENCE: All ages
RUNNING TIME: 80 minutes
STARRING: Arnold Schwarzenegger, Sinbad, Phil Hartman, Rita Wilson, Robert Conrad, Jake Lloyd, and Jim Belushi
DIRECTOR: Brian Levant
EXECUTIVE PRODUCER: Richard Vane
PRODUCERS: Chris Columbus, Mark Radcliffe, and Michael Barnathan
WRITER: Randy Kornfield
DISTRIBUTOR: 20th Century Fox
BRIEF SUMMARY:
Fast-paced, *Jingle All the Way* stars Arnold Schwarzenegger as Howard, a workaholic father who ventures out on Christmas Eve to buy Turbo Man. The toy store clerks laugh at him and say the doll hasn't been available since Thanksgiving. Howard meets a crazed mailman named Myron, played by Sinbad, who also wants the doll for his own son. Myron

offers to partner with Howard, but Howard says no. From then on, Myron and Howard go from one escapade to another in search of the toy. Through some daring-do and a last battle against Myron dressed as Turbo Man's arch-villain, Howard is able to come through on promises to his son and wife.

This movie is sometimes over the top, especially with its slapstick violence and sexual innuendo, but is otherwise well executed in every way. The driving force is Howard's quest to fulfill a promise to his son. Another important theme is pre-serving the family, and so adultery is shunned. Regrettably, the movie makes fun of fathers and social virtues. Christians won't mind the fact that the movie mocks Santa Claus, Rudolf, and commercialism, but Howard's son's hero worship is not replaced by faith in Jesus (who is the reason for the season) but by father worship. Furthermore, the humor is based on mockery and satire, not on biblical virtues.

CONTENT ANALYSIS: (B, C, L, V, A, D) Moral worldview where parental responsibility and fatherly love triumph over adulterous advances and child neglect, and positive portrayal of prayer; four obscenities and several overt sexual references; moderate action and mean-spirited slapstick violence including chases, tripping, bomb threat, man punches mean reindeer, and Ninja Santa threatens; alcohol use; and break-ing, entering, stealing, and fraud rebuked.

A Real Action Hero

THE LAST LIEUTENANT

Quality: ★☆☆☆   Acceptability: −1

WARNING CODES:
Language: ***
Violence: **
Sex: **
Nudity: *

RATING: Not rated
GENRE: War drama
INTENDED AUDIENCE: Adults
RUNNING TIME: 102 minutes
LANGUAGE: Norwegian
STARRING: Espen Skjonberg, Lars Andreas Larssen, and Gard B. Eidsvold
DIRECTORS: Hans Petter Moland and Bjorn Sundquist
PRODUCER: Harald Ohrvik
WRITER: Axel Hellstenius
DISTRIBUTOR: Seventh Arts Releasing
BRIEF SUMMARY:
The Last Lieutenant is a work of art from Norway about a commanding sol-dier who resists the Germans during World War II in spite of overwhelming odds. Compassionate, powerful, and deeply moving, it demonstrates a real action hero. This man is Thor Espedal, a sixtyish retired sea captain. In 1940 he hears of an impending invasion by the National Socialist Germans (Nazis) and decides to dust off his uniform to enlist. At the headquarters in Oslo, his superior officers surrender, but Thor won't accept this at all. He flees to high ground, recruits a battalion, and fights. At first successful, German war planes eventu-ally bomb the base. The group disbands as Thor reserves one last moment of defiance towards the enemy.

This movie presents extreme courage and sacrifice. Thor represents an unlikely hero, but his age and wisdom compel him to stand fast in both his principles and methods. He is committed to his cause even when others have lost hope. Like *Braveheart*, *The Last Lieutenant* has a great deal of violence as the Norwegians try to maintain dignity through defeat. Nevertheless, it shows men who don't sit back and watch their country being destroyed, but fight in the face of impos-sible odds in the name of dignity, honor, and freedom.

CONTENT ANALYSIS: (CC, B, LLL, VV, SS, N, M) Biblical worldview of courage and heroism with positive portrayals of the Lord's Prayer; twenty-five obscenities and five profanities; moderate violence with images of war, including shooting, images of corpses, knifing, abduction at gunpoint, bombing, attempted firing squad murder, attempted suicide, and tank runs over man implied; one brief clothed sex scene; upper male nudity; despair and hopeless situations.

The Nature of True Justice

LONE STAR

Quality: ☆☆☆☆   Acceptability: –2

WARNING CODES:

Language: ***
Violence: **
Sex: **
Nudity: None

RATING: R
GENRE: Drama
INTENDED AUDIENCE: Adults
RUNNING TIME: 130 minutes
STARRING: Chris Cooper, Elizabeth Pena, Joe Morton, Ron Canada, Clifton James, Kris Kristofferson, Matthew McConaughey, Miriam Colon, and Frances McDormand
DIRECTOR: John Sayles
EXECUTIVE PRODUCER: John Sloss
PRODUCERS: Maggie Renzi and Paul Miller
WRITER: John Sayles
DISTRIBUTOR: Sony Pictures Classics

BRIEF SUMMARY:
The discovery of Charley Wade's skeleton in the Texas desert begins an investigation into the victim's identity and the identity of his killer in Lone Star. The investigation soon reveals that Charley's death isn't the only skeleton that has been long-buried. Sheriff Charley Wade disappeared one night in 1957. Everyone has long suspected that he was killed by his deputy, Buddy Deeds, who subsequently became sheriff. The discovery of the skeleton leads the present sheriff of Rio country, Buddy's son, Sam, to seek the truth about the incident and about his father. He learns much more than he bargained for, which involves Sam's high school lover and Colonel Delmore Payne.

Lone Star is an engrossing film. Writer-director John Sayles has done a masterful job of keeping the audience's attention while he unravels a complicated storyline with numerous characters, flashbacks, and subplots. The actors are thoroughly convincing, and the production quality is superlative. Kris Kristofferson particularly performs well as the evil Charley Wade. However, viewers should be forewarned that the violence is shocking and graphic, though not gory. The worldview promotes moral relativism, and there are enough objectionable elements to warrant a caution to adults regarding this thought-provoking motion picture. Even so, Lone Star is the most thought-provoking movie of the year. It raises serious questions as to the nature of evil and justice.

CONTENT ANALYSIS: (Pa, B, LLL, VV, SS, A, D, M) Pagan worldview with moral elements; twelve obscenities, thirteen profanities, and seven vulgarities; two cold-blooded murders and violence in bar; fornication depicted and incest; alcohol use; drug abuse implied; and gambling and smuggling people across border.

Crawling, Creeping, or Captivating

MICROCOSMOS

Quality: ☆☆☆☆   Acceptability: +2

WARNING CODES:

Language: None
Violence: *
Sex: None
Nudity: None

RATING: G
GENRE: Documentary

INTENDED AUDIENCE: All ages
RUNNING TIME: 77 minutes
NARRATOR: Kristin Scott Thomas
DIRECTORS: Claude Nuridsany and Marie Pernennou
EXECUTIVE PRODUCERS: Michel Faure, Philippe Gautier, Andre Lazare, and Patrick Lancelot
PRODUCERS: Jacques Perrin, Christophe Barratier, and Yvette Mallet
DISTRIBUTOR: Miramax Films/ Buena Vista (Disney)
BRIEF SUMMARY: As the opening sequences sweep down from blue skies to earth, *Microcosmos* prepares you for a journey of the undiscovered. This documentary of nature's smallest is an exquisite experience of what some bugs do to pass the day away. From busy ants scurrying to harden their anthills to slimy slugs slithering out of their cocoons, the moments are all precious and magnificent. These are the super-stars of this documentary—crawling, creeping, or just plain captivating. They eat their own cocoons, they fight to defend their abode or simply to show who's mightier. They flaunt their gos-samer wings, take night swims, or sim-ply blend into their environment.

With only some minor narration, *Microcosmos* leaves you to enjoy its revela-tions. A brilliant soundtrack and crisp, precise editing combine to make this doc-umentary both witty and eye-opening. In between its loving and roving eye on the bugs of this world, the documentary splashes colors on the screen by showing fields of flowers burst open in splendor. As vines unfurl and raindrops pelt down, their magnification takes hues and shapes unfamiliar to the naked eye. Rated G, but some scenes showing natural laws of sur-vival might have to be explained to very young children. Otherwise, *Microcosmos* is an exhilarating experience in nature.

CONTENT ANALYSIS: (E, V) Environmentalist worldview featuring nature's insect world; some natural vio-lence including natural predatory instincts such as a spider wrapping prey in its web, stag beetles fight it out to a fatal end, and a pheasant kicking and eating bugs; and snail mating.

Deeper Than Physical Attraction

THE MIRROR HAS TWO FACES

Quality: ☆☆☆☆   Acceptability: –2

WARNING CODES:
  Language: *
  Violence: None
  Sex: ***
  Nudity: None
RATING: R
GENRE: Romantic comedy
INTENDED AUDIENCE: Adults
RUNNING TIME: 126 minutes
STARRING: Barbra Streisand, Jeff Bridges, Pierce Brosnan, George Segal, Mimi Rogers, Brenda Vaccaro, and Lauren Bacall
DIRECTOR: Barbra Streisand
EXECUTIVE PRODUCER: Cis Corman
PRODUCERS: Barbra Streisand and Arnon Milchan
WRITER: Richard LaGravenese
DISTRIBUTOR: TriStar Pictures/ Sony
BRIEF SUMMARY:
In *The Mirror Has Two Faces,* Rose Morgan, played by Barbra Streisand, longs for passion and romantic love. Her life becomes intertwined with fellow Columbia University professor Gregory Larkin, who theorizes that male-female liaisons should be founded on common goals and companionship rather than on physical attraction. Based on this practi-cal approach, he persuades Rose to marry him. The characters find that their per-sonality traits balance each other, and Rose helps Gregory in the classroom. The complications grow, however, when Rose can't fight her romantic feelings for

Gregory anymore. When she undergoes a major change, he is thrown completely off balance and must determine whether companionship is enough for a successful marriage.

The movie touchingly portrays relationships with all their awkwardness, vulnerability, and complexity. Ms. Streisand does a superb job both in front of and behind the camera. Unfortunately, the movie feeds the frequently held belief that finding the right person and falling passionately in love will bring true happiness, rather than basing happiness on a relationship with God. Sex is mentioned throughout the movie, and marriage is, for the most part, portrayed negatively. Negative religious references also are included. Despite these concerns, the movie shows that successful relationships can be based on qualities deeper than physical attraction.

CONTENT ANALYSIS: (Ro, Ho, L, SSS, A, D, M) Romantic worldview where passionate love is portrayed as the source of happiness; two profanities, five obscenities, two vulgarities, and one blasphemy; extensive references to sex including adultery and a lesbian orgy dream, phone sex portrayed, adultery depicted, sexless marriage depicted including husband rejecting sexual advances from wife, body kissing, and fondling between husband and wife; alcohol use and drunkenness; references to Valium and smoking; and lying and references to homosexuality.

Saved by the Bible

MISSION IMPOSSIBLE

Quality: ☆☆☆☆   Acceptability: −1

WARNING CODES:
  Language: ***
  Violence: **
  Sex: None
  Nudity: None
RATING: PG-13
GENRE: Action/Adventure

INTENDED AUDIENCE: Teens and adults
RUNNING TIME: 110 minutes
STARRING: Tom Cruise, Jon Voight, Henry Czerny, Emmanuelle Beart, Jean Reno, and Vanessa Redgrave
DIRECTOR: Brian De Palma
EXECUTIVE PRODUCER: Paul Hitchcock
PRODUCERS: Tom Cruise and Paul Wagner
WRITERS: David Koepp and Stephen Zaillian
BASED ON: The TV series created by Bruce Geller
WRITERS: David Koepp and Robert Towne
DISTRIBUTOR: Paramount Pictures
BRIEF SUMMARY:
Mission Impossible, the movie, opens with the MI team trying to flush out a scoundrel who is trying to steal a list of all the classified CIA undercover agents in Eastern Europe. In the process, several of the Mission Impossible team lose their lives and we find out that Ethan Hunt has been pegged as the possible mole in the heart of the intelligence community. Ethan knows that he is not, but he must find a way to vindicate himself. He decides to steal the list of covert agents by teaming up with other agents who have been disavowed. Hot on Cruise's tail is Kittridge, the top man at Mission Impossible. Through brain, brawn, and the Bible, Ethan outwits his adversaries and flushes out the real mole in an exciting finale.

Mission Impossible is well written, well produced, and well directed. The movie forgoes any sex, and the violence is pure action adventure. The movie moves quickly and keeps you on the edge of your seat. It relies to a large degree on the cleverness of the situation and the audience trying to figure out who is a good guy, who is a bad guy, and whether the whole thing isn't just one big sting operation. The major flaw in the film is an excess of profanity, although there are several positive references to God and the Bible. Tom Cruise has produced an intriguing spy thriller.

CONTENT ANALYSIS: (B, C, LLL, VV, A, D, M) Moral worldview where truth wins out, Scripture is quoted, and the Bible saves the hero in a unique way; twenty-three obscenities and eleven profanities; action violence where the actual bloody event is not shown, but the consequences of stabbings, shootings, and explosions are shown in a mild way; many life-threatening, cliff-hanger-type scenes where the person survives; drinking; smoking; and lying, deception, and fraud.

Righteous Humor

MUPPET TREASURE ISLAND

Quality: ☆☆☆   Acceptability: +3

WARNING CODES:
  Language: None
  Violence: *
  Sex: None
  Nudity: None
RATING: G
GENRE: Fantasy
INTENDED AUDIENCE: All ages
RUNNING TIME: 95 minutes
STARRING: Tim Curry, Kevin Bishop, and Billy Connolly
VOICES: Frank Oz, Dave Goelz, and Steve Whitmire
DIRECTOR: Brian Henson
EXECUTIVE PRODUCER: Frank Oz
PRODUCERS: Martin G. Baker and Brian Henson
WRITERS: Jerry Juhl and Kirk R. Thatcher
DISTRIBUTOR: Walt Disney Pictures/Buena Vista
BRIEF SUMMARY:
Muppet Treasure Island is another rollicking Muppet adventure that makes fun use of all the Muppet characters. The story follows the outline of Robert Louis Stevenson's classic tale. Opening at the isolated Benbow Inn, Jim Hawkins, Gonzo, and Rizzo attempt to serve the seedy group of pirates and cutthroats. One customer, Billy Bones, keeps blathering about a hidden treasure. When Billy expires, he gives Jim Captain Flint's famous treasure map. As pirates destroy the inn, Jim, Gonzo, and Rizzo escape to find Squire Trelawney (Fozzie Bear). The squire grants them one of his ships, captained by Mr. Smollett (Kermit the Frog), so they can find the treasure. Unbeknownst to our heroes, the cook is none other than Long John Silver. Long John's evil ways are revealed when they arrive at Treasure Island. After harrowing adventures, Jim and the crew are saved by their wits and the help of a jungle goddess, played by Miss Piggy.

As in many Muppet adventures, this movie contains positive references to prayer, God, and the Bible. In fact, it has a stirring, though humorous, sermon by Long John Silver condemning blasphemy. There is no real violence, but there is lots of adventure and slapstick comedy. Children will love this friendly adventure that will instruct them in good virtues, teamwork, and the value of love.

CONTENT ANALYSIS: (C, V, M) Christian worldview lifting up prayer and the Bible and presenting love as the answer to all problems; slapstick violence that is clearly not intended to hurt anyone, although some of the Muppet characters get bent out of shape; and skeletons and eerie settings.

Love Will Overcome

ONCE UPON A TIME . . . WHEN WE WERE COLORED

Quality: ☆☆☆   Acceptability: +2

WARNING CODES:
  Language: *
  Violence: *
  Sex: *

Nudity: None

RATING: PG

GENRE: Historical drama

INTENDED AUDIENCE: All ages

RUNNING TIME: 110 minutes

STARRING: Al Freeman Jr., Phylicia Rashad, Leon, Paula Kelly, Bernie Casey, Isaac Hayes, Polly Bergen, and Richard Roundtree

DIRECTOR: Tim Reid

EXECUTIVE PRODUCER: Butch Lewis

PRODUCERS: Michael Bennett and Tim Reid

WRITER: Paul W. Cooper

BASED ON: The novel by Clifton Taulbert

DISTRIBUTOR: Republic Pictures

BRIEF SUMMARY:

Once Upon a Time ... When We Were Colored, based upon the critically acclaimed book, chronicles the early life of its author Clifton Taulbert in Glen Allen, Mississippi. In the deep South in the 1950s and early 1960s, education means segregation. Clifton's first formal lesson from Poppa Taulbert at age five is to learn to recognize what a *W* and a *C* look like, so he can tell the difference between such things as restrooms and water fountains that are for "Whites only" and those that are for the "Colored." He quickly learns the difference between tolerance and intolerance by comparing what he understands from his close-knit community with the racial intolerance he experiences on the other side of the railroad tracks.

We too have a learning experience as we watch the swelling tide that led to the civil rights movement. Production quality is generally fine in this independent movie directed by Tim Reid and starring a cast of excellent actors. The producers did a fine job of creating the look and feel of the era. This movie is worth seeing, as it contains only moderately questionable elements while it promotes Christianity, family loyalty, personal responsibility, and a biblical worldview.

CONTENT ANALYSIS: (B, C, L, V, S, A, M) Moral biblical worldview with positive references to God and many positive depictions of Christianity; positive portrayals of community; six vulgarities (mostly use of the *N* word in reference to blacks); KKK parade, seductive fondling and dancing results in a juke joint fight involving a razor, broken bottle, and a baseball bat as weapons; implied fornication; boys ogle women dancing in carnival girlie show; alcohol consumption in juke joint; boy steals money but promises to pay it back; and birth of baby in cotton fields.

God Answers Prayer

THE PREACHER'S WIFE

Quality: ☆☆☆☆   Acceptability: +3

WARNING CODES:

Language: *

Violence: None

Sex: None

Nudity: None

RATING: PG

GENRE: Drama

INTENDED AUDIENCE: All ages

STARRING: Denzel Washington, Whitney Houston, Courtney B. Vance, Gregory Hines, Jennifer Lewis, and Loretta Devine

DIRECTOR: Penny Marshall

EXECUTIVE PRODUCERS: Penny Marshall, Elliott Abbott, and Robert Greenhut

PRODUCER: Samuel Goldwyn Jr.

WRITERS: Natalie Maulden and Allan Scott

BASED ON: The movie *The Bishop's Wife*

DISTRIBUTOR: Touchstone Pictures/Walt Disney Company/Buena Vista

BRIEF SUMMARY:

In *The Preacher's Wife*, Henry Biggs, the pastor of a run-down, inner-city church, is burned out. He has given everything he has in service to God. The last straw is that a greedy developer, Joe Hamilton, has bought the mortgage on the church and wants to turn it into a mall. In desperation, Henry utters one last prayer to God. Suddenly the angel Dudley, played by Denzel Washington, falls out of heaven. The good-natured but sometimes inept Dudley attempts to help, and eventually, he gets everyone to do their part. However, the big question is, "Will Joe Hamilton destroy the church and will this be Henry's last Christmas sermon?"

A remake of *The Bishop's Wife*, this superb movie contains winsome dialogue, strong theological references to Jesus Christ; the Christmas story told in Bible readings, song, and drama; constant references to God; biblical references to the church holding the neighborhood together, rebuking temptation, upholding the law of God, honoring marriage, commending prayer, lifting up salvation, and extolling forgiveness. It is flawed only by the *It's a Wonderful Life*-type angel explanation, but this is counterbalanced by clear references to God's law and grace. Movies don't get much better than this one. It is an emotional roller coaster that leads us to confront the true meaning of faith and love.

CONTENT ANALYSIS: (CCC, B, L, A, D, FR, M) Very strong Christian worldview with many references to God, including songs about Jesus, pictures of Jesus, the Christmas story, and prayer to Jesus, temptation rebuked, greed rebuked, marriage upheld, prayer commended, slightly flawed by the *Wonderful Life*-type angel who was a deceased man who comes back as an angel in answer to a prayer; one use of the word "hell," and several appeals to God; smoking rebuked; some drinking; and a quick robbery scene.

Every Parent's Worst Nightmare

RANSOM

Quality: ☆☆☆☆   Acceptability: −2

WARNING CODES:
Language: ***
Violence: ***
Sex: *
Nudity: None

RATING: R
GENRE: Thriller
INTENDED AUDIENCE: Adults
STARRING: Mel Gibson, Rene Russo, Brawley Nolte, Gary Sinise, Delroy Lindo, and Lili Taylor
DIRECTOR: Ron Howard
PRODUCERS: Scott Rudin, Brian Grazer, and B. Kipling Hagopian
WRITER: Alex Ignon
DISTRIBUTOR: Touchstone Pictures/Buena Vista (Disney)
BRIEF SUMMARY:

In *Ransom*, Tom Mullen has reached the pinnacle of success. He has built a small charter airlines company into an aviation empire. He seems to be a nice guy who lives in a beautiful New York City penthouse with his beautiful wife and his son, Sean. When Sean is kidnapped, we find out that Tom has enemies. These kidnappers are every parent's worst nightmare. One is a cop, who is driven by envy to destroy Tom. The FBI seems impotent in their attempts to help Tom. At first Tom goes along with the kidnapper's demands. Then he decides to stand up to the kidnapper and offers the ransom to anyone who will find the kidnapper and turn him in to the police. A roller coaster of intense brutality and emotion brings us to a surprising climax.

While suspenseful and action packed, the movie is filled with obscenities and profanities, not only from the villain, but from the heroes. Tom finally realizes he has to do what is right. Both he and his wife come to the point where they cry out to God. The direction is taut and tense. The violence is bloody.

CONTENT ANALYSIS: (B, C, LLL, VVV, S, A, D, M) Moral worldview of standing up to evil with several prayers for God's help; 108 obscenities and 23 profanities, mostly emotional appeals to

God; extreme violence including kidnapping, hitting, bloody bullet wounds, falling through glass, being hit by a car, and threats of violence; one bedroom scene cutaway; drinking; smoking; and kidnapping and deceit.

Seeking Retribution

THE ROCK

Quality: ☆☆☆   Acceptability: −2

WARNING CODES:
  Language: ***
  Violence: ***
  Sex: *
  Nudity: None
RATING: R
GENRE: Action/Adventure
INTENDED AUDIENCE: Adults
STARRING: Nicolas Cage, Ed Harris, Sean Connery, and William Forsythe
  DIRECTOR: Michael Bay
  EXECUTIVE PRODUCERS: William Stuart, Sean Connery, and Louis A. Stroller
  PRODUCERS: Don Simpson and Jerry Bruckheimer
  WRITERS: David Weisberg, Douglas S. Cook, and Mark Rosner
  DISTRIBUTOR: Hollywood Pictures/Walt Disney Company/Buena Vista
  BRIEF SUMMARY:
  In *The Rock,* Marine general Francis X. Hummel seeks retribution for men who died in secret operations. Seeking one hundred million dollars from the U.S. Government, General Hummel steals fifteen VX gas rockets and takes eighty-one prisoners on Alcatraz Island. He threatens to fire three toxic rockets on San Francisco unless his demands are met. The United States refuses to netogotiate, and two plans are developed. Plan A involves sending a team of Navy SEALS along with a chemical weapons expert, Stanley Goodspeed, and an Alcatraz escapee,

Patrick Mason, to deactivate the missiles. If Plan A is not successful, the military will resort to Plan B, which involves incinerating the island. Through a series of mishaps, the president orders Plan B. Now Goodspeed and Mason must defend themselves against Hummel and disarm all three rockets before they are all blown to bits.

The Rock is an entertaining action movie and moves along with nail-biting suspense and nonstop action. Nevertheless, there exists an enormous chasm of believability. This is pure escapism and any attempt to justify the events and characters as anything but cogs in an entertainment vehicle is futile. During the mission, many lives are lost through various means. Furthermore, both the good guys and the bad guys use foul language.

CONTENT ANALYSIS: (Pa, LLL, VVV, S, A, D, M) Pagan worldview of man seeking justice through vengeance; ninety obscenities and fifteen profanities; extreme violence including man killed by breaking neck, man shot with rocket out of window, two men killed by poison gas where their faces melt, man impaled on pipe, terrorist threats, and extensive machine gunfire resulting in twelve deaths; briefly depicted sex scene; alcohol use; and smoking.

Emotional Healing

SHINE

Quality: ☆☆☆☆   Acceptability: −1

WARNING CODES:
  Language: *
  Violence: *
  Sex: *
  Nudity: *
RATING: PG-13
GENRE: Drama
INTENDED AUDIENCE: Adults
RUNNING TIME: 100 minutes
STARRING: Armin Mueller-Stahl,

Noah Taylor, Geoffrey Rush, Lynn Redgrave, and John Gielgud
DIRECTOR: Scott Hicks
PRODUCER: Jane Scott
WRITER: Jan Sardi
DISTRIBUTOR: Fine Line Features
BRIEF SUMMARY:
Shine is based on the life of David Helfgott, an exceptionally talented boy who is pushed relentlessly by his father, Elias, to be a better pianist than anyone else. Elias forces all David's family to be musicians and denies them any freedom to make decisions for themselves. David competes in music competitions and begins to win recognition, but when he is offered an opportunity to study in the United States, his father denies him this chance. Instead, David accepts a music scholarship to an English university, even though it means being utterly disowned by his father. Later, David plays a concert with such indescribable passion that it results in David suffering a brain seizure. The remainder of the film concerns David's journey back to emotional healing and success.

Sin bears consequences, and we see that Elias, as well as David, suffer immensely for his treatment and rejection of his son. Yet, years afterward, Elias returns to acknowledge David. Add to these a positive portrayal of Judaism and secondary characters who act kindly toward David, even during his lowest moments, and you have a very uplifting theatrical experience. There are two scenes of violence upon David by his father that are quite scary. There is a brief scene of seminude dancers and two shots of male rear nudity in a nonsexual connotation. *Shine* is not a Christian film by any means, but is good filmmaking and a moral film that honors the human spirit.

CONTENT ANALYSIS: (BB, O, L, V, S, N, A, D) Moral worldview tainted by one character consulting an astrological chart; one obscenity; two depictions of child abuse with fists and wet towel; brief depiction of clothed sexual petting; brief image of seminude female dancers and two instances of naturalistic rear male nudity; alcohol use; and smoking.

Talent Is a Gift

SPACE JAM

Quality: ☆☆☆☆   Acceptability: +1

WARNING CODES:
  Language: *
  Violence: *
  Sex: None
  Nudity: None
RATING: PG
GENRE: Fantasy
INTENDED AUDIENCE: All ages
RUNNING TIME: 85 minutes
STARRING: Michael Jordan, Bugs Bunny, Wayne Knight, and Theresa Randle
DIRECTOR: Joe Pytka
EXECUTIVE PRODUCERS: David Falk and Ken Ross
PRODUCER: Ivan Reitman
WRITERS: Leo Benvenuti, Steve Rudnick, Timothy Harris, and Herschel Weingrod
DISTRIBUTOR: Warner Brothers
BRIEF SUMMARY:
Director Joe Pytka takes the wacky relationship between humans and "toons" to Moron Mountain, an outer space amusement park run by an overbearing boss. The boss finds that attendance is dropping off so he sends his little aliens to earth to capture the Looney Toon characters. Needless to say, Bugs Bunny is not going to be hauled away into space so easily. He challenges the little aliens to a basketball game, only to find out that they have the power to steal the talent and size of the top players in the NBA. The toons are distressed until they draft Michael Jordan to play against this MonStar squad from outer space. With the survival of toon-town at

stake, this ultimate game is waged by Michael Jordan and his friends.

Space Jam is a fast-paced, fun movie. Sometimes the pacing is so fast that you don't have time to enjoy the humor. It is punctuated by prayers and a church scene, and marred by an all-too-believable séance scene. Even so, this is a good-natured movie that stays away from the scatological humor that one would expect from this loony crowd.

CONTENT ANALYSIS: (B, O, L, V, M) Moral worldview with prayer and church scenes marred by brief, comic séance scene; seven uses of the word "butt" as well as two other mild vulgarities and a few mild vulgar animation sequences; slapstick violence but nothing extreme; and monster basketball.

Incarnational Allegory

THE SPITFIRE GRILL

Quality: ☆☆☆☆   Acceptability: –1

WARNING CODES:
  Language: **
  Violence: *
  Sex: *
  Nudity: None
RATING: PG-13
GENRE: Drama
INTENDED AUDIENCE: Older teens and adults
STARRING: Alison Elliott, Ellen Burstyn, Marcia Gay Harden, and Will Patton
DIRECTOR: Lee David Zlotoff
EXECUTIVE PRODUCER: Warren G. Stitt
PRODUCER: Forrest Murray
WRITER: Lee David Zlotoff
DISTRIBUTOR: Castle Rock Entertainment
BRIEF SUMMARY:
In *The Spitfire Grill*, Percy Talbot seeks healing from a painful past in Gilead, Maine. She finds friendship, mystery, confidence, and potential romance at the grill run by Hannah Ferguson. Throughout the movie, several characters demonstrate their need for healing and restoration. The movie has some positive moral attributes regarding friendship and church as a place of quiet reflection. *Spitfire Grill* is an emotive, Christian allegory, full of biblical analogies in the manner of sacramental and incarnational theology.

The movie is well acted and the plot is engrossing. The scenery of the movie, shot in Northeast Vermont, adds a touch of splendor to the production. Containing mild violence, mild foul language, and references to abuse, caution is advised for younger teenagers and children. Financed by a Roman Catholic order, *The Spitfire Grill* won the Sundance Film Festival Audience Award. When some Sundance organizers found out the movie was financed by a Christian group, they became very upset, although it is clear that the order kept the movie as low-keyed and allegorical as possible to avoid appearing too religious. It is refreshing to note that this movie, despite naysayers, has drawn an audience and has presented them with a redemptive story. We hope that it will sow seeds of redemption in the hearts of those who see it.

CONTENT ANALYSIS: (CC, B, Pa, LL, V, S, A, D, M) Christian worldview focusing on forgiveness, sacrifice, and welcoming the stranger, as well as the healing and restoration that comes from forgiveness, as demonstrated through circumstance and human interaction with positive reference to church and some minor references to American Indian lore; four profanities, twelve obscenities, one vulgarity, mild criticism of spouse, reference in church to the heroine's past history of child abuse, rape by stepfather, reference to pregnancy, and baby's death, off-color remarks, and gossiping rebuked; mild violence including slap during an argument, handling of guns and reference to murder with a razor; alcohol and reference to drunkenness; smoking; and incarceration portrayed and reference to solitary confinement.

Self-Sacrifice

STAR TREK: FIRST CONTACT

Quality: ✰✰✰✰   Acceptability: –1

WARNING CODES:
  Language: *
  Violence: **
  Sex: *
  Nudity: None
RATING: PG-13
GENRE: Science fiction
INTENDED AUDIENCE: Teens and adults
RUNNING TIME: 110 minutes
STARRING: Patrick Stewart, Jonathan Frakes, Brent Spiner, LeVar Burton, Michael Dorn, Gates McFadden, Marina Sirtis, Alfre Woodard, and James Cromwell
DIRECTOR: Jonathan Frakes
EXECUTIVE PRODUCER: Martin Hornstein
PRODUCER: Rick Berman
WRITERS: Brannon Braga and Ronald D. Moore
BASED ON: The TV series created by Gene Roddenberry
DISTRIBUTOR: Paramount Pictures
BRIEF SUMMARY:
Star Trek: First Contact is the eighth movie based on the popular TV series. Captain Picard and the crew of the Enterprise discover that the evil cyber-villains, the Borg, have entered Federation Space. The Enterprise blows up their ship, but a Borg contingent goes back in time to destroy a missile complex base on earth. The base holds a scientist and his rocket ship, which will lead to "first contact"—the first meeting between humans and beings from another planet. This meeting ultimately yields the birth of the United Federation of Planets. If the Borg succeed, they can alter the future and erase their enemies. If they lose, the future of mankind is saved.

This movie has all the elements that you would expect from a Star Trek movie—great ensemble acting, special effects, horrible villains, and philosophical themes. The goal of the Borg is to assimilate all life-forms into their own through brainwashing and cyber-fication. They all think the same and individuals are non-existent. Their worldview is similar to Communism, and the movie has anti-Communism themes. Star Trek: First Contact has violence, scary situations, and some foul language. This movie serves as a suitable launching pad for future film projects by the Next Generation crew.

CONTENT ANALYSIS: (B, AC, L, VV, S, A, M) Moral worldview extolling teamwork and self-sacrifice and rebuking revenge and Communism; seven obscenities and two exclamatory profanities; moderate violence including explosions, laser gunfire, threats with knives, and mass destruction of starships; mild sexual suggestiveness; alcohol use and drunkenness; and kidnapping.

The Responsibility of Fame

THAT THING YOU DO

Quality: ✰✰✰✰   Acceptability: +1

WARNING CODES:
  Language: **
  Violence: None
  Sex: None
  Nudity: None
RATING: PG
GENRE: Comedy
INTENDED AUDIENCE: Older children to adults
RUNNING TIME: 105 minutes
STARRING: Tom Everett Scott, Liv Tyler, Johnathon Schaech, Steve Zahn, Ethan Embry, Charlize Theron, and Tom Hanks
DIRECTOR: Tom Hanks

PRODUCERS: Gary Goetzman, Jonathan Demme, and Edward Saxon

WRITER: Tom Hanks

DISTRIBUTOR: 20th Century Fox

BRIEF SUMMARY:

That Thing You Do, written and directed by Tom Hanks, documents the rise of a fictional band, The Wonders, from Erie, Pennsylvania. It shows the excitement and challenges of being in a band when rock was young. Guy Patterson quits the long hours at his family business and joins Jimmy, Lenny, and the nameless bass player to form The Wonders. Winning a local talent contest, they become popular around Erie. They meet manager Mr. White, played by Tom Hanks, who represents Play-Tone records. With Mr. White's savvy skills, The Wonders rise to the top of the charts and gain a TV appearance in Hollywood. Will they go on to greater success or will they be a one-hit wonder?

Tom Hanks does not disappoint. His affable style, affection for the period, and wily sense of humor pervades this exceptionally well-produced movie. The greatest theme of this movie is the struggle between creative talent and possessive, power-hungry recording companies. The worldview of this movie is mildly Christian. Churchgoing, serving the church, and not working on Sunday are featured. *That Thing You Do* is only marred by a few obscenities and profanities.

CONTENT ANALYSIS: (C, LL, A, D, Ab, M) Mild Christian worldview with capitalistic elements; seven obscenities and three exclamatory profanities; alcohol use; smoking; and a mild jab at a Youth for Christ rally and mild rebellion themes.

Brotherly Love

A TIME TO KILL

Quality: ☆☆☆☆   Acceptability: −2

WARNING CODES:

Language: ***

Violence: ***

Sex: None

Nudity: None

RATING: R

GENRE: Drama

INTENDED AUDIENCE: Older teens and adults

STARRING: Sandra Bullock, Samuel L. Jackson, Matthew McConaughey, Kevin Spacey, and Donald Sutherland

DIRECTOR: Joel Schumacher

PRODUCERS: Arnon Milchan, John Grisham, and Hunt Lowry

WRITER: Akiva Goldsman

BASED ON: The novel by John Grisham

DISTRIBUTOR: Warner Brothers

BRIEF SUMMARY:

A Time to Kill is a carefully crafted attempt at surgically removing the cancer of racism. It is the story of Carl Lee Hailey, a father whose young daughter is cruelly attacked by two drunk white men out to harass the black community. It is also the story of a young lawyer, Jake Brigance, who defends Hailey after he murders these white rapists in the courthouse. Around this courtroom drama swirls a tornado of racist passions. On one side is the KKK, reestablished in the wake of Carl Lee's vigilante justice. On the other side are the NAACP and the black church, who are trying to use the case for their own purposes. We soon learn that all men are sinners, including Jake, who took this case at the expense of all of his loved ones.

Novelist John Grisham's faith is the foundation of this story, but there are those in the film who misuse and abuse this faith and the film seems to condone vigilantism as it plumbs the depths of racism. The movie doesn't deal with the fact that Jesus died for our sins, but it has moments of forgiveness. Regrettably, the violence is raw, though not exploited. The language is rough, but Jesus' name is not misused. *A Time to Kill* contains something to upset everyone, and yet at its core it tells us that we are all called to love our brothers.

CONTENT ANALYSIS: (C, LLL, VVV, A, D, M) Christian worldview that examines the issues of man's law, God's law and grace, and includes negative portraits of black and white individuals and groups that try to use Christianity for their own purposes; forty-one obscenities and four profanities; extreme violence including an off-camera rape of little girl, shootings, clubbing, hangings, torching, a man burns in his clan outfit, a woman is hung from a post to die, houses burn, man is beaten up, man is knifed, woman is beaten up, woman's blouse is torn off; and a man has to remove pants for medical treatment; alcohol use; smoking; and racism including cross burning, deceit, and misuse of funds.

Mass Destruction

TWISTER

Quality: ☆☆☆   Acceptability: −1

WARNING CODES:
  Language: ***
  Violence: **
  Sex: None
  Nudity: None
RATING: PG-13
GENRE: Thriller
INTENDED AUDIENCE: Families
RUNNING TIME: 116 minutes
STARRING: Helen Hunt, Bill Paxton, Jami Gertz, and Cary Elwes
DIRECTOR: Jan De Bont
PRODUCERS: Kathleen Kennedy, Ian Bryce, and Michael Crichton
WRITERS: Michael Crichton and Anne-Marie Martin
DISTRIBUTORS: Warner Brothers and Universal Pictures
BRIEF SUMMARY:
In *Twister,* Jo Harding and her crew of young scientists live to chase down unpredictable tornadoes so they can develop the scientific tools to better predict these destructive forces. Jo's estranged husband, meteorologist Bill Harding, tries to get Jo to sign their divorce papers so he can marry Melissa, and ends up joining in one last chase. Soon, the conniving Dr. Jonas Miller throws down a challenge to Jo and Bill to get to the big one first. Jo's team and Dr. Miller's team just miss several opportunities to use their tracking devices. When the big one finally comes, mass destruction ensues.

The special-effects team has created a sense of doom, but the direction fails to achieve a frightening edge. Perhaps this is because, unlike the animal villains of *Jaws* and *Jurrasic Park,* who were consciously seeking their human prey, tornadoes cannot will themselves to pursue the hero and heroine. The most disturbing aspect of the movie is that our hero, Bill, constantly takes the Lord's name in vain. Few parents want their children mouthing these words. Regrettably, *Twister* suffers from structural and credibility problems, but those who like disaster movies may find some merit in it.

CONTENT ANALYSIS: (Pa, R, LLL, VV, A, D, M) Pagan worldview with Romantic elements; thirty-one obscenities, eighteen profanities, and three vulgarities; extensive violence from tornadoes including houses, trucks, cars, and cattle laid waste with loss of life, man sucked up into tornado, fighting, and shoving; alcohol; and smoking.

Honesty Prevails

THE WHITE BALLOON

Quality: ☆☆☆☆   Acceptability: +3

WARNING CODES:
  Language: None
  Violence: None
  Sex: None
  Nudity: None
RATING: Not rated

GENRE: Comedy/Drama
INTENDED AUDIENCE: All ages
RUNNING TIME: 85 minutes
LANGUAGE: Persian
STARRING: Alda Mohammadkhani, Mohsen Kalifi, Fereshteh Sadr Orfani, Anna Bourkowska, Mohammad Shahani, and Mohammad Bahktiari
DIRECTOR: Jafar Panahi
PRODUCER: Jafar Panahi
WRITER: Abbas Kiarostami
DISTRIBUTOR: October Films
BRIEF SUMMARY:
The White Balloon is the story of a seven-year-old girl named Razieh, who wants a new goldfish. The one she likes dances in its bowl and is fatter than the one she has at home. It is the eve of a New Year in Teheran, and a goldfish is symbolic of the celebrations. She cajoles her mother into giving her the money, with strict instructions to bring home the change. Along the way to the goldfish shop, Razieh is distracted by a couple of snake charmers and would have lost her money to them, but with her sheer determination she demands her money back. To a curious little girl like Razieh, the fascinations of the city are many and, distracted again, she drops the money into an iron grate. Razieh enlists the help of many interesting characters to retrieve the money, spelling real charm and allure.

The director's keen eye and feel for his characters capture their nuances and gestures. There is not a mean bone in this story. It does have a dishonest boy and dishonest snake charmers. Otherwise, *The White Balloon* has a strong moral, family, and community sense, where kindliness and honesty prevail. The film's innocence is as refreshing and alluring as the wide-eyed innocence of little Razieh. With no strong language, violence, sex, or nudity, *The White Balloon* is simply charming.

CONTENT ANALYSIS: (B, M) Moral worldview focusing on family and a caring community; two small incidences where a young boy lies about wanting goldfish for his mother, but sells them and snake charmers discuss cheating a young girl.

Ferocious Storm

WHITE SQUALL

Quality: ☆☆☆☆   Acceptability: −2

WARNING CODES:
  Language: ***
  Violence: **
  Sex: *
  Nudity: *
RATING: PG-13
GENRE: Action/Adventure
INTENDED AUDIENCE: Teens and adults
RUNNING TIME: 130 minutes
STARRING: Jeff Bridges, Caroline Goodall, John Savage, and Scott Wolf
DIRECTOR: Ridley Scott
EXECUTIVE PRODUCER: Ridley Scott
PRODUCERS: Mimi Polk Gitlin and Rocky Lang
WRITER: Todd Robinson
DISTRIBUTOR: Hollywood Pictures/Buena Vista (Disney)
BRIEF SUMMARY:
White Squall is a tour de force of drama, action, and cinematography. Narrated by Chuck Gieg, it is the story of the square-rigged brigantine, the *Albatross*. In the fall of 1960, thirteen select young men were admitted as students aboard the vessel in the Ocean Academy. On this craft, not only would they learn reading, writing, and arithmetic, but they would also become united as a crew, each contributing to the spit and polish of a worthy seafaring vessel. Helming the ship is Sheldon or "Skipper" (played by the able Jeff Bridges). He is a no-nonsense captain that doesn't tolerate slackers or phobias. As these men travel through the Caribbean and the South Pacific, each

faces certain challenges such as fear of heights, sexual awareness, relationship with parents, and, most of all, a ferocious storm, or white squall.

This is a very entertaining and well-crafted movie. Every performance is believable, and each young man clearly defines his character. Each shot is saturated with color and well-thought-out composition. This movie shows real-life heroism and friendship. The audience will ride a fantastic, if sometimes scary, voyage. It is a powerful coming-of-age story that regrettably has some violence, bad language, and sexual themes.

CONTENT ANALYSIS: (H, B, LLL, VV, S, N, A, D, M) Humanist worldview with moral elements of courage, commitment, service, and sacrifice; nineteen obscenities and six profanities; urination and vomiting; moderate violence including wrestling, fighting, threats, man shoots dolphin and man clubs dolphin, shipwreck with casualties, injuries and implied drowning; one attempted sexual encounter with prostitute, one implied act of fornication, and some sexual talk; extensive upper-male natural nudity; alcohol use; smoking; and cheating and lying.

☆☆☆ THE BEST 1996 FILMS FOR FAMILIES ☆☆☆

Headline	Title
God Answers Prayer	*The Preacher's Wife*
God's Love Prevails	*The Hunchback of Notre Dame*
Rescued from Evil	*101 Dalmations*
Love One Another	*Harriet the Spy*
Talent Is a Gift	*Space Jam*
Honesty Prevails	*The White Balloon*
Righteous Humor	*Muppet Treasure Island*
The Responsibility of Reality	*The Adventures of Pinocchio*
Teamwork, Honesty, and Self-Sacrifice	*D3: The Mighty Ducks*
Friendship Triumphs	*James and the Giant Peach*

☆☆☆ THE BEST 1996 FILMS FOR MATURE AUDIENCES ☆☆☆

Headline	Title
Love Will Overcome	*Once Upon a Time ... When We Were Colored*
Saved by the Bible	*Mission Impossible*
Incarnational Allegory	*The Spitfire Grill*
Rejoice in All Circumstances	*Cold Comfort Farm*
Brotherly Love	*A Time to Kill*
Lest We Forget History	*Anne Frank Remembered*
Self-Sacrifice	*Star Trek: First Contact*
Noble Responsibilities	*Emma*
A Plethora of Biblical References	*Independence Day*
The Responsibility of Fame	*That Thing You Do*

☆☆☆ THE TWENTY MOST UNBEARABLE FILMS OF 1996 ☆☆☆

Headline	Title
Worst Attempt to Teach Children Witchcraft	*The Craft*
Worst Attempt at Sexploitation	*Striptease*
Worst Blasphemous Sequel	*John Carpenter's Escape from LA*
Worst Propaganda for Perversion	*The Birdcage*
Worst Attempt to Peddle Obscenity as Free Speech	*The People vs. Larry Flint*
Worst Lesbian Violence	*Bound*
Worst Mix of Occultism, Sex, and Violence	*Tales from the Crypt Presents Bordello of Blood*
Worst Hood Movie	*Phat Beach*
Worst Politically Correct Sarcasm	*The Last Supper*
Worst Marxist Blather	*The Crucible*
Worst Homosexual Propaganda	*The Celluloid Closet*
Worst Gangster Movie	*The Funeral*
Worst Anti-Family Movie	*The Stupids*
Worst Sexual Predators	*Stealing Beauty*
Worst Comic-Book Sexploitation	*Barb Wire*
Worst Remake	*The Island of Dr. Moreau*
Worst Import	*Little Indian, Big City*
Worst Comedy	*The Nutty Professor*
Worst Voyeurism	*Breaking the Waves*
Worst Anti-Catholic Bigotry	*The Glimmer Man*

They Found Each Other at Church

AIR BUD

Quality: ☆☆☆☆   Acceptability: +2

WARNING CODES:
  Language: *
  Violence: *
  Sex: None
  Nudity: None

RATING: PG
GENRE: Comedy
INTENDED AUDIENCE: All ages
RUNNING TIME: 98 minutes
STARRING: Kevin Zegers, Wendy Makkena, Michael Jeter, Bill Cobbs, and Eric Christmas
DIRECTOR: Charles Martin Smith
PRODUCERS: Robert Vince and William Vince
EXECUTIVE PRODUCERS: Michael Strange and Anne Vince
WRITERS: Paul Tamasy and Aaron Mendelsohn
DISTRIBUTOR: Walt Disney Pictures/Buena Vista Pictures Distribution
BRIEF SUMMARY:

In *Air Bud*, a basketball-shooting golden retriever inspires his boy owner and his high school basketball team to win the state championship. *Air Bud* opens with Mrs. Framm arriving with her withdrawn twelve-year-old son, Josh, and young daughter in a small Washington town where she hopes to rebuild their lives following the untimely death of her husband. Coming home from school, Josh discovers Buddy, a golden retriever who has run away from his abusive master, Norm Snively. Josh adopts him as a pet. Through hard work, Josh makes the school basketball team. When they discover Buddy's uncanny ability to accurately shoot a basketball, the team makes him their mascot. Buddy's antics inspire them and draw the attention of his former owner, who tries to exploit Buddy's newly discovered talent for TV commercials. Josh rescues Buddy from Snively and sets the dog free, just in time to rally the team in the state championship game.

A family film in the best sense, *Air Bud* provides parents with several scenes to use in discussing good family values with their children: selflessness, teamwork, hard work, good stewardship, and family togetherness. With a charming canine lead, *Air Bud* is a worthwhile movie that richly rewards the family who views it together. This surprising, thoroughly winsome comedy with genuine emotion boasts a likable cast and strong moral values, with almost no objectionable elements.

CONTENT ANALYSIS: (B, C, L, V, A, M) Biblical worldview promoting teamwork, sacrifice, family, and joyful living with triumph over selfishness, self-aggrandizement, and winning at all costs; three profanities; implied animal abuse; alcoholism; and miscellaneous immorality including man insults boy, boy destroys property in slapstick comedy, and boy steals dog to rescue him from abusive owner.

Willing to Risk One's Life for Others

AIR FORCE ONE

Quality: ☆☆☆☆   Acceptability: −2

WARNING CODES:
  Language: * * *
  Violence: * * *

Sex: None
Nudity: None

RATING: R
GENRE: Action/Adventure
INTENDED AUDIENCE: Adults
RUNNING TIME: 118 minutes
STARRING: Harrison Ford, Gary
Oldman, and Glenn Close
DIRECTOR: Wolfgang Petersen
PRODUCERS: Wolfgang Petersen
and Gail Katz
EXECUTIVE PRODUCERS: Thomas
A. Bliss, Marc Abraham, and David
Lester
WRITER: Andrew W. Marlowe
DISTRIBUTOR: Columbia Pic-
tures/Sony Pictures Entertainment
BRIEF SUMMARY:

In *Air Force One*, the president of the
United States, James Marshall (Harrison
Ford), must personally combat a group of
Russian terrorists who hijack Air Force
One. Faking his own escape in Air Force
One's escape pod, President James
Marshall personally takes on the terrorists
one by one in the jet cargo hold. They capture him and threaten to execute his
daughter unless he calls the Russian president to demand that he release the murderous, reactionary General Radek from a
grim Russian prison cell. The movie ends
with extravagant pyrotechnic explosions,
a spectacular rescue, and a plane crash.

Air Force One is Harrison Ford's tour
de force as an actor playing a heroic persona. It probably represents the pinnacle
of his long career in such notable films as
Indiana Jones, Star Wars, and *The Fugitive.*
Even though it is improbable that the
Secret Service would let Russian terrorists
with fake identifications board the president's jet, *Air Force One* delivers an
engrossing story, with moments of white-
knuckle tension and an emotionally satisfying conclusion. With a creative premise,
riveting acting by Harrison Ford, good
music and dialogue, and excellent cinematography, *Air Force One* has superlative production value. The movie also
upholds patriotism, with the president as

soldier-hero. However, beware of the
many killings.

CONTENT ANALYSIS: (BB, LLL,
VVV, A, M) Moral biblical worldview of
a president who is willing to sacrifice
himself for others, with strong biblical
and patriotic elements; eighteen obscenities and fourteen profanities (mainly
exclamatory); thirty killings by machine
gun, man attacks man with knife, man
strangles man, man threatens woman
with pistol to her head, and man falls
out of airplane without parachute; alcohol; and betrayal of the president.

The Gospel Gem Within

AMISTAD

Quality: ☆☆☆☆   Acceptability: −2

WARNING CODES:
  Language: None
  Violence: * * *
  Sex: None
  Nudity: * *

RATING: R
GENRE: Historical drama
INTENDED AUDIENCE: Adults
RUNNING TIME: 154 minutes
STARRING: Djimon Hounsou,
Morgan Freeman, Anthony Hopkins,
Matthew McConaughey, Nigel
Hawthorne, and Peter Postlethwaite
DIRECTOR: Steven Spielberg
PRODUCERS: Steven Spielberg,
Debbie Allen, and Colin Wilson
EXECUTIVE PRODUCERS: Walter
Parkes and Laurie MacDonald
WRITER: David Franzoni
DISTRIBUTOR: DreamWorks Pictures
BRIEF SUMMARY:

Amistad is a moving and uplifting,
but at times violent, true story of heroes
battling overwhelming odds to win
their freedom. It tells the true story of a
group of Africans who, in 1839, revolt
against the masters of a Spanish slave
ship, *La Amistad*, but are imprisoned in
Connecticut after being captured by the

U.S. Navy. The leader of the revolt, Cinque, and the other Africans are put on trial for murder. Eventually the case reaches the U.S. Supreme Court, where former President John Quincy Adams (Anthony Hopkins) delivers a stirring closing argument.

Director Steven Spielberg handles this morality tale with his usual flair and includes a powerful depiction of the life, death, resurrection, and ascension of Jesus Christ. The Christ story gives hope and comfort to two of the embattled Africans. Viewers should be warned, however, that although the film contains no obscenities or profanities, it does include glimpses of female and male nudity, some terrible violence, and a minor reference to ancestor worship. On the other hand, *Amistad* contains a rare historical balance. *Amistad* is an excellent and quietly powerful movie.

CONTENT ANALYSIS: (BB, CC, P, Pa, NN, VVV) Moral worldview with strong Christian elements including a positive depiction of the life, death, resurrection, and ascension of Jesus Christ, plus a patriotic speech that regrettably includes a diluted reference to ancestor worship; naturalistic male and female nudity; and extensive violence during scenes on slave ships (one group of Africans is graphically drowned; two African men are whipped; slave traders beat men, women, and children; brutal fight between Africans and slave traders where one slave-trading Spaniard's throat is cut, another Spaniard has sword thrust through his belly, and several Africans are stabbed, shot, or punched).

Demonic Attack and Answered Prayer

ANASTASIA

Quality: ☆☆☆☆   Acceptability: +1

WARNING CODES:
Language: None
Violence: *
Sex: *

Nudity: None
RATING: G
GENRE: Animated historical fantasy
INTENDED AUDIENCE: All ages
RUNNING TIME: 94 minutes
VOICES: Meg Ryan, John Cusack, Kelsey Grammer, Christopher Lloyd, Hank Azaria, Bernadette Peters, and Kirsten Dunst
DIRECTORS: Don Bluth and Gary Goldman
PRODUCERS: Don Bluth and Gary Goldman
EXECUTIVE PRODUCER: Maureen Donley
WRITERS: Susan Gauthier, Bruce Graham, Bob Tzudiker, and Noni White
BASED ON: The play by Marcelle Maurette
DISTRIBUTOR: 20th Century Fox
BRIEF SUMMARY:
Anastasia is the romantic story of the lone surviving heir to the Romanov throne who is searching for her family, which was destroyed by the evil Rasputin at the start of the Russian Revolution. *Anastasia* opens with the Czar's mother, the dowager empress, telling the audience how wonderful life was for the royal Romanov family before the evil Rasputin entered the imperial court. At a ball, the empress gives Anastasia a music box with a key that says, "Together in Paris." Rasputin enters and curses the Czar. The Russian Revolution follows, and the kitchen boy, Dimitri, saves the empress and Anastasia. In the confusion, Anastasia is separated from her grandmother. Ten years later, Anya emerges from an orphanage. When Dimitri sees Anya, he thinks he has found an Anastasia look-alike who can help him claim the reward offered by the empress. Meanwhile, Rasputin heads back to Earth from Limbo to kill Anastasia. The story comes to a climax when the empress, Anastasia, and Dimitri realize the truth about love and family.

Don Bluth, who gave us *An American Tale*, has produced a superb animated film. The historical side of *Anastasia* enhances the romance and will leave many viewers a little teary-eyed. Regrettably, the movie has some scenes that are too frightening for little children. There is no mention of God in the movie to balance the evil, supernatural Rasputin. *Anastasia* is magnificent entertainment that parents and children can enjoy if parents help their children develop discernment.

CONTENT ANALYSIS: (Ro, C, V, S, A, D, M) Romantic worldview with some answered prayer and redemptive elements; some intense animated violence including battles with Rasputin, demons attack a train, and a final battle with Rasputin and a demonic horse; frightening grotesqueries including Rasputin losing his body parts in Limbo (which caused a little girl in the screening audience to cry); some very mild sexual innuendo; alcohol use; and lying and cheating.

The Woes of Adultery

ANNA KARENINA

Quality: ☆☆☆   Acceptability: −2

WARNING CODES:
  Language: None
  Violence: * *
  Sex: * *
  Nudity: * *
RATING: R
GENRE: Epic drama
INTENDED AUDIENCE: Adults
RUNNING TIME: 110 minutes
STARRING: Sophie Marceau, Sean Bean, Alfred Molina, Mia Kirshner, and James Fox
  DIRECTOR: Bernard Rose
  PRODUCER: Bruce Davey
  EXECUTIVE PRODUCER: Stephen McEveety
  WRITER: Bernard Rose

BASED ON: The novel by Leo Tolstoy
DISTRIBUTOR: Warner Brothers
BRIEF SUMMARY:
The latest film rendition of Leo Tolstoy's *Anna Karenina* has great scope and captures the essence of the novel, but fails to achieve the emotional high of the 1935 Greta Garbo classic. The movie opens with Levin proposing to Kitty, but she is enamored with Count Vronsky and declines Levin's offer of marriage. When the count sees Anna Karenina, he feels lust at first sight. Count Vronsky pursues Anna, eventually winning her sexual favors and destroying her marriage. Levin eventually wins Kitty to be his wife and finds God. Anna and the count's affair ends in disaster.

This movie is an extremely strong statement against adultery, but it drags the audience through the adulterous gutter to get to the point. It also ends on a very clear Christian note, extolling prayer, confessing to God, asking God for forgiveness, and seeking the truth that can be found only in faith in Jesus Christ. Along the way, however, there is fornication, nudity, suicide, violence, and pain. The flaw is that the work tries to capture too much of Tolstoy's story and therefore loses some of the book's emotional intensity. Furthermore, the adultery could have been portrayed off-screen, and the movie would have been just as powerful.

CONTENT ANALYSIS: (CCC, Ab, VV, SS, NN, A, D) Strong Christian worldview illustrating the battle between romantic philosophy and Christianity, showing that the wages of adultery is death, though marred by some anti-biblical and anti-Christian comments; discreet but moderate violence such as man being hit by train, woman diving under train, a bloody scene of a wounded horse being shot, birth scene, and man playing Russian roulette with gun; adultery, fornication, and aftermath of army orgy with long shot of soldiers entangled with women; rear male nudity, upper and rear female nudity, and suggestive clothing; drinking; and smoking and opium use.

God's Grace

THE APOSTLE

Quality: ★★★☆   Acceptability: +1

WARNING CODES:

Language: *
Violence: * *
Sex: *
Nudity: None

RATING: PG-13

GENRE: Drama

INTENDED AUDIENCE: Teens and adults

RUNNING TIME: 148 minutes

STARRING: Robert Duvall, Farrah Fawcett, Miranda Richardson, Todd Allen, John Beasley, June Carter Cash, Billy Bob Thornton, Walt Goggins, and Billy Joe Shaver

DIRECTOR: Robert Duvall

PRODUCERS: Robert Carliner and Steven Brown

EXECUTIVE PRODUCER: Robert Duvall

WRITER: Robert Duvall

DISTRIBUTOR: October Films Release

BRIEF SUMMARY:

The Apostle is an affirmative portrait of Christians and evangelism. Robert Duvall is the lead actor, director, producer, and writer for this movie about a preacher coming to terms with his own sins. When Pentecostal preacher Sonny Dewey's wife, Jessie, leaves him for a young preacher named Horace, Sonny loses control and hits Horace with a baseball bat. Sonny runs to a small town in Louisiana, where he starts a new church and dubs himself the "Apostle." Even so, Sonny knows the law will catch up with him. Ever faithful to God, Sonny knows that in his frailties he will continue to work for God wherever he is.

God is clearly the hero in *The Apostle*, which shakes and shouts the glory of God. Robert Duvall spares very little in portraying the passions and earnestness of God-loving people. The movie contains a positive affirmation of the Christian faith and a strong Christian worldview. There are, however, touches of human weaknesses: Sonny's arrogance and violence; and Jessie's adultery and revenge. Also, Sonny exhibits few signs of repentance. These characteristics show that man is fallible and that all grace is from God. Duvall's performance is engaging and moving. *The Apostle* is one of the few films that trumpets the power and grace of God and portrays a vivid portrait of sawdust trail Pentecostalism.

CONTENT ANALYSIS: (B, CCC, L, VV, S, M) Redemptive Christian worldview with intense evangelical and Pentecostal elements glorifying Jesus, acknowledging him as Savior, encouraging church attendance, sermons, hymn singing, and extensive praising of God, marred by fallen preacher theme and little repentance; five vulgarities and two profanities; some violence including a car accident, a minister hitting a man with a bat, punching a man in a fistfight, and man pushes wife and pulls her hair; an implied adulterous sexual situation; and miscellaneous immorality involving running away from the law, arrogance, a violent temper, marital breakdown, and separation.

Remnant Theology

BATMAN AND ROBIN

Quality: ★★★☆   Acceptability: −1

WARNING CODES:

Language: *
Violence: * * *
Sex: *
Nudity: None

RATING: PG-13

GENRE: Fantasy

INTENDED AUDIENCE: Teens and adults

STARRING: George Clooney, Chris O'Donnell, Arnold Schwarzenegger, Uma Thurman, and Alicia Silverstone

DIRECTOR: Joel Schumacher

EXECUTIVE PRODUCERS: Benjamin Melniker and Michael E. Uslan

PRODUCER: Peter MacGregor-Scott

WRITER: Akiva Goldsman

BASED ON: The comic book by Bob Kane

DISTRIBUTOR: Warner Brothers

BRIEF SUMMARY:

Batman and Robin is a leather-clad morality tale set in a dark retro-futuristic world. In this fourth cinematic outing, Batman fights Mr. Freeze, who accidentally changed his molecular structure so that he could only survive at freezing temperatures. Meanwhile, a female environmentalist in the jungle gets turned into a human plant known as Poison Ivy. She heads to Gotham City to tell Bruce Wayne that he has to clean up the environment, or else. Also, Barbara, the niece of Wayne's butler Alfred, comes to Wayne Manor emotionally scarred by the accidental deaths of her parents. With the stage set, Batman, Robin, and Barbara (becoming Batgirl) battle Poison Ivy and Mr. Freeze over Gotham City.

The stylish direction, intelligent dialogue, powerful action, and excellent special effects keep us emotionally involved throughout all the illogical twists and turns in this movie. By now, parents should be well aware that the Batman series is dark. In spite of this, the movie contains almost no obscene language and many moral messages. Batman and Robin discuss the need to support and trust each other and are interested in preserving law and order. They are opposed by a psychotic environmentalist and the loony biochemist. Batman tells Mr. Freeze that he must not avenge the death of his wife because vengeance will only destroy him.

The movie is opposed to political correctness: Alfred feels honored to be able to serve Mr. Wayne; Barbara says she wants to be called "Batgirl," even though Batman tells her that it isn't politically correct; and Batman tells Poison Ivy that people are more important than plants. For those who like allegory, the remnant theology of Batman, Robin, and Alfred's redemptive presence in the midst of a dark, fallen world will give them much to discuss. There is a lot of action violence, but few deaths. However, there are some frightening scenes that make this movie inappropriate for young children.

CONTENT ANALYSIS: (BB, C, L, VVV, S, M) Moral and redemptive worldview in the midst of a dark, fallen world; four mild expletives; constant bloodless, comic-book violence with people frozen, beaten, tossed around, falling from buildings, and crashing through cars and buildings, and many special effects situations; lots of sexual innuendo, especially from Poison Ivy— most of it too sophisticated for children to understand; many moral messages; and many dark, bizarre images.

Hope and Courage

CATS DON'T DANCE

Quality: ☆☆☆☆   Acceptability: +2

WARNING CODES:
  Language: None
  Violence: *
  Sex: None
  Nudity: None

RATING: G

GENRE: Animated musical

INTENDED AUDIENCE: Children

RUNNING TIME: 70 minutes

VOICES: Scott Bakula, Jasmine Guy, Natalie Cole, George Kennedy, Hal Holbrook, Rene Auberjonois, John Rhys-Davies, Kathy Najimy, Betty Lou Gerson, and Don Knotts

DIRECTOR: Mark Dindal

PRODUCERS: David Kirschner and Paul Gertz

EXECUTIVE PRODUCERS: David Steinberg, Charles L. Richardson, and Sandy Russell Gartin

WRITERS: Robert Gannaway, Cliff Ruby, Elana Lesser, and Theresa Pettengill

DISTRIBUTOR: Turner Feature Animation

BRIEF SUMMARY:

Cats Don't Dance is a funny, musical cartoon send-up of 1930s Hollywood, featuring a motley crew of animal acto-wanna-bes. They are dismayed to learn that they are not able to fulfill their dreams because the movie studios will only accept human actors and actresses. Led by Danny, a cat from Kokomo, the animals overcome the mean-spirited scheming of Darla, the spoiled starlet. After a series of adventures and musical numbers, the animals improvise an audition for the big boss, Mr. Mammoth, and gain their much-deserved fame.

Cats Don't Dance tells the inside story of the entertainment industry. With great animation, good music, funny yet stereotyped characters, and a basically moral message, *Cats Don't Dance* makes a fun afternoon matinee. However, it must be noted that the positive moral message is somewhat diminished by several instances of seeking revenge. Furthermore, the romantic theme of *Cats Don't Dance* teaches that one will be happy by doing what one loves most. Of course, this self-centered approach to happiness will only end in despair. If one really wants to be happy, one must do what God wants, which he makes very clear in his written Word. However, given this discretionary caution, this is a fun animated musical.

CONTENT ANALYSIS: (Ro, B, V, M) Romantic worldview with a strong moral message; cartoon action violence; and revenge.

Uncovering True Lies

CONSPIRACY THEORY

Quality: ★★★☆   Acceptability: −1

WARNING CODES:

 Language: * *
 Violence: * *
 Sex: None
 Nudity: None

RATING: R

GENRE: Thriller

INTENDED AUDIENCE: Older teens and adults

RUNNING TIME: 135 minutes

STARRING: Mel Gibson, Julia Roberts, and Patrick Stewart

DIRECTOR: Richard Donner

PRODUCERS: Joel Silver and Richard Donner

EXECUTIVE PRODUCER: Jim Van Wyck

WRITER: Brian Helgeland

DISTRIBUTOR: Warner Brothers

BRIEF SUMMARY:

Featuring a top-notch, energetic cast and slick photography, *Conspiracy Theory* contends that the government secretly trains assassins with unethical drug and shock therapy, ultimately yielding an engaging, satisfying yarn. In *Conspiracy Theory*, Mel Gibson plays Jerry Fletcher, a New York cab driver who spouts off wild conspiracy theories to his customers. Also, he tries to protect the lovely Alice Sutton, played by Julia Roberts, who works for the Justice Department. Troubles arise when he announces in his newsletter that the government secretly trains assassins with unethical drug and shock therapy. Jerry is abducted and interrogated by Dr. Jonas. Jerry escapes, but he and Alice must flee from the conspirators posing as the CIA and FBI.

The filmmakers have added enough of a comic touch to the movie to let us know that they are not taking themselves too seriously. Gibson delivers a tour de force character who balances over-the-edge dementia with intelligence and an endearing sweetness and chivalry. *Conspiracy Theory* mixes a variety of movie metaphors, styles, and genres, openly borrowing from and paying tribute to the likes of John Frankenheimer's *The Manchurian Candidate* and Alfred Hitchcock's *The Man Who Knew Too Much.* Although *Conspiracy Theory* offers no real exposé of the one-world cabal, a small percentage of the viewers may be encouraged to dig deeper. The movie represents a tense, intelligent, and largely moral viewing experience with little foul language, no sex, and no nudity.

CONTENT ANALYSIS: (BB, Ro, LL, VV, D, M) Moral worldview of covert government experimentation with moral elements; nine obscenities and three profanities; moderate violence including shooting, torture, man bites man's nose, man falls down stairs, abduction, and punching; smoking; alcohol use; and miscellaneous immorality including corrupt government officials, brainwashing, and paranoia.

Redemptive Moments

THE EDGE

Quality: ☆☆☆☆   Acceptability: –1

WARNING CODES:
Language: None
Violence: *
Sex: None
Nudity: None
RATING: R
GENRE: Action/Drama
INTENDED AUDIENCE: Adults
RUNNING TIME: 117 minutes
STARRING: Anthony Hopkins, Alec Baldwin, Elle Macpherson, and Harold Perrineau
DIRECTOR: Lee Tamahori
PRODUCER: Art Linson
EXECUTIVE PRODUCER: Lloyd Phillips

WRITER: David Mamet
DISTRIBUTOR: 20th Century Fox
BRIEF SUMMARY:

In an era of high concept movies, it is a joy to come across *The Edge*, a brilliant piece of directing, writing, and acting. *The Edge* tells the story of a brilliant but unimaginative billionaire bookworm named Charles, played by Anthony Hopkins, who is stranded in the Alaskan wilderness with a photographer who wants his wife and his money. His wife, Mickey, is a young fashion model who drags him to Alaska to celebrate his birthday. Leaving his wife at a lodge, Charles flies with fashion photographer Bob into the wilderness. The small plane is hit by migrating geese and crashes into a frigid lake. The pilot dies, and Bob, Charles, and Bob's assistant, Steve, are faced with the need to survive. Stalked by a man-eating bear that kills Steve, they must find a way back to civilization. When Bob tries to kill him, Charles manifests real grace, and Bob eventually manifests repentance.

This is a magnificently photographed film. It contains tons of action and emotion, and yet it retains writer David Mamet's characteristic deft portraits of human nature. Regrettably, an excessive number of exclamations, profanities, and obscenities are uttered at the most violent moments, but beneath the language this is a movie devoid of explicit sex or pornoviolence. This movie finds the best in people and redemptive moments that are rare in Hollywood filmmaking.

CONTENT ANALYSIS: (CC, LLL, V, A, D, M) Redemptive worldview; forty-five obscenities and nine profanities; action violence including plane crash, several bear attacks, man cuts himself with a hunting knife by mistake, man falls into bear trap, spike goes through man's leg, and other nature movie-type violent incidents; alcohol use; smoking; and deceit and fraud.

Most Vapid Reduction of Faith

CONTACT

Quality: ☆☆☆☆   Acceptability: −2

WARNING CODES:
Language: **
Violence: *
Sex: *
Nudity: **

RATING: PG-13
GENRE: Science fiction
INTENDED AUDIENCE: Older teens and adults
RUNNING TIME: 120 minutes
STARRING: Jodie Foster, Matthew McConaughey, John Hurt, James Woods, Tom Skerritt, David Morse, Rob Lowe, and Angela Bassett
DIRECTOR: Robert Zemeckis
PRODUCERS: Robert Zemeckis and Steve Starkey
EXECUTIVE PRODUCERS: Joan Bradshaw and Lynda Obst
WRITERS: James V. Hart and Michael Goldenberg
BASED ON: The novel by Carl Sagan
DISTRIBUTOR: Warner Brothers
BRIEF SUMMARY:
Contact will give pseudo-intellectuals much food for thought while it disappoints the average moviegoer and offends Christians. Ellie Arroway, played by Jodie Foster, was taught how to use a ham radio by her father. As a Harvard-trained radio astronomer, Ellie's mission in life is searching for extraterrestrials. Her nemesis, Dr. Drummel, seems intent on thwarting her. Just when all seems lost, she detects a signal coming from the Vega system at the center of the universe. Thus, she battles it out with Dr. Drummel to see who will get to travel to Vega to meet the aliens, who turn out to be a letdown.

According to Carl Sagan's materialistic vision, salvation is not from God coming to earth to give us eternal life but from aliens telling us that there are other aliens out there. This small vision is at the heart of *Contact*. This film could have been redeemed if it had been devoid of Christian bashing, sex, and foul language. In the movie, Jodie Foster seems anguished while Matthew McConaughey seems too mellow. The movie is materialist drivel, crying out for true faith and a real God. *Contact* could be advertised as "Forrest Gump's sister meets L. Ron Hubbard."

CONTENT ANALYSIS: (E, AC, C, LL, V, NN, S, A, D, M) Evolutionary, scientific materialism worldview with many scenes bashing Christians, although a major character purportedly represents a man of faith; thirteen obscenities and six profanities; violent trips through the imagined wormholes of space and a deadly explosion; upper female and upper male nudity; implied fornication; alcohol use; smoking; and fraud.

Standing Up to Bad Cops

COP LAND

Quality: ☆☆☆☆   Acceptability: −2

WARNING CODES:
Language: * * *
Violence: * *
Sex: None
Nudity: None

RATING: R
GENRE: Detective
INTENDED AUDIENCE: Adults
RUNNING TIME: 105 minutes
STARRING: Sylvester Stallone, Harvey Keitel, Ray Liotta, Robert De Niro, Peter Berg, Janeane Garofalo, Robert Patrick, and Michael Rapaport
DIRECTOR: James Mangold
PRODUCERS: Cary Woods, Cathy Konrad, and Ezra Swerdlow
EXECUTIVE PRODUCERS: Bob Weinstein, Harvey Weinstein, and Meryl Poster

WRITER: James Mangold
DISTRIBUTOR: Miramax Films
BRIEF SUMMARY:
Cop Land opens as NYPD officer Murray Babitch accidentally kills two black drivers on the George Washington Memorial Bridge. Fearing police brutality charges, Murray's uncle Ray Donlan concocts a plan implying that Murray committed suicide. Across the water in Garrison, New Jersey, local sheriff Freddy Heflin, played by Sylvester Stallone, spends his days in quiet desperation. A man who wanted to be in the NYPD, he lost eligibility when, years ago, he lost his hearing in one ear. Freddy overlooks the antics of the many New York policemen that keep their homes in Garrison. What really happened to Babitch attracts internal affairs investigator Moe Tilden, played by Robert De Niro. Now the small-town sheriff and big-city investigator join forces to expose the corruption, while endangering their own lives and betraying their friends.

Cop Land is an ambitious, energetic, and engaging morality tale of police corruption, lost hopes, and courageous actions. Stallone portrays a humanity that hasn't been seen from him since *Rocky*. Although violent and containing rough language, this movie contains many commendable moral elements including fighting evil and prayer. *Cop Land* also confronts the differences between childhood dreams and adult realities. *Cop Land* may be criticized for its simplistic good-guys-bad-guys plot, but in these morally confused times its very simplicity endears us to its story.

CONTENT ANALYSIS: (C, B, LLL, VV, A, D, M) Mild Christian worldview recognizing Christ and prayer, with many moral elements including sacrifice and doing the right thing in the face of incredible obstacles; sixty-seven obscenities and six profanities; brief but brutal violence including car crash, shooting, threats with gun, fistfighting, attempted forced drowning, implied arson, image of burn victim, man shot in ear, and man falls to death; alcohol use; smoking; and miscellaneous immorality including major themes of police corruption and lying.

Get Me to the Church on Time

FLUBBER

Quality: ☆☆☆☆   Acceptability: +1

WARNING CODES:
  Language: *
  Violence: *
  Sex: None
  Nudity: *
RATING: PG
GENRE: Fantasy/Comedy
INTENDED AUDIENCE: All ages
RUNNING TIME: 90 minutes
STARRING: Robin Williams, Marcia Gay Harden, Christopher McDonald, and Raymond Barry
DIRECTOR: Les Mayfield
PRODUCERS: John Hughes and Ricardo Mestres
EXECUTIVE PRODUCER: David Nicksay
WRITERS: John Hughes and Bill Walsh
DISTRIBUTOR: Walt Disney Pictures/Buena Vista Pictures Distribution
BRIEF SUMMARY:
In *Flubber,* Robin Williams stars as Professor Philip Brainard, a professor who creates an animated, energy-filled compound that just may be the answer to the financial troubles of Medfield College where he teaches. Brainard has forgotten two dates to marry his sweetheart, Sara, the president of the financially troubled school. Evil financier Chester Hoenicker bankrolls Medfield College and plans to pull the money so he can take over the school. On their next wedding day, Phil invents Flubber, a green, morphable mass that even

seems alive. When Sara realizes that Phil has stood her up again, she tells him it is over. Phil tries to win back Sara by showing her the Flubber, but she is unimpressed. Chester discovers that Phil has made a financially promising discovery and sends some goons to steal Flubber. Phil and Sara jump into his Flubber-powered flying car and undertake a frantic Flubber-recovery plan.

Children will enjoy the special effects and the mayhem that results when Flubber flies out of control, although they may get bored at the beginning of the movie, which takes at least twenty minutes to set up the characters. Adults will like *Flubber* because it is a safe picture. Christian marriage is extolled, fornication is discouraged, and hard work is demonstrated. Objectionable material is minor, including a scatological reference and action violence.

CONTENT ANALYSIS: (CC, Ro, L, V, N, M) Moderate Christian, moral worldview where Christian marriage is extolled, fornication is rebuked, sacrifice and hard work are rewarded, and evil is brought to justice, with a romantic subplot; two profanities; action slapstick violence, including man hit by golf ball, man hit with bowling ball, lots of Flubber flying around and breaking things, man falls out of window unharmed, woman punches man, robot hits man, man hits robot, and explosions; upper male nudity and implied nude modeling; and some minor miscellaneous immorality including man accidentally swallowing Flubber, which is excreted comically, a dishonest practice by man, and man becomes too attached to his own creations.

Life Reevaluation

FOR RICHER OR POORER

Quality: ☆☆☆☆   Acceptability: −1

WARNING CODES:
Language: * * *
Violence: *
Sex: None
Nudity: None
RATING: PG
GENRE: Comedy
INTENDED AUDIENCE: Teens and adults
RUNNING TIME: 114 minutes
STARRING: Tim Allen, Kirstie Alley, Jay O. Sanders, Michael Lerner, and Wayne Knight
DIRECTOR: Bryan Spicer
PRODUCERS: Sid Sheinberg, Bill Sheinberg, and Jon Sheinberg
EXECUTIVE PRODUCERS: Richard Baker, Rick Messina, and Gayle Fraser-Baigelman
WRITERS: Jana Howington and Steve LuKanic
DISTRIBUTOR: Universal Pictures
BRIEF SUMMARY:
Combining slapstick violence, a big helping of *Witness*, and some biblical morality, *For Richer or Poorer* is another Tim Allen silver screen comedy. Brad and Caroline Sexton have wealth and power, but their marriage is troubled. When their accountant lies about their finances, the IRS comes after Brad and Caroline. Fleeing the IRS, they stumble into an Amish community. There they decide to pose as an Amish couple until they can solve their problems. As they live with the Amish, they learn the true meaning of life and struggle with their feelings toward each other.

For Richer or Poorer has plenty of farm-life slapstick comedy. The humor never makes fun of the Amish, just the Sextons' response to them. The movie is well executed. The biblical worldview is evident in prayer, forgiveness, marital reconciliation, reaping-what-you-sow, repentance, willingness to pay the consequences for one's actions, and self-sacrifice. The movie is marred by excessive foul language, but mainly for comic response. This is not a light comedy for the whole family but a redemptive message about the importance of marriage.

CONTENT ANALYSIS: (C, B, LLL, V, A, D, M) Mild Christian worldview with prayer, forgiveness, marital reconciliation, reaping-what-you-sow, repentance for dishonesty, willingness to pay the consequences for actions, and self-sacrifice elements; twenty-seven obscenities, ten profanities, and seventeen vulgarities; slapstick violence including shooting, car chases, and crashes; marital sex implied by a squeaking bed noise; alcohol use; smoking; and car theft.

High-Stakes Urban Adventure

THE GAME

Quality: ☆☆☆☆   Acceptability: −2

WARNING CODES:
   Language: * * *
   Violence: * *
   Sex: *
   Nudity: *
RATING: R
GENRE: Thriller
INTENDED AUDIENCE: Adults
RUNNING TIME: 128 minutes
STARRING: Michael Douglas, Sean Penn, Deborah Kara Unger, James Rebhorn, Carroll Baker, Peter Donat, and Armin Mueller-Stahl
   DIRECTOR: David Fincher
   PRODUCERS: Steve Golin and Cean Chaffin
   WRITERS: John Brancato and Michael Ferris
   DISTRIBUTOR: Polygram Filmed Entertainment
BRIEF SUMMARY:
In *The Game*, Michael Douglas plays the highly successful businessman Nicholas Van Orton, who thinks that all is going wrong in a high-tech, high-concept adventure game given to him by his brother, Conrad, played by Sean Penn. When he plays the game, Nicholas experiences a series of trials that unravel his ordered life. His rich clothes are ruined.

His home is defaced. He is drugged, robbed, and left for dead in Mexico. Finally he learns that all his money has been stolen from all his accounts. Nicholas believes the leaders of the game are nothing more than a front for a huge scam operation. Finally, when Nicholas believes that he has turned the tables on the game organizers, a series of surprise events shows him that the game was designed to teach him what he needed to learn: humility, humanity, and a contrite heart.

Like *Seven*, also directed by David Fincher, this movie is dark, terrifying, and goes through a series of tragedies ultimately closing in on a shocking and surprising ending. Unlike *Seven*, the film concludes, not with death, but with lessons learned and lives intact. The game serves as a series of trials resulting in Nicholas learning life's most important lesson—that to truly live life, you need to die to self and learn to value others more than yourself. The severity of such a game is very disturbing. The employees of the game impose some very serious and potentially dangerous pressure on Nicholas. Stylistically, the movie is only flawed by a few slow moments between the different trials facing Nicholas. In every other respect, the movie is well constructed and executed. This adults-only thriller earns its R-rating through attempted violence and foul language.

   CONTENT ANALYSIS: (B, CC, LLL, VV, S, N, A, D, M) Moral worldview with strong redemptive elements including a man learning humility and forgiveness; thirty-two obscenities and five profanities; moderate action violence including chases, dog bites, car crashes into water, shooting without deaths, and threats with gun; brief images of pornographic video on television; woman in underwear; alcohol use; smoking and images of cocaine; and miscellaneous immorality including implied suicide in the past and attempted suicide.

Another Kind of Swinger

GEORGE OF THE JUNGLE

Quality: ☆☆☆☆   Acceptability: −1

WARNING CODES:
  Language: * *
  Violence: * *
  Sex: * *
  Nudity: *
RATING: PG
GENRE: Romantic comedy
INTENDED AUDIENCE: All ages
RUNNING TIME: 91 minutes
STARRING: Brendan Fraser, Leslie Mann, John Cleese, and Thomas Haden Church
DIRECTOR: Sam Weisman
PRODUCERS: David Hoberman, Jordan Kerner, and Jon Avnet
EXECUTIVE PRODUCER: C. Tad Devlin
WRITERS: Dana Olsen and Audrey Wells
BASED ON: Characters by Jay Ward
DISTRIBUTOR: Walt Disney Pictures/Walt Disney Company/Buena Vista Distribution
BRIEF SUMMARY:
George of the Jungle is a lightweight parody of the *Tarzan* story. The movie opens with Ursula Stanhope, a wealthy heiress, indulging her romantic fantasies by taking an African safari. Her betrothed, the effete Lyle Van De Groot, finds her in the jungle and wants to take her back to civilized society, but she wants to find the legendary great white ape. Ursula and Lyle experience a mock lion attack just before George shows up to rescue the beautiful Ursula from his lion friend. Lyle vows revenge and wounds George. Ursula takes George back to San Francisco to care for him. Back in the jungle, Lyle's goons capture Ape. With the help of his animal friends, George heads back to Africa, saves Ape, trounces Lyle, and marries Ursula.

An intentional parody of the noble savage, *George of the Jungle* has its funny moments. Regrettably, its humor is too often scatological or sexual. This movie has neither the wonderful silly humor of the cartoon series, nor the grandeur of *The Jungle Book*. Instead, it is too earnest. It is a B movie without the vision and originality that could captivate audiences.

CONTENT ANALYSIS: (Ro, LL, VV, SS, N, A, D) Parody of a romantic worldview; six obscenities and five profanities; slapstick violence including pratfalls, blows to the groin, childish torture, and lots of running into trees (no blood); frequent sexual innuendo and sexual humor including bestiality; loincloths and upper male nudity; alcohol use; and smoking.

Empty-Handed

GOOD WILL HUNTING

Quality: ☆☆☆   Acceptability: −2

WARNING CODES:
  Language: * * *
  Violence: *
  Sex: *
  Nudity: None
RATING: R
GENRE: Drama
INTENDED AUDIENCE: Adults
RELEASE DATE: December 1997
RUNNING TIME: 140 minutes
STARRING: Robin Williams, Matt Damon, Ben Affleck, and Minnie Driver
DIRECTOR: Gus Van Sant
PRODUCER: Lawrence Bender
EXECUTIVE PRODUCERS: Bob and Harvey Weinstein, Jonathan Gordon, and Su Armstrong
WRITERS: Matt Damon and Ben Affleck
DISTRIBUTOR: Miramax Films
BRIEF SUMMARY:
Good Will Hunting opens as MIT math professor Lambeau poses a difficult math problem to his students. Janitor Will

Hunting sees the problem on the chalk-board and anonymously solves it. A genius, Will spends his time working blue collar jobs and brawling with his poor friends from the south side of Boston. One night, Will supports his friend Chuckie against the intellectual disdain of a conceited Harvard man and demonstrates such intellect that he wins premed Skylar's affection. Professor Lambeau tracks Will down in a courtroom and offers to be Will's legal guardian as long as Will gets therapy. Therapist Sean McGuire challenges Will to find a real job and a real relationship. Regrettably, Will starts off by bedding Skylar.

Because of this premature intimacy, Will's relationship with Skylar is disappointing. A paean to humanist ideology, *Good Will Hunting* has an excessive amount of foul language. Minnie Driver is effective as the premed student who falls for Will. She has the maturity to call him on his fears but the folly to jump into bed with him. Director Gus Van Sant's avant-garde use of color filters and foul language doesn't fit the feel-good premise about a promising bad boy who turns good.

CONTENT ANALYSIS: (H, Ro, LLL, V, S, A) Humanist worldview with romantic elements about a brilliant but rebellious young man who finds love through psychotherapy; nineteen profanities and two hundred obscenities, with sexual jokes; man hits woman; implied and depicted sex; and alcohol use.

The Making of a Hero

HERCULES

Quality: ☆☆☆☆   Acceptability: +1

WARNING CODES:
Language: *
Violence: *
Sex: None
Nudity: *
RATING: G

GENRE: Animated comedy
INTENDED AUDIENCE: All ages
RUNNING TIME: 90 minutes
VOICES: Danny DeVito, Tate Donovan, Susan Egan, Matt Frewer, Bobcat Goldthwait, Paul Shaffer, Rip Torn, James Woods, and Charlton Heston
DIRECTORS: John Musker and Ron Clements
PRODUCERS: Alice Dewey, John Musker, and Ron Clements
WRITERS: John Musker, Ron Clements, Donald McEnery, Bob Shaw, and Irene Mecchi
DISTRIBUTOR: Walt Disney Pictures/Buena Vista Pictures Distribution
BRIEF SUMMARY:
Disney's *Hercules* plays with ancient Greek myths and creates a spoof of American sports merchandising. Hercules realizes that moneymaking deals and beating up Hydras do not make a hero. Hercules is a half-man/half-god born of Zeus, the chief god on Mount Olympus. The god of the underworld, Hades, kidnaps baby Hercules and almost renders him mortal. Baby Hercules is adopted by a mortal couple and grows up to fall in love with Meg, who unwillingly works for Hades. Hades uses Meg to persuade Hercules to surrender his strength. Hercules does, and Hades sends four Titans to battle Zeus. Thus, Hercules must rescue Meg and his father.

A proper Christian understanding of this myth is that it is just a story, and that the Bible is the only source for faith and moral instruction. It is important to tell children that there is only one true God—not multiple gods as shown in *Hercules*. The movie does have some clear biblical allegories and values and shows that heroism isn't measured by your stats but by selfless behavior. Some parents will be concerned with the scary monsters. Others will be concerned by Meg's sassy nature. Overall, *Hercules* is a light, action-oriented Disney movie.

CONTENT ANALYSIS: (B, FR, C, L, V, N, D, M) Ultimately moral worldview set in a world of false religions and gods with prayer to Zeus, statements that this story is "the gospel truth," and Christological allegory; two mild profanities; mild slapstick violence including falling pillars, silly physical training sequences, and a few scary, bloodless battle sequences where Hercules fights a Minotaur, a Cyclops, an army of Titans, and cuts the heads off a multi-headed Hydra; buxom heroine acts flirtatious, and reference to man being unfaithful to woman; dresses with slits up the sides; and cigar smoking.

A Boy's Home Is His Castle

HOME ALONE 3

Quality: ☆☆☆☆   Acceptability: −1

RATING: PG
GENRE: Comedy
INTENDED AUDIENCE: All ages
WARNING CODES:

Language: *
Violence: * *
Sex: *
Nudity: None

RUNNING TIME: 102 minutes
STARRING: Alex D. Linz, Olek Krupa, Rya Kihlstedt, Lenny Von Dohlen, David Thornton, Kevin Kilner, Marian Seldes, and Haviland Morris
DIRECTOR: Raja Gosnell
PRODUCERS: John Hughes and Hilton Green
EXECUTIVE PRODUCER: Ricardo Mestres
WRITER: John Hughes
DISTRIBUTOR: 20th Century Fox
BRIEF SUMMARY:
Home Alone 3 uses the same elements as the first two movies to construct an entertaining movie. Eight-year-old Alex Pruitt comes down with chicken pox. Meanwhile, four spies steal U.S. stealth technology and place the stolen chip in a toy car to sneak it by airport x-ray machines. By mistake, Alex's neighbor, Mrs. Hess, picks up the bag with the toy, and so the chase begins. Back home, Mrs. Hess finds the toy and gives it to Alex. Alex notices the thieves searching the neighborhood, but by the time the police arrive the thieves have left. The police caution Alex about false alarms. When it is clear that the thieves are coming to his house, Alex arranges to inflict pain on these smugglers—after all, it's his home, and he's going to protect it.

The sight-gags in Home Alone 3 are well executed, but some of the slapstick violence goes too far. Although protecting our home, honesty, compassion for the elderly, and other good values are presented in this movie, many people may complain that the gags are too scatological and painful. Home Alone 3 may be dynamite entertainment for children of all ages, but the painful gags may wear thin on parents.

CONTENT ANALYSIS: (B, L, VV, S) Moral worldview with some redemptive elements; three borderline exclamatory profanities; constant slapstick violence from electrocution that blows off the seat of a man's pants, falling into freezing pool, numerous other falling gags, objects hitting people in the head, spray-painting eyes, and many hits to the groin; suggestive bathing suit posters in boy's room and some very mildly suggestive sexual gags.

Hero Caught in the Middle

THE JACKAL

Quality: ☆☆☆☆   Acceptability: −2

WARNING CODES:
Language: * *
Violence: * * *
Sex: None
Nudity: *

RATING: R
GENRE: Thriller
INTENDED AUDIENCE: Older teens and adults

RUNNING TIME: 123 minutes

STARRING: Richard Gere, Bruce Willis, Sidney Poitier, Diane Venora, Mathilda May, and Tess Harper

DIRECTOR: Michael Caton-Jones

PRODUCERS: James Jacks, Sean Daniel, Michael Caton-Jones, and Kevin Jarre

EXECUTIVE PRODUCERS: Terence Clegg, Hal Lieberman, Gary Levinsohn, and Mark Gordon

WRITER: Chuck Pfarrer

BASED ON: The novel *The Day of the Jackal* by Frederick Forsyth

DISTRIBUTOR: Universal Pictures

BRIEF SUMMARY:

The Jackal is a brilliant though R-rated retooling of author Frederick Forsyth's twenty-five-year-old thriller *The Day of the Jackal*. Richard Gere plays an ex-IRA soldier enlisted by the FBI and a Russian major to track down a cruel assassin, played by Bruce Willis. Gere and Willis give two of the best performances of their usually lackluster careers in this tense and exciting but flawed movie. Sidney Poitier and Diane Venora also shine in their roles. The movie is a marvelous modern retelling of the quintessential American story of the Western hero who must defend a family, children, and a woman from dark, savage forces threatening to destroy them. *The Jackal* is tainted by unnecessary, gratuitous violence, foul language, and a mild homosexual scene, but has an overall moral worldview. This is true especially at the end, when the movie upholds marital fidelity, self-sacrifice to protect the lives of others, and a biblical punishment for evildoers. The biblical punishment is shown by the fact that two of the villain's victims carry out his final punishment. The justice they deliver is a justice borne out of self-defense, not out of revenge, as in some action films.

CONTENT ANALYSIS: (B, I, P, Ho, LL, VVV, N, A, D, M) Moral and sometimes biblical worldview spoiled by gratuitous foul language, especially in two scenes in the beginning and middle of the movie; twenty obscenities, three profanities, one vulgarity, and one curse; excessive blood and brutality, fight in Russian bar ends in one shooting death, man murdered by ax in head, man tortured briefly by Russian police, man gets arm shot off and then is murdered by machine gun, one murder by poison, four cops slain brutally, another man murdered by two gunshots in chest, at least two people wounded, and miscellaneous gunfire, chasing and punching; scene in a homosexual bar with two mild kisses; natural upper male nudity and two women in revealing bikinis; alcohol use; smoking; miscellaneous immorality such as villain's cruel behavior including kidnapping, stealing, and forgery and no condemnation of previous immorality by hero who was active in the IRA but claims he did not bomb or deliberately kill civilians.

Restoring the Family

JUNGLE 2 JUNGLE

Quality: ☆☆☆☆   Acceptability: −1

WARNING CODES:

Language: *
Violence: *
Sex: None
Nudity: None

RATING: PG

GENRE: Comedy

INTENDED AUDIENCE: All ages

RUNNING TIME: 100 minutes

STARRING: Tim Allen, Sam Huntington, JoBeth Williams, Lolita Davidovich, Martin Short, Valerie Mahaffey, and Leelee Sobieski

DIRECTOR: John Pasquin

PRODUCER: Brian Reilly

EXECUTIVE PRODUCERS: Richard Baker, Rick Messina, and Brad Krevoy

WRITERS: Bruce A. Evans and Raymond Gideon

BASED ON: The play "Un Indien dans la Ville" by Herve Palud, Thierry Lhermitte, Igor Aptekman, and Philippe Bruneau de la Salle

DISTRIBUTOR: Walt Disney Pictures/Buena Vista Pictures Distribution

BRIEF SUMMARY:

Jungle 2 Jungle is a funny noble-savage yarn based on a French play. The movie opens with Michael Cromwell, played by Tim Allen, giving ulcers to his partner, Richard, played by Martin Short, by buying coffee futures at a high price. Michael then hops on a plane for the jungles of South America so he can finalize his divorce from a wife he hasn't seen for twelve years. When he gets to the remote native village, he finds out that he has a thirteen-year-old son named Mimi. Mimi goes back to New York with Michael and experiences all sorts of adventures. When Michael crosses the Russian mafia, Mimi saves the day and then heads home to South America. Michael realizes that selfishness is not a virtue and comes to the conclusion that he wants his family.

The pacing and jungle-versus-civilization humor combine to solicit frequent laughter. There are moments, however, when the supporting cast seems to be window dressing. Furthermore, there is too much bathroom humor, and too many mild profanities. Although there are no sexual relationships shown, it is implied that Michael is living with his fiancée. On the other hand, this is a very funny movie wherein Michael comes to realize that he would prefer to be a father and a husband rather than a wealthy commodities broker.

CONTENT ANALYSIS: (Ro, B, L, V, A, D) Classic romantic worldview featuring noble savage combined with moral elements; four exclamatory profanities and six obscenities and vulgarities; slapstick violence including chase by a spider, chase by crocodile, attack by snake, falling through banister, and a lightweight fight scene; revealing dresses; alcohol use; and smoking.

Learning to Love

KOLYA

Quality: ☆☆☆☆   Acceptability: −1

WARNING CODES:

Language: * *
Violence: None
Sex: *
Nudity: *

RATING: PG-13
GENRE: Drama
INTENDED AUDIENCE: Older children to adults
RUNNING TIME: 120 minutes
LANGUAGE: Czech
STARRING: Zdenek Sverak, Andrej Chalimon, and Libuse Safrankova
DIRECTOR: Jan Sverak
PRODUCERS: Eric Abraham and Jan Sverak
WRITER: Zdenek Sverak
DISTRIBUTOR: Miramax Films
BRIEF SUMMARY:

Winner of the Best Foreign Film award at a Golden Globes ceremony, the Czech film *Kolya* is truly deserving of its accolades. Beautifully acted, deeply moving, and artistically stunning, this foreign language film is set in Prague on the eve of the 1989 Velvet Revolution. Franta Louka is a fifty-five-year-old "confirmed bachelor" and cellist. In need of money, he reluctantly agrees to marry a friend's distant Russian niece for pay. The niece turns out to be young and beautiful, but she also has a five-year-old son named Kolya. To Louka's chagrin, his new young wife emigrates to Germany and leaves her little boy behind. The musician is transformed by his new responsibility.

This film not only tells the story of an old, corrupt man and an innocent child but also chronicles the collision of two cultures. The film gently and subtly suggests that humanity would do well to remember that its political enemies are populated by individuals, some of whom are innocent children. With breathtaking cinematography, the film is rich with symbolism. Despite those positive messages, however, the film presents morally ambiguous and reprehensible situations, such as the "fake marriage," some obscenities, and implied fornication. This film would best appeal to a mature audience, especially those who enjoy cinematic art.

CONTENT ANALYSIS: (B, LL, S, N, A) Moral worldview where values of family, love, and personal responsibility triumph over hedonistic pleasures; two obscenities, three profanities, and six vulgarities; implied fornication, adultery, and sexual innuendo; naked baby in bath; and alcohol use.

How to Love Your Child

LEAVE IT TO BEAVER

Quality: ☆☆☆☆   Acceptability: +3

WARNING CODES:
  Language: None
  Violence: *
  Sex: *
  Nudity: None
RATING: PG
GENRE: Comedy
INTENDED AUDIENCE: Families
RUNNING TIME: 95 minutes
STARRING: Cameron Finley, Christopher McDonald, Janine Turner, and Erik von Dettin
  DIRECTOR: Andy Cadiff
  PRODUCER: Robert Simonds
  EXECUTIVE PRODUCERS: Lynn Arost, David Helpern, and Ben Myron
  WRITERS: Brian Levant and Lon Diamond
  BASED ON: The TV series created by Bob Mosher and Joe Connelly
  DISTRIBUTOR: Universal Pictures
  BRIEF SUMMARY:
  In the movie Leave It to Beaver, Theodore (Beaver) Cleaver endures several boyish mishaps as he tries to win his father's respect. Beaver is a short, sincere eight-year-old who looks up to his elder brother, Wally. Regrettably, try as he might, Beaver just can't seem live up to his father's expectations. Small of stature, Beaver has a hard time at football practice. In the one game where the coach lets him play, which his father is watching, he flubs the play and passes the football to a smart-aleck opposing player who called for the pass. Even worse, he forfeits the shiny new bike his dad buys him to the town bully. How can he make his dad proud now?

Most of the appeal of Leave It to Beaver derives from its thrust toward family bonding implicit in its premise: What can a son do to obtain his father's love? Happily, in Leave It to Beaver, Ward Cleaver learns how he can give unconditional love to his son—a fortuitous lesson for audiences of all ages and stages. With high production value, appealing storyline, wholesome family interaction, and beautiful symphonic music based on the TV show melody, Leave It to Beaver is an entertaining, fun movie the whole family will enjoy. This movie leaves the viewer feeling warm and cuddly.

CONTENT ANALYSIS: (B, C, Ro, S) Biblical worldview of a boy trying to please his father with redemptive and Romantic elements; boy falls out of second-story window and boy steals bike; and twelve-year-old boy kisses twelve-year-old girl.

Tell the Truth

LIAR, LIAR

Quality: ☆☆☆   Acceptability: −2

WARNING CODES:
  Language: * * *
  Violence: *
  Sex: * *
  Nudity: None
RATING: PG-13
GENRE: Comedy

INTENDED AUDIENCE: Older teens and adults

RUNNING TIME: 100 minutes

STARRING: Jim Carrey, Justin Cooper, and Maura Tierney

DIRECTOR: Tom Shadyac

PRODUCER: Brian Grazer

EXECUTIVE PRODUCERS: James D. Brubaker and Michael Bostick

WRITERS: Paul Guay and Stephen Mazur

DISTRIBUTOR: Universal Pictures

BRIEF SUMMARY:

Liar, Liar is the story of Fletcher Reed, a self-absorbed defense attorney portrayed by "comedian of a thousand faces" Jim Carrey. Divorced and consumed with his career, Fletcher finds it impossible to live without lying. One lie leads to another and his ex-wife, Audrey, and young son, Max, find it increasingly impossible to believe anything he says. Realizing his dad isn't coming to his birthday party, Max makes a wish that his dad wouldn't be able to tell a lie for one day—a wish that comes true. The comedy that ensues is classic Jim Carrey. As his life comes tumbling down in one day, Fletcher realizes that he is about to lose something more precious than his career: his son. The story teaches Fletcher not how to love but how to be real and to tell the truth.

Regrettably, Mr. Carrey's humor is excessively vulgar and coarse, and is not appropriate for younger audiences. This scatological humor detracts from an otherwise funny, entertaining, and morally uplifting film. However, Fletcher tells the truth because of a birthday wish of his son. This is magical thinking, not answered prayer. *Liar, Liar* isn't for the whole family, but it does teach us to tell the truth.

CONTENT ANALYSIS: (B, LLL, V, SS, M) Moral worldview where telling the truth and taking care of family is encouraged; sixteen obscenities, seventeen vulgarities, and two profanities; man bruises and beats himself up; implied fornication, sexual talk, sexual situations, and some sexual innuendo; and miscellaneous immorality including traffic violations and lying.

Humorless Blues Brothers Bust Alien Bug

MEN IN BLACK

Quality: ☆☆☆☆   Acceptability: −3

WARNING CODES:

Language: * * *

Violence: * * *

Sex: *

Nudity: None

RATING: PG-13

GENRE: Science fiction

INTENDED AUDIENCE: Teens and adults

RUNNING TIME: 98 minutes

STARRING: Tommy Lee Jones, Will Smith, Linda Fiorentino, and Rip Torn

DIRECTOR: Barry Sonnenfeld

PRODUCERS: Walter F. Parkes and Laurie MacDonald

EXECUTIVE PRODUCER: Steven Spielberg

WRITER: Ed Solomon

BASED ON: The comic book by Lowell Cunningham

DISTRIBUTOR: Columbia Pictures

BRIEF SUMMARY:

Men in Black may be a sophist's dream, but it is a moral American's nightmare. With abundant foul language, this is an in-your-face, Blues-Brothers-go-alien-busting story. Based on an obscure comic book, *Men in Black* features a super-secret agency that keeps aliens in line. These are not illegal immigrants but ugly extraterrestrials who are living on Earth as a result of an intergalactic agreement wherein Earth has offered to serve as a safe zone for political refugees from other galaxies. When Men-in-Black agent K has to find a new partner, he chooses New York police officer James Edwards, who becomes agent J. Agents J and K have to stop an invading bug who threatens to destroy the galaxy. As they do so, the audience is confronted by foul language, wisecracks, grotesqueries, slime, and cynicism.

The acting, dialogue, and direction in this sci-fi film noir are excellent. The New Age worldview with its cynical attitude is perverse. There are no real heroes in *Men in Black* because life is not valued. Instead, these protagonists are merely able men doing a dirty job in a decadent universe. People without God may enjoy this parody of alien invasion movies, but most will find it repulsive.

CONTENT ANALYSIS: (Pa, O, LLL, VVV, S, D, M) Cynical, nihilistic worldview with New Age view of reality; fifty-two obscenities and six profanities; constant violence including removing a man's skin, breaking people into pieces, swallowing a man whole, dropping a woman from a tower, and throwing a body against a car—all heightened by shocking, horrific creatures; sexual innuendo, extensive disturbing birth scene, and hints of necrophilia; smoking; and removing people's memories.

Manners

MR. MAGOO

Quality: ☆☆☆☆   Acceptability: +1

WARNING CODES:
  Language: **
  Violence: None
  Sex: *
  Nudity: *
RATING: PG
GENRE: Comedy
INTENDED AUDIENCE: All ages
RUNNING TIME: 97 minutes
STARRING: Leslie Nielsen, Kelly Lynch, Ernie Hudson, Stephen Tobolowsky, Nick Chinlund, and Malcolm McDowell
  DIRECTOR: Stanley Tong
  PRODUCER: Ben Myron
  EXECUTIVE PRODUCERS: Henry G. Saperstein, Andre Morgan, and Robert L. Rosen
  WRITERS: Pat Proft and Tom Sherohman
  DISTRIBUTOR: Walt Disney Pictures/Buena Vista Pictures Distribution
  BRIEF SUMMARY:
  Leslie Nielsen does a great job of recreating the cartoon Mr. Magoo as a live-action persona in Walt Disney's *Mr. Magoo*. Quincy Magoo has donated a new wing to the museum to house, among other treasures, the famous "Star of Kuristan" ruby. At the gala opening, Magoo and his nephew, Waldo, meet Stacey, the beautiful ambassador from Kuristan. Master criminal Cloquet hires two thieves to steal the ruby so he can sell it to the highest bidding international gangster. Unknown to him, Magoo gets possession of the ruby, and the thieves want it back. The FBI and the CIA think that Magoo engineered the theft, so they join the chase. With the brilliant protection of his stalwart bulldog, Angus, and the assistance of Waldo, Magoo attempts to recover the jewel.

Mr. Magoo is a fun movie. Generally the humor is very clean and wholesome. There are a few off-color jokes and inappropriate slapstick humor scenes. Many of the best laughs belong to Angus, a great animal actor. With a slight caution, Magoo is funny Hollywood holiday fare. The credits apologize to people who are visually challenged. Of course, there are points where the storyline seems contrived, but, after all, this is a cartoon that has come to life.

CONTENT ANALYSIS: (B, C, LL, S, N, A, M) Moral worldview with a shot of the famous statue of Jesus watching over Rio de Janeiro; seven obscenities; lots of slapstick violence, most of it lightweight, bumbling, Magoo-type humor, one scatological scene when a fishing hook gets caught on a man's pants, several martial arts fight scenes, and two falls that look painful to sensitive parts of the body; lightweight sexual innuendo where

Magoo thinks that woman thief is attracted to him and Magoo tries to kiss her, but she gives him a fish to kiss; tight-fitting clothes on women and amply endowed women in bathing suits; alcohol use; and theft, lying, mistaken identity, and Magoo dresses as bride to recover stolen gem.

Service above Self

MRS. BROWN

Quality: ☆☆☆☆   Acceptability: −1

WARNING CODES:
  Language: *
  Violence: *
  Sex: None
  Nudity: *
RATING: PG
GENRE: Drama
INTENDED AUDIENCE: Teens and adults
RUNNING TIME: 103 minutes
STARRING: Judi Dench, Billy Connolly, Geoffrey Palmer, Antony Sher, and Gerald Butler
DIRECTOR: John Madden
PRODUCER: Sarah Curtis
EXECUTIVE PRODUCERS: Douglas Rae, Andrea Calderwood, and Rebecca Eaton
WRITER: Jeremy Brock
DISTRIBUTOR: Miramax Films
BRIEF SUMMARY:
In *Mrs. Brown*, John Brown, faithful retainer to Queen Victoria, helps pull the queen out of a long depression that started when her beloved husband, Prince Albert, died in 1861. Her inconsolable grief has driven her to spend years of seclusion on the Isle of Wight and in Balmoral Castle in Scotland. In a desperate effort to penetrate her depression, the queen's family summons John Brown, a plainspoken Scot servant, who had been a favorite of Prince Albert's. Brown sizes up the situation quickly, and after crossing verbal swords with the queen, he per-

suades her to get some air, with him as guide.

This fascinating clash of personalities and the deep friendship that subsequently develops is the substance of *Mrs. Brown*, a first-rate production from the makers of *Masterpiece Theatre*. This is indeed a masterpiece. With Oscar-caliber performances, *Mrs. Brown* scrupulously avoids adding sleaze to this story. In fact, while Brown's weakness for alcohol is honestly portrayed, this film highlights a virtue rarely seen in contemporary movies: a devotion to duty and service that transcends personal interest. With uncommon intelligence and value, *Mrs. Brown* is a fascinating history lesson and a moving portrait of a man who truly honored service above self.

CONTENT ANALYSIS: (B, L, V, N, A) Biblical worldview of a royal servant who valued service above self; three obscenities and two profanities; man pummeled by assailants; rear male naturalistic nudity from a distance; and alcohol use.

Doing the Right Thing

MY BEST FRIEND'S WEDDING

Quality: ☆☆☆☆   Acceptability: −1

WARNING CODES:
  Language: *
  Violence: None
  Sex: *
  Nudity: None
RATING: PG-13
GENRE: Comedy
INTENDED AUDIENCE: Older teens and Adults
STARRING: Julia Roberts, Dermot Mulroney, Cameron Diaz, and Rupert Everett
DIRECTOR: P. J. Hogan
PRODUCERS: Jerry Zucker and Ronald Bass

EXECUTIVE PRODUCERS: Gil Netter and Patricia Whitcher
WRITER: Ronald Bass
DISTRIBUTOR: TriStar Pictures
BRIEF SUMMARY:

My Best Friend's Wedding is a fresh, clever comedy that diverges from typical Hollywood romantic-comedy formula. Julia Roberts portrays Julianne Potter, a self-absorbed food critic who has had poor romantic relationships. One night she receives an unexpected phone call from her best friend, sportswriter Michael O'Neal. Julianne assumes that he is calling to make good on their past agreement, to marry each other if both were still single at age twenty-eight. Prepared to reject him, she is instead greeted with the news that her "betrothed" is marrying someone else. Suddenly she is hurled into a jealous tailspin and is convinced that Michael is the love of her life. With the help of her homosexual editor, George, she sets out to thwart Michael's marriage and proclaim her undying love for Michael.

Just as *My Best Friend's Wedding* threatens to deteriorate into a dark revenge comedy, the film is saved by Everett as George, giving piercing and calming commentary to Julianne. His dry wit contrasts with Julianne's mounting hysteria. The movie contains relatively little profanity, no violence, and no sex. George is homosexual, but this fact is not belabored. The acting is excellent. This amusing movie is a cut above most Hollywood offerings, but still propagates the fallacy that romantic love is the supreme and ultimate love.

CONTENT ANALYSIS: (Ro, L, S, A, D, M) Romantic worldview with moral observations and a moral conclusion; five obscenities and one profanity; a brief shove; sexual innuendo and implied fornication taking place in the past; alcohol use and abuse; smoking; and vengeance themes and homosexual character.

Cute, Warm, and Furry

NAPOLEON

Quality: ☆☆   Acceptability: +3

WARNING CODES:
  Language: None
  Violence: None
  Sex: None
  Nudity: None
RATING: G
GENRE: Family/Adventure
INTENDED AUDIENCE: Children
RUNNING TIME: 70 minutes
VOICES: Jamie Croft, Phillip Quast, and Carole Skinner
DIRECTOR: Mario Andreacchio
PRODUCERS: Michael Bourchier and Mario Andreacchio
EXECUTIVE PRODUCERS: Ron Saunders and Masato Hara
WRITERS: Michael Bourchier, Mario Andreacchio, and Mark Saltzman
DISTRIBUTOR: Samuel Goldwyn
BRIEF SUMMARY:

Napoleon is an adorable, tenderhearted animal adventure. Golden retriever puppy Napoleon takes a balloon ride into the outback, where he faces many dangers and meets many animal friends as he makes his way home. Napoleon lives in a nice home in the suburbs of Sydney, Australia. He wants to explore the world and gets upset when his mother calls him by his real name, Muffin. At a birthday party for his young master, he climbs into a basket that is tied to helium balloons, and the basket's tether to the ground breaks. He is blown to the edge of the outback where a helpful galah bird, "Birdo," pops Napoleon's balloons so that he can get down. Through a series of adventures, he learns that there is no place like home. With the help of a sea turtle, he tries to make it back home to his mother.

This film was made with tender loving care. It doesn't employ any modern techniques of moving the animals' lips. Most of the animal scenes are superb, and the script is clearly aimed at children so there is no intense jeopardy. Containing very mild action violence, no foul language, no sex, and no nudity, *Napoleon* is a wonderful opportunity to watch a good movie with your children.

CONTENT ANALYSIS: (B, V, M) Moral worldview; some nature violence and a feral cat who tries to attack a puppy and a penguin; and running away from home is reprimanded.

God-fearing Gambling Misfits

OSCAR AND LUCINDA

Quality: ✰✰✰✰   Acceptability: −2

WARNING CODES:

   Language: *
   Violence: * *
   Sex: *
   Nudity: * *

RATING: R
GENRE: Christian historical drama
INTENDED AUDIENCE: Adults
RUNNING TIME: 131 minutes
STARRING: Ralph Fiennes, Cate Blanchett, Ciaran Hinds, and Tom Wilkinson
   DIRECTOR: Gillian Armstrong
   PRODUCERS: Robin Dalton and Timothy White
   WRITER: Laura Jones
   BASED ON: The novel by Peter Carey
   DISTRIBUTOR: Fox Searchlight Pictures
   BRIEF SUMMARY:
Oscar and Lucinda is a quirky though lavishly produced romantic drama about a couple who share love and a passion for gambling in mid-nineteenth-century Australia. Oscar is oppressed by his stern preacher father, and runs away to become an Anglican minister. Shunned by his fellow students at Oxford, Oscar develops a taste for gambling. Soon Oscar realizes

that he must leave his gambling past and decides to sail to Australia to become a missionary. On the ship, he meets an Australian glass heiress named Lucinda. Oscar falls in love with Lucinda and promises to make her a glass church and deliver it to a Christian outpost in Northern Australia. The trip proves to be tragic.

Oscar and Lucinda comments on social mores, industrial development, religious practices, and repression. Oscar is shown to be repulsed by the rigid Victorian religious constraints, though he wants to follow God, whom he genuinely loves. He prays often, sings hymns, and reads the Bible. Lucinda is an outcast and an eccentric. *Oscar and Lucinda* has beautiful photography, lavish costumes, detailed art direction, and an original story. However, the obvious pain in the lives of the two protagonists is demonstrated by guilt, fear, violence, and some sexual situations.

CONTENT ANALYSIS: (CCC, Ab, L, VV, S, NN, A, D, M) Strong Christian worldview severely marred by anti-Christian thoughts and behaviors, intense fear in main character and compulsive gambling; three obscenities; moderate violence including man smacks boy, image of dead man hanging, brief but bloody killing with hatchet, dogfight implied, shooting, kicking, punching, and implied drowning; one brief depiction of woman fornicating with half-conscious man; rear male nudity, and naturalistic shots of nude Australian Aborigines; alcohol use; smoking; and miscellaneous immorality including implied prostitution, gambling, and overly strict parents.

Amazing Grace in the Midst of Horror

PARADISE ROAD

Quality: ✰✰✰✰   Acceptability: −2

WARNING CODES:
   Language: *
   Violence: * * *

Sex: None
Nudity: * *
RATING: R
GENRE: Christian historical drama
INTENDED AUDIENCE: Adults
RUNNING TIME: 121 minutes
STARRING: Glenn Close, Frances McDormand, and Pauline Collins
DIRECTOR: Bruce Beresford
PRODUCERS: Sue Milliken and Greg Coote
EXECUTIVE PRODUCERS: Andrew Yap and Graham Burke
WRITER: Bruce Beresford
DISTRIBUTOR: Fox Searchlight
BRIEF SUMMARY:
From the director of *Driving Miss Daisy* comes a thought-provoking morality tale filled with strong Christian content called *Paradise Road*. In 1942 Singapore, a high-society party is disturbed by a Japanese air attack. Immediately the women and children are evacuated, including an English woman named Adrienne and an Australian named Daisy. Their ship is bombed by the Japanese, and the women swim to shore. They are taken to a POW camp and the two decide, at the risk of punishment, to form an orchestra, using their voices as instruments. Faced with Japanese death threats and life-threatening disease, the women give more than thirty performances until the end of the war.

The set design and locations are excellent, the script is impeccable, and the acting is superb. This movie has a great number of strong female roles where each woman has dignity, courage, and integrity. Most impressive are the complex roles of the spiritual leaders. Viewers need to be warned that the strength and beauty of the women are in stark contrast to the brutality of the Japanese. There are many depicted moments of horror against the women, including torture, slapping, and killing. *Paradise Road* stands as a worthy insight into this pivotal point in history.

CONTENT ANALYSIS: (CCC, L, VVV, NN, A, D, M) Strong Christian worldview featuring Catholic nun and Christian missionary woman in Japanese prisoner of war camp; two obscenities and one profanity; extensive acts-of-war violence including shooting, bombing, beatings, torture, woman doused with gasoline and set on fire, image of severed head, and brutal treatment of women and children; rear male nudity and rear and upper female nudity; alcohol use; smoking; and destruction due to war.

An Eye for an Eye

PEACEMAKER

Quality: ☆☆☆☆   Acceptability: −2

WARNING CODES:
Language: * * *
Violence: * * *
Sex: None
Nudity: None

RATING: R
GENRE: Action/Adventure
INTENDED AUDIENCE: Older teens and adults
RUNNING TIME: 125 minutes
STARRING: George Clooney, Nicole Kidman, Armin Mueller-Stahl, Marcel Iures, Alexander Baluev, and Rene Medvesek
DIRECTOR: Mimi Leder
PRODUCERS: Walter Parkes and Branko Lustig
EXECUTIVE PRODUCERS: Michael Grillo and Laurie MacDonald
WRITER: Michael Schiffer
BASED ON: An article by Leslie Cockburn and Andrew Cockburn
DISTRIBUTOR: DreamWorks Pictures
BRIEF SUMMARY:
Reminiscent of James Bond flicks, *The Peacemaker* is a taut, tense tale of international terrorism. The movie tells the story of a Russian general who steals ten nuclear warheads in order to make a for-

tune. The general engineers a spectacular high-speed theft of the warheads as they speed through the Ural Mountains on a steam train. After off-loading the warheads to another speeding train, the general has one of the warheads rigged to explode after the abandoned steam train collides head-on with a passenger train further down the track. In Washington D.C., nuclear scientist Dr. Julia Kelly is ordered to team up with wheeler-dealer U.S. Army Special Forces Lieutenant Colonel Thomas Devoe to find the smugglers. Tom organizes some soldiers to illegally fly into Russian airspace to recover the weapons. When they do, they find that one weapon is headed for Manhattan.

This is a well-directed movie. George Clooney and Nicole Kidman do a good job. There are some plot points that seem, if not impossible, highly improbable. The movie tries to tug at all the right emotions. Regrettably, these emotional moments are dissipated beneath the withering barrage of violent deaths and vile language. Furthermore, after a while the intensity of the action starts to numb the senses.

CONTENT ANALYSIS: (B, C, LLL, VVV, A, D, M) Moral worldview with several references to Christianity marred by an indiscriminate use of violence and an excess of foul language; thirty obscenities and thirteen profanities; extreme violence, including massive death in a train crash, a nuclear bomb explosion, a car fight that involves the crushing and mutilation of people, pistol whipping, and point-blank executions; alcohol use; smoking; and bribery as a tool of international relations.

The Grief of a Child

PONETTE

Quality: ☆☆☆☆   Acceptability: −1

WARNING CODES:
Language: None
Violence: None

Sex: None
Nudity: None

RATING: Not rated
GENRE: Drama
INTENDED AUDIENCE: Adults
RUNNING TIME: 92 minutes
LANGUAGE: French
STARRING: Mary Trintignant, Xavier Beauvois, and Victoire Thivisol
DIRECTOR: Jacques Doillon
PRODUCER: Alain Sarde
WRITER: Jacques Doillon
DISTRIBUTOR: Arrow Releasing
BRIEF SUMMARY:
The French film *Ponette* dares to explore universal questions about God and his role in our lives through the eyes of a four-year-old child. The story opens with Ponette sucking her thumb as it protrudes from a cast binding her wrist. She was injured in a car accident that claimed her mother's life. Her father is overwhelmed by caring for his daughter, so he takes her to live with her aunt and two young cousins. Ponette's relatives commence to pummel her with their wildly divergent versions of the "truth" about death, God, and the afterlife. Her aunt offers her some Christian truths. The film chronicles Ponette's search, limited by her four-year-old mind, for the truth about these issues.

Ponette's struggle emerges as a metaphor for the universal human struggle to find truth. Her childish conversations and inability to grasp the concepts of death, God, and the afterlife are analogous to our own feeble attempts as adults to grapple with such issues while mired in human frailty. The film is intensely thought-provoking and will strike a deep chord in any viewer who has wrestled with such questions. The movie's religious themes are enhanced by recurring crucifixion imagery. Ultimately, the movie states that Ponette must "learn to be happy," which implies that peace and happiness can be mentally willed without God's help.

CONTENT ANALYSIS: (FRFRFR, CCC, A) Many conflicting false ideas about God, faith, and the afterlife, with several strong Christian elements including prayer, discussions of Christ, and the resurrection tale of Christ explicitly told; and alcohol use.

Choosing What Is Right

THE RAINMAKER

Quality: ☆☆☆☆   Acceptability: –2

WARNING CODES:
  Language: None
  Violence: * * *
  Sex: * *
  Nudity: None
  RATING: PG-13
  GENRE: Drama
  INTENDED AUDIENCE: Older teens and adults
  RUNNING TIME: 133 minutes
  STARRING: Matt Damon, Danny Glover, Claire Danes, Jon Voight, Mary Kay Place, Mickey Rourke, Johnny Whitworth, and Danny DeVito
  DIRECTOR: Francis Ford Coppola
  PRODUCER: Steven Reuther, Michael Douglas, and Fred Fuchs
  EXECUTIVE PRODUCER: Francis Ford Coppola
  WRITER: Francis Ford Coppola
  BASED ON: The novel by John Grisham
  DISTRIBUTOR: Paramount Pictures
  BRIEF SUMMARY:
In *The Rainmaker*, based on the novel by John Grisham, Rudy (Matt Damon) is fresh out of law school and ready to practice. He becomes an ambulance chaser, representing hurt clients and dealing with insurance companies. Rudy and Deck Shiffler (Danny DeVito) open their own law firm. Their first case is overwhelming for the inexperienced Rudy. A client has been denied a potentially life-saving bone marrow transplant. Rudy runs up against several obstacles, including a mysterious executive memorandum. The odds begin to turn in Rudy's favor when a former civil rights judge is assigned to the case.

The Rainmaker is a positive morality tale, which includes the fight for justice against seemingly insurmountable odds, the emphasis on choosing to do what is right over corrupt pursuits of wealth, and positive portrayals of family, love, and courage. The acting is superb; the dialogue is witty; and the plot is emotive. Rudy and Deck are heroes who fight for the truth but, regrettably, are forced to bend the rules at times to achieve their goal. Eventually the pressures of the legal system force Rudy to reconsider his career as a lawyer. This is a very idealistic movie that has some unpleasant, gritty situations.

CONTENT ANALYSIS: (BB, LL, VVV, SS, A, D, MM) Moral worldview where underdog lawyers take on corrupt insurance firm; two profanities, twenty-one obscenities, name-calling, and references to getting drunk, rape, and child molesters; excessive violence including violent fight with aluminum baseball bat, choking, fistfighting, and physically and verbally abusive behavior; adulterous kissing and touching, crude sexual joke, references to fornication, and obsession with sex; alcohol use; smoking; and miscellaneous immorality including lying, stealing, divorce, and deception.

In the Trenches of a Racial War

ROSEWOOD

Quality: ☆☆☆☆   Acceptability: –2

WARNING CODES:
  Language: * * *
  Violence: * * *
  Sex: * * *
  Nudity: * * *
  RATING: R

GENRE: Historical drama
INTENDED AUDIENCE: Adults
RUNNING TIME: 140 minutes
STARRING: Jon Voight, Ving Rhames, Don Cheadle, Bruce McGill, Loren Dean, and Michael Rooker
DIRECTOR: John Singleton
PRODUCER: Jon Peters
EXECUTIVE PRODUCER: Tracy Barone
WRITER: Gregory Poirier
DISTRIBUTOR: Warner Brothers
BRIEF SUMMARY:
Rosewood is a historical drama based on the true story of a small, thriving black community in Florida in the 1920s. When a woman from a struggling white community lies and says she was assaulted by a black man, a racial war is ignited with raw hostility, graphic violence, and innocent victims. In this racial war, we see human nature at its best and worst. White mobs indiscriminately hunt and kill African Americans as if they are animals. The story centers around two adversaries, Mann, a black World War I veteran, and John Wright, the lone white shopkeeper and resident of Rosewood.

This movie has many positive Christian elements. Wright's wife has a strong faith and is willing to risk her life to take a stand against violence. Other positive Christian elements include an emphasis on loving families, a positive portrayal of prayer, and gospel music. On the negative side, some whites leave a baptism service with their guns to participate in racial violence, and one blames God for establishing a social order of white supremacy. The film manipulates moviegoers into feeling good about revenge, even though that revenge is man's, not God's. This thought-provoking movie for adult viewers has nudity, sexual situations, and many racial slurs.

CONTENT ANALYSIS: (Pa, Ab, CC, LLL, VVV, SSS, NNN, A, D, M) Pagan worldview with extensive racist language and violence, but also including many strong Christian references; ten profanities, eight obscenities, and fifty-six vulgarities; extensive violence including lynchings, fatal shootings including shooting a crippled man, beating a woman after an adulterous affair, group beatings, arson, reference to body parts being cut off, reference to rape, reference to cockfight, reference to babies being killed, portrayal of Ku Klux Klan, and children forced to view violence; graphic adulterous sex; extensive male and female nudity; alcohol abuse; smoking; and lying and corrupt court and law enforcement officials.

Classic Animal Adventure

THE SECOND JUNGLE BOOK: MOWGLI AND BALOO

Quality: ☆☆☆   Acceptability: +2

WARNING CODES:
   Language: *
   Violence: *
   Sex: None
   Nudity: None

RATING: PG
GENRE: Animal adventure
INTENDED AUDIENCE: All ages
RUNNING TIME: 87 minutes
STARRING: Jamie Williams, Bill Campbell, Roddy McDowall, and David Paul Francis
DIRECTOR: Duncan McLachlan
PRODUCER: Raju Patel
EXECUTIVE PRODUCERS: Sharad Patel and Mark Damon
WRITERS: Bayard Johnson and Matthew Horton
BASED ON: The classic tale by Rudyard Kipling
DISTRIBUTOR: TriStar Pictures
BRIEF SUMMARY:
The Second Jungle Book: Mowgli and Baloo is a prequel to Disney's *Jungle Book*.

Here, we find Mowgli as a ten-year-old wild child who lives in the 1890s jungles of India with his adopted animal family: Grey Wolf; Baloo, the bear; and Bagheera, the black panther. Two monkeys, known as Bandars, are trying to capture Mowgli to bring him to their lost city so they can learn to live as humans. While escaping the Bandars, Mowgli runs into a talent scout for an American circus, named Harrison. Harrison wants to capture Mowgli and put him on display in the U.S. When Mowgli escapes, Harrison hires a sinister and mismatched gang to chase Mowgli to the lost city.

This is a fun adventure yarn. It has no sex or foul language except for one exclamatory profanity. The jungle is beautiful, the animals are endearing, and Jamie Williams is terrific. The filmmakers were careful to keep the animal attacks from becoming too threatening. This is good for children, but may leave adults a little restless. The major flaw is a romantic presupposition that Mowgli is a noble savage who is kin to the animals. Otherwise, this is an exciting, classic children's adventure yarn.

CONTENT ANALYSIS: (Ro, B, L, V, D) Romantic worldview with moral elements; one exclamatory profanity; nature adventure violence including python attack, pit of cobras, monkey attack, and tiger attack, with little or no harm caused in each instance; and smoking.

A Fallen Star

SELENA

Quality: ☆☆☆   Acceptability: +1

WARNING CODES:
  Language: *
  Violence: *
  Sex: None
  Nudity: None
RATING: PG
GENRE: Historical drama
INTENDED AUDIENCE: Teens and adults

RUNNING TIME: 125 minutes
STARRING: Jennifer Lopez, Edward James Olmos, Jon Seda, Constance Marie, and Jacob Vargas
DIRECTOR: Gregory Nava
PRODUCERS: Moctesuma Esparza and Robert Katz
EXECUTIVE PRODUCER: Abraham Quintanilla Jr.
WRITER: Gregory Nava
DISTRIBUTOR: Warner Brothers
BRIEF SUMMARY:
Selena is the true story of the rise, success, and tragic end of Selena Quintanilla Perez, a twenty-three-year-old, Mexican American pop star who broke through racial and social barriers to become a huge success in America and south of the border. Selena's father, Abraham, takes Selena to first one gig and then another so that she can make a name for herself. Selena meets Chris Perez, a wild-haired rocker guitarist who joins the band. Selena and Chris elope. The story takes a sour turn when it is discovered that Selena's fan club manager, Yolanda, has been stealing money. Yolanda snaps, culminating in the well-known shooting death of Selena, bringing this sweet success story to a premature and tragic ending.

While the movie can be commended for remaining true to the facts of the story, the overall production quality suffers from mediocrity. The film drags in many places, and while the leads perform adequately, the supporting cast does not. Overall, the film is an uplifting story that encourages mutual love and respect in family relationships. It further encourages a solid work ethic with a commitment toward accomplishing goals and fulfilling dreams. There is never any question of Selena's love and respect for her father. Having very few obscenities, no sex, and no nudity, it provides a moral insight into the life of a promising talent.

CONTENT ANALYSIS: (C, L, V, M) Christian worldview of family with some rebellion themes; two obscenities and one profanity; mild violence including implied murder; and casual drinking.

Overcoming Bondage

SHALL WE DANCE?

Quality: ☆☆☆☆   Acceptability: –1

WARNING CODES:

Language: *
Violence: None
Sex: *
Nudity: None

RATING: PG
GENRE: Comedy/Drama
INTENDED AUDIENCE: Adults
RUNNING TIME: 118 minutes
LANGUAGE: Japanese
STARRING: Koji Yakusho, Tamiyo
Kusakari, Naoto Takenaka, and Eriko
Watanabe
DIRECTOR: Masayuki Suo
PRODUCERS: Shoji Masui and Yuji
Ogata
EXECUTIVE PRODUCERS:
Hiroyuki Kato, Seiji Urushido, Shigeru
Ohno, Kazuhiro Igarashi, and Tetsuya
Ikeda
WRITER: Masayuki Suo
DISTRIBUTOR: Miramax Films
BRIEF SUMMARY:
Shall We Dance is a touching story of a
man who is overburdened by his life
until he discovers joy through dance les-
sons. This story about a common man in
Japan contrasts the strict Japanese work
habits, truncated family life, and lack of
communication between husband and
wife, with the joy of dancing. When the
hero decides to take ballroom dancing
lessons, he has already broken a social
code. When he actually derives joy from
the dancing, he discovers a sense of freedom that he had lost through years of
personal and family responsibility. His
initial infatuation with the beautiful but
sad dancing instructor becomes a chaste
friendship, where they give each other a
renewed motivation for living their
respective lives.

Everyone can identify with this story
of triumph over some of the excessive
burdens that society imposes on us. Its
characters are totally likable, and their
inner struggles are common to everyone.
The relationship of the two main characters encourages morality and responsibility, rather than self-gratification. They
take strength from each other to continue
building their own lives with greater
purpose—a moral perspective that gives
the movie its own strength. A couple of
overexaggerated slapstick situations and
characterizations detract from the story,
but these do not overshadow the otherwise sensitive and moving treatment of a
subject that will touch lives everywhere.
Shall We Dance won all thirteen Japanese
Academy Awards and was an audience
favorite at the 1996 Cannes Film Festival.

CONTENT ANALYSIS: (BB, L, S, A)
Moral worldview looking to dance as a
liberator of self, with moral elements of
family and husband's duty to his family;
three vulgarities; married man is
attracted to a young, beautiful, single
woman and takes dancing lessons with
her; and alcohol use.

Boys to Men

SHILOH

Quality: ☆☆☆   Acceptability: +2

WARNING CODES:

Language: *
Violence: *
Sex: None
Nudity: None

RATING: PG
GENRE: Adventure
INTENDED AUDIENCE: Families
RUNNING TIME: 93 Minutes
STARRING: Michael Moriarty, Blake
Heron, Scott Wilson, Ann Dowd, Bonnie
Bartlett, and Rod Steiger
DIRECTOR: Dale Rosenbloom
PRODUCERS: Zane W. Levitt, Dale
Rosenbloom, and Mark Yellen

EXECUTIVE PRODUCERS: Carl Borack and Mark Yellen
WRITER: Dale Rosenbloom
BASED ON: The novel by Phyllis Reynolds Naylor
DISTRIBUTOR: Legacy Films
BRIEF SUMMARY:

In *Shiloh*, a young boy, Marty, lives with his loving family in rural West Virginia. As Marty goes to town looking for work, an abused beagle named Shiloh follows him home. Marty wants to keep the dog, but the dog belongs to his neighbor, Judd. Marty's dad, Ray (Michael Moriarity), wants his son to respect another man's property and insists on returning the dog. Marty knows Judd abuses his animals. When the dog runs away again, Marty must decide whether to honor his dad and return the dog, thus sentencing the dog to many abuses, or find some way to save the adorable hound.

Marty is a good boy who helps his family, respects his parents, and wants to do the right thing in a difficult situation. He works hard to earn the dog. Marty's family is strong. To say this is merely a boy-and-his-dog movie, safe for families, would be like saying David fighting Goliath, the story told in 1 Samuel 17, is about a boy and his slingshot. This uncommonly intelligent film can generate a healthy discussion among family members of all ages regarding the issues of honesty, character, respect, and love. The acting is superb and the cinematography breathtaking. Support this kind of moviemaking, and you will not be disappointed!

CONTENT ANALYSIS: (B, L, V, A, M) Biblical, family-oriented worldview with respect, honesty, hard work, and sacrificial love, love for family and for neighbor, and respect for God's creatures, marred by a young boy hiding a dog; two vulgarities; man kicks dog several times, hits dog with butt of gun, threatens to kill dog, dog fight (no animal was harmed in the making of the film), man shoots raccoon, man treats boy harshly; and man drinks beer.

Food, Family, and Love

SOUL FOOD

Quality: ☆☆☆   Acceptability: −2

WARNING CODES:
  Language: * *
  Violence: *
  Sex: * * *
  Nudity: *
RATING: R
GENRE: Drama
INTENDED AUDIENCE: Adults
RUNNING TIME: 112 minutes
STARRING: Vanessa Williams, Vivica A. Fox, Nia Long, Michael Beach, Mekhi Pfifer, Jeffrey Sams, Irma P. Hall, and Brandon Hammond
DIRECTOR: George Tillman Jr.
PRODUCERS: Tracey E. Edmonds and Robert Teitel
EXECUTIVE PRODUCER: Kenneth "Babyface" Edmonds
WRITER: George Tillman Jr.
DISTRIBUTOR: 20th Century Fox
BRIEF SUMMARY:

In *Soul Food*, the death of kindly matriarch Mama Joe (Irma P. Hall) unleashes latent quarreling among her three daughters in a suburban Chicago African American family. Mama Joe believed that calling together the members of her fractious family each week for a Sunday afternoon banquet would build family cohesiveness. Regrettably, succumbing to diabetes, she lapses into a coma. Meanwhile, Mama Joe's three daughters, Teri, Maxine, and Bird, encounter domestic troubles including adultery, envy, and strife. The threads of the family's quilt threaten to unravel. Before she dies, Mama Joe tells her grandson, Ahmad, that she wants him to do something for her. What can ten-year-old Ahmad possibly do to bring peace to his quarreling uncles and aunts? The movie concludes with a surprisingly creative and emotionally satisfying ending.

Soul Food is distinguished by good acting, a good screenplay, and good directing. This movie uplifts the importance of family, although it is marred by crude language and depicted sex. *Soul Food* yet manages to serve up a visual banquet even with the banter, bickering, and blunt honesty of family gatherings. Strong allusions to Jesus Christ in the visiting pastor's prayer before the meals enhance the Christian nature of this film.

CONTENT ANALYSIS: (B, CC, LL, V, N, SSS, M) Moral worldview with outstanding Christian elements including a kindly African American matriarch who presides over dinners attended by quarreling daughters and their husbands; eighteen obscenities, six profanities, and four vulgarities; man threatens man with gun, woman threatens man with kitchen knife; upper front and lower rear male nudity; depicted but not graphic intercourse between married couple, and depicted fornication between a man and his mistress; and miscellaneous immorality.

Melancholy Vision

THE SWEET HEREAFTER

Quality: ✰✰✰✰   Acceptability: −2

WARNING CODES:
Language: *
Violence: *
Sex: * *
Nudity: * *
RATING: R
GENRE: Drama
INTENDED AUDIENCE: Adults
RUNNING TIME: 112 minutes
STARRING: Ian Holm, Sarah Polley, Bruce Greenwood, Tom McCamus, Gabrielle Rose, and Alberta Watson
DIRECTOR: Atom Egoyan
PRODUCERS: Camelia Frieberg and Atom Egoyan
EXECUTIVE PRODUCERS: Robert Lantos and Andras Hamori
WRITER: Atom Egoyan
BASED ON: The novel by Russell Banks
DISTRIBUTOR: Fine Line Features
BRIEF SUMMARY:
The Sweet Hereafter expertly tells the story of the aftermath of a school bus tragedy in a small Canadian town in which all the parents in the town except two lose their school-age children. Talented British actor Ian Holm plays an attorney who tries to get the parents to join a class-action lawsuit. Bruce Greenwood plays a morally flawed father who wants nothing to do with the lawsuit. Sarah Polley turns in a fine performance as the teenager of another father who has been committing incest with his daughter.

This complex art film, written and directed by Egyptian native Atom Egoyan, may be slow and confusing for those people not used to movies that jump back and forth in time. Egoyan presents a relentlessly melancholy vision of family tragedy, sexual sin, and loss in *The Sweet Hereafter*. He appears to validate several important moral principles in this movie. Egoyan strongly suggests, for example, that sexual sin has bad emotional consequences. Regrettably, he offers no solutions regarding how to truly cope with family tragedy, sexual sin, and loss. In fact, none of the characters in the movie are shown attending a church, praying to God, or opening a Bible, despite the religious overtones of the title and subject matter.

CONTENT ANALYSIS: (Pa, B, L, V, SS, NN, A, D, M) Pagan worldview with some moral principles supported such as not trying to capitalize financially on a tragedy and that sexual sin has bad emotional consequences; five obscenities; one violent school bus wreck; implied incest, depicted adultery, and an incestuous kiss; partial female nudity including female in underwear; alcohol use; tobacco use and references to drug use; and miscellaneous immorality such as lying and gossiping.

Female Rebel without a Cause

TITANIC

Quality: ✮✮✮   Acceptability: −2

WARNING CODES:

Language: * * *
Violence: * *
Sex: *
Nudity: * *

RATING: PG-13
GENRE: Historical drama
INTENDED AUDIENCE: Older teens and adults
RUNNING TIME: 187 minutes
STARRING: Leonardo DiCaprio, Kate Winslet, Billy Zane, Kathy Bates, Frances Fisher, Bernard Hill, Jonathan Hyde, Danny Nucci, David Warner, Gloria Stuart, and Bill Paxton
DIRECTOR: James Cameron
PRODUCERS: James Cameron and Jon Landau
EXECUTIVE PRODUCER: Rae Sanchini
WRITER: James Cameron
DISTRIBUTORS: Paramount Pictures and 20th Century Fox
BRIEF SUMMARY:
After all the hype, the delayed release, and the overbudgeting, *Titanic* is pure entertainment. Survivor Rose DeWitt Bukater (modeled on artist Beatrice Wood) recounts the tragedy. When diver-researcher Brock Lovett and his crew search the wreckage for a famed jewel, they find a safe containing a drawing of a young nude woman wearing the jewel. They locate the woman, Rose, now 101 years old, who tells of her adventure on the *Titanic* when she abandoned her fiancé for a young rogue artist named Jack, who saved her life as the ship sank.

Titanic is extremely photogenic, with lavish costumes, colorful sets, and superb special effects. Regrettably, Leonardo DiCaprio and Kate Winslet are too modern for the period. While everyone can enjoy the beauty of the set and appreciate the tragedy, moral Americans may be offended at the foul language, brief upper female nudity, implied fornication, and some scary scenes. On the other hand, families protect families, a Christian church service is held, and a priest recites prayers and the Bible. *Titanic* is not for children. Those who are not offended by the foul language, nudity, and fornication may be moved by this tragic tale.

CONTENT ANALYSIS: (Ro, B, C, LLL, VV, S, NN, A, D, M) Romantic worldview of luxury liner at sea and a young couple's forbidden love affair, with some Christian elements such as bravery, care for family, prayer, church scene, and Scripture reading; twenty-three obscenities (mostly mild), fourteen exclamatory profanities, and woman gives lewd gesture; moderate violence including implied drowning, threats with gun, attempted murder by shooting, man commits suicide by shooting, passengers and crew fall to their deaths, implied electrocution, and man slaps woman; implied fornication; female nudity and drawings of naked woman; alcohol use; smoking; and miscellaneous immorality including lying, obsessive behavior, and gambling.

ULEE'S GOLD

Quality: ✮✮✮✮   Acceptability: −1

WARNING CODES:

Language: * *
Violence: * *
Sex: None
Nudity: None

RATING: R
GENRE: Drama
INTENDED AUDIENCE: Adults

RUNNING TIME: 115 minutes

STARRING: Peter Fonda, Patricia Richardson, Jessica Biel, J. Kenneth Campbell, Christine Dunford, and Steven Flynn

DIRECTOR: Victor Nunez

PRODUCERS: Sam Gowan and Peter Saraf

EXECUTIVE PRODUCERS: Edward Saxon, John Sloss, and Valerie Thomas

WRITER: Victor Nunez

DISTRIBUTOR: Orion Pictures

BRIEF SUMMARY:

Praised at the 1997 Sundance Film Festival, *Ulee's Gold* stars Peter Fonda as Ulee Jackson, a beekeeper in Florida. He copes with raising his two granddaughters, Penny and Casey, because his son, Jimmy, is imprisoned and his daughter-in-law, Helen, has been absent for two years. One day, Ulee goes to rescue Helen from Jimmy's crime partner, Bill. Bill demands money for Helen and says that unless the money is delivered in a week, he will kill Helen and the granddaughters. Without casualties, Ulee is able to redeem his family and justice prevails.

Ulee's Gold has many images and themes of redemption, love, and forgiveness. Ulee works hard to provide for his family and even risks his own life to keep his family safe. His loving neighbor, Connie Hope, provides practical assistance. Casey goes from a rebellious teenager to a caring young lady. Penny demonstrates grace to her mother. Jimmy confesses his sins and asks to be accepted back into the family. The movie is rated R because the criminals use harsh language and Helen is seen in the throes of a drug overdose, but there is no sex, no nudity, and little violence. This character-driven story is about family and the lengths that one man will go to preserve and restore it. Ulee Jackson is a screen hero and his story is worth watching.

CONTENT ANALYSIS: (CCC, BB, LL, VV, A, D, M) Strong Christian worldview with many redemptive acts; fifteen obscenities, two vulgarities, and two profanities; moderate violence including threats with guns, men bind and gag women, and man stabs man in back; alcohol use; smoking, and woman withdraws from drugs; and miscellaneous immorality including rebellious attitudes.

More Media Manipulation

WAG THE DOG

Quality: ☆☆☆   Acceptability: −2

WARNING CODES:
  Language: * * *
  Violence: *
  Sex: None
  Nudity: *

RATING: R

GENRE: Satiric political drama

INTENDED AUDIENCE: Adults

RUNNING TIME: 110 minutes

STARRING: Dustin Hoffman, Robert De Niro, Denis Leary, Jim Belushi, Anne Heche, Willie Nelson, Andrea Martin, Woody Harrelson, and Kirsten Dunst

DIRECTOR: Barry Levinson

PRODUCERS: Barry Levinson, Dustin Hoffman, Robert De Niro, and Jane Rosenthal

EXECUTIVE PRODUCER: Ezra Swerdlow

WRITERS: Hilary Henkin and David Mamet

DISTRIBUTOR: New Line Cinema

BRIEF SUMMARY:

Wag the Dog stars Dustin Hoffman and Robert De Niro as men who fabricate a war and televise it to divert attention away from an indiscreet president desiring reelection. Hoffman plays a Hollywood producer named Stanley, who is hired by a presidential spin doctor named Conrad (played by De Niro), to create a fictional war between the U.S. and Albania. Stanley creates bogus news footage and even theme songs. Conrad and Stanley invent a story about a U.S. serviceman trapped in Albania who is rescued by a presidential order. Lies pile up on lies, events change, but the creative team rolls with the events until election day.

Wag the Dog is a frightening commentary on media manipulation. Much of the humor in this movie comes from the depths that these folks will sink to, to create a complete fabrication about the integrity of the presidency. The movie suggests that the president's own advisors, the CIA, and the media can be swayed to propagate lies. This movie doesn't endorse corruption, it just says that it can happen and gives an example in a comical manner. Containing many obscenities, it has no explicit sex, violence, or nudity as it exposes practices that are ultimately damaging America.

CONTENT ANALYSIS: (H, AP, LLL, V, N, A, D, M) Humanist worldview of political corruption and deception; thirty-nine obscenities and eight profanities; mild violence including implied shooting and implied murder; image of couple in bed talking; upper male nudity and woman in underwear; alcohol use; smoking; and miscellaneous immorality including lying, using people for ill-gotten gain, and discussion of purported sexual act of the president with a minor.

Genteel Cruelty

WASHINGTON SQUARE

Quality: ☆☆☆☆   Acceptability: +2

WARNING CODES:
  Language: None
  Violence: None
  Sex: None
  Nudity: None
RATING: PG
GENRE: Drama
INTENDED AUDIENCE: Teens and adults
RUNNING TIME: 115 minutes

STARRING: Jennifer Jason Leigh, Albert Finney, Ben Chaplin, and Maggie Smith
DIRECTOR: Agnieszka Holland
PRODUCERS: Roger Birnbaum and Julie Bergman Sender
EXECUTIVE PRODUCER: Randy Ostrow
WRITER: Carol Doyle
BASED ON: The novel by Henry James
DISTRIBUTOR: Hollywood Pictures/Buena Vista Pictures Distribution/Walt Disney Company
BRIEF SUMMARY:
In *Washington Square*, the exquisite retelling of the Henry James's tragic classic, Jennifer Jason Leigh plays Catherine Sloper, the daughter of a rich, pompous mid-nineteenth-century New York City doctor. A widower who has never gotten over the death of his wife, Dr. Sloper maintains tight control over Catherine and resents any suitor's intrusions into her world. When Catherine meets Morris Townsend at her sister's wedding, she allows herself to fall in love. However, Dr. Sloper refuses Morris's petition to marry his daughter and tells Catherine that he believes that Townsend only wants the Sloper fortune. Catherine agrees to accompany her father to Europe. When Dr. Sloper confronts her with his low opinion of her fiancée on a Swiss mountaintop, she defends Morris, and so Dr. Sloper calls her unfit to live in place of her deceased mother. The seeds of the impending tragedy have been sown, and the film concludes with a dignified but tragic ending.

Graced by a wonderful script, marvelous speeches, and finely shaded, emotionally nuanced acting, *Washington Square* is a resounding cinematic triumph. A period piece that compares favorably to its great film precedent, William Wyler's *The Heiress*, *Washington Square* well warrants time spent watching it.

CONTENT ANALYSIS: (Ro, B, C, FM, A) Chaste, Romantic worldview of unlucky would-be lovers in nineteenth-century New York, with biblical and free-market elements; and alcohol consumption.

Love in the Midst of War

WELCOME TO SARAJEVO

Quality: ☆☆☆☆   Acceptability: −1

WARNING CODES:
  Language: * *
  Violence: * *
  Sex: *
  Nudity: None
RATING: R
GENRE: War drama
INTENDED AUDIENCE: Adults
RUNNING TIME: 100 minutes
STARRING: Stephen Dillane, Woody Harrelson, Marisa Tomei, Kerry Fox, and Emily Lloyd
DIRECTOR: Michael Winterbottom
PRODUCERS: Graham Broadbent and Ismet Arnautalic
EXECUTIVE PRODUCER: Paul Sarony
WRITER: Frank Cottrell Boyce
BASED ON: The novel *Natasha's Story* by Michael Nicholson
DISTRIBUTOR: Miramax Films
BRIEF SUMMARY:
Welcome to Sarajevo tells the story of one man's awakening to his humanity in the midst of man's inhumanity. Michael Henderson is a British television reporter based in Sarajevo during the Serbian siege. Michael reports on the wounded, dead, and dying. He is upset by an American reporter who walks down the street to pick up a sniper victim and carry her into a church. Michael refuses to videotape the valiant scene and is scooped by the other networks. Even so, the American's act of compassion transforms Michael. He starts to take interest in the children of Sarajevo. He promises one nine-year-old girl that she will escape to England. Eventually he faces many obstacles to rescue this little girl.

Welcome to Sarajevo combines documentary footage with drama so the movie appears to have been shot in the midst of the siege. The acting is subdued and realistic, and the storyline is very emotional. There are hints of Christianity, although it is clear that there are many so-called Christians who are commiting war crimes. There is compassion for the Bosnians, but only brief references to the Christian-Muslim conflict. This film shows compassion at work when Michael rescues a young girl from this very violent war.

CONTENT ANALYSIS: (C, LL, VV, S, A, D) Mild Christian worldview about a reporter who learns to care for the civilians caught in a horrendous war; thirteen obscenities and five profanities; war violence including shots of bloody massacres, wounded people, murdered babies, and the atrocities of war; very mild sexual innuendo and husband and wife in bed; alcohol use; and smoking and drug use.

Pursuing a Dream

WILD AMERICA

Quality: ☆☆☆☆   Acceptability: +1

WARNING CODES:
  Language: **
  Violence: *
  Sex: None
  Nudity: *
RATING: G
GENRE: Adventure/Drama
INTENDED AUDIENCE: All ages
RUNNING TIME: 100 minutes
STARRING: Jonathan Taylor Thomas, Devon Sawa, Scott Bairstow, Jamey Sheridan, and Frances Fisher
DIRECTOR: William Dear
PRODUCERS: James G. Robinson, Irby Smith, and Mark Stouffer

EXECUTIVE PRODUCERS: Gary Barber, Steve Tisch, and Bill Todman Jr.

WRITER: David Michael Wieger

BASED ON: The novel by Mark Stouffer

DISTRIBUTOR: Warner Brothers

BRIEF SUMMARY:

Wild America is the true story of three Stouffer brothers who leave home in 1967 to spend the summer photographing wild animals in the American West. Young Marty cleans car parts in his father's backyard garage. His desire to photograph animals sets up a confrontation with his strict but loving father, who has worked hard to bequeath his carburetor parts company to his three sons. His father also mistrusts the financial prospects of their dream of photographing wild animals. After his mother intercedes, his father relents and lends money to Marty to buy a camera. The boys go out west, photograph bears in a cave, and return home to a bedridden father. The film concludes with an emotionally satisfying climax at a high school auditorium that their mother has rented for a showing of the brothers' wild animal adventure film.

A straight-up adventure film, *Wild America* depicts strong family values and exciting action sequences with almost no immorality. Tightly directed, the action is engrossing and believable. It is the kind of film that ought to be viewed by American audiences, who are starved for this kind of good, clean, Hardy Boys-type adventure, which champions the values of hard work, telling the truth, and self-reliance.

CONTENT ANALYSIS: (B, LL, V, N, D) Moral worldview of father wrestling with whether or not to let his three sons pursue their dream to photograph wild animals; twenty-one obscenities and three exclamatory profanities; some frightening experiences in the wild; one brief image of upper female nudity and many shots of upper male nudity; and smoking by father.

The Genteel versus the Common

THE WIND IN THE WILLOWS

Quality: ☆☆☆   Acceptability: +1

WARNING CODES:

Language: None
Violence: *
Sex: None
Nudity: None

RATING: PG

GENRE: Fantasy

INTENDED AUDIENCE: All ages

RUNNING TIME: 90 minutes

STARRING: Steve Coogan, Eric Idle, Terry Jones, Anthony Sher, Nicol Williamson, and John Cleese

DIRECTOR: Terry Jones

PRODUCERS: John Goldstone and Jake Eberts

EXECUTIVE PRODUCER: John Goldstone

WRITER: Terry Jones

BASED ON: The novel by Kenneth Grahame

DISTRIBUTOR: Columbia Pictures

BRIEF SUMMARY:

The screen adaptation of *The Wind in the Willows* by members of the Monty Python troupe is an imaginative fantasy where actors with minimal makeup portray animals. Mole, Rat, and Badger must save the day from mean weasels who are trying to steal Toad Hall from the profligate Mr. Toad. When Mole's tidy little underground Victorian home is destroyed by the weasels, Mole enlists the aid of Rat and Mr. Toad, the ne'er-do-well heir of the great Toad Hall. Regrettably, Toad is squandering his family fortune to indulge his lust for modern gadgets. Toad explains to his friends that he has sold the meadow in order to buy a motorcar. The weasels intend to take over Toad Hall and the river, eventually outlawing everything except their new dog-food factory that will use the river animals as feed. Thus

Toad, Rat, Mole, and Badger have to save the river.

This wonderful fantasy makes many moral points about cooperation, responsibility, courage, and civility. It portrays the weasels as greedy and cruel developers. It portrays Toad as a foolish heir who must come to grips with his responsibilities. In the movie, the sun talks, clocks talk and fantasy reigns. Regrettably, however, Toad is never reprimanded for escaping from jail, and stealing a train so he can get back to save Toad Hall. *The Wind in the Willows* will entertain children throughout the world who need good, fun, moral entertainment.

CONTENT ANALYSIS: (Ro, C, B, V, A, D, M) Romantic anti-modernity and pro-civility worldview with sincere repentance and forgiveness; some slapstick violence, some threats of violence and some dark scenes that may be frightening to little children; some debauchery in banquet scene; and miscellaneous immorality including man escapes from jail disguised as a woman, theft of car and train, and some lying.

Where Three Become None

THE WINGS OF THE DOVE

Quality: ☆☆☆☆   Acceptability: −2

WARNING CODES:

Language: *
Violence: None
Sex: * *
Nudity: * *

RATING: R
GENRE: Drama
INTENDED AUDIENCE: Adults
RUNNING TIME: 101 minutes
STARRING: Helena Bonham Carter, Linus Roache, Alison Elliott, Elizabeth McGovern, and Charlotte Rampling
DIRECTOR: Iain Softley
PRODUCERS: David Parfitt and Stephen Evans

EXECUTIVE PRODUCERS: Bob Weinstein, Harvey Weinstein, and Paul Feldsher
WRITER: Hossein Amini
BASED ON: The novel by Henry James
DISTRIBUTOR: Miramax Films
BRIEF SUMMARY:

The Wings of a Dove is the third adaptation of a work by nineteenth-century American expatriate Henry James in less than a year. It is a beautiful and precise story about how one woman connives to win a man she loves and ends up empty-handed. Helena Bonham Carter plays Kate, who lives in London in 1910. Kate is born into nobility, but is attracted to journalist Merton Densher. If Kate were ever to make her love for Merton public, she would lose her inheritance. The arrival of the dying American heiress, Millie, inspires Kate to plot to win Merton and Millie's money. When Kate invites Merton to join Millie and her on a vacation in Venice, unexpected consequences arise, causing Kate's plan to crumble.

The audience's sympathies are divided between despising Kate's perverted plans and having compassion for her because of the cruel social order in which she is trapped. She defies the social order by loving Merton and breaks the moral order by hoping to benefit from the death of Millie. Near the end, this morality tale has a brief but graphic sex scene, where Merton and Kate try to make love, but end up making resolutions that alienate them forever.

CONTENT ANALYSIS: (B, Pa, L, SS, NN, A, D, M) Moral worldview constantly challenged by selfish desires resulting in a bitter ending; one profanity; heavy kissing, brief clothed act of fornication and brief act of unclothed fornication; brief full female and full male nudity (no genitalia) and paintings of nudes; alcohol use and drunkenness; smoking and brief depicted opium use; and lying, devious plans, and selfish attitudes.

Los Angeles Erupts

VOLCANO

Quality: ☆☆☆☆   Acceptability: −1

WARNING CODES:
  Language: * *
  Violence: *
  Sex: None
  Nudity: None
RATING: PG-13
GENRE: Action/Drama
INTENDED AUDIENCE: Older children and adults
RUNNING TIME: 95 minutes
STARRING: Tommy Lee Jones, Anne Heche, Gaby Hoffman, and Don Cheadle
DIRECTOR: Mick Jackson
PRODUCERS: Neal H. Moritz and Andrew Z. Davis
EXECUTIVE PRODUCER: Lauren Shuler Donner
WRITERS: Jerome Armstrong and Billy Ray
DISTRIBUTOR: 20th Century Fox
BRIEF SUMMARY:
In *Volcano,* after an earthquake, a volcano erupts from the La Brea tar pits in Los Angeles and sends hot lava flowing out onto the streets. Under Mick Jackson's able direction, the film explodes onto the screen with ninety-five minutes of nonstop action. Tommy Lee Jones plays Los Angeles Office of Emergency Management chief Mike Roark, who comes on the scene of some strange geological events that the scientists can't explain. Soon he is battling a volcano that erupts and creates havoc.

This movie is nonstop action and very moral. Two minor characters explicitly quote from Scripture. One minor character, who is loading priceless Bosch paintings into a truck outside a city museum, declares that the paintings are priceless because they deal with "man's inclination to sin, in defiance of God's will." Another man tells a fireman that Matthew 7:26 is his favorite verse, because it deals with a man building his house on sand. *Volcano* is an inspiring and exciting picture, marred by some scurrilous language.

CONTENT ANALYSIS: (B, CC, LL, V, O) Biblical worldview with heroic overtones and Christian elements; thirteen obscenities and seven profanities; men burned to death, man expires in lava flow, and multiple car accidents; and radio references to astrology.

☆☆☆ THE BEST 1997 FILMS FOR FAMILIES ☆☆☆

Headline	Title
They Found Each Other at Church	*Air Bud*
Demonic Attack and Answered Prayer	*Anastasia*
Hope and Courage	*Cats Don't Dance*
Get Me to the Church on Time	*Flubber*
Manners	*Mr. Magoo*
How to Love Your Child	*Leave It to Beaver*
Pursuing a Dream	*Wild America*
Restoring the Family	*Jungle 2 Jungle*
Service above Self	*Mrs. Brown*
Remnant Theology	*Batman and Robin*

★★★ THE BEST 1997 FILMS FOR MATURE AUDIENCES ★★★

Headline	Title
The Gospel Gem Within	*Amistad*
Amazing Grace in the Midst of Horror	*Paradise Road*
God's Grace	*The Apostle*
Willing to Risk One's Life for Others	*Air Force One*
Love and Forgiveness	*Ulee's Gold*
Redemptive Moments	*The Edge*
Choosing What Is Right	*The Rainmaker*
Uncovering True Lies	*Conspiracy Theory*
Doing the Right Thing	*My Best Friend's Wedding*
Overcoming Bondage	*Shall We Dance?*

★★★ THE TWENTY MOST UNBEARABLE FILMS OF 1997 ★★★

Headline	Title
Worst Psychopathic Promotion of Violence	*Scream 2*
Worst Wicked Combination of Occultism, Christianity, and Pedophilia	*Eve's Bayou*
Worst Demonic Sci-Fi	*Event Horizon*
Worst Anti-Christian Children's Movies (tie)	*The Education of Little Tree* and *Fairytale—A True Story*
Worst Insidious Homosexual Propaganda	*In and Out*
Worst Vapid Reduction of Faith	*Contact*
Worst Blatant Peddling of Pornography	*Boogie Nights*
Worst Attack on God's Law	*Commandments*
Worst Dirty Old Man	*Deconstructing Harry*
Worst Promotion of Satan	*Devil's Advocate*
Worst Feminist Diatribe	*G. I. Jane*
Worst Sexual Idolatry	*Kama Sutra, a Tale of Love*
Worst Attack on Christianity Promoting Gaea Worship	*Fire Down Below*
Worst Promotion of Necromancy	*Kissed*
Worst Promotion of Demonic Religious Beliefs (tie)	*Kundun* and *Seven Years in Tibet*
Worst Anti-Morality Propaganda	*Midnight in the Garden of Good and Evil*
Worst Exhibitionism	*Private Parts*
Worst Promotion of Nazis in Space	*Starship Troopers*
Worst Brew of Sex and Violence	*Crash*
Worst Promotion of 1960s Libertinism	*Father's Day*

Crawling with Fun

ANTZ

Quality: ✰✰✰✰   Acceptability: +2

WARNING CODES:
   Language: *
   Violence: * *
   Sex: None
   Nudity: None
RATING: PG
GENRE: Animated comedy
INTENDED AUDIENCE: Ages eight and up
RUNNING TIME: 77 minutes
VOICES: Woody Allen, Sylvester Stallone, Sharon Stone, Gene Hackman, Dan Aykroyd, Anne Bancroft, Jennifer Lopez, Danny Glover, Jane Curtin, and Christopher Walken
DIRECTORS: Eric Darnell and Tim Johnson
PRODUCERS: Brad Lewis, Aron Warner, and Patty Wooton
EXECUTIVE PRODUCERS: Penney Finkelman-Cox, Sandra Rabins, and Carl Rosendahl
WRITERS: Todd Alcott, Chris Weitz, and Paul Weitz
DISTRIBUTOR: DreamWorks Pictures
BRIEF SUMMARY:

In *Antz*, a neurotic New York worker ant named Z is tired of conformity and longs for individuality when he meets a beautiful female ant who turns out to be the spoiled daughter of the queen ant. Z tries to find help for his angst. Therapy does not supply a solution, but the beautiful princess certainly does. They are accidentally ejected from the colony and encounter a myriad of obstacles in the outside world. When the princess is kidnapped, Z returns to the colony just in time to save everyone from the evil plans of a corrupt general. Valor, courage, and love ultimately win the day.

Antz is a superb piece of computer animation. The voices and matching caricatures of Woody Allen and the rest of the cast render a convincing, enticing invitation to an unexplored yet familiar domain. Although it has some violence, scary moments, and mild foul language, good defeats evil in *Antz*. The movie's moral, anti-Communist worldview takes a Christian stance in its solution to Z's internal battle whether to serve the community or his own individual desires and needs. Z learns that the individual has obligations toward the community, and the community has obligations toward the individual. This is a biblical viewpoint founded on the nature of the Holy Trinity, three persons in one God, the divine foundation for both the Many and the One.

CONTENT ANALYSIS: (BB, ACAC, CC, L, VV, AA, M) Moral worldview of good versus evil and anti-Communist theme with strong, positive implications for Christian theology and philosophy; seven mild obscenities, two mild exclamatory profanities, a couple of mild vulgarities, and a reference to the rear end of an aphid; mild slapstick violence, a fight in an ant saloon, scary war scenes of ant army fighting big termites who spit acid, with mild homage to *Saving Private Ryan*, ant leader tries to drown colony of ants, and humans use magnifying glass and flyswatter to kill bugs; one passing reference to "erotic fantasies" and brief discussions about ants having lots of children; bugs wear no clothes; alcohol use and drunkenness; and bureaucrat plots to commit mass murder and become dictator.

Not Yet

ARMAGEDDON

Quality: ☆☆☆☆   Acceptability: −1

WARNING CODES:
Language: * * *
Violence: * *
Sex: *
Nudity: *

RATING: PG-13
GENRE: Science fiction
INTENDED AUDIENCE: Teens and adults
RUNNING TIME: 145 minutes
STARRING: Bruce Willis, Ben Affleck, Liv Tyler, Billy Bob Thornton, Peter Stormare, and Steve Buscemi
DIRECTOR: Michael Bay
PRODUCERS: Jerry Bruckheimer, Gale Anne Hurd, and Michael Bay
EXECUTIVE PRODUCERS: Jonathan Hensleigh, Jim Van Wyck, and Chad Oman
WRITERS: Jonathan Hensleigh and J. J. Abrams
DISTRIBUTOR: Touchstone Pictures/Buena Vista Pictures Distribution/Walt Disney Company
BRIEF SUMMARY:
Armageddon possesses more hormones, more of an attitude, and less of the philosophic musings of *Deep Impact*. When a meteor shower hits New York, NASA finds out that there is a giant asteroid headed for Earth. The director of NASA, Dan Truman, states the asteroid will decimate the Earth in twenty days. NASA sends two crews in two new space shuttles to drill into the asteroid and plant a nuclear bomb. NASA hires the best driller in the world— Harry Stamper. Stamper brings his misfits to accomplish the mighty deed and save the planet from destruction.

Although the story is predictable, the character development and scripting is so good that this roller coaster keeps the audience on the edge of their seats. Reconciliation scenes, romantic scenes, and good-old-boy scenes all provide the necessary cadence to keep the emotions on edge. Aside from the few nods at evolution, there is much prayer, quoting of the Bible, and praise to Jesus. If it wasn't for the mild foul language and a bar scene with a crewman with an overactive libido, this would be a very acceptable film. Regrettably, however, *Armageddon* posits that man triumphs over the apocalypse.

CONTENT ANALYSIS: (Pa, Ev, CC, LLL, VV, S, N, A, D, M) Eclectic worldview with evolutionary elements, pagan elements, anti-biblical elements, and moral and Christian elements including sacrificing oneself for others and appeals to Jesus and God, with the humanist premise that man triumphs over prophecy; thirty obscenities and ten profanities (mostly mild); lots of action special effects, with violence such as hurtling meteors, crashing spaceships, breaking apart oil rigs with consequent injury to people, but very little blood and gore and only brief man-to-man combat including shoving and pointing a gun at someone; implied fornication; revealing clothing and bar scene with women in revealing clothing; alcohol use; smoking; and disobedience to authority and rebellious attitudes that are rebuked and resolved.

Helpful Lilliputians

THE BORROWERS

Quality: ☆☆☆☆   Acceptability: +2

WARNING CODES:
Language: *
Violence: *
Sex: None
Nudity: None

RATING: PG
GENRE: Family/Fantasy
INTENDED AUDIENCE: Children and adults
RUNNING TIME: 87 Minutes

STARRING: John Goodman, Doon Mackichan, Jim Broadbent, Mark Williams, Bradley Pierce, Celia Imire, and Aden Gillett

DIRECTOR: Peter Hewitt

PRODUCERS: Tim Bevan, Rachel Talalay, and Eric Fellner

EXECUTIVE PRODUCER: Walt de Faria

WRITERS: Gavin Scott and John Kamps

BASED ON: The book by Mary Norton

DISTRIBUTOR: Polygram Filmed Entertainment

BRIEF SUMMARY:

In *The Borrowers*, a family of miniature people who exist on borrowed knickknacks and live under the floorboards of the first floor of a house, come to the family's rescue when an evil banker unjustly evicts them from their heritage. Pete discovers and befriends a whole family of miniature people, the Clocks (also called the Borrowers), who purloin household knickknacks temporarily as they maintain their diminutive existence under the floorboards of the Lenders' first floor, trying not to be squished. Through a series of comical misadventures, the Borrowers help to right the wrongs caused by the greedy lawyer and enable the Lender family to keep their house.

The Borrowers is a magical tale of innocent imagination with wholesome, delightful humor and family-friendly themes. Special effects enhance the story, but don't overwhelm it. For example, Pop Clock pulls himself up the side of the kitchen table with a miniature hook and needle. He teaches his children to obey the Borrowers Code of Rules: "Be quiet, cautious, and inconspicuous. Never be seen, never be heard, and never be squished." Funny, imaginative, wholesome, and delightful, *The Borrowers* will bring joy and mirth to the whole family.

CONTENT ANALYSIS: (Ro, B, L, V) Romantic worldview of magical minia-ture people coming to the rescue of unjustly dispossessed homeowners, with biblical elements of good overcoming evil; one obscenity and a miniature boy falls into dog feces; and some fantasy violence including truck running over miniature boy who survives, termite gun accidentally turned on man, miniature boy and girl take acrobatic falls down drainpipes, kitchen appliances fall on man, and miniature girl falls into milk bottle.

A Fun Epic of Miniature Proportions

A BUG'S LIFE

Quality: ☆☆☆☆   Acceptability: +3

WARNING CODES:

Language: None
Violence: * *
Sex: None
Nudity: None

RATING: G

GENRE: Animated comedy

INTENDED AUDIENCE: All ages

RUNNING TIME: 70 minutes

VOICES: Dave Foley, Kevin Spacey, Julia Louis-Dreyfus, Phyllis Diller, Roddy McDowall, David Hyde Pierce, Jonathan Harris, and John Ratzenberger

DIRECTOR: John Lasseter

CODIRECTOR: Andrew Stanton

PRODUCERS: Darla Anderson and Kevin Reher

WRITERS: Donald McEnery, Andrew Stanton, and Bob Shaw

DISTRIBUTOR: Walt Disney Pictures/Buena Vista Pictures Distribution/Walt Disney Company

BRIEF SUMMARY:

Pixar Studios and Walt Disney's *A Bug's Life* is the story of a persistent ant who saves his colony from a menacing villain. This time the villain is a grasshopper named Hopper, who leads a band of other grasshoppers to extort food. An inventive worker ant named Flik enlists a group of circus bugs to fend off the evil horde in a story reminiscent of Japanese filmmaker Kurosawa's *Seven Samurai*, and Italian filmmaker Federico Fellini's *La Strada* about inept circus performers.

A Bug's Life is marvelous family filmmaking. Audiences will probably find the circus bugs the most enjoyable aspect of this movie. Their interaction among each other and with the other characters really brings the movie to life. *A Bug's Life* extols the values of courage, teamwork, hope, perseverance, community, and individual effort. Flik, the hero ant, shows tremendous courage in standing up for the weak against a bigger, stronger villain, leading to a rousing, heartwarming finish. Computer animation takes another leap forward in this movie. Director John Lasseter and his staff of writers, animators, and computer technicians create an elaborate alternate reality that is fun to watch.

CONTENT ANALYSIS: (BB, VV, A, M) Moderately moral worldview of good and evil; moderate action violence including grasshoppers forcing ants to collect food for them, ant hits rock, circus bugs accidentally scorch flea, birds chase bugs to eat them, and evil grasshopper hits ants and threatens child ant; mild transgender humor about male ladybug; bugs drink alcohol-like drinks in bar settings and mean grasshoppers drink alcohol-like drinks in Mexican-style saloon; lying rebuked; some references to magical thinking from a washed-up mantis, and rebuked intolerance for someone who doesn't fit in with the crowd.

Justice Sometimes Has Its Price

A CIVIL ACTION

Quality: ☆☆☆☆   Acceptability: −1

WARNING CODES:
Language: *
Violence: *
Sex: None
Nudity: None

RATING: PG-13
GENRE: Drama
INTENDED AUDIENCE: Teens and adults
RUNNING TIME: 113 minutes
STARRING: John Travolta, Robert Duvall, William H. Macy, Tony Shalhoub, Kathleen Quinlan, John Lithgow, and Dan Hedaya
DIRECTOR: Steven Zaillian
PRODUCERS: Scott Rudin, Robert Redford, and Rachel Pfeffer
EXECUTIVE PRODUCERS: Steven Zaillian and David Wisnievitz
WRITER: Steven Zaillian
BASED ON: The book by Jonathan Harr
DISTRIBUTOR: Touchstone Pictures/Buena Vista Pictures Distribution/Walt Disney Company
BRIEF SUMMARY:
Based on a true story, *A Civil Action* stars John Travolta as personal injury lawyer Jan Schlichtmann, a rich, polished bachelor who gives up all his material possessions to pursue a case where water pollution killed several children in a New England community. In trying the case, Jan butts heads with the lawyer of a huge corporation, played by Robert Duvall in one of his best performances.

Courtroom dramas can be among the most confining, predictable movies. Famed screenwriter Steven Zaillian (*Schindler's List* and *Searching for Bobby Fischer*, two of the best movies in recent years) overcomes the limitations of the genre in *A Civil Action*. This is a mesmerizing movie with lots of wonderful acting, including Travolta as the slick lawyer with the conscience he didn't know he had. Despite the environmentalism in this movie, which seems to favor a bloated federal government, *A Civil Action* contains some strong moral aspects of fighting for truth, goodness, and justice at great personal cost. It also keeps the foul language to a real minimum and includes no sexual immorality, nudity, or excessive violence.

CONTENT ANALYSIS: (BB, E, So, L, V, A, D, M) Moral worldview with an environmentalist plot problem and socialist elements that in one key scene reflect nihilism; five obscenities and four profanities; mild threats of violence, tearing apart an office in frustration, and arguing; alcohol use; smoking; and local companies lie to cover up their pollution of local drinking water but personal injury lawyer goes after big companies because they have money, then relies on federal government when he loses case due to his own pride and mismanagement.

Moving Family Tribute

DEEP IMPACT

Quality: ★★★☆   Acceptability: −1

WARNING CODES:
Language: * *
Violence: *
Sex: *
Nudity: None
RATING: PG-13
GENRE: Science fiction
INTENDED AUDIENCE: Older children to adults
RUNNING TIME: 121 minutes
STARRING: Robert Duvall, Téa Leoni, Morgan Freeman, Elijah Wood, Maximilian Schell, Ron Eldard, Vanessa Redgrave, and Leelee Sobieski
DIRECTOR: Mimi Leder
PRODUCERS: Richard D. Zanuck and David Brown
EXECUTIVE PRODUCERS: Steven Spielberg, Walter Parkes, and Joan Bradshaw
WRITERS: Bruce Joel Rubin and Michael Tolkin
DISTRIBUTORS: Paramount Pictures and DreamWorks Pictures
BRIEF SUMMARY:
Deep Impact is an exciting disaster movie and a dramatic celebration of the traditional ties that bind families together. In the movie, the U.S. government learns that a large comet will hit Earth and destroy all life. It works secretly with Russia to build a spaceship to break up the comet, but a young TV news reporter named Jenny Lerner finds out about the comet. The president, played by Morgan Freeman, decides to tell everything to the nation and the world. He announces that veteran astronaut Spurgeon Tanner, played by Robert Duvall, will lead the spaceship's expedition.

Deep Impact is a celebration of heroic self-sacrifice and the traditional ties that bind families together. As people prepare to meet their doom, the movie focuses on the reactions of several American families: the families of the astronauts, the reporter's estranged relationship with her father, and the families of two teenagers in love. Those who support traditional family values may be particularly moved by the reconciliation scene between the reporter and her father. They also will like the president's reference to God answering people's prayer and the final scenes between the astronauts and their families. The movie, however, has some gratuitous foul language, a flippant remark about sex from a teenager, and shots of people being swept away by tidal waves.

CONTENT ANALYSIS: (BB, CC, H, Fe, LL, V, S, A, D, M) Moderately moral worldview that pays tribute to traditional family relationships and heroic self-sacrifice, including reference to God and a quotation from 1 Corinthians 13; sixteen obscenities and eleven profanities (mostly exclamatory); mild action violence of explosions on comet and on spaceship, video news shots of looters/protestors, suicide, and tidal wave from small comet devastates cities, killing millions, with medium- and long-distance shots of people getting horribly swept away; one senseless verbal reference to juvenile sex; alcohol use; smoking; and feminist images of daycare center at work and minor humanist themes of government deciding people's fate by lottery.

Movie Malpractice

DR. DOLITTLE

Quality: ☆☆   Acceptability: −1

WARNING CODES:
  Language: * *
  Violence: *
  Sex: *
  Nudity: *

RATING: PG-13
GENRE: Comedy
INTENDED AUDIENCE: Children and adults
RUNNING TIME: 86 minutes
STARRING: Eddie Murphy, Kristen Wilson, Ossie Davis, Oliver Platt, Peter Boyle, Kyla Pratt, Norm Macdonald, Chris Rock, and Albert Brooks
DIRECTOR: Betty Thomas
PRODUCERS: John Davis, Joseph M. Singer, and David T. Friendly
EXECUTIVE PRODUCERS: Sue Baden-Powell and Jenno Topping
WRITERS: Nat Mauldin and Larry Levin
DISTRIBUTOR: 20th Century Fox
BRIEF SUMMARY:
Comedian Eddie Murphy applies his brand of comic attitude to a beloved character in children's literature in *Dr. Dolittle*. Murphy plays John Dolittle, a doctor who's about to accept a lucrative deal with a major HMO. John has suppressed his unique gift of talking with animals, but the gift returns just as he is about to sign the HMO deal. Animals start to flock to him, seeking medical attention and even psychological advice. They disrupt his well-planned life, including his family. Eventually he and his family have to decide how they will respond to the crisis.

Dr. Dolittle is a fine vehicle for Murphy's talents, but the comedy is uneven and fails to build to a cohesive, hilarious climax. Although children will love to watch the animals in this movie and enjoy some of their antics, the movie includes an abundance of crude scatological references and mild scatological obscenities, especially during the movie's first half. For an Eddie Murphy film, *Dr. Dolittle* is mild; for a children's movie, it is still too much. Thus, while the movie contains a mildly moral worldview that rebukes greed and extols family togetherness, *Dr. Dolittle* deserves a caution for concerned parents and their children.

CONTENT ANALYSIS: (B, Ro, E, LL, V, S, N, AA) Mildly moral worldview where greed is rebuked and a man's family learns to accept his unique gift, with mild romanticist and environmental elements; one strong obscenity, thirteen mild obscenities, one strong profanity, one mild profanity, several vulgarities, and one blasphemy where a reverend and his belief in exorcism are mocked; man hits man with door and man punches man in nose; one scene where a husband and wife plan sex and several sexual innuendos; one scene of partial rear female nudity; and alcohol use and drunkenness.

The Virgin Queen?

ELIZABETH

Quality: ☆☆☆   Acceptability: −4

WARNING CODES:
  Language: *
  Violence: * * *
  Sex: * * *
  Nudity: * *

RATING: R
GENRE: Historical drama
INTENDED AUDIENCE: Adults
RUNNING TIME: 124 minutes
STARRING: Cate Blanchett, Geoffrey Rush, Joseph Fiennes, Christopher Eccleston, and Richard Attenborough
DIRECTOR: Shekhar Kapur
PRODUCERS: Alison Owen, Eric Fellner, and Tim Bevan
WRITER: Michael Hirst
DISTRIBUTOR: Gramercy Pictures
BRIEF SUMMARY:
Elizabeth is an R-rated revisionist view of what happened in the early years of

the reign of Queen Elizabeth I in sixteenth-century England. Containing excessive violence, sexual content, and nudity, this movie portrays Elizabeth as a weak woman who wants merely to play with her paramour and who fails to grasp the basic principles of the Christian faith for which she was willing to die in real life. The real Elizabeth was a strong woman and a profound Protestant theologian who was willing to die for her faith and to avoid compromising affairs.

Many modern pagans cannot imagine that anyone could ever be a virgin their whole life. Thus, the creators behind the movie *Elizabeth* envision a Queen Elizabeth I, the long-reigning Virgin Queen of sixteenth-century England, as a woman who must give up her young lover for the good of England. Queen Elizabeth, played by Cate Blanchett, decides she must remain unmarried in order to protect herself and serve her country. She also must use the head of her secret service to smoke out some traitors and assassinate another queen in Scotland.

Despite its pagan view of sex, politics, and sixteenth-century religious conflict, *Elizabeth* is not without its positive qualities as a movie. It sympathizes with the predicament of Elizabeth who, in order to protect herself and help her country, must focus completely on her public life. The movie seems to honor her decision even as it brings a note of sadness to the story. Also, despite its critical view of some of the religious leaders of the day, the movie does not attack essential Christian beliefs or the Bible.

CONTENT ANALYSIS: (Pa, B, C, L, VVV, SSS, NN, A, RHRHRH, M) Mild pagan worldview of religious and political battles in sixteenth-century England and of famous queen who gives up her private life to serve her country, plus some moral and Christian elements;

four mild obscenities and one mild profanity plus one crude sexual remark; moderately gory scenes of battlefield of corpses and corpse of woman killed by poisoned dress that cut into her flesh, excessively violent scenes of three Protestant "heretics" burned at stake, heads on sticks and brief torture scene of Roman Catholic assassin/priest; several scenes of depicted and implied fornication and adultery; upper female and male nudity; alcohol use; strong revisionist history about the Protestant Reformation and England; and Roman Catholic queen persecutes Protestants, Pope allegedly uses priest to try to assassinate a Protestant queen, Protestant queen allegedly gets revenge by killing off treasonous rivals, and noble Frenchman dresses in women's clothes in one scene.

If the Slipper Fits

EVER AFTER

Quality: ☆☆☆☆   Acceptability: +1

WARNING CODES:
  Language: None
  Violence: *
  Sex: None
  Nudity: None
RATING: PG-13
GENRE: Historical fantasy
INTENDED AUDIENCE: Teens and adults
RUNNING TIME: 122 minutes
STARRING: Drew Barrymore, Anjelica Huston, Dougray Scott, and Jeanne Moreau
DIRECTOR: Andy Tennant
PRODUCERS: Mireille Soria and Tracey Trench
WRITERS: Susannah Grant, Andy Tennant, and Rick Parks
DISTRIBUTOR: 20th Century Fox
BRIEF SUMMARY:
Ever After turns the classic Cinderella story into an imaginative, entertaining

masterpiece without magic or fairy god-mothers. In sixteenth-century France, servants prepare for the arrival of their lord, Auguste, and his new bride, Rodmilla. His first wife died while giving birth to his daughter, Danielle. Rodmilla is accompanied by her two daughters. When Auguste dies suddenly, Danielle is raised as a servant by Rodmilla. Years later, young Prince Henry discovers Danielle and is impressed by her spirit. The king offers the prince an opportunity to find a bride before the masked ball or marry a Spanish princess. Rodmilla introduces her daughters to the prince, but subjects Danielle to heavy work and ridicule. The climax is surprising, unique, and satisfying.

This is not just one of five hundred fairy-tale versions of Cinderella; instead, it is a very realistic fantasy with no magic and no fairy godmother. The dialogue is exquisite, full of humor, pathos, and profound insight into the human condition. There are strong positive references to God and powerful references to responsibility. Regrettably, there are a sprinkling of obscenities and some exclamations. *Ever After* is a film that people need to discover, and once they do it will help them to live happily ever after.

CONTENT ANALYSIS: (CC, L, V, M) Finely tuned Christian worldview with an appeal to God, references to God, lies rebuked, and moral principles taught; three exclamations invoking God, and four mild obscenities; swordplay, punching, and seeing the effect of a whipping; several kisses; and cruel stepmother utters death threats.

Here, Lizard, Lizard

GODZILLA

Quality: ☆☆☆☆   Acceptability: −1

WARNING CODES:
  Language: * * *

Violence: * *
  Sex: None
  Nudity: None
RATING: PG-13
GENRE: Science fiction
INTENDED AUDIENCE: Older children and adults
RUNNING TIME: 140 minutes
STARRING: Matthew Broderick, Jean Reno, Maria Pitillo, and Hank Azaria
  DIRECTOR: Roland Emmerich
  PRODUCER: Dean Devlin
  EXECUTIVE PRODUCERS: Roland Emmerich, Ute Emmerich, and William Fay
  WRITERS: Dean Devlin and Roland Emmerich
  DISTRIBUTOR: TriStar Pictures
  BRIEF SUMMARY:
Roland Emmerich and Dean Devlin, the brains behind the successful films *Stargate* and *Independence Day,* turn their golden touch on Japanese monster movies in the eagerly awaited American version of *Godzilla.* This time, Godzilla is the creation of nuclear testing by the French government in Polynesia. He is headed for New York City to lay a bunch of eggs. Fortunately, nuclear biologist Nick Tatopoulos, played by Matthew Broderick, helps a group of French Secret Service men destroy the monster's lair and trap Godzilla so that the United States Air Force can kill him.

Godzilla lacks the depth and characterizations of Devlin and Emmerich's earlier hits, but it packs an immensely powerful punch in its action sequences. Regrettably, however, *Godzilla* is filled with foul language. Although most of the expletives are mild, there are so many of them that the movie gets our highest rating for excessive foul language. The movie also lacks the prayers and patriotism of Emmerich and Devlin's last movie, *Independence Day,* which earned a Movieguide Award for Ten Best 1996 Films for Mature Audiences.

The film does, however, condemn lying and stealing to get ahead. In doing so, it explicitly decries the old adage, "Nice guys finish last."

CONTENT: (B, H, E, LLL, VV, M) Mild moral worldview with humanist and environmental elements; three strong obscenities, twenty-one mild obscenities, six profanities, and six vulgarities; intense action violence and scary suspense (Godzilla and his young eat a few people but there is no gore); drinking; smoking; and a female journalist is goaded into stealing to get a hot story.

Seeking Renewal and Restoration

HOPE FLOATS

Quality: ☆☆☆☆   Acceptability: −1

WARNING CODES:
  Language: None
  Violence: *
  Sex: * *
  Nudity: None
RATING: PG-13
GENRE: Romantic drama
INTENDED AUDIENCE: Young adults
RUNNING TIME: 100 minutes
STARRING: Sandra Bullock, Harry Connick Jr., Gena Rowlands, and Mae Whitman
  DIRECTOR: Forest Whitaker
  PRODUCER: Lynda Obst
  EXECUTIVE PRODUCERS: Sandra Bullock and Mary McLaglen
  WRITER: Steven Rogers
  DISTRIBUTOR: 20th Century Fox
  BRIEF SUMMARY:
In the poignant and moving *Hope Floats*, Sandra Bullock turns in a powerful performance as a woman spurned by the news of her husband's infidelity with her best friend. As Birdee Pruitt, Bullock returns to her Texas hometown to find healing, grace, and renewal. Married to her high school sweetheart for many years, Birdee discovers that her husband,

Bill, and her best friend, Connie, are having an affair. Devastated, Birdee takes her nine-year-old daughter, Bernice, and returns to her mother's house in Texas. Birdee, a former beauty queen, has to adjust to being a single mom while struggling with the humiliation of her husband's affair. Meanwhile, Bernice is having a difficult time being away from her father and has trouble making friends. Birdee's mother tries to get Birdee together with Justin, who had a crush on Birdee in high school.

Hope Floats speaks about marriage and love and how one copes with its pressures and problems. This film focuses on the breakup of the nuclear family due to betrayal and infidelity. *Hope Floats* portrays the healing process that the rejected spouse goes through from hitting rock bottom to regaining self-confidence. It also depicts the anguish that children experience. *Hope Floats* raises some good issues for discussion. It clearly presents the negative consequences and destructiveness of infidelity, while affirming the value of support, love, and stability.

CONTENT ANALYSIS: (Ro, B, V, SS, A, D) Romantic worldview with moral elements; very mild violence including a big child hitting a smaller child; one scene of implied sex and adultery themes; alcohol use; and smoking.

Grace and Healing

THE HORSE WHISPERER

Quality: ☆☆☆☆   Acceptability: +1

WARNING CODES:
  Language: *
  Violence: *
  Sex: *
  Nudity: None
RATING: PG-13
GENRE: Drama
INTENDED AUDIENCE: Older teens and adults

RUNNING TIME: 165 minutes

STARRING: Robert Redford, Kristin Scott Thomas, Sam Neill, Dianne Wiest, Scarlett Johansson, and Chris Cooper

DIRECTOR: Robert Redford

PRODUCERS: Robert Redford and Patrick Markey

EXECUTIVE PRODUCER: Rachel Pfeffer

WRITERS: Eric Roth and Richard LaGravenese

BASED ON: The novel by Nicholas Evans

DISTRIBUTOR: Touchstone Pictures

BRIEF SUMMARY:

Robert Redford directs the movie adaptation of the popular novel *The Horse Whisperer*. One frosty winter morning, thirteen-year-old Grace gets into a terrible accident while riding her horse Pilgrim. Grace's mother, Annie, decides to help Grace and Pilgrim by taking them across the country to see horse specialist Tom Booker, played by Redford. So starts a long, arduous rehabilitation program with the goal of calming Pilgrim and Grace. Meanwhile, Tom develops an adulterous attraction towards Annie. As Booker's work nears completion, Annie discusses her differences with her husband and makes a choice that will dramatically affect their future.

The Horse Whisperer is filled with grace, love, patience, and sacrifices made to achieve personal healing. It is filled with examples and behaviors of health and Christ-likeness. Life is mentioned as a gift from God. The gospel of Christ is preached on the radio. At the Booker home, grace is given before meals. Moral troubles occur when Annie and Tom become attracted to one another but, while an adulterous kiss is shared, she makes moral and correct choices. An expertly crafted movie from an American film icon, it is a sensitive, beautiful, honorable movie with lots to recommend it and a great deal of integrity and grace.

CONTENT ANALYSIS: (CC, BBB, Ev, Pa, L, V, S, A, M) Strong moral and Christian worldview featuring theme of restoration, with prayers, listening to Christian radio, recognition that life is a gift from God, and extensive acts of patience, love, hospitality, and healing; one evolutionary statement, five obscenities, and four profanities; brutal but brief violence tastefully photographed of a truck accident that injures girl and a horse and kills another girl; an adulterous kiss and sexual tension; alcohol use; tobacco use; and arguing and difficult family conflict scenes.

Great Holiday Entertainment

I'LL BE HOME FOR CHRISTMAS

Quality: ☆☆☆☆   Acceptability: +2

WARNING CODES:
   Language: *
   Violence: None
   Sex: None
   Nudity: *

RATING: PG

GENRE: Comedy

INTENDED AUDIENCE: Ages seven and up

RUNNING TIME: 86 minutes

STARRING: Jonathan Taylor Thomas, Jessica Biel, Adam LaVorgna, Gary Cole, Eve Gordan, Lauren Maltby, and Andrew Lauer

DIRECTOR: Arlene Sanford

PRODUCERS: David Hoberman and Tracey Trench

EXECUTIVE PRODUCER: Robin French

WRITERS: Tom Nursall and Harris Goldberg

BASED ON: A story by Michael Allin

DISTRIBUTOR: Walt Disney Pictures/Buena Vista Pictures Distribution/Walt Disney Company

BRIEF SUMMARY:

A delightful comedy about a scheming college student who learns the errors of his ways, *I'll Be Home for Christmas* stars Jonathan Taylor Thomas of TV's *Home Improvement*. Thomas plays selfish Jake Wilkinson, who wakes up days before Christmas to find himself stranded in the California desert. Jake is the butt of a practical joke by some football players, who think he double-crossed them and glued a Santa Claus hat and beard on his head. Jake must find a way to get back to his family in New York by Christmas Eve and catch up with his girlfriend.

The PG rating for this entertaining, heartwarming movie comes more from Jake's conniving ways and the dangerous practical joke played on him than from its very mild foul language. Although there are only two references to Jesus Christ, who is the real reason for the season, the movie has no distasteful sexual references and plenty of positive family values. Jake changes his selfish ways, learns to help others, and reconciles with his stepmother and father in a charming and uplifting way. A delightful script, tight direction, and enjoyable performances help make this movie one of the best holiday comedies.

CONTENT ANALYSIS: (BB, L, N, DD, M) Moderately moral worldview of selfish character who repents and changes his immoral ways; one possible obscenity silently mouthed, three mild exclamatory profanities, and four mild vulgarities; kissing, reference to what it would be like to wake up to someone after marriage, single man buys plane tickets for beach vacation with girlfriend, and single man wrongly thinks rival might have slept with girlfriend but woman forced man to wear sweaters, coats, and mittens while they shared a hotel bed; upper male nudity, and hero pulls towel off college student who has just taken a shower but object blocks the view; jocks drug college student and leave him stranded to get revenge; and miscellaneous immorality such as lying, stealing, cheating on test,

practical jokes, parent tries to bribe child, and placing value of material objects and personal happiness above family obligations and duties to others, most of which are effectively rebuked during the movie; plus one offhand comment that illegitimately compares so-called "homophobia" with racism and sexism.

Grace versus Law

LES MISERABLES

Quality: ☆☆☆☆   Acceptability: +1

WARNING CODES:
  Language: *
  Violence: * *
  Sex: None
  Nudity: None

RATING: PG-13
GENRE: Historical drama
INTENDED AUDIENCE: Teens and adults
RUNNING TIME: 129 minutes
STARRING: Liam Neeson, Geoffrey Rush, Uma Thurman, Claire Danes, Hans Matheson, Reine Brynolfsson, and Peter Vaughan
DIRECTOR: Bille August
PRODUCERS: Sarah Radclyffe and James Gorman
WRITER: Rafael Yglesias
BASED ON: The novel by Victor Hugo
DISTRIBUTOR: Columbia Pictures
BRIEF SUMMARY:
Victor Hugo's great redemptive story, *Les Miserables*, has once more been magnificently adapted to the big screen. When convict Jean Valjean, played by Liam Neeson, is released from prison, he seeks shelter at the home of a poor bishop. Jean steals the bishop's silverware and is caught by the police. Rather than condemning Jean, the bishop gives him two silver candlesticks and tells him to sin no more. Valjean repents, prospers, and even becomes mayor, but Inspector Javert begins an endless pursuit to expose

Valjean and bring him to justice for jumping parole. Valjean takes in a former prostitute named Fantine. When Fantine dies, Valjean raises her daughter, Cosette, as his own. When the French Revolution begins, Javert has his opportunity to seize Valjean again.

This classic tale explores the struggle of grace versus law, forgiveness versus justice, love versus hatred, and peace versus war. It is filled with redemptive images, theology, and prayers. When a policeman calls Fantine a whore, Valjean says she is God's creation. When Javert thinks he has denounced Valjean unjustly, Valjean, as mayor, tells Javert, "I order you to forgive yourself." This version of *Les Miserables* is remarkably restrained in showing grotesqueries. *Les Miserables* stands out as one of the all-time great movies.

CONTENT ANALYSIS: (CCC, C, P, L, VV, A, M) Strong Christian worldview filled with redemption, grace, prayers, forgiveness, and patriotic elements; nine vulgarities; moderate violence including hitting, shooting, charging with swords, images of war without gore, execution by firing squad, explosions, horse-drawn wagon crashes, and suicide by implied drowning; implied prostitution; brief alcohol use; and miscellaneous immorality including strong elements of unforgiveness and hard-heartedness.

Magical Masterpiece

LIFE IS BEAUTIFUL

Quality: ✰✰✰✰   Acceptability: +3

WARNING CODES:
  Language: None
  Violence: *
  Sex: None
  Nudity: None
RATING: PG-13
GENRE: Comedy/Drama
INTENDED AUDIENCE: Older children to adults

RUNNING TIME: 119 minutes
LANGUAGE: Italian
STARRING: Roberto Benigni, Nicoletta Braschi, Giorgio Cantarini, Giustino Durano, Sergio Bustric, and Horst Buchholz
DIRECTOR: Roberto Benigni
PRODUCERS: Elda Ferri and Gianluigi Braschi
WRITERS: Vincenzo Cerami and Roberto Benigni
DISTRIBUTOR: Miramax Films
BRIEF SUMMARY:
Life Is Beautiful is a hilarious, heartwrenching, and terrifying but family-friendly masterpiece of Italian cinema. Comic genius Roberto Benigni stars, writes, and directs this modern fable about a Jewish man who uses wit and imagination to help his wife and child survive the horrors of the Jewish Holocaust during World War II. In the endearing, hilarious first half of the movie, Roberto plays Guido, who humorously woos and marries a Roman Catholic schoolteacher, Dora. In the harrowing, heartbreaking second half of the movie, set in a concentration camp, Guido uses his wit and imagination to protect the life and innocence of his son, Joshua, and to reach out to his beloved Dora, who is imprisoned in another building.

Life Is Beautiful is a wonderful story of love, romance, wit, humor, survival, sacrifice, and the indomitable human spirit. Christians should be very pleased with its strong moral worldview, its gentle blend of comedy and fantasy, the complete absence of foul language and sexual immorality, and its lack of nudity. Unlike other movies about the Holocaust, *Life Is Beautiful* has no scenes of depicted violence. The violence of the Nazis is implied by other dramatic means. *Life Is Beautiful* is a modern classic that will endure for years to come.

CONTENT ANALYSIS: (BBB, C, V, A, D, M) Strong moral worldview of life in an Italian city in the late 1930s and of the

Jewish Holocaust in Italy in the mid-1940s with minor Christian elements; some very mild slapstick violence, Nazi soldier takes person behind wall for murder but the audience only hears short burst of machine-gun fire and surrealistic long-distance shot of Holocaust corpses in fog; some alcohol use; some smoking; and anti-Semitism and Fascism.

Family Ingenuity

LOST IN SPACE

Quality: ☆☆☆   Acceptability: −1

WARNING CODES:
  Language: * *
  Violence: * *
  Sex: None
  Nudity: None
RATING: PG-13
GENRE: Science fiction
INTENDED AUDIENCE: Older children to adults
RUNNING TIME: 120 minutes
STARRING: Gary Oldman, William Hurt, Matt LeBlanc, Mimi Rogers, Heather Graham, Lacey Chabert, Jack Johnson, and Jared Harris
DIRECTOR: Stephen Hopkins
PRODUCERS: Mark W. Koch, Stephen Hopkins, Akiva Goldsman, and Carla Fry
EXECUTIVE PRODUCERS: Mace Neufeld, Bob Rehme, Richard Saperstein, and Michael de Luca
WRITER: Akiva Goldsman
DISTRIBUTOR: New Line Cinema
BRIEF SUMMARY:
Lost in Space, like many modern spectacles, is short on rich writing and logic but grand on thrills and fun. Also, Lost in Space speaks for preserving the families of the future and encourages family relationships and biblical morality. The movie begins in the year 2058 with Major Don West assigned to fly the Jupiter 2 to Alpha Prime, the only other habitable planet in the galaxy. The nations of Earth have stopped fighting and have joined together to colonize space. In twenty years, all of the fossil fuels will be gone and the Earth's inhabitants will need another home, so the Robinson family, led by Professor John Robinson (William Hurt) is commissioned to perform a recognizance mission. Problems ensue when villain Dr. Zach Smith sabotages the mission.

Lost in Space is carefully crafted and marketed to reach a big audience. On most accounts it delivers. The special effects are impressive. The sounds and sights surprise. The story weakens near the middle and remains slightly confusing. Moral Americans will be pleased at the constant theme of family togetherness. Love and forgiveness are displayed, sexual advances are rebuked, and foul language is rebuked. Furthermore, the violence is tame and action oriented.

CONTENT ANALYSIS: (BB, I, E, LL, VV, M) Strong moral worldview of preserving and protecting family with sexual advance rebuked and swearing rebuked, as well as internationalist and environmentalist elements; ten mostly mild obscenities, some sexual remarks; moderate action violence including starships shooting, explosions, attack by space spiders, and several scary situations; and miscellaneous immorality including lying and sabotage.

Snips and Snails

LITTLE MEN

Quality: ☆☆   Acceptability: +3

WARNING CODES:
  Language: *
  Violence: *
  Sex: None
  Nudity: None
RATING: PG

GENRE: Drama
INTENDED AUDIENCE: All ages
RUNNING TIME: 105 minutes
STARRING: Mariel Hemingway, Michael Caloz, Ben Cook, and Chris Sarandon
DIRECTOR: Rodney Gibbons
PRODUCERS: Pierre David and Franco Battista
EXECUTIVE PRODUCERS: Meyer Shwarzstein and Tom Berry
WRITER: Mark Evan Schwartz
BASED ON: The novel by Louisa May Alcott
DISTRIBUTOR: Legacy Releasing
BRIEF SUMMARY:
Little Men, based on Louisa May Alcott's classic, has great Christian content but modest production value. The story begins in Boston, where two street urchins steal some bread from a vendor. Nat is caught, but the real culprit, Dan, gets away. Nat is taken to Plumfield, a home for boys run by the grown-up Jo from *Little Women*, played by Mariel Hemingway, and her professor husband, Dr. Fritz Bhaer. Nat instantly takes to the fun, protection, and camaraderie of the home, though he has a problem with lying. Dan shows up and desires to be admitted. Dan disobeys and is sent away. Dan returns, a horse gets out of line, a girl shows up to live at Plumfield, and a beloved adult passes away.

Little Men is filled with so much Christian content that it is almost a Sunday school lesson. It teaches children to tell the truth, say their prayers, obey their elders, and work hard. The adults are kind but strict. Mariel Hemingway seems a little severe as Jo. The art direction and photography, while warm and cozy, are not lush and rich as they were in *Little Women*. Nevertheless, *Little Men* is a welcome addition to the silver screen.

CONTENT ANALYSIS: (CCC, L, V, A, D, M) Strong Christian worldview emphasizing prayer, honesty, charity, faith, hard work, goodness, discipline, and Christian hymn singing; two pro-fanities, both rebuked; mild action violence including pillow fighting, boxing that turns into an angry fistfight, and attempted stabbing; brief alcohol use; pipe and cigar smoking; and miscellaneous immorality including rebellion, stealing, unintentional fire starting, arguing, and pride.

Childhood in Paris

MADELINE

Quality: ☆☆☆   Acceptability: +3

WARNING CODES:
  Language: *
  Violence: *
  Sex: None
  Nudity: None

RATING: PG
GENRE: Comedy
INTENDED AUDIENCE: Children
RUNNING TIME: 85 minutes
STARRING: Frances McDormand, Nigel Hawthorne, Hatty Jones, Ben Daniels, Arturo Venegas, and Stephane Audran
DIRECTOR: Daisy von Scherler Mayer
PRODUCERS: Saul Cooper, Pancho Kohner, and Allyn Stewart
EXECUTIVE PRODUCER: Stanley R. Jaffe
WRITERS: Malia Scotch Marmo, Mark Levin, and Jennifer Flackett
BASED ON: The book by Ludwig Bemelmans
DISTRIBUTOR: TriStar Pictures
BRIEF SUMMARY:
The book *Madeline* was first written and illustrated in 1939. Now the movie version brings to life this story of a precocious girl, her friends, their benevolent nun teacher Miss Clavel, and the owner of their school, Lord Covington. At the start, Madeline gets her appendix removed. Then Lord Covington tells Miss Clavel he is going to close the school. Pepito, the son of the Spanish ambassador, moves in next door and matches wits with Madeline.

Madeline falls into the Seine River, but a dog rescues her. Eventually bumbling circus performers kidnap Madeline and Pepito. In the end, Madeline makes a touching, last-minute effort to save the school.

Madeline has many moral elements. Miss Clavel prays often. She tells Pepito's tutor that she prays on her day off. Madeline is more precocious and active than rebellious. She has a good heart and doesn't do anything explicitly wrong. In fact, she learns many lessons. The Paris cityscapes are very beautiful. The story introduces the audience to some French history, French architecture, and some fine art. This movie easily could have been rated G with the removal of two foul words. It is very clean, wholesome, and family friendly.

CONTENT ANALYSIS: (C, BBB, L, V, M) Mild Christian worldview with Christian prayers and thanking the Lord, and many moral elements including love, patience, understanding, perseverance, and asking forgiveness; two profanities, four mild French obscenities, and a few name-callings; girl falling into river and girls run away from mice; and miscellaneous immorality including girl kidnapped, boy kicks over statue, man steps in dog excrement, girl threatens to run away, a minor element of false religion, and some lying rebuked.

Replacing Tyranny with Goodness

THE MAN IN THE IRON MASK

Quality: ☆☆☆☆   Acceptability: +1

WARNING CODES:
   Language: *
   Violence: * *
   Sex: * *
   Nudity: *
RATING: PG-13
GENRE: Historical action/
Adventure

INTENDED AUDIENCE: Teens and adults
RUNNING TIME: 127 minutes
STARRING: Leonardo DiCaprio, Jeremy Irons, John Malkovich, Gerard Depardieu, Anne Parillaud, Gabriel Byrne, and Judith Godreche
DIRECTOR: Randall Wallace
PRODUCERS: Randall Wallace and Russ Smith
EXECUTIVE PRODUCER: Alan Ladd Jr.
WRITER: Randall Wallace
BASED ON: The novel by Alexander Dumas
DISTRIBUTOR: Metro Goldwyn-Mayer/United Artists
BRIEF SUMMARY:
Filled with Christian principles, *The Man in the Iron Mask* relates an epic adventure of the Three Musketeers. The year is 1622 in Paris, France, ruled by heartless King Louis XIV, played by Leonardo DiCaprio. The king is deaf to the cries of his people. The former musketeers, Aramis, Athos, and Porthos, have left the service of the king, but Captain D'Artagnan still stands guard, hopeful that Louis will reform. When Louis steals a woman away from her beloved, killing the son of Athos, the musketeers plan to replace the king with a prisoner whose face has been hidden behind an iron mask. Misfortune, danger, and swordplay mark the remainder of the movie.

This movie has action, humor, lavish costumes, scenic locations, and drama, and is filled with commendable lines and situations extolling Christian prayer, faith, goodness, family love, laying down one's life for another, and other redemptive elements. *The Man in the Iron Mask* shows that service and loyalty to the King of Kings is more important than service to an earthly despot. The violence is moderate, but there are some sexual situations and an implied adulterous relationship, though no depicted fornication or nudity. *The Man in the Iron Mask* demonstrates the triumph of goodness over injustice.

CONTENT ANALYSIS: (CCC, Pa, L, VV, SS, N, A, D, M) Strong Christian worldview extolling Christian prayer, faith, commitment, telling the truth, goodness in leadership, family love, laying down your life for another, and other redemptive elements with some pagan ideas; three obscenities; moderate action violence including swordplay, shooting, stabbing, explosions, attempted suicide, and suicide by hanging; an implied adulterous relationship, fornication implied with bedroom scenes and some sexual noises, and several brief scenes of lusty, seductive women; upper male nudity and women in cleavage-revealing corsets; alcohol use; smoking; and lying, treachery, and rebellion.

Masked Champion

THE MASK OF ZORRO

Quality: ✰✰✰✰   Acceptability: −1

WARNING CODES:
  Language: *
  Violence: * *
  Sex: None
  Nudity: *
RATING: PG-13
GENRE: Adventure
INTENDED AUDIENCE: Teens and adults
RUNNING TIME: 135 minutes
STARRING: Antonio Banderas, Anthony Hopkins, Catherine Zeta-Jones, Stuart Wilson, and Matt Letscher
DIRECTOR: Martin Campbell
PRODUCERS: Doug Claybourne and David Foster
EXECUTIVE PRODUCERS: Steven Spielberg, Walter F. Parkes, and Laurie MacDonald
WRITERS: John Eskow, Ted Elliott, and Terry Rossio
DISTRIBUTOR: TriStar Pictures

BRIEF SUMMARY:
Zorro returns to the big screen for the first time in over forty years in the rousing and entertaining *Mask of Zorro.* This handsome production features the fight for control of Mexico and California. Anthony Hopkins plays Don Diego de la Vega, who fought Spanish oppression in California as the legendary romantic hero Zorro, aided by young Alejandro. Spanish governor Don Montero arrests Don Diego, murders his beautiful wife, and kidnaps their infant daughter, Elena. Don Diego is thrown into prison, and Alejandro turns to a life of crime. Twenty years later, Zorro escapes from prison and enlists the grown Alejandro, played by Antonio Banderas, as the new Zorro to win back Elena and free the people from Montero's oppression.

The Mask of Zorro includes lots of swashbuckling and a very tight plot. Zorro uses his sword to disable, disarm, and embarrass his foes. There is a lot of swordplay but not a lot of killing, although there is one grotesque scene of a man's head in a jar. The first Zorro is a loving family man. The second Zorro, although he flirts with Elena, doesn't dally with her and ultimately marries her. He is an old-fashioned hero. Location photography, music, and costuming add authenticity to this period tale. This adaptation of the masked swordsman story is a handsome, accomplished work.

CONTENT ANALYSIS: (C, B, Ro, L, VV, N, AA, D, M) Light Christian worldview of Catholic community with prayers and church attendance, moral elements of righting wrongs and doing good, and romantic elements; two mild profanities and some name-calling; grotesque scene of a head and hand in a jar, and extensive action violence including swordplay, stabbing, man thrown against wall, man falls down a cliff, crowd riots, punching, decapitation implied, criminal commits suicide, shooting, and explosions; sexual innuendo, including a sensuous dance sequence; Zorro cuts the top off a woman's dress, but no female nudity shown, rear male nudity, and upper male nudity; alcohol use and brief image of drunken man; smoking; and lying, cheating, stealing, and egomania, most of which are rebuked.

What Causes Fights and Quarrels

MEN WITH GUNS

Quality: ☆☆☆☆   Acceptability: −1

WARNING CODES:
  Language: * *
  Violence: *
  Sex: None
  Nudity: *
RATING: R
GENRE: Drama
INTENDED AUDIENCE: Adults
RUNNING TIME: 128 minutes
LANUAGE: Spanish
STARRING: Federico Luppi, Damian Delgado, Dan Rivera Gonzalez, Tania Cruz, Damian Alcazar, and Mandy Patinkin
  DIRECTOR: John Sayles
  PRODUCERS: R. Paul Miller and Maggie Renzi
  EXECUTIVE PRODUCERS: Lou Gonda, Jody Patton, and John Sloss
  WRITER: John Sayles
  DISTRIBUTOR: Sony Pictures Classics
  BRIEF SUMMARY:
  In the Spanish language movie *Men with Guns,* director John Sayles presents intelligent storytelling, a passionate reserve, a moral hunger, an in-depth familiarity with Christian values, and an idealistic hope tempered by a very realistic view of mankind. In Mexico City, Dr. Humberto Fuentes has just lost his wife. Dr. Fuentes wants to find out how his legacy is doing. His legacy is the young student doctors he trained to go into the jungle to help the Indians. He discovers that each of his students who went into the jungle has been killed. In each case, it doesn't matter whether it was the army or the guerrillas who killed them—it was men with guns, trying to exercise power over the impoverished people whom the young doctors were trying to help.

  Although Sayles shows the sinfulness of man in *Men with Guns,* he cuts away from the actual act of violence to allow the viewer's imagination to do justice to the story. The movie is clearly anti-government, but it does not promote licentiousness; rather, it is a search for the good that is very hard to find. Ultimately, Sayles is asking extremely moral questions and trying to get at the Truth whom he himself needs to know.

  CONTENT ANALYSIS: (Ro, BB, C, LL, V, N, A, D, M) Romantic worldview with many strong moral and redemptive elements and many overt references to Jesus Christ, counterbalanced by references to materialism, humanism, liberation theology, and priest's loss of faith; twenty-two obscenities; references to violence, scenes of the aftermath of violence and scenes leading up to the point of violence (murder, execution, and rape) without depicting the vile act itself; upper male nudity; alcohol use; smoking; and miscellaneous immorality including lying, theft, and fraud.

A Spoonful of Sugar

MIGHTY JOE YOUNG

Quality: ☆☆☆☆   Acceptability: +1

WARNING CODES:
  Language: * *
  Violence: * *
  Sex: None
  Nudity: None
RATING: PG
GENRE: Fantasy
INTENDED AUDIENCE: Older children and adults
RUNNING TIME: 115 minutes

STARRING: Bill Paxton, Charlize Theron, Rade Ser Bedzija, Naveen Andrews, Regina King, and David Paymer

DIRECTOR: Ron Underwood

PRODUCERS: Ted Hartley and Tom Jacobson

EXECUTIVE PRODUCER: Gail Katz

WRITERS: Mark Rosenthal and Lawrence Konner

BASED ON: The original RKO picture *Mighty Joe Young*

DISTRIBUTOR: Walt Disney Pictures

BRIEF SUMMARY:

Mighty Joe Young is not a monster movie; rather, it is a fantasy thrill ride about a big gorilla with a big heart. Jill Young takes care of a large, fifteen-foot-tall gorilla named Joe, whose mother was killed along with Jill's mother twenty years earlier by an evil poacher. Zoologist Gregg O'Hara convinces Jill to take Joe to California to keep him safe, but the evil poacher tracks Joe, leading to a final showdown and a scary moment where a child is threatened by a raging fire in an amusement park.

Although the details have changed, *Mighty Joe Young* follows the pattern of the original 1949 fantasy. Unlike *King Kong*, who is just a Hollywood ape, Joe is a compassionate gorilla. Thus, this story also has a clear environmentalist message. This message is very low key, however. *Mighty Joe Young* is a cut above recent Disney wildlife action adventure films, yet parents need to point out some of the philosophical flaws to their children, after enjoying a very entertaining movie. Appropriate for children seven years and up, this movie contains some violence, a few very mild obscenities, and scary scenes.

CONTENT ANALYSIS: (E, BB, Pa, Ev, LL, VV, A, D, M) Environmentalist worldview with strong moral points as well as some paganism and evolutionary elements; eight mild profanities all of which are exclamatory, and three very mild obscenities; moderate violence that was not glamorized though sometimes heartbreaking, such as the death of Mighty Joe Young's mother and Jill Young's mother, also some violence to physical property and an out-of-control fire, children threatened by fire, and threatening gorilla, a man's finger is bitten by gorilla, and man eventually killed by gorilla; a rapport between Joe and Jill and some kissing; some alcohol; some smoking; and evil rebuked.

Mixed Messages

MULAN

Quality: ☆☆☆☆   Acceptability: −4

WARNING CODES:

Language: None
Violence: *
Sex: None
Nudity: None

RATING: G

GENRE: Animated adventure

INTENDED AUDIENCE: Children and adults

RUNNING TIME: 102 minutes

VOICES: Ming-Na Wen, Lea Salonga, Soon-Tek Oh, Eddie Murphy, B. D. Wong, James Shigeta, Pat Morita, George Takei, James Hong, Harvey Fierstein, June Foray, and Donny Osmond

DIRECTORS: Barry Cook and Tony Bancroft

PRODUCER: Pam Coats

WRITERS: Rita Hsiao, Christopher Sanders, Philip Lazebnik, Raymond Singer, and Eugenia Bostwick-Singer

DISTRIBUTOR: Buena Vista Pictures Distribution/Walt Disney Pictures/Walt Disney Company

BRIEF SUMMARY:

Based on an ancient Chinese legend about a young woman who poses as a soldier to save her father's life, Walt Disney Pictures' animated adventure *Mulan* is visually striking, funny, exciting, and very moving at times. It is the story of a young woman who doesn't quite fit her traditional society's mold of a dutiful, husband-seeking daughter. When her slightly crippled father is drafted to fight an evil invader, Mulan poses (without his knowledge) as a man to go in his place. Her family's ghostly "ancestors" unknowingly send a sarcastic dragon, voiced by funnyman Eddie Murphy, to watch over Mulan. This begins a series of adventures, leading from an army training camp to a snowy mountain pass and the inside of the emperor's beautiful palace.

Mulan clearly has a strong moral worldview that upholds the importance of family, courage, self-sacrifice, responsibility, honor, freedom, and country. It also demonstrates the value of honoring one's parents. Regrettably, it includes scenes of ancestor worship and spirits of dead people coming alive, and a disturbing homosexual subtext. That subtext contains two lines that mock those of us who are concerned about modern society's acceptance of homosexual cross-dressing and other similar perversions that undermine the traditional moral values of the Bible.

CONTENT ANALYSIS: (BB, FRFR, OO, Ho, V, Fe, M) Moderately strong moral worldview about the importance of family, honor, and country, coupled with elements of false religion, occultism, spiritism, and a pro-homosexual subtext; army of evil aggressors fight a small band of soldiers protecting their country including explosions and brief swordplay, and some martial arts and swordplay during film's climax; and pro-feminist subtext of women in combat, superstitious beliefs in "good luck" crickets, and women told to hold their tongues in presence of men.

Big Entertainment

MY GIANT

Quality: ☆☆☆   Acceptability: −1

WARNING CODES:
  Language: * * *

Violence: *
Sex: None
Nudity: None
RATING: PG
GENRE: Romantic comedy/Buddy movie
INTENDED AUDIENCE: All ages
RUNNING TIME: 97 minutes
STARRING: Billy Crystal, Gheorghe Muresan, and Kathleen Quinlan
DIRECTOR: Michael Lehman
PRODUCER: Billy Crystal
EXECUTIVE PRODUCER: Peter Schindler
WRITERS: Billy Crystal and David Seltzer
DISTRIBUTOR: Castle Rock Entertainment
BRIEF SUMMARY:
My Giant is the story of the relationship that develops between Sammy, a second-rate talent agent from Chicago (Billy Crystal), and Max, a seven-foot-seven-inch giant from Romania. When Sammy asks God to save him during a terrifying car wreck in Romania, he envisions the enormous hands of God personally carrying him to heaven. He wakes up in a monastery where he meets Max, the giant who pulled him from his car. Max loves God, who protects him from the ridicule of those who treat him as a freak. Sammy makes a deal with Max. If Max lets Sammy put him in the movies, he will take Max to find his long-lost love. An unfortunate turn of events causes Sammy to change how he views his family and the life God has given him. Sammy learns that reconciliation comes through forgiveness, that joy springs forth from love, and that giving is more blessed than receiving.

A family-friendly movie with a biblical worldview and redemptive elements of Christian forgiveness, *My Giant* has several mild obscenities, a few profanities, and a vomiting scene, but it shows that God answers our prayers. It also implies that God, in using Max to save

Sammy from dying, can give us all true meaning and purpose in our lives.

CONTENT ANALYSIS: (BB, CC, ReRe, LLL, V, A, M) Biblical, Christian world-view with acknowledgment of existence of a personal God who protects us and has a purpose for our lives, with stress placed on the importance of loving God and confessing our sins, repenting and seeking forgiveness, as well as redemptive Christian values with emphasis on trust, helping others, selflessness, importance of family and friends, and marital reconcili-ation; seventeen obscenities and six pro-fanities; minor action violence in wrestling match between giant and seven midgets and fistfight with two thugs, in which one is knocked out and one is hurled through the air; shocking, repulsive scene of loud burp and projectile vomiting from over-consumption of wine; and lying and deceit used to protect another from hurt and to promote joy and hope.

True Crime Drama

THE NEWTON BOYS

Quality: ✰✰✰✰   Acceptability: −2

WARNING CODES:
    Language: * * *
    Violence: * *
    Sex: None
    Nudity: None
RATING: R
GENRE: Historical gangster movie
INTENDED AUDIENCE: Older teens and adults
RUNNING TIME: 125 minutes
STARRING: Matthew McCon-aughey, Ethan Hawke, Vincent D'Onofrio, Skeet Ulrich, Julianna Margulies, and Dwight Yoakam
DIRECTOR: Richard Linklater
PRODUCER: Anne Walker-McBay
WRITERS: Richard Linklater, Claude Stanush, and Clark Lee Walker
BASED ON: The novel by Claude Stanush

DISTRIBUTOR: 20th Century Fox
BRIEF SUMMARY:
The Newton Boys is a historical gang-ster movie about America's most suc-cessful bank robbers, four brothers who, from 1919 to 1924, robbed over eighty banks. Featuring a bravado cast, authen-tic sets and costumes, great music, and keen direction, the movie is a fine piece of historical drama. It gives an inside look at how these brothers continued their wrongdoing for so long and how they got off relatively easy once they were captured. Leading the brothers is Matthew McConaughey as the eldest brother, Willis. Tired of picking cotton, Willis rallies his brothers to rob banks. They cap their five-year spree by a heist that gets them arrested. Because of Willis's cunning and charm, the boys only receive a few years in jail, and all of them live to a ripe old age.

The Newton Boys does not depict gra-tuitous violence. Indeed, the Newton brothers boasted that they never killed a man in the course of their bank robbing. Although they remained unrepentant until their dying day, these men gave money to the Salvation Army and recog-nized prayer. Solid storytelling without much violence, *The Newton Boys* is flawed by excessive foul language and, of course, by the fact that it glorifies criminals.

CONTENT ANALYSIS: (Pa, CC, LLL, VV, A, D, M) Pagan worldview of unre-pentant criminals with some Christian elements of hymn singing, prayer, and Bible quoting; forty-one obscenities and twenty-two profanities; moderate vio-lence including fistfighting, shooting without deaths but bloodletting and explosions; chasing women and kissing; alcohol use; smoking; and lying, cheat-ing, and stealing.

An Emotional Journey

ONE TRUE THING

Quality: ✰✰✰✰   Acceptability: −2

WARNING CODES:

    Language: * *
    Violence: *
    Sex: *
    Nudity: None
RATING: R
GENRE: Drama
INTENDED AUDIENCE: Adults
RUNNING TIME: 126 minutes
STARRING: Meryl Streep, Renee
Zellweger, William Hurt, Tom Everett
Scott, Lauren Graham, and Nicky Katt
DIRECTOR: Carl Franklin
PRODUCERS: Harry Ufland and
Jesse Beaton
EXECUTIVE PRODUCERS: William
W. Wilson III and Leslie Morgan
WRITER: Karen Croner
BASED ON: The novel by Anna
Quindlen
DISTRIBUTOR: Universal Pictures
BRIEF SUMMARY:

In *One True Thing*, Renee Zellweger
plays a determined journalist who must
put her career on hold to return home
and care for her dying mother. In the
movie, a Northeastern family takes a
momentous emotional journey when it
is forced to come face-to-face with the
prospect of losing a loved one to cancer.
The story begins with Meryl Streep
playing domestic mom Kate, dressed
up like Dorothy from *The Wizard of Oz*
at a costume party for her husband's
fiftieth birthday. The audience soon
learns that Kate is not physically well,
stricken with cancer, and her health
slides rapidly in the months to come.
Kate's husband, George, enlists their
daughter Ellen to take care of Kate.
Ellen learns to accept her mother's
domestic lifestyle. Long-hidden family
secrets are revealed at Kate's worst
moment, culminating in the possibility
of euthanasia.

While Streep and Hurt act solidly,
Zellweger strikes a powerhouse performance. Carl Franklin's direction gives
a straightforward, no-frills exposition.
There are also positive Christian values
in this movie including self-sacrifice,
prayer, and hymn singing. However, this
is definitely a philosophically liberal
movie. All of the men are ineffective or
insignificant. Plus, the ugly aspect of
euthanasia is explored and would have
occurred if the would-be mercy killers
had had enough courage to do it.

CONTENT ANALYSIS: (Pa, C, LL, V,
S, A, D, M) Pagan worldview of cultur-
ally Christian family dealing with dying
family member, including self-sacrifice,
prayer before dinner, and singing "Silent
Night"; six obscenities and four profanities; implied suicide; implied adultery;
smoking; drinking; and implied corrupt
boss, anger, and attempted euthanasia.

Laughter Is the Best Medicine

PATCH ADAMS

Quality: ☆☆☆   Acceptability: −1

WARNING CODES:

    Language: * * *
    Violence: *
    Sex: None
    Nudity: None
RATING: PG-13
GENRE: Comedy
INTENDED AUDIENCE: Older
teens and adults
RUNNING TIME: 122 minutes
STARRING: Robin Williams, Monica
Potter, Daniel London, Philip Seymour
Hoffman, and Bob Gunton
DIRECTOR: Tom Shadyac
PRODUCERS: Barry Kemp, Mike
Farrell, Marvin Minoff, and Charles
Newirth
EXECUTIVE PRODUCERS: Marsha
Garces Williams and Tom Shadyac
WRITER: Steve Oedekerk
DISTRIBUTOR: Universal Pictures
BRIEF SUMMARY:
Laughter is the best medicine. At least
that is what medical student Patch Adams

believes. Based on a true story and featuring Robin Williams, *Patch Adams* provides lots of love and warmth, and champions Christ-like attitudes and behaviors in challenging modern medical treatment and impersonal institutes of medicine. It is only flawed by obscenity use, a very crude visual joke, and some minor production problems.

In 1969, Adams admits himself into a mental institution for suicidal depression. In the institute he finds boring, uncaring medical staff, not a good atmosphere for someone trying to get over depression. Adams finds his own cure—he helps other patients laugh and find joy through playfulness. Christening himself "Patch," Adams enrolls in medical school. He finds romantic love, faces expulsion, and opens his own clinic.

Patch Adams is a remarkable and poignant movie. Although the movie has some strong foul language, the title character makes several biblical references, joins in a Christian funeral, and wrestles with God in prayer after a terrible accident. As Patch, Robin Williams offers one of his best comic performances since *Aladdin*. The major theme of *Patch Adams* is enduring and true—it is far more important to actually care for people, get to know them, find out their dreams, and give them joy, than to see them merely as case studies for illnesses. Laughter can indeed be the best medicine because joy is a gift from the Holy Spirit.

CONTENT ANALYSIS: (BB, C, Pa, LLL, A, D, M) Moral, biblical worldview of loving others despite differences and treating people as individuals, with a few strong Christian elements including Scripture reading at funeral, sacrifice, and prayers, but some mild immoral behavior and mild New Age references; twenty-four obscenities, many mild, and three exclamatory profanities; implied murder; very crude visual joke about female medical exams; social drinking; smoking; and grisly images of cuts and sores, plus disturbing images of cancer patients and people dying.

Joyous Affirmation

THE PARENT TRAP

Quality: ☆☆☆☆   Acceptability: +1

WARNING CODES:
  Language: * *
  Violence: *
  Sex: *
  Nudity: None
RATING: PG
GENRE: Comedy
INTENDED AUDIENCE: All ages
RUNNING TIME: 124 minutes
STARRING: Dennis Quaid, Natasha Richardson, Lindsay Lohan, and Elaine Hendrix
DIRECTOR: Nancy Meyers
PRODUCER: Charles Shyer
WRITERS: David Swift, Nancy Meyers, and Charles Shyer
DISTRIBUTOR: Walt Disney Pictures/Buena Vista Pictures Distribution/Walt Disney Company
BRIEF SUMMARY:
The remake of *The Parent Trap* is even better than the delightful original. Little Hallie Parker and Annie James meet at camp and slowly discover that they are identical twins, separated at birth when their parents, Nick Parker and Elizabeth James, split up. Once they discover their identity, their goal is to bring their parents together, and the butler, the nanny, and their grandfather help them do just that. The foil is Nick Parker's new love interest, Meredith Blake, played with venom by Elaine Hendrix.

What makes this movie work is the fine sense of timing and comic sensibility. The movie affirms marriage, the need for both parents, and moral values that most Americans hold dear. Even the butler and the nanny make the right moral choices, although they also provide comic relief for several of the scenes. The only troubling parts of the movie are one practical joke played on Meredith, where she almost swallows a lizard, and several exclamations that invoke God. In the final analysis, *The Parent Trap* deserves many kudos as adorable, funny, winsome, moral, life-affirming, family-affirming, family-friendly entertainment.

CONTENT ANALYSIS: (C, LL, V, S, AA, D, M) Christian worldview affirming marriage, family, and God; one obscenity (mild) and eleven exclamations invoking God but not said in a profaning manner; lots of practical camp jokes including pratfalls and being hit by water balloons, scary ear-piercing, practical jokes including woman almost swallows lizard, and fencing scene with full regulation padding; suggested practical joke of camp girls taking another girl's clothes; some kissing, petting, and sexual innuendo; one parent has a vineyard so wine is a central element of the plot and one scene of drunkenness is mildly rebuked; and miscellaneous immorality including telling borderline lies and dealing in deception to bring parents together that is not rebuked.

Teaching the Parrot

PAULIE

Quality: ☆☆☆☆   Acceptability: +1

WARNING CODES:

Language: *
Violence: *
Sex: None
Nudity: None

RATING: PG
GENRE: Comedy
INTENDED AUDIENCE: Older children to adults
RUNNING TIME: 91 minutes
STARRING: Gena Rowlands, Tony Shalhoub, Cheech Marin, Bruce Davison, Hallie Kate Eisenberg, and Jay Mohr

DIRECTOR: John Roberts
PRODUCERS: Mark Gordon, Gary Levinsohn, and Allison Lyon Segan
EXECUTIVE PRODUCER: Ginny Nugent
WRITER: Laurie Craig
DISTRIBUTOR: DreamWorks
BRIEF SUMMARY:
A movie for ages eight and up, *Paulie* is about a talking parrot who learns morals and values as he experiences different owners and travels across America. Set in a gritty, realistic world, Paulie learns some good lessons in this coming-of-age parrot story, which is flawed by only one blatant profanity and some dark aspects to its story.

A Russian professor immigrant named Misha takes a job as a janitor at a laboratory that is trying to find a communications link between people and animals. In the basement of the laboratory, he discovers a parrot named Paulie who can talk, not just repeat words. Paulie tells Misha that he belonged to a young girl named Marie. Paulie also tells Misha about how he learned to talk and how he made his way to Los Angeles. Misha takes pity on Paulie and decides to spring him from his laboratory prison.

When caught stealing, Paulie says that nobody ever taught him that stealing was wrong, but learns that it is. He also learns to be polite and to love. Misha learns he must speak up at the right time, while Paulie learns that he must not talk too much. Greed and evil are exposed, and crime is rebuked. Only two things detract from this morality tale: one blatant profanity and the stark realism. Therefore, *Paulie* is not a movie for little children. It is a movie with a big heart and deserves better than being depreciated by profanity.

CONTENT ANALYSIS: (B, E, L, V, M) Moral worldview with slight environmentalist tinge; one blatant profanity; mild action violence; and parrot being taught to steal as well as being taught moral lessons.

Through the Looking Glass

PLEASANTVILLE

Quality: ✰✰✰✰   Acceptability: −4

WARNING CODES:
  Language: * * *
  Violence: * *
  Sex: * *
  Nudity: *
RATING: PG-13
GENRE: Fantasy/Comedy
INTENDED AUDIENCE: Teens and adults
RUNNING TIME: 116 minutes
STARRING: Tobey Maguire, Reese Witherspoon, Jeff Daniels, Joan Allen, William H. Macy, and J. T. Walsh
  DIRECTOR: Gary Ross
  PRODUCERS: Robert John Degus, Jon Kilik, and Gary Ross
  EXECUTIVE PRODUCERS: Michael De Luca, Mary Parent, and Steve Soderbergh
  WRITER: Gary Ross
  DISTRIBUTOR: New Line Cinema
  BRIEF SUMMARY:
Pleasantville is a contemporary fable contrasting today's jaded society with a fictional 1950s town, ultimately teaching the costs and joys of freedom of expression and individuality. The movie tells the story of a modern teenager and his sister, who miraculously enter the world of a 1950s television situation comedy. There, they begin to tell the townspeople that they don't have to fit a mold, that they can make their own decisions. When people accept their advice, they turn from black and white to color, which results in a few minor riots and uproars.

Pleasantville is an enchanting and delightful movie. Gary Ross, the screenwriter of *Big* and the politically correct *Dave*, presents an exhilarating yet thought-provoking scenario in his directorial debut. *Pleasantville* endorses free speech, freedom of choice, and facing inevitable change. Regretfully, the cata-

lyst for this change is illicit sex between two teenagers. Also, other sexual themes are explored, and many exclamatory profanities are uttered. *Pleasantville* doesn't mock 1950s morality, but mocks stagnation.

The movie not only advocates change, which is not of itself a moral issue, it also advocates abolishing traditional mores. For example, when the characters in *Pleasantville* fornicate or publicly display nude paintings of someone else's wife, they are magically transformed from Philco monochrome to Trinitron brilliance. This movie advocates a self-contradictory, therefore false, moral relativism. It also accepts the new-Marxist view of psychological/sexual/social repression developed by the Frankfurt School.

CONTENT ANALYSIS: (RoRo, AbAb, PaPa, B, LLL, VV, SS, N, A, D, M) Romantic worldview with anti-biblical elements extolling immorality passing as free will and freedom with abuses of freedom; nine obscenities, eighteen exclamatory profanities, and five stronger profanities; town trashes store, boy punches boy, and vandalism; brief images of arms and legs hanging out of convertible cars implying fornication, sexual flirtation, masturbation implied, and adulterous kiss depicted where unknowing fictional characters don't know of its immoral implications; contemporary teenage girls going without bras and paintings of nude women displayed; alcohol use; smoking; and miscellaneous immorality including rioting.

A Revisionist *All the King's Men*

PRIMARY COLORS

Quality: ✰✰   Acceptability: −4

WARNING CODES:
  Language: * * *
  Violence: *
  Sex: * * *
  Nudity: * *

RATING: R
GENRE: Drama
INTENDED AUDIENCE: Adults
RUNNING TIME: 134 minutes
STARRING: John Travolta, Emma Thompson, Billy Bob Thornton, Kathy Bates, Adrian Lester, Maura Tierney, and Larry Hagman
DIRECTOR: Mike Nichols
PRODUCER: Mike Nichols
EXECUTIVE PRODUCERS: Neil Machlis and Jonathan D. Drake
WRITER: Elaine May
BASED ON: The book by Joe Klein
DISTRIBUTOR: Universal Pictures
BRIEF SUMMARY:
Filled with 130 obscenities and 38 profanities, *Primary Colors* is a movie about adulterous Southern governor Jack Stanton, who will do anything to gain the power of the presidency of the United States. Based in part on the scathing novel by Joe Klein, the movie is full of homosexuality, infidelity, suicide, unfaithfulness, and deceit. *Primary Colors* attempts to portray Stanton as a noble politician who refuses to do negative campaign ads despite receiving negative barbs from his opponents. Lying, cheating, and adultery are okay, so long as Stanton doesn't participate in negative campaigning. The movie is also peppered with scenes where Stanton pays lip-service to God through statements such as "God bless." These scenes endorse politicians who trivialize God and use religion to gain political power. The movie contends that Stanton's sins are irrelevant when compared to his "compassion" for the people.

The cinematic quality of the movie is poor. Lighting, settings, and photography are deficient. Reportedly, President Clinton exchanged favors with star John Travolta to obtain a more favorable rewrite of Joe Klein's original novel. According to *George* magazine, Clinton helped the cultic Church of Scientology get a more favorable hearing by the German government, which has banned Scientology in Germany.

CONTENT ANALYSIS: (HH, AbAb, PCPC, HoHo, LLL, V, SSS, NN, Fe, FM, I, RH, D, A) Humanist, anti-biblical, politically correct worldview that endorses sexual immorality, adultery, homosexuality, bisexuality, and people who trivialize God and religion to gain political power; 130 obscenities, 38 profanities and 10 vulgarities; suicide with handgun, plus a couple of slapping scenes; implied homosexual and bisexual sex, on-screen lesbian kiss, and implied adulterous sex; men and women in underwear and in bed with upper male nudity; alcohol use; drug and references to substance abuse; and feminism, internationalist elements, and revisionist history.

Let Your Family Go

THE PRINCE OF EGYPT

Quality: ☆☆☆☆   Acceptability: +4

WARNING CODES:
  Language: None
  Violence: *
  Sex: None
  Nudity: *
RATING: G
GENRE: Animated biblical epic
INTENDED AUDIENCE: Ages seven and up
RUNNING TIME: 90 minutes
VOICES: Val Kilmer, Sandra Bullock, Ralph Fiennes, Danny Glover, Jeff Goldblum, Steve Martin, Helen Mirren, Michelle Pfeiffer, Patrick Stewart, and Martin Short
DIRECTORS: Brenda Chapman, Steve Hickner, and Simon Wells
PRODUCERS: Penny Finkelman-Cox and Sandra Rabins
WRITERS: Kelly Asbury and Lorna Cook
DISTRIBUTOR: DreamWorks
BRIEF SUMMARY:
Magnificent entertainment, *The Prince of Egypt* takes animated movies to a new

level as it dramatizes the biblical story of Moses and his call from God to lead the Israelites out of Egypt. By the grace of God, Moses is rescued from Pharaoh's command to kill the firstborn of Israel. Ironically, he is brought up in Pharaoh's home as one of his sons. Eventually God confronts Moses in the burning bush. Finally God defeats the false gods of Egypt and frees his chosen people.

Magnificent, groundbreaking art, music, story, and direction combine to make *The Prince of Egypt* an entertaining masterpiece. Although the movie contains some scary scenes, it contains nothing that little children can't watch as long as parents are involved. *The Prince of Egypt* proclaims the sovereignty of God and his miraculous involvement with mankind. It shows the need for virtue, integrity, character, and the Ten Commandments. The movie also clearly shows God acting in history. It foreshadows the Prince of Peace, who leads all those who ask out of their contemporary bondage into freedom in the kingdom of God. *The Prince of Egypt* is entertainment at its best.

CONTENT ANALYSIS: (CCC, BBB, V, N, M) Very clear, God-honoring, theocentric, biblical worldview where God is the hero behind the scenes and false religions are exposed and rebuked; violence done very effectively but tastefully so that the audience knows that the firstborn are being killed and that the angel of death is passing by but don't see the gruesome act of violence, water turns into blood, and many plagues and boils; pictures of children being thrown into the river clearly showing that they are little baby boys, but nothing excessive or salacious; some suggestive clothing, one shot up a man's tunic revealing underwear, one shot of buxom woman behind veil who turns out to be servant who was bound and gagged; and clear portrayal of Egyptian religion and a little suggestive humor.

Quest for Disney Audience

QUEST FOR CAMELOT

Quality: ☆☆☆   Acceptability: +2

WARNING CODES:
  Language: None
  Violence: * *
  Sex: None
  Nudity: None

RATING: G
GENRE: Animated adventure
INTENDED AUDIENCE: All ages
RUNNING TIME: 78 minutes
VOICES: Jessalyn Gilsig, Bryan White, Andrea Corr, Cary Elwes, Gary Oldman, Eric Idle, Don Rickles, Jane Seymour, Pierce Brosnan, Bronson Pinchot, and Celine Dion
DIRECTOR: Frederik Du Chau
PRODUCERS: Dalisa Cooper Cohen and Frank Gladstone
WRITERS: Kirk DeMicco, William Schifrin, Jacqueline Feather, and David Seidler
BASED ON: The novel *The King's Damsel* by Vera Chapman
DISTRIBUTOR: Warner Brothers
BRIEF SUMMARY:
Quest for Camelot is a Warner Brothers animated movie featuring song and dance numbers, lots of action, and a little romance. The story revolves around King Arthur and the Knights of the Round Table. The heroine is a teenage girl named Kayley, who dreams of joining the knights around the Round Table in place of her late father, Sir Lionel. The safety of Camelot is assured as long as Arthur is on the throne and his sword, Excalibur, is in his hand. One day Sir Ruber declares his desire to gain the throne. He steals Excalibur and creates a troop of mechanical warriors out of the townspeople. Kayley and a blind young man use skill, ingenuity, and courage to save their beloved city.

The animation is good, but not spectacular. Voice talent is solid. Songs are average but sweet. The overarching themes of the story are preservation of truth, freedom, and peace. *Quest for Camelot* does have some moral errors and mild reasons for concern. Kayley displays some feminist views. Arthur sees Camelot as a social utopia. However, these minor themes are quickly glossed over and greater themes are more fully explored. *Quest for Camelot* is a fine effort by Warner Brothers.

CONTENT ANALYSIS: (B, Pa, Fe, VV, M) Light, moral worldview emphasizing liberty, freedom, peace, and love with the inclusion of a prayer and some magical and feminist elements; moderate action violence including some scary scenes, chase scenes, fights with swords, spear throwing, and siege on castle; and miscellaneous immorality including megalomania, stealing, brief image of slain men, sword stolen, fire-breathing dragons, magic potion, and betrayal.

Happy Trails to Heaven

THE RIDE

Quality: ✰✰✰✰   Acceptability: +4

WARNING CODES:
   Language: None
   Violence: *
   Sex: None
   Nudity: None
RATING: PG
GENRE: Christian Western
INTENDED AUDIENCE: All ages
RUNNING TIME: 101 minutes
STARRING: Michael Biehn, Brock Peirce, and Jennifer Blanc
DIRECTOR: Michael O. Sajbel
PRODUCER: Laurie Leinonen
EXECUTIVE PRODUCER: John Shepherd
WRITER: Michael O. Sajbel
DISTRIBUTOR: World Wide Pictures
BRIEF SUMMARY:
The Ride is one of the best-crafted movies from World Wide Pictures.

Smokey Banks is a rodeo champion whose carousing has taken him out of the winner's circle. When Smokey fails a bull ride, gets beaten up for a loan, and has his trailer repossessed, he explodes and knocks out the tow-truck driver who is taking his trailer. Eventually he is thrown in jail. One of his fans, Danny from the Saguaro Boys' Ranch for orphaned and troubled children, convinces the police to have Smokey serve his sentence at the ranch. Though Smokey wants no part of this, he becomes involved in the life of Danny, who is dying of cancer. Eventually Smokey has to deal with God and his disappointment with himself.

The Ride is a captivating story. These people are believable in a profound way that Hollywood seldom captures. The dialogue is sparse and well written. The acting is excellent. Unlike older Billy Graham films, the tent prayer meeting at the rodeo, with Franklin Graham, is not the end of the story. The premise is played out and the story is told in a way that will fulfill audience expectations and help them to know God.

CONTENT ANALYSIS: (CCC, V, A, D) Christian worldview with evangelism—a morality tale; a couple of fight scenes; drinking; smoking; and playing cards.

Babies in a Pickle

THE RUGRATS MOVIE

Quality: ✰✰✰   Acceptability: +1

WARNING CODES:
   Language: None
   Violence: * *
   Sex: None
   Nudity: *
RATING: G
GENRE: Animated comedy
INTENDED AUDIENCE: Ages six and up
RUNNING TIME: 85 minutes
VOICES: E. G. Daily, Christine Cavanaugh, Kath Soucie, Cheryl Chase,

Tim Curry, Whoopi Goldberg, and David Spade

DIRECTORS: Norton Virgien and Igor Kovalyov

PRODUCERS: Arlene Klasky and Gabor Csupo

EXECUTIVE PRODUCERS: Albie Hecht and Debby Beece

WRITERS: David N. Weiss and J. David Stem

DISTRIBUTOR: Paramount and Nickelodeon

BRIEF SUMMARY:

Nickelodeon's popular cartoon series about a group of adventurous babies hits the silver screen in *The Rugrats Movie*. Tommy, Chuckie, and the gang get lost in the woods and must take care of Tommy's new brother, Dylan, when a dinosaur toy goes haywire and a van crashes. The babies face a band of crazy monkeys, a thunderstorm, and a hungry wolf in this energy-packed adventure that is a little too frenetic for small children.

The Rugrats Movie is too fast-paced for very small children, but older children may enjoy the crazy journey the babies take. Much of the charm relies on the quirky voices of Tommy, Chuckie, and the twins, voiced by E. G. Daily, Christine Cavanaugh, and Kath Soucie. Although the movie fittingly has no foul language or sex in it, it does have discussions and references to babies messing their diapers, a scene where babies in a maternity ward urinate to form a rainbow in the air, and some moderate action and slapstick cartoon violence. Responsibility and love win out in the end, however, so there are some positive moral messages in the text of this colorful animated movie.

CONTENT ANALYSIS: (BB, VV, N, M) Mild moral worldview teaching love for others and responsibility; babies mention "Bod," baby-talk for God; discussions and references to babies urinating and messing their diapers with "poop" and scene of babies in maternity ward urinating to form a rainbow in the air; moderate action and slapstick cartoon violence such as monkeys wreck train, newborn baby hits other kids with rattle and bottle, truck filled with mattresses crashes with babies inside, babies take scary rides on land and water in dinosaur toy, one baby falls into water and is in danger of drowning, family dog fights off scary wolf, and flying machine crashes; rear male nudity of baby; and miscellaneous immorality such as grandparent falls asleep while watching children, sibling rivalry, arguing, and babies have mistaken magical thinking about a perceived wizard whom they call a "lizard," but truth is revealed to audience.

Unnecessary Roughness!

SAVING PRIVATE RYAN

Quality: ☆☆☆   Acceptability: −3

WARNING CODES:
  Language: * * *
  Violence: * * *
  Sex: *
  Nudity: None

RATING: R

GENRE: War movie/Historical epic

INTENDED AUDIENCE: Older teens and adults

RUNNING TIME: 164 minutes

STARRING: Tom Hanks, Edward Burns, Tom Sizemore, Matt Damon, Jeremy Davies, Adam Goldberg, Barry Pepper, Giovanni Ribisi, Vin Diesel, and Ted Danson

DIRECTOR: Steven Spielberg

PRODUCERS: Steven Spielberg, Ian Bruce, Mark Gordon, and Gary Levinsohn

WRITER: Robert Rodat

DISTRIBUTOR: DreamWorks

BRIEF SUMMARY:

Filled with excessive violence and foul language, Steven Spielberg's "realistic" World War II epic about the Normandy invasion, *Saving Private Ryan*, contains a mild moral worldview with positive references to God and some Christian elements. In this movie about D day, a squad of American soldiers is sent behind enemy lines to retrieve Private Ryan because he is the only surviving member of a family of four brothers. Led by Tom Hanks as Captain John Miller, the squad begins to question the morality of their mission as they engage the Nazis in two minor skirmishes and a big battle sequence at the end.

The major moral message of *Saving Private Ryan* is an important one: Americans must lead morally upright, socially responsible lives to earn the freedom that their ancestors bought with their lives. Spielberg develops this message brilliantly. Regrettably, he also includes excessive violence to depict the horrors of war. Also, he adds excessive, unnecessary foul language and dilutes the religious beliefs of the real American soldiers in that conflict. However, Spielberg does include a few brief references to God and Christianity. Despite the violence, the opening battle is intense and mesmerizing. It gives proper weight to the sacrifices American soldiers made at Omaha Beach on 6 June 1944. Regrettably, the movie's characters and climax fail to be completely engrossing.

CONTENT ANALYSIS: (B, Ab, H, C, LLL, VVV, S, D, RHRH, M) Mild moral worldview with positive references to God, combined with immoral, humanist, and Christian elements, but there is no talk of one's ultimate salvation; sixty-seven obscenities, twenty-one profanities, and several vulgarities, including some sexual references; extreme graphic war violence including gruesome, bloody scenes of bodies ripped open, limbs torn off, men on fire, and gunshot wounds, plus many explosions; two soldiers tell bawdy stories of sexual encounters; smoking; revisionist history of American Christians during World War II; and miscellaneous immorality

such as Americans killing three soldiers trying to surrender and German soldier lies to save his neck.

Trivializing Our Greatest Writer

SHAKESPEARE IN LOVE

Quality: ☆☆☆☆   Acceptability: −2

WARNING CODES:
   Language: *
   Violence: *
   Sex: * * *
   Nudity: * *

RATING: R
GENRE: Romantic comedy
INTENDED AUDIENCE: Adults
RUNNING TIME: 122 minutes
STARRING: Gwyneth Paltrow, Joseph Fiennes, Geoffrey Rush, Colin Firth, Ben Affleck, and Judi Dench
DIRECTOR: John Madden
PRODUCERS: David Parritt, Donna Gigliotti, Harvey Weinstein, Edward Zwick, and Marc Norman
EXECUTIVE PRODUCERS: Bob Weinstein and Julie Goldstein
WRITERS: Marc Norman and Tom Stoppard
DISTRIBUTOR: Miramax Films
BRIEF SUMMARY:
Bawdy, romantic, and funny, period movie *Shakespeare in Love* details an imagined experience by the young bard himself, which inspires him to write "Romeo and Juliet." In 1593, new playwright William Shakespeare is working on a big moneymaking comedy called "Romeo and Ethel." Soon he meets a young woman named Lady Viola, and passion arises. Complications occur when Shakespeare discovers that Lady Viola must marry Lord Wessex. Now a tragedy, the performance brings unlikely guests and cast changes and unpleasant pressures on the forbidden romance.

Shakespeare in Love is a fictional examination of what might have been, mixing factual characters with fictional characters. This movie contains excessive scenes of depicted fornication, with revealing nudity. These scenes become even more unsettling when the movie reveals that Shakespeare already has a wife and children, who live in Stratford. Thus the movie's basic premise ultimately trashes the bard's reputation and legacy, slandering the moral character of our greatest writer, who by the historical record, was a devout Protestant Christian. However, when a death occurs, Shakespeare mourns and repents with loud cries to Jesus Christ for forgiveness. This is a rare recognition of God and his Holy Order in an otherwise hedonistic movie.

CONTENT ANALYSIS: (RoRoRo, Pa, Fe, Ho, C, L, V, SSS, NN, A, DD, M) Strong romantic worldview of literary inspiration with pagan elements, feminist elements, homosexual elements, and one strong appeal to Jesus for forgiveness; three obscenities and three exclamatory profanities; light action violence including men sword fight with no injuries, implied murder by stabbing, falls, duel with knives, man's feet held above flaming hot coals, two acts of depicted adultery and two acts of depicted fornication; upper male nudity and upper female nudity; alcohol use and drunkenness; smoking; and lying, cheating, deception, and cross-dressing for theatrical parts.

Uncommon Faith and Love

SIMON BIRCH

Quality: ✰✰✰✰   Acceptability: +1

WARNING CODES:
  Language: * *
  Violence: *
  Sex: None
  Nudity: None
RATING: PG
GENRE: Drama
INTENDED AUDIENCE: Older children and adults
RUNNING TIME: 120 minutes

STARRING: Joseph Mazzello, Oliver Platt, David Strathairn, Ian Michael Smith, Dana Ivey, Ashley Judd, and Jim Carrey
DIRECTOR: Mark Steven Johnson
PRODUCERS: Laurence Mark and Roger Birnbaum
EXECUTIVE PRODUCER: John Baldecchi
WRITER: Mark Steven Johnson
INSPIRED BY: The novel *A Prayer for Owen Meany* by John Irving
DISTRIBUTOR: Hollywood Pictures
BRIEF SUMMARY:
Simon Birch is a fictional remembrance of a remarkable dwarf boy, Simon, who demonstrates great faith in God and becomes a hero and instrument of God's grace. Twelve-year-old Simon Birch thinks he will be used as a hero by God and befriends twelve-year-old Joe, who seeks to find his biological father. Both Simon and Joe feel like outsiders, but Joe's mother, Rebecca, constantly shows love to them. One day an unexpected event causes tragedy. From that point the destinies of the two boys become linked as both try to find the one thing they are missing. For Joe, it is the identity of his biological father. For Simon, it is the special purpose God has in mind, which only a small miracle like he can fulfill. On a church excursion, they find the answers to their questions.

In *Simon Birch*, Simon represents a sort of modern-day holy fool who confronts the Pharisees of his day, the ineffectual religious leaders who have no heart, compassion, or Christ-like spirit. The movie has more than a few obscenities and profanities, plus some inappropriate behaviors by the two boys. Every year one movie shows a greater insight into God, faith, Christ, and the human condition than all others. This year *Simon Birch* may be that movie. It teaches matters of faith in a uniquely wonderful, well-acted, charming, and moving way.

CONTENT ANALYSIS: (CCC, BBB, LL, V, A, D, M) Strong Christian worldview emphasizing faith in God, character's belief that God has made him special, prayer, offering thanks to God, discussions of spiritual matters, church attendance, expressions of love, Scripture reading, and inclusion of Christian services, with a couple negative portrayals of Christian leaders; fourteen obscenities (some mild), six profanities, several vulgarities, and one foul gesture; mild violence including breaking and entering, smashing a window, woman accidentally killed by baseball, kicking, and scary bus crash; sexual attraction and boy grabbing girl's breasts implied; adult alcohol use; adults smoke; and a few rebellious attitudes.

The Future of Violent Toys

SMALL SOLDIERS

Quality: ☆☆☆   Acceptability: −1

WARNING CODES:
Language: * *
Violence: * * *
Sex: None
Nudity: None
RATING: PG-13
GENRE: Fantasy/Action
INTENDED AUDIENCE: Older children to adults
RUNNING TIME: 105 minutes
STARRING: David Cross, Jay Mohr, Denis Leary, Gregory Smith, Kirsten Dunst, Phil Hartman, and Tommy Lee Jones as the voice of Chip Hazard
DIRECTOR: Joe Dante
PRODUCERS: Michael Finnell and Colin Wilson
EXECUTIVE PRODUCER: Walter Parkes
WRITERS: Gavin Scott, Adam Rifkin, Ted Elliott, and Terry Rossio
DISTRIBUTOR: DreamWorks Pictures
BRIEF SUMMARY:
Small Soldiers is a dark, violent, and sometimes funny movie delivering lots of action and scares revolving around the possible future of violent toys. The movie starts with two toy designers creating action figures that play back with their owners. Munitions microprocessing chips from the defense department are installed in the toys. The result is the Commando Elite—roughneck, unrelenting fighters led by Chip Hazard, and peaceful, grotesque monsters called the Gorgonites, led by Archer. Teenage toy-store keeper Alan and his neighbor Christy keep a haven for the Gorgonites, and the Commando Elite perform an all-out assault on their home and families.

Though the action involves toys and shows no bloodletting, Small Soldiers employs some of the same tactics found in the most graphic war films, including many obscenities. The toys are unrelenting, fearsome, and sadistic. They cause great harm to the Abernathy and Fimple families. The special effects are admirable, but it seems that every summer the writing of summer action movies gets more and more clichéd and dull. While it has some moral elements of trust and pro-family, the movie seems to gloss over violence in the media and violence with toys and games.

CONTENT ANALYSIS: (Pa, B, LL, VVV, A, D) Pagan worldview of combative toys with some moral elements of confessing wrongdoing, preserving family, trust, and familial love; thirteen obscenities (mostly mild), three profanities (mild), and numerous vulgarities and name-calling; heavy and sometimes scary action violence including toy cuts boy, toy ties up girl, toys knock out parents with sleeping pills, toys attack home with an all-out assault, toys burn boy's pant leg, and girl mows toys down with mower, toys become electrocuted, some war violence on television, and humans fight back; brief alcohol use by parents; and miscellaneous immorality including stealing, former rebellious behaviors implied, and some eerie images of mutant female dolls.

Clever Corporate Intrigue

THE SPANISH PRISONER

Quality: ☆☆☆   Acceptability: +1

WARNING CODES:
  Language: None
  Violence: *
  Sex: None
  Nudity: None
RATING: PG
GENRE: Mystery
INTENDED AUDIENCE: Adults
RUNNING TIME: 112 minutes
STARRING: Campbell Scott, Rebecca Pidgeon, Steve Martin, Ben Gazzara, Ricky Jay, and Felicity Huffman
  DIRECTOR: David Mamet
  PRODUCER: Jean Doumanian
  EXECUTIVE PRODUCER: J. E. Beaucaire
  WRITER: David Mamet
  DISTRIBUTOR: Sony Pictures Classics
  BRIEF SUMMARY:
  In *The Spanish Prisoner,* Joe Ross, a brilliant engineer, develops a top-secret invention to make a fortune for his company, but runs into a sinister conspiracy to steal the process to the invention. Tricked into delivering the only copy of the process to Jimmy Bell, a mysterious jet-setting businessman who stands him up at a prearranged meeting, Joe goes to colleagues he thought were friends but discovers that they too are somehow involved in the conspiracy. Joe pursues company secretary Susan Ricci to a New York ferry, where the movie's surprising climax occurs.
  With minimal foul language, minimal violence, no sex, but full of clever plot twists and a surprise ending, *The Spanish Prisoner* harks back to the good old days of Alfred Hitchcock's Hollywood whodunits with clever execution and sustained suspense. It uses clever storytelling and clipped dialogue set around 1990s corporate intrigue to depict a mystery that keeps the audience guessing the whole time. *The Spanish Prisoner* will delight moral audiences with classic and clever detective storytelling. The only problem might be the main character's failure to seek God's help in his crisis.
  CONTENT ANALYSIS: (H, BB, V, M) Humanist worldview with strong moral elements of a brilliant engineer who falls victim to corporate shenanigans; one profanity; scene of dead man sitting with knife in his stomach and man fires drug bullet at other man; and betrayal and evil scheming.

Overcoming Moral Dilemmas

STAR TREK: INSURRECTION

Quality: ☆☆☆   Acceptability: +1

WARNING CODES:
  Language: *
  Violence: * *
  Sex: None
  Nudity: *
RATING: PG
GENRE: Science fiction
INTENDED AUDIENCE: Ages eight and up
RUNNING TIME: 103 minutes
STARRING: Patrick Stewart, Jonathan Frakes, Brent Spiner, LeVar Burton, Michael Dorn, Gates McFadden, Marina Sirtis, F. Murray Abraham, and Donna Murphy
  DIRECTOR: Jonathan Frakes
  PRODUCER: Rick Berman
  EXECUTIVE PRODUCER: Martin Hornstein
  WRITER: Michael Piller
  DISTRIBUTOR: Paramount Pictures
  BRIEF SUMMARY:
  In the ninth movie of the *Star Trek* franchise, Captain Picard and the gang from the starship *Enterprise* learn a disturbing and puzzling fact. A cultural survey team reports that their android friend Lieutenant Commander Data, played once again with charm by Brent Spiner, has gone berserk while the team is study-

ing a peaceful race of humanoids called the Ba'ku. When Captain Picard, played by Patrick Stewart in another commanding performance, investigates, he uncovers an evil plot behind the survey team. Soon, Picard and his crew are forced to choose between disobeying a direct order and violating one of the basic principles of the society they serve.

Star Trek: Insurrection has plenty of action to keep fans of the series enthralled. It also lets each of the main characters have his or her delightful moment in the cinematic sunshine. Finally, it has a moderately moral worldview of self-sacrifice and good battling evil, plus a morally redemptive element in which one of the villains eventually decides to help the good guys. Only a brief bubble-bath scene between two heterosexual characters, three mildly obscene words, some violence, and a few mildly scary aliens make this movie cautionary for younger children.

CONTENT ANALYSIS: (BB, C, H, Pa, L, VV, N, A, M) Moderately moral worldview of self-sacrifice and battling evil, with a morally redemptive element as well as minor humanist and pagan elements; two mild obscenities and one moderately strong obscenity; moderate action violence such as laser weapon battles in outer space and on land, evil beings hunt down people from peaceful village, rock slide, explosions, hand-to-hand combat, and man uses special machine to stretch man's face and skull to murder him; man and woman sit together in sexy but short bubble-bath scene and man lays head in woman's lap on futuristic couch/bed; alcohol use; and a few mildly scary aliens and moments.

Old-Fashioned Romance

STILL BREATHING

Quality: ★★★☆   Acceptability: −1

WARNING CODES:
  Language: None
  Violence: *
  Sex: *
  Nudity: None
RATING: PG-13
GENRE: Romantic comedy/Drama
INTENDED AUDIENCE: Older teens and adults
RUNNING TIME: 108 minutes
STARRING: Brendan Fraser, Joanna Going, Celeste Holm, Ann Magnuson, and Lou Rawls
DIRECTOR: Jim Robinson
PRODUCERS: Jim Robinson and Marshall Persinger
EXECUTIVE PRODUCER: Joyce Schweickert
WRITER: Jim Robinson
DISTRIBUTOR: October Films
BRIEF SUMMARY:
Still Breathing, the first feature written and directed by Jim Robinson, treats audiences with a refreshing look at love in the 1990s. The scene opens with an attractive but conniving young woman named Roz, played by Joanna Going, walking to her car on a desolate Hollywood street where she is met by a man pointing a gun. The would-be robber is suddenly hit by a car that skids away into the night. Roz calls 911 at a pay phone in front of the Formosa Café. At that same moment in San Antonio, Texas, a sweet-natured young man named Fletcher (played by Brendan Fraser), who has been determined to find his one true love, has a fragmentary, mysterious dream of Roz in front of the café. Waking up, he believes that she is the one meant to be his soul mate. Fletcher pursues Roz as the movie contrasts his innocent life with her complicated, deceptive life. Will Fletcher break down Roz's emotional defenses?

Still Breathing is devoid of any foul language, explicit violence, sex, or nudity.

Director and writer Jim Robinson combines clever dialogue, humor, and passion with strong character development to draw the audience into the story. *Still Breathing* is not explicitly moral, nor does it seem to take a strong moral stance, and it is marred by some implied nominalism.

CONTENT ANALYSIS: (RO, Pa, B, V, S, M, Pa) Romantic worldview with moral and nominalistic elements; some sensual and sexual innuendos and subject matter; one scene of man pulling gun to rob woman and then getting hit by car; depiction of beginning of sexual seduction that is not completed and indication that woman has slept around; woman starts to take off blouse; man uses strange dream to find woman living in another state; and conning people out of money.

Politically Correct Abuse

THERE'S SOMETHING ABOUT MARY

Quality: ✫✫✫   Acceptability: −3

WARNING CODES:
  Language: * * *
  Violence: * *
  Sex: * * *
  Nudity: * * *
RATING: R
GENRE: Romantic comedy
INTENDED AUDIENCE: Adults
RUNNING TIME: 111 minutes
STARRING: Cameron Diaz, Matt Dillon, and Ben Stiller
DIRECTORS: Peter and Bobby Farrelly
PRODUCERS: Frank Beddor, Michael Steinberg, Charles B. Wessler, and Bradley Thomas
EXECUTIVE PRODUCERS: Robert Miller, Marcus Hu, Jon Gerrans, and Daryl Roth
WRITERS: Ed Decter, John J. Straus, Peter Farrelly, and Bobby Farrelly
DISTRIBUTOR: 20th Century Fox

BRIEF SUMMARY:
There's Something About Mary is a sophomoric fantasy that pushes a perverse agenda while cynically masquerading as a warmhearted love story. Ben Stiller plays a former high school nerd named Ted, who hires a smarmy private detective to find the love of his life—the kind, foulmouthed, naïve, and beautiful Mary, played by Cameron Diaz. The detective, played by Matt Dillon, falls in love with Mary himself and tries to foil Ted's attempts to find her. Ted faces numerous other obstacles along the way, such as getting picked up by the police for murder. All of this is done in a cynical manner, with disgusting characters coming in and out of the storyline continuously.

The Farrelly brothers foist lowbrow, dumb wackiness and perversion on the movie audience. The production values in the movie are mixed. Feigning a good-natured and fun tone, the movie contains many intentionally offensive elements, including mocking the handicapped, mocking family and marriage, advocating auto-eroticism, cruelty to animals, exposing private parts, racial stereotyping, and self-hatred, sophomoric lust masquerading as love, continual use of an obscenity, and scenes of suggested oral sexual perversion and gross masturbation. Tacky and tasteless, *There's Something About Mary* uses raunchy humor as a means to pervert morality, love, and decency.

CONTENT ANALYSIS: (RoRo, PaPa, AbAbAb, B, PC, LLL, VV, SSS, NNN, A, DD, MMM) Politically correct romantic worldview with homosexual and pagan elements; eighty-three obscenities and fourteen profanities; man punches man, man pushes handicapped people down, dog bites man in private parts, dog mauls man, man electroshocks dogs, man burns dog, man beats dog, man gets sexual member caught in zipper, handicapped man beats man, phony handicapped man painfully struggles with crutches, police detective slams man's head against desk, several fistfights, and talk of mutilation; woman thinks male discharge is hair gel, man displays testicles caught in zipper, foot fetish, three instances of partially depicted oral sex, perverse sex, dog licks woman's lips, homosexual sexual activity, breasts fondled, homosexuality advocated, voyeurism, masturbation advocated, and masturbation scene; exposed female breasts, strip-club dancers, exposed male testicles, references to private parts, and elderly female breasts displayed and manipulated; alcohol use; marijuana smoking and speed administered to unknowing woman and dog; and racist comments, homosexuality mocked, handicapped mocked, men mocked, marriage mocked, and cynical humor.

Escaping Personal Restrictions

THE TRUMAN SHOW

Quality: ✰✰✰✰   Acceptability: +1

WARNING CODES:
  Language: *
  Violence: *
  Sex: None
  Nudity: None
RATING: PG
GENRE: Fantasy
INTENDED AUDIENCE: Teens and adults
RUNNING TIME: 104 minutes
STARRING: Jim Carrey, Laura Linney, Noah Emmerich, Holland Taylor, and Ed Harris
DIRECTOR: Peter Weir
PRODUCERS: Edward S. Feldman, Adam Schroeder, and Scott Rudin
WRITER: Andrew Niccol
DISTRIBUTOR: Paramount Pictures
BRIEF SUMMARY:
In Jim Carrey's movie The Truman Show, he turns his funny bone into a panic button as he plays a man trying to escape a twenty-four-hour-a-day TV broadcast program that focuses only on him. The producer of The Truman Show thinks he has all factors controlled. He handpicked Truman from the womb, broadcast his birth, and placed him in a fictional town contained in a huge sound-stage. There are five thousand hidden cameras scattered throughout the town, capturing Truman's every move. All of the townspeople are actors, who sometimes are fed lines from the producer. When Truman remembers a girlfriend who told him that this is all a lie, Truman tries to escape and find the real world.

Creative, ambitious, and containing wonderful set design, The Truman Show is an original, moral, and insightful story about personal freedom. Truman's liberation is tied to an appeal to God by the one girl who told him the truth. The most important aspect of The Truman Show is the metaphors and allegories within it. The movie gives us clues and forces us to ask questions that may lead to some important answers and perhaps the most important One of all. One must ask who is the director/producer character in the movie supposed to be—God or the adversary? What is reality? What awaits Truman beyond the exit? What is freedom? This movie doesn't have any sex, foul language is restricted, and the only violence is action oriented.

CONTENT ANALYSIS: (B, CC, L, V, A, M) Light, moral worldview with Christian allegorical elements and emphasizing the value of freedom and individual choice with reference to God; four obscenities and two profanities; mild action violence including chase scenes and attempted drowning; alcohol use; and miscellaneous immorality including massive deception on individual.

A False Heaven and Hell

WHAT DREAMS MAY COME

Quality: ✰✰✰✰   Acceptability: −4

WARNING CODES:

Language: * *
Violence: *
Sex: None
Nudity: *

RATING: PG-13
GENRE: Fantasy
INTENDED AUDIENCE: Older teens and adults
RUNNING TIME: 106 minutes
STARRING: Robin Williams, Cuba Gooding Jr., Annabella Sciorra, and Max von Sydow
DIRECTOR: Vincent Ward
PRODUCERS: Barnet Bain and Stephen Simon
EXECUTIVE PRODUCERS: Ted Field, Frederica Huggins, and Scott Kroopf
WRITER: Ron Bass
BASED ON: The novel by Richard Matheson
DISTRIBUTOR: Polygram Films
BRIEF SUMMARY:
In *What Dreams May Come*, Robin Williams plays a man who dies in a car crash, travels to heaven, and then journeys to hell to rescue his recently departed wife. *What Dreams May Come* probes the question, "Would you go to hell to rescue the person you love?" The story begins with the young doctor, Chris, played by Robin Williams, meeting the love of his life, Annie. Thirteen years later, the married couple's two children die in a car crash, and then Chris dies in a car crash. Chris is taken to heaven by an angelic guide named Albert, played by Cuba Gooding Jr. When Annie commits suicide and goes to hell, Chris decides to rescue her, but the powers of hell are strong and he faces the possibility of being trapped there forever.

The good news is that this movie recognizes heaven, hell, and a loving God. A great many of the beautiful, supernatural depictions seem to be inspired by the artwork of Christian artists. However, *What Dreams May Come* fails to tell people that the only way to heaven is through faith in Jesus Christ. Furthermore, the movie conveys that people can be reincarnated if they wish, an idea that contradicts the Bible. Also, while it does recognize God, it doesn't depict him on the throne of judgment. Finally, the movie falsely affirms the possibility of rescuing someone from hell.

CONTENT ANALYSIS: (RoRo, C, AbAb, FR, LL, V, N, M) Extreme romantic worldview with some Christian elements including Scripture reading, heaven, hell, a loving God, and many anti-Christian elements such as the ability to travel from heaven to hell and implied ability to reincarnate, and false-religious elements of a journey through the supernatural; ten obscenities and four profanities; mild violence including brief, scary car accident and implied suicide; brief rear female naturalistic nudity; and miscellaneous immorality including scary images of hell.

Open Your Eyes

WIDE AWAKE

Quality: ☆☆☆☆   Acceptability: +3

WARNING CODES:

Language: *
Violence: *
Sex: None
Nudity: None

RATING: PG
GENRE: Comedy/Drama
INTENDED AUDIENCE: Families
RUNNING TIME: 90 minutes
STARRING: Joseph Cross, Rosie O'Donnell, Denis Leary, Dana Delany, Robert Loggia, Timothy Reifsnyder, Heather Casler, and Dan Lauria
DIRECTOR: M. Night Shyamalan
PRODUCERS: Cary Woods and Cathy Konrad

EXECUTIVE PRODUCERS: Randy Ostrow, Bob Weinstein, Harvey Weinstein, and Meryl Poster

WRITER: M. Night Shyamalan

DISTRIBUTOR: Miramax Films

BRIEF SUMMARY:

In *Wide Awake*, Joseph Cross plays Joshua A. Beal, a young fifth grader in a Roman Catholic school who searches for God to make sure that his late beloved grandfather is okay. Joshua Beal is a young boy who lives in Philadelphia. Joshua has just lost his grandfather to cancer. "I'm going on a mission," Joshua tells his friend Dave. "I'm going to look for God to make sure my grandpa's okay." Joshua asks the adults around him how to find God as he tries out for the football team, meets a girl named Hope, and gets stuck in a turnstile. Throughout, there are flashbacks of Joshua with his grandfather. "Always," his grandfather notes, "hold onto your faith. Faith will get you through." Even so, Joshua has doubts. Eventually a miraculous experience gives Joshua new hope.

Wide Awake shows that God has been with Joshua throughout his search. Joshua learns to find God in the memories he has of his grandfather and in his experiences with other people. He discovers that he is made in God's image and that, although like everyone else he has a sinful nature, he continues to reflect that image in all his relationships. This entertaining movie is filled with remarkable scenes of Christian forgiveness, compassion, faith, and worship. The touching portrayal of God, the children's performances, and the refreshing look at life make *Wide Awake* an ideal movie for the whole family.

CONTENT ANALYSIS: (CCC, BB, FR, L, V, D, M) Christian worldview with many moral elements, several positive references to Christian worship, prayer, and Christian symbols, and some

scenes of typical childhood rebellion, but also including two references to false religions; eight obscenities and one mild profanity; mild violence involving a bully; references to pipe smoking; and miscellaneous immorality such as leaving school without permission, turning off alarm, disrupting field trip, and lineup in hallway.

X-Citing Thriller

THE X-FILES

Quality: ☆☆☆   Acceptability: –1

WARNING CODES:

Language: * *
Violence: * *
Sex: None
Nudity: None

RATING: PG-13

GENRE: Science fiction/Thriller

INTENDED AUDIENCE: Older children to adults

RUNNING TIME: 122 minutes

STARRING: David Duchovny, Gillian Anderson, Martin Landau, William B. Davis, John Neville, and Armin Mueller-Stahl

DIRECTOR: Rob Bowman

PRODUCERS: Chris Carter and Daniel Sackheim

WRITER: Chris Carter

DISTRIBUTOR: 20th Century Fox

BRIEF SUMMARY:

The X-Files movie is an exciting but surprisingly mundane science fiction thriller about two FBI agents battling a secret conspiracy of powerful men who are helping a mysterious, unseen race of alien invaders. The story focuses on two FBI agents named Mulder and Scully, who battle a global conspiracy of government insiders and businessmen. The secret cabal hides the activities of mysterious aliens from another planet who are trying to colonize Earth. The aliens are secretly breeding a dangerous alien mutant while the human conspirators secretly create a vaccine against the aliens' deadly blood. The story is mostly a cat-and-mouse chase in which Mulder and Scully continue their investigation while they try to keep each other alive.

The tense ending of *The X-Files* is a bit anti-climactic because the alien monsters are revealed early in the film. The two leads, David Duchovny and Gillian Anderson, make compelling heroes. Their appealing quality lends weight to the moderately strong moral worldview of *The X-Files*, which takes a solid stance in favor of goodness, truth, liberty, and self-sacrifice. *The X-Files* has a strong moral worldview of good heroes battling evil, lacks excessive foul language and violence, and has no implied or depicted sex.

CONTENT ANALYSIS: (BB, H, Ev, LL, VV, M) Moderately strong moral worldview of good versus evil and heroes battling globalist conspirators with humanist, evolution elements regarding science fiction aliens; eight obscenities and five profanities, nearly all exclamatory; moderate action violence—alien attacks two cavemen, alien attacks scientist, aliens try to grab heroes, man grazes other man's head with gunshot, man shoots driver, one off-screen murder, bomb explodes in car killing one man, and brief shots of corpses destroyed by aliens; a reference to natural nudity; and men selfishly conspire to enslave humans and use people as hosts for alien parasite.

Love Letters in the Wire

YOU'VE GOT MAIL

Quality: ✰✰✰✰   Acceptability: –1

WARNING CODES:
  Language: * *
  Violence: None
  Sex: *
  Nudity: None

RATING: PG
GENRE: Romantic comedy
INTENDED AUDIENCE: Older teens and adults
RUNNING TIME: 118 minutes
STARRING: Tom Hanks, Meg Ryan, Parker Posey, Jean Stapleton, Dave Chappelle, Steve Zahn, and Greg Kinnear
DIRECTOR: Nora Ephron
PRODUCERS: Lauren Shuler Donner and Nora Ephron
EXECUTIVE PRODUCERS: Delia Ephron, Julie Durk, and G. Mac Brown
WRITERS: Nora Ephron and Delia Ephron
DISTRIBUTOR: Warner Brothers
BRIEF SUMMARY:
You've Got Mail is a remake of the Jimmy Stewart movie *The Shop Around the Corner*. It reunites *Sleepless in Seattle* stars Tom Hanks and Meg Ryan with writer-director Nora Ephron. Hanks plays Joe Fox, an aggressive business-man who has built an empire of book superstores. Ryan plays Kathleen Kelly, who owns a smaller bookstore around the corner. While the two anonymously build a relationship through the Internet, they square off against each other in business. Eventually Joe discovers Kathleen's identity and must figure out how he can reveal himself and reconcile with her instead of losing her forever.

This movie has all the ingredients for a genuine hit. Hanks and Ryan perform with flair. Ephron's script displays great insight into the human condition. Pure entertainment, it focuses more on Joe trying to restore his image to Kathleen than it does on romance and love. Though a relatively clean adult comedy, *You've Got Mail* has some foul language and does not rebuke the live-in relation-ships Joe and Kathleen have before they hook up. The movie does suggest, how-ever, that the Internet should not be a substitute for human interaction and that patience, tact, love, and empathy can save the day and save a relationship.

CONTENT ANALYSIS: (B, Ro, Pa, LL, S, A, D, M) Light, moral worldview where kindness, compassion, and trust triumph over impersonal business practices, mixed with strong romantic and some pagan elements; nine mostly mild obscenities and four exclamatory profanities; two unmarried couples live together and a mention of "cybersex"; alcohol use; minor characters smoke; and in jest woman asks her deceased mother what to do.

☆☆☆ THE BEST 1998 FILMS FOR FAMILIES ☆☆☆

Headline	Title
Let Your Family Go	*The Prince of Egypt*
A Fun Epic of Miniature Proportions	*A Bug's Life*
Joyous Affirmation	*The Parent Trap*
If the Slipper Fits	*Ever After*
Crawling with Fun	*Antz*
Open Your Eyes	*Wide Awake*
Helpful Lilliputians	*The Borrowers*
A Spoonful of Sugar	*Mighty Joe Young*
Masked Champion	*The Mask of Zorro*
Childhood in Paris	*Madeline*

☆☆☆ THE BEST 1998 FILMS FOR MATURE AUDIENCES ☆☆☆

Headline	Title
Uncommon Faith and Love	*Simon Birch*
Justice Sometimes Has Its Price	*A Civil Action*
Escaping Personal Restrictions	*The Truman Show*
Moving Family Tribute	*Deep Impact*
Grace versus Law	*Les Miserables*
Magical Masterpiece	*Life Is Beautiful*
Grace and Healing	*The Horse Whisperer*
Not Yet	*Armageddon*
What Causes Fights and Quarrels	*Men with Guns*
Replacing Tyranny with Goodness	*The Man in the Iron Mask*

✰✰✰ THE TWENTY MOST UNBEARABLE FILMS OF 1998 ✰✰✰

Headline	Title
Worst Politically Correct Banality	*There's Something About Mary*
Worst Spiritism	*Beloved*
Worst Occultism for Children	*Blade*
Worst Teaching Children to Kill	*The Butcher Boy*
Worst New Age, False Religion	*What Dreams May Come*
Worst Promotion of Anti-Christian Occultism	*Practical Magic*
Worst Pedophilia (tie)	*Happiness* and *Lolita*
Worst Anti-Christian Sex Farce	*Orgazmo*
Worst Perversion	*The Opposite of Sex*
Worst Pro-Suicide Propaganda for Teenagers	*Dead Man on Campus*
Worst Revisionist Histories (tie)	*Elizabeth* and *Shakespeare in Love*
Worst Revisionist Propaganda	*Pleasantville*
Worst Infomercial for Political Correctness	*Primary Colors*
Worst Anti-Jewish Feminism	*A Price above Rubies*
Worst Anti-Christian Revisionist History	*Dangerous Beauty*
Worst Darwinian Individualism	*Ayn Rand: A Sense of Life*
Worst Sleaze	*Baseketball*
Worst Drug Promotion	*Fear and Loathing in Las Vegas*
Worst Content	*Very Bad Things*
Worst Dumbest	*Krippendorf's Tribe*

Private Lives

42 UP

Quality: ☆☆☆   Acceptability: +1

WARNING CODES:
   Language: *
   Violence: None
   Sex: None
   Nudity: None

RATING: Not rated
GENRE: Documentary
INTENDED AUDIENCE: Older children and adults
RUNNING TIME: 133 minutes
DIRECTOR: Michael Apted
PRODUCER: Michael Apted
EXECUTIVE PRODUCERS: Ruth Pitt and Stephen Lambert
DISTRIBUTOR: First Run Features
BRIEF SUMMARY:
The movie *42 Up* is an intriguing documentary chronicling the lives of a group of British-born forty-two-year-olds who have been visited by a film crew every seven years since the age of seven (1964). Michael Apted produced and directed all but the first of this series of movies, with each movie revealing the latest twists and turns of these everyday people. Viewers listen and watch as their youthful hopes and dreams are contrasted with the realities of the present, including their personal failures, losses, joys, and successes.

This movie contains three mild profanities and two mild obscenities, as well as scenes of smoking, people drinking in a tavern, and brief scenes of people gambling at the dog races. There is no nudity or sexuality, but there are several conversations about failed marriages, one couple choosing to live together unmarried, and one brief discussion of infidelity. However, the bad consequences of these actions are not hidden. There are also many redeeming conversations about love, commitment, appreciation for parents and children, miraculous restorative faith, and a scene of one of the subjects praying in church. Thus, *42 Up* is a good movie, designed to attract older children and adults.

CONTENT ANALYSIS: (BB, CC, Ro, L, A, D, M) Moral worldview with some Christian elements including redemptive conversations and reference to miraculous faith; three mild profanities and two mild obscenities, plus discussion of failed marriages and brief allusion to one instance of adultery; one couple chooses to live together unmarried and a brief allusion to adultery; alcohol use; smoking; and gambling and evidence of the British class system.

Learning to Share and Care

THE ADVENTURES OF ELMO IN GROUCHLAND

Quality: ☆☆☆   Acceptability: +2

WARNING CODES:
   Language: None
   Violence: *
   Sex: None
   Nudity: None

RATING: G
GENRE: Fantasy
INTENDED AUDIENCE: Children
RUNNING TIME: 70 minutes
STARRING: The *Sesame Street* characters, Vanessa Williams, and Mandy Patinkin
DIRECTOR: Gary Halvorson

PRODUCERS: Alex Rockwell and Marjorie Kalins

EXECUTIVE PRODUCERS: Brian Henson, Stephanie Allain, and Martin G. Baker

WRITERS: Mitchell Kriegman and Joseph Mazzarino

DISTRIBUTOR: Columbia Pictures/Sony

BRIEF SUMMARY:

The Adventures of Elmo in Grouchland features the lovable *Sesame Street* character Elmo in his debut. Bert and Ernie introduce Elmo and occasionally interrupt the action to help explain some of the plot twists. Elmo loves his fuzzy, well-worn blue blanket better than anything in the whole world. One day, Elmo loses his blanket in Oscar the Grouch's garbage-can home. Elmo goes after it, but accidentally falls down another porthole into Grouchland. In Grouchland, Elmo goes on a journey to retrieve his stolen, treasured blanket from the greedy Huxley, played by Mandy Patinkin, the Broadway star from TV's *Chicago Hope.*

There is very little objectionable material in this movie. The villain isn't too mean, and his henchmen are actually benevolent bugs. There is little violence, and it is all action oriented. There is no sexual content, and foul language is limited to a few flatulence-type noises. The lesson here is loud and clear: Share your possessions and don't be greedy. A well-produced movie with adequate special effects, nice but not extravagant music, and a clearly explained plot, *The Adventures of Elmo in Grouchland* should keep the young at heart more than entertained.

CONTENT ANALYSIS: (BBB, V, M) Mainly moral worldview promoting sharing and caring and rebuking greed; a few burps and a few characters make flatulent noises with their mouths; mild action including an out of control skater, a few collisions, a big chicken chases after Elmo, and Elmo breaks into Oscar the Grouch's home; the "Queen of Trash"

wears an unrevealing leotard outfit; stealing rebuked and lying rebuked.

Sticking Together in Crisis

AGNES BROWNE

Quality: ☆☆☆   Acceptability: −2

WARNING CODES:

Language: ***
Violence: *
Sex: *
Nudity: None

RATING: R

GENRE: Drama

INTENDED AUDIENCE: Older teens and young adults

RUNNING TIME: 91 minutes

STARRING: Anjelica Huston, Marion O'Dwyer, Ray Winstone, Arno Chevrier, and Tom Jones

DIRECTOR: Anjelica Huston

PRODUCERS: Anjelica Huston, Arthur Lappin, Jim Sheridan, and Greg Smith

EXECUTIVE PRODUCERS: Gerry Browne, Laurie Mansfield, Morgan O'Sullivan, and Tom Palmieri

WRITERS: John Goldsmith and Brendan O'Carroll

BASED ON: The novel *The Mammy* by Brendan O'Carroll

DISTRIBUTOR: October Films

BRIEF SUMMARY: Anjelica Huston directs herself as the title character in *Agnes Browne*, set in 1967. Agnes must borrow money to bury her recently deceased husband. With seven children to feed, her job as a sidewalk fruit saleswoman hardly makes ends meet, but hard work, Christian faith, and the love of her friend Marion help her get by just fine. Her struggles in the story include talking to her oldest son about puberty and fending off a would-be suitor. When a loan shark threatens to steal her furniture, her prayer for a miracle yields help from a famous musician and hope for a better future.

Agnes Browne is written well, with many warm, wonderful lines. Agnes goes to a church that prays the Lord's Prayer. She works hard and asks God for a miracle. When a friend dies, however, she tells her deceased friend to petition God for a miracle. Also, her culture and class allow her to swear at her children. *Agnes Browne* isn't remarkable cinema, but it is a remarkable story of love that made it to the big screen. A pleasant, feel-good movie, it is spoiled by foul language and misguided prayers.

CONTENT ANALYSIS: (CC, FR, LLL, V, S, A, DD, M) Christian worldview of practicing Catholic Irish family that prays, attends church, thanks God, asks God to bless others, sticks together through a crisis, and seeks God for a miracle, and false religious element where woman asks deceased woman to petition God; twenty-six obscenities, sixteen profanities, several regional, colloquial vulgarities, and mother regularly swears at her children; mild violence including pulling a boy's ear, man punches boy in stomach and boy slaps man's face; kissing and some talk by women asking if another woman misses sex; woman in lingerie; alcohol use; many characters smoking including children; and mean, unforgiving loan shark character.

Most Perverse Marxist Attack on the Family

AMERICAN BEAUTY

Quality: ☆☆   Acceptability: −4

WARNING CODES:

Language: ***
Violence: ***
Sex: ***
Nudity: **

RATING: R
GENRE: Drama
INTENDED AUDIENCE: Adults
RUNNING TIME: 118 minutes
STARRING: Kevin Spacey, Annette Benning, Scott Bakula, Peter Gallagher, Thora Birch, and Wes Bentley

DIRECTOR: Sam Mendes
PRODUCERS: Bruce Cohen and Dan Jinks
WRITER: Alan Ball
DISTRIBUTOR: DreamWorks SKG
BRIEF SUMMARY:

American Beauty is a perverse attack on the good, the true, and the beautiful. A rebellious teenage girl named Jane tells her friend Ricky that she hates her dad because he is a geek. He asks her if she wants her dad dead. She says yes. Her father, Lester Burnham, is going through an early midlife crisis. His wife, Carolyn, dominates him and only wants material success. Lester becomes enamored with a high school cheerleader and decides to make big changes in his life after smoking dope with Ricky. Meanwhile, Carolyn has an adulterous affair with a charismatic business competitor. All of this comes to a head when Lester is shot after trying to fornicate with Angela who is in high school.

Filled with violence, sex, adoration of drugs, and rebellious attitudes, *American Beauty* perverts everything that is beautiful into ugliness. Morality is denigrated and demonized. Everything about this movie is warped, especially the ending, where Lester seemingly goes to heaven after indulging in many sins. The only bright spot is when Lester decides not to fornicate with Angela. Otherwise, every message in this movie is immoral or condones immorality.

CONTENT ANALYSIS: (PaPaPa, AbAbAb, HoHo, LLL, VVV, SSS, NN, AAA, DDD, MMM) Pagan worldview with strong anti-moral, pro-homosexual elements; fifty-five obscenities and twelve profanities; extreme violence including father beats and kicks son, young man videos dead bird, man has head blown open with blood all over the place, and discussions of violence; adultery, pedophilia, fornication, masturbation, and homosexuality; female nudity and several upper nudity shots, male nudity with no genitalia shown; alcohol abuse; extreme marijuana use and pushing marijuana use; and lying, cheating, blackmail, Peeping Tom, and encourages teenage rebellion.

A Search for a Suitable Sweetheart

THE BACHELOR

Quality: ☆☆☆   Acceptability: −1

WARNING CODES:
   Language: **
   Violence: None
   Sex: None
   Nudity: None
RATING: PG-13
GENRE: Romantic comedy
INTENDED AUDIENCE: Older teens and adults
RUNNING TIME: 97 minutes
STARRING: Chris O'Donnell, Renee Zellweger, Artie Lange, and Hal Holbrook
DIRECTOR: Gary Sinyor
PRODUCERS: Bing Howenstein and Lloyd Segan
EXECUTIVE PRODUCER: Chris O'Donnell
WRITER: Steve Cohen
BASED ON: The silent movie *Seven Chances* (1925) with Buster Keaton
DISTRIBUTOR: New Line Cinema
BRIEF SUMMARY:
In *The Bachelor,* Chris O'Donnell stars as Jimmie, a young man who decides to marry his longtime girlfriend Ann, played by Renee Zellweger. Jimmie fears commitment, however, and Ann tells him he needs to grow up. When Jimmie's grandfather dies, he leaves him with a one-hundred-million-dollar inheritance, but only if he gets married before his next birthday, which just happens to be the following day. Jimmie is thus faced with finding a bride before it is too late. Meanwhile, a priest talks to Jimmie about marriage. The man became a priest after his wife died. "Marriage was one of the best things I ever did," the priest says, while telling Jimmie about his grandchildren. Jimmie finally understands the positive side of marriage, but it may be too late.

Like *Runaway Bride,* the institution of marriage is promoted, not pelted, in *The Bachelor.* It's a funny, charming movie with no sex. Although viewers should exercise caution due to several obscenities, profanities, lewd remarks, and lewd references, the movie has a positive outlook on marrying the right person for the right reasons, a refreshing attitude compared to most of the other romantic comedies Hollywood is making.

CONTENT ANALYSIS: (BB, Ro, CC, LL, AA, M) Mostly moral worldview with some romantic and Christian worldview elements including a mostly positive, faithful view of marriage, characters make decisions based on love and emotions, and main character gets advice on commitment and love from a priest who is viewed in a good light; nineteen obscenities, six profanities, and several lewd remarks and references; reference to main character's sexual relationship; woman shown in lingerie; alcohol use and abuse including drunkenness; and greed rebuked.

Not-So-Holy Innocent

BICENTENNIAL MAN

Quality: ☆☆☆   Acceptability: −1

WARNING CODES:
   Language: **
   Violence: *
   Sex: None
   Nudity: None
RATING: PG
GENRE: Comedy/Fantasy
INTENDED AUDIENCE: Older children and adults
RUNNING TIME: 133 minutes
STARRING: Robin Williams, Sam Neill, Embeth Davidtz, Wendy Crewson, and Oliver Platt

DIRECTOR: Chris Columbus

PRODUCERS: Wolfgang Petersen, Gail Katz, Laurence Mark, Neal Miller, Chris Columbus, Mark Radcliffe, and Michael Barnathan

EXECUTIVE PRODUCER: Dan Kolsrud

WRITER: Nicholas Kazan

BASED ON: A short story by Isaac Asimov

DISTRIBUTOR: Touchstone Pictures/Buena Vista/Disney

BRIEF SUMMARY:

In *Bicentennial Man,* sometime in the near future, Mr. Martin accepts the delivery of his new robot, Andrew, played by Robin Williams. Mr. Martin discovers that Andrew has a unique personality and incredible learning capacity. Andrew's creative talents make him wealthy. Years later, Andrew falls in love with Mr. Martin's great-granddaughter and decides to become human. They couple and, as she ages, he figures out that he must die in order to be really human.

Regrettably, *Bicentennial Man* is flawed by poor story development. If *Bicentennial Man* had just focused on its first storyline, it would have been very entertaining and redemptive. In this first storyline, Andrew discovers that he is unique, leaves his home, and then returns when he discovers that love and family are more important than freedom. In the second storyline, Andrew seeks his own kind. By the third storyline, Andrew just wants to become another human being and interprets humanness in terms of sexual gratification. Seeking marriage with a human being, Andrew gets pretty preachy about why he should be considered human. There is a politically correct message, which undermines the better aspects of the movie.

CONTENT ANALYSIS: (Pa, FR, PC, C, B, LL, S, A, MM) Vague New Age worldview about a robot trying to become a human being and implication that he goes to Hollywood heaven upon death, plus politically correct elements that everybody is human, featuring statements like "How can we tell the difference between robots with real human parts from an actual human?" as well as moral and redemptive elements; thirteen obscenities and four profanities; implied fornication and mild discussion of sex; alcohol use; and teaching a robot to swear, euthanasia, and woman marries robot.

Less Bloody, Just As Profane

THE BLAIR WITCH PROJECT

Quality: ☆☆   Acceptability: −3

WARNING CODES:
  Language: ***
  Violence: **
  Sex: None
  Nudity: None

RATING: R

GENRE: Horror

INTENDED AUDIENCE: Older teens and adults

RUNNING TIME: 81 minutes

STARRING: Heather Donahue, Michael Williams, and Joshua Leonard

DIRECTORS: Daniel Myrick and Eduardo Sanchez

PRODUCERS: Gregg Hale and Robin Cowie

EXECUTIVE PRODUCERS: Bob Eick and Kevin J. Foxe

WRITERS: Daniel Myrick and Eduardo Sanchez

DISTRIBUTOR: Artisan Entertainment

BRIEF SUMMARY:

The premise of *The Blair Witch Project,* a low-budget horror movie, is that three student filmmakers enter Maryland's Blair Hills Forest to make a documentary on the legendary Blair Witch, a seldom seen, ghostly presence with a two-hundred-year history of brutal murder. The students get lost in the woods and are hunted by unseen forces, who make vague, scary noises at night and leave signs of ill omen in the morning. The students turn to lots of cursing and hysterical arguing when things don't go their way. After one of them disappears and is apparently murdered, the remaining two happen upon an abandoned two-story cabin.

The Blair Witch Project has none of the gore, brutality, or torture of today's teen horror movies. It may not appeal, therefore, to teenagers whose idea of horror is some TV star-turned-scream-queen running around in a tight T-shirt while a psycho-killer's on the loose. *Blair Witch* does have, however, a moderately strong occult worldview where evil demonic forces are physically and mentally stronger than human beings and even God. No one gains any victory whatsoever against these evil forces. Also, the three "heroes" are hedonistic, pagan characters with little moral awareness.

CONTENT ANALYSIS: (OO, Ab, LLL, VV, AA, DD, M) Moderately strong occult worldview where the demonic world of evil "ghosts" is physically and mentally stronger than human beings and, perhaps, God, with some anti-biblical elements; 212 obscenities, 19 profanities, 1 blasphemy, and 2 obscene gestures; mild acts of violence depicted, such as two people hit on head from behind and some slapping and hitting, but very intense, terrifying story plus gruesome references to past violence; alcohol use and drunkenness; smoking and reference to marijuana; and lots of pointless arguing and hedonistic attitudes by main characters.

Triumph in the Midst of Poverty

CHILDREN OF HEAVEN

Quality: ☆☆☆　　　Acceptability: +3

WARNING CODES:
　Language: *

Violence: None
Sex: None
Nudity: None

RATING: PG
GENRE: Drama
INTENDED AUDIENCE: All ages
RUNNING TIME: 87 minutes
LANGUAGE: Farsi
STARRING: Amir Farrokh Hashemian, Bahareh Seddiqi, and Amir Naji
DIRECTOR: Majid Majidi
PRODUCERS: Amir Esfandiari and Mohammad Esfandiari
WRITER: Majid Majidi
DISTRIBUTOR: Miramax Films
BRIEF SUMMARY:
Children of Heaven is winsome, life affirming, and moral. Nine-year-old Ali and his sister, Zohre, live in a poor section of Teheran. One day Ali retrieves his sister's recently repaired, beaten-up, pink shoes from a decrepit shoemaker. At the grocery, Ali loses the shoes. Zohre asks, "How am I going to go to school without shoes?" Ali says that they can share his sneakers. Day after day, they try to make do. Ali learns that there is an upcoming marathon where the third place prize is a new pair of sneakers. His weeks of running to school help him in the race, but some shoving causes the triumphant ending to be filled with pathos and mystery.

Truly, these are children of heaven. Although they have so little, they love each other deeply. Ali and his sister are brilliant. To get two little children to be so sincere, honest, and open is a work of genius. In the midst of poverty, this film affirms life, love, family, and compassion. The trials and tribulations are real-life events, yet the movie is always captivating, more so than many effects-laden action adventure films. This gem deserves to be seen and appreciated.

CONTENT ANALYSIS: (B, L) Moral worldview; and two very lightweight obscenities.

Rotten to the Core

THE CIDER HOUSE RULES

Quality: ☆☆☆   Acceptability: −4

WARNING CODES:
  Language: *
  Violence: **
  Sex: **
  Nudity: **
RATING: PG-13
GENRE: Drama
INTENDED AUDIENCE: Teens and adults
RUNNING TIME: 131 minutes
STARRING: Tobey Maguire, Charlize Theron, Delroy Lindo, Paul Rudd, Michael Caine, Erykah Badu, Kieran Culkin, Kate Nelligan, and Heavy D
DIRECTOR: Lasse Hallstrom
PRODUCERS: Richard N. Gladstein, Alan C. Blomquist, and Leslie Holleran
EXECUTIVE PRODUCERS: Bobby Cohen, Meryl Poster, Bob Weinstein, and Harvey Weinstein
  WRITER: John Irving
DISTRIBUTOR: Miramax Films/ Buena Vista (Disney)
BRIEF SUMMARY:
The Cider House Rules uses a homespun approach to celebrate the "virtues" of abortion. Homer Wells is a young man growing up in an orphanage in rural Maine. Dr. Larch runs the orphanage and serves as a surrogate father to his charges. Dr. Larch performs abortions, which Homer insists is wrong. In time, Homer moves away from the orphanage, commits adultery, and is faced with a chance to do his own abortion. Eventually, Homer returns to the orphanage and assumes Dr. Larch's position as head of the abortion mill/orphanage.

The Cider House Rules is offensive on many levels. It insidiously manipulates viewers with blatant symbolism, heart-tugging scenes, and votes for anarchy. Homer goes back home, just as so many white liberals go home after they've assuaged their guilt by serving in a soup kitchen for an evening. Another bothersome element is the theme of incest. Premarital sex and unwed pregnancy are also rampant, despite the World War II setting. Moviegoers would be ill-advised to view this two-hour valentine to abortion advocates.

CONTENT ANALYSIS: (AbAbAb, PCPCPC, PaPaPa, RHRH, L, VV, SS, NN, DD, M) Strong anti-biblical, politically correct, pagan worldview espousing endless pro-abortion preaching plus historical revisionism of American society in World War II; seven obscenities and two profanities; murder by stabbing, fistfighting, and gory view of stitches; depicted adultery and implied incest; rear male and rear female nudity; drug abuse (ether) and smoking; and deceit and lying.

Saved at Sea

DEEP BLUE SEA

Quality: ☆☆☆   Acceptability: −2

WARNING CODES:
  Language: ***
  Violence: ***
  Sex: None
  Nudity: None
RATING: R
GENRE: Horror/Science fiction
INTENDED AUDIENCE: Older teens and adults
RUNNING TIME: 105 minutes
STARRING: Samuel L. Jackson, LL Cool J, Saffron Burrows, Thomas Jane, Jacqueline McKenzie, Michael Rapaport, and Stellan Skarsgard
DIRECTOR: Renny Harlin
PRODUCERS: Akiva Goldsman, Tony Ludwig, and Alan Riche
EXECUTIVE PRODUCERS: Duncan Henderson and Bruce Berman

WRITERS: Duncan Kennedy, Donna Powers, and Wayne Powers
DISTRIBUTOR: Warner Brothers
BRIEF SUMMARY:

In *Deep Blue Sea*, three scientifically enhanced sharks endanger the people on a floating laboratory. When the smartest shark bites off the arm of one of the scientists and irreparably damages the whole facility, the people, including a resourceful cook played by rapper LL Cool J, must avoid the sharks while climbing and swimming to safety. This generates lots of exciting action, narrow escapes, and some gruesome deaths. It also generates some corny dialogue, but the movie has its tongue firmly planted in its cheek, so it's better just to sit back and enjoy the excitement of this popcorn movie.

Deep Blue Sea has a strong Christian worldview, centered on the Christian faith of the cook, the movie's most heroic character. He uses his faith to help the people survive, makes reference to Daniel in the lion's den, and prays to God for help. At a crucial, tense moment, he leads several other survivors in a prayer while reciting part of the twenty-third Psalm. This is one of the strongest Christian action movies in quite some time. Regrettably, *Deep Blue Sea* includes plenty of R-rated foul language and lots of gory, scary action violence.

CONTENT ANALYSIS: (CCC, BB, PaPa, Ab, LLL, VVV, A, D, M) Strong Christian worldview with moral elements where the strongest, most heroic character is a Christian who uses prayer and his faith in God to survive and to help others survive, plus pagan elements, especially in the use of foul language and gruesome action violence, and a couple of anti-biblical elements; thirty-two obscenities and four profanities plus an obscene gesture; extreme and intense action violence including shark bites off man's arm, shots of arm's bloody stump, shark flings man's body against glass, many shark attacks where several people

get torn apart, swallowed, eaten, and bitten, with blood, and sharks get blown up into bloody pieces; woman shown in underwear; alcohol use and Christian refers to his past bouts with liquor; smoking; and lying rebuked, psychological blackmail rebuked, and woman scientist rebuked for using unethical means to find a cure for senility.

Flawed Brilliance

A DOG OF FLANDERS

Quality: ☆☆☆   Acceptability: +1

WARNING CODES:
  Language: *
  Violence: *
  Sex: *
  Nudity: None
RATING: PG
GENRE: Drama
INTENDED AUDIENCE: All ages
RUNNING TIME: 100 minutes
STARRING: Jon Voight, Jesse James, Jeremy James Kissner, Cheryl Ladd, Jack Warden, Farren Monet, Bruce McGill, Steven Hartley, and Andrew Bicknell
DIRECTOR: Kevin Brodie
PRODUCER: Frank Yablans
EXECUTIVE PRODUCERS: Martin J. Barab, Larry Mortorff, and Mark Damon
WRITERS: Kevin Brodie and Robert Singer
BASED ON: The children's book by Louisa de la Ramée
DISTRIBUTOR: Warner Brothers
BRIEF SUMMARY:

A Dog of Flanders is an excellent family movie that manages to overcome several problems to become perhaps one of the best Christian-friendly movies released so far this year by a major studio. Nello is a young boy born into a challenging world, a small Flemish town in the early 1800s. Orphaned as a toddler and living with his kindly grandfather,

Nello must overcome the chains of poverty to pursue his dream of becoming a great artist. Circumstances threaten to crush Nello's dream, including a false accusation of arson. He finds that only acts of compassion, confession, and forgiveness, followed by an act of God, can save him.

Despite its positive qualities, *A Dog of Flanders* contains some mild foul language, a scene with a fortune-teller reading palms, and some pagan elements regarding magical thinking and death. These negative elements seem to be overcome by the movie's Christian worldview and its strong moral elements. These positive aspects culminate in a wonderful scene at the end of the movie where a bright burst of sunlight reveals a beautiful painting in which Jesus Christ is being taken down from the cross. The painting is the sacred object that Nello most wants to see.

CONTENT ANALYSIS: (CC, BBB, Ro, O, Pa, L, V, S, AA, D, M) Christian worldview of forgiveness and redemption with strong moral qualities (including positive references to God and a painting of Christ's crucifixion that plays a crucial role in the story), marred by mildly romantic view of self-expression, a scene with a fortune-teller reading palms, and some pagan elements regarding magical thinking and death; four mild obscenities and three mild profanities, which are more like short prayers and words of thanks; mild violence, mostly off-screen, such as man beats dog and leaves him for dead, man attacks child and other man with axe, man falls down steps and suffers mortal head wound, and people fight accidental barn fire; implied adultery in barn; alcohol use and drunkenness; smoking; and villain commits adultery, which clearly has terrible consequences, villain falsely accuses boy of arson, implied illegitimate birth, rich people capitalize on poor boy's misfortunes, children have a streak of rebellion in them, and greed is rebuked and redeemed.

Mocking Hounds from Hell

DOGMA

Quality: ☆☆   Acceptability: −4

WARNING CODES:
  Language: ***
  Violence: ***
  Sex: *
  Nudity: *
RATING: R
GENRE: Comedy/Fantasy
INTENDED AUDIENCE: Adults
RUNNING TIME: 125 minutes
STARRING: Ben Affleck, George Carlin, Matt Damon, Linda Fiorentino, Janeane Garofalo, Salma Hayek, Jason Mewes, Jason Lee, Alan Rickman, Chris Rock, and Kevin Smith
  DIRECTOR: Kevin Smith
  PRODUCER: Scott Mosier
  WRITER: Kevin Smith
  DISTRIBUTOR: Lions Gate Films
  BRIEF SUMMARY:
In *Dogma,* an abortion clinic worker is joined by unorthodox apostles, prophets, and even a muse to stop two fallen angels who want to destroy creation. The two demons want to return to heaven when a Roman Catholic cardinal announces that confession will no longer be required, but sinners can merely pass under a special gate for absolution. Letting the demons pass under the gate will destroy creation, the story says. A motley crew of heroes faces off with the two demons. They get help from a wimpy female god, bringing the whole crazy situation to a lackluster conclusion.

Perhaps no movie since *The Last Temptation of Christ* has received so much criticism from the Christian community as *Dogma,* by director Kevin Smith. A fickle, female god, angels that can be redeemed, and other heretical elements eventually overshadow some accurate theology in this violent, obscenity-filled, and ultimately blasphemous story. The movie bogs down at the end and mainly seems to be a showcase for Kevin Smith's erratic talents. Mr. Smith seems to be a man wrestling with his own Christian faith, but he obviously has a lot to learn about the true nature of God.

CONTENT ANALYSIS: (FRFRFR, PCPC, CCC, AbAbAb, LLL, VVV, S, N, A, DD, MM) Mainly false religious worldview with some politically correct notions and lots of Christian, anti-Christian, and anti-Catholic content; ninety-four obscenities and thirteen profanities; moderate violence including shooting, angel threatens with broken bottle, man throws angel off train, fallen angels beat up man, fallen angel stabs woman in back to death, man hits fallen angel with golf club, implied massacre of many people by fallen angel, man shoots angel's wings off, and fallen angel explodes; one male character continually makes sexual advances toward women, and some sexual humor; rear male nudity, angels show humans their genderless groin areas and female angel dances at strip club in bikini; alcohol use; smoking and brief image of marijuana use; and toilet overflows and creates a demon made out of excrement.

The Faithful Runner

ENDURANCE

Quality: ☆☆☆☆   Acceptability: +3

WARNING CODES:
Language: None
Violence: *
Sex: None
Nudity: *
RATED: PG
GENRE: Documentary/Drama
INTENDED AUDIENCE: All ages
RUNNING TIME: 83 minutes
STARRING: Haile Gebrselassie, Bekele Gebrselassie, Assefa Gebrselassie, and Shawanness Gebrselassie
DIRECTOR: Leslie Woodhead
PRODUCERS: Terrence Malik, Ed Pressman, and Max Palevsky
WRITER: Leslie Woodhead
DISTRIBUTOR: Hollywood Pictures/Buena Vista/Walt Disney
BRIEF SUMMARY:
Endurance is the true story of a man named Haile, the son of a poor Ethiopian farmer who leaves the family farm to join a running club in his nation's capital. "I have to work hard, but without God, all my efforts are useless," intones the friendly, soft-spoken Haile. After watching his mother die and fighting with his father about pursuing his dream of running, Haile eventually gets to the 1996 Olympic Games in Atlanta, where he wins the 10,000-meter race.

Majestic, yet down-to-earth in scope, *Endurance* was clearly the undiscovered jewel of the Telluride Film Festival. Containing Scripture readings from the New Testament, a baptism scene in a Coptic Orthodox Church, and other Christian elements, it tells the story of a Third-World runner who implements his faith in Jesus Christ and wins a spectacular triumph through faith and hard work. Not since 1983's *Chariots of Fire* has an American-distributed film so closely linked the enormous human effort needed to win an international running contest with overt faith in Jesus Christ. *Endurance* may well requite the movie appetite of those who enjoyed that earlier masterpiece.

CONTENT ANALYSIS: (CCC, FR, V, N) Strong Christian worldview where main character reads Scripture and attributes athletic victory to God's intervention, with one scene of totemism; father hits son and schoolteacher hits student; and upper male nudity in ethnic context.

Mayhem Rules

FIGHT CLUB

Quality: ☆☆☆☆   Acceptability: −4

WARNING CODES:

Language: ***
Violence: ***
Sex: **
Nudity: ***

RATING: R
GENRE: Drama
INTENDED AUDIENCE: Adults
RUNNING TIME: 141 minutes
STARRING: Brad Pitt, Edward Norton, Helena Bonham Carter, Meat Loaf Aday, and Jared Leto
DIRECTOR: David Fincher
PRODUCERS: Art Linson, Cean Chaffin, and Ross Grayson Bell
EXECUTIVE PRODUCER: Arnon Milchan
WRITER: Jim Uhls
BASED ON: The novel by Chuck Palahniuk
DISTRIBUTOR: 20th Century Fox
BRIEF SUMMARY:
Fight Club is bizarre, kinetic, and full of camera tricks and deeply disturbed material. It is perhaps the next cult movie to entice would-be vigilantes to repeated viewings. The narrator, played by Edward Norton, has a cushy job and a cushy apartment. Bored, he becomes addicted to self-help groups. One day, the narrator's apartment blows up, and he moves into a dilapidated old house with a stranger named Tyler Durden, played by Brad Pitt. The narrator and Tyler start Fight Club. When the group plans mass destruction, the narrator tries to find Tyler to stop him, but discovers a shocking, surprise revelation.

This is not a simple cops-and-robbers movie. After Columbine and the rise of vigilantism in America, this movie is completely irresponsible. Though Tyler is eventually shut down, he causes lots of damage, including death. Some cinephiles may love the snazzy cinematography and the script, which is full of wry humor, off-beat statements, and crazy details, but in *Fight Club*, the narrator trades one false life for another, resulting in tragedy. Filled with violence and an abandonment of reason for falsehood, this ranks as one of the most dangerous movies released this year.

CONTENT ANALYSIS: (AbAbAb, LLL, VVV, SS, NNN, A, D, MMM) Anarchistic, nihilist worldview that distorts truth, resulting in complete mayhem with jabs at Christian-based support groups, man picks fight with priest and sprays Bible with mace, and man tells man that God doesn't like him; fifty-five obscenities and nine profanities; massive amounts of violence including many bloody, brutal fistfights, car accident, shooting, explosions, man burns man's hand with chemicals, and dream of scary plane crash; depicted fornication and pornography use; obscured full female nudity and brief but graphic image of male genitalia; alcohol use; smoking; and addiction to support groups, man urinates into food, stealing, disturbing images of advanced stages of dementia.

Space Cadets

GALAXY QUEST

Quality: ☆☆☆   Acceptability: +1

WARNING CODES:

Language: **
Violence: **
Sex: *
Nudity: *

RATING: PG
GENRE: Science fiction/Comedy
INTENDED AUDIENCE: Older children and adults
RUNNING TIME: 102 minutes
STARRING: Tim Allen, Sigourney Weaver, Alan Rickman, Tony Shalhoub, Daryl Mitchell, and Sam Rockwell
DIRECTOR: Dean Parisot
PRODUCERS: Suzan Ellis, Mark Johnson, and Charles Newirth
WRITERS: Robert Gordon and David Howard
DISTRIBUTOR: DreamWorks SKG

BRIEF SUMMARY:

Galaxy Quest is a spoof of science fiction TV programs that works. Tim Allen and Sigourney Weaver play two TV actors in a canceled science fiction show who get the chance to do the real thing when a group of real aliens asks for their help and their TV crew. At first, Tim's character is excited to be involved, but reality literally smacks him in the face when they are confronted by the evil, lizard-like Sarris. This leads to more thrills, chills, and comic situations.

Humor abounds in *Galaxy Quest*. Excellent jabs at TV series like *Star Trek* grace the screen. The story includes many funny situations based on the characters and the obstacles they face, and the movie has lots of adventure and space battles to enjoy. Furthermore, there are some key moral points about honesty and pride in *Galaxy Quest*. Jason has to get over his ego, humble himself, and learn how to love others. Only a few mild, off-color bits, some foul language, and story glitches spoil the fun. *Galaxy Quest* deserves only a mild caution for family audiences, especially those with young children.

CONTENT ANALYSIS: (BB, Pa, LL, VV, S, N, AA, D, M) Moral worldview about honesty and pride, including some mild references to God, with a few pagan elements and some gray areas; twelve obscenities, one strong profanity, and five mild profanities, some exclamatory, some "thank God" in a positive sense; sometimes cartoonish action violence with aliens dying, splatting against the windshield, threats of violence, implied torture, ugly aliens, and people dying in space, but nothing salacious; some kissing and implied sex between alien and human; natural upper male nudity, plus brief lewdness and some cleavage; alcohol use and drunkenness; smoking; and fanatic sci-fi fans, ugly food made of bugs and other grotesqueries, and bickering.

A Modern Spanish Classic

THE GRANDFATHER

Quality: ☆☆☆☆   Acceptability: +2

WARNING CODES:

 Language: *
 Violence: *
 Sex: None
 Nudity: None

RATING: PG
GENRE: Historical drama
INTENDED AUDIENCE: Adults
RUNNING TIME: 145 minutes
LANGUAGE: Spanish
STARRING: Fernando Fernán Gómez, Rafael Alonso, Cayetana Guillén Cuervo, and Agustín González
DIRECTOR: José Luis Garci
PRODUCERS: Luis María Delgado, Valentin Penero, and Enrique Quintana
WRITERS: José Luis Garci and Horacio Valcárcel
BASED ON: The novel by Benito Peréz-Galdós
DISTRIBUTOR: Miramax Films
BRIEF SUMMARY:

The Grandfather is a magnificent Spanish historical tale about the true meaning of honor, family, and love. The movie opens with Countess Lucrecia rejecting her paramour. Her daughters live in the country on the former estate of their grandfather, Count Don Rodrigo. His former servants now run the estate because he lost all his wealth while searching for gold in the Americas. Lucrecia holds the title to the remaining properties. The count wants to pass on his honor to his natural descendants, but Lucrecia opposes him and even tries to imprison him in the old monastery.

All of this sets the stage for one of the most magnificent movies ever made. This story is on a par with *Don Quixote*. *The Grandfather* considers the great issues in life and comes to some wonderful conclusions. The countryside, the oceans, and the estates are beautiful. The dialogue is profound. The acting is superbly realistic. *The Grandfather* exposes man's foibles and says man is created in the image of God. Well worth watching, it will have a very limited release but deserves recognition. It is a movie that you'll want to see again and again.

CONTENT ANALYSIS: (CCC, Ro, B, L, S, A, D, M) Christian worldview with romantic elements and moral elements that discusses honor versus love and has profound philosophical themes; one obscenity and one profanity; threats of violence but none consummated; discussion of adultery and infidelity; alcohol use; smoking; and immorality rebuked.

The Holy Giant

THE GREEN MILE

Quality: ☆☆☆☆   Acceptability: −2

WARNING CODES:

Language: ***
Violence: **
Sex: *
Nudity: *

RATING: R
GENRE: Spiritual drama
INTENDED AUDIENCE: Adults
RUNNING TIME: 170 minutes
STARRING: Tom Hanks, Michael Clarke Duncan, Bonnie Hunt, David Morse, Michael Jeter, Graham Greene, Harry Dean Stanton, and Gary Sinise
DIRECTOR: Frank Darabont
PRODUCERS: Frank Darabont and David Valdes
WRITER: Frank Darabont
BASED ON: The novel by Stephen King
DISTRIBUTOR: Warner Brothers
BRIEF SUMMARY:
The Green Mile offers dramatic and spiritual substance with powerful performances and a wonderful recognition of faith, repentance, and divine healing.

Tom Hanks plays Paul, the chief prison guard of a death-row section called "the green mile." One day, an enormous man named John arrives on death row, having been convicted of killing two small girls. John soon displays a miraculous ability to heal others. As prisoners come and go, Paul and John develop a respectful friendship. In the end, as John nears his appointed time for the electric chair, Paul finds out who really killed the two girls and receives his own miracle.

Although the movie is three hours long, Tom Hanks and the supporting cast give powerhouse performances. There are many strong Christian references to faith in God, churchgoing, faithfulness in marriage, and recognition that healing power may come from God. Despite several theological problems and some violence and strong foul language, grace abounds in this movie. *The Green Mile* can be likened to *Dead Man Walking*, where grace enlightens the lives of criminals and jailers alike. Those who love metaphor, incarnational theology, and movie evangelism will appreciate *The Green Mile*.

CONTENT ANALYSIS: (CCC, O, FR, LLL, VV, S, N, M) Strong spiritual worldview from a Christian perspective about heroic, benevolent, churchgoing, faithful prison boss and his relationship with a man who holds miraculous healing powers accredited to Christ, with several utterances of thanks to God, appeals to God for mercy on souls of death-row prisoners, talk of repentance, hero talks about his fear of hell, hero talks about being fearful before God's judgment throne, and a brief superstitious, idolatrous comment made by a minor character about a St. Christopher medal having powers to keep one safe, a sadistic, evil supporting character who receives his just punishment, and a false, religious element suggesting that supernatural powers can be transferred simply by touching, rather than receiving it from

God; forty-five obscenities, fourteen profanities, a few racial slurs, a few sexual references; and several scenes of urination, including prisoner urinates on guard's shoe; moderate violence including an implied murder of two young girls, brief shooting resulting in death, sadistic prison guard breaks prisoner's fingers by clubbing, a few smacks and slaps to the face, punching, brief scene of electrocution, and another graphic, drawn-out scene of electrocution involving burning; implied sex between married couple and brief sounds of their sexual encounter, evil prisoner makes some sexual remarks of intent toward guard, and sadistic guard looks at pornographic drawings; rear male nudity and upper male nudity; and brief image of two dead girls, prisoner spits on prison guard, and burning.

Bear Adventure

GRIZZLY FALLS

Quality: ★★★☆   Acceptability: +2
WARNING CODES:
Language: *
Violence: **
Sex: None
Nudity: None
RATING: PG
GENRE: Historical adventure
INTENDED AUDIENCE: All ages
RUNNING TIME: 94 minutes
STARRING: Bryan Brown, Tom Jackson, Oliver Tobias, Daniel Clark, and Richard Harris
DIRECTOR: Stewart Raffill
PRODUCERS: Peter R. Simpson and Allan Scott
EXECUTIVE PRODUCERS: Mark Damon, Raylan Jensen, and Georges Campana
WRITER: Richard Beattie
BASED ON: A story by Stuart Margolin

DISTRIBUTOR: Providence Entertainment
BRIEF SUMMARY:
Grizzly Falls is a well-made adventure story that harkens back to the adventures of yesteryear. In a proper Victorian home in Chicago, the mother of a young boy named Harry longs for her adventurer husband to come home. The man doesn't because he is on a quest. Harry's mother dies, and eventually Harry's father returns and takes him into the American wilderness. His father assembles an Indian guide named Joshua and some rough backwoodsmen so that he can be the first man to trap and not kill a grizzly. When Harry's father captures a grizzly's cubs, the bear kidnaps Harry. The rest of this exciting movie involves Harry's father trying to find his son, and Harry learning to live in the wilderness.

Grizzly Falls is a well-produced movie, both exciting and captivating. The characters are real and interesting. Probably the only question mark is the friendship that Harry strikes up with the grizzly. This is, after all, a dangerous wild animal. With only a few obscenities and some action violence, *Grizzly Falls* has a strong moral worldview as well as a bear that seems too good to be true.

CONTENT ANALYSIS: (BB, C, O, L, VV, A, M) Strong moral worldview with a mention of faith and one mention of magical compass as well as a bear that seems too good to be true; four obscenities and three mild profanities; adventure violence including bear mauls dogs, bear attacks man, animals are shot, men get hit by falling log and break bones, not too bloody but sometimes intense; boy's mother dies peacefully; alcohol use and barroom scene; and gambling and rough backwoodsmen.

You Auto See It

HANDS ON A HARD BODY

Quality: ★★★☆   Acceptability: +3

WARNING CODES:

Language: *
Violence: None
Sex: None
Nudity: None

RATING: PG
GENRE: Documentary
INTENDED AUDIENCE: All ages
RUNNING TIME: 97 minutes
DIRECTOR: S. R. Bindler
PRODUCERS: S. R. Bindler, Todd Gustawes, and Chapin Wilson
EXECUTIVE PRODUCER: Matthew McConaughey
BRIEF SUMMARY:

Hands on a Hard Body is not the title of a prurient sex comedy; rather, it is a documentary about twenty-four people who compete in the "Hands on a Hard Body" contest in Texas to win a Nissan pickup truck. The contest involves keeping your hands on the truck until everyone else has dropped out—which may take days! The low-budget documentary has won many audience awards. Grainy and rough, it tells the fascinating story of twenty-four people who will stand for hours with their hands on this truck to try to win something that they need badly. One of the contestants won the contest in 1993 for keeping his hands on the truck for eighty-three hours. Several of the contestants are Christians.

It is hard to explain why this is such a riveting movie. These people are nice to each other, but even so, they experience the slings and arrows of the human condition at its most basic level. The audience learns to appreciate these people after a while. What seems silly becomes captivating. Maybe this movie will instill commitment, endurance, character, and dignity in your children. Beware, however, of the title. The term "hard body" has been used for salacious movies, so make sure you look for *Hands on a Hard Body*.

CONTENT ANALYSIS: (BB, CC, L, D) Moral worldview with a lot of Christian content; very little obscene language; and some cigarette smoking.

Setting the Captive Free

THE HURRICANE

Quality: ☆☆☆☆   Acceptability: −2

WARNING CODES:

Language: ***
Violence: **
Sex: *
Nudity: *

RATING: R
GENRE: Drama
INTENDED AUDIENCE: Older teens and adults
RUNNING TIME: 160 minutes
STARRING: Denzel Washington, John Hannah, Deborah Kara Unger, Liev Schreiber, Vicellous Reon Shannon, David Paymer, Dan Hedaya, and Rod Steiger
DIRECTOR: Norman Jewison
PRODUCERS: Armyan Berstein, Norman Jewison, and John Ketcham
EXECUTIVE PRODUCERS: Marc Abraham, Irving Azoff, Thomas A. Bliss, Rudy Langlais, Tom Rosenberg, and William Teitler
WRITERS: Armyan Bernstein and Dan Gordon
BASED ON: The books *The 16th Round* by Rubin "Hurricane" Carter and *Lazarus and the Hurricane* by Sam Chaiton and Harry Swinton
DISTRIBUTOR: Universal Pictures
BRIEF SUMMARY:

The Hurricane is a powerful, moral movie, starring Denzel Washington as boxer Rubin "Hurricane" Carter. It fictionalizes Hurricane's two major jail terms and the friends who eventually help set him free. The story begins with Rubin as an eleven-year-old boy. He is put into a juvenile delinquent center for violently defending a friend against sexual assault. On his release, he hones himself into a championship boxer, only to be framed for a murder he says he didn't commit. After nearly twenty years in a New Jersey prison, he is finally granted freedom when a boy, inspired by Carter's autobiography, travels from Canada to fight for Rubin until he is free.

As Carter, Denzel Washington brilliantly goes from hate to love, unforgiveness to forgiveness, and hopelessness to hopefulness. In two important scenes, he receives strength from the Bible. *The Hurricane* advocates justice, love, kindness, and self-sacrifice. Objectionable content includes a child-molesting villain, strong foul language, some troublesome politically correct historical revisionism, and brief images of a bloody murder scene. Despite these serious problems, the core of this controversial drama lies in Carter's metamorphosis from darkness to light, with the movie allowing Scripture to season and define Rubin's story.

CONTENT ANALYSIS: (BBB, CC, RH, PC, Pa, LLL, VV, S, N, A, D, MM) Strong moral worldview espousing justice, love, kindness, and self-sacrifice, with some strong Christian content including Scripture quoting and redemptive elements of sacrificial love setting another free, plus some troublesome historical revisionism, political correctness, and pagan elements of hatred and racial discrimination, which are rebuked; forty-eight obscenities, six profanities, and a few racial slurs; moderate violence including shooting, boy throws bottle at man's head, brief image of police beating man, and scary scene of car accident; an adult man makes sexual advances toward small boy, and some adulterous flirtation between opposite sex adults; upper male nudity; alcohol use; smoking; and stealing, racism, intense arguing, and images of two corpses.

No Man Is Good; No, Not One

AN IDEAL HUSBAND

Quality: ☆☆☆☆   Acceptability: −1

WARNING CODES:
   Language: *
   Violence: None
   Sex: *
   Nudity: **
RATING: PG-13
GENRE: Comedy
INTENDED AUDIENCE: Teens and adults
RUNNING TIME: 95 minutes
STARRING: Rupert Everett, Julianne Moore, Minnie Driver, Cate Blanchett, and Jeremy Northam
DIRECTOR: Oliver Parker
PRODUCERS: Bruce Davey, Uri Fruchtmann, Barnaby Thompson, Nicky Kentish Barnes, and Paul L. Tucker
EXECUTIVE PRODUCERS: Andrea Calderwood, Ralph Kamp, and Susan B. Landau
WRITER: Oliver Parker
BASED ON: The play by Oscar Wilde
DISTRIBUTOR: Miramax Films
BRIEF SUMMARY:

An Ideal Husband proves the ideal comedy, thanks to its respectful adaptation of Oscar Wilde's original play. Rupert Everett plays Lord Arthur Goring, a wealthy bachelor who spends most of his time admiring himself in the mirror and charming the ladies of his upper-crust social circle. His leisurely life suddenly becomes complicated when an old flame returns to town—the scheming Mrs. Laura Cheveley. Mrs. Cheveley possesses a letter proving that Lord Goring's friend, Sir Robert Chiltern, bought his way into Parliament. She attempts to blackmail Sir Robert. Fearing public castigation and his wife's contempt, he must decide whether to expose his long-buried sins or commit new ones to conceal his past.

If all of this sounds complicated, it is. But the plot unfolds in unexpected ways that thrill rather than bewilder. Rupert Everett's hilarious turn is delightful. The best part of *An Ideal Husband* is its clever dialogue. Wilde's rapier wit is hilarious and compassionate. The likable characters become hopelessly mired in their own deceit. It is a perpetual pleasure to watch them wriggle, struggling to extricate themselves. In the end, love and honesty win out and moral ideals triumph.

CONTENT ANALYSIS: (B, L, S, NN, AA, D, M) Somewhat moral worldview with morality winning over idolatry and deceit; three obscenities and one profanity; subtly implied fornication and man fondles widow's breast; a very brief flash of a nude woman in the background in the opening scenes and upper male nudity; alcohol use and vaguely implied alcohol abuse; smoking; and deceit, lying, and blackmail.

Getting the Inside Dope

THE INSIDER

Quality: ★★★☆   Acceptability: −2

WARNING CODES:
  Language: ***
  Violence: None
  Sex: None
  Nudity: None
RATING: R
GENRE: Drama
INTENDED AUDIENCE: Adults
RUNNING TIME: 158 minutes
STARRING: Al Pacino, Russell Crowe, Christopher Plummer, Diane Venora, Philip Baker Hall, Lindsay Crouse, and Debi Mazar
DIRECTOR: Michael Mann
PRODUCERS: Michael Mann and Pieter Jan Brugge
WRITERS: Eric Roth and Michael Mann
DISTRIBUTOR: Touchstone Pictures/Buena Vista Pictures Distribution/Walt Disney Company
BRIEF SUMMARY:
The Insider is a well produced, acted, directed, and photographed movie about a 60 Minutes producer who helps a scientist blow the whistle on some nefarious activities in the large tobacco companies. Harassed by the scientist's former company, a large tobacco firm, both the producer and the scientist fight to expose the truth behind the chemical makeup in tobacco products. The scientist becomes a key figure in federal and state government lawsuits against "Big Tobacco," but CBS lawyers briefly put the kibosh on a scheduled interview with the intense scientist. This leads to interesting questions about journalistic ethics and corporate machinations.

Playing like an edge-of-your-seat political thriller, The Insider nevertheless has a mild socialist worldview with politically correct elements and a tone of historical revisionism, despite its positive moral qualities. It fails to reveal the Marxist past of the 60 Minutes producer's college training. It also fails to consider the dangers of letting Big Brother government harass businesses in order to extort money from them, money that will be used to pay for huge social programs. Such social programs seem to be just as addictive as the nicotine in any cigarette.

CONTENT ANALYSIS: (So, H, PC, RH, B, LLL, A, D, M) Mild socialist humanist worldview of leftist journalist manipulating humanist scientist into becoming a whistle-blower on large, controversial smoking companies, plus some political correctness, historical revisionism, and moral elements regarding truth, product liability, and ethical issues about TV journalism and business practices; sixty-two mostly strong obscenities, one strong profanity, and at least one mild profanity; implied and depicted threats of violence; alcohol use; smoking; and wife fails to support husband who takes a principled stand against corruption and deceit.

The Greatest Hero Ever Assembled

INSPECTOR GADGET

Quality: ★★☆   Acceptability: +2

WARNING CODES:

Language: *
Violence: *
Sex: None
Nudity: None

RATING: PG
GENRE: Fantasy/Comedy
INTENDED AUDIENCE: All ages
RUNNING TIME: 85 minutes
STARRING: Matthew Broderick, Rupert Everett, Joely Fisher, Michelle Trachtenberg, and Dabney Coleman
DIRECTOR: David Kellogg
PRODUCERS: Jordan Kerner, Roger Birnbaum, and Andy Heyward
EXECUTIVE PRODUCERS: Jon Avnet, Barry Bernardi, Aaron Meyerson, and Jonathan Glickman
WRITERS: Kerry Ehrin, Zak Penn, and Audrey Wells
DISTRIBUTOR: Walt Disney Pictures/Buena Vista
BRIEF SUMMARY:
Disney's live-action movie, *Inspector Gadget*, is a good-hearted movie with many positive virtues and lots of good special effects, but it never gets beyond its cartoon roots. It tells the story of a virtuous security man named John Brown who wants to do good, but doesn't have what it takes. When the villain tries to steal some secrets about developing a robotic policeman, John gets terribly injured. Brenda, the daughter of the deceased inventor of the robotic policeman, decides to reconstruct John as the robotic Inspector Gadget. Eventually, Inspector Gadget must fight a mean robotic version of himself and the villain.

There are a lot of fantastic special effects that help propel the action and provide humor. There is redemption, love triumphs over evil, miracles happen, and the good guys win. Regrettably, however, these parts don't seem to make a whole. The movie also includes four very mild profanities and a mocking reference to Eastern religion with a scatological joke. Otherwise, *Inspector Gadget* is as clean as his police whistle.

CONTENT ANALYSIS: (CC, Pa, L, V, M) Christian worldview with some pagan elements; four exclamatory profanities; action cartoon violence; mildly frightening scenes with villains including explosions, blows on body parts, pratfalls, and frightening situations; romantic attraction; and good triumphs over evil.

From War to Peace

THE IRON GIANT

Quality: ☆☆☆☆   Acceptability: +1

WARNING CODES:

Language: **
Violence: *
Sex: None
Nudity: None

RATING: PG
GENRE: Animated science fiction
INTENDED AUDIENCE: All ages
RUNNING TIME: 90 minutes
VOICES: Vin Diesel, Jennifer Aniston, Harry Connick Jr., Cloris Leachman, Eli Marienthal, Christopher McDonald, John Mahoney, and M. Emmet Walsh
DIRECTOR: Brad Bird
PRODUCER: Allison Abbate
EXECUTIVE PRODUCER: Des McAnuff
WRITERS: Brad Bird and Tim McCanlies
BASED ON: The children's book by Ted Hughes
DISTRIBUTOR: Warner Brothers
BRIEF SUMMARY:
The animated cartoon, *The Iron Giant*, opens with a giant robot falling to Earth. The year is 1957, Sputnik has just been launched by the evil Soviet empire, and fear of invasion is running rampant. One Washington insider takes the threat seriously and travels to a small Maine town to find out what's happening. Meanwhile, little Hogarth Hughes tracks down the iron giant, who is eating the town's metal objects. He finds out that this giant is not

a bad sort. Yet, when the military arrives with guns blazing, the iron giant retaliates. Love, however, overcomes the giant's programming to kill, and the ending has powerful emotional resonance.

This is one of the most exciting animated movies ever made. There are a lot of positive things going on here. Clearly, it's Hogarth's love that gets the giant to choose the right path. However, poor usage and terminology muddle this positive message. The story includes a strange mixture of Christian, New Age, politically correct, environmental, and other worldviews. Even so, love overcomes evil and death. Therefore, the story works in spite of its politically correct concepts and some unnecessary profanities.

CONTENT ANALYSIS: (BB, CC, Pa, H, E, FR, LL, V, M) Very mixed worldview with moral, Christian, pagan, environmental, humanist, and false religious elements combined; six profanities and six obscenities; cartoon violence including giant robot electrocuted, army being blasted and disintegrated, giant robot being hit by train, giant robot hit by nuclear warhead, boy falling and getting hit, and a mean national security agent; an espresso joke, a mild, veiled bathroom joke, some evasion of the truth by boy in attempt to hide giant robot, plus false teaching about the soul and false teaching about guns.

Grace-Full Romance

JUST THE TICKET

Quality: ☆☆☆   Acceptability: −1

WARNING CODES:
  Language: ***
  Violence: *
  Sex: *
  Nudity: None

RATING: R
GENRE: Romantic comedy
INTENDED AUDIENCE: Older teens and adults

RUNNING TIME: 112 minutes
STARRING: Andy Garcia, Andie MacDowell, Richard Bradford, Andre Blake, Elizabeth Ashley, and Ron Leibman
DIRECTOR: Richard Wenk
PRODUCERS: Gary Lucchesi and Andy Garcia
EXECUTIVE PRODUCERS: Andie MacDowell and Yoram Pelman
WRITER: Richard Wenk
DISTRIBUTOR: United Artists/ Metro Goldwyn-Mayer
BRIEF SUMMARY:

In *Just the Ticket*, Andy Garcia plays Gary, an eccentric Roman Catholic man trying to woo back the love of his life, Linda, played by Andie MacDowell. Gary lives from day to day as a ticket scalper, and Linda has just been accepted into the exclusive Cordon Bleu school for chefs in France. That gives Gary only three weeks to scalp a bunch of tickets to the Pope's scheduled appearance at Yankee Stadium in New York City, to offer Linda a better life.

Gary clearly believes in God, despite his problematic lifestyle. He goes to confession several times, although once he brings a beer. Gary also thanks God openly when he finds out that the Pope is coming to town, and has a crucifix hanging on his wall. The turning point in the movie occurs when Gary unexpectedly comes face-to-face with the Pope, who blesses him. This blessing turns out to be prescient, for Gary does in fact land on his feet only by an act of pure grace, not through his own efforts. Thus, despite some unbiblical elements and strong foul language, the movie recognizes the presence of God and his unseen hand in our lives.

CONTENT ANALYSIS: (CC, Pa, Ab, LLL, V, S, A, DD, M) Moderately strong Christian worldview with pagan and unbiblical elements; twenty-four obscenities and three profanities; mild violence such as men punching man; implied fornication; woman comes out of shower wrapped in a towel; alcohol use; implied drug use; and ticket scalping, bringing a beer to church, and an irresponsible lifestyle partially rebuked.

Healing Broken Relationships

MAGNOLIA

Quality: ★★★☆   Acceptability: −2

WARNING CODES:
  Language: ***
  Violence: **
  Sex: **
  Nudity: **
RATING: R
GENRE: Drama/Satire
INTENDED AUDIENCE: Adults
RUNNING TIME: 186 minutes
STARRING: Tom Cruise, Julianne Moore, John C. Reilly, Melora Walters, William H. Macy, Jason Robards, Philip Seymour Hoffman, Jeremy Blackman, and Henry Gibson
DIRECTOR: Paul Thomas Anderson
PRODUCER: Joanne Sellar
EXECUTIVE PRODUCERS: Michael De Luca and Lynn Harris
WRITER: Paul Thomas Anderson
DISTRIBUTOR: New Line Cinema
BRIEF SUMMARY:
In the three-hour opus *Magnolia* by Paul Thomas Anderson, two fathers try to reconcile with their older children and one young child becomes alienated from his dad. Meanwhile, a healthcare worker tries to fulfill one dying father's last request for reconciliation, and a Christian policeman becomes attracted to one of the older children, a woman who, unknown to him, has a drug problem. Those stories culminate in a bizarre miracle of biblical proportions. *Magnolia* even gives this miracle a Bible reference. The whole affair results in scenes of catharsis, repentance, forgiveness, redemption, and a smile of hope.

One of the best-directed and most original movies of the year, *Magnolia* has an apparent Christian worldview, partly because the Christian policeman seems to be one of the two main heroic characters in the movie. The movie actually ends with a positive resolution to his relationship with the drug addict. *Magnolia*'s scenes of repentance, forgiveness, and redemption, however, are marred by lots of strong foul language, some early sex scenes, a bad image of fathers (one of whom is repentant), and some violence. An R-rated movie for adults only, it thus rates a strong, extreme caution.

CONTENT ANALYSIS: (CC, PaPaPa, Ab, LLL, VV, SS, NN, AA, DD, Ho, MM) Christian worldview with elements of repentance, forgiveness, implied redemption, and a heroic Christian character who prays silently in one scene before a crucifix and talks to God in other scenes, plus very strong pagan content by lost, sinful characters; about 240 mostly strong obscenities, 34 mostly strong profanities, and lewd descriptions by major villainous character about seducing women; moderate level of dramatic violence such as man killed by accidental shotgun firing, screaming, angry man overturns table, angry man throws chair, three attempted suicides, policeman handcuffs irate woman to couch, several vehicles crash, and bizarre natural phenomenon smashes cars, hits houses and breaks windows, and dog dies off-screen after accidentally eating some medical drugs; briefly depicted sex scenes, implied fornication, possible incest discussed, and strong sexual references; upper and rear male nudity, upper female nudity on TV, and obscured upper female nudity through shower glass; alcohol use and drunkenness; smoking and heavy drug use, but drug use is rebuked; man expresses homosexual desires for muscle-bound bartender; and adult issues regarding adultery, taking advantage of children to earn money, spousal abandonment, returning stolen money, and incest, combined with elements of repentance, forgiveness, and implied redemption.

Violent Allegory

THE MATRIX

Quality: ☆☆☆☆   Acceptability: −2

WARNING CODES:

Language: ***
Violence: ***
Sex: None
Nudity: *

RATING: R

GENRE: Science fiction

INTENDED AUDIENCE: Older teens and adults

RUNNING TIME: 136 minutes

STARRING: Keanu Reeves, Laurence Fishburne, Carrie-Anne Moss, Hugo Weaving, and Joe Pantoliano

DIRECTOR: Andy Wachowski and Larry Wachowski

PRODUCER: Joel Silver

EXECUTIVE PRODUCERS: Barrie Osborne, Andrew Mason, Andy Wachowski, Larry Wachowski, Erwin Stoff, and Bruce Berman

WRITERS: Andy Wachowski and Larry Wachowski

DISTRIBUTOR: Warner Brothers

BRIEF SUMMARY:

Hong Kong action thrillers continue their influence in Hollywood with the science fiction thriller *The Matrix*, starring Keanu Reeves. Reeves plays a messianic hero and computer hacker named Neo, who must defeat the dehumanized, evil agents of a mysterious power known as "The Matrix." Joining Neo is a charismatic black leader named Morpheus, played by Laurence Fishburne, and a sexy but lethal female hacker named Trinity, played by Carrie-Anne Moss. Extreme action violence, including brutal martial arts combat and automatic weapons fire, leads to a rousing victory over evil.

Despite its strong foul language and a couple of overlong action sequences, *The Matrix* is a unique blend of martial arts action, cops-and-robbers thriller, science fiction fantasy, special effects, and moral/religious philosophy. *The Matrix* uses an explicit Christian allegory to support a moral worldview where good triumphs over evil. Neo is a messianic hero who sacrifices himself to save humanity. At one point, Trinity's love brings him back to life. This scene deliberately reminds one metaphorically of the love of the Father who literally brought Jesus Christ back to life in the Resurrection, the historical lynchpin of the Christian faith.

CONTENT ANALYSIS: (PaPa, BB, CC, LLL, VVV, N, A, D, O, Fe, MM) Eclectic worldview with Christian, moral, and pagan elements, vaguely New Age regarding violence and philosophy about virtual computer world and real world; twenty-five obscenities and fourteen profanities, mostly exclamatory and a few that are also appeals to God, plus four obscenities heard in song over final credits; extreme action violence, with a little gore, including several brutal martial arts battles, evil secret agents get police to chase and shoot heroes, two main heroes storm office building in a hail of bullets to rescue leader, explosions, minor heroes betrayed and murdered, movie shows how evil intelligent machines hook up human bodies, placing them in vat of goo to harvest their electrical energy as a replacement for solar power; reference to sex in virtual computer world; upper male nudity and brief rear male nudity, plus woman in low-cut red dress and woman in tight-fitting clothes; alcohol use; smoking; people go to vaguely occult seer called "The Oracle" who "reads" their future but no mention of where prophet gets her power, and boy with shaved head mentally bends spoon in virtual computer world; mildly feminist images of women doing macho combat but men do most of the brutal martial arts combat; and evil villains pose as secret agents to oppress humans but are defeated, evil agent expresses hatred for humanity, talk of fate is rebuked, and virtual computer world is described at the end as "a world without rules and controls, beyond boundaries, a world where anything is possible."

Banishing the Monster

THE MUMMY

Quality: ☆☆☆   Acceptability: −3

WARNING CODES:
  Language: ***
  Violence: ***
  Sex: None
  Nudity: *
RATING: PG-13
GENRE: Horror/Action/Adventure
INTENDED AUDIENCE: Teens and adults
RUNNING TIME: 126 minutes
STARRING: Brendan Fraser, Rachel Weisz, John Hannah, Arnold Vosloo, Ardeth Bay, Kevin J. O'Connor, and Jonathan Hyde
DIRECTOR: Stephen Sommers
PRODUCERS: James Jacks and Sean Daniel
WRITER: Stephen Sommers
DISTRIBUTOR: Universal Pictures
BRIEF SUMMARY:
The newest remake of *The Mummy* is an entertaining but intense and scary action story with a strong occult worldview. A beautiful Egyptologist and her brother enlist the aid of an American adventurer and the leader of an ancient order of royal bodyguards to defeat the occult powers of an evil Egyptian high priest. The priest's mummified body is brought back to life when the woman reads an incantation from the Egyptian Book of the Dead. The heroes must battle a huge sandstorm, locusts, and an army of mummies and skeletons in order to defeat the villain.

The Mummy is a visually striking combination of Indiana Jones, *Poltergeist* movies, *Lawrence of Arabia*, and a Hollywood Western with six-guns blazing! It all becomes a little too overwhelming and jumbled at times. Also, the heroes use occult means to defeat the occult villain. In horror movies from the golden age of Hollywood, the heroes used Christianity, specifically the Cross of Christ, to defeat the occult. This triumph of the demonic is only mitigated by some moral elements of fighting against a great evil force, a couple of positive references to God, and strong, noble images of unselfish sacrifice.

CONTENT ANALYSIS: (OOO, FRFR, B, H, Pa, Ab, LLL, VVV, N, AA, D, MM) Strong occult worldview where good guys use occult means to defeat totally evil occult villain, plus false religion elements, moral elements of taking a stand against total evil and references to biblical plagues in Exodus and to Allah (the Muslim and Arab name for God, but no references to Muhammed or the Koran), three of the four main good guys are humanists, statues and other references to pagan Egyptian gods and religion, and anti-biblical elements in one scene with scheming coward ineffectually using the Cross and the Star of David to stop villain; twenty-three mostly mild obscenities, five mild profanities, and one strong exclamatory profanity; lots of scary action violence, mostly against evil occult villain, including huge desert battle scene between soldiers, many gunfights, "good" guys set boat on fire to stop ignorant secular humanists, black bugs (scarabs) come alive to eat human flesh, sword fights against mummies and nasty skeletons animated from the dead by occult means, and villain uses occult powers to wreak havoc, such as sending biblical plagues on people, creating huge windstorm, and mummifying good guys and other people; some kissing; ancient Egyptian queen dressed in revealing clothing; alcohol use and scenes of drunkenness; smoking; and many scary scenes, looting graves, greed, adultery, burying people alive, and missionary seems to have given up calling to search for treasure while drinking too much at times.

Kermit and Company Get Funky

MUPPETS FROM SPACE

Quality: ☆☆☆☆   Acceptability: +2

WARNING CODES:
  Language: *
  Violence: *
  Sex: None
  Nudity: None
RATING: G
GENRE: Comedy
INTENDED AUDIENCE: All ages
RUNNING TIME: 88 minutes
STARRING: Jeffrey Tambor, Andie McDowell, Rob Schneider, and Ray Liotta
VOICES: Brian Henson, Frank Oz, Dave Goelz, and Bill Barretta
DIRECTOR: Tim Hill
PRODUCERS: Brian Henson and Martin G. Baker
EXECUTIVE PRODUCERS: Kristine Belson and Stephanie Allain
WRITERS: Jerry Juhl, Joseph Mazzarino, and Ken Kaufman
DISTRIBUTOR: Columbia Pictures
BRIEF SUMMARY:
Muppets from Space recaptures the zaniness of the old Muppets TV series from the 1970s. It tells how Gonzo attempts to rendezvous with the alien creatures from his native planet. Government agents interrupt his plans, however, by kidnapping Gonzo and Rizzo the rat while Kermit the frog leads a group of Muppets to rescue their friends. Also, Miss Piggy takes over a TV show about UFOs and aliens and becomes part of the rescue effort.

A genuinely funny, toe-tapping family movie with popular tunes from the seventies, *Muppets from Space* provides an entertaining look at the large house where all the Muppets live, including the Swedish chef and a peppy little king prawn named Pepe. It contains positive moral messages that overcome some minor politically correct pagan elements about cultural identity. In fact, Gonzo ultimately learns that cultural identity isn't everything. Also, the other Muppets learn to face physical danger and evil to rescue their friends. They learn about the importance of listening to and standing by your friends, even in the midst of apparent failure. Mostly, however, *Muppets from Space* is a chance to spend an entertaining time with some silly, goofy characters.

CONTENT ANALYSIS: (BB, PC, Pa, L, V, M) Moral worldview with some minor, politically correct pagan elements about self-esteem and cultural identity; two very mild obscenities and one mild exclamatory profanity; mild slapstick violence and threats with gun; Miss Piggy does her Mae West shtick; Miss Piggy uses scientist's perfume concoction to make people friendly; and some mild and borderline problems such as poker gambling, kidnapping, getting angry, aliens move objects around by unseen magical force, a comment about always having "alien tendencies" covertly spoofs homosexual political correctness (some children and adults may not get the intent behind the joke, however), Gonzo dreams of being turned away from the Ark by Noah, and odd mention of evolution ("cosmic knowledge" fish say they're "highly evolved" but act stupid, thereby perhaps spoofing Darwin and New Age believers).

The Power of Music

MUSIC OF THE HEART

Quality: ☆☆☆☆   Acceptability: −1

WARNING CODES:
  Language: **
  Violence: None
  Sex: *
  Nudity: None

RATING: PG
GENRE: Drama
INTENDED AUDIENCES: Older children and adults
RUNNING TIME: 134 minutes
STARRING: Meryl Streep, Aidan Quinn, Angela Bassett, Gloria Estefan, Jane Leeves, Keiran Culkin, and Jay O. Sanders
DIRECTOR: Wes Craven
PRODUCERS: Marianne Maddalena, Walter Scheuer, Allan Miller, and Susan Kaplan
EXECUTIVE PRODUCERS: Bob Weinstein, Harvey Weinstein, and Amy Slotnick
WRITER: Pamela Gray
DISTRIBUTOR: Miramax Films/ Buena Vista (Disney)
BRIEF SUMMARY:

Departing completely from the horror films that made him famous, Wes Craven helms *Music of the Heart*, based on the inspirational true story of music teacher Roberta Guaspari, played by Meryl Streep. When her husband leaves her, she applies for a teaching position at an inner-city elementary school in Harlem, New York, and is accepted. Using fifty of her own violins, she starts to train these underprivileged and undisciplined children in the study of violin. She eventually places the needs of her own two children and her students ahead of her own.

This inspiring film will captivate the soul of both young and old. It demonstrates the influence individuals can have on children's lives. More than sixteen hundred youths have been trained through Roberta's programs over the past sixteen years. This is a story of persevering when your world is crumbling, of family sticking beside one another and fighting back when the establishment tells you that your plans are over. It is an inspirational story of regaining one's own self-worth by accomplishing personal dreams lost long ago and by helping others. Very moral, it is marred by two obscenities, two profanities, and an implied adulterous relationship.

CONTENT ANALYSIS: (BB, Pa, LL, S, A, M) Moderately strong moral worldview, promoting discipline, family, love, commitment, perseverance, music, teaching, and care, with some pagan elements of adultery implied; two mostly mild profanities and two obscenities; and adultery and stealing rebuked.

A Minor Christian Gem

NATURALLY NATIVE

Quality: ☆☆☆   Acceptability: –1

WARNING CODES:
  Language: **
  Violence: *
  Sex: *
  Nudity: *

RATING: PG-13
GENRE: Drama
INTENDED AUDIENCE: Older teenagers and adults
RUNNING TIME: 108 minutes
STARRING: Valerie Red-Horse, Irene Bedard, Kimberly Norris Guerrero, Pato Hoffmann, and Max Gail
DIRECTORS: Jennifer Wynne Farmer and Valerie Red-Horse
PRODUCERS: Valerie Red-Horse, Dawn Jackson, and Yvonne Russo
WRITER: Valerie Red-Horse
DISTRIBUTOR: Mashantucket Pequot Tribal Nation
BRIEF SUMMARY:

In *Naturally Native*, three Christian sisters, who happen to also be Native Americans, use prayer to help them start a business together and reunite with their tribal extended family at a Mission Indian reservation. The eldest of the three sisters leads them in prayer at a few crucial moments, but must overcome her own battle with the alcoholism she inherited from her mother. An answered prayer from God helps the three sisters in the movie's resolution.

Naturally Native is a charming, touching, and sometimes humorous story of family, God, and cultural traditions working together to overcome obstacles. At one point the sisters even rebuke a potential investor, who happens to be an occult fortune-teller who believes in reincarnation. Mild caution is advised, however, because of some foul language, mild sexual content, a disturbing but mild scene of violence, and minor worldview problems, including some political correctness. Happily, prayers to God and strong moral values play important roles in the scenes where these problems occur. This is truly a unique independent movie financed totally by an Indian tribe in Connecticut. As such, it serves as a wonderful role model for the Christian community as a whole.

CONTENT ANALYSIS: (CC, BB, CapCap, Pa, PC, LL, V, S, N, AA, M) Christian worldview with moral principles expressed, insensitive palm reader is rebuked, prayers are said, and an answered prayer reunites three Native American sisters with their extended family and gains them personal success, plus strong pro-capitalist and anti-tax, anti-government sentiments expressed and some vestiges of pagan Native American religion and political correctness, but no mention of pagan deities in English dialogue (the movie does not translate some Native American chants); two strong obscenities, seven mild obscenities, four mild exclamatory profanities, and two strong exclamatory profanities; woman punches man and blind date forces physical attentions on young woman, then hits her, knocks her to ground, and kicks her when she tries to fight him off; married couple shown in bed together after implied two nights of passion, and hugging and kissing in bathtub prior to one such night; upper male nudity, including during bathtub scene, shots of cleavage and woman in sexy underwear; alcohol use and drunkenness plus references to mother who died of alcoholism; and Indian gaming approved by heroines, woman tries to find mate through computer, woman has trouble controlling her anger, and sisters go to government bureaucrat for business loan.

Rocket Boys to Men

OCTOBER SKY

Quality: ☆☆☆☆   Acceptability: −1

WARNING CODES:
  Language: ***
  Violence: *
  Sex: None
  Nudity: *
RATING: PG
GENRE: Drama
INTENDED AUDIENCE: Ages twelve and up
RUNNING TIME: 107 minutes
STARRING: Jake Gyllenhaal, Chris Cooper, Laura Dern, and Chris Owen
DIRECTOR: Joe Johnston
PRODUCERS: Charles Gordon and Larry Franco
EXECUTIVE PRODUCERS: Marc Sternberg and Peter Cramer
WRITER: Lewis Colick
BASED ON: The book *Rocket Boys* by Homer H. Hickam Jr.
DISTRIBUTOR: Universal Pictures
BRIEF SUMMARY:
For pure entertainment value, there are few American directors today who can match the talent of Joe Johnston, who made *The Rocketeer*. With *October Sky*, Johnston's talent has matured to include realistic human drama in a family setting. Based on a true story, the movie is about a West Virginia teenager named Homer who in 1957 starts building homemade rockets with his friends so that they can eventually win a prize at the state science fair. Homer's father is the major obstacle the "rocket boys" face in their goal to escape the confined world of their mining hometown.

Many family dramas rely on conflict between parents and children. Naturally, this leads such dramas to sometimes show rebelliousness of children against parents and mistreatment of children by parents. This is the case with *October Sky*, but the movie also argues in favor of reconciliation and mutual support and respect among family members. This wholesome quality to this well-crafted movie is marred, however, by more than thirty obscenities and a line of dialogue about teenage premarital sex that is not rebuked. Even so, director Joe Johnston and his team succeed in creating a wonderful and vivid depiction of an historic time and place.

CONTENT ANALYSIS: (BB, C, Pa, LLL, V, N, A, D, Pa, M) Moderately moral, pro-family worldview with one brief shot of people closing a prayer with "in Christ's name" and one "Thank God" uttered; thirty-two obscenities and three profanities, plus a couple minor vulgarities; mild violence with rockets exploding and chasing people or hitting building, man shoves other man away from minor coal cave-in, and man dies from major off-screen cave-in, plus father and son argue; boy tells another boy he'll now have trouble losing his virginity and teenage couple sits in parked car in one brief shot but are interrupted; upper male nudity; alcohol use and boys use moonshine to keep rockets from exploding; smoking; some pagan elements; and labor unrest and father shows favoritism toward one son over another but disfavored son shows rebellious character that is not really rebuked, though the movie argues in favor of reconciliation and mutual support among family members.

Cracking the Bible Code

THE OMEGA CODE

Quality: ☆☆   Acceptability: +2

WARNING CODES:
Language: None

Violence: **
Sex: None
Nudity: None
RATING: PG-13
GENRE: Action/Adventure
INTENDED AUDIENCE: Teens and adults
RUNNING TIME: 99 minutes
STARRING: Casper Van Dien, Michael York, Michael Ironside, and Catherine Oxenberg
DIRECTOR: Robert Marcarelli
PRODUCER: Matthew Crouch
EXECUTIVE PRODUCER: Paul F. Crouch Sr.
WRITERS: Hollis Barton and Stephan Blinn
DISTRIBUTOR: Providence Entertainment
BRIEF SUMMARY:
The Omega Code explodes across the screen with a special-effects-laden apocalyptic story. The storyline is well known. A professor of mythology, Dr. Gillen Lane, has a strong cult following for his self-realization psychobabble. His marriage, however, is on the rocks, and he would like to repair it. Instead, he gets drawn into the orbit of Dr. Stone Alexander, the Antichrist who is preparing to take over the world. The plot device that moves this all along is the Bible Code. The plot progresses pretty much according to premillennial theology.

Christians who like Bible prophecy may enjoy this movie. Everybody who is involved should be commended for the look of the movie and the pacing of this action-oriented plot. Yet, the script does not develop a strong sense of jeopardy, and the characters need much better development. However, young teenagers and many others may appreciate the constant action and adventure. Several people at the screening quibbled with the theology, but one need not believe in the Bible Code to appreciate the movie. It is, after all, fiction with a gospel message. As such, the church should support it.

CONTENT ANALYSIS: (CC, VV, A, D, M) Christian worldview with some arguable philosophic and theological points; action adventure violence including shooting, man's head with bloody wound, bird eating dead body of animal, explosions, and frightening visions; some hugs and kisses; alcohol use; smoking; and deception.

Instrument of Fate

THE RED VIOLIN

Quality: ✰✰✰✰   Acceptability: –2

WARNING CODES:
   Language: *
   Violence: *
   Sex: ***
   Nudity: ***
RATING: Not rated
GENRE: Drama
INTENDED AUDIENCE: Adults
RUNNING TIME: 130 minutes
STARRING: Samuel L. Jackson, Don McKellar, Carlo Cecchi, Irene Grazioli, Jean-Luc Bideau, Christoph Koncz, Jason Flemyng, Greta Scacchi, Sylvia Chang, and Colm Feore
   DIRECTOR: Francois Girard
   PRODUCER: Niv Fichman
   WRITERS: Francois Girard and Don McKellar
   DISTRIBUTOR: Lions Gate Films
   BRIEF SUMMARY:
Strange, detailed, visually spectacular, epic, poignant, and beautiful only begin to describe a fascinating art house movie called *The Red Violin*. The movie begins in present-day Montreal with an auction for the mysterious, magical "red violin." The story then goes back in time to 1681 in Italy, where master violinmaker Nicolo Bussoti tells his pregnant wife, Anna, that he will give his best violin to their newborn son. Anna and her child, however, die during labor. Over the next three hundred years, the violin passes to Vienna, England, China, and then to Montreal. In the process, the violin becomes an idol to its users.

Figuratively and cinematically, this movie is all over the map. It is an opulent costume drama, a political thriller, and a sleek modern mystery. Always beautiful and frequently haunting, its passionate music provides a thread for the story. Morally, this movie is about obsession and contains some brief but graphic sexual scenes. Regrettably, the movie also gives credence to the power of tarot cards and the violin's own magical powers. Even so, *The Red Violin* provides an epic viewing experience, showing a wide range of characters, time periods, and locations in celebration of a beautiful instrument.

CONTENT ANALYSIS: (RoRo, OO, BB, L, V, SSS, NNN, A, D, M) Romantic worldview of high drama involving the owners of a red violin over the centuries with occult elements of tarot card used as plot-driving device and moral elements including Jesuits caring for orphans, students playing sacred music, and risking life for beauty; three obscenities and one profanity; mild violence including threat of suicide, implied war violence during Chinese revolution, and image of corpse; strong sexuality including implied fornication, scene of graphic fornication, and heavy kissing; full male and full female nudity (no genitalia); alcohol use; smoking; and superstitious beliefs, deception, and stealing.

Character in the Midst of Hell

RIDE WITH THE DEVIL

Quality: ✰✰✰✰   Acceptability: –2

WARNING CODES:
   Language: ***
   Violence: ***
   Sex: *
   Nudity: *
RATING: R
GENRE: Historical Civil War drama

INTENDED AUDIENCE: Older teens and adults

RUNNING TIME: 134 minutes

STARRING: Tobey Maguire, Skeet Ulrich, James Caviezel, Jonathan Rhys Meyers, Simon Baker, Jeffrey Wright, and Jewel

DIRECTOR: Ang Lee

PRODUCERS: Ted Hope, Robert F. Colesberry, and James Schamus

WRITER: James Schamus

BASED ON: The novel *Woe to Live On* by Daniel Woodrell

DISTRIBUTOR: USA Films

BRIEF SUMMARY:

The Civil War movie *Ride with the Devil* follows a small group of young Southern guerrilla fighters across seasons and battles, witnessing through their eyes the unpredictable violence, the vulnerability of civilians, and the total war of guerrilla armies. Amid all the mayhem and death, friendship, loyalty, and generosity survive—even a sense of humor. Furthermore, in the end, there is resurrection as the young men reach turning points in the fighting and in themselves.

This is classic filmmaking with a sure and steady hand and a strong moral worldview. No razzle-dazzle here, no self-conscious use of the camera, no tricks. The filmmakers even got the jargon right. It's a rare Hollywood event, a story of substance told with genuine artistry. Considering what gets "green-lighted" these days, it's nothing short of a miracle that this movie was made, and made with an outstanding cast of newcomers and unknowns at that. Containing only one slight anachronism, *Ride with the Devil* is not only first-class entertainment; it's a liberating experience. Extreme caution is necessary, however, due to the violence, which is almost unavoidable in a movie of this nature.

CONTENT ANALYSIS: (BBB, CC, AB, LLL, VVV, S, N, A, D, M) Moral worldview with Christian elements as well as some immoral elements; thirty-three obscenities and one profanity; extreme violence running the gamut from battle scenes, shootings, murders, assassinations, bones stick out, and blood, guts, and gore in a Civil War context; implied fornication, which leads in a unique way to marriage; brief upper female nudity during breast-feeding scene and mild references to body parts; drinking; smoking; and carousing, deception, jealousy, envy, and cruelty.

Getting the Right Man

RUNAWAY BRIDE

Quality: ☆☆☆☆   Acceptability: +1

WARNING CODES:

   Language: *
   Violence: *
   Sex: None
   Nudity: None

RATING: PG

GENRE: Romantic comedy

INTENDED AUDIENCE: All ages

RUNNING TIME: 116 minutes

STARRING: Julia Roberts, Richard Gere, and Joan Cusack

DIRECTOR: Garry Marshall

PRODUCERS: Ted Field, Tom Rosenberg, Scott Kroopf, and Robert Cort

EXECUTIVE PRODUCERS: Ted Tannenbaum, David Madden, and Gary Lucchesi

WRITERS: Josann McGibbon and Sara Parriott

DISTRIBUTOR: Paramount Pictures

BRIEF SUMMARY:

Runaway Bride, the reteaming of Julia Roberts and Richard Gere, is a triumph. Clean by Hollywood standards, there are only two mild obscenities and some off-color humor, but no nudity or sexual immorality. Julia Roberts as Maggie Carpenter inspires men to the point of matrimony but can't seem to commit herself fully to a relationship, so she turns around and runs at the final moment. Gere, as Ike, a columnist, grabs Maggie's story and embellishes it. Happily engaged for the fourth time, Maggie is furious at the article and gets Ike fired. Ike takes a trip to Maggie's small town to recover his job. Slowly they discover each other.

Once you get used to its sweet, cutesy tone, this movie warms the heart. It's a romantic comedy in the tradition of the old Hollywood romances, where the protagonists fall in love because of each other, not out of lust and circumstance. *Runaway Bride* celebrates rather than denigrates the institution of marriage. The movie also contains a contented, godly Catholic priest with charm and integrity. *Runaway Bride* plays it straight down the middle in a predictable but warm, light, romantic way.

CONTENT ANALYSIS: (CC, H, RoRo, BB, L, V, A) Moderately strong Christian worldview where true love rules the day, with humanist elements of man healing himself plus a positive, godly Roman Catholic priest portrayed with morality and integrity, and a few romantic elements; two mild obscenities, three vulgarities, and some off-color humor; minor violence where man punches man; implied chastity; and alcohol use.

A Boy and His Dog

SHILOH 2: SHILOH SEASON

Quality: ☆☆☆   Acceptability: +3

WARNING CODES:
  Language: *
  Violence: *
  Sex: None
  Nudity: None

RATING: PG
GENRE: Drama
INTENDED AUDIENCE: Ages nine and up
RUNNING TIME: 96 minutes
STARRING: Zachary Browne, Michael Moriarty, Scott Wilson, Rod Steiger, Ann Dowd, and Frannie
DIRECTOR: Sandy Tung
PRODUCERS: Carl Borack and Dale Rosenbloom

EXECUTIVE PRODUCER: Seth Willenson
WRITER: Dale Rosenbloom
BASED ON: The novel by Phyllis Reynolds Naylor
DISTRIBUTOR: Legacy Releasing
BRIEF SUMMARY:
In *Shiloh 2: Shiloh Season*, twelve-year-old Marty Preston must protect his whole family from the mean-tempered former owner of his beloved dog, Shiloh. The owner, whose name is Judd, still thinks of Shiloh as his own dog and is drinking more heavily. Judd falsely accuses Marty and his father of plotting against him. Marty eventually decides to win the man's friendship through acts of love and kindness, while also asking God for help, a biblical theme that makes this enjoyable movie a unique family film.

Judd presents quite a scary figure in the first half of *Shiloh 2*. Thus, the intended audience seems to be age nine or older. The second half advocates lots of good moral values, however. The characters pursue truth, rebuke gossip, show kindness, and repay evil with good. Although neither Jesus Christ nor the Bible are mentioned, Marty asks God to change Judd. Marty then proceeds to use biblical principles to help get Judd to change. This gives a strong redemptive aspect to the second half of the story. Fine acting by Scott Wilson as Judd adds greatly to the scenes of conflict, confrontation, and redemption in this more enjoyable second part of the Shiloh story.

CONTENT ANALYSIS: (BB, CC, L, V, AA, M) Strong moral worldview about overcoming evil with good including a redemptive prayer to God for help in changing a man's sinful behavior, though Jesus Christ is not mentioned; five mild obscenities and one mild profanity; very mild off-screen violence with sound effects such as man shoots squirrel and man wrecks truck, plus threats of violence and dogs chase girl, with one biting her ankle; alcohol use and drunkenness; and children spy on man, gossiping, and man falsely accuses other people, all of which are effectively and strongly rebuked by dialogue and by depicted behavior.

Dead Wrong

THE SIXTH SENSE

Quality: ☆☆☆   Acceptability: −4

WARNING CODES:
  Language: *
  Violence: **
  Sex: None
  Nudity: *
RATING: PG-13
GENRE: Thriller
INTENDED AUDIENCE: Older teens and adults
  RUNNING TIME: 114 minutes
  STARRING: Bruce Willis, Haley Joel Osment, Toni Collette, and Olivia Williams
  DIRECTOR: M. Night Shyamalan
  PRODUCERS: Frank Marshall, Kathleen Kennedy, and Barry Mendel
  EXECUTIVE PRODUCER: Sam Mercer
  WRITER: M. Night Shyamalan
  DISTRIBUTOR: Hollywood Pictures/ Buena Vista/Disney
  BRIEF SUMMARY:
The Sixth Sense is a psychological thriller that assumes the dead walk among us. It begins with Bruce Willis as Dr. Crowe celebrating his latest professional achievement at home. Dr. Crowe is not completely satisfied with his success because he feels he has failed some of his former patients. When Cole, a reticent young boy who is going through troubling psychological trauma, comes along, Dr. Crowe jumps at the chance to redeem himself. It seems Cole is capable of seeing, hearing, and even touching dead people who exist all around him. Through all the counseling, Dr. Crowe's marriage seems to be unraveling under all the strain.

The Sixth Sense is reminiscent of movies such as *Ghost* than more straight-up ghost movies like *Poltergeist*. Along with some of the typical roller-coaster-ride chills common to the horror film genre, this movie also has a human, melancholic dimension to it that makes it more intelligent and satisfying than the typical thriller. Nevertheless, the occult premise is false, and Cole even uses religious icons to ward off spirits of dead people. *The Sixth Sense* also contains some moderate violent material.

CONTENT ANALYSIS: (OOO, FRFRFR, L, VV, N) Occult false religious worldview postulating that the spirits of the dead walk among us with occult elements where boy protects himself from the dead with religious icons; one obscenity; mild action violence including shooting, poisoning, and implied car crash; and upper male nudity.

Most Vile, Childhood-Killing Movie

SOUTH PARK: BIGGER, LONGER, AND UNCUT

Quality: ☆☆   Acceptability: −4

WARNING CODES:
  Language: ***
  Violence: ***
  Sex: ***
  Nudity: ***
RATING: R
GENRE: Animated pornography
INTENDED AUDIENCE: Adults
RUNNING TIME: 80 minutes
VOICES: Jesse Howell, George Clooney, Brent Spiner, Minnie Driver, Dave Foley, Eric Idle, Stewart Copeland, and Mike Judge
  DIRECTOR: Trey Parker
  PRODUCERS: Trey Parker and Matt Stone
  EXECUTIVE PRODUCERS: Scott Rudin and Adam Schroeder
  WRITERS: Trey Parker, Matt Stone, and Pam Brady

DISTRIBUTOR: Paramount Pictures
BRIEF SUMMARY:

South Park: Bigger, Longer, and Uncut is intentionally vile, with the most abhorrent content in the history of mainstream moviemaking. In this pornographic cartoon, Stan rounds up his friends to avoid church so they can go see the latest Terrence and Philip movie where Terrence and Philip tell them to f– their uncles and do other obscene things. The mothers of South Park get outraged and start a war against Canada for producing the movie when their children imitate Terrence and Philip. Eventually, a major war takes place, blood spurts, and Satan comes from hell to take over the Earth but is convinced to go back while Kenny goes to a perverted heaven.

This is a blasphemous, evil movie. The point is that the world's children should be allowed to see *South Park* and that adults should let children engage in vile actions and foul language. Jews, blacks, and homosexuals are mocked, while morality and God are completely vilified in this feature-length cartoon, which includes 340 obscenities, sodomy, extreme violence, and foul images.

CONTENT ANALYSIS: (AbAbAb, LLL, VVV, SSS, NNN, A, DD, MMM) Anti-Christian, anti-God, anti-morality, intentionally immoral, with the most vile content in the history of mainstream moviemaking; 340 counted obscenities (there may be more that are muddled), 14 profanities, and many disgusting bodily functions, including vomiting; bloody violence including ripping out heart, ripping body parts apart, splattering blood, and putting heart in microwave oven; extreme sex including homosexuality and pedophilia; extreme nudity including pictures of male and female genitalia, and jokes about the same; smoking by young boy and drug use including hash pipe; and rebellion, theft, lying, cheating, and a surplus of other depraved content.

Wagner in Space

STAR WARS EPISODE I: THE PHANTOM MENACE

Quality: ☆☆☆☆   Acceptability: –1

WARNING CODES:
  Language: *
  Violence: **
  Sex: None
  Nudity: None
RATING: PG
GENRE: Science fiction
INTENDED AUDIENCE: All ages
RUNNING TIME: 133 minutes
STARRING: Liam Neeson, Jake Lloyd, Natalie Portman, and Ewan McGregor
DIRECTOR: George Lucas
PRODUCER: Rick McCallum
EXECUTIVE PRODUCER: George Lucas
WRITER: George Lucas
DISTRIBUTOR: 20th Century Fox
BRIEF SUMMARY:

In the *Star Wars Episode I*, the galactic republic has turned into a bureaucratic nightmare. Senator Palpatine, a secret villain calling himself Darth Sidious, is trying to consolidate his power. Two Jedi knights, Qui-Gon Jinn and Obi-Wan Kenobi, are sent to a planet as ambassadors to solve the political dispute. After rescuing the queen, they are forced to land on a desert planet. There, they find a young slave boy, Anakin Skywalker, who exhibits extraordinary ability to use the "Force." Battles occur, sword fights take place, and there is great loss and surprising triumph in the first episode of this imaginative space opera.

Star Wars is an epic symphony based on mythic concepts. Throughout this story, in the midst of exciting action adventure and humorous asides, George Lucas reveals mythic elements. There are constant references to be mindful of the living Force, which is personalized in this episode. In terms of action and plot, *The Phantom Menace* is comfortably PG with many moral and some redemptive elements. What is threatening is the nominalistic, New Age philosophy that creeps into this movie too frequently. Concerned parents whose children demand to see it should see *Star Wars* with their children to help them think through the movie's theology.

CONTENT ANALYSIS: (PaPa, BB, C, OO, L, VV, M) New Age pagan world-view with strong moral and redemptive elements; many mythic teachings and some occult elements where characters have magical powers, including ESP, mind control, and foretelling the future without the power of the Holy Spirit; one mild obscenity; lots of action and violence including light-saber fights, man cut in half off-screen then falls, army attacks, many droids destroyed, people wounded, but very little blood and gore; someone steps in creature dung, and villain manipulates political situation to gain power.

A Wonderful Gift of Grace

THE STRAIGHT STORY

Quality: ✰✰✰✰   Acceptability: +2

WARNING CODES:
  Language: *
  Violence: *
  Sex: None
  Nudity: None
RATING: G
GENRE: Drama
INTENDED AUDIENCE: All ages
RUNNING TIME: 111 minutes
STARRING: Richard Farnsworth, Sissy Spacek, and Harry Dean Stanton
DIRECTOR: David Lynch
PRODUCERS: Neal Edelstein, Alain Sarde, and Mary Sweeney
EXECUTIVE PRODUCER: Pierre Edelman
WRITERS: David Lynch and John Roach

DISTRIBUTOR: Walt Disney Pictures/Buena Vista Distribution
BRIEF SUMMARY:
The Straight Story is a powerful, understated, beautifully crafted work of grace. This true story tells about an over-seventy-year-old, self-reliant man of the Plains named Alvin Straight, played by Richard Farnsworth. Alvin lives in Laurens, Iowa, with his daughter Rose, who is mentally challenged, though she has an exceptional memory. After falling in his kitchen, he hears that his estranged brother Lyle has had a stroke. Alvin decides that he needs to visit his brother who lives more than 360 miles away in Mt. Zion, Wisconsin. He doesn't have a driver's license, doesn't have much money, and doesn't like public transportation, so he decides to ride his lawnmower to Mt. Zion. Along the way, Alvin helps all those he meets understand biblical truth. His journey itself affirms life, forgiveness, and humility.

Director David Lynch's craftsmanship is so fine that the film is unbelievably lifelike and captivating. This is a family film with mature themes. In spite of Alvin's old buddies using some mild swear words, this work will show brothers and sisters the importance of reconciliation. *The Straight Story* is a modern parable that deserves much praise.

CONTENT ANALYSIS: (CC, BBB, L, V, A, D, M) Redemptive worldview about a man reconciling with his brother with biblical illustrations and references to the Bible; two profanities and one mild obscenity; frightening storms, the thud of a man collapsing in a kitchen, vivid sounds of war, and other suspenseful events illustrated only by sound; some alcohol use; heavy smoking; and consistent, life-affirming morality.

Nutty Fairy Tale Comes Alive

STUART LITTLE

Quality: ✰✰✰✰   Acceptability: +2

WARNING CODES:

Language: *
Violence: *
Sex: None
Nudity: None

RATING: PG
GENRE: Fantasy/Comedy
INTENDED AUDIENCE: All ages
RUNNING TIME: 84 minutes
STARRING: Geena Davis, Hugh Laurie, and Jonathan Lipnicki
VOICES: Michael J. Fox, Nathan Lane, Chazz Palminteri, Steve Zahn, Jennifer Tilly, and Bruno Kirby
DIRECTOR: Rob Minkoff
PRODUCER: Douglas Wick
EXECUTIVE PRODUCERS: Jeff Franklin and Steve Waterman
WRITERS: M. Night Shyamalan and Gregory J. Brooker
BASED ON: The novel by E. B. White
DISTRIBUTOR: Columbia Pictures/Sony Pictures Entertainment
BRIEF SUMMARY:

In *Stuart Little*, a human family in New York City adopts a little white mouse named Stuart, who has trouble fitting in despite his big, courageous heart. The parents' human son at first shuns the new addition to the family, but the two become close friends during a toy boat race in Central Park. Things get a little hairy for Stuart when a group of alley cats decide to "scratch him out." Stuart's new family becomes distraught looking for him, but help from an unexpected source soon arrives for the plucky little fellow.

Stuart Little is a cute family movie with excellent special effects that make the action come alive. It is also wonderfully nutty at times. The children at the screening seemed to enjoy the story and the characters. Michael J. Fox does a marvelous job as the voice of Stuart. Nathan Lane gives his usual sarcastic performance as Snowball the house cat, and Geena Davis is positively endearing as Mrs. Little. The pro-family and redemptive messages in the movie are marred only by four mild obscenities and a very mild possible nod to the politically correct philosophies behind today's identity politics.

CONTENT ANALYSIS: (BB, C, PC, L, V, M) Moral worldview about supporting and looking out for family members plus redemptive element of potentially sacrificing your own life for the safety of another, and very mild political correctness reminding one of identity politics of the far left, but done in the context of a moral universe; four mild obscenities, mouse character says "Oh, dear" several times when disturbed or in trouble and bullying cats pass gas; mild family movie violence such as intelligent mouse falls down laundry chute and almost drowns in washer, house cat tries to eat mouse, conceited little boy crashes his toy boat into toy boats of other kids during race, alley cats chase mouse to "scratch him out," and toy car and cats fall into water; and villainous characters deceive the hero and his adoptive family.

Flies through the Air with the Greatest of Ease

TARZAN

Quality: ☆☆☆☆   Acceptability: +1

WARNING CODES:

Language: *
Violence: **
Sex: None
Nudity: *

RATING: G
GENRE: Animated adventure
INTENDED AUDIENCE: All ages
RUNNING TIME: 82 minutes
VOICES: Tony Goldwyn, Glenn Close, Rosie O'Donnell, Minnie Driver, Nigel Hawthorne, Brian Blessed, Lance Henriksen, and Wayne Knight
DIRECTORS: Chris Buck and Kevin Lima

PRODUCERS: Bonnie Arnold and Phil Collins

WRITER: Tab Murphy

BASED ON: The novel by Edgar Rice Burroughs

DISTRIBUTOR: Walt Disney Pictures/Walt Disney Company/Buena Vista Distribution

BRIEF SUMMARY:

Disney's *Tarzan* is the first animated feature to focus on the legendary jungle hero. A catastrophic shipwreck leaves a young couple and their infant son, Tarzan, stranded on the shores of a hostile jungle. The leopard Sabor leaves Tarzan an orphan, and a gorilla mother adopts him after she loses her baby to Sabor. Tarzan matures into an athletic man who kills Sabor. When other humans arrive—including Jane, the beautiful daughter of a professor—Tarzan must decide whether to stay with his gorilla family or return to civilization.

Artistically, there is a lot to appreciate about *Tarzan*. Using a 3-D technique, the movie shows Tarzan moving through the jungle like no live actor could ever do, all to the beat of Phil Collins's effective music. *Tarzan* is a moral story in which the characters constantly talk about family love and self-sacrifice. However, the movie also includes two references to evolution; the villain proves to be another greedy white man wishing to exploit the jungle; and the professor and Jane "go native," preferring the jungle to civilization. To correct for these elements, parents may want to spend a media-wise moment with their children if they allow them to see *Tarzan*.

CONTENT ANALYSIS: (BB, Pa, E, PC, L, VV, N, A, M) Mild moral worldview of taking care of family with a "going native" conclusion and mild pro-environmental political correctness implied with gun-happy, greedy English villain who wants to exploit gorillas; one use of the word "heck"; moderate action violence including implied leopard attacking and eating gorilla baby and human man and wife, Tarzan fights with leopard and it is implied that he stabs him to death, ship burns and sinks, implied death by accidental hanging in heat of battle, and man shoots at gorillas but misses; Jane is excited at seeing Tarzan and being near him; man constantly in loincloth; villain drinks wine; and a little scatological humor where ape sniffs baby diaper and a joke about emotional constipation.

Warm and Savory

TEA WITH MUSSOLINI

Quality: ☆☆☆☆   Acceptability: −1

WARNING CODES:

Language: **
Violence: *
Sex: **
Nudity: *

RATING: PG

GENRE: Drama

INTENDED AUDIENCE: Teens and adults

RUNNING TIME: 117 minutes

STARRING: Cher, Judi Dench, Joan Plowright, Maggie Smith, Lily Tomlin, Charlie Lucas, and Baird Wallace

DIRECTOR: Franco Zeffirelli

PRODUCERS: Ricardo Tozzi, Giovannella Zannoni, and Clive Parsons

EXECUTIVE PRODUCER: Marco Chimenz

WRITERS: John Mortimer and Franco Zeffirelli

DISTRIBUTOR: MGM

BRIEF SUMMARY:

In the movie *Tea with Mussolini*, Franco Zeffirelli crafts a delightful tale about love, friendship, art, and triumph during World War II in Florence, Italy. Somewhat of an autobiographical story, the movie begins in 1935. The father of a boy whose English mother has died doesn't want anything to do with him. A kind Englishwoman named Mary takes in little Luca. Mary is part of a women's group called the *Scorpioni*, or "Scorpions," because they sting with wit. When the war begins the women are rounded up. Now Luca returns to Florence from boarding school and becomes involved in dangerous schemes to save the lives of his beloved friends.

Tea with Mussolini is worth savoring. The Florentine cityscapes are beautiful; and the costuming, lighting, camera work, and acting are excellent. The script, however, is sometimes a little overzealous. Regrettably, there is some obscenity and profanity use, and a homosexual character seems unnecessary, but the themes and lessons in this story are its most savory delight. They concern friendship, sacrifice, and love for beauty. Zeffirelli doesn't make movies frequently, but he has been making remarkable movies for a long time. We hope that he will make many more.

CONTENT ANALYSIS: (BBB, C, Ho, LL, V, SS, N, A, D) Strong moral worldview of friendship and sacrifice during World War II, with several appeals to God and references to God; seven obscenities (mostly mild) and seven profanities; mild violence including Fascists smash windows and destroy property and threats with guns; implied fornication, implied homosexual character cross-dresses as young man to avoid the Fascists, and brief, mild sexual innuendo; naturalistic upper male nudity; alcohol use; and smoking.

Faith Matters

THE THIRD MIRACLE

Quality: ☆☆☆☆   Acceptability: −2

WARNING CODES:

Language: **
Violence: *
Sex: *
Nudity: **

RATING: R
GENRE: Drama
INTENDED AUDIENCE: Older teens and adults
STARRING: Ed Harris, Anne Heche, and Armin Meuller-Stahl
DIRECTOR: Agnieszka Holland
PRODUCERS: Fred Fuchs and Steven Haft
EXECUTIVE PRODUCERS: Ashok Amritraj, Francis Coppola, and Elie Samaha
WRITERS: Richard Vetere and John Romano
DISTRIBUTOR: Sony Pictures Classics
BRIEF SUMMARY:

The Third Miracle is a powerful and uplifting movie that explores issues of Christian faith. Ed Harris plays a lapsed Roman Catholic priest, Frank Shore, who finds a kind of personal redemption when he sets out to seek the truth about the alleged miracles of a deeply devout laywoman. Anne Heche plays the woman's unsaintly daughter who tempts him. After experiencing a miracle himself, Father Frank decides to defend the laywoman's bid for sainthood against the formidable Archbishop Werner, who doubts that an ordinary housewife can be a saint.

The Third Miracle contains references to sinful behavior, including swearing, prostitution, drugs, child abuse, murder, and church politics, but doesn't push a "miracles are within us all" humanistic stance. It contends that miracles are truly from a higher power, implicitly God, though it does not focus on who God is. While tackling issues of faith and doubt, the movie successfully draws viewers into experiencing the anguish and joy of Father Frank's journey, leaving them with a sense of mystery and hope. Rarely has the tension between faith and reason, miracles and reality, and sinfulness and redemption been treated with more reverence and skill.

CONTENT ANALYSIS: (BB, CC, Ab, LL, V, S, NN, AA, DD, M) Although not explicitly Christian, contains many elements of a biblical and Christian worldview, with some naturalistic portrayals of sinful people, including religious leaders; four profanities and nine obscenities; mild war bombing scenes, dead man with bleeding head wound, very brief and blurry cigarette burning on arm of child, and blood streaming down a statue of Mary; implied solicitation of prostitution and implied fornication; nude upper backside of cripple and of man after implied fornication; some casual alcohol drinking, and one instance of mild drunkenness; implied morphine use in the background; and brief images of demonic drawings.

To Infinity and Beyond

TOY STORY 2

Quality: ☆☆☆☆   Acceptability: +4

WARNING CODES:
Language: None
Violence: *
Sex: None
Nudity: None

RATING: G
GENRE: Animated action/Comedy
INTENDED AUDIENCE: All ages
RUNNING TIME: 92 minutes
VOICES: Tom Hanks, Tim Allen, Joan Cusack, Kelsey Grammer, Don Rickles, Jim Varney, Wallace Shawn, John Ratzenberger, Annie Potts, Wayne Knight, and John Morris
DIRECTOR: John Lasseter
CODIRECTORS: Lee Unkrich and Ash Brannon
PRODUCERS: Helene Plotkin and Karen Robert Jackson
EXECUTIVE PRODUCER: Sarah McArthur
WRITERS: Andrew Stanton, Rita Hsiao, Doug Chamberlin, and Chris Webb

BASED ON: An original story by John Lasseter, Pete Docter, Ash Brannon, and Andrew Stanton
DISTRIBUTOR: Walt Disney Pictures/Buena Vista Pictures Distribution/Walt Disney Company
BRIEF SUMMARY:
In the original *Toy Story*, Woody the cowboy had to rescue the new "big man in the toy box," Buzz Lightyear. In *Toy Story 2*, it is good-hearted Woody who gets himself stolen by a toy collector. Buzz, Hamm the piggy bank, Mr. Potato Head, and Slinky Dog head out to rescue Woody. Woody gets placed next to his old pals from his glory days of being a children's television cowboy star. These pals are extremely happy to see Woody because now they can be sold to a museum where children will actually be able to look at them. Meanwhile, Buzz and the gang encounter many obstacles in rescuing Woody. Eventually, Woody realizes that having a loving friendship is more important than fame.

This major premise is combined with many great story elements including love, compassion, forgiveness, and reconciliation. Moreover, these well-crafted themes have strong references to great films. This movie has a solid structure. It not only presents a fast-paced, funny adventure story but also pulls at the heartstrings. The story builds jeopardy without stressing evil. *Toy Story 2* is the type of movie you would like to keep for infinity and beyond!

CONTENT ANALYSIS: (BBB, CC, V, M) Very moral redemptive worldview with some Christian references such as "God bless you," a reference to the prodigal son's return, and an emphasis on loving one another and giving up one's life not only for one's friends but also for one's enemies; one airline baggage sticker on a toy's derriere says "Butte" (as in Butte, Montana) but the *e* is partially obscured, and one flatulence joke; Mr. and Mrs. Potato Head enjoy kissing each other, and some romantic references; some action cartoon-type violence including a battle with Emperor Zurg (although all the weapons are harmless), plus some perilous situations including elevator shaft, traffic accidents while toys try to get across street, and airplane danger; and stealing and deception by villainous characters, but generally great content.

Planes, Trains, and Gadgets

WILD WILD WEST

Quality: ☆☆☆   Acceptability: –2

WARNING CODES:
  Language: **
  Violence: **
  Sex: **
  Nudity: **
RATING: PG-13
GENRE: Science fiction/Western
INTENDED AUDIENCE: Older teens and adults
RUNNING TIME: 100 minutes
STARRING: Will Smith, Kevin Kline, Kenneth Branagh, Salma Hayek, and Ted Levine
DIRECTOR: Barry Sonnenfeld
PRODUCERS: Jon Peters and Barry Sonnenfeld
EXECUTIVE PRODUCERS: Bill Todman Jr., Joel Simon, Kim LeMasters, Tracy Glaser, and Barry Josephson
WRITERS: S. S. Wilson, Brent Maddock, Jeffrey Price, and Peter S. Seaman
DISTRIBUTOR: Warner Brothers
BRIEF SUMMARY:
Wild Wild West is a big, flamboyant, simply plotted, and merely serviceable adaptation of the popular television series, which aims to please all members of the family, and barely makes it. Will Smith plays James T. West, a government agent who shoots first, second, third, and may ask a few questions later. He is part-nered with another government agent, Artemus Gordon, played by Kevin Kline, who is a master of disguise and a clever inventor. President Grant sends them to track down the diabolical Dr. Loveless.

Moral elements in this movie include bravery, patriotism, singing "The Battle Hymn of the Republic," respect for brain over brawn, and recognition of God in the building of America. Violence is also generally action oriented, and not bloody. However, morally objectionable elements in this family-oriented movie include prostitutes, heavy kissing by our naked hero that implies the start of fornication, and some crude sexual humor. *Wild Wild West* is very splashy with lots of action, charismatic heroes, and a good amount of humor, but its enjoyment lasts only as long as it is playing.

CONTENT ANALYSIS: (B, C, Pa, LL, VV, SS, NN, A, D, M) Mild moral worldview of protecting the U.S. president from evil with Christian element of recognizing God as the builder of America and singing "Battle Hymn of Republic"; pagan elements of brothels and bars; fourteen obscenities, three profanities, and several racial slurs by villain against hero; lots of action violence including chases, fight scenes, evil man blows up buildings and trains, heroes fall into mud, villain falls to death (impact not shown), implied villain electrocution, slapping, threats with gun, and brief more intense violence where super-tank shoots many people dead and man is decapitated by a flying saw blade; depicted heavy kissing in hot tub (implying foreplay to fornication), some mild sexual humor and innuendo, man touches fake disguise breasts and jokes about touching "my breasts," crossdressing for disguise purposes, implied prostitution with "entertainer" girls, image of bondage gear in brothel, lots of cleavage shots, upper male nudity, implied nudity of couple in hot tub, brief image of rear female nudity through hole in pajama bottoms; smoking cigars; alcohol use in bars; and suggested bestiality in one brief incident set in a brothel.

Let Right Be Done

THE WINSLOW BOY

Quality: ✰✰✰✰   Acceptability: +3

WARNING CODES:

Language: *
Violence: None
Sex: None
Nudity: None

RATING: G
GENRE: Melodrama
INTENDED AUDIENCE: All ages
RUNNING TIME: 110 minutes
STARRING: Nigel Hawthorne, Jeremy Northam, Rebecca Pidgeon, Gemma Jones, and Guy Edwards
DIRECTOR: David Mamet
EXECUTIVE PRODUCER: Sarah Green
WRITER: David Mamet
BASED ON: The play by Terence Rattigan
DISTRIBUTOR: Sony Pictures Classics
BRIEF SUMMARY:
The Winslow Boy is a very good, G-rated drama based on a famous play by celebrated British playwright Terence Rattigan. It tells the real-life story of a young naval cadet in 1910 England who is accused of stealing a five-shilling postal order. The cadet's family hires a famous lawyer to defend him, but the fight places a heavy toll on the family's well-being. The father's health deteriorates, the publicity disrupts the family's home, and the daughter's engagement with a young man is broken.

Director David Mamet pays close attention to period detail to transport the audience back in time to 1910. *The Winslow Boy* brings up several questions of justice. Was the pursuit of justice and truth worth the cost? Since the pivotal argument in the Parliamentary debate quotes Jesus as a final resort, is it possible that the story is saying that one has to give up everything before one can turn to the only One who can win the case and cause right to be done? The movie stimulates much thinking on these issues, leaving them open for the audience to ponder. *The Winslow Boy* is a worthwhile dramatic experience, and requires several viewings.

CONTENT ANALYSIS: (CC, B, H, L, D, Fe) Christian worldview of justice where the pivotal argument winning the Winslow case (that the powerless must be protected against the powerful king) is summed up in Jesus' statement "Whatever you do to the least of these, you do to me," with some humanist and moral elements; one obscenity and two appeals to God; and issues of women's suffrage in the early 1900s.

☆☆☆ THE BEST 1999 FILMS FOR FAMILIES ☆☆☆

Headline	Title
To Infinity and Beyond	*Toy Story 2*
Let Right Be Done	*The Winslow Boy*
Exciting Animation	*Tarzan*
Nutty Fairy Tale Comes Alive	*Stuart Little*
Kermit and Company Get Funky	*Muppets from Space*
The Faithful Runner	*Endurance*
Rocket Boys to Men	*October Sky*
From War to Peace	*The Iron Giant*
Space Cadets	*Galaxy Quest*
Helping Others	*Star Wars I: The Phantom Menace*

☆☆☆ THE BEST 1999 FILMS FOR MATURE AUDIENCES ☆☆☆

Headline	Title
A Wonderful Gift of Grace	*The Straight Story*
Getting the Right Man	*Runaway Bride*
No Man Is Good; No, Not One	*An Ideal Husband*
A Modern Spanish Classic	*The Grandfather*
The Holy Giant	*The Green Mile*
Getting the Inside Dope	*The Insider*
Warm and Savory	*Tea with Mussolini*
Character in the Midst of Hell	*Ride with the Devil*
The Power of Music	*Music of the Heart*
Setting the Captive Free	*The Hurricane*

☆☆☆ THE TWENTY MOST UNBEARABLE FILMS OF 1999 ☆☆☆

Headline	Title
Worst Vile, Anti-Child Movie	*South Park: Bigger, Longer, and Uncut*
Worst Revisionist History	*The Messenger: The Story of Joan of Arc*
Worst Attack on the Family	*American Beauty*
Worst Blasphemy	*Dogma*
Worst Pro-Abortion Movie	*The Cider House Rules*
Worst Exploitation of Teenage Incest	*Cruel Intentions*
Worst Promotion of Gratuitous Violence	*Fight Club*
Worst Call to Teenage Fornication	*American Pie*
Worst Promotion of Spiritism	*The Sixth Sense*
Worst Waste of Potential	*Being John Malkovich*
Worst Pro-Lesbian Movie	*Better Than Chocolate*
Worst Self-Deception	*Boys Don't Cry*
Worst Propaganda	*Cradle Will Rock*
Worst Sex Offenders	*Eight Millimeter*
Worst Soulless Sex Award	*Eyes Wide Shut*
Worst Darwinism	*Instinct*
Worst Religious Animation	*Princess Mononoke*
Worst False Religion	*Pokemon: The First Movie*
Worst Winsome Wicked Witch	*Sleepy Hollow*
Worst Homosexual Serial Killer's Dream	*The Talented Mr. Ripley*

Every Dog Has Her Day

102 DALMATIANS

Quality: ☆☆☆   Acceptability: +1

WARNING CODES:

Language: None
Violence: *
Sex: None
Nudity: None

RATING: G
GENRE: Comedy
INTENDED AUDIENCE: All ages
RUNNING TIME: 99 minutes
STARRING: Glenn Close, Alice Evans, Ioan Gruffudd, Gerard Depardieu, Tim McInnerny, and the voice of Eric Idle
DIRECTOR: Kevin Lima
PRODUCER: Edward S. Feldman
WRITERS: Kristen Buckley, Brian Regan, Bob Tzudiker, and Noni White
BASED ON: The novel by Dodie Smith
DISTRIBUTOR: Walt Disney Pictures/Buena Vista Distribution/Walt Disney Company
BRIEF SUMMARY:

In Disney's live-action comedy *102 Dalmatians*—a sequel to *101 Dalmations*—the reformation of dognapper Cruella De Vil, played again by Glenn Close, goes awry, leading to more shenanigans involving a bunch of dogs and, this time, a daffy parrot as well. The top dog in the new story is a Dalmatian puppy named "Oddball," who doesn't have any spots. Once again Glenn Close plays Cruella De Vil, the fashion-conscious villain of the first movie. A behavioral psychologist apparently has modified Cruella's nasty streak, but Cruella's probation officer, Chloe Simon, has her suspicions. Her suspicions grow when Chloe's three Dalmatian puppies, including Oddball, disappear. Has Cruella changed back her spots?

This movie has a mild Christian worldview with moral elements. As such, it shows that psychological reprogramming, or behavior modification, cannot stop a person from sinning. The movie doesn't show, however, that a renewed spiritual relationship with God and Jesus Christ can indeed transform people into better citizens. This positive worldview is also marred by wacky environmentalist ideas equating animals with humans, some unrebuked cheating, and a crude outfit. Although the movie's pacing is spotty, children probably will enjoy watching the antics of Cruella and the animals just as much as they did in the previous movie. The final shots of Cruella may be worth the entire price of admission.

CONTENT ANALYSIS: (C, BB, EE, V, Ho, A, M) Mild Christian worldview with moral elements showing that psychological reprogramming cannot stop a person from sinning, marred by some wacky environmentalist views and some miscellaneous immorality that is not rebuked; cat burps after implied eating of canary or parakeet; slapstick violence such as pratfalls, animals tug at clothes, animal activists pour blood on person wearing fur, and woman falls into goop and machinery, plus other mild violence such as fighting; fashion designer wears furry tiger's head on his crotch in one scene; very mild homosexual innuendo; very mild alcohol reference in restaurant scene; and dognapping rebuked, villain frames man rebuked and psychological behavior modification rebuked, but parrot and dogs resort to cheating to win tug-of-war contest with man—a bad message to send to children and, in this day and age, election officials.

Moose and Squirrel Save the Day

THE ADVENTURES OF ROCKY AND BULLWINKLE

Quality: ☆☆☆   Acceptability: +1

WARNING CODES:
  Language: *
  Violence: *
  Sex: None
  Nudity: None
RATING: PG
GENRE: Animated/Live-action fantasy
INTENDED AUDIENCE: All ages
RUNNING TIME: 90 minutes
STARRING: Robert De Niro, Janeane Garofolo, Rene Russo, Jason Alexander, and Randy Quaid
DIRECTOR: Des McAnuff
PRODUCERS: Jane Rosenthal and Robert De Niro
EXECUTIVE PRODUCERS: Tiffany Ward and David Nicksay
WRITER: Kenneth Lonergan
BASED ON: Characters created by Jay Ward
DISTRIBUTOR: Universal Pictures
BRIEF SUMMARY:
In *The Adventures of Rocky and Bullwinkle,* Rocky the flying squirrel and his dim-witted pal, Bullwinkle the moose, foil the plan of a witless group of spies to take over America. An FBI agent brings Rocky and Bullwinkle to the real world of human beings to foil the plan to take over America. Rocky and Bullwinkle have mere hours to get from Hollywood to New York to thwart this diabolical plan. Their nemesis, Fearless Leader, sends his two witless henchmen, Boris and Natasha, to stop them. They try everything, including a degeneration machine. Along the way there are many gags and funny slapstick bits, and many stars appear to enliven the plot.

In spite of its witty moments, *The Adventures of Rocky and Bullwinkle* does not have the care and the craftsmanship of *Toy Story 2* and *Chicken Run*. Nor does it have quite the freshness and wit of the television series. Although the movie overtly tells viewers several times that lying, cheating, and stealing are wrong, somebody saw fit to put a strong obscenity and some other unnecessary exclamations in the movie. Everyone tries hard, however, and *The Adventures of Rocky and Bullwinkle* is full of enough laughs to make it a worthwhile entertainment excursion.

CONTENT ANALYSIS: (BB, C, L, V, D, M) Moral worldview with a reference to prayer and a rebuttal of various immoral actions, somewhat marred by unnecessary foul language; two obscenities and three exclamatory profanities; slapstick fantasy violence, including characters falling off water tower, cartoon characters flattened under bus, and cartoon characters fall into ground, but very little real violence; smoking by Fearless Leader; and lying, cheating, and stealing are all rebuked.

Entertaining and Thoughtful Exposé

ALMOST FAMOUS

Quality: ☆☆☆   Acceptability: −2

WARNING CODES:
  Language: * * *
  Violence: None
  Sex: *
  Nudity: *
RATING: R
GENRE: Comedy/Satire
INTENDED AUDIENCE: Teens and adults
RUNNING TIME: 123 minutes
STARRING: Patrick Fugit, Billy Crudup, Kate Hudson, Frances McDormand, Jason Lee, Anna Paquin, and Philip Seymour Hoffman

DIRECTOR: Cameron Crowe
PRODUCERS: Cameron Crowe and Ian Bryce
WRITER: Cameron Crowe
DISTRIBUTOR: DreamWorks Pictures
SUMMARY:
Almost Famous is an autobiographical movie about screenwriter and director Cameron Crowe's days as a fifteen-year-old rock journalist for *Rolling Stone* magazine. The protagonist, fifteen-year-old William Miller, lives with his single mother, but is smart enough to be nearing his high school graduation. Against her better judgment, William's mother allows him to go on a lucrative assignment from the prestigious *Rolling Stone* magazine, to tour with a new band called Stillwater. For the most part, William retains his mother's sense of moral integrity and develops close friendships with the lead guitarist and a young female groupie. In the process, William comes of age, dark truths are revealed, and everyone learns some life lessons.

The subject matter of *Almost Famous* is problematic, but the director, Cameron Crowe, does not focus on the sleazier aspects of the wild life of a rock band, including the strong foul language. He is more interested in the redemptive aspects of his story. In fact, the most important lesson William learns is that having moral integrity is better than trying to be "cool" like the rock stars he idolizes. Ultimately, *Almost Famous* is a very entertaining, insightful piece, though marred by some very objectionable elements.

CONTENT ANALYSIS: (BB, C, PaPa, LLL, S, N, A, DD, M) Moral worldview stressing moral integrity with redemptive elements including brief references to Jesus and God in a couple songs on the soundtrack and pagan elements depicting wild rock-and-roll milieu in a slightly satirical fashion; at least thirty-one mostly strong obscenities, ten mild profanities, and one strong profanity plus some obscene gestures and implied vomiting; mild violence; vaguely implied fornication amid depicted revelry, groupies decide to "deflower" fifteen-year-old, and reference to oral sex; brief upper male and female nudity; alcohol use depicted; smoking, brief marijuana use, man takes LSD and jumps into pool from roof, and woman takes an overdose of pills but a friend tries to save her life; and adultery, lying, and teenage rebellion.

Exquisitely Woven Redemptive Masterpiece

THE BASKET

Quality: ☆☆☆☆   Acceptability: +3

WARNING CODES:
  Language: *
  Violence: *
  Sex: None
  Nudity: None

RATING: PG
GENRE: Historical drama
INTENDED AUDIENCE: All ages
RUNNING TIME: 105 minutes
STARRING: Peter Coyote, Karen Allen, Robert Karl Burke, Amber Willenborg, Jock MacDonald, Tony Lincoln, and Ellen Travolta
DIRECTOR: Rich Cowan
EXECUTIVE PRODUCERS: Marc Dahlstrom, Dave Holcomb, Greg Rathvon, and Dave Tanner
WRITERS: Don Caron, Rich Cowan, Frank Swoboda, and Tessa Swoboda
DISTRIBUTOR: North by Northwest Entertainment
BRIEF SUMMARY:
The Basket is a redemptive masterpiece. Made in Spokane, Washington, of all places, this movie has drawn rave reviews from everyone. Starring Peter Coyote and Karen Allen, it tells the story of a new schoolteacher in a small town in the American Northwest during World War I,

who uses opera and the new game of basketball to help a pair of German orphans facing discrimination. The story includes a strong Christian pastor who takes the orphans into his home. Eventually, the big game comes and virtue, redemption, and self-sacrifice triumph in a way that has never been seen before in a movie whose central motif is a sports game.

The Basket is one of the most wholesome, uplifting movies ever released. The quality of the production rivals a big-budget Hollywood movie. Better yet, the emotional orchestration of the characters is perfectly balanced with the brilliantly nuanced plot. It deserves more than rave reviews from secular critics, it deserves attention from everyone who wants to commend the good. If you like exciting, character-driven dramas, *The Basket* will more than meet your expectations. It is a profound, redemptive movie that all ages can enjoy.

CONTENT ANALYSIS: (CCC, BBB, L, V, M) Strong redemptive worldview with strong pastor and many moral virtues, although to get there you have to overcome prejudice and alienation; three mild obscenities; some children scuffle, wartime flashbacks with people being shot but not gruesome, various images of soldier who lost his leg, and threat of violence; alcohol use; and gambling partially rebuked, bigotry, and prejudice overcome.

Romantic Pirouettes

BILLY ELLIOT

Quality: ★☆☆☆   Acceptability: –2

WARNING CODES:
   Language: * * *
   Violence: * *
   Sex: None
   Nudity: *
RATING: R
GENRE: Drama
INTENDED AUDIENCE: Older teens and adults

RUNNING TIME: 110 minutes
STARRING: Jamie Bell, Gary Lewis, Julie Walters, Jean Heywood, Jamie Draven, and Stuart Wells
DIRECTOR: Stephen Daldry
PRODUCERS: Greg Brenman and Jon Finn
EXECUTIVE PRODUCERS: Natascha Wharton, Charles Brand, Tessa Ross, and David M. Thompson
WRITER: Lee Hall
DISTRIBUTOR: Universal Focus/ Universal Studios
BRIEF SUMMARY:
Young newcomer Jamie Bell stars in *Billy Elliot*, a movie about a working-class, eleven-year-old boy in England who escapes his harsh social environment by recognizing and using his talent for ballet. His coal-mining, recently widowed father, however, is too busy feeding the family and taking part in a strike at the local government-run mine to take much notice of Billy's needs. When he finds out about the ballet, the father becomes worried that his son is taking up a profession that he thinks is designed only for girls and men filled with perverted homosexual lust. Billy tries to break through the walls of his father's prejudice, as well as his own doubts and fears.

Billy Elliot in many ways is a poignant and often humorous family drama. Family situations lie at the heart of this well-produced, well-acted movie, which chugs along rather nicely, especially in the entertaining and original dance numbers. Jamie Bell in the title role is a true find. All of these positive aspects are somewhat derailed, however, by much strong foul language and by the movie's Marxist political correctness. That irrational, evil philosophy promotes a pro-homosexuality ideology that appears at times in the story.

CONTENT ANALYSIS: (RoRo, B, C, PCPC, ACap, Ho, LLL, VV, N, A, D, MM) Romantic worldview of working-class boy overcoming social obstacles to pursue his dreams, with moral and redemptive elements concerning his clash and ultimate reconciliation with his father, marred by politically correct anti-capitalist moments and politically correct references to homosexuality and cross-dressing; sixty-eight mostly strong obscenities and seven profanities; angry strike rallies, with eggs thrown at bus and strike riots with police chasing and beating one man in one scene; young friend of eleven-year-old hero is homosexual cross-dresser who kisses him on the cheek and boy visits teacher's daughter, who lightly strokes his cheek; upper male nudity; alcohol use; smoking; and deception, stealing, rebellion, arguments, spying on one's parent, and talking back.

Christian Fiction Comes to Hollywood

BLESS THE CHILD

Quality: ☆☆☆   Acceptability: −2

WARNING CODES:

Language: *
Violence: * * *
Sex: None
Nudity: None

RATING: R
GENRE: Spiritual warfare/Fantasy
INTENDED AUDIENCE: Adults
RUNNING TIME: 110 minutes
STARRING: Kim Basinger, Jimmy Smits, Rufus Sewell, Ian Holm, Angela Bettis, and Christina Ricci
DIRECTOR: Chuck Russell
PRODUCER: Mace Neufeld
EXECUTIVE PRODUCERS: Bruce Davey, Robert Rehme, and Lis Kern
WRITERS: Tom Rickman, Clifford Green, and Ellen Green
BASED ON: The novel by Cathy Cash Spellman
DISTRIBUTOR: Paramount Pictures

BRIEF SUMMARY:

Bless the Child is a strong Christian allegory of God ordaining a child in our present times to witness to him. Opposing the Christian guardians of the child are Satanists who are trying to convert the child to the devil or kill her. Produced by many Hollywood friends, *Bless the Child* opens as a Christmas star appears and Maggie (played by Kim Basinger) is told that a special child will be born. Her drug-addict sister abandons her baby, Cody, to Maggie. As the years progress, it becomes clear that Cody is special. Eventually, children born on the same day as Cody are killed in a slaughter of the innocents. FBI agent John Travis discovers that Satanists, calling themselves New Dawn and led by Eric Stark, are trying to find Cody. Stark either must convert Cody to the devil, or sacrifice her. In the spiritual battle, demons appear, vermin attack, and violence occurs.

Bless the Child is a blatant Christian allegory with a few Catholic trappings. The movie testifies that Jesus is God incarnate. Although there is no sex or nudity in *Bless the Child*, the intense violence is compounded because it involves a young child. Therefore, this is not a movie for children. The production values of the movie are good, and the special effects are terrific. *Bless the Child* has brought Christian allegory to the big screen and deserves the enthusiastic support of the Christian community.

CONTENT ANALYSIS: (CCC, BBB, L, VVV, A, DD, M) Strong moral Christian worldview; nine obscenities; extreme violence including a woman's head falls off after decapitation, knitting needles jammed into eyes, rats attack woman, demons and Satanists beat people, vagrant man set on fire and burned to death, car demolitions, woman injected with drugs while child watches, man shoots other men and bullets explode, woman stabs man with knife, threats of violence including child sacrifice, and child being told to jump off roof; discussions of profligate lifestyle; alcohol use; smoking and drug use; and many Christian symbols, allegories, and metaphors, as well as many satanic symbols depicted as evil.

Riding the Waves of Life

CAST AWAY

Quality: ✰✰✰   Acceptability: −1

WARNING CODES:
  Language: *
  Violence: * *
  Sex: None
  Nudity: *
RATING: PG-13
GENRE: Adventure
INTENDED AUDIENCE: Teens and adults
RUNNING TIME: 87 minutes
STARRING: Tom Hanks and Helen Hunt
DIRECTOR: Robert Zemeckis
PRODUCERS: Steve Starkey, Tom Hanks, Robert Zemekis, and Jack Rapke
EXECUTIVE PRODUCER: Joan Bradshaw
WRITER: William Broyles Jr.
DISTRIBUTOR: 20th Century Fox
BRIEF SUMMARY:
In *Cast Away*, Tom Hanks plays Chuck Noland, an international troubleshooter for Federal Express, whose plane crashes over the Pacific Ocean. Chuck Noland's life has been ruled by the clock, and now he has to survive for four years on a desert island. After many harrowing experiences, he survives a difficult journey on a wooden raft and comes back to find out that the world is not what he expected.

Cast Away is easy to criticize. Tom Hanks does a superb job, but some of the minor characters are slightly stilted, and the plot does not run smoothly. Furthermore, much of the movie seems like an advertisement for Federal Express. The most disappointing part of the movie, however, is that it ends on an existential, fatalistic note. It is clear that Chuck is supposed to learn some lessons, such as Hollywood's favorite theme that there is more to life than work. Of course, there's also more to life than no work on a desert island. There are some slight Christian hints in the movie, but they are very slight. On the other hand, the cinematography is beautiful, and the special effects are superb.

CONTENT ANALYSIS: (B, C, H, L, VV, N, A, D, M) Vaguely moral worldview with very slight Christian content, as well as some totemism, humanism, and existential fatalism; five lightweight exclamatory profanities and four obscenities; action violence including frightening storm, flight attendant gets hit on head, producing copious amounts of blood, plane sinks into ocean, man rides out storm, man gets cut and bruised, man gashes leg on coral, and man knocks out his own impacted tooth with a rock and an ice-skate blade; kissing; upper male nudity and man in underwear; drinking; smoking; and man takes pride that he stole or borrowed a little child's bike to complete his Federal Express delivery, man lies about his wife, and man talks to totem that he creates.

Cartoon Caper with Jaunty Jiggles

CHARLIE'S ANGELS

Quality: ✰✰✰   Acceptability: −1

WARNING CODES:
  Language: * *
  Violence: * *
  Sex: *
  Nudity: *
RATING: PG-13
GENRE: Action/Adventure
INTENDED AUDIENCE: Teens and young adults

RUNNING TIME: 98 minutes

STARRING: Drew Barrymore, Lucy Liu, Cameron Diaz, Bill Murray, Tim Curry, Crispin Glover, Sam Rockwell, Kelly Lynch, and the voice of John Forsythe

DIRECTOR: McG

PRODUCERS: Drew Barrymore, Leonard Goldberg, and Nancy Juvonen

EXECUTIVE PRODUCERS: Joseph Caracciolo, Aaron Spelling, Betty Thomas, and Jenno Topping

WRITERS: Ryan Rowe, Ed Solomon, and John August

BASED ON: The TV series

DISTRIBUTOR: Columbia Pictures/Sony

BRIEF SUMMARY:

The story of *Charlie's Angels* is not really important. Suffice it to say that it involves three beautiful women who go undercover to stop an evil plot involving kidnapping, stolen software, satellite technology, industrial espionage, violation of individual privacy, and revenge. Drew Barrymore, Cameron Diaz, and Lucy Liu play the three heroines, while Bill Murray plays their comic sidekick.

Charlie's Angels is a fairly entertaining and amusing action flick. It's a cartoon caper that doesn't take itself too seriously. For instance, at one point the movie shows the heroines dressed undercover as Japanese massage experts, to the tune of the jaunty eighties hit, "I Think I'm Turning Japanese." In these respects, *Charlie's Angels* may remind many viewers of the classic 1960s spy movie *Our Man Flint,* starring the venerable James Coburn. The moral aspects of the story are undercut, however, by some foul language, sexual innuendo, implied sexual immorality, nudity, and a worldview with slightly humanist, feminist, and politically correct implications. Therefore, be cautious about letting children see this PG-13 movie, especially if the child is a precocious teenage boy with raging hormones and an undeveloped biblical worldview.

CONTENT ANALYSIS: (H, Fe, PC, Pa, Ab, B, LL, VV, S, N, A, D, M) Slightly humanist worldview with some slightly feminist, politically correct ideals and some pagan, hedonistic attitudes regarding sexual promiscuity and some moral values about fighting evil and protecting the ones you love, including puns about angels and about having faith in a father figure; nine obscenities, seven mild profanities, two strong profanities, and an obscene gesture; moderate cartoon action violence such as martial arts fighting, chase scenes, attempted murders, explosions, and man tries to shoot woman dead; implied fornication and sexual innuendos; some female nudity, such as woman seduces man by revealing plenty of cleavage, woman wrapped in bedsheets, and nude woman tumbles down hill with the most revealing parts blurred or obscured; alcohol use; smoking; and stealing, betrayal, and revenge rebuked.

Egg-cellent Moral Comedy

CHICKEN RUN

Quality: ☆☆☆☆   Acceptability: +3

WARNING CODES:
  Language: *
  Violence: *
  Sex: None
  Nudity: None

RATING: G

GENRE: Animated comedy

INTENDED AUDIENCE: All ages

RUNNING TIME: 85 minutes

VOICES: Mel Gibson, Julia Sawalha, Jane Horrocks, Lynn Ferguson, and Miranda Richardson

DIRECTORS: Peter Lord and Nick Park

PRODUCERS: Peter Lord, David Sproxton, and Nick Park

EXECUTIVE PRODUCERS: Jake Eberts, Jeffrey Katzenberg, and Michael Rose

WRITER: Karey Kirkpatrick
BASED ON: An original story by Peter Lord and Nick Park
DISTRIBUTOR: DreamWorks
BRIEF SUMMARY:

Chicken Run, an egg-cellent cartoon comedy from DreamWorks, tells the story of a group of hens dedicated to escaping a chicken farm before they get the ax. All of their attempts fall short until a "flying rooster" named Rocky (voiced by Mel Gibson) lands on their front coop and promises to help them. Rocky is an obnoxious and arrogant American bird. He immediately attracts the attention of the entire clutch, and the hens obey his every word as he takes them through exercises in preparation to fly over the fences that restrain them. However, Rocky moves through his own moral abyss, knowing full well that he cannot actually fly. Things come to a head when the farmers, Mr. and Mrs. Tweedy, build an enormous chicken-pie-making machine. In the words of Mrs. Tweedy, "Chickens go in, pies come out."

Chicken Run is a brilliantly crafted, funny movie filled with many moral elements and witty spoofs. In the tradition of the *Toy Story* movies, this movie is as enjoyable (if not more so) for adult viewers as it is for young. Its clever dialogue and exquisite, laborious, and beautiful claymation will amaze the entire family.

CONTENT ANALYSIS: (BBB, C, L, V) Moral worldview with many moral elements including prayer, honesty, and loyalty; some references to "bum" in the English sense of the word; slapstick, cartoon violence perpetrated against villains, some implied violence, ferocious dogs, and some threats of violence against the chickens; and nothing else potentially objectionable.

A Flawed Theological Lesson

CHOCOLAT

Quality: ✩✩✩✩   Acceptability: −2

WARNING CODES:
  Language: * *
  Violence: *
  Sex: *
  Nudity: * *
RATING: PG-13
GENRE: Romantic comedy
INTENDED AUDIENCE: Teens and adults
RUNNING TIME: 121 minutes
STARRING: Juliette Binoche, Alfred Molina, Judi Dench, Johnny Depp, Carrie-Anne Moss, Lena Olin, and Peter Stormare
DIRECTOR: Lasse Hallstrom
PRODUCERS: David Brown, Kit Golden, and Leslie Holleran
EXECUTIVE PRODUCERS: Bob Weinstein, Harvey Weinstein, Alan C. Blomquist, and Meryl Poster
WRITER: Robert Nelson Jacobs
BASED ON: The novel by Joanne Harris
DISTRIBUTOR: Miramax Films/ Walt Disney Company
BRIEF SUMMARY:

In the story of *Chocolat*, a legalistic Roman Catholic mayor and a pagan woman, who opens a magical chocolate shop in his French town, clash, leading to a battle of wills affecting everyone around them. This movie has an apparent romantic worldview with pagan religious content and some occult, politically correct, and anti-Christian elements, including a nascent liberal notion about the deity of Jesus Christ, all of which are nearly overcome by a strong Christian sense of the proper roles of law and grace.

In *Chocolat*, Alfred Molina plays a noble count named Paul, a legalistic Roman Catholic mayor of a small town in France. Vianne, a mysterious, beautiful woman of South American and French descent, played by Juliette Binoche, opens up a chocolate store during Lent, a holy period of Christian abstinence. This outrages Paul because it offends his fanatic moralism. It sets off a battle of wills that affects the whole town, as well as another unusual outsider played by Johnny Depp.

Chocolat is an interesting, richly made parable. It is a flawed theological lesson about the Christian doctrine of law and grace, including the gospel of Jesus Christ. Part of that lesson is delivered by the young Catholic priest in the story. *Chocolat,* however, does not fully rebuke the romantic, pagan, occult, and other anti-Christian notions in its story, which includes some brief sexual content and nudity. There are also some politically correct elements that may lead many viewers to take a wrong approach to the movie's Christian content. Still, near the end of the story the movie clearly shows that a pagan, sometimes occult, lifestyle has not been able to fully satisfy either Vianne or her young daughter.

CONTENT ANALYSIS: (RoRo, PaPa, O, PC, Ab, CC, LL, V, S, NN, AA, DD, MM) Apparent romantic worldview with pagan religious content (such as references to a planned fertility celebration during Easter and a small chocolate statue of a fertility goddess, which is not worshiped, however) and some occult, politically correct, and anti-Christian elements, all of which are nearly overcome by a strong Christian sense of the proper roles of law and grace, an element that is finally expressed by a young, inexperienced Roman Catholic priest, though in a general, theologically liberal way that may be open to politically correct, heretical interpretations; eleven mostly mild obscenities, two strong profanities, and three mild profanities, plus woman admits she reads salacious literature; mild violence such as drunken, wife-beating husband tries to force wife to come back home, arsonist pours gasoline to set fire to burn two homes, homes shown burning, man breaks down door, man hit over head by frying pan, and man destroys store goods in fit of rage; implied sex between married couple after husband eats candy laced with some kind of aphrodisiac, nude engaged couple embrace erotically on bed, implied fornication, and man puts suspender back on shoulder after exiting tent where he was kissing a woman; partial sexual nudity in one scene; alcohol use and drunkenness; woman makes herbal chocolates that affect people's behavior in a way that loosens their inhibitions; and miscellaneous immorality, such as wife-beating, legalism, gambling, rootlessness, arson, and stealing, most of which are rebuked at some point.

Love Triumphs over Enlightenment

CROUCHING TIGER, HIDDEN DRAGON

Quality: ☆☆☆☆   Acceptability: −2

WARNING CODES:
  Language: *
  Violence: * *
  Sex: * *
  Nudity: *
RATING: PG-13
GENRE: Martial arts/Fantasy
INTENDED AUDIENCE: Teens and adults
RUNNING TIME: 120 minutes
LANGUAGE: Mandarin
STARRING: Chow Yun-Fat, Michelle Yeoh, Zhang Zi Yi, Chang Chen, Cheng Pei Pei, and Lung Sihung
DIRECTOR: Ang Lee
PRODUCERS: Hsu Li Kong, William Kong, and Ang Lee
WRITERS: James Schamus, Tsai Ku Jung, and Wang Hui Ling
DISTRIBUTORS: Columbia Pictures/Sony Entertainment and Warner Brothers
BRIEF SUMMARY:
With *Crouching Tiger, Hidden Dragon,* director Ang Lee, of *Sense and Sensibility* fame, tackles the mythic martial arts genre so famous in China. Set in the Qing dynasty, the movie opens with the famous

Wudan fighter Li Bu Bai telling Lady Shu Lien that he is giving up fighting and the Green Destiny sword. Li asks Shu Lien to take the sword to Sir Te. At Sir Te's home, Governor Yu arrives to marry off his daughter En. A thief, presumed to be the Jade Fox, steals the famous sword, flying from rooftop to rooftop and executing incredible martial arts moves. Master Li and Shu Lien must recover the sword. In the process, love triumphs over enlightenment.

Although there is much martial arts fighting, there's very little bloodshed, and the movie is more of a martial arts ballet than a kung-fu film. It explores the mythic themes of love and enlightenment, family and duty, morals and revenge. Eastern mysticism is refuted by the romantic plotline. An ardent Taoist would be upset that love is given prominence over self-realization. There is only one obscene word, but, regrettably, there are two relatively discreet love scenes.

CONTENT ANALYSIS: (RoRo, FRFR, BB, L, VV, S, N) Romantic worldview with strong Eastern religious elements including dualism as well as strong moral considerations with a pointed emphasis on family, true love, virtue, and observing the rules for one's own good; one obscenity; lots of martial arts action violence, but very little blood or consequences, though there are terrific sword fights, martial arts fights over rooftops and in treetops, balletic fighting, a few wounds, a few killings, and a woman jumps off mountain to fulfill legend, but not gory or bloody; fornication and foreplay while clothed or covered; and revealing dress and situations.

Laurels for Lizards

DINOSAUR

Quality: ☆☆☆☆   Acceptability: +1

WARNING CODES:
  Language: None

Violence: * *
Sex: None
Nudity: None
RATING: PG
GENRE: Animated fantasy
INTENDED AUDIENCE: Older children and adults
RUNNING TIME: 82 minutes
VOICES: D. B. Sweeney, Julianna Margulies, Alfre Woodard, Ossie Davis, Max Casella, Della Reese, Joan Plowright, and Samuel E. Wright
DIRECTORS: Ralph Zondag and Eric Leighton
PRODUCERS: Pam Marsden and Baker Bloodworth
WRITERS: John Harrison and Robert Nelson Jacobs
BASED ON: An original screenplay by Walon Green
DISTRIBUTOR: Walt Disney Pictures
BRIEF SUMMARY:
Dinosaur tells how one dinosaur helps save a group of other dinosaurs and a family of friendly lemur monkeys from various dangers after a meteor destroys part of the Earth. The lemur monkeys, accompanied by their adopted veggie-dinosaur son and brother, Aladar, meet a herd of veggie dinosaurs, who are looking for a green "nesting" valley that they migrated to before a large meteor destroyed part of their planet, presumably Earth, including the island home of Aladar and the monkeys. The herd must fight off thirst, hunger, and some meat-eating dinosaurs. Aladar's wisdom and courage saves them from these dangers.

Although *Dinosaur* includes some story elements favoring an evolutionary worldview and political correctness, it contains mostly a moral worldview. *Dinosaur* not only teaches taking care of those who are weaker and standing up to bullies, it also ironically includes some statements against the evolution concept of "survival of the fittest." Furthermore, it has redemptive elements of sacrificing oneself for the welfare of others, even to the point of death. Finally, although some of its action violence may scare small children and there are two scenes with baby dinosaur dung, this is a great-looking, well-produced movie that's very enjoyable, if sometimes predictable and familiar. Teaching children to be media-wise is advised.

CONTENT ANALYSIS: (BB, C, Ev, PC, VV) A moral worldview that teaches monogamous heterosexuality, taking care of those who are weaker, standing up to bullies, and includes some anti-Darwinian statements rejecting the tra-ditional notion of survival of the fittest, with redemptive elements of sacrificing oneself for the welfare of others, even to the point of possible death, plus some elements favoring an evolutionary worldview regarding huge meteor hit-ting Earth, and being kind to outsiders and misfits; two scenes where baby dinosaurs relieve themselves; action vio-lence that may be scary for small chil-dren, such as carnivorous dinosaurs chase veggie-eating, talking dinosaurs, dinosaurs trampled but not to the point of significant injury, dinosaurs fight, one dinosaur grabs another one with its teeth to eat it, and images of razor-sharp teeth that sometimes snap; and lemur monkey refers to himself as a "love monkey" and asks female lemurs if they want to play "monkey in the middle."

Getting in Touch with Your Outer Child

DISNEY'S THE KID

Quality: ☆☆☆☆   Acceptability: +3

WARNING CODES:
  Language: *
  Violence: *
  Sex: None
  Nudity: None
RATING: PG
GENRE: Comedy
INTENDED AUDIENCE: Families

RUNNING TIME: 101 minutes
STARRING: Bruce Willis, Spencer Breslin, Emily Mortimer, Lily Tomlin, and Jean Smart
DIRECTOR: Jon Turteltaub
PRODUCERS: Jon Turteltaub, Christina Steinberg, and Hunt Lowry
EXECUTIVE PRODUCERS: Arnold Rifkin and David Willis
WRITER: Audrey Wells
DISTRIBUTOR: Walt Disney Pic-tures/Buena Vista
BRIEF SUMMARY:
Disney's The Kid stars Bruce Willis as a forty-year-old man named Russ, who realizes he must literally get in touch with his inner child to make his life worthwhile. By strange circumstances, Russ encounters his eight-year-old self, whom he is deeply disappointed to see is chubby and dull. It is, however, the child who is more disappointed by the person Russ has become—a man who lives alone without a wife, a family, or even a dog. After much prodding, the man realizes the boy is there to help him (not the other way around) and under-stands what he must do—change his ways, refocus his life, marry his girl-friend, and purchase a dog.

Disney's The Kid is a funny, fluffy, and moral feel-good movie with very little objectionable content. Rated PG for some mild foul language, this is a skill-fully written, refreshing movie that man-ages to overcome its reliance on psychological solutions to life's prob-lems. The discerning viewer, who under-stands the movie's minor flaws and can put up with some implausible situations, will enjoy it, so long as he or she remem-bers that Jesus Christ is our real hope and salvation.

CONTENT ANALYSIS: (BB, Pa, L, V, A, D, M) Moral worldview with many moral elements including personal transformation, kindness, and generos-ity slightly marred by psychological sal-vation message and unexplained fantasy elements; four mild obscenities, three exclamatory appeals to God, and many unkind and even abusive statements by the lead character; school yard fight, boxing practice, and other minor violence; some alcohol; antidepressant drug; and lying, cheating, and meanness rebuked.

The Joy of Christmas Offers Hope and Redemption

DR. SUESS' HOW THE GRINCH STOLE CHRISTMAS

Quality: ☆☆☆☆   Acceptability: +1

WARNING CODES:
Language: None
Violence: *
Sex: None
Nudity: *

RATING: PG
GENRE: Fantasy
INTENDED AUDIENCE: All ages
RUNNING TIME: 105 minutes
STARRING: Jim Carrey, Jeffrey Tambor, Christine Baranski, Bill Irwin, Molly Shannon, and Taylor Momsen
DIRECTOR: Ron Howard
PRODUCERS: Brian Grazer and Ron Howard
EXECUTIVE PRODUCER: Todd Hallowell
WRITERS: Jeffrey Price and Peter S. Seaman
BASED ON: The book by Dr. Seuss
DISTRIBUTOR: Universal Pictures
BRIEF SUMMARY:
Dr. Seuss' How the Grinch Stole Christmas stars funnyman Jim Carrey as the nasty Grinch who finds out that he does have a heart after all. The outline of the movie follows the story from the classic children's book and TV cartoon. Adding to the fun in this version, however, is Cindy Lou Who, who finds out that the Grinch had a tough childhood, so she gets the other Whos to invite the Grinch to their Christmas celebration. Things go wrong, however, and the Grinch feels rejected and plots to steal all the Christmas presents in Whoville.

How the Grinch Stole Christmas is an entertaining family fantasy. This movie retains the central message that there's more to Christmas than presents, and augments it with tremendous visual and special effects. Although the story includes some romantic worldview elements, it is clear that there is sin in Whoville and that people need repentance and forgiveness. The production values here are a wonderful treat, but many people may be disappointed about the lack of specific references to Jesus Christ in this Christmas offering. The movie also includes some infrequent scatological humor and some slapstick violence that parents should warn their children not to imitate.

CONTENT ANALYSIS: (BB, CC, Ro, V, A, M) Moral worldview with redemptive content and discussion about Christmas, marred by some romantic worldview notions and very lightweight and infrequent scatological humor; some scatological humor including Grinch places mistletoe near his rear-end, Grinch gives sleeping man having a romantic dream the rear of a dog to kiss, and Grinch falls on top of woman with low-cut dress; slapstick violence including monster pops out of Grinch cave that turns out to be a carnival-like dummy with a dog barking into a megaphone, Grinch eats glass, Grinch hits himself with mallet as a sedative, Grinch places his head between monkey banging cymbals to avoid the sounds of Christmas, and Grinch has termites in his teeth; some sexual references including Christmas party where keys are being exchanged, Martha May Whovier makes sexual references, and Grinch falls on top of her with his head on her chest; Martha May wears suggestive outfits; Grinch eats wine bottle but does not drink alcohol and later takes a swig from a bottle labeled "XXX"; and Grinch overcomes self-pity, anger, meanness, and vengefulness.

Overcoming Oppression

EAST-WEST

Quality: ☆☆☆☆   Acceptability: −2

WARNING CODES:
  Language: *
  Violence: *
  Sex: *
  Nudity: * *
RATING: PG-13
GENRE: Drama
INTENDED AUDIENCE: Older
teens and adults
RUNNING TIME: 121 minutes
LANGUAGE: French
STARRING: Sandrine Bonnaire, Oleg
Menchikov, Serguei Bodrov Jr., and
Catherine Deneuve
  DIRECTOR: Regis Wargnier
  PRODUCER: Yves Marmion
  WRITERS: Roustam Ibraguimbek,
Serguei Bodrov, Louis Gardel, and
Regis Wargnier
  DISTRIBUTOR: Sony Pictures
Classics
SUMMARY:
The French movie *East-West* is a hard
but rewarding look at the struggle to
keep hope alive during Stalinist Russia,
centering upon the lives of the return
émigré family of Alexei Golovine, his
French wife Marie, and their son Serioja.
A doctor returns to the Soviet Union to
help rebuild the country after World War
II, but must sacrifice his ideals to keep
his family out of the labor camps. When
his wife's attempts to escape to freedom
fail, the doctor risks his own life to help
her and his son escape. He realizes there
is a price to pay for the freedom of others, and his love drives him to make an
ultimate sacrifice.
East-West features wonderful acting.
The skills needed to convey the subtle
and often unspoken emotions are a treat
to watch. The grim reality of life under
Stalin is communicated with the mini-

mum of violence—just enough for the
gravity of the Golovine's situation to hit
home. There are, however, some sexual
situations and brief foul language. A
complex movie, *East-West* exposes viewers to elemental instincts of survival,
love, and freedom. While it doesn't
involve Christianity in the answer, the
movie pays deep respect to the power of
love and hope in overcoming oppression.
  CONTENT ANALYSIS: (BB, C, H, L,
V, S, NN, A, M) Moral worldview, though
not explicitly Christian, with redemptive
elements of sacrifice and some humanistic elements, more critical of oppression
than the political nature of Communism;
very few obscenities, mainly referring
derogatorily to women during an interrogation scene; one shooting death without
blood and two brief interrogation scenes
with slapping of woman; one scene of
implied sex with brief backside nudity,
and two extramarital affairs depicted,
including living with a mistress; rear
nudity and woman exposes bra briefly;
some subdued social drinking and some
scenes of mild drunkenness; and some
questionable   immoral   relationships,
including a public affair and a hidden
affair, plus some deception revolving
around plots to escape.

Unconditional Love Defeats Selfishness

THE EMPEROR'S NEW GROOVE

Quality: ☆☆☆☆   Acceptability: +1

WARNING CODES:
  Language: None
  Violence: *
  Sex: None
  Nudity: None
RATING: G
GENRE: Animated comedy
INTENDED AUDIENCE: All ages
RUNNING TIME: 78 minutes
VOICES: David Spade, John
Goodman, Eartha Kitt, Patrick
Warburton, and Wendie Malick

DIRECTOR: Mark Dindal
PRODUCER: Randy Fullmer
EXECUTIVE PRODUCER: Don Hahn
WRITER: David Reynolds
DISTRIBUTOR: Walt Disney Pictures
BRIEF SUMMARY:

The Emperor's New Groove is set in a mythical kingdom in the Peruvian Andes. The story follows the misadventures of an arrogant young emperor named Kuzco, voiced by David Spade. His power-hungry female advisor, Yzma, voiced by Eartha Kitt, transforms Kuzco into a llama. Stranded in the jungle, Kuzco's only chance is a good-hearted peasant named Pacha, voiced by John Goodman. Meanwhile, Yzma and her loony, dullwitted assistant, Kronk, track Kuzco to finish him off. Everything comes to a wonderful, clever ending that will have viewers on the edge of their seats, laughing with joy.

Director Mark Dindal and producer Randy Fullmer have assembled a talented cast and crew to create a wacky ride through a colorful cartoon world. Their team imbues the characters with a brilliant array of entertaining character traits. They make the story come alive with energy, humor, and adventure, marred only by mild cartoon violence, children dreaming of their father in danger, and very mild sexual innuendo. Best of all, *The Emperor's New Groove* teaches valuable moral lessons in an entertaining fashion. Included with these lessons are some redemptive elements of forgiveness, repentance, and unconditional love.

CONTENT ANALYSIS: (BBB, C, Ro, Pa, V, S, Ho, A, M) Strong moral worldview with redemptive elements of forgiveness, repentance, and unconditional brotherly love (including a comment that "the wicked shall receive their just rewards from above") as well as some romantic elements and mild, implicit New Age pagan psychic elements when children dream of their father in danger; plenty of funny slapstick cartoon violence, including spills, falls, chases, and comical attempts to poison someone to death and some scary images, such as sharp teeth and glowing eyes of a den of black panthers who chase and trap man; some mild cartoon sexual references including two men accidentally kiss and male llama dresses as wife of his friend to escape disclosure with waiter saying, "Bless you for coming out in public"; alcohol use; and conceit rebuked, arrogance rebuked, callousness rebuked, tyranny rebuked, murder foiled and rebuked, possible homosexual subtext regarding Boy Scouts, and woman mixes secret potions, but movie indicates potions are weird cartoon science rather than an occult practice.

Flawed Case Study

ERIN BROCKOVICH

Quality: ✮✮✮✮   Acceptability: –2

WARNING CODES:
  Language: * * *
  Violence: *
  Sex: *
  Nudity: * *
RATING: R
GENRE: Drama
INTENDED AUDIENCE: Older teens and adults
RUNNING TIME: 130 minutes
STARRING: Julia Roberts, Albert Finney, Aaron Eckhart, Marg Helgenberger, Peter Coyote, and Conchata Ferrell
DIRECTOR: Steven Soderbergh
PRODUCERS: Danny DeVito, Michael Shamberg, and Stacey Sher
EXECUTIVE PRODUCERS: John Hardy and Carla Santos Shamberg
WRITER: Susannah Grant
DISTRIBUTORS: Universal Pictures and Columbia Pictures/Sony
BRIEF SUMMARY:

In *Erin Brockovich*, Julia Roberts plays the true story of a twice-divorced single mother who finds herself leading the charge against a power company in California whose pollution seriously damaged the health of nearly an entire desert town. After Erin shames her lawyer into giving her a job, she convinces her lawyer to allow her to investigate the case. He welcomes the chance to get the brash young woman out of his hair. Surprisingly, however, she discovers the cover-up involving contaminated water and helps put together a solid lawsuit.

Reportedly, the real Erin Brockovich not only uses lots of strong foul language, as in this movie, but she also enjoys wearing low-cut clothes and very short dresses. Much of the humor in the movie involves how Erin uses her body and her speech to get people to do things for her and the case, especially the men she encounters. Roberts plays these qualities to the hilt, yet expresses genuine concern for the plight of the townspeople. The director and the rest of the cast and crew, especially Albert Finney as the lawyer, add greatly to the proceedings. These and other qualities somewhat mitigate the movie's abundance of objectionable content.

CONTENT ANALYSIS: (H, Fe, B, LLL, V, S, NN, A, D, M) Humanist worldview with feminist and moral elements; eighty-four obscenities and eighteen profanities; very brief mild violence including speeding car slams into rear of other car; implied fornication; upper male nudity, woman in underwear in one bedroom scene and woman wears revealing clothes throughout most of movie; alcohol use; smoking; and business corruption and pollution.

Heart-Rending Moral Themes

THE FAMILY MAN

Quality: ☆☆☆☆   Acceptability: −1

WARNING CODES:
  Language: * * *

  Violence: *
  Sex: * *
  Nudity: * *
RATING: PG-13
GENRE: Fantasy
INTENDED AUDIENCE: Teens and adults
RUNNING TIME: 146 minutes
STARRING: Nicholas Cage, Téa Leoni, Jeremy Priven, and Don Cheadle
DIRECTOR: Brett Ratner
PRODUCERS: Marc Abraham, Tony Ludwig, Alan Riche, and Howard Rosenman
EXECUTIVE PRODUCERS: Thomas A. Bliss and Andrew Z. Davis
WRITERS: David Diamond and David Weissman
DISTRIBUTOR: Universal Pictures
BRIEF SUMMARY:
In *The Family Man*, Nicholas Cage plays Jack Campbell, a Scrooge-like businessman who finds out what his life could have been thanks to an angel-like character. Instead of waking up in his penthouse on Christmas morning, he wakes up married with two kids. Jack is incredibly disappointed by this mundane, middle-class life. By the end of his brief glimpse of what life could've been, he discovers, of course, the real values of life.

The Family Man is a heart-rending movie. Very well written, it makes you laugh and cry. Better yet, it's an intentionally moral movie. It wants to prove that everyone needs love, marriage, children, and that these things are much more important than fame or fortune, and it does prove its case. Its spiritual underpinnings are much more vague, however. There are many lightweight profanities. Also, there's a conscious earthiness to even the good choices. Drinking is part and parcel to family life, sex is thrilling, especially with your wife, and adultery is beguiling. *The Family Man* will strike a responsive chord in many people. It is too bad that it didn't have more courage to proclaim its convictions with more integrity.

CONTENT ANALYSIS: (BB, C, H, LLL, V, SS, NN, AA, D) Very moral worldview with slight Christian references and significant humanist content; seventeen obscenities and twenty-two light profanities, many of which are exclamations; and baby relieves himself on father; threat of violence; clearly implied fornication and adultery considered but rejected; upper male nudity, shadow female nudity fairly explicit in shower, nude doll on bar, and nude baby; alcohol use and drunkenness; and smoking.

Mixed Blessings

FANTASIA 2000

Quality: ☆☆☆   Acceptability: +1

WARNING CODES:
  Language: None
  Violence: *
  Sex: None
  Nudity: None
RATING: G
GENRE: Animated musical
INTENDED AUDIENCE: All ages
RUNNING TIME: 81 minutes
VOICES: Steve Martin, Quincy Jones, Bette Midler, Itzhak Perlman, James Earl Jones, Angela Lansbury, and Penn and Teller
SUPERVISING DIRECTOR: Hendel Butoy
DIRECTORS: Pixote Hunt, Hendel Butoy, Eric Goldberg, James Algar, Francis Glebas, Gaetan Brizzi, Paul Brizzi, and Don Hahn
PRODUCER: Donald W. Ernst
EXECUTIVE PRODUCER: Roy Edward Disney
DISTRIBUTOR: Walt Disney Pictures (Buena Vista/Touchstone/Hollywood Pictures/Miramax Films)

BRIEF SUMMARY:
Fantasia 2000 by Disney uses the IMAX large-screen format to create seven new cartoon segments and to bring back an old favorite, "The Sorcerer's Apprentice." In the eight segments, butterfly shapes flitter to the sounds of Beethoven's Fifth Symphony, flying whales float to the majestic music of Respighi's "Pines of Rome," city dwellers rush about to the tunes of Gershwin's "Rhapsody in Blue," and animals march to Noah's Ark to the wonderful motifs of "Pomp and Circumstance." Regrettably, however, the last segment is a pagan ode to the creative powers of a demonic nature sprite. This lends a politically correct air of pluralism to the movie, which also includes a dynamic Noah's Ark sequence that features Donald Duck and Daisy.

Fantasia 2000 uses the big IMAX format well to tell its stories, especially when the screen is filled with butterflies, whales, animals, and broomsticks. The movie could have included some brighter colors and sharper geometric shapes, however. Also, despite the strong Noah's Ark segment, *Fantasia 2000* could have used some Bach, some Mozart, some waltzes by Strauss, and better writing to enliven the mix. Furthermore, some of the images will frighten younger children, so parents beware.

CONTENT ANALYSIS: (PC, BBB, PaPaPa, FRFRFR, OO, C, V, M) Pluralistic worldview with strong biblical and moral elements mixed with strong pagan, false religious elements and a strong scary sequence about occult magic, plus some minor redemptive qualities; mild high-art cartoon violence such as crowd runs past doorman, spinning him around, toy soldier knocked out of window, toy soldier flips villain into fire, flamingos accidentally wrap necks around branch, Mickey Mouse chops up marching broomstick with ax, and volcano turns forest into ash; henpecked husband escapes wife to dance with showgirls at nightclub; and stealing donut and apple.

Without a Hurt, the Heart Is Hollow

THE FANTASTICKS

Quality: ☆☆☆☆   Acceptability: −1

WARNING CODES:

Language: *
Violence: *
Sex: None
Nudity: *

RATING: PG
GENRE: Musical/Romance
INTENDED AUDIENCE: Older children and adults
RUNNING TIME: 87 minutes
STARRING: Joel Grey, Jean Louisa Kelly, Joe McIntyre, Jonathan Morris, Brad Sullivan, and Barnard Hughes
DIRECTOR: Michael Ritchie
PRODUCERS: Michael Ritchie and Linne Radmib
WRITERS: Tom Jones and Harvey Schmidt
BASED ON: The play by Tom Jones and Harvey Schmidt
DISTRIBUTOR: Metro Goldwyn-Mayer/United Artists
BRIEF SUMMARY:
The Fantasticks is a long-delayed movie version of the famous stage musical about two young lovers who become jaded about their romance. The movie version is set in a beautiful rural landscape in 1920s Arizona. Luisa and Matt go in search of romance and adventure at a local carnival, but come back to one another with a deeper, wiser love.

Director Michael Ritchie takes a wistful approach to the story's happy ending that lingers. It's a feeling of nostalgia and yearning that's summed up in the melancholy, provocative verse from the play's signature song, "Try to Remember," which says, "Without a hurt, the heart is hollow." The landscape vistas in The Fantasticks are easy on the eyes. The three performers involved in the lovers' triangle, Joe McIntyre as Matt, Jean Louisa Kelly as Luisa, and Jonathan Morris as a magician, have wonderful voices that complement the famous melodies, although McIntyre's acting is not up to the level of Morris's and Kelly's. There's only one bawdy scene that makes The Fantasticks not quite family friendly. It's a burlesque scene at the carnival where Matt encounters a clown who crudely leers while exposing some fake breasts.

CONTENT ANALYSIS: (Ro, B, L, V, N, A, D, M) Romantic worldview with moral elements, including allusion to the prodigal son story in the New Testament; two mild obscenities and three mild exclamatory profanities; slapstick violence and men wrestle and battle with swords; allusions to lust of the eyes and rape; upper female nudity on stage prop while man gives a lascivious leer; alcohol use; man is drugged; and fathers conspire to have man pretend to abduct young woman so that her lover can save her and become the hero in her eyes.

Rocky Road to Virtue

THE FLINTSTONES IN VIVA ROCK VEGAS

Quality: ☆☆☆   Acceptability: +1

WARNING CODES:

Language: None
Violence: *
Sex: None
Nudity: None

RATING: PG
GENRE: Fantasy
INTENDED AUDIENCE: All ages
RUNNING TIME: 91 minutes
STARRING: Kristen Johnson, Mark Addy, Stephen Baldwin, Jane Krakowski, Alan Cumming, and Joan Collins
DIRECTOR: Brian Levant

PRODUCERS: Bruce Cohen and Steven Spielberg

EXECUTIVE PRODUCERS: Joseph Barbera, William Hanna, and Dennis E. Jones

WRITERS: Harry Elfont, Deborah Kaplan, Jim Cash, and Jack Epps Jr.

BASED ON: The animated series by Hanna-Barbera Productions

DISTRIBUTOR: Universal Pictures

BRIEF SUMMARY:

The Flintstones in Viva Rock Vegas tells how Fred and Wilma and Barney and Betty get together, with help from an alien who is studying the mating habits of humans. Wilma is tired of her life of wealth and security. She leaves home, ending up as waitress Betty's roommate. Fred and Barney go to the burger joint where Betty works. They meet Betty and Wilma and fall in love with them. Wilma brings Fred, Barney, and Betty to her home for her father's birthday, which they destroy in comic style. Chip Rockefeller invites them to his new casino so that he can make a fool out of Fred and Barney and win Wilma's hand in marriage, because he needs Wilma's money to pay off his debts.

Viva Rock Vegas takes a slightly rocky road to virtue. Moral principles are upheld in the end, including honesty, marriage, decency, and hard work. Regrettably, getting to this high-minded ending involves some low-life humor and some politically correct class envy. Included among the slapstick humor are scatological jokes and homosexual jokes, including a cross-dressing sequence. Although the plot is complex, most children will just enjoy the slapstick roller-coaster ride.

CONTENT ANALYSIS: (BB, PC, Ho, V, A, M) Ultimately moral worldview with some class biases as well as some scatological humor and homosexual humor; some scatological references to bodily functions; cartoon-type violence with man getting rammed into the ground by a large rock, man falling from a Ferris wheel and making a large indentation in the ground, man punches and knocks another man out and several other visual slapstick jokes; strong homosexual sight gags including opening alien sequence where aliens reproduce by splitting into two, alien comes to Earth to view mating habits of earthlings, Barney falls from top bunk onto Fred so alien thinks they're mating, and several heterosexual sight gags including provocatively dressed femme fatal as well as some lightweight romance including kissing; cross-dressing as showgirls to escape security forces and some revealing costumes; suggested alcohol use; and other sight gags like dinosaur passing gas, plus gambling, deception, greed, avarice, and envy, which are all clearly rebuked.

Making Time for Family

FREQUENCY

Quality: ✩✩✩   Acceptability: –1

WARNING CODES:
  Language: * * *
  Violence: * *
  Sex: None
  Nudity: None

RATING: PG-13

GENRE: Science fiction/Thriller

INTENDED AUDIENCE: Teens and adults

RUNNING TIME: 111 minutes

STARRING: Dennis Quaid, James Caviezel, Andre Braugher, Elizabeth Mitchell, and Noah Emmerich

DIRECTOR: Gregory Hoblit

PRODUCERS: Hawk Koch and Gregory Hoblit

EXECUTIVE PRODUCERS: Robert Shaye and Richard Saperstein

WRITER: Toby Emmerich

DISTRIBUTOR: New Line Cinema

BRIEF SUMMARY:

In the time-travel thriller *Frequency*, a unique solar flare allows a policeman in

1999 to communicate with his long-dead father in 1969 via the father's ham radio. The son gives the father some special information that saves his father's life. Regrettably, it unleashes a serial killer who will eventually claim the life of the son's mother. Father and son race against time to stop the killer before he claims another victim.

Frequency is an entertaining, pro-family thriller with an interesting take on the age-old science fiction concept of time travel. Its moral worldview suggests not only that family bonds transcend time but also that every little decision we make can have vast consequences for those who are closest and dearest to us. Another worthy quality in this movie is the concern that both father and son express, not just for the life of the mother, but also for the lives of the other victims of the serial killer. This is a well-directed, well-written movie, marred only by some foul language and some violence. It can lead to some valuable discussions between parents and their teenage children about family and life-and-death issues.

CONTENT ANALYSIS: (BB, LLL, VV, A, D, M) Moral worldview stressing family bonds and human life; thirty-one obscenities and fifteen profanities; moderate violence including fires, explosions, fireman saves woman's life, man beaten up, gunshots fired, man's hand shot off, and brief images of skeleton and a woman's corpse; alcohol use; smoking; and murderer steals driver's license to plant incriminating evidence.

Searching for Salvation

GEORGE WASHINGTON

Quality: ☆☆☆☆   Acceptability: +1

WARNING CODES:
Language: * *
Violence: * *
Sex: * *
Nudity: None

RATING: Not rated
GENRE: Stream-of-consciousness drama
INTENDED AUDIENCE: Teens and adults
RUNNING TIME: 89 minutes
STARRING: Candace Evanofski, Donald Holden, and Curtis Cotton III
DIRECTOR: David Gordon Green
PRODUCERS: David Gordon Green, Sacha W. Mueller, and Lisa Muskrat
WRITER: David Gordon Green
DISTRIBUTOR: Cowboy Booking International
BRIEF SUMMARY:

George Washington is a brilliant, enigmatic stream-of-consciousness feature film by twenty-five-year-old filmmaker David Gordon Green. The movie focuses on a group of racially mixed children, including George, Nasio, Buddy, Vernon, and Sonya, who see the beauty in the fallen world around them, where death and decay are part of the very fabric of life. In the story, an accidental death upsets the children's world and spurs George first to seek to be a hero and then to seek salvation from Jesus Christ.

George Washington is a small film that will probably not reach big audiences. It had trouble finding a distributor. Audiences who will respond to its spiritual themes may be upset by the life-and-death issues of the movie, including little children talking about sexual activity and using obscenities. There is an air of hyper-realism here that is transformed by director Green into a lyrical insight into mankind. Hopes and fears, good and bad, and life and death happen, and the most real moment is when the title character cries out for salvation.

CONTENT ANALYSIS: (CCC, BB, LL, VV, SS, D, M) Christian worldview with moral imperatives limited only by the fallenness of man; twelve obscenities and one exclamatory profanity; girl draws on wall with dog feces, and discussions about going to the bathroom;

boy slips on bathroom floor, hits head and dies, boy almost drowns in pool, man kills dog off-screen, punching and shoving among boys, and threats of violence; discussions of sexual activity among girls, some of whom are very young, kissing, discussions of dog sexually attacking child; smoking; and children lie and cover up boy's death.

A.D. without J.C.

GLADIATOR

Quality: ☆☆☆   Acceptability: −3

WARNING CODES:
  Language: *
  Violence: * * *
  Sex: *
  Nudity: *
RATING: R
GENRE: Historical action/
Adventure
INTENDED AUDIENCE: Teens and adults
RUNNING TIME: 150 minutes
STARRING: Russell Crowe, Joaquin Phoenix, Richard Harris, Connie Nielsen, and Oliver Reed
DIRECTOR: Ridley Scott
PRODUCERS: David H. Franzoni, Steven Spielberg, and Douglas Wick
EXECUTIVE PRODUCER: Branko Lustig
WRITERS: David H. Franzoni, John Logan, and William Nicholson
DISTRIBUTOR: DreamWorks
BRIEF SUMMARY:
Russell Crowe stars as Maximus in *Gladiator,* a revisionist history of how Emperor Commodus brutalizes ancient Rome until he is overthrown. In the story, Maximus is a Roman general who willingly serves the famous Stoic emperor, Marcus Aurelius. Marcus plans to name Maximus his successor, but his evil son, Commodus, murders Marcus, takes the crown for himself, and tries to get rid of Maximus. Maximus survives to become a great gladiator. Taken to Rome, Maximus finally gets his chance to overthrow the tyrant.

Gladiator is almost a four-star movie, with fine acting and high production values. Although vengeance is Maximus's motivation, he exhibits several virtues, not the least of which is mercy when killing is unnecessary. Furthermore, the movie makes clear that the blood-sport of the Colosseum is distracting and destroying Rome. It rebukes dictatorship and mobocracy, and commends republican government. However, it seems as if the filmmakers are toying with the audience, attracting them with a violent "blood-and-guts" epic while positing virtues in the dialogue. Worse, although the movie is set in A.D. 180, the "year of our Lord," the Lord of heaven and earth, Jesus Christ, whose love and sacrifice triumphed over the corrupt Roman Empire, is never mentioned. This movie is not really suitable for teenagers.

CONTENT ANALYSIS: (PaPa, BB, C, RHRH, L, VVV, S, N, A, D, MMM) Pagan worldview with many moral, redemptive, and revisionist history elements as well as evil rebuked; three mild obscenities and chants of worship to Roman gods; extreme violence including decapitation, blood spurting, bodies cut in half, arms and legs hacked to pieces, constant violence in warfare and gladiatorial games, threats of violence, patricide, and attempted patricide; suggestions of incest and discussions of homosexuality; upper male nudity; alcohol use; potions; and deception, greed, envy, and gambling.

Compelling Apocalypse

LEFT BEHIND

Quality: ☆☆☆   Acceptability: +4

WARNING CODES:
  Language: None
  Violence: *
  Sex: None
  Nudity: None

RATING: PG
GENRE: Science fiction
INTENDED AUDIENCE: All ages
RUNNING TIME: 97 minutes
STARRING: Kirk Cameron, Brad
Johnson, Chelsea Noble, and Clarence
Gilyard
DIRECTOR: Vic Sarin
PRODUCERS: Peter Lalonde, Paul
Lalonde, Joe Goodman, and Ralph
Winter
EXECUTIVE PRODUCERS: Peter
Lalonde, Paul Lalonde, Bobby Neutz,
and Ron Booth
WRITERS: Allan McElroy, Paul
Lalonde, and Joe Goodman
BASED ON: The novel by Tim
LaHaye and Jerry B. Jenkins
DISTRIBUTOR: Cloud Ten Pictures
SUMMARY:
Left Behind is an apocalyptic fantasy
about two men and a pastor fighting the
evil machinations of the Antichrist. Kirk
Cameron plays Buck in *Left Behind*,
based on the best-selling novel by Tim
LaHaye and Jerry B. Jenkins. Buck is a
TV reporter reporting from Israel when
a massive enemy air attack miraculously
stops. Later, as Buck is flying to Europe
to find out what happened, people disappear from the plane, and the pilot,
Captain Steele, turns the plane back to
Chicago. In Chicago, Buck stays with
Captain Steele, who finds that his wife
and son have disappeared. In searching
for his family, Steel discovers the truth,
with the help of a pastor who's been
"left behind." Buck also discovers the
truth just before he's drawn into the
orbit of the secretary general of the
United Nations.
Left Behind is crafted with a very careful, deft touch. It involves the audience
in the storyline of the people. Kirk
Cameron's vulnerability, though unlike
the Buck of the book, makes the movie
very compelling. He is an everyman
caught in circumstances beyond his control. The characters are well drawn. *Left*

Behind presents the gospel of Jesus Christ
in a very entertaining, powerful, and
winsome way.
CONTENT ANALYSIS: (CCC, BBB, V,
A, D, M) Strong Christian worldview
that presents the gospel of Jesus Christ in
a powerful, winsome way as well as
many moral principles including reaffirming marriage and family; some
exclamatory appeals to God; violence
that is treated in a discreet manner,
including people disappearing as a result
of so-called "rapture," car crashes, man
shoots man at point-blank range but
camera does not show blood and gore,
some threats of violence as well as some
war scenes, all done within a PG-rating;
brief alcohol use; smoking; and pre-tribu-
lation, premillennial eschatology.

Touching the Face of God

THE LEGEND OF BAGGER VANCE

Quality: ☆☆☆☆   Acceptability: −1

WARNING CODES:
Language: * * *
Violence: *
Sex: *
Nudity: None
RATING: PG-13
GENRE: Drama/Spiritual allegory
INTENDED AUDIENCE: Older chil-
dren and adults
RUNNING TIME: 126 minutes
STARRING: Will Smith, Matt Damon,
Charlize Theron, Bruce McGill, and Joel
Gretsch
DIRECTOR: Robert Redford
PRODUCERS: Robert Redford,
Michael Nozik, and Jake Eberts
EXECUTIVE PRODUCER: Karen
Tenkhoff
WRITER: Jeremy Leven
BASED ON: The novel by Steven
Pressfield
DISTRIBUTOR: DreamWorks
Pictures

BRIEF SUMMARY:

The Legend of Bagger Vance is about a caddy who becomes a spiritual guide and guardian angel for a troubled young man, played by Matt Damon, who finds redemption on the golf course. Matt Damon plays Captain Junuh, a World War I veteran who disappears after a horrible experience on the battlefields of Europe. Junuh becomes a local hero with great, but perhaps unfounded, expectations when his rich ex-fiancée, played by Charlize Theron, gets him to play in a golf tournament with two actual professional champions. Smith plays the caddy, Bagger Vance, who helps Junuh rediscover the gifts that God gave him when he was born.

Bagger Vance is a wonderful parable about God, marred by some foul language and sexual content. It also has some brief dialogue that may strike many as too reminiscent of New Age philosophy. The rest of the movie, however, has a strong theistic worldview, combined with some redemptive elements. It also extols the virtues of honesty, integrity, and honoring one's parents. In all, *The Legend of Bagger Vance* is one of the best, most spiritually uplifting movies of the year. Caution is recommended, however, because of the foul language and sexual content.

CONTENT ANALYSIS: (BBB, C, Pa, FR, Ro, LLL, V, S, M) Strong theistic worldview that plays like a theophany and extols honesty and integrity with redemptive elements and some New Age pagan sentiments about becoming one with the universe in one scene, plus some romantic elements regarding using your feelings rather than your mental faculties; nineteen obscenities and eight profanities, including a few strong exclamatory ones; mild World War I violence as troops advance amid explosions followed by men falling dead and some images of corpses, but nothing really graphic, and man commits suicide off-screen; implied fornication and depicted seduction scene

when woman seems willing to trade sex for a big personal favor; woman in underwear in two scenes; alcohol use; smoking; and gambling, man expresses despair, another man expresses nihilistic thought, and boy ashamed of his father when he has to become a street sweeper to make ends meet during the Great Depression.

Powerful Parable

MERCY STREETS

Quality: ☆☆☆☆   Acceptability: +4

WARNING CODES:
  Language: *
  Violence: *
  Sex: None
  Nudity: None

RATING: PG-13
GENRE: Crime drama
INTENDED AUDIENCE: Older children and adults
RUNNING TIME: 100 minutes
STARRING: David White, Eric Roberts, Cynthia Watros, Shiek Mahmud-Bey, Robert La Sardo, Stacy Keach, and Lawrence Taylor
DIRECTOR: Jon Gunn
PRODUCERS: Kevin Downes, Bobby Downes, Geoff Ludlow, Jon Gunn, David White, and Travis Mann
EXECUTIVE PRODUCERS: Marta Wells, Dan Wells, Greg Bowerman, and Karen Bowerman
WRITERS: John Mann and Jon Gunn
DISTRIBUTOR: Providence Entertainment
BRIEF SUMMARY:

The crime drama *Mercy Streets* is a Christian parable about an ex-con and his twin brother, a pastor, who learn about God's love and grace when confronted by the villainous plans of a con man and kidnapper. The movie opens with John, played by David White, getting out of prison. Eric Roberts plays Rome, who greets John with an offer of another con. John wants to get out of crime, but he thinks he needs money to do so, and Rome is convincing, especially with a dead body in his trunk. Eventually, John escapes Rome's clutches and ends up on the doorstep of his twin brother, Jeremiah, a pastor. When Rome mistakes Jeremiah for John and kidnaps him, the switch in roles teaches each one of the brothers something about God's love and grace.

Mercy Streets is a breakthrough movie that treats the gritty underside of life in a powerful way without resorting to cheap stereotyping, foul language, or excessive violence. Instead of a movie that will lead teenagers to think that crime pays, *Mercy Streets* leads them to the Truth. Breaking away from the biblical epic mold, it tells a Christian parable in a convincing, captivating way. As such, it is a masterful piece of moviemaking with a strong gospel message that compares favorably with Hollywood fare.

CONTENT ANALYSIS: (CCC, BBB, L, V, A, M) Strong Christian worldview with many moral elements; one light obscenity; mild violence heightened by threats of violence with slapping, chopping meat as a threat, visualizing a mock murder, and several shootings that are done in a very discreet manner; some kissing; and lying, cheating, kidnapping, counterfeiting, and stealing rebuked.

Funny, but Flawed

MISS CONGENIALITY

Quality: ★★★   Acceptability: –2

WARNING CODES:
  Language: * * *
  Violence: * *
  Sex: *
  Nudity: *
RATING: PG-13
GENRE: Comedy
INTENDED AUDIENCE: Older teens and adults
RUNNING TIME: 117 minutes

STARRING: Sandra Bullock, Michael Caine, Benjamin Bratt, Candice Bergen, William Shatner, and Ernie Hudson
DIRECTOR: Donald Petrie
PRODUCER: Sandra Bullock
EXECUTIVE PRODUCERS: Bruce Berman, Marc Lawrence, and Ginger Sledge
WRITERS: Marc Lawrence, Katie Ford, and Caryn Lucas
DISTRIBUTOR: Castle Rock/ Warner Brothers
BRIEF SUMMARY:
In *Miss Congeniality*, a female FBI agent who's just "one of the guys" is chosen to go undercover as a beauty pageant contestant, but she needs a makeover. Though the case she has been assigned to is tough, the tougher task will be her ability to pull it off.

Miss Congeniality takes the audience into the silly whirlwind of beauty pageants, exposing their truths and misconceptions. The storyline moves along, though snagging on a few silly plot points and "bumbling" villains. Sandra Bullock plays her role as Gracie with spunk and hilarious facial expressions. These add to the silliness of the movie, but take away from any semi-dramatic scenes. Despite the movie's many laughs, however, there are some questionable elements that blemish it. Things brought to the surface, such as one character's abrasive treatment of another and Gracie's personal struggles, are never explored. Even though the movie is a comedy, these defects seem to keep things on a level that is more silly than funny. This is an entertaining movie, but beware of a mild romantic worldview, plenty of foul language, and other questionable content.

CONTENT ANALYSIS: (Ro, B, Pa, Ab, Ho, LLL, VV, S, N, AA, D, MM) Mild romantic worldview of characters in an idealistic story with some moral elements of justice being served, pagan elements of eclectic behavior, character yells profanity then says prayer aloud to stay undercover, and two homosexual characters, one who states a pro-lesbian slogan; twelve obscenities, seven profanities, seven exclamatory profanities, and some sexual references; boy attempts to punch girl, hitting post instead, girl punches and kicks boys, woman throws a fit by kicking and slamming things, explosions, woman slaps man on back of head, man choking, men point guns at each other, man holds knife to woman's throat, struggle with guns, and scenes of punching and kicking for defense; some references to sexual activity among girls and talk of intentions for fornication; upper male nudity and some skimpy clothing; bar scene, alcohol use, and drunkenness; smoking; and joking about bulimia, and character plots destruction.

A Quest for Redemption

MISSION: IMPOSSIBLE 2 (M:I-2)

Quality: ☆☆☆☆   Acceptability: −1

WARNING CODES:
Language: * *
Violence: * * *
Sex: *
Nudity: *

RATING: PG-13
GENRE: Spy/Action/Adventure
INTENDED AUDIENCE: Older children and adults
RUNNING TIME: 126 minutes
STARRING: Tom Cruise, Thandie Newton, Ving Rhames, Dougray Scott, and Anthony Hopkins
DIRECTOR: John Woo
PRODUCERS: Tom Cruise and Paula Wagner
EXECUTIVE PRODUCERS: Terence Chang and Paul Hitchcock
WRITER: Robert Towne
DISTRIBUTOR: Paramount Pictures
BRIEF SUMMARY:
M:I-2, the sequel to the hit *Mission: Impossible*, features lots of pumped-up action, with Tom Cruise again playing special agent Ethan Hunt, who must stop a rogue agent from unleashing a deadly virus. Caught in the crossfire is an international female thief, played by Thandie Newton. Both Ethan and the rogue agent are in love with the beautiful thief, making for difficult complications. In the end, Ethan's quest for the deadly virus also becomes a quest to save her life and repair the damage between them.

Hong Kong-trained action director John Woo confessed recently that he is a Christian. He uses several Christian symbols to identify Tom Cruise's character with a saintly quest for redemption and virtue. Woo's Christian worldview, and the relationship between the hero and the damsel in distress, help make *M:I-2* an above-average action thriller. Also, although the action is strong and intense, it never exceeds the boundaries of the movie's PG-13 rating. The hero, in fact, shows appropriate moral restraint in his fighting. Finally, the amount of foul language is lower and milder than usual, as is the obligatory sexual content.

CONTENT ANALYSIS: (CC, BB, Pa, LL, VVV, S, N, A, D, M) Redemptive Christian worldview with moral elements and hero identified with saintly virtues and with images of Christ crucified, plus brief immoral pagan attitudes regarding sexuality; sixteen obscenities, mostly mild, and one mild exclamatory profanity; two scenes with mild sexual innuendo; strong action violence including shoot-outs, chase scenes, and fistfights plus gruesome images of deadly virus that causes bleeding from eyes, mouth, and nose; implied fornication and man unwittingly puts woman into compromising position; upper male nudity and implied female nudity; alcohol use; smoking; and stealing.

Poignant Pup

MY DOG SKIP

Quality: ☆☆☆☆   Acceptability: +2

WARNING CODES:

Language: **
Violence: *
Sex: None
Nudity: None

RATING: PG
GENRE: Drama
INTENDED AUDIENCE: Older children and adults
RUNNING TIME: 92 minutes
STARRING: Kevin Bacon, Mark Beech, Frankie Muniz, Diane Lane, Luke Wilson, and Harry Connick Jr.
DIRECTOR: Jay Russell
PRODUCERS: John Lee Hancock, Broderick Johnson, Mark Johnson, and Andrew A. Kosove
EXECUTIVE PRODUCER: Mary P. Ewing
WRITER: Gail Gilchriest
BASED ON: A novel by Willie Morris
DISTRIBUTOR: Warner Brothers
BRIEF SUMMARY:
In the family movie *My Dog Skip*, eight-year-old Willie Morris lives in Yazoo, Mississippi, in 1942. Willie is an only child, the son of an overly protective father. Willie's great hero is Dink Jenkens, the star athlete who lives next door. On his birthday, Willie's mother gives Willie a dog, against her husband's advice. Willie and Skip become inseparable. Willie discovers moonshiners using an old grave to hide their alcohol. One day, when Willie takes out his frustration on Skip, Skip runs away, getting locked in the moonshiners' tomb. This crisis helps Willie become a man.

My Dog Skip is an elegant tale, with great character studies. It also has positive references to faith and everyday concerns. Everyone involved should be commended because it is one of the best-constructed family movies, hampered only by some lightweight vulgarities. Probably the only missing ingredient is a sense of simple fun for younger children that would make it more accessible to Willie's contemporaries in the audience. Even so, *My Dog Skip* is a faithful, hopeful, and uplifting coming-of-age movie that children and adults will love.

CONTENT ANALYSIS: (BB, C, H, LL, V, A, D, M) Moral worldview with a positive reference to God, a picture of the sacred heart of Jesus, as well as some minor humanist elements; eleven obscenities, a reference to fear causing someone to relieve themselves in their clothes and implicitly rebuked minor references to sissy and anti-black statements; minor violence such as dog gets slapped, boy gets pushed around by bullies, bullies gang up on boy, bootleggers threaten boy, bootleggers hit dog with shovel off-screen, deer shot, and dog attacks Adolph Hitler dummy in crotch area; incipient romance of two children; alcohol use; smoking; and references to witch in graveyard to scare young boy.

A Wacky Road toward Salvation

O BROTHER, WHERE ART THOU?

Quality: ☆☆☆☆   Acceptability: −2

WARNING CODES:

Language: * * *
Violence: * * *
Sex: *
Nudity: None

RATING: PG-13
GENRE: Musical comedy
INTENDED AUDIENCE: Older children and adults
RUNNING TIME: 107 minutes
STARRING: George Clooney, John Turturro, Tim Blake Nelson, Holly Hunter, Charles Durning, Michael Badalucco, and John Goodman
DIRECTOR: Joel Coen
PRODUCER: Ethan Coen
EXECUTIVE PRODUCERS: Tim Bevan and Eric Fellner
WRITERS: Ethan and Joel Cohen
BASED ON: Homer's epic Greek poem *The Odyssey*

DISTRIBUTOR: Touchstone Pictures/Buena Vista/Disney

BRIEF SUMMARY:

O Brother, Where Art Thou is a wacky musical comedy set in Mississippi during the Great Depression, where three escaped prisoners from a chain gang find fame, fortune, and perhaps even salvation. Starring George Clooney as the talkative, know-it-all leader of the prisoners, this movie is loosely based on Homer's poem, *The Odyssey.* During a series of bizarre situations and strange encounters, two of the prisoners seem to find Christ, but Clooney's character remains dubious. Even so, the movie ends with a miracle from God after pleas to him for help, mercy, and forgiveness, followed by a spiritually uplifting gospel song.

Joel and Ethan Coen, the filmmakers behind *Fargo,* made this movie. Some viewers may not like their flair for wacky humor and bizarre characters, but the movie is well made and well acted. *O Brother, Where Art Thou* also includes plenty of foul language and some shocking, but brief, violent images, such as a speeding vehicle ramming a cow. On the positive side, however, the movie happily affirms that God can indeed work miracles if you call upon him and that the spiritual joys of being a Christian and singing a gospel song uplift one's spirit.

CONTENT ANALYSIS: (CC, Ab, H, O, LLL, VVV, S, A, D, MM) Christian, redemptive worldview with baptism scene, light salvation scenes, God answers cries for mercy, help, and forgiveness in the movie's climax and elsewhere, and strong gospel-oriented folksy music, marred by a borderline irreverent tone, some immoral behavior, and backsliding, including man with humanist, disbelieving attitude, but man is rebuked by others for his humanist attitude, plus three women appear to have magical powers in one scene (corresponding to scene in *The Odyssey* wherein ship sails near female creatures whose singing lures ships onto rocks); forty-eight mostly mild obscenities, fifteen strong profanities, and four mild profanities; strong violence in a couple scenes, such as "Babyface" Nelson shoots cow with machine gun, speeding car hits cow, and large man uses big tree branch to club two men, plus some general gunfire and legal authorities set fire to barn to smoke out escaped prisoners; women in skimpy outfits seduce men with song that puts them to sleep; alcohol use; smoking; and miscellaneous immorality done mostly for comic effect such as escapes from chain-gang prison farm, stealing, bank robbery, car theft, betrayal, baptized men slide back into criminal behavior but apparently go clean at the end and find fame and fortune, KKK lynching rally shown but then disrupted by heroes, political corruption, satanic villain, man says he sold his soul to the devil, and a couple of minor villains use religion for evil ends but are clearly rebuked and defeated.

Soul-Searching Warfare

THE PATRIOT

Quality: ☆☆☆☆   Acceptability: −2

WARNING CODES:
Language: *
Violence: * * *
Sex: None
Nudity: None

RATING: R

GENRE: Historical epic

INTENDED AUDIENCE: Older children and adults

RUNNING TIME: 162 minutes

STARRING: Mel Gibson, Heath Ledger, Joely Richardson, Jason Isaacs, Chris Cooper, Tcheky Karyo, Rene Auberjonois, Lisa Brenner, and Tom Wilkinson

DIRECTOR: Roland Emmerich

PRODUCERS: Dean Devlin, Mark Gordon, and Gary Levinsohn

EXECUTIVE PRODUCERS: Roland Emmerich, Ute Emmerich, and William Fay

WRITER: Robert Rodat

DISTRIBUTOR: Columbia Pictures/Sony

BRIEF SUMMARY:

The Patriot stars Mel Gibson as a family man named Benjamin Mark, who wrestles with his desire for revenge and the just cause of the American War for Independence in the late 1700s. The cruel British Colonel Tavington, played impeccably by Jason Isaacs, shoots Ben's fifteen-year-old son, Thomas, as Ben's oldest son, Gabriel, is led away captive. Ben's fury is unleashed, and taking his two youngest boys, he goes into the woods to fight a guerilla war, slaughtering the British and rescuing Gabriel. Ben continues to wrestle with his sinful desire for vengeance and the worthiness of the Revolutionary cause. Eventually, he sees that he needs to stay the course, and rejects vengeance to take up the flag.

The violent battle scenes may concern older moviegoers, while younger moviegoers might chafe at the soul-searching, but the heart of this movie is faith. Prayer runs throughout the film, and the Cross of Jesus Christ is lifted up. *The Patriot* is a terrific, engrossing movie. One can only hope that this soul-searching and pain will lead many to search for the God to whom Ben prays so often in this story.

CONTENT ANALYSIS: (CCC, PP, LL, VVV, A, M) Christian worldview with strong moral, patriotic overtones dealing with the problem of sin, redemption, freedom, family, principles, pride, and a just cause; thirteen obscenities and one calling upon God in a spiritual context; extreme violence in battlefield situations, including people's body parts being blown off, a child being shot, several scenes of people dying, and townspeople being burned in a church by British army; two lingering kisses; alcohol use; and plunder and the impact of the brutality of war on civilians.

Changing the World

PAY IT FORWARD

Quality: ☆☆☆☆   Acceptability: −1

WARNING CODES:

Language: * * *

Violence: * *

Sex: *

Nudity: *

RATING: PG-13

GENRE: Drama

INTENDED AUDIENCE: Teens and adults

RUNNING TIME: 124 minutes

STARRING: Haley Joel Osment, Kevin Spacey, Helen Hunt, Jon Bon Jovi, and Angie Dickinson

DIRECTOR: Mimi Leder

PRODUCERS: Peter Abrams, Robert L. Levy, and Steven Reuther

EXECUTIVE PRODUCERS: Mary McLaglen and Jonathan Treisman

WRITER: Leslie Dixon

BASED ON: The novel by Catherine Ryan Hyde

DISTRIBUTOR: Warner Brothers

BRIEF SUMMARY:

To "pay it forward" means to return a favor to someone other than the person who did you the favor. Academy Award winners Helen Hunt and Kevin Spacey, together with Haley Joel Osment, star in this redemptive, dramatic tale. Spacey plays a teacher who inspires Osment's character to do random acts of kindness.

Pay It Forward is a well-written gem that carries out a lofty idea in a realistic way. Though the directing is weak, the acting by the veteran cast makes the plot come alive with fantastic character development. Interestingly enough, the ability of movies to provoke imitative behavior may work in a positive manner with this movie. The idea of paying a favor back by doing something for other people rather than the one who paid you the favor, is a reflection of what Christ has done for us. He has paid the price for our sins, and we, in turn, are to tell others this good news so that others may come to him. Regrettably, this PG-13 movie contains foul language, alcohol abuse, and implied fornication. Due to these elements, as well as some tense family scenes, caution is recommended for older children.

CONTENT ANALYSIS: (BBB, C, Pa, Ro, LLL, VV, S, N, AAA, DD, M) Strong moral worldview of boy who desires the right things despite being surrounded by family problems, and teacher cares for students with some redemptive, pagan, and romantic elements; thirty obscenities (some of which are rebuked), eight profanities, and one racial slur; vehicle smashes into other vehicle, man breaks window with gun, man holds woman hostage with gun, police point guns at armed man, some tense family situations of arguing, man fires gun at wall to scare woman, mother slaps son, man grabs man and shoves him into restroom after man tries to entice boy, man breaks window and steals audio equipment, boys tease other boy, man's chest and face scarred from burns, woman contemplates suicide on bridge, and depicted stab wound with knife; implied fornication and kissing; partial nudity of couple and many skimpy outfits; alcohol use, abuse, and alcoholism; implied heroin use and depicted marijuana use; and lying.

Power versus Persistence

THE PERFECT STORM

Quality: ✰✰✰   Acceptability: −2

WARNING CODES:
  Language: * * *
  Violence: * *
  Sex: None
  Nudity: *
RATING: PG-13
GENRE: Action/Drama

INTENDED AUDIENCE: Older teens and adults
RUNNING TIME: 123 minutes
STARRING: George Clooney, Mark Wahlberg, Diane Lane, William Fichtner, John C. Reilly, and Mary Elizabeth Mastrantonio
DIRECTOR: Wolfgang Petersen
PRODUCERS: Gail Katz, Wolfgang Petersen, and Paula Weinstein
EXECUTIVE PRODUCERS: Duncan Henderson and Barry Levinson
WRITERS: Sebastian Junger and William D. Wittliff
BASED ON: The book by Sebastian Junger
DISTRIBUTOR: Warner Brothers
BRIEF SUMMARY:
The Perfect Storm is loosely based on the real-life story of six men aboard a fishing vessel that ended up caught in the middle of two colliding storms. Director Wolfgang Petersen (of *Das Boot* and *Air Force One*) helms *The Perfect Storm*. George Clooney stars as Captain Billy Tyne, leader of the crew aboard the *Andrea Gail*. As they find great success further out, Captain Billy informs the crew that there is a large storm in their path. The crew decides to go for it, knowing that the ride will be rough. They underestimate the strength of the storm, however. Cut off from the mainland, the crew fights a desperate battle against wind and sea.

The special effects in *The Perfect Storm* are tremendous. Hollywood pretty boys Clooney and Wahlberg are mostly genuine when portraying the lives of fishermen as gruff, not glamorous. Pagan elements of strong foul language, smoking, a lot of alcohol use, and brief drunkenness mar the movie, however. There is also some action violence. Even so, the movie's worldview is mostly a moral one. Enemies are brought together, crew members risk their lives for one another, and prayer is mentioned.

CONTENT ANALYSIS: (BB, Pa, Ab, LLL, VV, N, AA, D, M) Mostly moral worldview of people pulling together despite their differences, with some pagan elements, plus blasphemous song heard in background; seventeen obscenities and thirteen profanities; woman has a brief, frightening dream of ocean storm, man gets into scuffle with another man, depictions of men gutting fish, fish being filled with ice, shark accidentally ends up on deck of ship with scary depictions of shark biting man's leg, man shoots shark, man accidentally hooked through hand and whisked out to sea, many scenes of people being thrown about on boats, helicopter crashes into water, scenes of implied drowning, and extremely violent storm; some kissing and a joking allusion to sex; upper male nudity; alcohol use and drunkenness; smoking; and a seemingly heartless, greedy character.

Beyond the Envelope

POLLOCK

Quality: ☆☆☆☆   Acceptability: −2

WARNING CODES:
   Language: * * *
   Violence: *
   Sex: * *
   Nudity: *

RATING: R
GENRE: Biography
INTENDED AUDIENCE: Adults
RUNNING TIME: 122 minutes
STARRING: Ed Harris, Marcia Gay Harden, Amy Madigan, Jennifer Connelly, and Jeffrey Tambor
DIRECTOR: Ed Harris
PRODUCERS: Fred Berner, Ed Harris, and John Kilik
EXECUTIVE PRODUCERS: Joseph Allen and Peter Brant
WRITERS: Barbara Turner and Susan J. Emshwiller
BASED ON: The book *An American Saga* by Steven Naifeh and Gregory White Smith

DISTRIBUTOR: Sony Pictures Classics
BRIEF SUMMARY:
   Ed Harris directs and stars in *Pollock,* one of the best movies made about the life of an artist. The movie follows Jackson Pollock from his life as a down-and-out artist; to his being discovered by his future wife, Lee Krasner, who promotes him to international fame; and then his final fall to self-destruction. By the end, Pollock is famous, but his manic depression has gotten the best of him. Always wanting the child that Krasner denied him, he starts having affairs and eventually kills himself and another woman in a senseless car crash after a drunken spree.

   Ed Harris has brought Jackson Pollock to life. Marcia Gay Harden as Krasner matches Ed Harris's Pollock turn for turn. For those who find Pollock's work unintelligible, the movie gives meaning to his abstractions. Transformed by reading Carl Jung, Pollock strives to reveal his subconscious, but going so deeply breaks all the artistic barriers. At the end of his life, Pollock becomes embittered, expressing his extremely spoiled state of mind, a state of mind cultivated by Krasner. She made his art a success, and then refused to allow him to grow up and take responsibility for his actions.

   CONTENT ANALYSIS: (HH, C, Ho, LLL, V, SS, N, AAA, DD, MM) Humanist worldview with an undertone of nihilism and one positive reference to a church wedding; forty-four obscenities, nine profanities, harsh anti-Semitic racial slurs directed by Pollock toward his wife, and Pollock relieves himself in wealthy woman's fireplace; several violent tantrums including breaking chair against post and a car accident; fornication, adultery, and a homosexual character; shadow nudity and various states of disrobing including upper male nudity; alcohol use with many scenes of drunken rage and intent to drink; heavy smoking and taking drugs; and lying, cheating, anger, and selfishness.

Victory on the Field and in the Heart

REMEMBER THE TITANS

Quality: ☆☆☆☆   Acceptability: +3

WARNING CODES:
  Language: None
  Violence: *
  Sex: None
  Nudity: *
RATING: PG
GENRE: Drama
INTENDED AUDIENCE: Older children and adults
RUNNING TIME: 113 minutes
STARRING: Denzel Washington, Will Patton, Donald Adeosun Faison, Hayden Panettiere, and Ryan Hurst
DIRECTOR: Boaz Yakin
PRODUCER: Jerry Bruckheimer
EXECUTIVE PRODUCERS: Michael Flynn and Mike Stenson
WRITER: Gregory Allen Howard
DISTRIBUTOR: Walt Disney Pictures/Walt Disney Company
BRIEF SUMMARY:
Based on a true story, *Remember the Titans* depicts the forced integration of an all-black high school with an all-white high school and its impact on football in 1971 Alexandria, Virginia. Denzel Washington stars as Herman Boone in *Remember the Titans*. Boone's a black coach given the head coach position at a formerly all-white school due to forced integration. Met with disdain, anger, and a divided football team of racial foes, Coach Boone must teach his players unity. Tempers flare but, little by little, confrontations turn into accomplishments not only for the team but also for Boone and the assistant white coach whose job he took. Amid the many trials that the players and coaches face, *Remember the Titans* makes it clear that the real victory lies in changed hearts.

Though the movie's racial theme is not always easy, the casting and performances by Washington, Will Patton as the assistant coach, and Donald Faison as one of the players are excellent. Despite a few minor questionable elements, this movie gives an important life lesson about exchanging hate for loyal friendships. It is a refreshing, uplifting, and often humorous look at the antics of high school football.

CONTENT ANALYSIS: (CCC, BBB, Ro, V, N, M) Strong Christian worldview with many moral elements of characters learning to overcome prejudice by building deep friendships, and other moral undertones including Christian elements such as implied team prayer with depicted "Amen," man says, "I'm not a savior, I'm a football coach," Christian character called "the Rev" who wants to be a pastor, recital of Isaiah 40:31 in a song, and romantic elements where some character actions are done on a whim; some racial epithets, depiction of boy vomiting and implied vomiting; football violence, young girl kicks man in shins, rioting with depicted bottle thrown through window, large group brawl later rebuked, depictions of bruises and black eyes, parents riot with depicted shouting and anger, rock thrown through family's window, and depicted car crash with bruises and scratches on character; upper male nudity in locker room; racism; and male kisses other male briefly, in a nonhomosexual context, as a joke.

Redemptive Allegory

RETURN TO ME

Quality: ☆☆☆   Acceptability: −1

WARNING CODES:
  Language: * *
  Violence: *
  Sex: None
  Nudity: None
RATING: PG
GENRE: Romantic comedy

INTENDED AUDIENCE: Older children to adults

RUNNING TIME: 120 minutes

STARRING: David Duchovny, Minnie Driver, Carroll O'Connor, Bonnie Hunt, David Alan Grier, and Jim Belushi

DIRECTOR: Bonnie Hunt

PRODUCER: Jennie Lew Tugend

EXECUTIVE PRODUCERS: C. O. Erickson and Melanie Greene

WRITERS: Bonnie Hunt and Don Lake

DISTRIBUTOR: Metro Goldwyn-Mayer/United Artists

BRIEF SUMMARY:

In *Return to Me*, David Duchovny of TV's *The X-Files* plays a man named Bob who must cope with life after losing his wife in a car accident. Bob is a bear to work with at his job, his house is a mess, he orders take-out food every night, and his social life isn't any better. Bob falls in love with Grace (Minnie Driver), a woman who unknowingly received his deceased wife's heart after a transplant. When the truth is later discovered, Bob is faced with the overwhelming situation of his past and present love.

Romantic comedies often take the brunt of a critic's force, and *Return to Me*, though standard, is not typical by any means. Though this story is quite unusual, the characters are portrayed with realistic strength, defying the usual sexual innuendos and advances. While Grace is ashamed of her surgical scar, an unknowing Bob is concerned with her inner beauty. Regrettably, *Return to Me* has some scars of its own, mainly several profanities and obscenities, including two used by a child. Ultimately, however, this movie is a strong, provocative Christian allegory.

CONTENT ANALYSIS: (CC, BB, LL, V, A, D, M) Christian allegory with many redemptive, moral, and faith-filled elements including a relationship based on true love and good moral character, mentions of "God's blessing" during emotional turmoil, images of church, and character asks, "What was God thinking?"; eight profanities, nine strong obscenities, and five mild obscenities; woman on stretcher with some blood, man has blood on tuxedo, and woman slaps man but apologizes; alcohol use; character always smokes cigar; and lying and gambling.

Heroism and Endurance

RETURN WITH HONOR

Quality: ☆☆☆☆   Acceptability: +1

WARNING CODES:

Language: *
Violence: *
Sex: None
Nudity: None

RATING: PG

GENRE: War documentary

INTENDED AUDIENCE: Older teens and adults

RUNNING TIME: 102 minutes

STARRING: Lt. Everett Alvarez, Lt. Comdr. Bob Shumaker, Comdr. Jeremiah Denton, Seaman Douglas Hegdahl, Lt. John "Mike" McGrath, and Senator John McCain

NARRATED BY: Tom Hanks

DIRECTORS: Freida Lee Mock and Terry Sanders

PRODUCERS: Freida Lee Mock and Terry Sanders

WRITERS: Freida Lee Mock, Terry Sanders, and Christine Z. Wiser

DISTRIBUTOR: Ocean Releasing

BRIEF SUMMARY:

U.S. soldiers held captive during the Vietnam War describe their ordeal through various interviews in *Return with Honor*. The Vietnam War has long been a controversial, multifaceted subject told by those who fought in it and those who protested it. However, in *Return with Honor* the surviving POWs, or prisoners of war, tell their story. This movie depicts the soldiers' ordeal and loyalty. The presence of these and other men who served as POWs is powerful as they describe their experiences with tears, pain, and even laughter and joy. Their courageous story is supported by war footage and in drawings by one of the former POWs.

Filmmakers Freida Lee Mock and Terry Sanders, who won an Oscar for *Maya Lin*, have established a perspective toward Vietnam that broadens awareness. Though this documentary contains one obscenity and some graphic descriptions, it explores the issue with respect and is highly recommended for its positive portrayal of a horrid ordeal. *Return with Honor* not only teaches, it instills respect for serving God and country, survival, heroism, and, ultimately, biblical values. Lt. Paul Galanti, a POW for six and one-half years, puts things into perspective for today: "There's no such thing as a bad day when there's a doorknob on the inside of the door."

CONTENT ANALYSIS: (BBB, L, V) Strong moral worldview where military personnel describe their experiences as prisoners during the Vietnam War; one obscenity in context; some violent descriptions and drawings of imprisonment and torture.

Comic Myth-Adventures

THE ROAD TO EL DORADO

Quality: ☆☆☆   Acceptability: +1

WARNING CODES:

Language: *
Violence: *
Sex: None
Nudity: *

RATING: PG
GENRE: Animated musical adventure
INTENDED AUDIENCE: Older children and adults
RUNNING TIME: 83 minutes

VOICES: Kevin Kline, Kenneth Branagh, Rosie Perez, Armand Assante, and Edward James Olmos
DIRECTORS: Eric "Bilbo" Bergeron and Don Paul
PRODUCERS: Bonne Radford and Brooke Breton
EXECUTIVE PRODUCER: Jeffrey Katzenberg
WRITERS: Ted Elliott and Terry Rossio
DISTRIBUTOR: DreamWorks
BRIEF SUMMARY:
In *The Road to El Dorado*, the colorful animated feature from DreamWorks, two con men, voiced by Kevin Kline and Kenneth Branagh, must save the golden city of El Dorado from an evil pagan priest and an army of Spanish conquistadors. After a series of comic misadventures, Tulio and Miguel discover El Dorado, where a power struggle is occurring between the tribal chieftain and the evil occult priest. With the help of a sexy tribal maiden, Tulio and Miguel pose as "gods" to take off with some of the city's gold. Complicating their plan is Tulio's growing feelings for the maiden and Miguel's growing friendship with the kindly tribespeople, not to mention the evil priest and the Spaniards.

The Road to El Dorado is a colorful, sometimes exciting movie, with lots of humor. The good-natured story is spoiled, however, by references to pagan religion and a scary monster conjured up by the evil priest, who is defeated by human effort. Despite these and other problems, such as some naturalistic nudity, the movie has several strong positive qualities. It teaches, for example, moral principles such as honesty, friendship, kindness, and respect for human life.

CONTENT ANALYSIS: (RoRo, BB, HH, RH, Pa, O, Ab, L, V, N, AA, D, M) Romantic worldview regarding primitive cultures and the nature of man, with many moral virtues plus humanist elements, revisionist history regarding the

Christian worldview of the Spanish conquistador, Cortes, and some pagan elements that are rebuked, such as occult pagan villain advocates human sacrifice and conjures demonic monster; three mild obscenities and a few mild profanities; action and slapstick violence such as sword fights, men jump into barrels, and men fight scary demonic monster; scantily clad heroine seduces, kisses, and embraces one hero; heroine wears sexy, revealing outfit and upper and rear male nudity in naturalistic contexts; alcohol use and drunkenness; smoking; and gambling and deceit from heroes, with deceit eventually being rebuked.

Exploring Moral Dilemmas

RULES OF ENGAGEMENT

Quality: ☆☆☆☆   Acceptability: −2

WARNING CODES:
Language: * * *
Violence: * * *
Sex: None
Nudity: None
RATING: R
GENRE: War film/Drama
INTENDED AUDIENCE: Older teens and adults
RUNNING TIME: 127 minutes
STARRING: Samuel L. Jackson, Tommy Lee Jones, Guy Pearce, Ben Kingsley, Bruce Greenwood, Anne Archer, Blair Underwood, Philip Baker Hall, and Dale Dye
DIRECTOR: William Friedkin
PRODUCERS: Richard D. Zanuck and Scott Rudin
EXECUTIVE PRODUCERS: Adam Schroeder and James Webb
WRITER: Stephen Gaghan
DISTRIBUTOR: Paramount Pictures
BRIEF SUMMARY:
In the military drama *Rules of Engagement*, Tommy Lee Jones plays a Marine attorney whom Samuel L. Jackson's Marine colonel chooses to defend when he is put on trial for a rescue mission that goes terribly wrong. The excitement seldom flags in this thrilling drama that intelligently explores the moral dilemmas American soldiers sometimes face when they serve their country in tense and often excruciating combat situations.

Rules of Engagement is a tailor-made movie for the powerhouse acting talents of Tommy Lee Jones of *The Fugitive*, Samuel L. Jackson of *Pulp Fiction*, and Guy Pearce of *L.A. Confidential*. *Rules of Engagement* has a strong moral worldview that honors the United States military and the people who serve in it. This is a very patriotic American movie that still manages to communicate universal themes that transcend any one country. Director William Friedkin deserves a lot of credit for how well this movie is made, as does screenwriter Stephen Gaghan. Some Muslim groups, however, may be upset by some of the content. Regrettably, also, the movie contains more than seventy-five strong obscenities and profanities and some very violent combat footage, though it's not as intense as *Saving Private Ryan*. Such content naturally requires extreme caution.

CONTENT ANALYSIS: (BB, PP, FR, LLL, VVV, AA, M) Moral worldview with patriotic elements that explores the moral dilemmas soldiers face in combat plus a few very brief references to Islamic religious slogans and Islamic terrorism; fifty-four mostly strong obscenities and twenty-six mostly strong profanities; very strong combat violence such as explosions and gunfire hitting bodies with blood spurting, plus bloody images of wounds and two men engage in brutal fistfight in a house; alcohol use and one scene of drunkenness; and villainous character hides evidence that would exonerate another man of a murder charge, but is defeated in the end, and another man lies to protect his career.

The Ripe Stuff

SPACE COWBOYS

Quality: ☆☆☆   Acceptability: –2

WARNING CODES:
  Language: * * *
  Violence: *
  Sex: None
  Nudity: *
RATING: PG-13
GENRE: Science fiction
INTENDED AUDIENCE: Teens and adults
RUNNING TIME: 130 minutes
STARRING: Clint Eastwood, Tommy Lee Jones, James Garner, Donald Sutherland, James Cromwell, Loren Dean, and William Devane
DIRECTOR: Clint Eastwood
PRODUCERS: Clint Eastwood and Andrew Lazar
EXECUTIVE PRODUCER: Tom Rooker
WRITERS: Ken Kaufman and Howard Klausner
DISTRIBUTOR: Warner Brothers
BRIEF SUMMARY:
Clint Eastwood directs *Space Cowboys*, in which he plays a former test pilot who, after forty years, finally gets a chance to go into space. He won't take it, however, unless he can surround himself with the only crew he trusts—a team of geriatric test pilots played by Tommy Lee Jones, James Garner, and Donald Sutherland.
Space Cowboys is another entertaining, fairly exciting movie from Clint Eastwood, although it is not among his best. Although laced with lots of foul language to cover the sentiment in the story with a macho sheen, the movie's tale of heroism and sacrifice has a symbolic Christian motif that gives it a mild Christian worldview. Regrettably, however, the foul language in the movie is enough to give it an extreme caution. Also, the movie makes no bones about the sexual interests of one of the team members. Despite this, *Space Cowboys* has a haunting final shot that adds much depth to the movie's moral theme of sacrifice. It also does great honor to the individuals who have given their lives to help develop America's space program. Their courage in the face of death enriches all our lives.

CONTENT ANALYSIS: (C, B, Pa, LLL, V, N, A, D, M) Mild Christian worldview with moral and pagan elements; seventy-five obscenities, seven strong profanities, and two mild profanities, plus young man vomits during wild plane ride; mild action violence including two fistfights, crashes in outer space, two men injured during crashes, and rockets blast off; a few sexual references; upper and rear male nudity during medical examinations with one man not shy about being fully nude in front of woman doctor; alcohol use; smoking; and miscellaneous immorality such as lying.

Little Tykes

THOMAS AND THE MAGIC RAILROAD

Quality: ☆☆   Acceptability: +1

WARNING CODES:
  Language: None
  Violence: *
  Sex: None
  Nudity: None
RATING: G
GENRE: Fantasy
INTENDED AUDIENCE: All ages
RUNNING TIME: 86 minutes
STARRING: Alec Baldwin, Peter Fonda, Mara Wilson, Didi Conn, Russell Means, Cody McMains, and the voice of John Bellis
DIRECTOR: Britt Allcroft
PRODUCER: Britt Allcroft
EXECUTIVE PRODUCERS: Brent Baum, Nancy Chapelle, Charles Falzon, and Barry London
WRITER: Britt Allcroft

BASED ON: The 1945 novel *The Three Railway Engines* by Rev. W. Awdry

DISTRIBUTOR: Destination Films

BRIEF SUMMARY:

Thomas and the Magic Railroad is a delightful little yarn for children. It tells the story of two worlds, a world with people and a world where trains, including the hero, Thomas the train, talk to each other. Traveling between these two worlds is Mr. Conductor, played by Alec Baldwin. Doll-sized, he has some magic gold dust that takes him between the worlds. Everyone must learn to work together to foil the evil plot of a diesel engine. Despite the low budget, the acting and direction in this movie are good, especially Alec Baldwin as Mr. Conductor. This is a whimsical Alec Baldwin that audiences have not seen before. Bravo!

Everyone in *Thomas and the Magic Railroad* learns many virtues. For instance, Mr. Conductor must learn not to give up, and another character must learn responsibility. Although there is a lot of magic, it is not the "you can become God" type of magic. The basic lesson is that "helping each other brings to life the magic in all of us." Children will enjoy *Thomas and the Magic Railroad*, but it is suggested that parents watch with their children to help them discern the best things the story is teaching.

CONTENT ANALYSIS: (B, Pa, V, M) Moral worldview with magical plot device; some violence including a diesel train engine with a mechanical shovel that attacks the other trains and people, people fall from great heights, and train falls from bridge; and dog gives human false information.

Sacrificial Love Is Tiggerific!

THE TIGGER MOVIE

Quality: ☆☆☆☆   Acceptability: +3

WARNING CODES:

Language: *

Violence: *

Sex: None

Nudity: None

RATING: G

GENRE: Animated comedy

INTENDED AUDIENCE: All ages

RUNNING TIME: 77 minutes

VOICES: John Hurt, Jim Cummings, Nikita Hopkins, Ken Sansom, John Fielder, Peter Cullen, Andre Stojka, Kath Soucie, and Tom Attenborough

DIRECTOR: Jun Falkenstein

PRODUCER: Cheryl Abood

WRITER: Jun Falkenstein

BASED ON: Characters created by A. A. Milne

DISTRIBUTOR: Walt Disney/Buena Vista/Walt Disney Company

BRIEF SUMMARY:

The Tigger Movie recaptures the cuddly spirit of Walt Disney's three featurettes about Winnie the Pooh and his friends, made in 1966, 1968, and 1974. In this, the first feature-length motion picture set in the Hundred Acre Wood, Tigger goes searching for his "gigantical, stripedy" family tree. He is sad that he doesn't have any other tiggers to go bouncing with him. His friends go out of their way to help him, but their efforts end in failure. Finally, a test of their friendship shows everyone what true caring really means.

The Tigger Movie is a fun picture that will not disappoint most fans of the *Winnie the Pooh* stories or the earlier *Winnie the Pooh* movies by Disney. Director Jun Falkenstein, who also wrote the script for *The Tigger Movie*, has taken great care in delineating Milne's famous characters. Their strengths and foibles drive the basic storyline and enrich the details. The voice talent also performs well. Best of all, the movie teaches the importance of having caring friends. There is even a message of sacrificial Christian love imbedded in the story. As Tigger himself might say, "That's tiggerific!"

CONTENT ANALYSIS: (BBB, C, L, V, M) Strong moral worldview with

Christian elements of caring, sacrifice, and friendship; one use of the word "heck" by Tigger; very mild slapstick violence (mostly pratfalls and near misses) plus mildly scary scene with big avalanche; and Tigger imagines meeting hundreds of other tiggers, including a Marilyn Monroe type whose skirt blows up like in the famous Monroe scene from *The Seven Year Itch* and including some female tiggers acting as dancing girls in old Hollywood-style musicals, but nothing really salacious.

Taking the High Road

A TIME FOR DRUNKEN HORSES

Quality: ☆☆☆☆   Acceptability: +2

WARNING CODES:
  Language: None
  Violence: *
  Sex: None
  Nudity: None

RATING: Not rated
GENRE: Drama
INTENDED AUDIENCE: All ages
RUNNING TIME: 80 minutes
LANGUAGE: Farsi
STARRING: Ayoub Ahmadi, Rojin Younessi, Amaneh Ekhtiar-dini, and Madi Ekhtiar-dini
DIRECTOR: Bahman Ghobadi
PRODUCER: Bahman Ghobadi
WRITER: Bahman Ghobadi
DISTRIBUTOR: Shooting Gallery Films
BRIEF SUMMARY:
A Time for Drunken Horses is a poor title for an incredibly powerful, moral movie about a Kurdish boy living on the border between Iran and Iraq who must battle incredible odds to save the life of his handicapped brother. A Cannes Film Festival award winner, the story focuses on little Ayoub, the eldest brother of a family of five siblings. Both he and his sister, Ameneh, care for their dwarf brother, Madi, who needs an operation. For a small payment, they will do anything, including carrying gigantic loads across cold mountains. Eventually, Ayoub decides to cross the mountains to sell the mule for his brother's operation. The caravan is ambushed, and the mules are too drunk to go forward. Abandoned by everyone, Ayoub puts Madi on his back and forges ahead through the landmine-strewn border in the face of terrible odds.

A Time for Drunken Horses is incredible storytelling. These people are not only real, but the director captures the reality of their life without any histrionics. The movie is beautifully filmed; lyrical, yet intense. These children continue to make moral choices. Even surrounded by harsh circumstances and barbaric people, they insist on doing the right thing. When Ayoub's sister cries out to God for healing for her brother, it captures the essence of the human condition.

CONTENT ANALYSIS: (BBB, V, A, M) Moral worldview; one slap, one scuffle between smugglers, sounds of machine gunfire, father comes home dead on the back of a mule, and little dwarf receives injections; alcohol fed to mules to help them survive the cold of winter and crossing the mountain passes; and little boy learns how to survive in a very difficult world where people lie and cheat but he remains honest.

Discovering a Higher Purpose

TITAN A.E.

Quality: ☆☆☆☆   Acceptability: +1

WARNING CODES:
  Language: None
  Violence: * *
  Sex: None
  Nudity: *

RATING: PG
GENRE: Animated science fiction
INTENDED AUDIENCE: Older children and adults

RUNNING TIME: 98 minutes

VOICES: Matt Damon, Drew Barrymore, Bill Pullman, Nathan Lane, Tone-Loc, John Leguizamo, Janeane Garofalo, and Ron Perlman

DIRECTORS: Don Bluth, Gary Goldman, and Art Vitello

PRODUCERS: Don Bluth, Gary Goldman, and David Kirschner

EXECUTIVE PRODUCER: Paul Gertz

WRITERS: Ben Edlund, John August, and Joss Whedon

BASED ON: The story by Hans Bauer and Randall McCormick

DISTRIBUTOR: 20th Century Fox

BRIEF SUMMARY:

Titan A.E., an animated science fiction movie for older children, tells the story of a young man who takes on the challenge of saving the human race from a legion of evil energy creatures. In the year 3028, the Drej, a legion of creatures consisting of pure energy, destroy the Earth. A professor narrowly escapes this destruction on the *Titan A.E.*, a ship holding enough DNA to create a new Earth. Fifteen years later, his son must find the hidden *Titan*, with the map encoded in his hand. Knowing he is the only one who can find the *Titan* before the Drej destroy it, he takes on the challenge to save the human race.

Titan A.E. is a redemptive story that takes elements of danger, action, romance, and comedy and uses them to create a world a thousand years from now. A couple of these elements may not be suitable for smaller children. Like *The Road to El Dorado*, this animated feature contains rear male nudity and some romantic situations. The movie's fight scenes are fairly tame, but contain some incidents of characters being wounded and hurt. The *Titan* spaceship is a type of Noah's Ark, containing the DNA from every Earth creature. The movie's positive qualities as a moral, heroic tale make this science fiction movie an action adventure that many will find entertaining.

CONTENT ANALYSIS: (CC, BB, Ro, Pa, V, N, MM) Strong redemptive worldview where character fights to save the human race, and many moral elements including man tries to save enemy, man makes solid friendships and risks life for friends, but characters have an idealistic view of Earth before it was destroyed and no acknowledgement of the Creator; moderate action violence, such as exchanges of gunfire, bug creature gets shot with depicted ooze remaining, ship explodes, many other explosions, guard is zapped several times, man pounds fists against walls, man dreams of being shot, woman shot in arm with brief depiction of blood, and man twists alien's neck, killing him; some mildly sensual moments; rear male nudity and woman shown in a towel; and lying, deceit, and bribery.

Redemptive Heroics

U-571

Quality: ☆☆☆☆   Acceptability: −1

WARNING CODES:
  Language: * * *
  Violence: * *
  Sex: None
  Nudity: None

RATING: PG-13

GENRE: War drama

INTENDED AUDIENCE: Teens and adults

RUNNING TIME: 115 minutes

STARRING: Matthew McConaughey, Harvey Keitel, Bill Paxton, Jon Bon Jovi, Jake Weber, and David Keith

DIRECTOR: Jonathan Mostow

PRODUCERS: Dino De Laurentiis and Martha De Laurentiis

EXECUTIVE PRODUCER: Hal Lieberman

WRITERS: Jonathan Mostow, Sam Montgomery, and David Ayer

DISTRIBUTOR: Universal Pictures

BRIEF SUMMARY:

The movie *U-571* is a rousing submarine movie about a group of American sailors who commandeer a damaged German submarine with an important decoding machine and must get safely back to England. Matthew McConaughey delivers an intense and strongly heroic yet vulnerable performance as the lieutenant who takes command in tragic circumstances. Although his character has a very bad habit of using some strong profanity, his performance is unforgettable as he leads the sailors through hostile waters to England.

This movie deftly returns a more old-fashioned and ultimately more honorable spirit to the World War II movie, even when compared to *Saving Private Ryan*. It also contains some redemptive elements. At one point, for instance, the Americans must release the body of one of their own dead men to fool a German battleship. "His body is gonna save our lives," one of the characters tells the other men. Adding to this redemptive worldview is the movie's tasteful but exciting use of wartime violence. Hence, this movie is truly a welcome relief, except for the PG-13 rated foul language. This regrettable aspect of the movie includes fourteen strong profanities. Though these profanities are exclamatory, they are really quite gratuitous.

CONTENT ANALYSIS: (CC, BBB, PP, LLL, VV, M) Redemptive worldview with strong moral elements including someone says "Godspeed" and patriotic elements; thirty-three obscenities, fourteen profanities, wartime violence, with many tense moments, explosions, gunfights, hand-to-hand combat, and National Socialist (Nazi) sailors murder survivors on raft, but movie cuts away from most of the gory details; a couple of mild verbal references to sailors sharing intimate moments with women while on shore leave; and Nazi sailors carry out Hitler's orders to murder all survivors of naval campaigns and panicked American sailor violates chain of command but is properly rebuked.

Dedication, Not Deceit

WHAT WOMEN WANT

Quality: ☆☆☆   Acceptability: −2

WARNING CODES:

  Language: * *

  Violence: *

  Sex: *

  Nudity: *

RATING: PG-13

GENRE: Romantic comedy

INTENDED AUDIENCE: Teens and adults

RUNNING TIME: 120 minutes

STARRING: Mel Gibson, Helen Hunt, Marisa Tomei, Bette Midler, and Alan Alda

DIRECTOR: Nancy Meyers

PRODUCERS: Susan Cartsonis, Bruce Davey, Gina Matthews, Nancy Meyers, and Matt Williams

EXECUTIVE PRODUCERS: Carmen Finestra, Stephen McEveety, and David McFadzean

WRITERS: Josh Goldsmith, Cathy Yuspa, and Diane Drake

DISTRIBUTOR: Paramount Pictures

BRIEF SUMMARY:

What Women Want, starring Mel Gibson as Nick and Helen Hunt as Darcy, tells the story of a man who accidentally receives the ability to hear what women are thinking. Nick is a chauvinistic advertising executive. When he accidentally receives the ability to hear what women are thinking, he tries to rid himself of the ability, but later embraces it, realizing that he can further his career by taking Darcy's thoughts and stating them as his own ideas before she even utters a word.

What Women Want considers the consequences of being able to "hear" what others are thinking. In many scenes, the man uses this ability for his personal benefit, leading to conniving and deceit. Yet there are other instances where he uses it to help others, including an unnoticed girl with suicidal thoughts. Eventually the experience changes the man, not only romantically, but relationally as well. This movie's strong moral resolution is regrettably marred, however, by elements of foul language, sexual references, and implied sex. These and the movie's inability to develop certain characters make the ending not as strong as it could have been. *What Women Want* is a funny movie that uses some questionable elements to tell the morality tale of a man who changes for the better.

CONTENT ANALYSIS: (BB, PaPa, O, LL, V, S, N, A, DD, M) Mostly moral worldview of a chauvinistic man who learns how to be caring toward women, with some pagan elements of eclectic behavior in relationships and mild occult element of man obtaining gift, possibly from God, of being able to hear what women are thinking; thirteen obscenities, three profanities, four exclamatory profanities, and some sexual terminology; mild violence including man slips and falls, man gets electrocuted, woman slaps man, and woman has suicidal thoughts; some sexual references, implied fornication, couple shown in bed after sex, sexual gesture, woman describes man as a "sex god," implied impotence, heavy kissing, and girl thinks about losing her virginity on prom night; obscured male nudity, women in lingerie, showgirl outfits that reveal cleavage; alcohol use; smoking, marijuana use and depicted prescription drugs intended for suicide; and man tries on various products for women including pantyhose, nail polish, etc., and girl's estranged relationship with father restored.

Kickin' It, Mutant Style

X-MEN

Quality: ☆☆☆   Acceptability: −1

WARNING CODES
  Language: * *
  Violence: * *
  Sex: None
  Nudity: *
RATING: PG
GENRE: Science fiction
INTENDED AUDIENCE: Teens and young adults
RUNNING TIME: 95 minutes
STARRING: Patrick Stewart, Ian McKellen, Halle Berry, Famke Janssen, James Marsden, Bruce Davison, Rebecca Romijn-Stamos, Ray Park, and Anna Paquin
DIRECTOR: Bryan Singer
PRODUCERS: Lauren Shuler Donner and Ralph Winter
EXECUTIVE PRODUCERS: Avi Arad, Stan Lee, Richard Donner, and Tom DeSanto
WRITER: David Hayter
BASED ON: The Marvel Comic Book series
DISTRIBUTOR: 20th Century Fox
BRIEF SUMMARY:
X-Men is the classic comic tale of the conflicts between two groups of genetically enhanced humans, aka mutants, and normal people. A young man named Erik, later Magneto, learns hatred in a 1944 concentration camp, a hatred he turns against the human race. Magneto believes that mankind and mutantkind can never be at peace. Meanwhile, Professor Charles Xavier bands together a group of mutants called the X-Men to use their powers to help mankind. Meanwhile, humans have developed a strong fear of mutants.

X-Men could have turned into a politically correct diatribe. Instead, some mutants are bad and some are good, while some humans are bad and some are good. There are a lot of moral lessons, including the unconditional forgiveness Professor X shows to his old friend Magneto, in the hopes that he will turn from his evil ways. Regrettably, *X-Men* is strongly evolutionary, which allows no room for true compassion and, in that sense, is contradictory. Furthermore, the movie has a humanist worldview with many moral, redemptive elements but also with some foul language and some questionable comments made about God. Even so, *X-Men* has many moral elements that can be culled from it with media wisdom.

CONTENT ANALYSIS: (HH, BB, C, EE, Ab, LL, VV, M) Humanist worldview with many moral and redemptive elements including forgiveness and self-sacrifice, with a strong conflicting evolutionary focus and some demeaning comments made about "God-fearing" people in specific and God in general; ten obscenities; strong action violence with man threatened with gun, man threatens people with adamantium retractable claws, car crashes, man gets thrown out of vehicle, man accidentally impales young girl with adamantium retractable claws, cage fighting, and lengthy scenes of violence between mutants; young people kiss; Mystique character is basically nude except for a coat of blue paint and some scales; and villain displays hatred toward others.

☆☆☆ THE BEST 2000 FILMS FOR FAMILIES ☆☆☆

Headline	Title
Exquisitely Woven Redemptive Masterpiece	*The Basket*
Egg-cellent Moral Comedy	*Chicken Run*
Victory on the Field and in the Heart	*Remember the Titans*
Poignant Pup	*My Dog Skip*
Getting in Touch with Your Outer Child	*Disney's The Kid*
Unconditional Love Defeats Selfishness	*The Emperor's New Groove*
Sacrificial Love Is Tiggerific!	*The Tigger Movie*
Discovering a Higher Purpose	*Titan A.E.*
Powerful Parable	*Mercy Streets*
The Joy of Christmas Offers Hope and Redemption	*How the Grinch Stole Christmas*

☆☆☆ THE BEST 2000 FILMS FOR MATURE AUDIENCES ☆☆☆

Headline	Title
Soul-Searching Warfare	*The Patriot*
Redemptive Allegory	*Return to Me*
Exploring Moral Dilemmas	*Rules of Engagement*
Redemptive Heroics	*U-571*
Heart-Rending Moral Themes	*The Family Man*
Heroism and Endurance	*Return with Honor*
Touching the Face of God	*The Legend of Bagger Vance*
A Quest for Redemption	*Mission: Impossible 2 (M:I-2)*
Overcoming Oppression	*East-West*
Searching for Salvation	*George Washington*

☆☆☆ THE TWENTY MOST UNBEARABLE FILMS OF 2000 ☆☆☆

Headline	Title
Worst Scientology Propaganda	*Battlefield Earth*
Worst Political Propaganda	*The Contender*
Worst Attempt to Demonize Our Children	*Little Nicky*
Worst Horror-Comedy	*Scary Movie*
Worst Calling Evil Good	*Quills*
Worst Neo-Marxist Movie	*Dancer in the Dark*
Worst One World Movie	*The Art of War*
Worst Hippy Movie	*The Beach*
Worst Horror Movie	*Blair Witch 2: Book of Shadows*
Worst Anarchic	*Cecil B. Demented*
Worst Evil Assault on Beauty	*The Cell*
Worst Anti-Christian Movie	*Cotton Mary*
Worst Comedy	*Drowning Mona*
Worst Stoner Movie	*Dude, Where's My Car?*
Worst Paganism	*Dungeons and Dragons*
Worst Psychic	*The Gift*
Worst Anti-Semitic Movie	*Kadosh*
Worst Perverse Movie	*Lies*
Worst Sci-Fi	*Mission to Mars*
Worst of the Worst of 2000	*Whipped*

Pathetic, Anti-Human Storytelling

A.I.

Quality: ✩✩✩   Acceptability: −4

WARNING CODES:

Language: *
Violence: ***
Sex: *
Nudity: *

RATING: PG-13
GENRE: Science fiction
INTENDED AUDIENCE: Older teens and adults
RUNNING TIME: 146 minutes
STARRING: Haley Joel Osment, Frances O'Connor, Jude Law, William Hurt, and Sam Robards
VOICES: Jack Angel, Meryl Streep, and Robin Williams
DIRECTOR: Steven Spielberg
PRODUCERS: Kathleen Kennedy, Steven Spielberg, and Bonnie Curtis
EXECUTIVE PRODUCERS: Ian Harlan and Walter Parkes
WRITER: Steven Spielberg
BASED ON: The short story "Supertoys Last All Summer Long" by Brian Aldiss
DISTRIBUTOR: Warner Brothers
BRIEF SUMMARY:

The protagonist in *A.I.*, Steven Spielberg's science fiction remake of the fairy tale *Pinocchio*, is a child robot named David, played by Haley Joel Osment of *The Sixth Sense*. A test couple is given David so that he can replace their sick real child, Martin, who's been frozen to wait for a life-giving cure. When Martin suddenly is cured, David accidentally endangers the mother, Monica, and Martin. David is scheduled to be taken apart and remade, but Monica can't bear to see that happen, so she abandons him in the forest and tells him to run away. There begins a lengthy series of fantastic, often disturbing, adventures where David tries to find out how he can become real, like Pinocchio did, so that his mother, Monica, can really love him.

A.I. is a visually dazzling, fairly entertaining, provocative work. It has a number of storytelling flaws, however, and a number of moral, philosophical, and spiritual flaws. The storytelling flaws prevent *A.I.* from becoming the truly entertaining, uplifting movie it wants to be. The other flaws make *A.I.* an ultimately abhorrent movie for committed Christians and other people who take the Bible, as the Word of God, seriously.

CONTENT ANALYSIS: (PaPa, EE, FRFR, HH, AbAb, PC, B, L, VVV, S, A, M) Solid pagan worldview with an alarmist environmentalism in a setting that diminishes God by including false religious notions and strong atheism that says that prayer does not work and God is probably not there, plus much talk about the need for love and a nurturing mother figure; at least one strong profanity and at least seven mild profanities; disturbing and scary scenes of violence such as scissors almost poke person's eye out, boy takes knife to child android's fleshy arm, boy nearly drowns, woman abandons child android, mechanical robots with human faces and/or limbs tortured and violently ripped apart or melted or burned, gunfire, implied murder as blood pools near woman corpse's head, and motorcycles with scary, snarling wolf faces; implied sexual activity by "gigolo" robot with human clients and gigolo robot entices young males with sexy holographic image of woman in lingerie, including posing image over one man's crotch; naturalistic nudity of male children, and professor orders female android to strip; alcohol use; and man apparently frames robot for murder, totalitarian government, and satire of man using religious reasons for a pro-human life stance.

Punch-Drunk

ALI

Quality: ☆   Acceptability: −2

WARNING CODES:
  Language: ***
  Violence: ***
  Sex: **
  Nudity: *
RATING: R
GENRE: Drama/Biography
INTENDED AUDIENCE: Teens and adults
RUNNING TIME: 152 minutes
STARRING: Will Smith, Jon Voight, Jamie Foxx, Mario Van Peebles, Ron Silver, and Mykelti Williamson
DIRECTOR: Michael Mann
PRODUCERS: Michael Mann, Jon Peters, Paul Ardaji, A. Kitman Ho, and James Lassiter
EXECUTIVE PRODUCERS: Howard Bingham, Graham King, and Lee Caplin
WRITERS: Eric Roth and Michael Mann
DISTRIBUTOR: Columbia Pictures/Sony
BRIEF SUMMARY:
Ali is a mess. *Ali* claims to tell the story of boxer Muhammed Ali, up to his fight with George Forman, when he regained his title. The movie is as punch-drunk as the ex-fighter became in his later years. *Ali* opens with young Cassius Clay encountering a gruesome newspaper photo of a lynched black man. Cassius works out with his boxing equipment and fights the undefeated Sonny Liston. The movie shows the controversies that followed Cassius when he decided to join the Black Muslims, changed his name, and refused to be drafted. Somewhere in all this, Ali befriends sportscaster Howard Cosell, gets divorced several times, and goes to Africa, where he meets Idi Amin, the leader who literally cannibalized his people. Finally, Ali beats up George Foreman, and the movie ends.

Ali is a tedious, boring, poorly edited example of bad filmmaking. Will Smith is okay as Muhammed Ali, but he does not have the charisma the real Ali had. Jon Voight has Howard Cosell's mannerisms down, but is too low key. Of course, there is plenty of boxing violence and some sexual immorality, but the movie forgets, or else edited out so as not to inflame people, the racist comments Ali often made about "white devils" when he converted to Islam.

CONTENT: (PaPa, FRFR, HH, PCPC, AbAb, C, B, LLL, VVV, SS, N, AA, D, M) Confused, eclectic, pointless worldview with much Muslim content, some anti-Muslim contents, much humanist content, some anti-Christian and anti-Jewish comments, some pro-Christian comments, some pro-black power comments, some anti-black power comments; twenty-two obscenities, four profanities, and one pointed blasphemy; lots of boxing violence with the now-overused *Rocky* effects of slow-motion punches combined with appropriate sound effects, some non-boxing violence including man slaps around his friend, Malcolm X gets shot several times at point-blank range, and rioting on the streets and rioting on TV, with cars burning and people beaten up; several scenes of fornication, serial marriages, and adultery, with Ali admitting that his weakness as a Muslim is his attraction to women; men in boxing trunks; drinking sometimes to get drunk; smoking; and much discussion of Islam, much ridicule of other people, positive portraits of Mobutu and Idi Amin, the man who literally cannibalized the people of Uganda in Africa, and unnecessary scene of Muhammed Ali going into cockpit of aircraft.

Web of Intrigue

ALONG CAME A SPIDER

Quality: ✰✰✰   Acceptability: –2

WARNING CODES:
  Language: * *
  Violence: * *
  Sex: None
  Nudity: None
RATING: R
GENRE: Suspense/Thriller
INTENDED AUDIENCE: Adults
RUNNING TIME: 103 minutes
STARRING: Morgan Freeman, Monica Potter, Michael Wincott, and Mika Boorem
  DIRECTOR: Lee Tamahori
  PRODUCERS: David Brown and Joe Wizan
  EXECUTIVE PRODUCERS: Morgan Freeman and Marty Hornstein
  WRITER: Marc Moss
  BASED ON: The novel by James Patterson
  DISTRIBUTOR: Paramount Pictures
  BRIEF SUMMARY:
  In *Along Came a Spider*, Morgan Freeman returns as Dr. Alex Cross, from the best-selling James Patterson novel. Cross, a retired police detective, teams with Secret Service Agent Jezzie Flannigan to match wits with a diabolical criminal in an apparent kidnapping case. Seeking redemption from previous failures, the hero and heroine join to fight their adversary, who is intent on committing "the crime of the century."
  Along Came a Spider may thrill audiences with its twists and turns and compelling characters. Freeman as Dr. Cross, Monica Potter as Agent Flannigan, Mika Boorem as the kidnapped girl, and Michael Wincott as the villain work well

together to create a suspenseful story. Unlike the first movie featuring Dr. Cross, *Kiss the Girls,* director Lee Tamahori and screenwriter Marc Moss take the best from the novel and throw in some surprises. *Along Came a Spider* includes some strong foul language and dark subject matter, however, that deserve a strong caution. Thus, although its moral worldview contains many scenes of courage and bravery as officers attempt to rescue a young abducted girl and protect others, its web of intrigue requires a finely tuned sense of media wisdom.
  CONTENT ANALYSIS: (BB, LL, VV, D, M) Moral worldview with many scenes of courage and bravery as officers attempt to rescue a young abducted girl and protect others; one profanity, six strong obscenities, five mild obscenities, and man caresses policewoman's leg while demanding crude sex (nothing happens, as police interrupt); some solid action violence such as automobile crash with brief bloody face shown, numerous deaths (including five shootings, one strangulation, and two fall from bridge), woman stabs man in leg in self-defense, and man uses taser gun to shock woman; man propositions policewoman; adults smoke; and child drugged and abducted as well as several scenes of child in imminent danger, theft, betrayal, and killer argues, "Forgiving yourself is one thing you cannot do."

Because of Our Past

AN AMERICAN RHAPSODY

Quality: ✰✰✰   Acceptability: –1

WARNING CODES:
  Language: *
  Violence: *
  Sex: None
  Nudity: None
RATING: PG-13
GENRE: Biographical drama

INTENDED AUDIENCE: Teens and adults

RUNNING TIME: 106 minutes

STARRING: Scarlett Johansson, Nastassja Kinski, Tony Goldwyn, Balazs Galko, and Zsuzsa Czinkoczi

DIRECTOR: Eva Gardos

PRODUCERS: Colleen Camp and Bonnie Timmermann

EXECUTIVE PRODUCERS: Jay Firestone, Adam Haight, and Andrew G. Vajna

WRITER: Eva Gardos

DISTRIBUTOR: Paramount Pictures Classics

BRIEF SUMMARY:

An American Rhapsody tells the autobiographical tale of a young girl in Communist Hungary who was separated from her parents, who had to leave her behind for several years so they could escape to freedom in the United States. Though low budget, this movie is a remarkable ode to those who braved death to flee to America.

Suzanne is a baby when her parents escape, inadvertently leaving her behind in Communist Hungary. Suzanne stays with foster parents until her parents find a way to bring her to America. When she arrives, she is homesick for her foster parents and wants to go back to Hungary. This leads to family tensions, which explode when she becomes a teenager. Eventually she returns to Hungary, where she learns about the horrors of Communism and what home really is.

Being a true story, the plot is slightly convoluted, but the power of *An American Rhapsody* lies in the characterizations. Scarlett Johansson as the teenage Suzanne gives a great performance until the movie nears its end, when she has to change from the rebellious teenager to the loving daughter. Nastassja Kinski, as her real mother, gives the performance of a lifetime. With only four lightweight obscenities, limited kisses, drinking, and obscured violence, *An American Rhapsody* is a remarkable ode to those who braved

death to flee to America. It is a message to all Americans to help us appreciate just how precious freedom is.

CONTENT ANALYSIS: (BBB, ACA-CAC, C, L, V, AA, D, M) Moral worldview with a strong anti-Communist perspective and redemptive elements; four light obscenities and two positive appeals to God; brief violence, including girl shoots gun at door, but repents, man shot by soldier in flashback sequence, escape through barbwire fence, with man cutting woman's hair to facilitate escape; kissing, tight clothes; lots of teenage drinking (condemned); lots of smoking; and girl rebels against mother but repents, Communists seize several homes, woman lies to Communist police to protect her children, grandmother takes child from foster parents, and child is reunited with true parents.

Clash of Worldviews

ATLANTIS: THE LOST EMPIRE

Quality: ☆☆☆   Acceptability: −1

WARNING CODES:
  Language: None
  Violence: **
  Sex: None
  Nudity: *

RATING: PG

GENRE: Animated action/Adventure

INTENDED AUDIENCE: Older children and adults

RUNNING TIME: 95 minutes

VOICES: Michael J. Fox, James Garner, Leonard Nimoy, Cree Summer, John Mahoney, David Ogden Stiers, Claudia Christian, Corey Burton, Don Novello , Phil Morris, Jim Varney, Jacqueline Obradors, and Florence Stanley

DIRECTORS: Gary Trousdale and Kirk Wise

PRODUCER: Don Hahn

ASSOCIATE PRODUCER: Kendra Haaland

WRITER: Tab Murphy
DISTRIBUTOR: Walt Disney Pictures
BRIEF SUMMARY:

The animated *Atlantis: The Lost Empire* is a unique blend of art, music, story, and characterization. The story follows Milo Thatch, a slightly naïve linguistics expert, and a colorful band of explorers. Milo's quest leads them to the depths of the ocean floor to find an ancient civilization that, at the height of its glory, was swept away without a trace by a giant tidal wave thousands of years ago.

Atlantis overwhelms the imagination with its sometimes stunning visual and auditory impact and with plenty of action. Voice, writing, and artistic talent combine to engage the audience. The depth of the characters adds to its emotional power. The movie teaches the value of honor, compassion, and relationships. A solid moral tone pervades much of the film, which also includes a crucial scene where the hero appears to pray. Regrettably, the movie also borrows from some occult, pagan theories about Atlantis being an advanced civilization powered by special energy crystals that the people worshiped. This gives the movie a confused, pluralistic worldview. This is another sign of the pluralistic paganism of our age, which tries so hard not to offend the sensibilities of non-Christians.

CONTENT ANALYSIS: (Pa, OO, BB, VV, M) Eclectic, purposely vague, pagan/pluralistic worldview that combines occult elements regarding the myth of Atlantis (including some of the occult trance "messages" from the so-called "sleeping prophet," Edgar Cayce) with moral, religious elements, including hero appears to pray before taking a "leap of faith," and ethical values are emphasized, such as keeping one's word, right and wrong action, teamwork, compassion, the importance of one's family and cultural legacy, and comments against human greed; one "fool" on screen in translation of Atlantean language, one "geez," and one man says, "Lord, give me strength," when another character does a silly behavior; solid cartoon action violence, such as huge mechanical sea monster attacks submarines and escape pods fire back with explosive torpedoes, fireflies burn property, threats with guns, lava threatens people, and climactic chase scene with gunfire from the villains and energy weapons from small flying vehicles; implied romance developing between hero and heroine; brief naturalistic nudity when man swims, some scant clothing on heroine when she swims, and woman wears low-cut seductive dress; and attempted theft, greed, and betrayal rebuked.

The Darker Side of Genius

A BEAUTIFUL MIND

Quality: ☆☆☆☆   Acceptability: −1

WARNING CODES:
  Language: *
  Violence: **
  Sex: *
  Nudity: None
RATING: PG-13
GENRE: Drama
INTENDED AUDIENCE: Older teens and adults
RUNNING TIME: 125 minutes
STARRING: Russell Crowe, Ed Harris, Jennifer Connelly, and Paul Bettany
DIRECTOR: Ron Howard
PRODUCERS: Brian Grazer and Ron Howard
EXECUTIVE PRODUCERS: Todd Hallowell and Karen Kehela
WRITER: Akiva Goldsman
BASED ON: The book by Sylvia Nasar
DISTRIBUTOR: Universal Pictures

BRIEF SUMMARY:

A Beautiful Mind tells the true story of Dr. John Nash, diagnosed as a paranoid-schizophrenic, who won a Nobel Prize for his work on game theory. Masterfully directed and well acted, this movie compellingly portrays the journey every person must take in the dark valley of conformity to find God's purposes for his or her life.

When Carnegie Scholarship genius John Nash enters Princeton in 1947, he is brilliant, arrogant, and rude. John's friends tell him that math will never lead to higher truth, but John wants to make his life count. One night in a bar while watching coeds, John comes up with a "game theory" that flies in the face of conventional wisdom. His findings earn him a prestigious job. Eventually the government asks John to decode Russian radio communications, but then John becomes delusional, and is hospitalized with mental illness. With his wife's help, John begins the slow road to recovery. When scholars latch onto his earlier writings, John receives the Nobel Prize. Softened by his experiences, John humbly receives his prize, acknowledging the sacrificial support of his wife.

A Beautiful Mind is a masterpiece. With typical, heart-gripping direction by Ron Howard *(Apollo 13)*, and with the broad acting skills of Russell Crowe, who must age from a college kid to an old man, the movie is masterfully presented. This is a cleverly portrayed but sobering look into the mindset of the mentally ill, and demonstrates the healing power of love.

CONTENT ANALYSIS: (BB, C, Ro, H, Ab, LL, VV, S, AA, D, M) Solid moral worldview contains redemptive and romantic elements as wife lays her life down in ultimate commitment to her mentally ill husband; some humanist worldview elements; eleven obscenities, seven strong profanities, and six mild profanities, as well as several instances of joking about fornication; a few violent scenes include protagonist

throwing desk through window, a car chase/shoot-out with bad guys, bloody wounds shown, man gets shock therapy, and footage of atomic bomb exploding; bed scene where wife makes sexual advances toward husband under covers, college boy speculating about fornication, and protagonist tries to pick up co-ed; alcohol use and abuse depicted, smoking depicted; and theme of mental illness portrayed with disturbing scenes of father leaving baby in tub too long, multiple delusions, shock treatments, and mockery by outsiders.

It Could Have Been

BLACK HAWK DOWN

Quality: ☆☆☆　　　　Acceptability: −3

WARNING CODES:
　Language: ***
　Violence: ***
　Sex: None
　Nudity: *
RATING: R
GENRE: War drama
INTENDED AUDIENCE: Older teens and adults
RUNNING TIME: 143 minutes
STARRING: Josh Hartnett, Ewan McGregor, Tom Sizemore, Eric Bana, William Fichtner, Ewen Bremner, Sam Shepard, Jeremy Piven, and Ioan Gruffudd
DIRECTOR: Ridley Scott
PRODUCERS: Jerry Bruckheimer and Ridley Scott
EXECUTIVE PRODUCERS: Simon West, Mike Stenson, Chad Oman, and Branko Lustig
WRITER: Ken Nola
BASED ON: The book by Mark Bowden
DISTRIBUTOR: Columbia Pictures
BRIEF SUMMARY:

Black Hawk Down describes the U.S. military tragedy that happened in Somalia on 3 October 1993. General

Garrison sends in some troops to capture some key lieutenants of the Somalian warlord, whose clan had been starving and killing 300,000 of his fellow Somalians. The Clinton administration decides that they should not bring any heavy armament. The whole capital, Mogadishu, is armed to the teeth against the Americans. The soldiers deploy and are sitting ducks. The rest of the movie shows the acts of valor and bravery on the part of many men as they try to get out of Mogadishu.

The bloodshed in *Black Hawk Down* is extreme. There is also plenty of strong foul language. Despite superb acting and compelling moments, the filmmakers do not have the courage of their convictions. They refuse to turn into villains either the Muslims or the American politicians who sent men into harm's way without adequate firepower. Clearly, *Black Hawk Down* is supposed to be jingoistic, but it would have been nice if the filmmakers had relied less on you-are-there factual content and more on dramatic structure and storytelling, which includes pointing fingers and having villains.

CONTENT ANALYSIS: (BB, M) Solid moral worldview with acts of valor, loyalty, and sacrifice set against the backdrop of a corrupt Islamic culture; eighty-seven mostly strong obscenities and thirteen profanities; extreme wartime violence that will affect even the most desensitized, including man's legs blown off while man is still alive, man's hand blown off, man picks up hand, blood spurting in person's mouth and face, painful operations with no anesthetic, gruesome killings, shootings, maimings, beatings, several crowd scenes of Somalians beating Americans to death, and explosions; minor alcohol use and medical use of drugs; and smoking.

Honor Secures Liberty

BLACK KNIGHT

Quality: ★☆☆☆   Acceptability: −1

WARNING CODES:
Language: ***
Violence: **
Sex: *
Nudity: None

RATING: PG-13
GENRE: Comedy/Fantasy
INTENDED AUDIENCE: Teens and adults
RUNNING TIME: 101 minutes
STARRING: Martin Lawrence, Marsha Thomason, Tom Wilkinson, Vincent Regan, Kevin Conway, and Jeannette Weegar
DIRECTOR: Gil Junger
PRODUCERS: Arnon Milchan, Darryl J. Quarles, Michael Green, and Paul Schiff
EXECUTIVE PRODUCERS: Martin Lawrence, Jeffrey Kwatinetz, Peaches Davis, and Jack Brodsky
WRITERS: Darryl J. Quarles, Peter Gaulke, and Gerry Swallow
DISTRIBUTOR: 20th Century Fox
BRIEF SUMMARY:
Comedian Martin Lawrence stars in *Black Knight* as Jamal Walker, a black man from Los Angeles who mysteriously travels back in time to medieval England. Jamal falls in love with a black lady-in-waiting (a Moor from North Africa), poses as Jamal Skywalker, the messenger from a French duke, and becomes friends with a dissolute former knight with a drinking problem. Jamal discovers that the evil king of England has stolen his crown. He uses his twenty-first-century street smarts and modern-day sports moves to help his new friends. In return, Jamal learns the meaning of honor, courage, and integrity.

Martin Lawrence does a good job as the comical hero. It is fun to watch him play both the funnyman and the courageous, feisty hero. Tom Wilkinson also does a fine job as Sir Knolte, who, with Jamal's encouragement, regains his own honor as a former knight. The rest of the cast is also good. Director Gil Junger shows a very deft hand at filming both the comedic and action scenes. In all, *Black Knight* is a funny comedy that contains some touching, heroic moments, but is spoiled by foul language and sexual content.

CONTENT ANALYSIS: (Ro, BB, PC, Fe, Ho, LLL, VV, S, AA, M) Light romantic worldview with a strong moral premise about winning liberty by being courageous, persistent, honorable, and full of integrity, plus some political correctness, feminism, and mild homosexual jokes; thirty-nine obscenities and some toilet humor; comical and action violence such as man falls into water, pratfalls, horse chases man, implied beheading, attempted beheading, fighting, boxing, wrestling, man thrusts another man's face into horse manure, medieval battle, arrows pierce soldiers, sword fighting, and villain slightly cuts woman's throat; implied fornication and other sexual references, kissing, and man takes off his pants because he thinks woman wants to get into bed with him; shot from behind of woman baring her chest; drunkenness; and lying.

The Importance of Faith

THE BODY

Quality: ☆☆☆   Acceptability: +1

WARNING CODES:
  Language: *
  Violence: * *
  Sex: None
  Nudity: None
RATING: PG-13
GENRE: Drama/Thriller
INTENDED AUDIENCE: Teens and adults
RUNNING TIME: 100 minutes
STARRING: Antonio Banderas, Olivia Williams, John Shrapnel, and Derek Jacobi
DIRECTOR: Jonas McCord

PRODUCER: Rudy Cohen
EXECUTIVE PRODUCERS: Mark Damon, Moshe Diamant, Dianm Sillan Isaacs, and Werner Koenig
WRITER: Jonas McCord
BASED ON: The novel by Richard Ben Sapir
DISTRIBUTOR: Lions Gate Films/ TriStar
BRIEF SUMMARY:
Antonio Banderas stars in *The Body* as a Roman Catholic priest, Father Matt Gutierrez, who investigates the discovery of an ancient crucified body in Jerusalem that may or may not be the body of Jesus Christ. A top Vatican cardinal assigns Father Matt to investigate the reported finding of a crucified body in a walled-off section of a rich man's tomb in Jerusalem. Israeli officials force the female archaeologist, who discovered the body, to work with Father Matt as he investigates her findings before she can publish her paper on them. Hampering their investigation are some Jewish and Arab radicals who desperately want to find out what's going on for political and religious reasons. Violence eventually erupts.

The Body ultimately affirms Christian faith in the resurrection and deity of Jesus Christ. It even uses an important Bible verse to do so: "Blessed are those who have not seen and yet have believed" (John 20:29). There are, however, some elements that require caution. For instance, Father Matt's experience confirms his belief that God has no place whatsoever in politics. There is also some violence and a few obscenities. Finally, the ending also questions the Roman Catholic hierarchy. Even so, *The Body* is an exciting thriller that takes several edge-of-your-seat twists and turns until it arrives at a pro-Christian ending that affirms faith in the Christ's resurrection and deity.

CONTENT ANALYSIS: (CC, Ab, PC, FR, L, VV, D, M) Christian worldview marred by anti-clerical content and protagonist expresses vague support for liberation theology, plus some side characters express false religious notions; five obscenities; action violence including terrorists bomb village square as a diversion to steal an object, gunfire between villains and police, small chase scene, villains kidnap children to use as extortion, a couple of other explosions during gunfire, man beaten up and stoned, and man questions his faith and commits suicide; woman lightly kisses Catholic priest's hand and lips after injurious incident that makes him question his faith; brief alcohol use; smoking; and stealing and manipulation.

Too Shrill

CATS AND DOGS

Quality: ☆☆   Acceptability: −1

WARNING CODES:
  Language: *
  Violence: ***
  Sex: None
  Nudity: None
RATING: PG
GENRE: Fantasy
INTENDED AUDIENCE: Older children and adults
RUNNING TIME: 97 minutes
STARRING: Jeff Goldblum, Elizabeth Perkins, and Alexander Pollock
VOICES: Toby Maguire, Alec Baldwin, Susan Sarandon, Joe Pantoliano, Michael Clarke Duncan, and Jon Lovitz
DIRECTOR: Lawrence Guterman
PRODUCERS: Andrew Lazar, Chris Defaria, Warren Zide, and Craig Perry
EXECUTIVE PRODUCERS: Bruce Berman, Chris Bender, and J. C. Spink
WRITERS: John Requa and Glenn Ficarra
DISTRIBUTOR: Warner Brothers
BRIEF SUMMARY:
Cats and Dogs is a pitch looking for a story, where talking, sentient dogs try to protect humans from a bunch of talking cats led by the evil Mr. Tinkles. It starts out with an extended chase scene where, of course, cats and dogs are fighting like cats and dogs. The level of violence, however, is more intense than the classic cartoons of Hollywood's heyday. The plot thickens when the dogs and cats talk and when a group of cats catnap a key canine secret agent. The dog spies have been protecting the Brody family because Mr. Brody, played by Jeff Goldblum, is trying to find a cure for people's allergic reactions to dogs. The dogs realize that if he finds this cure, they can do a better job of protecting the humans from the evil cats. Meanwhile, Mr. Tinkles, a cat, is organizing his takeover of the world. He sends in a bunch of cats to destroy Mr. Brody's lab, which is only protected by a puppy. The plot goes on and on from there, punctuated by an increasing level of violence and a constant barrage of scatological humor.

Cats and Dogs suffers from predictable plot points, tired clichés, lack of character development, and over-the-top acting. Its violence and toilet humor is unacceptable for children under twelve.

CONTENT ANALYSIS: (EvEv, L, VVV, M) Anthropomorphic, evolutionary worldview featuring sentient cats and dogs; four exclamatory profanities and several verbal and visual vulgarities; dogs marking their territory, flatulence, dog sniffing, and dogs drinking from toilets; over-the-top cartoon violence with dog hitting its head against a tree, dog crashing through a window (twice), biting, scratching, very violent and ugly ninja cats, very violent and ugly Russian cat, exploding bone, cat grenade that sends out spikes that destroy room, bombs, ninja knives, cat abuses comatose man, cat abuses other cats, and factory explodes; and weak father figure.

Good Movie, Mate!

CROCODILE DUNDEE IN LOS ANGELES

Quality: ☆☆☆☆   Acceptability: −1

WARNING CODES:
  Language: * *
  Violence: *
  Sex: *
  Nudity: *
RATING: PG
GENRE: Comedy
INTENDED AUDIENCE: Older children and adults
RUNNING TIME: 95 minutes
STARRING: Paul Hogan, Linda Kozlowski, Jere Burns, Serge Cockburn, Paul Rodriguez, Alec Wilson, Jonathan Banks, and Aida Turturro
DIRECTOR: Simon Wincer
PRODUCERS: Lance Hool and Paul Hogan
EXECUTIVE PRODUCERS: Kathy Morgan, Steve Robbins, and Jim Reeve
WRITERS: Matthew Berry and Eric Abrams
BASED ON: Characters created by Paul Hogan
DISTRIBUTOR: Paramount Pictures
BRIEF SUMMARY:
Crocodile Dundee in Los Angeles sends the Australian crocodile hunter to Los Angeles with his family, where he runs into a host of funny escapades. Like the first movie on which it's based, *Crocodile Dundee in Los Angeles* starts in the Australian outback. Sue Charleton and Mick "Crocodile" Dundee live in Walkabout Creek with their nine-year-old son, Mikey. Sue's newspaper tycoon father asks her to fill in for the bureau chief of his Los Angeles outlet, who has died under suspicious circumstances. Mick thinks it's a good time to expose Mikey to the world outside Walkabout Creek. So the family packs their bags and heads for L.A., where Mick does the tourist thing and eventually becomes embroiled in Sue's investigation of her colleague's death.

Crocodile Dundee in Los Angeles is a highly entertaining addition to this series, and is probably tamer and more family friendly than the other two movies. If you like the character of Crocodile Dundee, you'll probably enjoy this movie immensely. It's like visiting an old friend who, though he may regale you with the same old stories, is still fun to be around. The movie contains some PG-rated material requiring a bit of caution, however. It also has a couple of minor worldview problems, but still manages to send a few positive messages along its very amiable way.

CONTENT ANALYSIS: (Ro, BB, Pa, Ho, LL, V, S, N, A, D) Romantic worldview with strong moral elements about fighting mean crooks, discovering truth, and protecting loved ones, plus a pagan reference to meditating for personal peace that turns into a joke, mystical Aboriginal power over animals, and lightweight, comic verbal references to homosexuality; twenty obscenities and the British vulgarity "bloody" and lizard dung; comic, adventure violence as bucolic hero battles huge crocodile and urban crooks, men hit with boards, man throws knife at villain to scare him, men wreck roof of car, and cars nearly crash; cohabitation without benefit of marriage but marriage is extolled at the end, and comments about physical attraction; brief upper male nudity and women wearing low-cut tops; alcohol use; smoking; and father tells boy to stay away from the pub after boy makes mildly crude remark about a woman's "nice" body.

One Giant Risk for Man

THE DISH

Quality: ☆☆☆   Acceptability: −1

WARNING CODES:
  Language: * *

Violence: None
Sex: None
Nudity: None

RATING: PG-13
GENRE: Comedy
INTENDED AUDIENCE: Teens and adults
RUNNING TIME: 104 minutes
STARRING: Sam Neill, Patrick Warburton, Kevin Harrington, Tom Long, Genevieve Mooy, Tayler Kane, and Bille Brown
DIRECTOR: Rob Sitch
PRODUCER: Michael Hirsh
WRITERS: Santo Cilauro, Tom Gleisner, Jane Kennedy, and Rob Sitch
DISTRIBUTOR: Warner Brothers
BRIEF SUMMARY:
The Dish was the largest grossing movie in Australia in the year it was released. The story is about the Australian crew of one of the two satellite dishes tracking *Apollo 11*, the first manned flight to land on the moon. Leading the crew is a man named Cliff, who's about to turn fifty-two and lost his wife the previous year. Although they have more bravado than expertise, they manage to overcome some comical mishaps and accomplish their mission.

The Dish is winsome and leaves the audience with a feeling of joy that these men were able to overcome incredible odds to place a man on the moon and bring him back. Sam Neill is particularly excellent as Cliff. However, it is sad that they covered up a mistake with a lie. They even discuss the fact that lying is wrong, but they do it to buy themselves time. Although the movie is devoid of sex and violence, there are a significant number of lightweight obscenities. *The Dish* also has some positive references to God, plus a terrific church scene with a sincere prayer by a typical Anglican priest at a crucial moment.

CONTENT ANALYSIS: (BB, CC, Ab, LL, A, D, M) Moral worldview with some positive references to God, a satiric view of politically correct socialist dogma, a terrific church scene but another major scene that condones lying; eighteen light obscenities as well as several uses of the word "bloody" with a strong Australian accent, and five exclamatory profanities; threat of disaster on the first moonwalk; alcohol; smoking; and lying as a major plot point.

Pathetically Gross

DR. DOLITTLE 2

Quality: ☆☆   Acceptability: −2

WARNING CODES:
  Language: ***
  Violence: *
  Sex: **
  Nudity: *

RATING: PG
GENRE: Comedy
INTENDED AUDIENCE: Older children and adults
RUNNING TIME: 100 minutes
STARRING: Eddie Murphy, Kristen Wilson, Raven-Symone, Kyla Pratt, Lil' Zane, Kevin Pollack, Jeffrey Jones, and the voices of Norm Macdonald, Lisa Kudrow, and Frankie Muniz
DIRECTOR: Steve Carr
PRODUCER: John Davis
EXECUTIVE PRODUCERS: Neil Machlis and Joe Singer
WRITER: Larry Levin
BASED ON: The books by Hugh Lofting
DISTRIBUTOR: 20th Century Fox
BRIEF SUMMARY:
Dr. Dolittle 2 opens in a winsome, humorous way. Dr. Dolittle has too many patients to attend, both human and animal. Instead of taking his family to Paris for some much-needed R and R, Dr. Dolittle tries to save a local forest from developers by finding a mate for an endangered bear named Ava. Dr. Dolittle finds a mate in Archie, a circus bear,

who's actually a big ham. The rest of the movie entails Dr. Dolittle trying to get Archie to become the bear that he should be, and about the developer who is trying to thwart these plans.

The filmmakers of *Dr. Dolittle 2* decide to finish off the romantic comedy between Ava and Archie abruptly and focus the end of the movie on the environmental battle. The trouble is, the audience cared about the former— which took up most of the movie—not the latter. Therefore, children stopped laughing and critics started mumbling that the movie was way too long. Running out of story and character development, the movie tries to hold the audience by increasing the bathroom humor and lightweight sexual references, which render the later half of the movie just plain offensive.

CONTENT ANALYSIS: (EEE, PaPa, PCPC, LLL, V, SS, N, A, M) Environmentalist worldview that blurs the line between human beings and animals and bashes developers; two profanities, twenty-three strong obscenities, with many scatological references such as flatulence and dog marks his territory to excess; slapstick violence, including man stung by bees, animal attacks, bear tranquilized, often involving bodily functions such as wolf marks its territory near the face of a dog; constant lightweight sexual references as Dr. Dolittle tries to get bears to mate, with many double entendres such as male bear says he'd like to see female bear wet; animals lick private parts to excess; alcohol use; and feng shui gag, racist gag about Mexican chameleon, and interspecies mating gags.

Against All Odds

THE ENDURANCE: SHACKLETON'S LEGENDARY ANTARCTIC EXPEDITION

Quality: ☆☆☆☆   Acceptability: +4

WARNING CODES:
Language: *
Violence: *
Sex: None
Nudity: None

RATING: G
GENRE: Documentary
INTENDED AUDIENCE: All ages
RUNNING TIME: 93 minutes
NARRATED BY: Liam Neeson
DIRECTOR: George Butler
PRODUCER: George Butler
EXECUTIVE PRODUCERS: Caroline Alexander, Paula Apsell, Mike Ryan, and Phyllis Ryan
WRITERS: Caroline Alexander and Joseph Dorman
BASED ON: The book by Caroline Alexander
DISTRIBUTOR: Cowboy Pictures
BRIEF SUMMARY:

The Endurance: Shackleton's Legendary Antarctic Expedition focuses on Ernest Shackleton's last great expedition to try to cross Antarctica in 1914. *Endurance* is a powerful G-rated documentary with a strongly moral point of view, not the least of which is Shackleton's tremendous moral leadership.

Shackleton put an ad in the English newspaper with the terms "low wages," "bitter cold," "return doubtful," and other such daunting warnings. As a result, five thousand men applied to go with him. He chose twenty-seven and headed out in August 1914, just days before the beginning of World War I. When their ship, *The Endurance*, arrived at the great bay in Antarctica on December 5, the ice was too thick to reach the continent. *The Endurance* was eventually crushed. Thwarted, Shackleton's new goal was to save his men at all costs. The movie portrays the harrowing tale of how he did that against tremendous obstacles, including mutiny, starvation, storms, and the loss of supplies.

Although not enough attention is paid to the spiritual life of Shackleton and his men, *The Endurance* is extremely moral. Shackleton is seen as a servant leader who kept the morale of his team together against all odds. Misdeeds are quickly rebuked. Forgiveness is freely offered. *The Endurance* deserves all the positive reviews it received.

CONTENT ANALYSIS: (BBB, C, L, V) Very strong moral worldview with very minor Christian element; one obscenity; and threat of mutiny, constant natural disasters that are very fearsome including ice flow, crushed boat, severe frostbite, hurricane, sleet, snow, starvation, men forced to kill dogs and puppies, and suggested execution of mutineer.

Spoonful of Sugar Makes the Witchcraft Go Down

HARRY POTTER AND THE SORCERER'S STONE

Quality: ☆☆☆   Acceptability: −4

WARNING CODES:
   Language: *
   Violence: *
   Sex: None
   Nudity: None
RATING: PG
GENRE: Fantasy
INTENDED AUDIENCE: All ages
RUNNING TIME: 150 minutes
STARRING: Daniel Radcliffe, Rupert Grint, Emma Watson, Ian Hart, Richard Harris, John Hurt, Richard Griffiths, and John Cleese
DIRECTOR: Chris Columbus
PRODUCER: David Heyman
EXECUTIVE PRODUCERS: Chris Columbus, Mark Radcliffe, Michael Barnathan, and Duncan Henderson
WRITER: Steve Kloves
BASED ON: The novel by J. K. Rowling
DISTRIBUTOR: Warner Brothers

BRIEF SUMMARY:
Harry Potter and the Sorcerer's Stone tells the story of an orphaned boy who's invited to attend the Hogwarts School of Witchcraft and Wizardry, where he finds the home and family he has never had. Harry undergoes a series of adventures with his newfound friends, Ron and Hermione. Eventually, they must do battle with the mysterious villain who killed Harry's parents, who wants to get his hands on some powerful magic that can make him immortal.

The production values in *Harry Potter and the Sorcerer's Stone* are state of the art. The movie almost perfectly depicts the fantasy elements from the book. Director Chris Columbus has done a marvelous job with the young actors, especially Daniel Radcliffe as Harry, and with the veteran adult actors as well. Like the book, however, the story of *Sorcerer's Stone* drags in the middle. Finally, despite some positive moral elements, the story's occult, pagan worldview adds an elitist works theology to its occultism and rewards the children for disobeying the school rules at Hogwarts and lying about it. Condemned by God throughout the Bible, witchcraft is a selfish, elitist form of gnosticism, an evil theology of secret, esoteric knowledge.

CONTENT ANALYSIS: (PaPaPa, OOO, B, C, L, VV, M) Very strong pagan worldview with very strong occult elements including witchcraft and ghosts, plus some moral, redemptive elements; two profanities and five obscenities; scary violence including troll tries to club children to death, large three-headed dog tries to viciously bite children, human-size chess pieces smash each other to pieces, chess piece attacks boy, vines try to strangle children, villain drinks animal's blood after apparently killing it, and rough rugby-style game on flying broomsticks includes blocking and checking children and teenagers into posts and knocking them off broomsticks so that they fall to the ground; use of magic is based on being angry and scared; and children constantly break school rules.

Love Brings People Together

I AM SAM

Quality: ✰✰✰✰   Acceptability: −1

WARNING CODES:
  Language: **
  Violence: *
  Sex: None
  Nudity: *
RATING: PG-13
GENRE: Drama/Comedy
INTENDED AUDIENCE: Teens and adults
RUNNING TIME: 132 minutes
STARRING: Sean Penn, Michelle Pfeiffer, Dakota Fanning, Laura Dern, Dianne Wiest, Brent Spiner, and Mary Steenburgen
DIRECTOR: Jessie Nelson
PRODUCERS: Jessie Nelson, Edward Zwick, Richard Solomon, and Marshall Herskovitz
EXECUTIVE PRODUCER: David Rubin
WRITERS: Jessie Nelson and Kristine Johnson
DISTRIBUTOR: New Line Cinema
BRIEF SUMMARY:
In the movie *I Am Sam,* Sam Dawson, played by Sean Penn, is a mentally handicapped man who gets a homeless girl pregnant when she seeks shelter in his apartment. When the mother abandons him and the child, Lucy, Sam must rely on a kindly neighbor's help to survive. All goes well for six years, until the child protection authorities at Lucy's school decide that Sam is not a fit father. A rich but troubled lawyer named Rita Harrison, played by Michelle Pfeiffer, is goaded by her coworkers to take Sam's case pro bono. This begins a series of ups and downs as Sam fights to regain custody of his beautiful, intelligent daughter.

Sean Penn does a tremendous job as Sam, whose simple compassion shines like a beacon through his clouded mind. Michelle Pfeiffer is also excellent as Rita, as is Dakota Fanning as Sam's daughter Lucy and Laura Dern as the woman who wants to adopt Lucy. Although laced with some foul language, *I Am Sam* is a moral, redemptive movie that shows that love can bring people together, even apparent enemies.

CONTENT ANALYSIS: (BBB, C, Ro, LL, V, N, D, M) Strong moral worldview with a couple of important, positive comments about God, including an answered prayer, plus some redemptive and romantic elements; five obscenities, eight strong profanities, and six mild profanities; brief dramatic violence such as pushing and soccer action; movie opens with birth of illegitimate child; naked baby in mild birthing scene; smoking; and miscellaneous immorality, such as reckless driving, road rage, woman abandons her child and the child's mentally handicapped father, and workaholic woman neglects her son.

Fun-Filled Family Matters

JIMMY NEUTRON: BOY GENIUS

Quality: ✰✰✰✰   Acceptability: +3

WARNING CODES:
  Language: *
  Violence: *
  Sex: None
  Nudity: None
RATING: G
GENRE: Animated science fiction/Comedy
INTENDED AUDIENCE: All ages
RUNNING TIME: 84 minutes
VOICES: Debi Derryberry, Patrick Stewart, Martin Short, Andrea Martin, Megan Cavanaugh, and Mark DeCarlo
DIRECTOR: John A. Davis
PRODUCERS: Steve Oedekerk, John A. Davis, and Albie Hecht
EXECUTIVE PRODUCERS: Julia

Pistor and Keith Alcorn

WRITERS: John A. Davis, David N. Weiss, J. David Stem, and Steve Oedekerk

DISTRIBUTOR: Paramount Pictures/Nickelodeon

BRIEF SUMMARY:

The G-rated animated movie *Jimmy Neutron: Boy Genius* is smart, funny, exciting, entertaining, and full of great moral messages that will have audiences cheering. When Jimmy and his friends decide to sneak out of the house to go to a new amusement park, they have so much fun that they wish they didn't have any parents. When their parents are kidnapped by aliens, however, Jimmy and his friends find out they not only need their parents, they actually want them back!

This simple introduction to the plot of *Jimmy Neutron* does not do the movie justice. There is much to commend in *Jimmy Neutron: Boy Genius*. It is a dramatically rich movie with layers and layers of good morals and good writing. It is funny and poignant at the same time. The animation is terrific, as is the voice acting. Despite some evolutionary comments, the movie has a strong moral worldview with many redemptive moments, including a pro-life message. *Jimmy Neutron* blasts off into the stratosphere of great family films.

CONTENT ANALYSIS: (BBB, C, Ev, L, V) Pro-family, moral worldview, with many redemptive moments and some evolutionary comments; two vulgarities and some very mild scatological humor; threat of human sacrifice to big chicken god, lots of cartoon action violence but the violence is not realistic; parents love each other; asthmatic boy needs to use inhaler; and pro-life message, be-careful-what-you-wish-for message, and a good warning about overindulgence.

Morality Trumps Adolescent Fantasy

JOE SOMEBODY

Quality: ☆☆☆   Acceptability: −1

WARNING CODES:

Language: ***
Violence: *
Sex: None
Nudity: *

RATING: PG

GENRE: Comedy

INTENDED AUDIENCE: Older children and up

RUNNING TIME: 97 minutes

STARRING: Tim Allen, Jim Belushi, Julie Bowen, Kelly Lynch, Hayden Panettiere, Patrick Warburton, and Greg Germann

DIRECTOR: John Pasquin

PRODUCERS: Arnold Kopelson, Anne Kopelson, Matthew Gross, Ken Atchity, and Brian Reilly

EXECUTIVE PRODUCERS: Arnon Milchan, Chi-Li Wong, and William Wilson III

WRITER: John Scott Shepherd

DISTRIBUTOR: 20th Century Fox

BRIEF SUMMARY:

Comic Tim Allen stars in *Joe Somebody* as a father who tries to restore his sense of self-respect by fighting the office bully who humiliated him in front of his daughter. Joe is a video specialist in Minneapolis who feels like a nobody. While taking his daughter, Natalie, to "bring-your-daughter-to-work day," Mark, the office bully, humiliates Joe in front of his daughter. When Joe tries to stand up to Mark, Mark slaps him twice. Joe slinks away, calls in sick, and takes his daughter back to school. The company suspends Mark and sends Meg, the office "wellness coordinator," to help Joe. Her advice backfires, however. Now all Joe wants is to challenge Mark to a fight while he takes self-defense classes from a has-been movie star played by Jim Belushi.

Joe Somebody is an often funny comedy that shows off Tim Allen's ability to play physical comedy. The scenes between him and Belushi are particularly humorous.

The story sometimes plays, however, like a series of vignettes. There's also some significant foul language that requires a caution for older children. All's well that ends well, however. Joe eventually learns the value of turning away from physical violence, and thus regains the respect of his daughter that he really wants.

CONTENT ANALYSIS: (BB, Pa, LLL, V, N, A, D, M) Moral worldview with some pagan elements; about twenty-six obscenities, three strong profanities, three mild profanities, and some light body humor; some violence, including bully twice slaps protagonist very hard, protagonist decides to get martial arts and boxing training, and some martial arts kicks and punches, including several comedic kicks to groin area; it is implied that divorced wife lives with her boyfriend; upper male nudity and women in nightgowns; alcohol use includes visit to karaoke bar; smoking; and cohabitation, gambling, bullying rebuked, and revenge rebuked.

The Ultimate Tourist Trap

JURASSIC PARK III

Quality: ✩✩✩✩   Acceptability: –1

WARNING CODES:

Language: **
Violence: **
Sex: None
Nudity: None

RATING: PG-13
GENRE: Science fiction/Horror
INTENDED AUDIENCE: Teens and adults
RUNNING TIME: 91 minutes
STARRING: Sam Neill, William H. Macy, Téa Leoni, Alessandor Nivola, Trevor Morgan, Michael Jeter, and Laura Dern
DIRECTOR: Joe Johnston
PRODUCERS: Kathleen Kennedy and Larry Franco

EXECUTIVE PRODUCER: Steven Spielberg
WRITERS: Peter Buchman, Alexander Payne, and Jim Taylor
BASED ON: Characters created by Michael Crichton
DISTRIBUTOR: Universal Pictures
BRIEF SUMMARY:

In *Jurassic Park III*, Dr. Alan Grant, played by Sam Neill, once again gets duped into traveling to one of the two dinosaur islands created by a genetic engineering company. This movie is a thrilling, redemptive action movie, but it includes some scary, intense violence and an awkward mix of evolution and God that may be too confusing for children.

After a brief prologue, *Jurassic Park III* opens with Dr. Grant accepting the proposal of wealthy adventurer Paul Kirby and his wife, Amanda, to accompany them on an aerial tour of the second dinosaur island created by a genetic engineering company. All is not what it seems, however. Eventually, Grant and his young protégé, Billy, are stranded on the island with the Kirbys and a pilot. The real reason for the Kirbys' visit to the island is revealed, followed by some surprising developments. Finally Dr. Grant is forced to learn the terrifying implications of his new theory about one species, the dreaded velociraptor.

Director Joe Johnston, of *October Sky*, has fashioned a completely thrilling action flick. *Jurassic Park III* also seems more redemptive and morally compelling than the other two *Jurassic Park* movies. Dr. Grant makes some brief comments supporting evolution, but he also makes some positive acknowledgements of God. Naturally, the movie includes plenty of intense, scary action violence. Therefore, this is not a movie for younger children, and it probably deserves a caution for older children.

CONTENT ANALYSIS: (BB, CC, Ev, Ro, LL, VV, M) Moral worldview with some redemptive elements plus two brief, somewhat positive references to God, marred by evolutionary concepts as well as a romantic notion regarding animals; five lightweight obscenities and twelve exclamatory profanities; scary, intense action violence with some blood that will be too much for children, such as terrifying dinosaurs often attack and try to kill or eat people, plus plane crash, two men explode junk plane with gun and boy in danger; and lying and subterfuge rebuked.

Spacey Cadet Bonds with Earthlings

K-PAX

Quality: ☆☆☆   Acceptability: –2

WARNING CODES:

Language: ***
Violence: *
Sex: None
Nudity: None

RATING: PG-13

GENRE: Drama/Science fiction

INTENDED AUDIENCE: Teens and adults

RUNNING TIME: 120 minutes

STARRING: Kevin Spacey, Jeff Bridges, Mary McCormack, Alfre Woodard, Peter Gerety, and David Patrick Kelly

DIRECTOR: Iain Softley

PRODUCERS: Lawrence Gordon, Lloyd Levin, and Robert F. Colesberry

EXECUTIVE PRODUCER: Susan G. Pollock

WRITER: Charles Leavitt

BASED ON: The novel by Gene Brewer

DISTRIBUTOR: Universal Pictures

BRIEF SUMMARY:

Kevin Spacey stars in K-Pax as a mysterious patient who is transferred into the psychiatric care of Dr. Mark Powell, played by Jeff Bridges. Resistant to drug therapy, the man insists he is a visitor from the distant planet, K-Pax. Dr. Powell finds this man, calling himself Prot, to be "the most convincing delusional" ever. Consumed with curing his patient and discovering the truth, Dr. Powell launches an investigation into Prot's beliefs, background, and private pain. Prot has a strange and wonderful effect on the other patients in the psych ward. Could he be who he says he is? Or is he a deeply disturbed man carrying a terrible secret?

Well acted and directed, K-Pax is fraught with intense themes, some foul language, and wacky false notions about reality. Even so, the messages of hope, redemption, and the importance of family make this an enjoyable mystery. The ending is open to interpretation and is therefore sure to disappoint a few. K-Pax may seem otherworldly but, ultimately, it promotes the value of healing more than scientific cures, reconciliation more than pride, and family more than fast-paced careers. It's a down-to-earth message for a society intent on moving at light-speed.

CONTENT ANALYSIS: (HH, BB, EvEv, Pa, C, Ab, LLL, V, A, D, M) Humanist worldview with moral as well as evolutionary elements that alternately attack and promote families, references that man lives only once, but must relive his mistakes as evolutionary life repeats itself for eons, man alleges alien planet where there is no need for marriages, families, or government, and where children are raised by all, one man searches for redemption and doesn't find it, another man doesn't search for redemption and finds partial redemption, mental patient reads passages from the Bible, including 1 Corinthians 13, and brief reference to Jesus Christ includes anti-Christian remark that even Christians do not follow his teachings; at least twenty-five mostly mild obscenities and several profanities; mild violent content includes mugging, implied choking, wrestling with patients, and strangulation of an evil attacker, talk of past suicide, and man shown walking into water to drown, plus oblique description of rape and murder, with flashback scenes obscuring victims and crime scene; brief kissing and talk of man getting girlfriend pregnant, and brief scene of married couple in bed; some cleavage; drinking; and intensely emotional scenes involving patient under hypnosis, danger to children, man shows psychiatrist that he needs to give his patients hope and not just drugs, and psychiatrist is a workaholic who neglects his family but finally partially realizes what's important in life.

Triumph over Taliban Terrors

KANDAHAR

Quality: ★★★☆   Acceptability: +2

WARNING CODES:
Language: *
Violence: *
Sex: None
Nudity: None
RATING: PG
GENRE: Drama
INTENDED AUDIENCE: Older children and up
RUNNING TIME: 85 minutes
LANGUAGE: Farsi
STARRING: Niloufar Pazira, Hassan Tantai, and Sadou Teymouri
DIRECTOR: Mohsen Makhmalbaf
PRODUCER: Mohsen Makhmalbaf
WRITER: Mohsen Makhmalbaf
DISTRIBUTOR: Avatar Films
BRIEF SUMMARY:
In *Kandahar*, a reporter receives a suicide announcement from her sister in Afghanistan and makes haste back to the war-torn nation to try and save her life. With disturbing clarity about Islam and the Taliban's devastating ways, this brilliantly performed foreign film presents a compelling challenge to all who have a heart to see the captives set free.

Kandahar tells the story of Nafas, a female journalist who fled the horrors of the Islamic fundamentalists of Afghanistan. As her family fled, her sister stepped on a mine that blew her legs off. Her father stayed behind to take care of the sister, and the rest of the family sought refuge in Canada. Years later, Nafas receives a desperate letter from her sister in Afghanistan, who has decided to commit suicide before the next eclipse. Nafas rushes back to her country to rescue her sister. Donning the burka, she finds herself interacting with both friend and foe, some who help and some who hinder her quest. In the process of experiencing first-hand the horrors of the Islamic regime, including imprisonment, her sacrificial love and hope remain strong.

This is a brilliant movie based on the real-life experience of the actress who plays Nafas. There is no foul language, merely a few appeals to God. There is no sex or violence, but there is the constant, intense threat of violence. *Kandahar* is worthwhile viewing for all those who need to understand the truth of Islam and so they can understand the liberating grace of Jesus Christ.

CONTENT ANALYSIS: (BB, Fe, FR, L, V, M) Moral worldview with some feminism but not politically correct or anti-moral, and very strong inference that Islam is wrong; several appeals to God and discussions of violence; constant jeopardy, threats of violence, many scenes of people who have lost legs and even arms to mines and other forms of violence, and fear of violence; and bandits, liars, thieves, and cheats.

Chivalry, Romance, and Destiny Meet

KATE AND LEOPOLD

Quality: ★★★☆   Acceptability: −1

WARNING CODES:
Language: ***
Violence: *

Sex: None
Nudity: None
RATING: PG-13
GENRE: Romantic comedy/
Fantasy
INTENDED AUDIENCE: Teens and
adults
RUNNING TIME: 105 minutes
STARRING: Meg Ryan, Hugh
Jackman, Liev Schreiber, and Breckin
Meyer
DIRECTOR: James Mangold
PRODUCER: Cathy Konrad
EXECUTIVE PRODUCER: Kerry
Orent
WRITERS: James Mangold and
Steven Rogers
DISTRIBUTOR: Miramax
BRIEF SUMMARY:

In *Kate and Leopold,* a royal English duke from 1870 falls through a time portal to 2002, where true love may await. *Kate and Leopold* starts out in 1870, where Leopold's uncle is ready for his nephew, a poverty-stricken English duke, to marry a wealthy American lady. The uncle arranges a fancy party in New York City, where Leopold must make his choice. While dancing, however, Leopold spots a man with an unusual device. He follows the man, Stuart, and finds him shooting photos of his elevator invention sketches in the study. When Leopold confronts him, Stuart bolts out the door, across town, and to the top of a large building, where he proceeds to jump off, taking Leopold with him through a time portal to the year 2002. Leopold has many hilarious reactions to the modern city, but maintains his regal deportment while exploring his new world. He falls in love with the beautiful Kate McKay, a harried, heartsick lady who is not sure whether to trust him. Will Leopold have to go back to the past empty-handed, or is there another way?

Kate and Leopold is a delightful, fun, romantic movie that will make the audience swoon and dream. It is an enthralling, old-fashioned romantic comedy that stresses truth, honesty, chivalry, and honor.

CONTENT ANALYSIS: (BB, Ro, LLL, V, A, D, M) Biblically oriented, moral worldview stressing truth, honesty, chivalry, upright intentions, quest for life and love through honorable means, mixed with some elements of romanticism where emotions rule behavior and some postmodern ideology with an emphasis on fate and inevitability; fifteen obscenities and fifteen profanities; references to dog waste and slightly veiled body humor; apparent fall from a building and some mild physical comedy, hint of suicide, action violence, such as man on a horse heroically chases down purse snatcher; suggestion of affair; some mild depictions of alcohol and smoking; and purse snatcher defeated.

Delightfully Redemptive

KINGDOM COME

Quality: ☆☆☆   Acceptability: −1

WARNING CODES:
Language: * *
Violence: *
Sex: *
Nudity: None
RATING: PG
GENRE: Comedy
INTENDED AUDIENCE: Teens and
adults
RUNNING TIME: 89 minutes
STARRING: LL Cool J, Whoopi
Goldberg, Viveca A. Fox, Loretta Devine,
Anthony Anderson, and Cedric the
Entertainer
DIRECTOR: Doug McHenry
PRODUCERS: John Morrissey and
Edward Bates
EXECUTIVE PRODUCERS: Rochelle
Bates and Lawrence Turman
WRITERS: David Dean Bottrell and
Jessie Jones

BASED ON: The play *Dearly Departed* by David Dean Bottrell and Jessie Jones

DISTRIBUTOR: Fox Searchlight Pictures

BRIEF SUMMARY:

Kingdom Come is a delightful, redemptive African American movie in the tradition of *To Sleep with Anger.* Whoopi Goldberg stars as Raynelle Slocumb, the matriarch of a family that gathers for the funeral of her husband. Slocumb lives in a mythical town, Lulu, where the church is the center. Her husband dies while she reads a letter explaining the gospel to him and quoting the Scripture, "But the day of the Lord will come like a thief" (2 Peter 3:10). As his relatives gather for the funeral they bring their problems, but turn to the Lord for help when they assemble for the funeral inside the church. Even a very rebellious son accepts Jesus Christ and quotes Scripture.

Kingdom Come is a low-budget movie, but the characters are so wonderful that, with all their flaws, it would be nice to be with them at that church service in Lulu. These people are not polished, but they are human and compelling. The direction has a light touch, so the audience won't feel that this movie is preaching at them. Also, the music is terrific. Regrettably, there is some foul language, flatulence, and some discussion about adultery and alcoholism, which are rebuked.

CONTENT ANALYSIS: (CCC, Pa, LL, V, S, AA, D, M) Very Christian worldview with answers to prayer, conversion, and a focus on Jesus Christ, mitigated by pagan lifestyle of son who is converted and of other characters who are not Christian; twenty-one obscenities and five borderline profanities, plus some dialogue about sex and flatulence; fistfight between brothers and threats of violence; references to sex, including adultery, married couples in bed, and scantily clad woman jumps into bed; alcohol use, including some alcoholism rebuked; smoking rebuked; and adultery, lying, and cheating rebuked.

Vanity Fair Revisited

A KNIGHT'S TALE

Quality: ✩✩✩   Acceptability: −1

WARNING CODES:
  Language: * *
  Violence: * *
  Sex: *
  Nudity: *

RATING: PG-13
GENRE: Action/Adventure
INTENDED AUDIENCE: Older children and up
RUNNING TIME: 132 minutes
STARRING: Heath Ledger, Rufus Sewell, Shanynn Sossamon, Paul Bettany, Mark Addy, and Alan Tudyk
DIRECTOR: Brian Helgeland
PRODUCERS: Brian Helgeland, Tim Van Rellim, and Todd Black
WRITER: Brian Helgeland
DISTRIBUTOR: Columbia Pictures/Sony
BRIEF SUMMARY:

Heath Ledger of *The Patriot* stars in *A Knight's Tale*, where he plays a commoner named William who enters a jousting tournament as a knight to help feed himself and his friends, even though his posing as a knight without a noble lineage puts his life in jeopardy. William falls for the witty Jocelyn. Jocelyn has kept her virtue because she doesn't want to be a medieval wife. The rotten Count Adhemar also has his eye set on Jocelyn and tries to defeat William's plans to win the grand tournament and take Jocelyn for himself.

A Knight's Tale is a warm, friendly, entertaining movie with lots of good things in it, including a great father-son relationship, a woman of virtue, bad behavior rebuked, and many positive references to God. However, the movie is flawed: it is too long; it tries in a very guarded way to push the envelope (even inserting a naturalistic nude scene); the jousting sequences are too tame; and the addition of rock music and modern dancing does not succeed. Even with all its flaws, however, *A Knight's Tale* entertains the audience with its tale of knights and Christian chivalry.

CONTENT ANALYSIS: (CC, BBB, Pa, Ab, LL, VV, S, N, A, M) Christian worldview with strong moral and redemptive elements as well as some pagan elements and some mild clerical humor; thirteen very lightweight obscenities and three lightweight profanities, with some church humor and borderline blasphemy; lots of action violence, especially in jousting matches, sword fights, some fistfights, very little blood, and some humorous violence; suggested fornication; full naturalistic male nudity, but no private parts shown, and very brief cleavage; alcohol use; and lying about the past rebuked, cheating rebuked, and gambling mocked and rebuked.

Masonic Drivel

LARA CROFT: TOMB RAIDER

Quality: ☆☆☆   Acceptability: −4

WARNING CODES:
  Language: *
  Violence: **
  Sex: None
  Nudity: *
RATING: PG-13
GENRE: Action/Adventure/Fantasy
INTENDED AUDIENCE: Older children to young adults
RUNNING TIME: 101 minutes
STARRING: Angelina Jolie, Iain Glen, Noah Taylor, Daniel Craig, Richard Johnson, Christopher Barrie, and Jon Voight
DIRECTOR: Simon West
PRODUCERS: Lawrence Gordon, Lloyd Levin, and Colin Wilson
EXECUTIVE PRODUCERS: Jeremy Heath-Smith and Stuart Baird
WRITERS: Patrick Massett and John Zinman
BASED ON: The video games developed by Core Design
DISTRIBUTOR: Paramount Pictures
BRIEF SUMMARY:
Lara Croft: Tomb Raider has some plot holes so big that it almost doesn't recover from its heroine falling into them. In the story, Angelina Jolie plays an adventuress who goes on a search for two pieces of a triangle that, when assembled, will make the owner god. A group of bad guys calling themselves the Illuminati want to find the artifact so that their leader can become god when all the planets align. Thus it is a race against time to see who is going to recover the pieces and either destroy it or become god.

Part travelogue, and filled with constant action violence, *Tomb Raider* does not have enough humor and character development to overcome the stupidity of the script. The direction is lackluster also. More important, although the foul language is kept to a minimum and the threat of a man becoming god is thwarted, the confused mix of occultism, Hinduism, Buddhism, and even a few references to Christianity gives the movie an abhorrent, pagan worldview. *Tomb Raider* would be totally insignificant if it did not rely on so many occult and false religious beliefs, which too many uninformed people take seriously.

CONTENT ANALYSIS: (PaPa, OOO, FRFR, C, L, VV, N, A, DD, M) Eclectic pagan worldview with a confused mix of occultism, Hinduism, Buddhism, and even a few references to Christianity; five obscenities and two profanities; constant action violence including fighting with horrific creatures, maniacal machines and evil men, lots of underlings die by machine gun, by monsters, by falling from heights, some blood when heroine grabs knife by blade, and villain gets stabbed, but movie keeps the blood to a minimum; kissing and references to sexuality; heroine in lingering shower scene, rear female nudity, tight-fitting, revealing clothing, and male nudity, but private parts not shown; alcohol use; smoking and suggestion of drug use by villain; and lying, cheating, fraud, and a surplus of tattoos.

Sugar and Spice

LEGALLY BLONDE

Quality: ✰✰✰   Acceptability: −1

WARNING CODES:
  Language: ***
  Violence: *
  Sex: *
  Nudity: None
RATING: PG-13
GENRE: Comedy
INTENDED AUDIENCE: Teens
RUNNING TIME: 96 minutes
STARRING: Reese Witherspoon, Selma Blair, Luke Wilson, Matthew Davis, Victor Garber, Jennifer Coolidge, Holland Taylor, and Raquel Welch
  DIRECTOR: Robert Luketic
  PRODUCERS: Ric Kidney and Marc E. Platt
  WRITERS: Karen McCullah Lutz and Kirsten Smith
  BASED ON: The book by Amanda Brown
  DISTRIBUTOR: Metro Goldwyn-Mayer/United Artists
  BRIEF SUMMARY:
  Underneath its garish pinks and contemporary sensibilities, Legally Blonde is an old-fashioned Hollywood teen comedy where moral virtue ultimately rules and the audience discovers once more that you can't judge a book by its cover. Reese Witherspoon plays pretty but slightly shallow Elle Woods, who fol-

lows her ex-boyfriend into Harvard Law School to try to win him back. Of course, at Harvard, Elle stands out like a pink flamingo in New England. She quickly realizes that she has to get with the program. Through determination and many moral principles, she overcomes.

There are some really funny scenes in Legally Blonde, as well as a few misses. With all its storytelling virtues and fine performances, however, including Witherspoon's brilliant turn, the movie wraps up too quickly, resulting in jumping conflict and a jarring ending. Although Legally Blonde affirms morality, loyalty, keeping your word, and many other virtues, it suffers from a lax attitude toward sexuality, drugs, and foul language. There are also a few jabs at Christianity and the obligatory, politically correct lesbian, but a lying homosexual witness is appropriately rebuked.

CONTENT ANALYSIS: (RoRo, BB, Ho, Ab, LLL, V, S, A, D, M) Moral premise with moral elements set in a romantic world with a couple of homosexual characters and significant anti-Christian elements; thirty light obscenities and seventeen mild profanities; woman stands up, hitting UPS man in the nose; kissing, professor tries to seduce student, homosexual characters, lesbian character, sexual references, and references to body parts; women in underwear, swimwear, and tight-fitting clothes, women doing a bend and lift maneuver, and revealing clothes; alcohol; smoking and discussion of drugs; and student keeps her word, student tries to do the right thing, student manipulates women, lying rebuked, homosexuality mocked, and sexual advances rebuked.

An Epic Challenge for a Small Creature

THE LORD OF THE RINGS: THE FELLOWSHIP OF THE RING

Quality: ✰✰✰✰   Acceptability: −1

WARNING CODES:

Language: None
Violence: ***
Sex: None
Nudity: None

RATING: PG-13

GENRE: Fantasy epic

INTENDED AUDIENCE: Older children and up

RUNNING TIME: 175 minutes

STARRING: Elijah Wood, Ian McKellen, Viggo Mortensen, Sean Astin, Liv Tyler, Cate Blanchett, John Rhys-Davies, Christopher Lee, Hugo Weaving, Ian Holm, and the voice of Andy Serkis as Gollum

DIRECTOR: Peter Jackson

PRODUCERS: Peter Jackson, Barrie M. Osborne, Fran Walsh, and Tim Sanders

EXECUTIVE PRODUCERS: Mark Ordesky, Bob Weinstein, Harvey Weinstein, Robert Shaye, and Michael Lynne

WRITERS: Fran Walsh, Philippa Boyens, and Peter Jackson

BASED ON: The books by J. R. R. Tolkien

DISTRIBUTOR: New Line Cinema

BRIEF SUMMARY:

In *The Fellowship of the Ring*, part one of *The Lord of the Rings*, a young Hobbit named Frodo has been entrusted with an ancient evil ring and must embark on an epic quest to destroy the Crack of Doom. With dazzling effects and a great moral story, part one of *The Lord of the Rings* is a must-see for fantasy fans, with a caution to parents of older children for strong sword-type violence and a brief occult element not in the book.

After a short prologue, the movie opens in a village in the shire in Middle Earth. A hobbit named Frodo, played by Elijah Wood, is a friendly, likeble chap who is thrust into an adventure not of his choosing. Gandalf, played magnificently by Ian McKellen, is a powerful wizard who helps him. Good-hearted Frodo must destroy an evil ring that has the power to unleash a hellish nightmare on relatively peaceful Middle Earth. Elves, hobbits, dwarfs, and humans must pull together in the face of monstrous odds to help Frodo complete his task.

Part one of *The Lord of the Rings* is a wonderful epic fantasy about good and evil, with top-notch actors, storyline, and special effects. The movie is clean, but there is plenty of sword-fighting violence that is, at times, a bit too strong for children. Happily, however, the filmmakers have left in plenty of Christian author J. R. R. Tolkien's biblical, allegorical references. Take your older children if they are mature enough to handle mystical creatures, scary monsters, and sword fighting.

CONTENT ANALYSIS: (BBB, CC, O, Pa, VVV, A, D, M) Strong moral worldview with redemptive Christian elements allegorically espousing the virtues of sacrifice, unity, kingdom purpose, loyalty, and perseverance; some occult elements with "magic" evil ring, elf queen with supernatural powers (but it is implied in other works that such powers are given to such beings by the Creator), and wizards use supernatural powers, which are not in the original book; strong violence includes lots of sword-fighting combat, a man is ambushed and shot with arrows, and creatures and monsters of all sorts are shot with arrows, skewered by spears, and hacked with axes and swords; implied alcohol use in visit to tavern; mild pipe-smoking; and good overcomes evil, plus oaths and spells spoken by wizards and other fantasy characters.

Can a Happy Ending Save the Majestic?

THE MAJESTIC

Quality: ☆☆   Acceptability: −4

WARNING CODES:

Language: ***
Violence: *
Sex: None
Nudity: *

RATING: PG

GENRE: Drama

INTENDED AUDIENCE: Older children to adults

RELEASE DATE: December 2001

STARRING: Jim Carrey, Martin Landau, Laurie Holden, David Ogden Stiers, James Whitmore, Hal Holbrook, Bob Balaban, and Bruce Campbell

DIRECTOR: Frank Darabont

PRODUCER: Frank Darabont

EXECUTIVE PRODUCER: Jim Behnke

WRITER: Michael Sloane

DISTRIBUTOR: Castle Rock Entertainment/Warner Brothers

BRIEF SUMMARY:

Jim Carrey stars in *The Majestic* as a young writer in 1951, Pete Appleton, who has just gotten his first big break in Hollywood. However, his contract is torn up when it's found that he once attended a Communist-front meeting while at college. Pete gets drunk and suffers amnesia in an accident. In a small town, a man named Harry Trimble, played by Martin Landau, recognizes Pete as his son, Luke, who went off to World War II nine years earlier. All seems to be going well, until Pete regains his memory and the FBI comes to subpoena him to testify on his Communist activities in Hollywood.

Despite another terrific performance by Carrey, much of *The Majestic* is dull, boring, and silly. It also contains a strong Marxist worldview that favors the Communist sympathizers in Hollywood during the thirties, forties, and fifties. In reality, these Marxists were not nice guys who were just misguided. They were political stooges of the Stalinist government in the Soviet Union, which murdered millions of people. They were the terrorist sympathizers of their day, and, like the terrorist sympathizers of Osama Bin Ladin, they should be condemned, not eulogized.

CONTENT ANALYSIS: (CoCoCo, PCPCPC, RHRHRH, B, P, Ro, LLL, V, N, AA, M) Strong Marxist revisionist history worldview with some positive references to God by one character, some patriotism, and an upbeat romantic ending; twenty-six obscenities and twenty profanities; violent car crash off bridge, with man hitting head against bridge with a sickening thud, and man gets punched; several kisses; upper male nudity in doctor's office; drinking to get drunk; and stereotypical villainous FBI and congressional characters.

Senseless Animation

MARCO POLO: RETURN TO XANADU

Quality: ☆   Acceptability: −4

WARNING CODES:

Language: None
Violence: **
Sex: None
Nudity: None

RATING: Not rated

GENRE: Animated adventure

INTENDED AUDIENCE: Children

VOICES: Paul Ainsley, Alan Altshuld, Elea Bartling, Nicholas Gonzalez, John C. Hyke, Michael Kostroff, Robert Kramer, Tim Owen, and Tony Pope

DIRECTOR: Ron Merk

PRODUCERS: Chris Holter, Igor Meglic, and Ron Merk

WRITERS: Chris Holter, Ron Merk, and Sheldon Moldoff

DISTRIBUTOR: Koan, Incorporated/The Tooniversal Company

BRIEF SUMMARY:

Marco Polo: Return to Xanadu is one of the most confused, poorly animated productions to appear on the big screen. The movie opens with a yogi named Babu on a flying carpet distorting the history of Marco Polo. Marco Polo visits Xanadu during the reign of Kublai Khan. Khan befriends Polo and gives him half of a magic medallion crafted by an ancient wizard. Some time later, a descendant also named Marco Polo is targeted by Foo Ling, the evil foe of the original Marco Polo. Marco journeys to Xanadu to reunite his portion of the medallion with the broken half. Along the way he receives advice from Babu, who claims that reality is all an illusion.

Marco Polo fails completely. The animation is worse than direct-to-video or even cartoons made on a daily basis for cable outlets. There are a host of unpleasant characters, including anti-Asian stereotypes. The movie's soundtrack is abysmal. The songs are painful. The movie is muddled, obscure, evil, and confused. False religious, revisionist, occult, and anti-Christian elements dominate this worthless production. One has to pity the people who actually spent time working on this production.

CONTENT ANALYSIS: (PaPaPa, FRFRFR, OOO, RoRo, RHRH, VV, D, M) Extreme Hindu worldview with extreme occult elements, romantic elements, and a revisionist view of history; scary characters, occult violence, cartoon violence including falling thousands of feet, sword fights, punches, beatings, drownings, and bombings; effete character and anti-Asian stereotyping; pipe-smoking; and characters change shapes and sizes.

Big Risks and Big Lessons

MAX KEEBLE'S BIG MOVE

Quality: ☆☆☆   Acceptability: +2

WARNING CODES:

Language: None
Violence: *
Sex: None
Nudity: None

RATING: PG
GENRE: Comedy
INTENDED AUDIENCE: Children

RUNNING TIME: 75 minutes
STARRING: Alex D. Linz, Larry Miller, Robert Carradine, and Nora Dunn
DIRECTOR: Tim Hill
PRODUCERS: Russell Hollander, Mike Karz, and Raymond Reed
EXECUTIVE PRODUCER: Guy Riedel
WRITERS: Jonathan Bernstein, Mark Blackwell, and James Greer
DISTRIBUTOR: Walt Disney/ Buena Vista
BRIEF SUMMARY:

In *Max Keeble's Big Move*, seventh grader Max learns he is moving away and spends his last week getting revenge on his tormentors, only to learn he's not moving after all and will now be left at the mercy of his victims.

Max Keeble dreams of vanquishing the bullies in superhero style. One bully dips him in mud and covers him in garbage, whereupon principal Jindraike singles out Max in front of the school. On the way home, a scary ice cream man attacks him with ice cream, and he finds out that Jindraike is threatening to level his favorite animal shelter. Just in time, Max finds out that his family will be moving to Chicago at the end of the week, which means that he can exact revenge on all these bullies—without consequence! Max devises an elaborate scheme whereby he gains some respect from his classmates, but alienates some true friends. When Max finds out he is not moving after all, he must find the strength to undo his misdeeds and turn his school around.

Max Keeble's Big Move is cute, funny, and acceptable for all except very young children, who may be frightened by the bullies. The movie contains some disrespectfulness and over-the-top adult characters, but it delivers some good laughs and great lessons about loyalty, returning good for evil, and facing one's fears with wisdom.

CONTENT ANALYSIS: (BB, Pa, V, M) Dominant moral worldview teaches the value of returning good for evil, maintaining loyalty to friends, perseverance, and boldness, as well as elements of pagan worldview with the ends justifying the means; mild schoolboy violence with bully pranks as protagonist is "tarred and feathered," harassed for lunch money, held in bathroom with possible head in toilet, and generally intimidated, plus a wild food fight in the cafeteria; and general sense of disrespectfulness to over-the-top authority figures.

Apocalyptic Visions

MEGIDDO: OMEGA CODE 2

Quality: ☆☆   Acceptability: +1

WARNING CODES:
  Language: *
  Violence: **
  Sex: None
  Nudity: None
RATING: PG-13
GENRE: Thriller/Apocalyptic fiction
INTENDED AUDIENCE: Older children and up
RUNNING TIME: 106 minutes
STARRING: Michael York, Michael Biehn, Diane Venora, Udo Kier, Greg Ellis, R. Lee Ermey, and David Hedison
DIRECTOR: Brian Trenchard-Smith
PRODUCERS: Matthew Crouch and Gary M. Bettman
EXECUTIVE PRODUCER: Paul Crouch
WRITERS: Hollis Barton, Stephan Blinn, and John Fasano
DISTRIBUTOR: TBN Films
BRIEF SUMMARY:
Megiddo: Omega Code 2 tells what happens with the Antichrist on his way to power and destruction at Armageddon. In *Megiddo*, Satan possesses the spirit of a troubled little boy named Stone Alexander. Stone tries to burn his baby brother, David, to death, so Stone's media-mogul father sends him off to military school in Europe. Years later, Stone (played by Michael York) has become chancellor of a world government in Europe, Russia, and Africa while his brother, David, played by Michael Biehn, has become Vice President of the United States of America. Using political subterfuge and murder, including slaying his father, Stone has gained control of the whole world except for the United States, Latin America, and China. David tries to stop his evil brother, the Antichrist. The stage is now set for Armageddon, but God is the only one who can win this battle.

Michael York and Michael Biehn deliver good performances. The special effects in *Megiddo* are pretty spectacular at times. Some lackluster expository dialogue and an awkward, hurried, dramatic structure damages the movie's first half, however. Still, *Megiddo* plainly shows that victory over evil is best achieved when people turn to God. This stirring message is better than most of what you'll see in Hollywood's blockbusters.

CONTENT ANALYSIS: (CCC, PPP, L, VV, A, D, M) Christian dispensationalist worldview with scenes of Black Mass, showing evil of demon-possessed Antichrist villain with supernatural powers, and a strong sense of patriotism; several light obscenities and some appeals to God; solid action violence such as huge battle between soldiers and tanks and airplanes, gunfire between government agents, villain throws father off balcony to murder him, evil child tries to burn his baby brother, children taunt child with burned dolls, and supernatural villain uses evil powers to kill people; alcohol use; brief smoking; and scary scenes that probably are too intense for young children, but God wins in the end. The movie is perfectly suitable for older children and teenagers.

Love and Fun Conquer Fear

MONSTERS, INC.

Quality: ☆☆☆☆   Acceptability: +1

WARNING CODES:
  Language: *
  Violence: **
  Sex: None
  Nudity: None
RATING: G
GENRE: Animated comedy
INTENDED AUDIENCE: Ages four and up
RUNNING TIME: 84 minutes
VOICES: John Goodman, James Coburn, Billy Crystal, Mary Gibbs, Frank Oz, Bonnie Hunt, and John Ratzenberger
  DIRECTOR: Pete Docter
  PRODUCER: Darla K. Anderson
  EXECUTIVE PRODUCERS: John Lasseter and Andrew Stanton
  WRITERS: Andrew Stanton and Daniel Gerson
  ORIGINAL STORY BY: Pete Docter, Jill Culton, Jeff Pidgeon, and Ralph Eggleston
  DISTRIBUTOR: Pixar/Walt Disney Pictures/Buena Vista
  BRIEF SUMMARY:
Monsters, Inc. is an animated fantasy from Pixar Animation Studios (the *Toy Story* studio) about two fanciful, lovable "monsters," who run into complications and an insidious plot when they try to return a little human child to her world. *Monsters, Inc.* is a hilarious, incredibly imaginative, and exciting animated movie.

Monsters, Inc. takes place in Monstropolis, a thriving company town where monsters of all shapes and sizes reside. James P. Sullivan ("Just call me Sulley") is the top kid-scaring monster for Monsters, Inc. Sulley's job is to jump out of closets to scare kids so that Monsters, Inc. can collect the power of children's screams. The company converts that power into electricity. When a little girl accidentally follows Sulley back into his world, Sulley and his friend Mike scheme to put the little girl, whom Sulley nicknames "Boo," back into her bedroom. They don't realize that the evil, chameleon-like Randall has insidious plans for the cute little human child.

Pixar has fashioned a hilarious, incredibly imaginative, and exciting family-friendly animated movie. *Monsters, Inc.* not only shows that fun and friendship conquer fear, it also shows that love conquers fear as well. This movie has lots of heart for the whole family. A very mild caution, however, for the youngest children, specifically ages two through four, due to some potentially frightening moments, although these moments are much milder than those of most movies.

CONTENT ANALYSIS: (BBB, CC, L, VV, M) Strong moral worldview with solid redemptive elements emanating from a nascent Christian worldview where love, laughter, and fun triumph over fear and nastiness; one "darn," some mild potty humor, and one burp; some scary, violent cartoon elements; and deceit, fear, and nastiness ultimately rebuked and overcome by love, laughter, fun, and friendship.

Red Windmill Surrealism

MOULIN ROUGE

Quality: ☆☆☆   Acceptability: −2

WARNING CODES:
  Language: None
  Violence: *
  Sex: * *
  Nudity: *
RATING: PG-13
GENRE: Musical drama
INTENDED AUDIENCE: Older teens and adults
RUNNING TIME: 126 minutes

STARRING: Nicole Kidman, Ewan McGregor, John Leguizamo, Jim Broadbent, and Richard Roxburgh

DIRECTOR: Baz Luhrmann

PRODUCERS: Martin Brown, Baz Luhrmann, and Fred Baron

WRITERS: Baz Luhrmann and Craig Pearce

DISTRIBUTOR: 20th Century Fox

BRIEF SUMMARY:

Set in the decadent world of the infamous homoerotic Paris nightclub around 1900, *Moulin Rouge* tells the story of a love triangle between a writer, a duke, and a courtesan who entertains people at the club. In the story, which is laced with new versions of popular songs, a writer named Christian, played by Ewan McGregor (the young Obi-Wan Kenobi in *The Phantom Menace*), searches for love. Nicole Kidman plays Satine, the city's most famous courtesan, who is in search of more fame. Her admirer, the Duke of Worchester, played by Richard Roxburgh, is in search of Satine. Eventually, the duke's obsession intervenes, leading to tragedy.

From the colorful and comedic cast of characters to the amazingly elaborate set designs, *Moulin Rouge* overloads the senses with sounds and images. These are combined with an edgy shooting style, digital editing effects, many comical sound effects, and unique renditions of modern songs from Madonna, Elton John, and the Beatles to *The Sound of Music*. The problem with all this, however, is that the movie's romantic worldview promotes erotic frenzy in the name of love. Although there are no profanities or obscenities, there is discussion about sex, much implied sexuality, some crude sexual references, and aggressive erotic dancing.

CONTENT ANALYSIS: (RoRoRo, B, V, SS, N, A, M) Strong romantic worldview promoting erotic frenzy in the name of love, done in a tongue-in-cheek way, with some moral elements; many sexual, erotic references; man manhandles women, man falls through roof, man hits man, many references to killing man; much eroticism such as erotic sex games played that insinuate orgasms, sexy green fairy flies around, metaphorically sexual conversation between man and woman, references to engaging in sex, man and woman lay on top of each other, woman seductively grasps at man's body, two men on one woman, sexually driven score with fast edgy edits stirring up sexual frenzy, and many sexually aggressive dances; dancing women lift their dresses exposing undergarments and showing partial upper nudity, plus partial body shots of women dancing erotically and two nude women in picture on wall; alcohol use implied; and movie depicts decadence.

On the Line . . . of Being Wholesome

ON THE LINE

Quality: ☆☆☆   Acceptability: +1

WARNING CODES:
  Language: *
  Violence: *
  Sex: None
  Nudity: *
RATING: PG
GENRE: Romantic comedy
INTENDED AUDIENCE: Teens
RUNNING TIME: 80 minutes
STARRING: Lance Bass, Joey Fatone, and Emmanuelle Chriqui
DIRECTOR: Eric Bross
PRODUCERS: Peter Abrams, Robert L. Levy, Wendy Thorlakson, and Rich Hall
EXECUTIVE PRODUCERS: Bob Osher, Jeremy Kramer, and Robbie Brenner
WRITERS: Eric Aronson and Paul Stanton
DISTRIBUTOR: Miramax Films/ Disney

BRIEF SUMMARY:

On the Line is the story of a young man who runs into problems searching for a girl he met on the commuter trains in Chicago. Aimed at teenage audiences, *On the Line* is a relatively clean, entertaining movie about young romance.

On the Line tells the story of Kevin, played by Lance Bass, who is known by his friends for being awkward around girls. After a trying day at work, he happens to find a girl (Emmanuelle Chriqui) that he can talk to easily without passing out. He forgets to ask her for her name and telephone number, however. Since he really likes her, he is committed to finding her again. Kevin distributes a simple "Are You Her?" bulletin to find the girl. A news reporter writes up the story, and a number of lovelorn girls respond. This causes frustration to Kevin, but a host of dates for Kevin's opportunistic friends. Young and old, male and female, everyone becomes interested in debating whether it is possible to fall in love at first sight.

With only three obscenities, no sex scenes, no rebellious piercings, no drug abuse, and no parental hatred themes, *On the Line* is a good movie for teenagers. It has a cute story full of good, clean fun. Best of all, the protagonist is a wholesome guy—moral, respectful, respectable, and forgiving. What a refreshing change!

CONTENT ANALYSIS: (BB, C, Pa, Ho, L, V, N, A, M) Moral worldview with protagonist credibly portrayed as a moral character, respectful and respectable, forgiving and restoring; New Age worldview ridiculed, homosexual theme comically addressed; three obscenities, some flatulence humor, and young man squirts mouthwash down his pants and acts like it stung him; brief mild violence such as protagonist knocks a friend out, person hit with a handbag, and amplifier falls from stage, injuring someone; brief homosexual references and some suggestive lyrics; assumed upper male nudity when character imagines himself naked onstage, plus female cleavage; alcohol use; and miscellaneous immorality such as coworker betrays hero by taking credit for his ideas on their marketing accounts and hero's response to the betrayal is forgiveness.

Demonic Occult Attack on Christianity and Christians

THE OTHERS

Quality: ☆☆☆   Acceptability: −4

WARNING CODES:

Language: *
Violence: **
Sex: *
Nudity: *

RATING: PG-13
GENRE: Horror/Ghost story
INTENDED AUDIENCE: Teens and adults
RUNNING TIME: 104 minutes
STARRING: Nicole Kidman, Fionnula Flanagan, Alakina Mann, and James Bentley
DIRECTOR: Alejandro Amenábar
PRODUCERS: Fernando Bovaira, Jose Luis Cuerda, and Sunmin Park
EXECUTIVE PRODUCERS: Tom Cruise, Paula Wagner, Bob Weinstein, Harvey Weinstein, and Rick Schwartz
WRITER: Alejandro Amenábar
DISTRIBUTOR: Dimension Films
BRIEF SUMMARY:

In *The Others*, Nicole Kidman plays Grace, a young woman waiting for her beloved husband to return from World War II. Grace has been raising her two young children alone in a cavernous Victorian mansion on the secluded Isle of Jersey near England. Isolated from the world, Grace is a fervent Christian, teaching her faith to her children who, she says, suffer from some terrible skin disease that requires them to refrain from sunlight. When three mysterious new servants arrive to replace the ones that inexplicably left, startling and supernatural events begin to unfold.

The Others doesn't ignore Christian beliefs. Far from it. Instead, its strong occult worldview overtly attacks the Christian beliefs of its conflicted heroine, Grace. The upshot of this worldview is that there is really no heaven or hell and that dead people continue to live and can achieve redemption for their sins on their own power and merit instead of Christ's. The movie's worldview rejects Christianity and contains false religious notions about redemption and the afterlife. Ultimately, *The Others* is an abhorrent movie, despite fine production values and some wonderful acting, especially by Alakina Mann and James Bentley as the two children.

CONTENT ANALYSIS: (OOO, AbAbAb, FRFRFR, L, VV, S, N, D, M) Strong demonic worldview attacks Christians and rejects Christianity to support the belief that the dead continue to live, but without a heaven or a hell, plus many false religious notions such as mother tells child to ask forgiveness from "the Virgin," mother describes eternal hell but calls it "limbo," and movie's worldview accepts the possibility of gaining personal redemption in the afterlife by using one's own power to forgive yourself rather the grace of God or Jesus Christ; one mild obscenity and three mild profanities plus appeals and expressions of gratitude to God; scary violence from "ghosts" and "poltergeists" (furniture moves and thumps, sounds of weeping), plus several jump scenes, spooky images of corpses, hallucinating mother tries to strangle one of her children, and description of murder and suicide; implied intercourse between husband and wife; brief partial nudity; smoking; and depiction of an occult séance.

Brotherhood of Heroes

PEARL HARBOR

Quality: ☆☆☆   Acceptability: −1

WARNING CODES:
Language: * * *
Violence: * *
Sex: *
Nudity: *
RATING: PG-13
GENRE: War movie/Historical romance
INTENDED AUDIENCE: Teens and adults
RUNNING TIME: 183 minutes
STARRING: Ben Affleck, Kate Beckinsale, Josh Hartnet, Cuba Gooding Jr., Alec Baldwin, Jon Voight, Tom Sizemore, and Dan Aykroyd
DIRECTOR: Michael Bay
PRODUCERS: Michael Bay and Jerry Bruckheimer
EXECUTIVE PRODUCERS: Barry Waldman, Bruce Hendricks, Randall Wallace, Scott Gardenhour, Chad Oman, and Mike Stenson
WRITER: Randall Wallace
DISTRIBUTOR: Touchstone/Buena Vista/Walt Disney Company
BRIEF SUMMARY:
In the World War II extravaganza *Pearl Harbor*, Ben Affleck and Josh Hartnett star as two childhood buddies, Rafe and Danny, who join the United States Air Force at the dawn of World War II. Rafe falls in love with a Navy nurse, Evelyn, but goes away to join an American squadron of volunteer pilots in England. When his plane crashes in the sea, Rafe is presumed drowned. Three months later in Pearl Harbor, Evelyn is still pining for Rafe when she decides to give her heart to Danny, who's also been assigned to Pearl. Their love affair is interrupted by Rafe's sudden reappearance and by explosive world events as Japan attacks the American fleet.

Pearl Harbor is a love letter to the "brotherhood of heroes" who survived the deadly Japanese attack on 7 December 1941 and went on to defeat National Socialism in Japan. Interwoven within this mythic story of tragedy and triumph is a sometimes hokey love triangle and a Saturday matinee tale of youthful heroics. Not always successful, *Pearl Harbor* is still a spectacular, redemptive piece of filmmaking. Regrettably, it contains plenty of foul language and some implied sexual immorality.

CONTENT ANALYSIS: (BB, PPP, CC, RH, Ro, Pa, LLL, VV, S, N, M) Moral worldview with strongly patriotic and solidly Christian, redemptive elements undermined by mild revisionist history, romantic elements, and some pagan elements including image of Japanese Buddhist shrine; about thirty-two obscenities, eleven strong profanities, and eighteen mild profanities; lots of action and war violence with slight blood including explosions, gunfire, planes chasing one another, boats sinking, planes crashing, and men drowning, plus some intense hospital scenes including burn victims and nurse uses finger to stop blood flow; implied fornication; partial nudity; alcohol use; smoking; and revenge and lust.

Confused Evolutionary Hype

PLANET OF THE APES

Quality: ☆☆   Acceptability: −4

WARNING CODES:
  Language: **
  Violence: **
  Sex: None
  Nudity: None
RATING: PG-13
GENRE: Science fiction
INTENDED AUDIENCE: Older children and adults
RUNNING TIME: 120 minutes
STARRING: Mark Wahlberg, Tim Roth, Helena Bonham Carter, Paul Giamatti, Estella Warren, and Michael Clarke Duncan
  DIRECTOR: Tim Burton
  PRODUCER: Richard D. Zanuck
  EXECUTIVE PRODUCER: Ralph Winter
WRITERS: William Broyles Jr., Lawrence Konner, and Mark Rosenthall
BASED ON: The novel by Pierre Boule
DISTRIBUTOR: 20th Century Fox
BRIEF SUMMARY:
Mark Wahlberg stars in this remake of *Planet of the Apes* as an American astronaut who crash-lands on a brutal, primal planet where apes are in charge and humans are hunted and enslaved by the tyrannical simians. Wahlberg plays Captain Leo Davidson. After Davidson is caught and enslaved, he befriends a female chimpanzee named Ari, played by Helena Bonham Carter. Ari wants to end the slavery of human beings, whom she sees as "separate but equal" to the apes. A mad chimpanzee general named Thade, played extravagantly by Tim Roth, has other ideas.

Planet of the Apes has some beautiful special effects and some slick filmmaking, but it is plagued by plot holes, story inconsistencies and self-contradictions, poor dialogue, over-the-top acting, an abhorrent worldview, and a very weak hero and lead actor. The worldview that eventually takes shape during this movie reveals a materialistic, evolutionary viewpoint about parallel universes marred by biological confusion and an attempt to mock human society, especially prayer, faith, conservative economics, and the movement supporting gun ownership. The "Twilight Zone" ending will leave many people scratching their heads, because it is inane and poorly executed.

CONTENT ANALYSIS: (HHH, EvEvEv, AbAb, PCPC, C, LL, VV, A, DD, M) Strong "multiverse," materialistic, evolutionary worldview with interspecies confusion, incoherent ontology and science, several scenes making fun of prayer and reducing faith to serial multiverse evolution, mocks conservative economics and the movement supporting gun control passes itself off as tolerant thinking, plus some incarnational allegorical elements; eight obscenities and four profanities; action violence such as talking apes capture, beat, and enslave talking humans, gunfire, explosions, spaceship crash-lands, fight scene when humans ride horses through ape encampment, and big battle between humans and apes; brief scene where chimpanzee female starts to seduce apparent mate in bed, sexual confusion among different primate species; chimpanzee female in slip with human-like breasts; implied alcohol use; hallucinogen; and slavery and attempted genocide rebuked.

Delightful Discovery

THE PRINCESS DIARIES

Quality: ☆☆☆☆   Acceptability: +3

WARNING CODES:

   Language: None
   Violence: *
   Sex: None
   Nudity: None

RATING: G
GENRE: Comedy
INTENDED AUDIENCE: All ages
RUNNING TIME: 114 minutes
STARRING: Anne Hathaway, Julie Andrews, Hector Elizondo, Heather Matarazzo, Caroline Goodall, Mandy Moore, Robert Schwartzman, and Erik Von Detten
   DIRECTOR: Garry Marshall
   PRODUCERS: Whitney Houston, Debra Martin Chase, and Mario Iscovich
   WRITER: Gina Wendkos
   BASED ON: The novel by Meg Cabot
   DISTRIBUTOR: Walt Disney Pictures/Buena Vista
   BRIEF SUMMARY:
The Princess Diaries is a G-rated modern fairy tale about a teenage girl in San Francisco who finds out that she is heir to the throne of a small European nation. The Princess Diaries is a wonderful, whole-some filmmaking gem—a movie that children and young teenagers will want to see over and over.

Newcomer Anne Hathaway stars in The Princess Diaries as Mia Thermopolis, an awkward, fifteen-year-old girl in San Francisco. One day Mia is stunned to learn that her grandmother has just shown up and wants to have tea with her. Mia is resentful. She feels that her father abandoned her and that her grandmother never took an interest in her. When she goes for tea, she finds out that her grandmother is Queen Clarisse Renaldi, played with aplomb by Julie Andrews. Queen Clarisse tells Mia that she is a princess and has to assume her rightful role, now that her father has died, or the Kingdom of Genovia will cease to exist. The Queen and her entourage have only two weeks to turn Mia into a real princess.

The Princess Diaries is a delightful discovery. This movie has been carefully crafted. The script is coherent. The plot is intriguing. The unexpected carries viewers along, and the acting is good. In fact, the whole process of turning Mia into a princess is a process of learning how to be responsible for your actions, live a virtuous life, and do the right thing in the face of adversity.

CONTENT ANALYSIS: (BB, C, Ro, PC, V, A, M) Christian moral worldview with very few romantic and politically correct notions and many moral messages, some mild humor mocking homosexuality, an appeal to God, and a positive statement about older brother joining the church as a priest; a nun says "for the love of God"; some minor slapstick violence but nobody really hurt; some teenage kissing, cheerleaders perform, and spoof of teenage girl bands; some revealing costumes; wine at dinner; and lying, abandonment, divorce, transvestism, selfishness, tattoos, and ear-piercing all rebuked, teenage romance frowned upon, and feng shui practices mocked.

Morality Eventually Overcomes Greed

RAT RACE

Quality: ☆☆☆☆   Acceptability: −2

WARNING CODES:

Language: ***
Violence: **
Sex: *
Nudity: *

RATING: PG-13
GENRE: Comedy
INTENDED AUDIENCE: Teens and adults
RUNNING TIME: 112 minutes
STARRING: Rowan Atkinson, Cuba Gooding Jr., Jon Lovitz, John Cleese, Wayne Knight, Whoopi Goldberg, Breckin Meyer, Amy Smart, Seth Green, Lanai Chapman, and Dave Thomas
DIRECTOR: Jerry Zucker
PRODUCERS: Jerry Zucker, Sean Daniel, and Janet Zucker
EXECUTIVE PRODUCERS: James Jacks and Richard Vane
WRITER: Andrew Breckman
DISTRIBUTOR: Paramount Pictures
BRIEF SUMMARY:

The story of *Rat Race* involves an eccentric, devious Las Vegas tycoon who lassos eleven people into a frantic, comedic race for two million dollars stashed seven hundred miles away in a locker in Silver City, New Mexico. An attorney, a mother, an Italian tourist, a female helicopter pilot, two slackers, a man and his family, and a professional football referee are among the cast of characters who populate this frantic, often hilarious comedy. *Rat Race* stars Whoopi Goldberg, John Cleese, Cuba Gooding Jr., Jon Lovitz, Rowan Atkinson, Wayne Knight, and relative newcomers Breckin Meyer, Seth Green, and Amy Smart.

Nearly all of the characters in *Rat Race* lie, cheat, steal, and do other immoral things to get there first for the money. Most of the time, however, these greedy acts land them in even more trouble. The story ends on a strong moral and very redemptive note. Regrettably, there is some really inappropriate foul language and some crude humor, especially three adult-oriented sexual jokes. There is also some slight ethnic humor, jokes about Wayne Knight carrying a heart for an emergency organ transplant, and humor regarding a group of mentally handicapped people on an outing.

CONTENT ANALYSIS: (B, Pa, Ho, C, LLL, VV, S, N, A, D, MM) Moral worldview exposing the frailties and sins of human beings with a moral, redemptive ending, but movie contains some crude humor, especially three sexual jokes, one of which is an oblique reference to pedophilia plus effeminate man dresses up as Lucille Ball in a busload of women dressed likewise for an *I Love Lucy* convention, person says "God bless you," and people are ironically compared to "the twelve apostles" when they finally do a good deed; twenty-two obscenities, one strong profanity/blasphemy, and three mild exclamatory profanities; lots of comic violence such as pratfalls, getting entangled in machinery, vehicle crashes, fighting, perilous hot-air balloon ride, man gets an electrical shock, and mishandling a heart being shipped for an organ transplant; cross-dressing character; man shows off his skin ring on his naked breast and woman does likewise, but movie only shows an obscured side view of her chest; alcohol use; smoking; and cheating, lying, deceit, stealing, gambling, and ethnic humor done in a comic vein, plus brief humor about a group of mentally handicapped people and an encounter with some Nazi skinheads.

A Lively Comedy for Christ

ROAD TO REDEMPTION

Quality: ☆☆☆   Acceptability: +4

WARNING CODES:

Language: None
Violence: *
Sex: None
Nudity: None

RATING: G
GENRE: Comedy
INTENDED AUDIENCE: Older children and adults
RUNNING TIME: 85 minutes
STARRING: Pat Hingle, Julie Condra, Leo Ross, Jay Underwood, Tony Longo, and Wes Studi
DIRECTOR: Bob Vernon
PRODUCER: John Shepherd
EXECUTIVE PRODUCER: Barry Werner
WRITER: Bob Vernon
DISTRIBUTOR: World Wide Pictures, Incoporated
BRIEF SUMMARY:

Road to Redemption is a lively, funny Christian comedy from World Wide Pictures, the movie ministry of the Billy Graham Evangelistic Association. The movie tells the comical story of Amanda, a spoiled young woman who gets in trouble after she and her boyfriend take money from her boss, a gangster. Amanda turns to her wealthy grandfather, a witty, kind, compassionate man with a weak heart and a strong faith in Jesus Christ. He agrees to give her the money to pay her debt, but only if she travels with him to his favorite fishing hole in Redemption, Montana, where they spent time when she was a little girl. Amanda's boss and his henchman drag her boyfriend into the search for her, and now they're hot on her trail.

Road to Redemption is a fast-paced comedy with wholesome values. An added bonus is the movie's wonderful, crisp color photography, quick editing, and strong, frequently comical performances. *Road to Redemption* is an entertaining way to introduce people to the serious message of the gospel of Jesus Christ. It deserves the church's full support.

CONTENT ANALYSIS: (CCC, BBB, V, M) Christian worldview in comedy about the redemption of a sinner, plus strong moral values overcome sinfulness; mild slapstick violence including thug punches man off-screen two times, car chase, several car accidents, man accidentally fires shotgun, train hits car, and people threatened with death unless they hand over stolen money; unmarried couple lives together; and mild miscellaneous immorality such as gambling, stealing, gangsterism, arson, and lying, but all of it is directly or indirectly rebuked by the Christian witness appearing in the story.

Canine Capers

SEE SPOT RUN

Quality: ☆☆☆   Acceptability: +1

WARNING CODES:

Language: *
Violence: *
Sex: None
Nudity: None

RATING: PG
GENRE: Comedy
INTENDED AUDIENCE: Older children and families
RUNNING TIME: 97 minutes
STARRING: David Arquette, Michael Clarke Duncan, Leslie Bibb, Paul Sorvino, Joe Viterelli, Angus T. Jones, and Anthony Anderson
DIRECTOR: John Whitesell
PRODUCERS: Robert Simonds, Tracey Trench, and Andrew Deane
EXECUTIVE PRODUCERS: Michael Alexander Miller and Bruce Berman
WRITERS: George Gallo, Gregory Poirier, Danny Baron, and Chris Faber
DISTRIBUTOR: Warner Brothers
BRIEF SUMMARY:

David Arquette stars in *See Spot Run* as a young mailman named Gordon, who has problems with a police dog, a boy, and some gangsters. Gordon ends up babysitting for the young son of a pretty girl who goes away on a nightmarish business trip that leaves her stranded. The son befriends a huge dog, who happens to be an FBI canine running from some gangsters who want to kill him. Further comical shenanigans ensue as the gangsters search for the dog, the FBI learns of the plot, and the mother tries to get back home before Gordon's irresponsibility endangers her son. What they all fail to realize, however, is that Gordon, James, and the dog are developing a bond that no one can break.

Despite some mild foul language and scatological humor, *See Spot Run* has a generally positive, good-natured, entertaining worldview. Things end happily, of course, but parents may also be concerned about one scene where Gordon feeds James some sugary cereals for breakfast, against his mother's dietary wishes for her son. Gordon learns his lesson, however, when James starts acting up with all the sugar inside him.

CONTENT ANALYSIS: (B, L, V, A, D, M) Moral worldview supporting love, maturity, responsibility, and judging people fairly, marred by some scatological and bathroom humor; nine mild obscenities plus some flatulence jokes and bathroom jokes about dogs and about dog biting off man's private parts; comic slapstick violence such as dog bites mob boss in his private parts, dogs chase mailman, gangsters try to kill FBI dog, men get electric shocks, mailman falls into dog feces, villain throws dog out window, dog fends off gangsters in pet store, men knock over store displays, and man falls off rainspout, ripping off his underwear; implied nudity under shirt; alcohol use; smoking cigars, and FBI agents retrieve what looks like a package of heroin; and irresponsibility and immaturity rebuked, and man feeds young boy sugary cereal.

The Joy of Movie Magic

SHADOW MAGIC

Quality: ☆☆☆☆   Acceptability: +3

WARNING CODES:
  Language: *
  Violence: *
  Sex: None
  Nudity: None

RATING: PG
GENRE: Historical drama
INTENDED AUDIENCE: All ages
RUNNING TIME: 115 minutes
STARRING: Jared Harris, Xia Yu, Xing Yufei, Liu Peiqi, Lu Liping, and Li Yusheng
DIRECTOR: Ann Hu
PRODUCER: Ann Hu
EXECUTIVE PRODUCERS: Charles Xue, Steve Chang, Chiu Shun-Ching, Han Sanping, Ulrich Felsberg, Eitan Hakami, and Katia Milani
WRITER: Ann Hu
DISTRIBUTOR: Sony Pictures Classics/Sony
BRIEF SUMMARY:
Shadow Magic is a valentine to the early days of cinema in Old China at the turn of the last century. *Shadow Magic* is delightful in every respect, with winsome characters and clearly defined morals.

Shadow Magic is a magical film that has nothing to do with the occult arts; rather, it is the fictionalized true story of the first motion picture introduced in Peking, China, in 1902. Liu Jinglun is the chief photographer at the Feng Tai Photo Shop. Captivated by an Englishman's motion picture camera and projector, Liu helps the Englishman seek fame and fortune using the new art medium. Liu's fascination endangers his relationship with the daughter of an opera star, who fears that his career is threatened by the "shadow magic" box.

Loyalty, honesty, and integrity are the subsidiary messages of the movie, but the primary message is that one should not be afraid of the future and not abandon the past. The joy of watching the moving images becomes the joy of capturing on film what Peking looked like at the turn of the century, knowing that it would all pass away. Filmmaker Ann Hu, who was persecuted by the Chinese Cultural Revolution as a young girl and fled to America, has done a masterful job.

CONTENT ANALYSIS: (BB, Ro, L, V, A, M) Moral worldview with a positive perspective on progress, a slight reference to following your heart and no mention of pagan Chinese religious beliefs; one obscenity; two scenes where a man is thrown out of a building but doesn't seem to be hurt, one scene where two friends scuffle, throwing punches that seem insignificant and rolling on the ground, and one scene where a projector burns up and a man hurts his leg; drinking; and lying that is rebuked.

Fractured Fairy Tale

SHREK

Quality: ☆☆☆☆   Acceptability: +1

WARNING CODES:
  Language: *
  Violence: *
  Sex: None
  Nudity: None
RATING: PG
GENRE: Animated fairy tale/ Comedy
INTENDED AUDIENCE: All ages
RUNNING TIME: 89 minutes
VOICES: Mike Myers, Cameron Diaz, Eddie Murphy, and John Lithgow
DIRECTORS: Andrew Adamson and Victoria Jensen
PRODUCERS: Aron Warner, John H. Williams, and Jeffrey Katzenberg
EXECUTIVE PRODUCERS: Penney Finkelman Cox and Sandra Rabins
WRITERS: Ted Elliott, Terry Rossio, Roger S. H. Schulman, and Joe Stillman

BASED ON: The children's book by William Steig
DISTRIBUTOR: DreamWorks Pictures
BRIEF SUMMARY:
Shrek is a fractured fairy tale about a smelly ogre who finds that it takes a princess with a punch to finally soften his heart. *Shrek* is a delightful computer-animated comedy with only a few minor elements to take the bloom off its family-friendly rose.

Shunned by the human townspeople around him, Shrek is a cynical, no-nonsense creature whose swamp has been overrun by annoying fairy-tale creatures, including the Seven Dwarfs. He sets out to make the evil king remove these creatures but finds himself on a quest to rescue a beautiful princess from a fire-breathing dragon instead. The princess packs a punch, however, that softens his heart.

Shrek is thoroughly enjoyable on nearly every level. The script is very funny, although it crosses the line in good taste a few times. Mike Myers as Shrek and Eddie Murphy as a talkative donkey make a delightful comic team. John Lithgow as the evil king and Cameron Diaz as the princess add a lot to this mix. In fact, the story of *Shrek* turns out to be quite a sweet, heart-warming morality tale about learning to love and be loved and looking beyond outward appearances to the inner beauty inside. The animation in *Shrek* is also superb. Not even a few PG elements can spoil all the fun.

CONTENT ANALYSIS: (BB, C, PC, O, L, V, M) Moral worldview about looking past people's outward appearance and about fighting tyranny, plus politically correct subtext and occult spell as a fairy-tale device to set up the story's positive moral conflicts; five mostly mild obscenities and profanities, plus creature passes gas, and a sexual double entendre; cartoon violence in a comical manner, such as protagonist fights soldiers, hero battles scary fire-breathing dragon to rescue princess, and monster gobbles up one person; kissing and romance; ogre bathes in mud; and surly attitudes, discrimination against social misfits rebuked in what may seem to some to be a slightly politically correct fashion, and tyranny rebuked.

Pint-Sized Secret Agents Save the Family

SPY KIDS

Quality: ✰✰✰   Acceptability: +1

WARNING CODES:
  Language: *
  Violence: *
  Sex: None
  Nudity: None

RATING: PG
GENRE: Comedy/Action
INTENDED AUDIENCE: All ages
RUNNING TIME: 86 minutes
STARRING: Antonio Banderas, Carla Cugino, Alexa Vega, Daryl Sabara, Alan Cumming, Teri Hatcher, and Tony Shalhoub
DIRECTOR: Robert Rodriguez
PRODUCERS: Elizabeth Avellan and Robert Rodriguez
EXECUTIVE PRODUCERS: Bob Weinstein, Harvey Weinstein, and Cary Granat
WRITER: Robert Rodriguez
DISTRIBUTOR: Dimension Films
BRIEF SUMMARY:
Spy Kids is a James Bond-type adventure for children, with a Hispanic flavor. For years, Ingrid Cortez has told her children the bedtime story "The Spies Who Fell in Love." Her children, Carmen and Juni, don't suspect that the spies in the fairy tale are actually their parents. Antonio Banderas stars as Gregorio Cortez, who still maintains his espionage contacts. When seven secret agents disappear, Gregorio comes out of retirement to discover what happened. The bad guys kidnap Ingrid and Gregorio, however.

Carmen and Juni spring into action to rescue their parents and save the world.

Spy Kids has several positive messages and a moral worldview. The dialogue explicitly states that keeping a family together is the most challenging task of all. Marriage and family require courage and hard work, the mother says at one point. The colorful set designs, special effects, and costumes in Spy Kids are quite imaginative. The frenetic action pace doesn't quite hold together at times, however. Not enough attention is paid to building to an appropriate climax. There are also some scary characters that may scare very little children. Even so, Spy Kids is a very imaginative and fun family movie.

CONTENT ANALYSIS: (BB, C, H, L, V, M) Moral worldview about defeating evil and the importance of family with a Christian wedding featuring a priest making the sign of the cross and a redemptive act, plus a brief offhand reference to the Cold War that may reflect internationalism; two mild exclamatory obscenities and two mild exclamatory profanities; many chases, slapstick violence, and some martial arts fighting, with scary moments of being chased by black hooded henchmen and by weird robots or androids who have big thumbs in place of heads, arms, and legs, plus fire singes woman's hair; family members hide secrets from one another; and some scary moments as children are chased by the villains who have kidnapped their parents.

The Old West Comes Alive

TEXAS RANGERS

Quality: ✰✰✰   Acceptability: −1

WARNING CODES:
  Language: **
  Violence: ***
  Sex: None
  Nudity: None

RATING: PG-13

GENRE: Western

INTENDED AUDIENCE: Teens and adults

RUNNING TIME: 93 minutes

STARRING: James Van Der Beek, Dylan McDermott, Usher Raymond, Ashton Kutcher, Rachel Leigh Cook, Randy Travis, Vincent Spano, and Tom Skerritt

DIRECTOR: Steve Miner

PRODUCERS: Alan Greisman and Frank Price

EXECUTIVE PRODUCERS: Bob Weinstein, Harvey Weinstein, and Cary Granat

WRITERS: Scott Busby and Martin Copeland

BASED ON: The book *Taming of the Neuces Strip* by George Durham

DISTRIBUTOR: Dimension Films

BRIEF SUMMARY:

Texas Rangers is an old-fashioned Western morality tale built on a strong Christian foundation, but revealing the violence of the Old West. After the Civil War, the Texas governor wants one man to head up the reconstituted Texas Rangers: Leander McNelly, a preacher and a lawman. Leander hires Lincoln Rogers Dunnison to write down his strategic briefings and reports. A Mexican bandit tries to goad the Mexican Army into taking Texas back by force. When he draws thirty Texas Rangers into a trap, Leander kills some prisoners rather than bring them back to justice. Lincoln objects. Eventually, good triumphs over evil, morality wins out, Leander rediscovers his Christian focus, and the meek inherit the earth.

Texas Rangers is an old-fashioned type of movie. It has a clear storyline, well-developed characters, and a strong moral punch. It's clear, however, that it was shot on a low budget. Although the leads do a good job with their roles, the thinness of the budget shows at times. Based on true stories, this movie should

be rediscovered, when it comes out on video, by parents who want their children to see a more accurate portrait of the Old West.

CONTENT ANALYSIS: (CC, BBB, LL, VVV, A, M) Christian worldview with a strong moral message mitigated by strong Western violence; fifteen light obscenities and six light profanities used by the bad guys; lots of Western violence but very little blood and gore such as several big battles where people get shot, several hangings, several point-blank shootings, and threats of violence; brief kissing and chaste romance; natural upper male nudity; alcohol use and medicinal alcohol use; lying rebuked and treachery rebuked.

Swan Out of Water

THE TRUMPET OF THE SWAN

Quality: ☆☆   Acceptability: +3

WARNING CODES:

  Language: None
  Violence: *
  Sex: None
  Nudity: None

RATING: G

GENRE: Animated fantasy

INTENDED AUDIENCE: All ages

RUNNING TIME: 75 minutes

VOICES: Jason Alexander, Mary Steenburgen, Reese Witherspoon, Carol Burnett, Dee Baker, and Joe Mantegna

DIRECTORS: Richard Rich and Terry L. Noss

PRODUCER: Lin Oliver

EXECUTIVE PRODUCER: Seldon O. Young

WRITER: Judy Rothman Rofe

BASED ON: The book by E. B. White

DISTRIBUTOR: TriStar Pictures/ Sony

BRIEF SUMMARY:

The Trumpet of the Swan is about a future trumpet swan Louie, who was born mute and is now on a mission searching for his voice. Father swan is overjoyed when his wife lays three eggs. The father, who is a bit bombastic due to his position as the chief trumpeter swan, immediately breaks into song. Two eggs hatch into girl swans, and finally his pride and joy, Louie, hatches. The parents soon find out that Louie is mute, a serious problem for a trumpeter. Louie goes to great lengths to find his voice. In the process, he learns how to read and write, becomes a pop sensation in Boston playing the trumpet, and tries to win the heart of Serena.

The Trumpet of the Swan is one of the cleanest children's movies in a long time. Bad attitudes and actions are clearly rebuked. Violence is held to a minimum. The problem with the movie is its entertainment value. Like some of director Richard Rich's previous works, the movie looks more like a Saturday morning cartoon. However, this is a movie that deserves wholehearted support. It's too bad that the commitment to family values didn't extend to a commitment to entertainment value.

CONTENT ANALYSIS: (BB, C, V, M) Moral worldview with two Christian references; two swans fight, boy almost goes over waterfall, swan gets scratched when shot by man, squirrels fight with unscrupulous manager; some romance between swans but nothing immoral; and father swan steals but is repentant when he finds out the consequences and makes restitution.

Romantic Conundrums

THE WEDDING PLANNER

Quality: ☆☆☆   Acceptability: −1

WARNING CODES:
 Language: * * *
 Violence: *
 Sex: None
 Nudity: *

RATING: PG-13
GENRE: Romantic comedy
INTENDED AUDIENCE: Teens and adults
RUNNING TIME: 104 minutes
STARRING: Jennifer Lopez, Matthew McConaughey, Alex Rocco, Justin Chambers, Bridgette Wilson, Judy Greer, and Joanna Gleason
DIRECTOR: Adam Shankman
PRODUCERS: Peter Abrams, Deborah Del Prete, Jennifer Gibgot, Robert L. Levy, and Gigi Pritzker
EXECUTIVE PRODUCERS: Moritz Borman, Guy East, Meg Ryan, Nina R. Sadowski, Chris Sievernich, and Nigel Sinclair
WRITERS: Pamela Falk and Michael Ellis
DISTRIBUTOR: Columbia Pictures/Sony
BRIEF SUMMARY:
The Wedding Planner is a romantic comedy set in San Francisco, where a wedding planner unknowingly falls in love with the groom of her rich new client. Mary, a no-nonsense wedding planner, ironically, has no love life of her own. One day she runs into a handsome young doctor, who turns out to be the fiancé of Mary's new client, and a series of humorous conflicts begins. Complicating matters is the fact that Mary's Italian immigrant father tries to set Mary up with a young man fresh off the boat from Italy.

The Wedding Planner is a breezy, relatively tame romantic comedy with a unique clash of characters. The quadrangle between Mary, Steve, Fran, and Mary's Italian suitor develops an entertaining series of problems that, regrettably, are resolved in a rather pedestrian way by the movie's abrupt ending. Mary handles the conflict between herself, Steve, and Fran in a moral way. *The Wedding Planner* is also free of sexual immorality. It contains, however, a significant number of mostly mild obscenities and profanities. It also has a scene involving drunkenness and some offensive jokes regarding a nude statue's private parts.

CONTENT ANALYSIS: (Ro, B, LLL, V, N, AA, M) Romantic worldview with some moral elements including a wedding at a church; sixteen obscenities and sixteen mild profanities; man pushes woman out of way of oncoming trash receptacle, horse runs out of control, and two people accidentally break a statue; couple tries to glue private part back on statue that is accidentally broken; naked statue shown for comic effect; alcohol use, couple appears tipsy from visiting winery and woman gets drunk when she accidentally runs into ex-fiancé; and lack of a full regard for the sacred importance of marriage.

☆☆☆ THE BEST 2001 FILMS FOR FAMILIES ☆☆☆

Headline	Title
Delightful Discovery	*The Princess Diaries*
Love and Fun Conquer Fear	*Monsters, Inc.*
Fun-Filled Family Matters	*Jimmy Neutron: Boy Genius*
The Joy of Movie Magic	*Shadow Magic*
Pint-Sized Secret Agents Save the Family	*Spy Kids*

☆☆☆ THE BEST 2001 FILMS FOR MATURE AUDIENCES ☆☆☆

Headline	Title
An Epic Challenge for a Small Creature	*The Lord of the Rings: Fellowship of the Ring*
The Darker Side of Genius	*A Beautiful Mind*
Because of Our Past	*An American Rhapsody*
Love Brings People Together	*I Am Sam*
The Ultimate Tourist Trap	*Jurassic Park III*
On the Line . . . of Being Wholesome	*On the Line*
Brotherhood of Heroes	*Pearl Harbor*
Triumph over Taliban Terrors	*Kandahar*

★★★ THE TWENTY MOST UNBEARABLE FILMS OF 2001 ★★★

Headline	Title
Most Bigoted Anti-Christian Satire	*Bubble Boy*
Worst Sugar-Coated Promotion of Witchcraft	*Harry Potter and the Sorcerer's Stone*
Raunchiest Popular Sex Fantasy	*American Pie 2*
Worst Marxist-Leninist Propaganda	*Enemy at the Gates*
Worst Gaia Propaganda	*Final Fantasy: The Spirits Within*
Worst Jack-the-Bodice-Ripper	*From Hell*
Worst Masonic Confusion	*Lara Croft: Tomb Raider*
Worst Pedophilia	*L.I.E.*
Worst Trivializing of Communist Threat	*The Majestic*
Worst Animation for Children	*Marco Polo: Return to Xanadu*
Most Confused Lesbianism	*Mulholland Drive*
Most Perverse and Disgusting	*Freddy Got Fingered*
Worst Foreign Film Containing Spiritualism	*The Brotherhood of the Wolf*
Most Racist	*How High*
Most Demonic Bigotry	*The Others*
Most Confused Evolutionary Hype	*Planet of the Apes*
Most Anti-Father	*The Royal Tenenbaums*
Worst Horror Spoof	*Scary Movie 2*
Worst Anti-Family Diatribe	*Sordid Lives*
Most Pathetic Anti-Human Storytelling	*A.I.*

He Who Remembers

ARARAT

Quality: ★★★★   Acceptability: –2

WARNING CODES:

Language: *
Violence: **
Sex: ***
Nudity: **

RATING: R
GENRE: Drama/History
INTENDED AUDIENCE: Adults
RUNNING TIME: 115 minutes
LANGUAGE: English with some Armenian, French, and German
STARRING: Christopher Plummer, David Alpay, Arsinée Khanjian, Charles Aznavour, Bruce Greenwood, Marie-Josée Croze, Simon Abkarian, and Elias Koteas
DIRECTOR: Atom Egoyan
PRODUCERS: Atom Egoyan and Robert Lantos
WRITER: Atom Egoyan
DISTRIBUTOR: Miramax Films (Disney)
BRIEF SUMMARY:

Ararat is a superb, profound movie by gifted director Atom Egoyan, which recounts the story of the Armenian holocaust, one of the worst cases of genocide in recorded history. The killing of the Armenians by the Turks started on 24 April 1915, in the Ottoman Empire and resulted in the killing of over 1.5 million people. This complex tale weaves the stories of Raffi, Celia, Edward, who is an established movie director, David, who is a Canadian customs agent, and others whose storylines come together.

Ararat is marred by a needless, prolonged sex scene. The wartime violence, rape, and stripping of the women can be excused as portraying the truth of history, but trimming the sex scene would have given the movie a greater audience. The movie also may serve to agitate people to take revenge. Several Turkish reporters and sympathizers were insulted by the movie, but it's a must-see movie for viewers who do not understand the history of the persecution of Christians and Jews by Muslims. Christians who see it, however, need to venture forth to spread the Good News of Jesus Christ, rather than the bad news of revenge.

CONTENT ANALYSIS: (CC, BB, Pa, L, VV, SSS, NN, A, D, M) Overt Christian worldview about the Armenian holocaust, in which Turkish Muslims slaughtered 1.5 million Christian Armenians in 1915, a reciting of the last few lines of the Lord's Prayer, many crosses and religious art and artifacts, a lot of moral messages, and an anti-homosexual subplot, as well as references to luck and to father's ghost that could refer to memory not poltergeists; five obscenities and three profanities; wartime violence including bombs exploding, people losing limbs, people shot, people beaten, and women raped; unnecessary adolescent sex scene and women raped in war; upper female nudity and women stripped and forced by Turkish soldiers to dance naked; alcohol; smoking; and lying to customs officer.

Truth Is Never Overrated

BIG FAT LIAR

Quality: ★★★   Acceptability: +1

WARNING CODES:

Language: *
Violence: *

Sex: None
Nudity: *

RATING: PG
GENRE: Comedy
INTENDED AUDIENCE: All ages
RUNNING TIME: 93 minutes
STARRING: Frankie Muniz, Paul
Giamatti, Amanda Bynes, Amanda
Detmer, and Lee Majors
    DIRECTOR: Shawn Levy
    PRODUCERS: Mike Tollin and Brian
Robbins
    EXECUTIVE PRODUCER: Michael
Goldman
    WRITERS: Dan Schneider
    DISTRIBUTOR: MCA/Universal
    BRIEF SUMMARY:
Big Fat Liar tells a story of mythic pro-
portions. A young fallen hero must travel
to a mythical land—in this case
Hollywood—to do battle with one of the
biggest monsters on the face of the
planet—a Hollywood studio executive.
Child actor Frankie Muniz plays Jason, a
fourteen-year-old caught in a lie who
must expose a cheating Hollywood studio executive, played by Paul Giamatti, in
order to restore his father's faith in him.
    Big Fat Liar is energetically filmed and
performed. Its story could use a little
help in the humor department, but Paul
Giamatti makes a funny villain, and
Frankie Muniz is a worthy, intelligent
hero with plenty of outrageous schemes
at his fingertips. Morally speaking,
Jason's scheming and practical jokes are
not something parents will want their
children to emulate. Still, truth wins out
in the end. This moral lesson comes
through strongly at the end. There are
also a couple of times when characters
look skyward, appealing to God for
help. *Big Fat Liar* deserves a mild caution, especially for younger children, but
is to be commended for its virtues.
    CONTENT ANALYSIS: (BB, L, V, N,
A, D, M) Moral worldview supports
telling the truth and honoring one's
father, rebukes lying and includes

appeals to God for help; about four light
obscenities, five mild profanities, and one
vulgarity; comic violence includes bullies
steal teenager's skateboard, teenager on
child's bike runs into limousine, man
jumps out of car, car bumps into another
car, children wrestle man, and implied
kick in the groin; boy poses as girl to fool
elderly, myopic woman; bare-chested
man in swimming trunks; alcohol use;
smoking cigar; and deception, lying ultimately rebuked, young teenager does
things without parental permission, practical jokes, stealing, and father tells son,
"Making up stories seems to be your
God-given talent."

Savior of the World

CHANGING LANES

Quality: ☆☆☆☆   Acceptability: –2

    WARNING CODES:
    Language: ***
    Violence: **
    Sex: None
    Nudity: None

RATING: R
GENRE: Drama/Thriller
INTENDED AUDIENCE: Older
teens and adults
    RUNNING TIME: 125 minutes
    STARRING: Ben Affleck, Samuel L.
Jackson, Kim Staunton, Toni Collette,
Sydney Pollack, William Hurt, and
Amanda Peet
    DIRECTOR: Roger Michell
    PRODUCER: Scott Rudin
    EXECUTIVE PRODUCERS: Ron
Bozman and Adam Schroeder
    WRITERS: Chap Taylor and Michael
Tolkin
    DISTRIBUTOR: Paramount Pictures
    BRIEF SUMMARY:
Changing Lanes is a redemptive drama
starring Samuel L. Jackson and Ben
Affleck as two men in New York City
who engage in a battle of wills when a
traffic accident on Good Friday entangles

their lives together. Gavin, a Wall Street lawyer played by Ben Affleck, is in such a hurry that he leaves an important court document at the scene of an auto accident with Doyle, an insurance salesman played by Samuel L. Jackson. Because of Gavin's rude behavior, Doyle misses an important custody hearing with his wife for their two sons. Doyle refuses to return the file, so Gavin hires a shady computer hacker to make it look like Doyle is bankrupt. The situation escalates from there until the movie's climax.

This description doesn't do justice to Chap Taylor and Michael Tolkin's brilliant script, nor to the nuances in Jackson's and Affleck's performances. Despite some strong foul language, this provocative and exciting movie ends on an uplifting, moral tone of forgiveness, charity, and reconciliation. Even more important, the filmmakers place their moral ending within a Christian context. There are several important references to God, prayer, and Jesus Christ, including Christ's sacrificial death. *Changing Lanes* is a different kind of dramatic thriller for discerning adults who are looking for a more redemptive experience at the local multiplex.

CONTENT ANALYSIS: (CCC, BBB, Pa, LLL, VV, A, D, M) Very strong Christian worldview contains strong moral elements and includes references to Jesus as the Savior of the world and a situation where God appears to answer a man's prayer; marred by some moral relativism and questioning of God's plan; twenty-one obscenities, four strong profanities, and three mild profanities; moderate violence includes auto accident, man punches two men in face, threats, security guards wrestle man to the ground, and man deliberately damages wheel on man's car, resulting in car crash; married man kisses former mistress or girlfriend's cheek; alcohol use and AA meeting briefly depicted; smoking; and lying, fraud, and deliberately setting off sprinklers in office building.

Climbing to New Heights

THE CLIMB

Quality: ☆☆☆☆   Acceptability: +3

WARNING CODES:
Language: None
Violence: *
Sex: None
Nudity: None

RATING: PG
GENRE: Action/Adventure
INTENDED AUDIENCE: Older children and adults
RUNNING TIME: 99 minutes
STARRING: Jason George, Ned Vaughn, Dabney Coleman, Kyli Santiago, Clifton Davis, and Todd Bridges
DIRECTOR: John Schmidt
PRODUCER: John Shepherd
EXECUTIVE PRODUCER: Roger Flessing
WRITERS: Robert Pierce and Patrick Egan
DISTRIBUTOR: World Wide Pictures
BRIEF SUMMARY:
The Climb tells a powerful story of a mountain climber whose sacrifice helps bring another climber to Jesus Christ. The story of *The Climb* starts with two mountain climbers rescuing a young man, who turns out to be the son of a wealthy owner of some superstores in Denver, Colorado. Derek is a hotshot African American (played magnificently by Jason George), who wants to do everything himself in an effort to get back at his father who abandoned him as a young man. Michael Harris (played sensitively by Ned Vaughn) is a committed Christian hurting from the loss of his wife. To repay Derek and Michael, the wealthy owner decides to sponsor them on a climbing expedition to a dangerous mountain in Chile that has claimed many lives. Getting to the mountain proves to be just as difficult as climbing it.

In spite of a small budget, *The Climb* tells a powerful story that will bring tears to many eyes. More interesting, it combines all four of Aristotle's four basic plots—man against nature, man against man, man against God or gods, and man against himself. Furthermore, these all seem to work together seamlessly. *The Climb* is a first-rate production and terrific entertainment that will take audiences to new heights.

CONTENT ANALYSIS: (CCC, V, AA) Strong Christian worldview; some dangerous climbing scenes and a fight scene; kissing and pregnancy out of wedlock; and alcohol use and drunkenness.

Hyper Time

CLOCKSTOPPERS

Quality: ★☆☆☆   Acceptability: −1

WARNING CODES:
  Language: *
  Violence: **
  Sex: None
  Nudity: None
RATING: PG
GENRE: Science fiction
INTENDED AUDIENCE: Older children and teens
RUNNING TIME: 92 minutes
STARRING: Jesse Bradford, French Stewart, Paula Garces, Michael Biehn, Robin Thomas, Garikayi Mutambirwa, and Julia Sweeney
  DIRECTOR: Jonathan Frakes
  PRODUCERS: Gale Anne Hurd and Julia Pistor
  EXECUTIVE PRODUCER: Albie Hecht
  WRITERS: Rob Hedden, J. David Stem, and David N. Weiss
  DISTRIBUTOR: Paramount Pictures
  BRIEF SUMMARY:
Clockstoppers is a well-written, fast-paced science fiction movie from Nickelodeon. Zak, the teenage son of a professor, finds a special watch sent to his father by another scientist. The watch is able to speed up people's metabolism, making it seem as if they can stop time itself. It soon becomes clear that somebody is after the watch. Zak enlists the help of a diplomat's beautiful daughter to save his father, who has been kidnapped by the bad guys.

Clockstoppers is a very entertaining diversion for teenagers. It skews too old for the younger crowd and may be too sweet for older teenagers, but it's got a great heart and great action adventure. The direction by Jonathan Frakes of *Star Trek* fame augments the well-constructed story. Paula Garces is superb as Francesca. Her relationship with Zak is as romantic as it is chaste. Jesse Bradford as Zak is surprisingly appealing in this difficult role. There are also lots of moral messages in this movie, including a strong affirmation of family, and even some clearly redemptive ones. Only an ambiguous message about stealing and some scatological humor slightly spoil the fun.

CONTENT ANALYSIS: (BBB, H, C, L, VV, A, M) Moral worldview with a regrettable lapse into pragmatism with regard to stealing things to solve the plot problem as well as strong family affirmation, strong father-son affirmation, rebuttal of easy sexual relationships, redemptive moments and thanks given to God twice, and good triumphs over evil; six vulgarities and scatological moments, including dog put in car to relieve itself, and reference to soiling one's own pants; action fight scenes including man pulled involuntarily through airport, car rams another car, people zap other people with guns that cause freezing, people caught in violent explosion, two people go over bridge in truck and land in water, and fighting; several kisses; girl shows midriff and walks into room in a towel; club scene; and kidnapping, thuggery, theft, and deception.

God Will Give Me Justice

THE COUNT OF MONTE CRISTO

Quality: ★★★☆   Acceptability: −1

WARNING CODES:
  Language: *
  Violence: **
  Sex: *
  Nudity: None
RATING: PG-13
GENRE: Drama/Thriller
INTENDED AUDIENCE: Teens and adults
RUNNING TIME: 131 minutes
STARRING: Guy Pearce, James Caviezel, Richard Harris, and Dagmara Dominczyk
DIRECTOR: Kevin Reynolds
PRODUCERS: Gary Barber, Roger Birnbaum, Jonathan Glickman, and Morgan O'Sullivan
EXECUTIVE PRODUCER: Chris Brigham
WRITER: Jay Wolpert
BASED ON: The novel by Alexandre Dumas
DISTRIBUTOR: Touchstone/Buena Vista/Disney
BRIEF SUMMARY:
The Count of Monte Cristo is the story of a young, naïve sailor who is wrongfully imprisoned and escapes to take revenge on his betrayers only to learn that there is a better way. Edmund Dantes is a commoner whose plans to marry the beautiful Mercedes are shattered when his best friend, the noble Mondego who wants Mercedes for himself, deceives him. Unlawfully sentenced to the island prison of Chateau D'If, Edmund must endure a thirteen-year nightmare. Over time, he abandons God and becomes consumed by revenge. With the help of another inmate, Faria, Edmund manages to escape and transform himself into the mysterious, wealthy "Count of Monte Cristo." He cleverly insinuates himself into French high society and sets about to destroy those who so cavalierly enslaved him.

Filled with Christian allegories that are slightly diminished by pragmatic perspective, *The Count of Monte Cristo* is entertaining, exciting, and thought provoking. The story and production values are masterful. Filled with Christian truths and a strong apologetic defense of the existence of God, this movie is marred by implied sexual activity and intense violence. *The Count of Monte Cristo* is a powerful, redemptive tale.

CONTENT ANALYSIS: (CCC, Pa, Ro, L, VV, S, AA, D, M) Christian worldview portraying an early-nineteenth-century story of humiliation before exaltation and many references to the justice and presence of God, marred by a revenge motif and some romantic elements; seven light obscenities and one borderline appeal to God as well as long discussion about the existence of God, in which one man scoffs at God; significant violence with several bloody sword fights, swords go through men twice, knife and gun fights, and cruel whippings; two short, veiled scenes implying fornication; underwater swimming scene where the man and woman seem to be nude, (hard to tell); alcohol abuse depicted; smoking depicted; and miscellaneous immorality such as lying, stealing, rude insults, talk of sordid affairs, and parental neglect.

Heroic Code-Breakers

ENIGMA

Quality: ★★★☆   Acceptability: −2

WARNING CODES:
  Language: **
  Violence: *
  Sex: **
  Nudity: **
RATING: R
GENRE: Thriller/Historical drama

INTENDED AUDIENCE: Older teens and adults

RUNNING TIME: 117 minutes

STARRING: Dougray Scott, Kate Winslet, Jeremy Northam, Saffron Burrows, Nikilaj Coster-Waldau, Tom Hollander, Colin Redgrave, Matthew MacFadyen, and Robert Pugh

DIRECTOR: Michael Apted

PRODUCERS: Lorne Michaels and Mick Jagger

EXECUTIVE PRODUCER: Victoria Pearman

WRITER: Tom Stoppard

BASED ON: The novel by Robert Harris

DISTRIBUTOR: Manhattan Pictures International

BRIEF SUMMARY:

Enigma is a thriller set in 1943 at Bletchley Park, Britain's top-secret code-breaking headquarters during World War II. *Enigma* begins as Nazi U-boats are chasing an Allied convoy crossing the Atlantic to help sustain the British war effort. Mathematician Tom Jericho (Dougray Scott) has been recalled to Bletchley after successfully breaking the German code years before. Now the German Navy has suddenly and inexplicably changed the code, and 141 Allied ships loaded with ten thousand men and crucial supplies are at terrible risk. The effort to break the new code is hampered by the search for a spy.

Enigma is a terrific story that is fast paced, wonderfully acted, and smart enough to keep viewers guessing until the very end (if they haven't read the novel). Secret Service agent Wigram and Jericho are caught up in a psychological war in the midst of the larger world war they are fighting. Kate Winslet is captivating as Hester, a reserved woman who blossoms into a bold and passionate partner to Jericho as they struggle together to understand the personal and patriotic betrayal of a friend. The movie's moral worldview is spoiled by a brief but intense sex scene.

CONTENT ANALYSIS: (BB, PP, C, H, LL, V, SS, NN, A, D, M) Moral worldview with strong themes of "greater good" and sacrifice portrayed as Allied Forces fight evil of Hitler and eventually uncover Russian massacre, patriotic worldview in wartime, negative view of traitors harming war effort, allusion to Allied cover-up of wartime atrocity for political purpose of winning war; main characters meet in church, which is depicted as a normal activity; humanistic focus on man's ability to break code with machines and sheer human intelligence alone; thirteen obscenities and profanities; a few violent scenes, mostly fistfights, more intense than graphic and bloody; very brief but intense scene of intercourse with partial nudity, movement, and sound; alcohol use; smoking; and intense scenes of psychological manipulation, confrontation, and betrayal.

Behind the Silver Screen

FESTIVAL IN CANNES

Quality: ☆☆☆☆   Acceptability: −1

WARNING CODES:
  Language: **
  Violence: None
  Sex: *
  Nudity: None

RATING: PG-13

GENRE: Drama

INTENDED AUDIENCE: Older teens and adults

RUNNING TIME: 99 minutes

STARRING: Maximilian Schell, Anouk Aimee, Greta Scacchi, Ron Silver, Rachel Bailit, William Shatner, Jeff Goldblum, and Faye Dunaway

DIRECTOR: Henry Jaglom

PRODUCER: John Goldstone

WRITER: Henry Jaglom

DISTRIBUTOR: Paramount Classics

BRIEF SUMMARY:

Festival in Cannes is a movie about the movie industry, featuring a story concerning aging female movie stars and the men around them. *Festival in Cannes* is one of the most real, poignant, disturbing, and depressing insights ever into the movie industry. A hustler inserts himself into the conversation of three women, including a former star named Alice Palmer, and informs them that he's going to fund their movie. He gets the funding but only if Alice changes her script to feature an aging movie star named Millie. The movie continues to play out, revealing the greed, envy, passion, depression, manipulations, lies, and the ultimate truth involved with all these various characters who embody the essence of the movie industry.

Festival in Cannes is probably director Henry Jaglom's best movie. Anouk Aimee and Greta Scacchi are marvelous in their roles as Alice and Millie. An aging Maximilian Schell adds plenty of stature to his role. Not since the movie *The Player* has a movie gotten so many things right about the movie industry. Vanity leads the women into forsaking their sense and sensibility. Pride leads the men into double dealing. Power corrupts and lust compels. Jaglom makes one moral point after another by exposing the sins of each of these characters.

CONTENT ANALYSIS: (H, BB, LL, S, A, D, M) Humanist worldview with strong moral points; seven obscenities and three profanities; kissing and discussions of sex, including adultery; stars in revealing dresses in the background; alcohol use; smoking; moral confusion; and confession.

Going by the Book

HART'S WAR

Quality: ☆☆☆☆   Acceptability: −1

WARNING CODES:
Language: ***
Violence: **
Sex: None

Nudity: *
RATING: R
GENRE: War/Courtroom drama
INTENDED AUDIENCE: Teens and adults
RUNNING TIME: 125 minutes
STARRING: Bruce Willis, Colin Farrell, Terrence Howard, Maurcel Iures, and Cole Hauser
DIRECTOR: Gregory Hoblit
PRODUCERS: David Ladd, David Foster, Gregory Hoblit, and Arnold Rifkin
EXECUTIVE PRODUCER: Wolfgang Glattes
WRITERS: Billy Ray and Terry George
BASED ON: The novel by John Katzenbach
DISTRIBUTOR: Metro Goldwyn-Mayer/United Artists
BRIEF SUMMARY:
Hart's War, starring Bruce Willis, tells a redemptive story of honor, duty, courage, and sacrifice, set within an American POW camp in Adolph Hitler's Germany during World War II. The story opens in December 1944. Lieutenant Hart, played by Colin Farrell, is a privileged U.S. officer captured by Adolph Hitler's National Socialist army. Colonel McNamara (Bruce Willis), the officer commanding Hart's POW camp, thinks Hart has lied about his interrogation by the Germany enemy. He appoints Hart to be the defense attorney of a black aviator who allegedly murdered a racist sergeant, but McNamara has some ulterior motives. The story comes to a powerful and riveting conclusion.

Hart's War is one of the most Christian movies of 2002, in a year that has proven to be one of the more Christian-oriented in recent memory. This moral, well-done movie extols duty, honor, courage, goodwill toward one's fellow man, and, above all, sacrifice and laying down one's life for others, including one's country. A book containing the Psalms and the New

Testament plays an important symbolic role in two major scenes toward the end. This Christian worldview reverberates deeply in the dramatic conclusion, despite some possible politically correct, revisionist history and strong foul language.

CONTENT ANALYSIS: (CCC, BBB, PPP, PC, RH, LLL, VV, N, A, D, M) Strong Christian worldview extols duty, honor, courage, goodwill toward one's fellow man, and, above all, sacrifice and laying down one's life for others, including one's country and fellow countrymen (with important scenes involving a book that has a New Testament and the Psalms in it); positive worldview overcomes some possible politically correct, revisionist history about racism; about twenty-four obscenities and six strong profanities, and a brief flatulence scene; solid wartime action violence including a couple of men shot in head, plane strafes train station, dogfight, implied murder, Germans hang Russian prisoners, brief images of corpses, and explosions; partial male nudity in POW setting; alcohol use; plenty of smoking; and lying, betrayal, treason, racism, National Socialist officers from Adolph Hitler's Germany mistreat POWs, and soldiers frame another soldier, mostly rebuked.

A Big Problem for a Big Head

HEY ARNOLD! THE MOVIE

Quality: ★★★☆   Acceptability: +1

WARNING CODES:
Language: None
Violence: **
Sex: None
Nudity: None
RATING: PG
GENRE: Animated comedy
INTENDED AUDIENCE: All ages
RUNNING TIME: 84 minutes
VOICES: Spencer Klein, Francesca Marie Smith, Jamil Smith, Dan Castellaneta, Paul Sorvino, Jennifer Jason Leigh, and Christopher Lloyd
DIRECTOR: Tuck Tucker
PRODUCERS: Craig Bartlett and Albie Hecht
EXECUTIVE PRODUCERS: Marjorie Cohn and Julie Pistor
WRITERS: Craig Bartlett and Steve Vikstein
BASED ON: Characters created by Craig Bartlett
DISTRIBUTOR: Paramount Pictures
BRIEF SUMMARY:

Hey Arnold! The Movie takes the beloved TV cartoon figure with the football-shaped head and places him in conflict with a revenge-minded developer who wants to tear down Arnold's neighborhood to build a new shopping mall. *Hey Arnold! The Movie* opens with Arnold learning that his neighborhood is scheduled for the wrecking ball. A mean-hearted developer named Scheck, who owns Future Tech Industries, wants to build a new shopping mall there. Even the boardinghouse where Arnold lives with his grandparents has got to go! As the clock ticks down for demolishing the neighborhood, Arnold discovers that the block is actually a national landmark from the American War for Independence. If he can locate the document that declares his block a historical site, Arnold can save the neighborhood.

Hey Arnold! has a lot of heart and is a very humorous, entertaining movie. The movie ends with an exciting ride on a runaway bus. Older children will enjoy watching Arnold and his friends defeat the oily villain Scheck, who has a secret motive of vengeance for tearing down the neighborhood. They will also enjoy Arnold's interaction with the people who live on his block, especially Arnold's nemesis, Helga, who has a love-hate relationship with him. Parents will be pleased that the movie has a couple of positive references to prayer and an important reference to God's providence.

CONTENT ANALYSIS: (BB, VV, M) Moral worldview with positive references to prayer, one of them in Hebrew, and girl character says, "Godspeed, Arnold"; adults say "heck" several times, and some toilet humor; significant cartoon violence, especially at the end, including people throw tomatoes, explosion, runaway bus crashes into things, and fighting; one big kiss and child says he needs to lie down, girl says she'll go with him, and he replies, "There's no time for that"; and lying, stealing, and revenge.

Blatant Parody

HOLLYWOOD ENDING

Quality: ☆☆☆☆   Acceptability: −2

WARNING CODES:
   Language: ***
   Violence: *
   Sex: *
   Nudity: None
RATING: PG-13
GENRE: Comedy
INTENDED AUDIENCE: Teens and adults
RUNNING TIME: 114 minutes
STARRING: Woody Allen, Téa Leoni, Treat Williams, Debra Messing, Mark Rydell, George Hamilton, and Tiffani Thiessen
DIRECTOR: Woody Allen
PRODUCER: Letty Aronson
EXECUTIVE PRODUCER: Stephen Tenenbaum
WRITER: Woody Allen
DISTRIBUTOR: DreamWorks
BRIEF SUMMARY:
In *Hollywood Ending*, Woody Allen stars as a neurotic, has-been director who goes blind on the eve of shooting his comeback movie. *Hollywood Ending* is extremely funny in places, one of Woody Allen's most humorous movies in a long time. Director Val Waxman (Allen) is given one last stab at glory by his ex-wife, who ran off with a slick Hollywood producer. On the eve of the shoot, however, Val goes psychosomatically blind. His agent convinces Val, however, to fake it by relying on the help of the translator for the Chinese cinematographer hired by Val. Comical complications result, but Val's main desire is to get back with his wife.

Unlike the very subtle and poignant *Festival in Cannes*, Woody has painted with broad brushstrokes a humorous portrait of vile Hollywood filmmaking practices. The humor comes from the contrast of the vileness in the reality and the moral constants that should be the norm. Sometimes, however, the immorality of the situations and characters overwhelms the moral principles of the movie's moral worldview. The acting is very good, and the direction is better than other movies Woody Allen has done lately. The scriptwriting is sharp, but there is just enough immorality to demand extreme caution.

CONTENT ANALYSIS: (BB, Pa, LLL, V, S, A, DD, M) Moral worldview with lots of immoral people, some of whom are rebuked, some of whom are just humorous characters, but some of whom seem to be affirmed in their immorality; a few positive references to God and many profane utterances including five obscenities, three strong profanities regarding Jesus, and twenty-four mild profanities; slapstick violence, including one fall off the second story of a set, many bumps into objects by blind director; female star offers herself to director, director discusses masturbation, adulterous relationship and implied fornication, but nothing portrayed except for a few kisses; woman in lingerie and low-cut clothing; alcohol; smoking, director takes pills, references to drug use by son; deception, dishonesty, breaking one's word, gossip, and tons of sarcasm.

Crimson Pride

HOMETOWN LEGEND

Quality: ☆☆☆☆   Acceptability: +2

WARNING CODES:

Language: *
Violence: **
Sex: None
Nudity: None

RATING: PG
GENRE: Sports drama
INTENDED AUDIENCE: Older children and adults
RUNNING TIME: 104 minutes
STARRING: Terry O'Quinn, Nick Cornish, Lacey Chabert, Kirk B. R. Woller, Ian Bohen, and Kelli Garner
DIRECTOR: James Anderson
PRODUCER: Dallas Jenkins
EXECUTIVE PRODUCERS: Jerry B. Jenkins, Bob Abramoff, Ron Booth, and Leslie McRay
WRITERS: Shawn Hoffman and Michael Patwin
DISTRIBUTOR: Jenkins Entertainment
BRIEF SUMMARY:
Hometown Legend is an entertaining sports movie about an underdog high school football team in Alabama that's trying to recover from a tragic past. *Hometown Legend* opens with Rachel Sawyer, a Southern girl in Athens, Alabama, praying to God to save the town high school, which county officials have decided to close. Elvis Jackson, an orphaned teenager, comes to town to try to win the football scholarship named after Coach Buster Schuler's son who died twelve years ago in a tragic accident on the field. Coach Schuler comes out of retirement to coach the football team one last time, but clashes with many of the players, including Elvis and Schuler's nephew, Brian, the star quarterback who also wants to get the scholarship. Rachel angers Elvis when he finds out that she's on a campaign to use the scholarship money to save the school.

Hometown Legend is a terrific, entertaining family movie that winsomely proclaims the values of prayer and faith. Terry O'Quinn gives an excellent performance as Coach Schuler who, in a crucial moment, flaunts the tyrannical U.S. Supreme Court to lead his team in prayer. Lacey Chabert and Nick Cornish as Rachel and Elvis also deliver appealing, earnest performances. *Hometown Legend* will win the hearts, minds, and souls of the audience.

CONTENT ANALYSIS: (CC, BB, L, VV, M). Christian worldview with prayers and appeals to God, and solid moral values taught; three obscenities and some vulgarities; plenty of football violence and some fighting, plus football coach gets angry and throws things; some kissing; some apparent alcohol use by adults; and selfishness and disunity strongly rebuked.

In Unity We Prevail

ICE AGE

Quality: ☆☆☆☆   Acceptability: +1

WARNING CODES:

Language: None
Violence: *
Sex: None
Nudity: *

RATING: PG
GENRE: Animated comedy
INTENDED AUDIENCE: Children and adults
RUNNING TIME: 75 minutes
VOICES: Ray Romano, Dennis Leary, and John Leguizamo
DIRECTOR: Chris Wedge
PRODUCER: Lori Forte
WRITER: Peter Ackerman
DISTRIBUTOR: 20th Century Fox
BRIEF SUMMARY:
Ice Age, an animated comedy, tells what happens when a mammoth and a sloth escaping the Ice Age are forced together to rescue a human baby, whose parents have been terrorized by a pack of saber-toothed tigers. One tiger, Diego, tries unsuccessfully to wrest the baby

out of the mammoth's trunk. The cat cannot go back to his pack without the child, so is forced to stay with the sloth and mammoth until he can steal the baby. He lies, saying that he knows where the baby's father is. In the end the tiger must decide whether he can really follow through with stealing the baby. Has his heart softened during the journey, or will his killer instinct win out?

Ice Age is fun. The animation is fantastic and the various voice talents add humor for adults. The movie has several politically correct, environmentalist elements however, countered by a strong endorsement of marriage, a life laid down for another, and a strong portrayal of the necessity of unity before victory. The slapstick violence and scary images require a caution for small children.

CONTENT ANALYSIS: (PC, E, Ev, B, C, Ho, V, N, M) Politically correct worldview stressing the environment and anti-hunting sentiments, and evolutionary portrayals; some moral, redemptive elements with mammoth preaching loyalty within marriage and another creature laying down life sacrificially, although disparaging humor is had at the expense of some birds who warn, "The end is near" and chant, "Doom on you"; a very subtle nod to homosexuality will go over children's heads; one "shut up" and some scatological humor; typical slapstick cartoon violence with characters getting heads tromped, hitting, tackling, falling, getting crushed, burned, some scary elements seen in passage through an ancient frozen pass featuring open-fanged, dinosaur-type creatures and ancient sea creatures, volcanic eruptions, avalanches, walls close in on creatures and human mother jumps over cliff and dies by drowning after saving her baby; nude baby; and lying and stealing.

Playing the Name Game

THE IMPORTANCE OF BEING EARNEST

Quality: ☆☆☆☆   Acceptability: +1

WARNING CODES:
  Language: None
  Violence: *
  Sex: None
  Nudity: *
RATING: PG
GENRE: Comedy/Satire
INTENDED AUDIENCE: Teens and adults
RUNNING TIME: 75 minutes
STARRING: Rupert Everett, Colin Firth, Frances O'Connor, Reese Witherspoon, Judi Dench, and Tom Wilkinson
DIRECTOR: Oliver Parker
PRODUCER: Barnaby Thompson
WRITER: Oliver Parker
BASED ON: The play by Oscar Wilde
DISTRIBUTOR: Miramax Films (Disney)
BRIEF SUMMARY:

In *The Importance of Being Earnest*, when two men in the same social circle both have an alter ego named Ernest, a comedy of mistaken identities soon erupts. In this remake of Oscar Wilde's satirical play, the eligible bachelor Jack Worthing lives a double life in late 1800s Victorian England. In his country manor, Worthing acts the serious landowner and gentleman who cares for his young niece. He often disappears, however, to the city to repair the damages wrought by his wayward younger brother, Ernest. The problem is that Jack *is* Ernest. Jack wishes to escape his lackluster country life, so he invents Ernest, who lives a more carefree lifestyle in London. There, he parties with a buddy named Algy, a financially troubled ladies' man with some secrets of his own. As Ernest, Jack woos the daughter of Algy's snooty aunt. Meanwhile, Algy discovers Jack's dual personas and launches a plan to become Ernest and woo Jack's lovely niece. A collision of Ernests is inevitable!

Through many laughs and farcical twists, *The Importance of Being Earnest* shows a tangled web of deception and the incredible hardship that it causes. Rupert Everett, Reese Witherspoon, Colin Firth, Frances O'Connor, and Judi Dench all do a marvelous job in keeping this complicated plot going.

CONTENT ANALYSIS: (B, Ro, V, N, A, D, M) Generally moral worldview with clear consequences shown for misdeeds such as lying and deception; secondary romantic worldview with emotion-based, fantasy-based decisions and outlooks; very mild violence with men being tough with each other; unplanned pregnancy referenced, plus a bit of natural nudity with buttocks and tattoo shown twice; alcohol suggested at bar scene; smoking depicted; and lying and deception.

Reviving a Dead Church

ITALIAN FOR BEGINNERS

Quality: ☆☆☆☆   Acceptability: +1

WARNING CODES:
Language: **
Violence: *
Sex: *
Nudity: None

RATING: R
GENRE: Drama/Comedy
INTENDED AUDIENCE: Teens and adults
RUNNING TIME: 100 minutes
LANGUAGE: Danish
STARRING: Anders W. Bethelsen, Ann Eleonora Jorgensen, Anette Stovelbaek, Peter Gantzler, Lars Kaalund, and Sara Indrio Jensen
DIRECTOR: Lone Scherfig
PRODUCER: Ib Tardini
WRITER: Lone Scherfig

DISTRIBUTOR: Miramax Films/Disney/Buena Vista
BRIEF SUMMARY:
Italian for Beginners is a life-affirming movie from Denmark that shows a Lutheran pastor reviving a dead church and transforming the lives of many townspeople. *Italian for Beginners* opens with Pastor Andreas being shown around the Danish church where he will serve as interim pastor. When Andreas preaches, there are only three people in the congregation, including the embittered former pastor who has lost his faith. Andreas runs into a group of troubled people taking Italian lessons. One by one, he ministers to the alienated, the needy, and the lost within his community. His love, compassion, and preaching combine to rebuild the church.

Italian for Beginners is a life-affirming, sacramental movie in the order of the famous *Tree of Wooden Clogs.* The problems are painful and intense, but the pastor's faith and compassion overcome these obstacles. The direction is superb. There are moments where the movie plays like a beautiful concert, and yet at all times it is humble and transparent. The acting is wonderful. There are a few lightweight obscenities and profanities, but they are mild. Most of the immoral behavior, of which there is very little, is rebuked. In fact, *Italian for Beginners* explicitly shows the power and presence of God.

CONTENT ANALYSIS: (CCC, BBB, Pa, LL, V, S, A, DD, M) Christian worldview emphasizes God's presence, faith, love, and forgiveness, but story features non-Christian characters and some immoral behavior; ten lightweight obscenities and two light profanities; dying woman in hospital scene, daughter turns up morphine drip on terminally ill mother, and woman slaps boyfriend; fornication suggested twice, but not shown; alcohol use; smoking; and lying rebuked, backbiting rebuked, and prayer extolled in answer.

LILO AND STITCH

Quality: ☆☆☆☆   Acceptability: +1

WARNING CODES:
  Language: *
  Violence: *
  Sex: None
  Nudity: *
RATING: PG
GENRE: Animated comedy/
Science fiction
INTENDED AUDIENCE: Older children to adults
RUNNING TIME: 85 minutes
FEATURING: The voices of Daveigh Chase, Jason Scott Lee, Tia Carrere, Kevin McDonald, Asheley Rose Orr, Ving Rhames, Chris Sanders, Kevin Michael Richardson, and David Ogden Stiers
DIRECTOR: Dean Deblois and Chris Sanders
WRITERS: Chris Sanders
DISTRIBUTOR: Walt Disney Pictures/Buena Vista
BRIEF SUMMARY:
Disney's animated comedy *Lilo and Stitch* is a delightful discovery. It is the story of two outcasts who find each other and, through many dangers and trials, change each other for the better and find love and *ohana*, the Hawaiian name for "family." Number 626, an illegal life-form created by an evil scientist in a distant galaxy, crash-lands in Hawaii, stumbles from the wreckage, and is promptly run over by a big truck that simultaneously strips him of his weapons, uniform, and consciousness. The next day, a lonely little girl, Lilo, and her sister, Nani, go to the animal shelter to get a puppy. Number 626 regains consciousness and quickly realizes he is being hunted by two galaxy bad guys and must escape. By posing as a puppy, #626 is grabbed up by Lilo, purchased, renamed "Stitch," and taken home by the girls. Lilo believes that *ohana* is the most important concept of all, and will not quit loving the mischievous Stitch, even though he is interested only in protecting his own hide. Hilarious antics ensue as Nani and Lilo try to teach Stitch how to fit in on the island.

Lilo and Stitch extols love, perseverance, commitment, faith, family, and redemption. Some action violence and references to evolution and voodoo make the movie inappropriate for younger children.

CONTENT ANALYSIS: (BBB, C, Ev, O, L, V, N, M) Strong moral worldview stressing the value of family, with heroine praying to God and some redemptive elements, yet light, comic references to evolution and voodoo; two very light obscenities; violence includes action and cartoon violence of spaceships exploding, brief fights, and lasers shooting; upper male nudity, people in swimsuits and female in bikini; and lying.

MINORITY REPORT

Quality: ☆☆☆☆   Acceptability: −2

WARNING CODES:
  Language: **
  Violence: ***
  Sex: **
  Nudity: *
RATING: PG-13
GENRE: Science fiction/Detective fiction
INTENDED AUDIENCE: Teens and adults
RUNNING TIME: 143 minutes
STARRING: Tom Cruise, Colin Farrell, Max von Sydow, Samantha Morton, Tim Blake Nelson, Peter Stormare, Steve Harris, and Kathryn Morris
DIRECTOR: Steven Spielberg

PRODUCERS: Gerald R. Molen, Bonnie Curtis, Walter F. Parkes, and Jan De Bont

EXECUTIVE PRODUCERS: Gary Goldman and Ronald Shusett

WRITERS: Scott Frank and Jon Cohen

BASED ON: The story by Philip K. Dick

DISTRIBUTOR: 20th Century Fox

BRIEF SUMMARY:

Tom Cruise stars in *Minority Report*, Steven Spielberg's new science fiction thriller about a policeman who becomes a murder suspect when a new system predicts that he will shoot a man to death in less than thirty-six hours. In *Minority Report*, three drug-abuse victims who are capable of seeing future events are used by the police to prevent future murders. Cruise plays detective John Anderton, leader of the Pre-Crime Unit in Washington, D.C., in the year 2054. When Cruise himself becomes a murder suspect, he escapes to find out whether the system is as flawless as he thought it was. Exciting chase scenes and elaborately choreographed fight scenes ensue as John also tries to discover who has set him up.

Minority Report is an intense, exciting science fiction thriller for mature audiences. It has a moral point of view with strong Christian allegorical elements, marred by some brief, gratuitous sexual references, drug content, several gruesome images, ambiguous suggestions of spiritism, and foul language. Despite its problematic moments, older viewers might find this movie worth seeing more than once, not only for Spielberg's brilliant cinematic vision but also for Tom Cruise's excellent performance, not to mention the fabulous supporting cast. In addition to being a well-constructed science fiction fantasy, *Minority Report* is also an archetypal film noir. Older teenagers and adults should exercise extreme caution regarding the movie's edgier material.

CONTENT ANALYSIS: (BB, CC, H, ACap, Pa, LL, VVV, SS, N, A, DD, M) Strong moral worldview with many redemptive elements and Christian allegorical elements, some light humanist qualities, and possible references to channeling and spiritism; eleven obscenities, four strong profanities, and eight mild profanities; much action violence plus some gory, extreme elements regarding stabbing and especially eye transplant, sonic gun fight, chase scenes, man jumps from car to car, vision of man about to stab his wife and her lover, fistfighting, wrestling, suicide, man shot in chest, visions of woman being drowned, electric shocks delivered via police stun-sticks, men with jetpacks crash through buildings, and gruesome images of detached eyeballs; brief depicted simulated sex in computerized hologram parlor and implied adultery; upper male nudity, image of woman's back and obscured upper female nudity through comatose woman's mesh medical outfit; alcohol use; drug use depicted; and murderer frames policeman, and Christian man is too ambitious and his moral conscience awakens too late, but he finds comfort in his religious faith at the end.

Celebrating One's Heritage

MY BIG FAT GREEK WEDDING

Quality: ☆☆☆   Acceptability: −1

WARNING CODES:

Language: **

Violence: *

Sex: *

Nudity: **

RATING: PG

GENRE: Romantic comedy

INTENDED AUDIENCE: Older teens and adults

RUNNING TIME: 95 minutes

STARRING: Nia Vardalos, John Corbett, Michael Constantine, Lainie Kazan, Andrea Martin, and Joey Fatone

DIRECTOR: Joel Zwick
PRODUCERS: Rita Wilson, Tom Hanks, and Gary Goetzman
EXECUTIVE PRODUCERS: Norm Watts, Paul Brooks, and Steven Shareshian
WRITER: Nia Vardalos
BASED ON: The one-woman show by Nia Vardalos
DISTRIBUTOR: Gold Circle Films and Home Box Office
BRIEF SUMMARY:
My Big Fat Greek Wedding is a big fat independent movie that celebrates one American woman's ethnic heritage, including the remnants of her family's Greek Orthodox Christian faith. At thirty, frumpy Toula Portokalos still lives with her parents and works at her father's Greek restaurant in Chicago's Greek section. After spying a handsome college teacher, Ian, at the restaurant, Toula decides she needs a makeover. She meets Ian again, and the two secretly begin a romantic relationship. This upsets her traditional-minded father, who thinks Toula should marry a Greek man and have Greek babies. The rest of the story tells how Toula and Ian manage to soften her father's heart and incorporate Ian into Toula's family, including the family's Greek Orthodox faith.

Although it is clear that Toula and Ian are not super-religious, *My Big Fat Greek Wedding* is a warmhearted, often amusing celebration of Toula's family heritage, including its Greek Orthodox Christian background. There is even a baptism scene where Ian gets baptized. *My Big Fat Greek Wedding* also contains, however, a moderate amount of mostly light foul language, a short sequence of implied premarital sex, and the stereotypical drinking of an alcoholic beverage brought over to America by Greek immigrants.

CONTENT ANALYSIS: (CC, B, Pa, LL, V, S, NN, A, D, M) Nominal Christian worldview celebrates marriage, family, cultural roots, and remnants of woman's nominal Greek Orthodox beliefs (includ-

ing a baptism and wedding scene), but with pagan, libertine view of premarital sex and a comical reference to Greek gods guarding a house; four light obscenities, one strong profanity, and nine light profanities; brief slapstick violence; implied fornication and passionate kissing; female cleavage and upper male nudity as man lies with girlfriend after sex, then he proposes marriage; alcohol use in ethnic party atmosphere and couple gets tipsy; smoking; and thirty-year-old Greek American woman still lives with her parents and lies to them about dating a non-Greek man, but she apologizes for lying.

Major League Dreams

THE ROOKIE

Quality: ☆☆☆☆   Acceptability: +1

WARNING CODES:
Language: *
Violence: None
Sex: None
Nudity: None
RATING: PG
GENRE: Drama
INTENDED AUDIENCE: Older children and adults
RUNNING TIME: 135 minutes
STARRING: Dennis Quaid, Rachel Griffiths, J. D. Evermore, Jay Hernandez, and Brian Cox
DIRECTOR: John Lee Hancock
EXECUTIVE PRODUCER: Philip Steuer
PRODUCERS: Mark Ciardi, Gordon Gray, and Mark Johnson
WRITER: Mike Rich
BASED ON: The life of Jimmy Morris
DISTRIBUTOR: Buena Vista/Walt Disney
BRIEF SUMMARY:
In *The Rookie*, pitcher Jimmy Morris, despite a lifetime of missed opportunities, now has a chance to leave his

small-town high school coaching job and pursue his lifelong dream to try out for the minor leagues and possibly go on to the majors. *The Rookie* stars Dennis Quaid in the title role as high school coach Jimmy Morris. Morris has undergone four surgeries on his shoulder, but his childhood dreams of baseball are still in him, and he practices alone at night. Jimmy had promised his wife and doctors that he wouldn't pitch, but one of his players is insistent, so he shocks everyone by throwing many unbelievable fastballs. Jimmy's players make a deal with their coach: If they move from being a losing team to winning the district title, then Jimmy will try out for the minor leagues. They win district, and Jimmy is faced with a decision. Should he teach baseball in a well-paying, respectable Texas school or risk it all on his big dream? Either decision could have far-reaching effects.

The Rookie contains heartfelt storytelling and excellent performances. It also extols the virtues of family, blessings, commitment, hope, and prayer. Dennis Quaid is perfect in his role as Jimmy Morris. His character is a wonderful husband, father, friend, and coach, not to mention a fine ballplayer. *The Rookie* is a telling example that biblically based, clean, pro-family movies can be the hottest ticket in town.

CONTENT ANALYSIS: (BBB, CC, Fe, L, A, M) Strong moral worldview espousing the virtues of strong families, strong fathers, prayer, the power of a blessing, and the necessity of teamwork; protagonist's house is next to a church, Catholic nuns bless the baseball field, coach prays audible prayers with team and silent prayer alone, wife shows undying support for her husband, even through loneliness and financial troubles, and father and son are restored through admission of mistakes and touching display of forgiveness; slight nod to feminism with protagonist's wife saying, "I'm a Texas woman, which means I don't need the help of a man to keep things runnin'!" (this comment meant to spur husband on to pursue his dreams); one mild obscenity; wife grabs protagonist's rear in the school office, embarrassing him; some alcohol use; and old Texas men gambling (with quarters), slightly rude bantering between the coach and players, and divorce depicted between protagonist's parents.

Godspeed, Peter

SPIDER-MAN

Quality: ☆☆☆☆   Acceptability: +1

WARNING CODES:
   Language: *
   Violence: **
   Sex: None
   Nudity: None
RATING: PG-13
GENRE: Action/Adventure/Science fiction
INTENDED AUDIENCE: Older children and up
RUNNING TIME: 120 minutes
STARRING: Tobey Maguire, Kirsten Dunst, Willem Dafoe, James Franco, Cliff Robertson, Rosemary Harris, and J. K. Simmons
DIRECTOR: Sam Raimi
PRODUCERS: Laura Ziskin and Ian Bryce
EXECUTIVE PRODUCERS: Avi Arad and Stan Lee
WRITER: David Koepp
BASED ON: The Marvel Comic Book series by Stan Lee and Steve Ditko
DISTRIBUTOR: Columbia Pictures/Sony
BRIEF SUMMARY:
Spider-Man is a live-action version of the famous comic book hero Peter Parker, who becomes a crime-fighting hero with superpowers when he's bitten by a genetically engineered spider. *Spider-Man* opens with Peter Parker telling the audience that this is a movie about a girl:

Peter Parker's neighbor, Mary Jane. A genetically engineered spider bites Peter, giving him superpowers, and a family tragedy convinces him that he has to use his powers to protect the innocent. Peter's transformation attracts Mary Jane. Meanwhile, the multimillionaire father of Peter's romantic rival becomes the Green Goblin, a schizophrenic with superhuman strength. The Green Goblin decides to destroy Peter as Spider-Man, and everything that Peter loves.

Spider-Man is very high-octane, with lots of tense action and exciting adventure, so much so that the premise (remember this story is about a girl) gets lost in the middle of the movie. The plot picks up rather quickly, however, and, better than that, there are many positive moral and redemptive messages, including the Lord's Prayer, lots of "God bless you's," and references to biblical wisdom. Tobey Maguire makes Spider-Man come alive. Willem Dafoe has some wonderful conflicted moments in this movie, but sometimes slips into mannerisms. Kirsten Dunst is good as Mary Jane. The action violence is too intense for younger children, however.

CONTENT ANALYSIS: (BBB, CC, Ev, LL, VV, S, A, D, M) Strongly moral worldview with overt Christian, redemptive content such as several "Thank God for you, Peter" and the whole Lord's Prayer recited as a person is attacked by the Green Goblin; minor references to genetic engineering speeding up evolution; ten light obscenities, six profanities, and one serious taking of the Lord's name in vain; lots of action violence with very little blood, including Peter Parker gets into a fistfight in school, gets bitten by a spider, raises money by entering an amateur wrestling match, and several serious battles between Peter and the Green Goblin, one where the Goblin cuts Peter's arm, which bleeds, and another where the Goblin impales himself; two kisses and gang threatens young girl;

low-cut outfits on female wrestlers and wet T-shirt on the love interest; alcohol use; smoking and drug use as part of an experiment; and many crimes thwarted by Spider-Man including stealing, breaking and entering, and beatings.

Radical Search for Freedom

SPIRIT: STALLION OF THE CIMARRON

Quality: ★★★★   Acceptability: −1

WARNING CODES:
   Language: None
   Violence: *
   Sex: None
   Nudity: None

RATING: G
GENRE: Animated fable
INTENDED AUDIENCE: All ages
RUNNING TIME: 83 minutes
VOICES: Matt Damon (narrator), James Cromwell, and Daniel Studi
   DIRECTORS: Kelly Asbury and Lorna Cook
   PRODUCERS: Mireille Soria and Jeffrey Katzenberg
   WRITER: John Fusco
   DISTRIBUTOR: DreamWorks
   BRIEF SUMMARY:
Spirit: Stallion of the Cimarron is an animated fable set in the Wild West about a wild mustang named Spirit who finds adventure and freedom amid the constrictive pressures brought to the land by the march of Western civilization. *Spirit* has a lot of heart, but it is not about the Holy Spirit; rather, it is about the romantic spirit of freedom. An Indian brave named Little Creek frees Spirit, a wild mustang, from the cruel treatment of an army colonel. Even though Little Creek befriends him, Spirit will not let Little Creek ride on his back. Eventually the cavalry attacks the Indian village and captures Spirit again. A powerful dramatic ending follows Spirit's next adventure.

The scripting of *Spirit* is so good that the test audiences applauded at several points in the movie and at the end. The music in *Spirit* does a very good job of sustaining the storyline, and the animation is wonderful, if stylized. *Spirit*, however, has a romantic worldview that inaccurately portrays Western civilization as mean, cruel, and repressive. *Spirit*, however, does not seek his freedom at the expense of everyone else. In fact, he tries valiantly to help others. Children will love this movie, but mediawise families should help their children think through the philosophical and historical problems in *Spirit*.

CONTENT ANALYSIS: (RoRo, RH, PC, B, C, V) Romantic worldview with some revisionist history, anti-Western civilization bias, rebellion against authority, and a radical search for freedom, mitigated by several moral, redemptive virtues including sacrificing oneself for others; one negative remark invoking Providence; and mild cartoon action violence includes horse being roped, riders thrown off horse, horses caught in wild river; gunshots, horses wounded, cavalry charges, Indian village attacked, locomotive tumbles down mountainside, mountain lion attacks young foals, mare giving birth, horse cornered in canyonlands, horse breaks out of fort, blacksmith kicked several times, and men get pushed against corral by horse.

A Great Little Story

STUART LITTLE 2

Quality: ☆☆☆☆   Acceptability: +3

WARNING CODES:
   Language: *
   Violence: *
   Sex: None
   Nudity: None
RATING: PG
GENRE: Fantasy/Comedy

INTENDED AUDIENCE: All ages
RUNNING TIME: 78 minutes
STARRING: Michael J. Fox, Nathan Lane, Jonathan Lipnicki, Geena Davis, Melanie Griffith, Hugh Laurie, James Woods, and Steve Zahn
DIRECTOR: Rob Minkoff
PRODUCERS: Lucy Fisher and Douglas Wick
EXECUTIVE PRODUCERS: Jeff Franklin, Steve Waterman, Rob Minkoff, Gail Lyon, and Jason Clark
WRITERS: Bruce Joel Rubin
BASED ON: Characters created by E. B. White
DISTRIBUTOR: Columbia Pictures/Sony
BRIEF SUMMARY:
Stuart Little 2 is a great story, with Stuart the mouse helping his new friend Margalo the bird escape the clutches of an evil falcon. When his brother, George, finds it more interesting to spend time with his friends than with his adopted mouse brother, Stuart, their father assures Stuart that every cloud has a silver lining and that he will find his own friends. Then, as Stuart is driving along in his little red roadster, a bird named Margalo falls into the seat next to him. Pursuing her is an evil falcon, the animal crime lord of the city. After they escape the falcon, Stuart invites Margalo to stay at the Little house, but Margalo is not the wounded bird she appears to be.

Stuart Little 2 is an incredibly entertaining movie. Every joke, which will not be revealed in this review, is on time and on target. Character arcs are clear. The suspense is exciting. The ingenuity is dramatic. Furthermore, the Little family is the type of family any child would want: They are loving, wise, and full of concern and hope. *Stuart Little 2* also contains an answered prayer. It is a must-see movie for families—as good as it gets.

CONTENT ANALYSIS: (CC, BB, L, V, M) Redemptive worldview with strong moral content, nun prays, reference to burning bush and Moses, a cat's prayer is answered, hero willing to lay down his life for others, hero gives beloved her freedom, but moral content slightly diminished by lying, which is rebuked, but perhaps not strongly enough; four mild obscenities; lots of action, cartoon-type violence, such as cat falls from building, mouse falls from building, mouse falls from airplane, falcon attacks bird, falcon attacks mouse; kiss while mouse and bird watch the movie *Vertigo* on TV; and cat wants to eat mouse and bird, and stealing is clearly rebuked.

The Milk of Christian Kindness

A WALK TO REMEMBER

Quality: ☆☆☆   Acceptability: +1

WARNING CODES:
  Language: **
  Violence: *
  Sex: *
  Nudity: None
RATING: PG
GENRE: Drama/Teen romance
INTENDED AUDIENCE: Teens and young adults
RUNNING TIME: 100 minutes
STARRING: Shane West, Mandy Moore, Peter Coyote, and Daryl Hannah
DIRECTOR: Adam Shankman
EXECUTIVE PRODUCERS: E. K. Gaylord II, Bill Johnson, Casey La Scala, and Edward L. McDonnell
PRODUCERS: Denise Di Novi and Hunt Lowry
WRITER: Karen Janszen
DISTRIBUTOR: Warner Brothers
BRIEF SUMMARY:
In *A Walk to Remember*, troubled teenaged boy, Landon, played by Shane West, finds his life changed as he falls in love with Jamie Sullivan, a Christian pastor's daughter, played by pop star Mandy Moore. *A Walk to Remember* is a romantic teenage tearjerker based on a novel by Nicholas Sparks. Landon Carter and his gang of fellow misfits open the story by hazing another high school student into their group, which results in physical harm to the boy. Though Landon evades arrest by lying to the police about his involvement in the incident, the school principal finds empty beer bottles as evidence of Landon's continued slide into debauchery. For disciplinary purposes, the principal assigns him to a theatre class and extra time at school on weekends as a tutor. There, Landon meets Jamie, a nerdy pastor's daughter with upstanding, uncompromising Christian morals. While doing his penance, Landon finds himself drawn into Jamie's moral universe.

Although there are some unresolved subplots, the production values in *A Walk to Remember* are high, and the actors all give very good performances. From a Christian standpoint, however, the most disappointing thing is the romantic notion that, somehow, human love can conquer what's bad and "save" someone from immorality. Still, the movie shows that Christian kindness can make a difference in other people's lives.

CONTENT ANALYSIS: (CC, BB, Ro, LL, V, A, M) Christian worldview with solid moral elements, including boy honors Christian girl's commitment to abstinence, but with some romantic notions regarding human love; nineteen obscenities, a couple of muffled profanities and some sexual vulgarities and innuendos, plus some implied urinating; gang of "tough kids" trespass, seriously hurt another teen during prank and leave him to be found by police, evading police, gang wrecks car, people lie, and brief fisticuffs; girl invites boy into her home while parents are away, insinuating they've done so before (he declines), fully clothed boy mocks sexual activity, plus passionate kissing; glimpse of altered image of thong bikini-clad model; and bitter conflict between boy and father who left both the boy and his mother (eventually forgiven) and the "good girl" purposely omits an important element of the full truth to her father.

Memories of Valor

WE WERE SOLDIERS

Quality: ☆☆☆☆   Acceptability: −2

WARNING CODES:
   Language: ***
   Violence: ***
   Sex: *
   Nudity: None

RATING: R
GENRE: Action/War movie/Drama
INTENDED AUDIENCE: Older teens and adults
RUNNING TIME: 135 minutes
STARRING: Mel Gibson, Sam Elliott, Madeleine Stowe, Greg Kinnear, Chris Klein, Keri Russell, Barry Pepper, Don Duong, and Ryan Hurst
DIRECTOR: Randall Wallace
PRODUCERS: Bruce Davey, Stephen McEveety, and Randall Wallace
EXECUTIVE PRODUCERS: Jim Lemley and Arne L. Schmidt
WRITER: Randall Wallace
BASED ON: The book We Were Soldiers Once . . . And Young by Lt. Gen. Harold Moore (Ret.) and Joseph L. Galloway
DISTRIBUTOR: Paramount Pictures
BRIEF SUMMARY:
We Were Soldiers is a true story starring Mel Gibson as Colonel Hal Moore, who led the first American helicopter troops into battle against the Communist North Vietnamese in 1965. We Were Soldiers is the first Vietnam movie to really honor the men who gave their lives in that difficult conflict. Mel Gibson plays the colonel, a devout Roman Catholic Christian with a Methodist wife and a gaggle of children. In 1965, Col. Moore's superiors order him to create a new combat tactic sending soldiers into combat quickly via helicopter and withdrawing them just as quickly. Moore finds out what everyone now knows, that the politicians were not committed to a full prosecution of the Vietnam War. On the ground in Vietnam, Moore sees immediately that the North Vietnamese are drawing his men into an ambush. A devastating battle ensues.

We Were Soldiers keeps you riveted to your seat. It's another massive undertaking from the team that produced the Oscar-winning movie Braveheart— Randall Wallace and Mel Gibson. Their Christian sympathies are clearly displayed in this patriotic, powerful movie, but the terrific battle sequences are complete with blood, obscenity, and profanity. Mel Gibson's character depends on God in a very personal way, however, which lifts this movie above the ordinary to become a transcendentally extraordinary and spiritually uplifting tale of courage, valor, and faith.

CONTENT ANALYSIS: (CCC, BBB, PPP, PC, LLL, VVV, S, A, D, M) Strong overt Christian worldview with Roman Catholic and Methodist references and strong references and appeals to Jesus Christ and the triune God of Christianity; strong American patriotism; very slight political correctness regarding the faith of non-Christians, but said in the vein of letting the Christian God be the ultimate judge of men's hearts; about thirty-three obscenities, six strong profanities, and three mild profanities; very strong, very bloody war violence such as men shot in throat, head, or chest, burn victim's skin on legs falls off to the bone, gaping burn scars on two men's faces, images of corpses and wounded men who are bleeding, surgeon's gown covered in blood, groups of soldiers shot or

napalmed severely, soldiers use bayo-
nets, and many explosions; married
couple tickle one another, kiss passionately, and hold one another closely in
bed; man in T-shirt and woman in nightgown; alcohol use; and smoking.

The normal charts rating the movies are not listed since this chapter only
includes those movies released in the first half of 2002.

CONCLUSION

Rejoice always, pray without ceasing, in everything give thanks; for this is the will of God in Christ Jesus for you.

1 Thessalonians 5:16–18 NKJV

It is our sincere hope and prayer that you have found this guide helpful to you, your family, and your friends. As you have discovered, there are good movies to see and there are movies to avoid.

We must exercise discretion and discernment in our entertainment choices, which comes through study of God's Word, prayer, and a sincere desire to walk according to God's will and under the guidance of his Holy Spirit. The key is to be careful, especially where your children are concerned, and remember Peter's admonition: "Just as he who called you is holy, so be holy yourselves in all you do; for it is written: 'Be holy, because I am holy'" (1 Peter 1:15–16).

What Can We Watch Tonight appeared first as *Movieguide: A Biblical Guide to Movies and Entertainment.* For a free sample of *Movieguide* please call 1-800-899-6684.

Please remember that you can make a difference. If Christians will stop supporting immoral, anti-Christian entertainment, producers will quickly change their approach, in order to regain our viewership and our dollars. In the case of movies, our economic support is easy to see: We spend money at the box office for a ticket. In the case of television, we pay when we wash, not when we watch. In other words, with TV we support immoral programs when we support advertisers that sponsor immoral programs.

The solution is simple:

- Support moral programs and movies aimed at the mass audience, not just those programs aimed at Christians, so that the producers who make those movies and programs will make more of the same.
- Boycott immoral movies and the advertisers who sponsor immoral television programs, and let the producer, advertisers, and other key persons know of your action and why.
- Witness to those involved in communications—whether that person is a video store owner, a ticket taker, a writer for the local paper, or a big-time producer.
- Encourage Christians to produce quality movies and television programs for the general public.
- Live exemplary, holy lives through the power of God's Spirit, so the mass media will be unable to find fault with us and will be convicted by the quality of our lives.

If you would like more information on what you can do, please call or write us. Also, join with us in praying that Christians will occupy the mass media for Jesus Christ and that the day will come when you will be able to take your family or friends to any theater and see an uplifting, wholesome movie. Until that day, we hope this guide will help you to choose the best in motion picture entertainment.

Submit yourselves to God. Resist the devil, and he will flee from you. Come near to God, and he will come near to you.... Humble yourselves before the Lord, and he will lift you up.

James 4:7–8, 10

May God bless you in all that you do.

ACTION ITEMS
You can also make a difference by

1. subscribing to *Movieguide*,
2. signing the Concerned Americans for Moral Entertainment pledge, and
3. joining the Christian Film and Television Commission™ ministry.

For more information, call or write:
Movieguide and Christian Film and Television Commission™
2510-G Las Posas Road, #502
Camarillo, CA 93010
(800) 899-6684

After reading this book, if you would like to subscribe to *Movieguide: A Biblical Guide to Movies and Entertainment*, a biweekly publication of Good News Communications that keeps you updated on current movies, please write or call us.

Also, if you would like to purchase any of the movies listed in this book on videotape, or you would like additional assistance, contact us at

MOVIEGUIDE
P.O. Box 9952
Atlanta, GA 30319
(770) 825-0084

EPILOGUE

Repent, then, and turn to God, so that your sins may be wiped out, that times of refreshing may come from the Lord, and that he may send the Christ, who has been appointed for you—even Jesus. He must remain in heaven until the time comes for God to restore everything, as he promised long ago through his holy prophets.

Acts 3:19–21

Father in heaven,

Thank you for making us part of your kingdom through the death and resurrection of your Son, Jesus the Christ. Thank you for entertainment, for joy, and for imagination.

Bless all who read this book. Grant us as your people discernment, courage, and wisdom to choose good entertainment and rebuke the bad.

Help us communicate this discernment to our friends and our families.

Help us most of all to lift up your holy name through the power of your Holy Spirit.

Thank you for all the blessings you have bestowed upon us.

Amen.

ACCEPTABILITY INDEX

+4

Adventures of Milo and Otis,The 91
Endurance, The:
  Shackleton's Legendary
  Antarctic Expedition 516
Eye of the Storm 165
Homeward Bound: The Incredible
  Journey 203
Jetsons: The Movie 110
Left Behind 482
Mercy Streets 484
Muppet Christmas Carol, The 177
Prince and the Pauper, The 116
Prince of Egypt, The.............................407
Quarrel, The..182
Ride, The 409
Road to Redemption 537
Sense and Sensibility 297
Shipwrecked 147
Toy Story 2 458
Weapons of the Spirit 120

+3

Beauty and the Beast.............................124
Beethoven 157
Black Beauty...230
Dark Horse 161
Dennis the Menace.................................196
Efficiency Expert....................................164
Endurance 432
For All Mankind 103
Free Willy...199
Gordy 238
In the Blood 109
Little Men 359
Sidekicks..220
Tom and Jerry: The Movie....................225
Where the Red Fern Grows: Part 2 187

+2

101 Dalmatians.....................................305

Adventures of Elmo
  in Grouchland, The..............................423
Air Bud 343
Aladdin...155
Antz 383
Avalon 93
Awakenings..94
Babe 269
Beethoven's 2nd....................................193
Blank Check...232
Borrowers, The 384
Cats Don't Dance...................................348
Cry the Beloved Country 275
D2: The Mighty Ducks 236
Daughters of the Dust...........................162
DuckTales: The Movie—
  Treasures of the Lost Lamp 99
Ele, My Friend 197
Emma 314
Ernest Goes to Jail................................100
Giant of Thunder Mountain, The 134
Grandfather, The 434
Grizzly Falls...436
Hometown Legend 555
Homeward Bound II: Lost
  in San Francisco 321
Hunchback of Notre Dame, The..........322
Honey, I Blew Up the Kid 170
I'll Be Home for Christmas 392
Inspector Gadget 439
Iron Will...243
It Takes Two...284
Jungle Book, The 243
Kandahar 522
Lassie 244
Lion King, The 245
Little Nemo: Adventures
  in Slumberland 173
Max Keeble's Big Move.........................529
Microcosmos...328
Mighty Ducks, The 175

Monkey Trouble....................................251
Mr. Holland's Opus 288
Muppets from Space.............................445
My Dog Skip.......................................486
Newsies 178
Omega Code, The 448
Once Upon a Forest 214
Once Upon a Time . . . When
    We Were Colored 331
Persuasion...292
Princess Caraboo................................253
Quest for Camelot 408
Remains of the Day, The 215
Richie Rich 256
Rock-A-Doodle...................................183
Santa Clause, The 258
Searching for Bobby Fischer.................218
Second Jungle Book, The: Mowgli and
    Baloo 369
Shiloh 371
Straight Story, The..............................454
Stuart Little.......................................454
Tall Tale 297
Time for Drunken Horses, A.................498

+1

102 Dalmatians...................................463
42 Up...423
Adventures of Pinocchio, The 305
Adventures of Rocky and Bullwinkle,
    The 464
Age of Innocence, The 191
Akira Kurosawa's Dreams 91
All I Want for Christmas 123
Amazing Panda Adventure, The 267
Anastasia 345
Andre...229
Angels in the Outfield.........................229
Anne Frank Remembered.....................306
Apostle, The 347
Baby's Day Out...................................230
Back to the Future III 94
Importance of Being Earnest, The.......557
Big Fat Liar 547
Body, The...512

China Cry...95
Cinema Paradiso 96
Corrina, Corrina.................................236
Curly Sue 128
Cyrano De Bergerac 97
D3: The Mighty Ducks 311
Day in October, A 162
Dear God 312
Dick Tracy 98
Dinosaur 472
Dog of Flanders, A 430
Dr. Seuss' How the Grinch
    Stole Christmas 474
Dunston Checks In..............................313
Emperor's New Groove, The 475
Enchanted April..................................164
Ever After...389
Fantasia 2000 478
Father of the Bride...............................131
First Knight..279
Flintstones in Viva
    Rock Vegas, The 479
Flubber 352
Forever Young 168
Galaxy Quest 433
George Washington..............................481
Gods Must Be Crazy II, The 105
Goofy Movie, A 282
Hamlet (1990) 106
Harriet the Spy...................................320
Hercules 356
Hey Arnold! The Movie.......................554
Home Alone..108
Hook 136
Horse Whisperer, The 391
Hunt for Red October, The...................109
I.Q. 242
Ice Age...556
Indian in the Cupboard, The 283
Iron Giant, The....................................440
Italian for Beginners 558
Les Miserables (1998) 393
Lilo and Stitch....................................559
Long Walk Home, The..........................110
Lorenzo's Oil 174

Man in the Iron Mask, The 397
Megiddo: Omega Code 2 530
Meteor Man, The..................................211
Mighty Joe Young 399
Miracle on 34th Street 250
Monsters, Inc. 531
Mountains of the Moon......................113
Mr. Magoo...362
My Father's Glory...............................138
My Girl 139
My Life 213
My Mother's Castle 138
Never Ending Story II:
   The Next Chapter 140
On the Line 533
Ox, The..179
Parent Trap, The.................................404
Paulie 405
Pebble and the Penguin, The..............291
Princess and the Goblin, The 252
Quigley Down Under 116
Return with Honor 493
Road to El Dorado, The......................494
Rocketeer, The.....................................146
Rookie, The 561
Rugrats Movie, The 409
Runaway Bride 450
Sandlot, The 216
Secret Garden, The 219
See Spot Run.......................................538
Selena 370
Shadowlands 219
Shrek..540
Simon Birch...412
Space Jam 335
Spanish Prisoner, The 414
Spider-Man 562
Spy Kids 541
Star Trek: Insurrection 414
Stranger Among Us, A 185
Tarzan..455
That Thing You Do 337
Thomas and the Magic Railroad 496
Three Men and a Little Lady 119
Titan A.E...498

To Sleep with Anger 119
Truman Show, The 417
Two Bits...299
Walk to Remember, A..........................565
Washington Square 376
While You Were Sleeping....................301
White Fang...152
Widow's Peak 263
Wild America 377
Wild Hearts Can't Be Broken..............152
Wind in the Willows, The 378

–1

Adventures of Huck Finn, The 191
Air Up There, The 192
Alive 193
American Rhapsody, An 507
Apollo 13 268
Armageddon...384
Atlantis: The Lost Empire....................508
Babyfever...231
Bachelor, The 426
Batman and Robin 347
Batman Forever 270
Benny and Joon 194
Bicentennial Man.................................426
Black Knight 511
Brady Bunch, The 271
Browning Version, The 233
Cast Away..468
Cats and Dogs 513
Charlie's Angels 468
Christopher Columbus:
   The Discovery..................................160
Civil Action, A.....................................386
Clockstoppers 550
Cold Comfort Farm 310
Conspiracy Theory 349
Cool Runnings 195
Count of Monte Cristo, The.................551
Crocodile Dundee in Los Angeles 514
Dead Man Walking..............................277
Deep Impact 387
Dish, The 514
Doctor, The..130

Dr. Dolittle 388

Edge, The...350

Entertaining Angels:
  The Dorothy Day Story 314

Evita 316

Family Man, The.......................................477

Family Thing, A...317

Fantasticks, The 479

Far Off Place, A 198

Festival in Cannes.....................................552

Fly Away Home 318

For Richer or Poorer..................................353

Forrest Gump 238

Frequency 480

Freshman, The 103

George of the Jungle 355

Gettysburg 201

Godzilla 390

Groundhog Day 201

Guarding Tess 239

Hart's War 553

Home Alone 2: Lost in New York 169

Hoop Dreams 240

Hope Floats 391

Howard's End 170

Hudsucker Proxy, The...............................240

I Am Sam 518

I Love Trouble..241

Ideal Husband, An 438

James and the Giant Peach..................324

Jane Eyre 325

Jingle All the Way.....................................326

Joe Somebody...519

Jumanji..285

Jungle 2 Jungle 358

Jurassic Park III 520

Just the Ticket..441

Kate and Leopold 522

Kingdom Come...523

Knight's Tale, A...524

Kolya 359

Last Lieutenant, The 327

Last of the Mohicans, The 171

Leap of Faith...172

Legally Blonde...526

Legend of Bagger Vance, The 483

Les Miserables (1995) 286

Lord of the Rings, The:
  The Fellowship of the Ring 526

Lost in Space 395

Lost in Yonkers..208

Love Affair...247

Madness of King George, The 248

Man Without a Face, The 209

Manhattan Murder Mystery 210

Mask of Zorro, The....................................398

Maverick..249

Memphis Belle 111

Men with Guns 399

Mission Impossible....................................330

Mission: Impossible 2 (M:I–2) 486

Mister Johnson 138

Month by the Lake, A................................287

Mr. Baseball 176

Mrs. Brown 363

Much Ado About Nothing.................212

Music of the Heart 445

My Best Friend's Wedding 363

My Big Fat Greek Wedding 560

Naturally Native 446

Nightmare Before Christmas, The.......214

October Sky...447

Of Mice and Men 179

Outbreak..290

Patch Adams 403

Pay It Forward 489

Pearl Harbor..534

Pocahontas 292

Ponette 367

Raise the Red Lantern 182

Regarding Henry 145

Return to Me..492

Reversal of Fortune 117

River Runs Through It, A.................183

Rudy...216

Sabrina 295

Safe Passage 257

Shall We Dance? 371

Shine..334

Sister Act..184

Sister Act II...........................221
Sleepless in Seattle 222
Small Soldiers 413
Spirit: Stallion of the Cimarron 563
Spitfire Grill, The...............336
Star Trek: First Contact 337
Step Kids 147
Still Breathing......................415
Strictly Ballroom.................222
Super Mario Bros..................223
Texas Rangers 541
Three Musketeers, The 224
Trial, The 226
Twister..................................339
Ulee's Gold 374
Volcano.................................380
Wedding Planner, The..........543
Welcome to Sarajevo 377
What About Bob? 151
X-Files, The...........................419
X-Men 501
You've Got Mail 420

−2

12 Monkeys 267
1492: Conquest of Paradise.................155
Agnes Browne 424
Air Force One.........................343
Ali..506
Almost an Angel 92
Almost Famous 464
Along Came a Spider 507
Amistad 344
Arachnophobia 92
Ararat....................................547
Barton Fink 123
Batman Returns.....................156
Big Night...............................307
Billy Elliot 466
Black Robe 126
Bless the Child.......................467
Bodyguard, The......................158
Braveheart 272
Brothers McMullen, The........273
Bullets Over Broadway 234

Changing Lanes 548
Citizen Ruth...........................308
City Slickers 127
Clear and Present Danger.....................234
Client, The.............................235
Commitments, The..................128
Contact 351
Crouching Tiger, Hidden Dragon 471
Cutting Edge, The...................160
Dances with Wolves.................97
Dangerous Minds 276
Dave 196
Deep Blue Sea.........................429
Distinguished Gentleman, The...........163
Doc Hollywood........................129
Dr. Dolittle 2..........................515
East-West 475
Edward Scissorhands................99
Enigma...................................551
Eraser 315
Erin Brockovich.......................476
Exorcist 3: Legion 101
Far and Away.........................166
Fargo 317
Feast of July...........................278
Few Good Men, A 167
Firm, The................................198
Flight of the Intruder 132
Forget Paris 279
Fugitive, The...........................200
Funny Bones 280
Game, The 354
Georgia 281
Get Shorty 282
Ghosts of Mississippi 319
Godfather, Part III, The.......................104
Good Will Hunting 355
Grand Canyon........................135
Green Mile, The 435
Grumpy Old Men 202
Hamlet (1996).........................319
Hollywood Ending 555
Horseman on the Roof, The..............322
Hurricane, The 437
In the Name of the Father 204

Inner Circle, The 136
Insider, The..439
Jackal, The 357
Jefferson in Paris 284
Jerry Maguire......................................325
Joy Luck Club, The...............................205
Jurassic Park 206
King of the Hill 206
K-Pax 521
Last Action Hero, The..........................207
Lethal Weapon 3..................................172
Liar, Liar...360
Little Man Tate.....................................137
Lone Star 328
Mac..209
Magnolia 442
Malcolm X..175
Mask, The...249
Matrix, The 443
Minority Report 559
Mirror Has Two Faces, The...................329
Miss Congeniality 485
Moulin Rouge 531
Mr. and Mrs. Bridge 112
Mr. Destiny..112
Mrs. Doubtfire 211
Murder in the First 289
My Cousin Vinny..................................178
Newton Boys, The 402
Nixon 289
O Brother, Where Art Thou? 487
One True Thing.....................................402
Only the Lonely 141
Oscar and Lucinda...............................365
Other People's Money 141
Paradise Road......................................365
Pathfinder..114
Patriot Games 180
Patriot, The 488
Peacemaker...366
Perfect Storm, The................................490
Player, The..181
Pollock 491
Postcards from the Edge 114
Pretty Woman 115

Prisoners of the Sun 143
Quiz Show...255
Rainmaker, The 368
Ransom...333
Rapture, The...144
Red Violin, The.....................................449
Restoration 294
Ride with the Devil 449
River Wild, The.....................................256
Rob Roy 294
Robin Hood: Prince of Thieves............145
Rock, The 334
Schindler's List 217
Shakespeare in Love.............................411
Soul Food 372
Space Cowboys 496
Speed 259
Stargate 260
Sweet Hereafter, The 373
Tatie Danielle 148
Teenage Mutant Ninja Turtles............118
Teenage Mutant Ninja Turtles II:
   The Secret of the Ooze 149
Third Miracle, The 457
Time to Kill, A......................................338
Titanic 374
Under Siege..185
Uranus 150
Wag the Dog 375
Waiting to Exhale 300
Waterworld 300
We Were Soldiers 566
What Women Want 500
White Hunter, Black Heart 121
White Squall..340
Wild Wild West.....................................459
Wings of the Dove, The.........................379
Witches, The 120
Wrestling Ernest Hemingway.............263

–3

Birdcage, The..308
Black Hawk Down 510
Blair Witch Project, The.......................427
Buffy the Vampire Slayer 159

Fisher King, The 132
Flatliners 102
Ghost 104
Gladiator 482
Glengarry Glen Ross 168
Men in Black 361
Mummy, The 444
Prince of Tides 143
Terminator 2: Judgment Day 149
There's Something About Mary 416

–4

A.I. 505
American Beauty 425
Bill and Ted's Bogus Journey 125
Cape Fear 126
Child's Play 2 95
Craft, The 311
Dogma 431
Doors, The 130
Elizabeth 388

Ferngully: The Last Rainforest 166
Guilty By Suspicion 135
Handmaid's Tale, The 107
Harry Potter and the
    Sorcerer's Stone 517
Lara Croft: Tomb Raider 525
Majestic, The 527
Marco Polo: Return to Xanadu 528
Mulan 400
Natural Born Killers 252
Others, The 533
People Under the Stairs 142
Planet of the Apes 535
Pleasantville 406
Primary Colors 406
Scarlet Letter, The 296
Sixth Sense, The 452
South Park: Bigger, Longer,
    and Uncut 452
What Dreams May Come 417

MPAA RATING INDEX

G

101 Dalmatians 305
102 Dalmatians 463
Adventures of Elmo
in Grouchland, The 423
Adventures of Milo And Otis, The 91
Adventures of Pinocchio, The 305
Aladdin 155
All I Want for Christmas 123
Anastasia 345
Babe 269
Balto 268
Beauty and the Beast 124
Black Beauty 230
Brief History of Time, A 157
Bug's Life, A 384
Cats Don't Dance 348
Chicken Run 468
DuckTales: The Movie—
Treasures of the Lost Lamp 99
Emperor's New Groove, The 475
Endurance, The:
Shackleton's Legendary
Antarctic Expedition 516
Fantasia 2000 478
Far Off Place, A 198
Ferngully: The Last Rainforest 166
For All Mankind 103
Giant of Thunder Mountain, The 134
Goofy Movie, A 282
Gordy 238
Hercules 356
Homeward Bound:
The Incredible Journey 203
Homeward Bound II:
Lost in San Francisco 321
Hunchback of Notre Dame, The 322
Jetsons: The Movie 110
Jimmy Neutron: Boy Genius 517
Lion King, The 245

Little Nemo: Adventures
in Slumberland 173
Little Princess, A 286
Microcosmos 328
Monsters, Inc. 531
Mulan 400
Muppet Christmas Carol, The 177
Muppet Treasure Island 331
Muppets from Space 445
My Father's Glory 138
My Mother's Castle 138
Napoleon 363
Once Upon a Forest 214
Pebble and the Penguin, The 291
Pocahontas 292
Prince and the Pauper, The 116
Prince of Egypt, The 407
Princess and the Goblin, The 252
Princess Diaries, The 535
Quest for Camelot 408
Road to Redemption 537
Rock-A-Doodle 183
Rugrats Movie, The 409
Secret Garden, The 219
Spirit: Stallion of the Cimarron 563
Straight Story, The 454
Swan Princess, The 260
Tarzan 455
Thomas and the Magic Railroad 496
Thumbelina 260
Tigger Movie, The 496
Tom and Jerry: The Movie 225
Toy Story 297
Toy Story 2 458
Trumpet of the Swan, The 542
Where the Red Fern Grows:
Part 2 187
Wild America 377
Wild Hearts Can't Be Broken 152
Winslow Boy, The 459

581

PG

Adventures of Huck Finn, The 191
Adventures of Rocky
   and Bullwinkle, The.........................464
Age of Innocence, The 191
Air Bud 343
Air Up There, The 192
Akira Kurosawa's Dreams 91
Almost an Angel 92
Amazing Panda Adventure, The 267
Andre...229
Angels in the Outfield........................229
Anne Frank Remembered....................306
Antz 383
Apollo 13 268
Atlantis: The Lost Empire....................508
Avalon 93
Baby's Day Out.....................................230
Back to the Future III 94
Basket, The 464
Beethoven 157
Beethoven's 2nd.....................................193
Benny and Joon 194
Bicentennial Man..................................426
Big Fat Liar 547
Blank Check..232
Borrowers, The 384
Brady Bunch, The 271
Casper...273
Cats and Dogs.......................................513
Climb, The..548
Clockstoppers 550
Cold Comfort Farm 310
Cool Runnings 195
Corrina, Corrina 236
Crocodile Dundee in Los Angeles 514
Curly Sue 128
Cutting Edge, The..................................160
Cyrano De Bergerac 97
D2: The Mighty Ducks 236
D3: The Mighty Ducks 311
Dark Horse...161
Day in October, A 162
Dear God..312
Dennis the Menace.................................195

Dick Tracy 98
Dinosaur 472
Distinguished Gentleman, The 163
Dog of Flanders, A 430
Dr. Dolittle 2 515
Dr. Seuss' How the Grinch Stole
   Christmas 474
Dunston Checks In.................................313
Efficiency Expert....................................164
Emma 314
Enchanted April......................................164
Ernest Goes to Jail.................................100
Fantasticks, The 479
Father of the Bride.................................131
Father of the Bride Part II 276
Flintstones in Viva
   Rock Vegas, The.................................479
Flintstones, The......................................236
Flubber 352
Fly Away Home 318
For Richer or Poorer.............................353
Forever Young 168
Free Willy 199
Freshman, The..103
Galaxy Quest 433
George of the Jungle 355
Gettysburg 201
Gods Must Be Crazy II, The 105
Grandfather, The 434
Grizzly Falls...436
Groundhog Day 201
Hamlet (1990) 106
Hands on a Hard Body.........................436
Harriet The Spy 320
Harry Potter and
   the Sorcerer's Stone 517
Hey Arnold! The Movie 554
Home Alone..108
Home Alone 2: Lost in New York 169
Hometown Legend 555
Honey, I Blew Up the Kid 170
Hook 136
Howard's End 170
Hudsucker Proxy, The..........................240
Hunt for Red October, The...................109

I Love Trouble 241
I.Q. 242
I'll Be Home for Christmas 392
Ice Age...556
Importance of Being Earnest, The.......557
In the Blood 109
Indian in the Cupboard, The 283
Inspector Gadget 439
Iron Giant, The................................440
Iron Will...243
It Takes Two....................................284
James and the Giant Peach..................324
Jane Eyre 325
Jingle All the Way 326
Joe Somebody..................................519
Jumanji...285
Jungle 2 Jungle 358
Jungle Book, The 243
Kandahar..522
Kingdom Come.................................523
Lassie...244
Leave It To Beaver 359
Left Behind 482
Lilo and Stitch..................................559
Little Man Tate.................................137
Little Men 395
Little Women 245
Long Walk Home, The.........................110
Lost in Yonkers 208
Madeline..395
Majestic, The 527
Manhattan Murder Mystery 210
Max Keeble's Big Move.......................529
Mighty Ducks, The 175
Mighty Joe Young 399
Miracle on 34th Street 250
Monkey Trouble.................................251
Month by the Lake, A..........................287
Mr. Holland's Opus 288
Mr. Magoo.......................................362
Mrs. Brown 363
Music of the Heart 445
My Big Fat Greek Wedding 560
My Dog Skip.....................................486
My Girl 139

My Life..213
Never Ending Story II:
   The Next Chapter 140
Newsies 178
Nightmare Before Christmas, The.......214
October Sky......................................447
On the Line 532
Once Upon A Time . . .
   When We Were Colored...................331
Parent Trap, The...............................404
Paulie 405
Persuasion 292
Preacher's Wife, The..........................332
Princess Caraboo 253
Raise The Red Lantern 182
Remains of the Day, The 215
Remember the Titans..........................491
Return to Me....................................492
Return with Honor 493
Richie Rich 256
Ride, The 408
Road to El Dorado, The 494
Rocketeer, The..................................146
Rookie, The......................................561
Runaway Bride 450
Sabrina 295
Sandlot, The 216
Santa Clause, The 258
Searching for Bobby Fischer................218
Second Jungle Book, The:
   Mowgli and Baloo...........................369
See Spot Run 538
Selena 370
Sense and Sensibility 297
Shadow Magic 538
Shadowlands 219
Shall We Dance? 371
Shiloh 371
Shiloh 2: Shiloh Season 450
Shipwrecked 147
Shrek..540
Sidekicks...220
Simon Birch......................................412
Sister Act...184
Sister Act II......................................221

Sleepless in Seattle 222
Space Jam 335
Spanish Prisoner, The 414
Spy Kids 541
Squanto: A Warrior's Tale 258
Star Trek: Insurrection 414
Star Wars Episode I:
　The Phantom Menace 452
Step Kids 147
Strictly Ballroom 222
Stuart Little 454
Stuart Little 2 563
Tall Tale 297
Teenage Mutant Ninja Turtles 118
Teenage Mutant Ninja Turtles II:
　The Secret of the Ooze 149
That Thing You Do 337
Three Men and a Little Lady 119
Three Musketeers, The 224
Titan A.E. 498
To Sleep with Anger 119
Truman Show, The 417
Two Bits 299
Walk to Remember, A 565
Washington Square 376
While You Were Sleeping 301
White Fang 152
White Hunter, Black Heart 121
Wide Awake 418
Widow's Peak 263
Wind in the Willows, The 378
Witches, The 120
You've Got Mail 420

PG–13

1492: Conquest of Paradise 155
A.I. 505
Alive 193
American Rhapsody, An 507
Apostle, The 347
Arachnophobia 92
Armageddon 384
Awakenings 94
Bachelor, The 426
Batman and Robin 347

Batman Forever 270
Batman Returns 156
Bill and Ted's Bogus Journey 125
Black Knight 511
Body, The 512
Bridges of Madison County, The 271
Buffy the Vampire Slayer 159
Cast Away 468
Charlie's Angels 468
China Cry 95
Christopher Columbus:
　The Discovery 160
Cider House Rules, The 428
City Slickers 127
Civil Action, A 386
Clear and Present Danger, A 234
Client, The 235
Clueless 274
Contact 351
Count of Monte Cristo, The 551
Crouching Tiger,
　Hidden Dragon 471
Cry the Beloved Country 275
Dances with Wolves 97
Dave 196
Deep Impact 387
Dish, The 514
Doc Hollywood 129
Doctor, The 130
Dr. Dolittle 388
East-West 475
Edward Scissorhands 99
Entertaining Angels:
　The Dorothy Day Story 314
Ever After 389
Evita 316
Family Man, The 477
Family Thing, A 317
Far and Away 166
Festival in Cannes 552
Field, The 100
First Knight 279
Flight of the Intruder 132
Forget Paris 279
Forrest Gump 238

Frequency 480
Fried Green Tomatoes 132
Fugitive, The 200
Ghost 104
Ghosts of Mississippi 319
Godzilla 390
Green Card 105
Grumpy Old Men 202
Guarding Tess 239
Guilty by Suspicion 135
Hamlet (1996) 319
Hollywood Ending 555
Hoop Dreams 240
Hope Floats 391
Horse Whisperer, The 391
I Am Sam 518
Ideal Husband, An 438
Jefferson in Paris 284
Jurassic Park 206
Jurassic Park III 520
Kate and Leopold 522
King of the Hill 206
Knight's Tale, A 524
Kolya 359
K-Pax 521
Lara Croft: Tomb Raider 525
Last Action Hero, The 207
Leap of Faith 172
Legally Blonde 526
Legend of Bagger Vance, The 483
Les Miserables (1998) 393
Liar, Liar 360
Life Is Beautiful 393
Lord of the Rings, The:
   The Fellowship of the Ring 526
Lorenzo's Oil 174
Lost in Space 395
Love Affair 247
Madness of King George, The 248
Malcolm X 175
Man in the Iron Mask, The 397
Man Without a Face, The 209
Mask of Zorro, The 398
Mask, The 249
Maverick 249

Megiddo: Omega Code 2 530
Memphis Belle 111
Men in Black 361
Mercy Streets 484
Meteor Man, The 211
Minority Report 559
Miss Congeniality 485
Mission Impossible 330
Mission: Impossible 2 (M:I–2) 486
Mister Johnson 138
Moulin Rouge 531
Mr. and Mrs. Bridge 112
Mr. Baseball 176
Mr. Destiny 112
Mrs. Doubtfire 211
Much Ado About Nothing 212
Mummy, The 444
My Best Friend's Wedding 363
Naturally Native 446
O Brother, Where Art Thou? 487
Of Mice and Men 179
Omega Code, The 448
Only the Lonely 141
Others, The 533
Patch Adams 403
Pay It Forward 489
Pearl Harbor 534
Perfect Storm, The 490
Planet of the Apes 535
Pleasantville 406
Quigley Down Under 116
Quiz Show 255
Rainmaker, The 368
Rat Race 536
Regarding Henry 145
River Runs Through It, A 183
River Wild, The 256
Robin Hood: Prince of Thieves 145
Rudy 216
Shine 334
Sixth Sense, The 452
Small Soldiers 413
Space Cowboys 496
Spider-Man 562
Spitfire Grill, The 336

Star Trek: First Contact 337

Stargate 260

Still Breathing......................................415

Stranger Among Us, A 185

Super Mario Bros.................................223

Tatie Danielle 148

Texas Rangers 541

Titanic 374

Trial, The 226

Twister...339

Volcano 380

Waterworld 300

Wedding Planner, The..........................543

What About Bob? 151

What Dreams May Come.......................417

What Women Want 500

White Squall...340

Wild Wild West 459

Wrestling Ernest Hemingway 263

X-Files, The..419

X-Men 501

R

12 Monkeys 267

Agnes Browne 424

Air Force One...343

Ali...506

Almost Famous 464

Along Came a Spider 507

American Beauty....................................425

Amistad 344

Anna Karenina......................................345

Ararat..547

Babyfever...231

Barton Fink 123

Big Night..307

Billy Elliot..466

Birdcage, The...308

Black Hawk Down 510

Black Robe 126

Blair Witch Project, The.......................427

Bless the Child.......................................467

Bodyguard, The......................................158

Braveheart 272

Brothers McMullen, The......................273

Browning Version, The 233

Bullets over Broadway 234

Cape Fear...126

Changing Lanes 548

Child's Play 2 95

Cinema Paradiso 96

Citizen Ruth..308

City Hall 308

Commitments, The................................128

Conspiracy Theory 349

Cop Land..350

Craft, The 311

Dangerous Minds 276

Dead Man Walking...............................277

Deep Blue Sea..429

Dogma..431

Doors, The 130

Edge, The..350

Elizabeth..388

Enigma...551

Eraser 315

Erin Brockovich.....................................476

Exorcist 3: Legion 101

Fargo 317

Feast of July...278

Few Good Men, A 167

Fight Club 432

Firm, The..198

Fisher King, The.....................................132

Flatliners 102

Funny Bones 280

Game, The 354

Georgia 281

Get Shorty 282

Gladiator 482

Glengarry Glen Ross.............................168

Godfather, Part III, The 104

Good Will Hunting 355

Grand Canyon.......................................135

Green Mile, The 435

Handmaid's Tale, The...........................107

Hart's War 553

Horseman on the Roof, The..................322

Hurricane, The 437

In the Line of Fire.................................203

In the Name of the Father 204
Inner Circle, The 136
Insider, The.......................................439
Italian for Beginners 558
Jackal, The 357
Jerry Maguire....................................325
Joy Luck Club, The.............................205
Just the Ticket...................................441
Last of the Mohicans, The 171
Les Miserables (1995) 286
Lethal Weapon 3................................172
Lone Star 328
Mac..209
Magnolia 442
Matrix, The 443
Men with Guns 399
Mirror Has Two Faces, The.................329
Mountains of the Moon.......................113
Murder in the First 289
My Cousin Vinny 178
Natural Born Killers 252
Newton Boys, The 402
Nixon 289
One True Thing..................................402
Oscar and Lucinda.............................365
Other People's Money.........................141
Outbreak...290
Paradise Road....................................365
Patriot Games 180
Patriot, The 488
Peacemaker.......................................366
People under the Stairs 142
Player, The..181
Pollock...491
Postcards from the Edge......................114
Pretty Woman 115
Primary Colors..................................406
Prince of Tides, The............................143
Prisoners of the Sun 143
Pulp Fiction.......................................253
Ransom...333
Rapture, The......................................144
Red Violin, The 449
Restoration 294
Reversal of Fortune 117
Ride with the Devil 449

Rob Roy...294
Rock, The...334
Rosewood...368
Rules of Engagement 494
Safe Passage 257
Saving Private Ryan 410
Scarlet Letter, The 296
Schindler's List 217
Shakespeare in Love............................411
Soul Food...372
South Park: Bigger, Longer,
    and Uncut.....................................452
Speed 259
Sweet Hereafter, The 373
Terminator 2: Judgment Day..............149
Thelma and Louise 149
There's Something About Mary..........416
Third Miracle, The 457
Time to Kill, A...................................338
Ulee's Gold 374
Under Siege..185
Unforgiven...185
Wag the Dog 375
Waiting to Exhale 300
We Were Soldiers 566
Welcome to Sarajevo 377
Wings of the Dove, The.......................379

NOT RATED

42 Up..423
Daughters of the Dust.........................162
Ele, My Friend 197
Eye of the Storm 165
George Washington..............................481
Last Lieutenant, The 327
Marco Polo: Return to Xanadu...........528
Ox, The..179
Pathfinder...114
Ponette 367
Quarrel, The 182
Time for Drunken Horses, A...............498
To Live 261
Uranus 150
Weapons of the Spirit 120
White Balloon, The..............................339

GENRE INDEX

Movies may be listed under more than one genre.

ADVENTURE

1492: Conquest of Paradise 155
Adventures of Huck Finn, The 191
Adventures of Milo and Otis, The 91
Adventures of Pinocchio, The 305
Air Force One..................................343
Amazing Panda Adventure, The 267
Atlantis: The Lost Empire..................508
Batman Forever 270
Batman Returns 156
Bill and Ted's Bogus Journey 125
Cast Away 468
Charlie's Angels 468
Clear and Present Danger, A 234
Climb, The......................................548
Count of Monte Cristo, The 551
Dances with Wolves............................97
Ele, My Friend 197
Eraser 315
Evita 316
Far Off Place, A 198
Flight of the Intruder 132
Free Willy..199
Fugitive, The 200
Giant of Thunder Mountain, The 134
Iron Will...243
Jungle Book, The 243
Knight's Tale, A...............................524
Lara Croft: Tomb Raider....................525
Lassie...244
Last of the Mohicans, The 171
Mask of Zorro..................................398
Meteor Man, The..............................211
Mission Impossible...........................330
Mission: Impossible 2 (M:I–2) 486
Mummy, The....................................444
Napoleon 363
Omega Code, The 448
Pathfinder.......................................114

Patriot Games 180
Peacemaker......................................366
Prince and the Pauper, The 116
Richie Rich 256
River Runs Through It, A...................183
River Wild, The................................256
Rob Roy 294
Robin Hood: Prince of Thieves............145
Rock, The...334
Second Jungle Book, The 369
Shiloh 371
Shipwrecked 147
Spanish Prisoner 414
Spider-Man 562
Three Musketeers, The 224
White Fang......................................152
White Squall.....................................340
Wild America 377
Wild Hearts Can't Be Broken..............152
X-Men..501

ANIMATION

Adventures of Rocky and
    Bullwinkle, The...........................464
Aladdin...155
Anastasia...345
Antz 383
Atlantis: The Lost Empire..................508
Balto 268
Beauty and the Beast 124
Bug's Life, A....................................384
Cats Don't Dance..............................348
Chicken Run 468
Dinosaur 472
DuckTales: The Movie—
    Treasures of the Lost Lamp 99
Emperor's New Groove, The 475
Fantasia 2000 478
Ferngully: The Last Rainforest 166

Goofy Movie, A 282
Hercules 356
Hey Arnold! the Movie 554
Hunchback of Notre Dame, The 322
Ice Age 556
Iron Giant, The 440
James and the Giant Peach 324
Jetsons: The Movie 110
Jimmy Neutron: Boy Genius 517
Lilo and Stitch 559
Lion King, The 245
Little Nemo: Adventures
    in Slumberland 173
Marco Polo: Return To Xanadu 528
Monsters, Inc. 531
Mulan 400
Nightmare Before Christmas, The 214
Once Upon a Forest 214
Pebble and the Penguin, The 291
Pocahontas 292
Prince and the Pauper, The 116
Prince of Egypt, The 407
Princess and the Goblin, The 252
Quest for Camelot 408
Road to El Dorado, The 494
Rock-A-Doodle 183
Rugrats Movie, The 409
Shrek 540
South Park: Bigger, Longer,
    and Uncut 452
Spirit: Stallion of the Cimarron 563
Swan Princess, The 260
Tarzan 455
Thumbelina 260
Tigger Movie, The 496
Titan A.E. 498
Tom and Jerry: The Movie 225
Toy Story 297
Toy Story 2 458
Trumpet of the Swan, The 542

COMEDY

101 Dalmatians 305
102 Dalmatians 463
Air Bud 343

Air Up There, The 192
Aladdin 155
All I Want for Christmas 123
Almost An Angel 92
Almost Famous 464
Angels in the Outfield 229
Antz 383
Arachnophobia 92
Babe 269
Baby's Day Out 230
Bachelor, The 426
Beethoven 157
Beethoven's 2nd 193
Importance of Being Earnest, The 557
Bicentennial Man 426
Big Fat Liar 547
Bill and Ted's Bogus Journey 125
Birdcage, The 308
Black Knight 511
Blank Check 232
Brady Bunch, The 271
Buffy the Vampire Slayer 159
Bug's Life, A 384
Bullets Over Broadway 234
Chicken Run 468
Chocolat 469
Citizen Ruth 308
City Slickers 127
Clueless 274
Cold Comfort Farm 310
Cool Runnings 195
Corrina, Corrina 236
Crocodile Dundee in Los Angeles 514
Curly Sue 128
D2: The Mighty Ducks 236
D3: The Mighty Ducks 311
Dave 196
Dear God 312
Dennis the Menace 195
Dish, The 514
Disney's the Kid 472
Distinguished Gentleman, The 163
Doc Hollywood 129
Dogma 431
Dr. Dolittle 388

Dr. Dolittle 2 515
Dunston Checks In 313
Efficiency Expert 164
Emperor's New Groove, The 475
Enchanted April 164
Ernest Goes to Jail 100
Father of the Bride 131
Father of the Bride Part II 276
Flintstones, The 236
Flubber 352
For Richer or Poorer 353
Forget Paris 279
Forrest Gump 238
Freshman, The 103
Funny Bones 280
Galaxy Quest 433
George of the Jungle 355
Get Shorty 282
Ghost 104
Gods Must Be Crazy II, The 105
Gordy 238
Green Card 105
Groundhog Day 201
Grumpy Old Men 202
Hercules 356
Hey Arnold! The Movie 554
Hollywood Ending 555
Home Alone 108
Home Alone 2: Lost in New York 169
Home Alone 3 356
Homeward Bound II:
    Lost in San Francisco 321
Honey, I Blew Up the Kid 170
Hudsucker Proxy, The 240
I Am Sam 518
I Love Trouble 241
I'll Be Home for Christmas 392
Ice Age 556
Ideal Husband, An 438
Inspector Gadget 439
I.Q. 242
Italian for Beginners 558
Jerry Maguire 325
Jetsons: The Movie 110
Jimmy Neutron: Boy Genius 517

Jingle All the Way 326
Joe Somebody 519
Jungle 2 Jungle 358
Just the Ticket 441
Kate and Leopold 522
Kingdom Come 523
Leave It To Beaver 359
Legally Blonde 526
Liar, Liar 360
Life Is Beautiful 393
Lilo and Stitch 559
Little Big League 245
Lost in Yonkers 208
Madeline 395
Manhattan Murder Mystery 210
Mask, The 249
Max Keeble's Big Move 529
Meteor Man, The 211
Mighty Ducks, The 175
Miracle on 34th Street 250
Mirror Has Two Faces, The 329
Miss Congeniality 485
Monkey Trouble 251
Monsters, Inc. 531
Month by the Lake, A 287
Mr. and Mrs. Bridge 112
Mr. Baseball 176
Mr. Destiny 112
Mr. Magoo 362
Mrs. Doubtfire 211
Much Ado About Nothing 212
Muppets from Space 445
My Best Friend's Wedding 363
My Big Fat Greek Wedding 560
My Cousin Vinny 178
My Giant 400
My Girl 139
Natural Born Killers 252
O Brother, Where Art Thou? 487
On the Line 532
Only the Lonely 141
Parent Trap, The 404
Patch Adams 403
Paulie 405
Player, The 181

Pleasantville 406

Postcards from the Edge 114

Pretty Woman 115

Princess Caraboo 253

Princess Diaries, The 535

Rat Race 536

Remains of the Day, The 215

Return to Me...492

Richie Rich 256

Road to Redemption 537

Rugrats Movie, The 409

Runaway Bride 450

Sabrina 295

Sandlot, The 216

Santa Clause, The 258

See Spot Run 538

Shakespeare in Love............................411

Shall We Dance? 371

Shrek..540

Sister Act..184

Sister Act II...221

Sleepless in Seattle 222

Spy Kids 541

Step Kids 147

Still Breathing......................................415

Strictly Ballroom 222

Stuart Little..454

Stuart Little 2.......................................563

Super Mario Bros. 223

Tatie Danielle 148

Teenage Mutant Ninja Turtles 118

Teenage Mutant Ninja Turtles II:

     The Secret of the Ooze 149

That Thing You Do 337

There's Something About Mary..........416

Three Men and a Little Lady 119

Tigger Movie, The 496

To Sleep With Anger 119

Toy Story 297

Toy Story 2 458

Trial, The 226

Wag the Dog 375

Wedding Planner, The..........................543

What About Bob? 151

What Women Want 500

While You Were Sleeping....................301

White Balloon, The...............................339

Wide Awake..418

Widow's Peak 263

You've Got Mail 420

DOCUMENTARY

42 Up..423

Anne Frank Remembered.....................306

Brief History of Time, A.......................157

Doors, The 130

Endurance 432

Endurance, The:

     Shackleton's Legendary

     Antarctic Expedition 516

For All Mankind 103

Hands on a Hard Body.........................436

Hoop Dreams 240

In the Blood 109

Microcosmos...328

Return with Honor 493

Weapons of the Spirit 120

DRAMA

1492: Conquest of Paradise.................155

Adventures of Huck Finn, The 191

Age of Innocence, The 191

Agnes Browne 424

Akira Kurosawa's Dreams 91

Ali...506

Alive 193

American Beauty....................................425

American Rhapsody, An 507

Amistad 344

Andre...229

Anna Karenina 345

Apollo 13 268

Apostle, The 347

Ararat..547

Avalon 93

Awakenings 94

Babyfever 231

Barton Fink 123

Basket, The 464

Beautiful Mind, A.................................508

Benny and Joon 194
Big Night...307
Billy Elliot 466
Black Beauty......................................230
Black Hawk Down 510
Black Robe 126
Body, The...512
Bodyguard, The 158
Braveheart 272
Bridges of Madison County, The 271
Brothers McMullen, The......................273
Browning Version, The 233
Changing Lanes 548
Children of Heaven 427
China Cry...95
Cider House Rules, The 428
Cinema Paradiso 96
City Hall 308
Civil Action, A...................................386
Client, The...235
Commitments, The...............................128
Corrina, Corrina 236
Count of Monte Cristo, The 551
Cry the Beloved Country 275
Cutting Edge, The...............................160
Dances with Wolves............................97
Dangerous Minds 276
Dark Horse 161
Daughters of the Dust.........................162
Day in October, A 162
Dead Man Walking.............................277
Dick Tracy 98
Doctor, The..130
Dog of Flanders, A 430
East-West 475
Edge, The..350
Edward Scissorhands 99
Efficiency Expert 164
Ele, My Friend 197
Elizabeth..388
Emma 314
Endurance..432
Enigma 551
Erin Brockovich..................................476
Ernest Hemingway 262

Eye of the Storm.................................165
Family Thing, A.................................317
Far and Away.....................................166
Far Off Place, A 198
Fargo 317
Feast of July.......................................278
Festival in Cannes..............................552
Few Good Men, A 167
Field, The..100
Fight Club 432
Firm, The..198
First Knight..279
Fisher King, The 132
Flatliners 102
Fly Away Home 318
Forever Young 168
Forrest Gump 238
Fried Green Tomatoes..........................132
George Washington.............................481
Georgia 281
Gettysburg 201
Ghosts of Mississippi 319
Glengarry Glen Ross............................168
Godfather, Part III, The 104
Good Will Hunting 355
Grand Canyon....................................135
Grandfather, The 434
Green Mile, The 435
Guarding Tess 239
Guilty By Suspicion............................135
Hamlet (1990) 106
Hamlet (1996) 319
Handmaid's Tale, The..........................107
Harriet the Spy...................................320
Hart's War 553
Hometown Legend 555
Homeward Bound:
    The Incredible Journey.....................203
Hope Floats 391
Horse Whisperer, The..........................391
Horseman on the Roof, The..................322
Howard's End 170
Hudsucker Proxy, The..........................240
Hurricane, The....................................437
I Am Sam 518

In the Name of the Father 204
Inner Circle, The 136
Insider, The................................439
It Takes Two................................284
Italian for Beginners 558
Jefferson in Paris 284
Joy Luck Club, The............................205
Kandahar................................522
King of the Hill 206
Kolya 359
K-Pax 521
Last Lieutenant, The 327
Last of the Mohicans, The 171
Leap of Faith................................172
Legend of Bagger Vance, The 483
Les Miserables (1995) 286
Les Miserables (1998) 393
Life Is Beautiful................................393
Little Man Tate................................137
Little Men 395
Little Women................................245
Lone Star 328
Long Walk Home, The......................110
Lorenzo's Oil................................174
Love Affair................................247
Mac................................209
Madness of King George, The 248
Magnolia 442
Majestic, The................................527
Malcolm X................................175
Man Without a Face, The 209
Memphis Belle 111
Men With Guns 399
Mercy Streets................................484
Mister Johnson 138
Moulin Rouge 531
Mountains of the Moon......................113
Mr. and Mrs. Bridge 112
Mr. Holland's Opus 288
Mrs. Brown................................363
Murder in the First 289
Music of the Heart 445
My Dog Skip................................486
My Father's Glory................................138
My Life................................213

My Mother's Castle 138
Naturally Native................................446
Nixon 289
October Sky................................447
Of Mice and Men................................179
Once Upon a Time . . .
    When We Were Colored..................331
One True Thing................................402
Oscar and Lucinda 365
Other People's Money 141
Outbreak................................290
Ox, The................................179
Paradise Road................................365
Pay It Forward................................489
Perfect Storm, The................................490
Persuasion................................292
Ponette 367
Postcards from the Edge......................114
Postman, The (Il Postino) 292
Preacher's Wife, The..........................332
Pretty Woman................................115
Primary Colors................................406
Prince of Tides, The..........................143
Prisoners of the Sun 143
Pulp Fiction................................253
Quarrel, The................................182
Quiz Show................................255
Rainmaker, The 368
Raise the Red Lantern 182
Rapture, The................................144
Red Violin, The................................449
Regarding Henry 145
Remember the Titans................................491
Restoration................................294
Reversal of Fortune 117
Ride with the Devil 449
River Runs Through It, A..................183
Robin Hood: Prince of Thieves..........145
Rookie, The................................561
Rosewood................................368
Rudy................................216
Rules of Engagement 494
Safe Passage 257
Scarlet Letter, The................................296
Schindler's List................................217

Searching for Bobby Fischer 218
Secret Garden, The 219
Selena 370
Sense and Sensibility 297
Shadow Magic.......................................538
Shadowlands 219
Shall We Dance? 371
Shiloh 2: Shiloh Season 450
Shine...334
Sidekicks 220
Simon Birch...412
Soul Food...372
Speed 259
Spitfire Grill, The 336
Squanto: A Warrior's Tale 258
Still Breathing 415
Straight Story, The...............................454
Stranger Among Us, A 185
Sweet Hereafter, The 373
Swing Kids...223
Tea with Mussolini...............................456
Thelma and Louise 149
Third Miracle, The 457
Time for Drunken Horses, A...............498
Time To Kill, A 338
Titanic 374
To Live 261
To Sleep with Anger 119
Trial, The 226
Two Bits..299
U-571 499
Ulee's Gold 374
Uranus 150
Volcano...380
Wag the Dog 375
Waiting to Exhale 300
Walk To Remember, A 565
Washington Square...............................376
We Were Soldiers 566
Welcome To Sarajevo............................377
Where the Red Fern Grows: Part 2.....187
White Balloon, The 339
White Hunter, Black Heart 121
Wide Awake...418
Widow's Peak 263

Wild America 377
Wild Hearts Can't Be Broken..............152
Wings of the Dove, The 379
Winslow Boy, The 459
Wrestling Ernest Hemingway 263

FANTASY

Adventures of Elmo
    in Grouchland, The....................423
Adventures of Rocky
    and Bullwinkle, The....................464
Akira Kurosawa's Dreams 91
Aladdin..155
Anastasia..345
Babe 269
Batman and Robin 347
Batman Forever 270
Beauty and the Beast............................124
Black Knight 511
Bless the Child.......................................467
Borrowers, The 384
Casper...273
Cats and Dogs 513
Crouching Tiger,
    Hidden Dragon............................471
Dick Tracy 98
Dinosaur 472
Dogma...431
Dr. Seuss' How the Grinch Stole
    Christmas 474
Edward Scissorhands..............................99
Ever After...389
Family Man, The....................................477
Flatliners 102
Flintstones in Viva
    Rock Vegas, The............................479
Flubber 352
Forever Young 168
Harry Potter and
    the Sorcerer's Stone 517
Homeward Bound II:
    Lost in San Francisco 321
Hook 136
Ice Age..556
Indian in the Cupboard, The..............283

Inspector Gadget 439
James and the Giant Peach..................324
Jumanji...285
Kate and Leopold 522
Lara Croft: Tomb Raider......................525
Last Action Hero, The..........................207
Lord of the Rings, The:
   The Fellowship of the Ring 526
Mask, The...249
Mighty Joe Young 399
Muppet Treasure Island 331
Never Ending Story II:
   The Next Chapter 140
Nightmare Before Christmas, The.......214
Pleasantville 406
Pocahontas 292
Princess and the Goblin, The 252
Santa Clause, The 258
Shrek..540
Small Soldiers 413
Space Jam 335
Stuart Little..454
Stuart Little 2...563
Super Mario Bros. 223
Tall Tale 297
Teenage Mutant Ninja Turtles.............118
Thomas and the Magic Railroad 496
Toy Story 297
Toy Story 2 458
Truman Show, The 417
Trumpet of the Swan, The 542
What Dreams May Come......................417
Wind in the Willows, The 378
Witches, The 120

HISTORICAL

Amistad 344
Anastasia...345
Anne Frank Remembered......................306
Apollo 13 268
Black Robe 126
Christopher Columbus:
   The Discovery 160
Count of Monte Cristo, The.................551
Elizabeth...388

Enigma 551
Ever After...389
Evita 316
Ghosts of Mississippi 319
Gladiator 482
Grandfather, The 434
Grizzly Falls 436
Jefferson in Paris 284
Les Miserables (1998) 393
Madness of King George, The 248
Man in the Iron Mask, The 397
Newton Boys, The 402
Once Upon a Time . . .
   When We Were Colored...................331
Oscar and Lucinda 365
Paradise Road...365
Patriot, The 488
Pearl Harbor...534
Pollock 491
Prince of Egypt, The..............................407
Ride with the Devil 449
Rosewood...368
Saving Private Ryan 410
Selena 370
Shadow Magic...538
Squanto: A Warrior's Tale 258
Swing Kids...223
Titanic 374

HORROR

Arachnophobia 92
Blair Witch Project, The.......................427
Child's Play 2 95
Deep Blue Sea...429
Exorcist 3: Legion 101
Flatliners 102
Ghost 104
Jurassic Park 206
Jurassic Park III 520
Mummy, The..444
Nightmare Before Christmas, The.......214
Others, The..533
People under the Stairs 142
Witches, The 120

INSPIRATION

Entertaining Angels:
  The Dorothy Day Story...................314
Prince of Egypt, The............................407

MUSICAL

Muppet Christmas Carol, The 177
Newsies 178

ROMANCE

Bachelor, The 426
Bridges of Madison County, The 271
Chocolat...469
Cyrano De Bergerac 97
Enchanted April...................................164
Fantasticks, The 479
Far Off Place, A 198
First Knight..279
Forget Paris..279
George of the Jungle 355
Ghost 104
Green Card 105
Hope Floats 391
I.Q. 242
Jane Eyre 325
Jerry Maguire.......................................325
Just the Ticket......................................441
Kate and Leopold 522
Last of the Mohicans, The 171
Little Women..245
Love Affair..247
Miracle on 34th Street 250
My Big Fat Greek Wedding 560
My Giant...400
On the Line 533
Only the Lonely 141
Pearl Harbor..534
Postman, The (Il Postino) 292
Pretty Woman 115
Princess Caraboo 253
Return to Me...492
Runaway Bride 450
Sabrina 295
Scarlet Letter, The 296
Shakespeare in Love.............................411

Sleepless in Seattle 222
Still Breathing......................................415
There's Something About Mary..........416
Walk to Remember, A...........................565
Wedding Planner, The..........................543
What Women Want 500
Where the Red Fern Grows: Part 2.....187
While You Were Sleeping.....................301
You've Got Mail 420

SATIRE

Almost Famous 464
Importance of Being Earnest, The.......557
Magnolia 442
Natural Born Killers 252
Wag the Dog 375

SCIENCE FICTION

12 Monkeys...267
A.I. 505
Armageddon..384
Back to the Future III 94
Bicentennial Man.................................426
Clockstoppers 550
Contact 351
Deep Blue Sea.......................................429
Deep Impact 387
Frequency 480
Galaxy Quest 433
Godzilla 390
Independence Day.................................323
Iron Giant, The.....................................440
Jurassic Park 206
Jurassic Park III 520
K-Pax 521
Left Behind 482
Lilo and Stitch......................................559
Lost in Space 395
Matrix, The 443
Men in Black 361
Minority Report 559
Planet of the Apes 535
Space Cowboys 496
Spider-Man 562
Star Trek: First Contact 337

Star Trek: Insurrection 414
Star Wars Episode I: The Phantom
   Menace 452
Stargate 260
Terminator 2: Judgment Day 149
Titan A.E. 498
Waterworld 300
Wild Wild West 459
X-Files, The 419
X-Men 501

THRILLER

Air Force One.......................................343
Along Came a Spider 507
Arachnophobia 92
Body, The 512
Bodyguard, The 158
Cape Fear...126
Changing Lanes 548
City Hall 308
Clear and Present Danger, A 234
Conspiracy Theory 349
Craft, The 311
Enigma 551
Frequency 480
Fugitive, The 200

Game, The 354
Hunt for Red October, The.................109
In the Line of Fire 203
Jackal, The 357
Lethal Weapon 3..................................172
Megiddo: Omega Code 2 530
Minority Report 559
Mission Impossible...............................330
Mission: Impossible 2 (M:I–2) 486
Patriot Games 180
Ransom..333
Sixth Sense, The 452
Twister...339
Under Siege 185
X-Files, The 419

WESTERN

Back to the Future III 94
Maverick..249
Quigley Down Under 116
Ride, The 409
Tall Tale 297
Texas Rangers 541
Unforgiven 185
Wild Wild West....................................459

MOVIE TITLES, ACTORS, AND DIRECTORS

12 Monkeys 267
42 Up...423
101 Dalmatians.................................305
102 Dalmatians.................................463
1492: Conquest of Paradise.................155

A.I...505
Abraham, F. Murray..........................414
Ackerman, Robert Allan: dir. 257
Adamson, Andrew: dir. 540
Adventures of Elmo
    in Grouchland, The......................423
Adventures of Huck Finn, The 191
Adventures of Milo and Otis, The 91
Adventures of Pinocchio, The 305
Adventures of Rocky
    and Bullwinkle, The......................464
Affleck, Ben 355, 384, 411,
                                         431, 534, 548
Age of Innocence, The 191
Agnes Browne 424
Agutter, Jenny 95
Aiello, Danny 309
Aimee, Anouk....................................552
Air Bud 343
Air Force One......................................343
Air Up There, The 192
Akira Kurosawa's Dreams 91
Aladdin..155
Alda, Alan..............................210, 500
Alexander, Jason..............313, 464, 542
Ali...506
Alive 193
All I Want for Christmas 123
Allcroft, Britt: dir. 496
Allen, Joan 218, 289, 406
Allen, Karen 207, 217, 465
Allen, Tim 258, 298, 353, 358,
                                         433, 458, 519
Allen, Woody 210, 383, 555
Allen, Woody: dir. 210, 234, 555

Alley, Kirstie..............................284, 353
Almost an Angel 92
Almost Famous 464
Along Came a Spider 507
Altman, Robert: dir.............................181
Amazing Panda Adventure, The 267
Ameche, Don.........................203, 236
Amenábar, Alejandro: dir. 533
American Beauty.................................425
American Rhapsody, An 507
Amistad 344
Amurri, Franco: dir. 251
Anastasia 345
Anderson, Anthony 538, 523
Anderson, Gillian 419
Anderson, James: dir........................556
Anderson, Paul Thomas: dir. 442
Andre..229
Andreacchio, Mario: dir...................364
Andrews, Julie 536
Angels In the Outfield 229
Aniston, Jennifer.............................440
Anne Frank Remembered 306
Anspaugh, David: dir. 216
Antz 383
Anwar, Gabrielle 153
Apollo 13 268
Apostle, The 347
Apted, Michael: dir...................423, 552
Arachnophobia 92
Ararat..547
Archer, Anne 180, 234, 495
Ardolino, Emile: dir.............119, 184
Arkin, Alan..............................146, 168
Armageddon..384
Armstrong, Gillian: dir. 247, 365
Arquette, David 538
Arquette, Rosanna..................132, 254
Ashley, Elizabeth 441
Assante, Armande............................155
Astin, Sean 111, 216, 527

Atkinson, Rowan.............................537
Atlantis: The Lost Empire...................508
Attenborough, Richard............206, 250
                                388, 497
Attenborough, Richard: dir. 220
Auberjonois, Rene 173, 348, 488
August, Bille: dir................................393
Austin, Michael: dir..........................253
Avalon..93
Avnet, Jon: dir. 133
Awakenings......................................94
Aykroyd, Dan....................139, 383, 534
Azaria, Hank.....................................390
Aznavour, Charles.............................547

Babe...269
Baby's Day Out................................230
Babyfever..231
Bacall, Lauren.............................123, 329
Bachelor, The..................................426
Back to the Future III...........................94
Bacon, Kevin 102, 167, 192, 289, 487
Baker, Carroll 354
Baker, Simon.....................................450
Bakula, Scott............................348, 425
Balaban, Bob.....................................528
Baldwin, Alec............109, 168, 319, 350
                                496, 513, 534
Baldwin, Stephen..............................479
Baldwin, William..............................102
Bale, Christian...................178, 224, 247
Ballard, Carroll: dir..........................318
Balsam, Martin..................................126
Bancroft, Anne 383
Bancroft, Tony: dir. 400
Banderas, Antonio...................316, 398,
                                512, 541
Baranski, Christine............................474
Barron, Steve: dir. 118, 306
Barrymore, Drew 389, 469
Barton Fink.....................................123
Basinger, Kim....................................467
Bass, Lance 532
Bassett, Angela..........175, 300, 351, 446
Bates, Alan..106

Bates, Kathy.......................133, 374, 407
Batman and Robin 347
Batman Forever................................270
Batman Returns...............................156
Bay, Michael: dir. 334, 384, 534
Bean, Sean..................101, 180, 232, 346
Beatty, Ned, ...216
Beatty, Warren 98, 247
Beatty, Warren: dir. 98
Beauty and the Beast.........................124
Beckinsale, Kate 310, 534
Beethoven 157
Beethoven's 2nd...............................193
Bellamy, Ralph 115
Belmondo, Jean-Paul.........................286
Belushi, Jim...............113, 129, 141, 291,
                                326, 375, 493, 519
Benigni, Roberto: dir. 394
Bening, Annette 135, 145, 247, 425
Benny and Joon 194
Benson, Robby 124
Berenger, Tom 101, 201
Berenson, Marisa 121
Beresford, Bruce: dir.........126, 138, 366
Bergen, Candice................................485
Bergman, Andrew: dir. 103
Berri, Claude: dir. 151
Berry, Halle 237, 501
Bethelsen, Anders W. 558
Bicentennial Man..............................426
Biel, Jessica 375, 392
Big Fat Liar 547
Big Night...307
Bill and Ted's Bogus Journey 125
Billy Elliot 466
Bindler, S. R.: dir. 437
Binoche, Juliette 322, 470
Birch, Thora 123, 180, 251, 425
Bird, Brad: dir....................................440
Birdcage, The...................................308
Black Beauty....................................231
Black Hawk Down 510
Black Knight....................................511
Black Robe 126
Blair Witch Project, The.....................427

Blair, Jon: dir. 306
Blanc, Michel 151
Blanchett, Cate 365, 388, 438, 527
Blank Check 232
Blatty, William Peter: dir. 101
Bless the Child 467
Blethyn, Brenda 183
Bluth, Don: dir. 184, 261
Body, The 512
Bodyguard, The 158
Bon Jovi, Jon 489, 499
Bonham Carter, Helena 106, 171,
379, 433, 535
Bonsall, Brian 232
Boorem, Mika 507
Borrowers, The 384
Bowen, Julie 519
Bowman, Rob: dir. 419
Boyle, Peter 258, 301, 388
Brady Bunch, The 271
Branagh, Kenneth 212, 320, 459
Branagh, Kenneth: dir. 212, 320
Brandauer, Klaus Maria 152
Brando, Marlon 103, 160
Bratt, Benjamin 485
Braugher, Andre 480
Braveheart 272
Bridges, Beau 220
Bridges, Jeff 132, 329, 340, 521
Bridges, Todd 549
Brimley, Wilford 187
Broadbent, Jim 234, 253, 263,
385, 532
Broderick, Matthew 103, 390, 440
Brodie, Kevin: dir. 430
Brody, Adrien 207
Brooks, Albert 388
Brooks, Foster 134
Brosnan, Pierce 138, 212, 247,
329, 408
Bross, Eric: dir. 532
Brothers McMullen, The 273
Brown, Bryan 143, 436
Browning Version, The 233
Buchholz, Horst 394

Buffy the Vampire Slayer 159
Bujold, Genevieve 306
Bullets Over Broadway 234
Bullock, Sandra 259, 263, 301,
338, 391, 407, 485
Burnett, Carol 542
Burnett, Charles: dir. 119
Burns, Edward: dir. 273
Burns, Edward 273, 410
Burrows, Saffron 429, 552
Burstyn, Ellen 336
Burton, LeVar 337, 414
Burton, Tim: dir. 100, 156, 535
Buscemi, Steve 317, 384
Busey, Gary 186
Butler, George: dir. 109, 516
Bynes, Amanda 548
Byrne, Gabriel 147, 247, 397

Caan, James 98, 315
Cadiff, Andy: dir. 360
Cage, Nicolas 239, 334, 477
Cain, Christopher: dir. 268
Caine, Michael 113, 177, 429, 485
Cameron, James: dir. 149, 374
Cameron, Kirk 483
Campbell, Bill 369
Campbell, Billy 146
Campbell, Bruce 528
Campbell, Glen 184
Campbell, Martin: dir. 398
Campbell, Neve 311
Candy, John 141, 195
Cape Fear 126
Capshaw, Kate 247
Carlin, George 431
Carney, Art 207
Caron, Leslie 280
Carr, Steve: dir. 515
Carradine, Robert 529
417, 474, 528
Carter Cash, June 347
Carter, Thomas: dir. 224
Casey, Bernie 332

Cassel, Seymore 152
Cast Away 468
Castellaneta, Dan............................554
Castle, Nick: dir. 196
Cates, Pheobe 253
Caton-Jones, Michael: dir........111, 129, 295, 358
Cats and Dogs 513
Cats Don't Dance..............................348
Caviezel, James 450, 480, 551
Cedric the Entertainer......................523
Chabert, Lacey 395, 556
Changing Lanes 548
Chapman, Brenda: dir......................407
Chappelle, Dave 420
Charlie's Angels 468
Chase, Daveigh 559
Chatiliez, Etienne: dir......................148
Cheadle, Don 369, 380, 477
Chechik, Jeremiah: dir..............194, 298
Chelsom, Peter: dir. 280
Cher 456
Cherry, John: dir..............................100
Child's Play 2 95
China Cry 95
Chriqui, Emmanuelle.......................533
Christie, Julie....................................320
Christopher Columbus:
  The Discovery................................160
Church, Thomas Haden 355
Cinema Paradiso 96
Citizen Ruth.......................................308
City Slickers 127
Civil Action, A..................................386
Clear and Present Danger...................234
Cleese, John 244, 261, 355, 378, 517, 537
Clements, Ron: dir. 156
Client, The...235
Clockstoppers 550
Clooney, George....348, 366, 452, 487, 490
Close, Glenn 106, 117, 305, 306, 344, 366, 463
Coburn, James....................250, 315, 531
Coen, Joel: dir. 123, 241, 317, 487

Cohen, Eli: dir. 182
Cold Comfort Farm 310
Cole, Natalie.....................................348
Coleman, Dabney 440, 549
Collette, Toni 164, 314, 452, 548
Collier, James: dir............................96
Collins, Joan 479
Columbus, Chris: dir........108, 141, 169, 212, 427, 517
Commitments, The...............................128
Conn, Didi 496
Connelly, Jennifer 146, 491, 509
Connery, Sean 109, 279, 334
Connick, Jr., Harry 111, 137, 391, 440, 487
Connolly, Billy..................................363
Conrad, Robert 326
Conspiracy Theory 349
Constantine, Michael 213, 560
Contact 351
Conway, Tim 312
Cook, Barry: dir................................400
Cool Runnings 195
Coolidge, Martha: dir.......................208
Cooper, Chris 328, 392, 447, 488
Coppola, Francis Ford: dir.......104, 368
Coppola, Sofia..................................104
Corbett, John 560
Cornell, John: dir. 92
Corrina, Corrina 236
Cosby, Bill 211
Costner, Kevin.............97, 145, 158, 301
Costner, Kevin: dir............................97
Count of Monte Cristo, The................551
Cowan, Rich: dir. 465
Cox, Brian 561
Coyote, Peter 465, 476, 565
Craft, The 311
Craven, Wes: dir.......................142, 446
Crawford, Michael 214
Crocodile Dundee in Los Angeles 514
Cromwell, James...............269, 337, 496
Cross, Ben 279
Crouching Tiger, Hidden Dragon 471
Crouse, Lindsay................................283

Crowe, Cameron: dir................326, 465
Crowe, Russell 439, 482, 509
Crudup, Billy 464
Cruise, Tom 166, 167, 199, 326,
                           330, 442, 486, 560
Cry the Beloved Country 275
Crystal, Billy......127, 280, 320, 401, 531
Crystal, Billy: dir.............................280
Cuaron, Alfonso: dir.........................287
Culkin, Macaulay 108, 139, 169, 256
Cumming, Alan 479, 541
Curly Sue 128
Curry, Tim................109, 166, 169, 225,
                           291, 331, 410, 469
Curtin, Jane.......................................383
Curtis, Jamie Lee 139, 168
Cusack, Joan......................236, 450, 458
Cusack, John......................234, 309, 345
Cutting Edge, The...............................160
Cyrano De Bergerac 97
Czerny, Henry 234, 330

D'Onofrio, Vincent, 181, 402
D2: The Mighty Ducks 236
D3: The Mighty Ducks 311
Dafoe, Willem 132, 234, 562
Daldry, Stephen: dir. 466
Dalton, Timothy................................146
Damon, Matt 355, 368, 410, 431, 483
Dance, Charles 207
Dances with Wolves 97
Danes, Claire 247, 368, 393
Dangerous Minds 276
Daniel, Rod: dir.................................194
Daniels, Jeff.........................93, 201, 259,
                           305, 318, 406
Danner, Blythe..........................112, 143
Danson, Ted 119
Dante, Joe: dir....................................413
Danza, Tony 229
Darabont, Frank: dir................435, 528
Dark Horse..161
Dash, Julie: dir...................................162
Daughters of the Dust.........................162
Dave 196

Davidovich, Lolita....................137, 358
Davidtz, Embeth...............278, 289, 426
Davis, Andrew: dir. 186, 200
Davis, Clifton 549
Davis, Geena 150, 564
Davis, John A.: dir. 518
Davis, Ossie...........................235, 388
Davison, Bruce...................................405
Day in October, A 162
Day-Lewis, Daniel............171, 192, 204
De Bont, Jan: dir.......................259, 339
De Niro, Robert.................94, 126, 135,
                           351, 375, 464
De Palma, Brian: dir. 330
Dead Man Walking...............................277
Dear God 312
Dear, William: dir....................229, 377
Deblois, Dean: dir. 559
Deep Blue Sea......................................429
Deep Impact 387
Deezen, Eddie 184
Delany, Dana 318, 418
DeMornay, Rebecca...........................225
Dempsey, Patrick...............................290
Dench, Judi 363, 411, 456, 470, 557
Deneuve, Catherine 475
Dennis the Menace...............................196
Depardieu, Gerard 97, 106, 151,
                           155, 320, 397, 463
Depp, Johnny 100, 194, 470
Dern, Laura 206, 308, 447, 518, 520
Derryberry, Debi................................518
Devane, William 496
DeVito, Danny 141, 156, 282,
                           356, 368
Diaz, Cameron 249, 363, 416,
                           469, 540
DiCaprio, Leonardo 374, 397
Dick Tracy 98
Dickinson, Angie 489
Diesel, Vin................................410, 440
Diller, Phyllis 385
Dillon, Matt 416
Dillon, Melinda 314
Dindal, Mark: dir....................348, 476

Dinosaur 472
Dish, The 514
Distinguished Gentleman, The 163
Doc Hollywood 129
Docter, Pete: dir. 531
Doctor, The 130
Dog of Flanders, A 430
Dogma 431
Doillon, Jacques: dir. 367
Dominczyk, Dagmara 551
Donat, Peter 354
Donner, Richard: dir. 173, 250, 349
Doors, The 130
Dorn, Michael 337, 414
Doug, Doug E. 195
Douglas, Michael 354
Dourif, Brad 101, 289
Downey, Jr., Robert 294
Dr. Dolittle 388
Dr. Dolittle 2 515
Dr. Suess' How the
  Grinch Stole Christmas 474
Dreyfus, Richard 115, 151, 208,
                                              288, 324
Driver, Minnie 307, 355, 438,
                                         452, 455, 493
Du Chau, Frederik: dir. 408
Duchovny, David 144, 419, 493
DuckTales: The Movie—
  Treasures of the Lost Lamp 99
Duffy, Karen 232
Dukakis, Olympia 241
Duke, Bill: dir. 221
Dunaway, Faye 107, 313, 552
Duncan, Michael Clarke 435,
                                         513, 535, 538
Duncan, Sandy 184, 261
Dunham, Duwayne: dir. 203
Dunn, Nora 529
Dunne, Griffin 147
Dunst, Kirsten 247, 285, 345,
                                         375, 413, 562
Dunston Checks In 313
Durning, Charles 98, 241, 242, 487
Dutton, Charles S. 216, 275

Duvall, Robert 107, 178, 263, 296,
                                         317, 347, 386, 387
Duvall, Robert: dir. 347
Dzundza, George 276

East-West 475
Eastwood, Clint 121, 186,
                                              204, 273, 496
Eastwood, Clint: dir. 121, 186,
                                                   273, 496
Ebersole, Christine 256
Edge, The 350
Edward Scissorhands 99
Edwards, Anthony 235
Efficiency Expert 164
Eggar, Samantha 161
Egoyan, Atom: dir. 373, 547
Eichorn, Lisa 207
Ele, My Friend 197
Elfman, Danny 214
Elizabeth 388
Elizondo, Hector 115, 536
Elliott, Chris 202
Elliott, Sam 201, 566
Ellis, David R.: dir. 321
Elwes, Cary 339, 244, 408
Emma 314
Emmerich, Noah 417, 480
Emmerich, Roland: dir. 260, 323,
                                                   390, 488
Emperor's New Groove, The 475
Enchanted April 164
Endurance 432
Endurance, The:
  Shackleton's Legendary
  Antarctic Expedition 516
Enigma 551
Entertaining Angels:
  The Dorothy Day Story 314
Ephron, Nora: dir. 421
Eraser 315
Erin Brockovich 476
Ermey, R. Lee 530
Ernest Goes to Jail 100
Estefan, Gloria 446

Estevez, Emilio..................176, 236, 312
Evans, David Mickey: dir. 217
Ever After.......................................389
Everett, Rupert................248, 313, 363, 438, 440, 557
Evita 316
Exorcist 3: Legion 101
Eye of the Storm 165

Fahey, Jeff..121
Falkenstein, Jun: dir. 497
Family Man, The............................477
Family Thing, A..............................317
Fanning, Dakota 518
Fantasia 2000 478
Fantasticks, The 479
Far and Away....................................166
Far Off Place, A 198
Fargo 317
Farina, Dennis.................................246
Farmer, Jennifer Wynne: dir. 446
Farnsworth, Richard 244, 454
Farrell, Colin 553, 560
Farrelly, Bobby: dir. 416
Farrelly, Peter: dir. 416
Farrow, Mia 263
Father of the Bride...............................131
Fatone, Joey 532, 560
Fawcett, Farrah 347
Feast of July.......................................278
Feldman, Corey...................................118
Ferngully: The Last Rainforest 166
Ferrer, Miguel....................................232
Festival in Cannes...............................552
Few Good Men, A 167
Fiedler, John 497
Field, Sally 203, 212, 238, 321
Fiennes, Joseph 388, 411
Fiennes, Ralph..........217, 255, 365, 407
Fierstein, Harvey 212, 234
Figgis, Mike: dir. 233
Fincher, David: dir...................354, 433
Finney, Albert.................233, 376, 476
Fiorentino, Linda 361, 431

Firm, The..198
First Knight......................................279
Firth, Colin 411, 557
Fishburne, Laurence.................218, 443
Fisher King, The.................................132
Flatliners 102
Fleming, Andrew: dir. 311
Flight of the Intruder 132
Flintstones in Viva Rock Vegas, The.................................479
Flubber 352
Fly Away Home 318
Foley, Dave 385, 452
Foley, James: dir. 168, 299
Fonda, Bridget 104, 129, 309
Fonda, Peter 375, 496
For All Mankind 103
For Richer or Poorer..........................353
Ford, Harrison 145, 180, 200, 234, 295, 344
Forever Young 168
Forget Paris 279
Forrest Gump 238
Forrest, Frederic..............................244
Forsythe, William 98, 334
Foster, Jodie 137, 250, 351
Foster, Jodie: dir. 137
Fox, Edward 287
Fox, James.......................180, 214, 346
Fox, Michael J.............94, 129, 203, 321, 455, 508, 564
Fox, Viveca A. 372, 523
Foxx, Jamie 506
Frakes, Jonathan 414
Frakes, Jonathan: dir. 337, 414, 550
Franklin, Carl: dir. 403
Fraser, Brendan 355, 415, 444
Free Willy...199
Freeman Jr., Al..........................175, 332
Freeman, Morgan 145, 186, 290, 344, 387, 507
Frequency 480
Freshman, The...................................103
Friedkin, William: dir. 495
Fugitive, The 199

Funny Bones 280
Furlong, Edward 149

Gabor, Eva 116
Galaxy Quest 433
Gallagher, Peter 181, 301, 425
Gambon, Michael 259
Game, The 354
Garci, José Luis: dir. 434
Garcia, Andy 104, 441
Gardos, Eva: dir. 508
Garner, James 250, 496
Garofalo, Janeane 351, 431, 464, 499
Gaup, Nils: dir. 114, 147
Gazzara, Ben 414
Gemes, Jozsef: dir. 253
George of the Jungle 355
George Washington 481
Georgia 281
Gere, Richard............115, 279, 358, 450
Get Shorty 282
Gettysburg 200
Ghobadi, Bahman: dir. 498
Ghost 104
Ghosts of Mississippi 319
Giamatti, Paul 535, 548
Giant of Thunder Mountain, The 134
Gibbons, Rodney: dir. 396
Gibbs, Mary......................................531
Gibson, Henry............................225, 442
Gibson, Mel 106, 168, 173, 210,
           250, 272, 292, 333, 349,
           469, 488, 500, 566
Gibson, Mel: dir. 210, 272
Gielgud, John 335
Gilliam, Terry: dir. 132, 267
Gilyard, Clarence..............................483
Girard, Francois: dir. 449
Gladiator 482
Glaser, Paul Michael: dir..........160, 192
Glen, John: dir. 160
Glengarry Glen Ross...........................168
Glenn, Scott 109, 298
Glover, Crispin..................................469

Glover, Danny ..119, 132, 135, 173, 229,
    368, 383, 407
Godfather, Part III, The 104
Gods Must Be Crazy II, The 105
Godzilla 390
Goldberg, Adam 410
Goldberg, Whoopi 104, 111, 181,
          184, 221, 236, 319,
          410, 523, 537
Goldblum, Jeff...206, 323, 407, 513, 552
Goldmam, Gary: dir. 261
Good Will Hunting 355
Gooding Jr., Cuba 290, 326, 418,
          534, 537
Goodman, John..................93, 123, 237,
          385, 475, 487, 531
Goofy Movie, A 282
Gordon-Levitt, Joseph 229
Gordy 238
Gosnell, Raja: dir...............................357
Gottfried, Gilbert 156
Graham, Heather...............................395
Grammer, Kelsey 458
Grand Canyon....................................135
Grandfather, The 434
Grant, Hugh 297, 215
Gray, Spalding 207
Green, David Gordon: dir. 481
Green Mile, The 435
Green, Seth 537
Greene, Graham 97, 435
Greenwood, Bruce............373, 495, 547
Grey, Joel...479
Grier, David Alan 493
Griffith, Melanie 185, 564
Griffiths, Rachel 561
Grizzly Falls.......................................436
Grodin, Charles..........................157, 194
Grosbard, Ulu: dir..............................281
Grosvenor, Charles: dir. 214
Groundhog Day 201
Grumpy Old Men 202
Guarding Tess 239
Guilty By Suspicion............................135
Gunn, Jon: dir....................................484

Guterman, Lawrence: dir. 513
Guttenberg, Steve 119, 284
Guy, Jasmine 348
Gwynne, Fred 178
Gyllenhaal, Jake...............................447

Hackman, Gene...............115, 186, 199,
                              282, 308, 383
Hagerty, Julie....................................151
Hagman, Larry 407
Haid, Charles: dir. 243
Haines, Randa: dir. 130, 263
Hall, Philip Baker 439, 495
Hallstrom, Lasse: dir. 429, 470
Halvorson, Gary: dir. 423
Hamilton, George 104, 129, 555
Hamilton, Linda.........................113, 149
Hamlet (1990) 106
Hamlet (1996) 319
Hancock, John Lee: dir.....................561
Handmaid's Tale, The..........................107
Hanks, Tom 222, 238, 268, 298,
                         337, 410, 420, 435,
                         458, 468, 493
Hanks, Tom: dir. 337
Hanna, William: dir. 110
Hannah, Daryl 565
Hanson, Curtis: dir. 256
Harden, Marcia Gay.257, 336, 352, 491
Hardwicke, Edward...........................220
Harlin, Renny: dir.............................429
Harrelson, Woody 129, 252, 375, 377
Harriet the Spy....................................320
Harris, Ed 168, 199, 268, 289,
                      334, 417, 457, 491, 509
Harris, Ed: dir. 491
Harris, Jonathan................................385
Harris, Phil 184
Harris, Richard 101, 180, 186,
                              263, 275, 436,
                              482, 517, 551
*Harry Potter and
  the Sorcerer's Stone* 517
Hart's War 553
Hartman, Phil............................326, 413

Hartnet, Josh 510, 534
Hata, Masami: dir. 173
Hata, Masanori: dir. 91
Hatcher, Teri 541
Hathaway, Anne 536
Hathcock, Bob: dir. 99
Hauer, Rutger....................................159
Hawke, Ethan 152, 193, 402
Hawthorne, Nigel............248, 344, 396,
                                      455, 460
Hayek, Salma 431, 459
Headly, Glenne 288
Heard, John 108, 169
Heche, Anne......................375, 380, 457
Hedaya, Dan 386
Hedren, Tippi.....................................308
Helgeland, Brian: dir..........................524
Helgenberger, Marg 476
Hemingway, Mariel 396
Hemmings, David: dir. 161
Henson, Brian 445
Henson, Brian: dir.....................177, 331
Hepburn, Katharine 247
Hercules 356
Herek, Stephen: dir..................176, 225,
                                      288, 305
Herrmann, Edward 256
Hershey, Barbara 224
Heston, Charlton 320
Hewitt, Peter: dir. 125, 385
Hey Arnold! The Movie......................554
Hickman, David: dir............................159
Hickner, Steve: dir. 407
Hicks, Scott: dir. 335
Hill, Bernard......................................374
Hill, Tim: dir. 445, 529
Hines, Gregory............................300, 332
Hingle, Pat 156, 538
Hoblit, Gregory: dir. 480, 553
Hoffman, Dustin.........98, 136, 290, 375
Hoffman, Michael: dir.........................294
Hoffman, Philip Seymour 403,
                                      442, 464
Hogan, P. J.: dir.................................363
Hogan, Paul............................92, 514

Holbrook, Hal 199, 348, 426, 528
Holland, Agnieszka: dir..........219, 376, 457
Hollywood Ending 555
Holm, Celeste...................................415
Holm, Ian...................106, 248, 373, 467
Home Alone....................................108
Home Alone 2: Lost in New York 169
Hometown Legend 555
Homeward Bound:
  The Incredible Journey.....................203
Homeward Bound II:
  Lost In San Francisco.......................321
Honey, I Blew Up the Kid 170
Hook 136
Hoop Dreams 240
Hope Floats 391
Hopkins, Anthony...........164, 171, 215,
                220, 226, 289, 344,
                350, 398, 486
Hopkins, Stephen: dir. 395
Hopper, Dennis...........................259, 301
Horse Whisperer, The.........................391
Horseman on the Roof, The................322
Hoskins, Bob 137, 223, 269, 289
Hounsou, Djimon..............................344
Houston, Whitney.............158, 300, 332
Howard, Ron: dir............166, 268, 333,
                474, 509
Howard's End 170
Howell, C. Thomas...........................201
Hu, Ann: dir. 539
Hudson, Kate 464
Hudsucker Proxy, The.........................240
Hughes, Bronwen: dir. 320
Hughes, John: dir............................129
Hulce, Tom 137
Hunchback of Notre Dame, The..........322
Hunt for Red October, The.................109
Hunt, Bonnie.................157, 194, 285,
                326, 435, 493, 531
Hunt, Bonnie: dir. 493
Hunt, Helen..............339, 468, 489, 500
Hunter, Holly, ...199, 487
Hurricane, The.................................437

Hurt, John..........101, 295, 351, 497, 517
Hurt, William 130, 325, 395,
                403, 548
Huston, Anjelica 121, 210, 389, 424
Huston, Anjelica: dir. 424
Hyde Pierce, David 385
Hytner, Nicholas: dir.......................248

I Am Sam 518
I Love Trouble................................241
I.Q. 242
I'll Be Home for Christmas 392
Ice Age..556
Ideal Husband, An 438
Idle, Eric............274, 378, 408, 452, 463
Importance of Being Earnest, The.......557
In the Blood 109
In the Name of the Father 204
Indian In the Cupboard, The..............283
Inner Circle, The 136
Insider, The...................................439
Inspector Gadget 439
Iron Giant, The................................440
Iron Will...243
Irons, Jeremy 117, 397
Ironside, Michael 448
Irvin, John: dir............................263, 287
Irwin, Bill..474
It Takes Two...................................284
Italian for Beginners 558
Ivory, James: dir., ...112, 171, 215, 285

Jackal, The 357
Jackman, Hugh 523
Jackson, Mick: dir. 158, 380
Jackson, Peter: dir. 527
Jackson, Samuel L.................254, 338,
                429, 449, 495, 548
Jacobi, Derek, ...320, 512
Jaglom, Henry: dir...................231, 552
James and the Giant Peach.................324
James, Clifton.................................328
James, Steve: dir.............................240
Jane Eyre 325
Janssen, Famke.................................501

Jefferson In Paris 284
Jerry Maguire 325
Jeter, Michael 301, 343, 435, 520
Jetsons: The Movie 110
Jewison, Norman: dir. 141, 437
Jingle All the Way 326
Joe Somebody 519
Joffe, Mark: dir. 164
Joffe, Roland: dir. 296
Johns, Glynis 301
Johnson, Ben 229
Johnson, Brad 132, 483
Johnson, Kristen 479
Johnson, Mark Steven: dir. 412
Johnson, Patrick Read: dir. 230
Johnston, Joe: dir., ...146, 285,
                                            447, 520
Jolie, Angelina 525
Jones, David: dir. 226
Jones, Dean 141, 157
Jones, James Earl 109, 180, 211,
                                   217, 234, 245,
                                   275, 316, 478
Jones, Jeffrey 515
Jones, Quincy 477
Jones, Terry 378
Jones, Terry: dir. 378
Jones, Tom 424
Jones, Tommy Lee 186, 200, 235,
                                   252, 270, 361, 380,
                                   413, 495, 496
Jordan, Michael 335
Joy Luck Club, The 205
Judd, Ashley 412
Jumanji 285
Junger, Gil: dir. 511
Jungle 2 Jungle 358
Jungle Book, The 243
Jurassic Park 206
Jurassic Park III 520
Just the Ticket 441

Kandahar 522
Kapur, Shekhar: dir. 388
Karyo, Tcheky 155, 488

Kasdan, Lawrence: dir. 135
Kate and Leopold 522
Kavner, Julie 94, 280
Kazan, Lainie 560
Keach, Stacy 484
Keaton, Diane 104, 131, 210, 278
Keaton, Michael 156, 212, 213
Keitel, Harvey 150, 184, 251,
                                   254, 351, 499
Keith, David 283, 499
Kellogg, David: dir. 440
Kennedy, George 348
Kidman, Nicole 166, 213, 270,
                                   366, 532, 533
Kiel, Richard...134
Kilmer, Val 130, 270, 407
King of the Hill 206
Kingdom Come....................................523
Kingsley, Ben, ...196, 217, 218, 495
Kinnear, Greg 295, 312, 420, 566
Kinnear, Roy...252
Kinski, Nastassja...................................508
Kirby, Bruno 103, 127, 455
Kleiser, Randall: dir. 152, 170
Kline, Kevin.....................135, 196, 253,
                                   322, 459, 494
Knight, Wayne 335, 353, 537
Knight's Tale, A....................................524
Koller, Xavier: dir....................................259
Kolya 359
Konchalovsky, Andrei: dir...............137
Kozlowski, Linda 92, 514
K-Pax 521
Kristofferson, Kris 328
Kurosawa, Akira: dir...........................91
Kwapis, Ken: dir. 313

Ladd, Cheryl 430
Lahti, Christine 130
Landau, Martin 306, 309, 419, 528
Lane, Diane...............................487, 490
Lane, Nathan.....245, 308, 455, 499, 564
Lang, Stephen 201, 268, 298
Lange, Jessica 126, 295
Langella, Frank 155, 196

Lansbury, Angela........................124, 478
LaPaglia, Anthony............................235
Lara Croft: Tomb Raider......................525
Larroquette, John............................256
Lasseter, John: dir. 298, 385, 458
Lassie...244
Last Action Hero, The.........................207
Last Lieutenant, The 327
Last of the Mohicans, The 171
Latifah, Queen 213
Lawrence, Joey...............................282
Lawrence, Martin.............................511
Leachman, Cloris.............................440
Leap of Faith...................................172
Leary, Denis...............375, 413, 418, 556
LeBlanc, Matt 395
Leder, Mimi: dir. 366, 387, 489
Ledger, Heath............................488, 524
Lee, Ang: dir. 297, 450, 471
Lee, Christopher 527
Lee, Jason..................................431, 464
Lee, Spike: dir.................................175
Left Behind 482
Legally Blonde.................................526
Legend of Bagger Vance, The 483
Leguizamo, John.......................532, 556
Lehman, Michael: dir. 401
Leigh, Jennifer Jason...............241, 281,
                                        376, 554
LeLouch, Claude: dir.........................286
Lemmon, Jack 168, 202, 320
Leoni, Téa...................387, 477, 520, 555
Lerner, Michael 232, 353
Les Misérables (1995) 286
Les Misérables (1998) 393
Lethal Weapon 3...............................172
Leto, Jared....................................433
Levant, Brian: dir. 157, 237, 326, 479
Levinson, Barry: dir....................93, 375
Levy, Shawn: dir. 548
Lewis, Jerry...................................280
Lewis, Juliette............................126, 252
Li, Gong 182, 262
Liar, Liar.......................................360
Libertini, Richard............................99

Lieberman, Robert: dir. 123, 312
Lilo and Stitch.................................559
Lima, Kevin: dir. 282, 463
Lindfors, Viveca..............................101
Lindo, Delroy 175, 333, 429
Linklater, Richard: dir. 402
Linney, Laura 417
Lion King, The 245
Liotta, Ray 236, 351
Lipnicki, Jonathan 564
Lithgow, John 111, 253, 386, 540
Little Man Tate................................137
Little Men 395
Little Nemo: Adventures
  in Slumberland 173
Liu, Lucy......................................469
LL Cool J 429, 523
Lloyd, Christopher..............94, 99, 196,
                                        229, 345, 554
Loc, Tone......................................232
Lone Star 328
Long Walk Home, The.........................110
Long, Nia 372
Long, Shelley..................................271
Lopez, Jennifer..................370, 383, 543
Lord of the Rings, The:
   The Fellowship of the Ring 526
Lord, Peter: dir. 469
Lorenzo's Oil 174
Lost in Space 395
Lost in Yonkers 208
Louis-Dreyfus, Julia 385
Love Affair.....................................247
Lovitz, Jon...........................113, 513, 537
Lowe, Rob, ...351
Lucas, George: dir............................453
Luhrmann, Baz: dir. 222, 532
Luketic, Robert: dir............................526
Lumet, Sidney: dir. 185
Lumley, Joanna 310, 324
Lynch, David: dir. 454
Lynch, Kelly 129, 362, 469, 519
Lynn, Jonathan: dir...................163, 178

Mac..209

Macdonald, Norm 388
MacDowell, Andie 106, 202, 441
MacLachlan, Kyle.............130, 226, 237
MacLaine, Shirley 115, 239, 263
Macpherson, Elle 350
Macy, Bill 289
Macy, William H. 317, 386,
                              406, 442, 520
Madden, John: dir. 363, 411
Madness of King George, The 248
Madonna...............................98, 316
Madsen, Kenneth: dir.......................162
Magnolia 442
Magnuson, Ann 415
Maguire, Tobey 406, 429, 450,
                              513, 562
Mahoney, John 123, 241
Majestic, The..527
Majidi, Majid: dir. 428
Majors, Lee 548
Makhmalbaf, Mohsen: dir. 522
Malcolm X.......................................175
Malick, Wendie 475
Malkovich, John.........................179, 397
Mamet, David: dir. 414, 460
Man In the Iron Mask, The................397
Man Without a Face, The 209
Mandrayar, Dharan: dir....................197
Mangold, James: dir. 351, 523
Manhattan Murder Mystery..............210
Mann, Michael: dir. 171, 439, 506
Mantegna, Joe 104, 218, 230,
                              280, 542
Marcarelli, Robert: dir. 165, 448
Marceau, Sophie 272, 346
Marco Polo: Return to Xanadu...........528
Margret, Ann.............................178, 202
Margulies, Julianna 402
Marin, Cheech.................................405
Marshall, Frank: dir....................93, 193
Marshall, Garry: dir................115, 312,
                              450, 536
Marshall, Penny: dir..................94, 332
Martin, Andrea 518, 560
Martin, Kellie 282

Martin, Steve 131, 135, 172,
                              278, 407, 414, 478
Mask of Zorro, The.............................398
Mask, The.......................................249
Masterson, Mary Stuart 133, 194
Mastrantonio, Mary Elizabeth.......145,
                              299, 490
Matrix, The, ...443
Matthau, Walter 196, 202, 242
Maverick..249
Max Keeble's Big Move........................529
Maxwell, Ronald F.: dir..................201
May, Jodhi.......................................171
Mayfield, Les: dir.....................250, 352
Mazar, Debi 439
Mazzello, Joseph...............220, 256, 412
McAnuff, Des: dir. 464
McCann, Chuck 99
McConaughey, Matthew 328, 338,
                              344, 351, 402,
                              499, 543
McCord, Jonas: dir...........................512
McCormack, Mary 521
McCullough, Jim: dir.......................187
McDermott, Dylan 250, 542
McDonald, Christopher..........150, 251,
                              255, 352, 360, 440
McDonald, Kevin 559
McDonnell, Mary 97, 135, 323
McDormand, Frances 317, 328,
                              366, 396, 464
McDowall, Roddy 369, 385
McDowell, Malcolm.........................362
McFadden, Gates......................337, 414
McG: dir.,.......................................469
McGill, Bruce...........................369, 483
McGoohan, Patrick..........................272
McGovern, Elizabeth 107, 207, 379
McGrath, Douglas: dir. 314
McGregor, Ewan..............453, 510, 532
McHenry, Doug: dir. 523
McKellar, Don 449
McKellen, Ian 310, 501, 527
McKeon, Doug..................................187
McLachlan, Duncan: dir. 340, 369

McTiernan, John: dir., 109................207

Meat Loaf...432

Megiddo: Omega Code 2.....................530

Memphis Belle.......................................111

Men in Black..361

Men with Guns......................................399

Menaul, Christopher: dir..................278

Mendes, Sam: dir..............................425

Mercy Streets...484

Merk, Ron: dir....................................528

Messing, Debra..................................555

Metcalf, Laurie...................................312

Meteor Man, The....................................211

Meyer, Breckin..........................523, 537

Meyers, Nancy: dir., 404..................500

Michell, Roger: dir...................292, 548

Micklin Silver, Joan: dir. 147

Microcosmos..328

Midler, Bette.............................478, 500

Mighty Ducks, The................................175

Mighty Joe Young..................................399

Milius, John: dir..................................132

Miller, George: dir.............140, 174, 229

Miller, Larry...............................236, 529

Miller, Penelope Ann.................103, 141

Miner, Steve: dir................153, 168, 542

Minkoff, Rob: dir. 455

Minority Report.....................................559

Miracle on 34th Street..........................250

Mirren, Helen............................248, 407

Mirror Has Two Faces, The.................329

Miss Congeniality................................485

Mission Impossible...............................330

Mission: Impossible 2 (M:I–2)..........486

Mister Johnson......................................138

Mitchum, Robert.................................126

Mock, Freida Lee: dir. 493

Modine, Matthew.......................111, 233

Molina, Alfred...................164, 346, 470

Monkey Trouble.....................................251

Monsters, Inc....531

Month By the Lake, A...........................287

Moore, Demi...............104, 167, 296, 322

Moore, Dudley..91

Moore, Julianne.................200, 438, 442

Moore, Mandy..........................536, 565

Moranis, Rick, 170.............................237

Moreau, Jeanne....................................389

Moriarty, Cathy....................................274

Morse, David............................351, 435

Mortensen, Viggo................................527

Morton, Samantha...............................560

Moss, Carrie-Anne..................443, 470

Mostow, Jonathan: dir.......................499

Moulin Rouge..531

Mountains of the Moon........................113

Mr. and Mrs. Bridge............................112

Mr. Baseball...176

Mr. Destiny..112

Mr. Holland's Opus.............................288

Mr. Magoo..362

Mrs. Brown..363

Mrs. Doubtfire......................................211

Much Ado About Nothing..................212

Mueller-Stahl, Armin........93, 334, 354, 366, 419, 457

Mulan..400

Mulroney, Dermot...............................363

Mummy, The..444

Muniz, Frankie..........................487, 548

Muppet Christmas Carol, The...........177

Muppets from Space.............................445

Murder in the First..............................289

Murphy, Brittany.................................275

Murphy, Eddie................163, 388, 400, 515, 540

Murray, Bill.....................151, 202, 469

Music of the Heart...............................445

Musker, John: dir. 156

My Best Friend's Wedding.................363

My Big Fat Greek Wedding................560

My Cousin Vinny................................178

My Dog Skip...486

My Father's Glory...............................138

My Girl..139

My Life..213

My Mother's Castle.............................138

Myers, Mike...540

Najimy, Kathy...................184, 221, 348

Natural Born Killers...........................252

Naturally Native.................................446
Nava, Gregory: dir............................370
Nealon, Kevin 123
Neeson, Liam 172, 217, 295, 393, 453
Neill, Sam 109, 206, 244, 294, 392, 426, 515, 520
Nelligan, Kate 143, 429
Nelson, Craig T. 319
Nelson, Jessie: dir. 236, 518
Nelson, Tim Blake 487, 560
Nelson, Willie..................................375
Neuwirth, Bebe.........................106, 306
Never Ending Story II:
   The Next Chapter 140
Neville, John..............................247, 419
Newell, Mike: dir. 164
Newhart, Bob 116
Newman, Paul 112, 241
Newsies 178
Newton Boys, The 402
Newton, Thandie....................285, 486
Nichols, Mike: dir. 115, 145, 308, 407
Nicholson, Jack 167
Nielsen, Connie 482
Nielsen, Leslie..............................123, 362
Nightmare Before Christmas, The.......214
Nixon 289
Noble, Chelsea 483
Noiret, Philippe 96, 151, 293
Nolte, Nick 126, 143, 174, 241, 285
Noonan, Chris: dir............................269
Norris, Aaron: dir. 220
Norris, Chuck...................................220
Northam, Jeremy 314, 438, 460, 552
Norton, Edward................................433
Noyce, Phillip: dir......................180, 234
Nunez, Victor: dir. 375
Nuridsany, Claude: dir. 329
Nuyen, France..............................96, 205
Nykvist, Sven: dir. 180

O Brother, Where Art Thou? 487
O'Connor, Carroll.............................493

O'Donnell, Chris...............133, 225, 270, 348, 426
O'Donnell, Rosie...............222, 237, 320, 418, 455
O'Hara, Catherine 108, 169, 214, 298
O'Hara, Maureen...............................141
October Sky....................................447
Of Mice and Men...............................179
Oldman, Gary 289, 296, 344, 395, 408
Olmos, Edward James 370
Olsen, Ashley 284
Olsen, Mary-Kate 284
Omega Code, The 448
On the Line 533
Once upon a Forest 214
Once upon a Time . . .
   When We Were Colored...................331
One True Thing.................................402
Only the Lonely 141
Ormond, Julia 279, 295
Orr, James: dir..................................113
Ortega, Kenny: dir. 178
Oscar and Lucinda.............................365
Osment, Haley Joel..........452, 489, 505
Other People's Money........................141
Others, The....................................533
Outbreak.......................................290
Ox, The...179
Oxenberg, Catherine 448
Oz, Frank 177, 331, 445, 531
Oz, Frank: dir. 151, 283

Pacino, Al.....................98, 104, 168, 299, 309, 439
Palance, Jack..............................127, 261
Palminteri, Chazz............................455
Paltrow, Gwyneth..............285, 314, 411
Panahi, Jafar: dir. 340
Panettiere, Hayden...................492, 519
Pantoliano, Joe 200, 230, 443, 513
Paquin, Anna............318, 325, 464, 501
Paradise Road.................................365
Parent Trap, The...............................404
Parisot, Dean: dir. 433

Park, Nick: dir. 469
Parker, Alan: dir. 128, 316
Parker, Mary-Louise................133, 135,
234, 235
Parker, Oliver: dir. 438, 557
Parker, Trey: dir.............................452
Pasquin, John: dir. 258, 358, 519
Patch Adams 403
Pathfinder..114
Patriot Games 180
Patriot, The 488
Patton, Will...............144, 336, 492
Paulie, ...405
Paxton, Bill 268, 339, 374,
400, 499
Pay It Forward 489
Payne, Alexander: dir.......................308
Peacemaker 366
Pearce, Guy 495, 551
Pearce, Richard: dir...........111, 172, 317
Pearl Harbor......................................534
Pebble and the Penguin, The...............291
Peck, Gregory.............................126, 141
Peet, Amanda, ...548
Penn, Sean 277, 354, 518
People Under the Stairs 142
Pepper, Barry....................................410
Perfect Storm, The...............................490
Perkins, Elizabeth...............93, 237, 250
Pernennou, Marie: dir. 329
Perry, Luke 159
Persuasion 292
Pesci, Joe 108, 169,
173, 178
Petersen, Wolfgang: dir...........204, 290,
344, 490
Petrie, Daniel: dir. 244
Petrie, Donald: dir. 202, 256, 485
Pfeiffer, Michelle..............156, 192, 276,
407, 518
Pfifer, Mekhi.....................................372
Phoenix, Joaquin...............................482
Piscopo, Joe 202
Pitt, Brad 150, 183, 267, 433
Place, Mary Kay......................308, 368

Planet of the Apes 535
Platt, Oliver 102, 225, 280,
298, 388, 412, 426
Player, The..181
Pleasantville 406
Plowright, Joan 93, 164, 196,
263, 305, 325,
456, 472
Plummer, Amanda 132, 254
Plummer, Christopher 184, 267,
439, 547
Pocahontas 292
Poitier, Sidney 358
Pollack, Kevin 92, 167, 515
Pollack, Sydney.................................548
Pollack, Sydney: dir..................199, 295
Pollock 491
Ponette 367
Portman, Natalie 453
Posey, Parker 420
Postcards from the Edge......................114
Potts, Annie 458
Pressman, Michael: dir.....................149
Preston, Kelly 325
Pretty Woman 115
Primary Colors....................................406
Prince and the Pauper, The 116
Prince of Egypt, The............................407
Prince of Tides 143
Princess and the Goblin, The 252
Princess Caraboo................................253
Prisoners of the Sun 143
Prosky, Robert....................106, 207, 216
Pryce, Jonathan 316
Pullman, Bill.....................222, 274, 301,
323, 499
Pytka, Joe: dir. 335

Quaid, Dennis 115, 404, 480, 561
Quaid, Randy.....................................464
Quarrel, The..182
Quest for Camelot 408
Quigley Down Under 116
Quinlan, Kathleen 130, 386, 401
Quinn, Aidan 93, 194, 446

Quinn, Anthony.........................141, 207
Quiz Show...255

Radcliffe, Daniel 517
Radford, Michael: dir. 293
Rae, Charlotte.....................................225
Rafelson, Bob: dir. 113
Raffill, Stewart: dir............................436
Raimi, Sam: dir...................................562
Rainmaker, The 368
Raise the Red Lantern 182
Ramis, Harold 247
Ramis, Harold: dir. 202
Rampling, Charlotte...........................379
Ransom...333
Rappeneau, Jean-Paul: dir. 97, 322
Rapture, The 144
Ratner, Brett: dir. 477
Ratzenberger, John 385, 458, 531
Rea, Stephen.......................................253
Red Violin, The....................................449
Redford, Robert 392
Redford, Robert: dir. 183, 255,
                                                        392, 483
Redgrave, Lynn...................................335
Redgrave, Vanessa...................171, 287,
                                                        330, 387
Red-Horse, Valerie 446
Red-Horse, Valerie: dir. 446
Reed, Oliver...............................280, 482
Reeve, Christopher.............................215
Reeves, Keanu...................212, 259, 443
Regarding Henry 145
Reid, Tim: dir......................................332
Reilly, John C.....................256, 442, 490
Reiner, Rob 234
Reiner, Rob: dir. 167, 319
Reinert, Al: dir.....................................103
Reinhold, Judge 258
Reitman, Ivan: dir...............................196
Remains of the Day, The 215
Renfro, Brad 235
Restoration 294
Return to Me..492
Return with Honor 493

Reversal of Fortune 117
Rey, Fernando 155
Reynolds, Burt 308
Reynolds, Kevin: dir..........145, 301, 551
Rhames, Ving, ...111, 369,
                                                        486, 559
Rhodes, Michael Ray: dir.................315
Rhys-Davies, John 348, 527
Ribisi, Giovanni 410
Ricci, Christina...........................274, 467
Rich, Richard: dir. 261, 542
Richardson, Miranda 164, 347, 469
Richardson, Natasha 107, 263, 404
Richie Rich 256
Rickles, Don 298, 408, 458
Rickman, Alan..................116, 145, 297,
                                                        431, 433
Ride with the Devil 449
Ride, The 409
Riegert, Peter......................................249
Ritchie, Michael: dir. 479
River Runs Through It, A...................183
River Wild, The 256
Road to El Dorado, The 494
Road to Redemption 537
Rob Roy..294
Robards, Jason 226, 246, 442
Robbins, Tim 181, 241, 242
Robbins, Tim: dir. 277
Robert, Yves: dir.................................139
Roberts, Eric 484
Roberts, John: dir. 405
Roberts, Julia 102, 115, 136,
                                                        241, 349, 363,
                                                        450, 476
Robertson, Cliff...........................153, 562
Robin Hood: Prince of Thieves............145
Robinson, James: dir.........................134
Robinson, Jim: dir. 415
Rocco, Marc: dir. 289
Rock, Chris 388
Rock, The 334
Rock-A-Doodle 183
Rocketeer, The......................................146
Rockwell, Sam............................433, 469

Rodriguez, Paul 514
Rodriguez, Robert: dir. 541
Roeg, Nicolas: dir............................121
Rogers, Marianne 134
Rogers, Mimi..................144, 161, 251,
329, 395
Roman, Phil: dir. 225
Romano, Ray....................................556
Romijn-Stamos, Rebecca 501
Roodt, Darrell James: dir. 275
Rookie, The.......................................561
Rooney, Mickey...............................173
Rose, Bernard: dir. 346
Rosenbloom, Dale: dir......................371
Ross, Gary: dir..................................406
Rossellini, Isabella 307
Roth, Tim 254, 295, 535
Roundtree, Richard 332
Rourke, Mickey................................368
Rowlands, Gena.....................391, 405
Rubens, Paul 159, 214
Rubin, Bruce Joel: dir. 213
Rudy..216
Ruehl, Mercedes 132, 208
Rugrats Movie, The 409
Runaway Bride 450
Rush, Geoffrey 335, 388, 393, 411
Russell, Charles: dir..........................315
Russell, Chuck: dir....................249, 467
Russell, Jay: dir................................487
Russell, Kurt....................................260
Russo, Rene 113, 173, 204,
282, 290, 333, 464
Ryan, Meg................130, 222, 242, 294,
345, 420, 523
Rydell, Mark.....................................555
Ryder, Winona..................100, 192, 247

Sabara, Daryl....................................541
Sabrina 295
Safe Passage 257
Sajbel, Michael O.: dir. 410
Salomon, Mikael: dir. 198
San Giacomo, Laura 115, 116
Sanders, Terry: dir. 493

Sandlot, The 216
Sanford, Arlene: dir. 392
Santa Clause, The 258
Sarandon, Chris 214, 396
Sarandon, Susan 150, 174, 235,
247, 257, 277, 513
Sarin, Vic: dir. 483
Sauvage, Pierre: dir. 120
Savage, Ben.....................................147
Savage, John....................................340
Sawa, Devon 377
Sayles, John: dir......................328, 399
Scacchi, Greta 181, 233, 285,
314, 449, 552
Scarlet Letter, The 296
Scheinman, Andrew: dir....................246
Schell, Maximilian.............198, 387, 552
Schepisi, Fred: dir. 176, 242
Scherfig, Lone: dir............................558
Schindler's List 217
Schlesinger, John: dir........................310
Schlondorff, Volker: dir.....................107
Schmidt, John: dir. 549
Schreiber, Liev..................307, 437, 523
Schroeder, Barbet: dir. 117
Schultz, Dwight................................111
Schumacher, Joel: dir...............102, 235,
270, 338, 348
Schwarzenegger, Arnold 149, 207,
315, 326, 348
Scofield, Paul.............................106, 255
Scorsese, Martin: dir.................126, 192
Scott, Campbell: dir. 307
Scott, Dougray 389, 486, 552
Scott, George C.........................101, 116
Scott, Ridley: dir..............150, 155, 340,
482, 510
Seagal, Steven 186
Searching for Bobby Fischer...............218
Second Jungle Book, The:
Mowgli and Baloo..........................369
Secret Garden, The 219
Sedgewick, Kyra 112
See Spot Run....................................538
Segal, George....................................329

Selena 370
Selick, Henry: dir. 214, 324
Sellecca, Connie 165
Selleck, Tom 116, 119, 160, 176
Sense and Sensibility 297
Sewell, Rufus.............................310, 524
Seymour, Jane 408
Shadowlands 219
Shadyac, Tom: dir. 361, 403
Shakespeare in Love............................411
Shalhoub, Tony 307, 386, 405,
                                         433, 541

Shall We Dance...................................371
Shandling, Gary................................247
Shankman, Adam: dir. 543, 565
Shannon, Molly..................................474
Shatner, William 485, 552
Shaw, Fiona.......................................113
Shawn, Wallace...........................282, 458
Sheedy, Ally.....................................141
Sheen, Charlie 225
Sheen, Martin 201, 314
Shepard, Sam 257, 510
Sheridan, Jim: dir. 101, 204
Shigeta, James 96
Shiloh 371
Shine..334
Shipwrecked 147
Shire, Talia 104
Short, Martin 131, 278, 291,
                                         358, 407, 518
Shrek...540
Shyamalan, M. Night: dir. 418, 452
Shyer, Charles: dir. 131, 241, 278
Siberling, Brad: dir. 274
Sidekicks...220
Silverstone, Alicia......................275, 348
Simon Birch.......................................412
Sinbad 321, 326
Singer, Bryan: dir. 501
Singleton, John: dir.............................369
Sinise, Gary 179, 238, 268, 333, 435
Sinise, Gary: dir..................................179
Sinyor, Gary: dir..................................426
Sirtis, Marina.....................................415

Sister Act..184
Sister Act II 221
Sitch, Rob: dir....................................515
Sixth Sense, The....................................452
Sizemore, Tom...........132, 410, 510, 534
Skarsgard, Stellan.....................180, 429
Skerritt, Tom.......................183, 351, 542
Slater, Christian................145, 166, 289
Sleepless in Seattle 222
Small Soldiers 413
Smith, Charles Martin: dir...............343
Smith, Ian Michael 412
Smith, John N.: dir.............................276
Smith, Kevin: dir................................431
Smith, Maggie..................184, 219, 221,
                                         376, 456
Smith, Will.........323, 361, 459, 483, 506
Smits, Jimmy 467
Sobieski, Leelee.........................358, 387
Soderbergh, Steven: dir............207, 476
Softley, Iain: dir., 379 521
Sommers, Stephen: dir. 191,
                                         244, 444
Sonnenfeld, Barry: dir. 282,
                                         361, 459
Sorvino, Paul...............98, 146, 538, 554
Soul Food..372
South Park: Bigger, Longer
    and Uncut......................................452
Space Cowboys 496
Space Jam 335
Spacek, Sissy..............................111, 454
Spacey, Kevin 168, 243, 290,
                                         338, 385, 425,
                                         489, 521
Spade, David............................410, 475
Spader, James 260
Spanish Prisoner, The 414
Speed 259
Spicer, Bryan: dir................................353
Spider-Man 562
Spielberg, Steven: dir. 136, 206,
                                         217, 344, 410,
                                         505, 560
Spiner, Brent.............337, 414, 452, 518

Spirit: Stallion of the Cimarron 563
Spitfire Grill, The 336
Spy Kids 541
Stallone, Sylvester 351, 383
Stanton, Harry Dean 435, 454
Stapleton, Jean 226, 420
Star Trek: First Contact 337
Star Trek: Insurrection 414
Stargate 260
Steenburgen, Mary 94, 518, 542
Steiger, Rod 371, 437, 451
Step Kids 147
Stern, Daniel......................108, 127, 169
Stewart, French 550
Stewart, Patrick.............337, 349, 407,
414, 501, 518
Stiers, David Ogden.........243, 528, 559
Still Breathing.....................................415
Stiller, Ben...416
Stoltz, Eric 111, 247, 254, 295
Stone, Oliver: dir., 130, 252..............289
Stone, Sharon 383
Stormare, Peter 317, 384, 470, 560
Stowe, Madeleine 171, 267, 566
Straight Story, The..............................454
Stranger Among Us, A 185
Streep, Meryl 115, 256, 273,
403, 446, 505
Streisand, Barbra 143, 329
Streisand, Barbra: dir.................143, 329
Strictly Ballroom................................222
Stuart Little..454
Suo, Masayuki: dir.............................371
Super Mario Bros. 223
Sutherland, Donald 159, 290,
338, 496
Sutherland, Kiefer 102, 167, 225
Sverak, Jan: dir. 359
Swayze, Patrick.........................104, 299
Sweeney, Julia 550
Sweet Hereafter, The 373

Takei, George.......................................143
Tall Tale 297
Tamahori, Lee: dir.......................350, 507

Tambor, Jeffrey 474, 491
Tandy, Jessica 133
Tarantino, Quentin: dir. 254
Tarzan...455
Tatie Danielle 148
Taylor, Elizabeth 237
Teenage Mutant Ninja Turtles............118
Teenage Mutant Ninja Turtles II:
The Secret of the Ooze 149
Tennant, Andy: dir.......................284, 389
Terminator 2: Judgment Day 149
Texas Rangers 541
That Thing You Do 337
There's Something About Mary..........416
Theron, Charlize 337, 400, 429, 483
Thewlis, David.....................................294
Third Miracle, The 457
Thomas and the Magic Railroad 496
Thomas, Betty: dir. 271, 388
Thomas, Jonathan Taylor 306,
377, 392
Thomas, Kristin Scott...............329, 392
Thompson, Caroline: dir................232
Thompson, Emma 171, 204, 212,
215, 297, 407
Thompson, Lea 94, 196
Thornton, Billy Bob 347, 384, 407
Three Men and a Little Lady 119
Three Musketeers, The 224
Thurman, Uma 254, 287, 348, 393
Tierney, Maura 361, 407
Tillman Jr., George: dir....................372
Tilly, Jennifer 234, 455
Time for Drunken Horses, A...............498
Time to Kill, A 338
Titan A.E...498
Titanic 374
To Sleep with Anger 119
Tobolowsky, Stephen 202, 362
Tolkin, Michael: dir.........................144
Tom and Jerry: The Movie...................225
Tomei, Marisa....................178, 377, 500
Tomlin, Lily 456, 473
Tong, Stanley: dir. 362
Torn, Rip 361

Tornatore, Giuseppe: dir. 96
Townsend, Robert 211
Townsend, Robert: dir. 211
Toy Story 298
Toy Story 2 458
Travis, Randy 542
Travolta, John 254, 282, 386, 407
Trenchard-Smith, Brian: dir. 530
Trial, The 226
Tripplehorn, Jeanne 199, 301
Trousdale, Gary: dir. 124, 508
Truman Show, The 417
Tucci, Stanley 307
Tucci, Stanley: dir. 307
Tucker, Tuck: dir. 554
Tung, Sandy: dir. 451
Tunney, Robin 311
Turteltaub, Jon: dir. 195, 301, 473
Turturro, John 123, 209, 255, 487
Turturro, John: dir. 209
Twister 339
Two Bits 299
Tyler, Liv 337, 384, 527
Tyson, Cicely 133

U-571 499
Ulee's Gold 374
Ullman, Tracey 234
Ulmann, Liv 180
Ulrich, Skeet 402, 450
Under Siege 185
Underwood, Blair 495
Underwood, Ron: dir. 127, 400
Uranus 150
Ustinov, Peter 174
Uys, Jamie: dir. 105

Vaccaro, Brenda 247, 329
Van Dien, Casper 448
Van Peebles, Mario 506
Van Sant, Gus: dir. 355
Vance, Courtney B. 191, 276, 332
Vardalos, Nia 560
Varney, Jim 100, 458
Vega, Alexa 541

Venora, Diane 358, 439, 530
Vereen, Ben 214
Vernon, Bob: dir. 538
Viterelli, Joe 538
Voight, Jon 330, 368, 369,
430, 506, 525, 534
Volcano 380
von Scherler Mayer, Daisy: dir. 396
von Sydow, Max 180, 418, 560
Vosloo, Arnold 444

Wachowski, Andy: dir. 443
Wachowski, Larry: dir. 443
Wag the Dog 375
Wahlberg, Mark 490, 535
Wainwright, Rupert: dir. 232
Waite, Ralph 321
Waiting to Exhale 300
Walk to Remember, A 565
Wallace, Randall: dir. 397, 566
Wallace, Stephen: dir. 143
Wallach, Eli 104
Walsh, M. Emmet 440
Walters, Julie 466
Wang, Wayne: dir. 205
Warburton, Patrick 475, 515, 519
Ward, Fred 181
Ward, Vincent: dir. 418
Warden, Jack 234, 301, 430
Wargnier, Regis: dir., ...475
Warner, David 149, 374
Warren, Christopher 156
Washington Square 376
Washington, Denzel 175, 332,
437, 492
Waterworld 300
Watson, Emma 517
We Were Soldiers 566
Weapons of the Spirit 120
Weaver, Sigourney 155, 196, 433
Weaving, Hugo 443, 527
Wedding Planner, The 543
Wedge, Chris: dir. 556
Weir, Peter: dir. 106, 417
Weisman, Sam: dir. 236, 355

Weisz, Rachel 444
Welch, Raquel 526
Welcome to Sarajevo 377
Wells, Simon: dir. 270, 407
Wen, Ming-Na...................................205
Wendt, George 135
Wenk, Richard: dir..........................441
West, Simon: dir. 525
Wettig, Patricia...............................135
Whaley, Frank 103, 130, 224, 242
What About Bob? 151
What Dreams May Come....................417
What Women Want 500
Where the Red Fern Grows: Part 2.....187
While You Were Sleeping.....................301
Whitaker, Forest: dir.................300, 391
White Fang....................................152
White Hunter, Black Heart 121
White Squall...................................340
Whitesell, John: dir. 538
Whitmore, James 528
Widow's Peak 263
Wiest, Dianne 100, 137, 234,
                                308, 392, 518
Wild America 377
Wild Hearts Can't Be Broken..............152
Wild Wild West.................................459
Wilkinson, Tom 365, 488, 511, 557
Williams, JoBeth...............................358
Williams, Robin 94, 132, 136, 156,
                    166, 212, 285, 308, 320,
                 352, 355, 403, 418, 426, 505
Williams, Treat 555
Williams, Vanessa.............315, 372, 423
Williamson, Mykelti.................238, 506
Williamson, Nicol..............................378
Willis, Bruce 254, 267, 358,
                          384, 452, 473, 553
Wilson, Hugh: dir. 239
Wilson, Luke 487, 526
Wilson, Rita 326
Wincer, Simon: dir. 116, 199, 514
Wind In the Willows, The 378
Winger, Debra 172, 220, 280
Wings of the Dove, The........................379

Winkler, Irwin: dir. 135
Winningham, Mare 281
Winslet, Kate 297, 320, 374, 552
Winstone, Ray 424
Winterbottom, Michael: dir. 377
Winters, Jonathan 237
Wise, Kirk: dir. 124, 508
Witches, The, ...120
Witherspoon, Reese.........198, 406, 526,
                                542, 557
Woo, John: dir....................................486
Wood, Elijah 168, 191, 387, 527
Woodard, Alfre 337, 521
Woods, James 319, 351, 564
Woodward, Edward..........................138
Woodward, Joanne 112
Worley, Jo Anne 282
Wrestling Ernest Hemingway 263
Wright, Robin...................................238

X-Files, The......................................419
X-Men...501

Yakin, Boaz: dir. 492
Yeoh, Michelle....................................471
Yimou, Zhang: dir.....................182, 262
Yoakam, Dwight................................402
York, Michael 448, 530
You've Got Mail 420
Yun-Fat, Chow 471

Zahn, Steve.................337, 420, 455, 564
Zaillian, Steven: dir. 218, 386
Zane, Billy...374
Zeffirelli, Franco: dir. 106, 325, 456
Zegers, Kevin 343
Zellweger, Renee 326, 403, 426
Zemeckis, Robert: dir. 94, 238,
                                351, 468
Zeta-Jones, Catherine........................398
Zi Yi, Zhang......................................471
Zieff, Howard: dir..............................139
Zlotoff, Lee David: dir. 336
Zucker, Jerry: dir..............104, 279, 537
Zwick, Joel: dir. 561

ACKNOWLEDGMENTS

This book was written by Dr. Ted Baehr with Dr. Tom Snyder. We would like to thank our intern Brian Shun and the many others who have contributed articles, excerpts, and reviews.

What Can We Watch Tonight is based on MOVIEGUIDE's reviews, which are copyrighted by Dr. Ted Baehr, and on the MOVIEGUIDE proprietary system of analysis and presentation.

"Whoever controls the media, controls the culture."

We want to hear from you. Please send your comments about this book to us in care of zreview@zondervan.com. Thank you.

GRAND RAPIDS, MICHIGAN 49530 USA

WWW.ZONDERVAN.COM